Oil Paintings in Public Ownership in the
Imperial War Museum

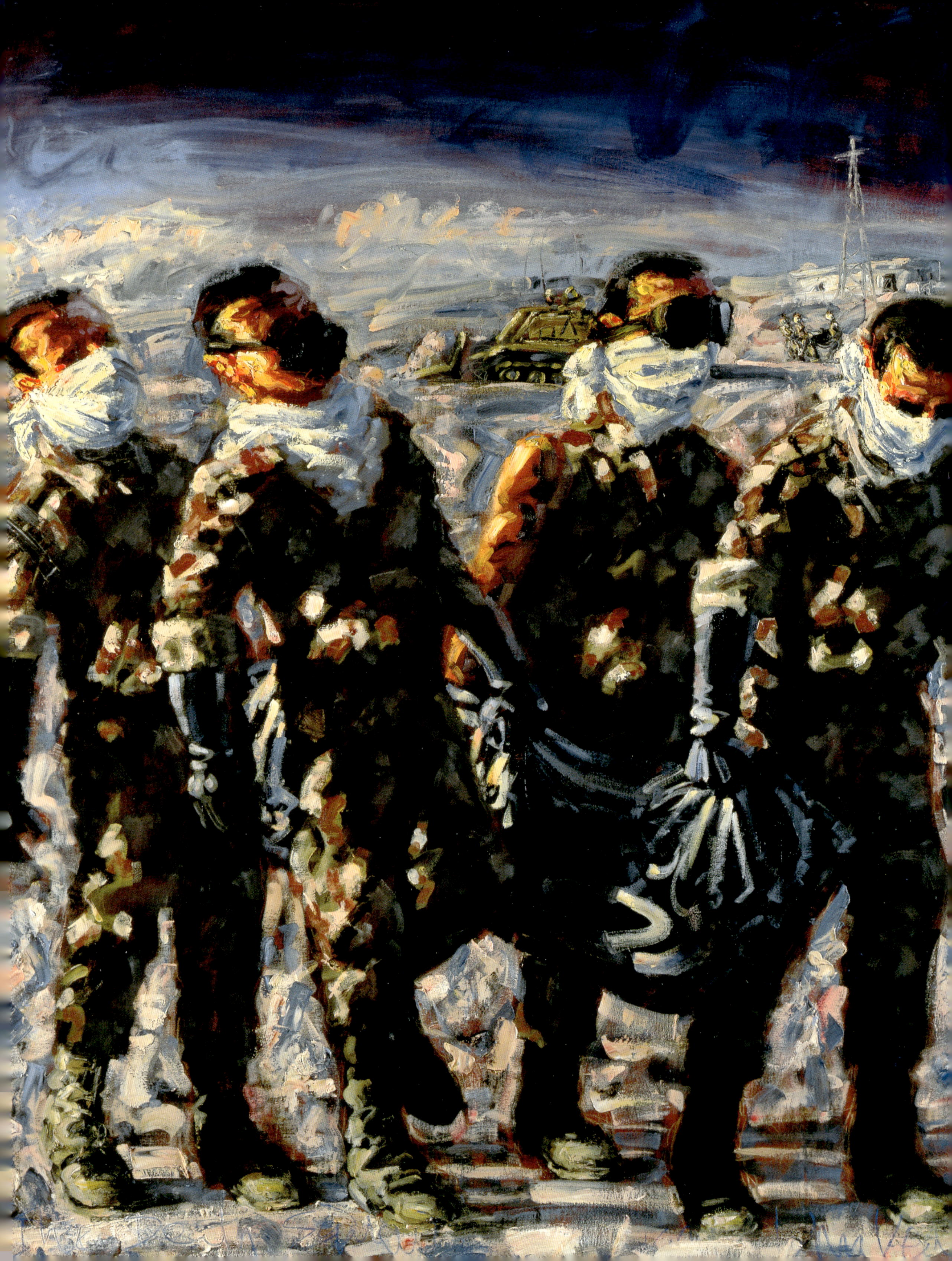

Oil Paintings in Public Ownership in the Imperial War Museum

The Public Catalogue Foundation

Andrew Ellis, Director
Sonia Roe, Editor
Andy Johnson, Photography

First published in 2006 by the Public Catalogue
Foundation, St Vincent House, 30 Orange Street,
London, WC2H 7HH

ISBN 1-904931-28-6 (hardback)
ISBN 1-904931-29-4 (paperback)

Photography: Andy Johnson

Designed by Jeffery Design, London

Distributed by the Public Catalogue Foundation,
St Vincent House, 30 Orange Street,
London, WC2H 7HH
Telephone 020 7747 5936

Printed and bound in the UK by Butler & Tanner
Ltd, Frome, Somerset

Cover image:

Orpen, William 1878–1931
Harvest (detail), 1918 (see p. 179)

Image opposite title page:

Keane, John, b.1954
Death Squad (detail), 1991 (see p. 118)

Back cover images (from top to bottom):

Howson, Peter b.1958
Cleansed 1994 (see p. 113)

Carline, Richard 1896–1956
Self Portrait in Uniform 1918 (see p. 27)

Nash, Paul 1889–1946
Battle of Britain 1941 (see p. 167)

Contents

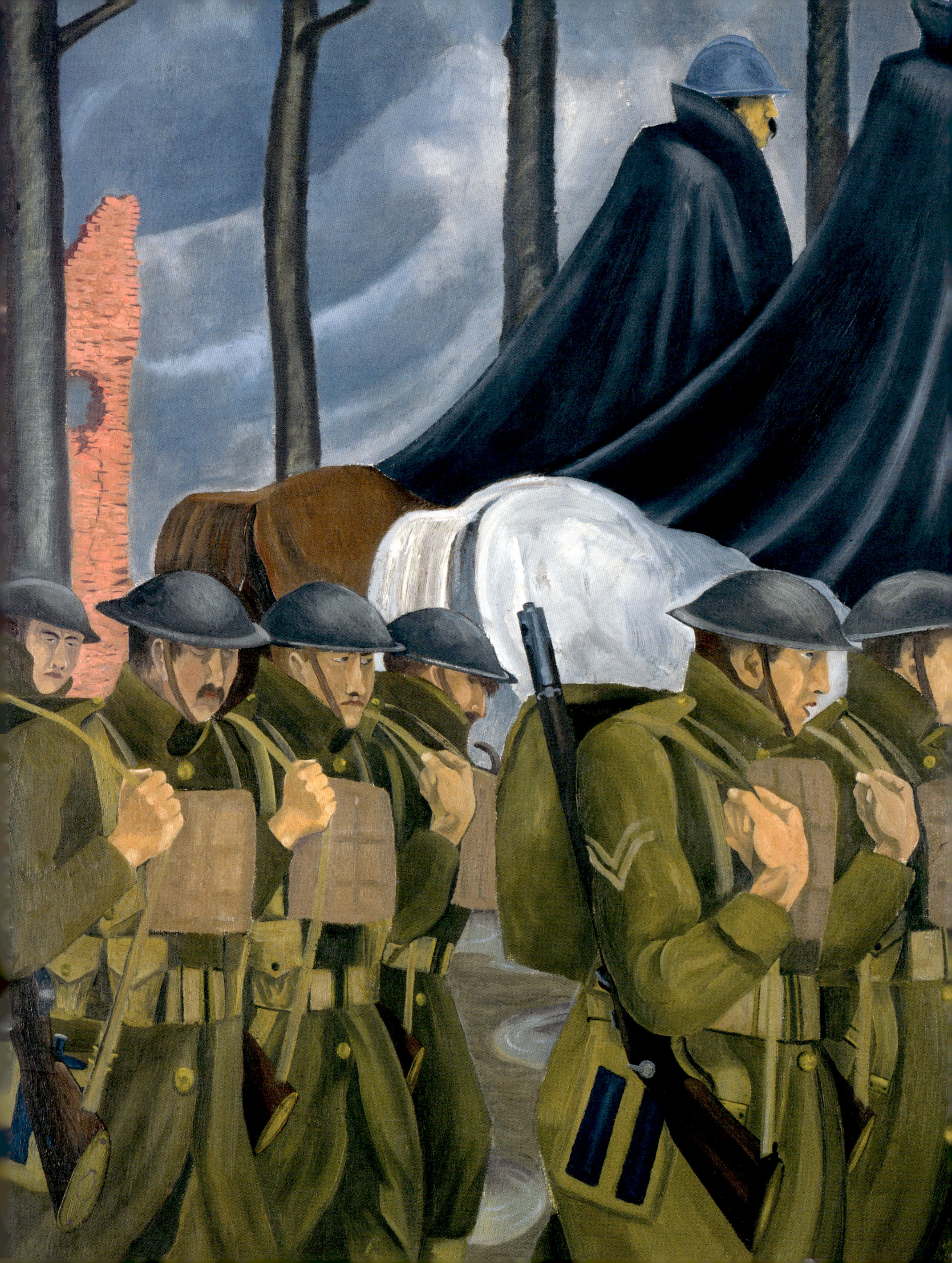

Foreword

The Trustees of the Public Catalogue Foundation are particularly pleased and proud to be publishing this volume of the oil paintings in the Imperial War Museum. The Foundation has, from the outset, been focused on the regions where the national collection is most at risk. The paintings in store in our national museums are less at any physical risk than at risk of being lost to the public eye and forgotten. The incongruity of this observation, viewed against the background of this collection being recognised in the 1920s as the most important collection of contemporary British Art in the country, eloquently illustrates our present predicament.

So, despite our focus on the regions, we must bring back to the public eye outstanding collections such as this. As it happens it falls happily into place after our Slade Catalogue which contains the foundation work of so many First World War British painters.

A visitor to the stacks of the Imperial War Museum needs courage and a strong heart. Few collections force the eye so insistently to deflect the visual so directly into the intellect. In a record that is essentially vile, the impasto of horror of many of the paintings has degraded with time into evil: it is the slow-release of shock from the home front images that has endured.

The World War One carnage changed so much, and the artist's vision with it. The destructive power of mechanised war obliterated the hedonism of sensation (to quote Kenneth McConkey) and gave birth to the images of World War Two where what shocks is less the trench than the Belsen. The coldness of modern warfare enters the visual vocabulary. Only with the images of contemporary warfare does the forgotten but unlost savagery of war begin again to pierce the official veil.

In the end, what unifies this collection is less its nationality or subject than a pervading sense of great dignity, which, in itself and perversely, inspires a deep sense of indignation.

Dr Alan Borg has been a mentor to the Foundation since its earliest moments and it is his influence, as a former director of the IWM, that led us to publish this catalogue. Publication would not have been possible, however, without the support of our key sponsor behind this catalogue and a previous one, RAB Capital plc, the investment management company founded by Philip Richards and Michael Alen-Buckley. Their generous and wide-ranging philanthropy is well-known. Lloyd Dorfman, who has long and brilliantly supported the arts through his business, Travelex, and Jonathan Lane, Managing Director of Shaftesbury plc also a long-standing supporter of the arts, have between them subscribed the balance. The Foundation and the British public are indebted to them all. As they are to Robert Crawford, Roger Tolson and all their colleagues at the Imperial War Museum for all their help in making this volume possible.

Fred Hohler, Chairman

Facing page: Nash, John Northcote, 1893–1977, *A French Highway* (detail), 1918, (p. 166)

The Public Catalogue Foundation

The United Kingdom holds in its galleries and civic buildings arguably the greatest publicly owned collection of oil paintings in the world. However, an alarming four in five of these paintings are not on view. Whilst many galleries make strenuous efforts to display their collections, too many paintings across the country are held in storage, usually because there are insufficient funds and space to show them. Furthermore, very few galleries have created a complete photographic record of their paintings, let alone a comprehensive illustrated catalogue of their collections. In short, what is publicly owned is not publicly accessible.

The Public Catalogue Foundation, a registered charity, has three aims. First, it intends to create a complete record of the nation's collection of oil, tempera and acrylic paintings in public ownership. Second, it intends to make this accessible to the public through a series of affordable catalogues and, after a suitable delay, through a free Internet website. Finally, it aims to raise funds through the sale of catalogues in gallery shops for the conservation and restoration of oil paintings in these collections and for gallery education.

The initial focus of the project is on collections outside London. Highlighting the richness and diversity of collections outside the capital should bring major benefits to regional collections around the country. The benefits also include a revenue stream for conservation, restoration, gallery education and the digitisation of collections' paintings, thereby allowing them to put the images on the Internet if they so desire. These substantial benefits to galleries around the country come at no financial cost to the collections themselves.

The project should be of enormous benefit and inspiration to students of art and to members of the general public with an interest in art. It will also provide a major source of material for scholarly research into art history.

Financial Supporters

The Public Catalogue Foundation would like to express its profound appreciation to the following organisations and individuals who have made the publication of this catalogue possible.

Donations of £10,000 or more

RAB Capital plc
Mr Lloyd Dorfman

Donations of £5,000 or more

Shaftesbury plc

Donations of £1,000 or more

P. F. Charitable Trust

National Supporters

The Bulldog Trust
The John S. Cohen Foundation
Hiscox plc
Stavros S. Niarchos Foundation

The Manifold Trust
The Monument Trust
P. F. Charitable Trust
Garfield Weston Foundation

National Sponsor

Christie's

Acknowledgements

The Public Catalogue Foundation would like to thank the individual artists and copyright holders for their permission to reproduce for free the paintings in this catalogue. Exhaustive efforts have been made to locate the copyright owners of all the images included within this catalogue and to meet their requirements. Copyright credit lines for copyright owners who have been traced are listed in the Further Information section.

The Public Catalogue Foundation would like to express its great appreciation to the following organisations for their great assistance in the preparation of this catalogue:

Bridgeman Art Library
Flowers East
Marlborough Fine Art
National Association of Decorative and Fine Art Societies (NADFAS)
National Gallery, London
National Portrait Gallery, London
Royal Academy of Arts, London
Tate

The Imperial War Museum would like to express its appreciation to the many individuals who have contributed so generously to their collection and those who continue to do so. They would also like to express their thanks to the following organisations which have so generously enabled them to acquire paintings featured in this catalogue:

William Beardmore
British Red Cross Society
Anthony d'Offay Gallery
Fulham Borough Council
Greater London Council
Guy's Hospital Medical and Dental Schools
Her Majesty the Queen
National Art Collections Fund
National Heritage Memorial Fund
National Lottery Fund
Order of St John of Jerusalem
Ross Gallery
Salonika Reunion Association
John Seagrim
The Long Range Desert Group Association
War Artists' Advisory Committee

Catalogue Scope and Organisation

Medium and Support

The principal focus of this series is oil paintings. However, tempera and acrylic are also included as well as mixed media, where oil is the predominant constituent. Paintings on all forms of support (e.g. canvas, panel, etc.) are included as long as the support is portable. The principal exclusions are miniatures, hatchments or other purely heraldic paintings and wall paintings *in situ*.

Public Ownership

Public ownership has been taken to mean any paintings that are directly owned by the public purse, made accessible to the public by means of public subsidy or generally perceived to be in public ownership. The term 'public' refers to both central government and local government. Paintings held by national museums, local authority museums, English Heritage and independent museums, where there is at least some form of public subsidy, are included. Paintings held in civic buildings such as local government offices, town halls, guildhalls, public libraries, universities, hospitals, crematoria, fire stations and police stations are also included. Paintings held in central government buildings as part of the Government Art Collection and MoD collections are not included in the county-by-county series but should be included later in the series on a national basis.

Geographical Boundaries of Catalogues

The geographical boundary of each county is the 'ceremonial county' boundary. This county definition includes all unitary authorities. Counties that have a particularly large number of paintings are divided between two or more catalogues on a geographical basis.

Criteria for Inclusion

As long as paintings meet the requirements above, all paintings are included irrespective of their condition and perceived quality. However, painting reproductions can only be included with the agreement of the participating collections and, where appropriate, the relevant copyright owner. It is rare that a collection forbids the inclusion of its paintings. Where this is the case and it is possible to obtain a list of paintings, this list is given in the Paintings Without Reproductions section. Where copyright consent is refused, the paintings are also listed in the Paintings Without Reproductions section. All paintings

in collections' stacks and stores are included, as well as those on display. Paintings which have been lent to other institutions, whether for short-term exhibition or long-term loan, are listed under the owner collection. In addition, paintings on long-term loan are also included under the borrowing institution when they are likely to remain there for at least another five years from the date of publication of this catalogue. Information relating to owners and borrowers is listed in the Further Information section.

Layout

Collections are grouped together under their home town. These locations are listed in alphabetical order. In some cases collections that are spread over a number of locations are included under a single owner collection. A number of collections, principally the larger ones, are preceded by curatorial forewords. Within each collection paintings are listed in order of artist surname. Where there is more than one painting by the same artist, the paintings are listed chronologically, according to their execution date.

The few paintings that are not accompanied by photographs are listed in the Paintings Without Reproductions section.

There is additional reference material in the Further Information section at the back of the catalogue. This gives the full names of artists, titles and media if it has not been possible to include these in full in the main section. It also provides acquisition credit lines and information about loans in and out, as well as copyright and photographic credits for each painting. Finally, there is an index of artists' surnames.

Key to Painting Information

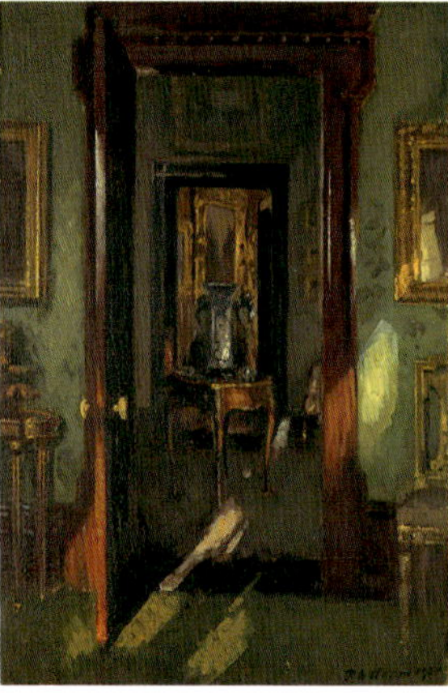

Almost all paintings are reproduced in the catalogue. Where this is not the case they are listed in the Paintings Without Reproductions section. Where paintings are missing or have been stolen, the best possible photograph on record has been reproduced. In some cases this may be black and white. Paintings that have been stolen are highlighted with a red border. Some paintings are shown with conservation tissue attached to parts of the painting surface.

Adam, Patrick William 1854–1929
Interior, Rutland Lodge: Vista through Open Doors 1920
oil on canvas 67.3 × 45.7
LEEAG.PA.1925.0671.LACF 🐝

Artist name This is shown as surname first. Where the artist is listed on the Getty Union List of Artist Names (ULAN), ULAN's preferred presentation of the name is always given. In a number of cases the name may not be a firm attribution and this is made clear. Where the artist name is not known, a school may be given instead. Where the school is not known, the painter name is listed as *unknown artist*. If the artist name is too long for the space, as much of the name is given as possible followed by (…). This indicates the full name is given at the rear of the catalogue in the Further Information section.

Painting title A painting followed by *(?)* indicates that the title is in doubt. Where the alternative title to the painting is considered to be better known than the original, the alternative title is given in parentheses. Where the collection has not given a painting a title, the publisher does so instead and marks this with an asterisk. If the title is too long for the space, as much of the title is given as possible followed by *(…)* and the full title is given in the Further Information section.

Medium and support Where the precise material used in the support is known, this is given.

Artist dates Where known, the years of birth and death of the artist are given. In some cases one or both dates may not be known with certainty, and this is marked. No date indicates that even an approximate date is not known. Where only the period in which the artist was active is known, these dates are given and preceded with the word *active*.

Execution date In some cases the precise year of execution may not be known for certain. Instead an approximate date will be given or no date at all.

Dimensions All measurements refer to the unframed painting and are given in cm with up to one decimal point. In all cases the height is shown before the width. Where the painting has been measured in its frame, the dimensions are estimates and are marked with (E). If the painting is circular, the single dimension is the diameter. If the painting is oval, the dimensions are height and width.

Collection inventory number In the case of paintings owned by museums, this number will always be the accession number. In all other cases it will be a unique inventory number of the owner institution. (P) indicates that a painting is a private loan. Details can be found in the Further Information section. The 🐝 symbol indicates that the reproduction is based on a Bridgeman Art Library transparency (go to www.bridgeman.co.uk) or that the Bridgeman administers the copyright for that artist.

Facing page: Thomson, Alfred Reginald, 1894–1979, *A Saline Bath, Royal Air Force Hospital* (detail), 1943, (p. 217)

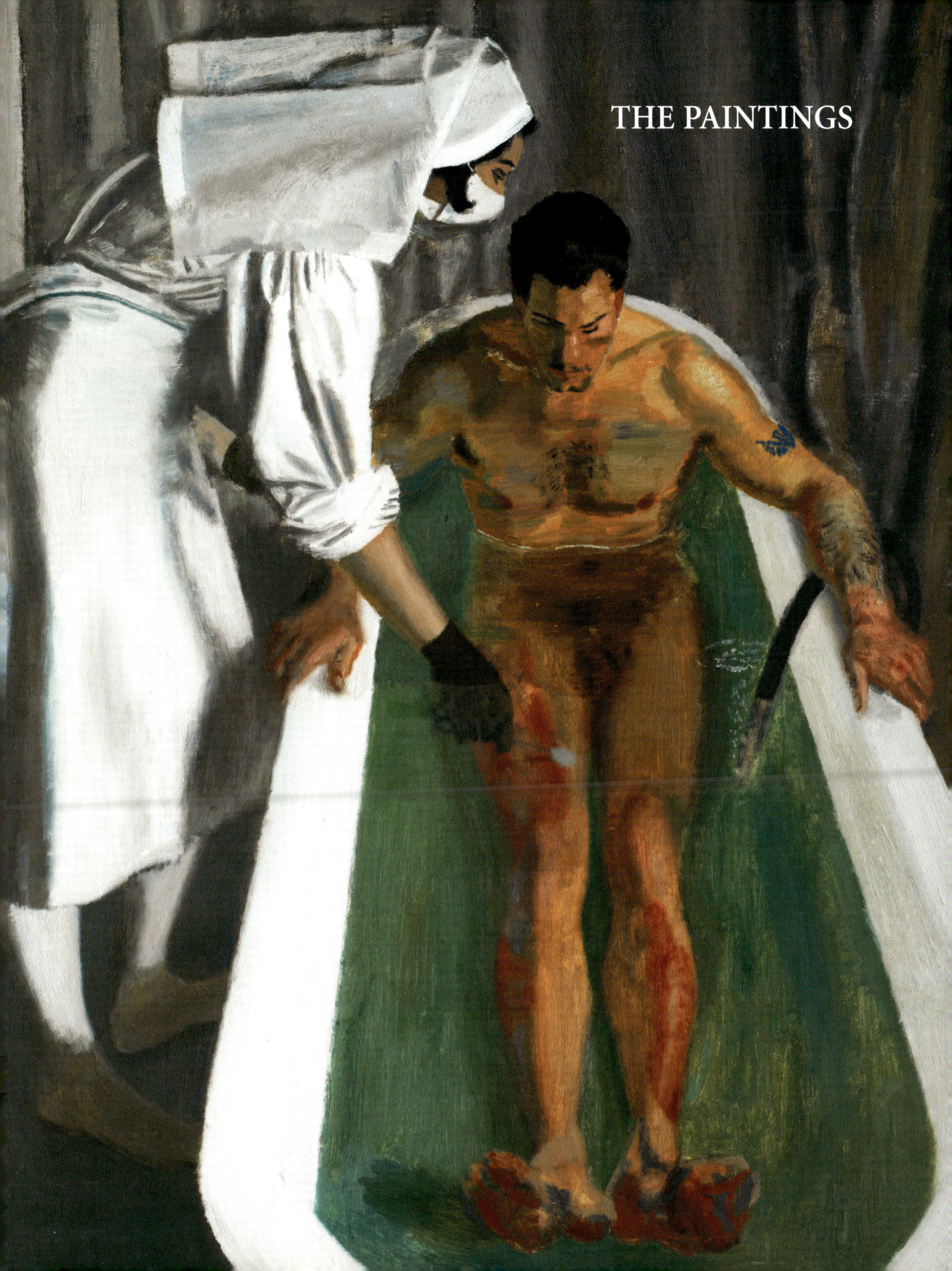
THE PAINTINGS

Imperial War Museum

That the Imperial War Museum should have a major collection of British art is both hugely surprising and entirely natural: surprising, that at times of compelling demands on national resources a collection of this scale should have been formed at all; natural, in that the Museum seeks to tell the story of all aspects of modern war and its impact on society, and the visual narratives of paintings are an important part of this mission. Although the subject matter is unusual and in many cases particular to the wars of the twentieth century and beyond, the paintings, like any others, seek to respond to the world around them. However, aesthetic judgements alone cannot do justice to a collection so intimately associated with such vital periods of national history. Looking again at the images reproduced here questions about the collection's true worth can be asked and answered afresh.

Two words that appear at the back of this catalogue give a clue to the sources of the collection: 'transferred' and 'commissioned' dominate the acquisition records. Although they gloss over the complexity of the war artist schemes, the variety of purposes and practices of the commissions, as well as the relationship between the commissioning bodies, they do give an indication of the scale of the fine art projects orchestrated by the British Government and the Imperial War Museum to respond to every aspect of war and its impact. These schemes were shaped and administered by a handful of individuals acting in the confidence that the schemes were both appropriate and justified at a time of national conflict. The earliest programme in the First World War, developed in 1916 under Charles Masterman, sought images for their propaganda value, acquiring the rights to reproduce paintings rather than the paintings themselves. Subsequently, John Lavery, James McBey and William Orpen all gave substantial collections to the Museum at the end of the War. More adventurous commissioning began with John Buchan as head of the Department of Information and when Lord Beaverbrook became the new Minister of Information in February 1917 the British War Memorials Committee was immediately established. Modelled on the scheme which Beaverbrook had been running from London on behalf of the Canadian Government, the committee sought to create a memorial to the Great War through paintings commissioned from the best artists of the day, including the most avant-garde.

At the outbreak of the Second World War, the Ministry of Information established the War Artists Advisory Committee on the lines of its First World War predecessors. Promoted and chaired by Sir Kenneth Clark, then Director of the National Gallery, the Committee sought 'to record the war at home and abroad', acquiring material from its own appointed artists as well as through independent submissions. Although there was an emphasis on working with figurative artists - Ben Nicholson, amongst others was not appointed - the scheme was again able to work with the major artists of the day. The Artistic Records Committee, established by the Museum in 1972, continued in these traditions. Although having greatly reduced resources, work by John Keane, 'official recorder' for the First Gulf War, and Peter Howson, sent to Bosnia, have been important additions to the collection.

The scale of aspiration for the various schemes is perhaps best measured by the intentions for their acquisitions. The British War Memorials programme drew its inspiration from Renaissance models of patronage: indeed, the canvas dimensions of Uccello's *Battle of San Romano* were identified as being most suitable for the subject matter. The paintings, which include Singer Sargent's *Gassed*, Paul Nash's *Menin Road* and Percy Wyndham Lewis's *A Battery Shelled*, were to be shown in their own pavilion either on Richmond Hill or at the Tate Gallery. Kenneth Clark's long-term agenda for the Second World War scheme was to change the status of the visual arts within British culture, firstly through a series of touring exhibitions that developed and exploited a growing interest in the visual arts, and then, at the end of the war, through the distribution of the 6,000 paintings acquired by the committee to galleries around the United Kingdom as well as overseas. The Imperial War Museum, established in 1917, had begun commissioning from its inception but with the failure of other options for the Ministry's First World War collection it became the recipient of this extraordinary government patronage, receiving nearly all their material and then over half of the War Artists Advisory Committee acquisitions. The 1,800 oils represented here are small part of a collection of over 20,000 works of art, including prints, original designs, art medals and illustrations.

Recognising the impact of the Great War on all aspects of society, and the importance of recording and measuring this, the schemes set out to create a unique portrait of a nation in the bloody trauma and social upheaval wrought by that war. In their very efforts to cover all aspects of the First World War, from the factory to the front, from citizens as manufacturers, directors, observers and dischargers of the weapons of war, to vulnerable victims of these same forces, the subject matter of war art was to change. No longer was it simply a paean of praise to military leaders, eulogies of personal sacrifice, or visions of national triumph on the battlefield. This war art looked resolutely at the daily life of the work place, the street and the city, as well as at the trenches, the mud and the long journey home. During the First World War the government programmes focussed more on warfare and its front-line logistics, and it was left to specialist committees of the Museum and the Royal Army Medical Corps to ensure that other aspects were recorded: socially liberated and independent women as portrayed by Flora Lion; the sheer scale and redeployment of industry seen in Anna Airy's canvas of the shoddily equipped Singer Factory in Glasgow - recently converted to armament production; and the painfully strange rehabilitation of disfigured soldiers exposed in Hodgson Lobley's portrayal of a toy workshop.

Government agencies as commissioners might have been expected to preclude criticism of the war. In practice, the messages in the resultant paintings were complex and questioning. Many images made social change and violence disturbingly clear, or gave a future outlook that was bleak to the point of despair. *Paths of Glory* by C. R. W. Nevinson was being purchased by the Museum even as the official censor sought to keep its image of forgotten and bloated dead soldiers off public display. The paintings illustrated here are not just of sacrifice, bravery, success, liberation and redemption; fear and failure, anxiety and death are also writ large.

What marked all these schemes was the importance of the eye-witness response and the quality of artistic vision. The most powerful voices from the First World War were both witness to and active in the atrocious events they described. Brothers Paul and John Nash served in the Artists Rifles, driving Paul's artistic visions from pastoral glade to the bloody copse of *We Are Making a New World*; Nevinson was an ambulance orderly; Eric Kennington served in the Kensingtons, and his image of exhausted soldiers, including himself, was genuinely felt and utterly shocking to its viewers. Others, such as Orpen, stayed long enough to be deeply affected by what they witnessed. Even the short visit Sargent made to the Front was enough to imbue his masterpiece, *Gassed*, with moral uncertainty.

The Second World War artists were less openly critical but even whilst recording the commonplace of the home front they reveal new social complexities and dangers. Evelyn Dunbar's painting of fishmongers distinguishes between different strata of society: those who wear uniform and those who queue. The children in Elsie Hewland's nursery school, exploring a new social world and learning at the craft table, mirror the experiences of their mothers and fathers elsewhere. The collapsing wall painted by Leonard Rosoman, an auxiliary fireman, captures the instantaneous destruction of the Blitz. Imagery ranges from the encoded world of John Piper's underground control rooms to Henry Carr's soldiers in North Africa, and from visions of new community in the shipbuilding cycle by Stanley Spencer to the moral vacuum of Belsen, with humanity reduced to detritus in Leslie Cole's and Doris Zinkeisen's paintings.

As well as providing a fascinating cross-section of British artistic practice at two key periods in the twentieth century – the development of Modernism and the neo-Romantic movement – the collection also demands to be judged against the best of British art. Indeed, at the end of the First World War, the Museum held the most important collection of contemporary British art in the country, lending many significant works to the Tate Gallery at Millbank. However, the collection's relationship to the immediate events of the day calls for a different set of values by which it should be assessed: George Lambourn's stark canvas of corpses in Calais might be little known but its message is coldly clear and demanding of our respect. On the other hand, *Battle of Britain* by Paul Nash is one of the great paintings of British art, visually engaging with its arabesque vapour trails and vast panorama, but its content, context and meaning are wrapped in and around the event it seeks to describe, a defining moment in the Second World War. The painting both captures the drama and scale of the conflict, and, as the Luftwaffe formations are broken and forced into sweeping lyrical manoeuvres before death, it tells assuredly of the victory of liberal culture over the social ordering of fascism. It is this visceral relationship with current or recent events that demands a different set of responses. Great art and history conjoined in this manner, and in the context of a Museum dedicated to recording the stories of individuals in wartime, creates a deeply moving and richly rewarding visual narrative, seen in print for the first time through the vision and publication of this catalogue.

Roger Tolson, Head of Art

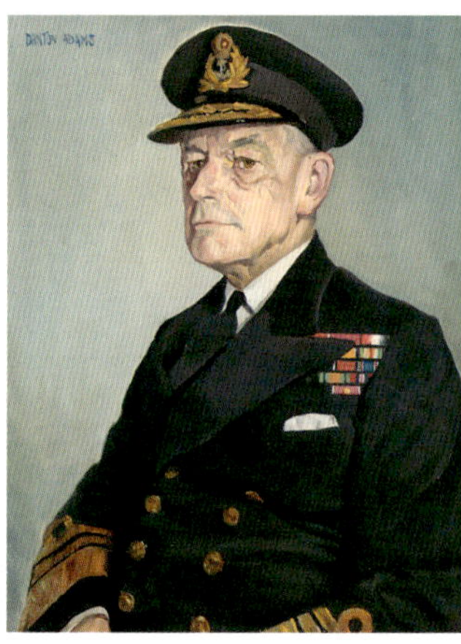

Adams, Danton 1904–1991
Vice Admiral Sir Arthur Dowding c.1950
oil on canvas 57.1 x 44.4
IWM ART LD 7265

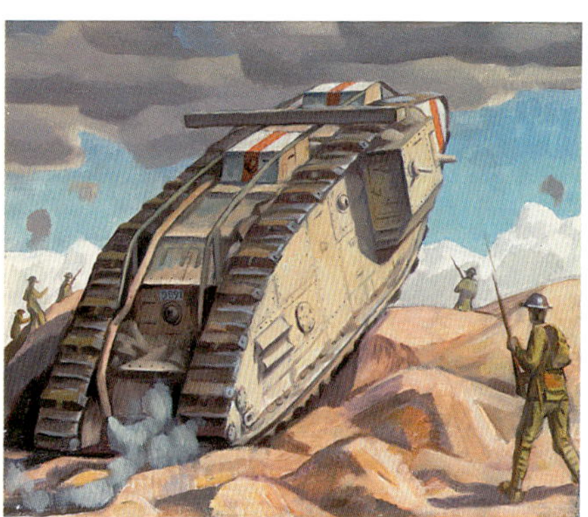

Adeney, William Bernard 1878–1966
A 'Mark V' Tank Going into Action 1918
oil on canvas 50.8 x 60.9
IWM ART 2267

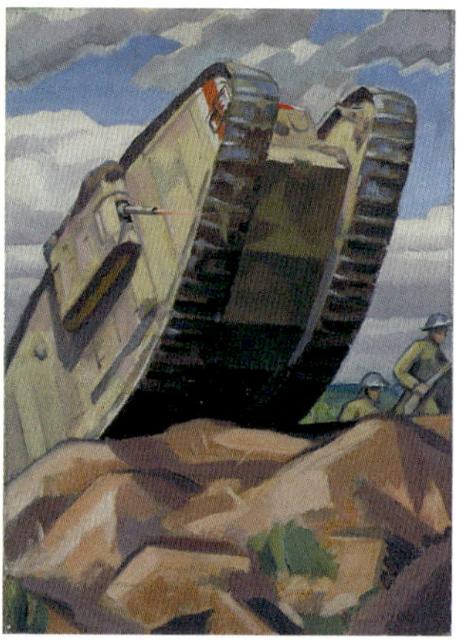

Adeney, William Bernard 1878–1966
The Advance 1918
oil on canvas 55.8 x 40.6
IWM ART 2707

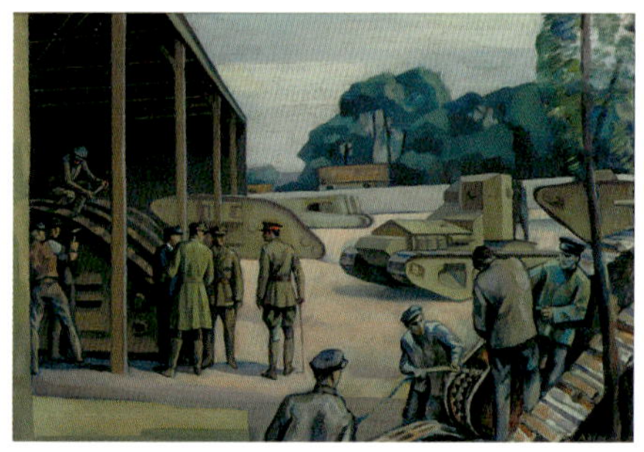

Adeney, William Bernard 1878–1966
*The Experimental Depot for Tanks, Dollis Hill,
North-West London* 1918
oil on canvas 60.9 x 91.4
IWM ART 1868

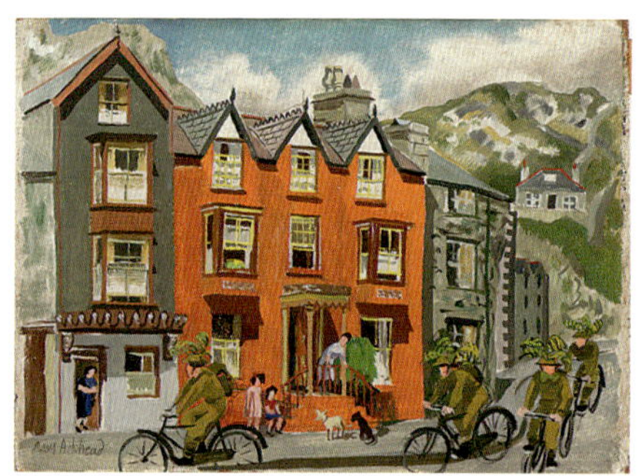

Adshead, Mary 1904–1995
Riding into Barmouth 1941
oil on board 25 x 35.9
IWM ART 16837

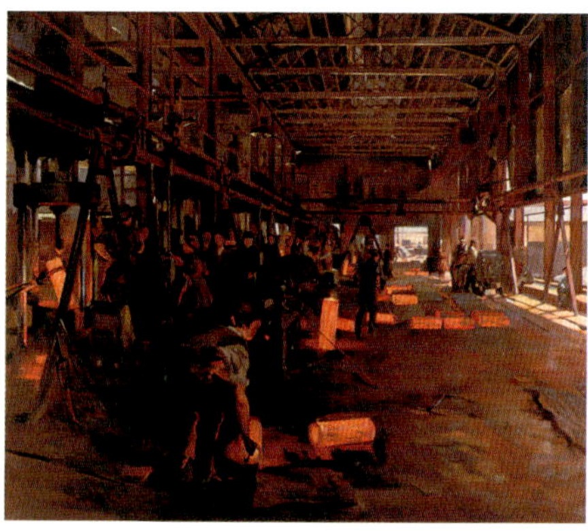

Airy, Anna 1882–1964
*A Shell Forge at a National Projectile Factory,
Hackney Marshes, London* 1918
oil on canvas 182.8 x 213.3
IWM ART 4032

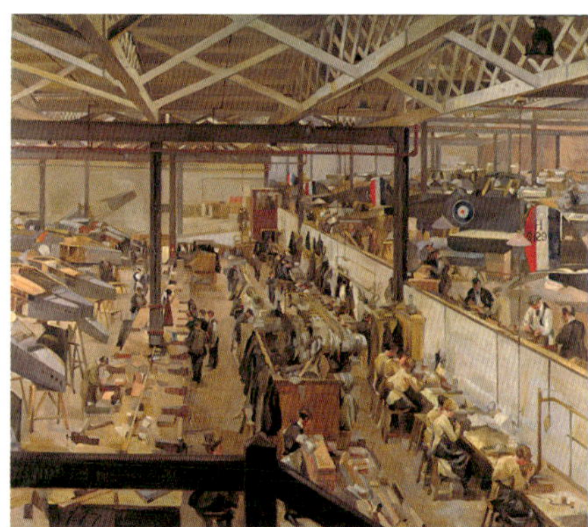

Airy, Anna 1882–1964
An Aircraft Assembly Shop, Hendon 1918
oil on canvas 182.8 x 213.3
IWM ART 1931

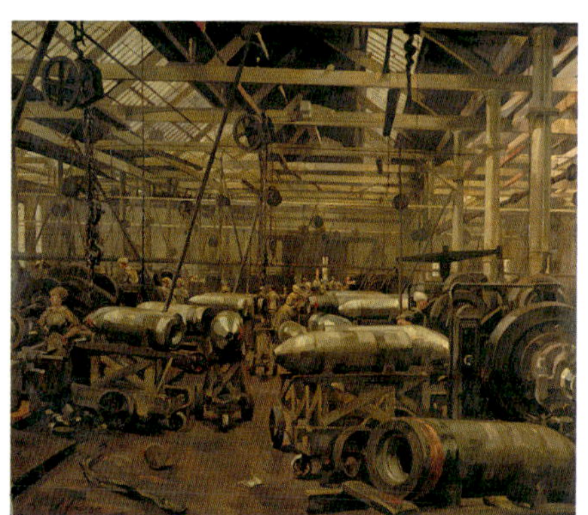

Airy, Anna 1882–1964
*Shop for Machining 15-Inch Shells: Singer
Manufacturing Company, Clydebank, Glasgow*
1918
oil on canvas 182.8 x 213.3
IWM ART 2271

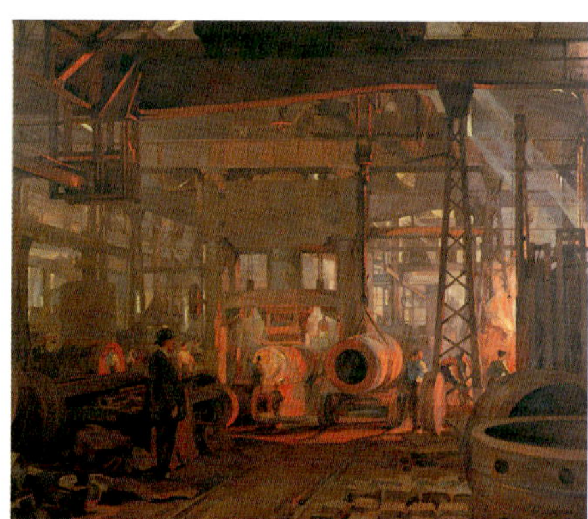

Airy, Anna 1882–1964
*The 'L' Press: Forging the Jacket of an 18-Inch
Gun, Armstrong-Whitworth Works, Openshaw*
1918
oil on canvas 183.8 x 214.5
IWM ART 2272

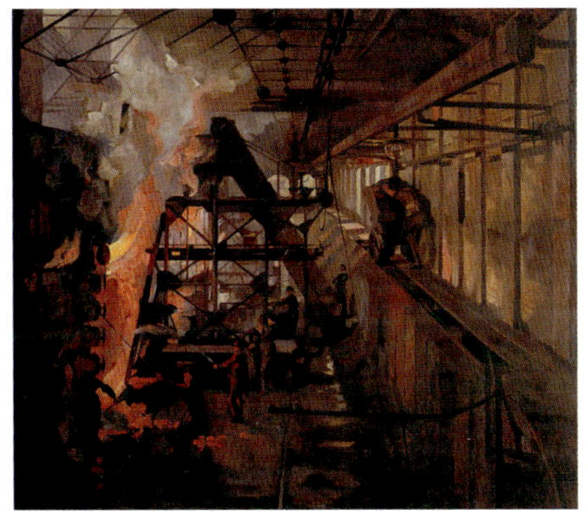

Airy, Anna 1882–1964
Women Working in a Gas Retort House: South Metropolitan Gas Company, London 1918
oil on canvas 184.7 x 217.1
IWM ART 2852

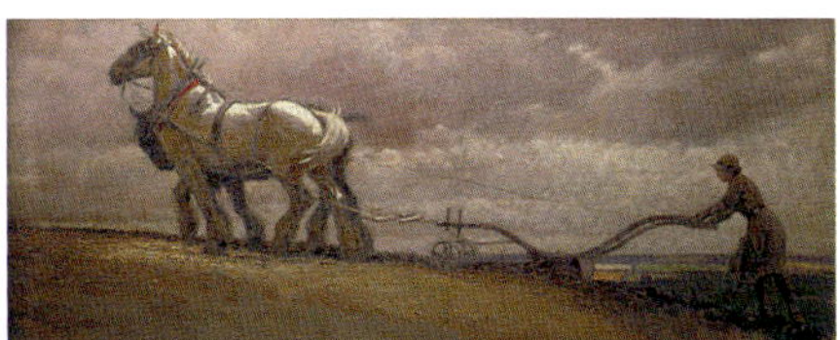

Aldin, Cecil 1870–1935
A Land Girl Ploughing c.1918
oil on canvas 91.4 x 228.6
IWM ART 2618

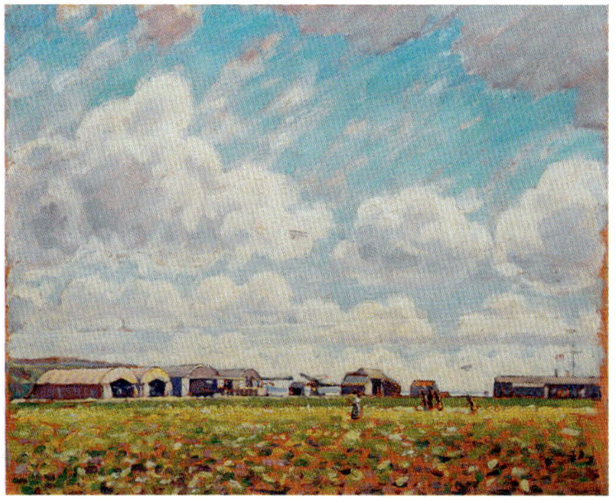

Allfree, Geoffrey Stephen 1889–1918
The Seaplane Station, Scapa Flow, Orkney 1917
oil on panel 32.3 x 40.6
IWM ART 151

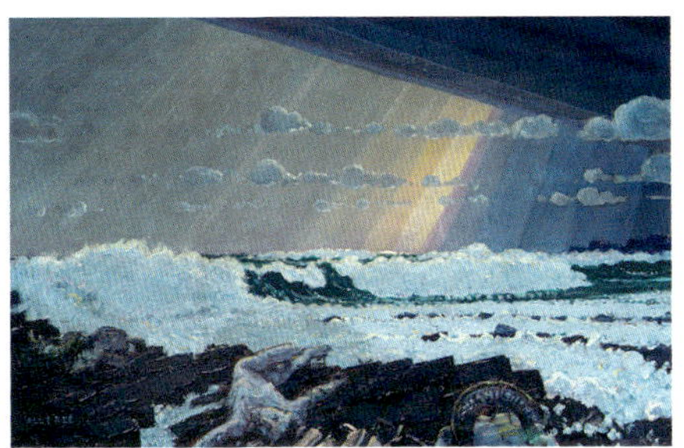

Allfree, Geoffrey Stephen 1889–1918
The Wreck of the 'Hampshire' c.1917–1918
oil on canvas 50.5 x 75.5
IWM ART 5252

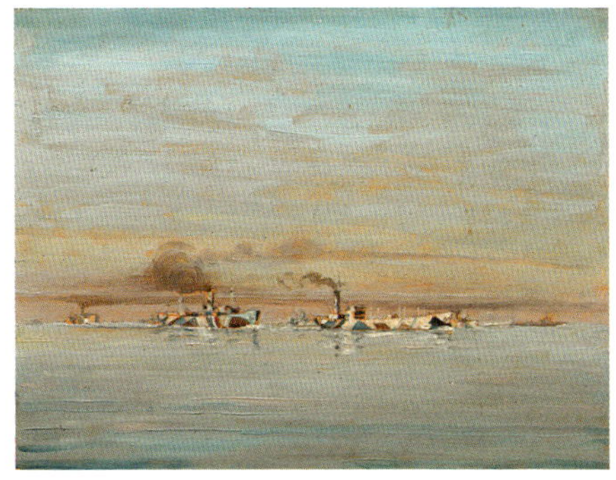

Allfree, Geoffrey Stephen 1889–1918
A Convoy in the Channel 1918
oil on panel 30.4 x 40.6 (E)
IWM ART 560

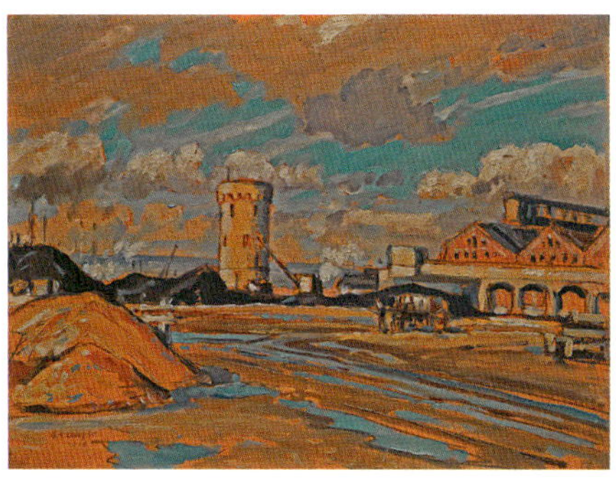

Allfree, Geoffrey Stephen 1889–1918
A Corner of a Dockyard 1918
oil on panel 30.4 x 40.6 (E)
IWM ART 561

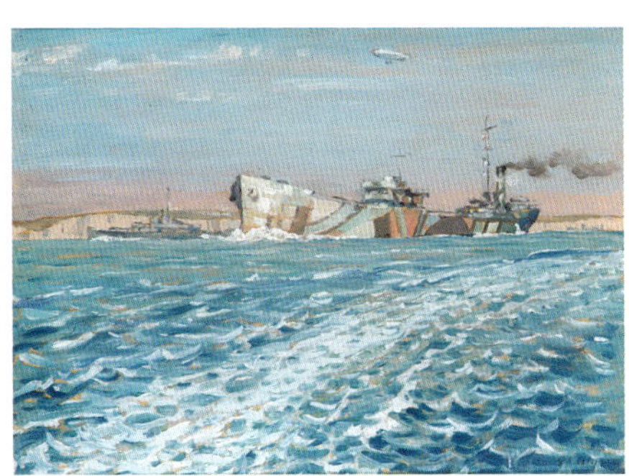

Allfree, Geoffrey Stephen 1889–1918
A Dazzled Oiler, with Escort 1918
oil on panel 31.7 x 41.9
IWM ART 567

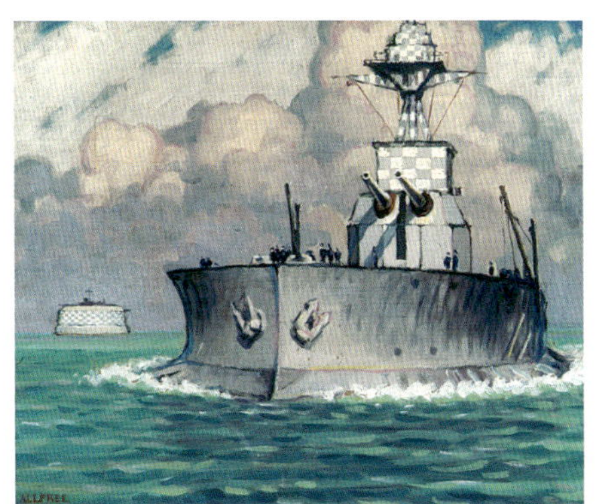

Allfree, Geoffrey Stephen 1889–1918
A Monitor 1918
oil on canvas 40.6 x 50.8
IWM ART 568

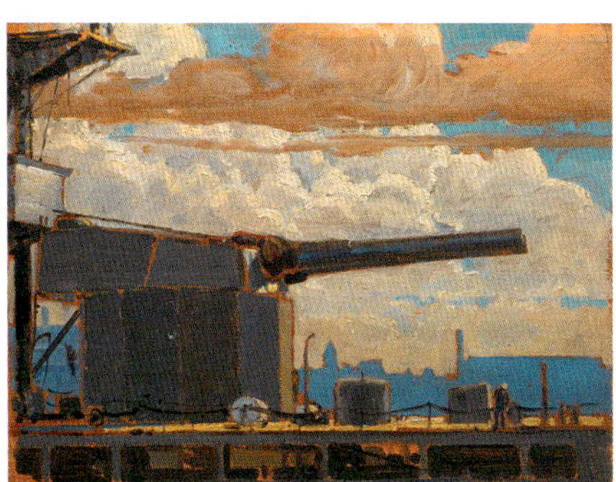

Allfree, Geoffrey Stephen 1889–1918
A Monitor's Turret 1918
oil on panel 30.4 x 40.6 (E)
IWM ART 564

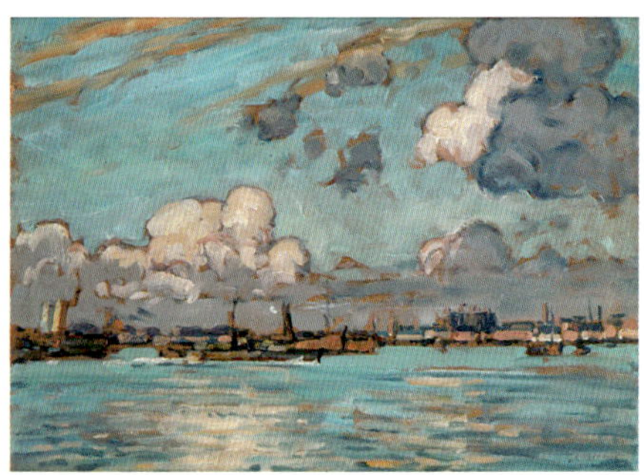

Allfree, Geoffrey Stephen 1889–1918
A Sketch in Portsmouth Harbour 1918
oil on panel 30.4 x 40.6 (E)
IWM ART 566

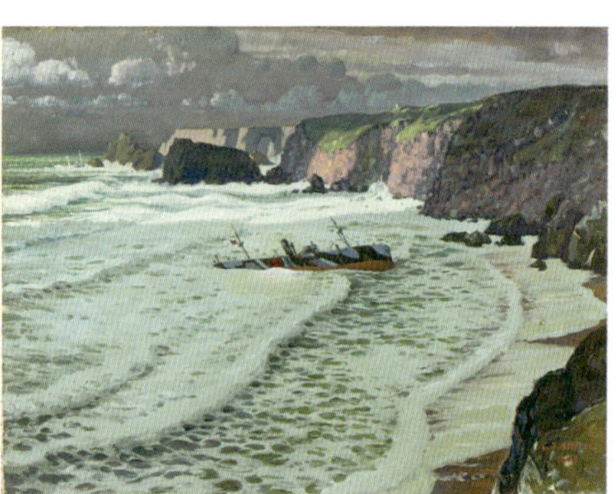

Allfree, Geoffrey Stephen 1889–1918
A Torpedoed Tramp Steamer off the Longships, Cornwall 1918
oil on canvas 45.7 x 60.9
IWM ART 2237

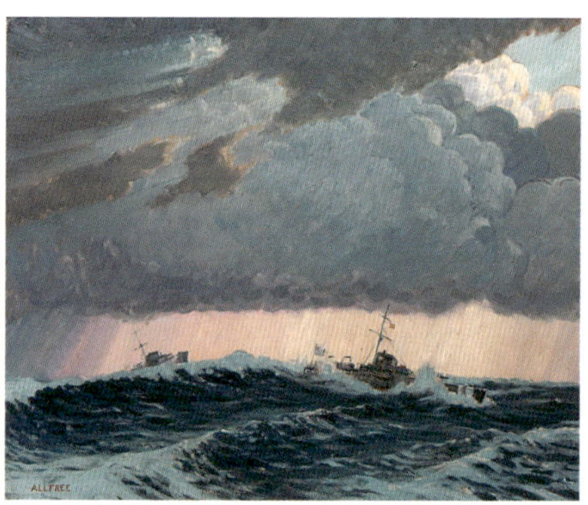

Allfree, Geoffrey Stephen 1889–1918
Motor Launches 1918
oil on canvas 64.7 x 76.2
IWM ART 1081

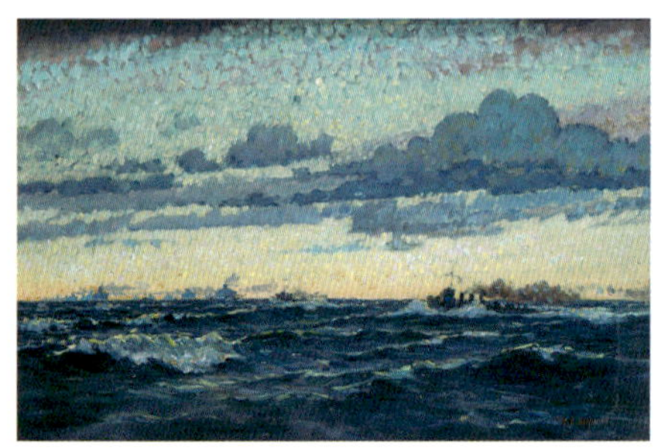

Allfree, Geoffrey Stephen 1889–1918
Seascape with Convoy and Evening Sky Effect 1918
oil on canvas 50.8 x 76.2
IWM ART 569

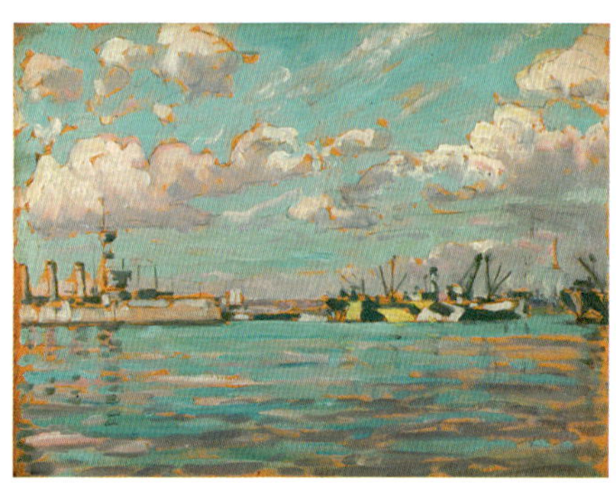

Allfree, Geoffrey Stephen 1889–1918
Ships in No.1 Basin 1918
oil on panel 30.4 x 40.6 (E)
IWM ART 565

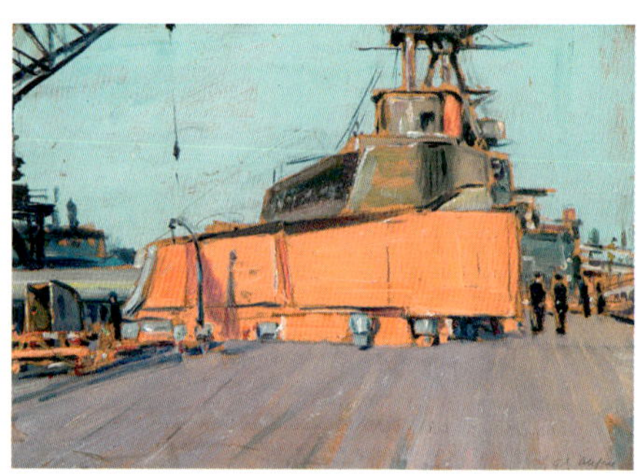

Allfree, Geoffrey Stephen 1889–1918
The Quarter-Deck of a Battleship 1918
oil on panel 30.4 x 40.6 (E)
IWM ART 562

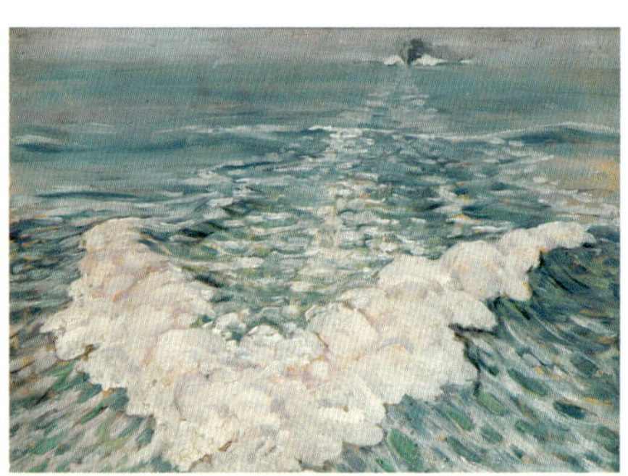

Allfree, Geoffrey Stephen 1889–1918
The Wake of a 'P' Boat 1918
oil on panel 30.4 x 40.6
IWM ART 563

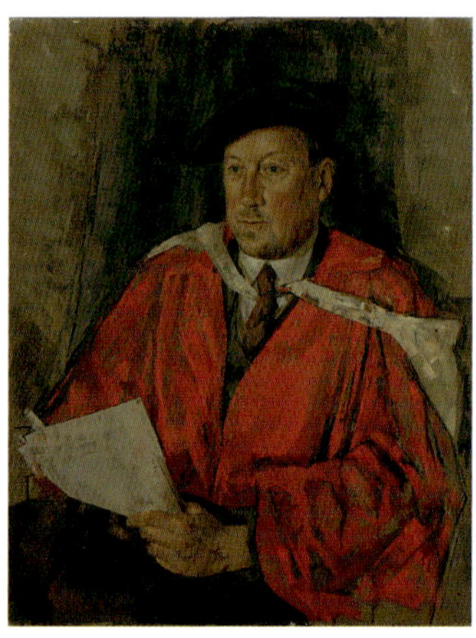

Appelbee, Leonard 1914–2000
Sir Robert Watson-Watt (1892–1973), CB, FRS, Radar Scientist 1945
oil on canvas 67.2 x 60.9
IWM ART LD 5744

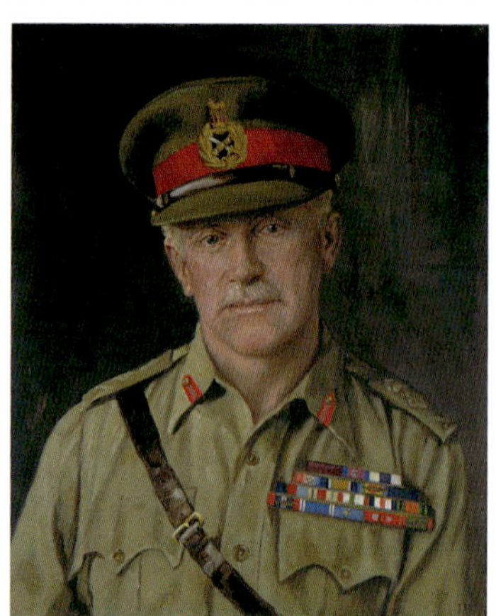

Aris, J. active 1940s
General Sir Richard Nugent O'Connor (1889–1981), KT, GCB, DSO, MC c.1940–1945
oil on canvas 60.9 x 50.8
IWM ART LD 7385

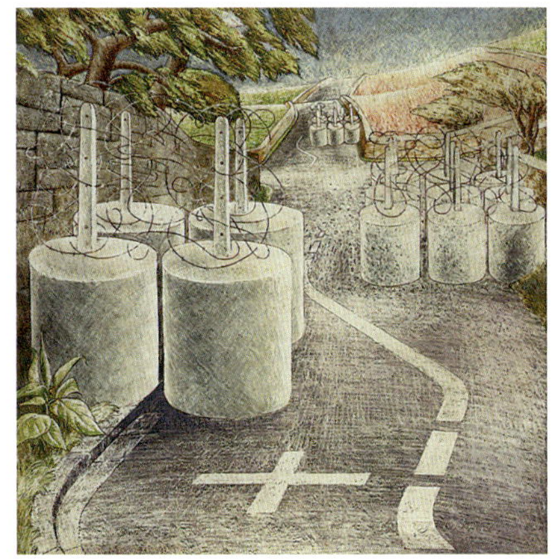

Armfield, Stuart 1916–2000
Anti-Invasion Obstacles on a Road 1940
tempera on board 33.5 x 33.5
IWM ART 15972

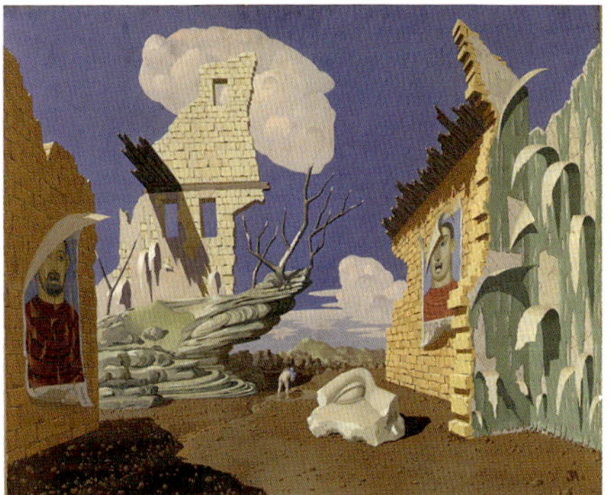

Armstrong, John 1893–1973
Pro Patria 1938
tempera on board 75.8 x 93.6
IWM ART 16547

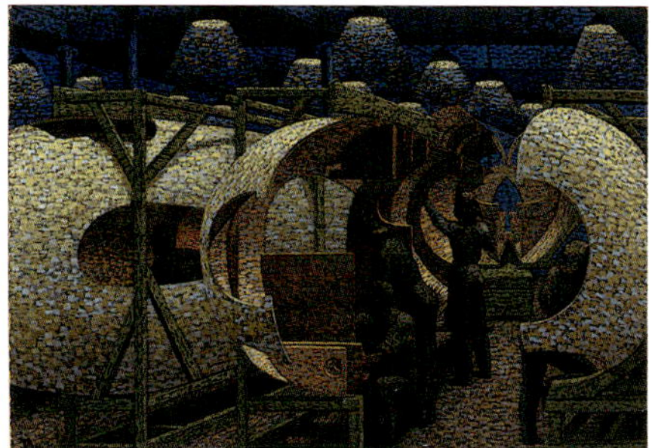

Armstrong, John 1893–1973
Building Mosquitoes 1943
tempera on panel 55.8 x 81.2
IWM ART LD 3359

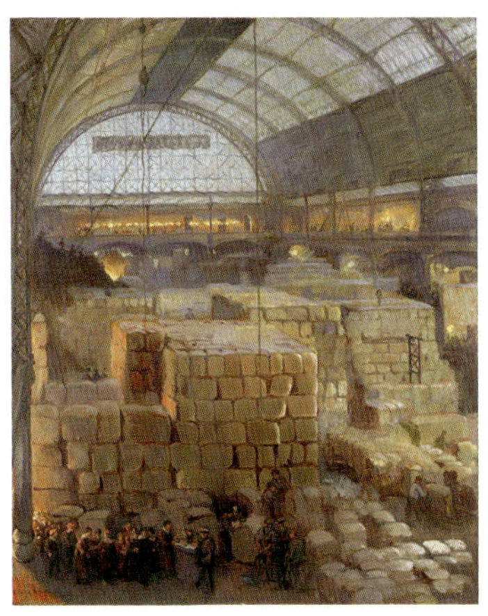

Atwood, Clare 1866–1962
Olympia in War Time: Royal Army Clothing Depot 1918
oil on canvas 60.9 x 50.8
IWM ART 2919

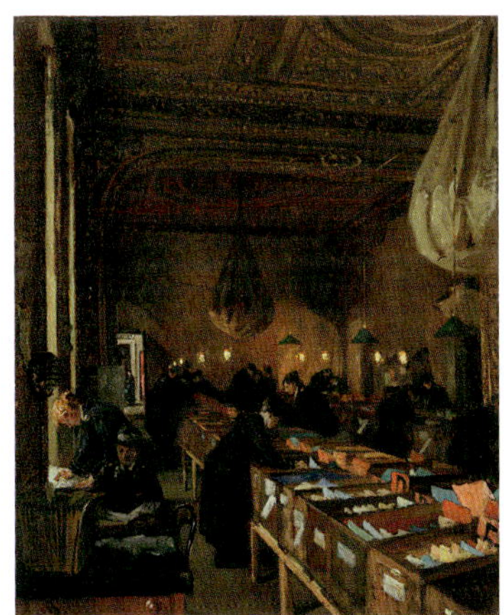

Atwood, Clare 1866–1962
Devonshire House, 1918: Voluntary Aid Detachment Workers Filing Papers in the Ballroom 1919
oil on canvas 76.3 x 63.5
IWM ART 2514

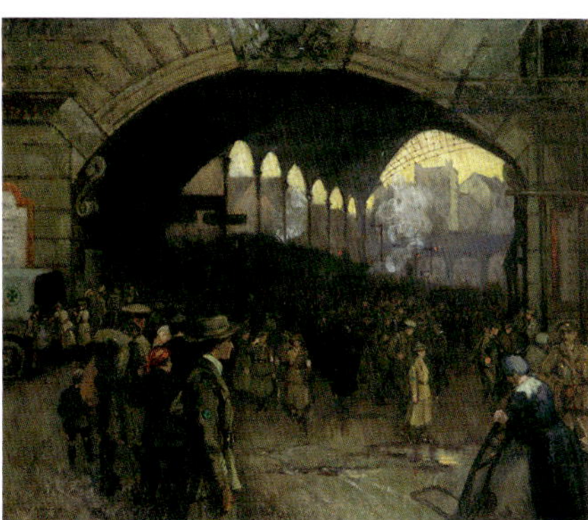

Atwood, Clare 1866–1962
Victoria Station, 1918: The Green Cross Corps (Women's Reserve Ambulance), Guiding Soldiers on Leave 1919
oil on canvas 63.5 x 76.2
IWM ART 2513

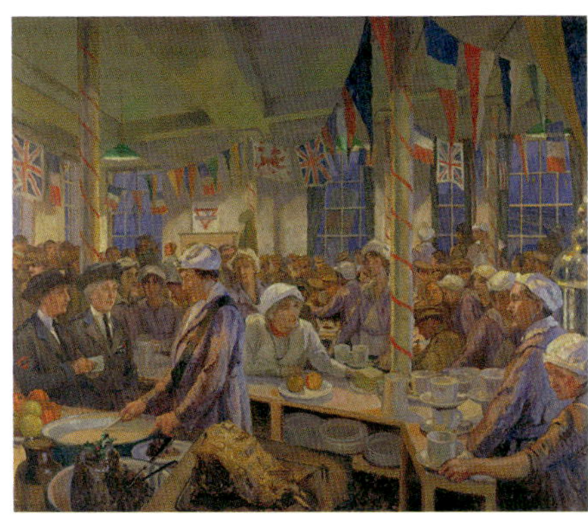

Atwood, Clare 1866–1962
Christmas Day in the London Bridge Young Men's Christian Association Canteen: Her Royal Highness Princess Helena (…) 1920
oil on canvas 152.4 x 182.8
IWM ART 3062

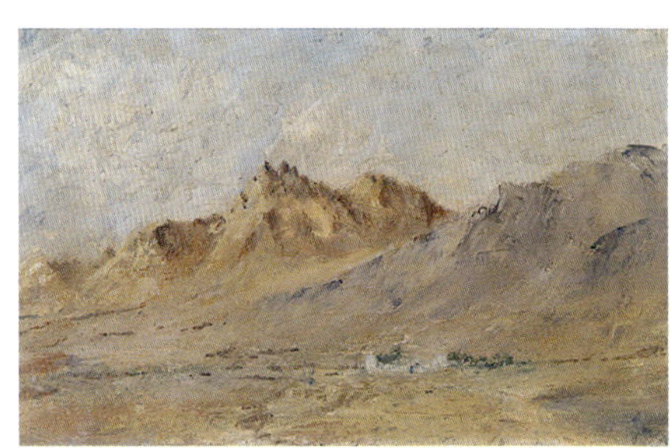

Auchinleck, Claude J. 1884–1981
Frontier Hills, Quetta, April 1954 1954
oil on board 24.1 x 40.6
IWM ART LD 6124

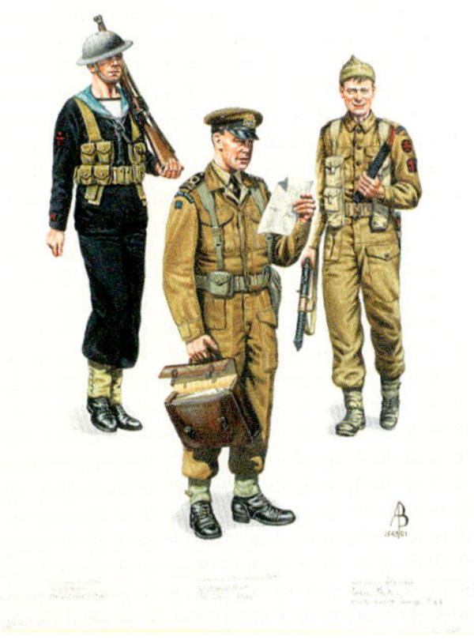

Baker, Alix b.1947
Royal Navy, World War Two: Leading Wire Man, Landing Party, Home Waters, 1940; Leading Seaman, Beach Party (…) 2000
acrylic on paper 38 x 27.2
IWM ART 17108 2

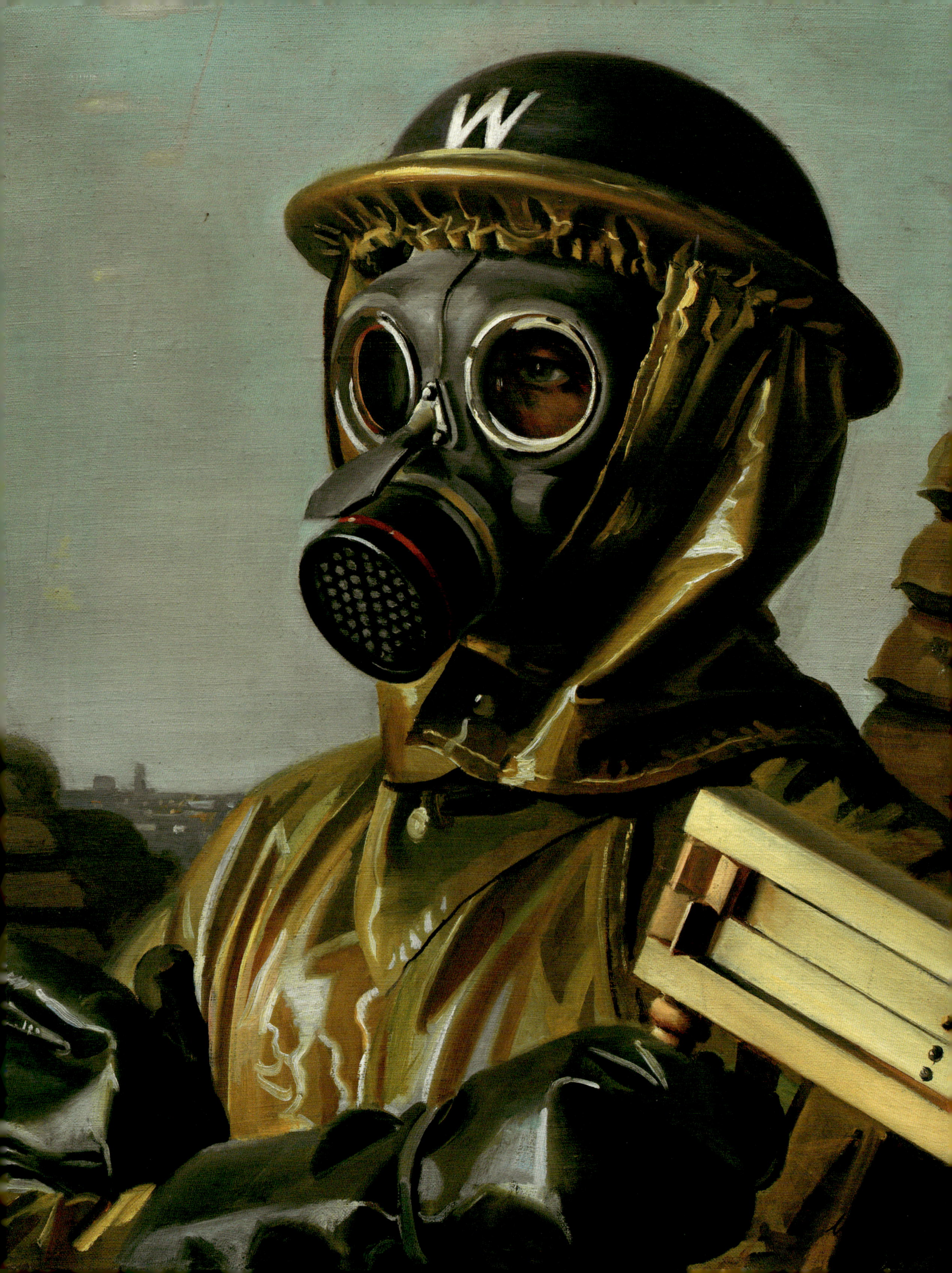

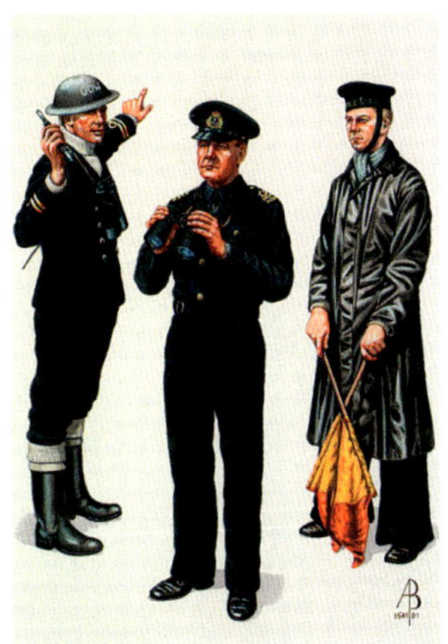

Baker, Alix b.1947
Royal Navy, World War Two: Lieutenant, Home Waters, 1941; Lieutenant Royal Naval Reserve, Home Waters, 1941 (…) 2000
acrylic on paper 38 x 27.2
IWM ART 17108 1

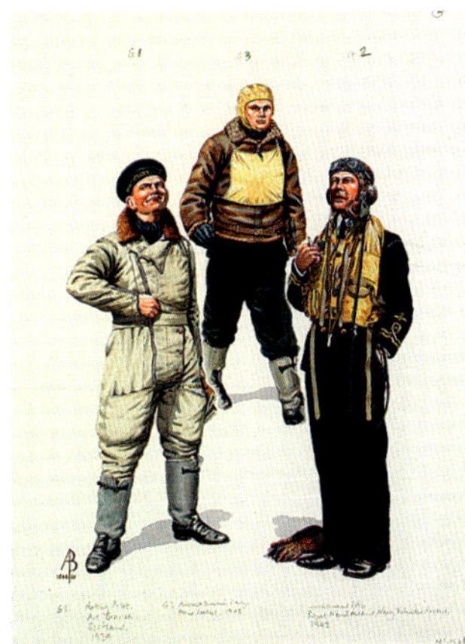

Baker, Alix b.1947
Air Branch, World War Two: Rating Pilot, Air Branch, Scotland, 1939; Lieutenant (A), Royal New Zealand Navy Volunteer (…) 2001
acrylic on paper 38 x 27.2 (E)
IWM ART 17108 7

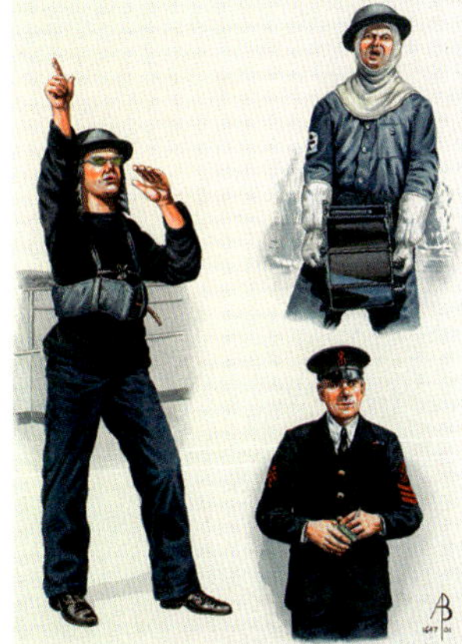

Baker, Alix b.1947
Anti-Aircraft Home Waters, Royal Navy, World War Two: Rating Home Waters, 1942; Anti-Aircraft Rating Third Class, Home (…) 2001
acrylic on paper 38 x 27.2
IWM ART 17108 6

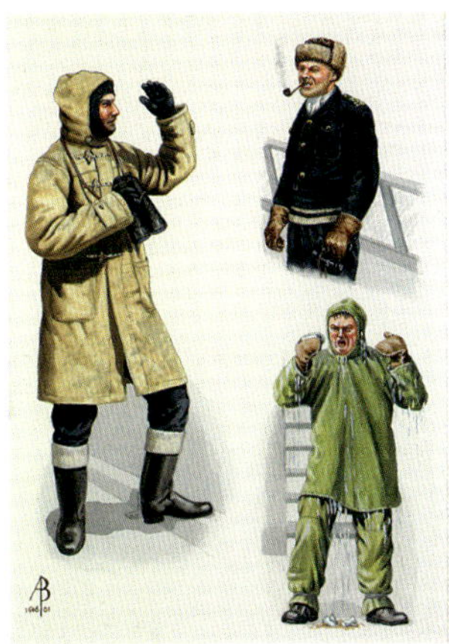

Baker, Alix b.1947
Northern Waters, Royal Navy, World War Two: Rating Northern Waters, 1943, Lieutenant, Royal Naval Volunteer Reserve (…) 2001
acrylic on paper 38 x 27.2
IWM ART 17108 5

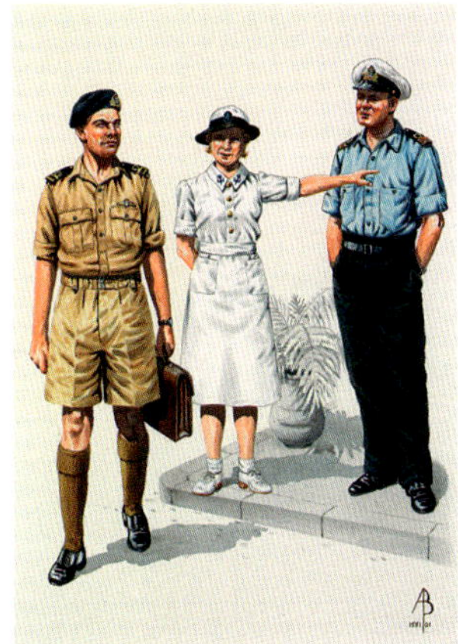

Baker, Alix b.1947
Pacific and Far East, Royal Navy, World War Two: Lieutenant Commander, Pacific, 1945; Women's Royal Naval Service (…) 2001
acrylic on paper 38 x 27.2
IWM ART 17108 10

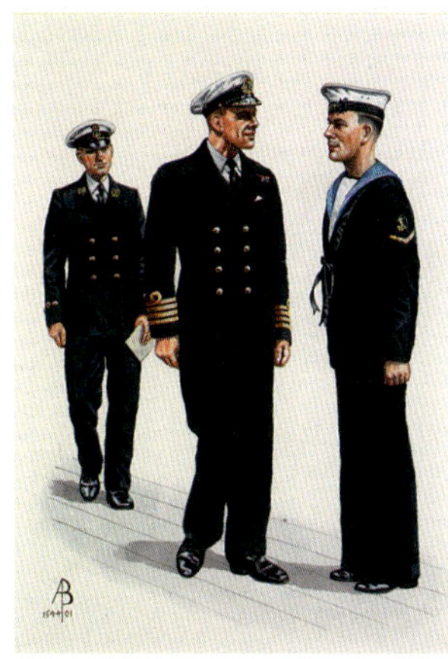

Baker, Alix b.1947
Royal Navy, 1939: Captain, Master at Arms, Leading Seaman 2001
acrylic on paper 38 x 27.2
IWM ART 17108 3

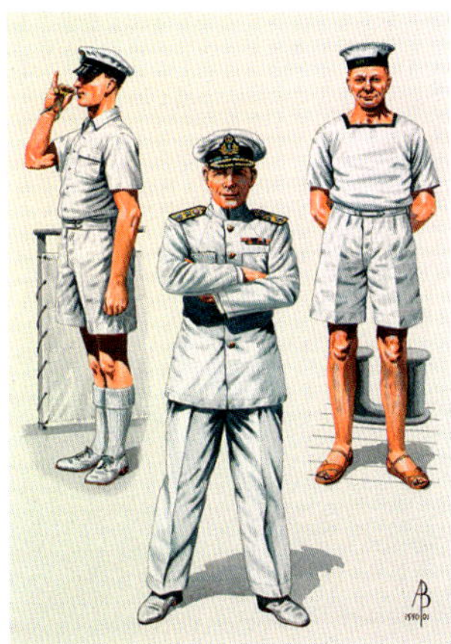

Baker, Alix b.1947
Royal Navy, Far East, World War Two: Petty Officer 1940, Rear Admiral, 1940; Rating, Far East, 1945 2001
acrylic on paper 38 x 27.2
IWM ART 17108 9

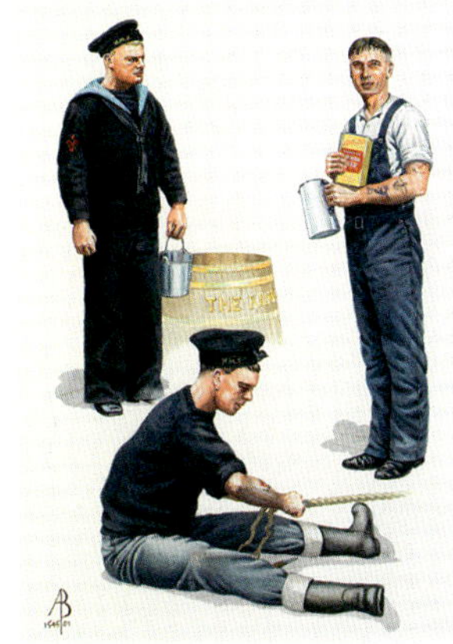

Baker, Alix b.1947
Royal Navy, World War Two: Visual Signalman, 1939; Rating (Overalls) Home Waters, 1944; Rating, Coastal (…) 2001
acrylic on paper 38 x 27.2
IWM ART 17108 4

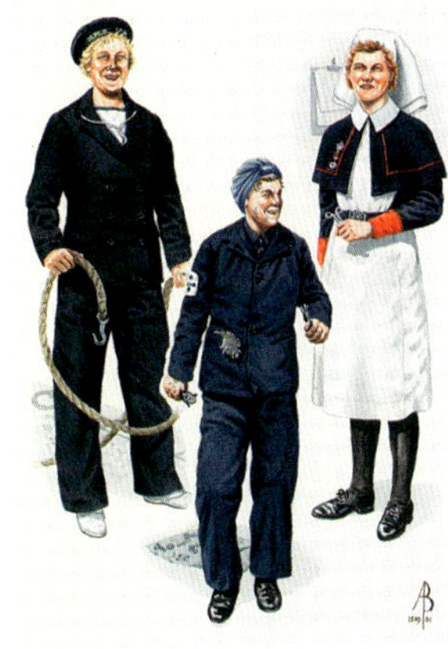

Baker, Alix b.1947
Women's Royal Naval Service and Queen Alexandra's Royal Naval Nursing Service: Women's Royal Naval Service (…) 2001
acrylic on paper 38 x 27.2
IWM ART 17108 8

Facing page: Brealey, William Ramsden, 1889–1949, *Gas Mask* (detail), 1939, (p. 24)

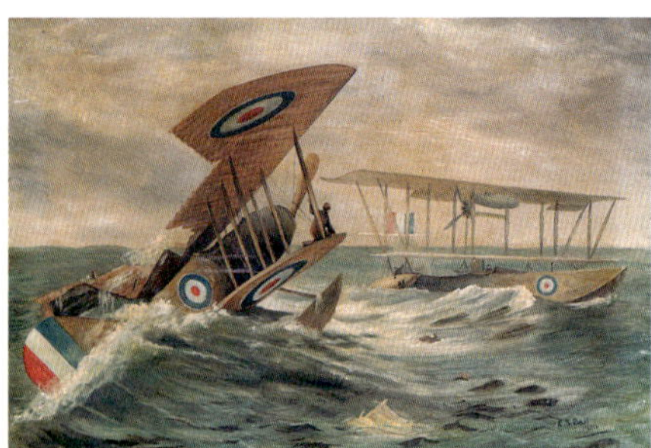

Ball, C. S. active 1920s
The Rescue 1920
oil on canvas 50.8 x 76.2
IWM ART 5601

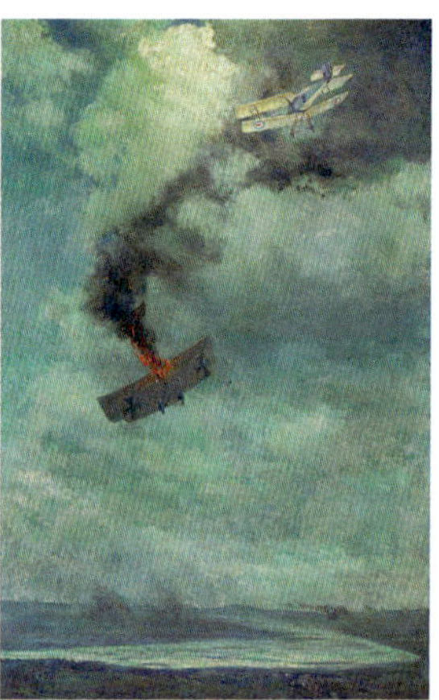

Barberis, Mario
British 'Nieuport Scout' Destroying an Enemy Biplane in Italy
oil on canvas 146 x 95.8
IWM ART 4202

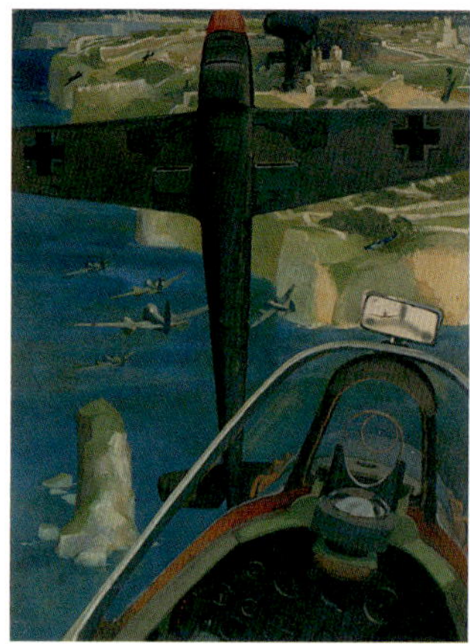

Barnham, Denis A. b.1920
Battle over Malta: Spitfire Attacking JU 88s but in a Dog-Fight with ME 109s 1942
oil on canvas 101.9 x 76.2
IWM ART LD 3960

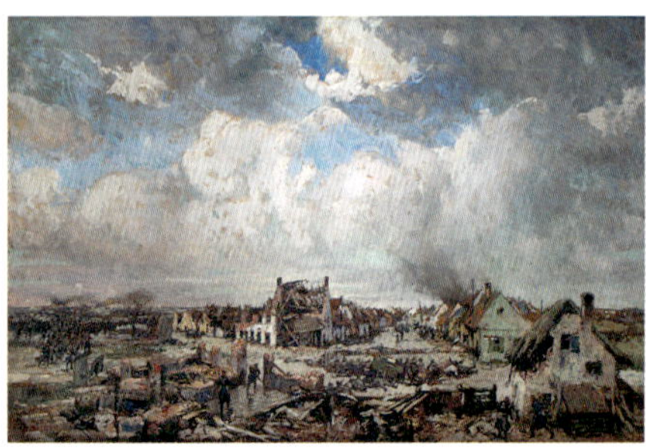

Bastien, Alfred 1873–1955
The Battle of Pervyse, 25 October 1914 1914
oil on canvas 147.3 x 195.5
IWM ART 4666

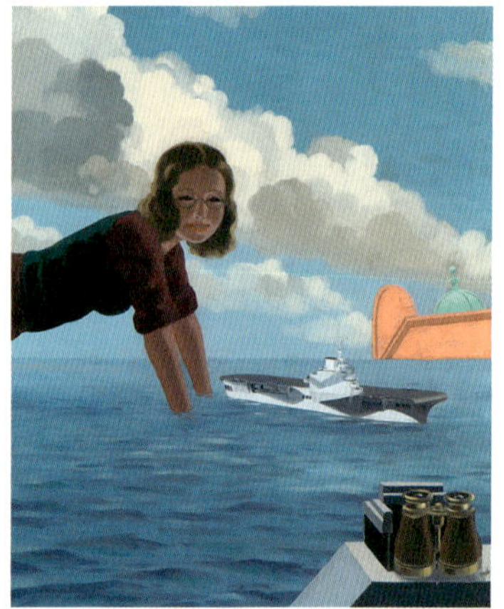

Bateman, John Yunge active 1943–1958
The Outside Viewing Tank: Directorate of Camouflage, Naval Section 1943
oil on canvas 66 x 55.2
IWM ART LD 2759

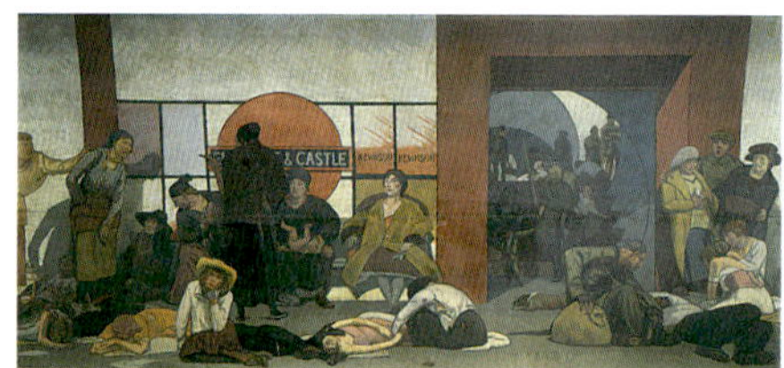

Bayes, Walter 1869–1956
The Underworld: Taking Cover in a Tube Station during a London Air Raid 1918
oil on canvas 254 x 548.6
IWM ART 935

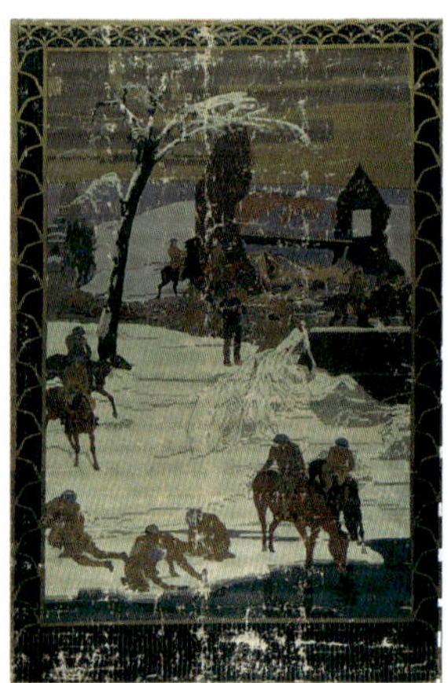

Bayes, Walter 1869–1956
The Road to Peace: Design for Tapestry 1919
oil on canvas 396.2 x 236.2
IWM ART 2753

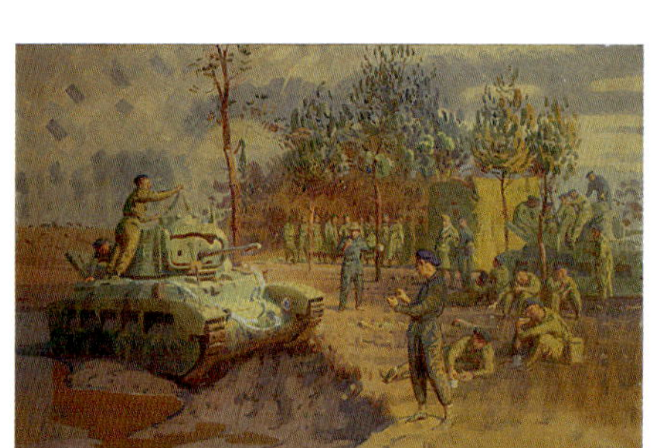

Bayes, Walter 1869–1956
The Armoured Fighting Vehicle School, Bovington: Lunch on the Driving Grounds 1940
oil on canvas 73.6 x 115.5
IWM ART LD 1157

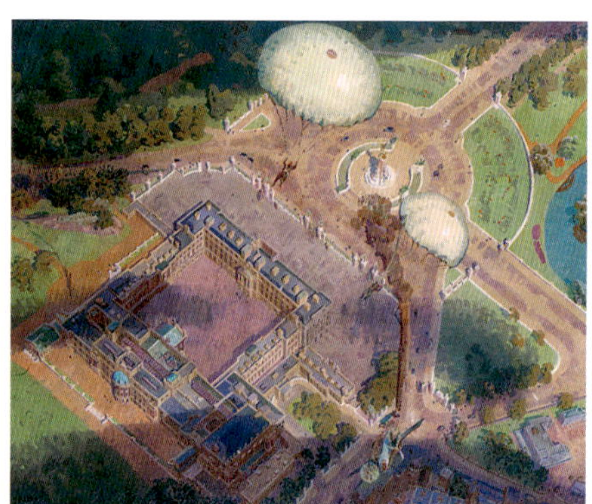

Bayes, Walter 1869–1956
Battle of Britain: Parachutists from an Enemy Aircraft Brought down in an Apparent Attempt to Bomb Buckingham Palace 1942
oil on canvas 119 x 140.9
IWM ART LD 2514

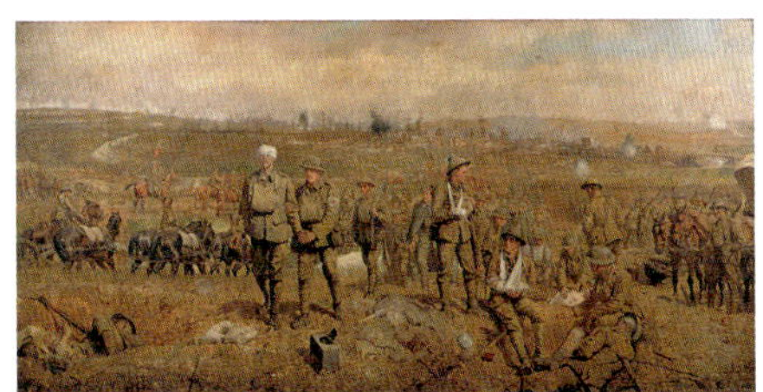

Beadle, James Prinsep 1863–1947
The Breaking of the Hindenburg Line 1918
oil on canvas 182.8 x 368.3
IWM ART 6296

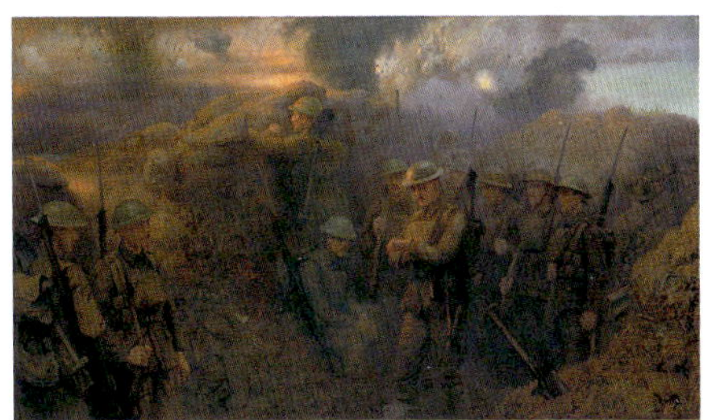

Beadle, James Prinsep 1863–1947
Zero Hour 1918
oil on canvas 107.9 x 185.4
IWM ART 5131

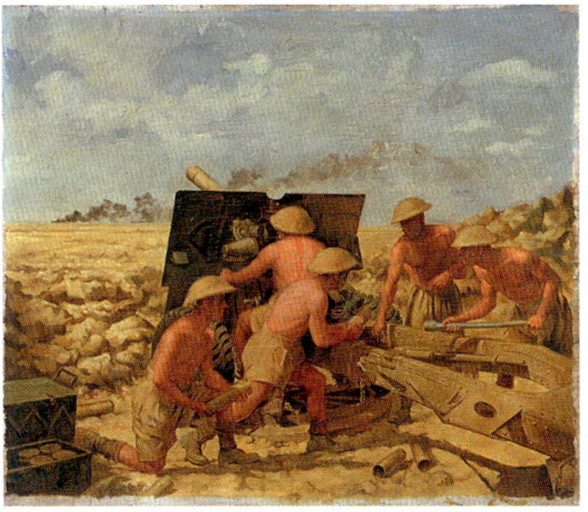

Berry, John b.1920
25-Pounder Gun and Team in Action on the El Alamein Front 1942
oil on panel 40.6 x 49.5
IWM ART LD 2788

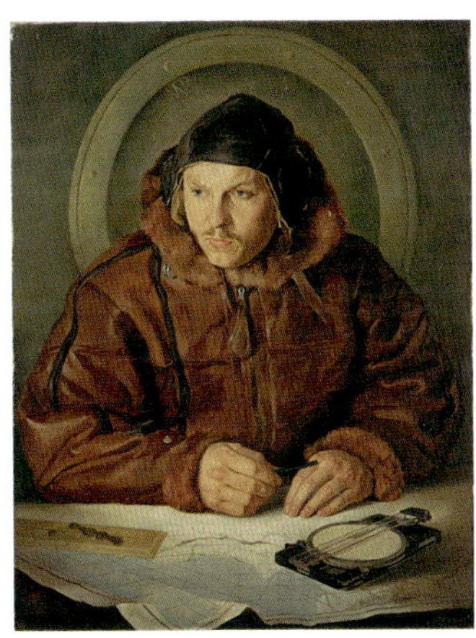

Berry, John b.1920
A Pathfinder 1943
oil on canvas 91.4 x 71.1
IWM ART LD 2939

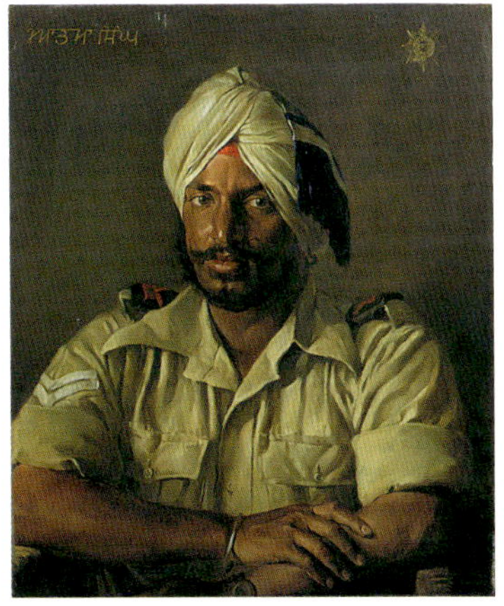

Berry, John b.1920
A Sikh: Atma Singh 1943
oil on canvas 76.2 x 63.5
IWM ART LD 3862

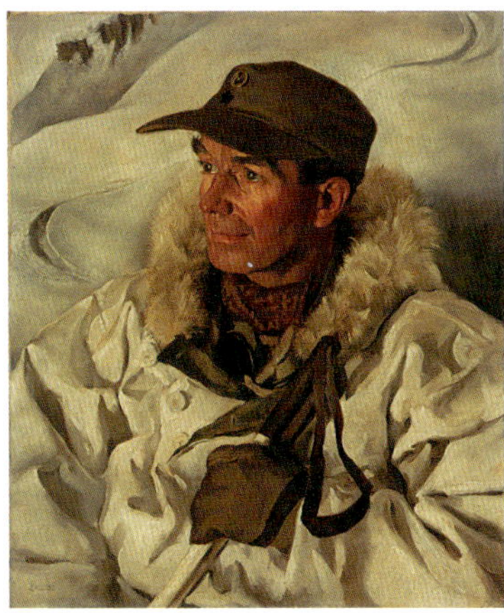

Berry, John b.1920
Major W. J. Riddell, Chief Instructor of the Mountaineer Wing of the Mountain Warfare School, Marine Expeditionary Force 1944
oil on canvas 58.4 x 50.8
IWM ART LD 3978

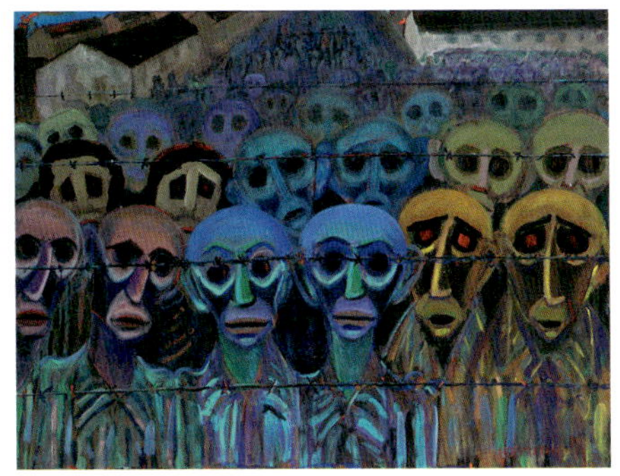

Birkin, Edith b.1927
A Camp of Twins: Auschwitz 1980–1982
oil on board 71.2 x 91.4
IWM ART 15588

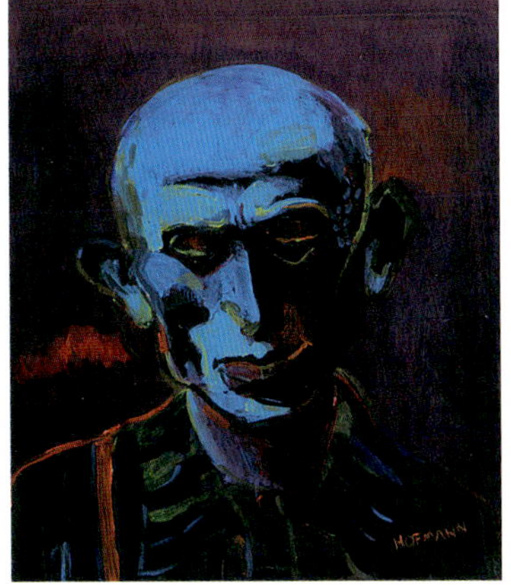

Birkin, Edith b.1927
Liberation Day 1980–1982
oil on board 53.3 x 45.7
IWM ART 15590

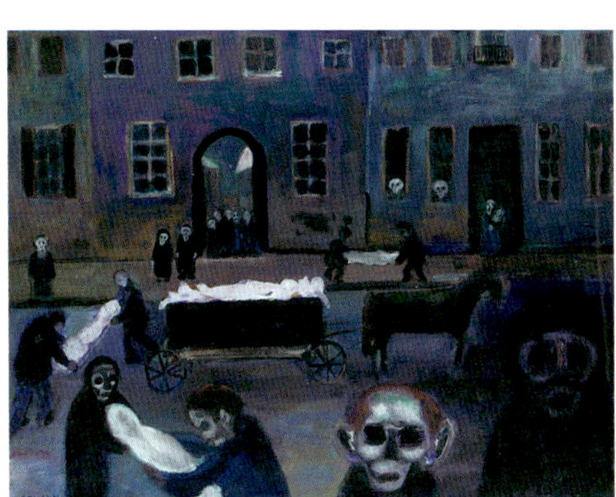

Birkin, Edith b.1927
The Death Cart: Lodz Ghetto 1980–1982
oil on board 71.2 x 91.4
IWM ART 15587

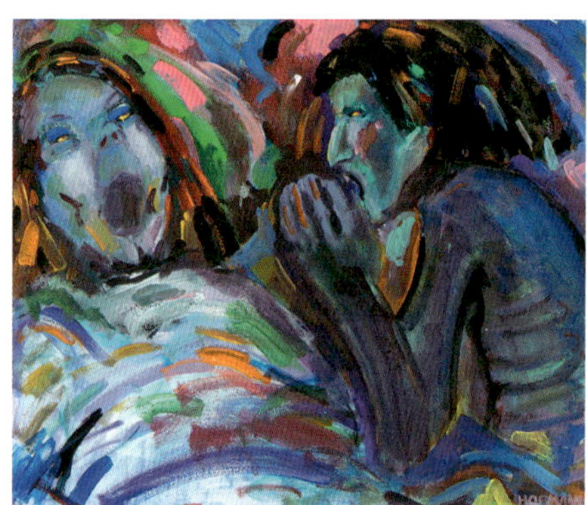

Birkin, Edith b.1927
The Last Gasp: Gas Chamber 1980–1982
oil on board 50.8 x 60.9
IWM ART 15589

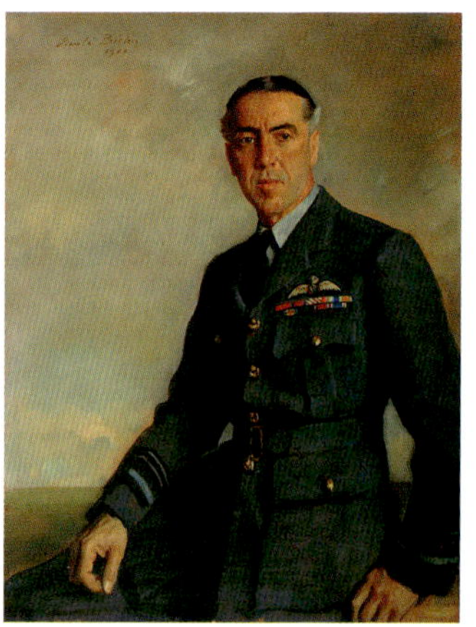

Birley, Oswald Hornby Joseph 1880–1952
*Air Marshal Sir Richard Peirse (1892–1970),
KCB, DSO, AFC* 1940
oil on canvas 137.1 x 88.9
IWM ART LD 689

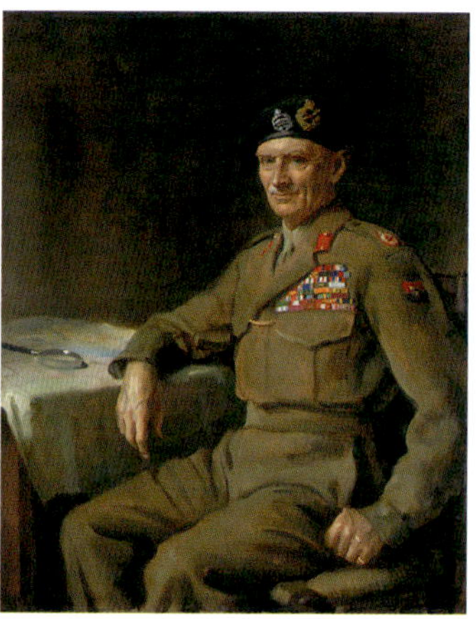

Birley, Oswald Hornby Joseph 1880–1952
*Field Marshal the Viscount Montgomery of
Alamein (1887–1976), KG, GCB, DSO* 1948
oil on canvas 127 x 88.9
IWM ART LD 5915

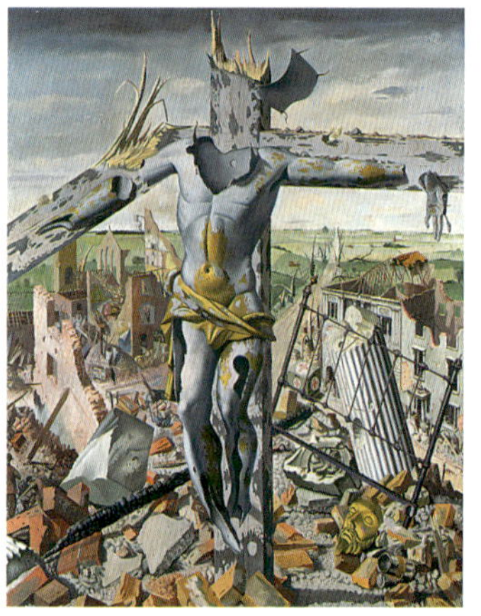

Blyth, Robert Henderson 1919–1970
In the Image of Man 1947
oil on canvas 127 x 101.6
IWM ART 16010

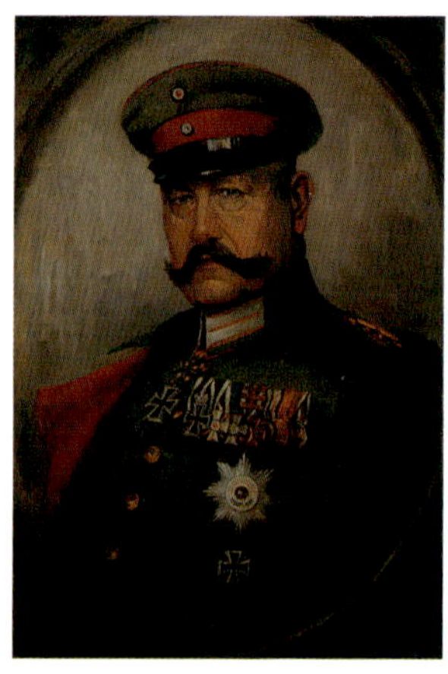

Böcher, August 1873–1961
*Field Marshal Von Hindenburg (1847–1934),
(formerly hung in the German battle cruiser
'Hindenburg')* c.1914–1918
oil on canvas 80 x 57.1
IWM ART 4216

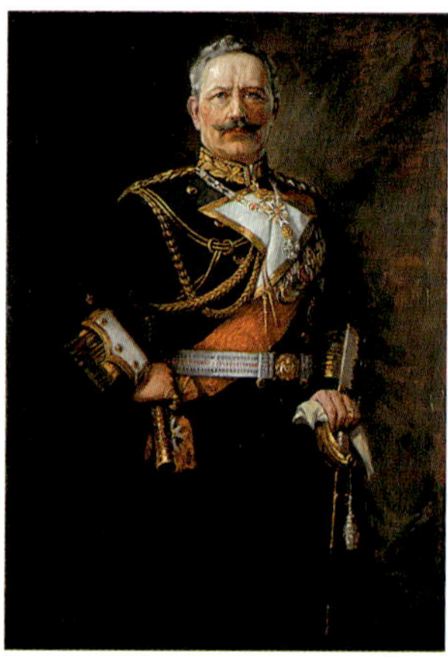

Böcher, August 1873–1961
Kaiser Wilhelm II (1859–1941) 1917
oil on canvas 104.7 x 76.2
IWM ART 5608

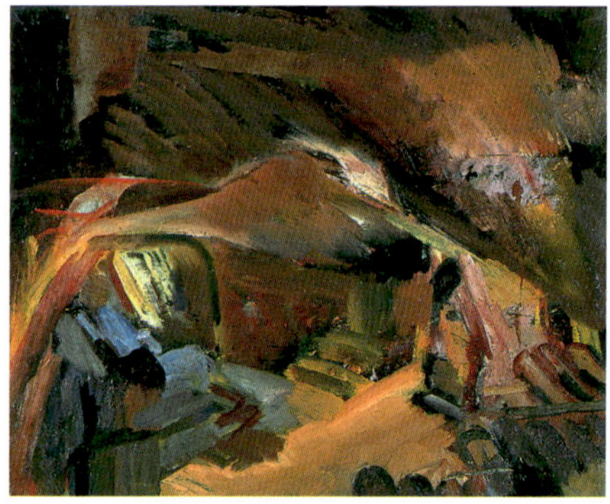

Bomberg, David 1890–1957
Bomb Store 1942
oil on canvas 59.6 x 75
IWM ART 16293

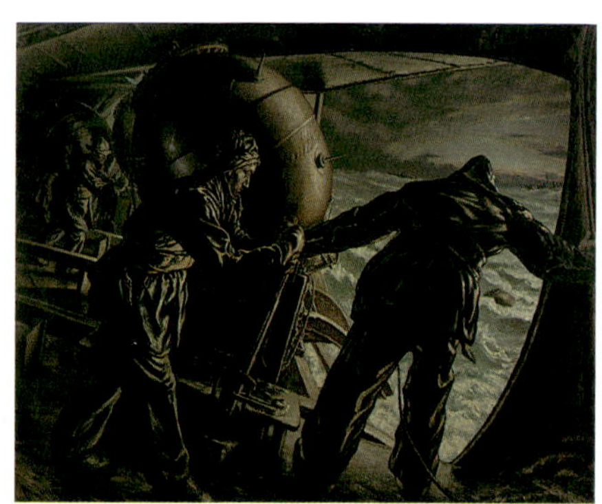

Bone, Muirhead 1876–1953
Winter Mine-Laying off Iceland c.1942
oil on canvas 127.9 x 160.6
IWM ART LD 1932

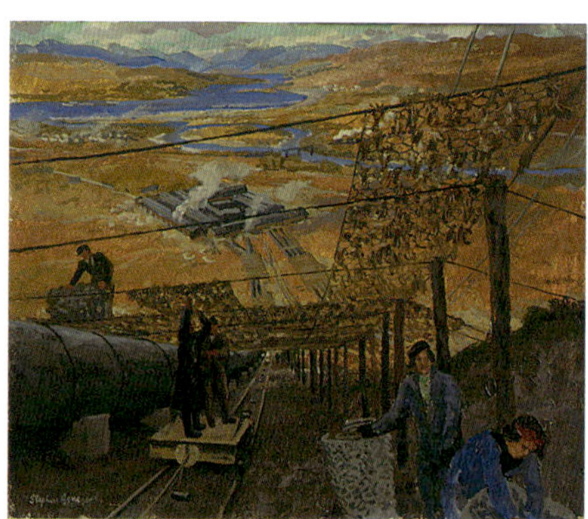

Bone, Stephen 1904–1958
*Camouflaging the Pipeline at the British
Aluminium Company's Works at Fort William,
October 1941* 1941
oil on card 49.5 x 59.6
IWM ART LD 1663

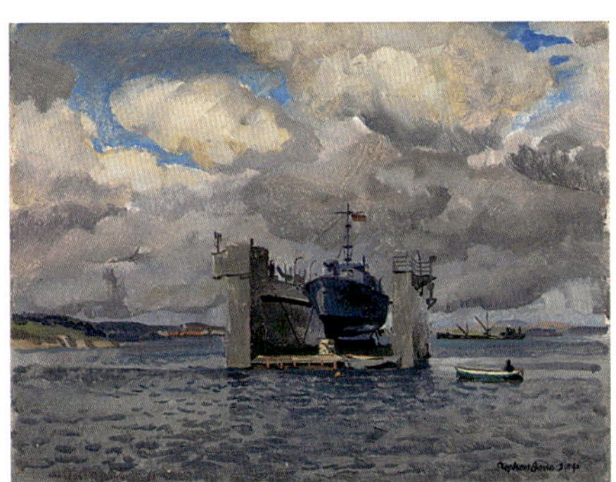

Bone, Stephen 1904–1958
*A Rescue Motor Launch in the Floating Dock,
Stornoway* 1942
oil on board 30.5 x 40.5
IWM ART LD 3115

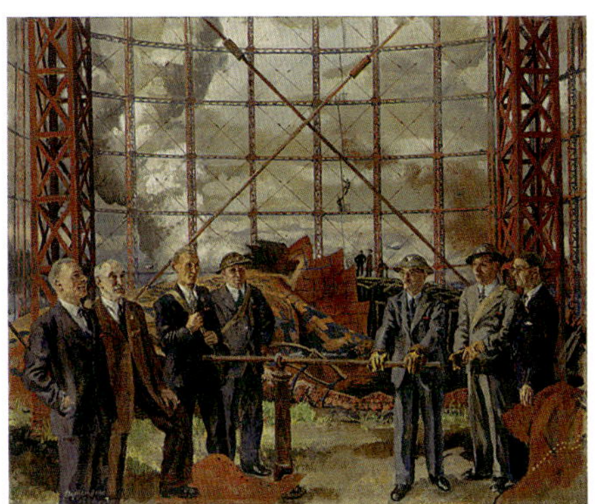

Bone, Stephen 1904–1958
Gas Workers 1942
oil on canvas 76.8 x 92
IWM ART LD 2430

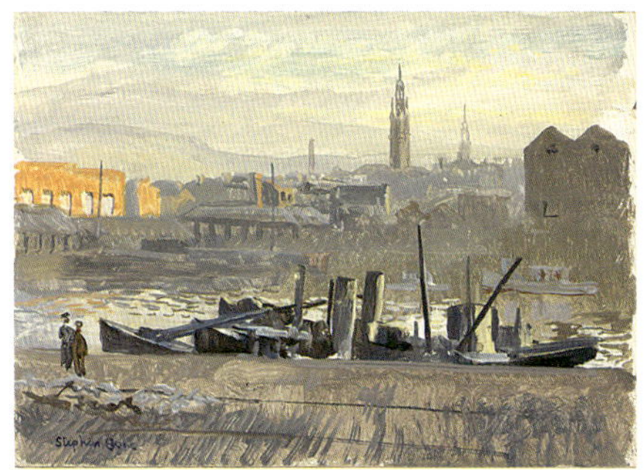

Bone, Stephen 1904–1958
*Drifters at Greenock with Hospital Launches
Beyond* c.1942–1944
oil on panel 25.1 x 35.5
IWM ART LD 4070

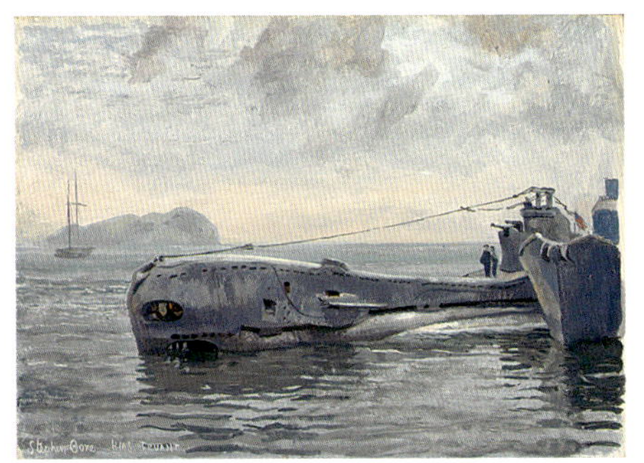

Bone, Stephen 1904–1958
'HMS Truant' c.1942–1944
oil on panel 25.4 x 35.5
IWM ART LD 4072

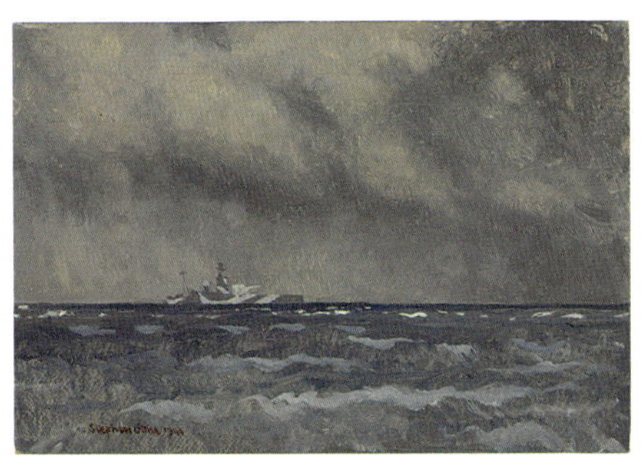

Bone, Stephen 1904–1958
Monitor: A Snowstorm Approaching
c.1942–1944
oil on panel 26.5 x 39.1
IWM ART LD 4075

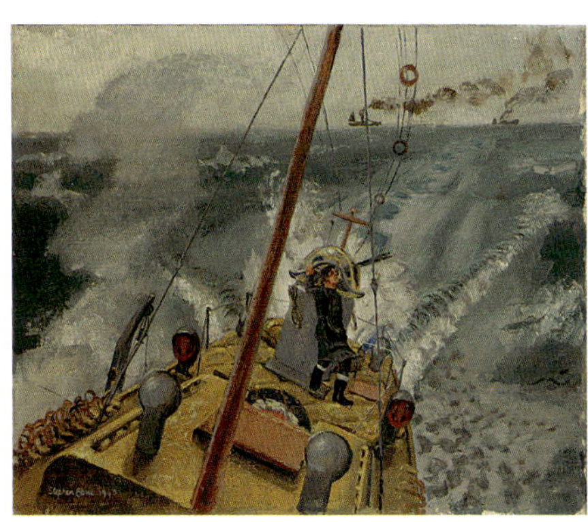

Bone, Stephen 1904–1958
Air-Sea Rescue 1943
oil on canvas 63.5 x 76.2
IWM ART LD 3213

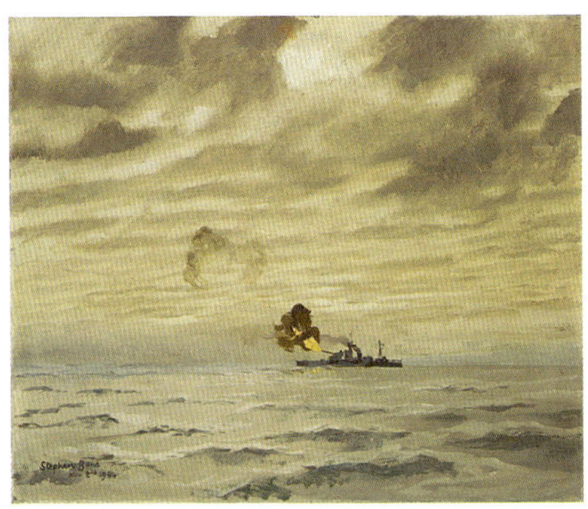

Bone, Stephen 1904–1958
'HMS Erebus' in Action off Walcheren 1943
oil on canvas 50.1 x 60.3
IWM ART LD 4706

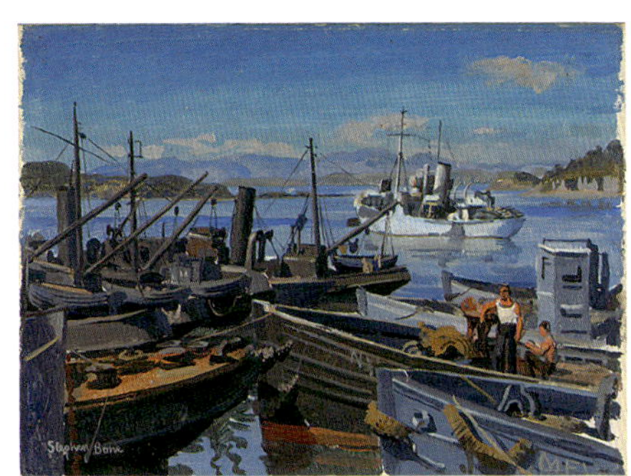

Bone, Stephen 1904–1958
'HMS Paul Rykens' and the Boat Pool, Oban
1943
oil on panel 24.7 x 34.2
IWM ART LD 3125

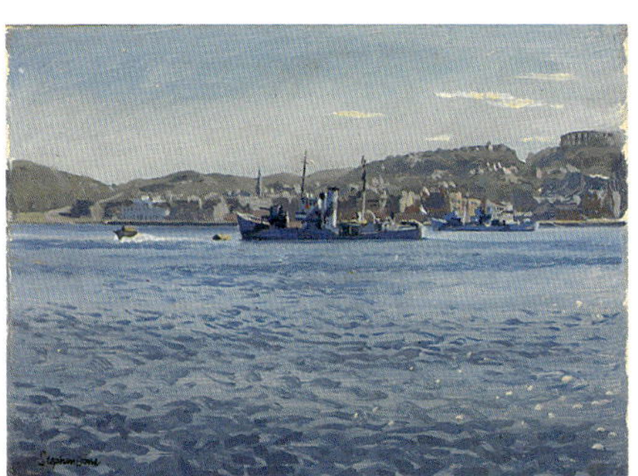

Bone, Stephen 1904–1958
*Oban Bay: Asdic Trawlers 'HMS Paul Rykens'
and 'HMS Southern Star'* 1943
oil on panel 25 x 35.5
IWM ART LD 3124

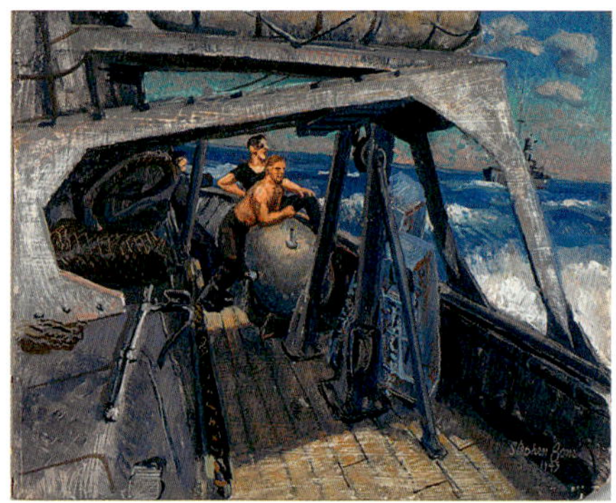

Bone, Stephen 1904–1958
*On Board a Minesweeper: Engine-Room Men
Take a Breath of Fresh Air* 1943
oil on panel 32.2 x 41
IWM ART LD 3275

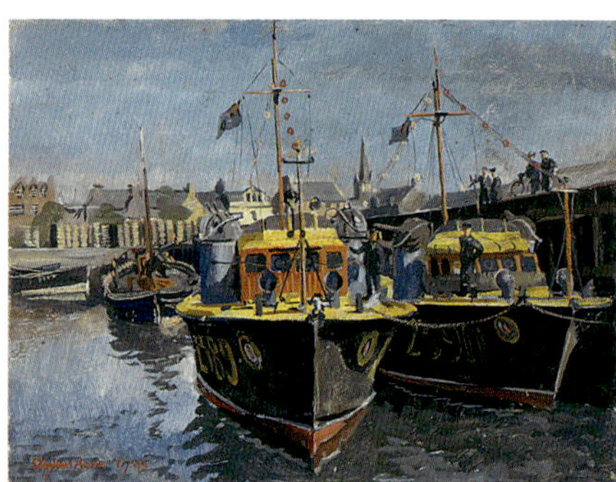

Bone, Stephen 1904–1958
*Royal Air Force Air Sea Rescue Launches,
Stornoway: The Fish Quay Beyond* 1943
oil on panel 30.2 x 40.5
IWM ART LD 3116

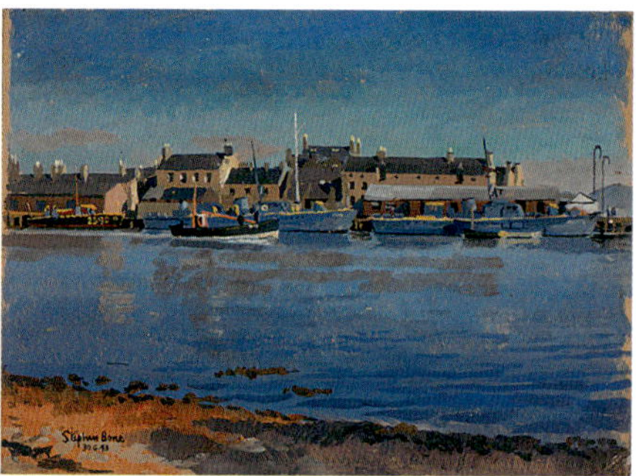

Bone, Stephen 1904–1958
*Royal Air Force Duty Boats and Naval Rescue
Launches at Stornoway: A Motor Drifter on Its
Way to the Fishing Grounds* 1943
oil on canvas board 26 x 35.5
IWM ART LD 3109

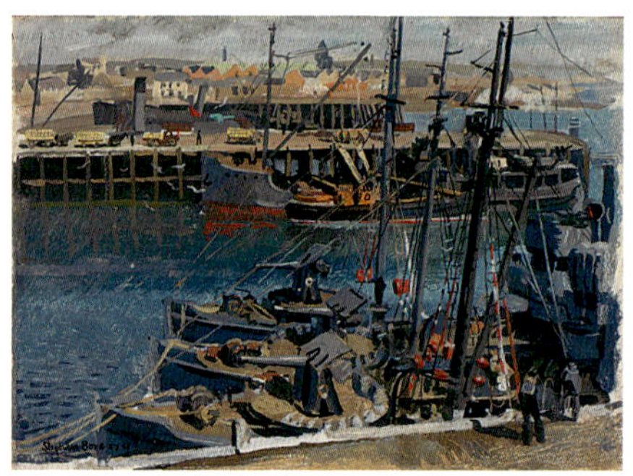

Bone, Stephen 1904–1958
*Stornoway: Armed Trawlers and a Coasting
Vessel Loading Kippers* 1943
oil on panel 25.4 x 35.5
IWM ART LD 3269

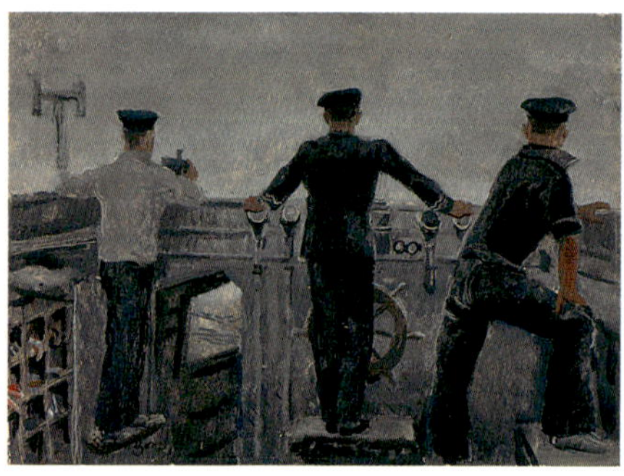

Bone, Stephen 1904–1958
A Motor Launch in a Fog 1943–1944
oil on panel 25.4 x 35.3
IWM ART LD 3264

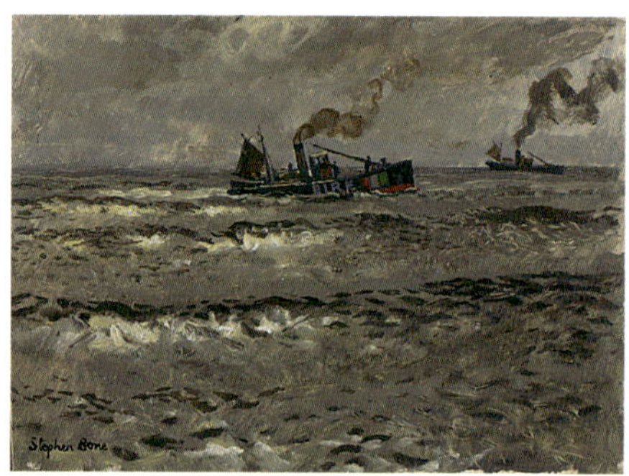

Bone, Stephen 1904–1958
A Neutral Drifter in the Minch 1943–1944
oil on board 25.2 x 34.6
IWM ART LD 3262

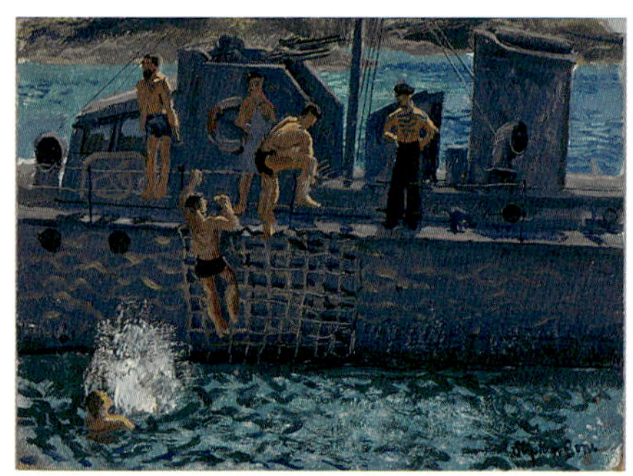

Bone, Stephen 1904–1958
Bathing from a Motor Launch 1943–1944
oil on panel 25.5 x 35.5
IWM ART LD 3267

Bone, Stephen 1904–1958
Convoy: The Rendezvous c.1943–1944
oil on panel 31 x 46.8
IWM ART LD 3278

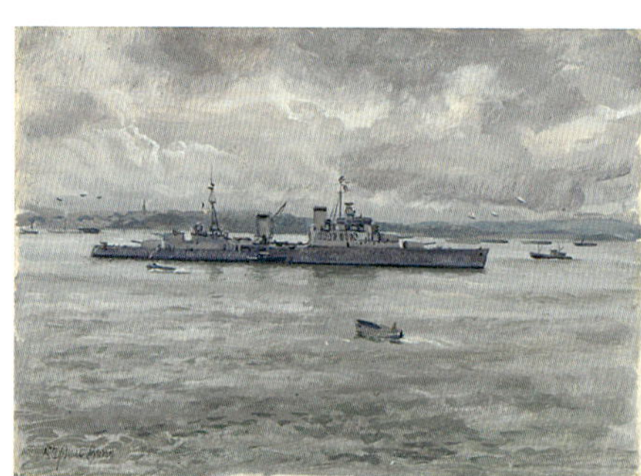

Bone, Stephen 1904–1958
'HMS Mauritius' c.1943–1944
oil on board 25 x 35.5
IWM ART LD 4373

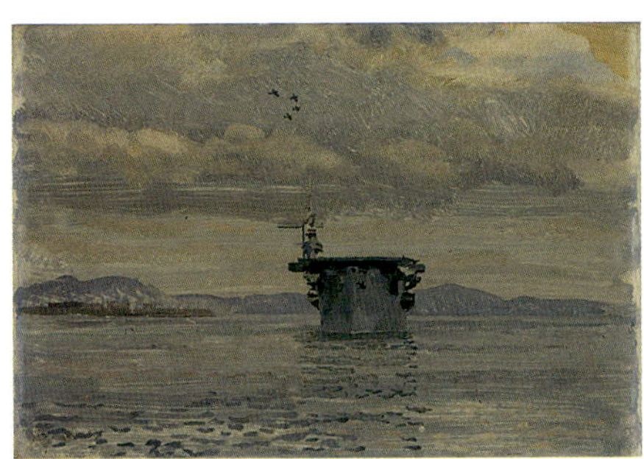

Bone, Stephen 1904–1958
*On Board an Escort Carrier: 'HMS Pursuer' in
Belfast Lough* c.1943–1944
oil on panel 24 x 35.7
IWM ART LD 3790

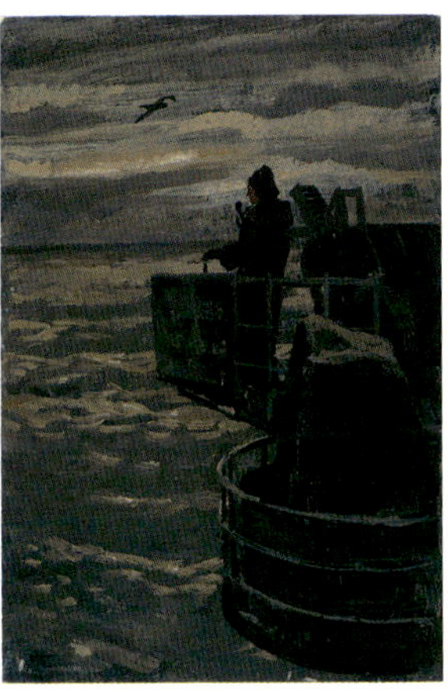

Bone, Stephen 1904–1958
*On Board an Escort Carrier: Lookout at Dawn,
'HMS Pursuer'* c.1943–1944
oil on panel 39.2 x 26.6
IWM ART LD 3793

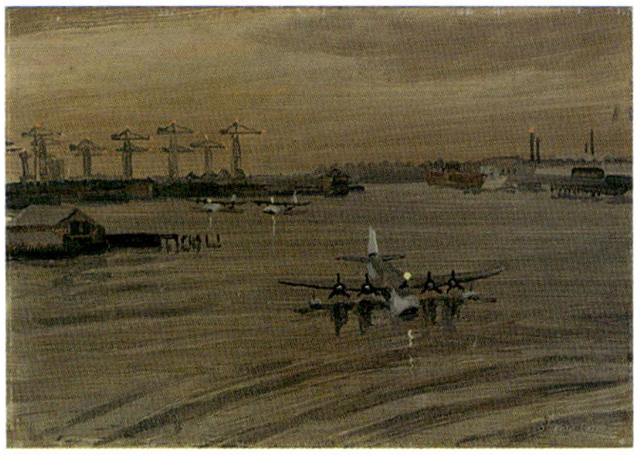

Bone, Stephen 1904–1958
*On Board an Escort Carrier: Winter Dusk in
Belfast Harbour; Sunderland Flying Boats*
c.1943–1944
oil on panel 26.6 x 39.3
IWM ART LD 3792

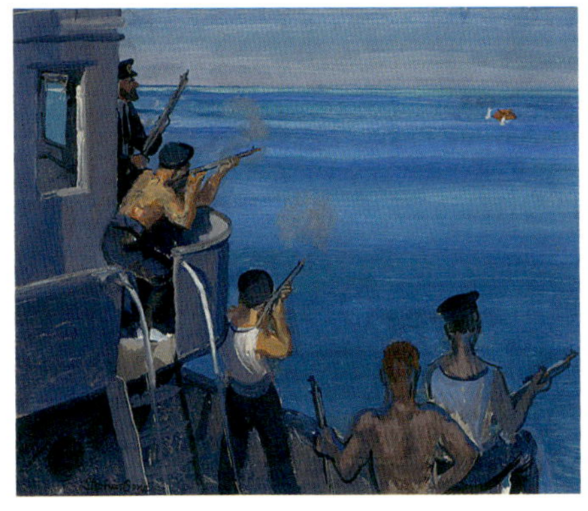

Bone, Stephen 1904–1958
Sinking a Floating Mine with Rifle Fire
c.1943–1944
oil on panel 32.8 x 38.8
IWM ART LD 3276

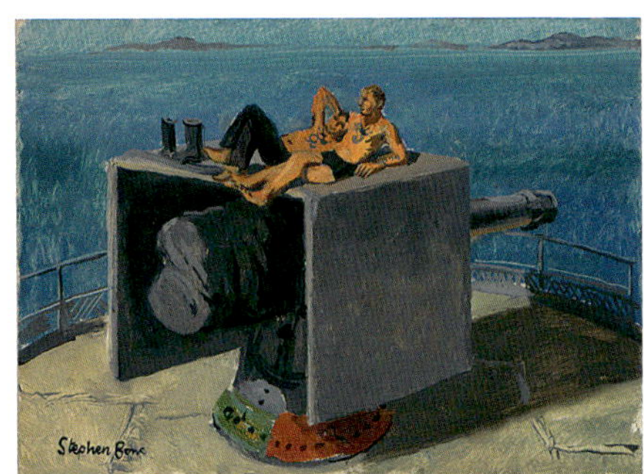

Bone, Stephen 1904–1958
Sunbathing on the Four-Inch Gun
c.1943–1944
oil on board 25.2 x 35.4
IWM ART LD 3270

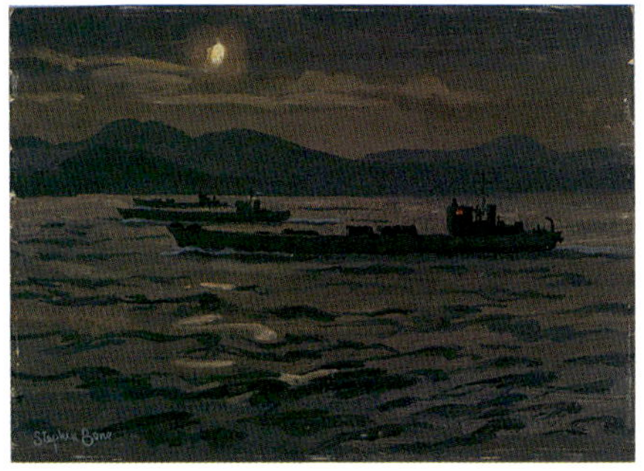

Bone, Stephen 1904–1958
Tank Landing Craft Just before Dawn
c.1943–1944
oil on panel 25 x 35.4
IWM ART LD 3279

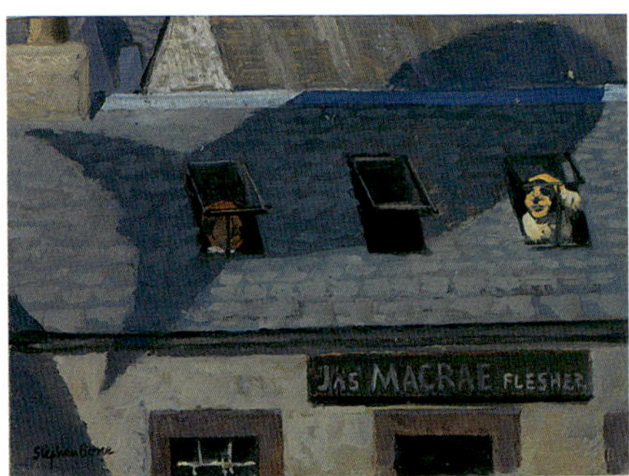

Bone, Stephen 1904–1958
The Shadow of a Balloon c.1943–1944
oil on panel 25 x 34.7
IWM ART LD 3281

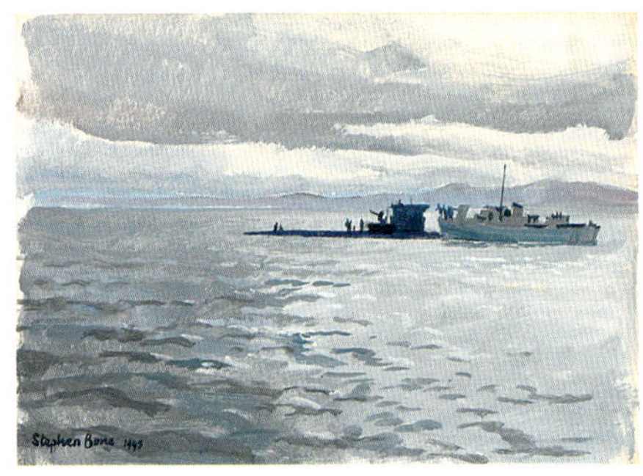

Bone, Stephen 1904–1958
*Boarding a German U-Boat at Loch Eriboll,
Sutherlandshire* c.1943–1945
oil on board 24.7 x 35.5
IWM ART LD 5369

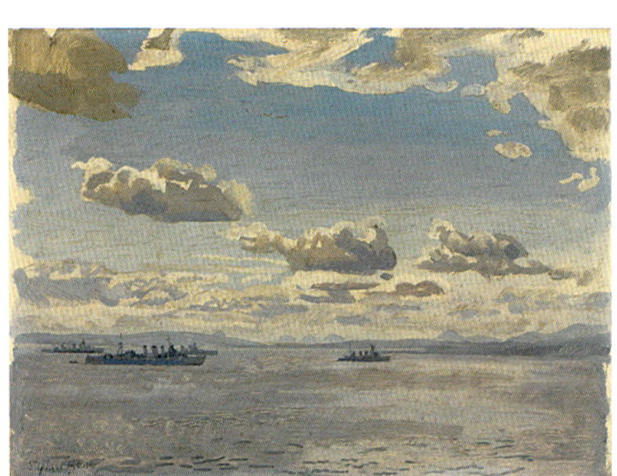

Bone, Stephen 1904–1958
Home Fleet Cruisers in the Firth of Forth
c.1943–1945
oil on panel 25.2 x 35
IWM ART LD 5368

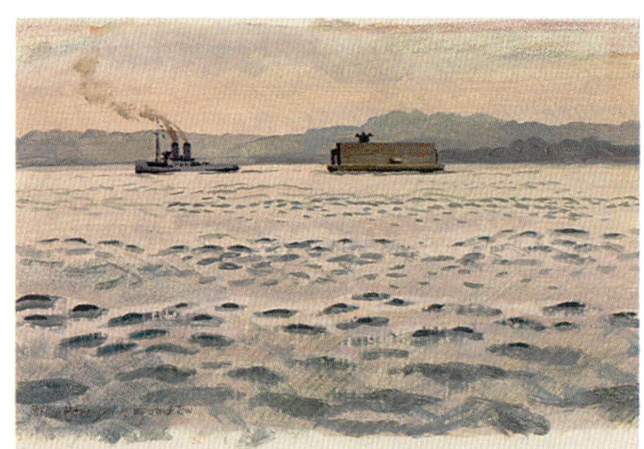

Bone, Stephen 1904–1958
*An Important Tow: A Caisson for Mulberry
Harbour Being Towed to Normandy* 1944
oil on panel 29.3 x 40.5
IWM ART LD 4453

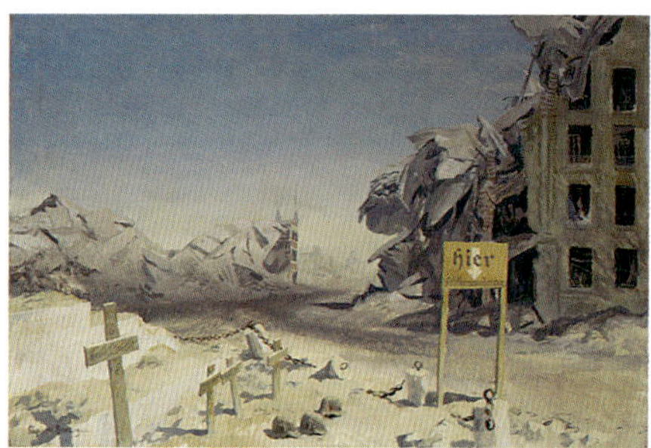

Bone, Stephen 1904–1958
Caen 1944
oil on canvas 49.5 x 74.9
IWM ART LD 4513

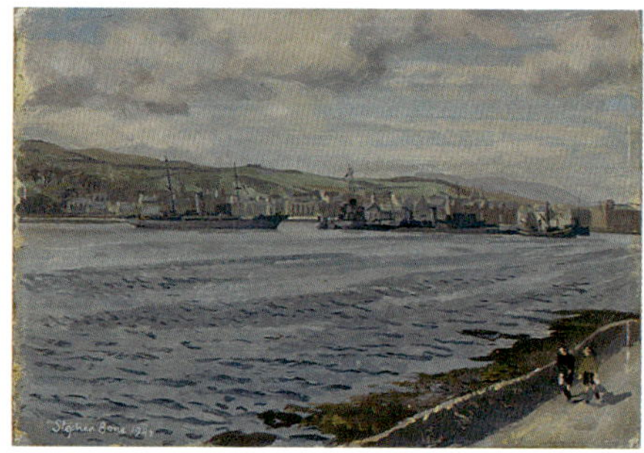

Bone, Stephen 1904–1958
*Campbeltown Harbour with 'HMS St
Modwyn' and 'HMS Samsonia'* 1944
oil on panel 24.3 x 35.5
IWM ART LD 4146

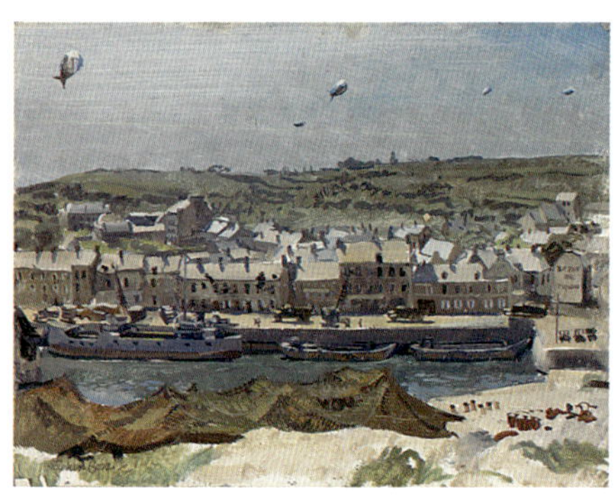

Bone, Stephen 1904–1958
Coasting Vessel and Barges at Port-en-Bessin
1944
oil on panel 30.1 x 40
IWM ART LD 4385

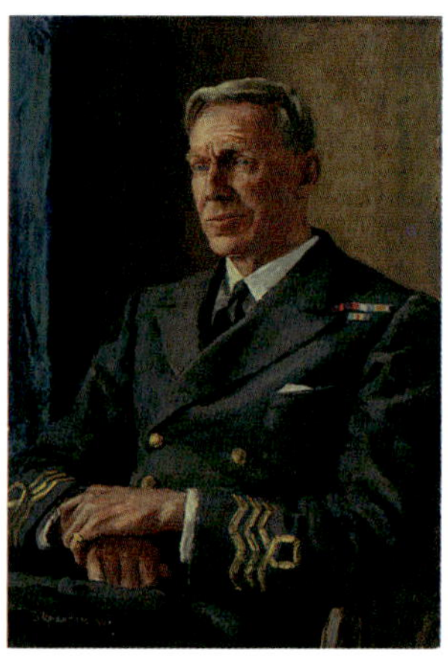

Bone, Stephen 1904–1958
*Commander E. G. Martin, OBE, Royal Naval
Volunteer Reserve* 1944
oil on panel 50.1 x 34.9
IWM ART LD 4077

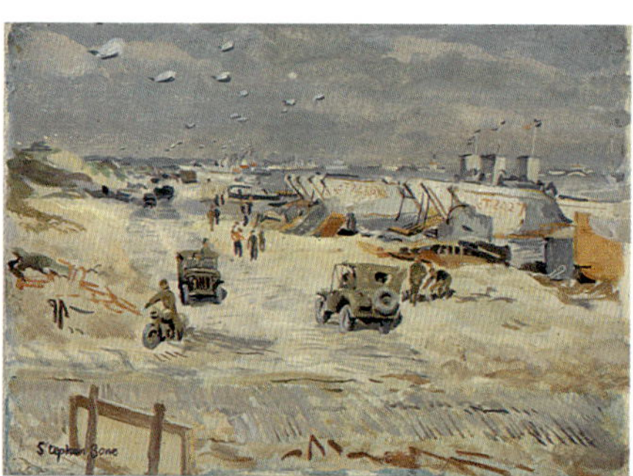

Bone, Stephen 1904–1958
Courseulles Beach 1944
oil on panel 24.9 x 35.2
IWM ART LD 5792

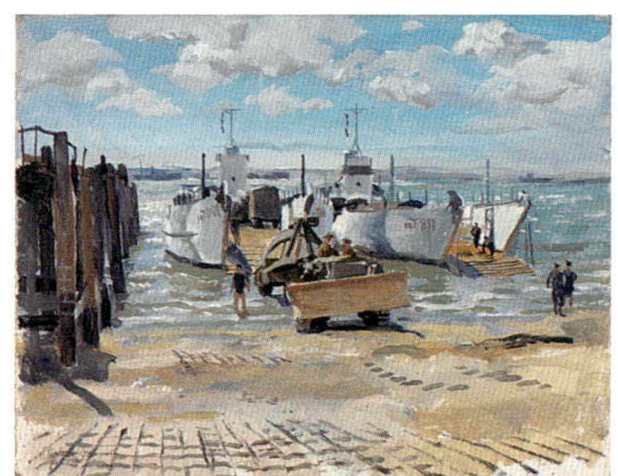

Bone, Stephen 1904–1958
Embarking Bulldozers 1944
oil on board 30.2 x 40.2
IWM ART LD 4380

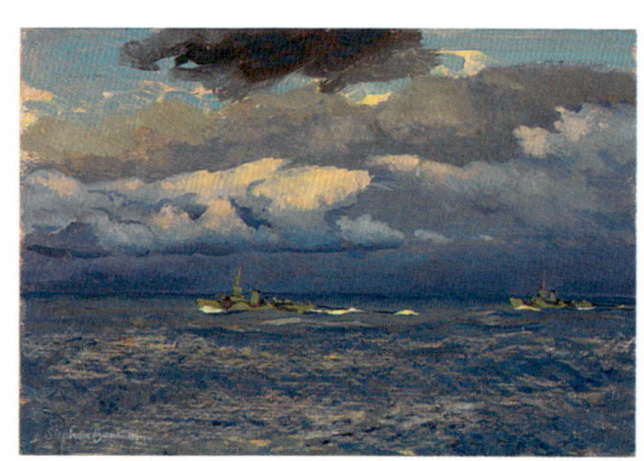

Bone, Stephen 1904–1958
*Fleet Minesweepers off Walcheren: Sunrise, 1
November 1944* 1944
oil on board 23.7 x 35.5
IWM ART LD 5440

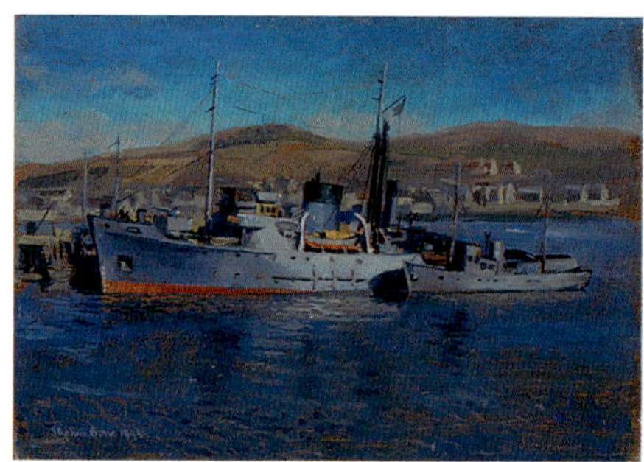

Bone, Stephen 1904–1958
HM Rescue Tug 'Samsonia' 1944
oil on panel 24.6 x 35.5
IWM ART LD 4071

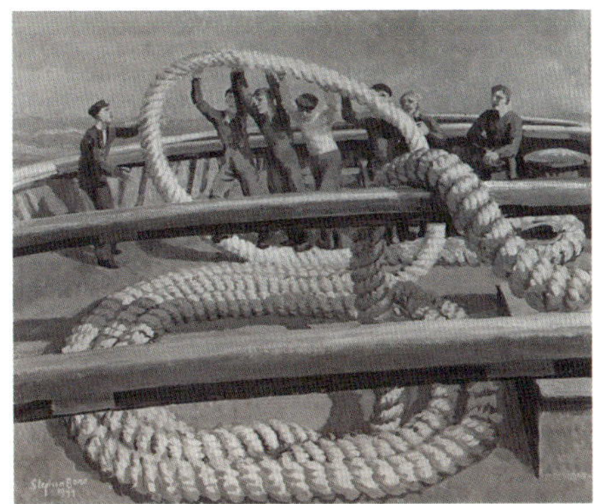

Bone, Stephen 1904–1958
HM Rescue Tug 'Samsonia': The 20 Inches Manilla Cable 1944
oil on canvas 50.1 x 60.3
IWM ART LD 4144

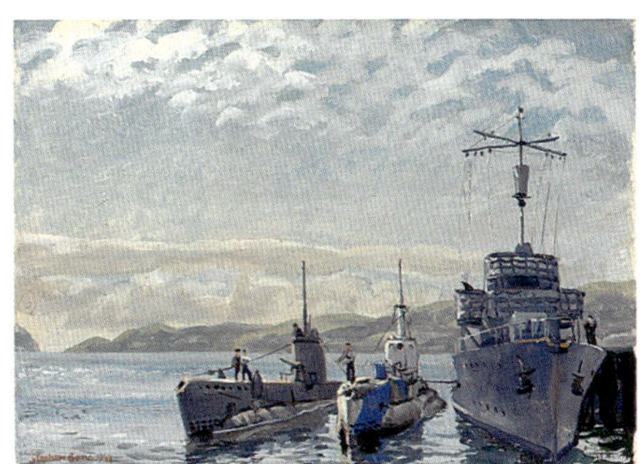

Bone, Stephen 1904–1958
HM Submarines 'Voracious', 'Sea-Lion' and 'La Cordelière' 1944
oil on panel 25.2 x 35.5
IWM ART LD 4068

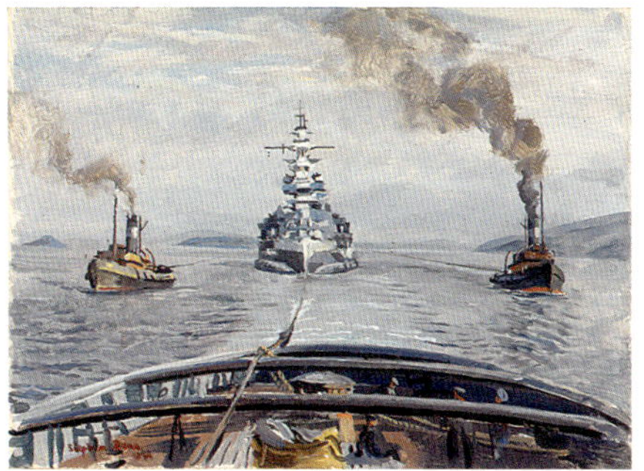

Bone, Stephen 1904–1958
'HMS Malaya' in Tow 1944
oil on panel 25.4 x 35.4
IWM ART LD 4145

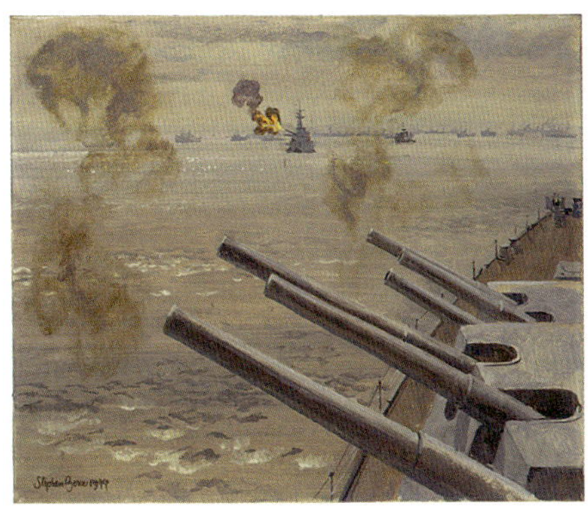

Bone, Stephen 1904–1958
'HMS Mauritius' and 'HMS Roberts' Bombarding Targets near Caen, 18 July 1944 1944
oil on canvas 49.2 x 59
IWM ART LD 4504

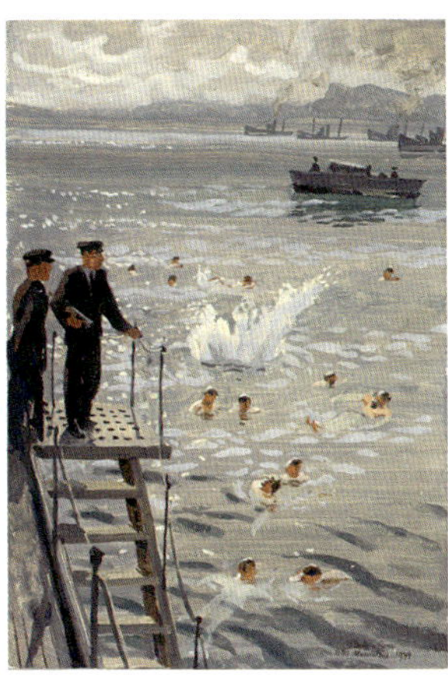

Bone, Stephen 1904–1958
'HMS Mauritius': Bathing, July 1944 1944
oil on paper 38.7 x 27.1
IWM ART LD 5786

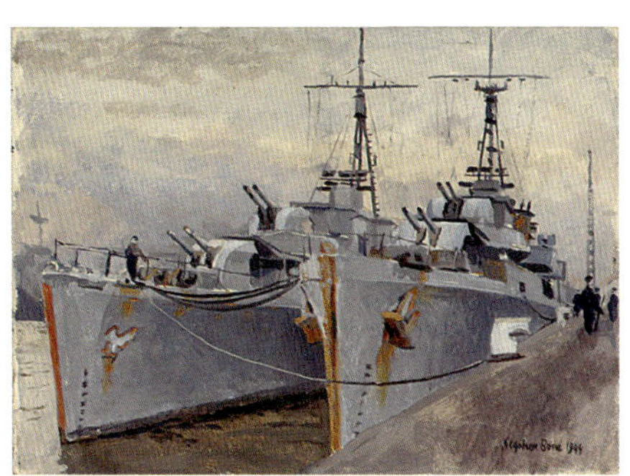

Bone, Stephen 1904–1958
'HMS Wildgoose' and 'HMS Starling' 1944
oil on panel 25.3 x 35.4
IWM ART LD 3878

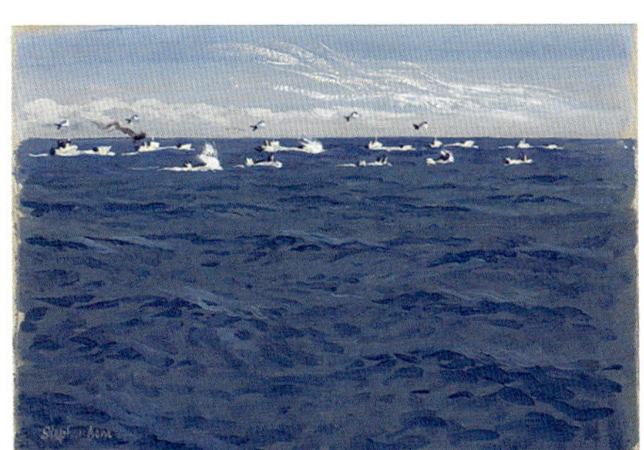

Bone, Stephen 1904–1958
Launch Control Trailer and Medium Landing Ship on Their Way to Normandy 1944
oil on panel 23.9 x 35.6
IWM ART LD 4774

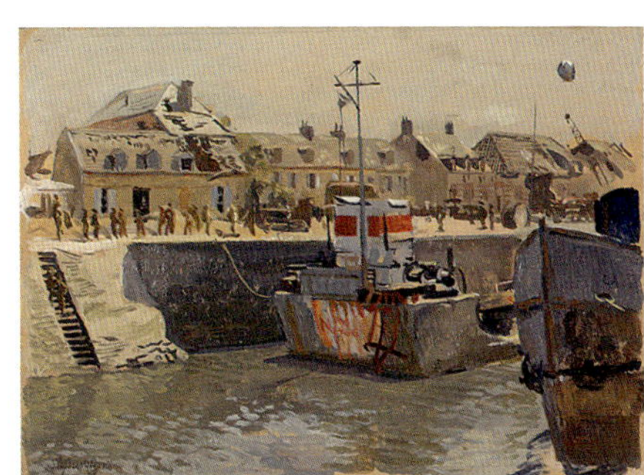

Bone, Stephen 1904–1958
Launch Control Trailer at Courseulles: Unloading Beer 1944
oil on panel 25 x 35.4
IWM ART LD 4383

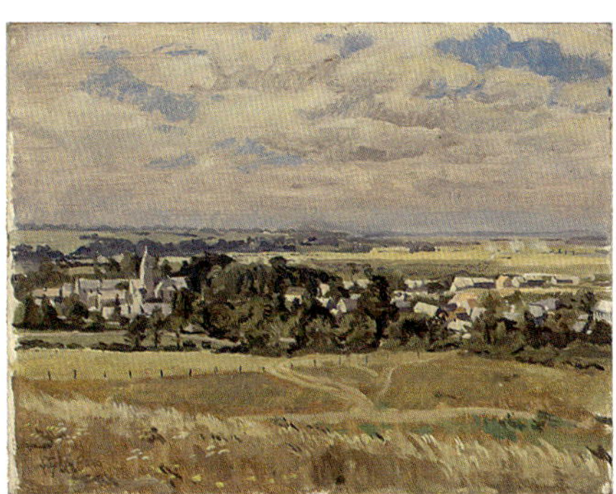

Bone, Stephen 1904–1958
Meuvaines, Calvados 1944
oil on panel 30.2 x 40.2
IWM ART LD 4387

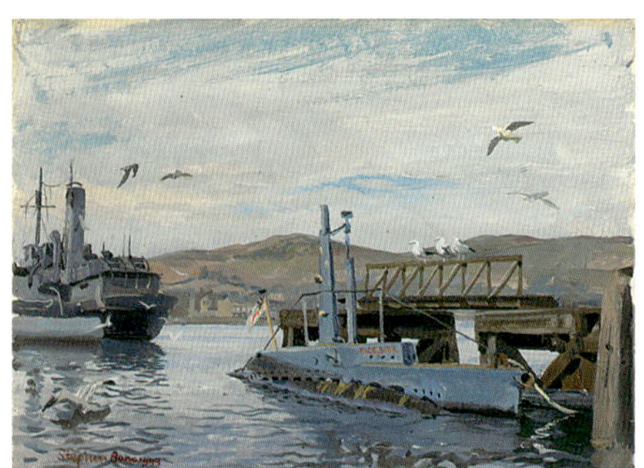

Bone, Stephen 1904–1958
Midget Submarine 'Excelsior' 1944
oil on panel 25.3 x 35.5
IWM ART LD 4066

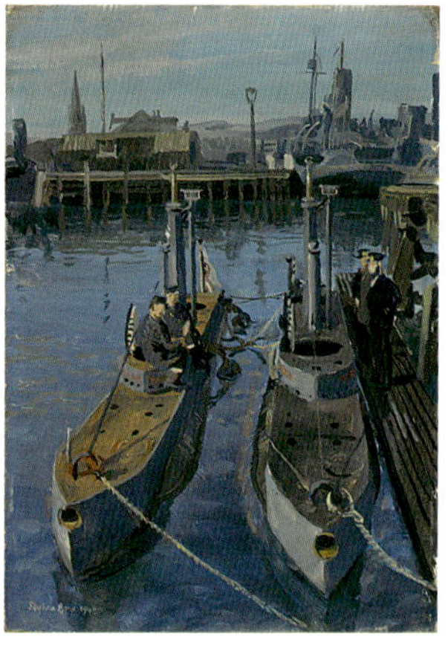

Bone, Stephen 1904–1958
Midget Submarines: 'Herald' and 'Excelsior'
1944
oil on panel 35.5 x 25.5
IWM ART LD 4065

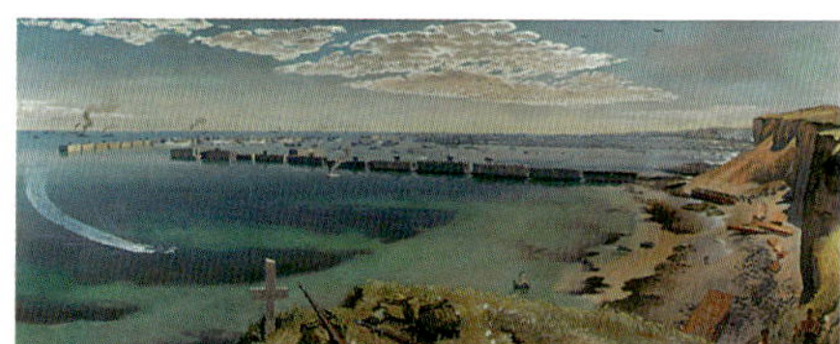

Bone, Stephen 1904–1958
Mulberry Harbour 1944
oil on canvas 76.2 x 182.8
IWM ART LD 5445

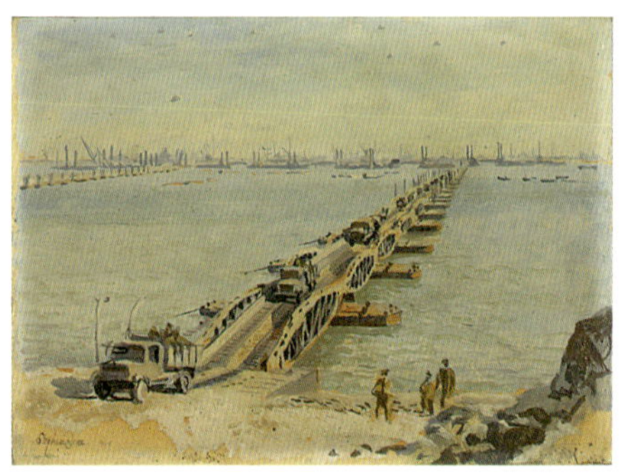

Bone, Stephen 1904–1958
Mulberry Harbour: Arromanches I 1944
oil on panel 25.4 x 34.5
IWM ART LD 4607

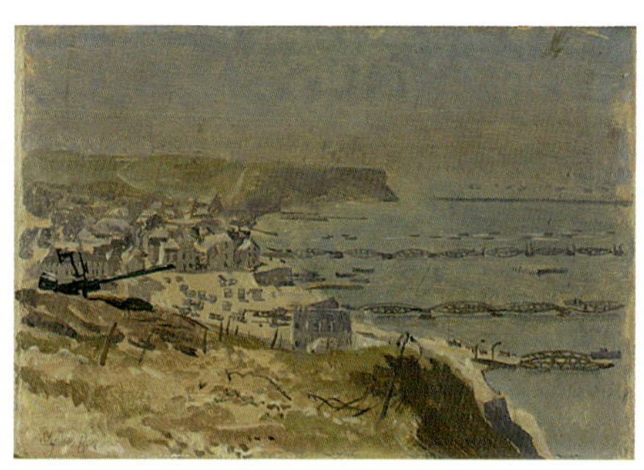

Bone, Stephen 1904–1958
Mulberry Harbour: Arromanches II 1944
oil on panel 23.8 x 35.4
IWM ART LD 4610

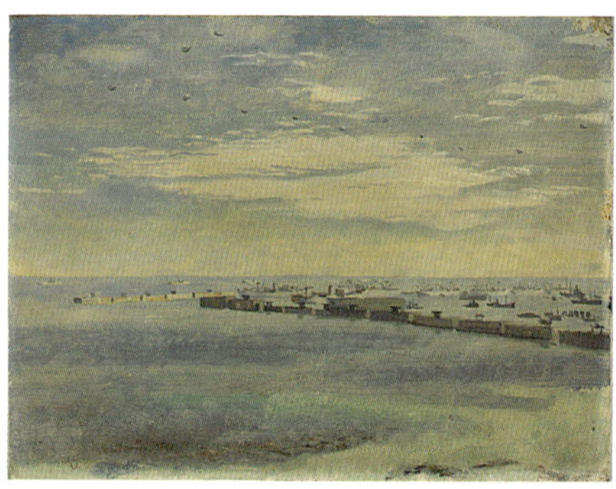

Bone, Stephen 1904–1958
Mulberry Harbour: Arromanches III 1944
oil on panel 29.9 x 40
IWM ART LD 4611

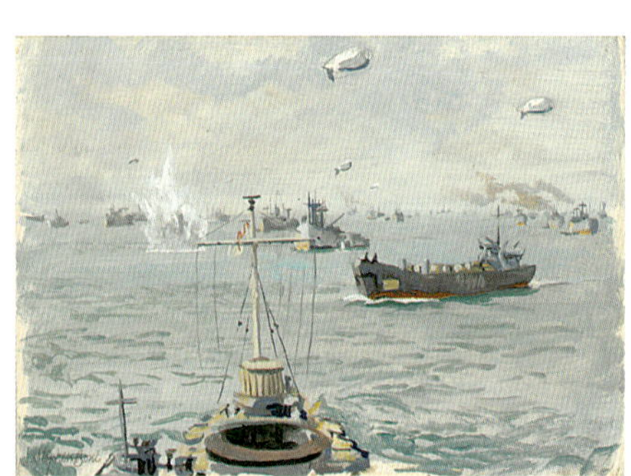

Bone, Stephen 1904–1958
Off the Normandy Beaches 1944
oil on board 25 x 35.7
IWM ART LD 4381

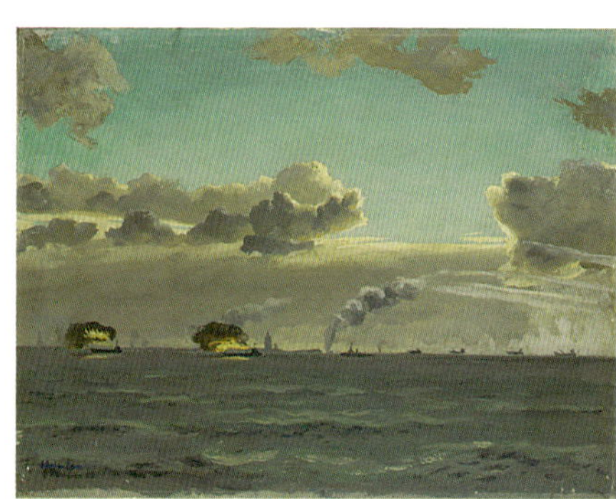

Bone, Stephen 1904–1958
Rocket Ships off Walcheren 1944
oil on canvas 45.4 x 60.3
IWM ART LD 4707

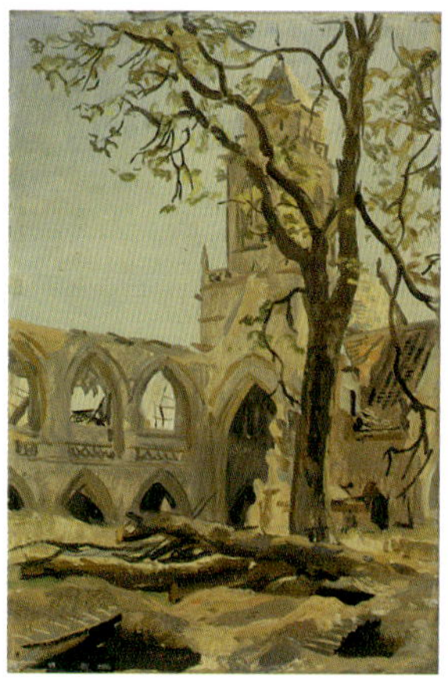

Bone, Stephen 1904–1958
Saint-Etienne-le-Vieux, Caen 1944
oil on panel 35.4 x 23.8
IWM ART LD 4386

Facing Page: McEvoy, Ambrose, 1878 –1927, *Petty Officer E. Pitcher, VC,* 1918 (p, 158)

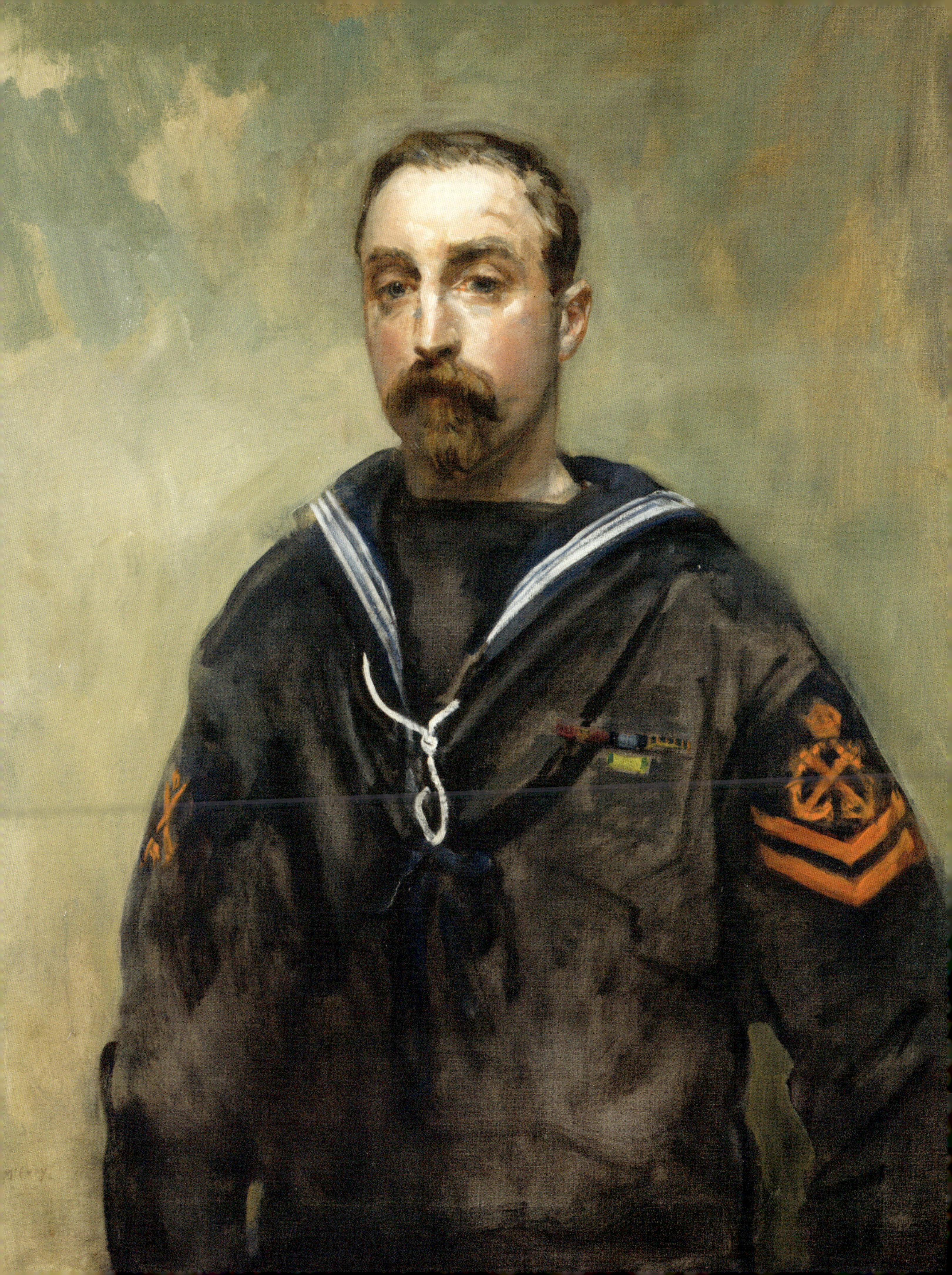

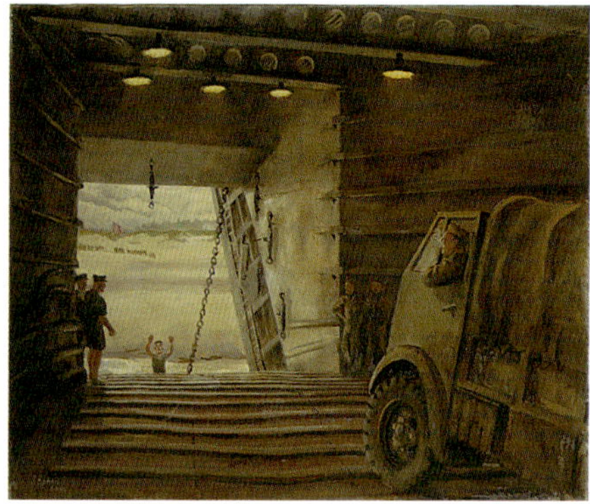

Bone, Stephen 1904–1958
The Gateway to Europe 1944
oil on canvas 61.5 x 74.2
IWM ART LD 4685

Bone, Stephen 1904–1958
'U' Class Submarine at Sea 1944
oil on panel 26.6 x 39.3
IWM ART LD 4069

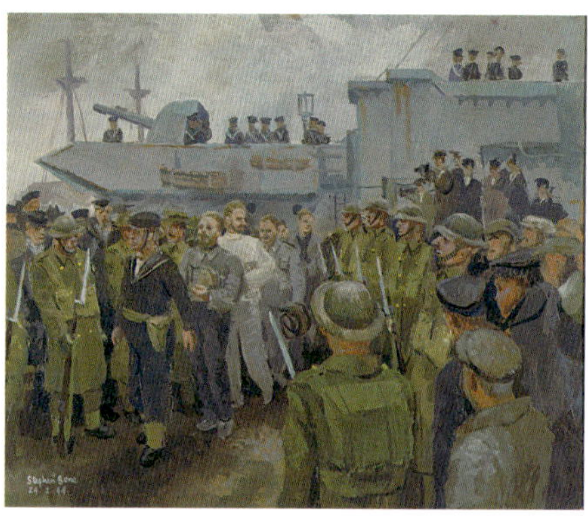

Bone, Stephen 1904–1958
*U-Boat Prisoners Landing from 'HMS
Starling', 24 February 1944* 1944
oil on canvas 50.8 x 60.9
IWM ART LD 3877

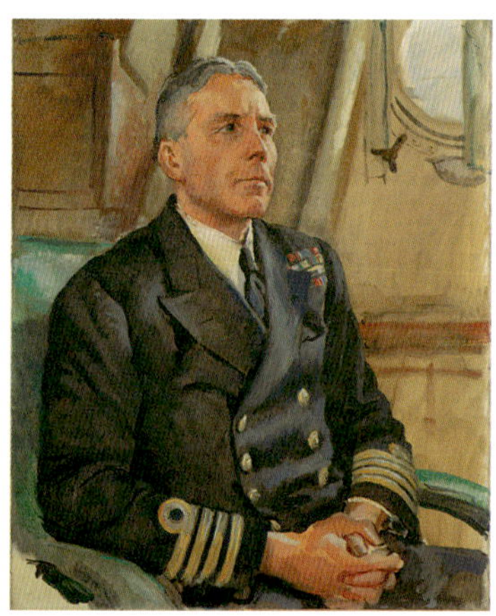

Bone, Stephen 1904–1958
*Captain W. G. Agnew, CB, CVO, DSO, of
'HMS Vanguard'* c.1944–1945
oil on canvas 76.2 x 63.5
IWM ART LD 5782

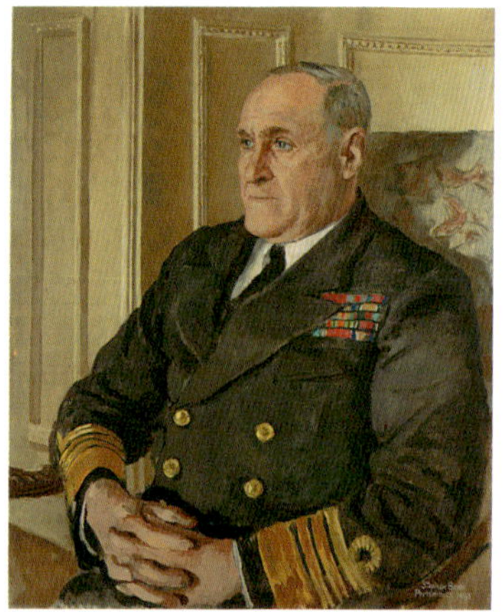

Bone, Stephen 1904–1958
*Admiral Sir Geoffrey Layton (1884–1964),
KCB, KCMG, DSO* 1945
oil on canvas 76.2 x 63.5
IWM ART LD 5673

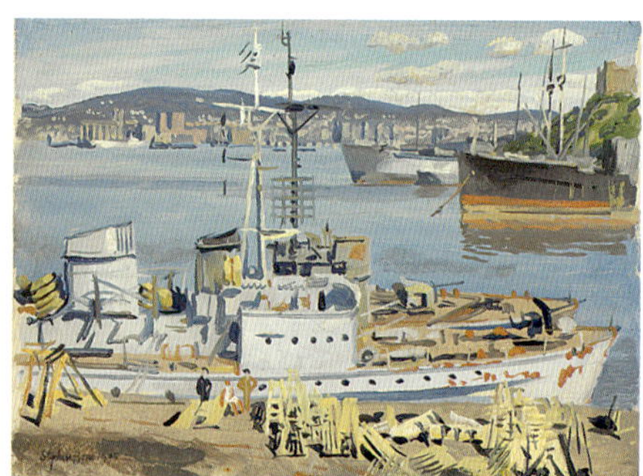

Bone, Stephen 1904–1958
*German Gunboats and Merchant Vessels
Interned at Sjursoya, near Oslo* 1945
oil on panel 25.1 x 35.3
IWM ART LD 5359

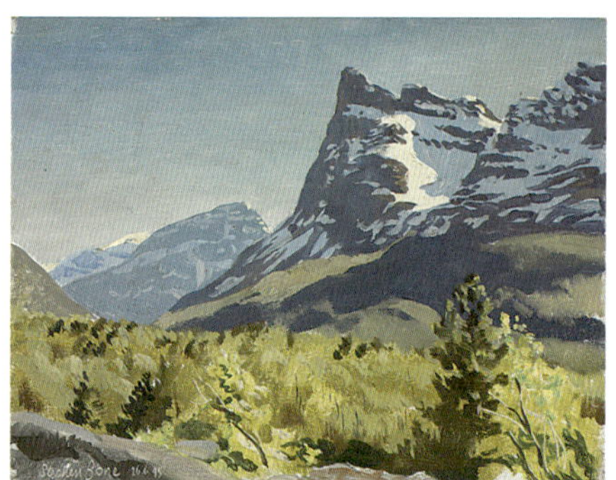

Bone, Stephen 1904–1958
Ottertind in Signaldal, Norway 1945
oil on panel 26.7 x 35
IWM ART LD 5338

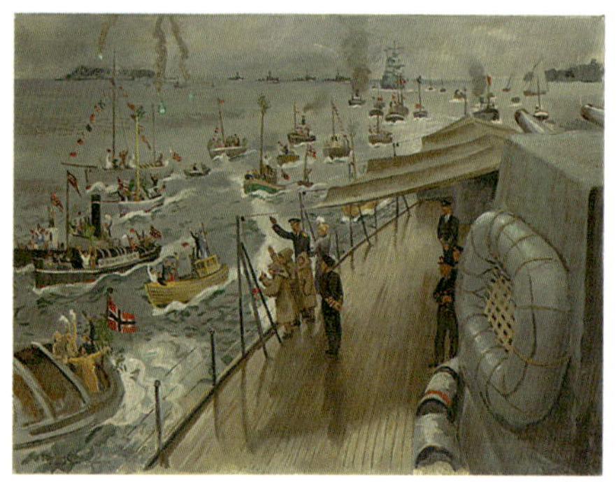

Bone, Stephen 1904–1958
*Return of the King of Norway in 'HMS
Norfolk'* 1945
oil on canvas 76.2 x 101.9
IWM ART LD 5446

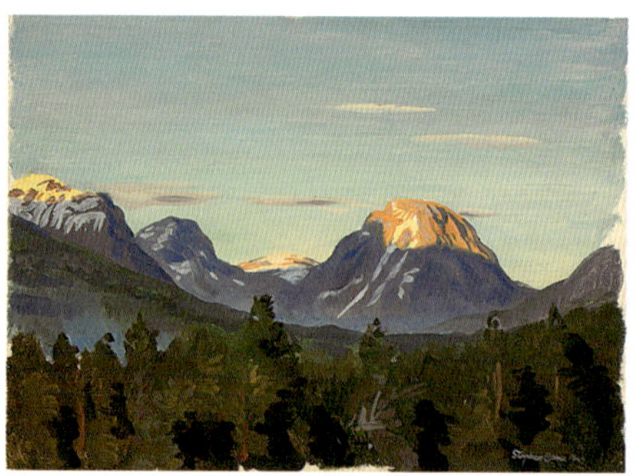

Bone, Stephen 1904–1958
The Midnight Sun 1945
oil on panel 25.2 x 35
IWM ART LD 5335

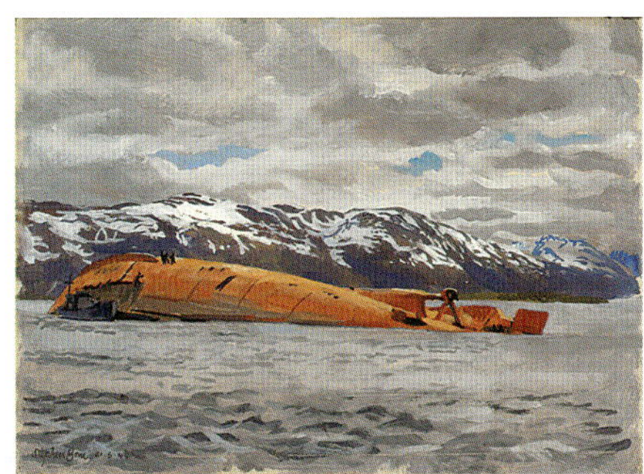

Bone, Stephen 1904–1958
The Wreck of the 'Tirpitz', June 1945 1945
oil on board 25.2 x 35.5
IWM ART LD 5441

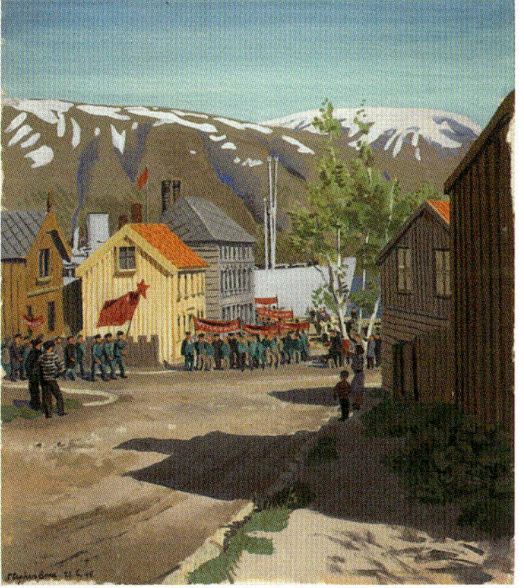

Bone, Stephen 1904–1958
Tromsø, 22 June 1945: Russian Ex-Prisoners Marching to the Murmansk Ship 1945
oil on paper 54.3 x 48.5
IWM ART LD 5443

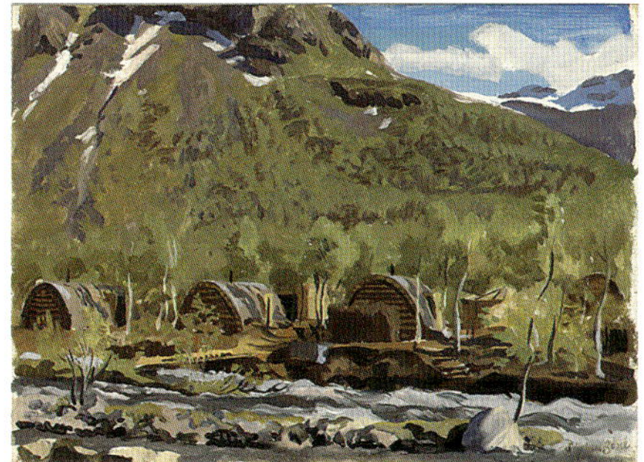

Bone, Stephen 1904–1958
A German Camp in Kitdal c.1945
oil on panel 25 x 35.4
IWM ART LD 5339

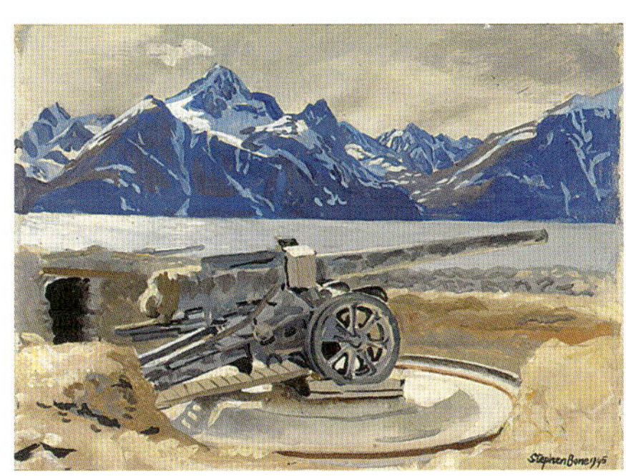

Bone, Stephen 1904–1958
German Guns at Djupvik: Lyngen Fjord c.1945
oil on panel 25.2 x 35.5
IWM ART LD 5340

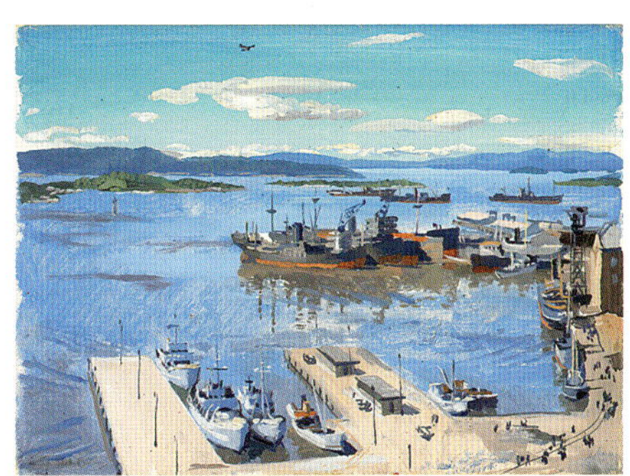

Bone, Stephen 1904–1958
Oslo Harbour with Minesweepers c.1945
oil on panel 25.1 x 35.3
IWM ART LD 5360

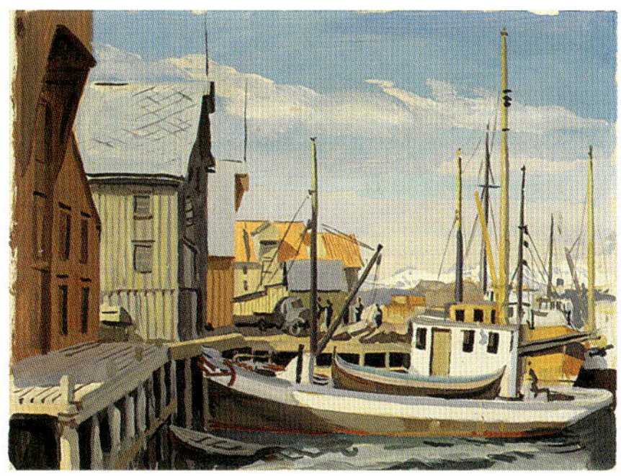

Bone, Stephen 1904–1958
Shipping at Tromsø c.1945
oil on paper 25.4 x 36.5
IWM ART LD 5350

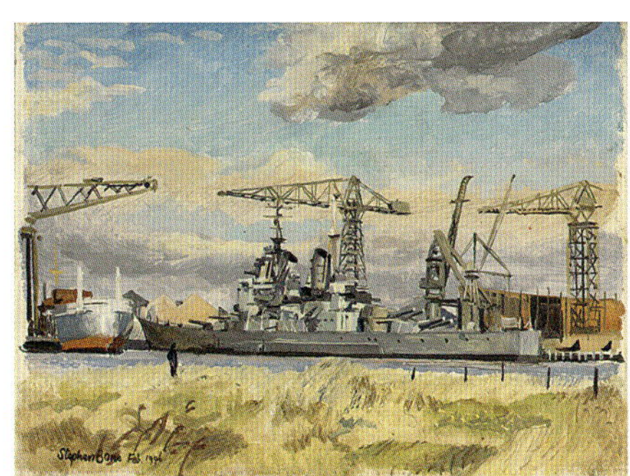

Bone, Stephen 1904–1958
'HMS Vanguard' from across the Clyde, February 1946 1946
oil on panel 25.6 x 35.5
IWM ART LD 5784

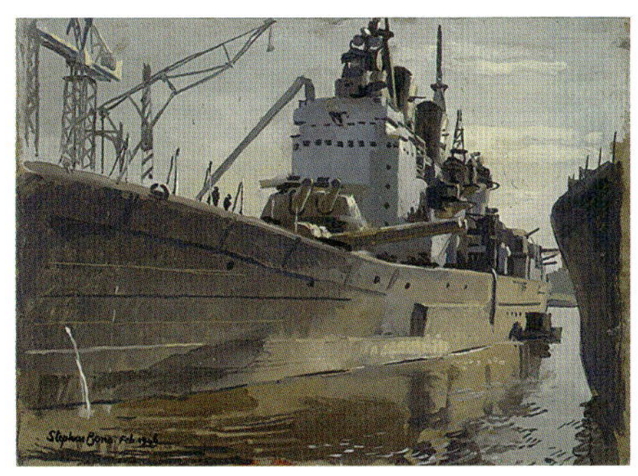

Bone, Stephen 1904–1958
'HMS Vanguard' in Dock, February 1946 1946
oil on panel 24.9 x 35.1
IWM ART LD 5785

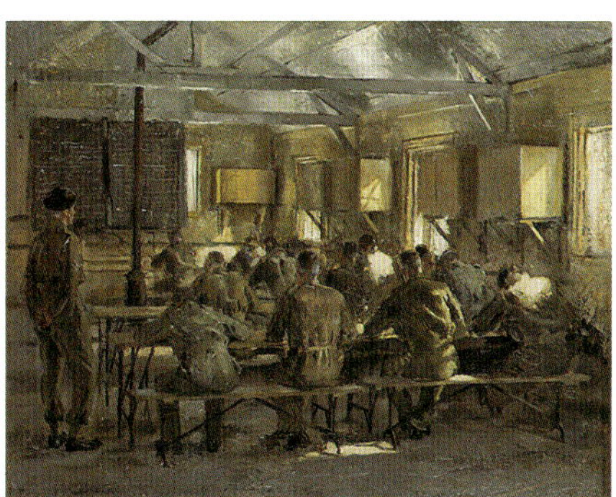

Boothroyd, Arthur Sharland b.1910
A Driving and Maintenance Class 1942
oil on panel 50.8 x 66
IWM ART LD 2978

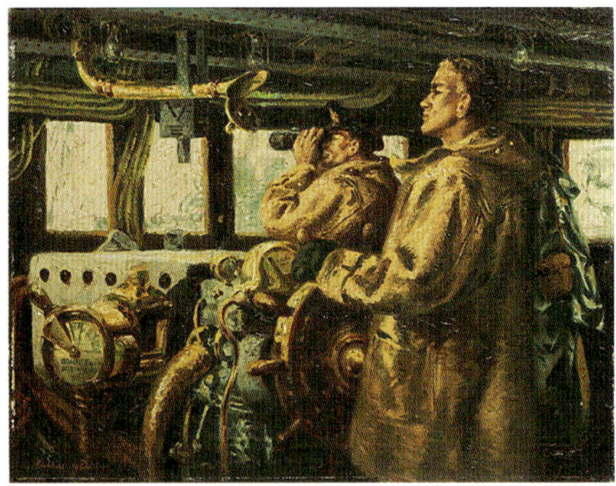

Brabbins, Oliver G. active 1930–1960
A Minesweeper's Wheelhouse 1944
oil on canvas 53.3 x 69.2
IWM ART LD 4525

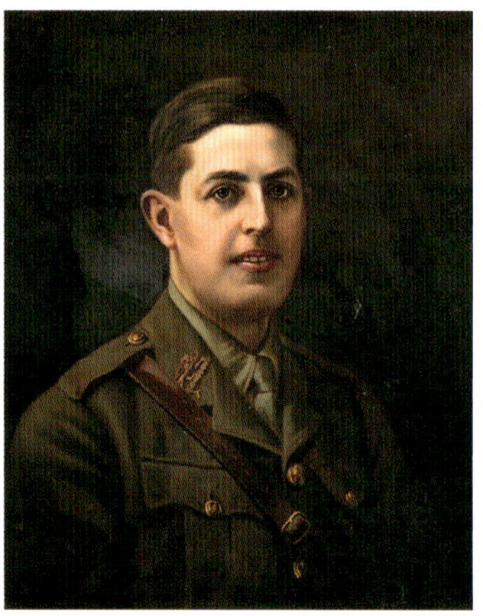

Braithwaite, Charles 1876–1941
George Braddyll Bigland of Bigland, Second Lieutenant, King's Own Royal Lancaster Regiment 1915
oil on canvas 60.9 x 50.8
IWM ART 4204

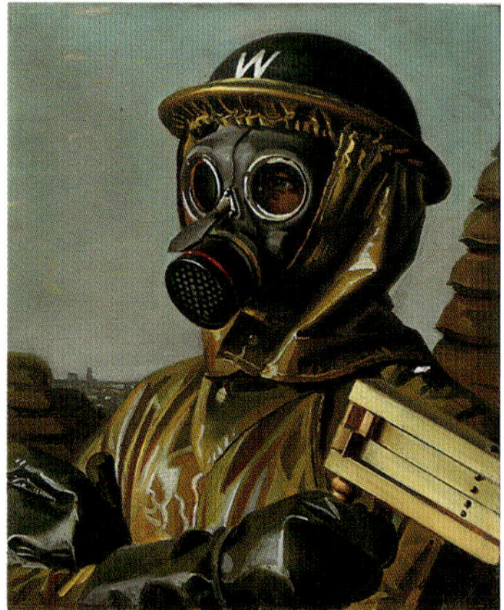

Brealey, William Ramsden 1889–1949
Gas Mask 1939
oil on canvas 60.9 x 50.8
IWM ART LD 1290

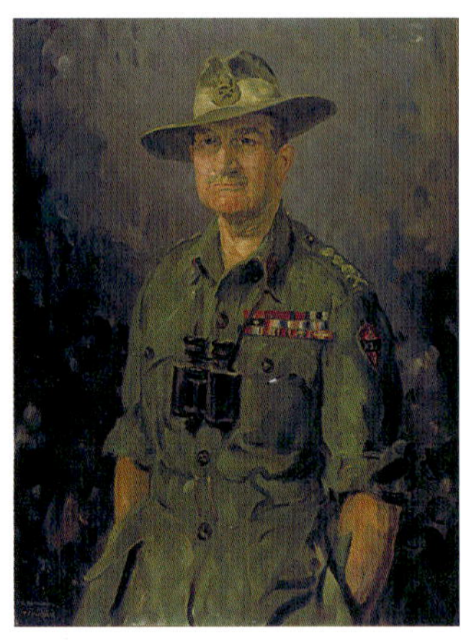

Browning, Amy Katherine 1881–1978
General Sir William Slim (1891–1970), GBE, KCB, DSO, MC 1961
oil on canvas 101.9 x 76.2
IWM ART LD 6011

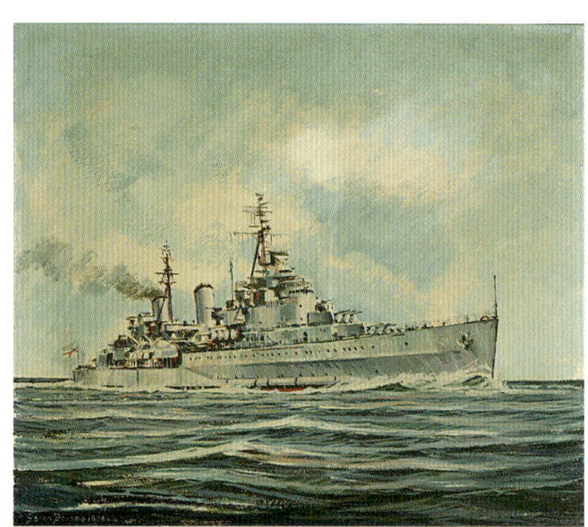

Brunoe, Søren 1916–1994
'HMS Belfast' at Sea
oil on canvas 59 x 69
IWM ART 16611

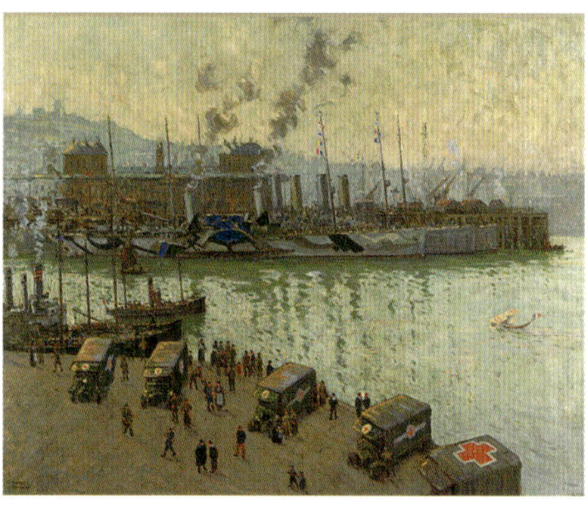

Bryant, Charles David Jones 1883–1937
Dazzled Leave Ships, Boulogne 1917
oil on canvas 101.9 x 127
IWM ART 1346

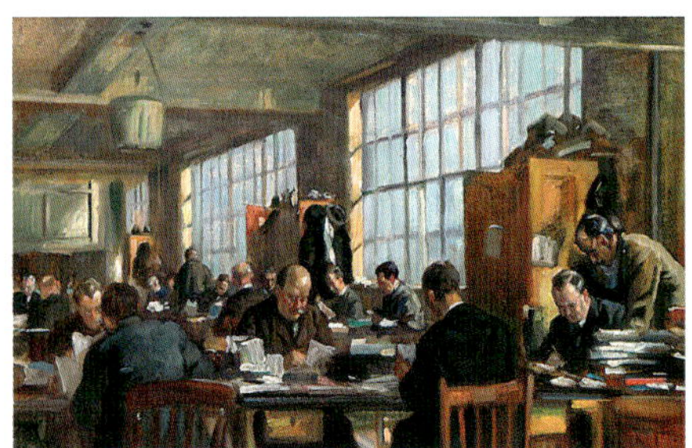

Bryce, Alexander Joshua Caleb 1868–1940
The Censorship: Strand House, Portugal Street, London 1918–1919
oil on canvas 50.8 x 76.2
IWM ART 1671

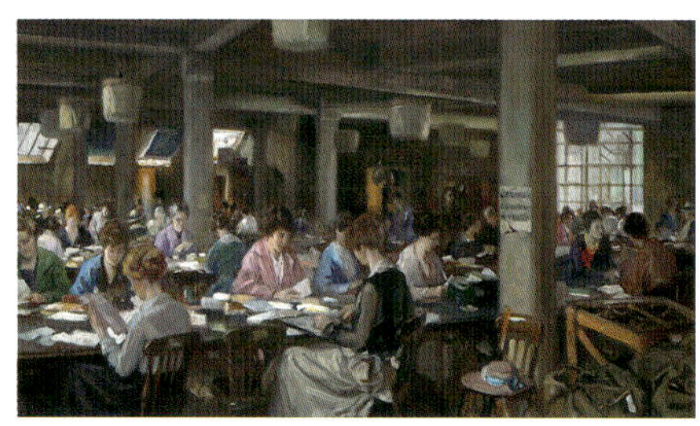

Bryce, Alexander Joshua Caleb 1868–1940
The Postal Censorship, Strand House: Censoring Letters to and from Enemy Prisoners of War; Colonel Creagh, (…) 1918–1919
oil on canvas 50.8 x 83.8
IWM ART 1990

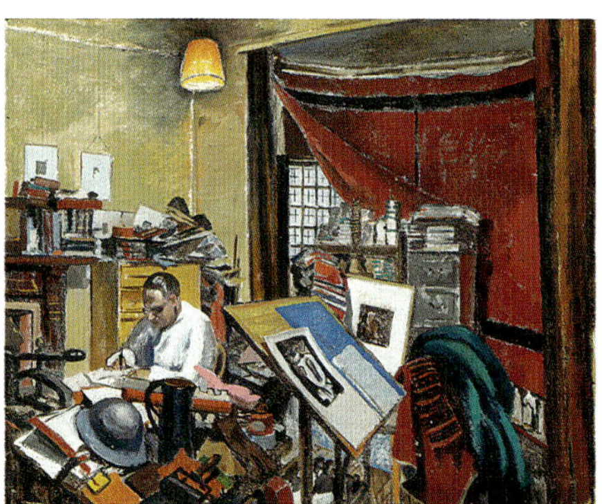

Buday, George 1907–1990
Self Portrait in the Studio c.1941
oil on board 50.8 x 71.1
IWM ART 17107

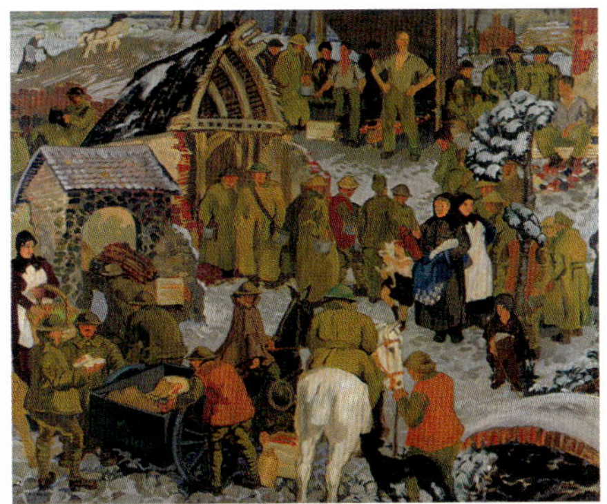

Budd, Herbert Ashwin 1881–1950
In Billets, Winter: Rations up 1921
oil on canvas 101.9 x 127
IWM ART 4664

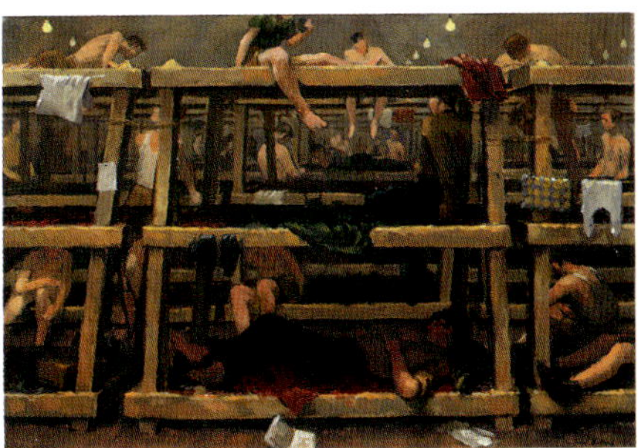

Bullard, Paul 1918–1996
British Prisoners of War, Italy 1946
oil on canvas 51.4 x 76.4
IWM ART 16315

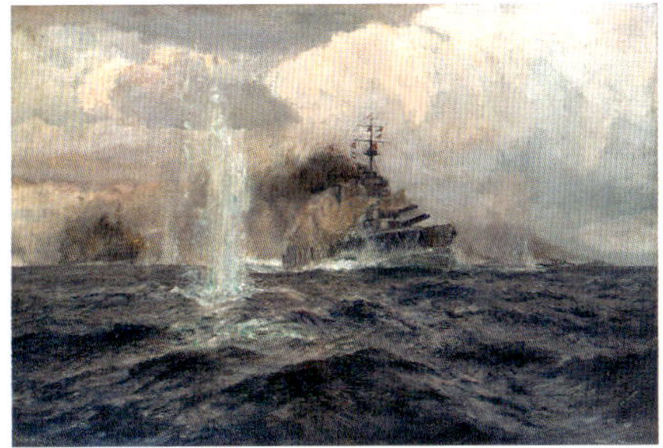

Burgess, Arthur James Wetherall
1879–1957
'HMS Lion' at the Dogger Bank Action 1915
oil on canvas 123.1 x 182.8
IWM ART 5205

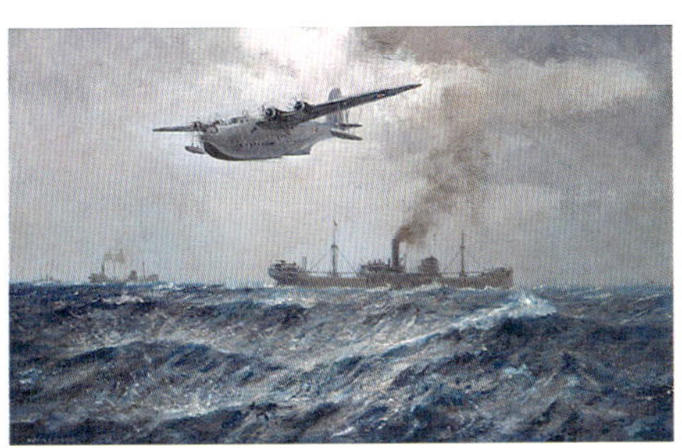

Burgess, Arthur James Wetherall
1879–1957
A Sunderland Flying-Boat on Patrol
c.1940–1945
oil on canvas 50.8 x 76.2
IWM ART LD 6003

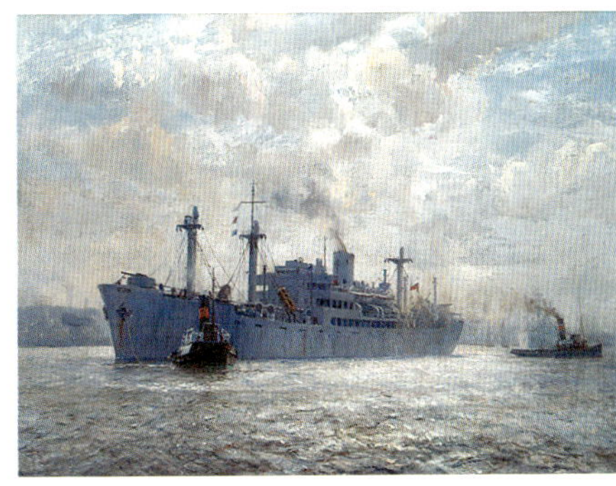

Burgess, Arthur James Wetherall
1879–1957
Freights to Pay the Debts of War c.1940–1945
oil on canvas 78.7 x 105.4
IWM ART LD 6004

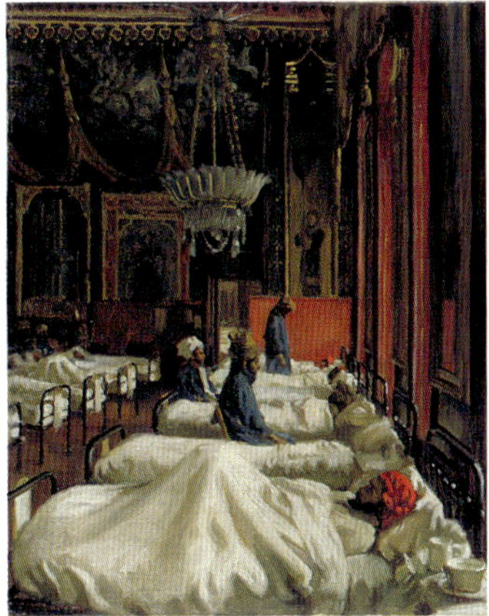

Burleigh, C. H. H. 1869–1956
*Interior of the Pavilion, Brighton: Indian Army
Wounded* c.1917
oil on canvas 55.8 x 45.7
IWM ART 116

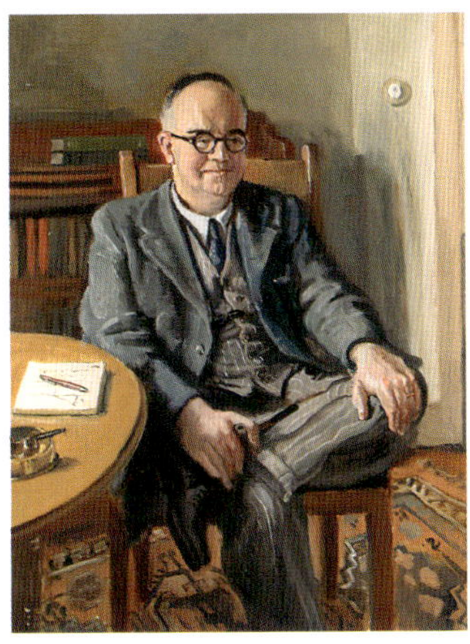

Burn, Rodney Joseph 1899–1984
*Dr R. E. Stradling (1891–1952), CB, MD, FRS,
Chief Scientific Adviser on Research and
Experiments to the Ministry of (…)* 1945
oil on canvas 91.4 x 71.1
IWM ART LD 3559

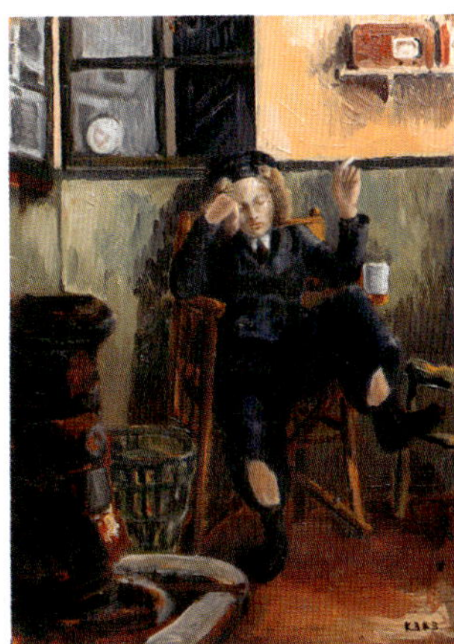

Burns, Kitty b.1925
*A Military Transport Type: Portrait of a
Women's Royal Naval Service Driver* 1945
oil on board 50.1 x 36.1
IWM ART LD 7234

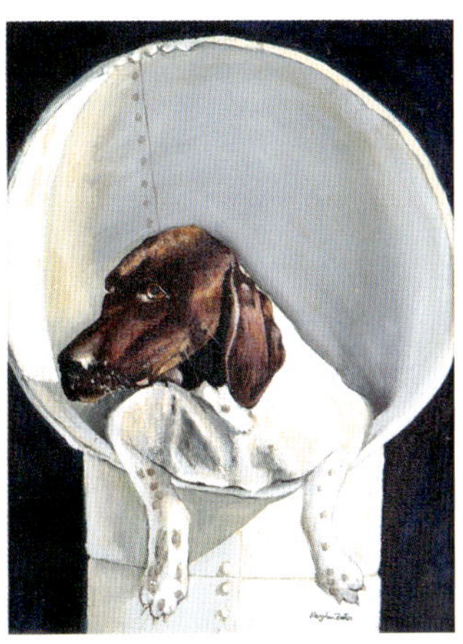

Burton, Mary Anne active 1960s
Judi: Ship's Mascot c.1960
oil on canvas 40.6 x 30.4
IWM ART LD 6680

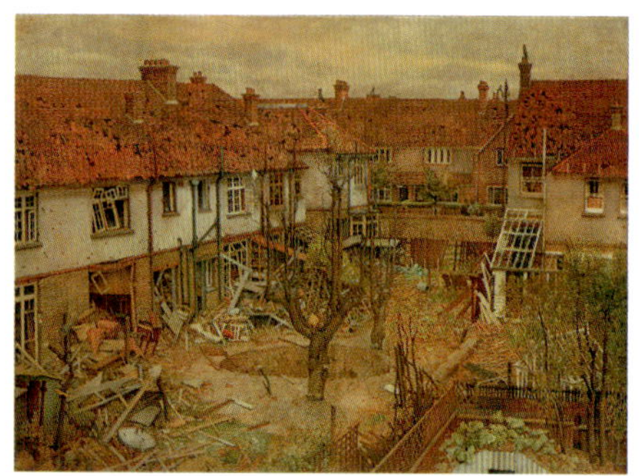

Bush, Harry 1883–1957
A Corner of Merton, 16 August 1940 1940
oil on canvas 93.9 x 127
IWM ART LD 6517

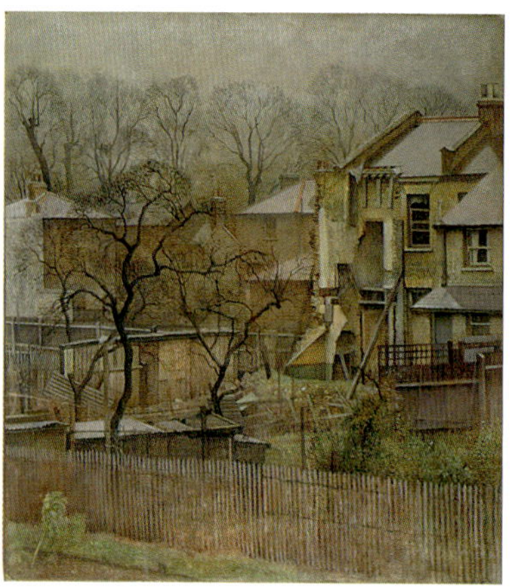

Bush, Harry 1883–1957
Bombed House, Merton 1940
oil on canvas 50.8 x 45.7
IWM ART 15662

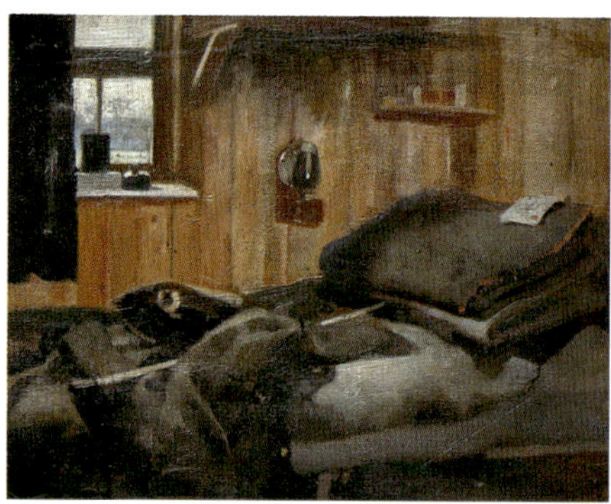

Bush, Harry 1883–1957
Interior of Barracks, 17 A. A. Coy, North Queensferry c.1940
oil on canvas 22.2 x 28.4
IWM ART 15696

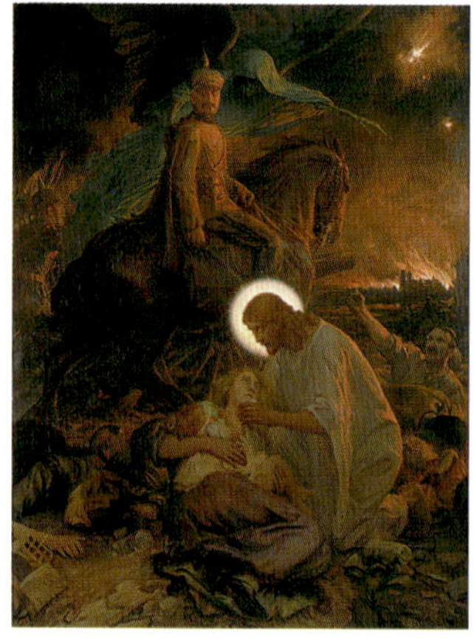

Butler, Charles Ernest 1864–c.1918
Blood and Iron 1916
oil on canvas 191 x 144.2
IWM ART 6492

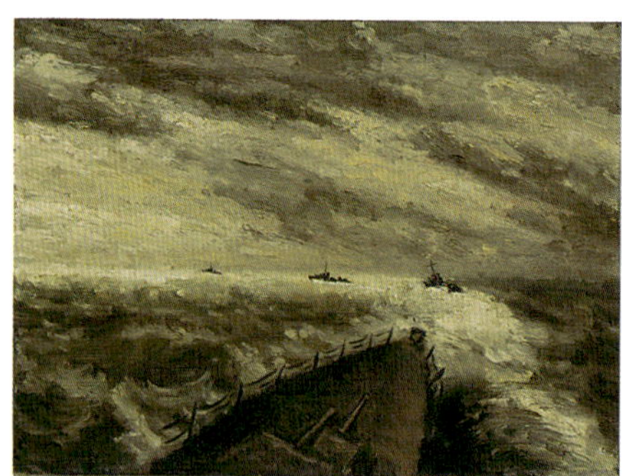

Butler, Robert D. F. b.1916
With a Destroyer Flotilla on an Offensive Patrol: 'HMS Worcester', 'HMS Eglington', 'HMS Quorn' and 'HMS Whitshed' 1942
oil on canvas 40.6 x 55.8
IWM ART LD 1206

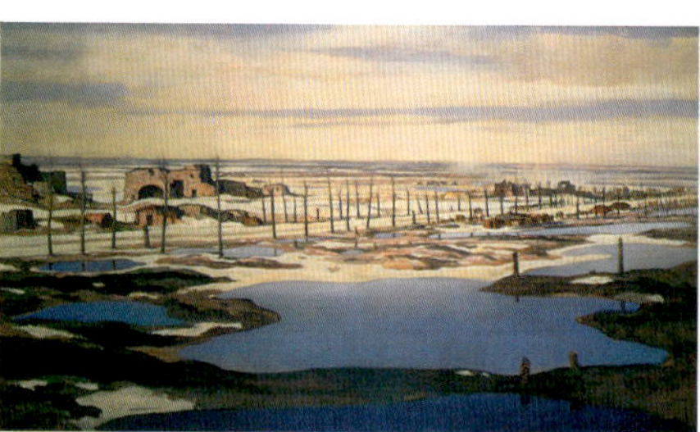

Cameron, David Young 1865–1945
The Battlefield of Ypres 1919
oil on canvas 182.8 x 317.5
IWM ART 2626

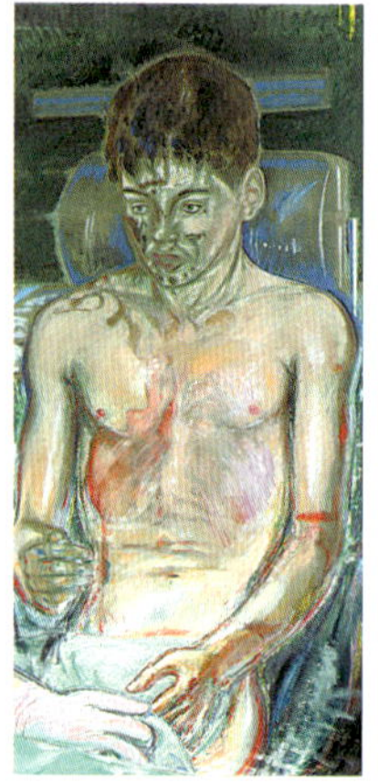

Camp, Jeffery b.1923
Burns 1987
oil on canvas 229 x 107.2
IWM ART 16228

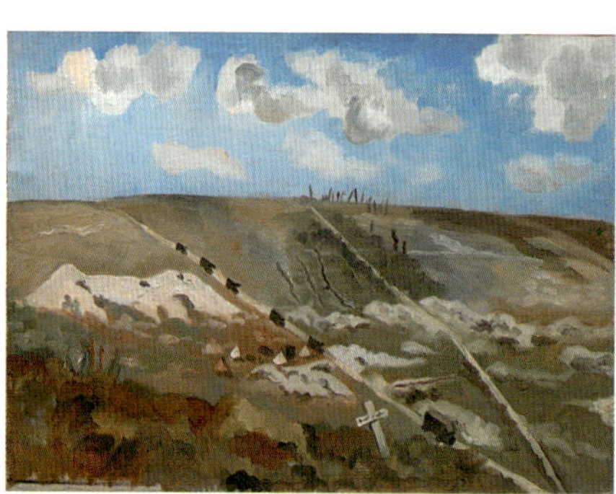

Carline, Richard 1896–1980
Albert: Bapaume Road 1918
oil on canvas 31.7 x 42.5
IWM ART 6344

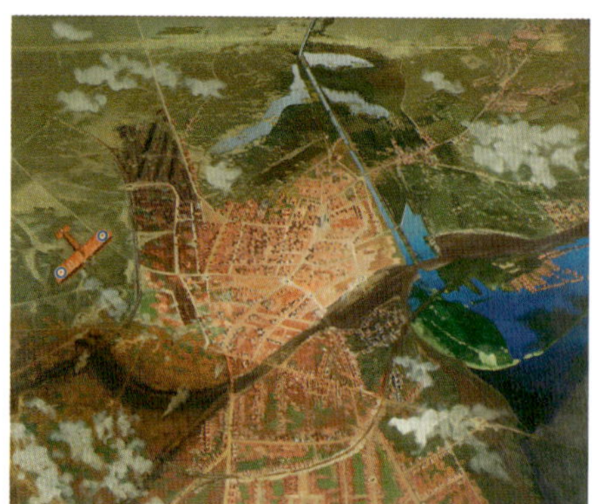

Carline, Richard 1896–1980
An Impression of Lens, France, Seen from an Aeroplane: The Anglo-German Front Line 1918
oil on canvas 109.2 x 127
IWM ART 2661

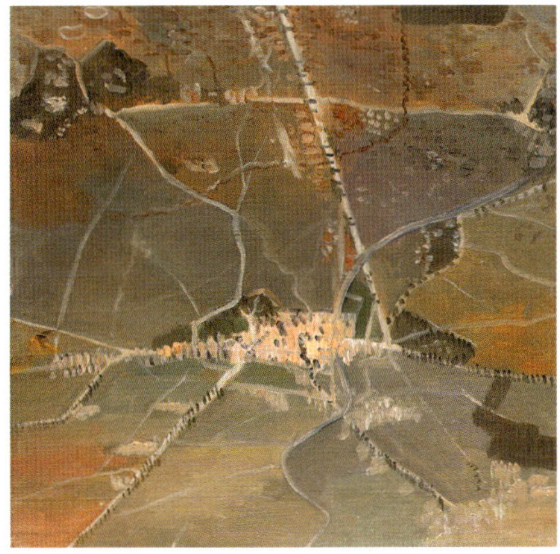

Carline, Richard 1896–1980
Bapaume Seen from an Aeroplane at 10,000 Feet 1918
oil on canvas 34.9 x 35.5
IWM ART 6347

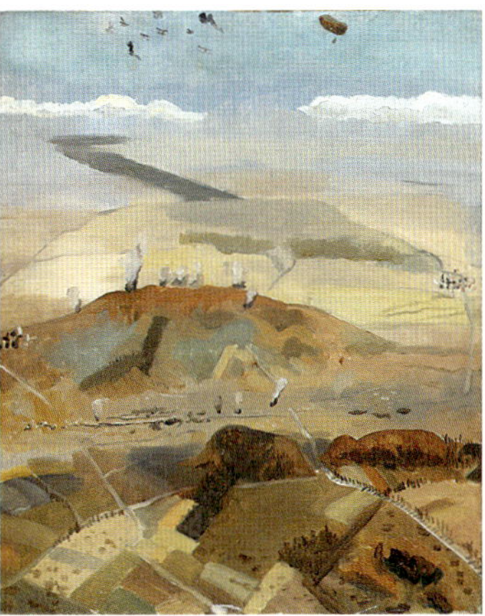

Carline, Richard 1896–1980
Kemmel Hill Seen from an Aeroplane 1918
oil on canvas 42.5 x 35.5
IWM ART 6343

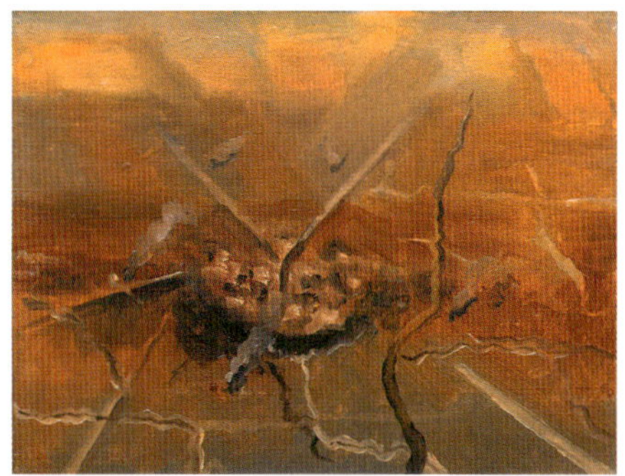

Carline, Richard 1896–1980
Lens from the Air 1918
oil on canvas 26 x 35.5
IWM ART 6341

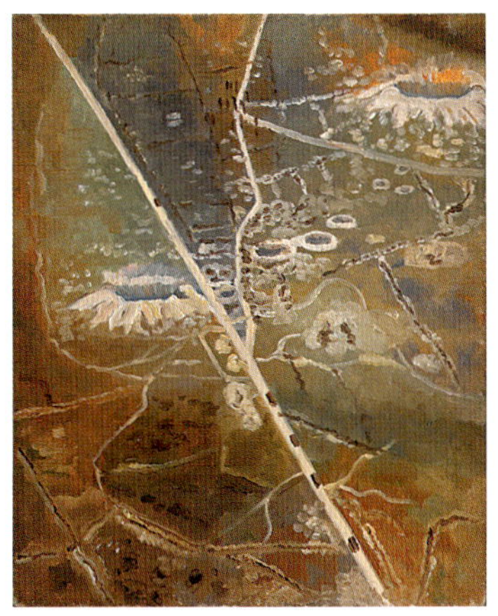

Carline, Richard 1896–1980
Mine Craters at Albert Seen from an Aeroplane 1918
oil on canvas 42.5 x 34.9
IWM ART 6346

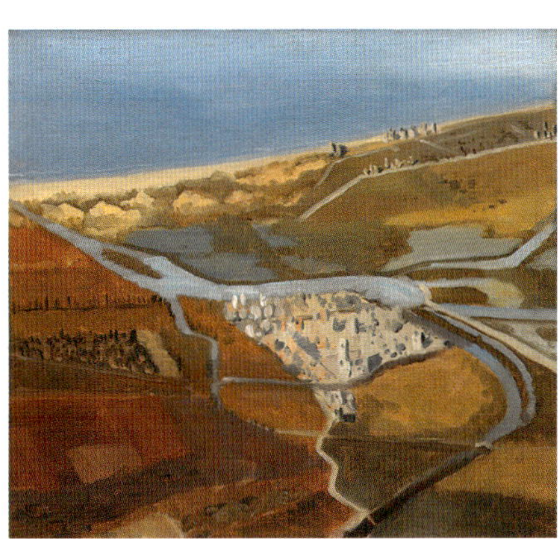

Carline, Richard 1896–1980
Nieuport and Seacoast Seen from an Aeroplane 1918
oil on canvas 35.5 x 39.3
IWM ART 6345

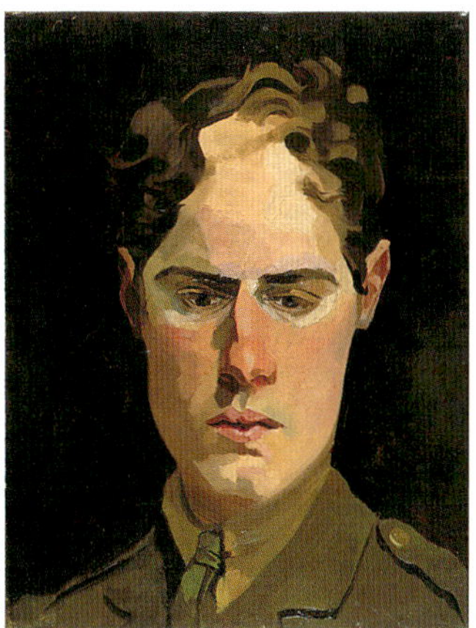

Carline, Richard 1896–1980
Self Portrait in Uniform 1918
oil on canvas 45.7 x 34.9
IWM ART 6170

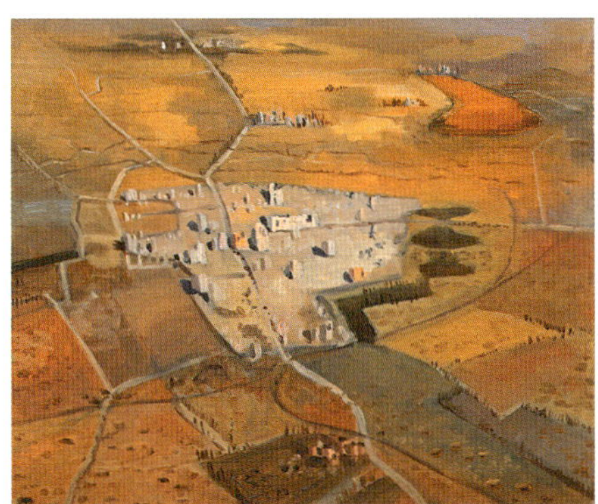

Carline, Richard 1896–1980
Ypres Seen from an Aeroplane 1918
oil on canvas 34.9 x 42.5
IWM ART 6342

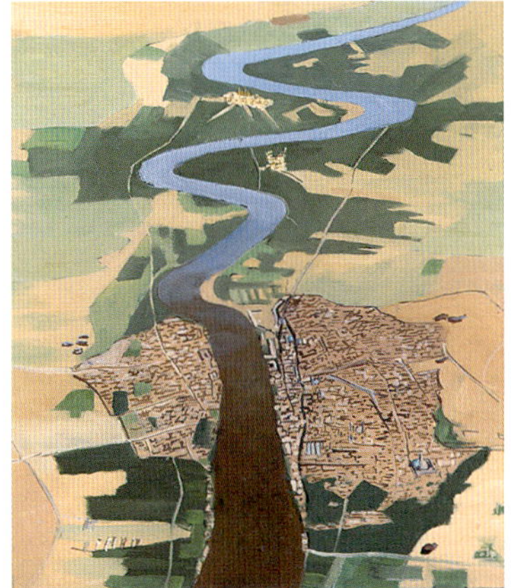

Carline, Richard 1896–1980
Baghdad 1919
oil on canvas 41.2 x 38.1
IWM ART 6348

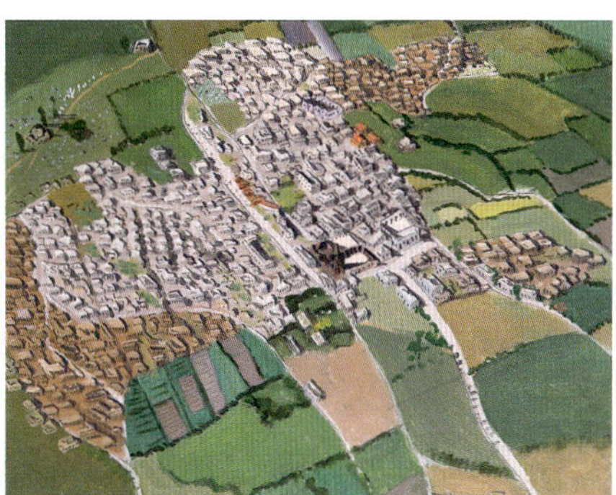

Carline, Richard 1896–1980
Gaza Seen from the Air, over British Lines on Ali Muntar Hill Looking towards the Sea 1919
oil on canvas 40.6 x 50.8
IWM ART 6350

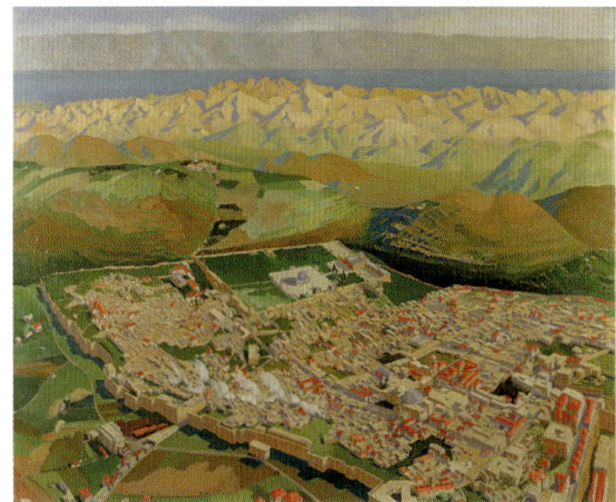

Carline, Richard 1896–1980
Jerusalem and the Dead Sea from an Aeroplane
1919
oil on canvas 105.4 x 130.8
IWM ART 3083

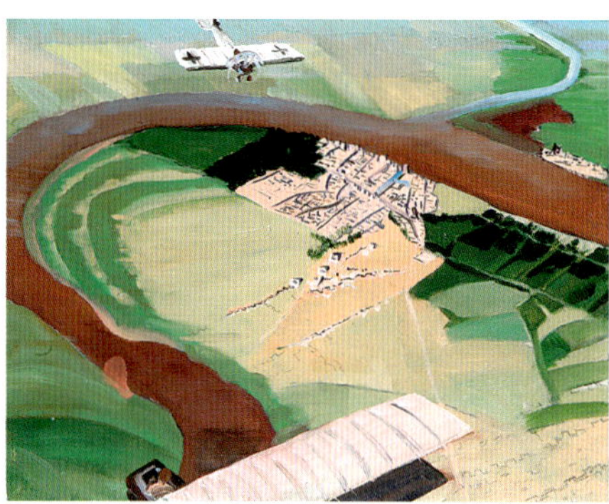

Carline, Richard 1896–1980
*Siege of Kut-el-Amara Seen from the Air:
British 'Maurice Farman' Aeroplane
Approaching, (…)* 1919
oil on canvas 37.4 x 48.2
IWM ART 6349

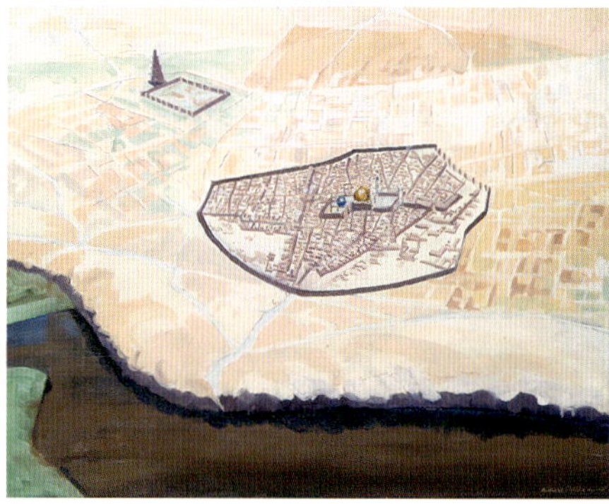

Carline, Richard 1896–1980
*The City of Samarrah and the Desert with
River Tigris* 1919
oil on canvas 50.1 x 63.5
IWM ART 6351

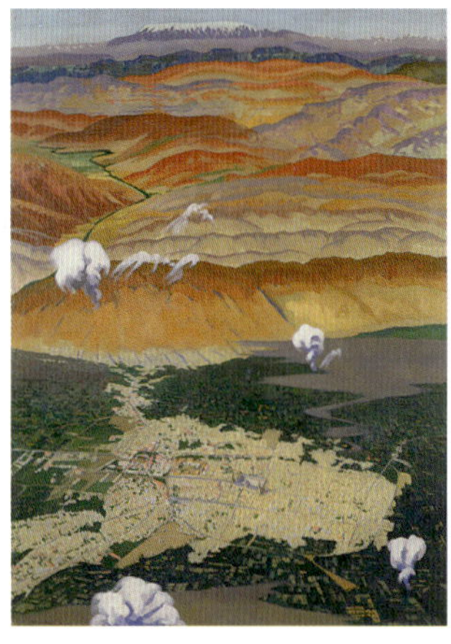

Carline, Richard 1896–1980
*Damascus and the Lebanon Mountains from
10,000 Feet* 1920
oil on canvas 143.5 x 105.4
IWM ART 3082

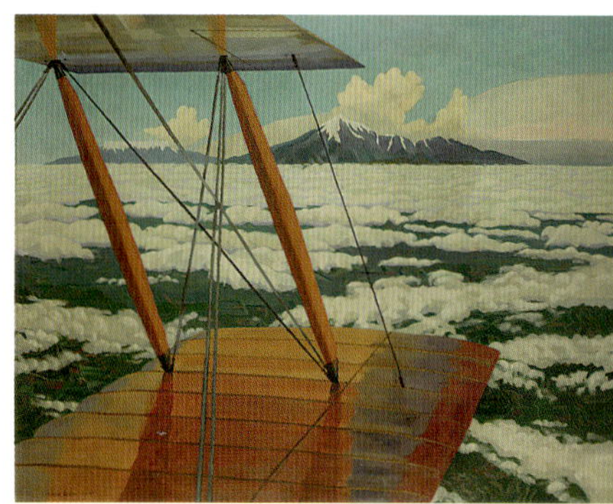

Carline, Richard 1896–1980
*Mount Hermon and Mount Sannin above the
Clouds* 1920
oil on canvas 107.9 x 138.4
IWM ART 3081

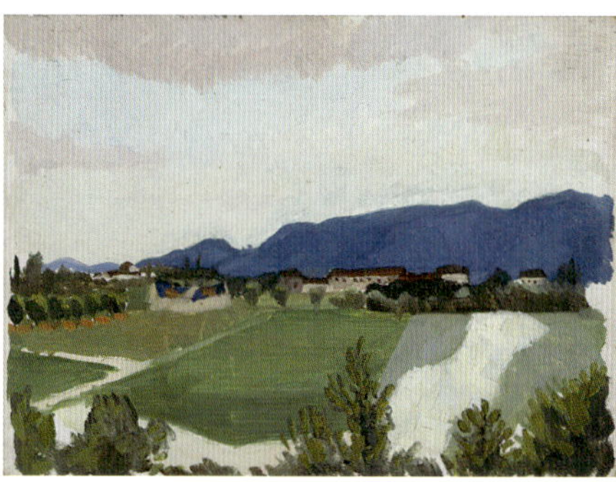

Carline, Sydney William 1888–1929
Aerodrome with Camouflaged Hangars 1918
oil on panel 32 x 41.5
IWM ART 4553

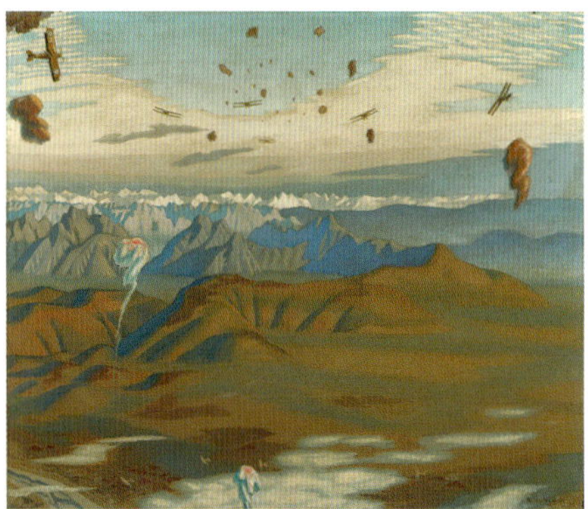

Carline, Sydney William 1888–1929
*Among the Anti-Aircraft Bursts at 20,000 Feet
above the Alps: A British Air Squadron
Crossing the Anglo-Austrian Line (…)* 1918
oil on canvas 76.2 x 91.4
IWM ART 2677

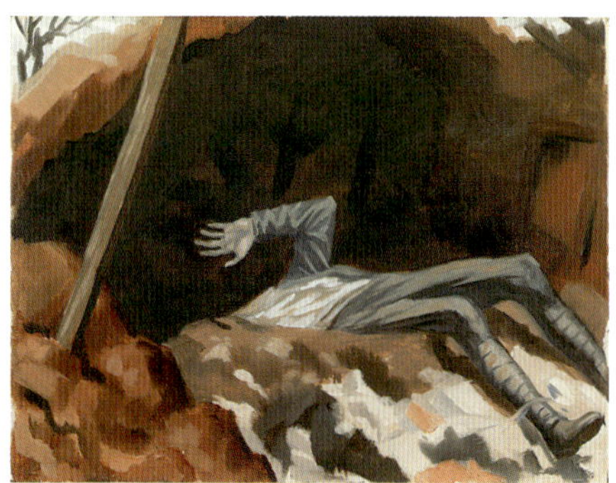

Carline, Sydney William 1888–1929
*Austrian Dugout beyond Mount Grappa after
the Italian Advance of October 1918* 1918
oil on canvas 30 x 40.5

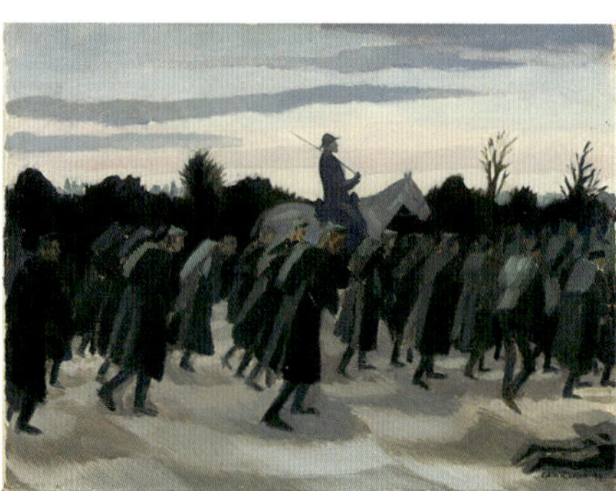

Carline, Sydney William 1888–1929
*Austrian Prisoners Driven in from the Austrian
Lines* 1918
oil on panel 29.8 x 40.6
IWM ART 2688

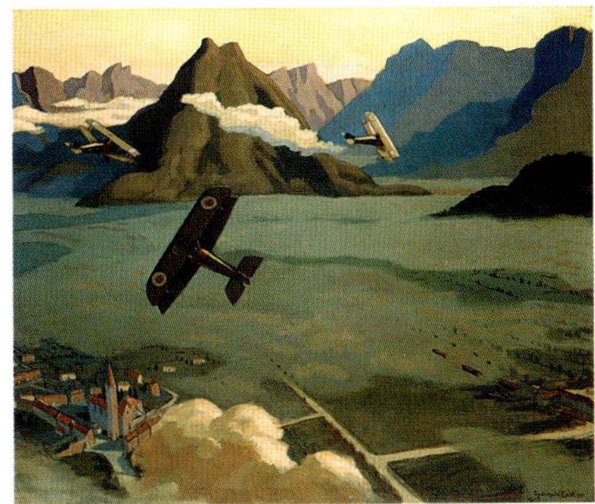

Carline, Sydney William 1888–1929
British Scouts Leaving Their Aerodrome on Patrol over the Asiago Plateau, Italy 1918
oil on canvas 76.2 x 91.4
IWM ART 2679

Carline, Sydney William 1888–1929
Italians Leaving Padua on Account of the Raids 1918
oil on board 30.5 x 40.6
IWM ART 4557

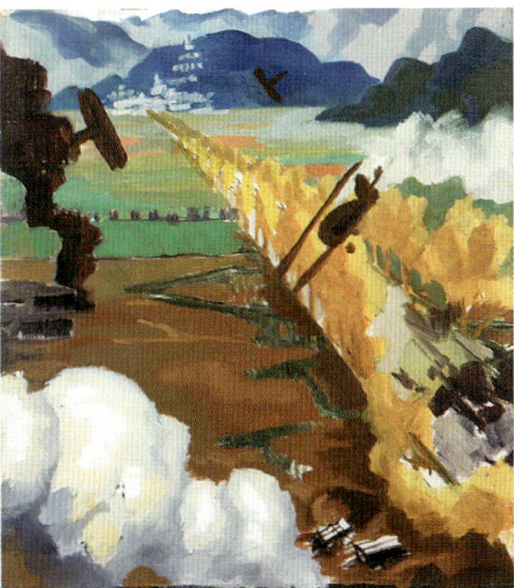

Carline, Sydney William 1888–1929
'Sopwith Camel' Patrol Attacking an Austrian Aerodrome near Sacile, Italy 1918
oil on board 38.7 x 35.3
IWM ART 4543

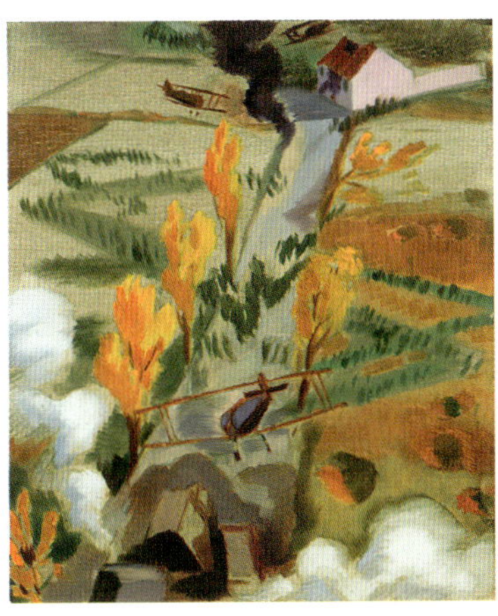

Carline, Sydney William 1888–1929
'Sopwith Camel' Patrol Attacking Austrian Troops Retreating along the Road to Udine, Italy 1918
oil on canvas 42 x 35.5
IWM ART 4544

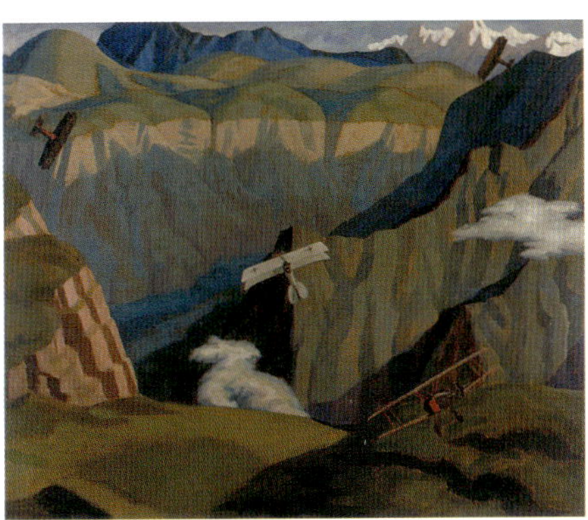

Carline, Sydney William 1888–1929
The Destruction of an Austrian Machine in the Gorge of the Brenta Valley, Italy 1918
oil on canvas 76.2 x 91.4
IWM ART 2678

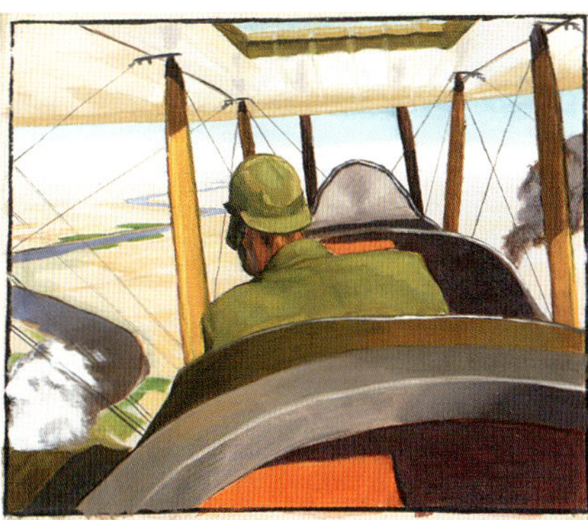

Carline, Sydney William 1888–1929
A British Pilot in a BE2c Approaching Hit along the Course of the River Euphrates, July 1919 1919
oil on canvas 40.2 x 47.8
IWM ART 4617

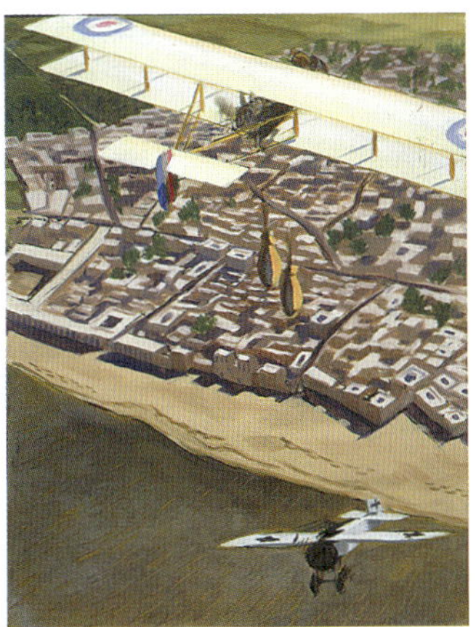

Carline, Sydney William 1888–1929
British 'Maurice Farman' Attacked by a German 'Fokker' While Dropping Sacks of Corn on Kut-el-Amara (…) 1919
oil on canvas 40.5 x 30.1
IWM ART 4628

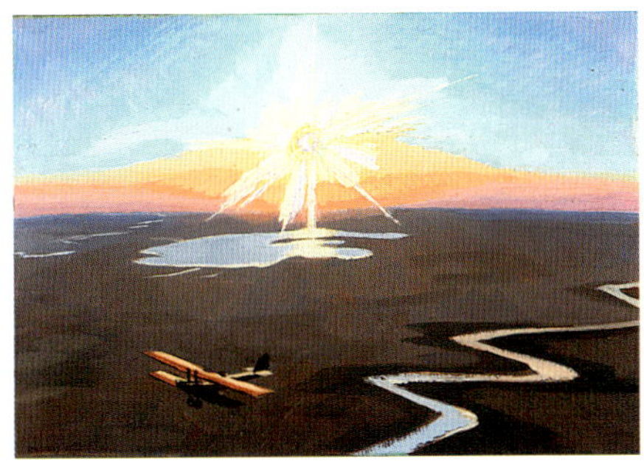

Carline, Sydney William 1888–1929
Flying over the Desert at Sunset, Mesopotamia 1919
oil on canvas 33.6 x 48.4
IWM ART 4623

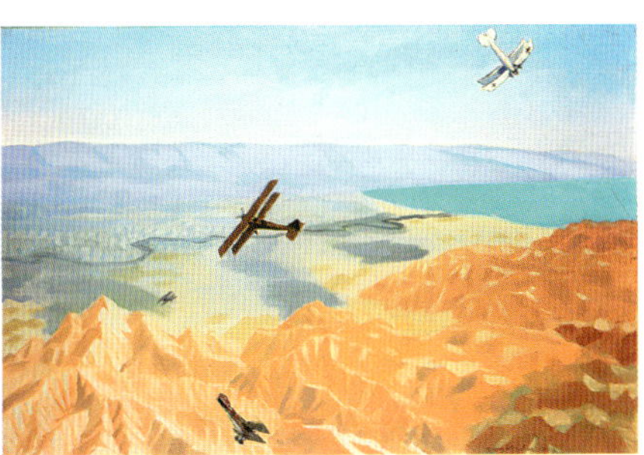

Carline, Sydney William 1888–1929
Study for 'The Dead Sea: An Enemy Aeroplane over the Dead Sea, Palestine' 1919
oil on canvas 44.2 x 67.4
IWM ART 4570

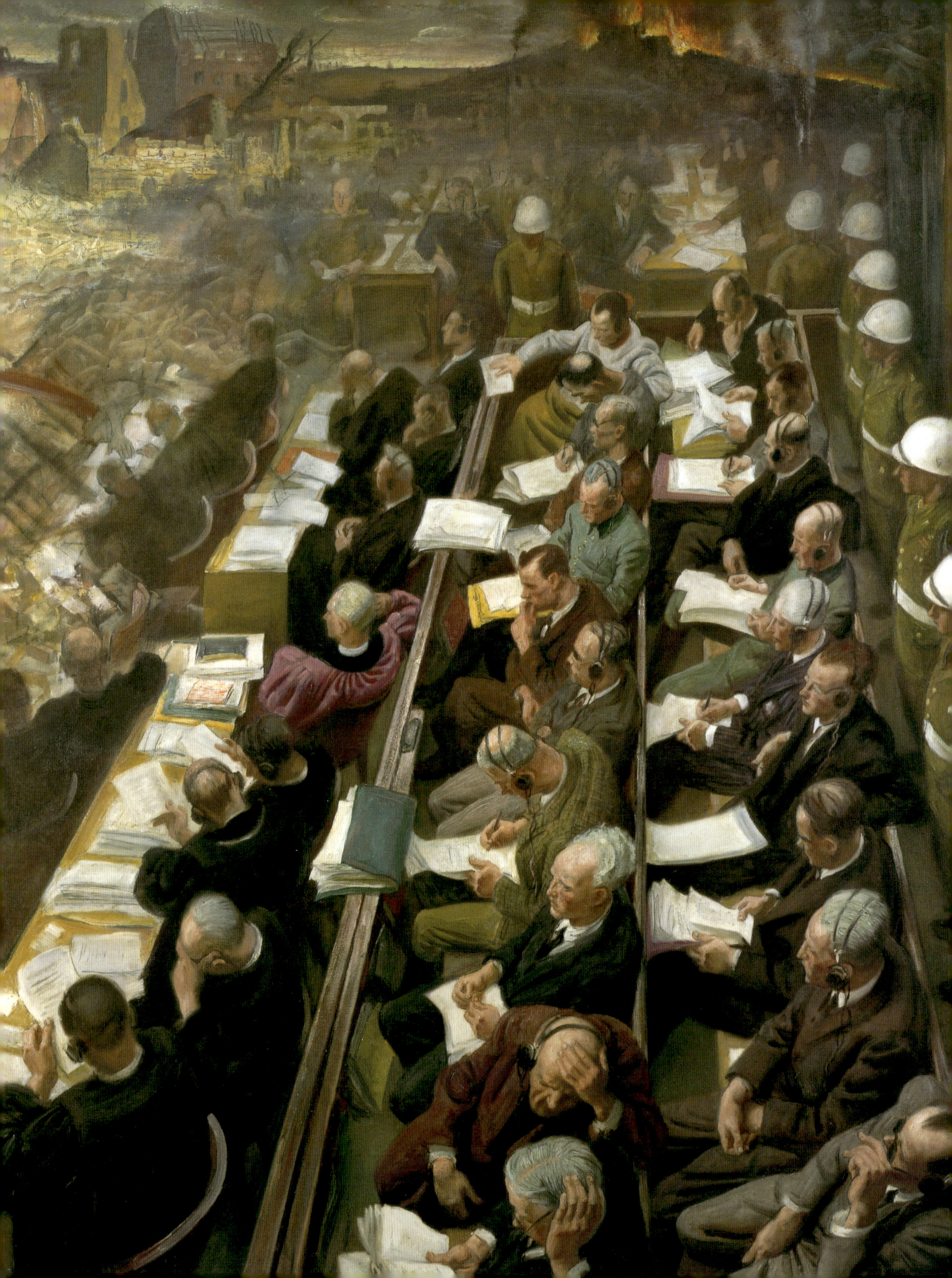

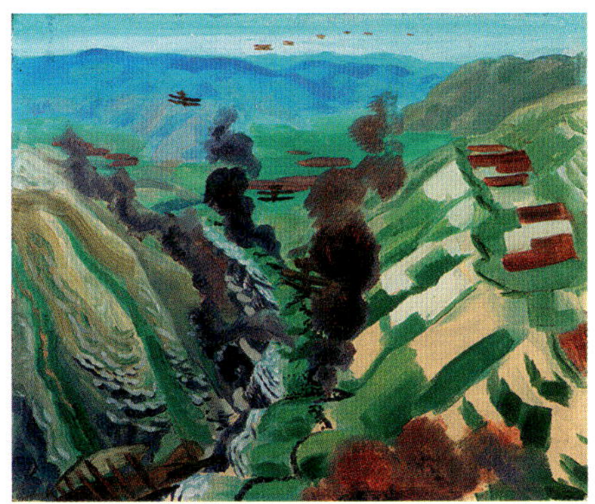

Carline, Sydney William 1888–1929
*Study for 'The Destruction of the Turkish
Transport in the Gorge of the Wadi Fara,
Palestine'* 1919
oil on canvas 33.8 x 41.7
IWM ART 4584

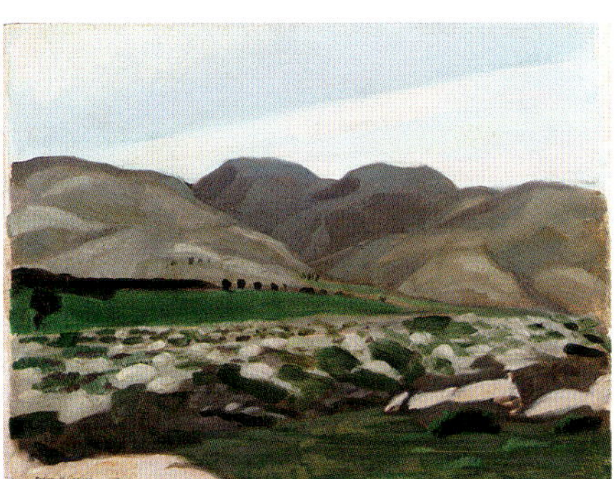

Carline, Sydney William 1888–1929
The Hills of Judea 1919
oil on canvas 30.2 x 40.3
IWM ART 4560

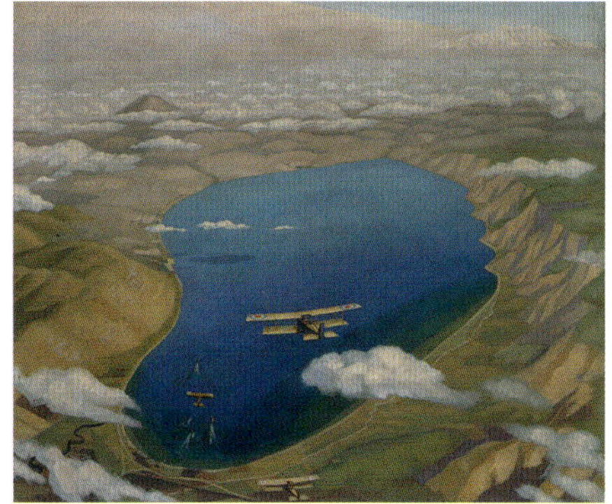

Carline, Sydney William 1888–1929
*The Sea of Galilee: Aeroplanes Attacking
Turkish Boats* 1919
oil on canvas 76.2 x 91.4
IWM ART 3080

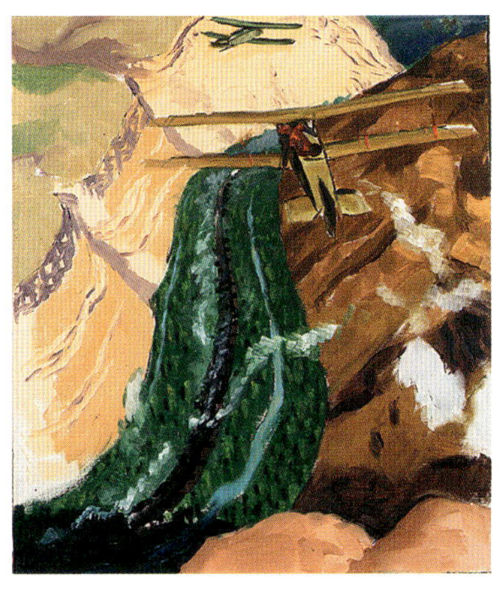

Carline, Sydney William 1888–1929
*Two British Planes Attacking the Turkish Army
Corps in the Gorge of the Wadi Baroda,
Lebanon, 30 September 1918* 1919
oil on canvas 57.4 x 37.2
IWM ART 4594

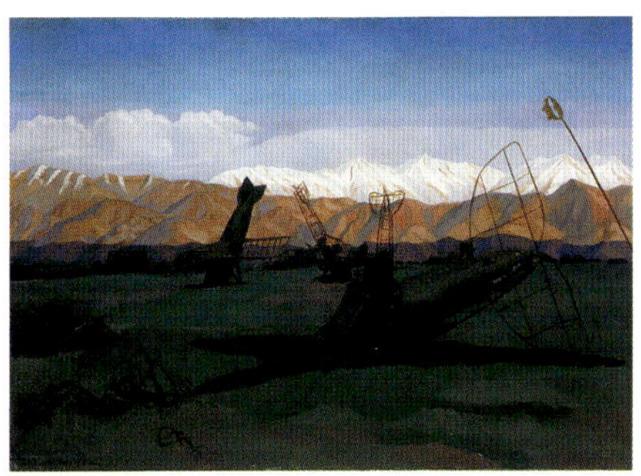

Carline, Sydney William 1888–1929
*A Destroyed Turkish Aerodrome at Rayak,
Lebanon, 1919* 1920
oil on canvas 76.2 x 106.6
IWM ART 3139

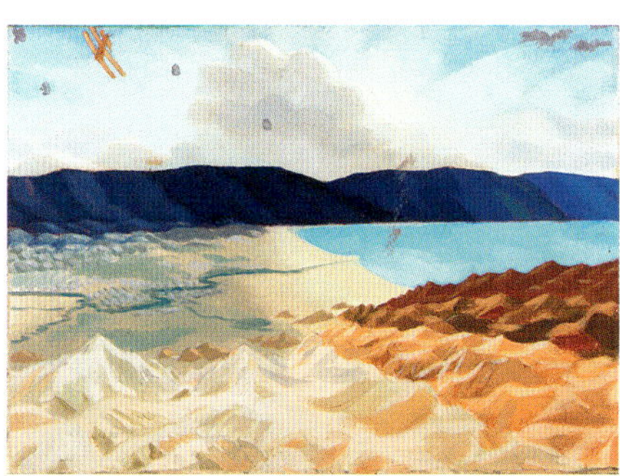

Carline, Sydney William 1888–1929
*Study for 'The Dead Sea: An Enemy Aeroplane
over the Dead Sea, Palestine'* 1920
oil on canvas 30.2 x 43
IWM ART 4583

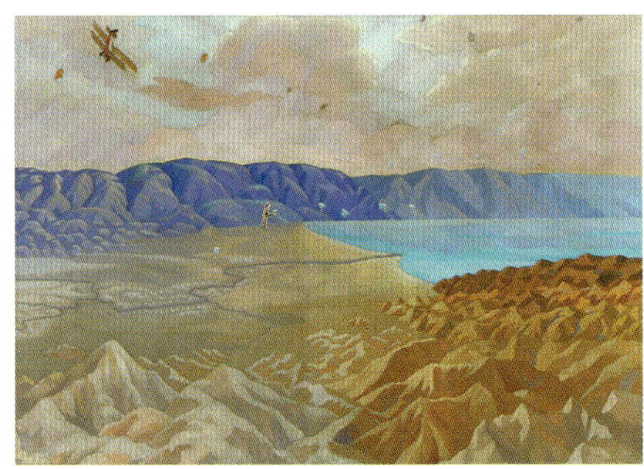

Carline, Sydney William 1888–1929
*The Dead Sea: An Enemy Aeroplane over the
Dead Sea, Palestine* 1920
oil on canvas 76.2 x 107.9
IWM ART 3079

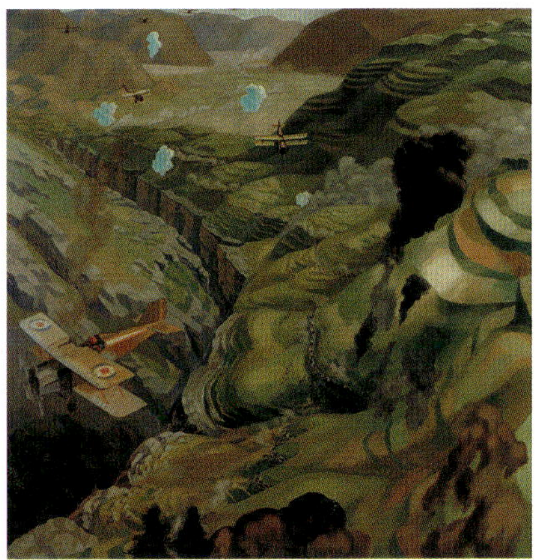

Carline, Sydney William 1888–1929
*The Destruction of the Turkish Transport in the
Gorge of the Wadi Fara, Palestine* 1920
oil on canvas 121.9 x 121.9
IWM ART 3138

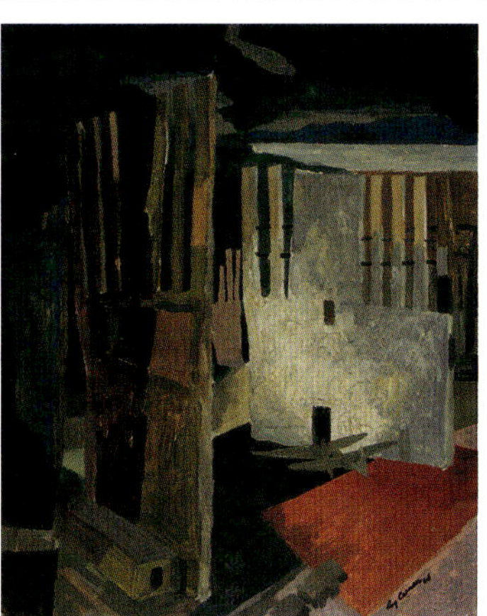

Carnon, Roy 1911–2002
Seletar, Singapore 1946
oil on board 78 x 65
IWM ART 16969

Facing page: Knight, Laura, 1877–1970, *The Nuremberg Trial* (detail), 1946, (p. 120)

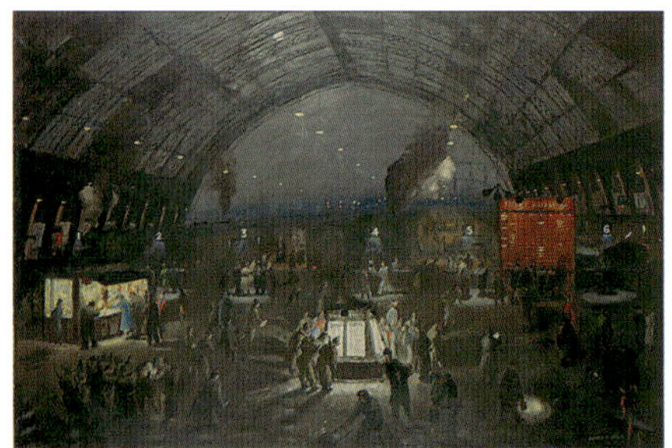

Carr, Henry Marvell 1894–1970
A Railway Terminus 1941
oil on canvas 99 x 149.8
IWM ART LD 1947

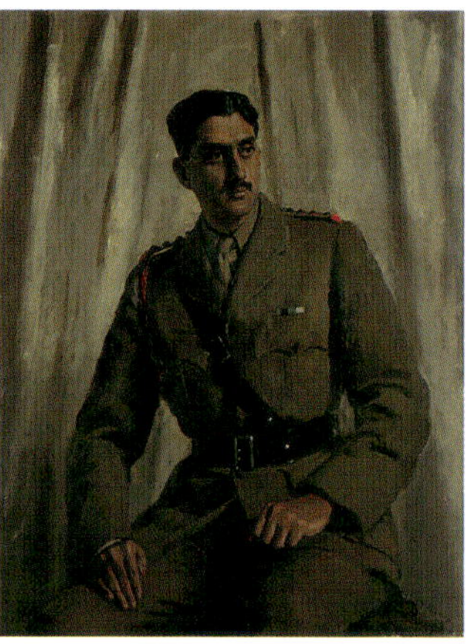

Carr, Henry Marvell 1894–1970
Captain Atal: Served at Keren, Eritrea 1941
oil on canvas 111.7 x 86.3
IWM ART LD 1212

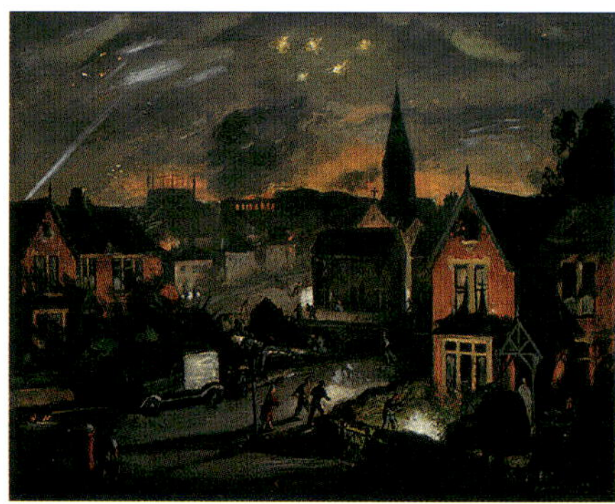

Carr, Henry Marvell 1894–1970
Incendiaries in a Suburb 1941
oil on canvas 72.8 x 91.8
IWM ART LD 1518

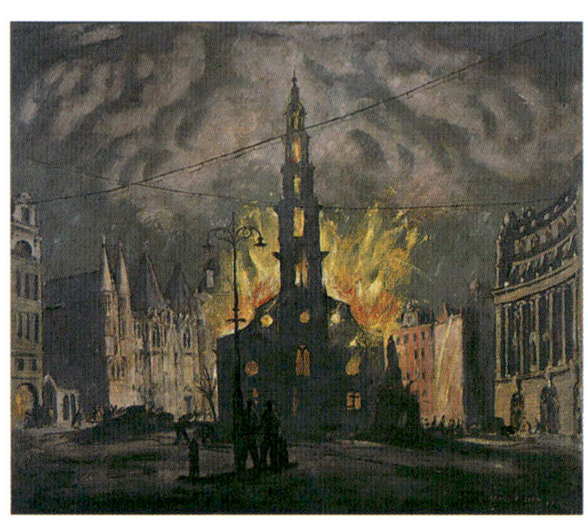

Carr, Henry Marvell 1894–1970
*St Clement Dane's Church on Fire after Being
Bombed* 1941
oil on canvas 76.2 x 91.4
IWM ART LD 1315

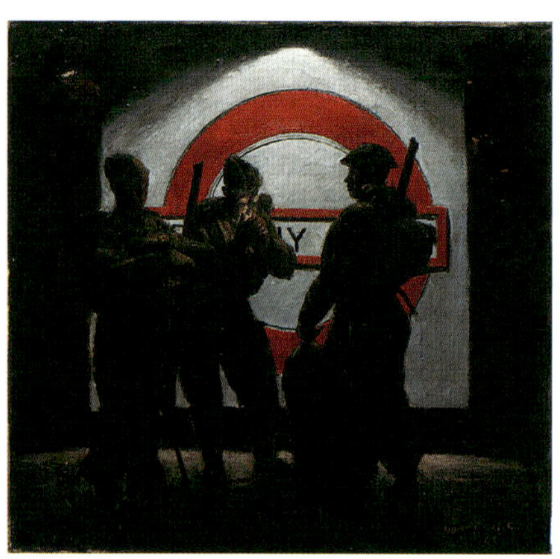

Carr, Henry Marvell 1894–1970
Familiar Silhouettes 1942
oil on canvas 50.8 x 53.9
IWM ART LD 1734

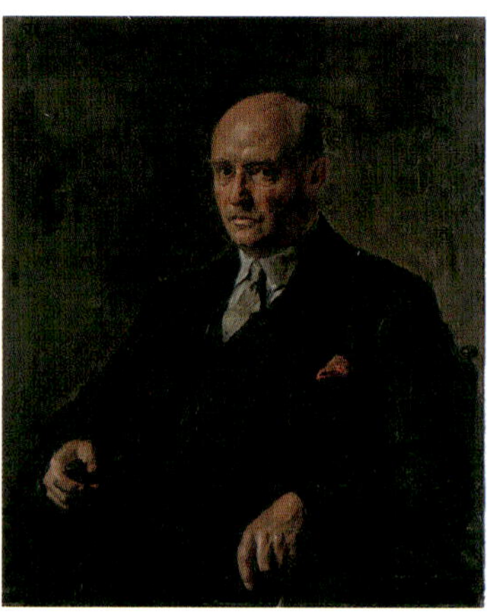

Carr, Henry Marvell 1894–1970
Sir Arthur Street, KCB, KBE, CMG, CIE, MC
1942
oil on canvas 91.4 x 76.2
IWM ART LD 2432

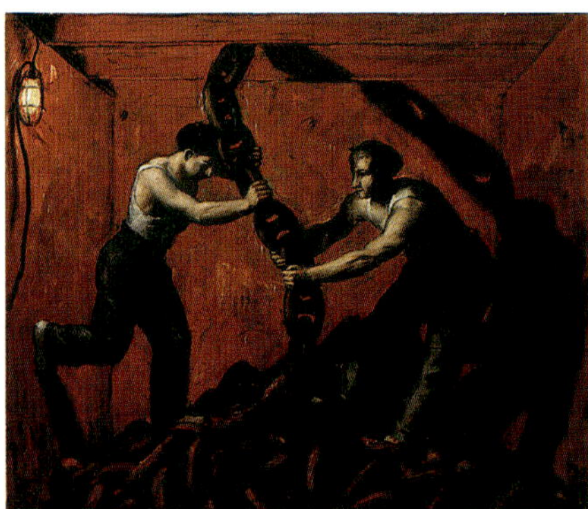

Carr, Henry Marvell 1894–1970
The Merchant Navy: The Chain Locker 1942
oil on canvas 76.5 x 91.6
IWM ART LD 2590

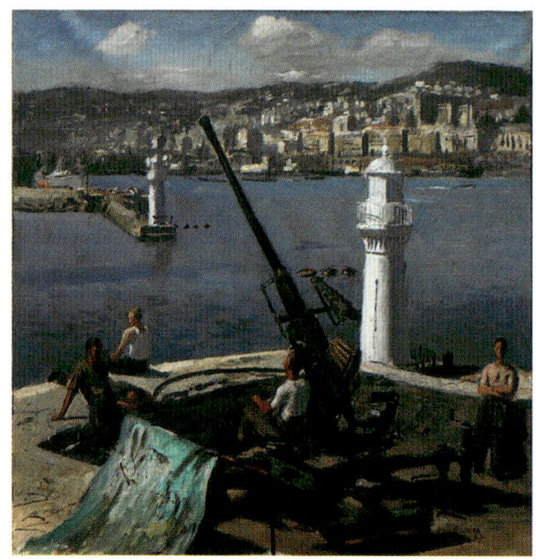

Carr, Henry Marvell 1894–1970
A Bofors Gun, Algiers 1943
oil on canvas 76.8 x 76
IWM ART LD 2964

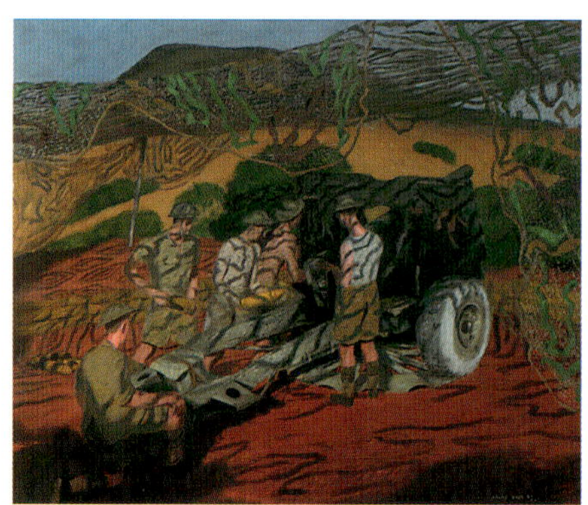

Carr, Henry Marvell 1894–1970
*A Camouflaged 25-Pounder Gun in Action
near Medjez-el-Bab with Djebel Djaffa, Tunis,
in the Background* 1943
oil on canvas 86.3 x 104.1
IWM ART LD 3231

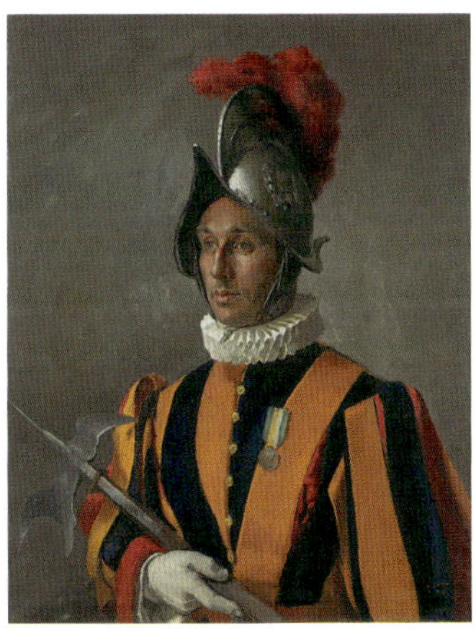

Carr, Henry Marvell 1894–1970
A Member of the Pope's Swiss Guard 1943
oil on canvas 99 x 78.7
IWM ART LD 4517

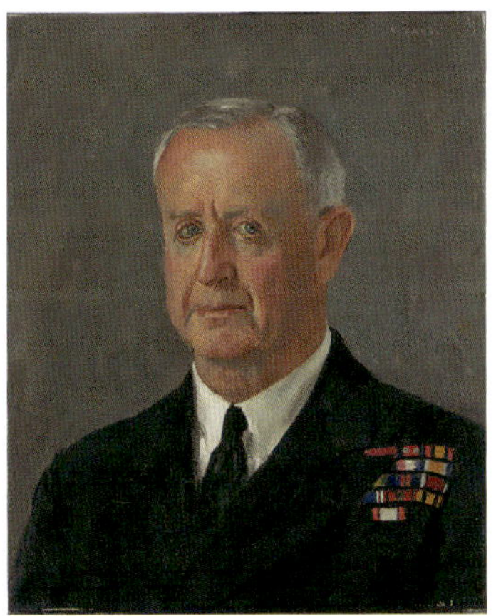

Carr, Henry Marvell 1894–1970
*Admiral of the Fleet, Sir Andrew Cunningham
(1890–1967), Bt, GCB, DSO* 1943
oil on canvas 53.3 x 44.4
IWM ART LD 2958

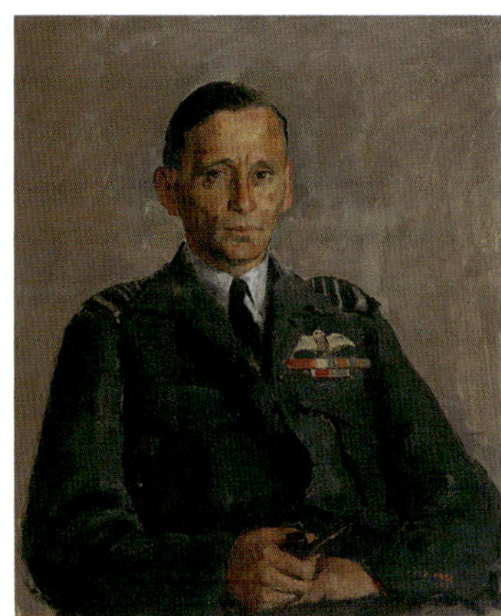

Carr, Henry Marvell 1894–1970
*Air Chief Marshal Sir Arthur Tedder
(1890–1967), GCB* 1943
oil on canvas 76.2 x 63.5
IWM ART LD 3054

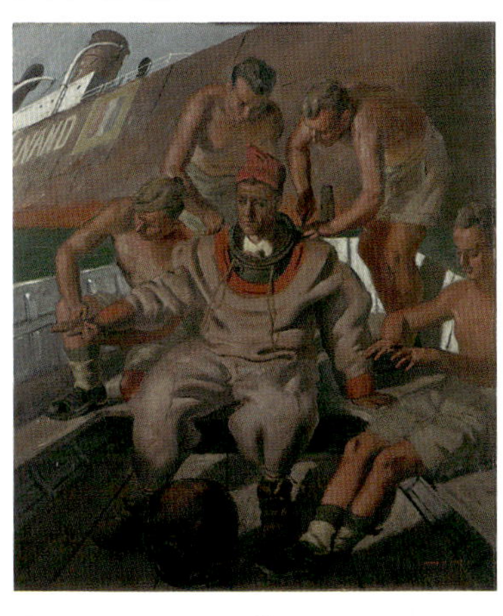

Carr, Henry Marvell 1894–1970
*Army Divers: Sappers of a Port Reconstruction
and Repair Group* 1943
oil on canvas 98.4 x 86.3
IWM ART LD 3396

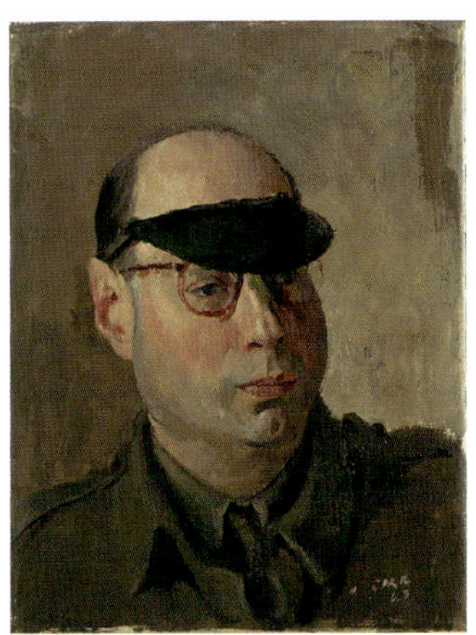

Carr, Henry Marvell 1894–1970
*Arthur E. Mann, War Correspondent, Mutual
Broadcasting Company of America* 1943
oil on canvas 45 x 34.9
IWM ART LD 2915

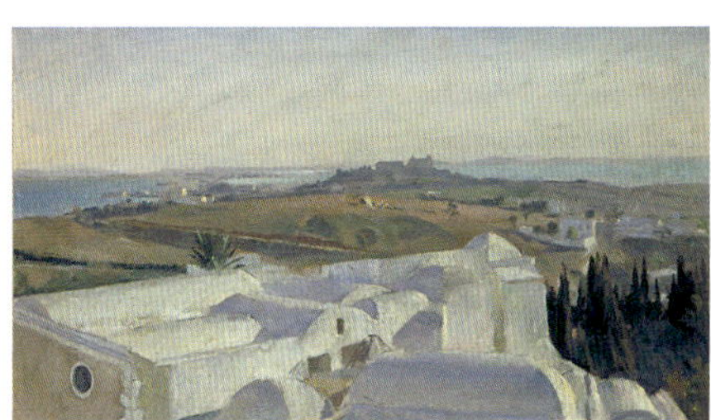

Carr, Henry Marvell 1894–1970
Carthage 1943
oil on canvas 50.8 x 91.4
IWM ART LD 3393

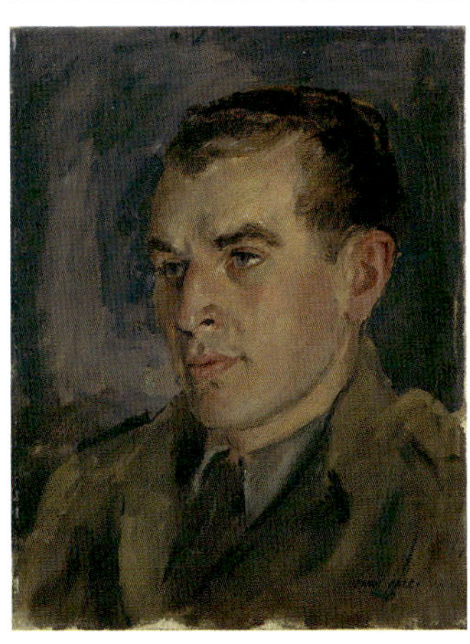

Carr, Henry Marvell 1894–1970
*Charles C. Collingwood, War Correspondent,
Columbia Broadcasting System of America*
1943
oil on canvas 45 x 34.9
IWM ART LD 2957

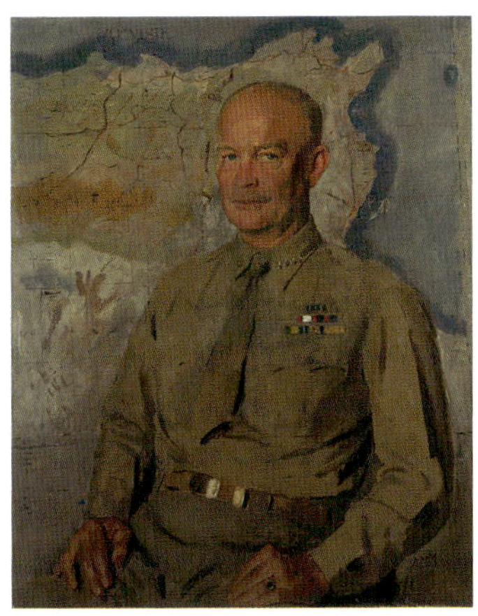

Carr, Henry Marvell 1894–1970
General Dwight D. Eisenhower (1890–1969)
1943
oil on canvas 93.3 x 75.5
IWM ART LD 2966

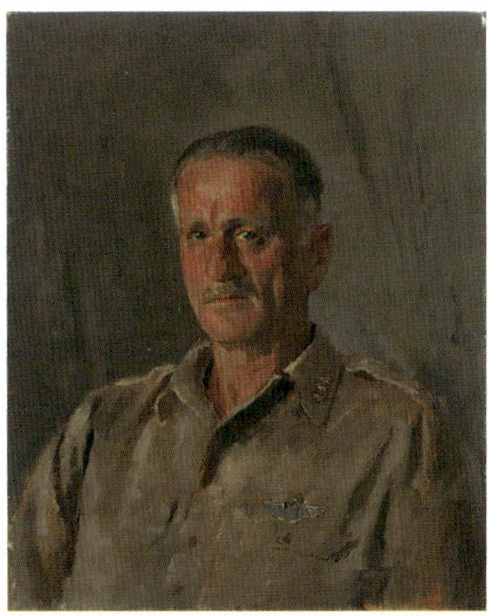

Carr, Henry Marvell 1894–1970
*General Spaatz (1891–1974), Air Commodore-
in-Chief, American Air Force* 1943
oil on canvas 63.5 x 53.3
IWM ART LD 3229

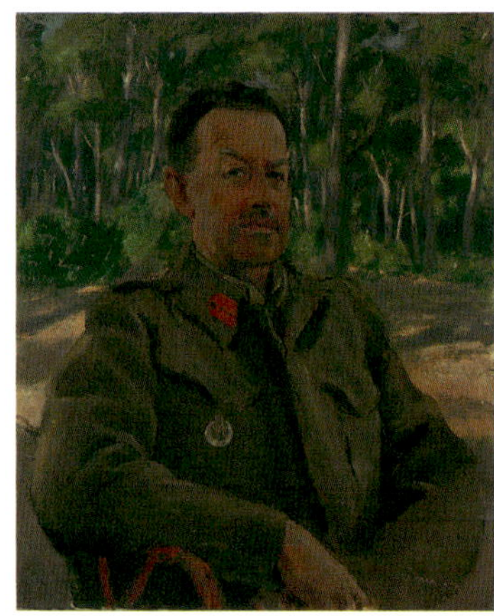

Carr, Henry Marvell 1894–1970
*General the Honourable Sir Harold Alexander
(1891–1969), GCB, CSI, DSO* 1943
oil on canvas 76 x 63
IWM ART LD 3073

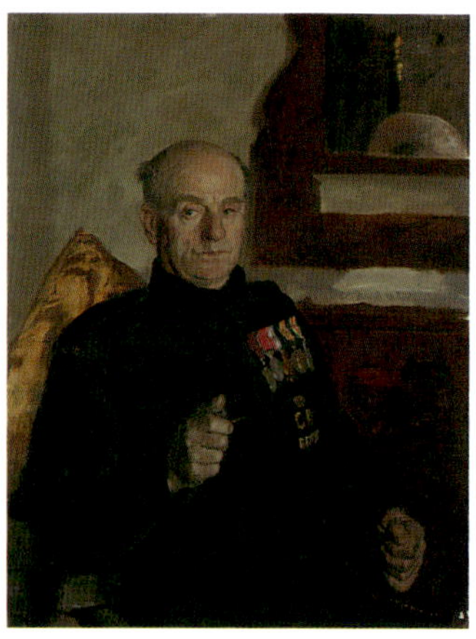

Carr, Henry Marvell 1894–1970
Henry Cox, CMG, BEM 1943
oil on canvas 91.4 x 71.1
IWM ART LD 2681

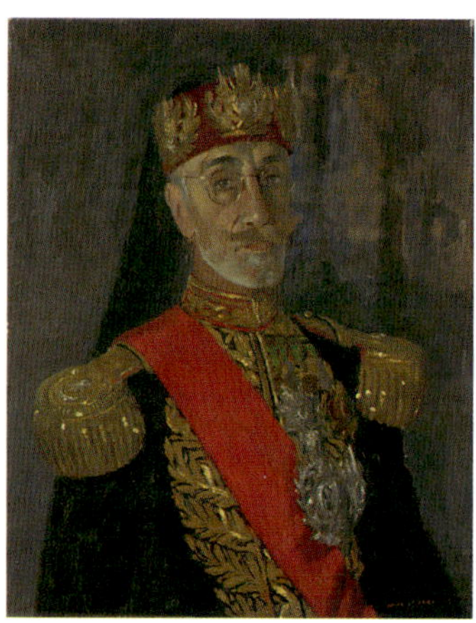

Carr, Henry Marvell 1894–1970
His Highness the Bey of Tunis 1943
oil on canvas 73.6 x 58.4
IWM ART LD 3394

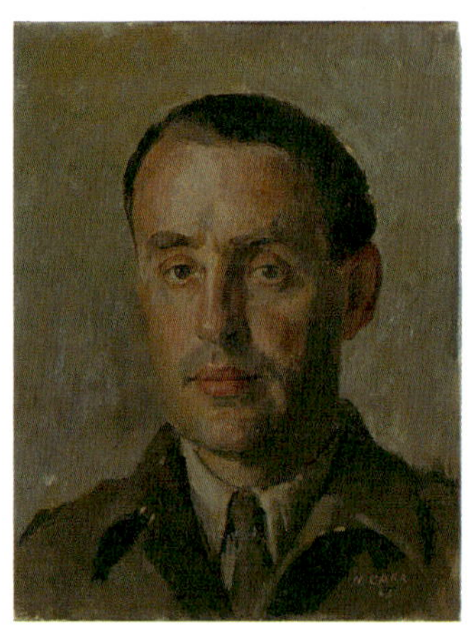

Carr, Henry Marvell 1894–1970
*Howard Marshall, War Correspondent, British
Broadcasting Corporation* 1943
oil on canvas 45 x 34.9
IWM ART LD 2860

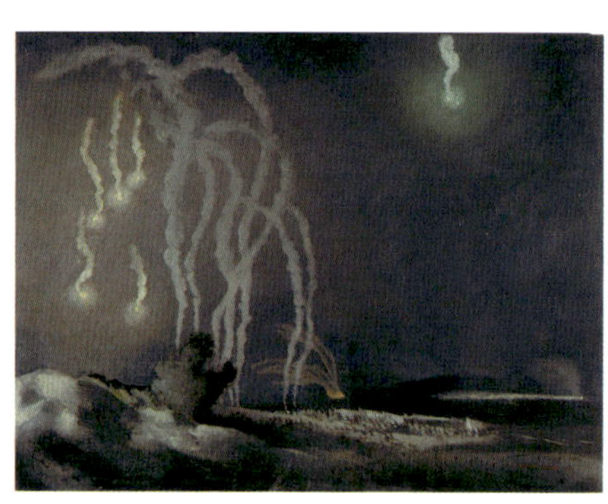

Carr, Henry Marvell 1894–1970
Infantry Landing Craft Disembarking Troops
1943
oil on canvas 67.3 x 90.1
IWM ART LD 3099

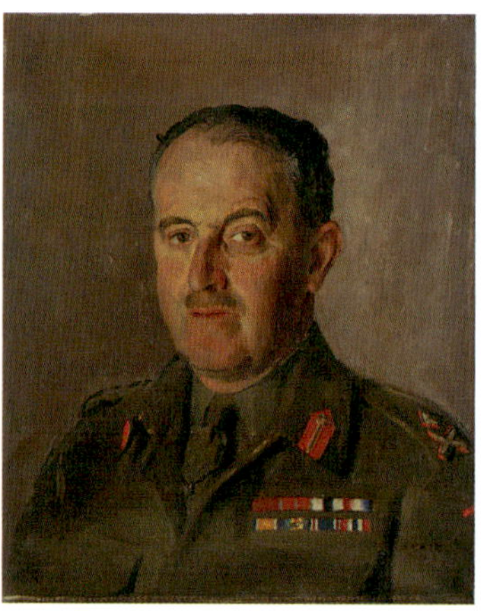

Carr, Henry Marvell 1894–1970
Major General H. M. Gale, CB, CBE, MC
1943
oil on canvas 57.4 x 47.9
IWM ART LD 2960

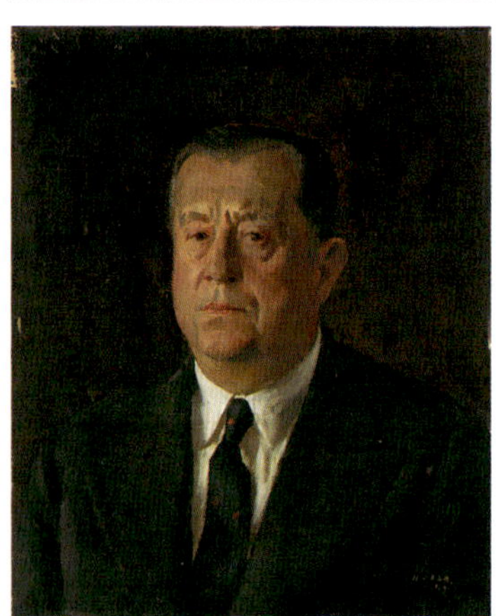

Carr, Henry Marvell 1894–1970
*Marcel Peyrouton (1887–1983), Governor
General, Algeria, 1943* 1943
oil on canvas 60.9 x 50.8
IWM ART LD 2961

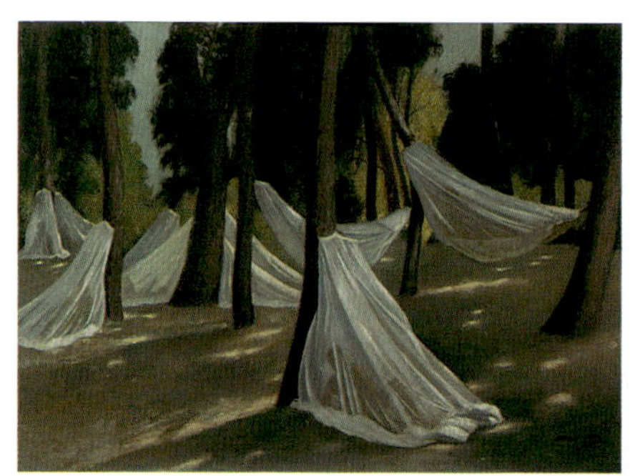

Carr, Henry Marvell 1894–1970
Mosquito Nets 1943
oil on canvas 73.6 x 104.1
IWM ART LD 3070

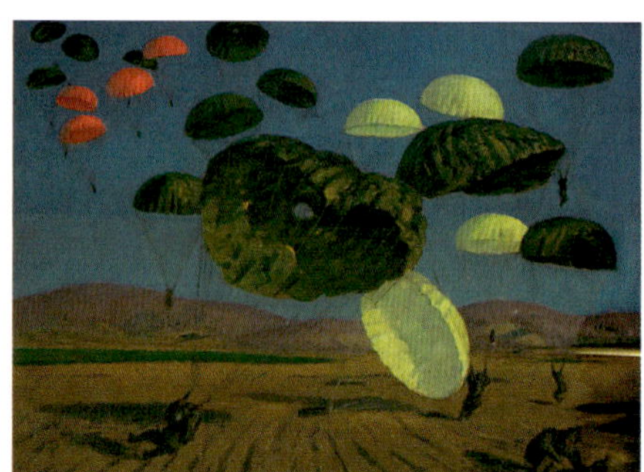

Carr, Henry Marvell 1894–1970
Parachute Drop 1943
oil on canvas 76.2 x 101.9
IWM ART LD 3072

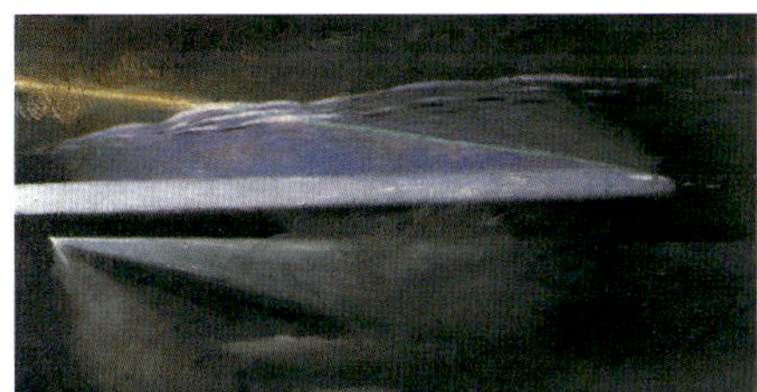

Carr, Henry Marvell 1894–1970
Searchlight on Infantry Landing Craft 1943
oil on canvas 53.3 x 104.1
IWM ART LD 3102

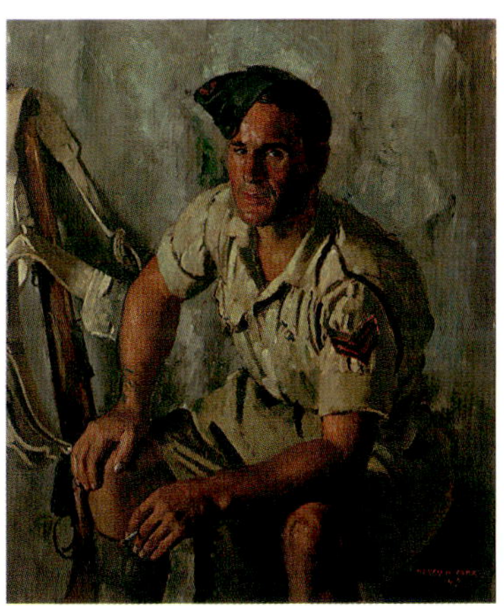

Carr, Henry Marvell 1894–1970
*Sergeant B. Montague: One of the Desert Rats
(7th Armoured Division)* 1943
oil on canvas 88.9 x 76.2
IWM ART LD 3465

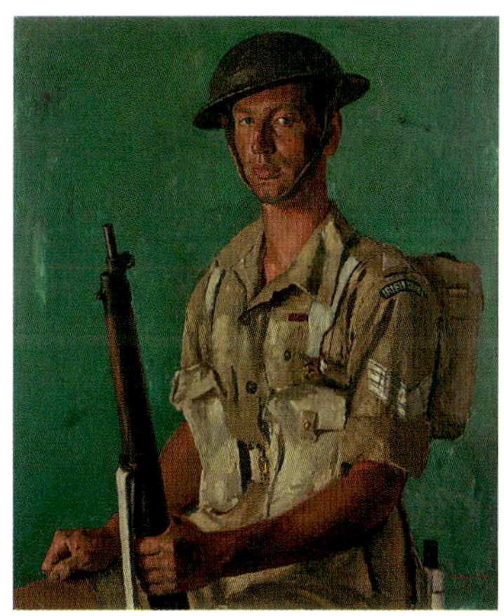

Carr, Henry Marvell 1894–1970
*Sergeant J. P. Kenneally, VC, First Battalion,
Irish Guards* 1943
oil on canvas 89.5 x 76.2
IWM ART LD 3395

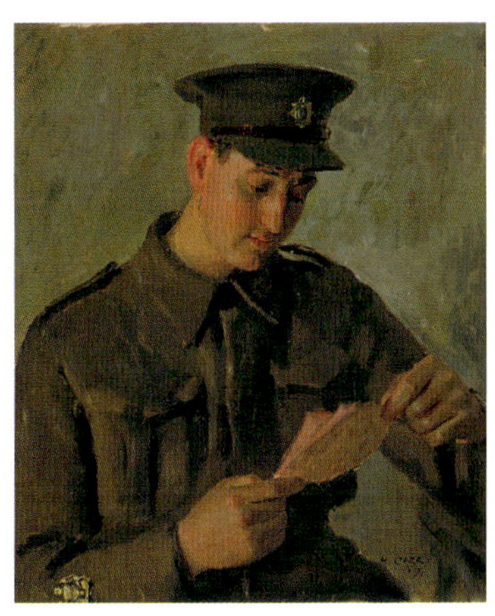

Carr, Henry Marvell 1894–1970
Staff Sergeant Major E. A. Billett 1943
oil on canvas 60.9 x 51.4
IWM ART LD 2962

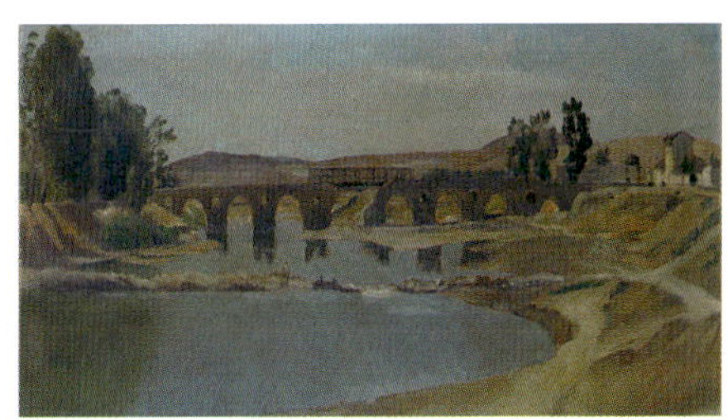

Carr, Henry Marvell 1894–1970
The Bailey Bridge at Medjez-el-Bab 1943
oil on canvas 48.2 x 87.6
IWM ART LD 3100

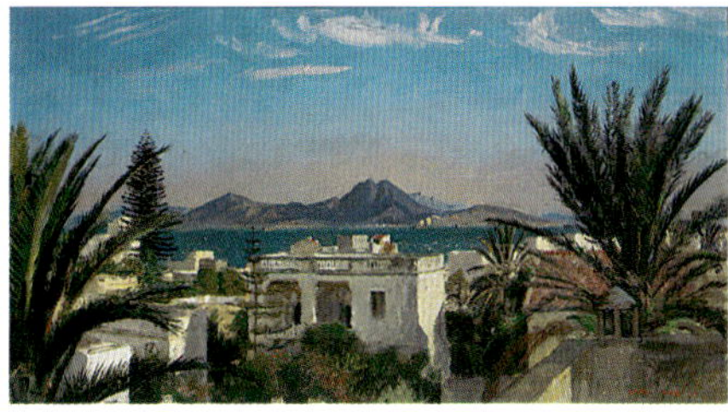

Carr, Henry Marvell 1894–1970
The Gulf of Carthage 1943
oil on canvas 46.9 x 86.3
IWM ART LD 3230

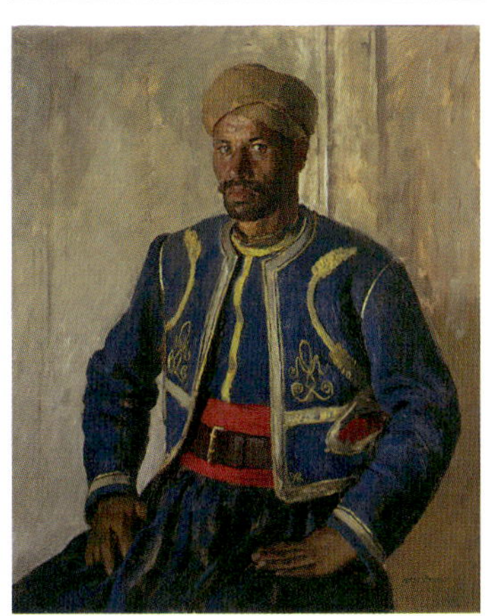

Carr, Henry Marvell 1894–1970
Tirailleur Algérien 1943
oil on canvas 90.1 x 74.9
IWM ART LD 3103

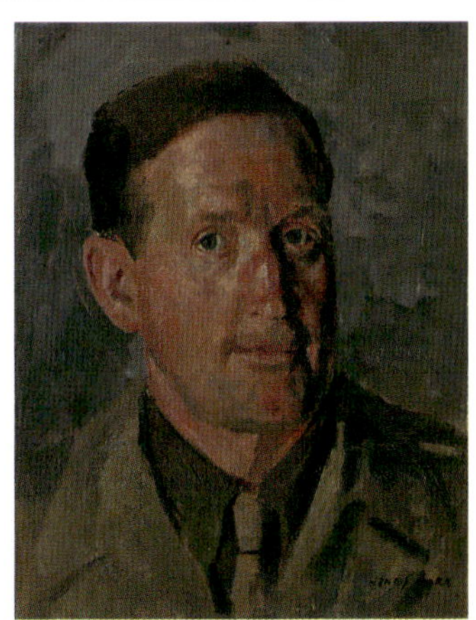

Carr, Henry Marvell 1894–1970
*William E. Mundy, Daily Telegraph War
Correspondent* 1943
oil on canvas 45 x 34.9
IWM ART LD 2956

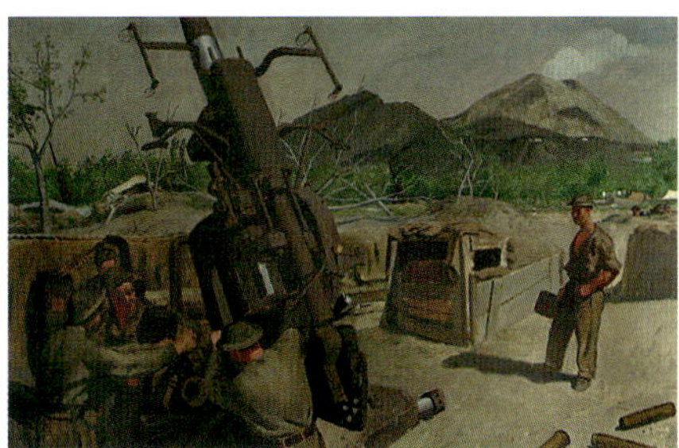

Carr, Henry Marvell 1894–1970
*A 3.7 Anti-Aircraft Gun of 393/72 Heavy Anti-
Aircraft Regiment, RA, CMF* 1944
oil on canvas 81.2 x 130.8
IWM ART LD 4064

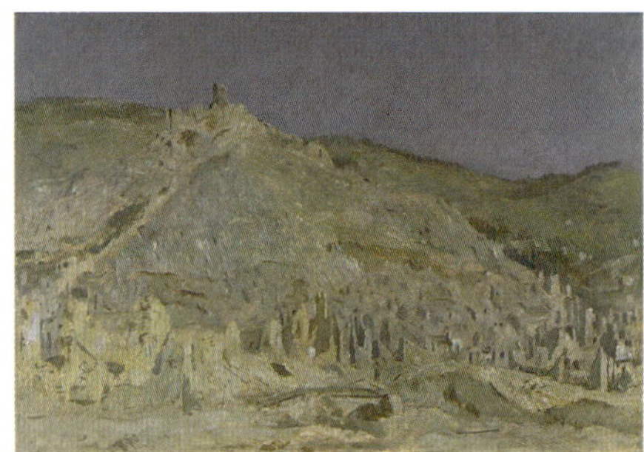

Carr, Henry Marvell 1894–1970
Cassino 1944
oil on canvas 50.8 x 74.9
IWM ART LD 4164

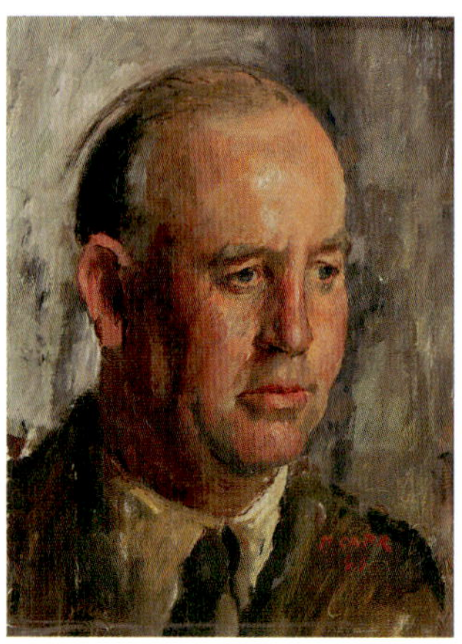

Carr, Henry Marvell 1894–1970
Edward Ardizzone (1900–1979), Official War Artist 1944
oil on canvas 40.6 x 30.4
IWM ART LD 4056

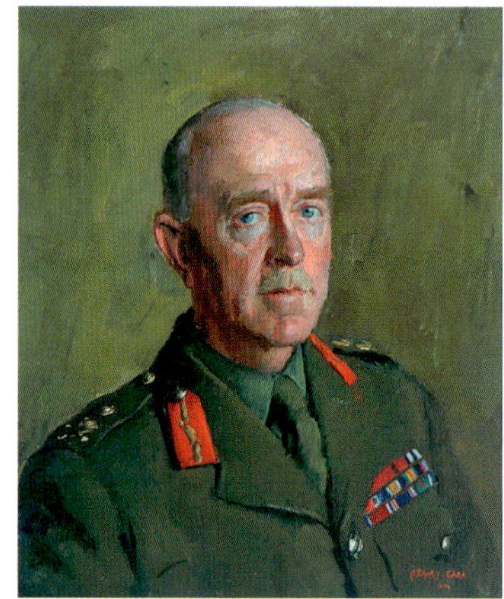

Carr, Henry Marvell 1894–1970
General Sir Harold Franklyn, KCB, DSO, MC 1944
oil on canvas 60.3 x 49.8
IWM ART LD 4806

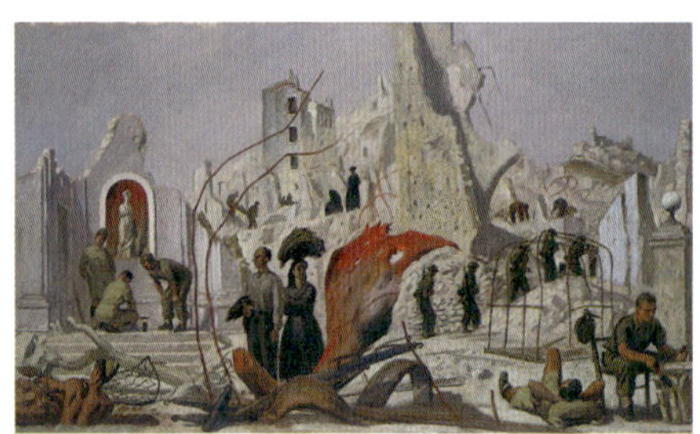

Carr, Henry Marvell 1894–1970
Liberation 1944
oil on canvas 99 x 170.1
IWM ART LD 4515

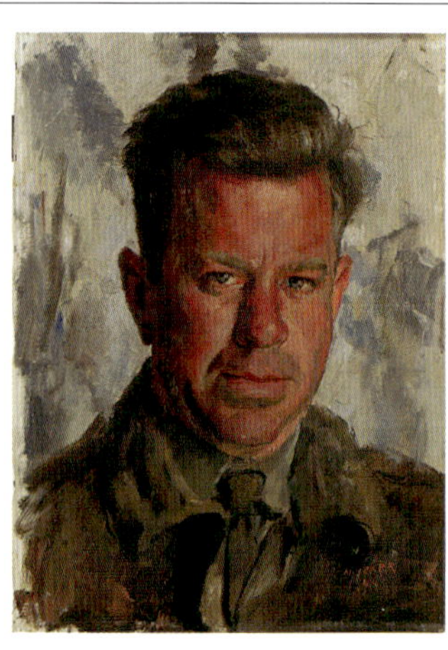

Carr, Henry Marvell 1894–1970
Lieutenant W. F. Smyth, Gunner Officer 1944
oil on canvas 43.8 x 32.3
IWM ART LD 4060

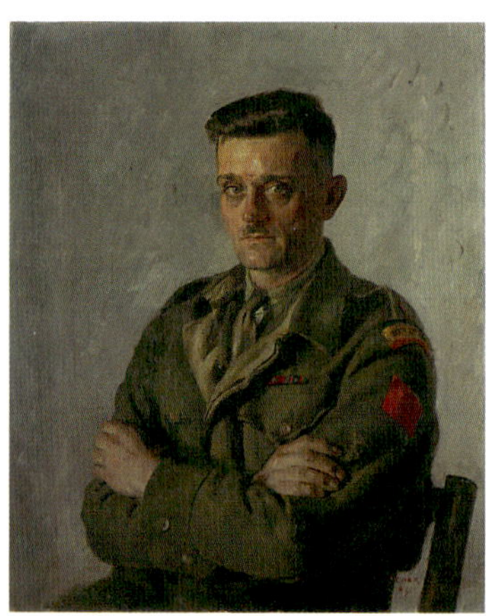

Carr, Henry Marvell 1894–1970
Major Paul Triquet, VC, of Cabano, Province of Quebec 1944
oil on canvas 74.6 x 61.9
IWM ART LD 3903

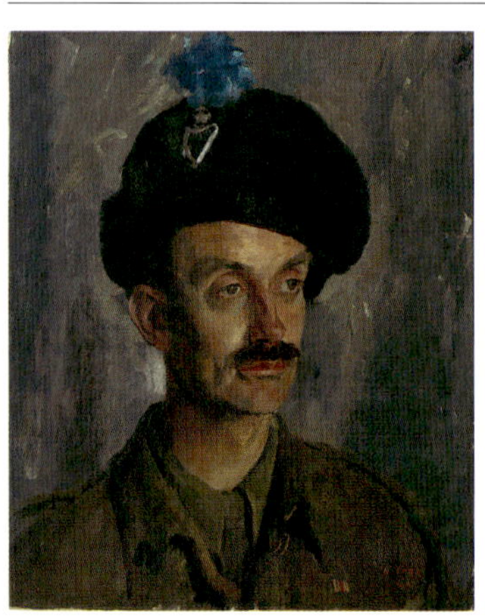

Carr, Henry Marvell 1894–1970
Major the Viscount Stopford, First Battalion, London Irish Rifles (Royal Ulster Rifles) 1944
oil on canvas 54.6 x 45.7
IWM ART LD 4058

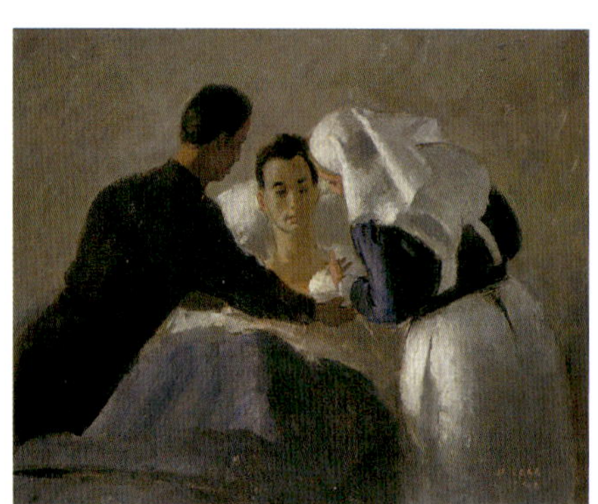

Carr, Henry Marvell 1894–1970
Nurse Giving an Injection of Penicilin to a Wounded Man, 15th Canadian General Hospital 1944
oil on canvas 40.6 x 50.8
IWM ART LD 3905

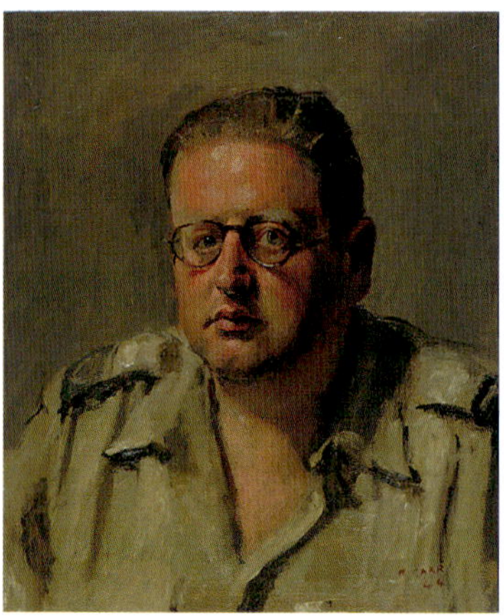

Carr, Henry Marvell 1894–1970
Paul Wyand, War Correspondent 1944
oil on canvas 53.9 x 45.4
IWM ART LD 4704

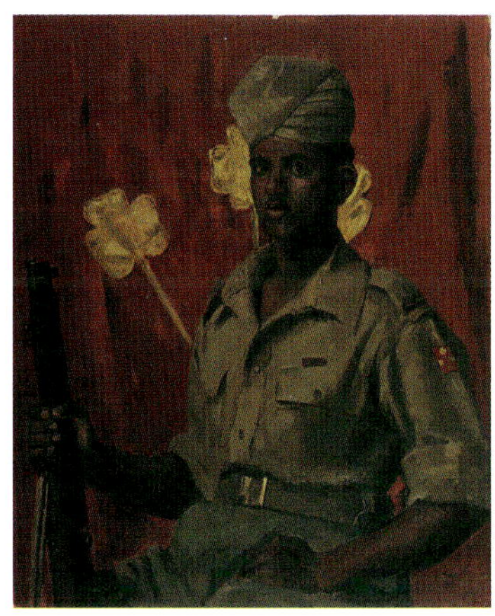

Carr, Henry Marvell 1894–1970
*Sepoy Kamal Ram (1924–1982), VC, 8th
Punjab Regiment* 1944
oil on canvas 90.1 x 74.9
IWM ART LD 4516

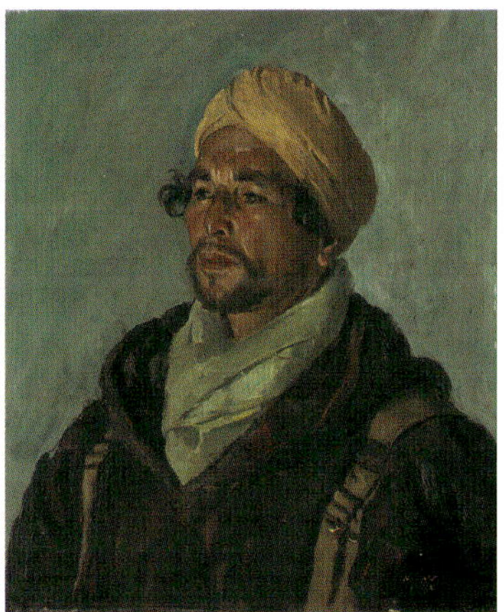

Carr, Henry Marvell 1894–1970
The Goumier 1944
oil on canvas 63.5 x 53.3
IWM ART LD 4059

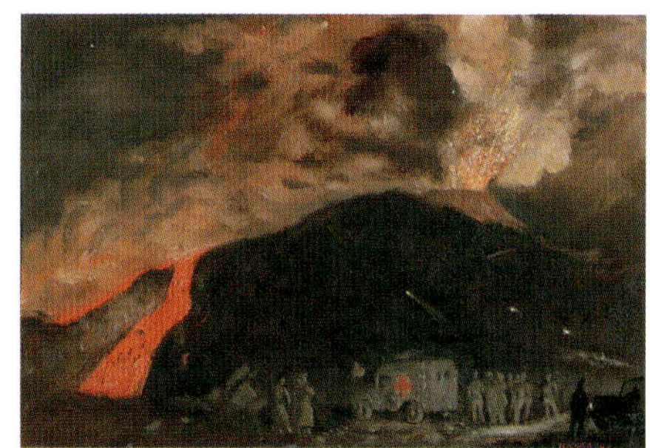

Carr, Henry Marvell 1894–1970
Vesuvius in Eruption, March 1944 1944
oil on canvas 36.8 x 54.6
IWM ART LD 3906

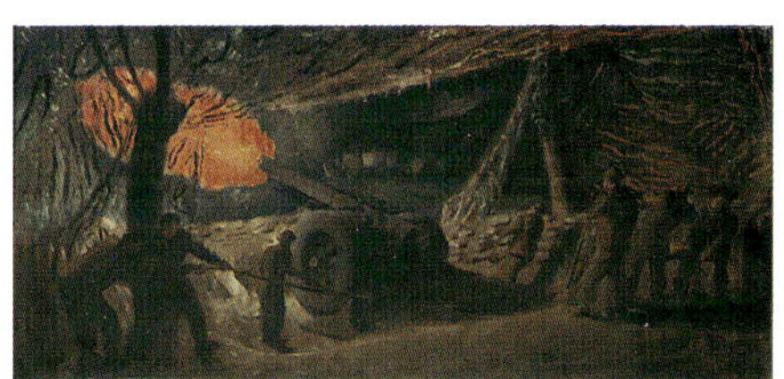

Carr, Henry Marvell 1894–1970
A 7.2 Gun Firing at Night c.1944
oil on canvas 33 x 70.4
IWM ART LD 4061

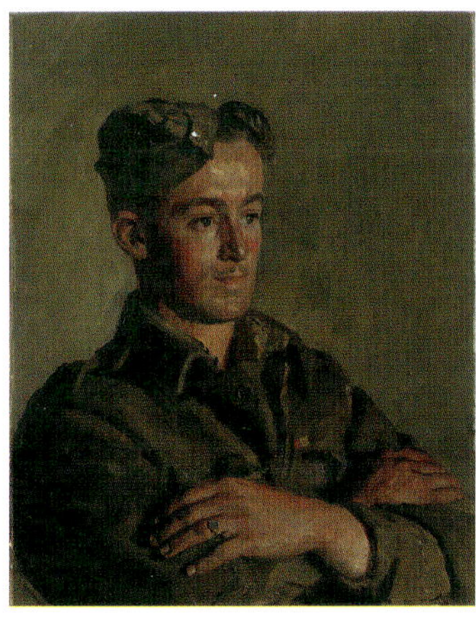

Carr, Henry Marvell 1894–1970
A Cockney Soldier c.1944
oil on canvas 61.5 x 49.5
IWM ART LD 3902

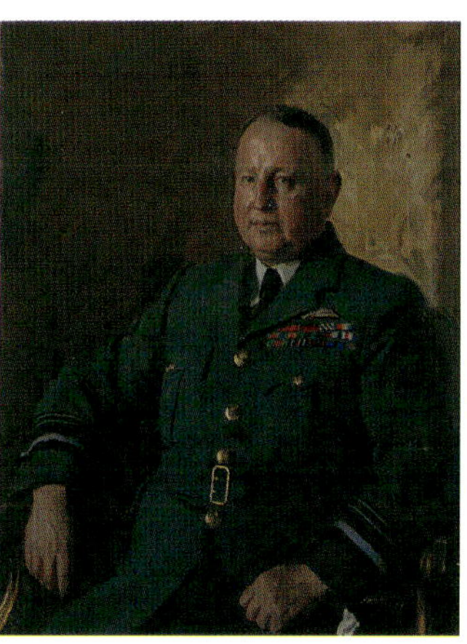

Carr, Henry Marvell 1894–1970
*Air Marshal Sir Leslie Hollinghurst, KBE, CB,
DFC* 1945
oil on canvas 91.4 x 71.1
IWM ART LD 5692

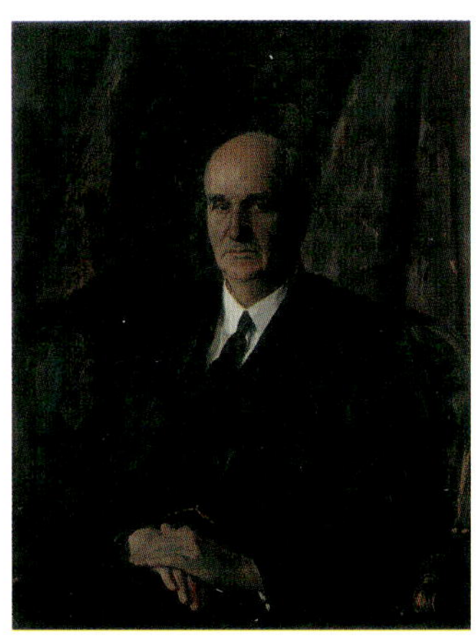

Carr, Henry Marvell 1894–1970
*Frederick Alexander Lindemann (1886–1957),
PC, FRS, First Baron Cherwell of Oxford* 1946
oil on canvas 91.4 x 71.1
IWM ART LD 5799

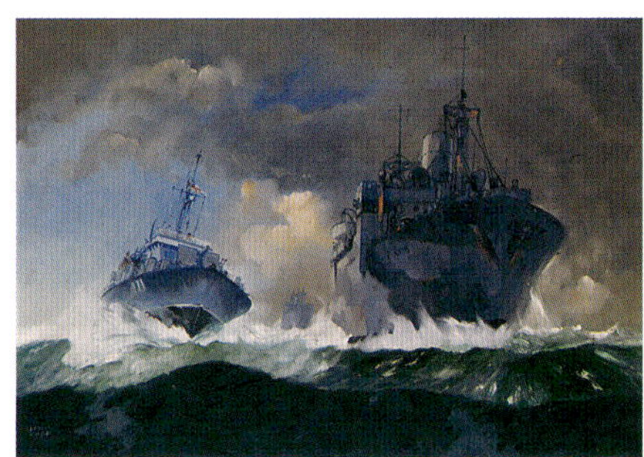

Carr, Leslie b.1891
The Navy's Little Ships on the High Seas
oil on board 53 x 76.5
IWM ART 17113

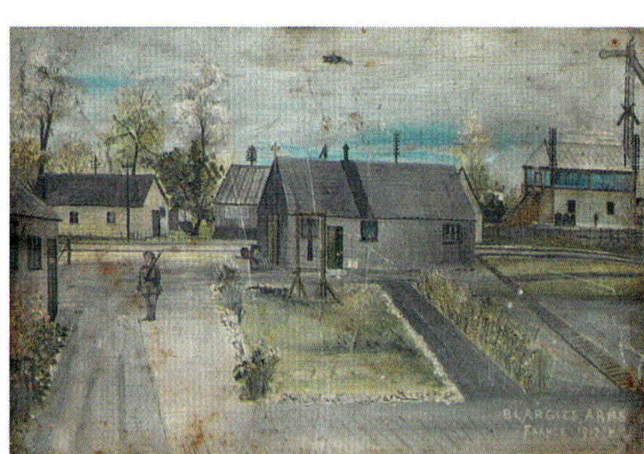

Chapman, H. M. active 1914–1918
Blargies, Arms, France 1917
oil on tin 20.6 x 30.6
IWM ART 16557 a

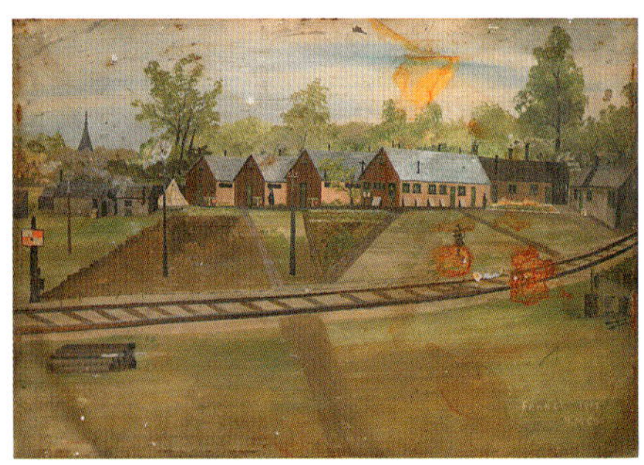

Chapman, H. M. active 1914–1918
France 1917
oil on tin 22.6 x 30.3
IWM ART 16557 b

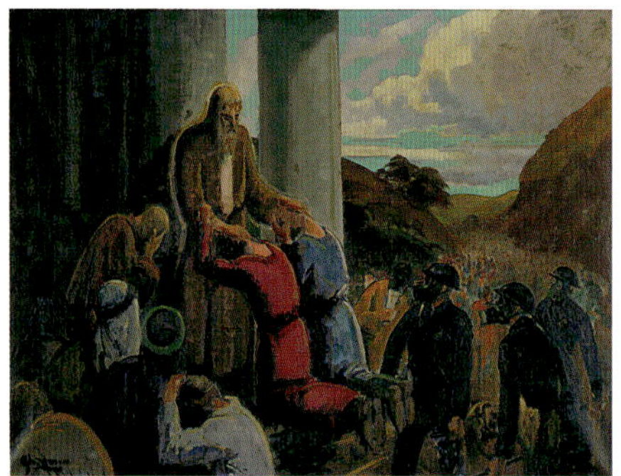

Chapman, Stephen active 1940s
Christ Receiving the Stretcher-Bearers
1940–1945
oil on canvas 91.4 x 121.9
IWM ART 15695

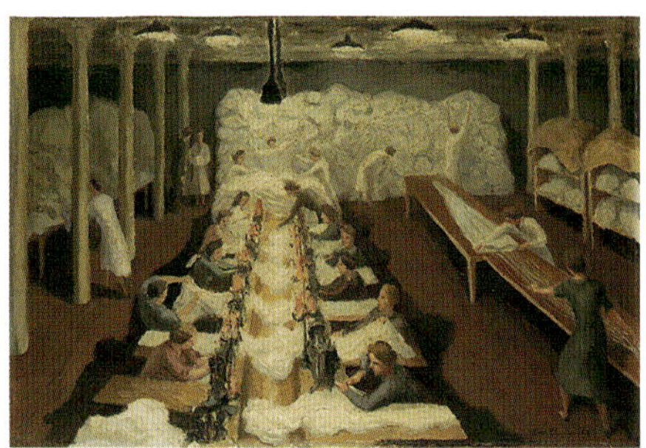

Charlton, Evan 1904–1984
A Parachute Factory 1943
oil on panel 51.1 x 76.2
IWM ART LD 2908

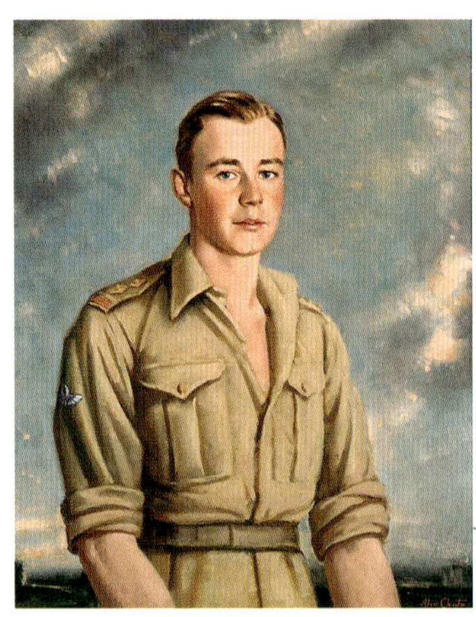

Christie, Alexander b.1901
*Simon Denis St Leger Fleming, Royal Horse
Artillery* 1946
oil on canvas 85.9 x 69.5
IWM ART 16556

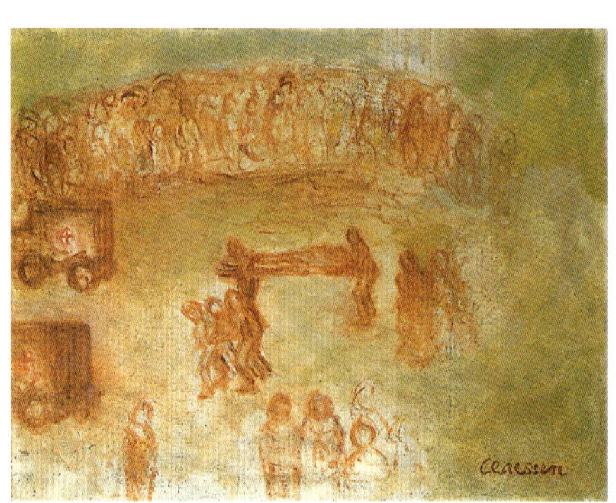

Claessen, George 1909–1999
ARP Practice: Dealing with Casualties
oil on canvas 49.8 x 66.6
IWM ART LD 4202

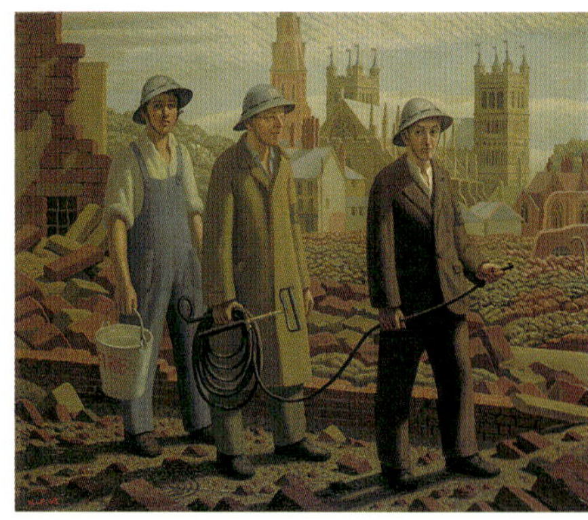

Clause, William Lionel 1887–1946
A Fire Guard Team, Exeter 1943
oil on canvas 64.1 x 76.2
IWM ART LD 3175

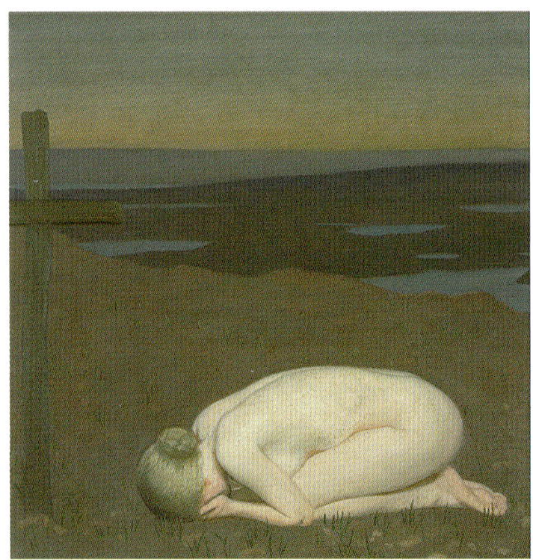

Clausen, George 1852–1944
Youth Mourning 1916
oil on canvas 91.4 x 91.4
IWM ART 4655

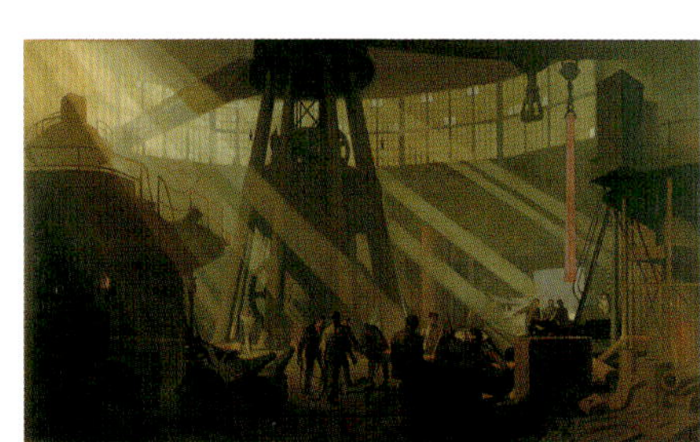

Clausen, George 1852–1944
In the Gun Factory at Woolwich Arsenal 1918
oil on canvas 182.8 x 317.5
IWM ART 1984

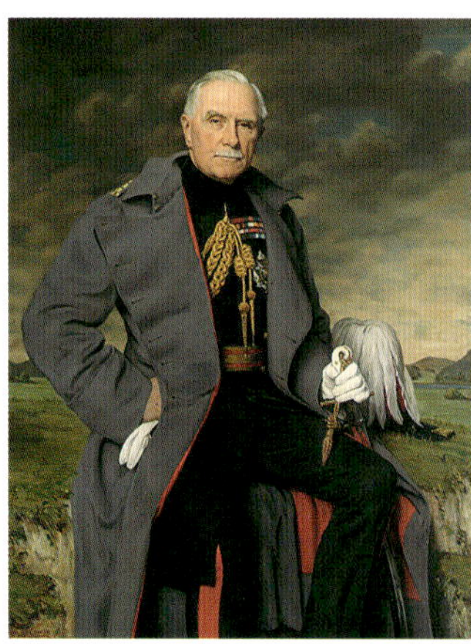

Codner, Maurice Frederick 1888–1958
*Field Marshal Lord Milne (1866–1948), GCB,
GCMG, DSO, DCL, LLD, K.St J.* 1936
oil on canvas 127 x 101.9
IWM ART 5201

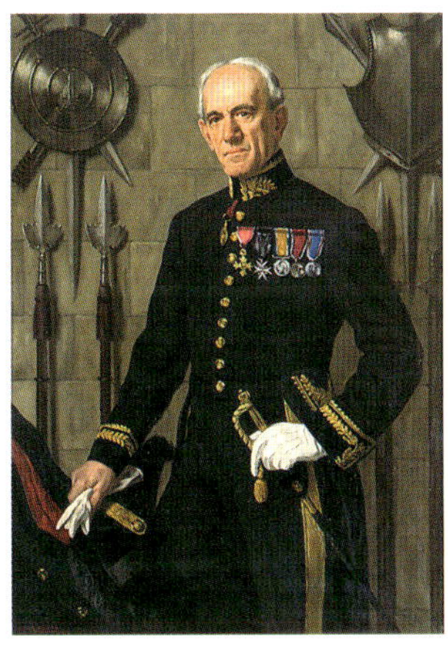

Codner, Maurice Frederick 1888–1958
Charles Ffoulkes (1868–1947), CB, CBE, First Curator and Secretary of the Imperial War Museum, in the Uniform of Master (…) 1937
oil on canvas 117.1 x 86.3
IWM ART 5066

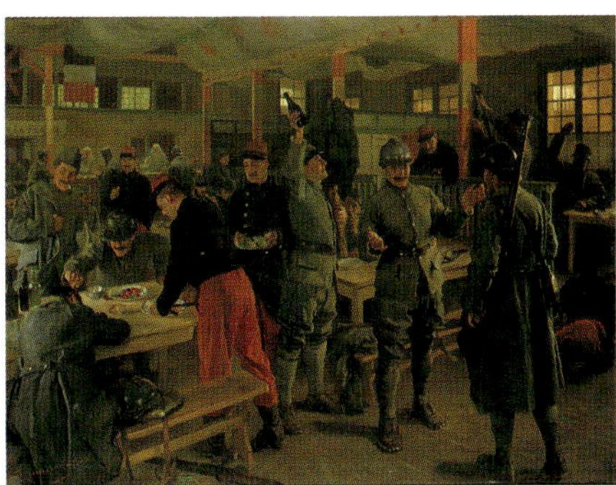

Codrington, Isabel 1874–1943
Cantine Franco-Britannique, Vitry-le-François 1919
oil on canvas 137.1 x 182.8
IWM ART 2622

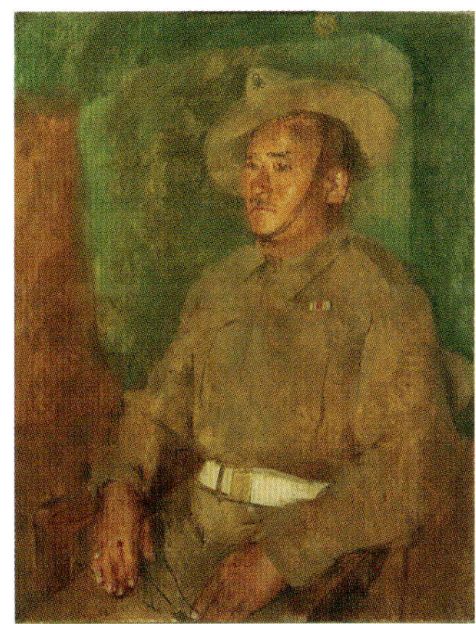

Coldstream, William Menzies 1908–1987
Havildar Kulbir Thapa, 2/3 Gurkha Regiment 1943
oil on canvas 91.4 x 71.7
IWM ART LD 3992

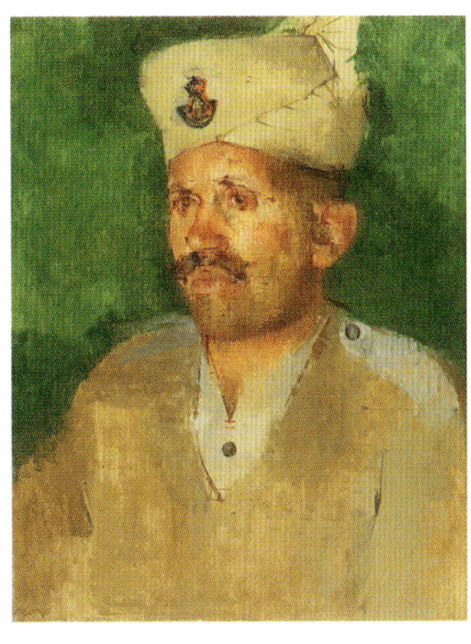

Coldstream, William Menzies 1908–1987
Rifleman Mangal Singh, 2/6 Rajput Rifles c.1943–1945
oil on canvas 60.9 x 48.2
IWM ART LD 3991

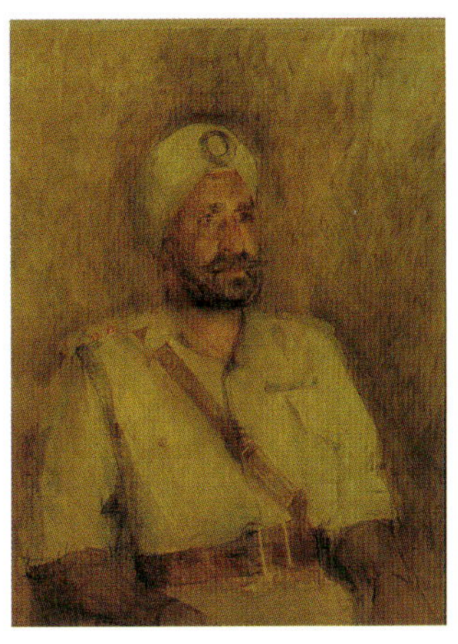

Coldstream, William Menzies 1908–1987
Subedar Jagat Singh, 2/11 Sikhs c.1943–1945
oil on canvas 91.4 x 68.5
IWM ART LD 3848

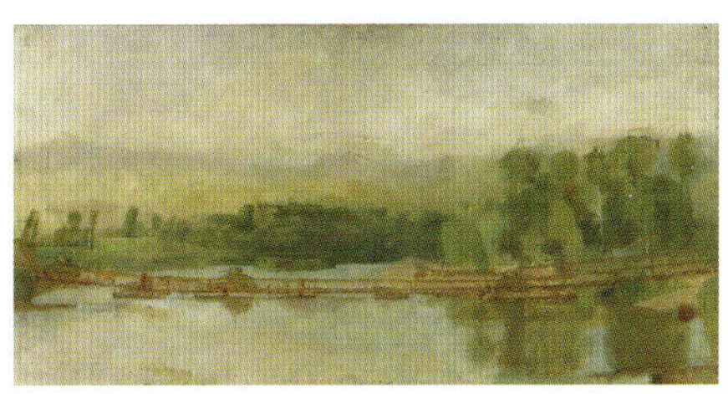

Coldstream, William Menzies 1908–1987
The Bailey Bridge Built by Royal Engineers over the Volturno River, Italy 1944
oil on canvas 30 x 60.9
IWM ART LD 4811

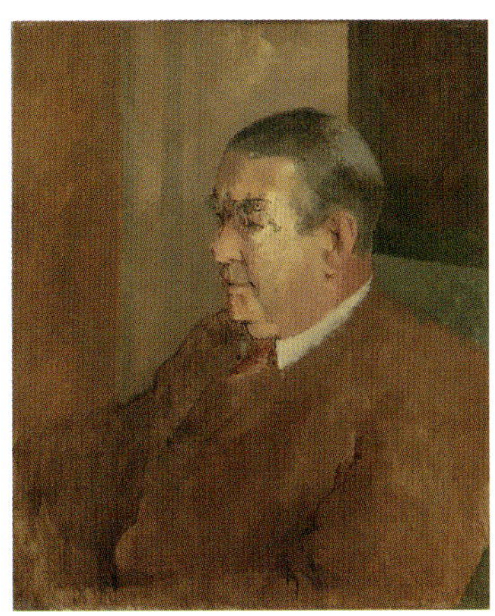

Coldstream, William Menzies 1908–1987
Sir Alwyn Crow, CBE, Director and Controller of Projectile Development (1940–1945) 1945–1947
oil on canvas 60.9 x 50.8
IWM ART LD 5774

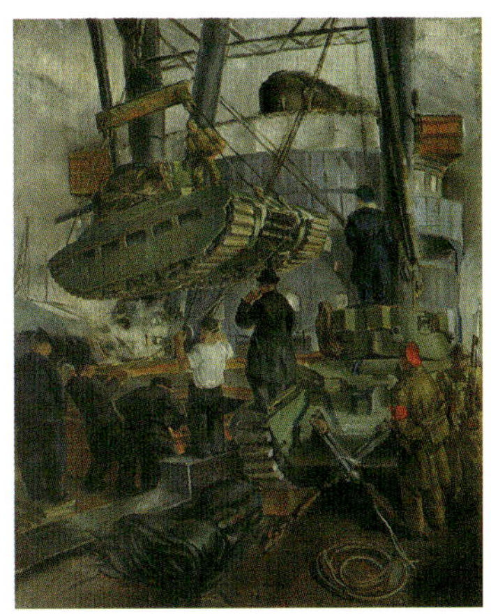

Cole, Leslie 1910–1976
Loading Tanks for Russia 1941
oil on canvas 48.2 x 41.2
IWM ART LD 1922

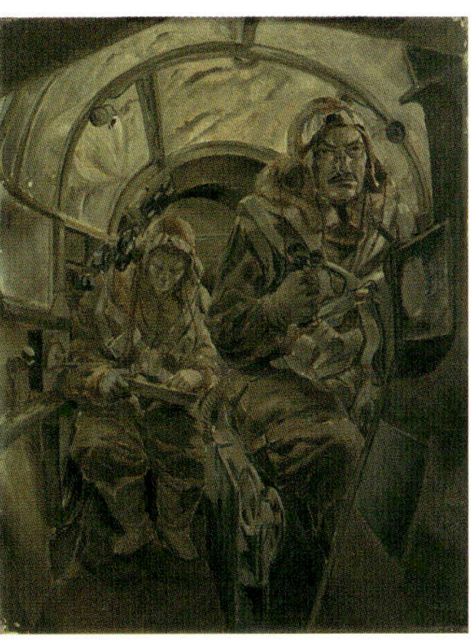

Cole, Leslie 1910–1976
The Interior of an Aircraft in Flight c.1941–1942
oil on canvas 50.8 x 40.6
IWM ART LD 1878

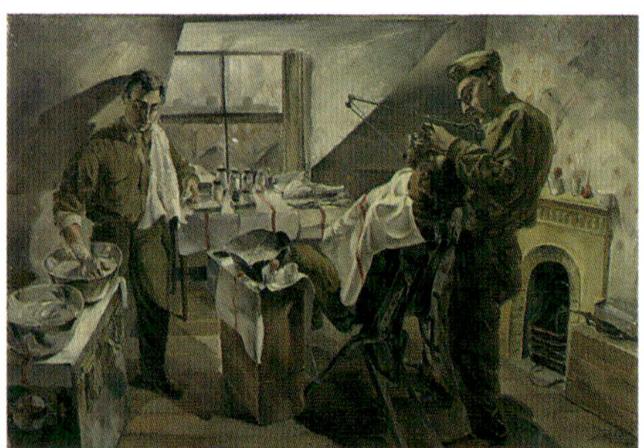

Cole, Leslie 1910–1976
16th US Medical Regiment: Field Dental Service Operating during an Attack 1942
oil on canvas 50.8 x 76.2
IWM ART LD 2735

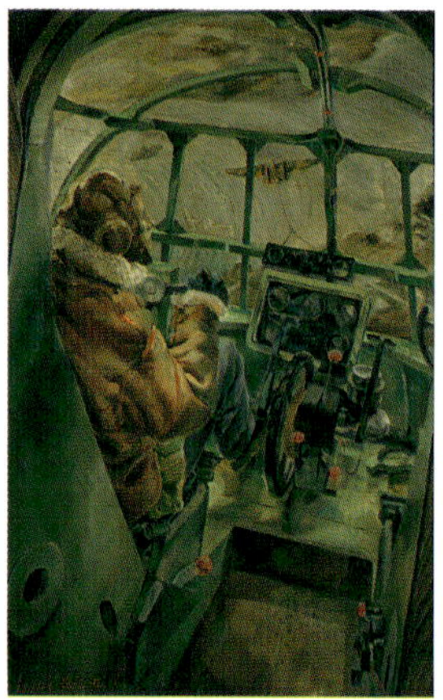

Cole, Leslie 1910–1976
A Glider Pilot at the Controls 1942
oil on canvas 76.2 x 50.8
IWM ART LD 2644

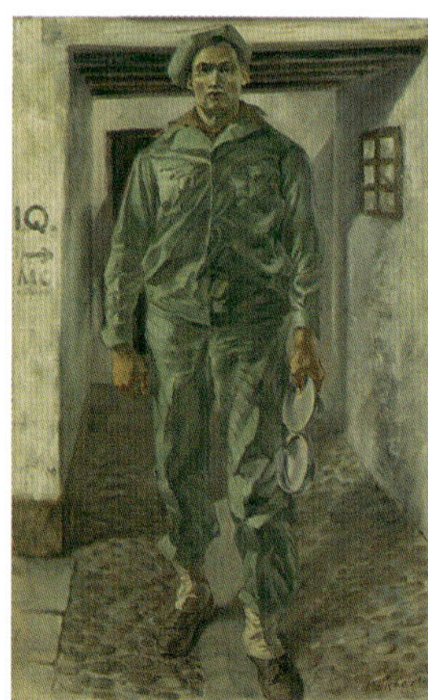

Cole, Leslie 1910–1976
An American Soldier in Fatigue Dress 1942
oil on canvas 55.8 x 35.5
IWM ART LD 2520

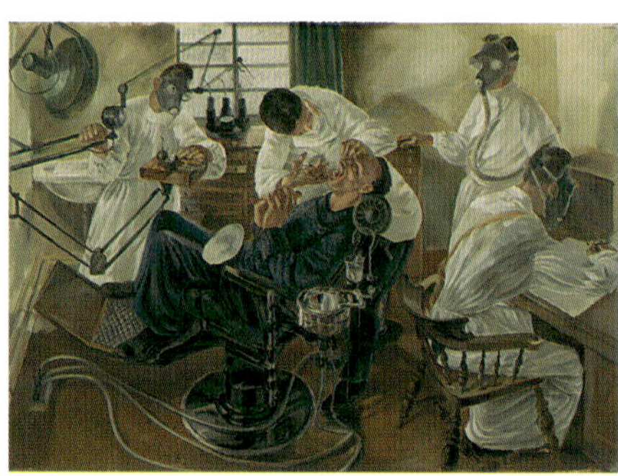

Cole, Leslie 1910–1976
Dentistry during the Hour of Gas Practice 1942
oil on canvas 53.3 x 76.2
IWM ART LD 2362

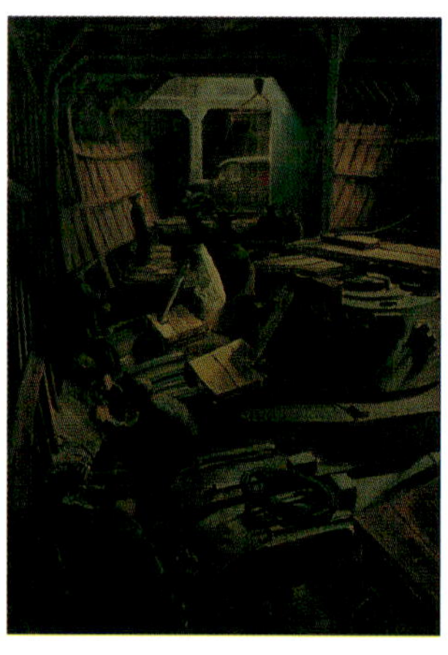

Cole, Leslie 1910–1976
Loading Tanks for Russia II 1942
oil on canvas 52.7 x 39.3
IWM ART LD 1969

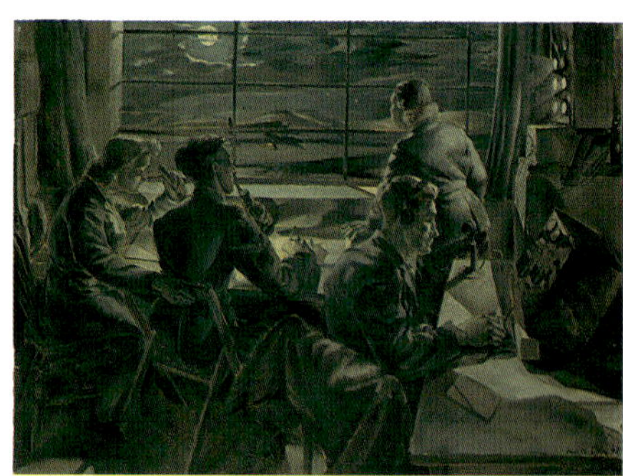

Cole, Leslie 1910–1976
Night Scene in a Watch Office 1942
oil on canvas 49.5 x 66.6
IWM ART LD 2503

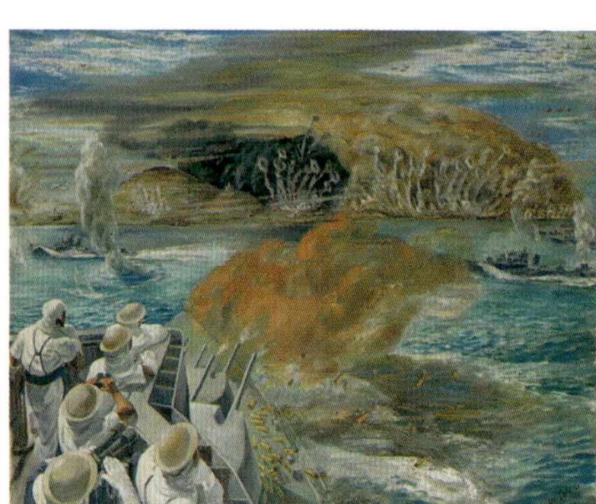

Cole, Leslie 1910–1976
Admiral C. H. J. Harcourt's Flagship 'HMS Newfoundland' in the Attack on Pantellaria 1943
oil on canvas 74.9 x 94.6
IWM ART LD 3555

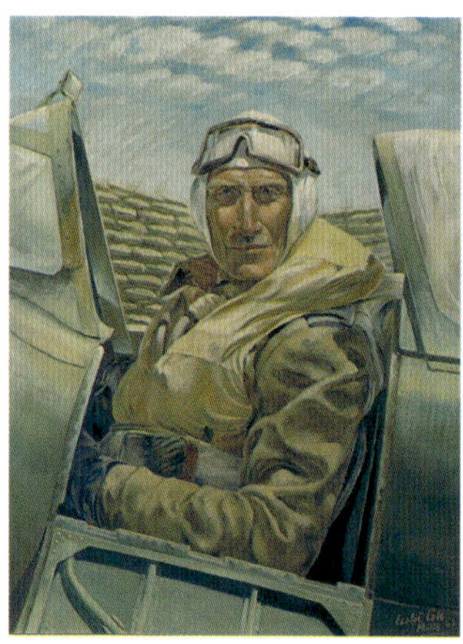

Cole, Leslie 1910–1976
Air Vice-Marshal Sir Keith Park (1892–1975), KBE, CB, MC, DFC, Air Officer Commanding Malta in His Plane 1943
oil on canvas 79.3 x 60.9
IWM ART LD 3258

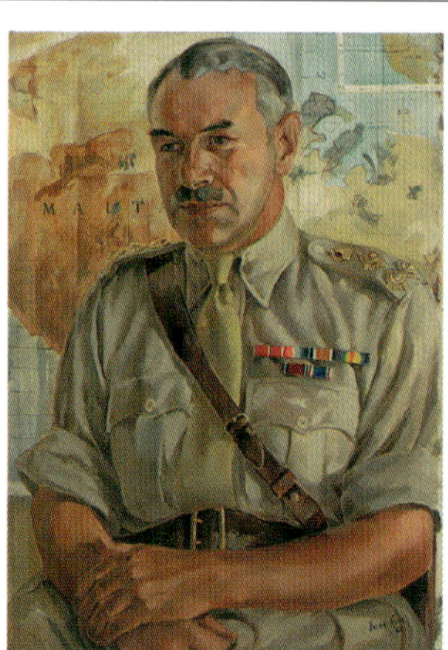

Cole, Leslie 1910–1976
Brigadier Ivan de la Bere, OBE, in Charge of Troops during the Siege of Malta 1943
oil on canvas board 66 x 47.3
IWM ART LD 3545

Facing page: Fergusson, John Duncan, 1874–1961, *Dockyard, Portsmouth* (detail), 1918, (p. 82)

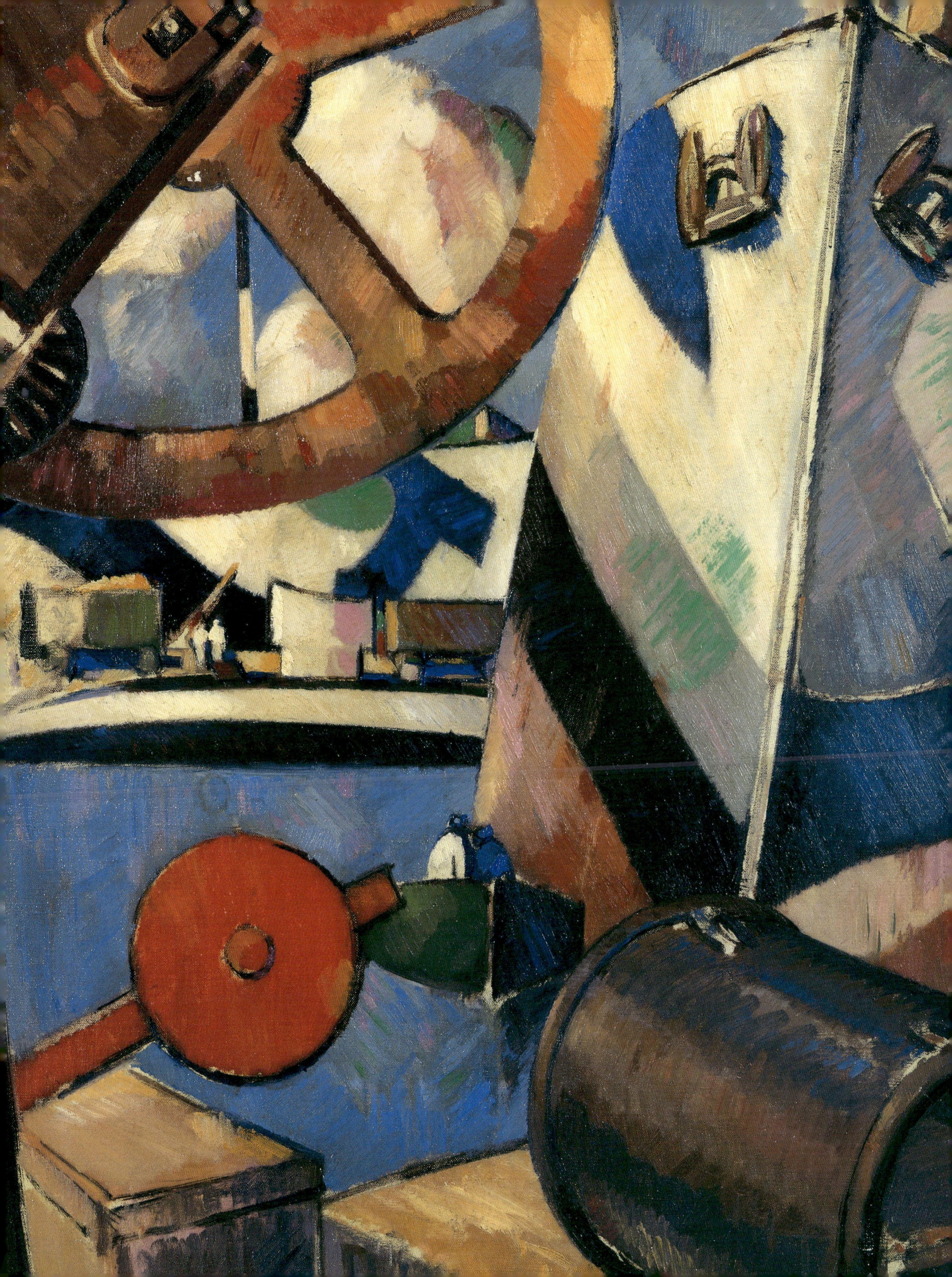

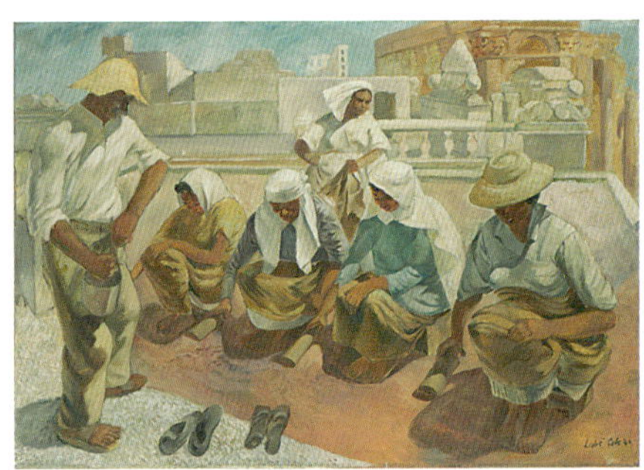

Cole, Leslie 1910–1976
*Diffone Workers Mending the Roof of the
Officers' Mess, Floriana* 1943
oil on canvas 57.1 x 82.5
IWM ART LD 3252

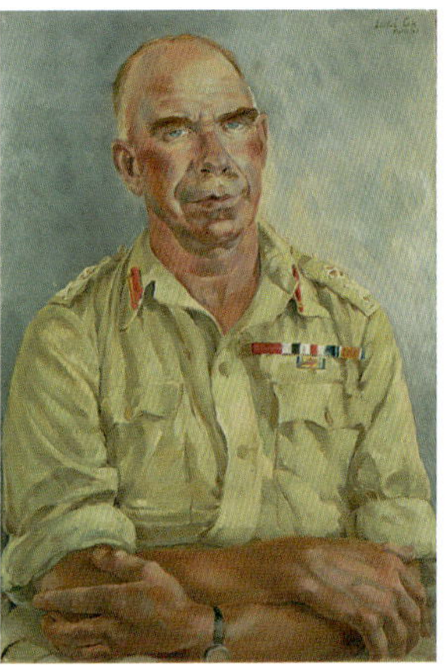

Cole, Leslie 1910–1976
Major General G. C. Kemp, CB, MC 1943
oil on canvas 63.5 x 43.8
IWM ART LD 3256

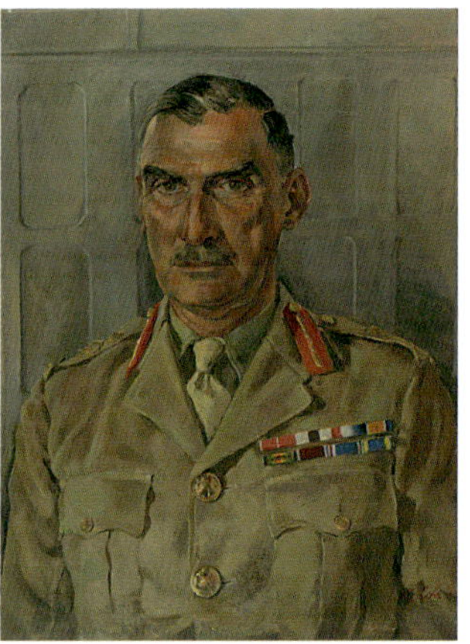

Cole, Leslie 1910–1976
*Major General W. H. Oxley, CBE, MC, General
Officer Commanding Troops in Malta* 1943
oil on canvas 65 x 48.2
IWM ART LD 3546

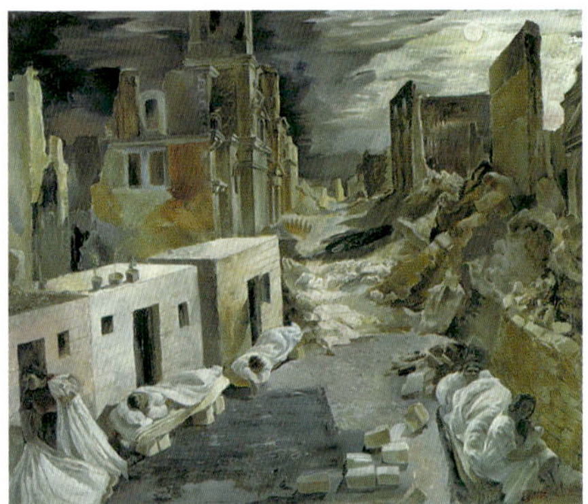

Cole, Leslie 1910–1976
*Malta: A Few People Sleep out among the
Debris* 1943
oil on canvas 76.2 x 93.9
IWM ART LD 3550

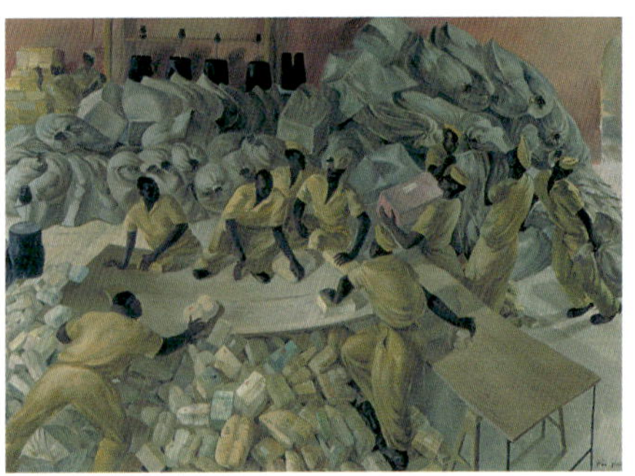

Cole, Leslie 1910–1976
*Malta Convoy: Basutos Deal with the Overflow
Mail on the Causeway, the Palace, Valletta*
1943
oil on canvas 64 x 90.8
IWM ART LD 3254

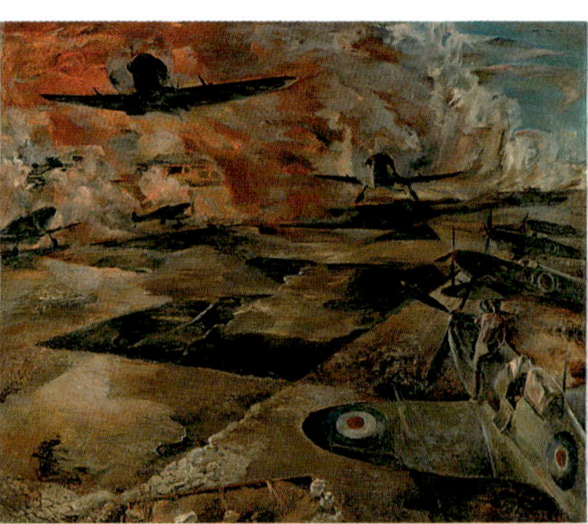

Cole, Leslie 1910–1976
*Malta: Fighters Take Off from Luca's Bombed
Runway* 1943
oil on canvas 76.2 x 91.4
IWM ART LD 3554

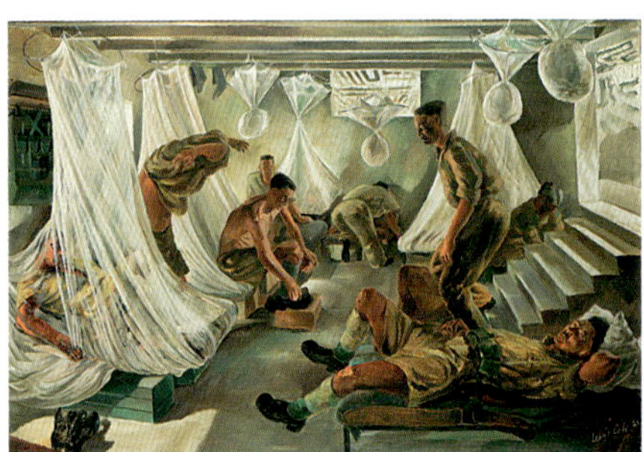

Cole, Leslie 1910–1976
*Malta: Gunners Resting Between Alerts at a
Heavy Anti-Aircraft Post* 1943
oil on canvas 60.9 x 91.4
IWM ART LD 3552

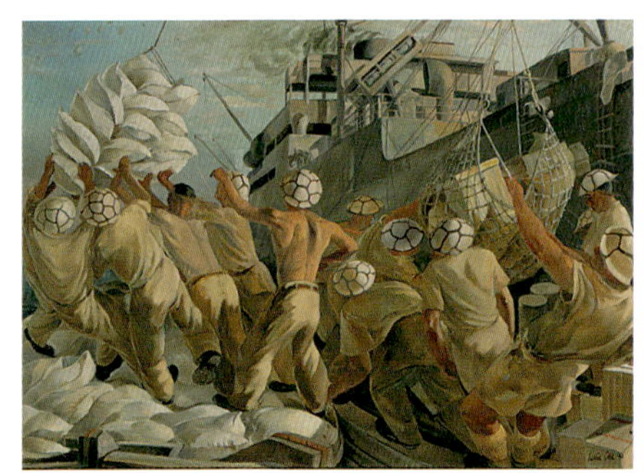

Cole, Leslie 1910–1976
*Malta: No Time to Lose, Soldier Dockers
Unloading a Convoy during a Raid* 1943
oil on canvas 64.2 x 91.6
IWM ART LD 3257

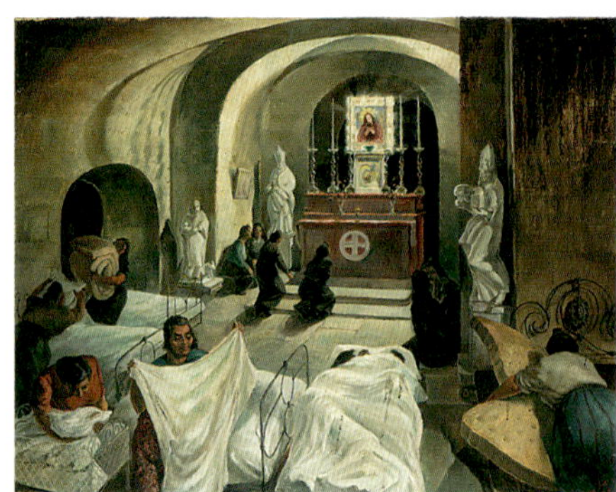

Cole, Leslie 1910–1976
*Malta: Preparing for the Night in the Crypt of
St Augustine's, Valletta* 1943
oil on canvas 69.2 x 93.9
IWM ART LD 3548

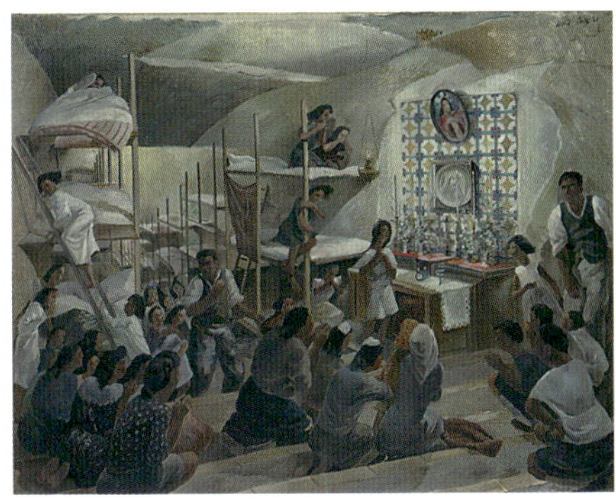

Cole, Leslie 1910–1976
Malta: Shelterers Praying during a Raid 1943
oil on canvas 71.1 x 91.4
IWM ART LD 3549

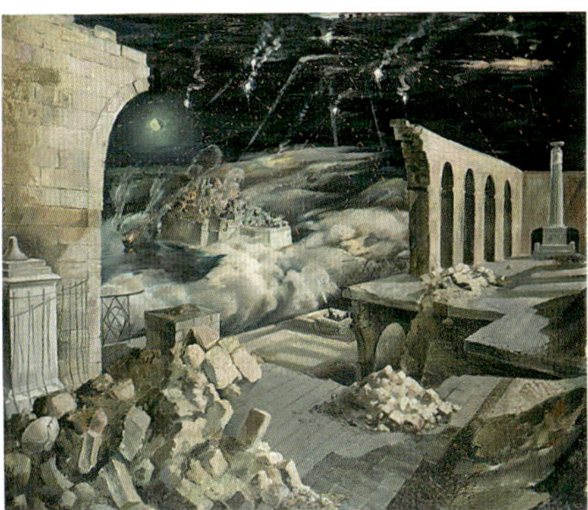

Cole, Leslie 1910–1976
Malta: The Harbour Barrage from the Upper Barracca 1943
oil on canvas 76.2 x 91.4
IWM ART LD 3551

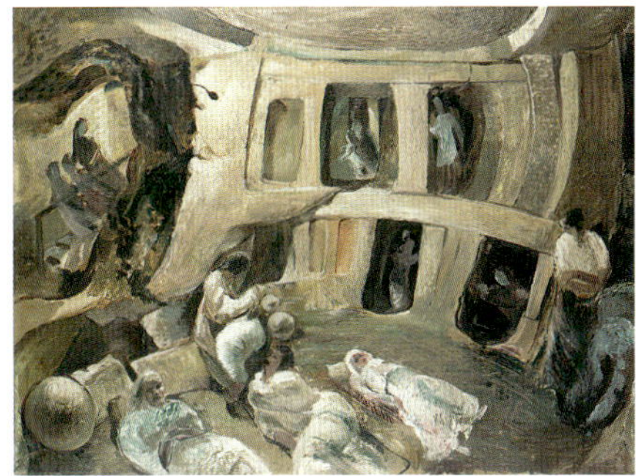

Cole, Leslie 1910–1976
Malta, the Hypogeum: People of Paula Sheltering during a Raid 1943
oil on canvas 67.3 x 91.4
IWM ART LD 3553

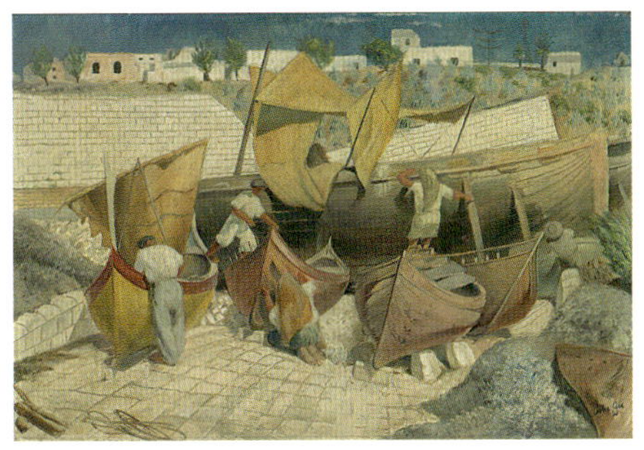

Cole, Leslie 1910–1976
Maltese Fishermen Mending Bombed Dghaisas and Other Boats 1943
oil on canvas 44.4 x 66
IWM ART LD 3240

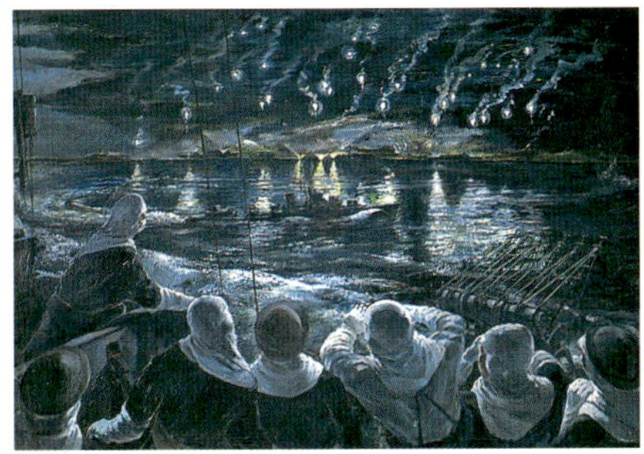

Cole, Leslie 1910–1976
Star Shells over Lampedusa during a Night Bombardment 1943
oil on canvas 58.4 x 83.1
IWM ART LD 3547

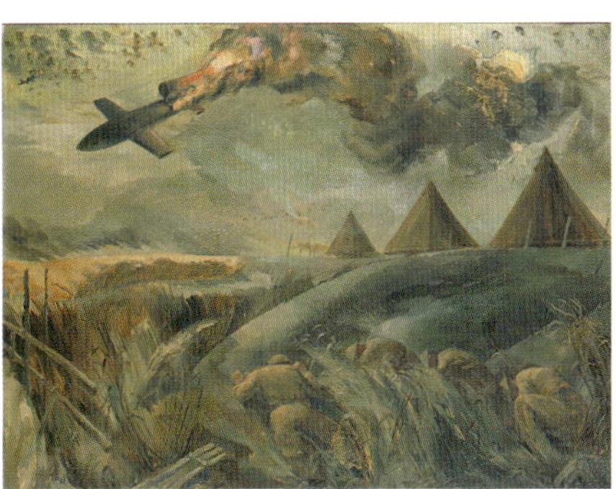

Cole, Leslie 1910–1976
Battle of London: Royal Marine Anti-Aircraft Gunners Bring down a Flying Bomb 1944
oil on canvas 66.6 x 90.1
IWM ART LD 4514

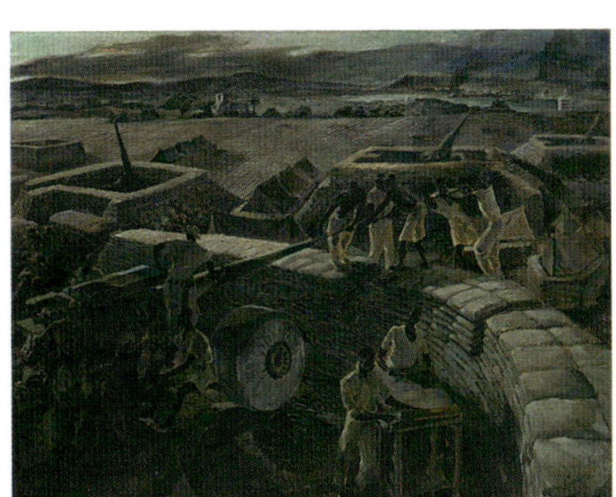

Cole, Leslie 1910–1976
Bechuanaland Boys Cleaning Anti-Aircraft Guns in the Twilight after Action, Syracuse, Sicily 1944
oil on canvas 68.5 x 89.5
IWM ART LD 4576

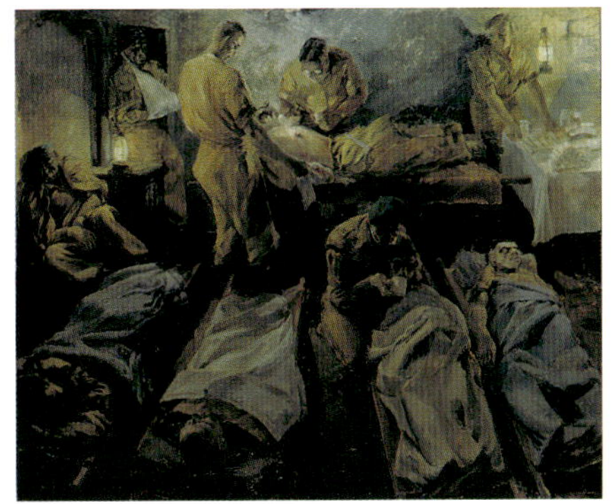

Cole, Leslie 1910–1976
Scene in a Regimental Aid Post: In a Filthy Cellar at Sallenelle, France, after an Action 1944
oil on canvas 66.6 x 82.5
IWM ART LD 4575

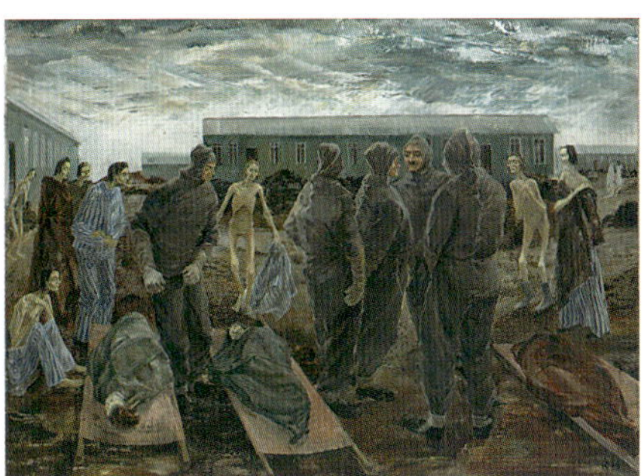

Cole, Leslie 1910–1976
Sick Women and the Hooded Men of Belsen 1944
oil on canvas 61.5 x 86.3
IWM ART LD 5017

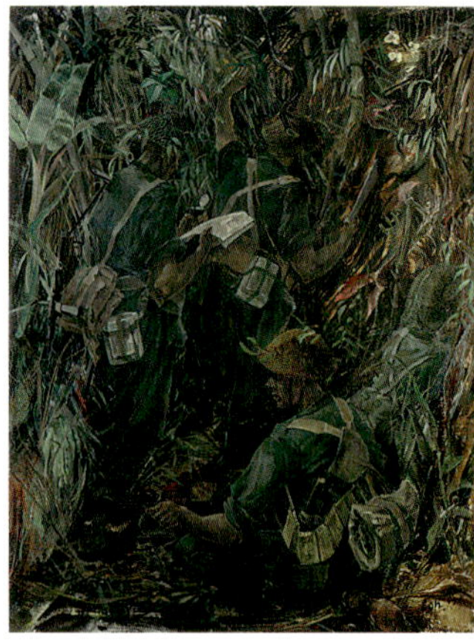

Cole, Leslie 1910–1976
14th Army: Men of the Royal Berkshire Regiment Form the Spearhead of a Patrol, Cutting through the Jungle (…) 1945
oil on canvas 88 x 67.7
IWM ART LD 5619

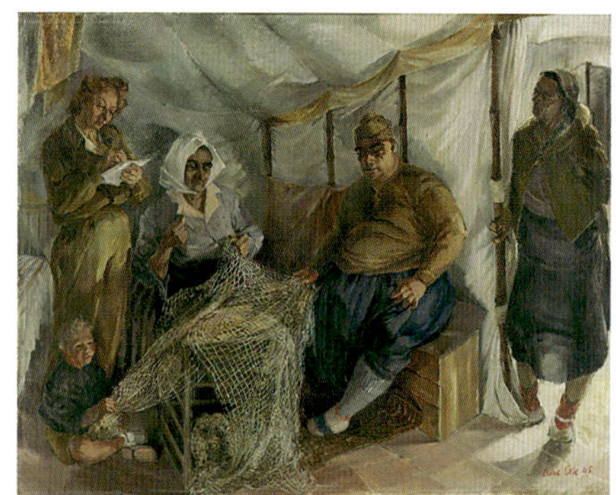

Cole, Leslie 1910–1976
A Greek Refugee Family from Samos at Moses Wells Encampment, Arabia, with Red Cross Workers 1945
oil on canvas 66 x 85
IWM ART LD 5041

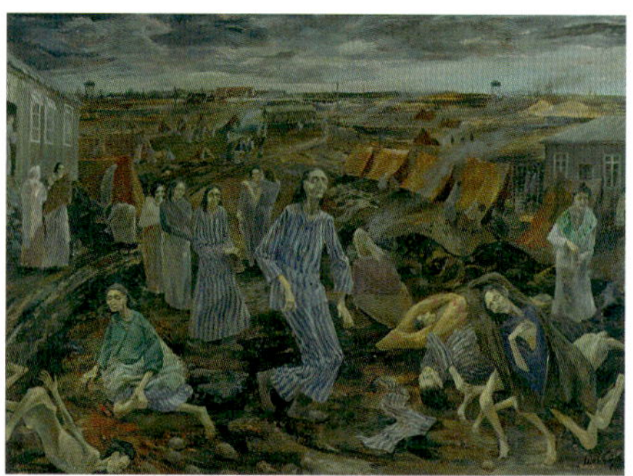

Cole, Leslie 1910–1976
Belsen Camp: The Compound for Women 1945
oil on canvas 66 x 90.1
IWM ART LD 5104

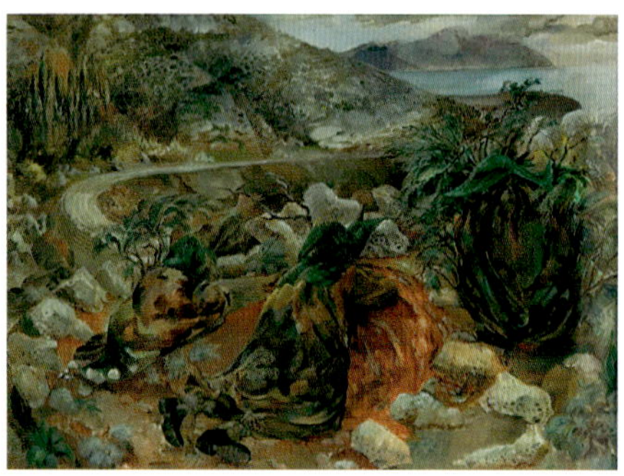

Cole, Leslie 1910–1976
British Snipers on the Island of Ubbea near Khakio, 10th Infantry Brigade 1945
oil on canvas 59.6 x 80
IWM ART LD 5040

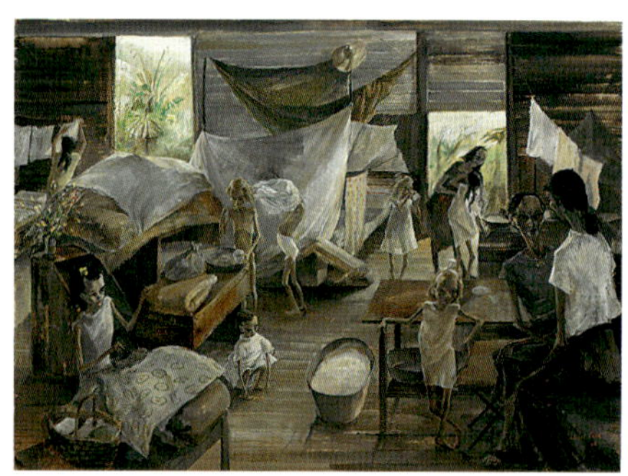

Cole, Leslie 1910–1976
British Women and Children Interned in a Japanese Prison Camp, Syme Road, Singapore 1945
oil on canvas 65.5 x 91.5
IWM ART LD 5620

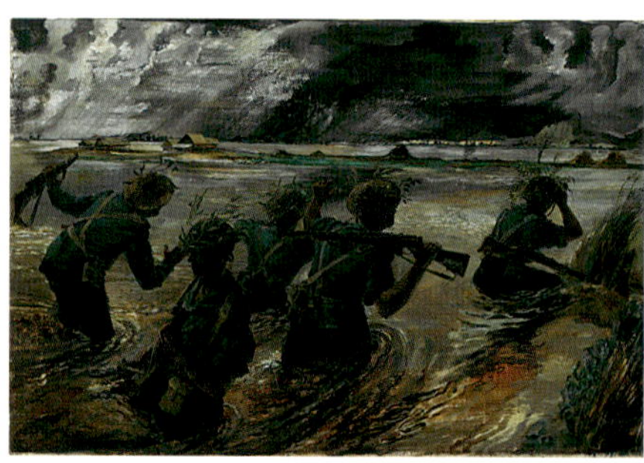

Cole, Leslie 1910–1976
Burma, 14th Army: The Battle of the Sittang Bend with Men of the Queen's Own (Royal West Kent) (…) 1945
oil on canvas 66 x 98
IWM ART LD 5617

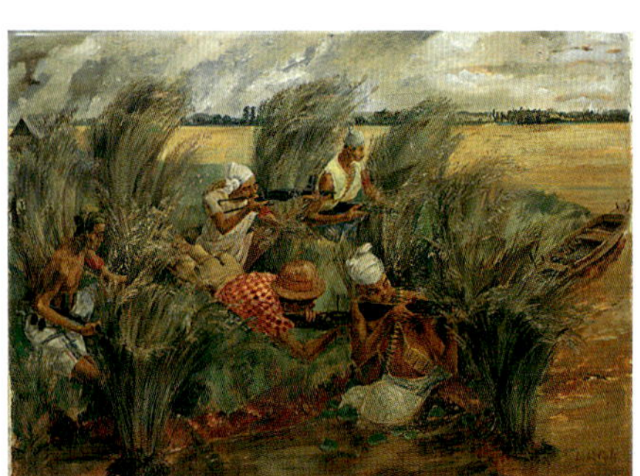

Cole, Leslie 1910–1976
Burmese Guerillas in Action 1945
oil on canvas 65.5 x 91.8
IWM ART LD 5687

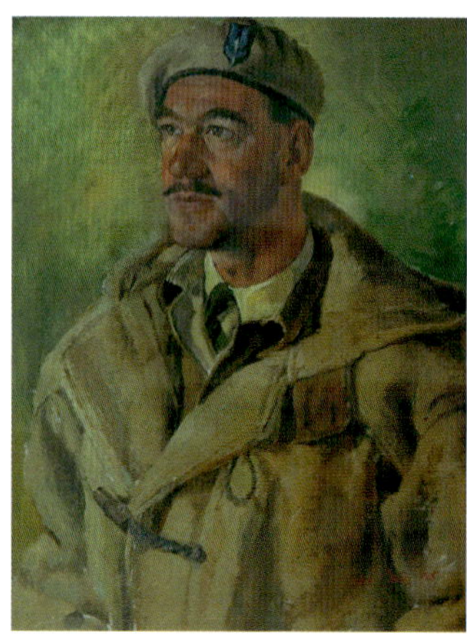

Cole, Leslie 1910–1976
Captain L. E. George, MC 1945
oil on canvas 67.3 x 52
IWM ART LD 4960

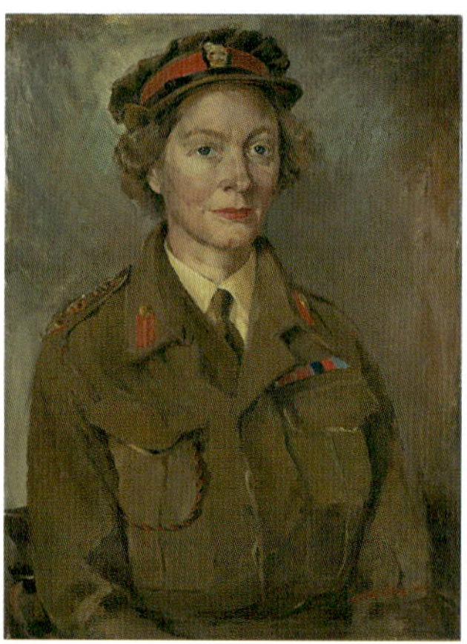

Cole, Leslie 1910–1976
Commandant Marjorie F. Wagstaffe, CBE, Deputy Director, Auxiliary Territorial Service, Middle East Forces 1945
oil on canvas 72.3 x 51.4
IWM ART LD 4959

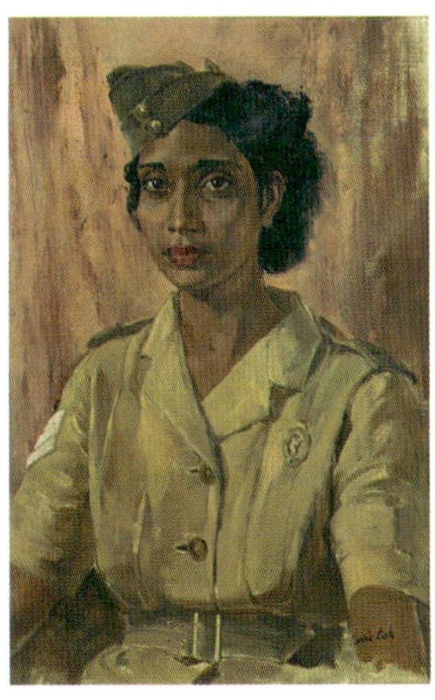

Cole, Leslie 1910–1976
Company Quartermaster, Sergeant Van Omoheusen of the Auxiliary Territorial Service, Ceylon 1945
oil on canvas 67.3 x 43.8
IWM ART LD 5688

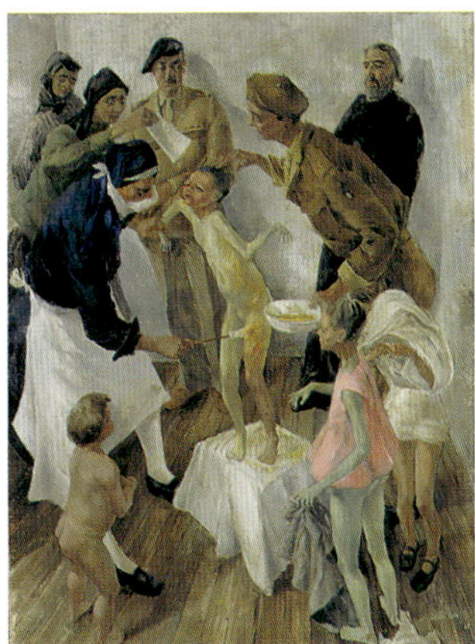

Cole, Leslie 1910–1976
Greece, an Orphanage: Curing Scabies with Anachryl 1945
oil on canvas 88.9 x 66
IWM ART LD 5057

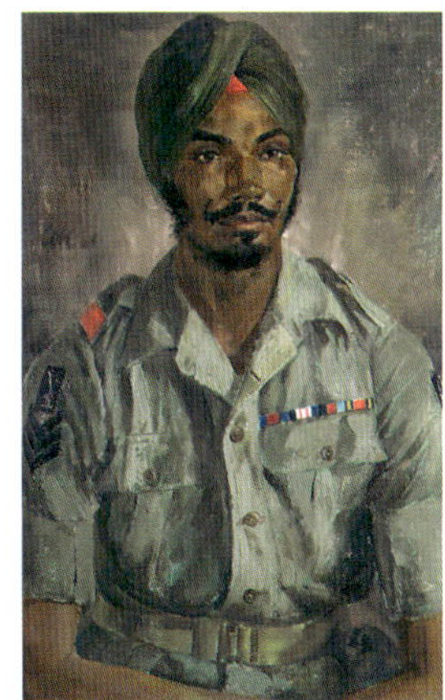

Cole, Leslie 1910–1976
Havildar Gurbakhsh Singh, IDSM 1945
oil on canvas 69.8 x 46.9
IWM ART LD 5616

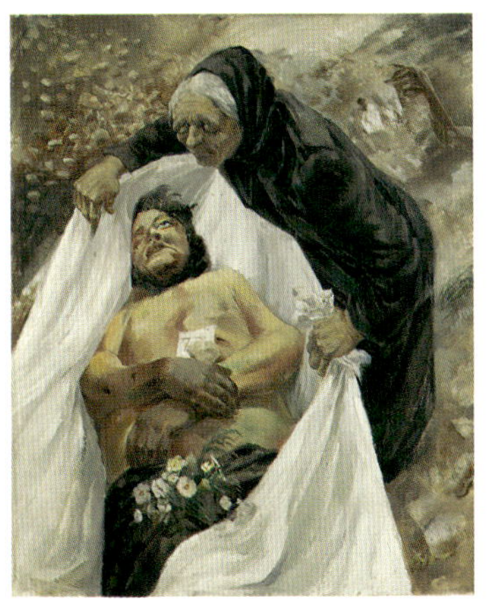

Cole, Leslie 1910–1976
Mother Mourning the Death of a Village Priest 1945
oil on canvas 59.6 x 48.8
IWM ART LD 5042

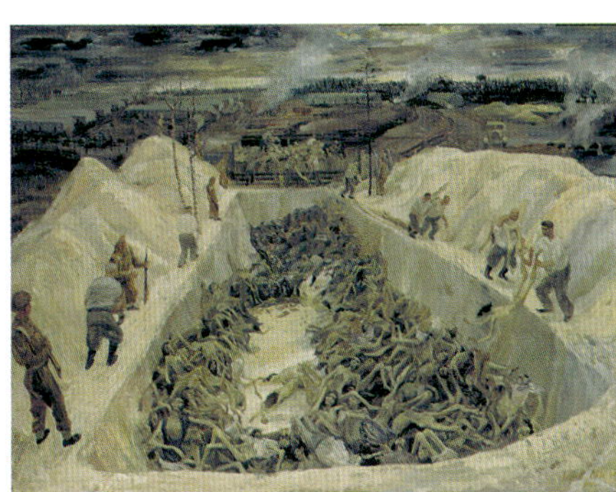

Cole, Leslie 1910–1976
One of the Death Pits, Belsen: SS Guards Collecting Bodies 1945
oil on canvas 62.2 x 90.1
IWM ART LD 5105

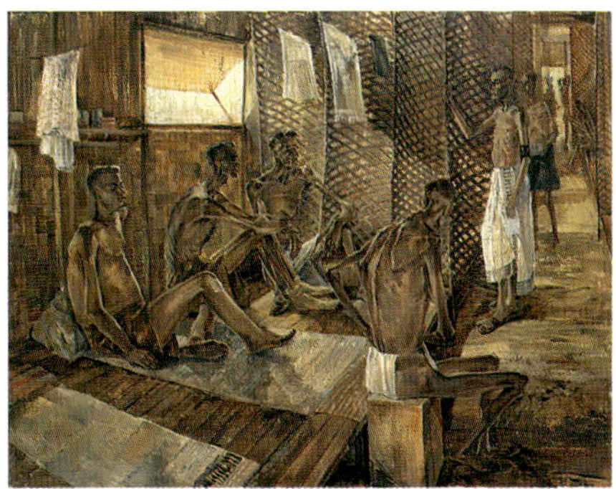

Cole, Leslie 1910–1976
Orderly on His Rounds in X Ward, Changi Gaol, Singapore, with Prisoners of War Suffering from Starvation and Beriberi 1945
oil on canvas 65.6 x 86.5
IWM ART LD 5618

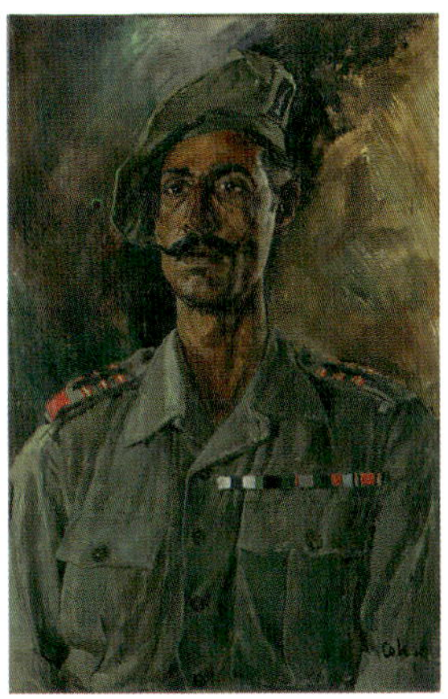

Cole, Leslie 1910–1976
Subedar-Major Musank Khan 1945
oil on canvas 67.3 x 43.1
IWM ART LD 5615

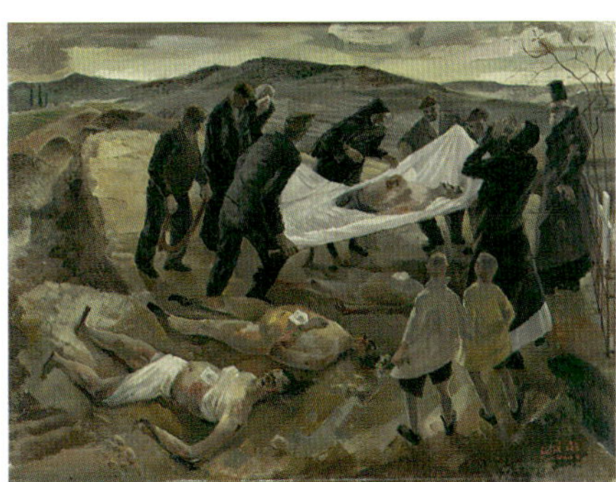

Cole, Leslie 1910–1976
The Greek Civil War: Relatives Mourn Their Dead at Peristeres 1945
oil on canvas 58.4 x 80.6
IWM ART LD 5039

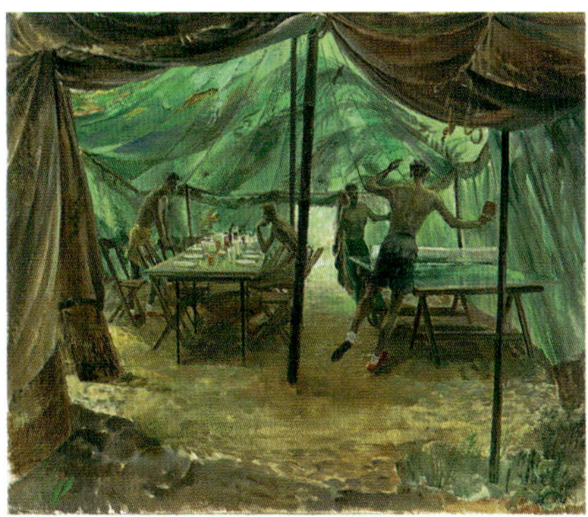

Cole, Leslie 1910–1976
Borneo: Officers' Mess, 3/8 Gurkha Regiment 1946
oil on canvas 50.8 x 60.9
IWM ART LD 5826

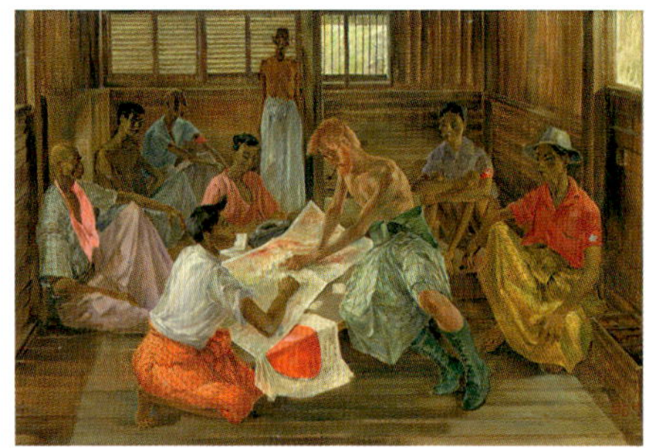

Cole, Leslie 1910–1976
*Burma, the Guerilla Headquarters: Sergeant
Brierley (Ex-Maquis) with Burmese Members
of Reindeer Force 136* 1946
oil on canvas 62.2 x 90.1
IWM ART LD 5823

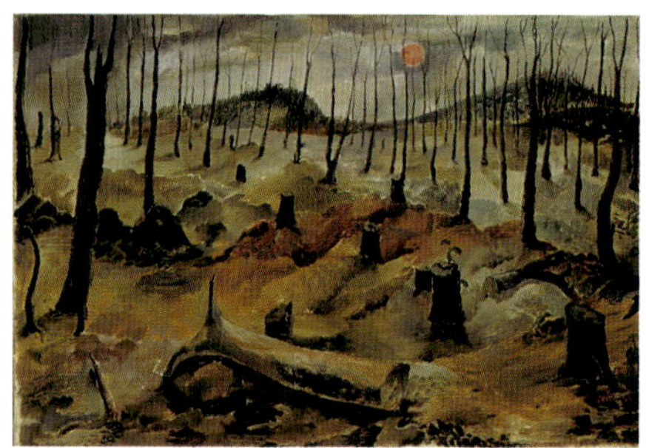

Cole, Leslie 1910–1976
Scorched Earth: Devastated Rubber Plantations
1946
oil on canvas 47.6 x 71.1
IWM ART LD 5828

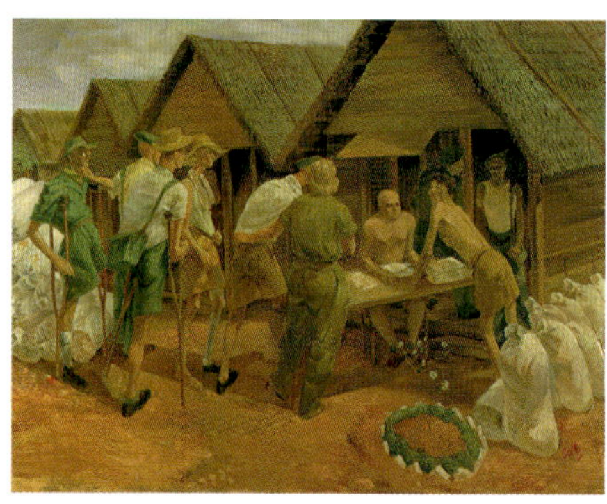

Cole, Leslie 1910–1976
*Singapore: Limbless Officers and Men Checking
out from Changi Gaol* 1946
oil on canvas 59 x 76.5
IWM ART LD 5824

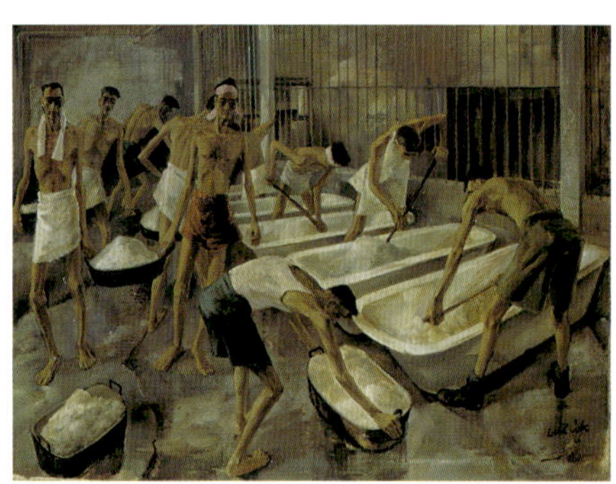

Cole, Leslie 1910–1976
*Singapore: The Cookhouse, Changi Gaol,
British Prisoners of War Prepare Their Main
Meal of Rice* 1946
oil on canvas 56 x 75.4
IWM ART LD 5825

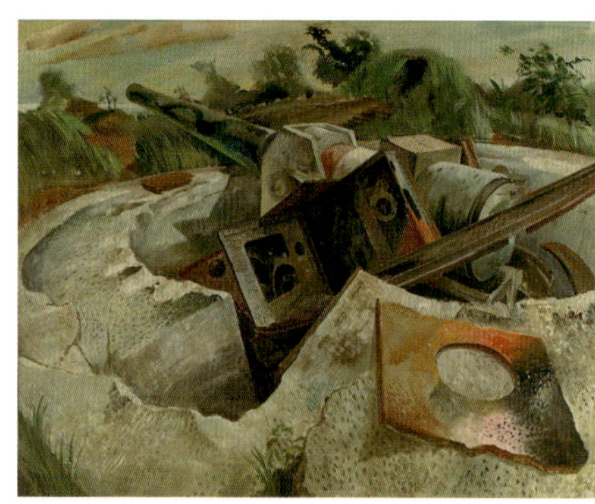

Cole, Leslie 1910–1976
*Singapore: The Remains of One of the Big
Defence Guns* 1946
oil on canvas 60.9 x 76.2
IWM ART LD 5827

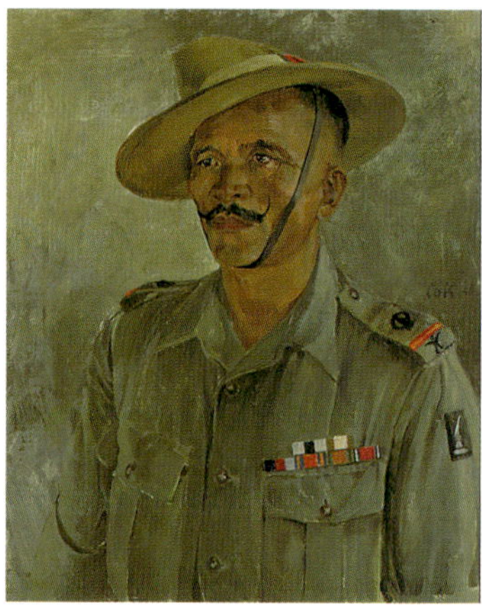

Cole, Leslie 1910–1976
Subedar-Major of the 3/8 Gurkhas 1946
oil on canvas 60.9 x 50.8
IWM ART LD 5829

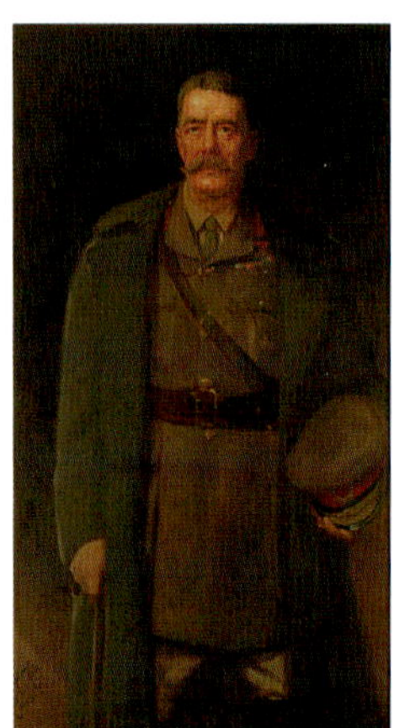

Cole, Philip Tennyson 1862–1939
Lord Kitchener of Khartoum (1850–1916)
c.1911–1914
oil on canvas 156.2 x 93.9
IWM ART 4229

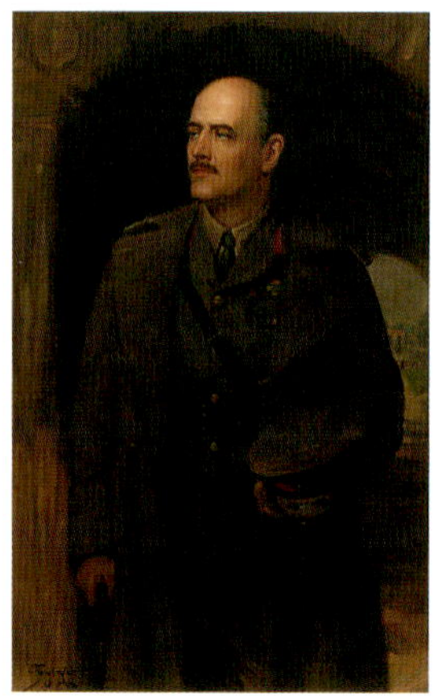

Cole, Philip Tennyson 1862–1939
*General Sir Edmund Allenby (1861–1936),
KCB* c.1917–1919
oil on canvas 141.6 x 90.8
IWM ART 4230

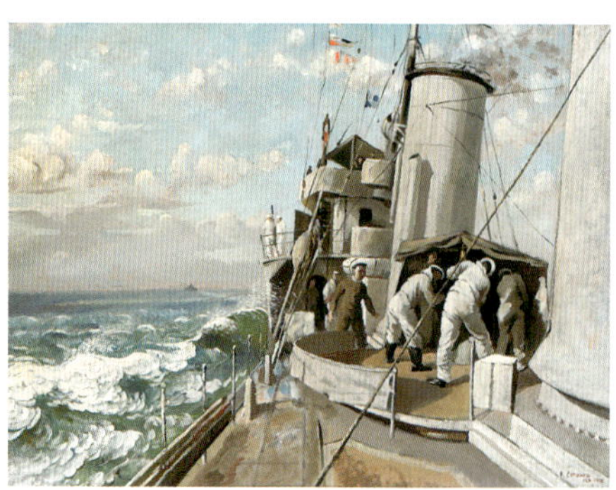

Connard, Philip 1875–1958
27 Knots: 'HMS Melampus' 1918
oil on canvas 71.1 x 91.4
IWM ART 1313

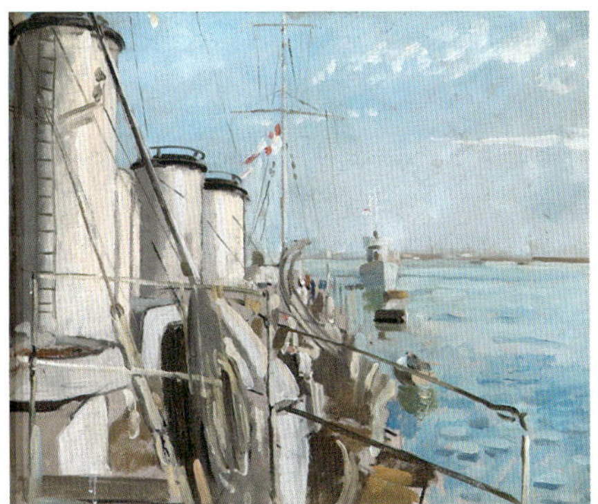

Connard, Philip 1875–1958
A Destroyer 1918
oil on panel 33 x 40.6
IWM ART 1287

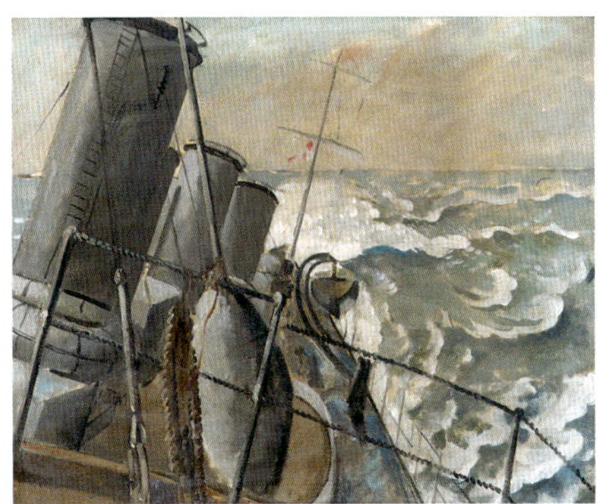

Connard, Philip 1875–1958
*A Destroyer in a Heavy Sea: From 'HMS
Melampus'* 1918
oil on canvas 50.8 x 60.9
IWM ART 1317

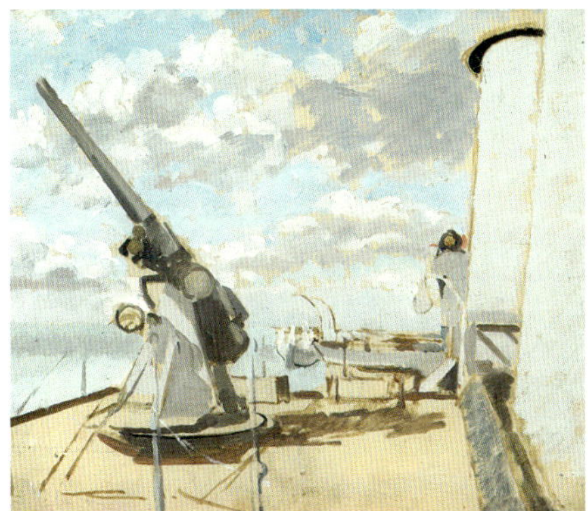

Connard, Philip 1875–1958
Anti-Aircraft Gun 1918
oil on canvas 33 x 40.6
IWM ART 1288

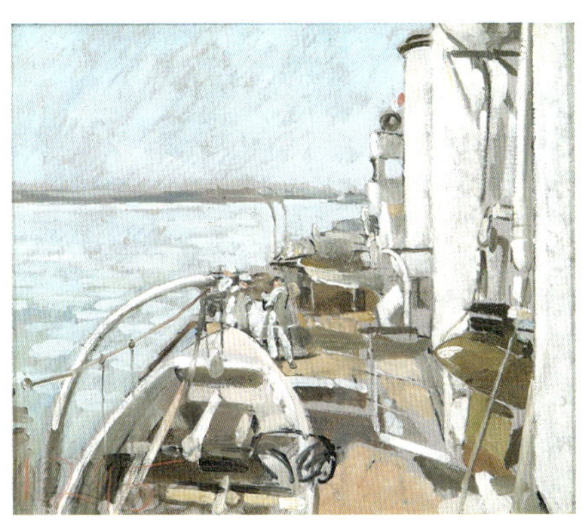

Connard, Philip 1875–1958
Between Decks 1918
oil on panel 33 x 40.6
IWM ART 1295

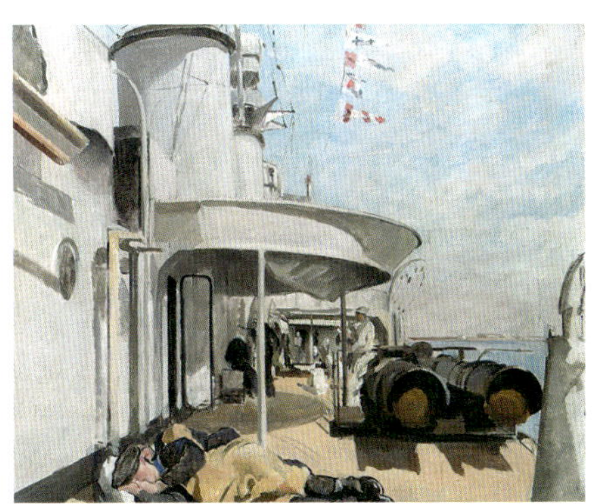

Connard, Philip 1875–1958
Between Decks, 'HMS Coventry' 1918
oil on canvas 63.5 x 76.2
IWM ART 1300

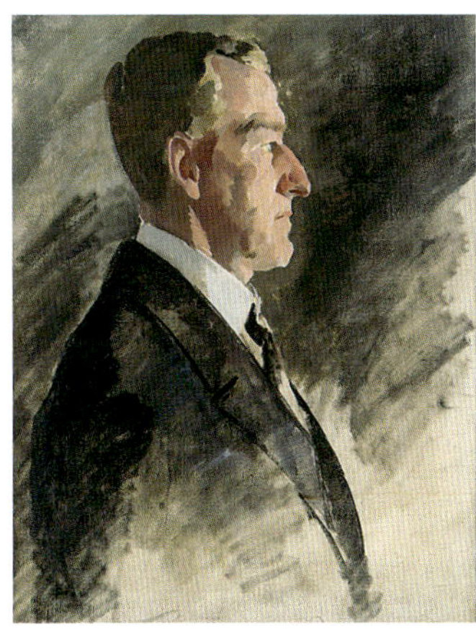

Connard, Philip 1875–1958
Captain P. Boyds, RN 1918
oil on canvas 60.9 x 50.8
IWM ART 4970

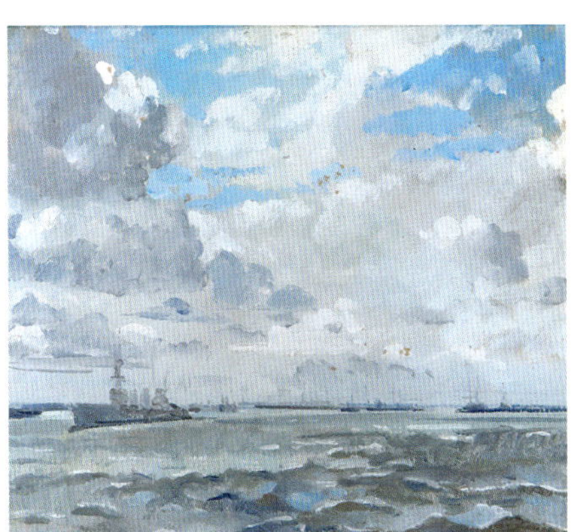

Connard, Philip 1875–1958
Cloud Shadows 1918
oil on panel 33 x 40.6
IWM ART 1320

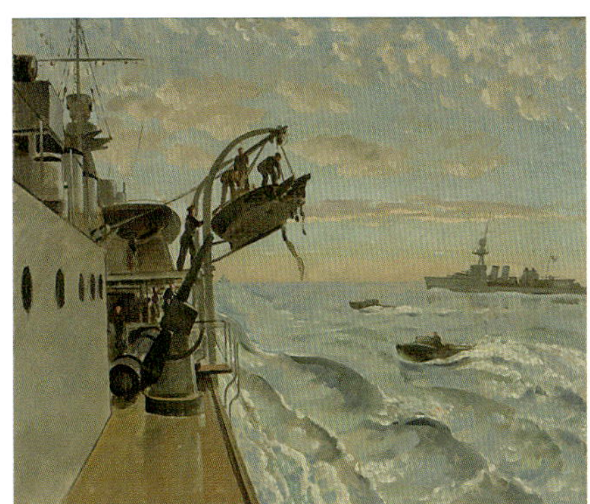

Connard, Philip 1875–1958
*Coastal Motor Boats off the Frisian Coast, 11
August 1918* 1918
oil on canvas 63.5 x 76.2
IWM ART 1299

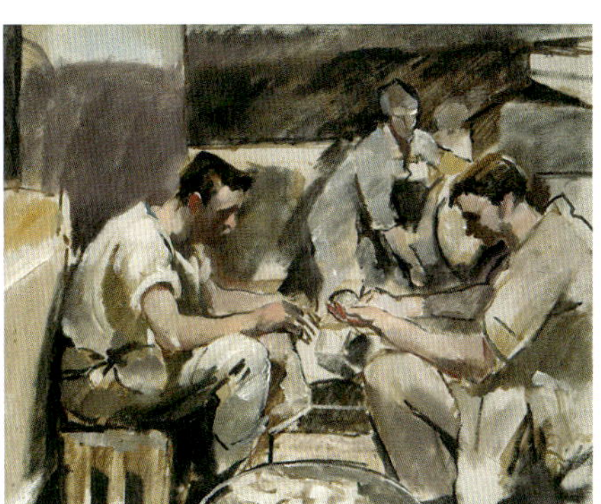

Connard, Philip 1875–1958
Cookhouse: 'HMS Maidstone' 1918
oil on canvas 50.8 x 60.9
IWM ART 4973

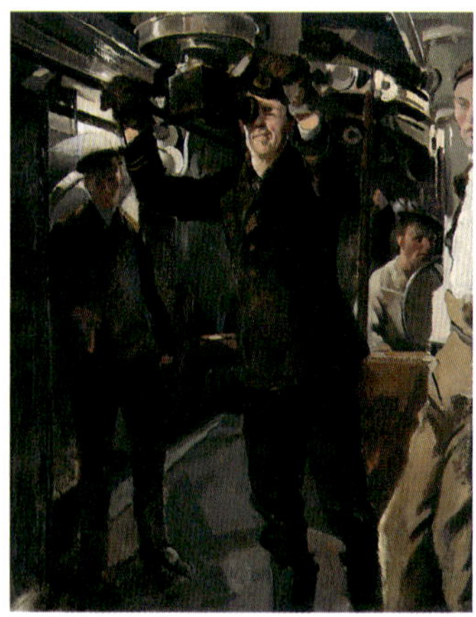

Connard, Philip 1875–1958
E.44 Making an Attack 1918
oil on canvas 60.9 x 50.8
IWM ART 1308

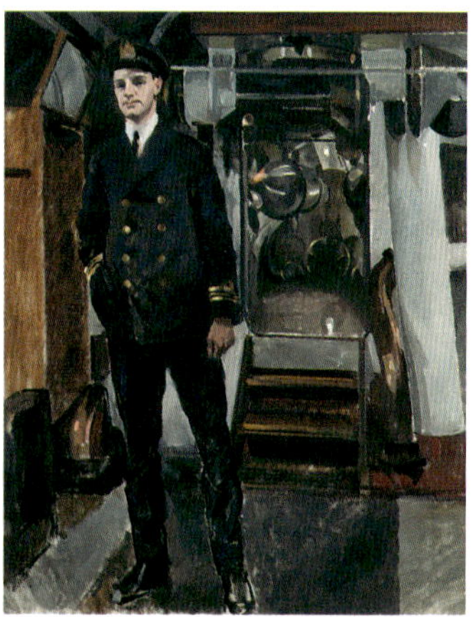

Connard, Philip 1875–1958
E.45: The Commander, Lieutenant-Commander J. E. Gaimes, DSO, RN 1918
oil on canvas 60.9 x 50.8
IWM ART 1304

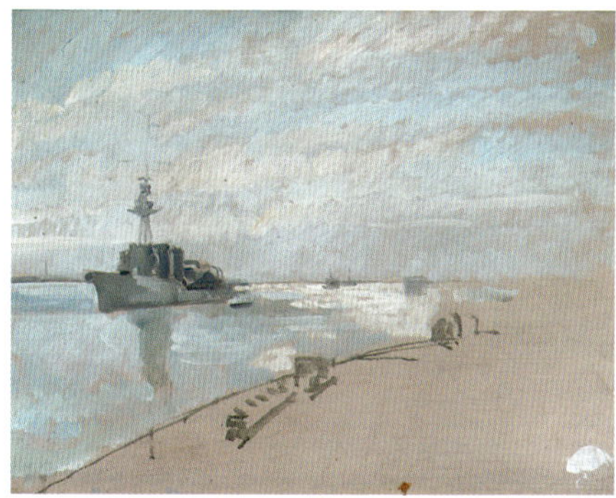

Connard, Philip 1875–1958
Evening 1918
oil on panel 30.4 x 40.6
IWM ART 1296

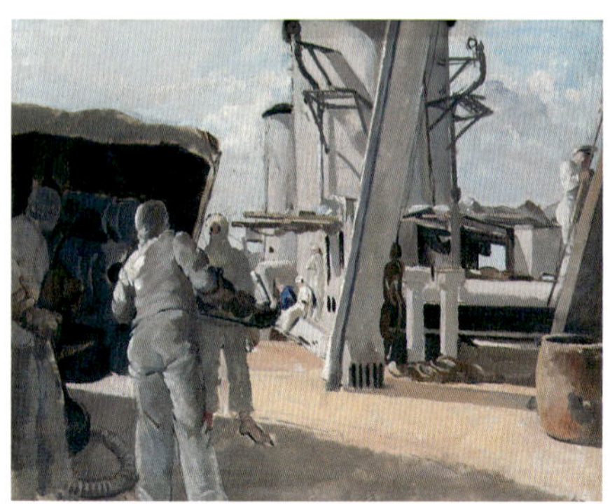

Connard, Philip 1875–1958
Gun Practice: 'HMS Canterbury' 1918
oil on canvas 50.8 x 60.9
IWM ART 1307

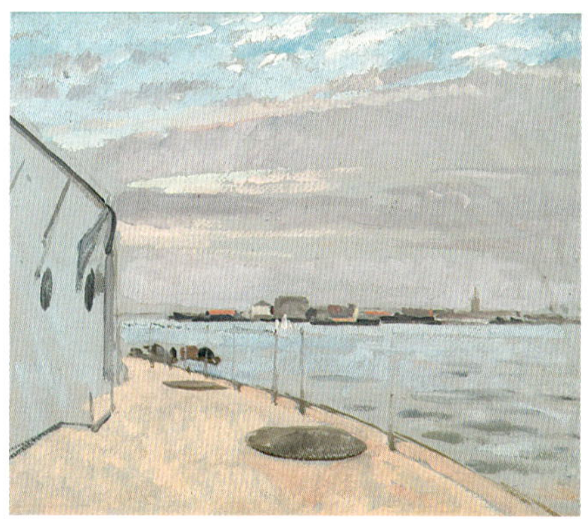

Connard, Philip 1875–1958
Harwich 1918
oil on panel 33 x 40.6
IWM ART 1292

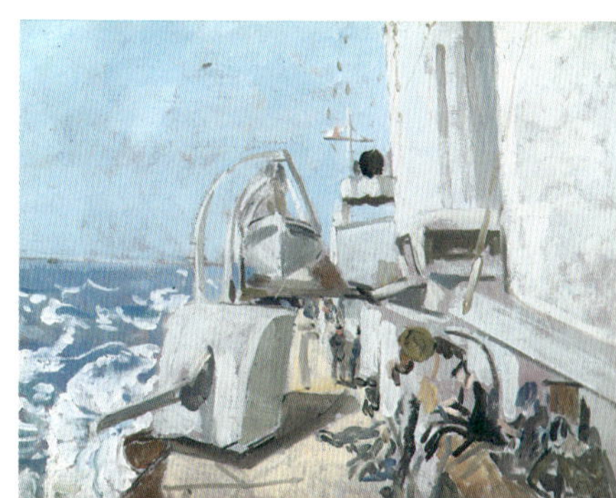

Connard, Philip 1875–1958
'HMS Canterbury' 1918
oil on panel 30.4 x 40.6
IWM ART 1282

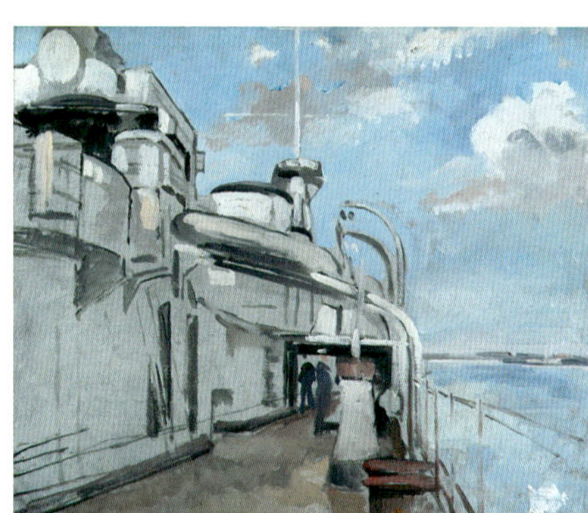

Connard, Philip 1875–1958
'HMS Canterbury' 1918
oil on panel 30.4 x 40.6
IWM ART 1285

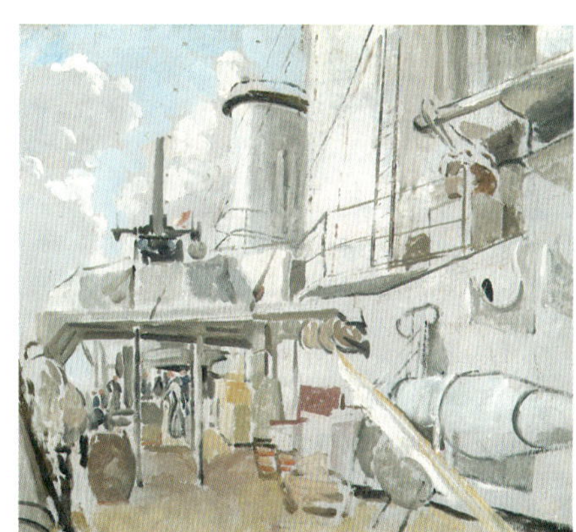

Connard, Philip 1875–1958
'HMS Curaçao' 1918
oil on panel 33 x 40.6
IWM ART 1298

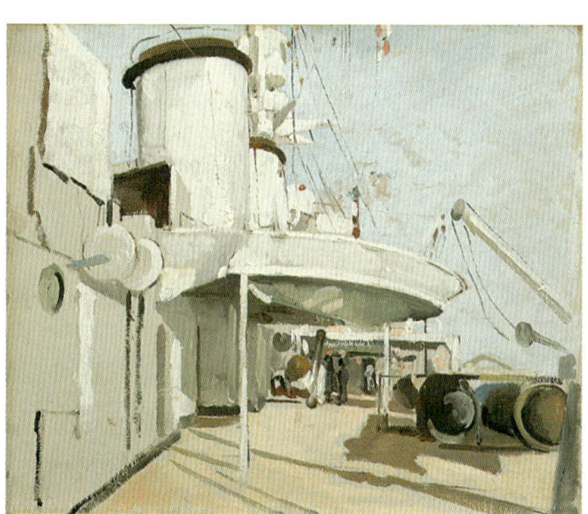

Connard, Philip 1875–1958
'HMS Curaçao' 1918
oil on panel 30.4 x 40.6
IWM ART 1312

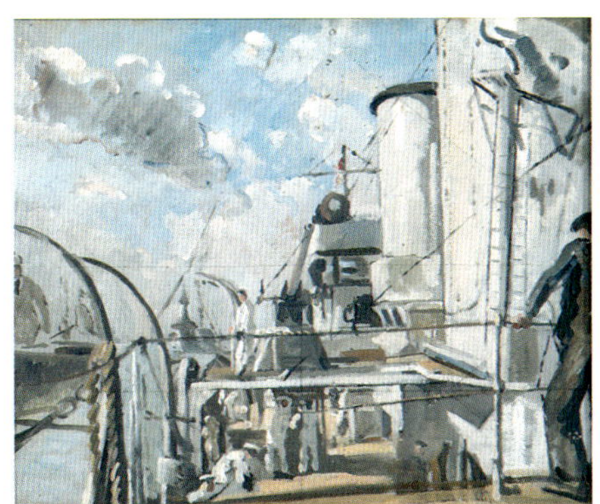

Connard, Philip 1875–1958
'HMS Curlew' 1918
oil on panel 30.4 x 40.6
IWM ART 1291

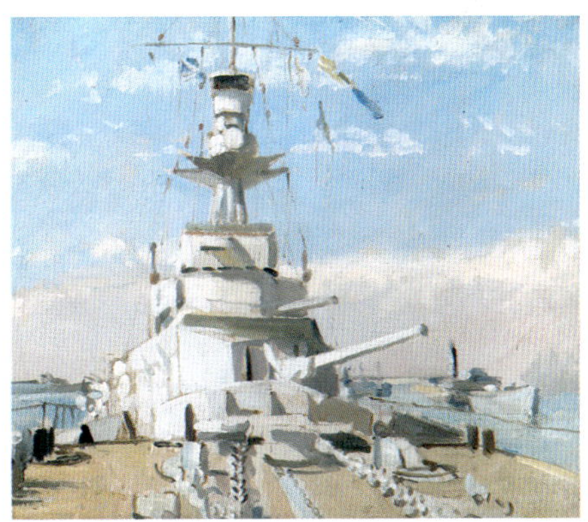

Connard, Philip 1875–1958
'HMS Curlew' 1918
oil on panel 33 x 40.6
IWM ART 1315

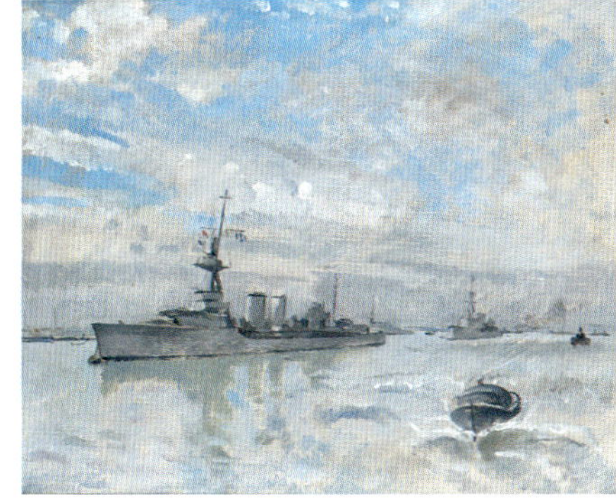

Connard, Philip 1875–1958
'HMS Danaë' 1918
oil on canvas 50.8 x 60.9
IWM ART 1303

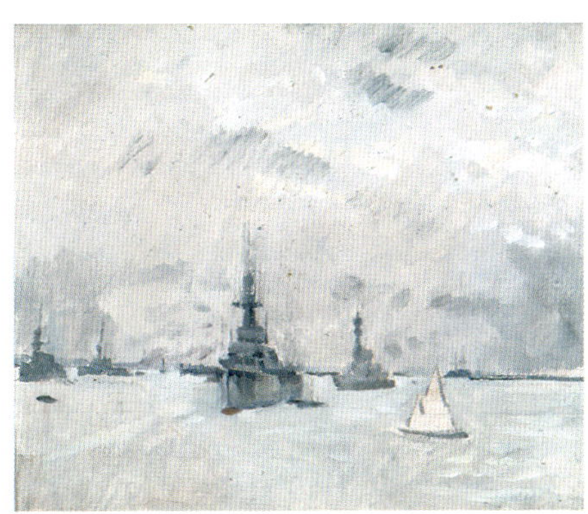

Connard, Philip 1875–1958
Light Cruisers 1918
oil on panel 33 x 40.6
IWM ART 1283

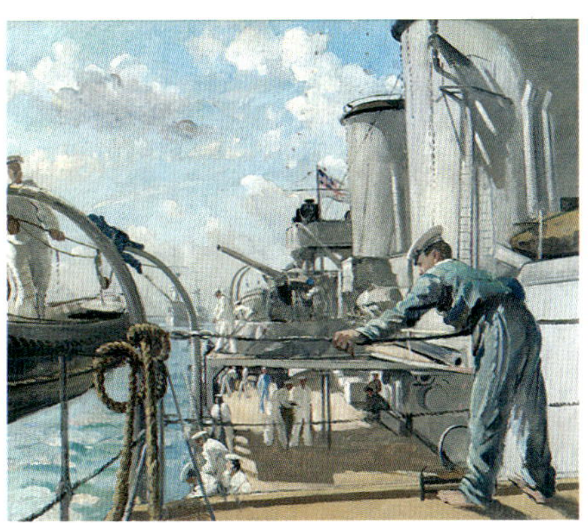

Connard, Philip 1875–1958
Lowering the Whaler: 'HMS Coventry' 1918
oil on canvas 63.5 x 76.2
IWM ART 1297

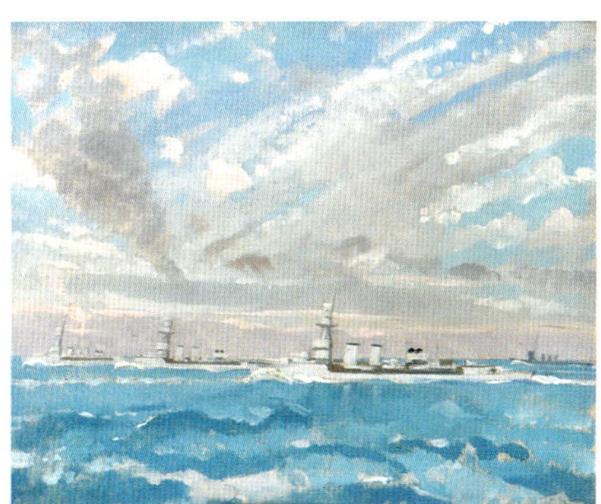

Connard, Philip 1875–1958
Near the South Dogger 1918
oil on canvas 50.8 x 60.9
IWM ART 1316

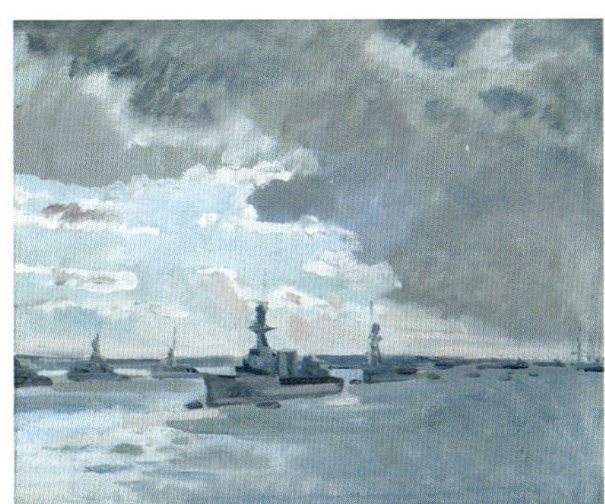

Connard, Philip 1875–1958
Off Harwich 1918
oil on panel 33 x 40.6
IWM ART 1286

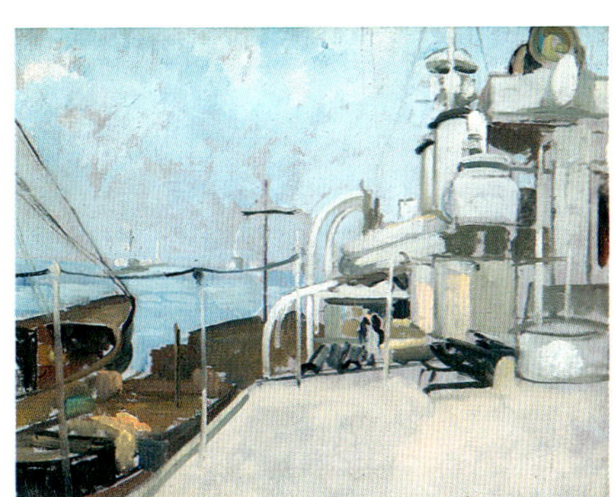

Connard, Philip 1875–1958
Oiler Alongside 1918
oil on panel 30.4 x 40.6
IWM ART 1289

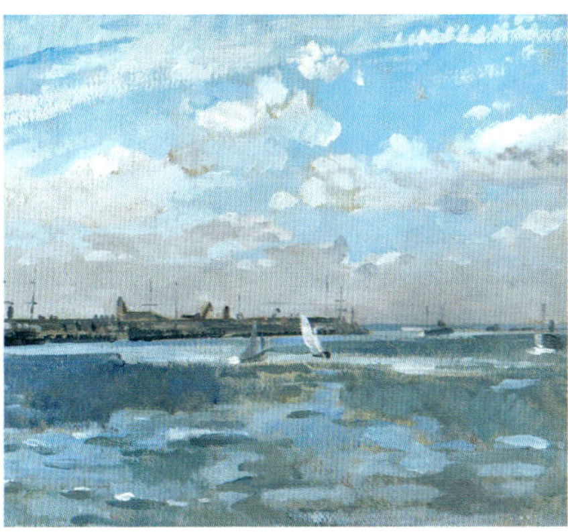

Connard, Philip 1875–1958
Parkestone 1918
oil on panel 33 x 40.6
IWM ART 1314

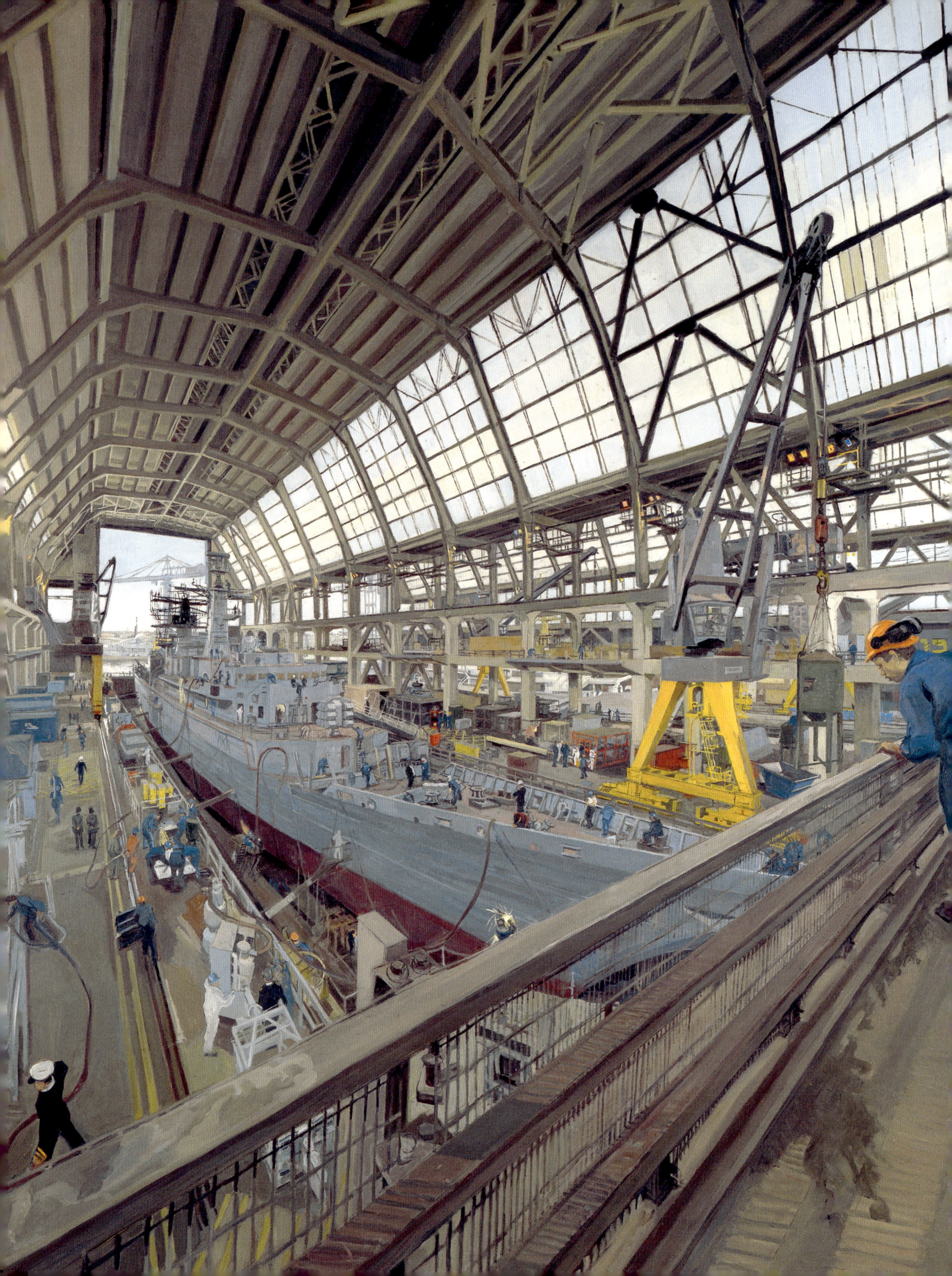

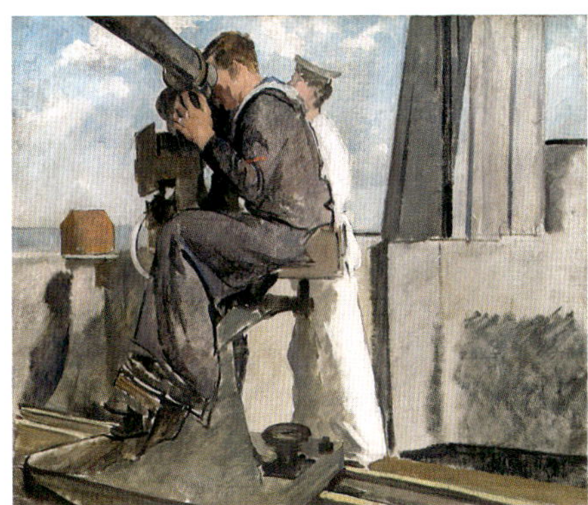

Connard, Philip 1875–1958
Rangefinder in Action, August 1918 1918
oil on canvas 63.5 x 76.2
IWM ART 4968

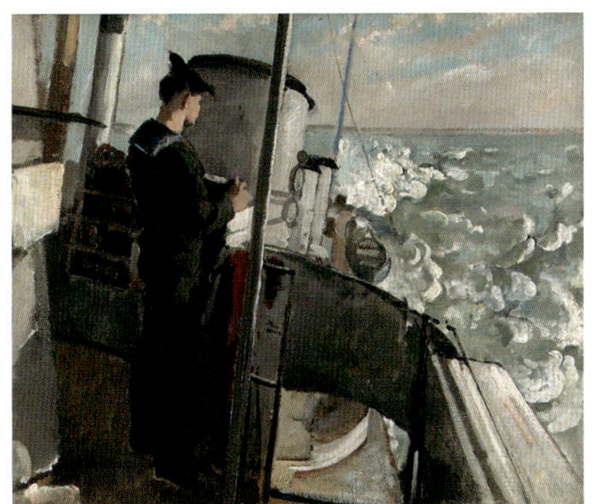

Connard, Philip 1875–1958
Sailor on the Bridge 1918
oil on canvas 50.8 x 60.9 (E)
IWM ART 4972

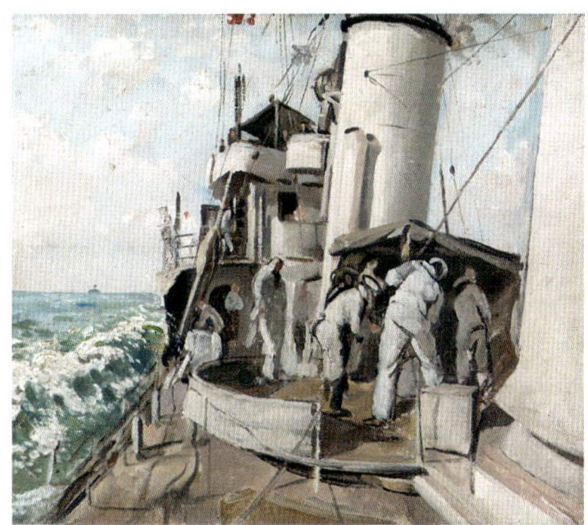

Connard, Philip 1875–1958
Sketch for '27 Knots: 'HMS Melampus'' 1918
oil on canvas 50.8 x 60.9 (E)
IWM ART 4969

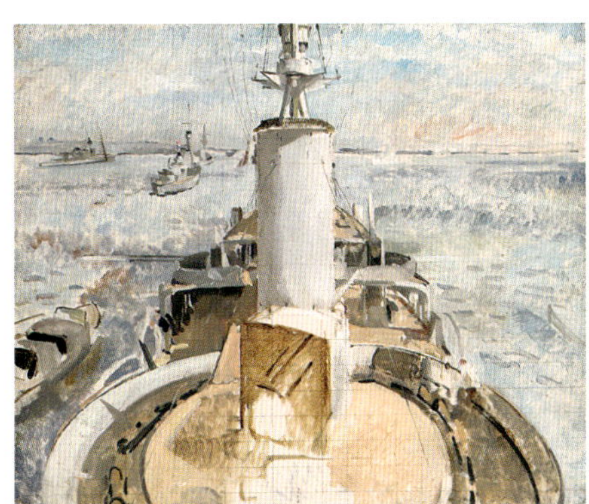

Connard, Philip 1875–1958
Sketch for 'The Harwich Force at Sea' 1918
oil on canvas 50.8 x 60.9
IWM ART 4971

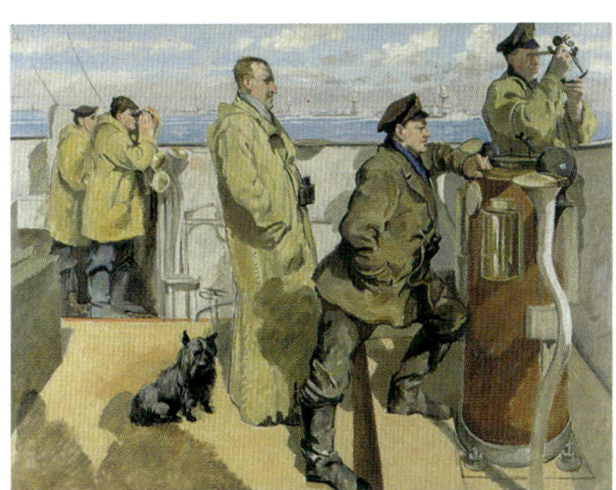

Connard, Philip 1875–1958
*St George's Day: Bridge of 'HMS Canterbury',
on Patrol Work when the Great Naval Raid on
Zeebrugge and Ostend Took Place* 1918
oil on canvas 76.2 x 101.9
IWM ART 1311

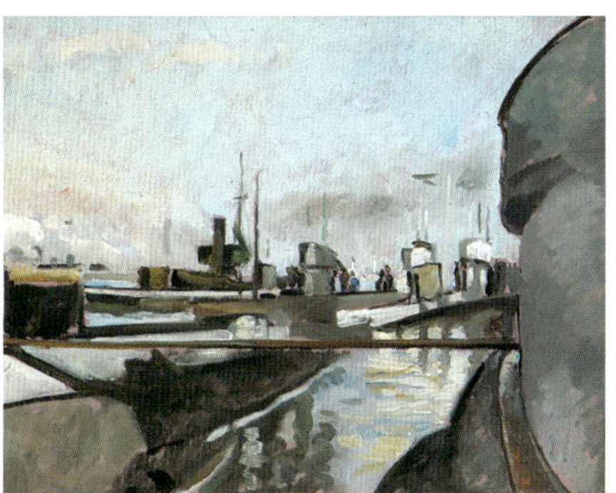

Connard, Philip 1875–1958
Submarines 1918
oil on panel 30.4 x 40.6
IWM ART 1284

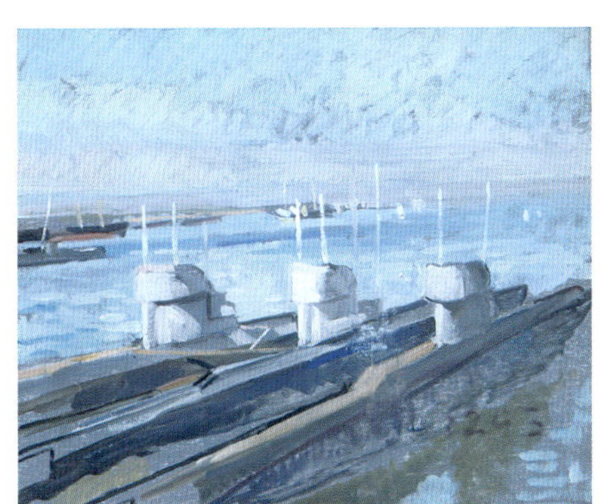

Connard, Philip 1875–1958
Submarines 1918
oil on panel 33 x 40.6 (E)
IWM ART 1293

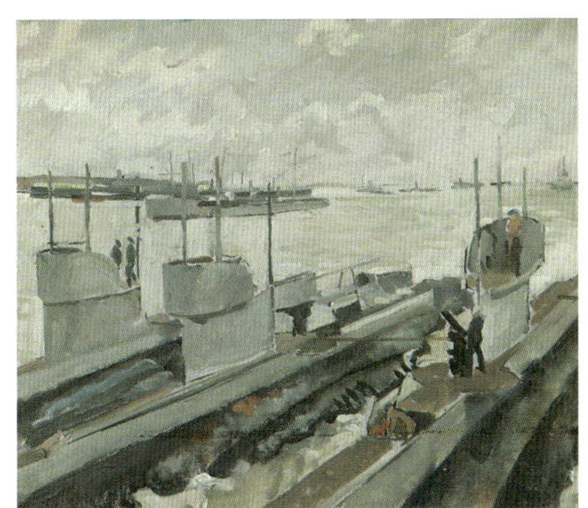

Connard, Philip 1875–1958
Submarines 1918
oil on panel 33 x 40.6 (E)
IWM ART 1319

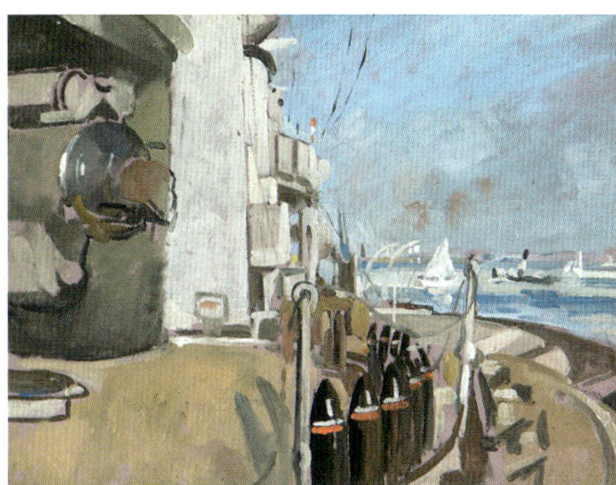

Connard, Philip 1875–1958
The Bandstand 1918
oil on panel 30.4 x 40.6
IWM ART 1290

Facing page: Wonnacott, John, b.1940, *Refit, Devonport* (detail), 1990, (p. 231)

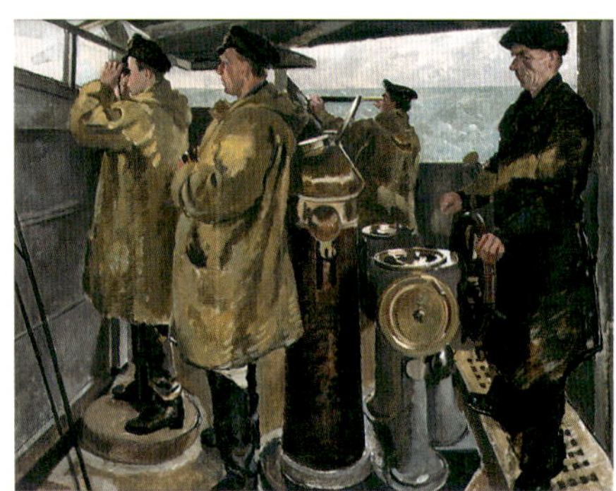

Connard, Philip 1875–1958
The Bridge, 'HMS Melampus' 1918
oil on canvas 71.1 x 91.4
IWM ART 1301

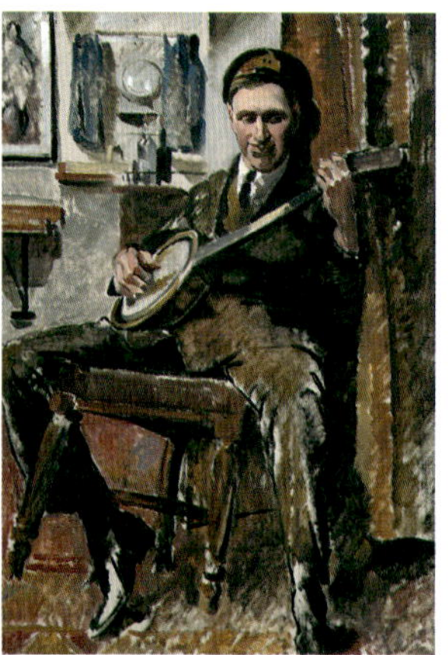

Connard, Philip 1875–1958
The Chief 1918
oil on canvas 71.1 x 50.8
IWM ART 1305

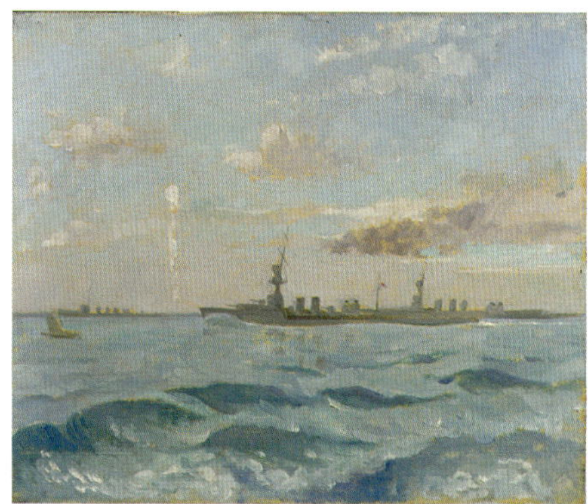

Connard, Philip 1875–1958
The Destruction of an Airship off the Frisian Coast, 11 August 1918 1918
oil on canvas 50.8 x 60.9
IWM ART 1321

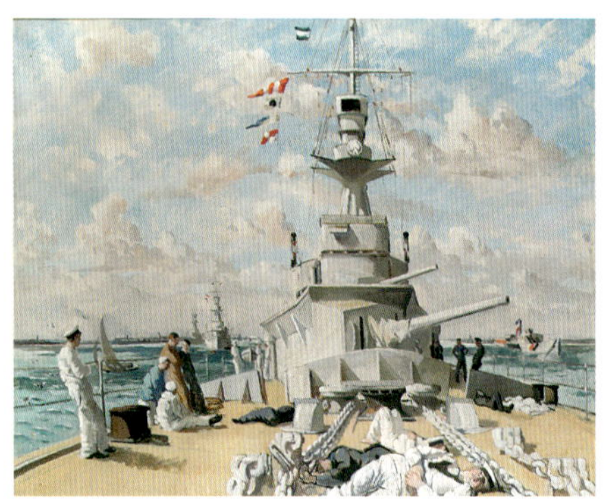

Connard, Philip 1875–1958
The Forecastle, 'HMS Curlew' 1918
oil on canvas 101.9 x 127
IWM ART 1306

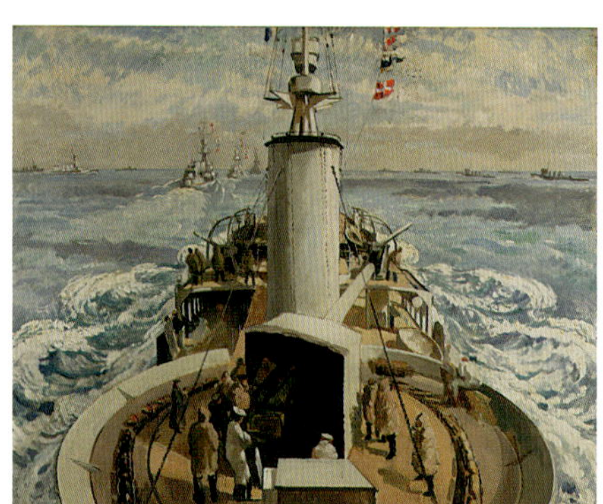

Connard, Philip 1875–1958
The Harwich Force at Sea 1918
oil on canvas 101.9 x 127
IWM ART 1302

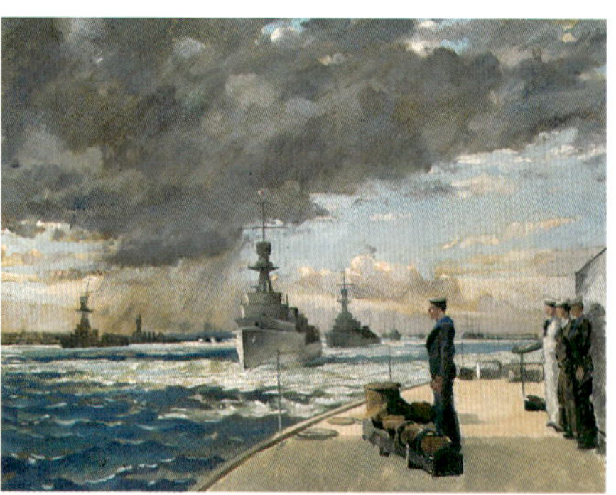

Connard, Philip 1875–1958
The Harwich Force Leaving for Sea 1918
oil on canvas 71.1 x 91.4
IWM ART 1318

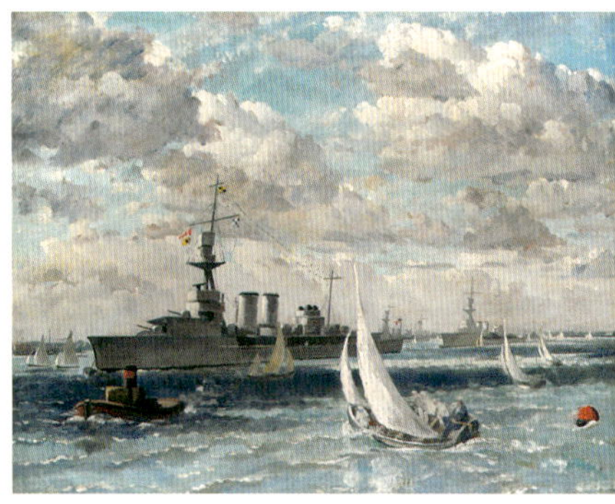

Connard, Philip 1875–1958
The Harwich Force: Sailing Race 1918
oil on canvas 101.9 x 127
IWM ART 1309

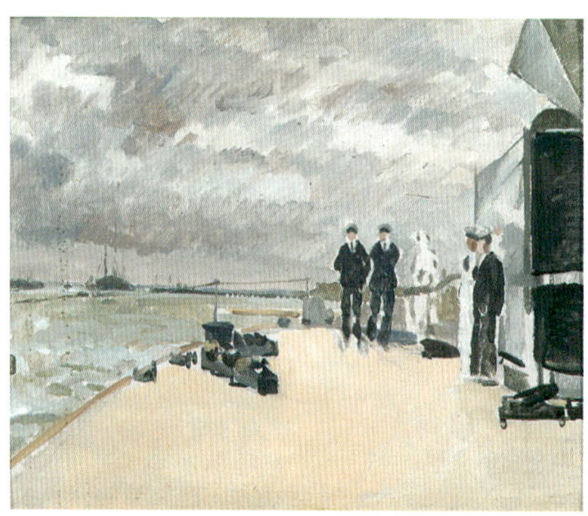

Connard, Philip 1875–1958
The Quarter-Deck 1918
oil on panel 33 x 40.6
IWM ART 1294

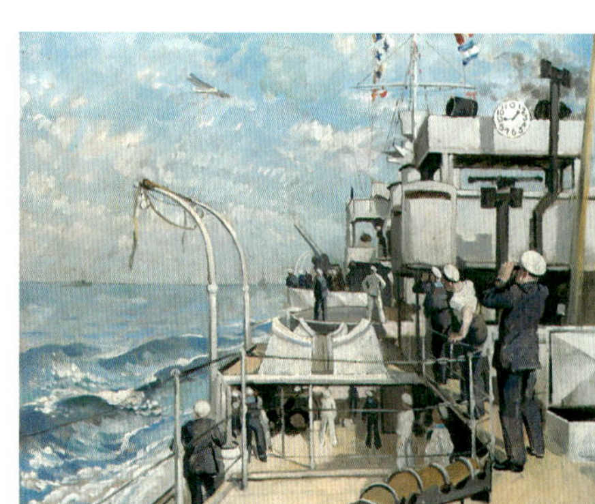

Connard, Philip 1875–1958
The Return of a 'Camel' off the Frisian Coast: 'HMS Curaçao', 11 August 1918 1918
oil on canvas 63.5 x 76.2
IWM ART 1310

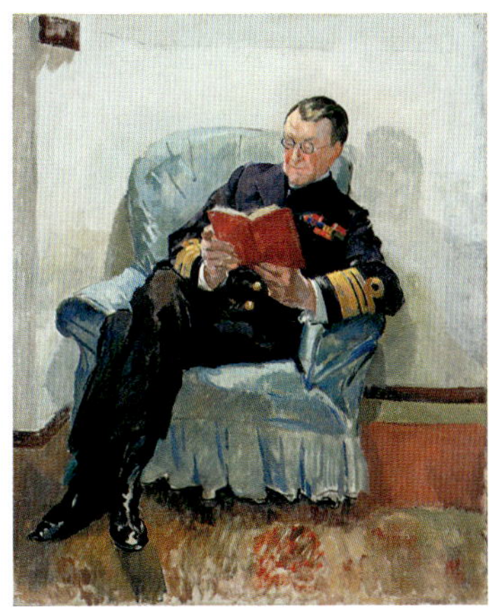

Connard, Philip 1875–1958
Vice Admiral the Honourable Sir Somerset A. Gough-Calthorpe (1864–1937), GCMG, KCB, CVO, on Board 'HMS Superb' (…) 1918
oil on canvas 76.2 x 63.5
IWM ART 2494

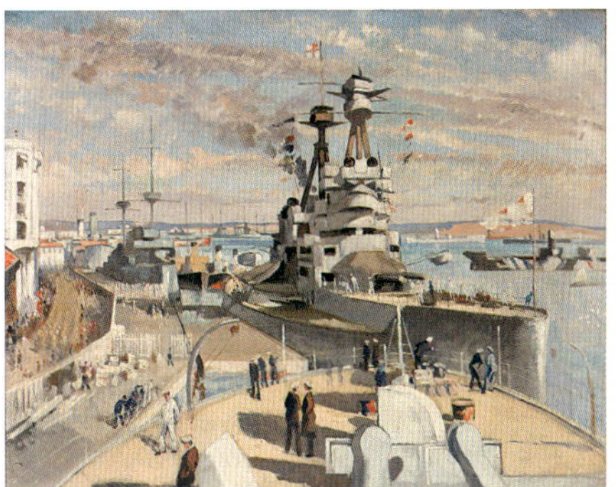

Connard, Philip 1875–1958
From 'HMS Caesar': 'HMS Superb' at Constantinople, 'HMS Lord Nelson' and the French 'Diderot' in the Distance (…) 1919
oil on canvas 71.1 x 88.9
IWM ART 2495

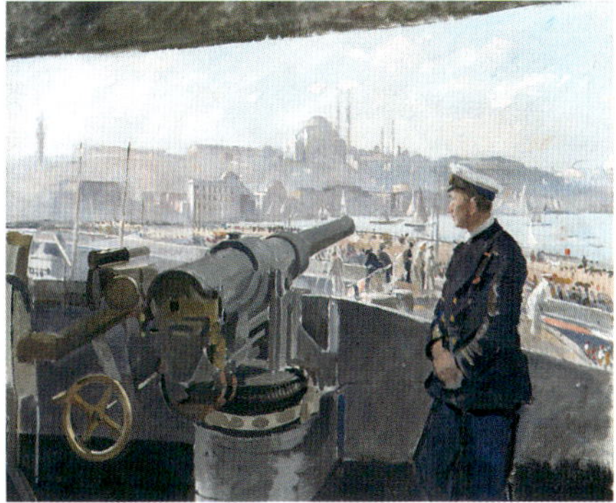

Connard, Philip 1875–1958
The Guns of 'HMS Caesar': Off Constantinople, Looking towards the Golden Horn 1919
oil on canvas 50.8 x 60.9
IWM ART 2460

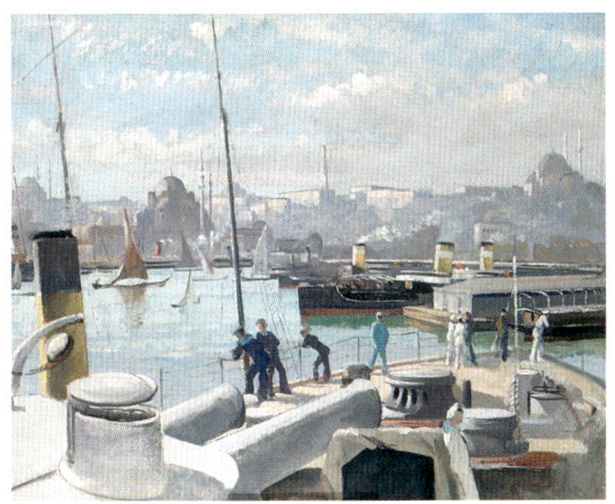

Connard, Philip 1875–1958
The Port of Constantinople: The Guns of 'HMS Caesar' 1919
oil on canvas 63.5 x 76.2
IWM ART 2496

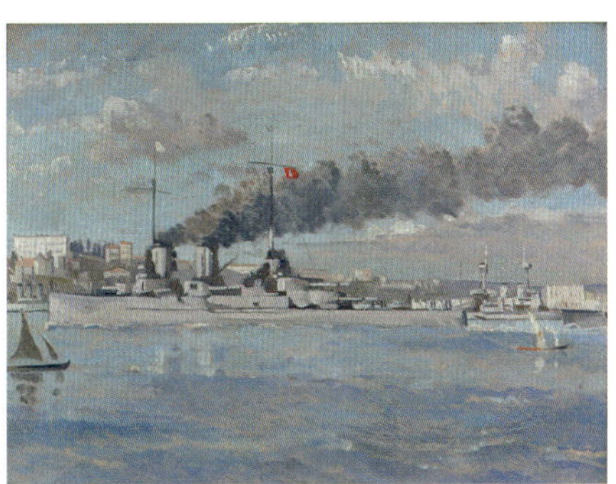

Connard, Philip 1875–1958
The Surrender of the 'Goeben': Passing the German Embassy, Constantinople, Flying the White Flag 1919
oil on canvas 50.8 x 68.5
IWM ART 2461

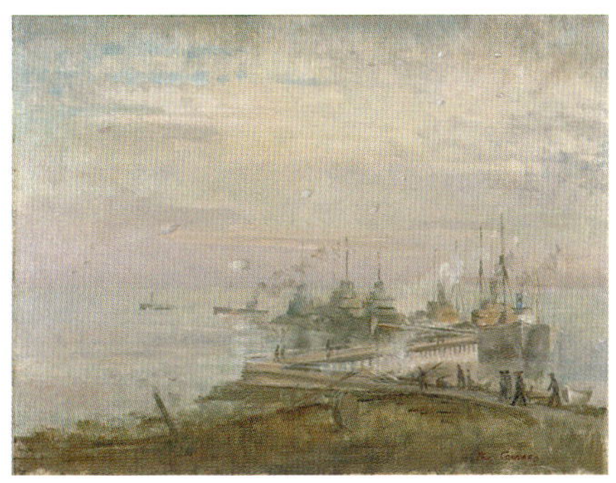

Connard, Philip 1875–1958
Balloon Barrage and Shipping 1940
oil on canvas 50.8 x 68.5
IWM ART LD 718

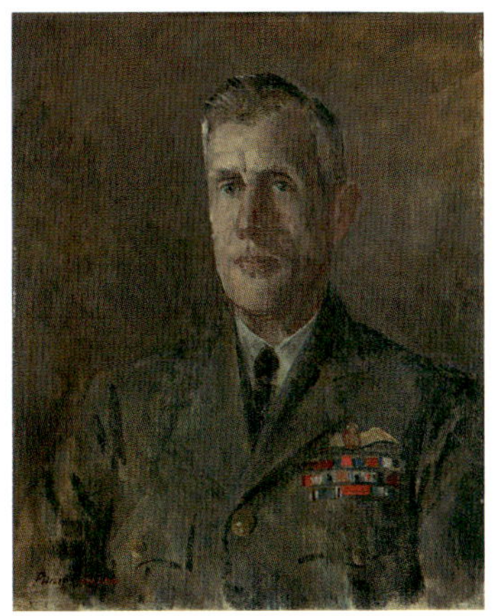

Connard, Philip 1875–1958
Air Chief Marshal Sir Edgar Ludlow-Hewitt (1886–1973), KCB, CMG, DSO, MC 1942
oil on canvas 60.9 x 50.8
IWM ART LD 2023

Connew, Joan V. b.1915
Blackout 1942
oil on canvas 50.8 x 76.2
IWM ART LD 2913

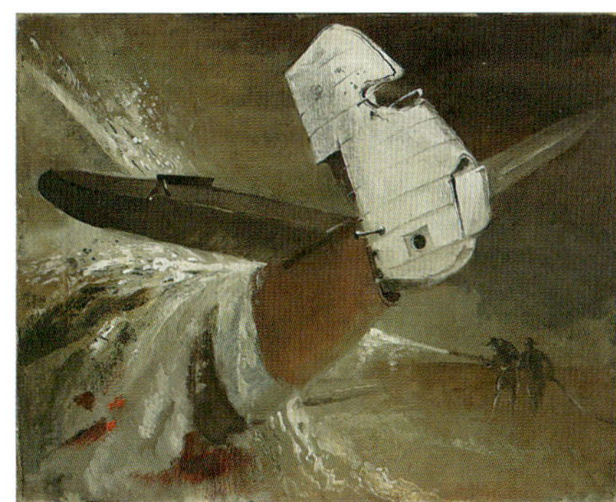

Cook, Frederick T. W. 1907–1982
Bristol Beaufighter I c.1944
oil on canvas 56 x 44.3
IWM ART 16125

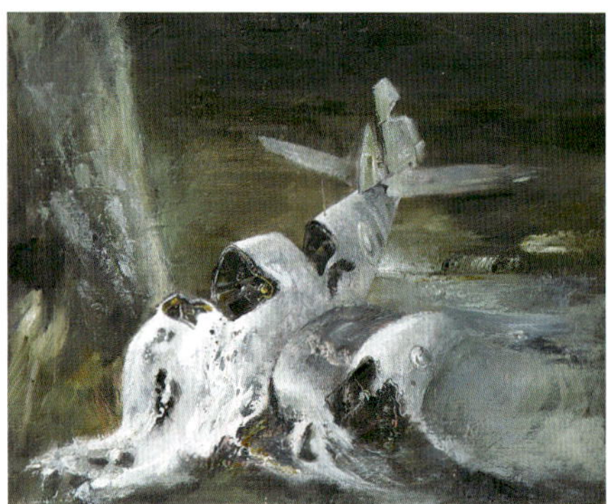

Cook, Frederick T. W. 1907–1982
Bristol Beaufighter II c.1944
oil on canvas 40.6 x 51
IWM ART 16126

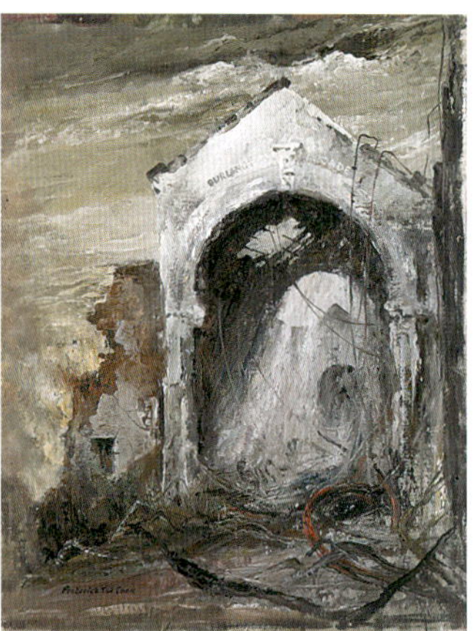

Cook, Frederick T. W. 1907–1982
Burlington Arcade c.1944
oil on panel 61.2 x 48.1
IWM ART 16122

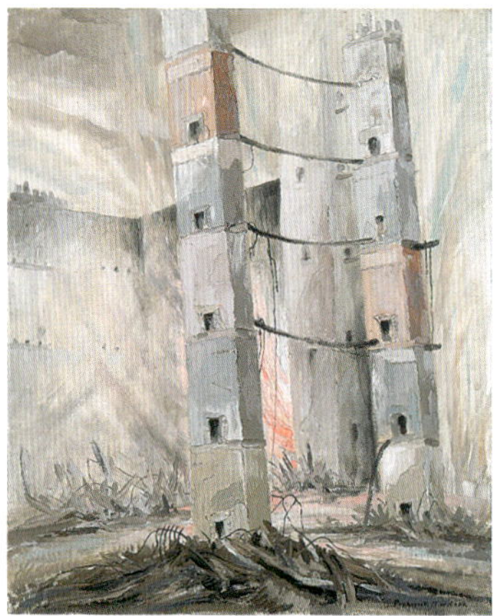

Cook, Frederick T. W. 1907–1982
Chancery Lane Fireplaces c.1944
oil on canvas 61 x 50.7
IWM ART 16124

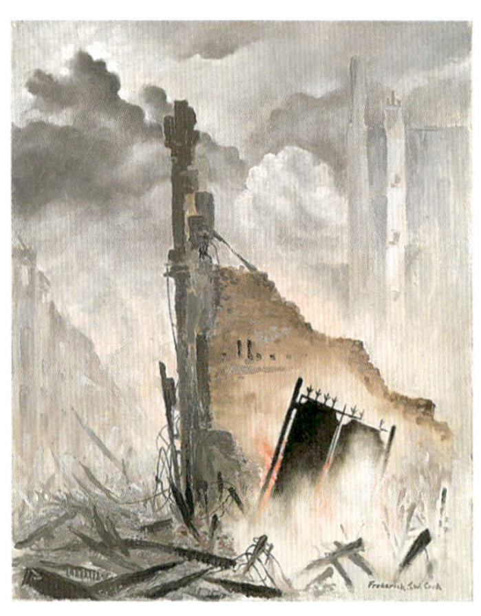

Cook, Frederick T. W. 1907–1982
Paternoster Row c.1944
oil on canvas 56.2 x 46
IWM ART 16123

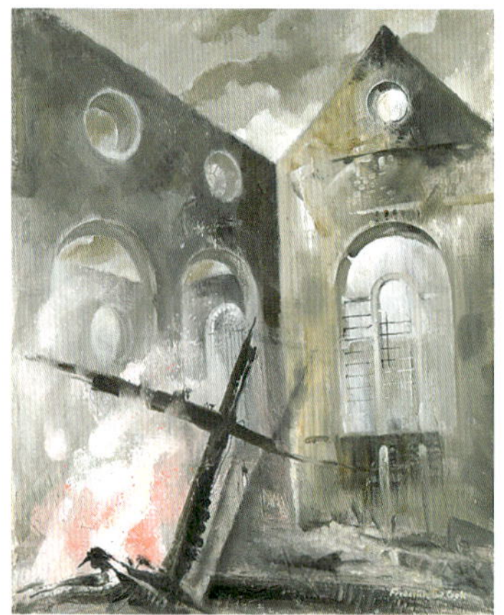

Cook, Frederick T. W. 1907–1982
St Bride's c.1944
oil on canvas 61 x 50.7
IWM ART 16121

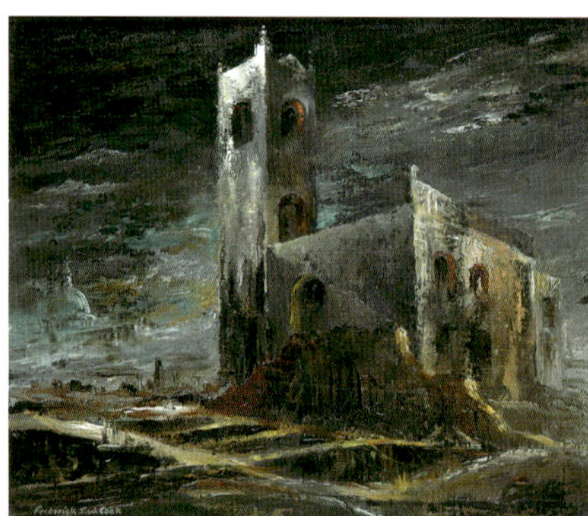

Cook, Frederick T. W. 1907–1982
St Nicholas Cole Abbey c.1944
oil on canvas 47.2 x 56.3
IWM ART 16120

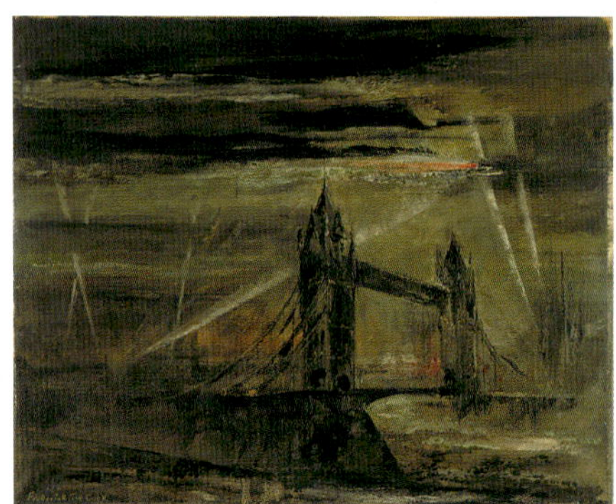

Cook, Frederick T. W. 1907–1982
A Flying Bomb over Tower Bridge 1944–1945
oil on canvas 39.3 x 49.5
IWM ART LD 4719

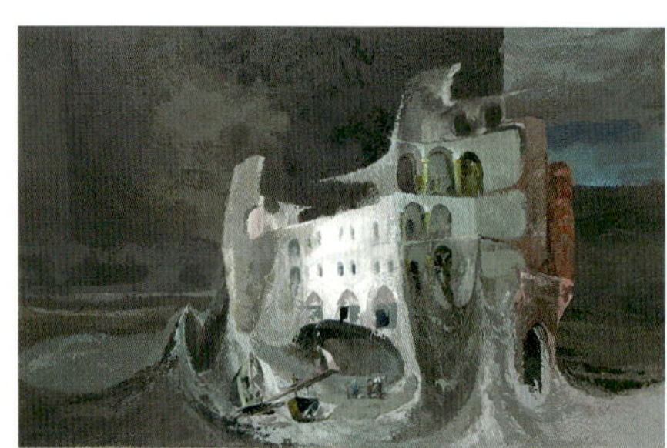

Cook, Frederick T. W. 1907–1982
Aftermath: The Prudential Building, Plymouth
1951
oil on canvas 76 x 91.5
IWM ART 16213

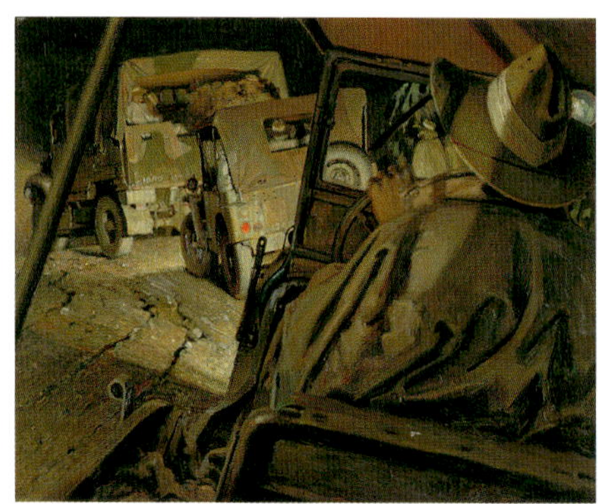

Cook, James 1904–1960
Australian Troops: Night Convoy c.1945
oil on board 42.9 x 54.4
IWM ART 16559

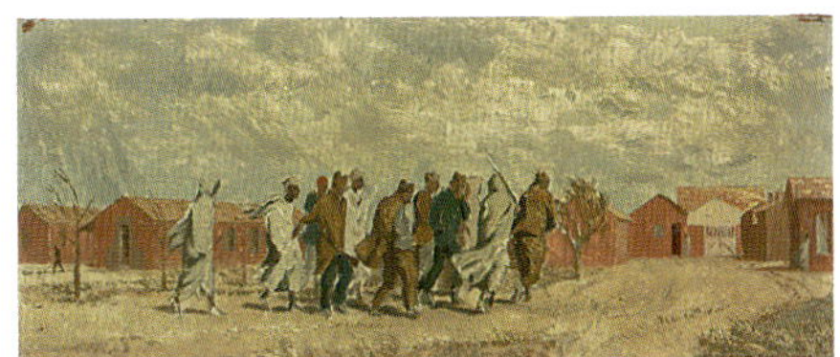

Cook, John Kingsley 1911–1994
*French and Arab Prisoners at Mecheria
Internment Camp, Algeria* 1942
oil on panel 27.3 x 65.4
IWM ART LD 2819

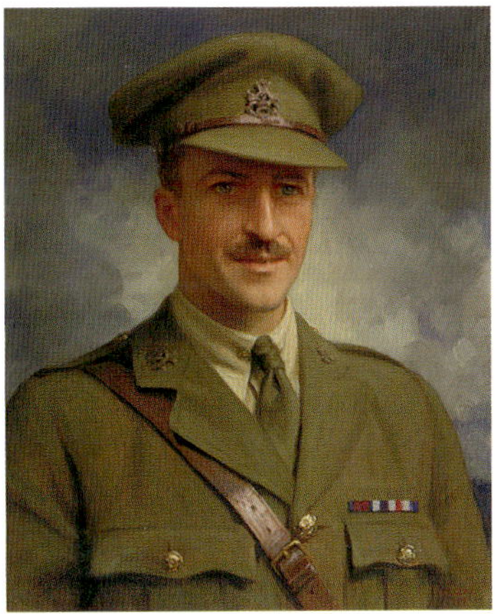

Cooke, Isaac 1846–1922
Lieutenant Colonel J. R. Webster, DSO, MC
1919
oil on canvas 76.2 x 60.9
IWM ART 6487

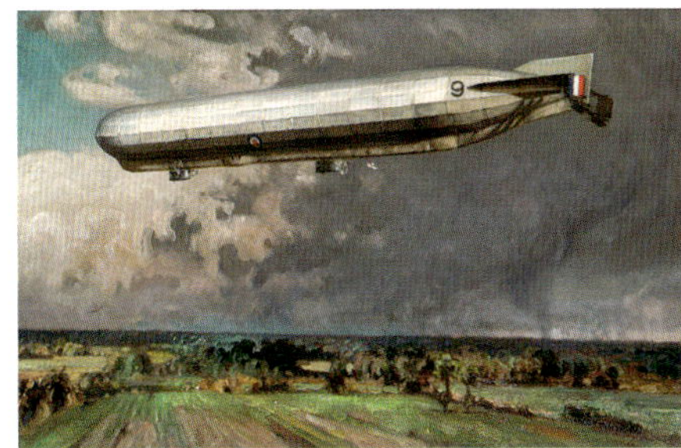

Cooper, Alfred Egerton 1883–1974
Airship 9 1918
oil on canvas 60.9 x 91.4 (E)
IWM ART 1462

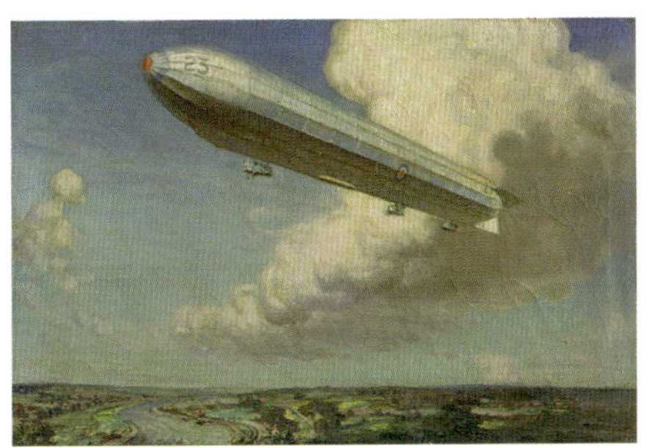

Cooper, Alfred Egerton 1883–1974
Airship 23 1918
oil on canvas 60.9 x 91.4 (E)
IWM ART 1461

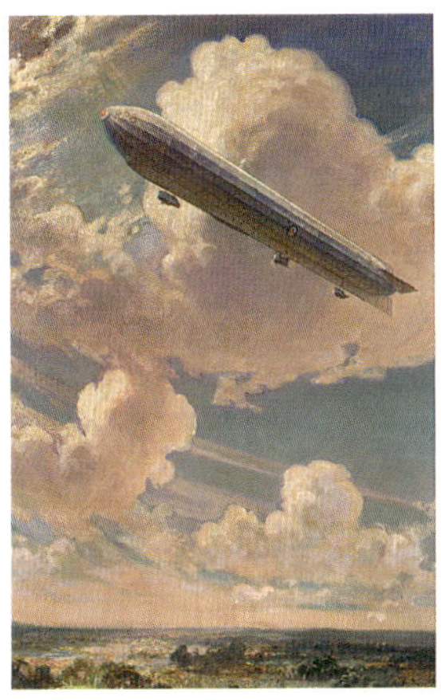

Cooper, Alfred Egerton 1883–1974
'Rigid 26' 1918
oil on canvas 91.1 x 60.6
IWM ART 1463

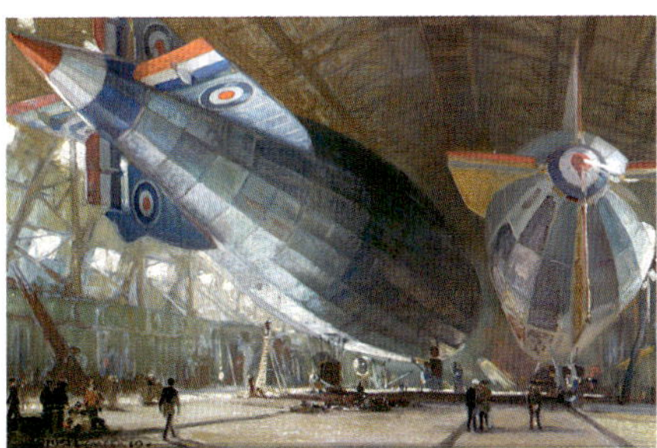

Cooper, Alfred Egerton 1883–1974
R.34 and R.29 in the Shed at East Fortune
1919
oil on canvas 60.9 x 91.4
IWM ART 4086

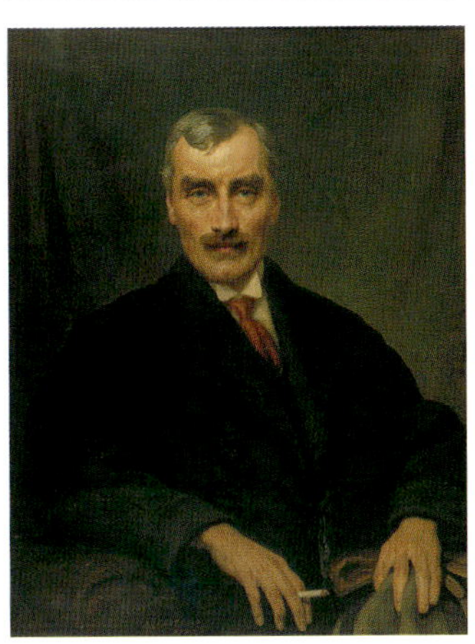

Cooper, Alfred Egerton 1883–1974
*Surgeon Major Arthur Martin-Leake
(1874–1953), VC, RAMC* 1921
oil on canvas 91.4 x 71.1
IWM ART 4069

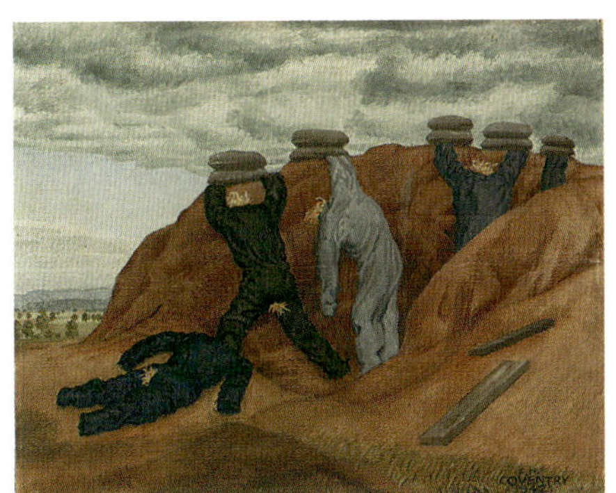

Coventry, Frederick Halford b.1905
Dummy Figures Used in Training 1942
oil on canvas 22.5 x 28.5
IWM ART LD 2468

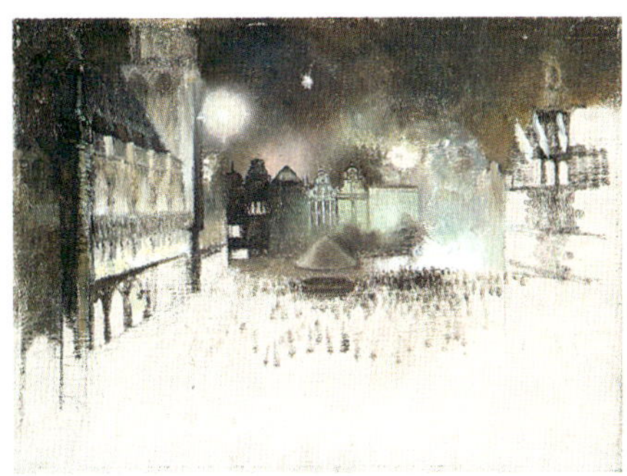

Cowern, Raymond Teague 1913–1986
Brussels: VE Day 3 1945
oil on canvas 34 x 47
IWM ART 16947

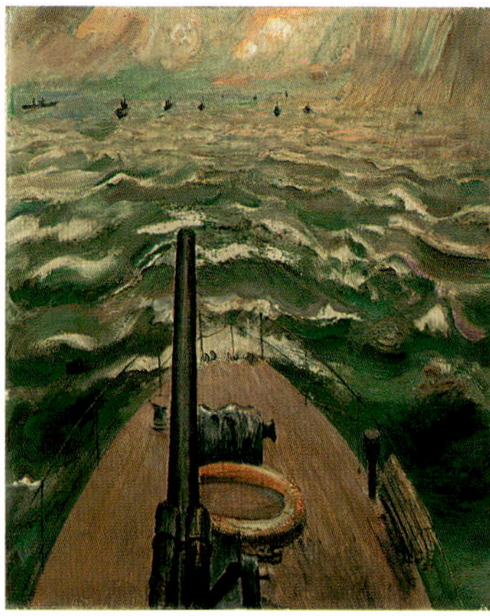

Coxon, Raymond James 1896–1997
Convoy 1942
oil on canvas 60.9 x 50.8
IWM ART LD 2161

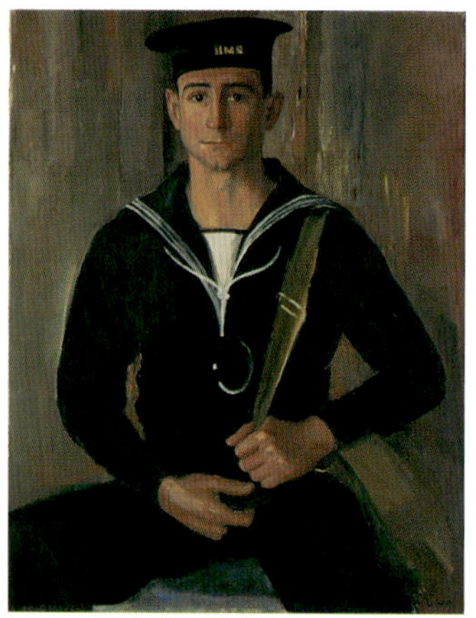

Coxon, Raymond James 1896–1997
Ordinary Seaman H. V. Cronyn, GM, RNVR, of 'HMS Mallard' 1943
oil on canvas 80.3 x 62.8
IWM ART LD 3266

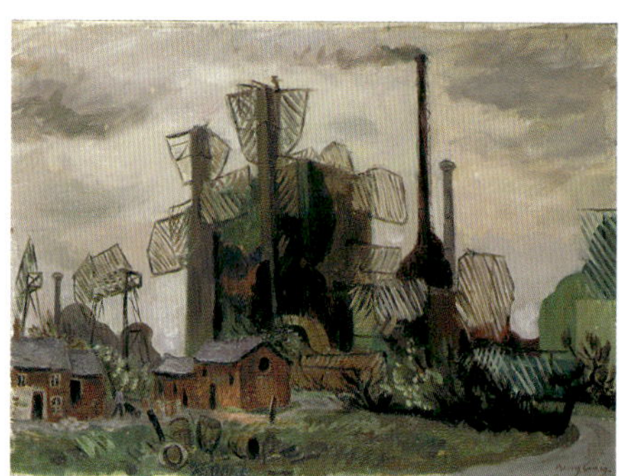

Craig, Barry 1902–1951
Camouflage Screens at a Cheshire Factory 1943
oil on canvas 54.6 x 74.9
IWM ART LD 3015

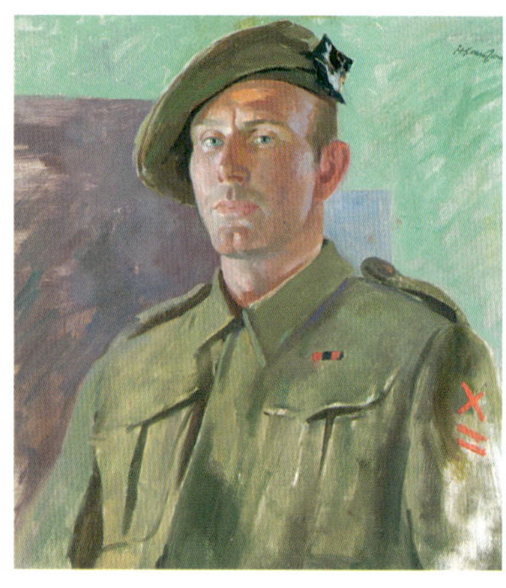

Crawford, Hugh Adam 1898–1982
Company Sergeant Major McLeod, DCM, Seaforth Highlanders, 51st Division 1942
oil on canvas 67.3 x 62.2
IWM ART LD 2132

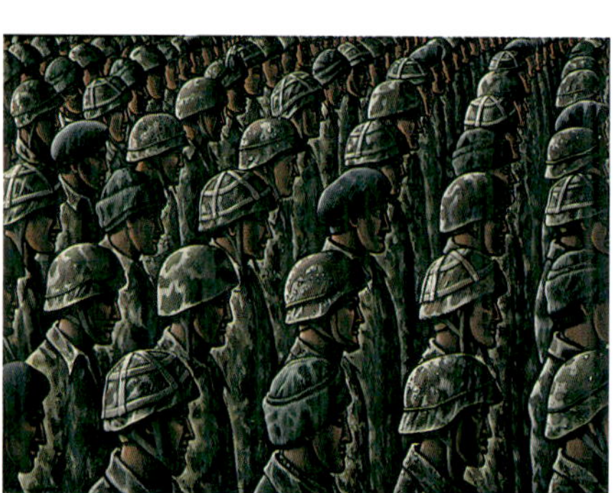

Crook, Pamela b.1945
Other Mothers' Sons 1991
acrylic on wood & canvas 91.5 x 127
IWM ART 16420

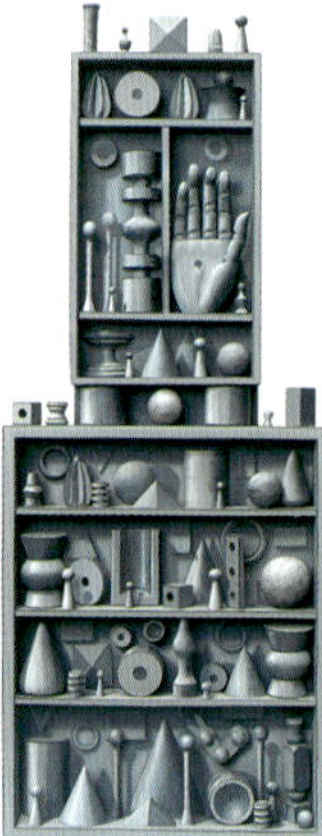

Crook, Pamela b.1945
The Naming of Parts 2003
acrylic on wood & objects 108 x 42.5
IWM ART 16846

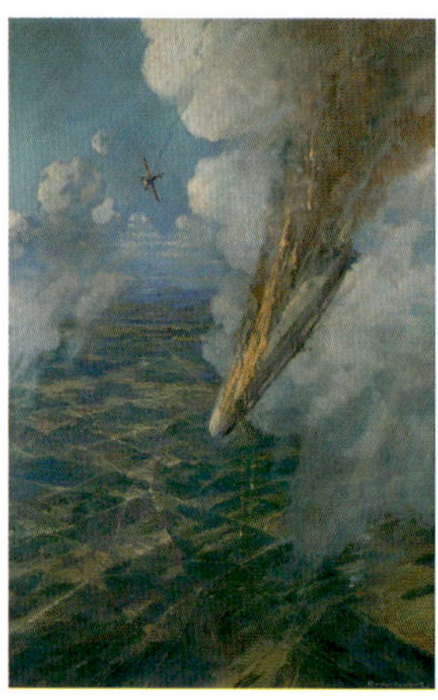

Crosby, Frederick Gordon 1885–1943
Lieutenant Warneford's Great Exploit: The First Zeppelin to Be Brought down by Allied Aircraft, 7 June 1915 1919
oil on canvas 182.8 x 121.9
IWM ART 3077

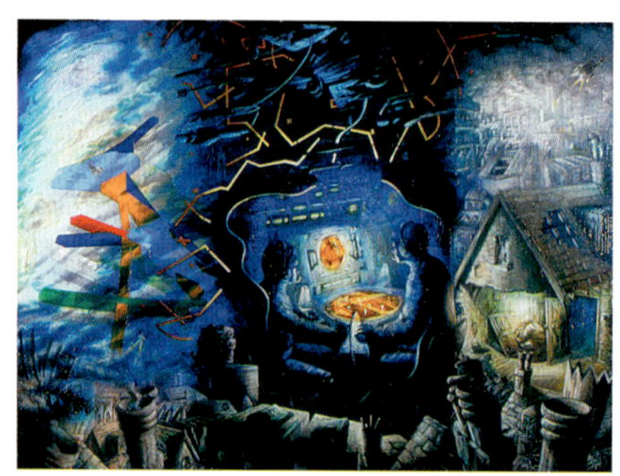

Crowley, Graham b.1950
Mainframe
acrylic on canvas 203.4 x 274.4
IWM ART 16330

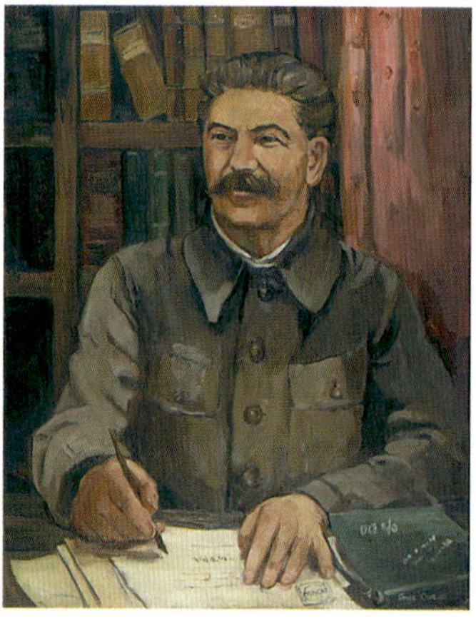

Cruttwell, Grace active 1903–1945
Joseph Stalin (1879–1953) c.1941–1945
oil on canvas 92.7 x 72.3
IWM ART LD 7213

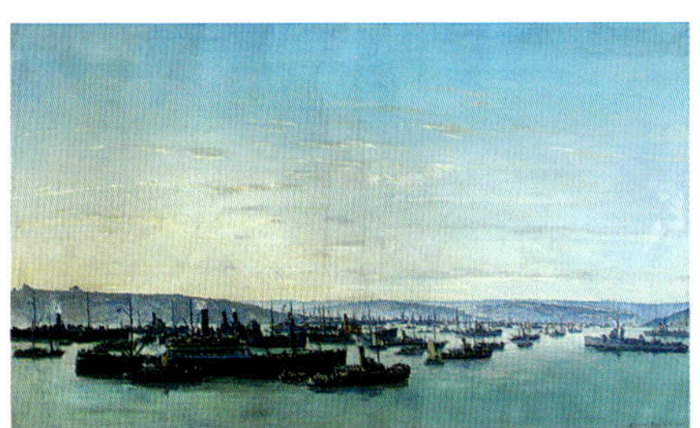

Cundall, Charles Ernest 1890–1971
Bordeaux Refugees at Falmouth 1940
oil on canvas 76.2 x 127
IWM ART LD 747

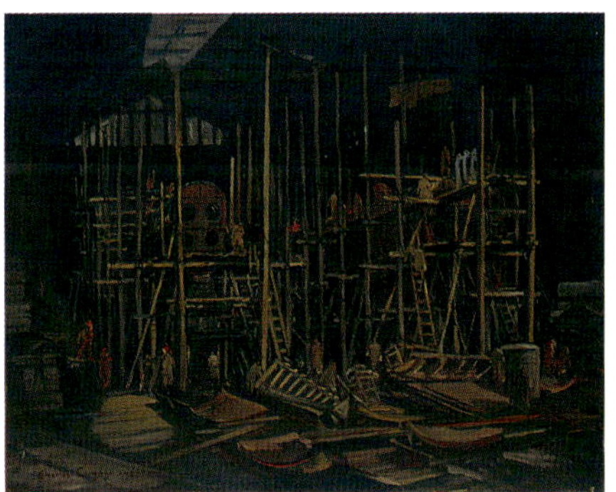

Cundall, Charles Ernest 1890–1971
Building Submarines 1940
oil on panel 50.8 x 66
IWM ART LD 749

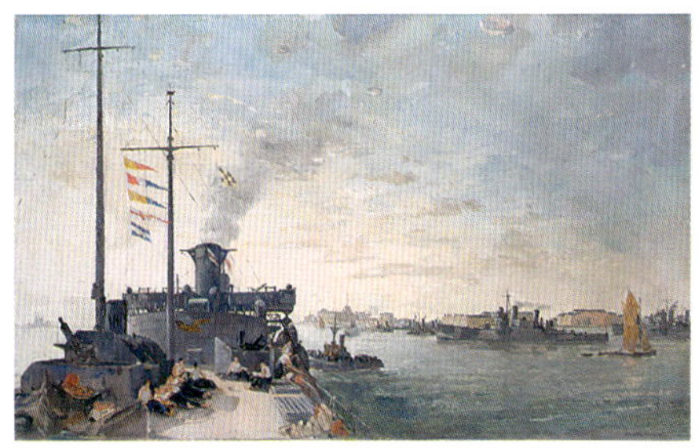

Cundall, Charles Ernest 1890–1971
Dunkirk Paddleboat 1940
oil on canvas 78.7 x 127
IWM ART LD 6049

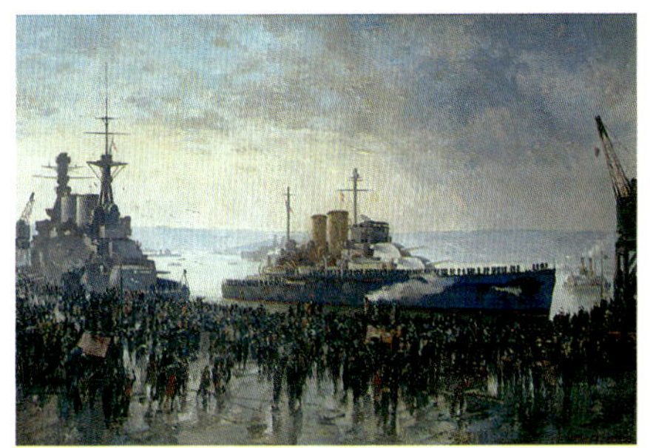

Cundall, Charles Ernest 1890–1971
'HMS Exeter' at Plymouth in 1940: Back from the Graf Spee Action 1940
oil on canvas 91.4 x 132
IWM ART LD 1848

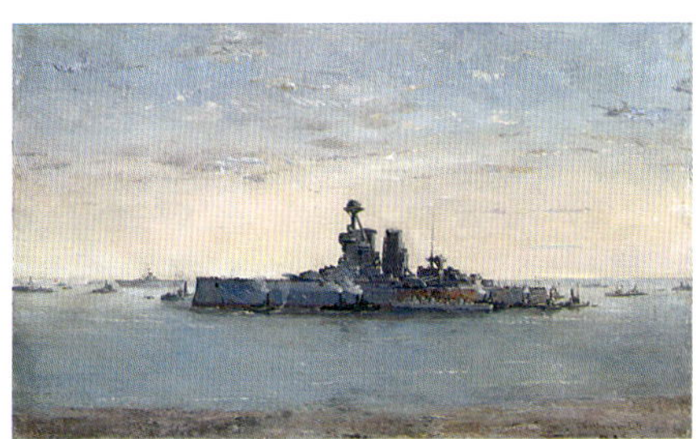

Cundall, Charles Ernest 1890–1971
'Iron Duke' 1940
oil on canvas 45.7 x 76.5
IWM ART LD 6050

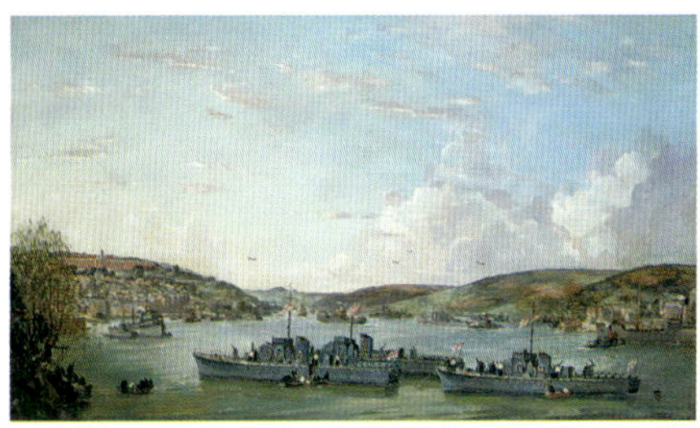

Cundall, Charles Ernest 1890–1971
Motor Launches, Dartmouth 1940
oil on canvas 65.7 x 124.4
IWM ART LD 1215

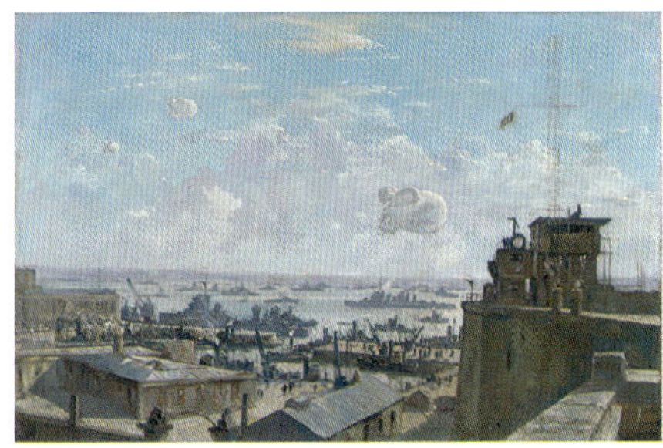

Cundall, Charles Ernest 1890–1971
Sheerness 1940
oil on canvas 58.4 x 91.4
IWM ART LD 745

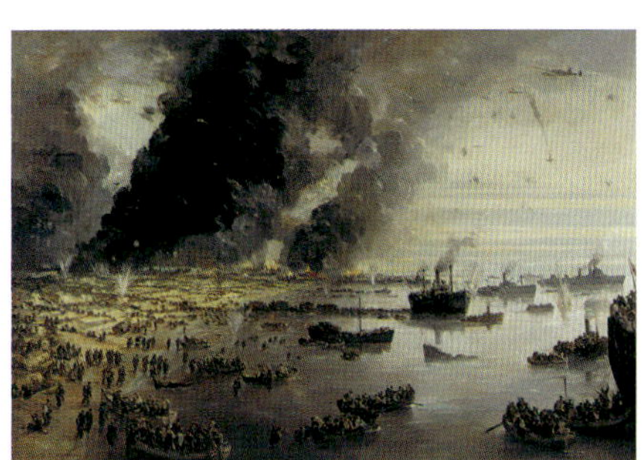

Cundall, Charles Ernest 1890–1971
The Withdrawal from Dunkirk, June 1940 1940
oil on canvas 101.8 x 152.8
IWM ART LD 305

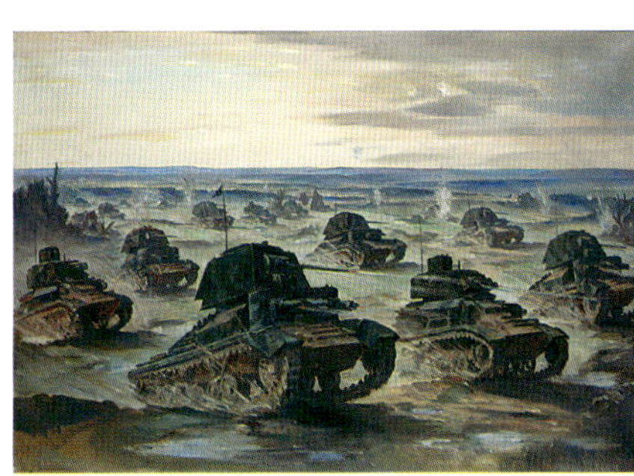

Cundall, Charles Ernest 1890–1971
Our Mechanised Army: Tanks in Action (Ministry of Information poster) c.1940–1942
oil on canvas 83.8 x 123.8
IWM ART LD 15

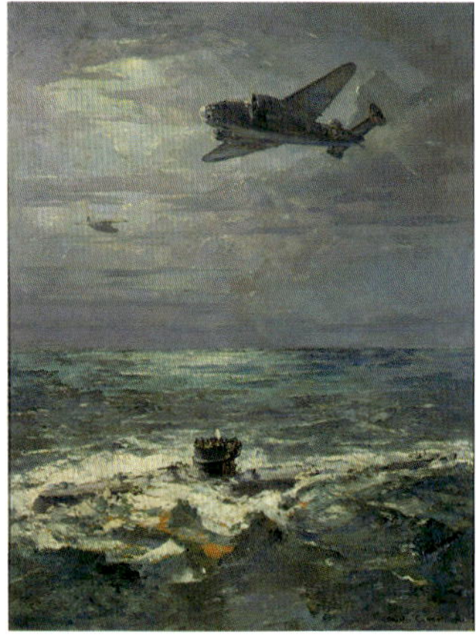

Cundall, Charles Ernest 1890–1971
A U-Boat Surrenders to a Hudson Aircraft
1941
oil on canvas 111.7 x 86.3
IWM ART LD 1561

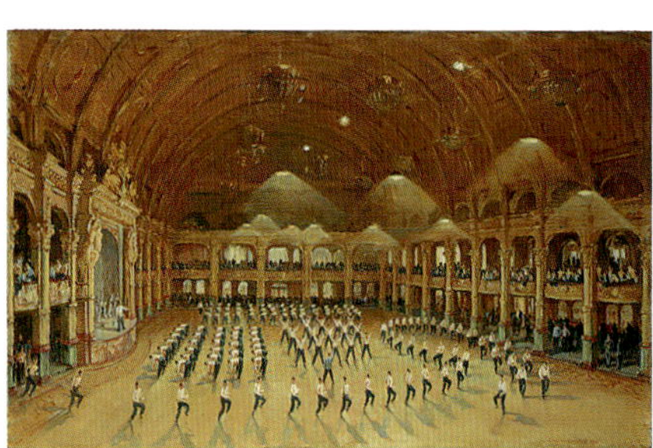

Cundall, Charles Ernest 1890–1971
Physical Training at a Royal Air Force Training Centre 1941
oil on canvas 76.2 x 121.9
IWM ART LD 904

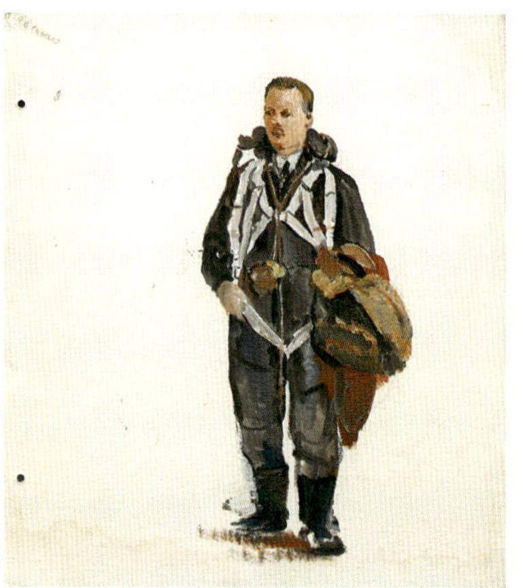

Cundall, Charles Ernest 1890–1971
A. B. Charles: Portrait of a Flyer 1941–1945
oil on paper 38.7 x 34.9
IWM ART LD 7257

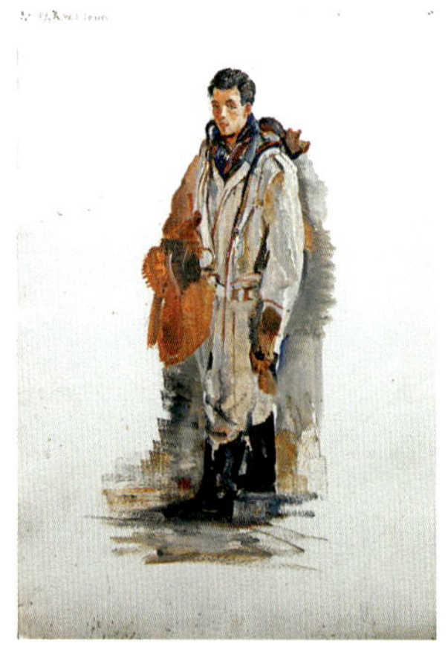

Cundall, Charles Ernest 1890–1971
Pilot Officer A. W. I. Jones: Portrait of a Flyer
1941–1945
oil on paper 52.7 x 36.8
IWM ART LD 7263

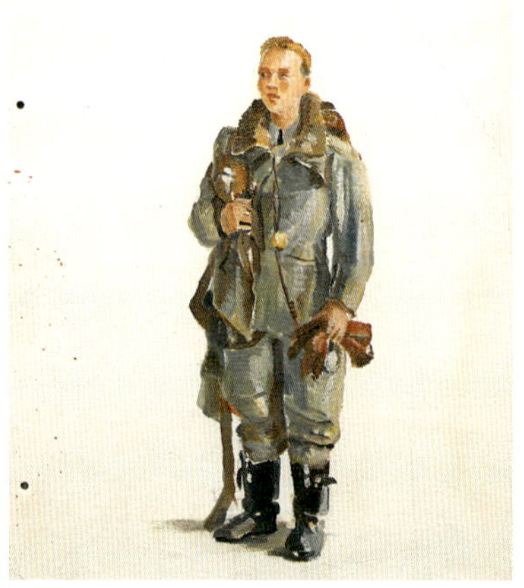

Cundall, Charles Ernest 1890–1971
Portrait of a Flyer II 1941–1945
oil on paper 40 x 34.9
IWM ART LD 7258

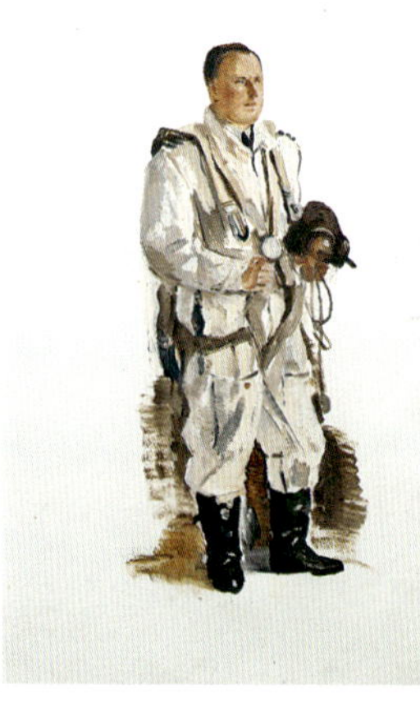

Cundall, Charles Ernest 1890–1971
Portrait of a Flyer III 1941–1945
oil on paper 46.9 x 29.2
IWM ART LD 7259

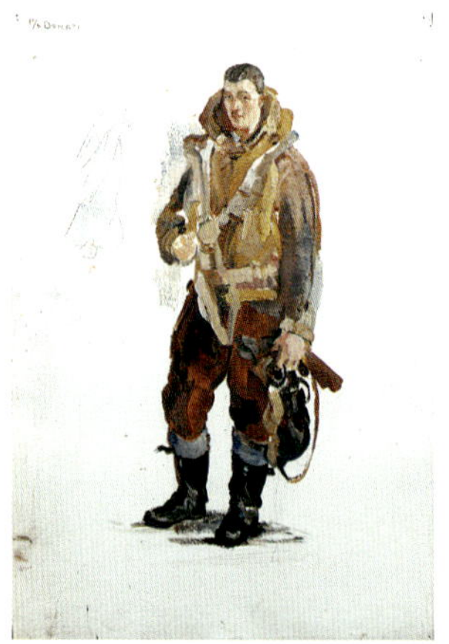

Cundall, Charles Ernest 1890–1971
Pilot Officer Donati: Portrait of a Flyer IV
1941–1945
oil on paper 53.3 x 36.1
IWM ART LD 7260

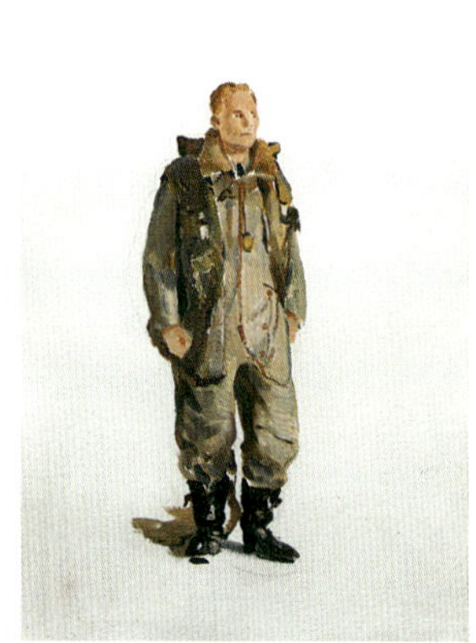

Cundall, Charles Ernest 1890–1971
Portrait of a Flyer V 1941–1945
oil on paper 51.4 x 36.1
IWM ART LD 7261

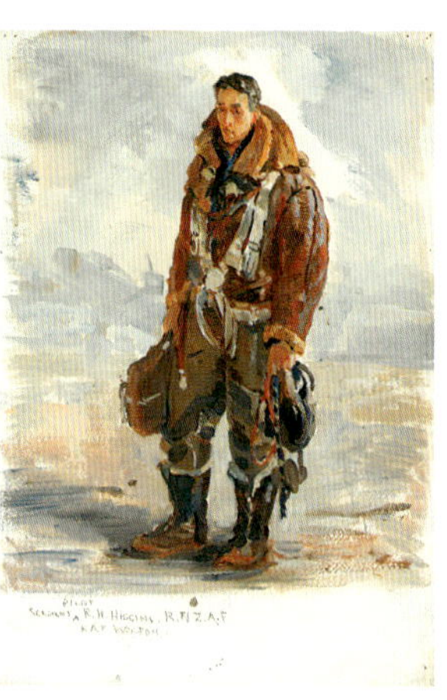

Cundall, Charles Ernest 1890–1971
Sergeant Pilot R. H. Higgins, Royal New Zealand Air Force, RAF Wyton 1941–1945
oil on paper 52 x 36.1
IWM ART LD 7262

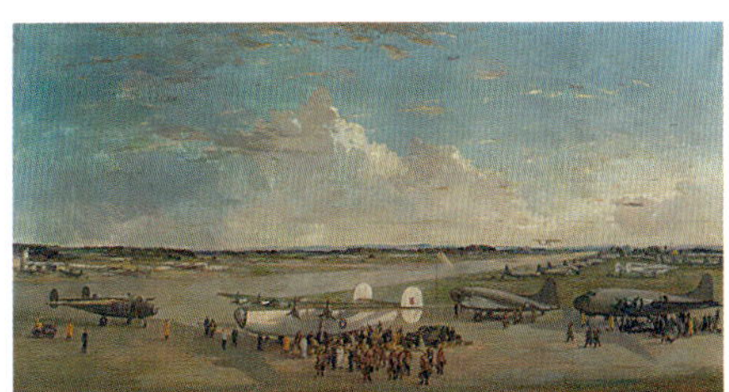

Cundall, Charles Ernest 1890–1971
Prestwick Airport 1942
oil on canvas 99 x 189.2
IWM ART LD 4803

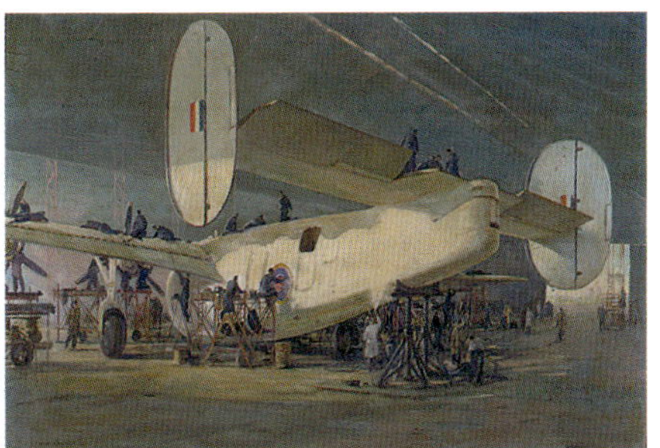

Cundall, Charles Ernest 1890–1971
Servicing a Liberator Aircraft 1942
oil on canvas 69.2 x 105.4
IWM ART LD 2485

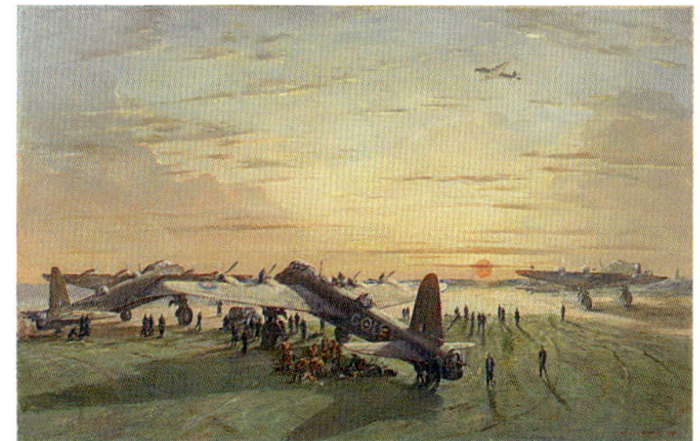

Cundall, Charles Ernest 1890–1971
Stirling Bomber Aircraft: Taken Off at Sunset
1942
oil on canvas 80 x 127
IWM ART LD 1849

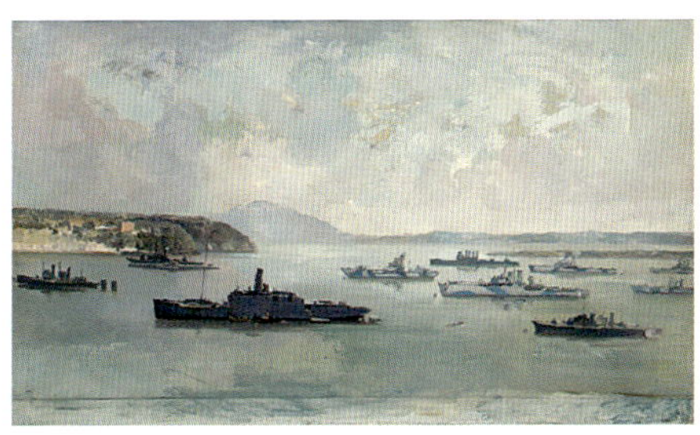

Cundall, Charles Ernest 1890–1971
Tobermory from the Admiral's Flagship 1942
oil on canvas 88.9 x 152.4
IWM ART LD 6052

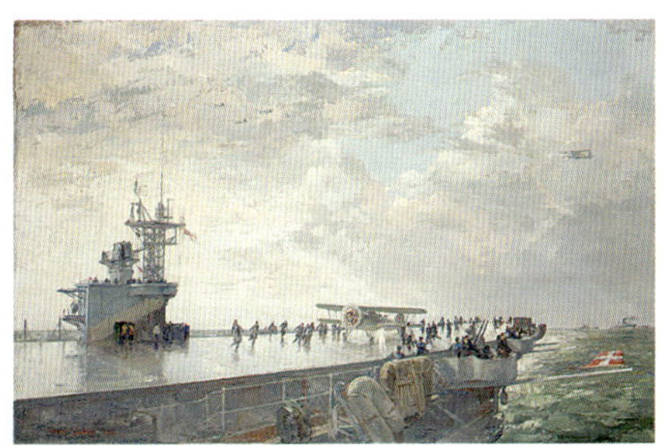

Cundall, Charles Ernest 1890–1971
Aircraft Carrier 1943
oil on canvas 86.3 x 133
IWM ART LD 3912

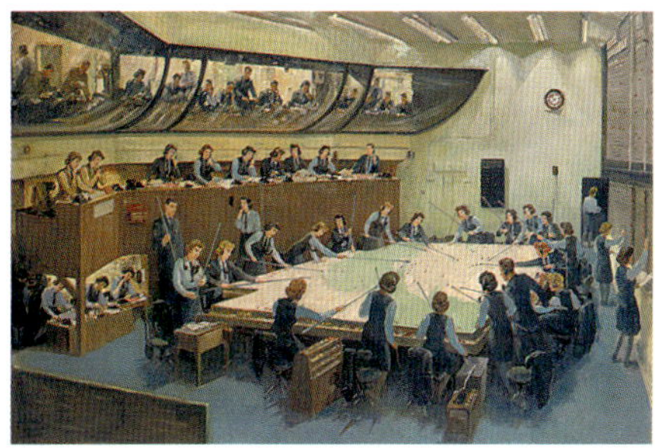

Cundall, Charles Ernest 1890–1971
*No.11 Fighter Group's Operations Room,
Uxbridge* 1943
oil on canvas 89.8 x 136.2
IWM ART LD 4140

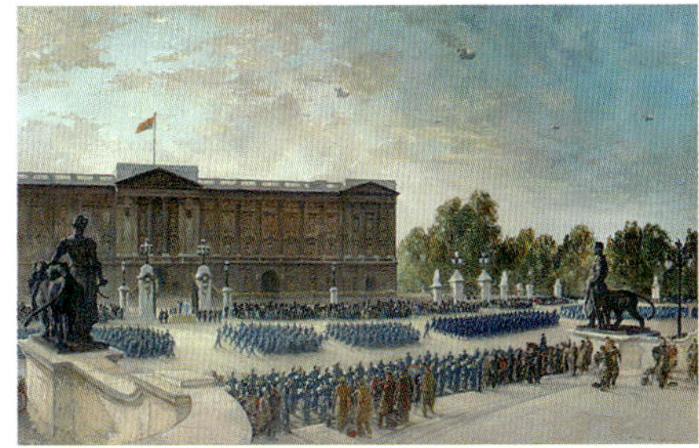

Cundall, Charles Ernest 1890–1971
*Royal Air Force Parade at Buckingham Palace:
Battle of Britain Anniversary* 1943
oil on canvas 96.5 x 152.4
IWM ART LD 3911

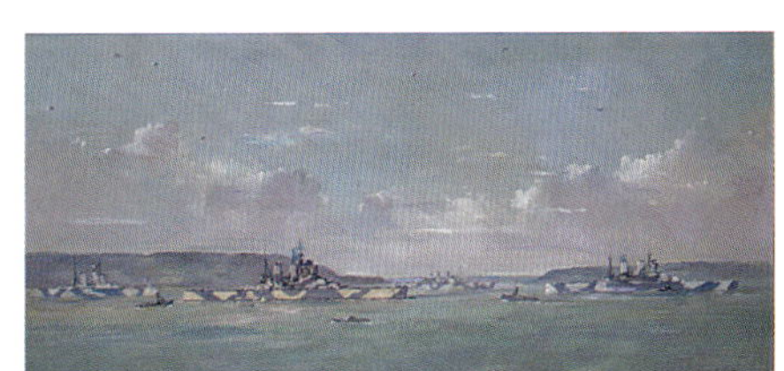

Cundall, Charles Ernest 1890–1971
Scapa Flow 1943
oil on canvas 63.5 x 137.1
IWM ART LD 6053

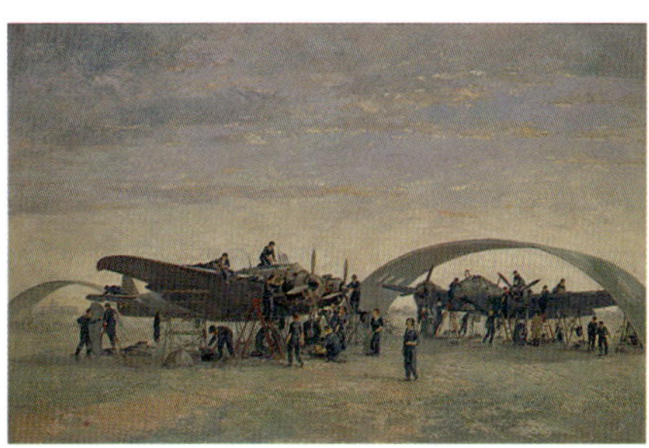

Cundall, Charles Ernest 1890–1971
Women's Auxiliary Air Force Mechanics 1943
oil on canvas 91.4 x 142.2
IWM ART LD 3913

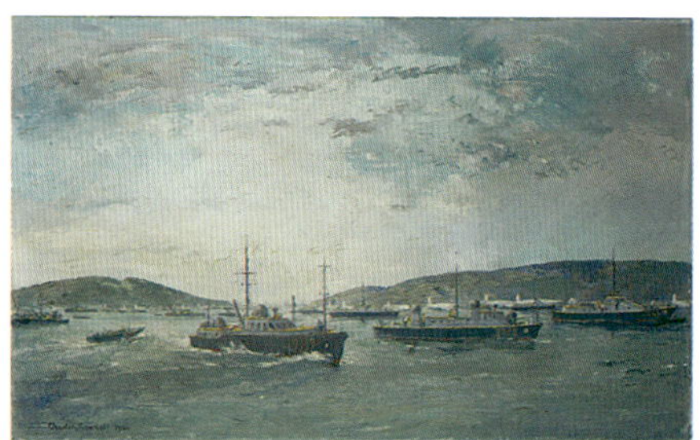

Cundall, Charles Ernest 1890–1971
Royal Air Force Marine Craft, Stranraer 1944
oil on canvas 59 x 98.4
IWM ART LD 4804

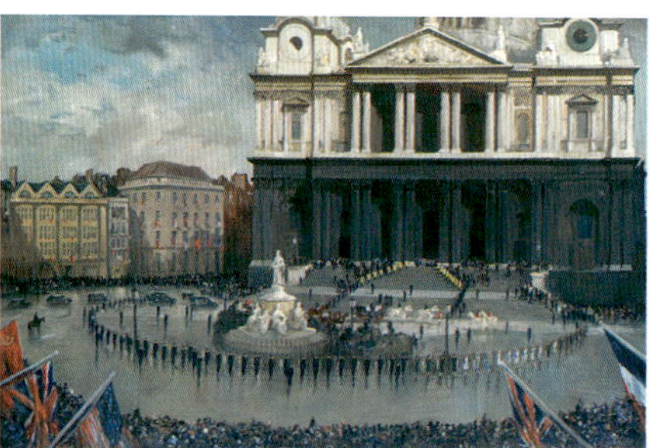

Cundall, Charles Ernest 1890–1971
*The Exterior of St Paul's Cathedral on
Thanksgiving Day, 13 May 1945* 1945
oil on canvas 121.9 x 182.8
IWM ART LD 5773

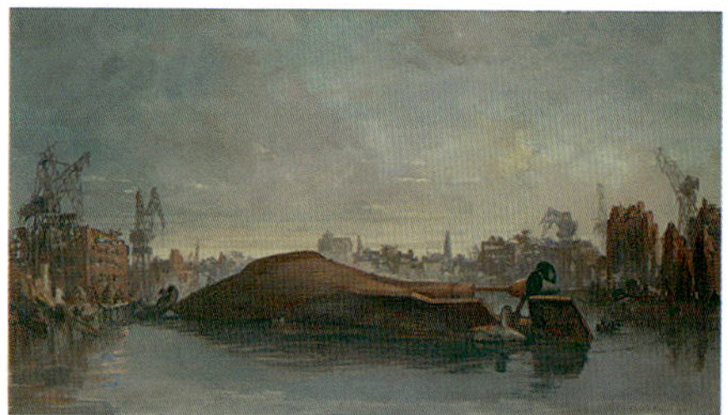

Cundall, Charles Ernest 1890–1971
*The German Heavy Cruiser 'Admiral Scheer' at
Kiel* 1945
oil on canvas 71.1 x 127
IWM ART LD 5679

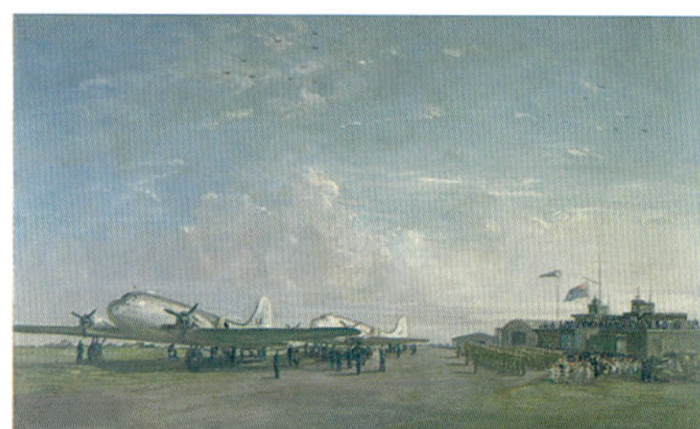

Cundall, Charles Ernest 1890–1971
The Royal Visit to Guernsey, 7 June 1945 1945
oil on canvas 76.2 x 127
IWM ART LD 5804

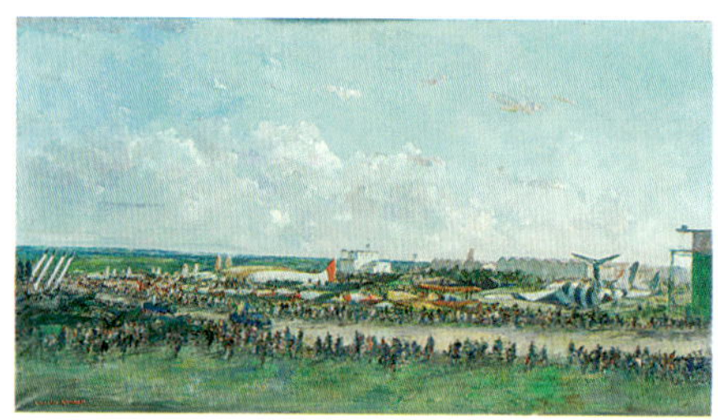

Cundall, Charles Ernest 1890–1971
*Visit of Her Majesty the Queen to RAF
Abingdon, 14 June 1968, to Celebrate the 50th
Anniversary of the Formation (…)* 1968
oil on canvas 49.5 x 90.8
IWM ART LD 6516

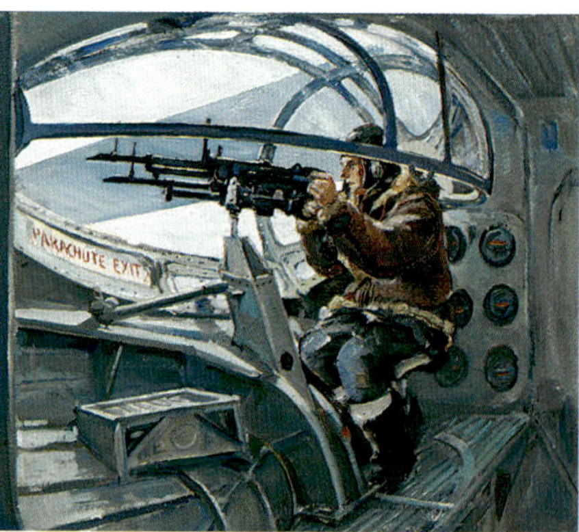

Cundall, Charles Ernest 1890–1971
Air Gunner Prepared for Action
oil on paper 36.3 x 40.3
IWM ART LD 6051

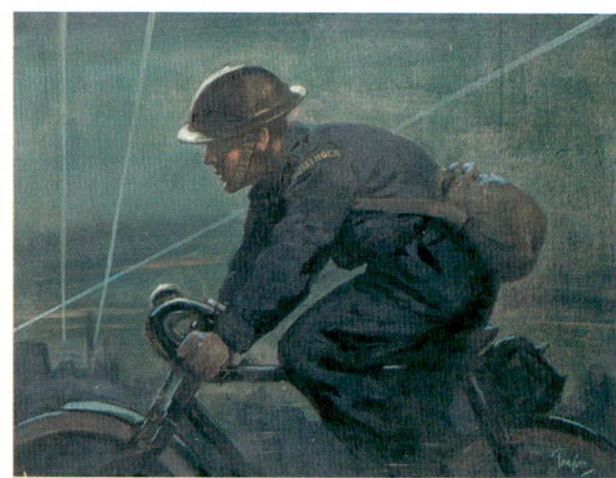

Curr, Thomas 1887–1958
A. R. P. Messenger c.1940–1945
oil on board 76.2 x 101.6
IWM ART 15864

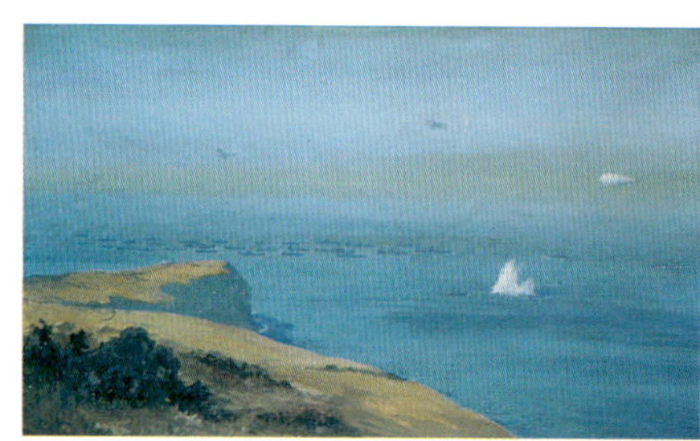

Dade, Ernest 1868–1936
A Convoy Passing Whitby High Lights c.1919
oil on canvas 76.2 x 127
IWM ART 1487

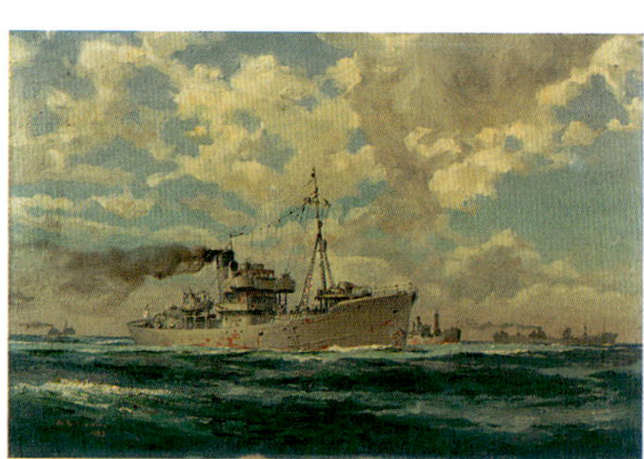

Daniels, Alfred b.1924
'HMS Greenfly' 1943
oil on burlap 55.8 x 84.4
IWM ART LD 3448

Facing page: Spencer, Stanley, 1891–1959, *Travoys Arriving with Wounded at a Dressing Station at Smol, Macedonia, September 1916*
(detail), 1919, (p. 214)

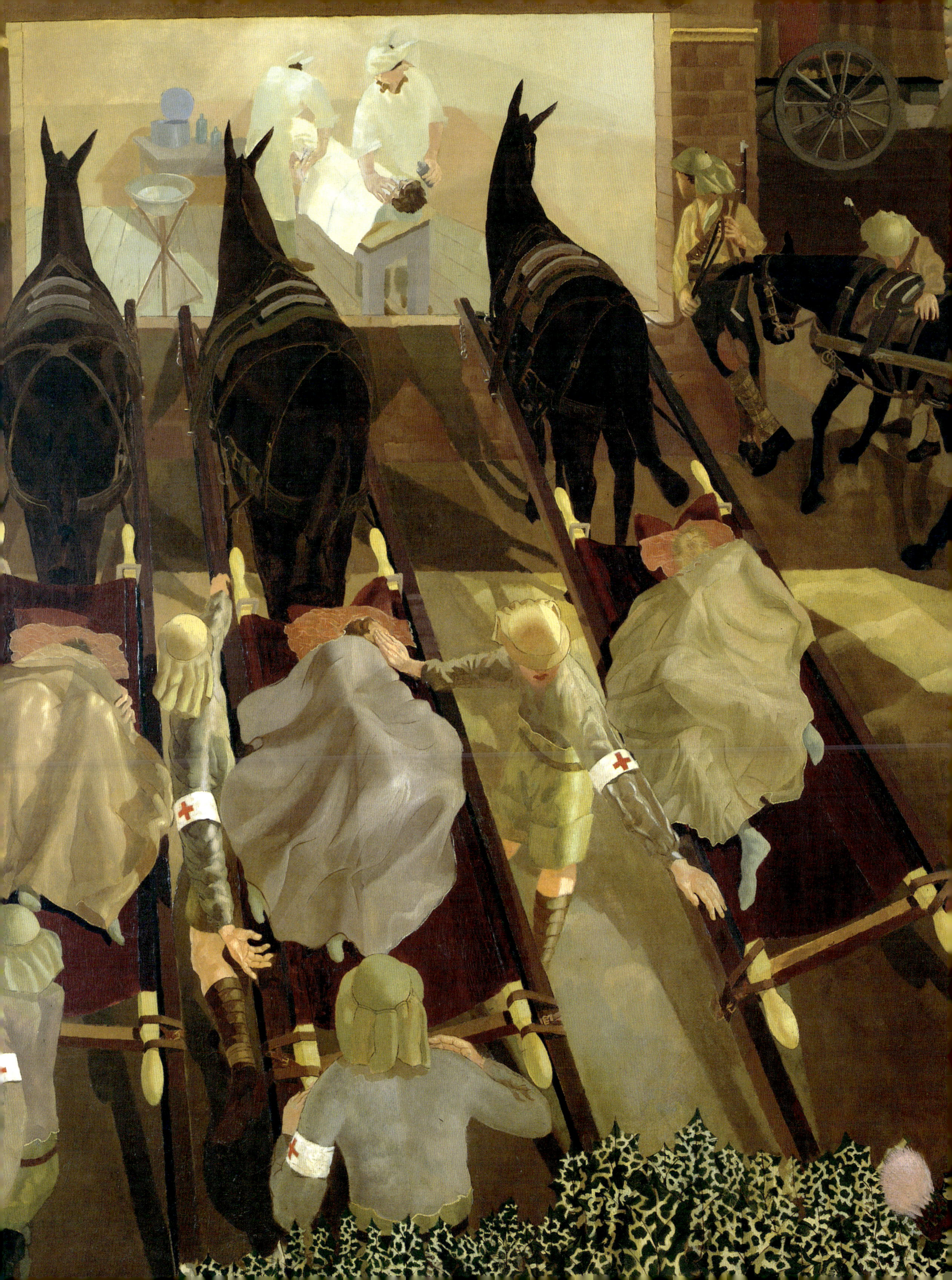

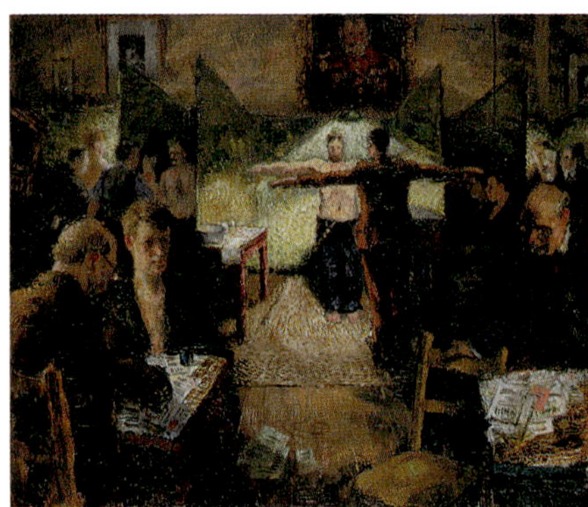

Daniels, Leonard 1909–1998
Medical Inspection 1942
oil on canvas 50.8 x 60.9
IWM ART LD 2504

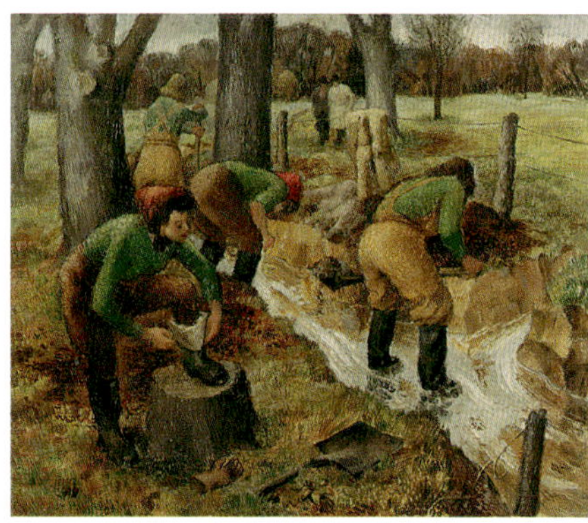

Daniels, Leonard 1909–1998
Women's Land Army: Ditching 1943
oil on canvas 50.8 x 60.9
IWM ART LD 2979

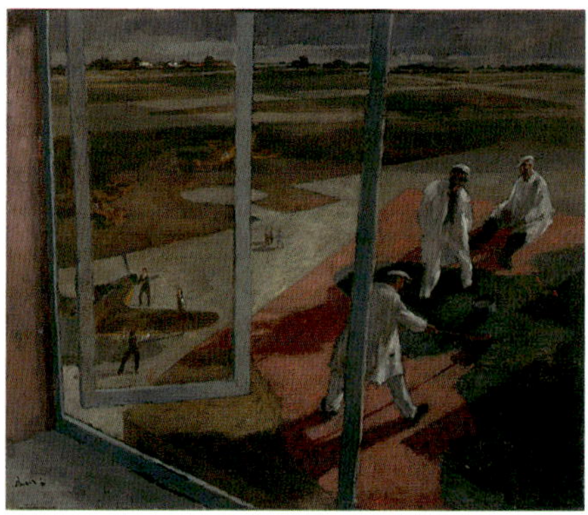

Darwin, Robin 1910–1974
Camouflaging a New Flight Shed 1941
oil on canvas 63.5 x 76.2
IWM ART LD 1211

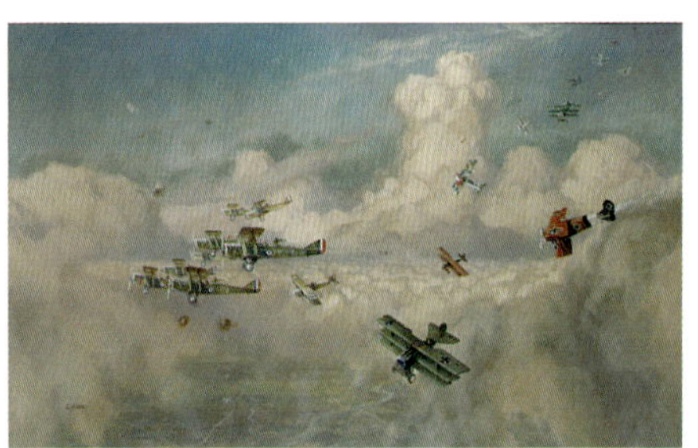

Davis, George Horace 1881–1963
Closing Up: A Bombing Formation of British Biplanes (DH9As) Closing Up to Beat off an Enemy Formation of 'Fokker' Triplanes 1919
oil on canvas 96.5 x 152.4
IWM ART 3071

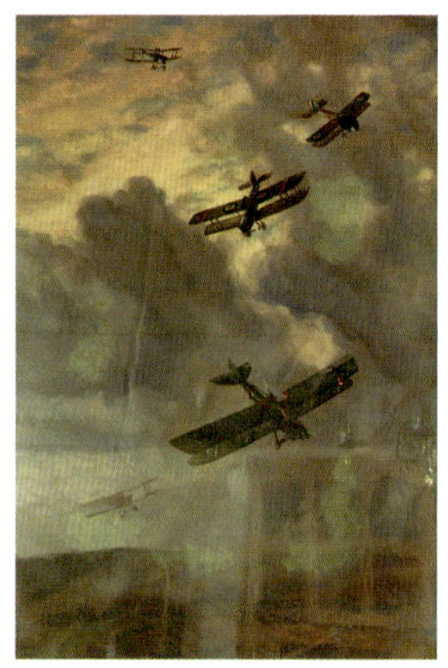

Davis, George Horace 1881–1963
Putting Out His Eyes: Tactics in Aerial Warfare 1919
oil on canvas 98.4 x 65.4
IWM ART 2296

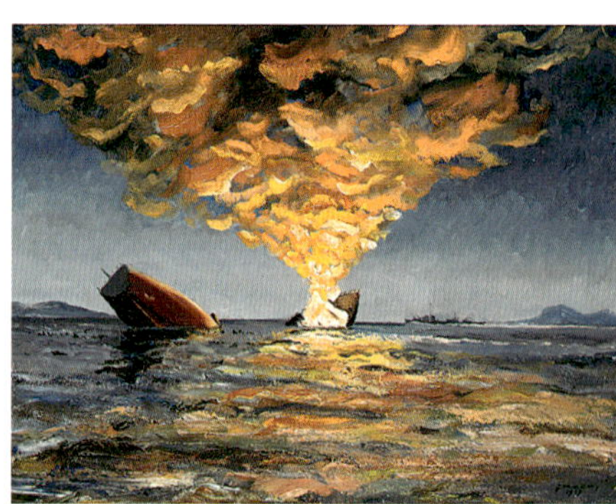

Davy, George Mark Oswald 1898–1983
The Sinking of 'HMS Eclipse' 1967
oil on canvas 54.6 x 69.8
IWM ART LD 6725

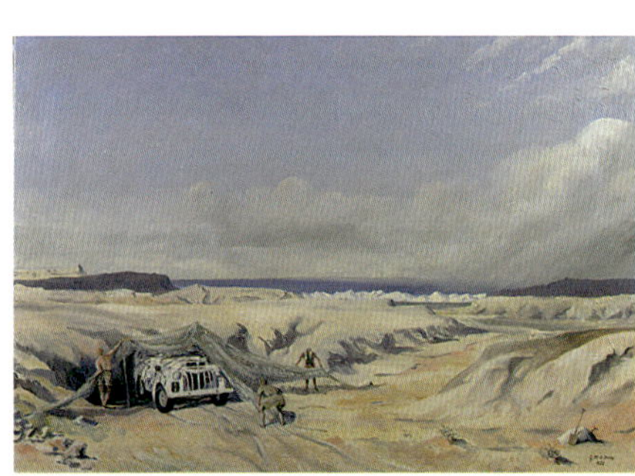

Davy, George Mark Oswald 1898–1983
Rhodesians on Road Watch, Libya 1973
oil on canvas 76.2 x 111.7
IWM ART LD 6721

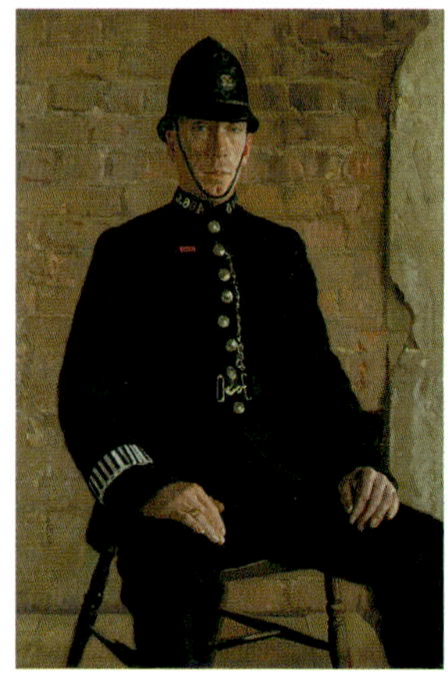

de Montmorency, Miles Fletcher 1893–1963
Police Constable W. H. Allen, GM 1942
oil on canvas 127 x 86.3
IWM ART LD 1999

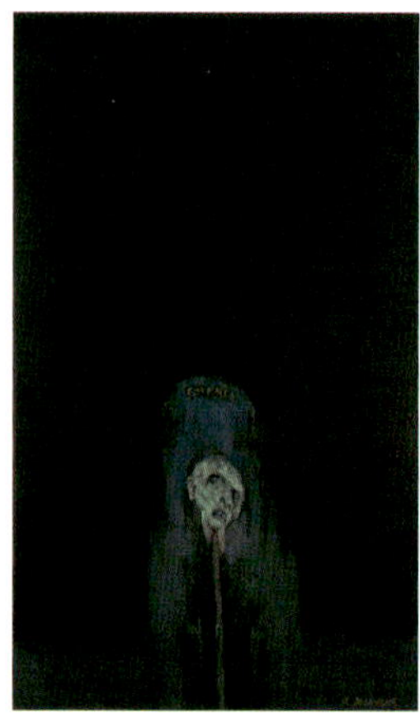

Delavigne, Ron b.1919
A Time of Silence 1998
oil on canvas 102.5 x 61
IWM ART 16848

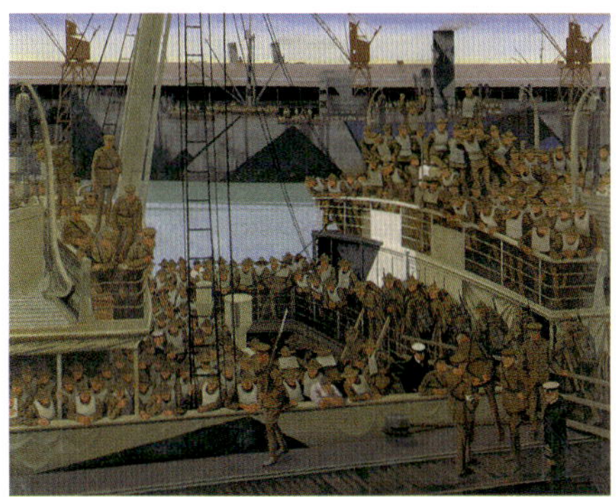

Derrick, Thomas 1885–1954
*American Troops at Southampton Embarking
for France* 1918–1919
oil on canvas 71.2 x 92.2
IWM ART 2323

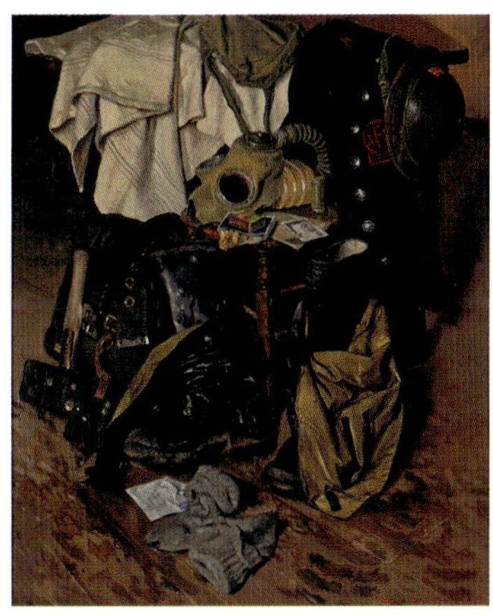

Dessau, Paul Lucien 1909–1999
And So to Bed 1941
oil on canvas 76 x 63
IWM ART 15863

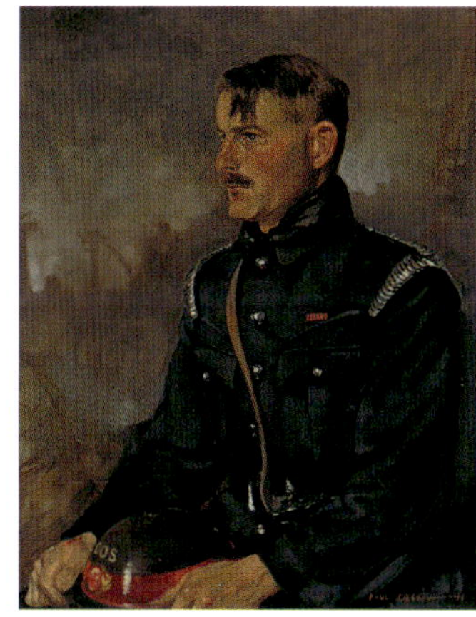

Dessau, Paul Lucien 1909–1999
G. V. Blackstone, GM, London Fire Force 1941
oil on canvas 76.2 x 60.9
IWM ART LD 1356

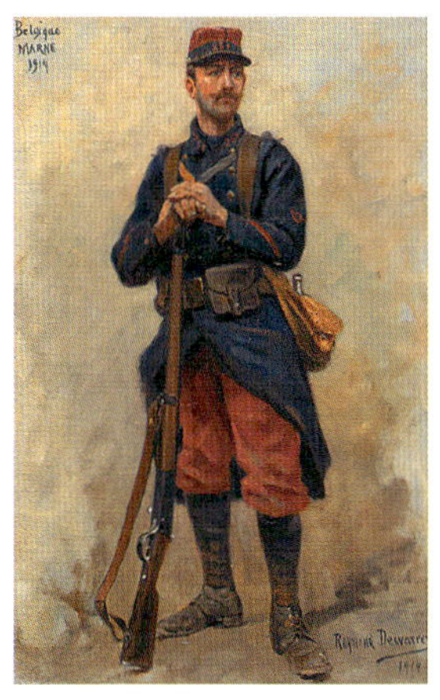

Desvarreux, Raymond 1876–1961
Belgique, Marne 1914
oil on canvas 40.6 x 27.9
IWM ART 5554

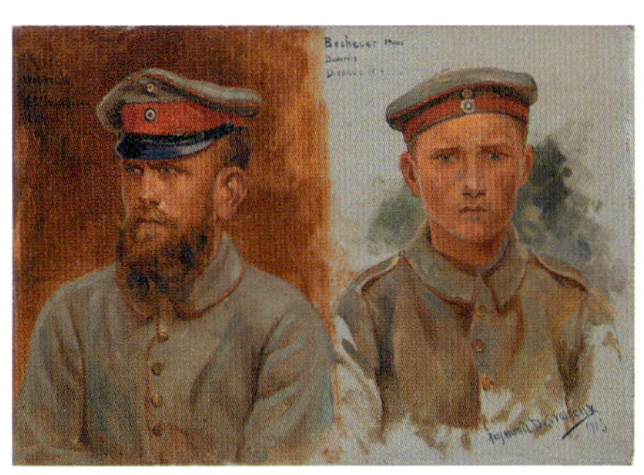

Desvarreux, Raymond 1876–1961
*Risse Waldeck, 55 Infanterie and Bechecer, 19
ans, Bavarois, 1914* 1915
oil on canvas 24.1 x 34.2
IWM ART 5562

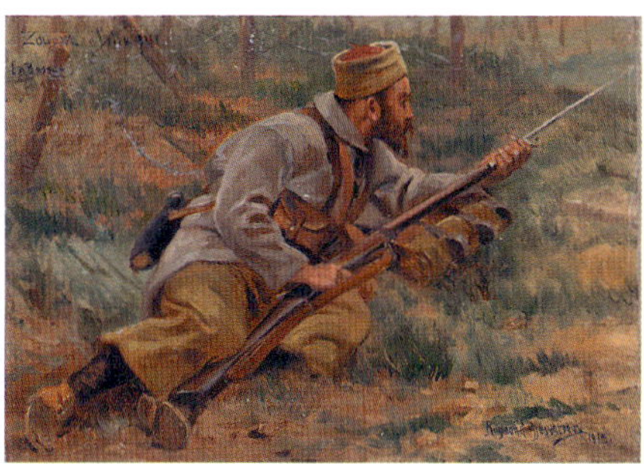

Desvarreux, Raymond 1876–1961
Zouave à l'attaque, la Bassée 1915
oil on canvas 24.1 x 34.9
IWM ART 5560

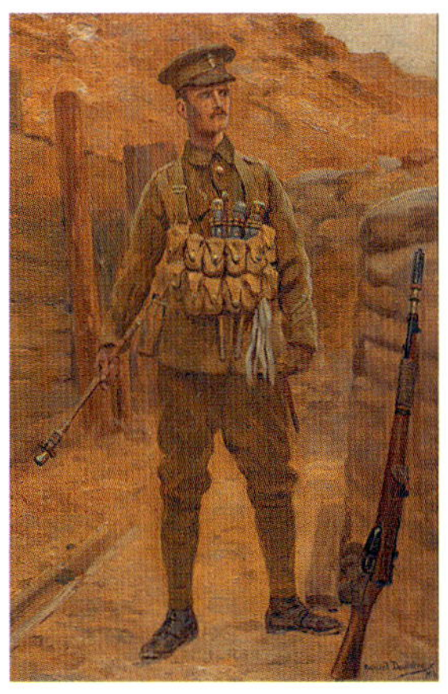

Desvarreux, Raymond 1876–1961
A British Soldier 1916
oil on canvas 40.6 x 27.3
IWM ART 5548

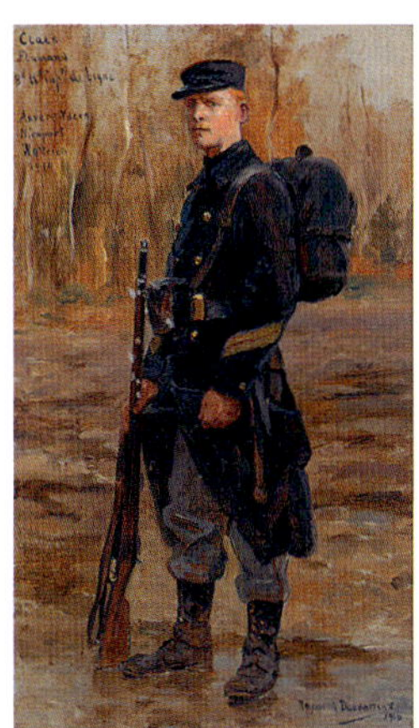

Desvarreux, Raymond 1876–1961
*Claes, Flamand: Huitième Régiment,
Infanterie de Ligne, Anvers, Ysers, Nieuport,
Watteren, 1914* 1916
oil on canvas 33 x 20.3
IWM ART 5558

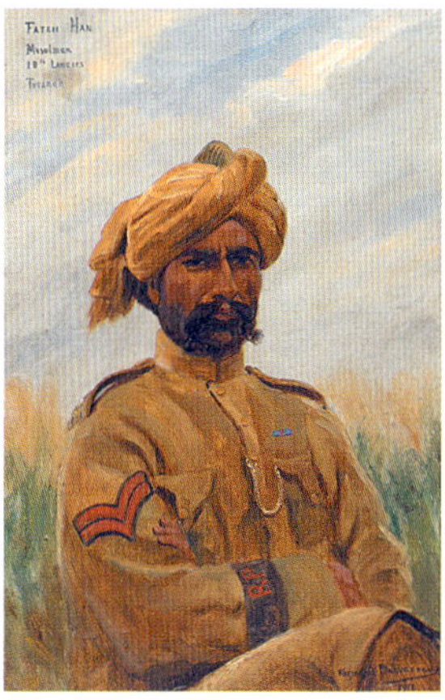

Desvarreux, Raymond 1876–1961
Fateh Han, Musulman: 18th Lancers, Tuvanah
1916
oil on canvas 40.6 x 27.3
IWM ART 5551

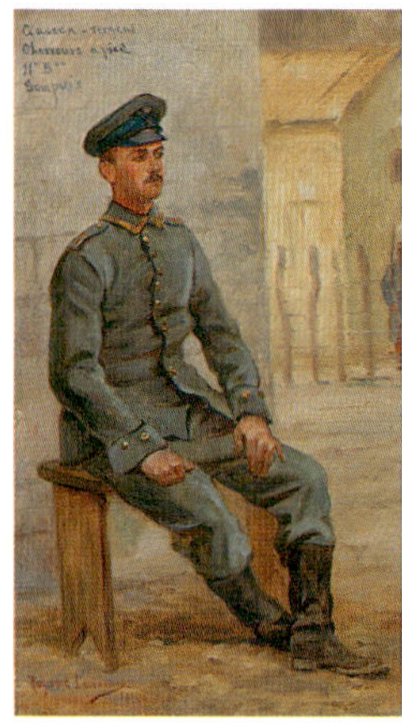

Desvarreux, Raymond 1876–1961
Gassen: Sergeant Classeurs à pied 1916
oil on canvas 33 x 20.3
IWM ART 5561

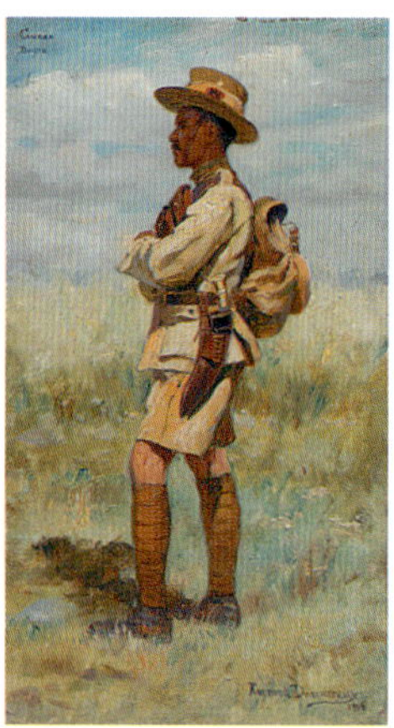

Desvarreux, Raymond 1876–1961
Gurkha, Dogra 1916
oil on canvas 30.4 x 20.3
IWM ART 5552

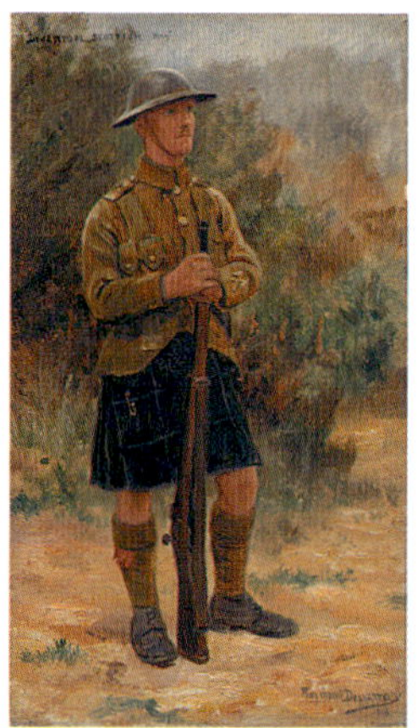

Desvarreux, Raymond 1876–1961
Liverpool Scottish Regiment 1916
oil on canvas 33 x 20.3
IWM ART 5549

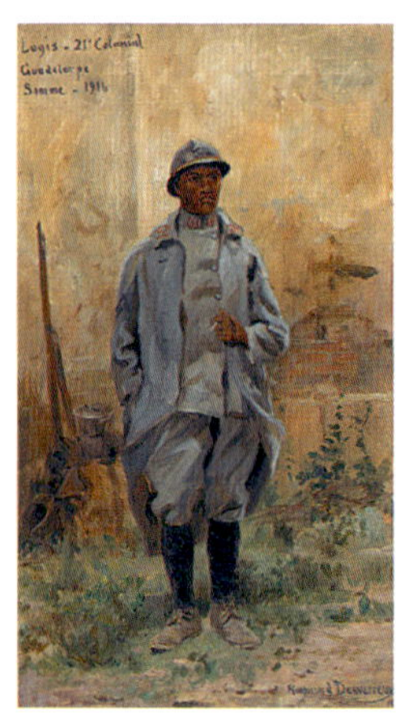

Desvarreux, Raymond 1876–1961
Logis: 21st Colonial Guadeloupe, Somme 1916
oil on canvas 30.7 x 18.5
IWM ART 5557

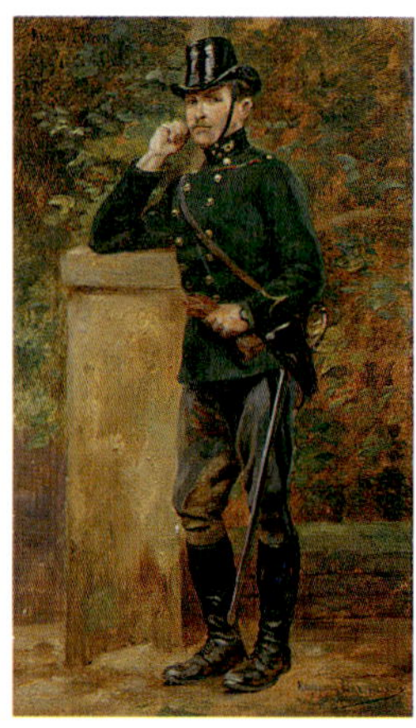

Desvarreux, Raymond 1876–1961
Major Peron 1916
oil on canvas 33 x 20.3
IWM ART 5559

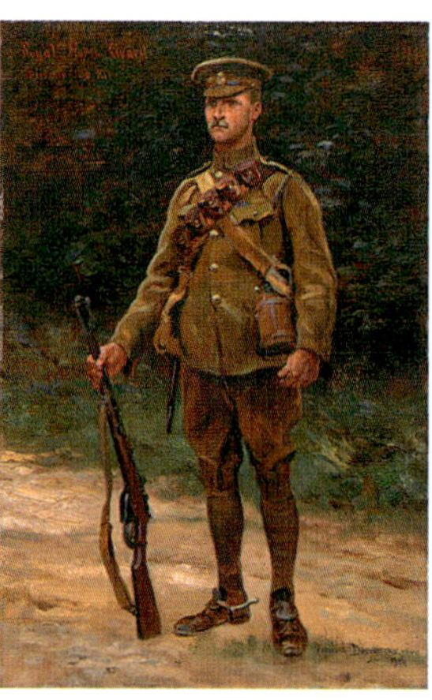

Desvarreux, Raymond 1876–1961
Royal Horse Guard: Dismounted Kit 1916
oil on canvas 40.6 x 26.6
IWM ART 5550

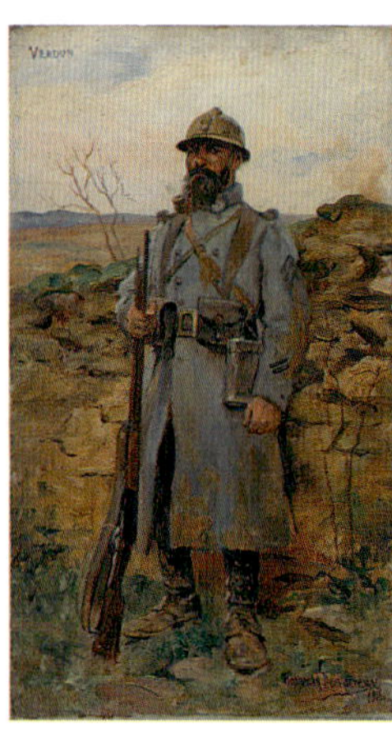

Desvarreux, Raymond 1876–1961
Verdun 1916
oil on canvas 33 x 19.6
IWM ART 5556

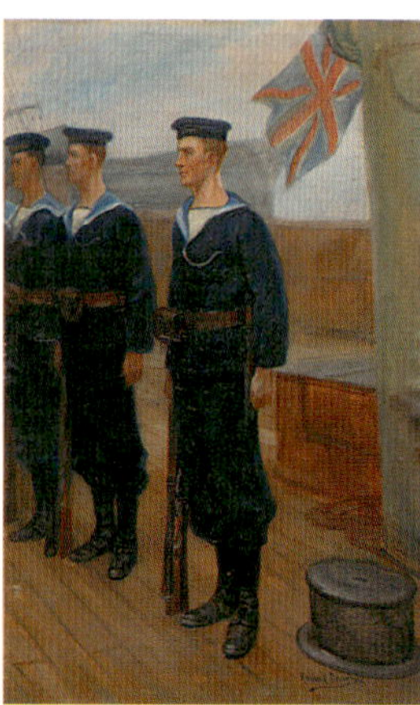

Desvarreux, Raymond 1876–1961
Three British Sailors c.1916–1918
oil on canvas 40.6 x 27.9 (E)
IWM ART 5547

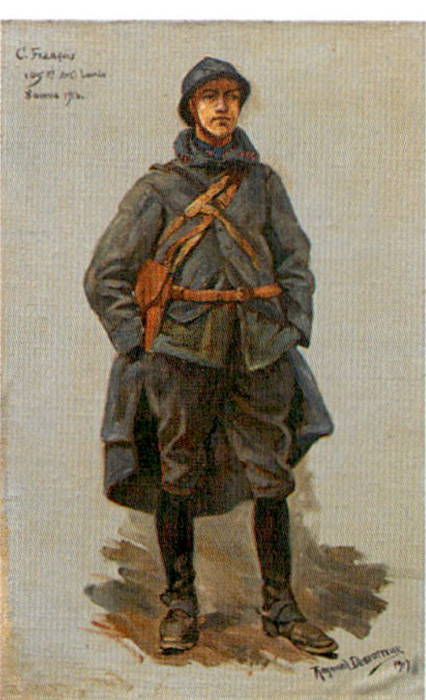

Desvarreux, Raymond 1876–1961
C. François: Somme, 1916 1917
oil on canvas 40.6 x 26.6
IWM ART 5546

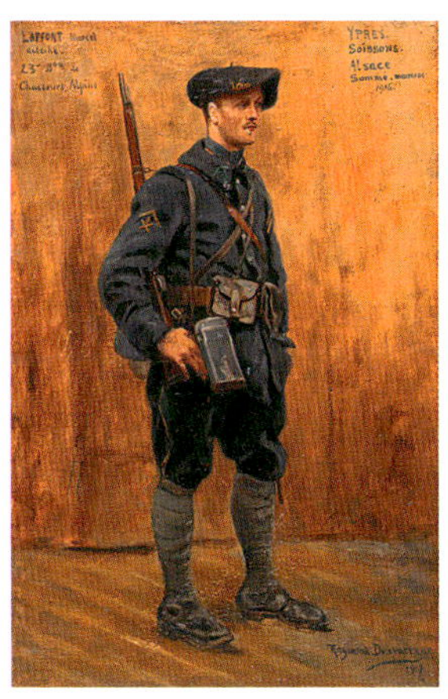

Desvarreux, Raymond 1876–1961
*Marcel Laffont, Ardèche, Chasseurs Alpins:
Ypres, Soissons, Alsace, Somme, Maureras,
1916* 1917
oil on canvas 40.6 x 27.3
IWM ART 5586

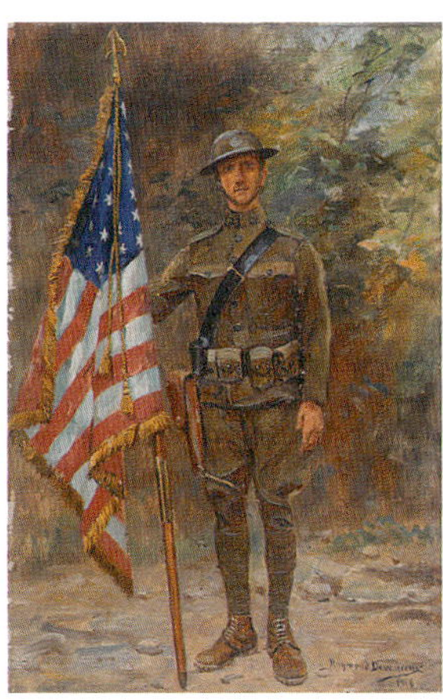

Desvarreux, Raymond 1876–1961
American Soldier 1918
oil on canvas 40.6 x 27.9 (E)
IWM ART 5553

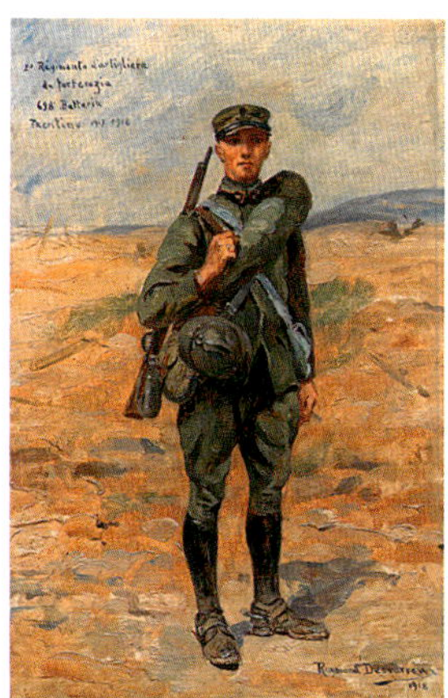

Desvarreux, Raymond 1876–1961
*Second Regimento d'Artiglieria da Forterezia:
698 Batteria Trentino (1917–1918)* 1918
oil on canvas 40 x 27.3
IWM ART 5585

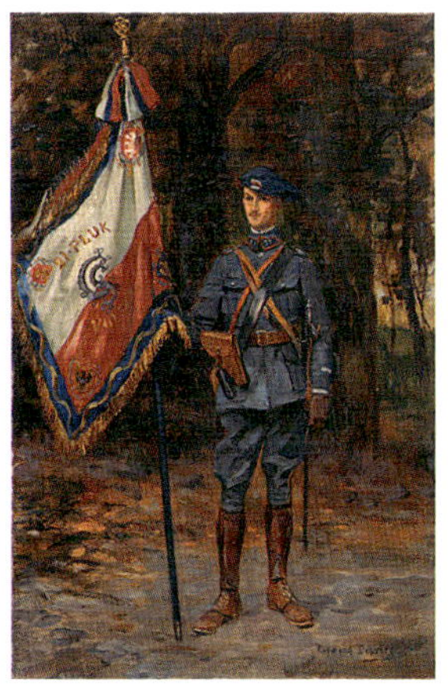

Desvarreux, Raymond 1876–1961
21 Pluk Volska, Senthe c.1927
oil on canvas 40 x 26.6
IWM ART 5545

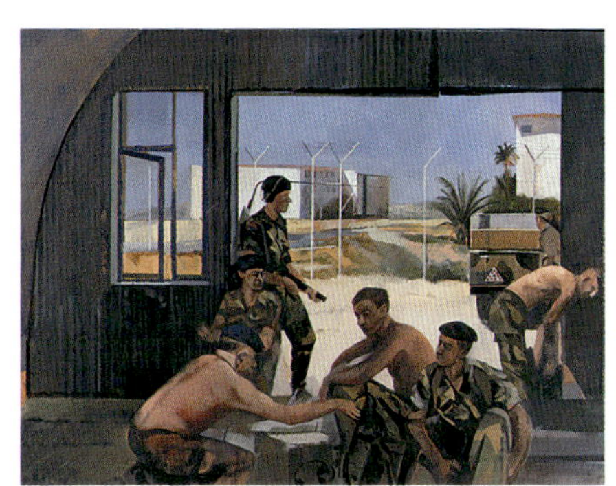

Devane, John b.1954
Military Compound, Episkopi, 'Cyprus' Series
1978
oil on canvas 91.4 x 121.9
IWM ART MW(A) 78

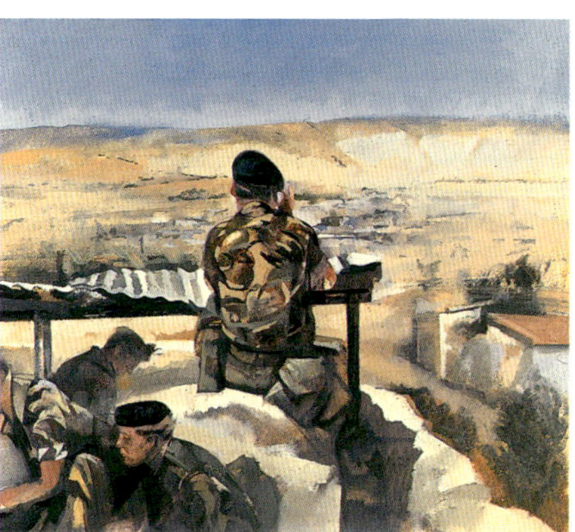

Devane, John b.1954
The Lookout, 'Cyprus' Series 1978
oil on canvas 71.1 x 86.3
IWM ART MW(A) 79

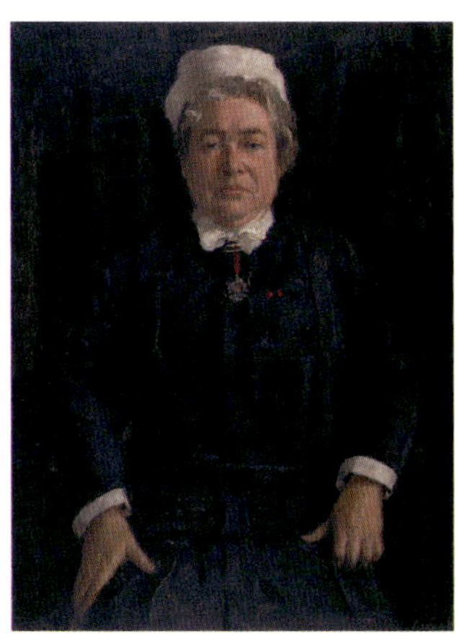

Devas, Anthony 1911–1958
*Miss M. S. Cochrane, Royal Regiment Canada:
State Registered Nurse, Matron, Charing Cross
Hospital* 1941
oil on canvas 101.9 x 76.2
IWM ART LD 1472 ❀

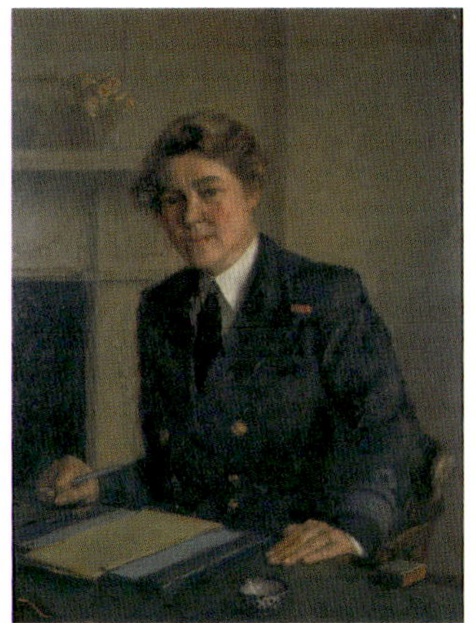

Devas, Anthony 1911–1958
Mrs Laughton Mathews, CBE 1943
oil on canvas 101.9 x 76.2
IWM ART LD 2736 ❀

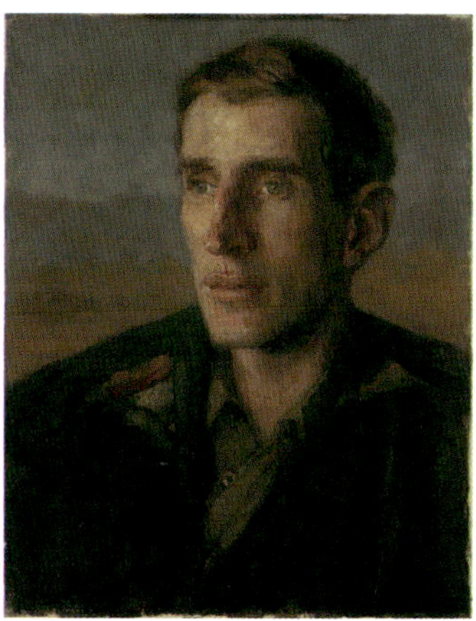

Devas, Anthony 1911–1958
Major Wilfred Thesiger (1910–2003), DSO
1944
oil on canvas 53.3 x 43.1
IWM ART LD 3836 ❀

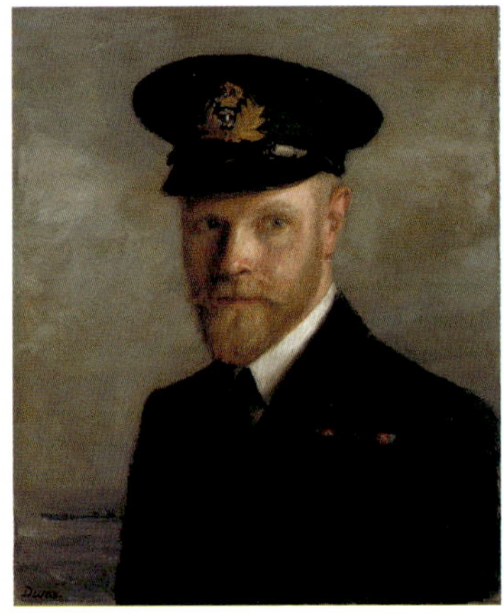

Devas, Anthony 1911–1958
*Lieutenant Commander G. E. Hunt, DSO,
DSC, RN* 1945
oil on canvas 60.9 x 50.8
IWM ART LD 5391

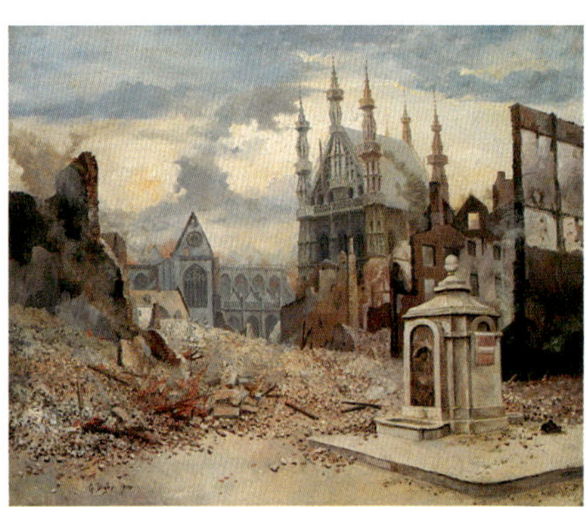

Digby, Grace 1895–c.1965
After the Shelling, Louvain 1914
oil on canvas 100.3 x 114.3
IWM ART 6158

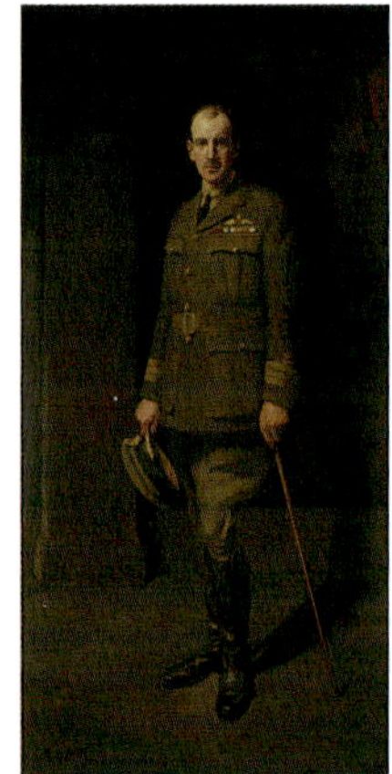

Dobson, Cowan 1894–1980
*Lieutenant Colonel Lionel Wilmot Brabazon
Rees (1884–1955), VC, OBE, MC, AFC, Royal
Artillery, Royal Flying Corps and (…)* 1918
oil on canvas 243.8 x 121.9
IWM ART 1468

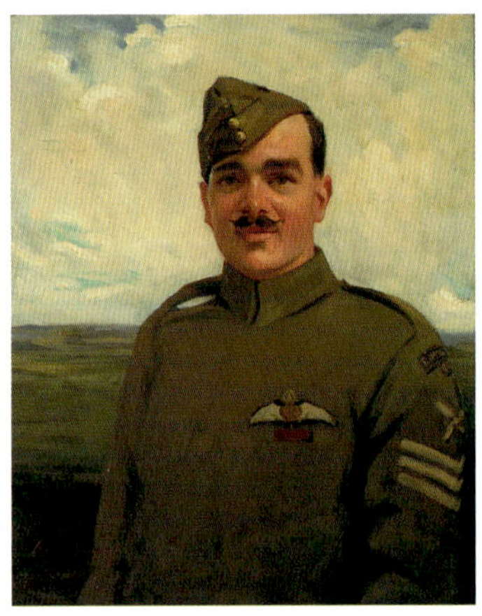

Dobson, Cowan 1894–1980
*Sergeant Mottershead (1893–1917), VC, DCM,
Royal Flying Corps* c.1918–1919
oil on canvas 76.2 x 63.5
IWM ART 2364

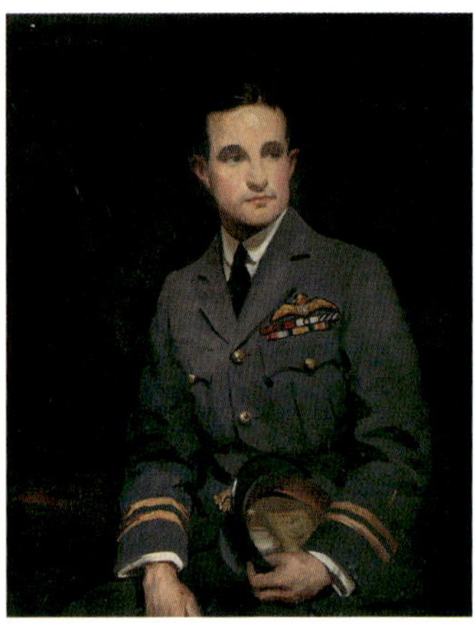

Dobson, Cowan 1894–1980
*Flight Lieutenant Andrew Weatherby
Beauchamp-Proctor (1894–1921), VC, DSO,
MC, DFC, Royal Air Force* 1920
oil on canvas 91.4 x 71.1
IWM ART 2880

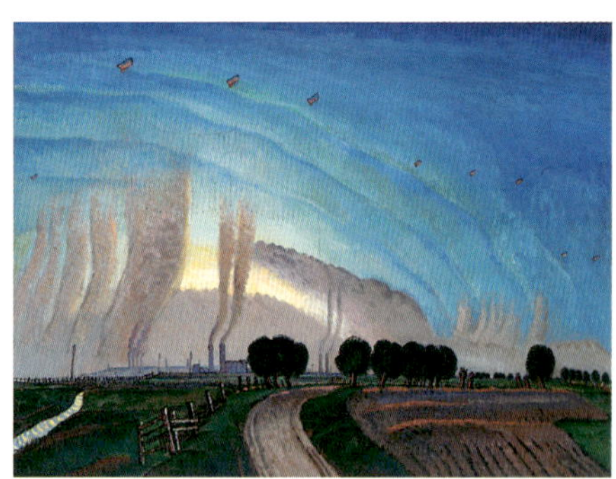

Dobson, Frank 1888–1963
The Balloon Apron 1918
oil on canvas 76.5 x 102
IWM ART 2001

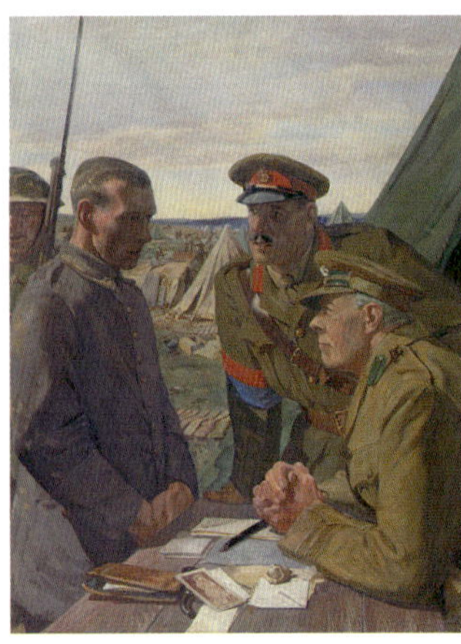

Dodd, Francis 1874–1949
Interrogation 1919
tempera on canvas 91.4 x 71.1
IWM ART 2234

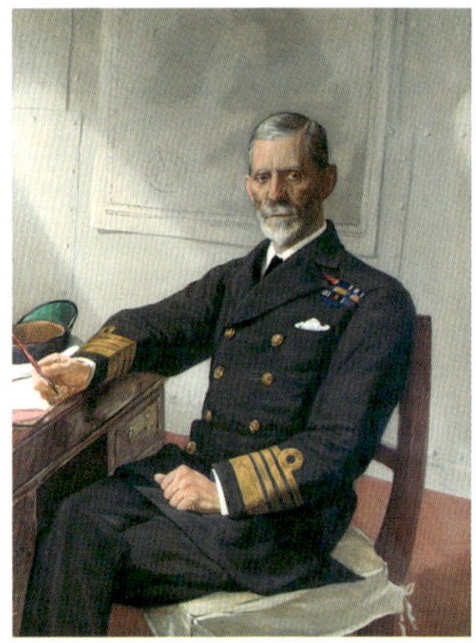

Dodd, Francis 1874–1949
*Admiral Sir Edward Eden Bradford, KCB,
CVO* 1920
oil on canvas 127 x 101.9
IWM ART 4038

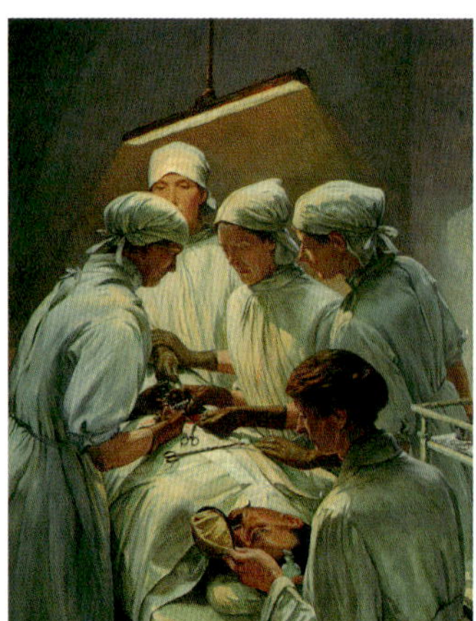

Dodd, Francis 1874–1949
*An Operation at the Military Hospital, Endell
Street: Dr L. Garrett, Dr Nora Murray, Dr W.
Buckley* 1920–1921
oil on canvas 121.9 x 96.5
IWM ART 4084

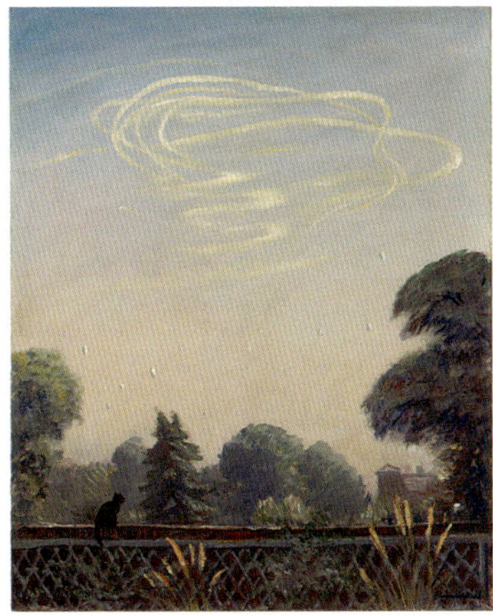

Dodd, Francis 1874–1949
An Aerial Battle 1940
oil on canvas 55.8 x 45.7
IWM ART LD 485

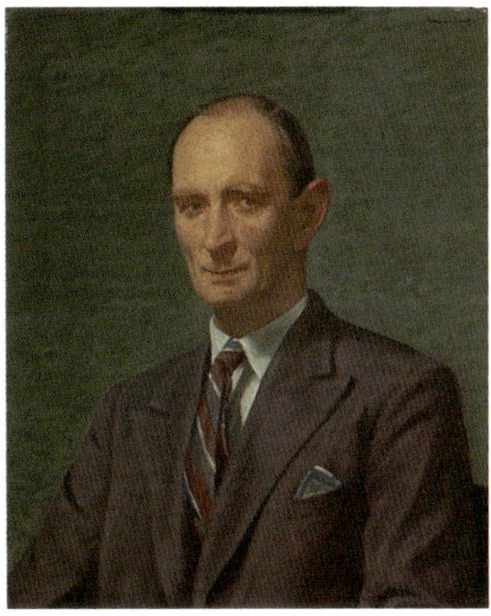

Dodd, Francis 1874–1949
*Wing Commander Eric John Hodsoll
(1894–1971), CB, Inspector General, Ministry
of Home Security* 1941
oil on canvas 60.9 x 50.8
IWM ART LD 1346

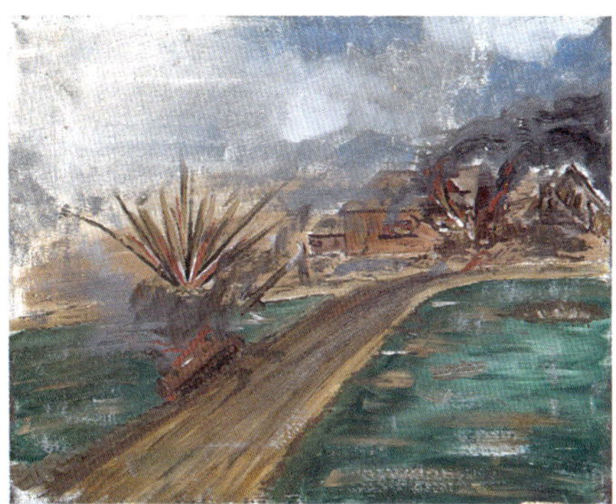

Dodd, Francis 1874–1949
Tank Attack on an Italian Village 1945
oil on canvas 32.2 x 40.4
IWM ART 16153

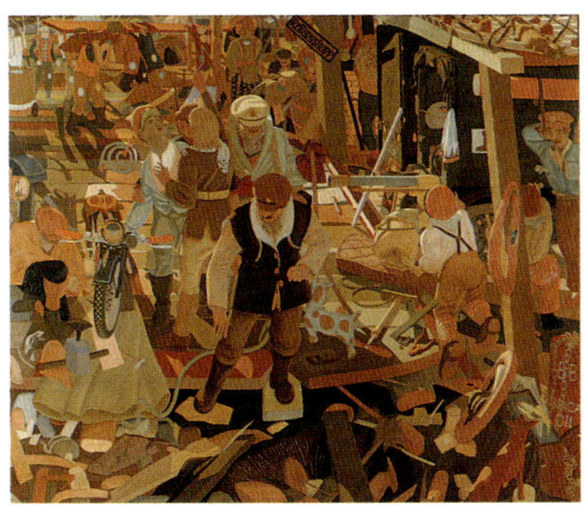

Dodgson, John Arthur 1890–1969
*Motor Transport Troops and German
Prisoners: Chaulnes, Autumn 1918* 1918
oil on canvas 182.8 x 220
IWM ART 4205

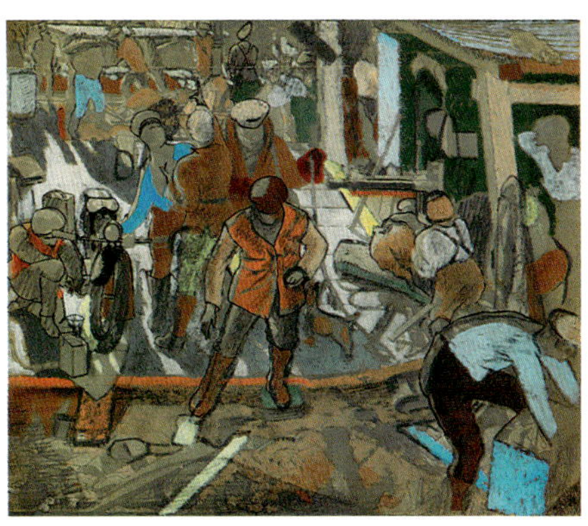

Dodgson, John Arthur 1890–1969
*Study for 'Motor Transport Troops and
German Prisoners: Chaulnes, Autumn 1918'*
1918
mixed media on paper 29.1 x 34.9
IWM ART 16669

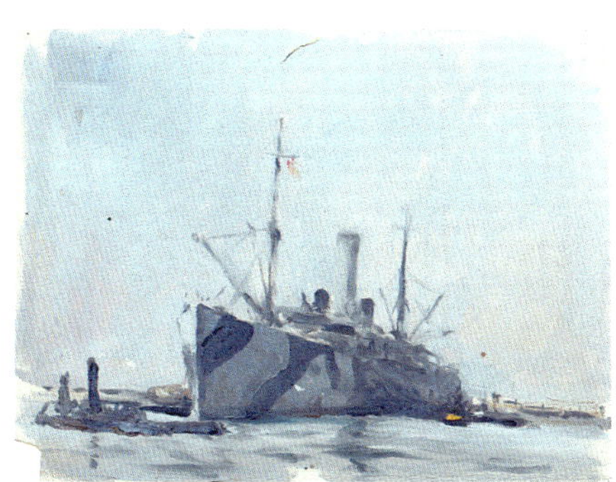

Douglas, Sholto Johnstone 1871–1958
Dazzled Steamer and Tug c.1919
oil on paper 29.8 x 40.6
IWM ART 3988

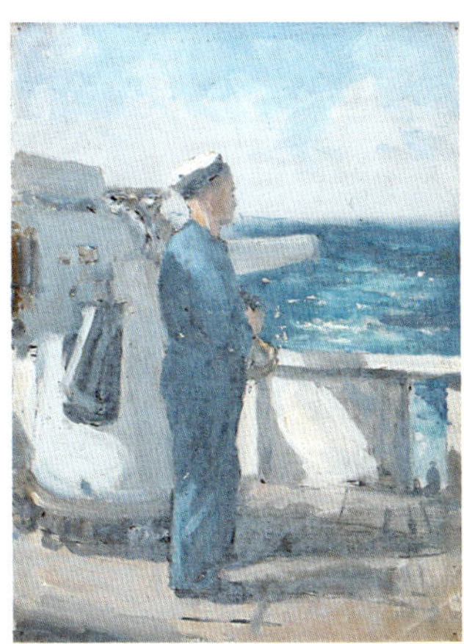

Douglas, Sholto Johnstone 1871–1958
*Defensively Equipped Merchant Ship Gunner
(Thornton A. Taylor)* c.1919
oil on canvas 40.6 x 30.4
IWM ART 3986

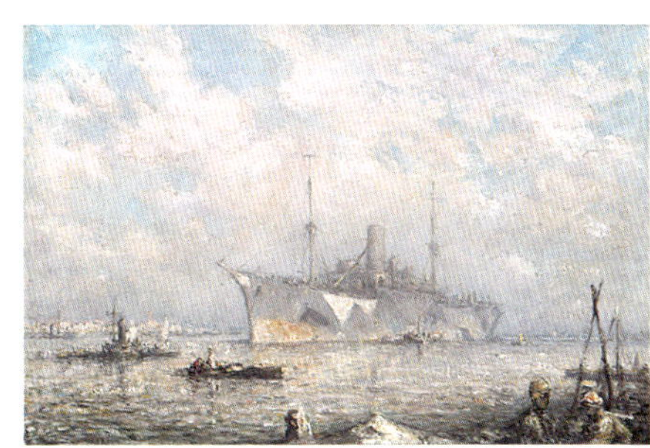

Douglas, Sholto Johnstone 1871–1958
'SS Ben Ledi' c.1919
oil on canvas 60.9 x 91.4
IWM ART 2295

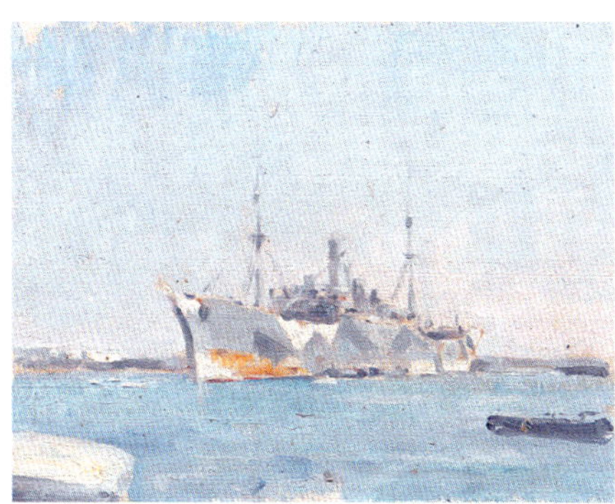

Douglas, Sholto Johnstone 1871–1958
'SS Ben Ledi' c.1919
oil on canvas 29.8 x 38.1
IWM ART 3978

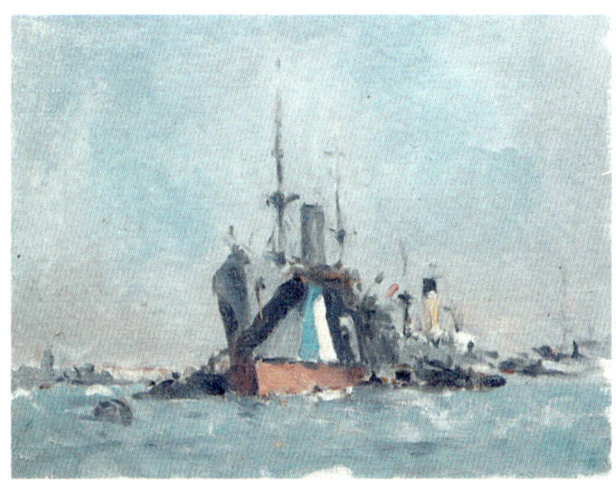

Douglas, Sholto Johnstone 1871–1958
'SS Ben Lomond' c.1919
oil on canvas 29.2 x 39.3
IWM ART 3982

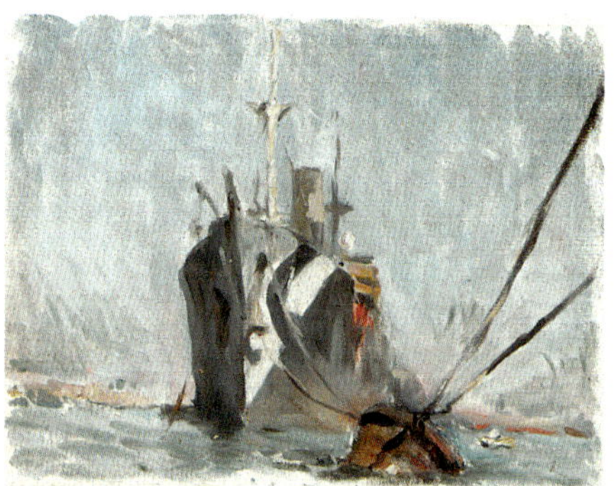

Douglas, Sholto Johnstone 1871–1958
'SS Ben Rinnes' c.1919
oil on canvas 29.2 x 39.3
IWM ART 3983

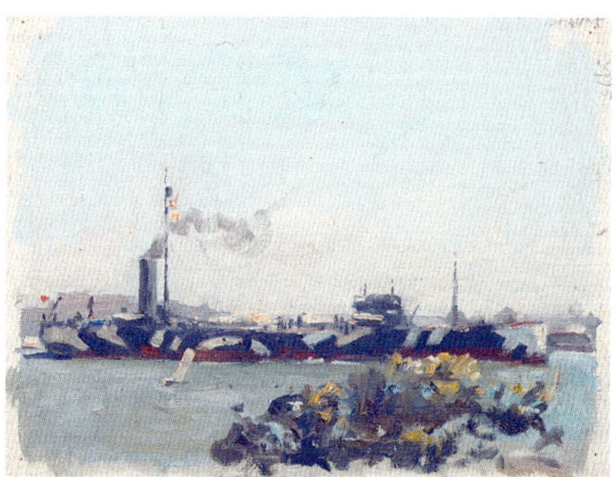

Douglas, Sholto Johnstone 1871–1958
'SS Birchleaf' c.1919
oil on canvas 29.2 x 39.3
IWM ART 3975

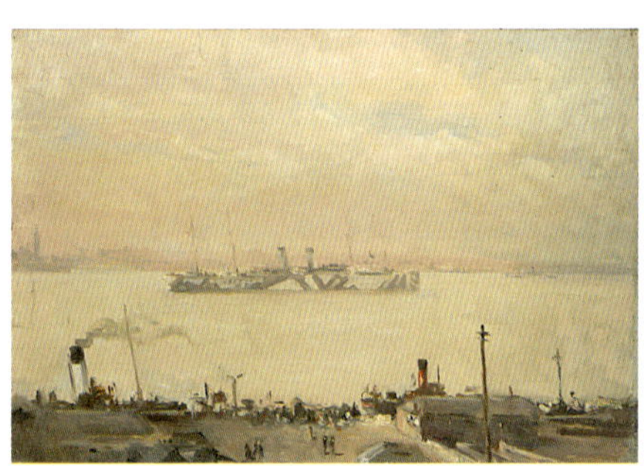

Douglas, Sholto Johnstone 1871–1958
*'SS Cedric', White Star Liner, Lying in the
Mersey with the Ferry Boat 'Iris' of Zeebrugge
Fame on the Left* c.1919
oil on canvas 60.9 x 91.4
IWM ART 1042

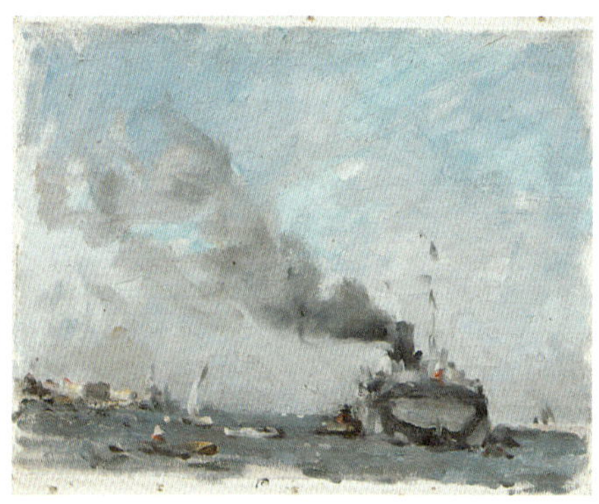

Douglas, Sholto Johnstone 1871–1958
'SS Circassia' c.1919
oil on canvas 29.2 x 38.7
IWM ART 3985

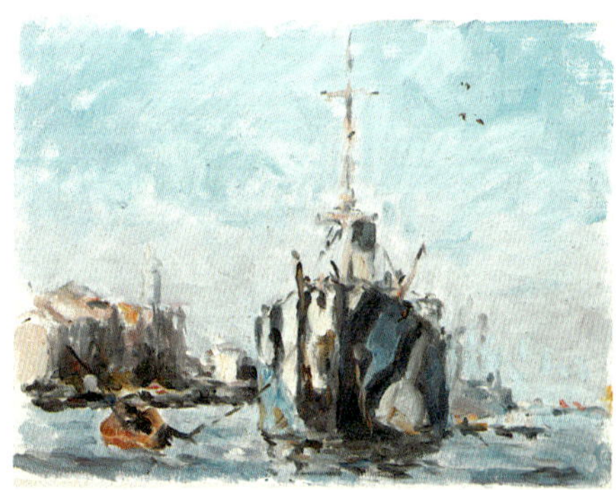

Douglas, Sholto Johnstone 1871–1958
'SS City of Oran' c.1919
oil on canvas 29.8 x 38.7
IWM ART 3977

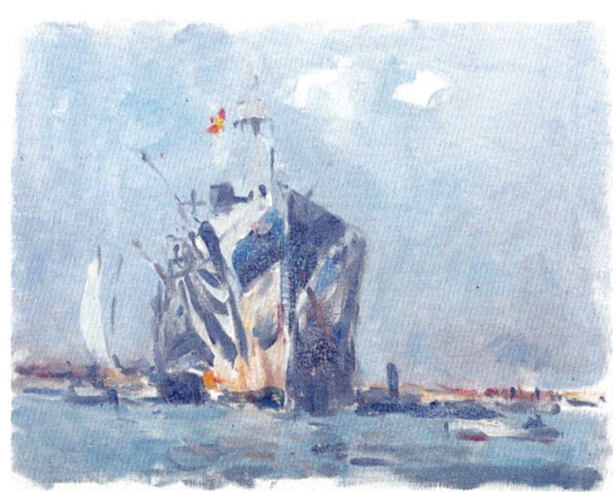

Douglas, Sholto Johnstone 1871–1958
'SS Huntscape' c.1919
oil on canvas 29.2 x 39.3
IWM ART 3976

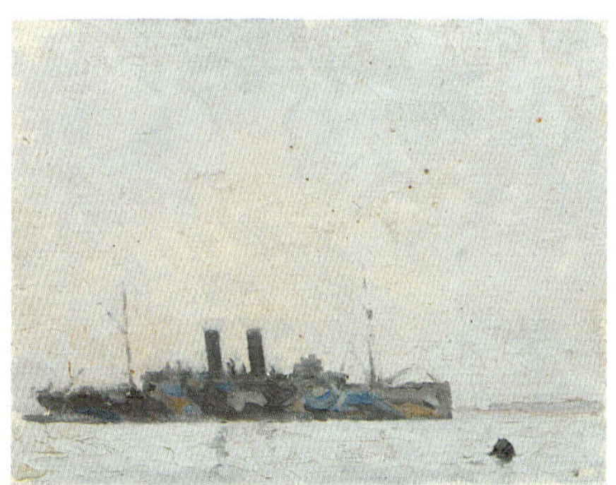

Douglas, Sholto Johnstone 1871–1958
'SS Kaiser-i-Hind' c.1919
oil on canvas 29.8 x 38.1
IWM ART 3974

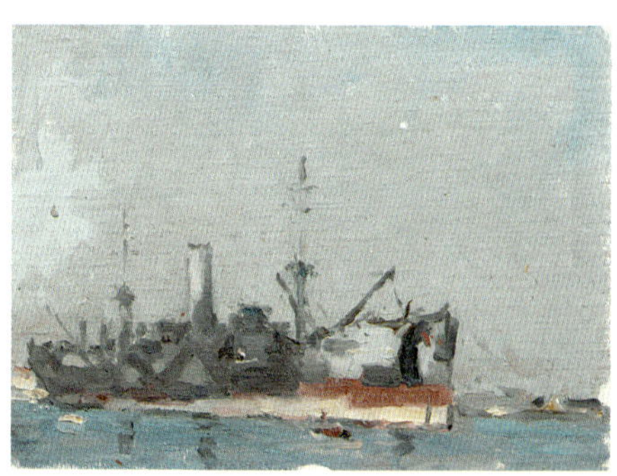

Douglas, Sholto Johnstone 1871–1958
'SS King John' c.1919
oil on canvas 29.8 x 39.3
IWM ART 3980

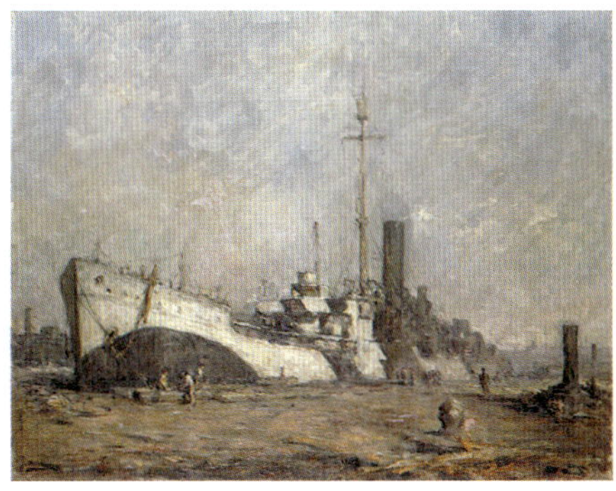

Douglas, Sholto Johnstone 1871–1958
'SS Lackawanna' c.1919
oil on canvas 86.3 x 113
IWM ART 1041

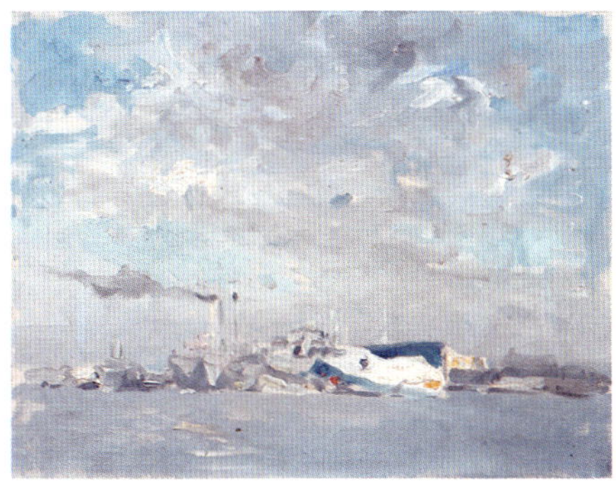

Douglas, Sholto Johnstone 1871–1958
'SS Natica' c.1919
oil on canvas 29.8 x 39.3
IWM ART 3973

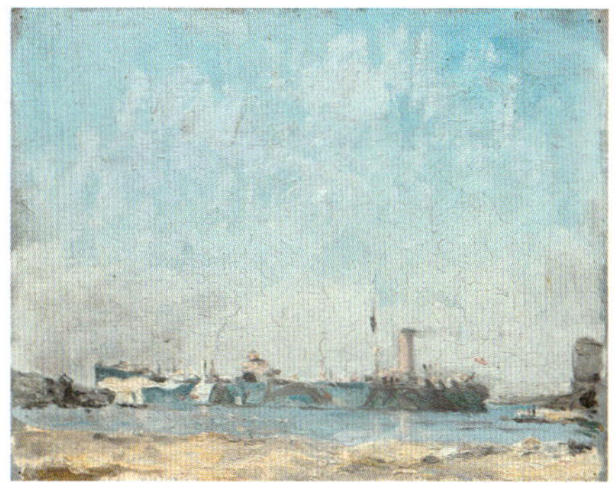

Douglas, Sholto Johnstone 1871–1958
'SS Natica' (Oiler) at Port Said c.1919
oil on canvas 33 x 42.5
IWM ART 3972

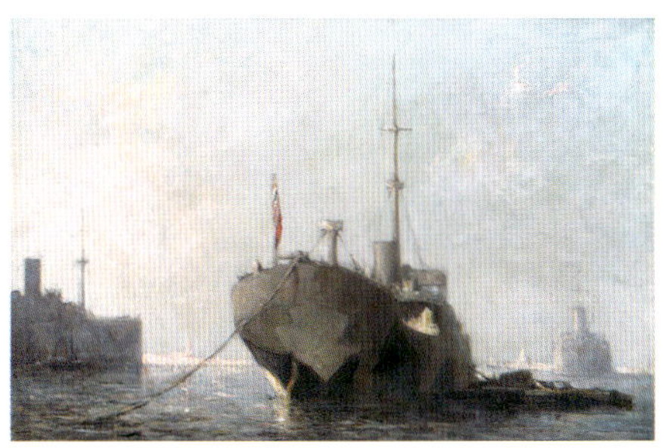

Douglas, Sholto Johnstone 1871–1958
'SS War Manor' c.1919
oil on canvas 60.9 x 91.4
IWM ART 2325

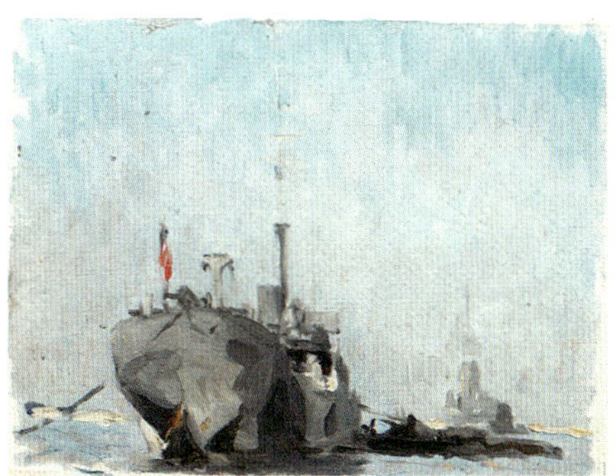

Douglas, Sholto Johnstone 1871–1958
'SS War Manor' c.1919
oil on canvas 29.2 x 39.3
IWM ART 3984

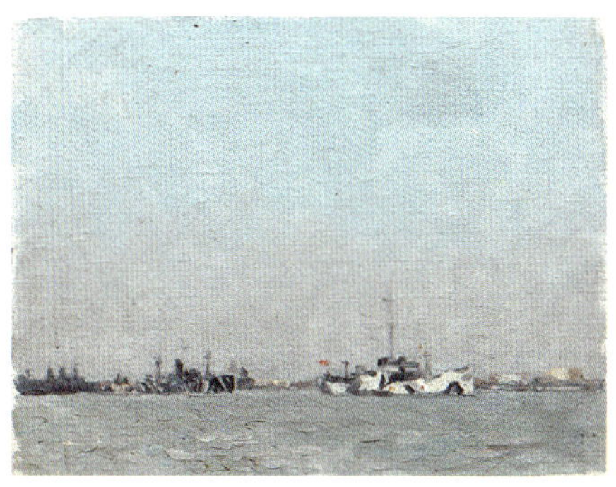

Douglas, Sholto Johnstone 1871–1958
'SS War Manor' and 'SS Clan Monroe' c.1919
oil on canvas 29.2 x 39.3
IWM ART 3981

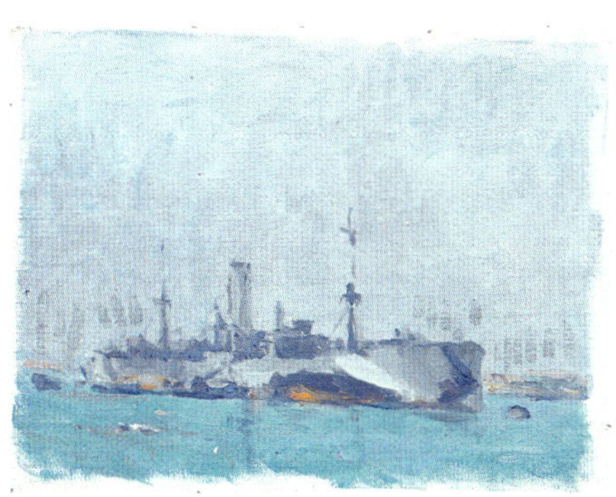

Douglas, Sholto Johnstone 1871–1958
'SS War Sword' c.1919
oil on canvas 29.8 x 38.7
IWM ART 3979

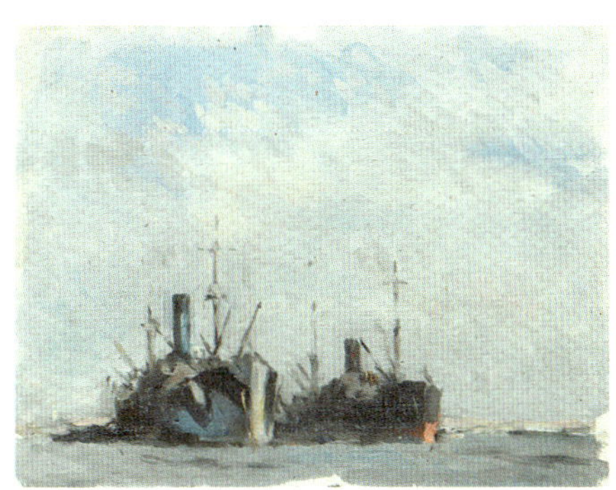

Douglas, Sholto Johnstone 1871–1958
Two Steamships, One Dazzled c.1919
oil on canvas 29.2 x 39.3
IWM ART 3987

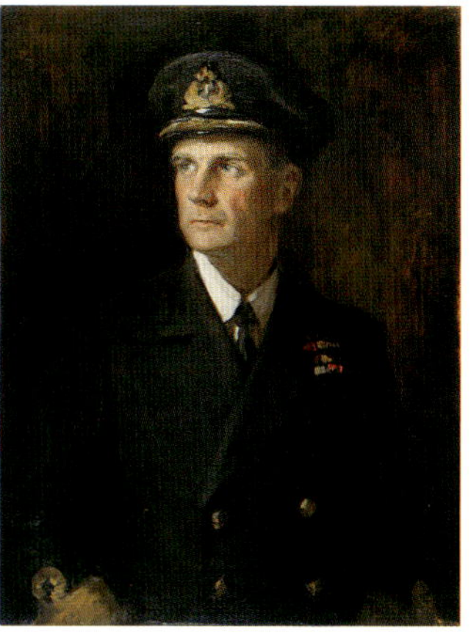

Douglas, Sholto Johnstone 1871–1958
Commodore Hugh J. Tweedie, CB 1920
oil on canvas 91.4 x 71.1
IWM ART 3068

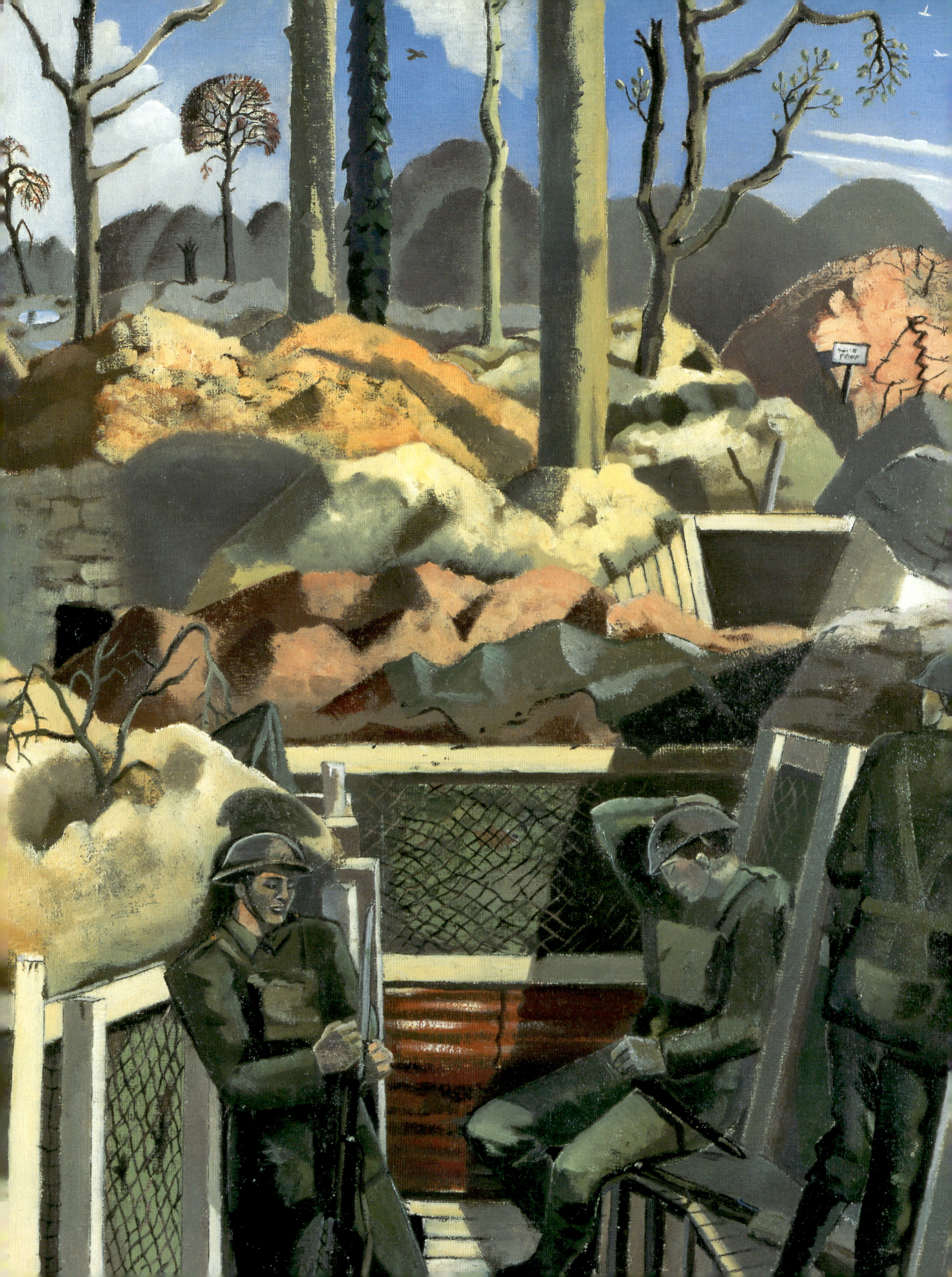

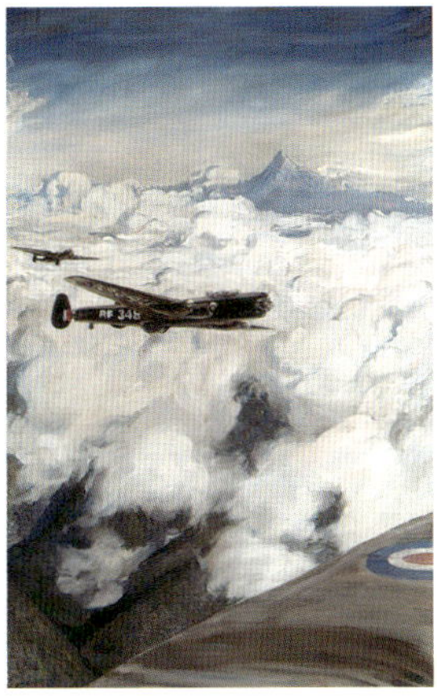

Drew, Pamela 1910–1989
Kenya: 'Lincolns' of No.49 Squadron Attacking Hideouts with Bombs, Mount Kenya Beyond
1955
oil on aluminium 91.4 x 60.9
IWM ART MW(A) 3

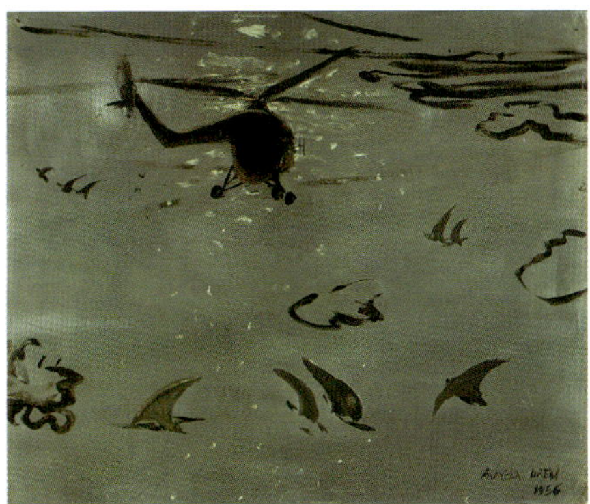

Drew, Pamela 1910–1989
'Bristol Sycamore', Port Said 1956
oil on aluminium 49.9 x 59.7
IWM ART 16401 2

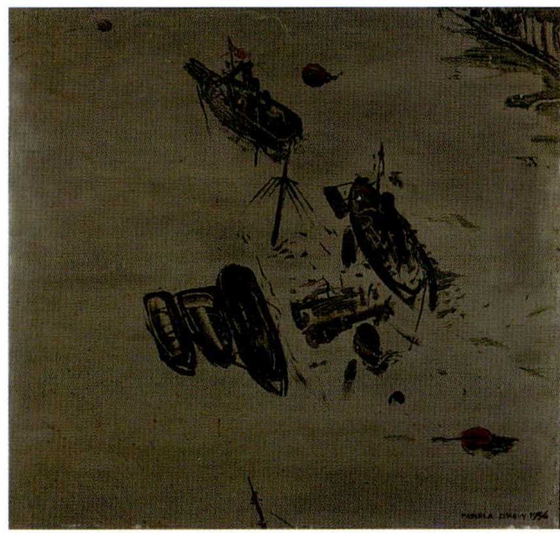

Drew, Pamela 1910–1989
Royal Navy Salvage, Port Said: Taken Over by the United Nations, November 1956 1956
oil on aluminium 56 x 61
IWM ART 16401 1

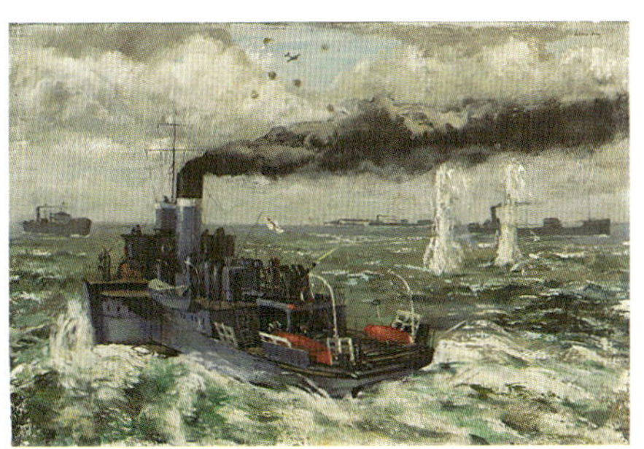

Dring, William D. 1904–1990
'HMS Lorna Doone' during an Attack on an East Coast Convoy 1943
oil on canvas 60.9 x 91.4
IWM ART LD 3297

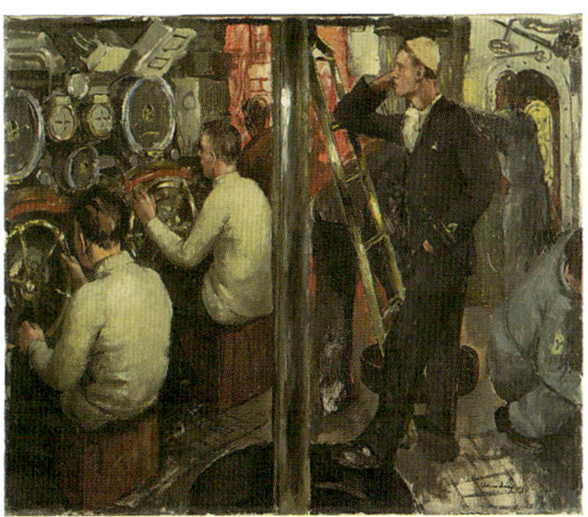

Dring, William D. 1904–1990
The Control Room in a Submarine during an Attack 1943
oil on canvas 50.8 x 60.9
IWM ART LD 2884

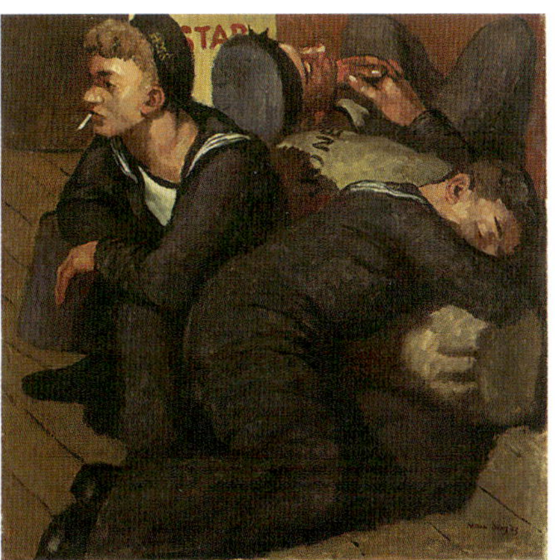

Dring, William D. 1904–1990
Waiting 1943
oil on canvas 73.6 x 76.2
IWM ART LD 2883

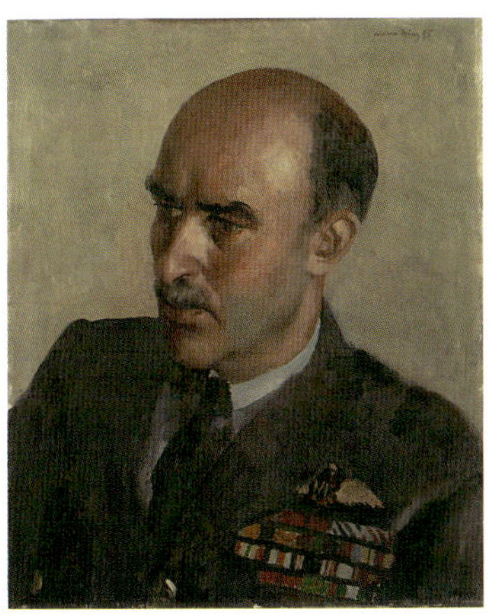

Dring, William D. 1904–1990
Air Marshal Sir James Robb (1895–1968), KBE, CB, DSO, DFC, AFC, Air Officer Commander-in-Chief, (…) 1945
oil on canvas 60.9 x 50.8
IWM ART LD 5729

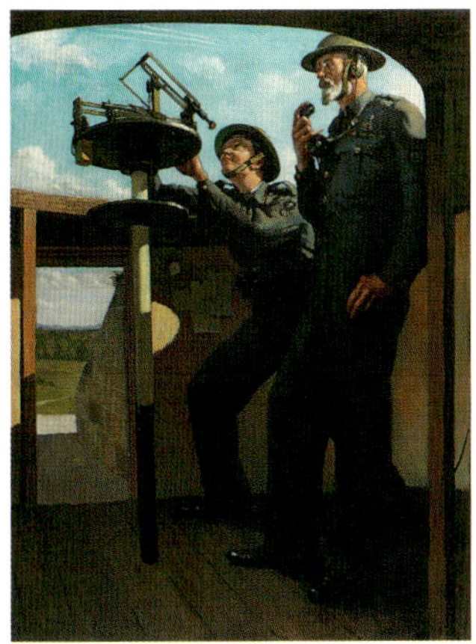

Dring, William D. 1904–1990
Leading Observer J. O. Isaacs and Chief Observer H. B. Harfield: Royal Observer Corps
1945
oil on canvas 121.9 x 91.4
IWM ART LD 5435

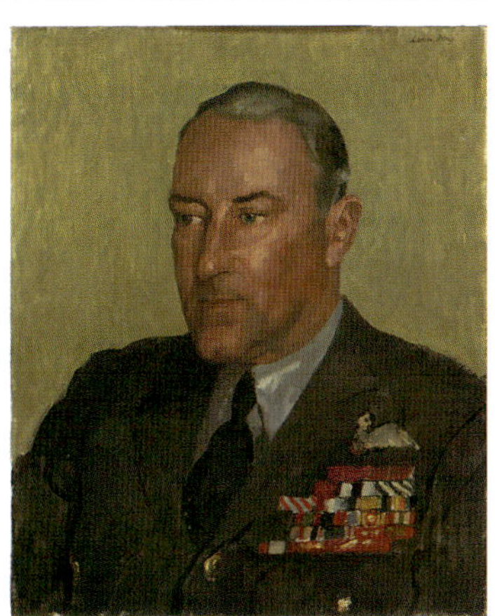

Dring, William D. 1904–1990
Air Marshal Sir Arthur Coningham (1895–1948), KCB, KBE, DSO, MC, DFC, AFC c.1945
oil on canvas 60.9 x 50.8
IWM ART LD 5868

Facing page: Nash, Paul, 1889–1946, *Spring in the Trenches, Ridge Wood, 1917* (detail), 1918, (p. 167)

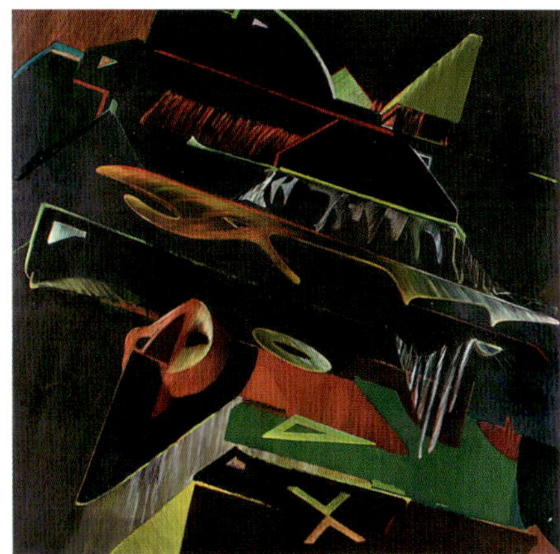

Dubsky, Mario 1939–1985
Battlefield Signals X Factor 1973–1977
oil on canvas 213.4 x 213.4
IWM ART 17103

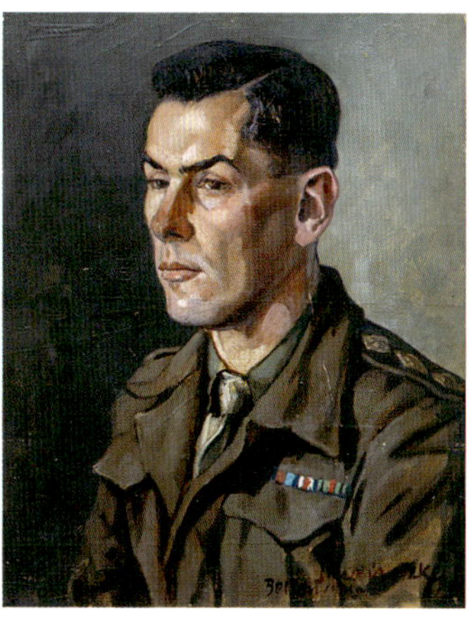

Dudinszky active 1940s
Captain Robert Wallis Dann 1945
oil on board 50 x 41
IWM ART 17110

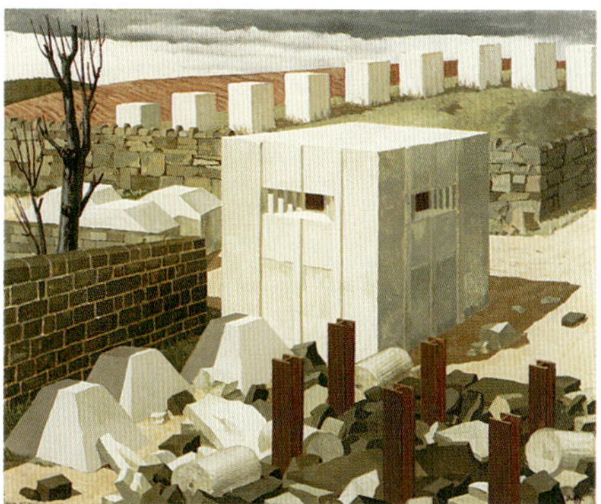

Duffy, Louis active c.1935–1950
A Blockhouse Somewhere in England 1943
oil on canvas 45.7 x 55.2
IWM ART LD 2906

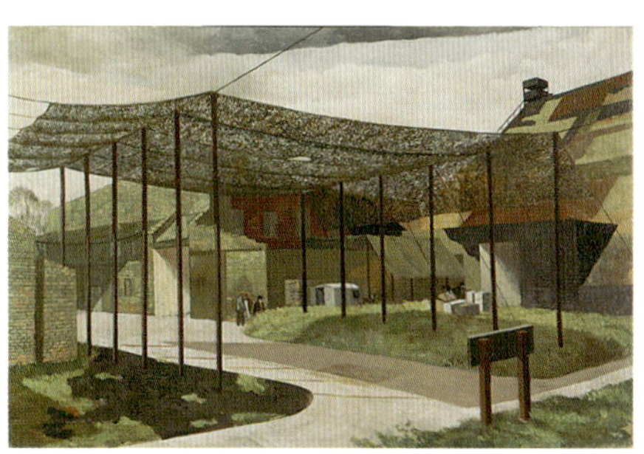

Duffy, Louis active c.1935–1950
Camouflage 1943
oil on canvas 50.1 x 76.2
IWM ART LD 2782

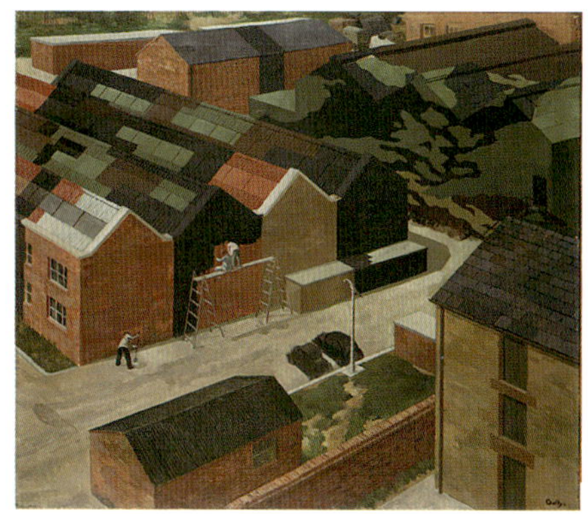

Duffy, Louis active c.1935–1950
The Entrance to a Factory 1943
oil on canvas 60.9 x 71.1
IWM ART LD 2783

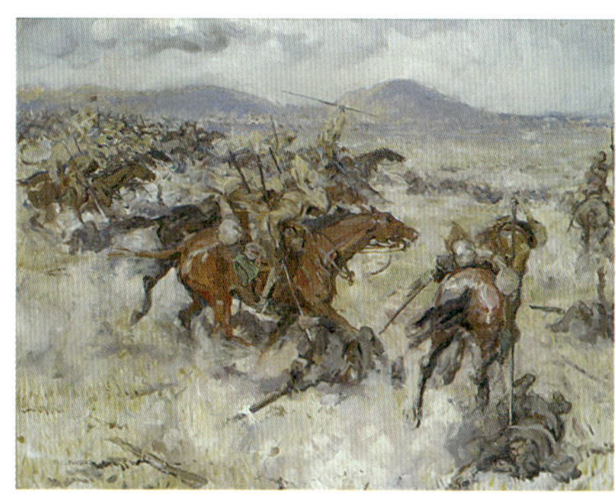

Dugdale, Thomas Cantrell 1880–1952
Charge of the Second Lancers at El Afuli in the Valley of Armageddon, 20 September 1918 1918
oil on canvas 71.1 x 91.4
IWM ART 2501

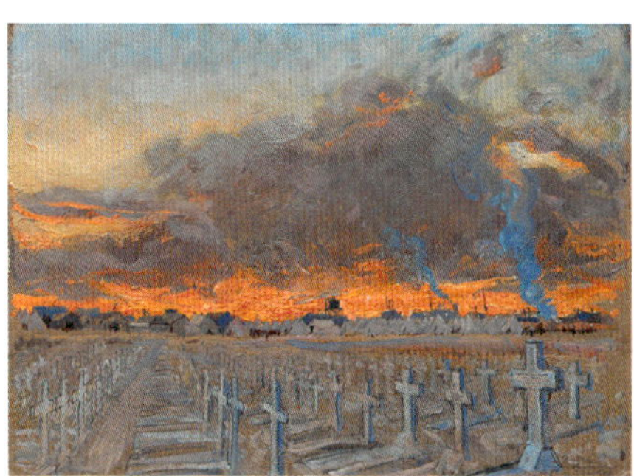

Dugdale, Thomas Cantrell 1880–1952
Graves at Kantara: The Last Day of 1918 1918
oil on panel 24.7 x 34.2
IWM ART 1865

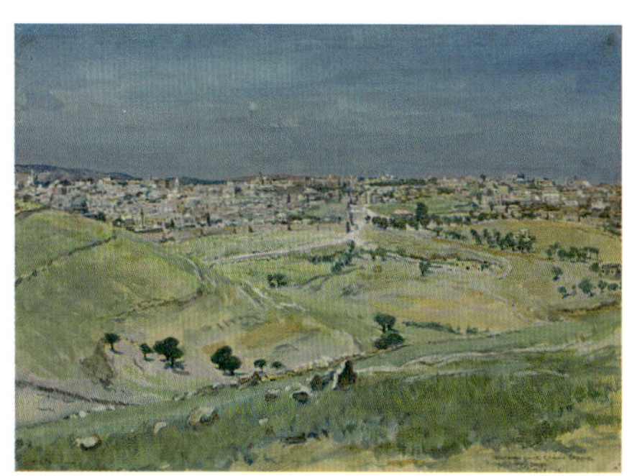

Dugdale, Thomas Cantrell 1880–1952
Jerusalem from the Mount of Olives: Gordon's Camel in the Middle Distance 1918
tempera on paper 24.7 x 34.9
IWM ART 1866

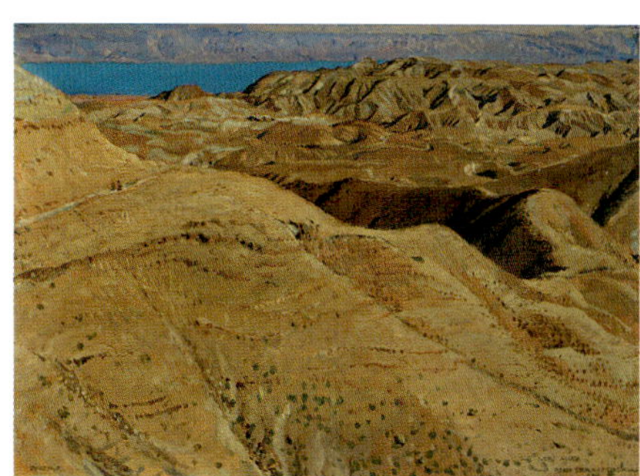

Dugdale, Thomas Cantrell 1880–1952
Nebi Musa (The Tomb of Moses) and the Dead Sea, from Talaat-ed-Dum 1918
oil on canvas board 24.7 x 34.9
IWM ART 1867

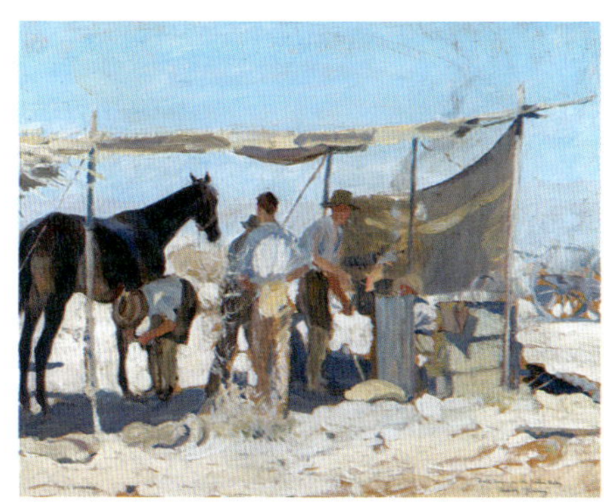

Dugdale, Thomas Cantrell 1880–1952
Shoeing under Difficulties, the Jordan Valley:
Field Forge in the Jordan Valley, Shoeing
'Jimmy' 1918
oil on panel 33 x 40.6
IWM ART 5220

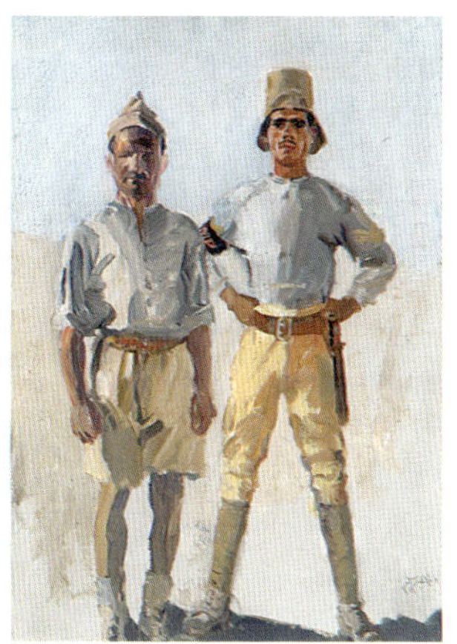

Dugdale, Thomas Cantrell 1880–1952
Military Policemen in Palestine c.1918
oil on canvas 34.2 x 24.1
IWM ART 6224

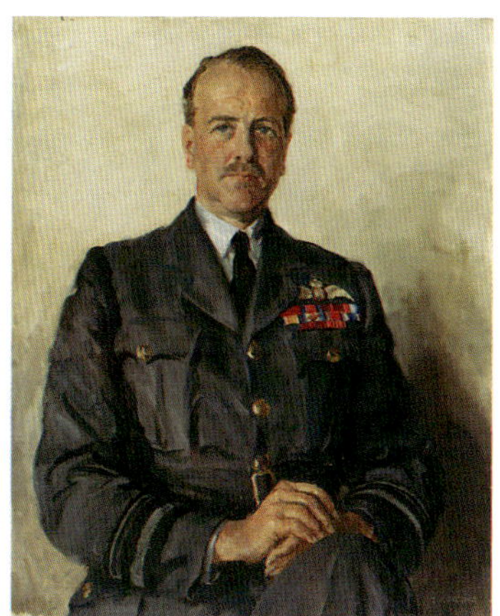

Dugdale, Thomas Cantrell 1880–1952
Air Vice-Marshal John Eustice Arthur Baldwin
(1892–1975), CB, DSO 1940
oil on canvas 91.4 x 76.2
IWM ART LD 669

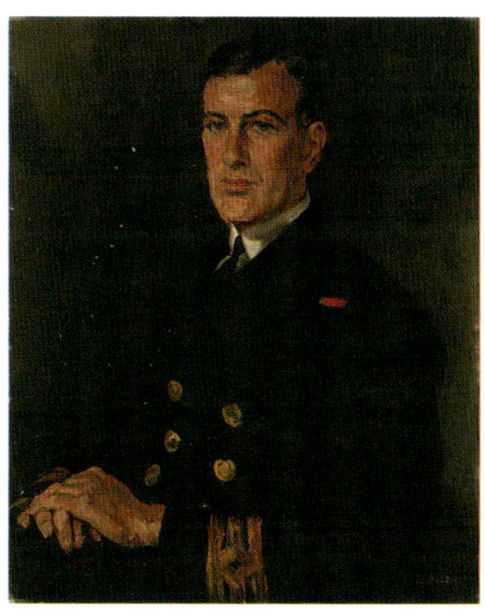

Dugdale, Thomas Cantrell 1880–1952
Chief Officer M. B. Copeland, OBE 1940
oil on canvas 76.2 x 63.5
IWM ART LD 908

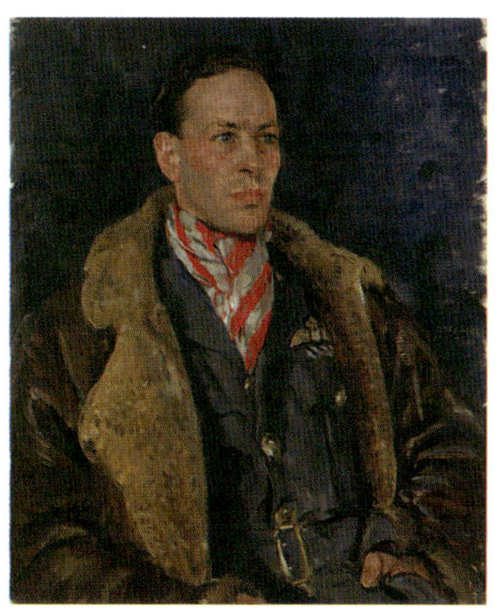

Dugdale, Thomas Cantrell 1880–1952
Squadron Leader George L. Denholm
(1909–1997), DFC 1940
oil on canvas 76.2 x 63.5
IWM ART LD 783

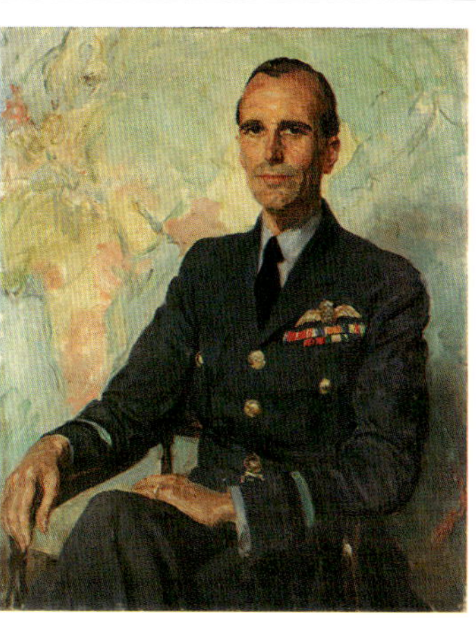

Dugdale, Thomas Cantrell 1880–1952
Air Commodore Robert Victor Goddard
(1897–1987), CBE 1941
oil on canvas 91.4 x 76.2
IWM ART LD 1520

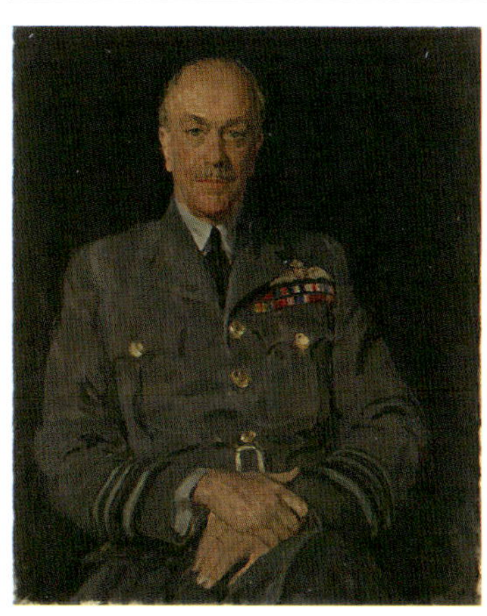

Dugdale, Thomas Cantrell 1880–1952
Air Marshal Sir Arthur Barratt, KCB, CMG,
MC 1941
oil on canvas 91.4 x 76.2
IWM ART LD 1210

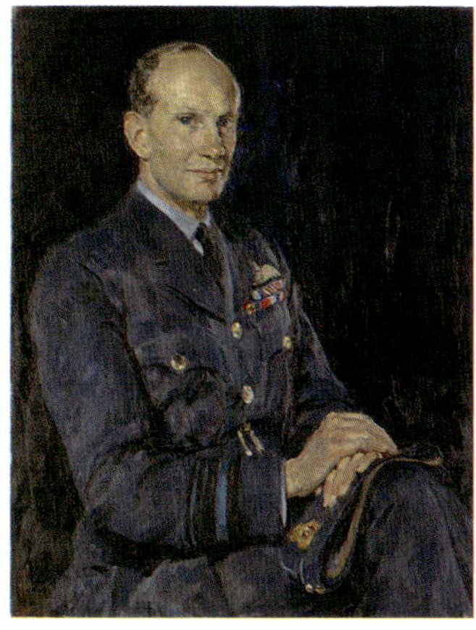

Dugdale, Thomas Cantrell 1880–1952
Air Vice-Marshal D. C. S. Evill, CB, DSC,
AFC 1941
oil on canvas 91.4 x 71.1
IWM ART LD 1651

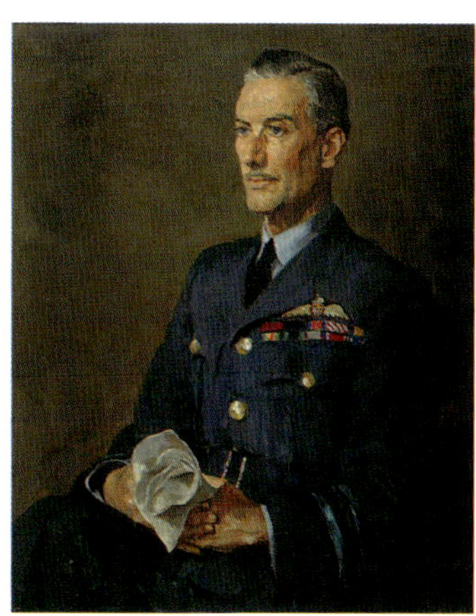

Dugdale, Thomas Cantrell 1880–1952
Air Vice-Marshal Norman Howard Bottomley
(1891–1970), CB, CIE, DSO, AFC 1941
oil on canvas 91.4 x 76.2
IWM ART LD 1650

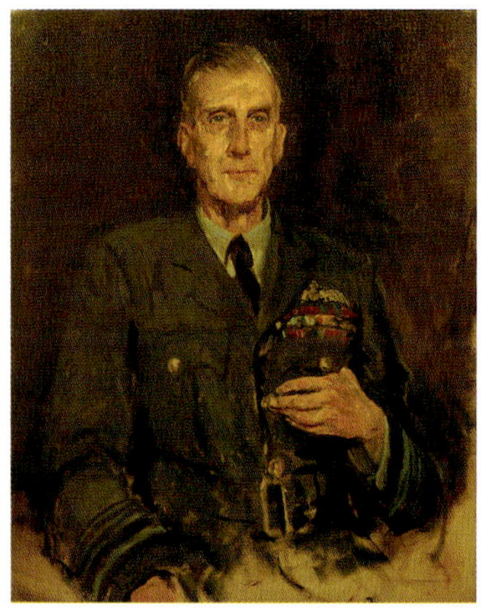

Dugdale, Thomas Cantrell 1880–1952
*Air Chief Marshal Sir Edgar Ludlow-Hewitt
(1886–1973), GCE, KCB, CMG, DSO, MC*
1945
oil on canvas 91.5 x 76.2
IWM ART LD 5727

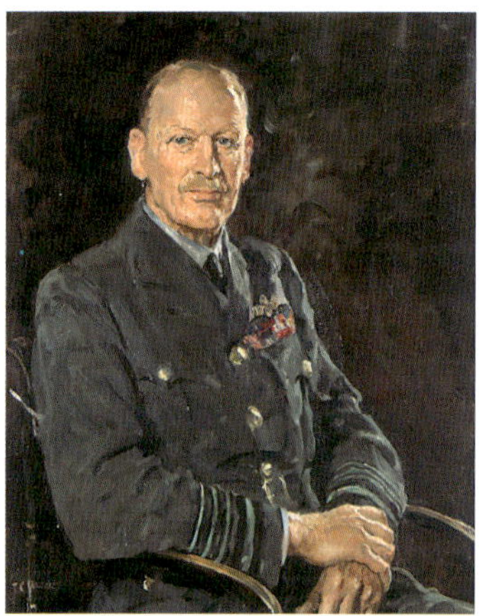

Dugdale, Thomas Cantrell 1880–1952
*Air Chief Marshal Sir Robert Brook-Popham,
GCVO, KCB, CMG, DSO, AFC* 1945
oil on canvas 90.1 x 76.2
IWM ART LD 5575

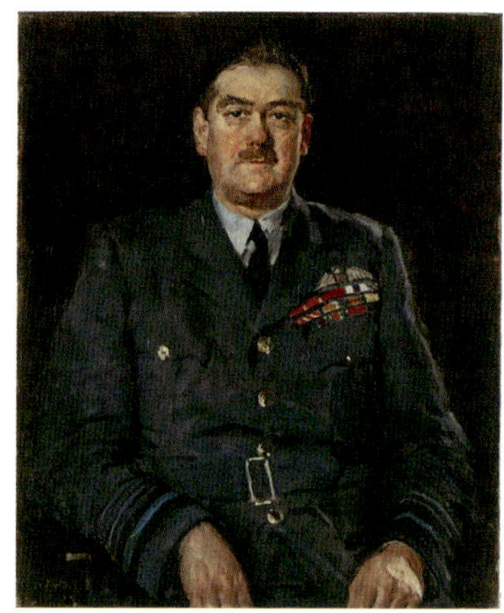

Dugdale, Thomas Cantrell 1880–1952
*Air Marshal Sir Robert Saundby (1896–1971),
KBE, CB, MC, DFC, AFC* 1945
oil on canvas 91.4 x 76.2
IWM ART LD 5728

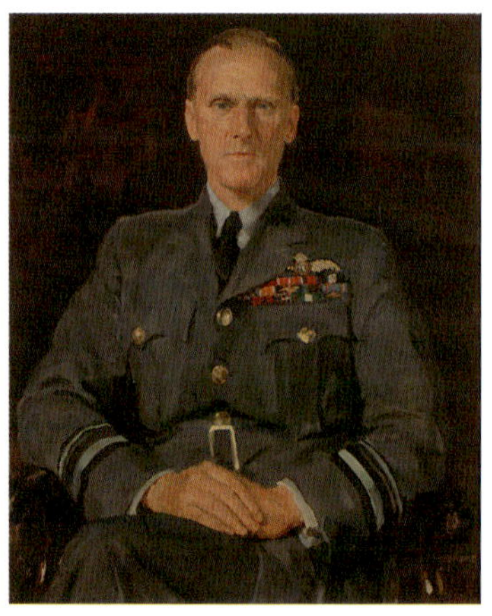

Dugdale, Thomas Cantrell 1880–1952
*Air Vice-Marshal Ronald Graham
(1896–1967), CB, CBE, DSO, DSC, DFC* 1945
oil on canvas 90.1 x 76.2
IWM ART LD 5574

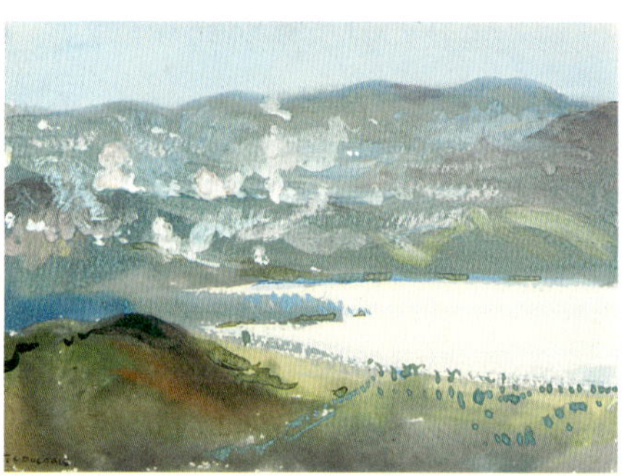

Dugdale, Thomas Cantrell 1880–1952
*Bombardment of Bulgar Trenches, Doiran,
Balkans: Pip Ridge and Grande and Petite
Couronnes*
tempera on paper 12.7 x 17.7
IWM ART 1864

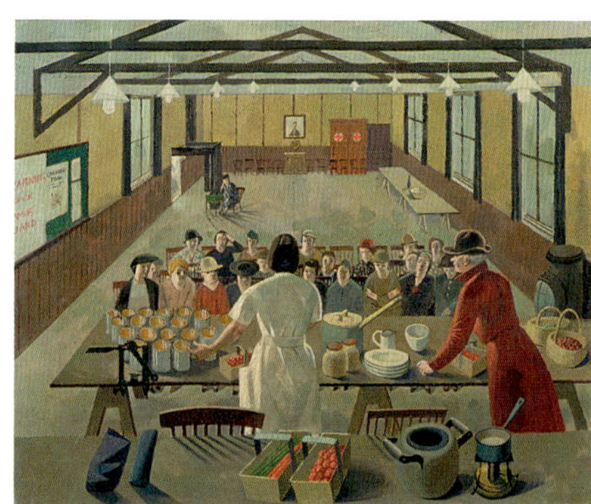

Dunbar, Evelyn Mary 1906–1960
A Canning Demonstration 1940
oil on canvas 50.8 x 60.9
IWM ART LD 765

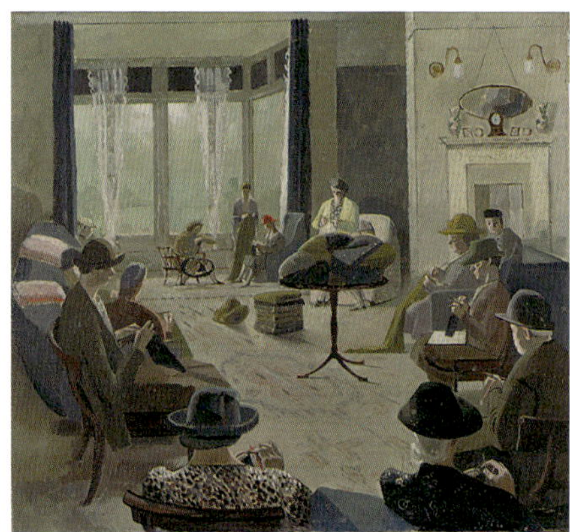

Dunbar, Evelyn Mary 1906–1960
A Knitting Party 1940
oil on canvas 45.7 x 50.8
IWM ART LD 768

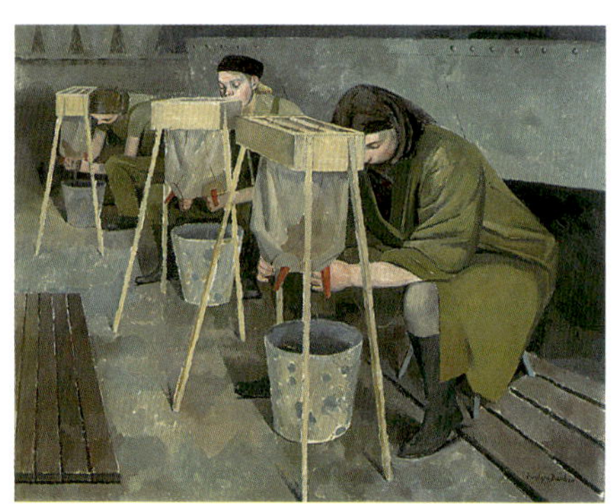

Dunbar, Evelyn Mary 1906–1960
Milking Practice with Artificial Udders 1940
oil on canvas 61.7 x 76.6
IWM ART LD 766

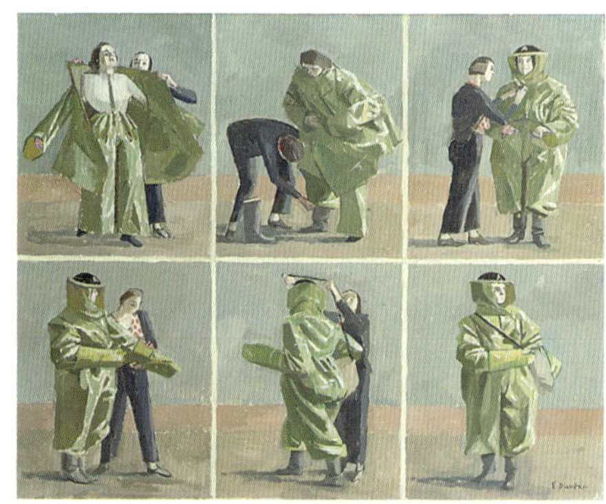

Dunbar, Evelyn Mary 1906–1960
Putting on Anti-Gas Protective Clothing 1940
oil on canvas 60.9 x 76.2
IWM ART LD 247

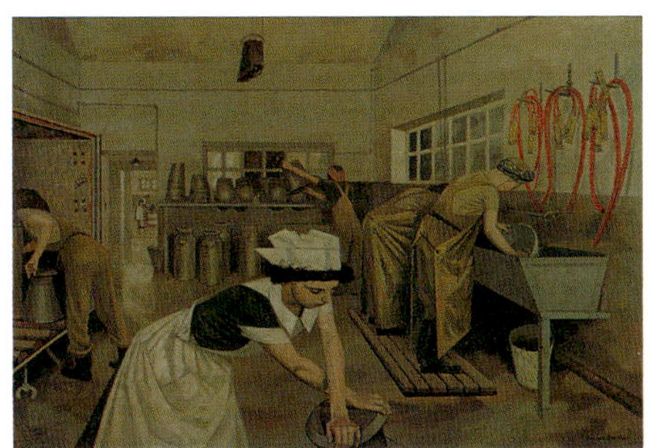

Dunbar, Evelyn Mary 1906–1960
Women's Land Army Dairy Training 1940
oil on canvas 50.8 x 76.2
IWM ART LD 767

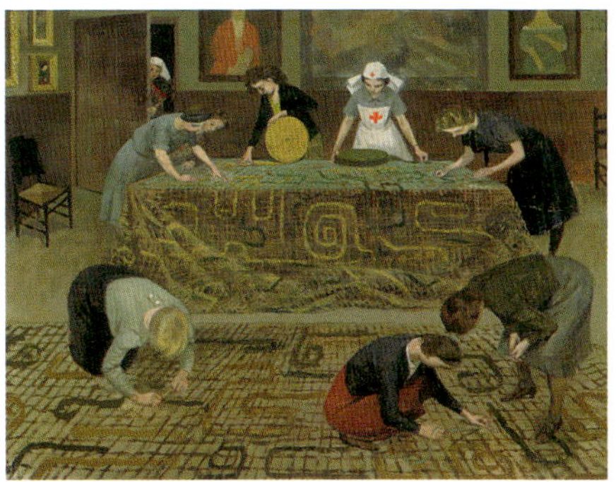

Dunbar, Evelyn Mary 1906–1960
Convalescent Nurses Making Camouflage Nets
1941
oil on canvas 45.8 x 61
IWM ART LD 1664

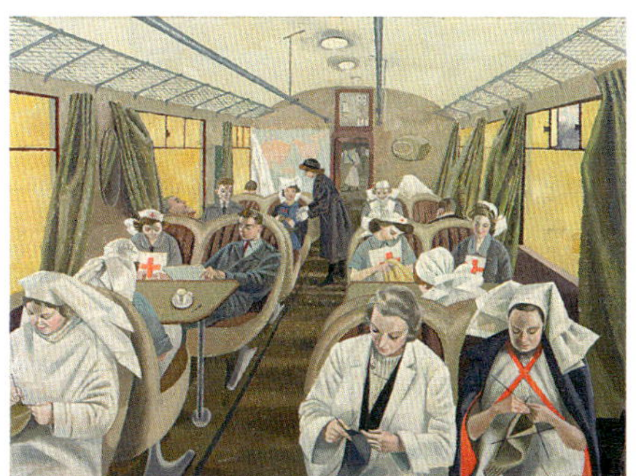

Dunbar, Evelyn Mary 1906–1960
*Standing-By on Train 21: A Civilian
Evacuation Train Ready to Evacuate Casualties
at Short Notice* 1941
oil on canvas 55.8 x 76.2
IWM ART LD 1858

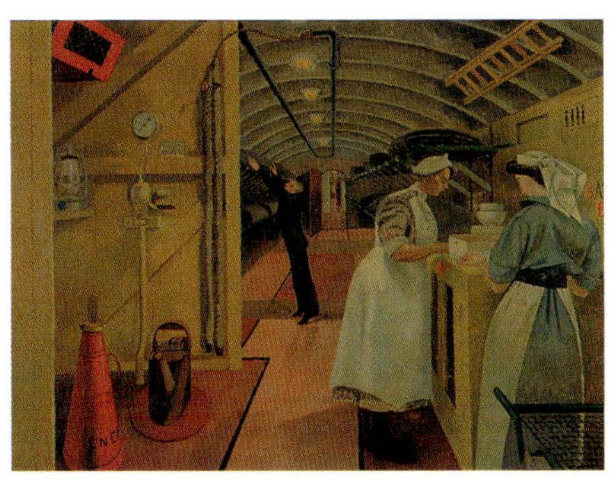

Dunbar, Evelyn Mary 1906–1960
Hospital Train 1942
oil on canvas 55.8 x 76.2
IWM ART LD 2477

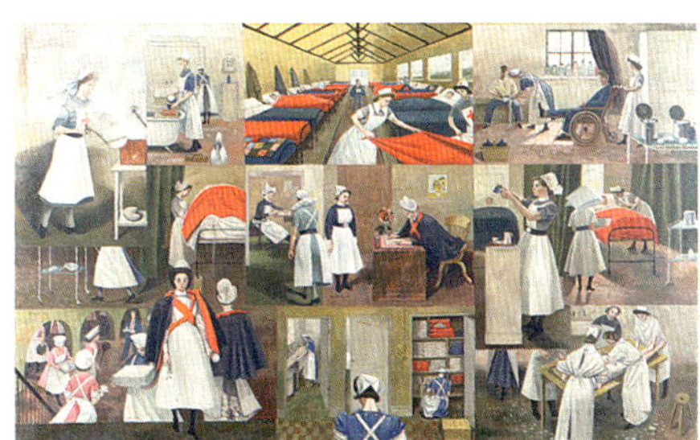

Dunbar, Evelyn Mary 1906–1960
St Thomas's Hospital in Evacuation Quarters
1942
oil on canvas 91.4 x 152.4
IWM ART LD 2478

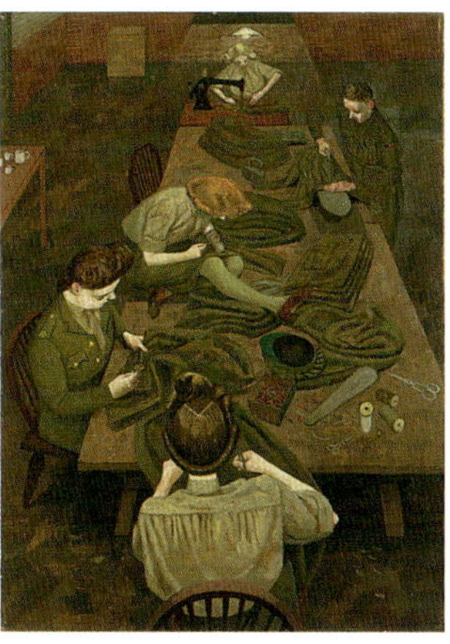

Dunbar, Evelyn Mary 1906–1960
*An Army Tailor and an Auxiliary Territorial
Service Tailoress* 1943
oil on canvas 60.9 x 45.7
IWM ART LD 3349

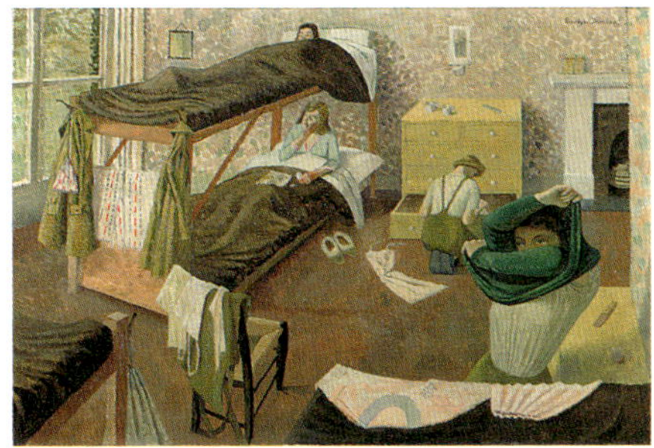

Dunbar, Evelyn Mary 1906–1960
Land Army Girls Going to Bed 1943
oil on canvas 50.8 x 76.2
IWM ART LD 3351

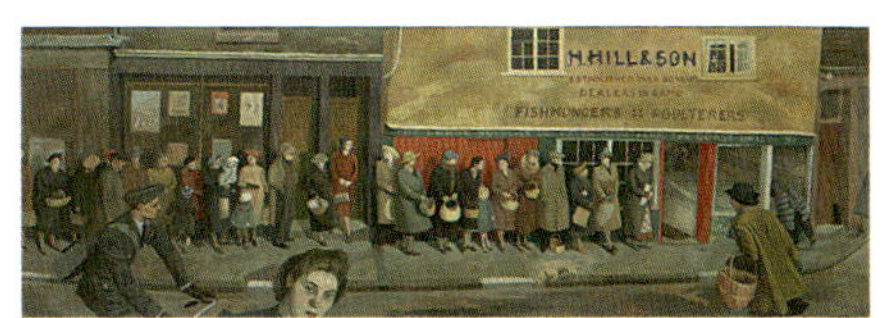

Dunbar, Evelyn Mary 1906–1960
The Queue at the Fish Shop 1944
oil on canvas 62.2 x 182.8
IWM ART LD 3987

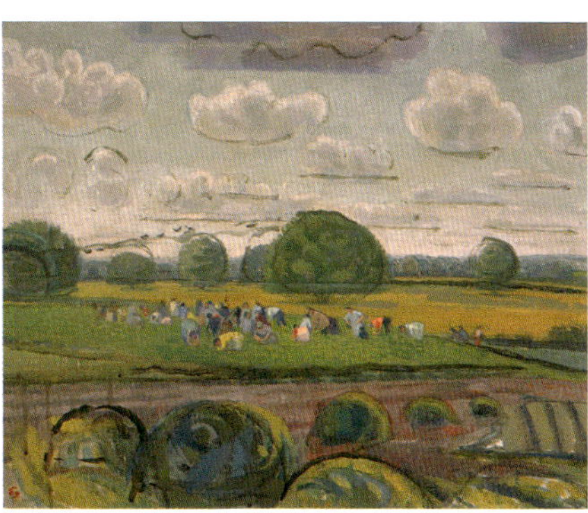

Dunbar, Evelyn Mary 1906–1960
Pea Picking at Rippers Cross Farm c.1945
oil on canvas 35.3 x 45.5
IWM ART 16452

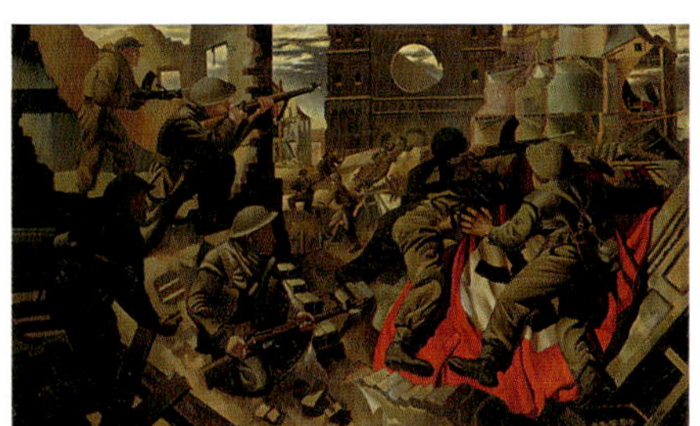

Eales, Edward A. active 1940s
Attack on a German Town 1945
oil on canvas 66 x 106.6
IWM ART LD 7279

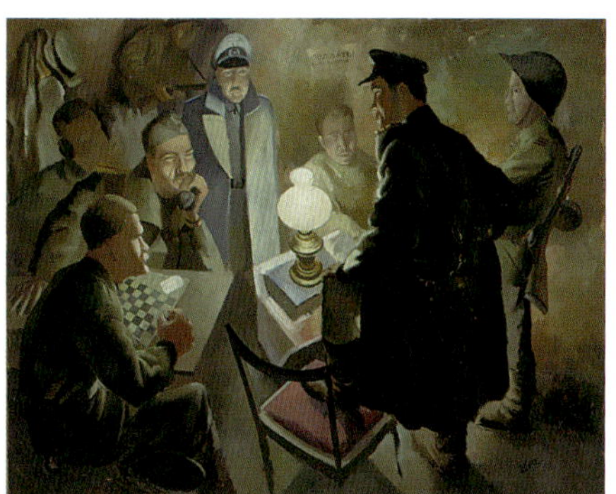

Eales, Edward A. active 1940s
A Captured German Officer Interrogated by Russian Soldiers c.1945
oil on canvas 60.9 x 76.2
IWM ART LD 7280

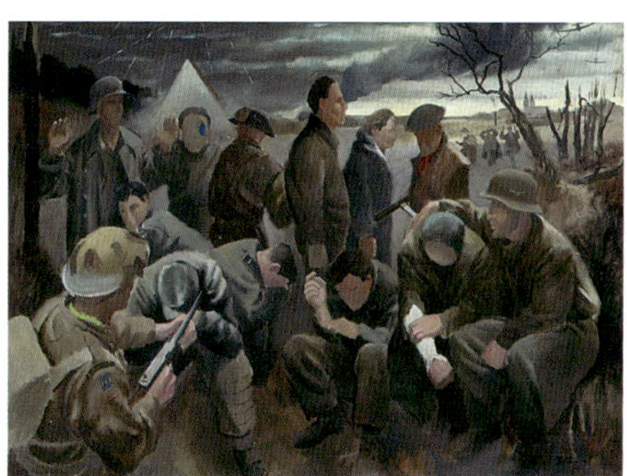

Eales, Edward A. active 1940s
Group of Prisoners c.1945
oil on canvas 60.9 x 81.2
IWM ART LD 7281

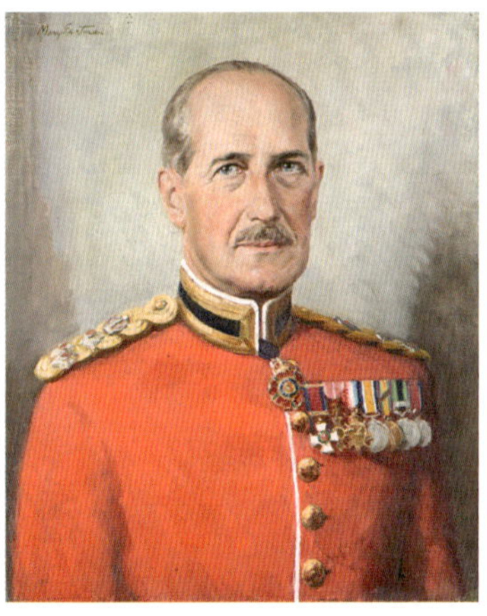

Eastman, Mary active c.1932–1979
Brooke-Smith c.1940–1945
oil on canvas 60.9 x 50.8
IWM ART LD 7264

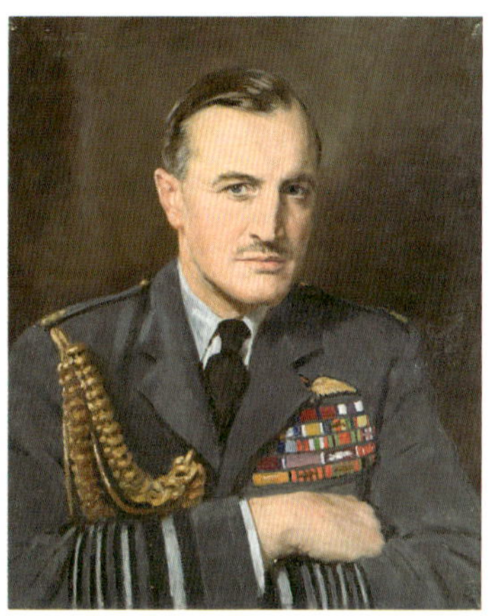

Eastman, Mary active c.1932–1979
Air Member for Personnel John C. Slessor (1897–1979) 1947
oil on canvas 60.3 x 50.8
IWM ART LD 6512

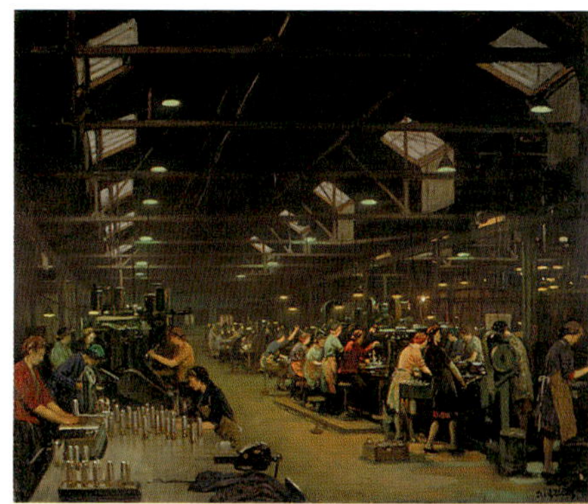

Elwell, Frederick William 1870–1958
A Munitions Factory 1944
oil on canvas 62.8 x 75.5 (E)
IWM ART LD 4908

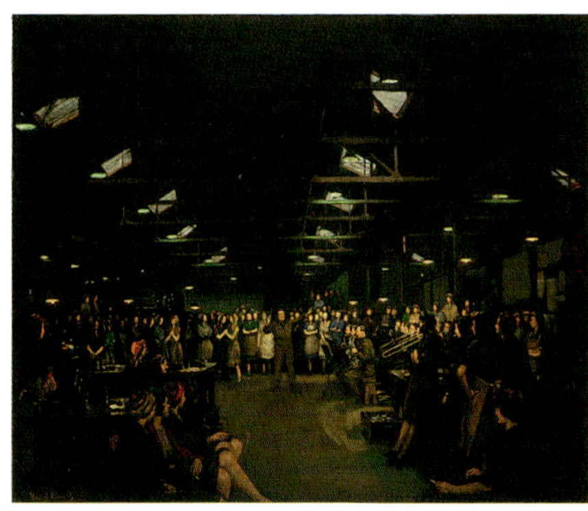

Elwell, Frederick William 1870–1958
A Musical Interlude 1944
oil on canvas 62.8 x 75.5 (E)
IWM ART LD 4909

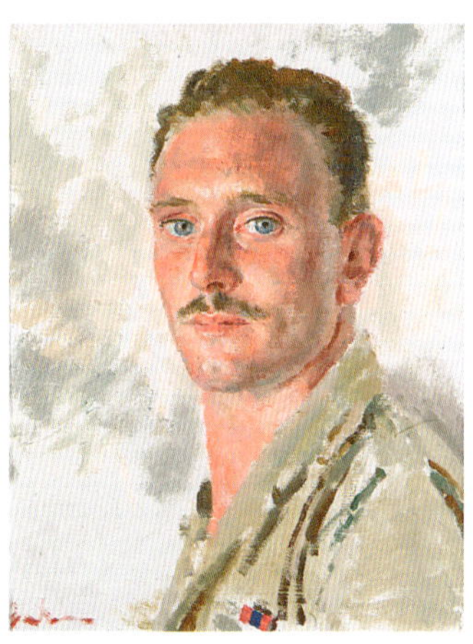

Elwes, Simon 1902–1975
Corporal Guise, DCM, Rifle Brigade 1942
oil on panel 50.8 x 40.6
IWM ART LD 2787

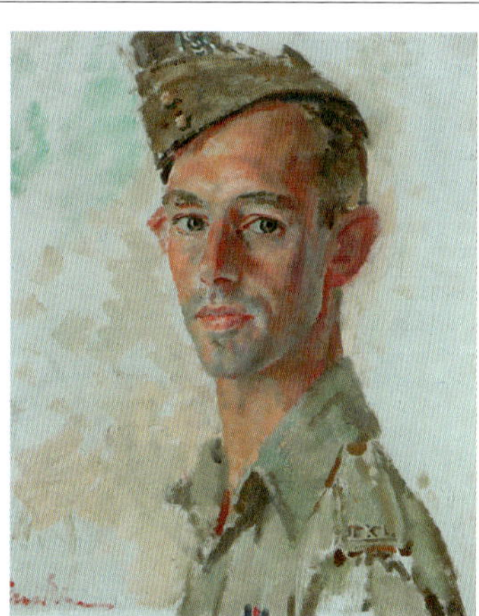

Elwes, Simon 1902–1975
Sergeant Edwards, 9th Queen's Royal Lancers 1942
oil on panel 52 x 44.4
IWM ART LD 2786

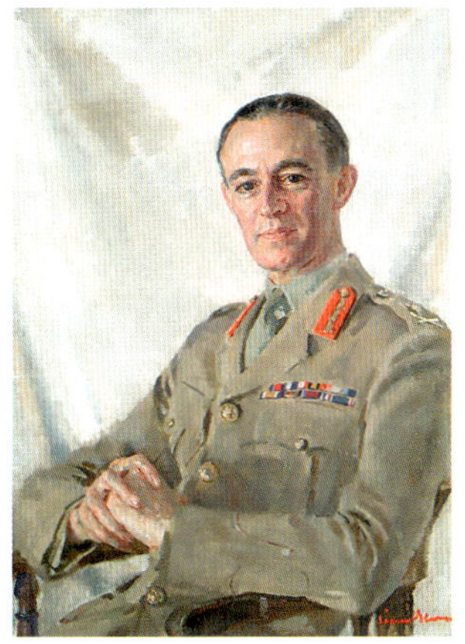

Elwes, Simon 1902–1975
Lieutenant General R. G. W. H. Stone CB,
DSO, MC, FRGS c.1942
oil on canvas 90.5 x 69
IWM ART 16667

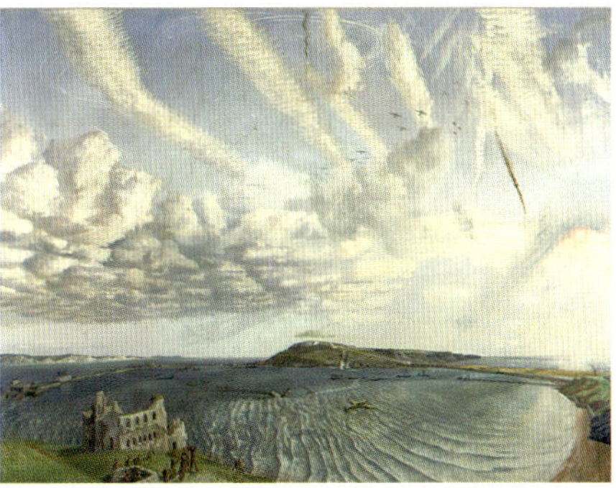

Eurich, Richard Ernst 1903–1992
Air Fight over Portland 1940
oil on canvas 76.2 x 101.9
IWM ART LD 769

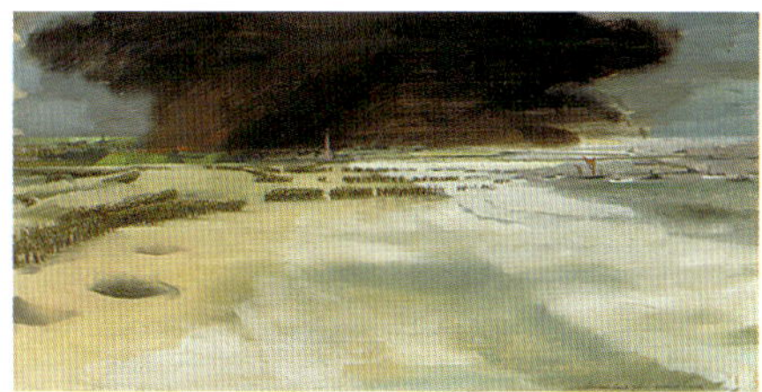

Eurich, Richard Ernst 1903–1992
Dunkirk Beaches 1940
oil on cardboard 22.8 x 45.7
IWM ART LD 2277

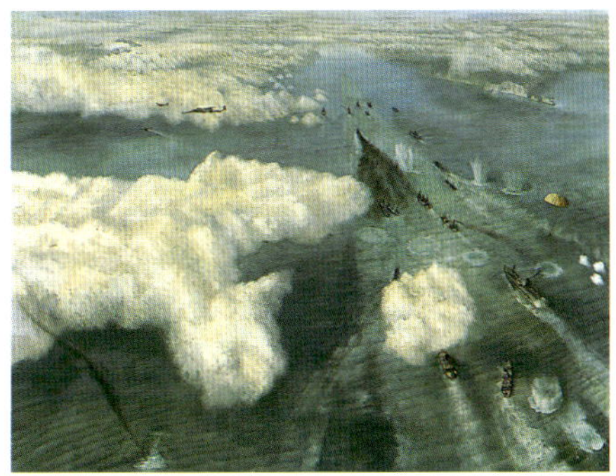

Eurich, Richard Ernst 1903–1992
Attack on a Convoy Seen from the Air 1941
oil on canvas 76 x 101.4
IWM ART LD 1326

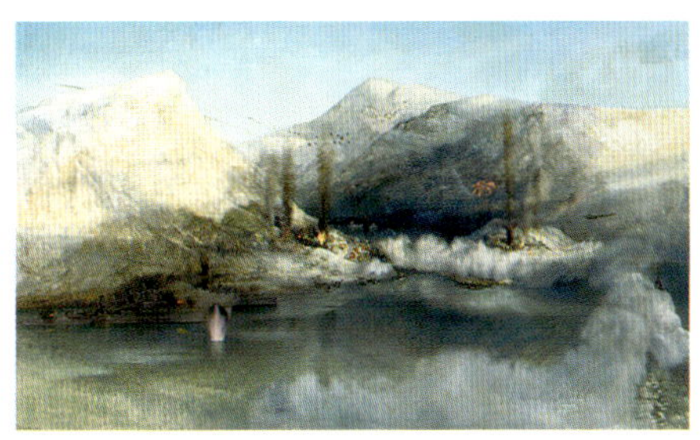

Eurich, Richard Ernst 1903–1992
The Raid of Vaagso, Norway, 26–27 December
1941 1941
oil on canvas 76.2 x 127
IWM ART LD 2298

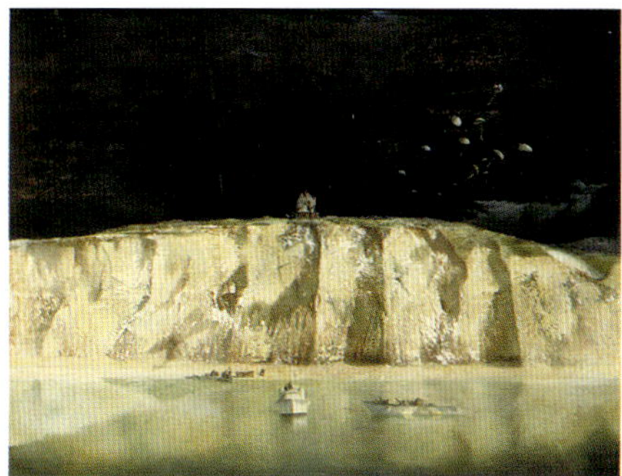

Eurich, Richard Ernst 1903–1992
The Raid on the Bruneval Radiolocation
Station, 27–28 February 1942 1942
oil on canvas 76.2 x 101.9
IWM ART LD 3475

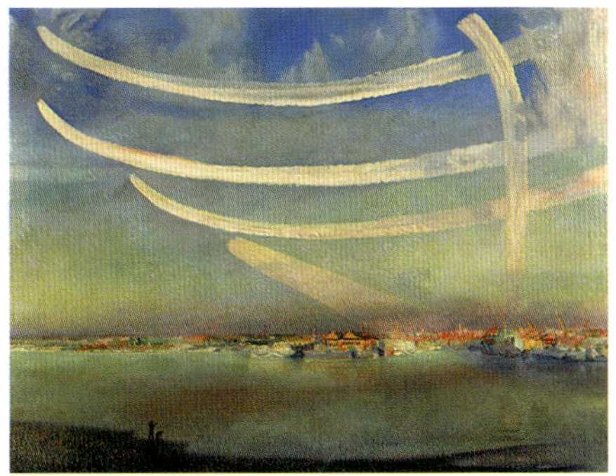

Eurich, Richard Ernst 1903–1992
'Fortresses' over Southampton Water 1943
oil on canvas 76.2 x 101.9
IWM ART LD 3958

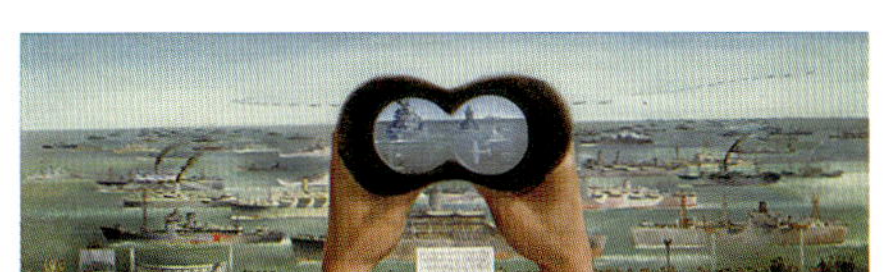

Eurich, Richard Ernst 1903–1992
The Great Convoy to North Africa 1943
oil on panel 36.8 x 127
IWM ART LD 3477

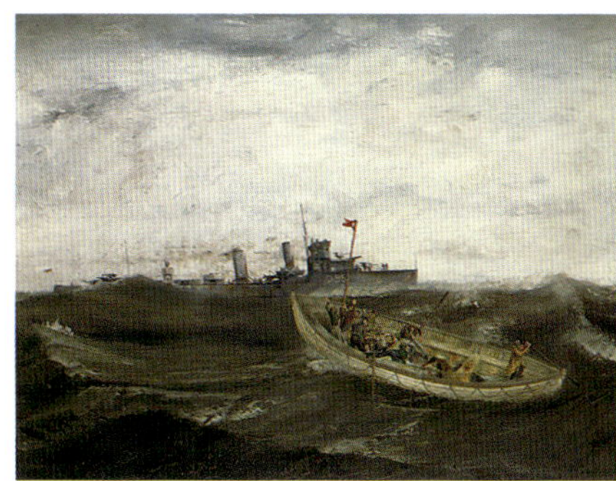

Eurich, Richard Ernst 1903–1992
A Destroyer Rescuing Survivors 1944
oil on canvas 76.2 x 101.9
IWM ART LD 2297

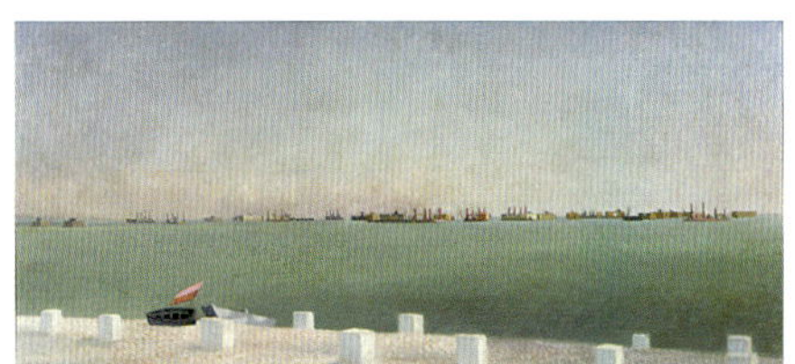

Eurich, Richard Ernst 1903–1992
*Mulberry: The Prefabricated Harbour
Assembled, Selsey Bill* 1944
oil on canvas 37.4 x 81.9
IWM ART LD 5189

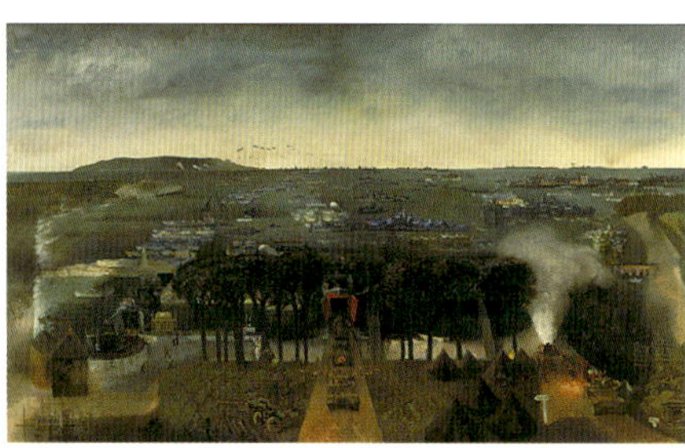

Eurich, Richard Ernst 1903–1992
Preparations for D-Day 1944
oil on canvas 76.2 x 127
IWM ART LD 4587

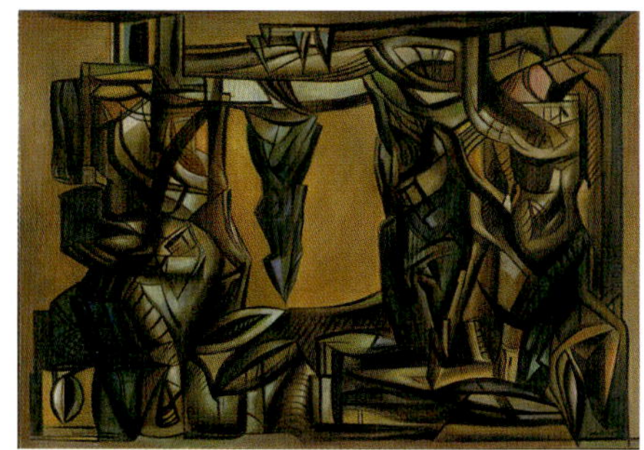

Evans, Merlyn Oliver 1910–1973
The Execution 1945
oil on canvas 82.2 x 119
IWM ART 15279

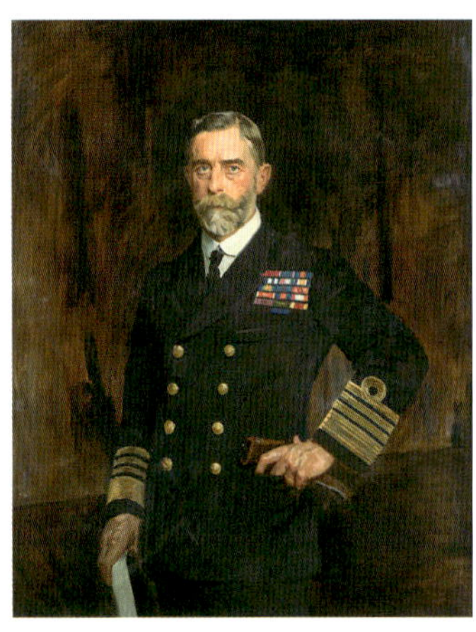

Eves, Reginald Grenville 1876–1941
*Admiral Sir Charles Madden (1906–2001),
GCB, GCVO, KCMG* 1922
oil on canvas 127 x 101.9
IWM ART 4177

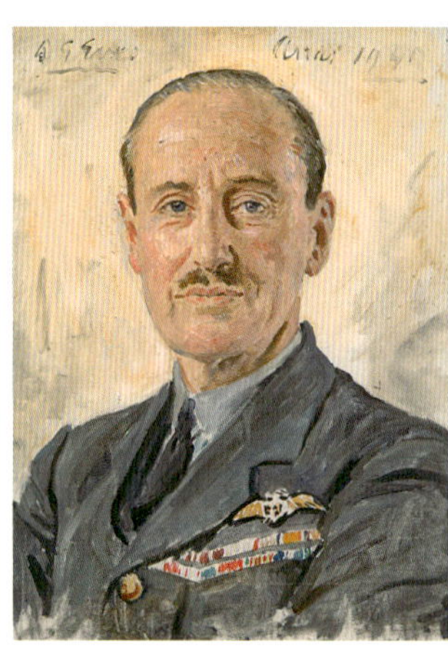

Eves, Reginald Grenville 1876–1941
Air Vice-Marshal C. H. Blount, OBE, MC
1940
oil on panel 50.8 x 40.6 (E)
IWM ART LD 1392

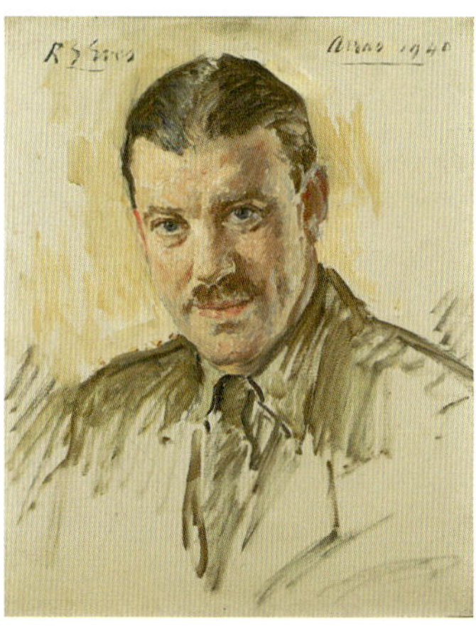

Eves, Reginald Grenville 1876–1941
*Captain Arthur William Milborne-
Swinnerton-Pilkington (1898–1952), MC*
1940
oil on panel 50.8 x 40.6 (E)
IWM ART LD 243

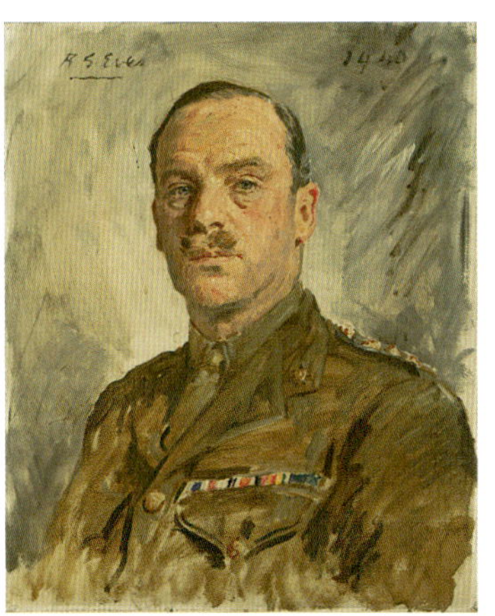

Eves, Reginald Grenville 1876–1941
Captain G. L. Hastings, MC 1940
oil on canvas 60.9 x 50.8
IWM ART LD 244

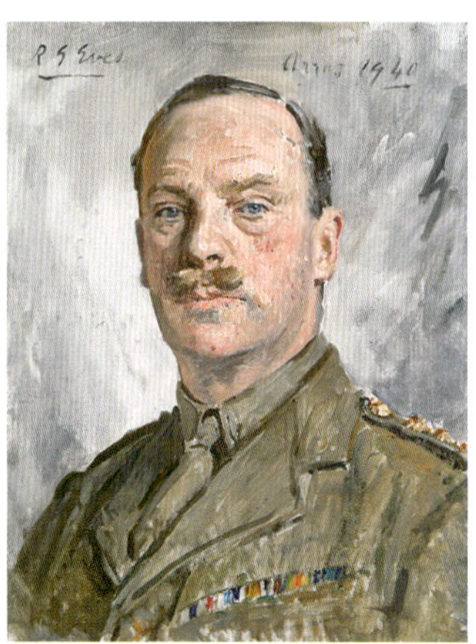

Eves, Reginald Grenville 1876–1941
Captain G. L. Hastings, MC 1940
oil on panel 50.8 x 40.6 (E)
IWM ART LD 1394

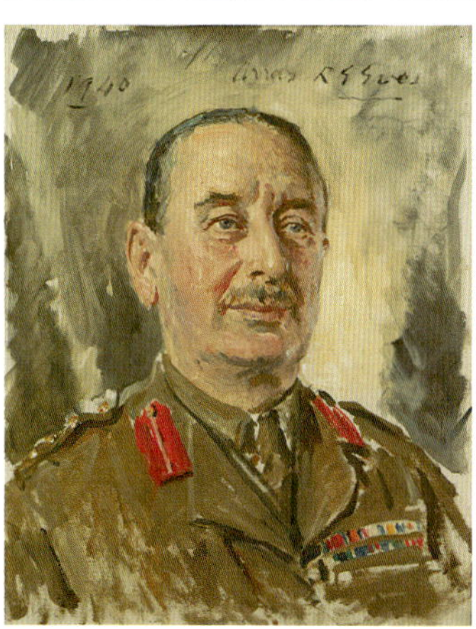

Eves, Reginald Grenville 1876–1941
Colonel H. Medlicott, DSO 1940
oil on panel 50.8 x 40.6 (E)
IWM ART LD 1390

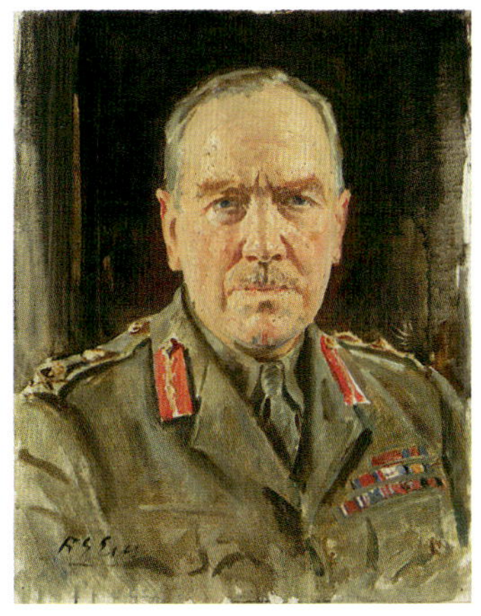

Eves, Reginald Grenville 1876–1941
General Sir Robert Gordon-Finlayson, KCB, CMG, DSO 1940
oil on panel 50.8 x 40.6
IWM ART LD 713

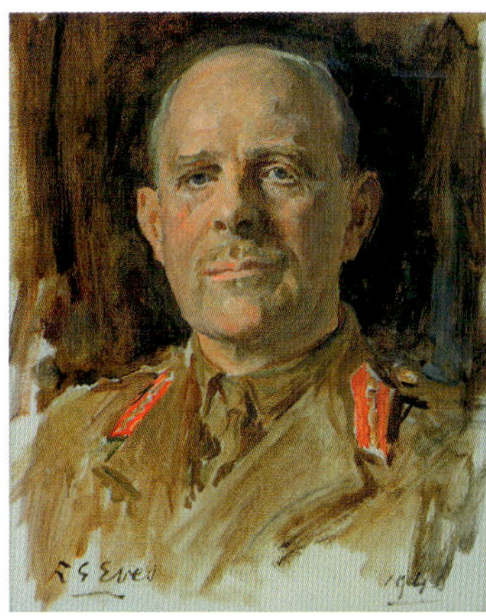

Eves, Reginald Grenville 1876–1941
General the Viscount Gort (1886–1946), VC, GCB, CBE, DSO, MVO, MC 1940
oil on canvas 50.8 x 40.6 (E)
IWM ART LD 616

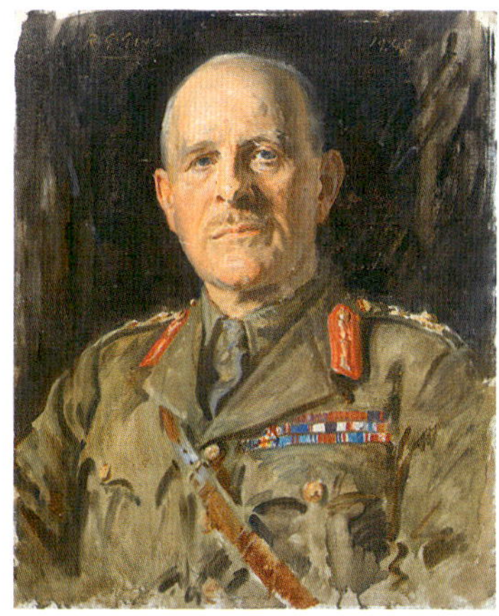

Eves, Reginald Grenville 1876–1941
General the Viscount Gort (1886–1946), VC, GCB, CBE, DSO, MVO, MC 1940
oil on panel 60.9 x 50.8
IWM ART LD 730

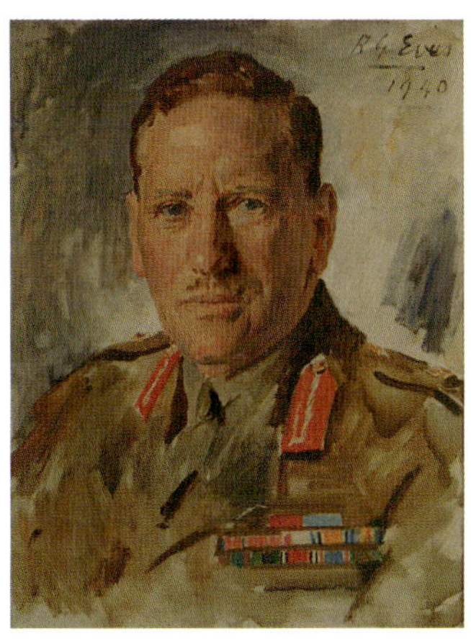

Eves, Reginald Grenville 1876–1941
Lieutenant General Claude J. E. Auchinleck (1884–1981), CB, CSI, DSO, OBE 1940
oil on panel 50.8 x 40.6 (E)
IWM ART LD 729

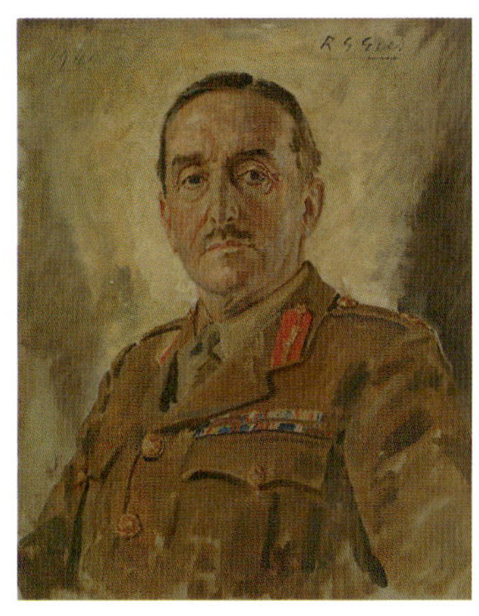

Eves, Reginald Grenville 1876–1941
Lieutenant General Sir Alan Brooke (1883–1963), KCB, DSO 1940
oil on canvas 60.9 x 50.8 (E)
IWM ART LD 241

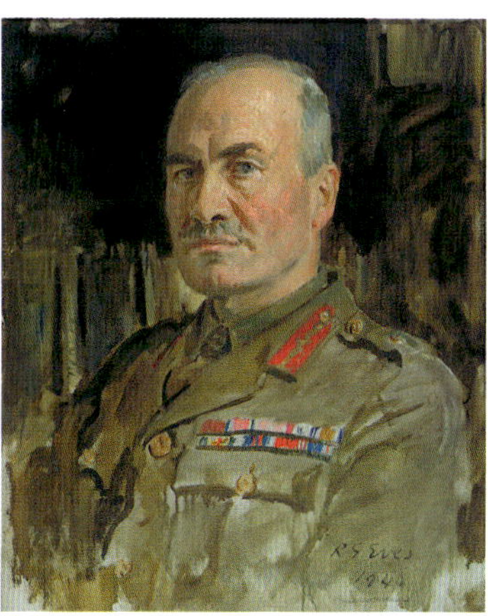

Eves, Reginald Grenville 1876–1941
Lieutenant General Sir Ronald Adam (1896–1979), Bt, CB, DSO, OBE 1940
oil on canvas 60.9 x 50.8
IWM ART LD 404

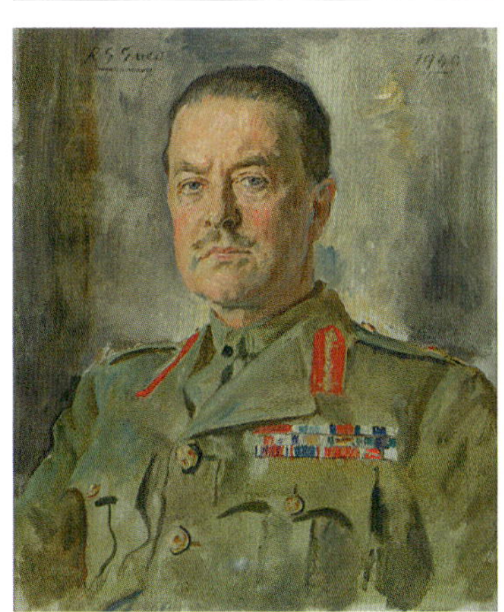

Eves, Reginald Grenville 1876–1941
Lieutenant General the Honourable H. R. Alexander, CB, CSI, DSO, MC 1940
oil on canvas 60.9 x 50.8
IWM ART LD 407

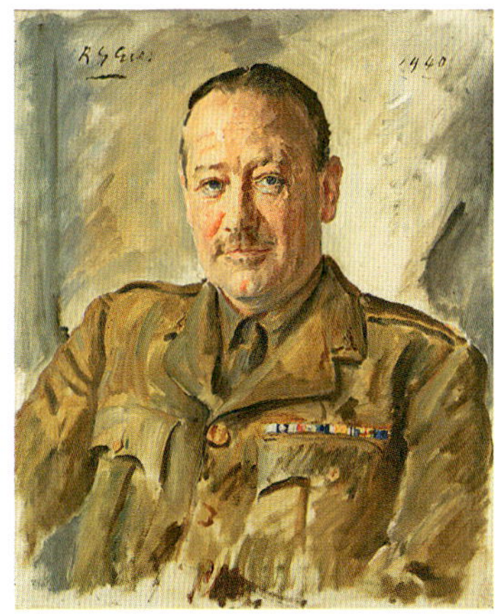

Eves, Reginald Grenville 1876–1941
Major C. Tremayne, MC, and Bar 1940
oil on canvas 60.9 x 50.8
IWM ART LD 246

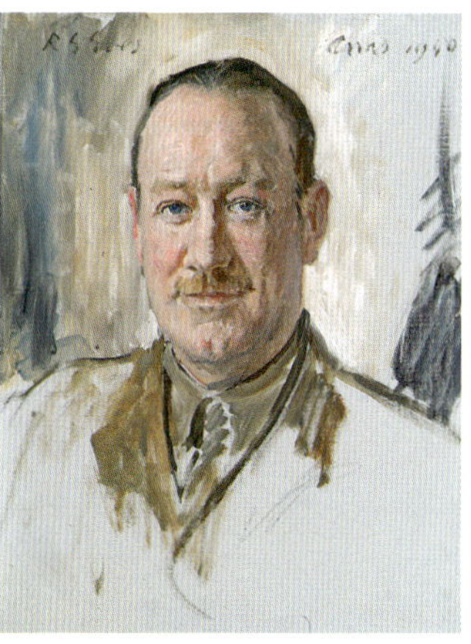

Eves, Reginald Grenville 1876–1941
Major C. Tremayne, MC and Bar 1940
oil on panel 50.8 x 40.6 (E)
IWM ART LD 1395

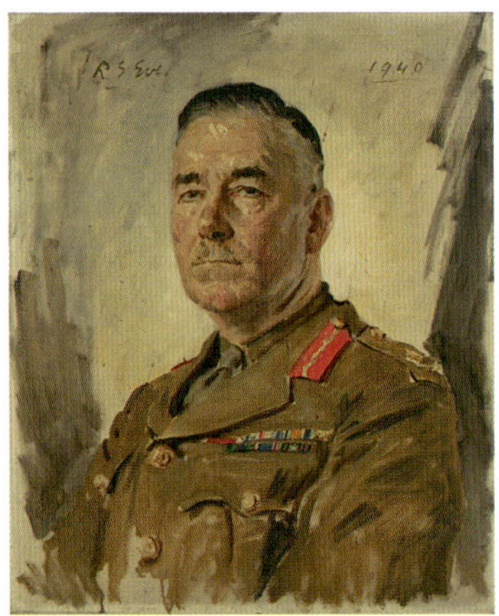

Eves, Reginald Grenville 1876–1941
*Major General Frank Noel Mason-Macfarlane
(1889–1953), CB, DSO, MC* 1940
oil on canvas 60.9 x 50.8
IWM ART LD 242

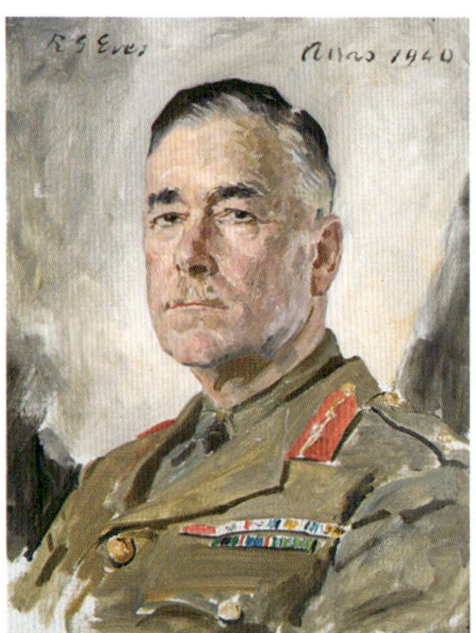

Eves, Reginald Grenville 1876–1941
*Major General Frank Noel Mason-Macfarlane
(1889–1953), CB, DSO, MC* 1940
oil on panel 50.8 x 40.6 (E)
IWM ART LD 1393

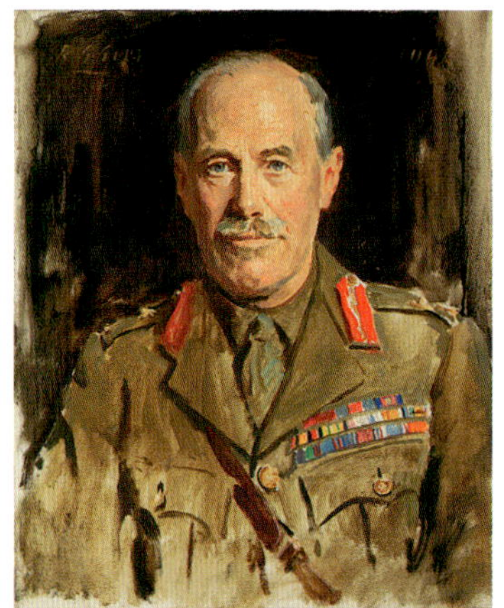

Eves, Reginald Grenville 1876–1941
*Major General W. N. Herbert, CB, CMG, DSO
and Bar* 1940
oil on canvas 60.9 x 50.8
IWM ART LD 405

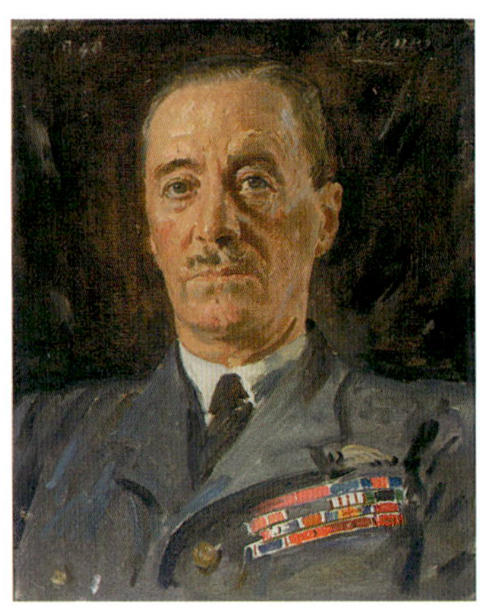

Eves, Reginald Grenville 1876–1941
*Sir Cyril Newall (1886–1963), GCB, CMG,
CBE* 1940
oil on panel 50.8 x 40.6
IWM ART LD 762

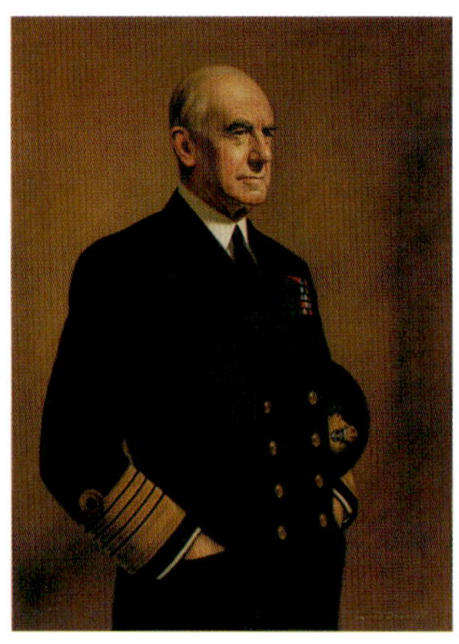

Ewart, David Shanks 1901–1965
*Admiral of the Fleet Sir Dudley Pound
(1877–1943), GCB, OM, GCVO* 1949
oil on canvas 101.9 x 76.2
IWM ART LD 5924

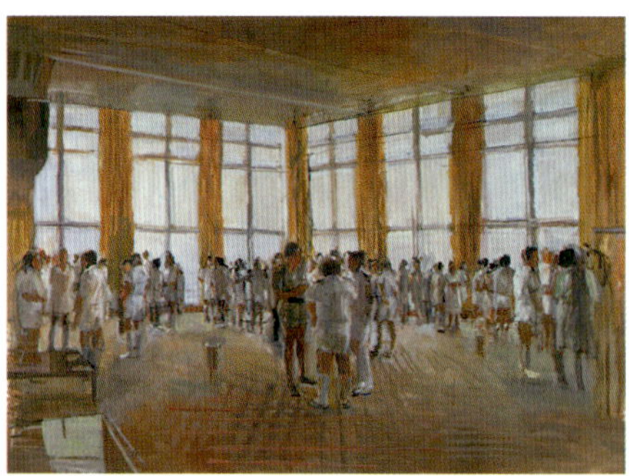

Eyton, Anthony John Plowden b.1923
*Reception for Australian and New Zealand
Naval Officers at 'HMS Tamar'* 1983
oil on canvas 132 x 183
IWM ART 15663

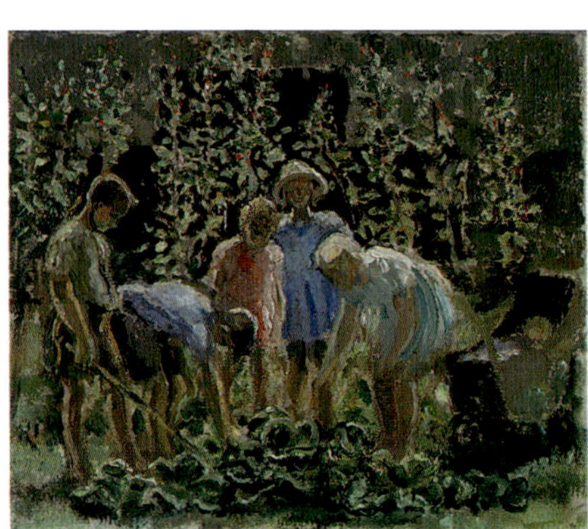

Faithfull, Leila 1896–1994
Evacuees Growing Cabbages 1940
oil on canvas 24.7 x 29.5
IWM ART LD 428

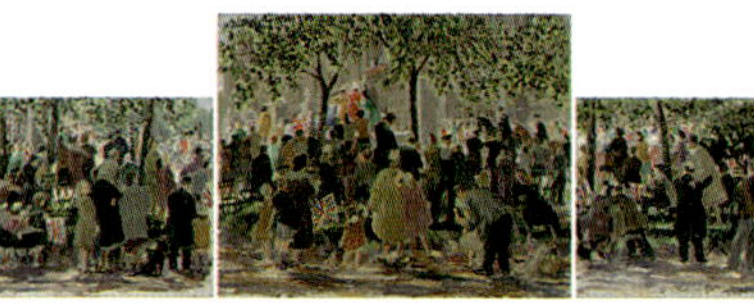

Faithfull, Leila 1896–1994
*VE-Day Celebrations outside Buckingham
Palace* 1945
oil on canvas 34.2 x 111.7
IWM ART LD 5202

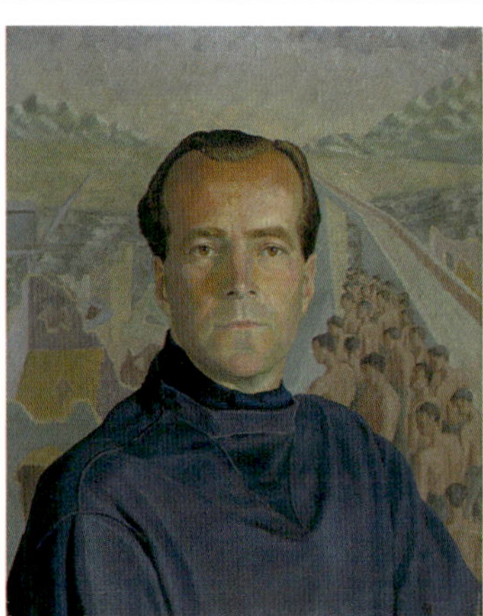

Feilding, David active 1940s
Robert Lush, a Prisoner of War 1945
oil on canvas 46 x 37.4
IWM ART LD 5403

Facing page: Dunbar, Evelyn Mary, 1906–1960, *Milking Practice with Artificial Udders* (detail), 1940, (p. 74)

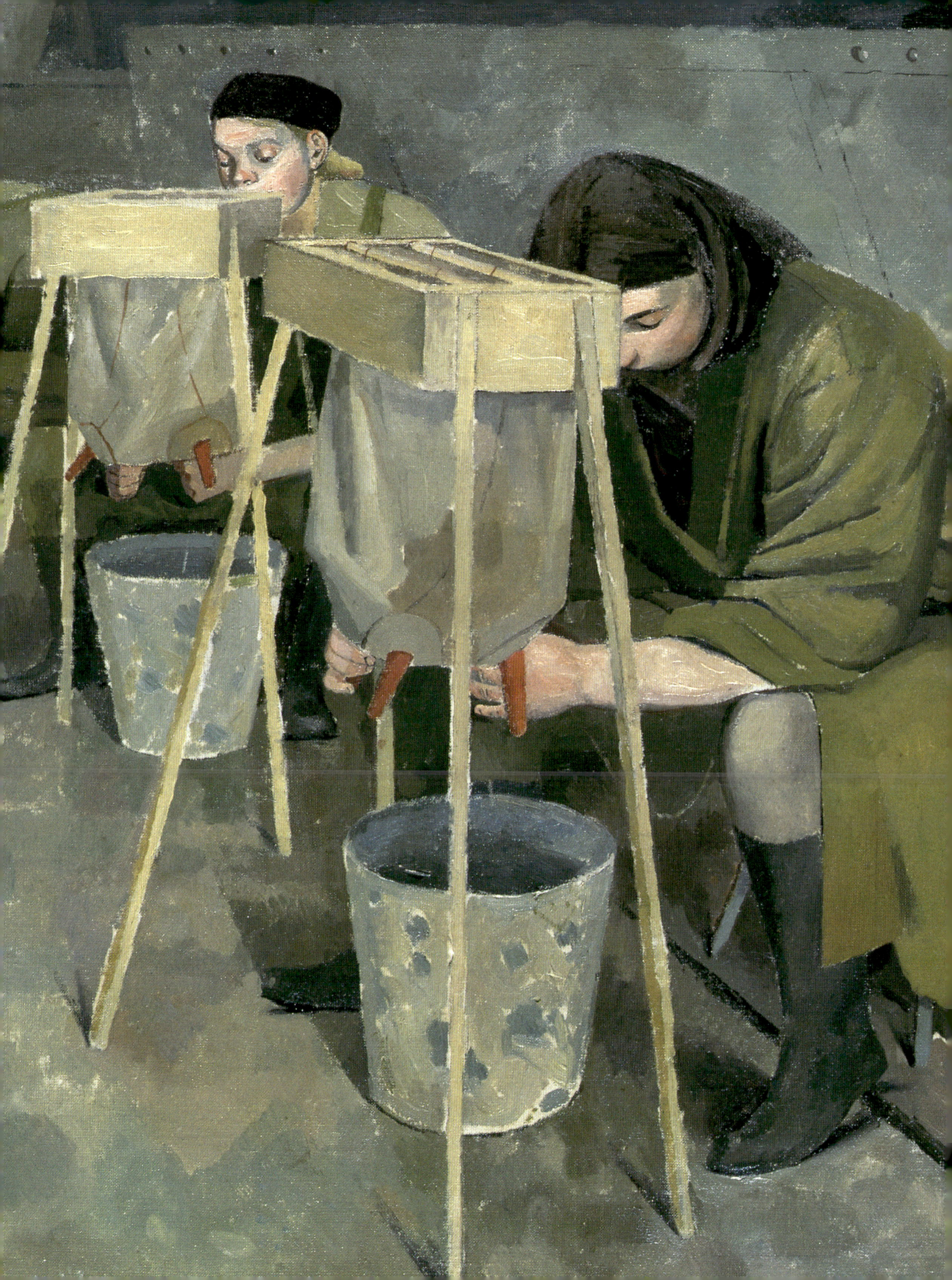

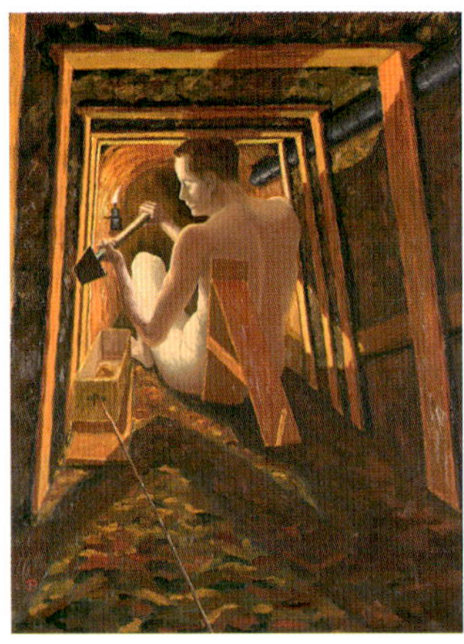

Feilding, David active 1940s
An Escape Tunnel Built by Prisoners of War
1946
oil on canvas 91.4 x 66
IWM ART LD 5877

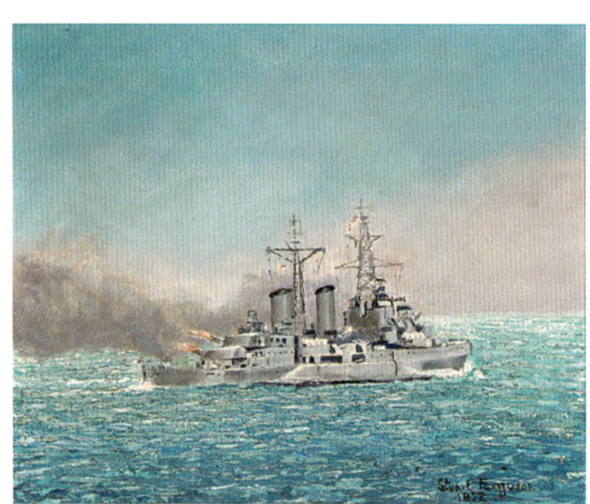

Ferguson, Stuart (Commander)
active 1970s
'HMS Belfast', Bay of Bengal 1972
oil on panel 50.2 x 60.9
IWM ART 16613

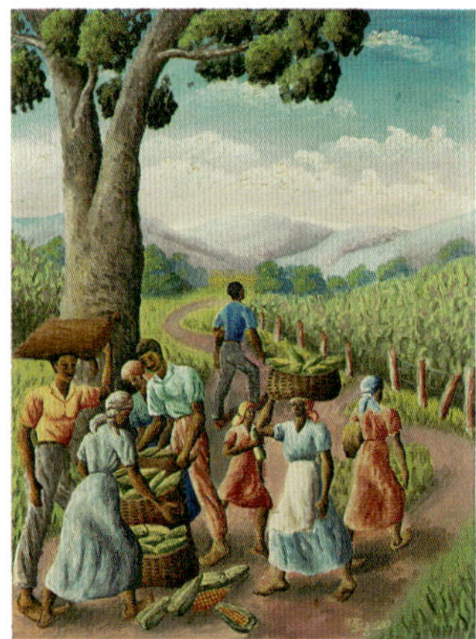

Ferguson, V. active 1940s
A Roadside Market Scene 1940s
oil on panel 54.2 x 40.6
IWM ART LD 3152

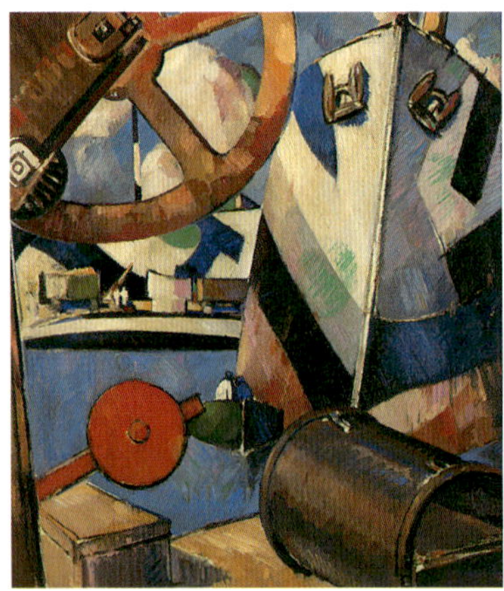

Fergusson, John Duncan 1874–1961
Dockyard, Portsmouth 1918
oil on canvas 77 x 68.8
IWM ART 5728

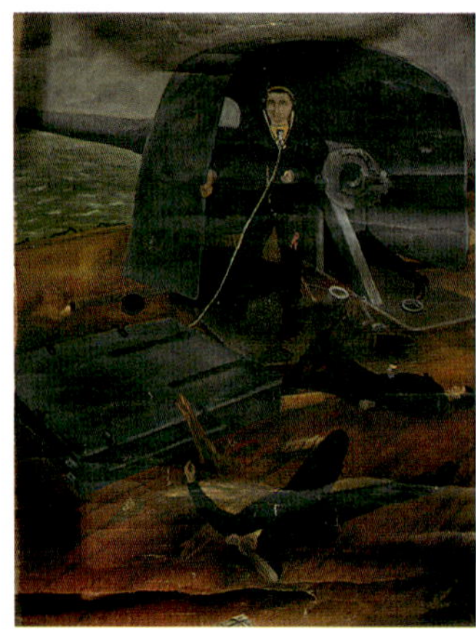

Feteridge, J. F. active 1914–1918
The FX Six-Inch Gun of 'HMS Chester' (Boy Jack Cornwall) 1917
oil on canvas 65.5 x 50.6
IWM ART 6458

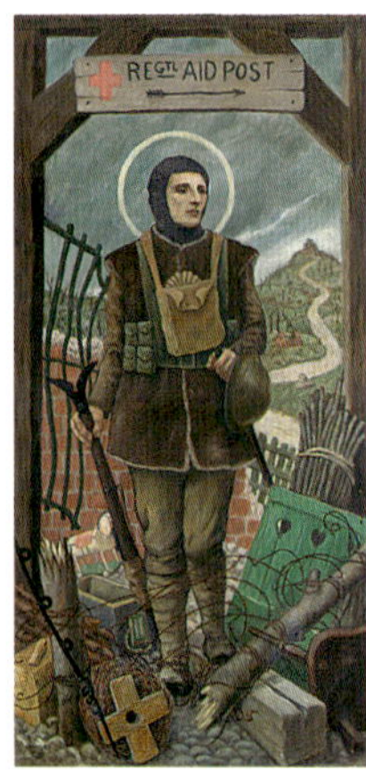

Ffoulkes, Charles 1868–1947
St George (1914–1918) 1933
oil on panel 121.2 x 60.9
IWM ART 5600

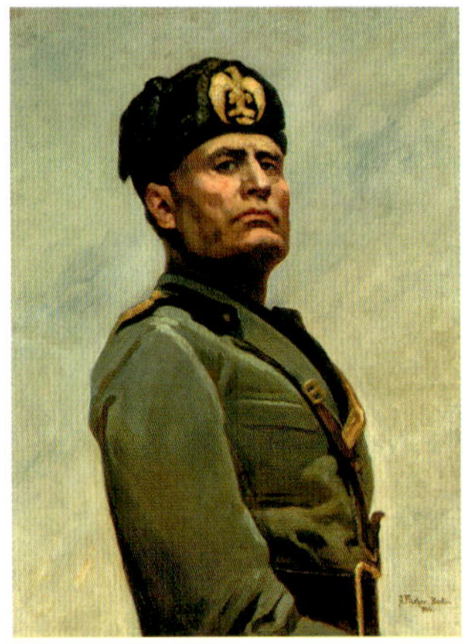

Fischer, Arthur 1872–1948
Benito Mussolini (1883–1945) 1934
oil on canvas 81.9 x 61.5
IWM ART LD 7283

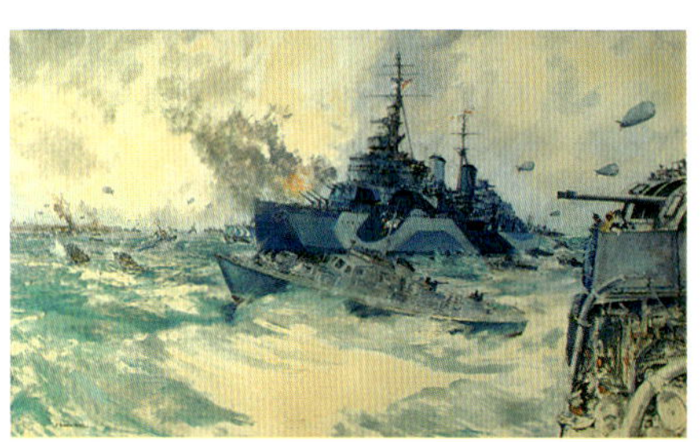

Flint, Francis Russell 1915–1977
'HMS Belfast', Normandy, 8 July 1944
c.1944–1945
oil on canvas 76.3 x 127
IWM ART 16569

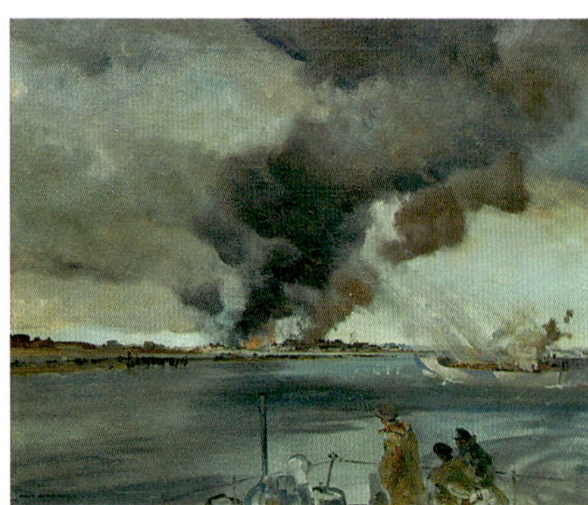

Flint, Francis Russell 1915–1977
A Rocket Ship Attacking at Walcheren 1945
oil on canvas 49.5 x 65
IWM ART LD 5464

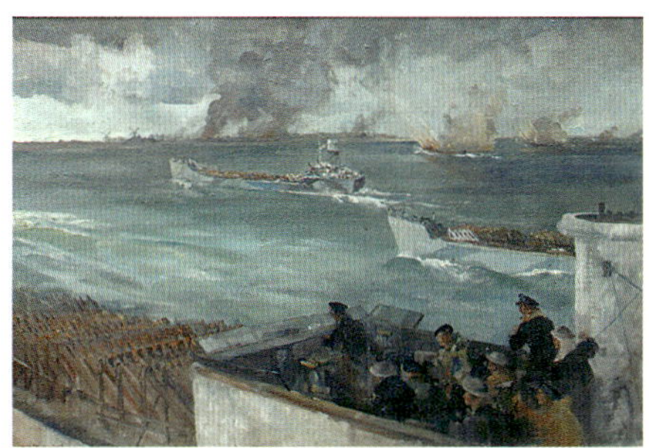

Flint, Francis Russell 1915–1977
Rocket Ships in Firing Position off Walcheren
1945
oil on canvas 49.5 x 60
IWM ART LD 5465

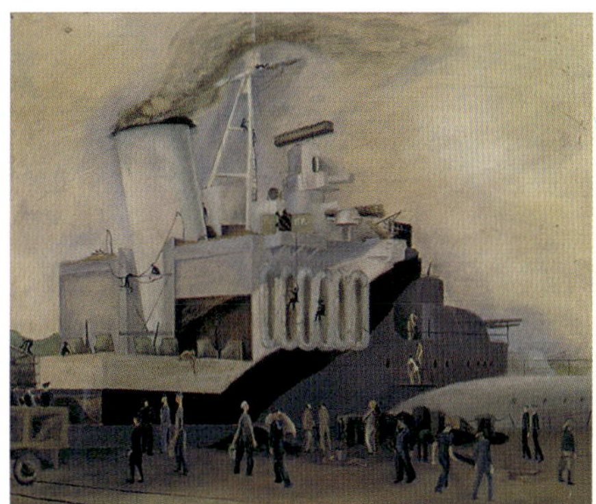

Foot, Victorine b.1920
Camouflaging a Cruiser in Dock 1943
oil on canvas 50.8 x 60.9
IWM ART LD 3016

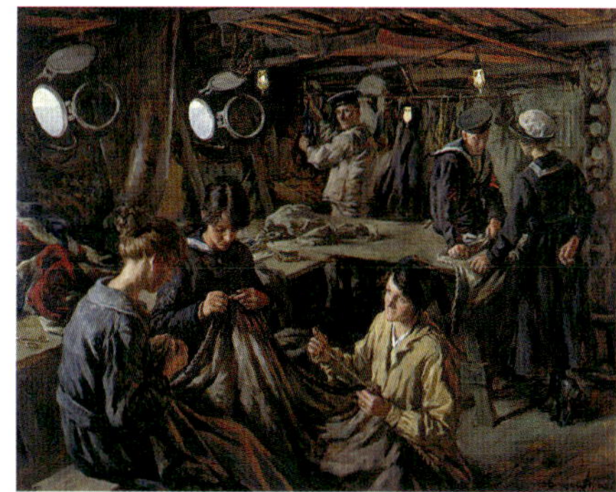

Forbes, Stanhope Alexander 1857–1947
Women's Royal Naval Service Ratings Sail-Making: Onboard 'HMS Essex' at Devonport
1918
oil on canvas 106.6 x 137.1
IWM ART 2621

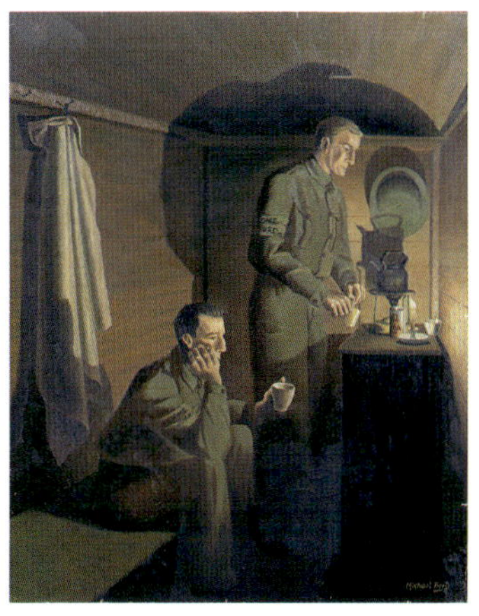

Ford, Michael b.1920
Home Guards Brewing Tea Just before Dawn
1941
oil on canvas 76.2 x 60.9
IWM ART LD 846

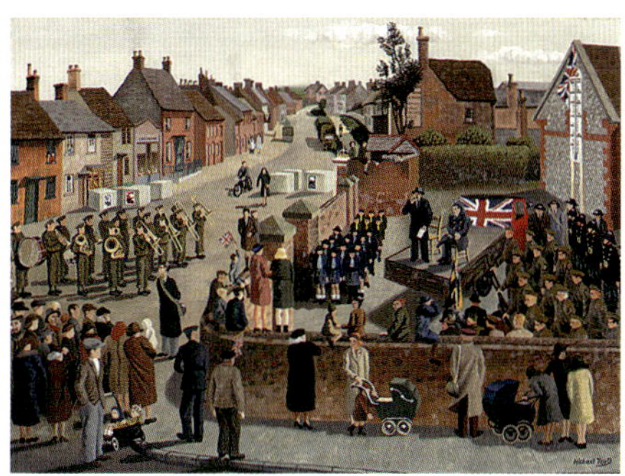

Ford, Michael b.1920
War Weapons Week in a Country Town 1941
oil on canvas 66 x 91.4
IWM ART LD 1291

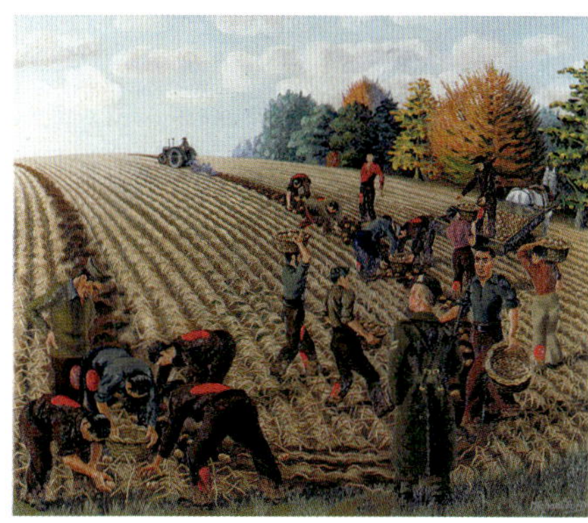

Ford, Michael b.1920
Italian Prisoners of War Working on the Land
1942
oil on canvas 76.2 x 91.4
IWM ART LD 1833

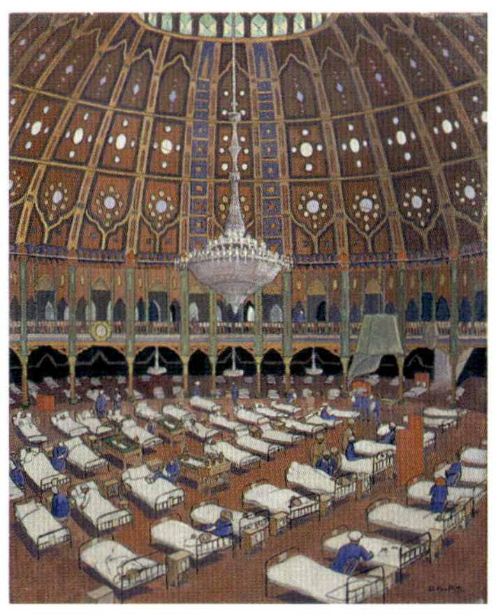

Fox-Pitt, Douglas 1864–1922
Indian Army Wounded in Hospital in the Dome, Brighton c.1919
oil on canvas 60.9 x 50.8
IWM ART 323

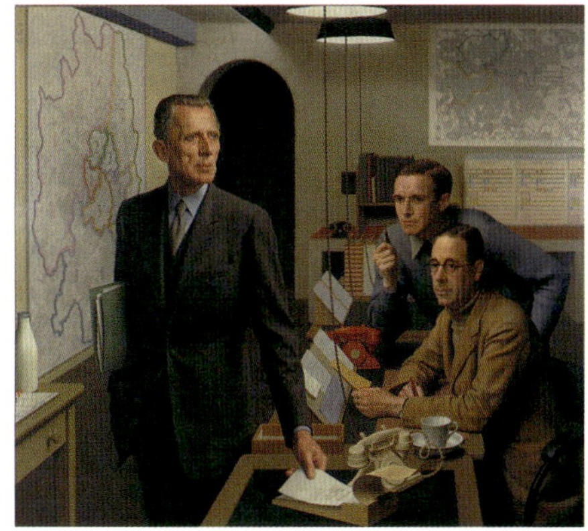

Frampton, Meredith 1894–1984
Sir Ernest Gowers (1880–1966), KCB, KBE, Senior Regional Commissioner for London, Lieutenant Colonel A. J. Child, (…) 1943
oil on canvas 148 x 168.5
IWM ART LD 2905

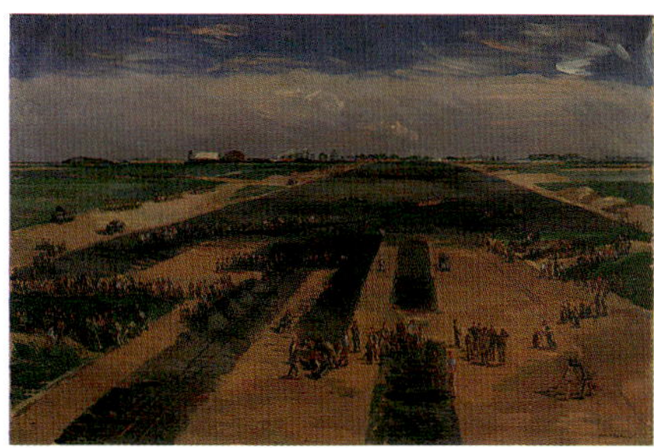

Freedman, Barnett 1901–1958
Aircraft Runway in Course of Construction at Thélus: Near Arras, May 1940 1940
oil on canvas 58.1 x 90.1
IWM ART LD 261

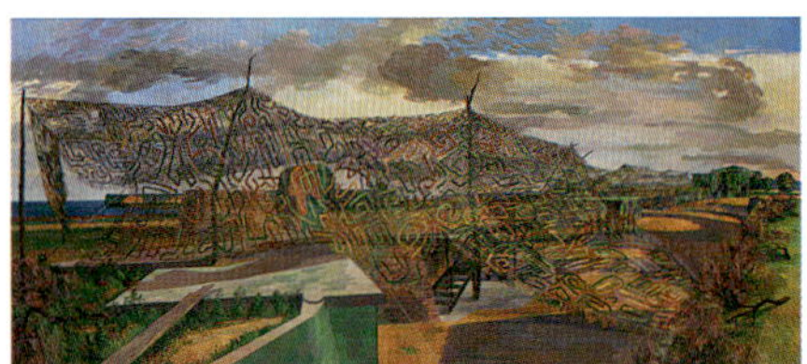

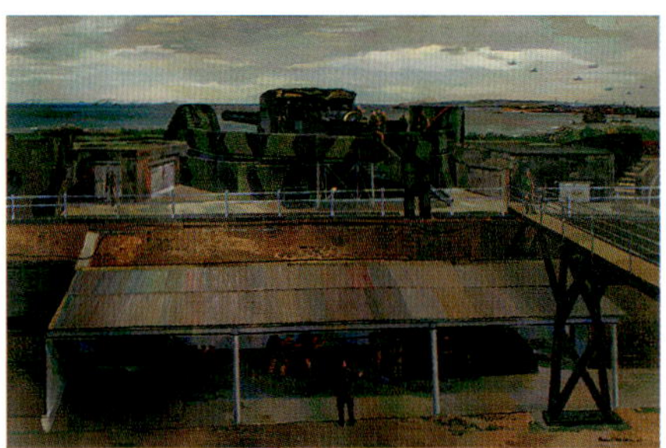

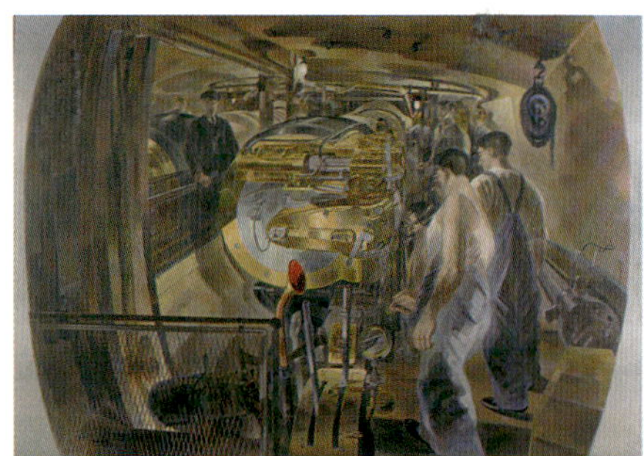

Freedman, Barnett 1901–1958
Coast Defence Battery, September 1940 1940
oil on canvas 109.8 x 245.1
IWM ART LD 838

Freedman, Barnett 1901–1958
The Gun 1940
oil on canvas 59 x 91.4
IWM ART LD 391

Freedman, Barnett 1901–1958
15-Inch Gun Turret, 'HMS Repulse' 1942
oil on canvas 200.6 x 292.1
IWM ART LD 2295

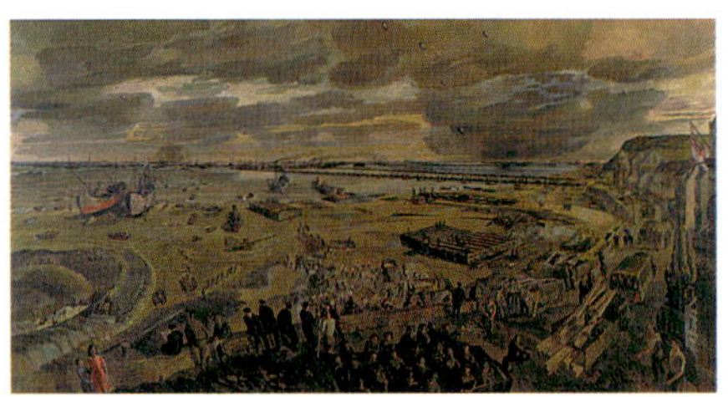

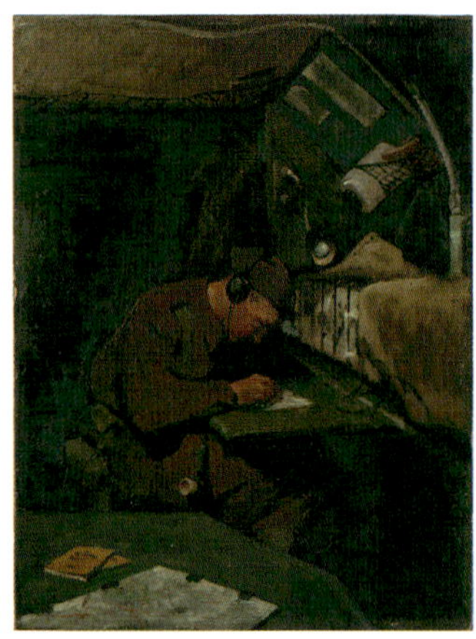

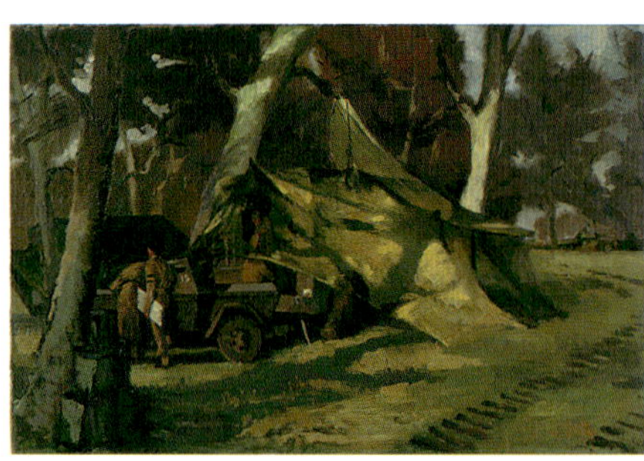

Freedman, Barnett 1901–1958
The Landing in Normandy, Arromanches: D-Day Plus 20, 26 June 1944 1944
oil on canvas 154.9 x 304.8
IWM ART LD 5816

Freeth, Thomas 1912–1997
A Wireless Operator in an Armoured Command Vehicle 1942
oil on canvas 45.7 x 35.5
IWM ART LD 2645

Freeth, Thomas 1912–1997
A Liaison Officer Arriving at the Headquarters of an Armoured Division 1943
oil on canvas 50.8 x 76.8
IWM ART LD 3287

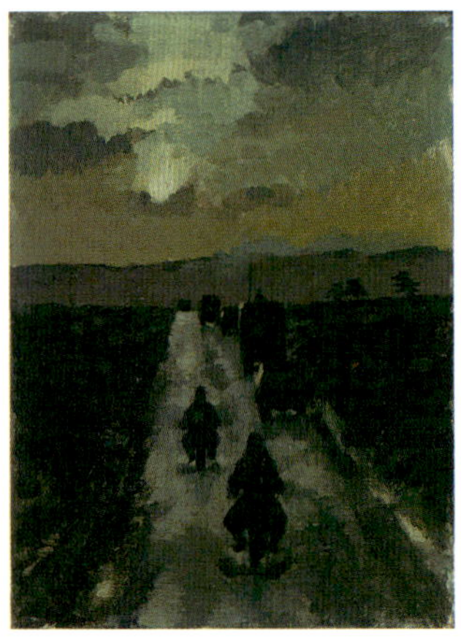

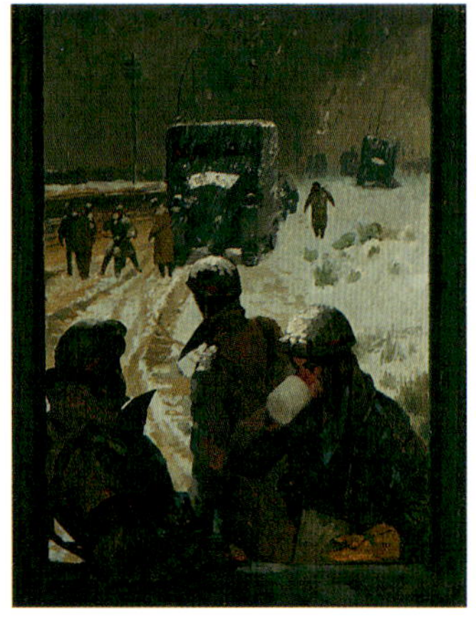

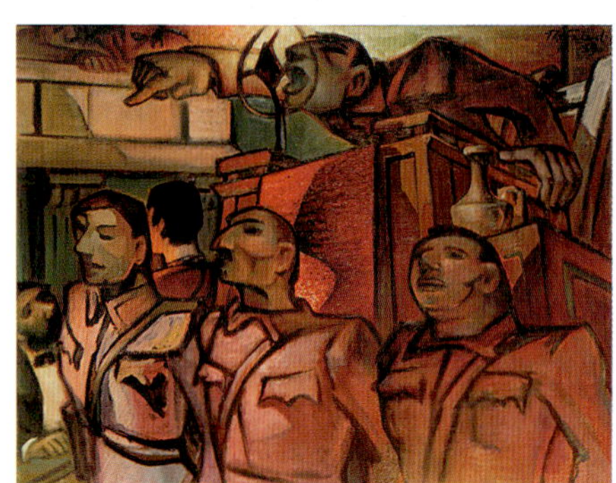

Freeth, Thomas 1912–1997
Divisional HQ in Convoy at First Light 1944
oil on canvas 29.8 x 22.2
IWM ART LD 4358

Freeth, Thomas 1912–1997
Twenty Minutes Halt: Divisional HQ in Convoy 1944
oil on canvas 75.5 x 60
IWM ART LD 4357

Fried, Theodore 1902–1980
Propagande 1939
oil on canvas 88.9 x 116.8
IWM ART LD 7208

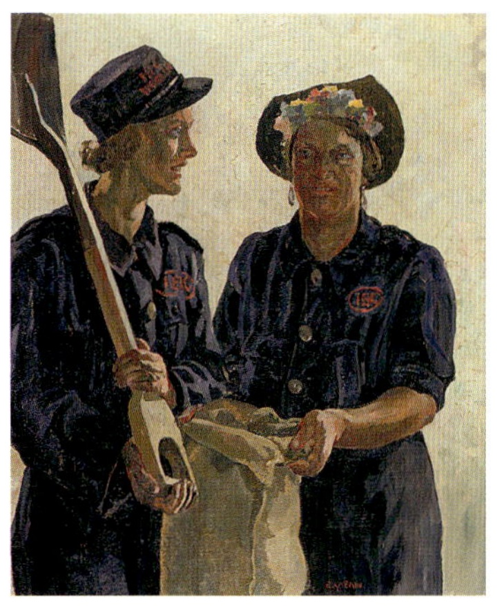

Gabain, Ethel 1883–1950
Sandbag Filling, Islington Borough Council
c.1941
oil on canvas 76.2 x 63.5
IWM ART LD 1443

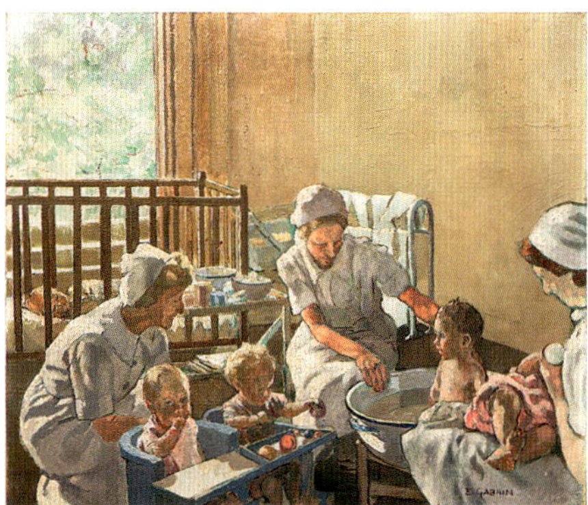

Gabain, Ethel 1883–1950
A Crèche c.1942
oil on canvas 50.8 x 60.9
IWM ART LD 2761

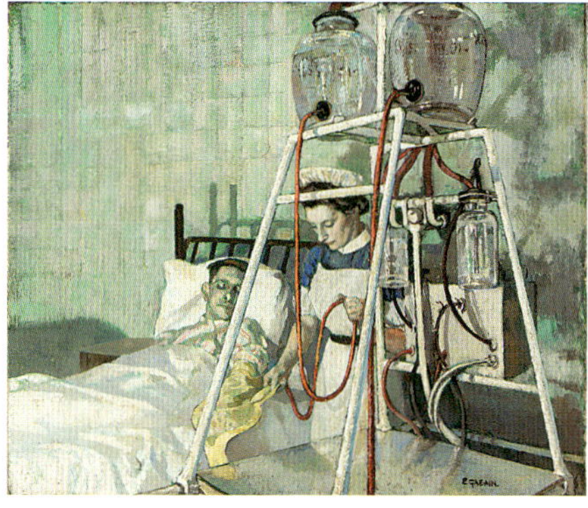

Gabain, Ethel 1883–1950
*A Bunyan-Stannard Irrigation Envelope for the
Treatment of Burns, Applied by Sister Roberts
in Middlesex Hospital* 1943
oil on canvas 62.2 x 74.9
IWM ART LD 3850

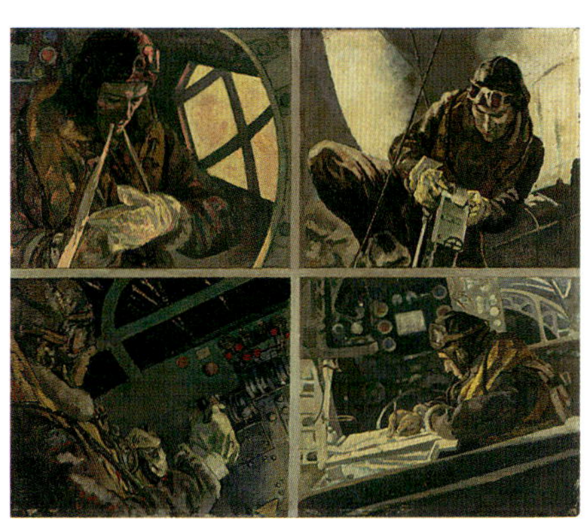

Gabain, Ethel 1883–1950
*A Bunyan-Stannard First Aid Envelope for
Protection against Infection in Burns, as Issued
to the Royal Air Force* c.1943
oil on panel 63.5 x 76.2
IWM ART LD 3849

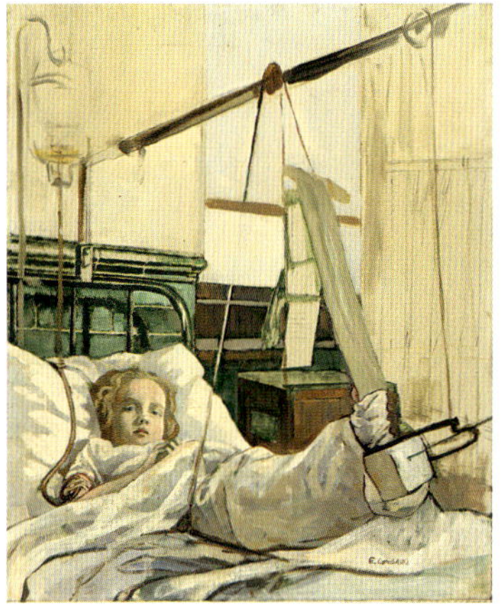

Gabain, Ethel 1883–1950
*A Child Bomb Victim Receiving Penicillin
Treatment* 1944
oil on canvas 76.2 x 63.5
IWM ART LD 5775

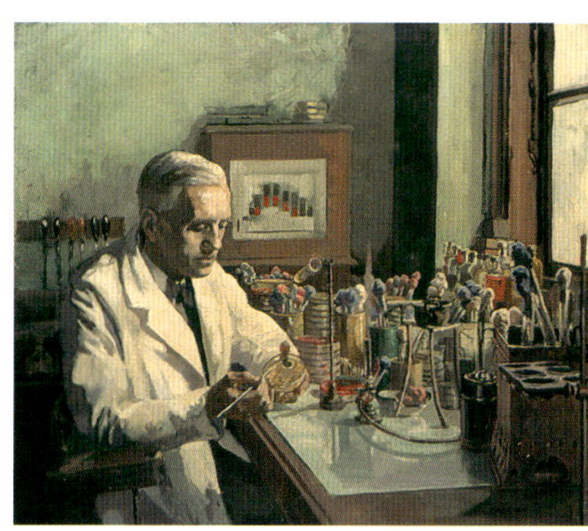

Gabain, Ethel 1883–1950
*Sir Alexander Fleming (1881–1955), FRS, the
Discoverer of Penicillin* 1944
oil on canvas 62.2 x 74.9
IWM ART LD 4217

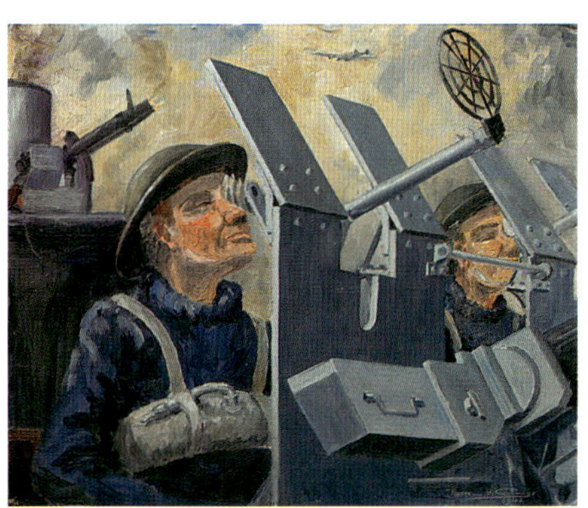

Gammage, Russell V. 1920–2001
Anti-Aircraft Gun and Crew 1942
oil on canvas 50.1 x 60.3
IWM ART LD 6160

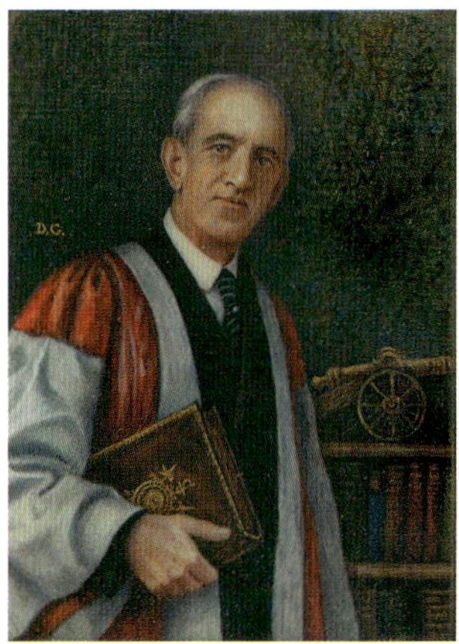

Garratt, Dorothy A. active 1912–1940
Dr Charles Ffoulkes, CB c.1920s
oil on card 12 x 9
IWM ART 16168

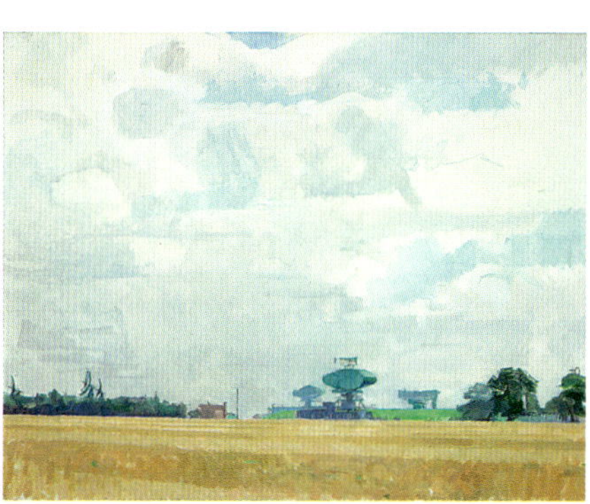

George, Patrick b.1923
Early Warning Radar Site, RAF Neatishead
1981
oil on canvas 77.5 x 100.5
IWM ART 15402

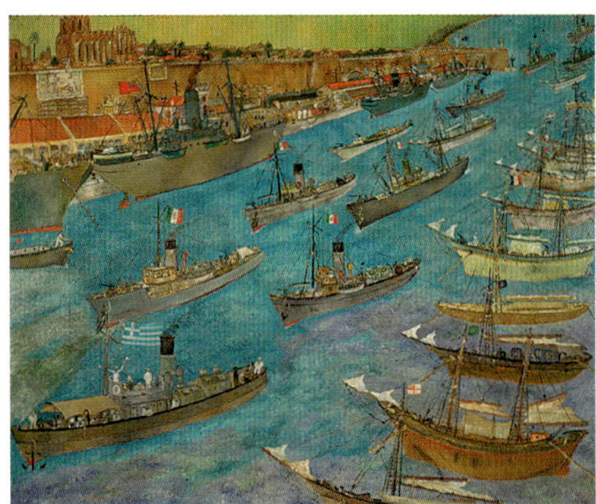

Georghiou, Georgios Polybius 1901–1972
*Italians Surrendering at Famagusta, Cyprus,
13 September 1943* 1943
oil on panel 100.3 x 121.9
IWM ART LD 5934

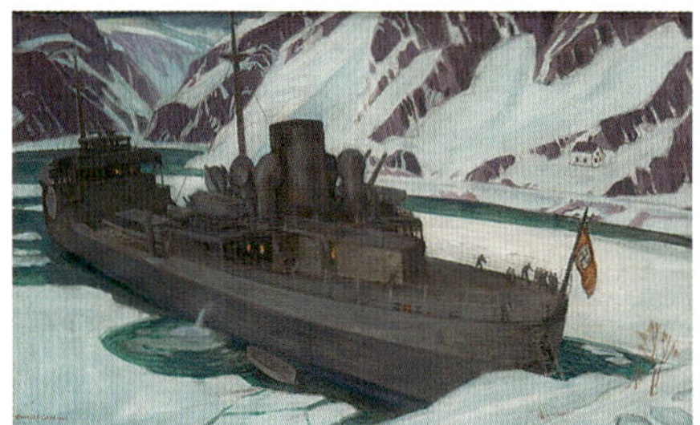

Gere, Charles March 1869–1957
The Standard Prison Ship 1940
oil on canvas 43 x 69.8
IWM ART LD 6358

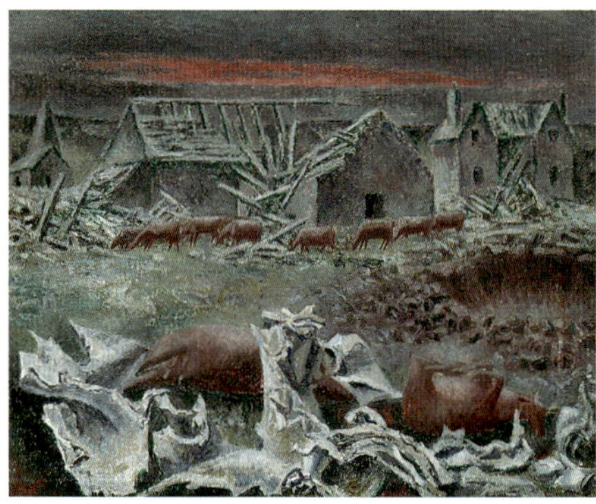

Gerrard, Kaff 1894–1970
Bomb Damage with Cows c.1944
oil on canvas 50.7 x 61
IWM ART 16413

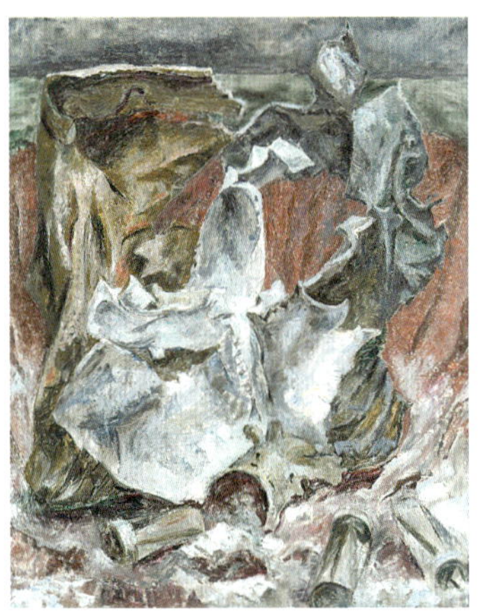

Gerrard, Kaff 1894–1970
Bomb Fragments with Incendiaries c.1944
oil on canvas 76 x 63.5
IWM ART 16411

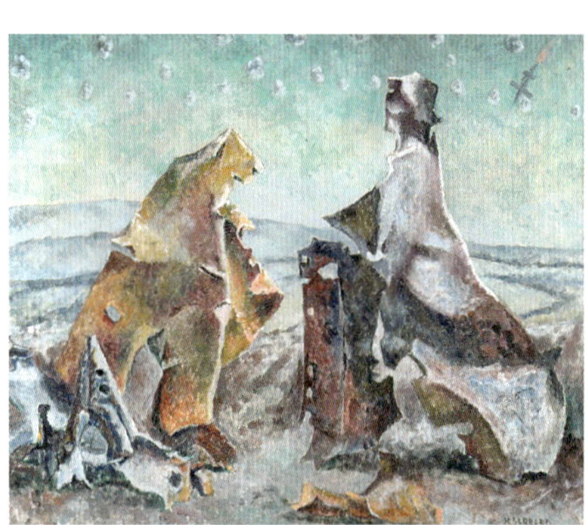

Gerrard, Kaff 1894–1970
Twisted Metal and Doodlebug c.1944
oil on canvas 63.7 x 76.5
IWM ART 16412

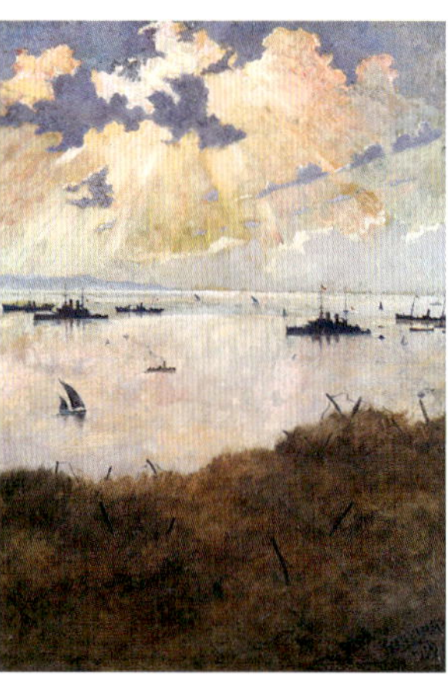

Gibbings, Robert 1889–1958
*Gallipoli: Sunset over Lemnos, 'HMS Triumph'
and 'HMS Swiftsure'* 1919
oil on canvas 74.9 x 54.6
IWM ART 2822

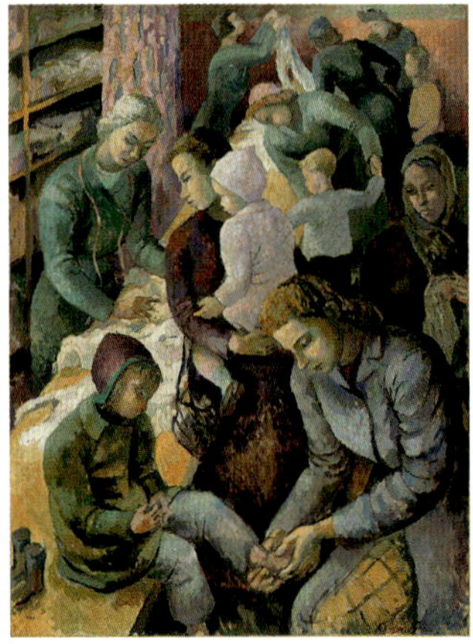

Gibbs, Evelyn 1905–1991
Women's Voluntary Services Clothing Exchange
1943
oil on canvas 101.9 x 76.2
IWM ART LD 3918

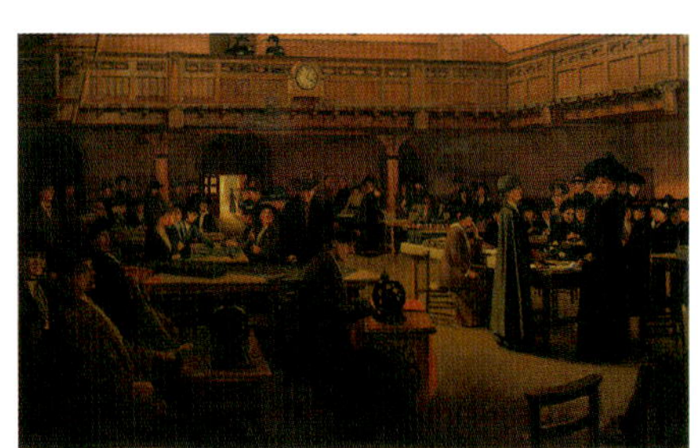

Gibbs, J. B. 1859–1935
Congleton War-Working Party 1917
oil on canvas 76.2 x 127
IWM ART 1628

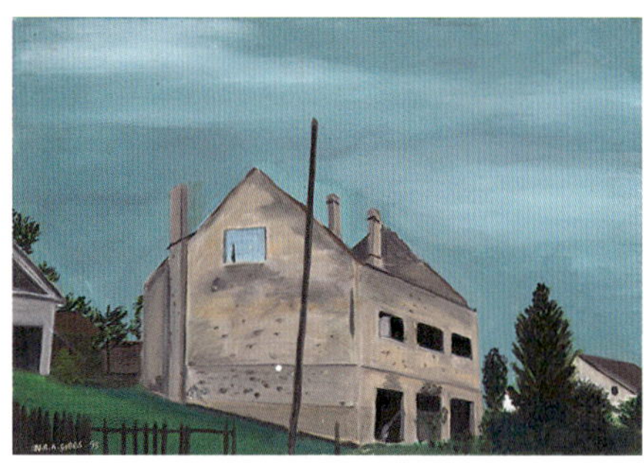

Gibbs, Nicholas b.1957
Ruins of War 1995
oil on canvas 45 x 66
IWM ART 17142

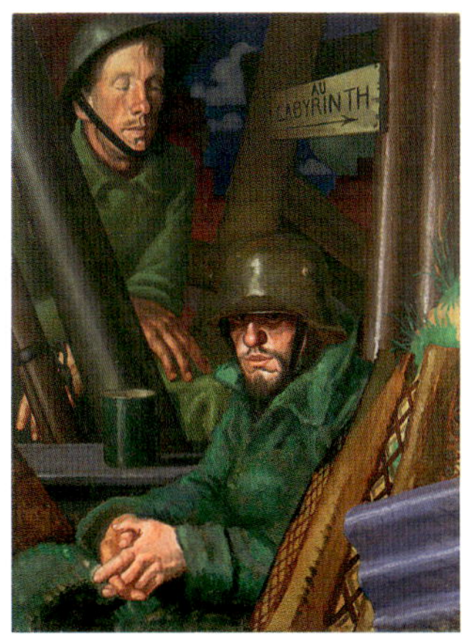

Gill, Colin Unwin 1892–1940
The Captive 1918
oil on canvas 101.9 x 76.2
IWM ART 1209

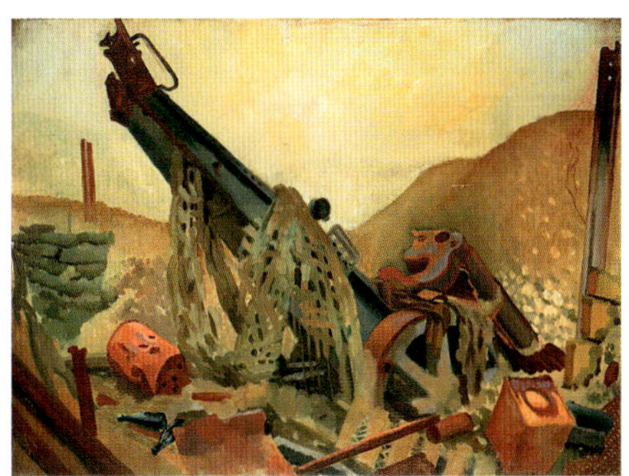

Gill, Colin Unwin 1892–1940
A Captured Howitzer at Fampoux 1919
oil on canvas 55.8 x 76.2
IWM ART 2279

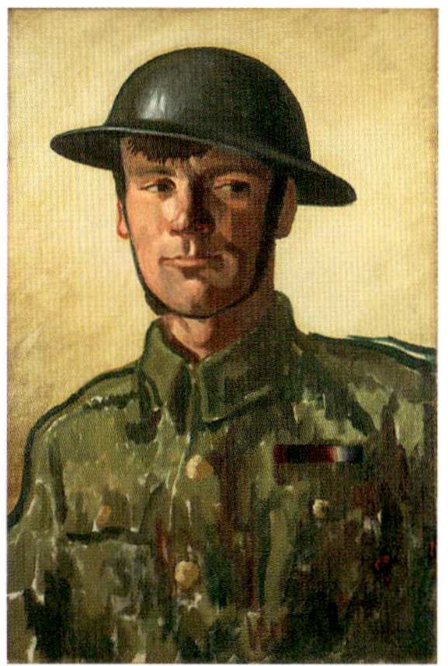

Gill, Colin Unwin 1892–1940
A Gunner 1919
oil on canvas 55.8 x 38.1
IWM ART 2281

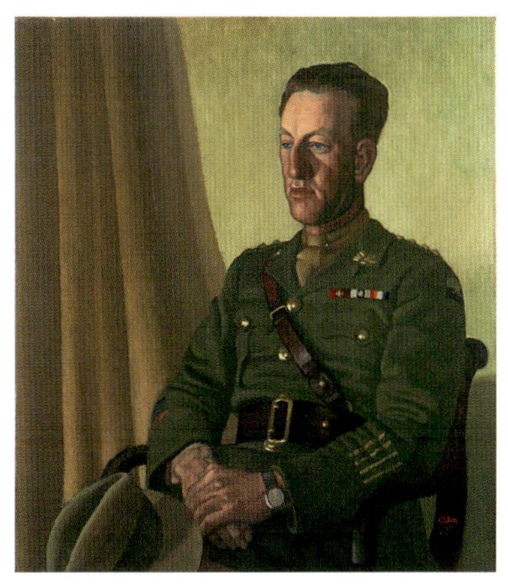

Gill, Colin Unwin 1892–1940
Captain Albert Jacka (1893–1932), VC, MC and Bar 1919
oil on canvas 91.4 x 81.2
IWM ART 1915

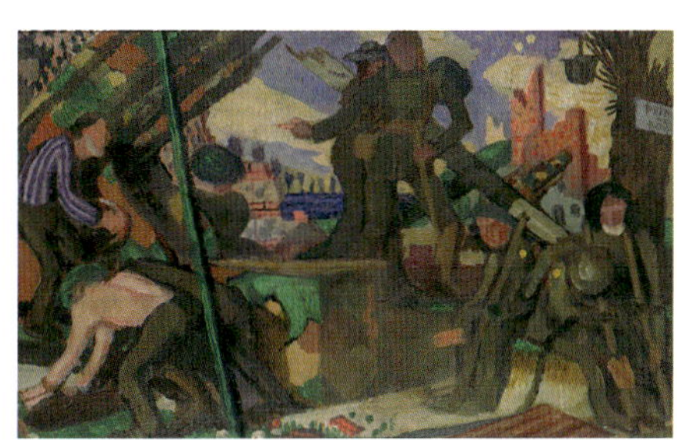

Gill, Colin Unwin 1892–1940
Design for 'Heavy Artillery' 1919
oil on panel 29.2 x 46.9
IWM ART 3896

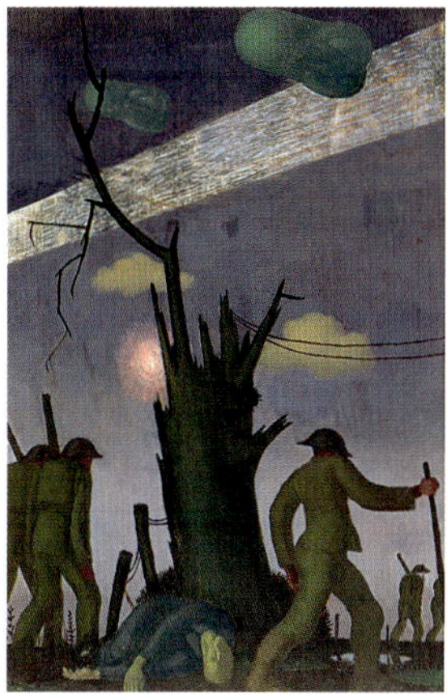

Gill, Colin Unwin 1892–1940
Evening after a Push 1919
oil on canvas 76.2 x 50.8
IWM ART 1210

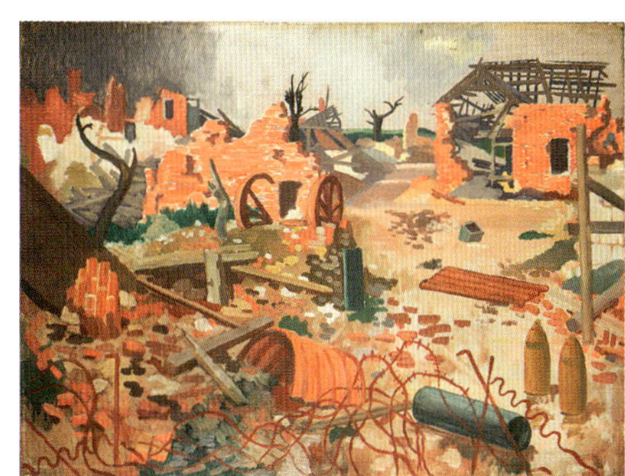

Gill, Colin Unwin 1892–1940
Fampoux 1919
oil on canvas 55.8 x 76.2
IWM ART 2280

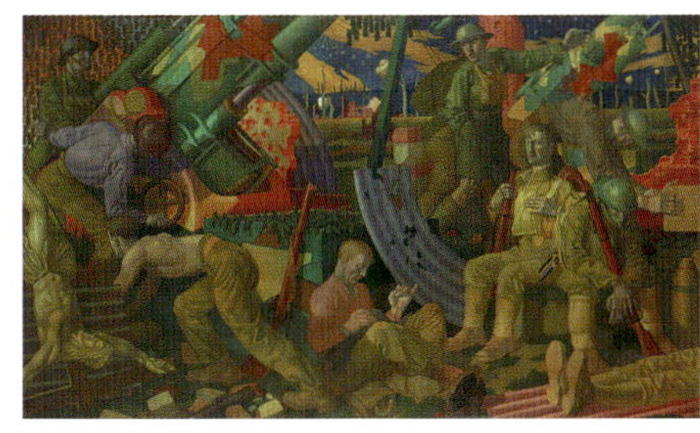

Gill, Colin Unwin 1892–1940
Heavy Artillery 1919
oil on canvas 182.8 x 317.5
IWM ART 2274

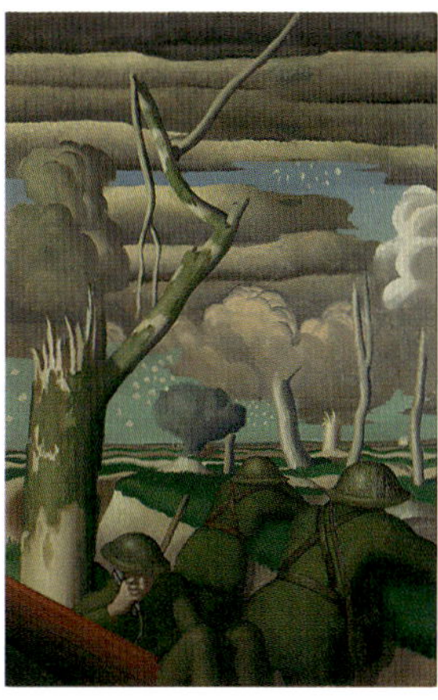

Gill, Colin Unwin 1892–1940
Observation of Fire: Gunner Officers Correcting Their Battery Fire by Field Telephone from a Disused Trench (…) 1919
oil on canvas 76.2 x 50.8
IWM ART 2297

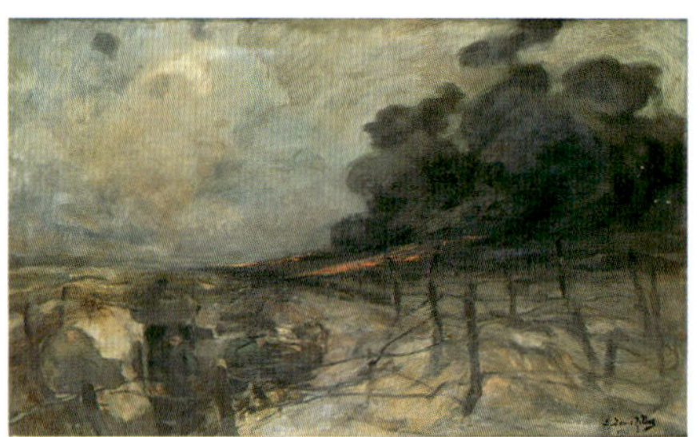

Gillot, Eugène Louis 1868–1925
An Attack by Flamethrowers 1918
oil on panel 48.2 x 80
IWM ART 876

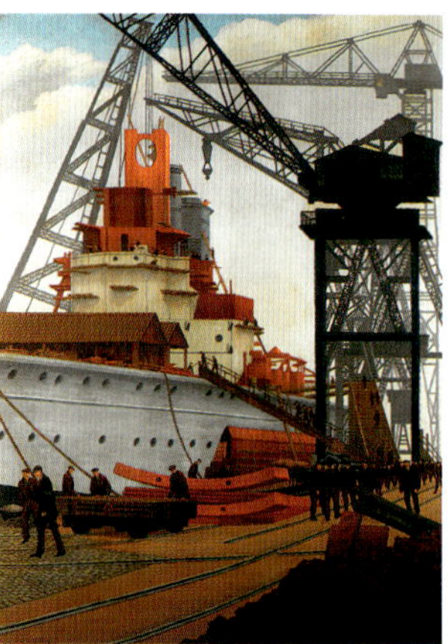

Ginner, Charles 1878–1952
Building a Battleship 1940
oil on canvas 83.8 x 60.9
IWM ART LD 252

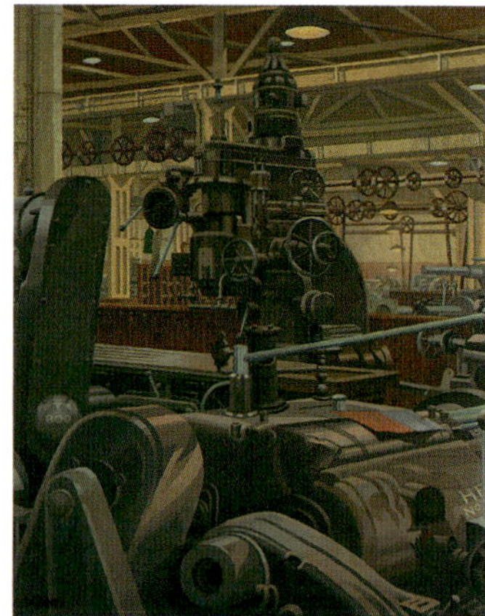

Ginner, Charles 1878–1952
Machine Tools for Russia 1942
oil on canvas 76.2 x 60.9
IWM ART LD 2809

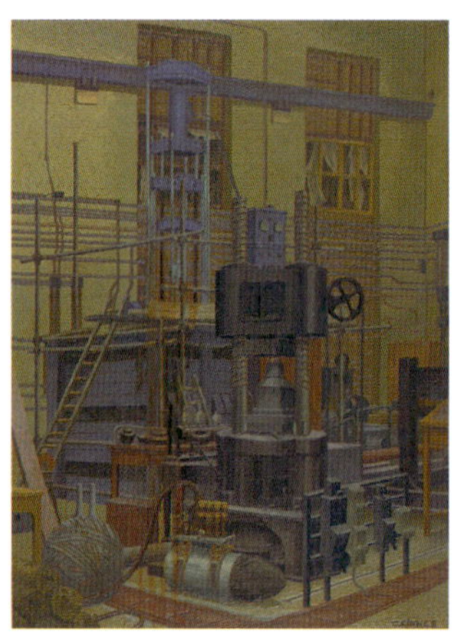

Ginner, Charles 1878–1952
The National Physical Laboratory, Teddington
1945
oil on canvas 76.2 x 55.8
IWM ART LD 5693

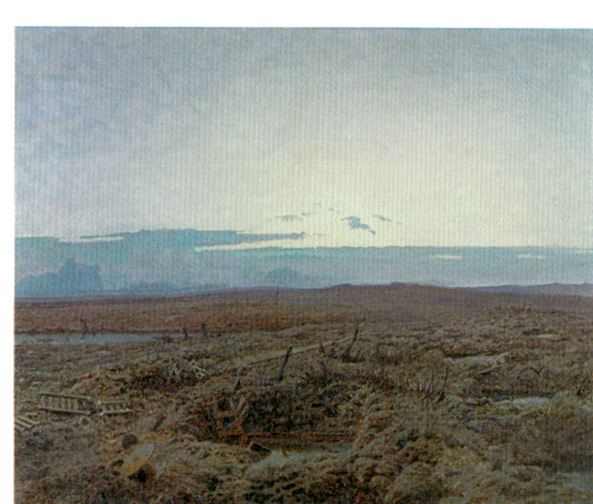

Ginnett, Louis 1875–1946
Ypres Salient, Dawn, February 1918 1918
oil on canvas 90.1 x 114.3
IWM ART 5207

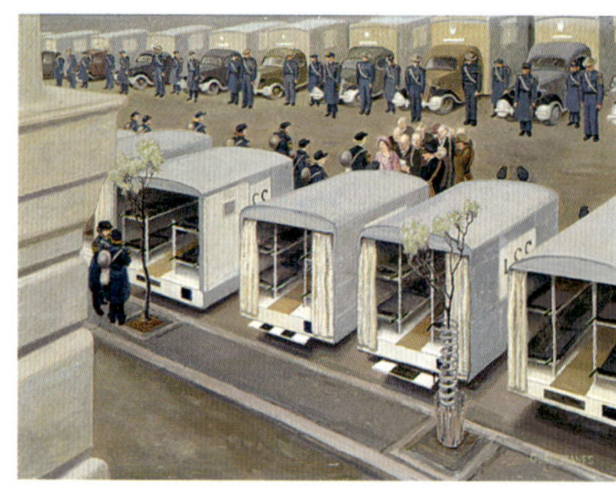

Gledstanes, Elsie 1891–1982
*Her Majesty the Queen Reviewing at County
Hall, May 1940* 1940
oil on canvas 45.8 x 61.1
IWM ART LD 6092

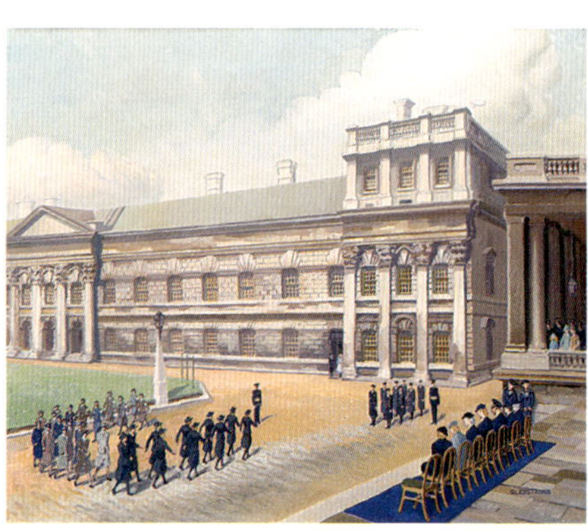

Gledstanes, Elsie 1891–1982
*The Duchess of Kent Reviewing Women's Royal
Naval Service Training, Summer 1940* 1940
oil on canvas 50.5 x 61
IWM ART LD 6063

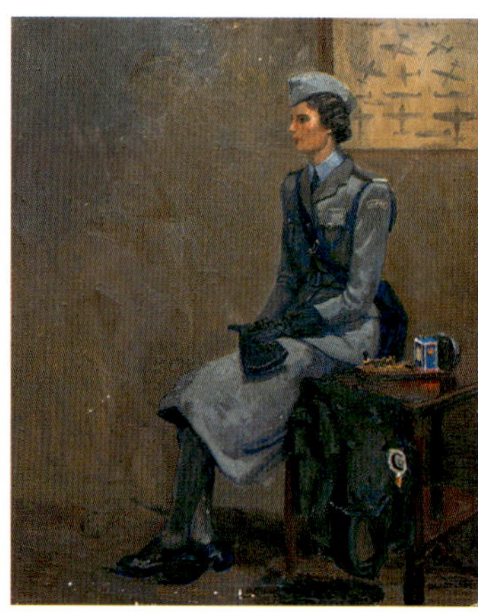

Gledstanes, Elsie 1891–1982
A Women's Royal Naval Service Officer c.1940
oil on canvas 60.8 x 51
IWM ART LD 6080

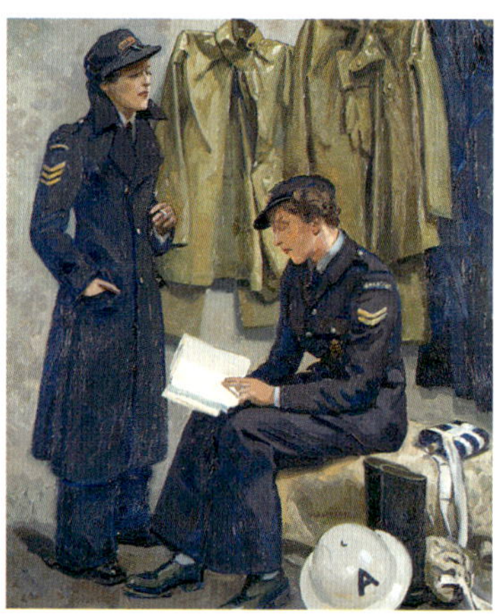

Gledstanes, Elsie 1891–1982
*Ambulance Drivers, Non-Commissioned
Officers* c.1940
oil on board 61 x 51
IWM ART LD 6090

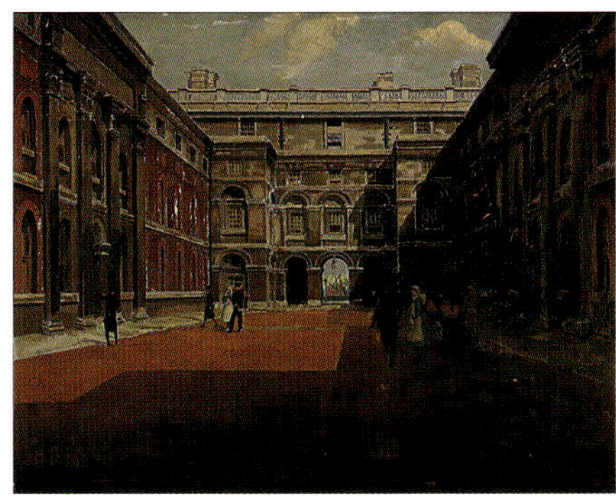

Gledstanes, Elsie 1891–1982
Courtyard, Queen Anne's House, Greenwich
c.1940
oil on board 60.8 x 77.1
IWM ART LD 6088

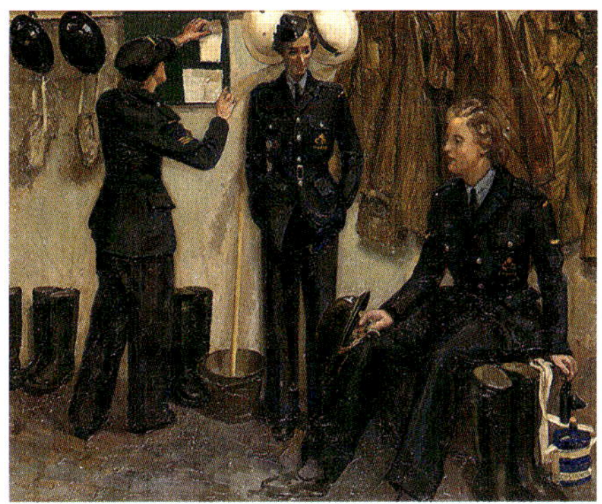

Gledstanes, Elsie 1891–1982
Drivers on Duty at an Ambulance Station
c.1940
oil on board 51 x 61
IWM ART LD 6091

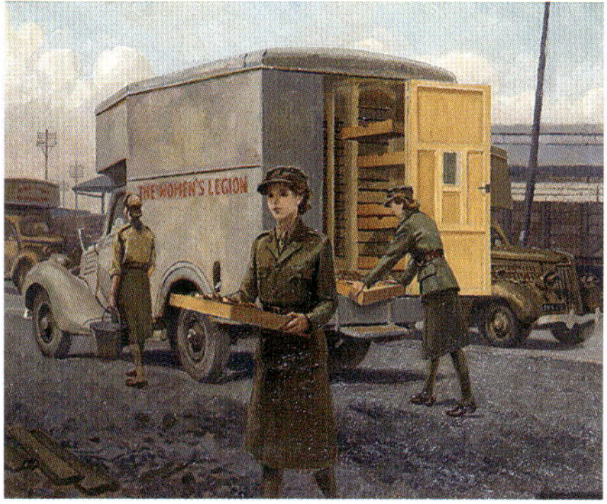

Gledstanes, Elsie 1891–1982
Food Van at the Royal Docks, London Women's Legion c.1940
oil on board 51 x 61
IWM ART LD 6093

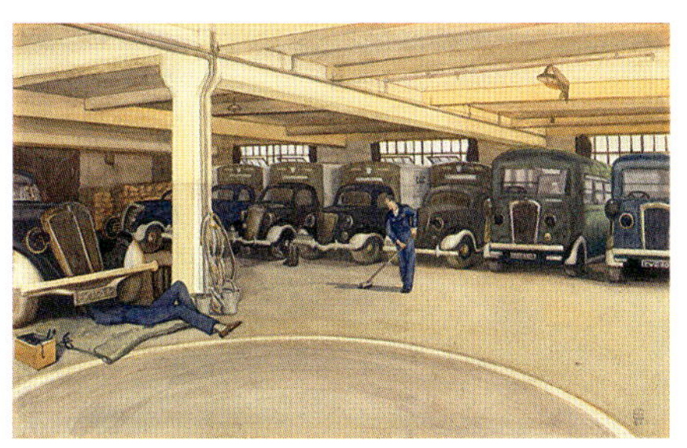

Gledstanes, Elsie 1891–1982
No.39a London Auxiliary Ambulance Station
c.1940
oil on card 29.1 x 47
IWM ART LD 6081

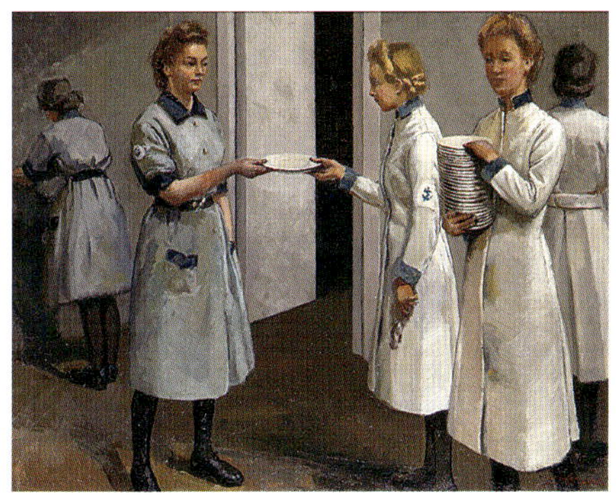

Gledstanes, Elsie 1891–1982
The Dirty Plate c.1940
oil on canvas 40.5 x 51
IWM ART LD 6089

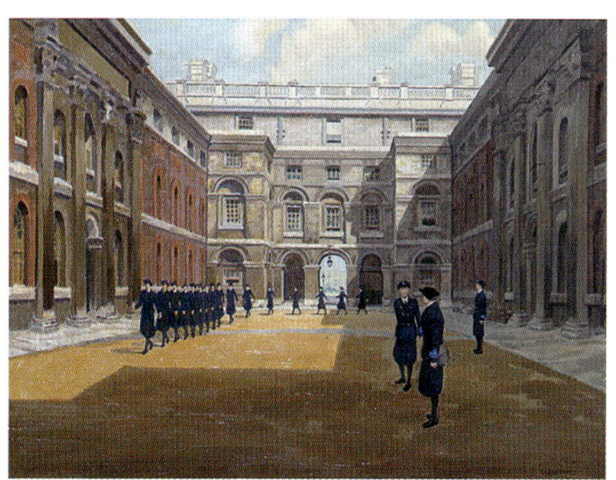

Gledstanes, Elsie 1891–1982
Women's Royal Naval Service Ratings Drill and Inspection in the Courtyard of Queen Anne's House, Greenwich
oil on board 59.7 x 76.3
IWM ART LD 6087

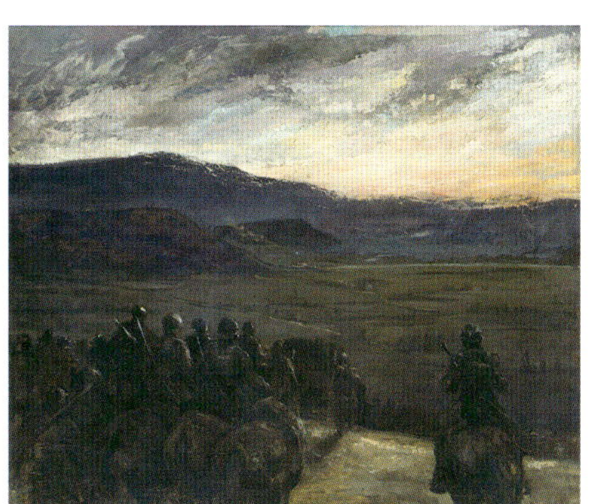

Gleichen, Helena 1873–1947
Troops Moving into Gorizia c.1917–1919
oil on canvas 107.9 x 126.3
IWM ART 5044

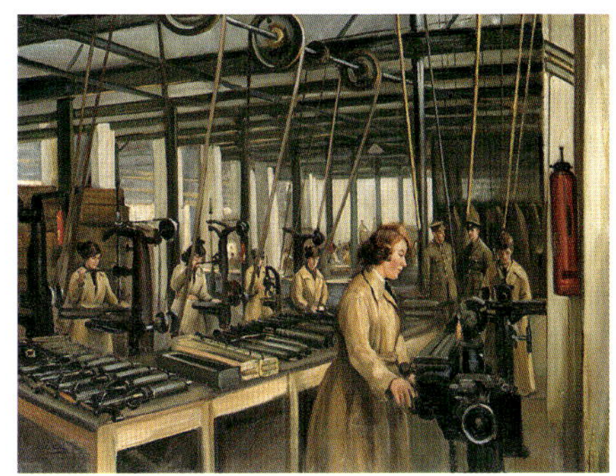

Glen, Graham active 1897–1919
Armament School, Uxbridge: Women's Royal Air Force at Work in Aerial Gun-Testing Shop
1918–1919
oil on canvas 71.1 x 91.4
IWM ART 2458

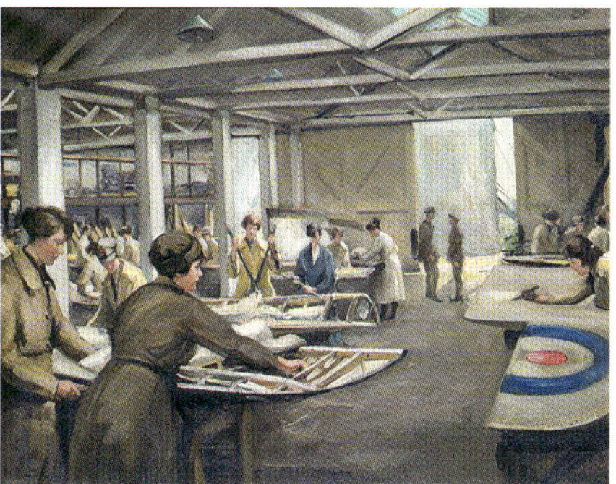

Glen, Graham active 1897–1919
No.1 Southern Aircraft Repair Depot, South Farnborough: Women's Royal Air Force at Work on Aeroplane Salvage 1918–1919
oil on canvas 71.1 x 91.4
IWM ART 2459

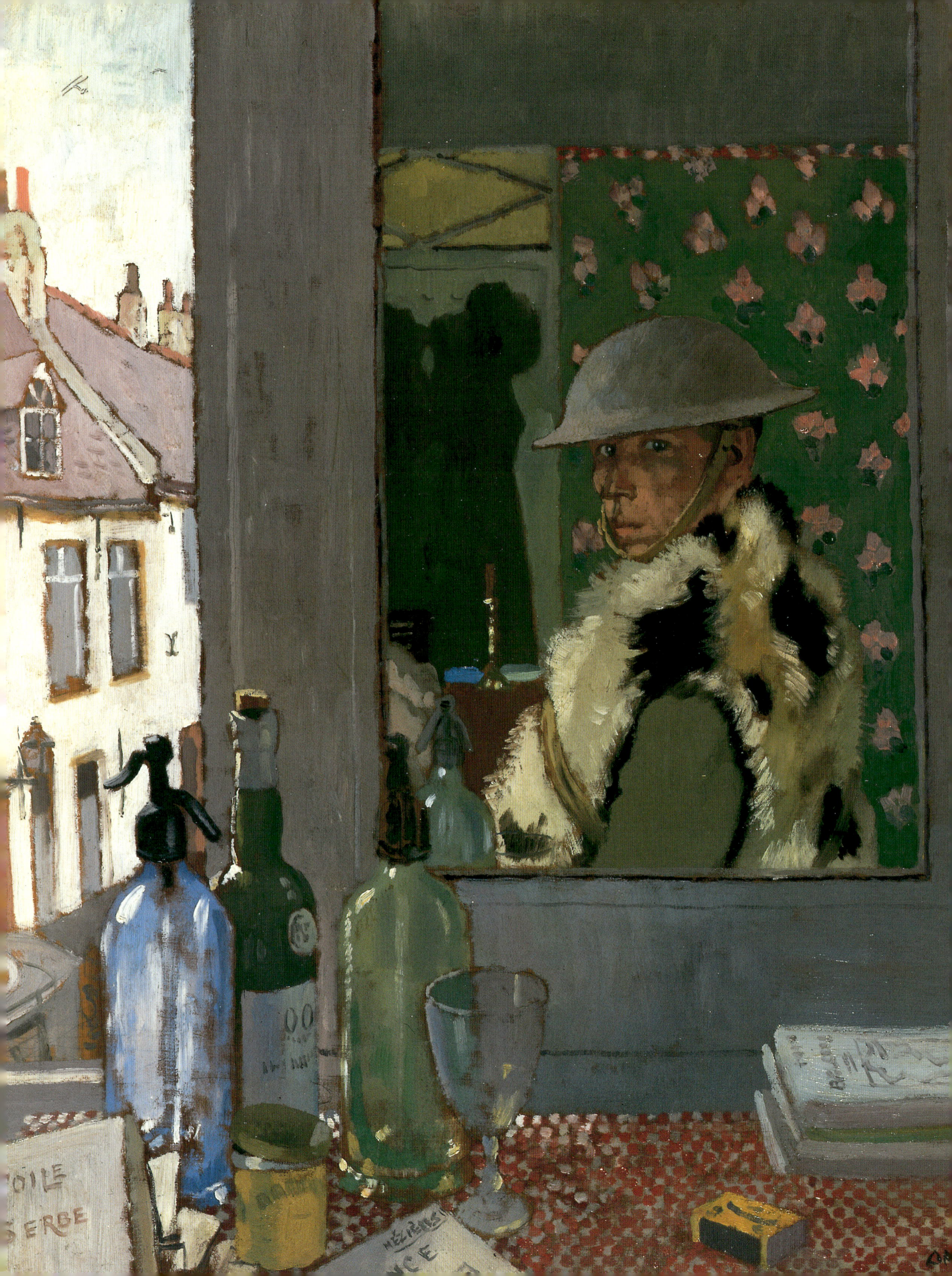

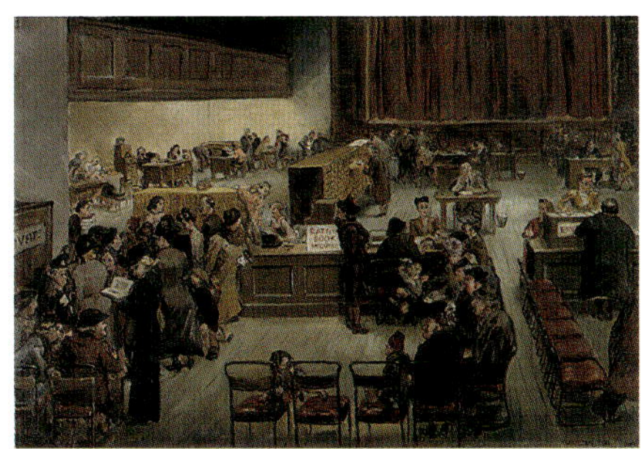

Golden, Grace Lydia 1904–1993
An Emergency Food Office 1941
oil on canvas 38.1 x 55.8
IWM ART LD 923

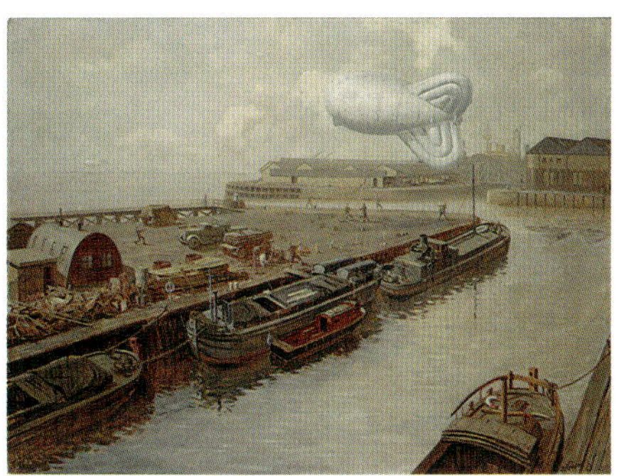

Goodin, Walter 1907–1992
A Barrage Balloon over a Dock at Hull c.1942
oil on panel 100.3 x 137.1
IWM ART LD 3008

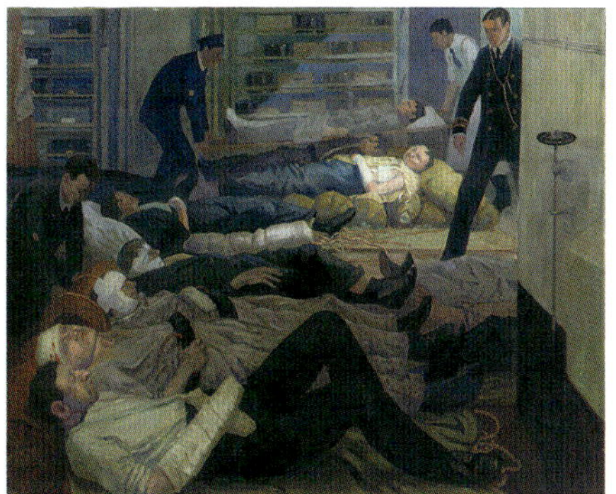

Gordon, Jan 1882–1944
'HMS Castor': Wounded, Received after the Battle of Jutland, 31 May 1916 1916
oil on panel 101.9 x 127 (E)
IWM ART 2781

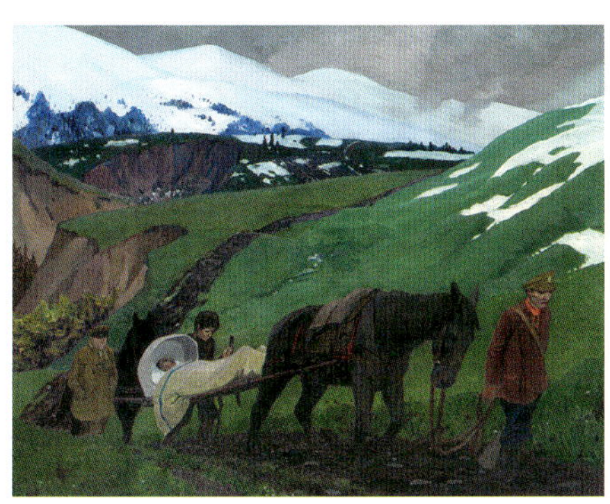

Gordon, Jan 1882–1944
Royal Navy Armoured Car Squadron: Transport of Wounded on the Turkish Front c.1918–1919
oil on canvas 101.9 x 127 (E)
IWM ART 4003

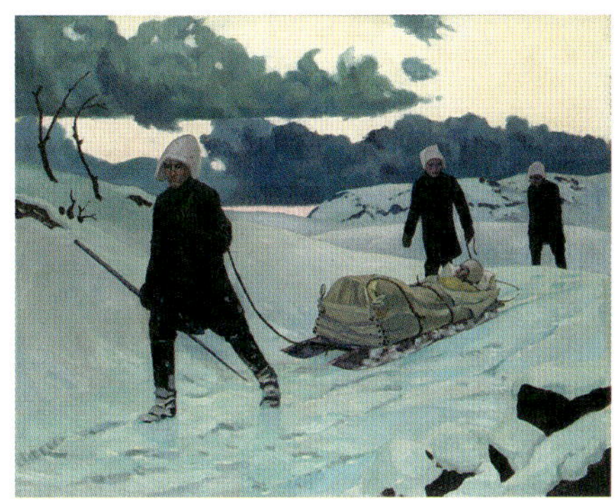

Gordon, Jan 1882–1944
Royal Navy Armoured Car Squadron: Winter Transport of Wounded at Alexandrovsk c.1918–1919
oil on canvas 101.9 x 127
IWM ART 4011

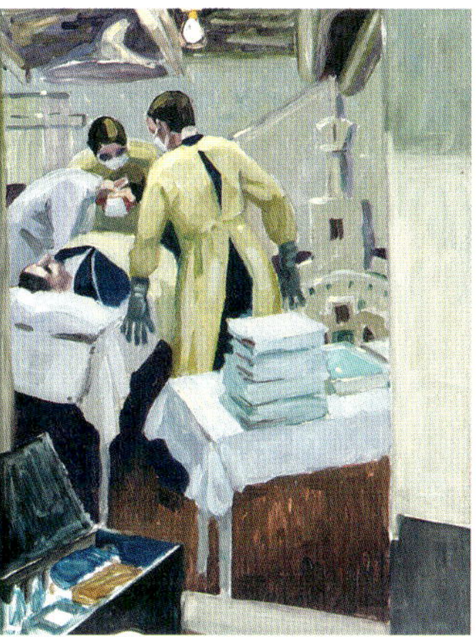

Gordon, Jan 1882–1944
The Dressing Station in a Man-of-War c.1918–1919
oil on panel 44.4 x 35.5
IWM ART 4017

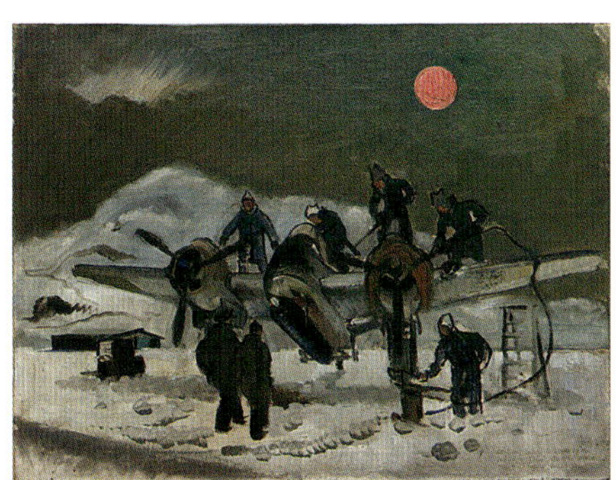

Gourdie, Thomas 1913–2005
De-Icing before a Strike off the Norwegian Coast, during which this Beaufighter was lost 1945
oil on canvas 45.5 x 60.7
IWM ART LD 4968

Gow, Andrew Carrick 1848–1920
The First Zeppelin Seen from Piccadilly Circus, 8 September 1915 1915
oil on canvas 66 x 45.7
IWM ART 5216

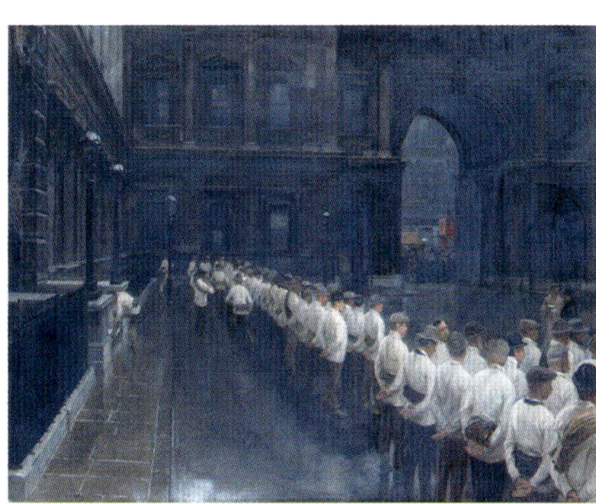

Gow, Andrew Carrick 1848–1920
Volunteers Drilling in the Courtyard of Burlington House 1915
oil on canvas 60.9 x 76.2
IWM ART 5217

Facing page: Orpen, William, 1878–1931, *Ready to Start: Self Portrait* (detail), 1917, (p. 176)

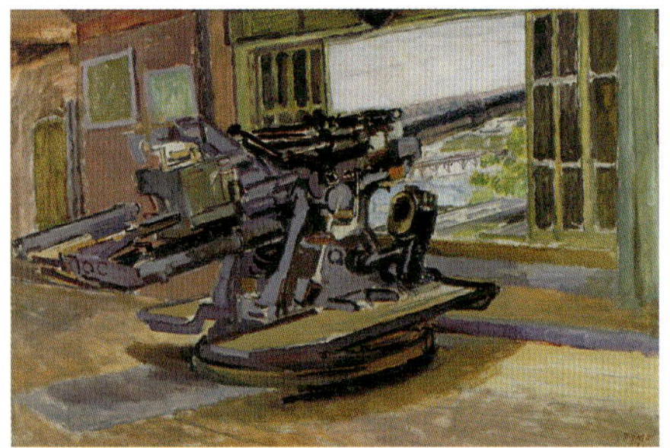

Grant, Duncan 1885–1978
Study for 'The Gunnery Lesson' 1940
oil on canvas 50.8 x 75.6
IWM ART 15547

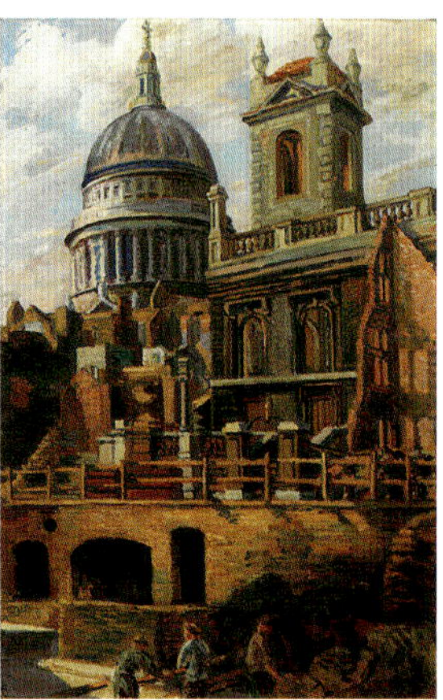

Grant, Duncan 1885–1978
St Paul's 1941
oil on canvas 91.6 x 61.4
IWM ART LD 1844

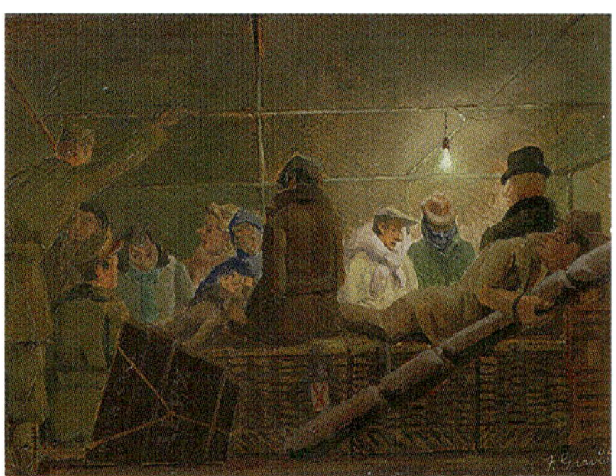

Graves, Frank 1913–2001
An Entertainments National Service Association Party Travels in a Canvas-Covered Lorry 1942
oil on panel 14.6 x 19.6
IWM ART LD 2868

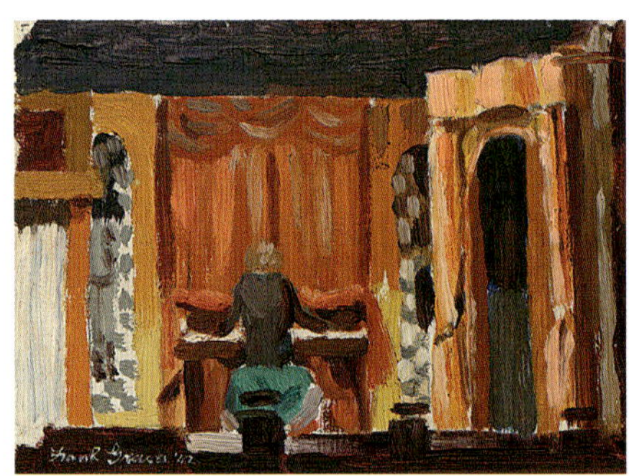

Graves, Frank 1913–2001
Ruth Earley Practises on Setting: Entertainments National Service Association Production, Garrison Theatre Stage 1942
oil on board 14.6 x 20.3
IWM ART LD 7198

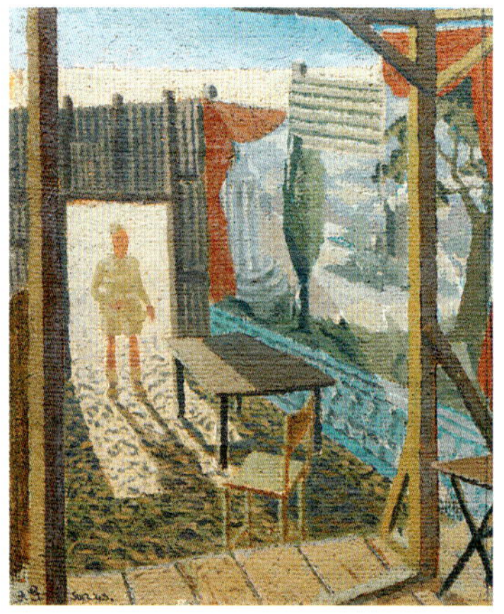

Graves, Frank 1913–2001
A Cinema in the Desert: Entertainments National Service Association, Suez 1943
oil on card 31.1 x 26
IWM ART LD 7195

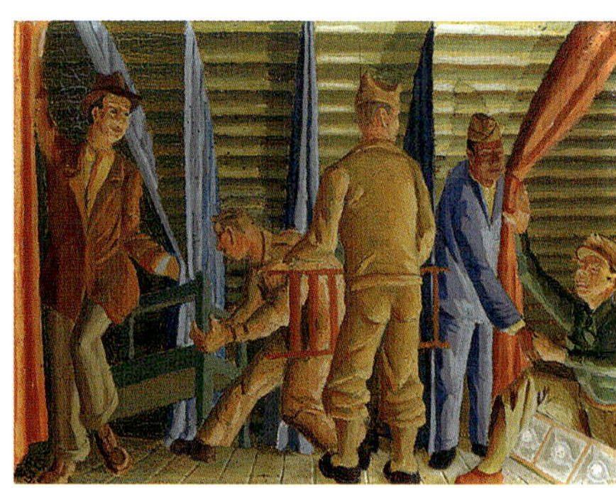

Graves, Frank 1913–2001
American Soldiers Prepare Nissen Hut Stage Prior to Entertainments National Service Association Show 1943
oil on board 14.6 x 19.6
IWM ART LD 7199

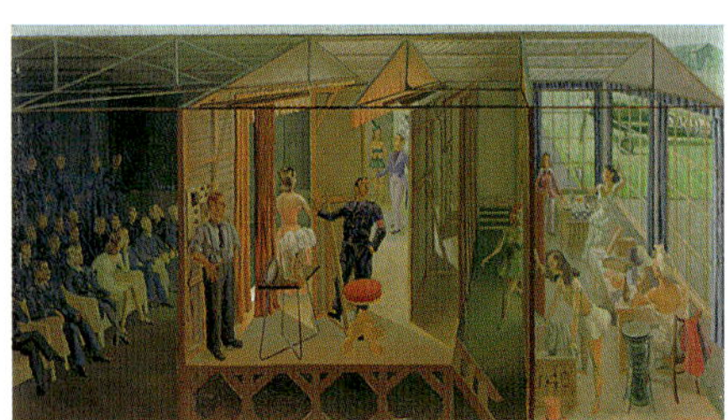

Graves, Frank 1913–2001
An Afternoon Show by an Entertainments National Service Association Company in a Navy Army and Air Force Institutes' (…) 1944
oil on panel 40 x 73
IWM ART LD 1690

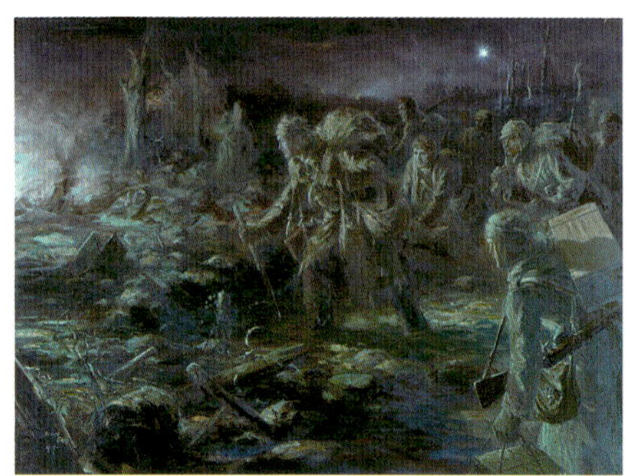

Gray, Joseph 1890–1962
A Ration Party of the 4th Black Watch at the Battle of Neuve Chapelle, 1915 1918–1919
oil on canvas 66 x 91.4
IWM ART 1917

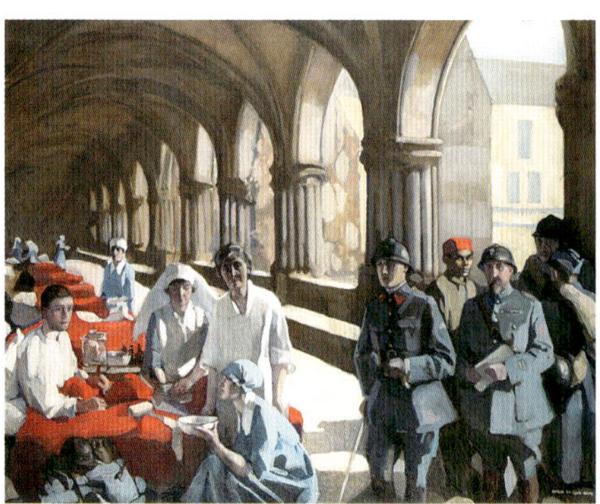

Gray, Norah Neilson 1882–1931
The Scottish Women's Hospital: In the Cloister of the Abbaye at Royaumont, Dr Frances Ivens Inspects a French Patient 1920
oil on canvas 114.3 x 139.7
IWM ART 3090

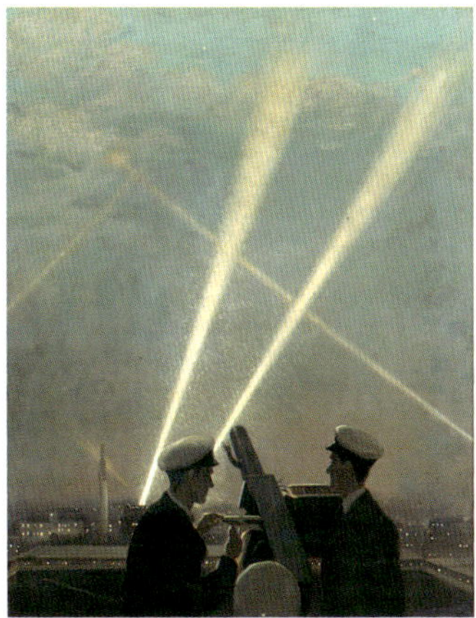

Gray, Ronald 1868–1951
*Evening Quarters: The Lookout at Cannon
Street Anti-Aircraft Station* 1917
oil on canvas 76.2 x 63.5
IWM ART 321

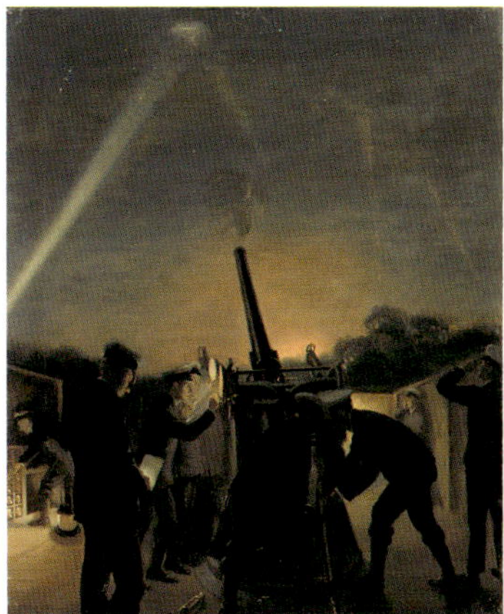

Gray, Ronald 1868–1951
King's Cross Anti-Aircraft Gun in Action 1917
oil on canvas 76.2 x 63.5
IWM ART 320

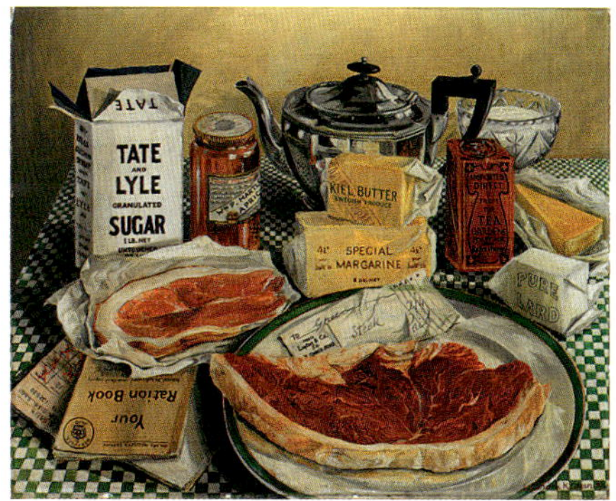

Green, Leonora Kathleen b.1901
Coupons Required 1941
oil on canvas 40.5 x 51
IWM ART 16344

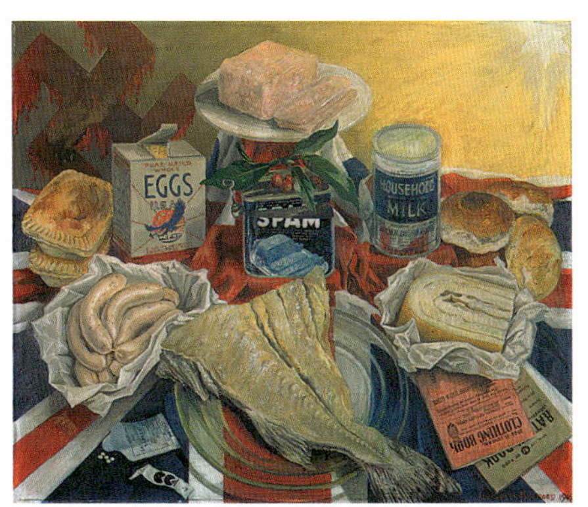

Green, Leonora Kathleen b.1901
Lest We Forget 1945
oil on canvas 51 x 61
IWM ART 16345

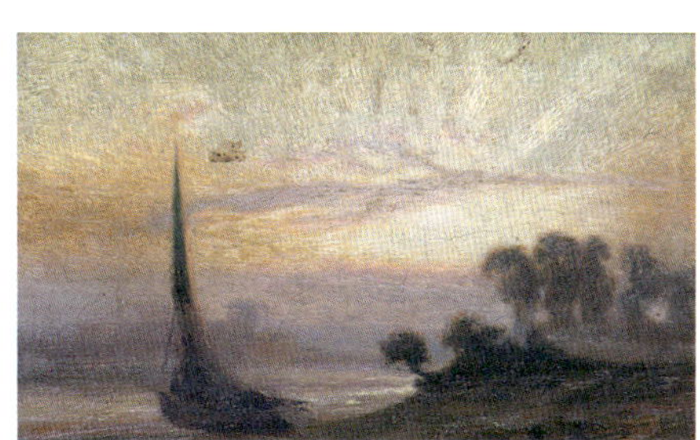

Greenwood, Walter Edmund
active 1914–1918
Sunset 1918
oil on canvas 20.3 x 33
IWM ART 5566

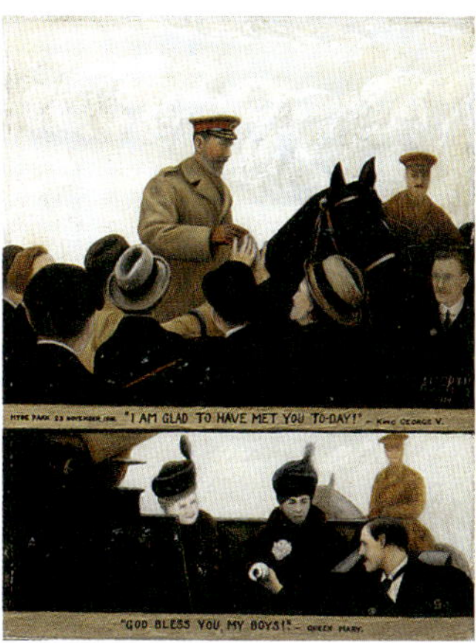

Groom, Arthur G. active 1914–1974
*Review of Silver Badge Men, Hyde Park, 23
November 1918* 1919
oil on panel 29.8 x 23.4
IWM ART 5538

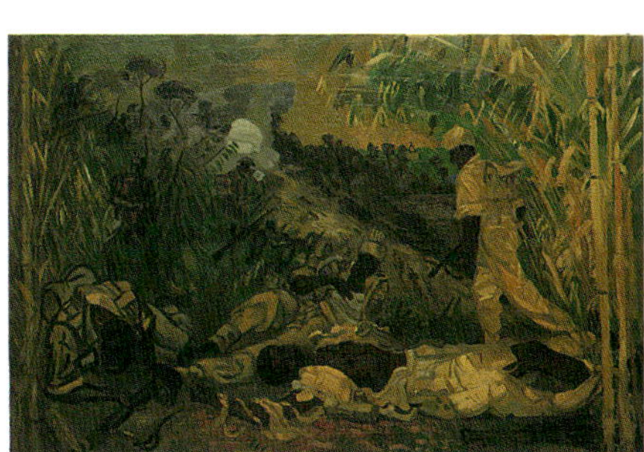

Gross, Anthony 1905–1984
*Arakan Campaign: The Battle of Rathedaung,
1943 with Six Rajputana Rifles Attacking Hill
North 75* 1944
oil on canvas 76.2 x 117.1
IWM ART LD 3771

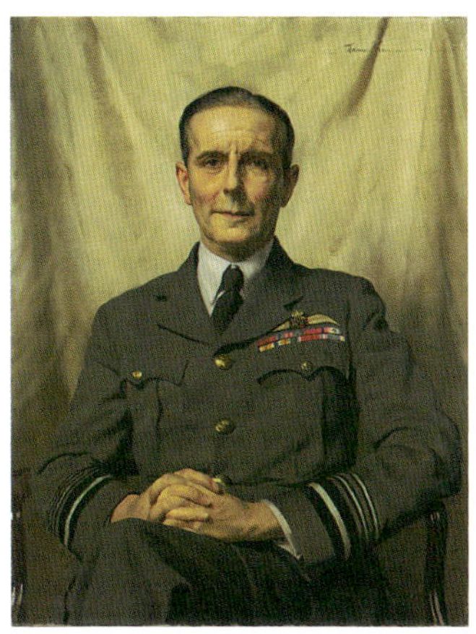

Gunn, Herbert James 1893–1964
*Air Marshal Sir Philip Joubert de la Ferté
(1887–1965), KCB, CMG, DSO* 1940
oil on canvas 91.4 x 71.1
IWM ART LD 764

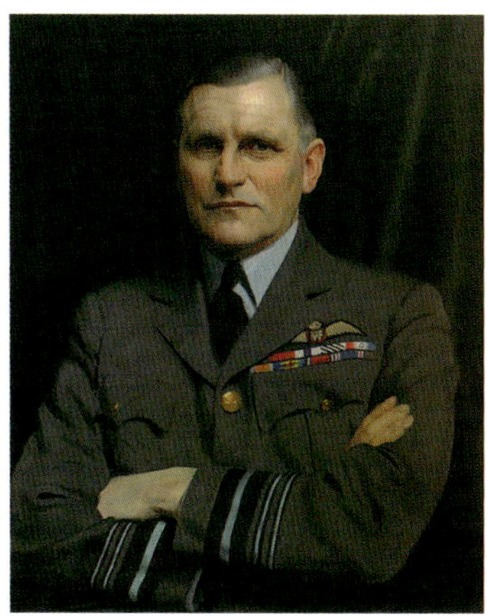

Gunn, Herbert James 1893–1964
*Air Marshal William Sholto Douglas
(1893–1969), CB, MC, DFC* 1940
oil on canvas 76.2 x 63.5
IWM ART LD 997

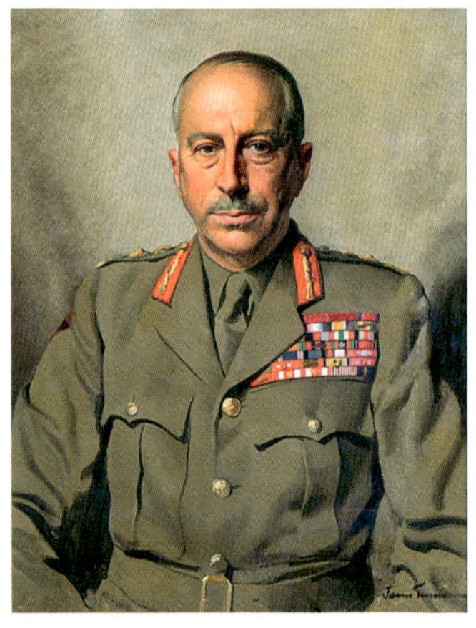

Gunn, Herbert James 1893–1964
*General Henry Graham Crerar (1888–1965),
CH, CB, DSO* 1941
oil on canvas 76.2 x 63.5
IWM ART LD 5932

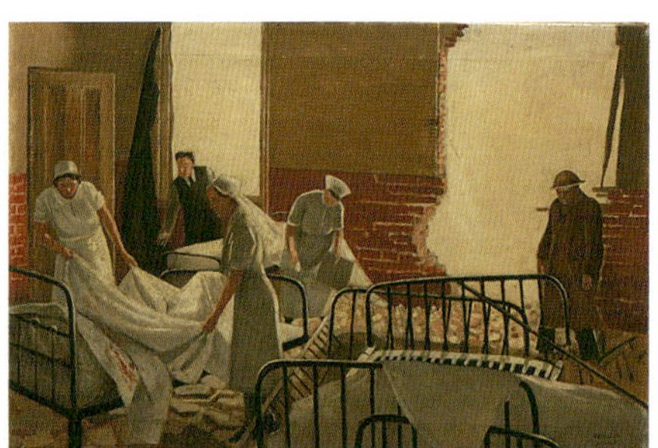

Guthrie, Kathleen 1905–1981
A Bombed Hospital Ward c.1940
oil on canvas 50.8 x 76.2
IWM ART LD 944

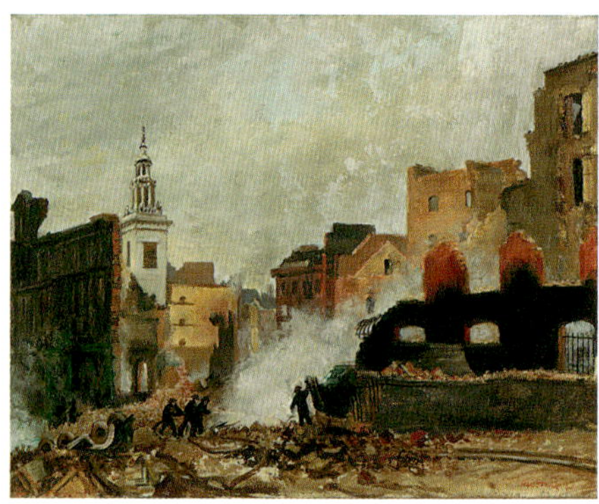

Hailstone, Bernard 1910–1987
An Evening in the City, April 1941 1941
oil on canvas 60.9 x 76.2
IWM ART LD 1354

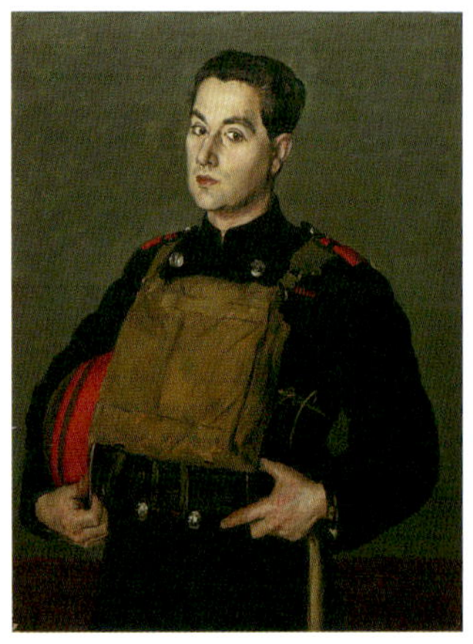

Hailstone, Bernard 1910–1987
*Andrew Nures Nabarro, GM, Leading Fireman,
Portsmouth Auxiliary Fire Service* 1941
oil on canvas 101.9 x 76.2
IWM ART LD 1906

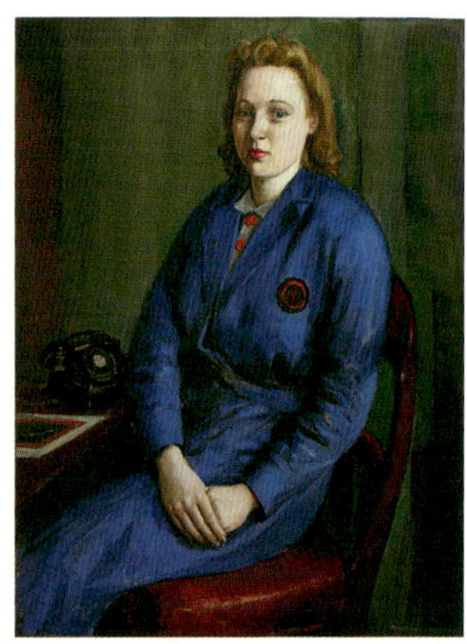

Hailstone, Bernard 1910–1987
*Barbara Mary Rendell, BEM, Auxiliary Fire
Service* 1941
oil on canvas 101.9 x 76.2
IWM ART LD 1912

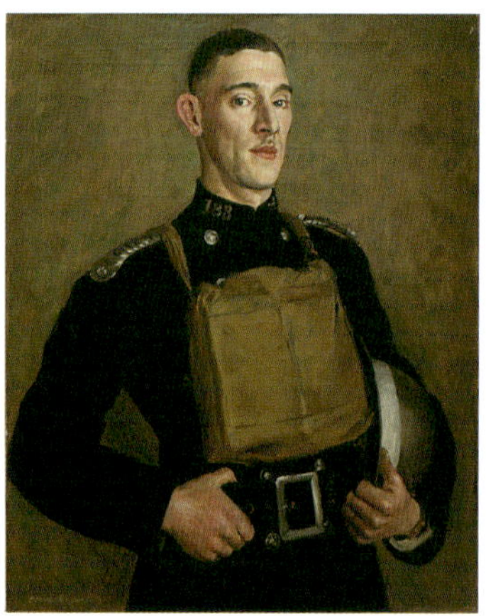

Hailstone, Bernard 1910–1987
*Frederick Charles Reville, GM, Bristol
Auxiliary Fire Service* 1941
oil on canvas 93.3 x 75.5
IWM ART LD 1907

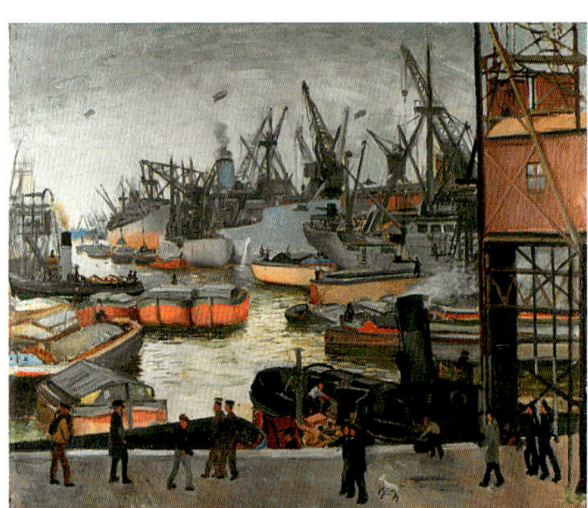

Hailstone, Bernard 1910–1987
Activity at a Hull Dock 1943
oil on canvas 63.5 x 76.2
IWM ART LD 3293

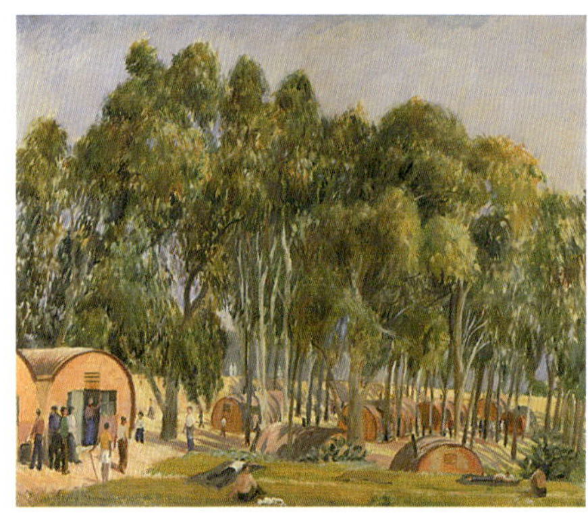

Hailstone, Bernard 1910–1987
Convoy Centre at Augusta, Sicily 1943
oil on canvas 63.5 x 76.2
IWM ART LD 3969

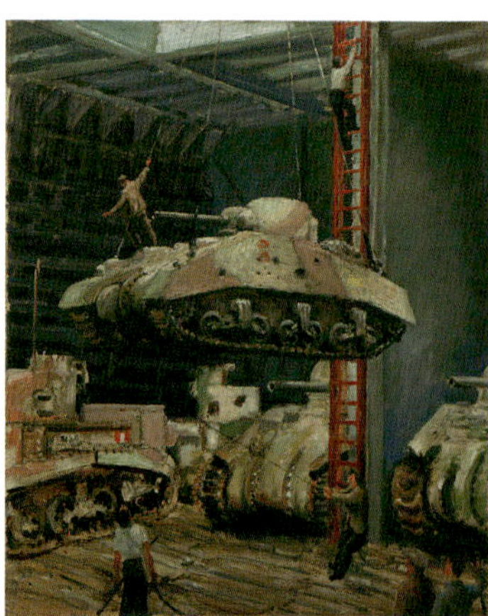

Hailstone, Bernard 1910–1987
*Damaged Tanks Being Lowered into the Hold
of a Merchant Ship* 1943
oil on canvas 60 x 50.1
IWM ART LD 4051

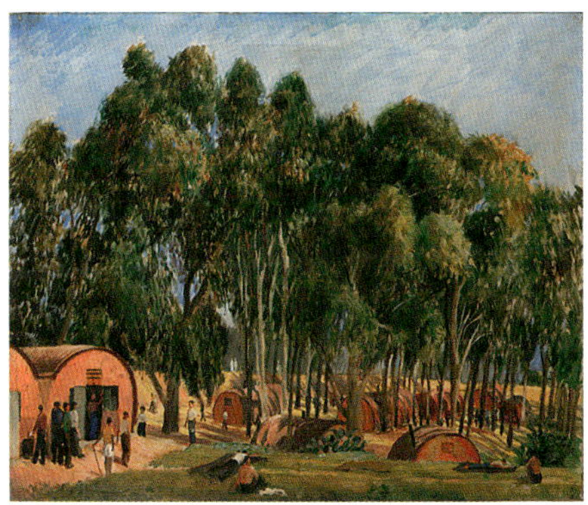

Hailstone, Bernard 1910–1987
Escaped Prisoners' Camp, Algiers 1943
oil on canvas 63.5 x 76.2
IWM ART LD 3968

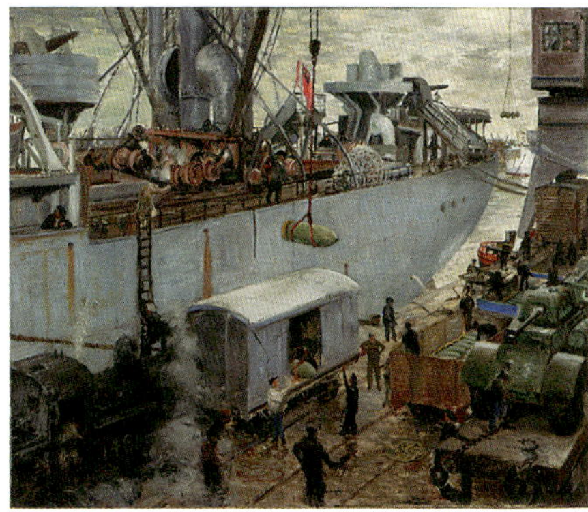

Hailstone, Bernard 1910–1987
Loading Ammuniton at Hull Docks 1943
oil on canvas 63.5 x 76.2
IWM ART LD 3107

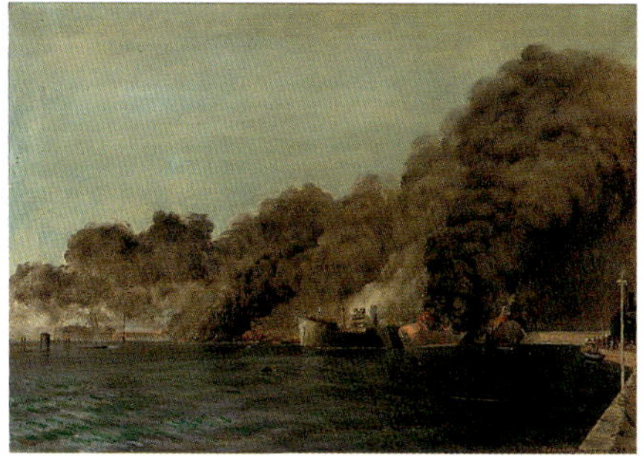

Hailstone, Bernard 1910–1987
The Morning after the Big Raid at Bari, Italy
1943
oil on canvas 61.5 x 88.2
IWM ART LD 4054

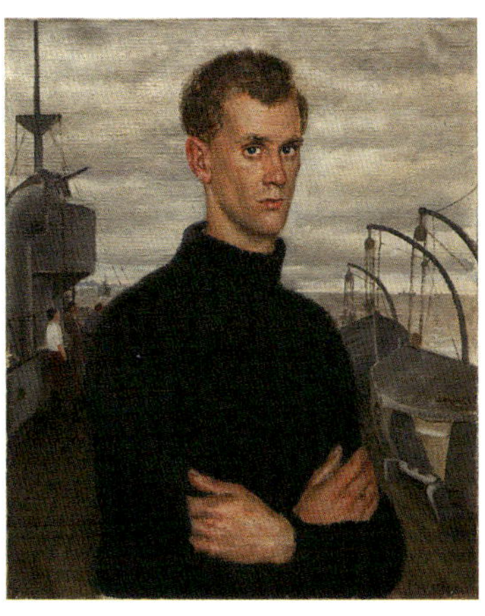

Hailstone, Bernard 1910–1987
Able Seaman Welcher 1944
oil on canvas 74.9 x 62.8
IWM ART LD 5076

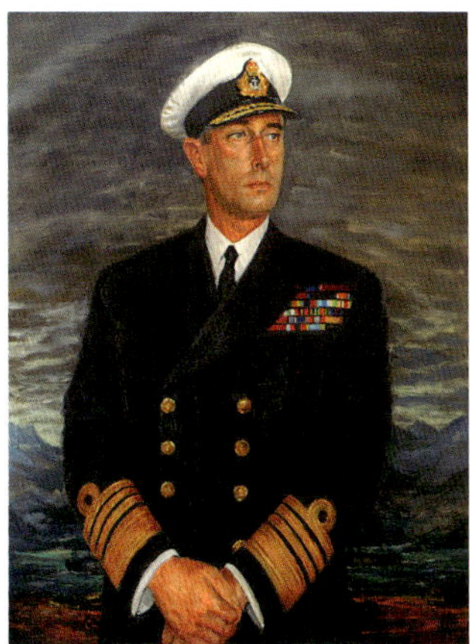

Hailstone, Bernard 1910–1987
*Admiral Lord Louis Mountbatten
(1900–1979), GCVO, KCB, DSO* 1944
oil on canvas 101.9 x 76.2
IWM ART LD 5840

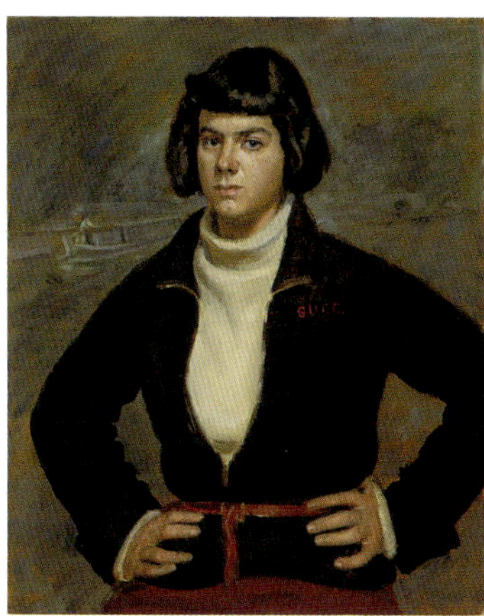

Hailstone, Bernard 1910–1987
Christian Vlasto, a Canal Boat Woman 1944
oil on canvas 75.5 x 62.2
IWM ART LD 4950

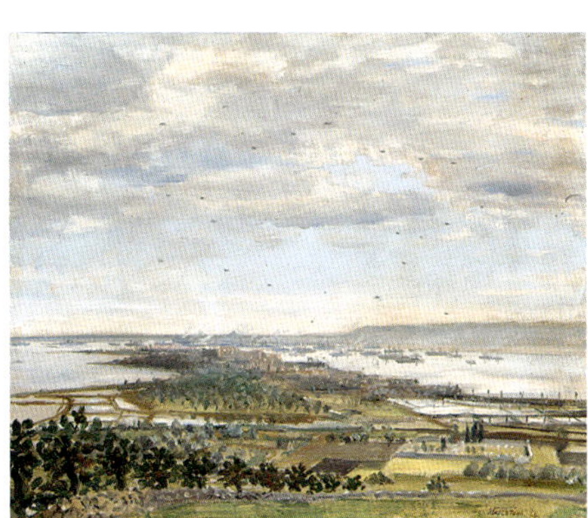

Hailstone, Bernard 1910–1987
Convoy from Malta 1944
oil on board 50.8 x 61
IWM ART 16759

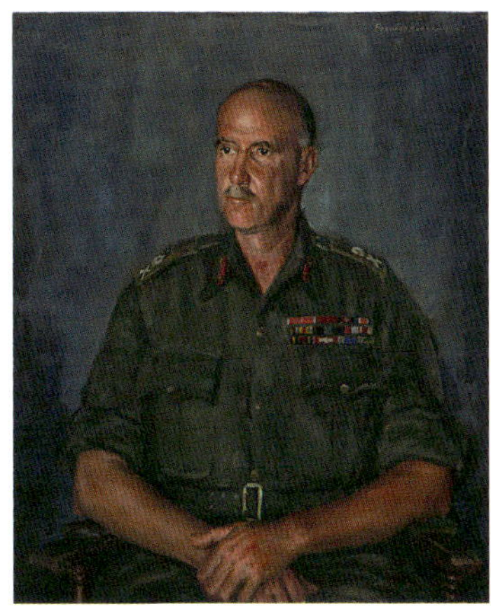

Hailstone, Bernard 1910–1987
*Lieutenant General Sir Frank Messervy (1893–
1974), KBE, CB, DSO and Bar* 1945
oil on canvas 76.2 x 63.5
IWM ART LD 5853

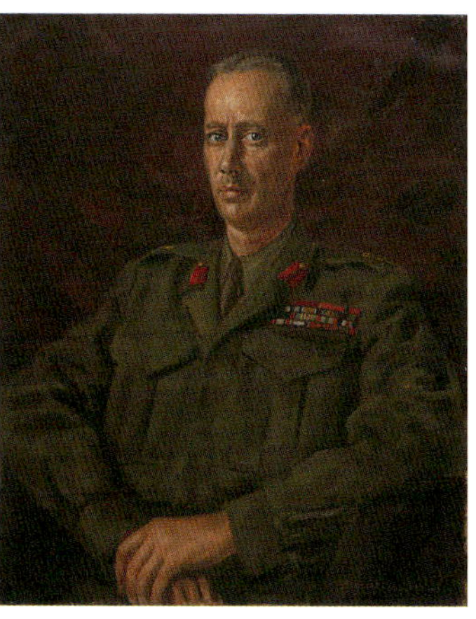

Hailstone, Bernard 1910–1987
*Lieutenant General Sir Miles Dempsey (1896–
1969), KCB, KBE, DSO, MC* 1945
oil on canvas 76.2 x 63.5
IWM ART LD 5856

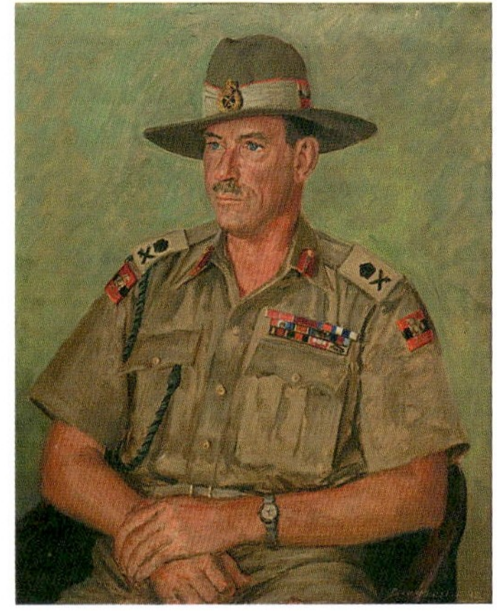

Hailstone, Bernard 1910–1987
*Lieutenant General Sir Montagu Stopford
(1892–1971), KBE, CB, DSO, MC* 1945
oil on canvas 76.2 x 63.5
IWM ART LD 5855

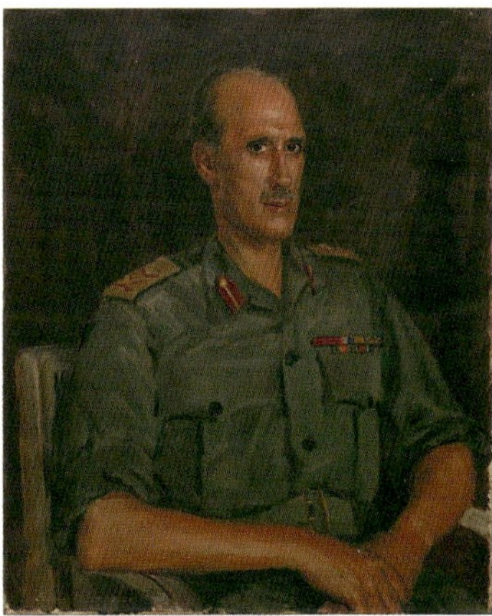

Hailstone, Bernard 1910–1987
Major General R. F. S. Denning, CB 1945
oil on canvas 76.2 x 63.5
IWM ART LD 5922

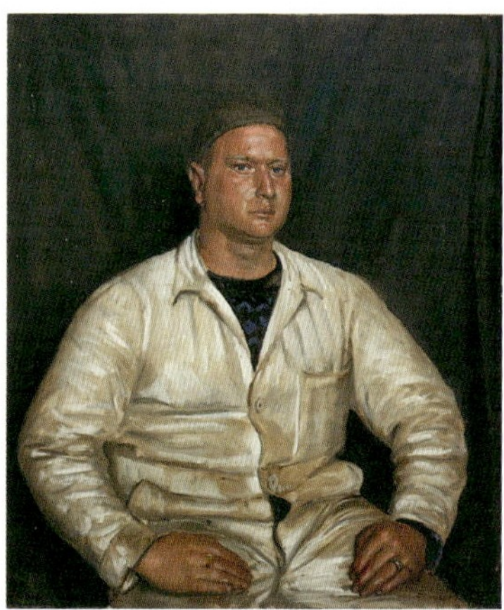

Hailstone, Bernard 1910–1987
*R. Dibnah, BEM, Motorman of the 'Nonsuch'
Blockade Runner* 1945
oil on canvas 88.9 x 75.5
IWM ART LD 5079

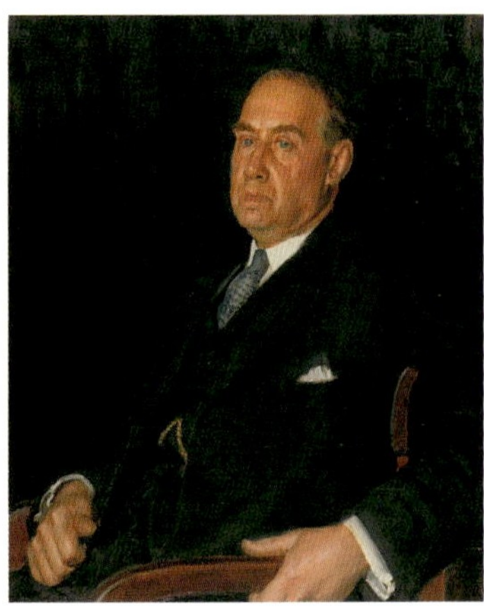

Hailstone, Bernard 1910–1987
Sir Edward Appleton (1892–1965), KCB, FRS
1945
oil on canvas 74.9 x 62.2
IWM ART LD 5580

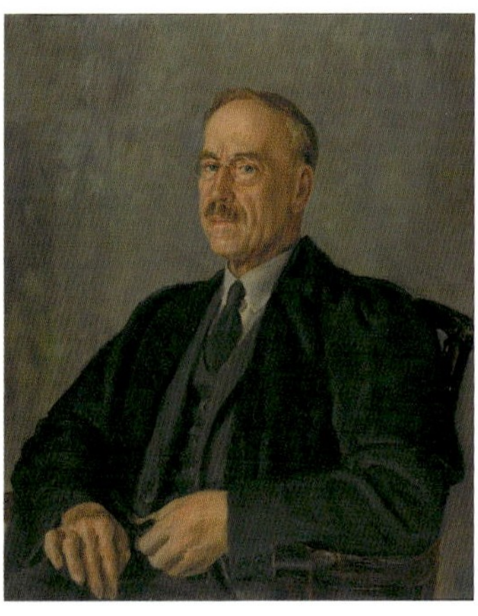

Hailstone, Bernard 1910–1987
*Sir Henry Tizard (1885–1959), KCB, AFC,
FRS* 1945
oil on canvas 74.9 x 62.2
IWM ART LD 5581

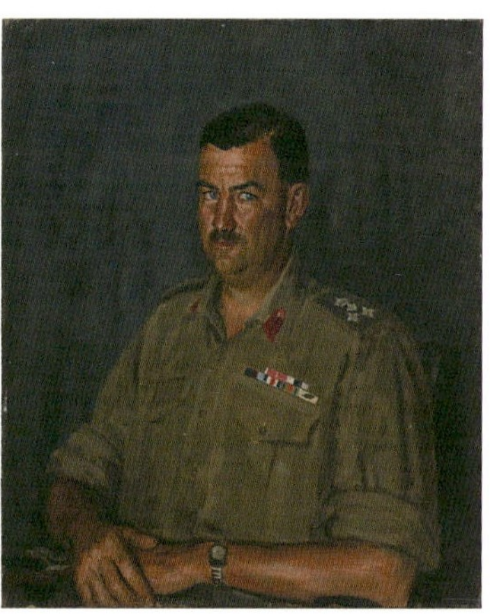

Hailstone, Bernard 1910–1987
*Brigadier C. P. Jones, CBE, MC, Malaya
Command* c.1945
oil on canvas 76.2 x 63.5
IWM ART LD 5854

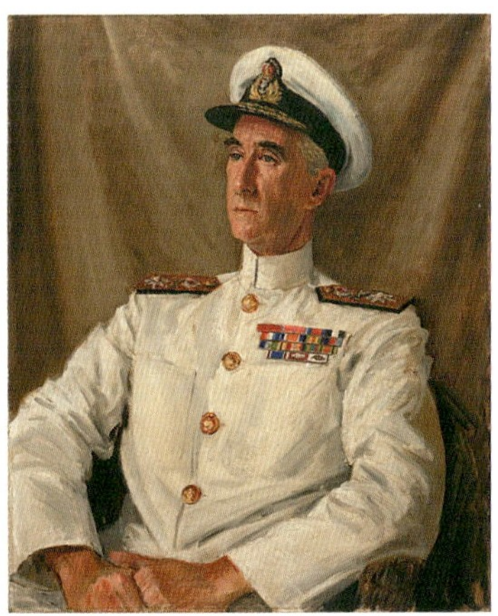

Hailstone, Bernard 1910–1987
*Rear Admiral C. E. Douglas-Pennant, CB,
CBE, DSO, DSC* c.1945
oil on canvas 76.2 x 63.5
IWM ART LD 5857

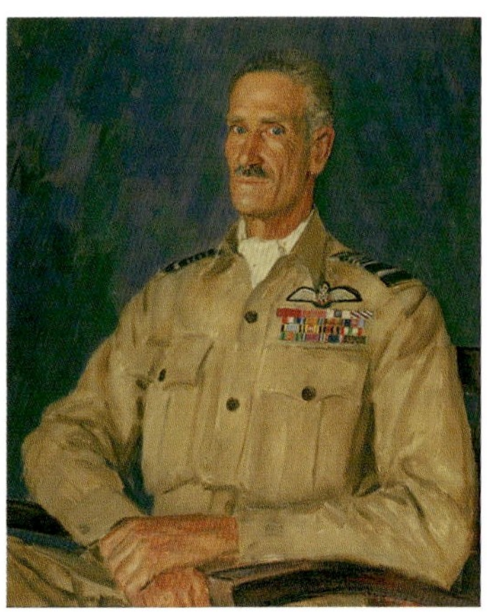

Hailstone, Bernard 1910–1987
*Air Chief Marshal Sir Keith Park (1892–1975),
KCB, KBE, MC, DFC* 1945–1946
oil on canvas 76.2 x 63.5
IWM ART LD 5921

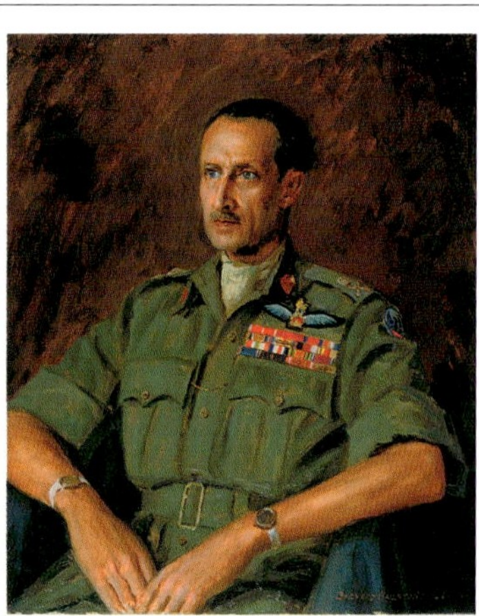

Hailstone, Bernard 1910–1987
*Lieutenant General Sir Frederick Browning
(1896–1965), KBE, CB, SO* 1946
oil on canvas 76.2 x 63.5
IWM ART LD 5923

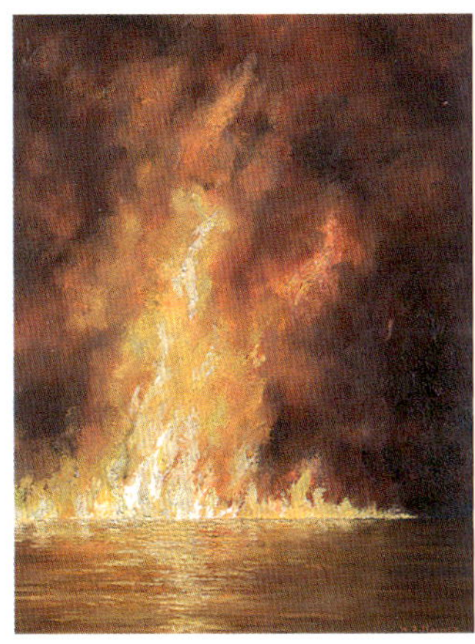

Haines, Wilfred Stanley 1905–1944
Burning Oil on a Slack Tide 1939–1944
oil on board 58.7 x 45.3
IWM ART 15180

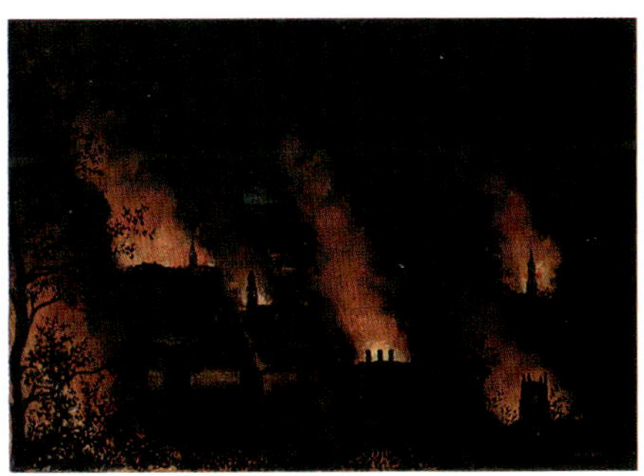

Haines, Wilfred Stanley 1905–1944
Fire Blitz on Bath 1942
oil on canvas 64.1 x 89.8
IWM ART LD 3052

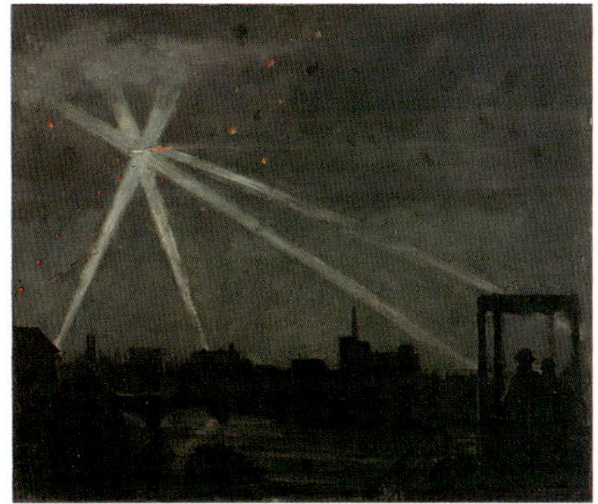

Haines, Wilfred Stanley 1905–1944
An Observation Post: Flying Bomb Raid 1944
oil on canvas 61.5 x 74.9
IWM ART LD 4720

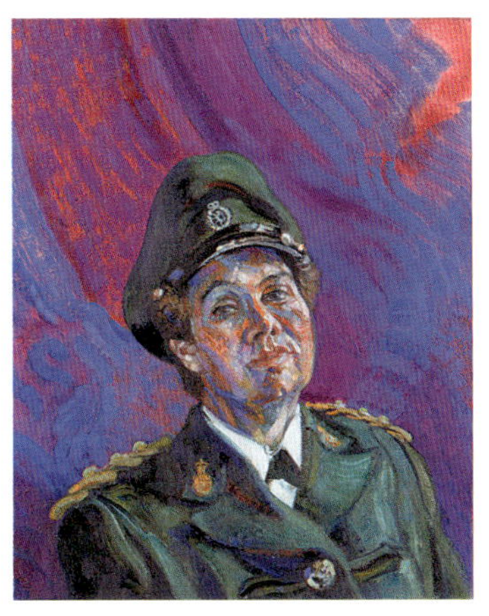

Hambling, Maggi b.1945
Captain E. P. Forster, Women's Royal Air Corps, Director of Music for the Women's Royal Air Corps Staff Band 1984
oil on canvas 56 x 46
IWM ART 15918

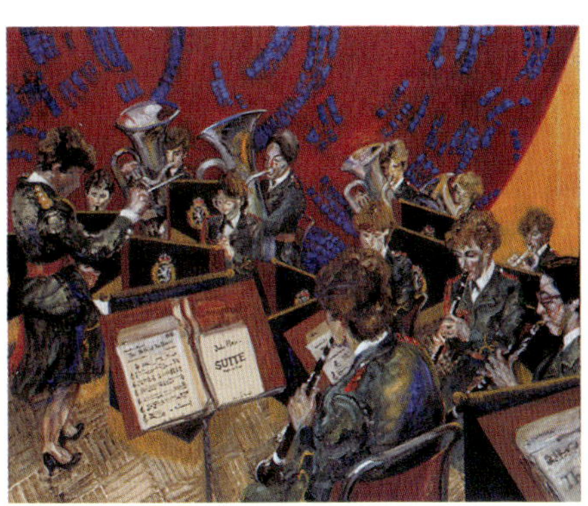

Hambling, Maggi b.1945
The Staff Band of the Women's Royal Army Corps 1984
oil on canvas 76.8 x 95
IWM ART 15917

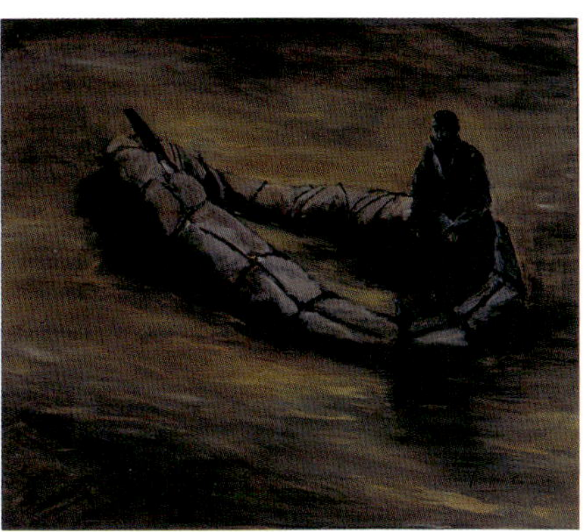

Hamilton, John 1919–1993
A Lone Survivor, Covered in Oil 1972–1978
oil on panel 60.9 x 71.1
IWM ART LD 7414

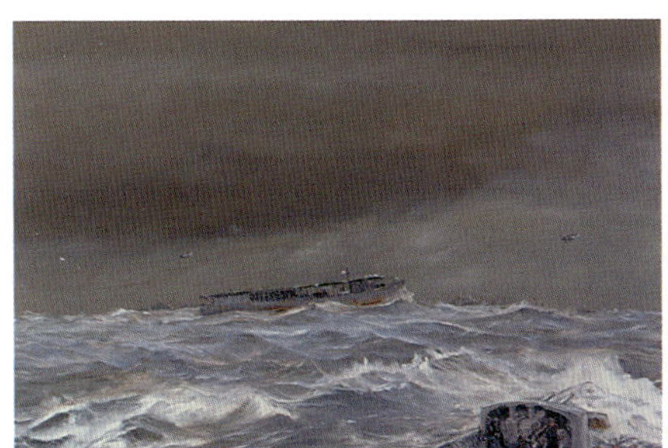

Hamilton, John 1919–1993
Air Cover: A Typical Escort Carrier, 'HMS Archer' on North Atlantic Escort Duty 1972–1978
oil on panel 60.9 x 91.4
IWM ART LD 7410

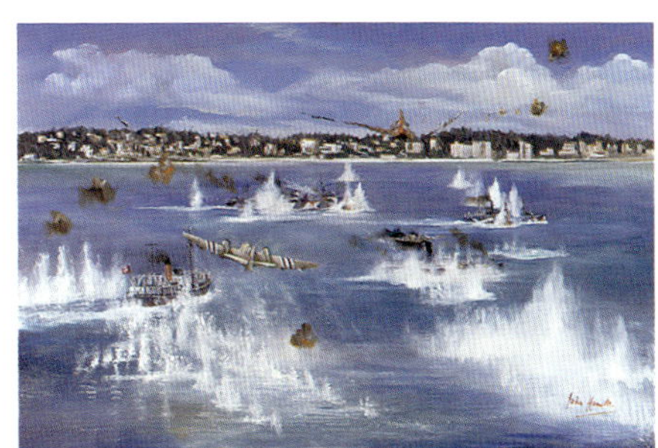

Hamilton, John 1919–1993
Aircraft Attacking Four Ships in the Mediterranean 1972–1978
oil on panel 60.9 x 91.4
IWM ART LD 7453

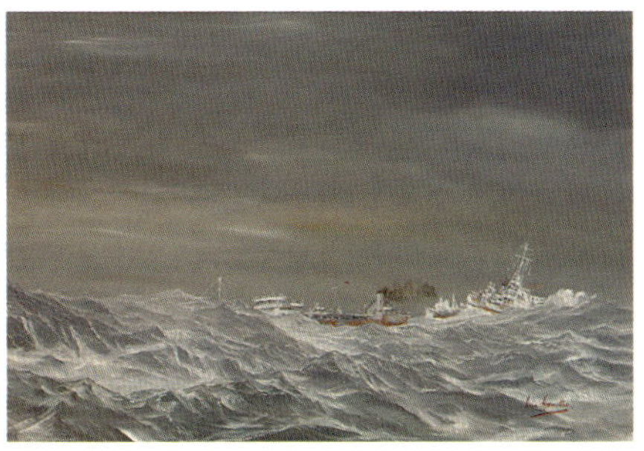

Hamilton, John 1919–1993
Arctic Gale 1972–1978
oil on panel 60.9 x 91.4
IWM ART LD 7395

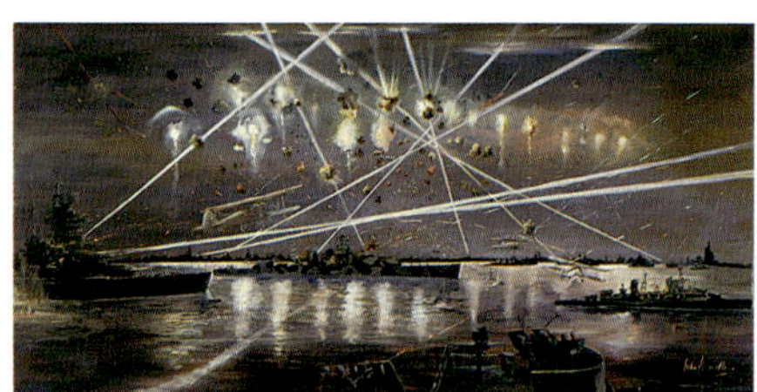

Hamilton, John 1919–1993
Attack on Taranto, 11 November 1940
1972–1978
oil on panel 60.9 x 121.9
IWM ART LD 7398

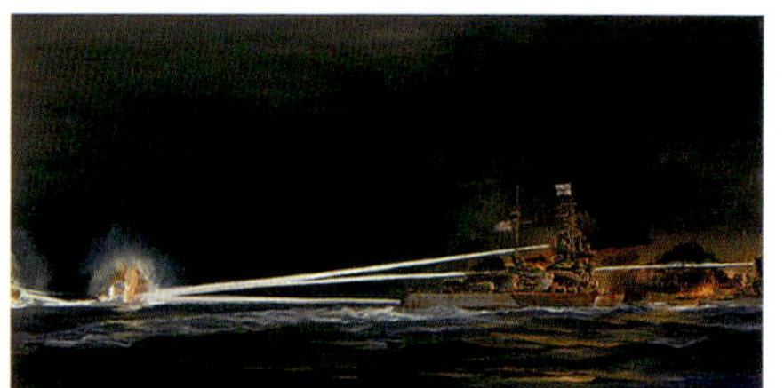

Hamilton, John 1919–1993
Battle of Matapan, 28 March 1941 1972–1978
oil on panel 60.9 x 121.9
IWM ART LD 7441

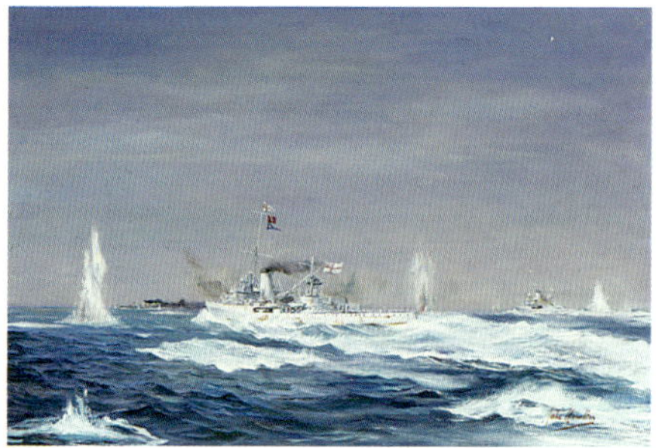

Hamilton, John 1919–1993
Battle of the River Plate 1972–1978
oil on panel 60.9 x 91.4
IWM ART LD 7394

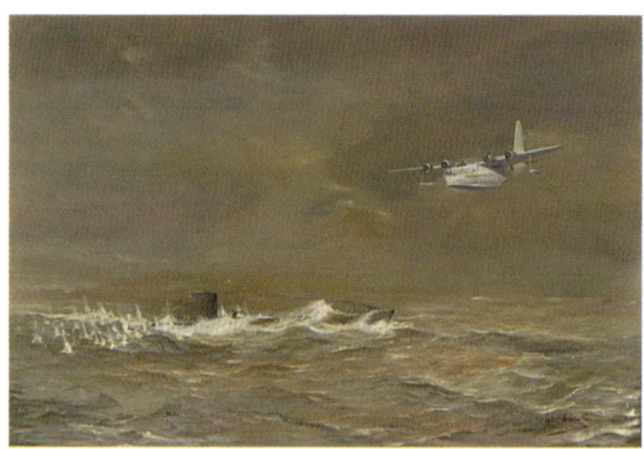

Hamilton, John 1919–1993
Caught on the Surface: A Short Sunderland Flying Boat Attacking a U-Boat 1972–1978
oil on panel 60.9 x 91.4
IWM ART LD 7412

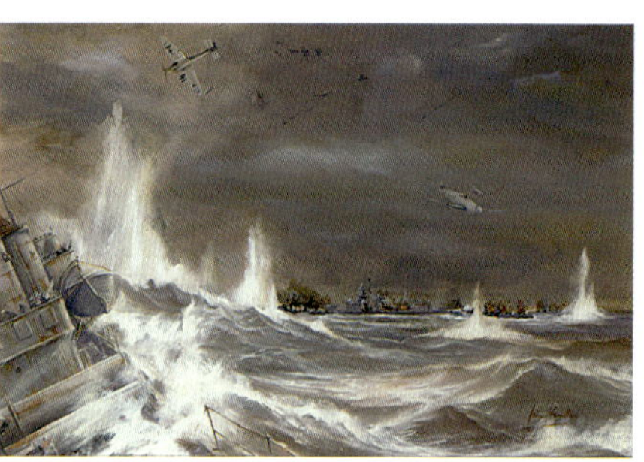

Hamilton, John 1919–1993
Channel Dash: The Attempt to Halt the Progress of the Battleships 'Scharnhorst' and 'Gneisenau' through the (…) 1972–1978
oil on panel 60.9 x 91.4
IWM ART LD 7448

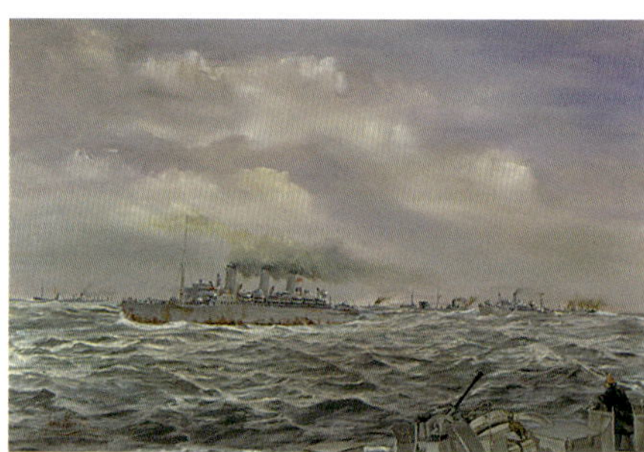

Hamilton, John 1919–1993
Convoy 1972–1978
oil on panel 60.9 x 91.4
IWM ART LD 7457

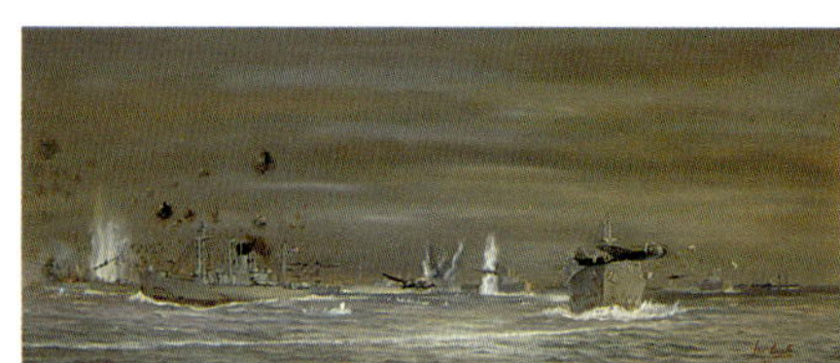

Hamilton, John 1919–1993
Convoy PQ18 Attacked by a Junkers 88 and Heinkel III Torpedo Bombers, 13 September 1942 1972–1978
oil on panel 50.8 x 121.9
IWM ART LD 7421

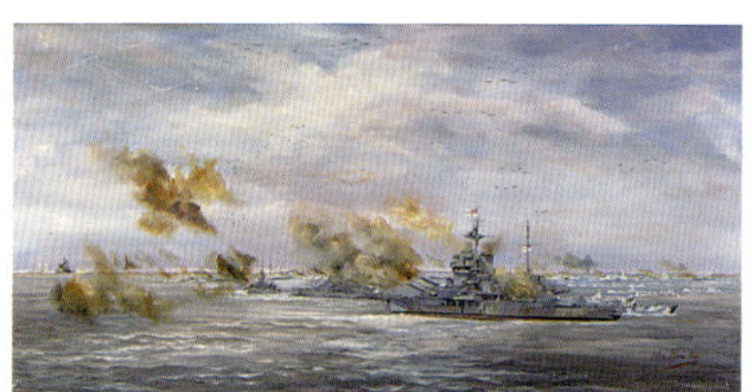

Hamilton, John 1919–1993
D-Day Naval Bombardment: 'HMS Ramillies', 'HMS Warspite' and Monitor 'HMS Roberts' Bombard the Beaches 1972–1978
oil on panel 60.9 x 121.9
IWM ART LD 7451

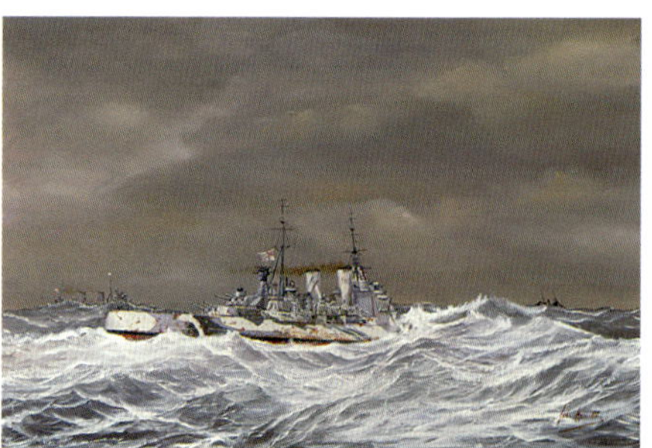

Hamilton, John 1919–1993
Distant Escort: The Cruisers 'HMS Sheffield' and 'HMS Jamaica' with the Battleship 'HMS Duke of York' Patrol (…) 1972–1978
oil on panel 60.9 x 91.4
IWM ART LD 7427

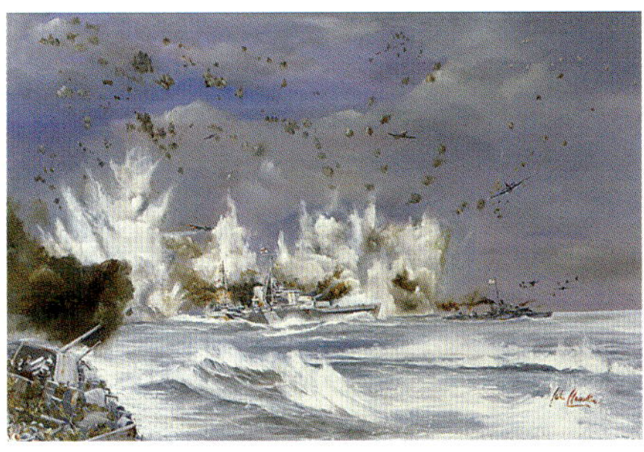

Hamilton, John 1919–1993
Evacuation of Crete: Cruisers 'HMS Orion' and 'HMS Kimberley' under Attack, May 1941
1972–1978
oil on panel 60.9 x 91.4
IWM ART LD 7433

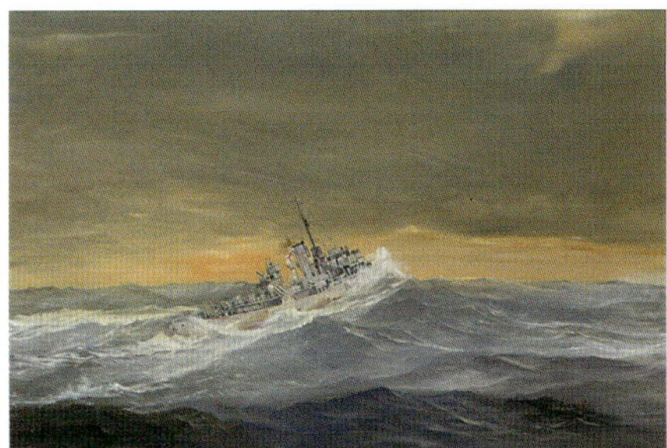

Hamilton, John 1919–1993
'HMC S Snowberry', a Flower Class Corvette of the Royal Canadian Navy 1972–1978
oil on panel 60.9 x 91.4
IWM ART LD 7400

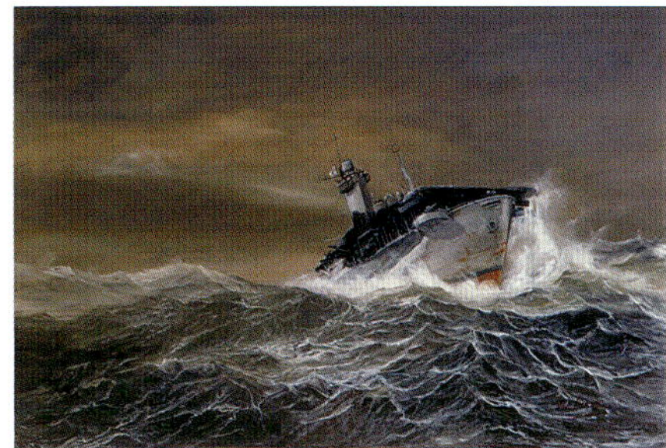

Hamilton, John 1919–1993
'HMS Biter' in an Arctic Gale 1972–1978
oil on panel 60.9 x 91.4
IWM ART LD 7428

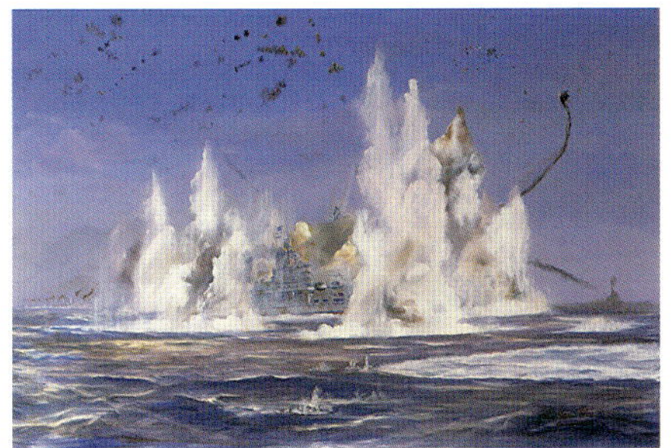

Hamilton, John 1919–1993
'HMS Illustrious' under Attack: Excess Convoy, January 1941 1972–1978
oil on panel 60.9 x 91.4
IWM ART LD 7439

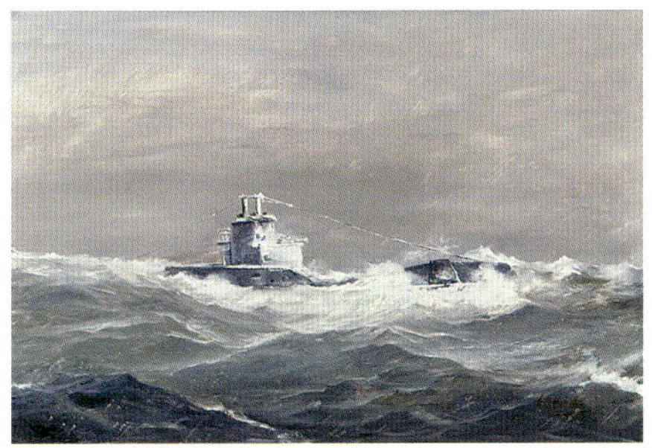

Hamilton, John 1919–1993
HMS Submarine 'Trident' on Patrol in Arctic Waters 1972–1978
oil on panel 60.9 x 91.4
IWM ART LD 7429

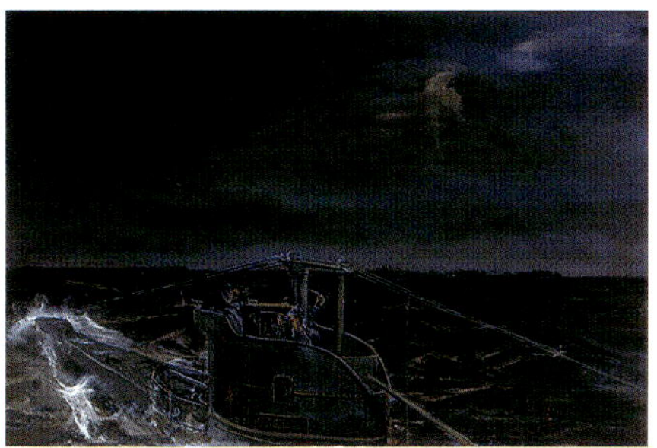

Hamilton, John 1919–1993
HMS Submarine 'Upholder' 1972–1978
oil on panel 60.9 x 91.4
IWM ART LD 7442

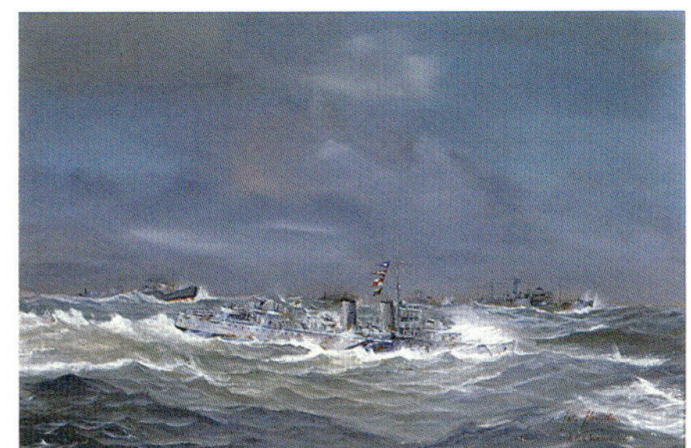

Hamilton, John 1919–1993
'HMS Wallace', 1940 1972–1978
oil on panel 60.9 x 91.4
IWM ART LD 7397

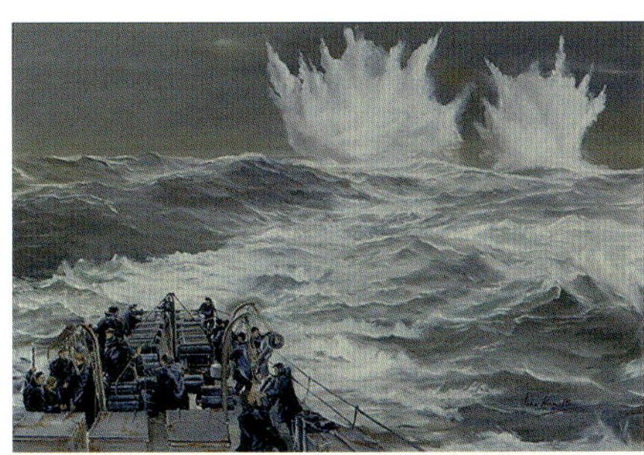

Hamilton, John 1919–1993
'HMS Woodpecker' 1972–1978
oil on panel 60.9 x 91.4
IWM ART LD 7406

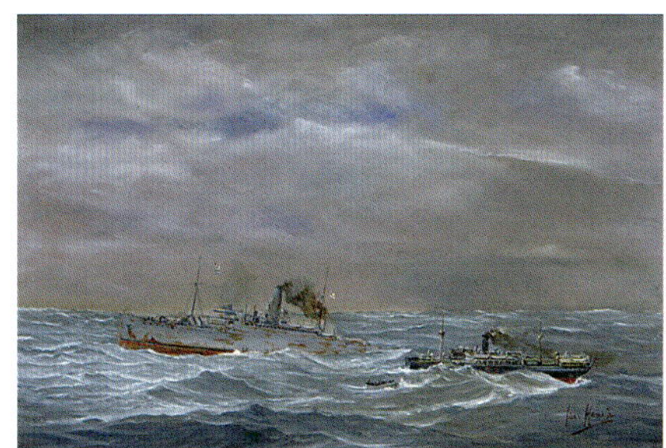

Hamilton, John 1919–1993
Large and Small Vessels and a Lifeboat
1972–1978
oil on panel 60.9 x 91.4
IWM ART LD 7454

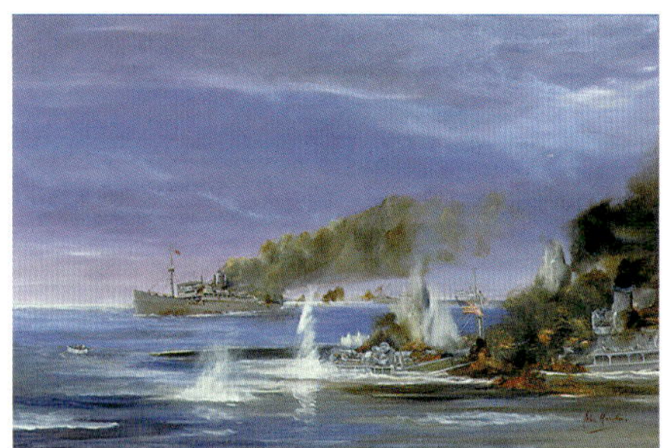

Hamilton, John 1919–1993
Last Stand of the 'SS Stephen Hopkins'
1972–1978
oil on panel 60.9 x 91.4
IWM ART LD 7445

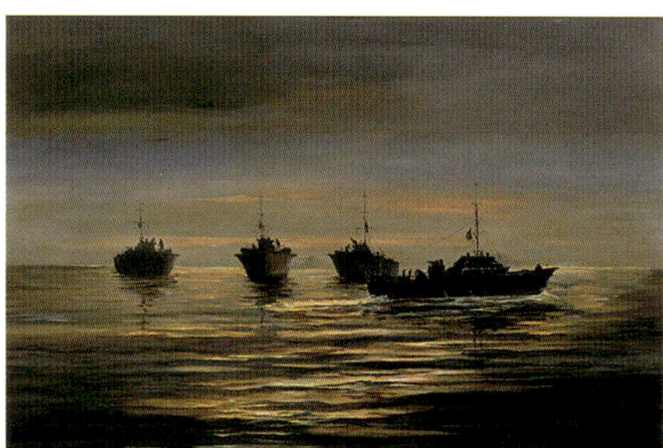

Hamilton, John 1919–1993
Listening: Motor Torpedo Boats of the Coastal Forces off the Enemy Coast 1972–1978
oil on panel 60.9 x 91.4
IWM ART LD 7449

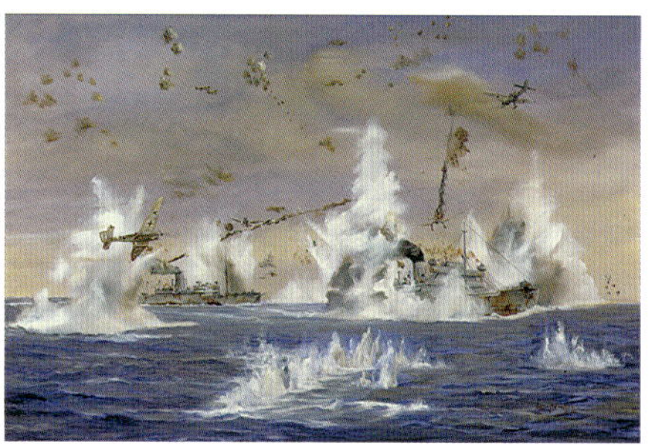

Hamilton, John 1919–1993
Malta Convoy: 'SS Brisbane Star' and 'SS Rochester Castle' 1972–1978
oil on panel 60.9 x 91.4
IWM ART LD 7437

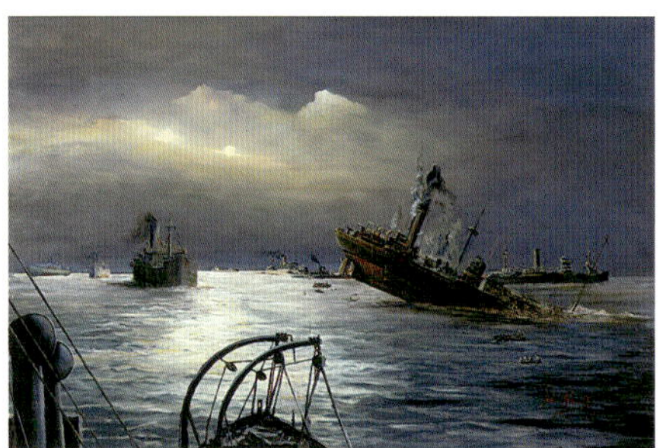

Hamilton, John 1919–1993
Mines in the Fairway 1972–1978
oil on panel 60.9 x 91.4
IWM ART LD 7447

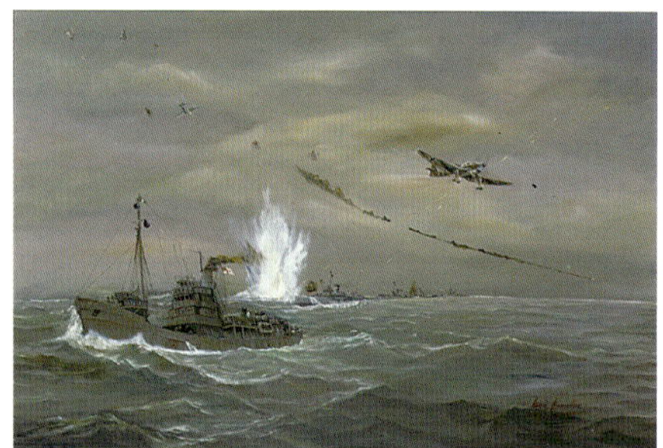

Hamilton, John 1919–1993
Minesweepers under Attack, Thames Estuary, October 1940 1972–1978
oil on panel 60.9 x 91.4
IWM ART LD 7446

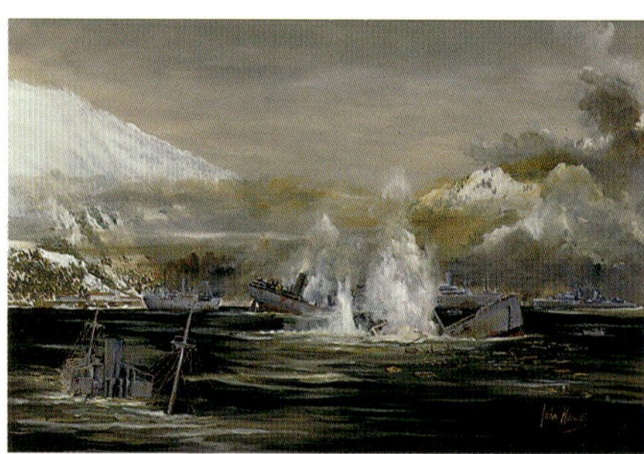

Hamilton, John 1919–1993
Narvik Harbour after the Destroyer Attack, 10 April 1940 1972–1978
oil on panel 60.9 x 91.4
IWM ART LD 7430

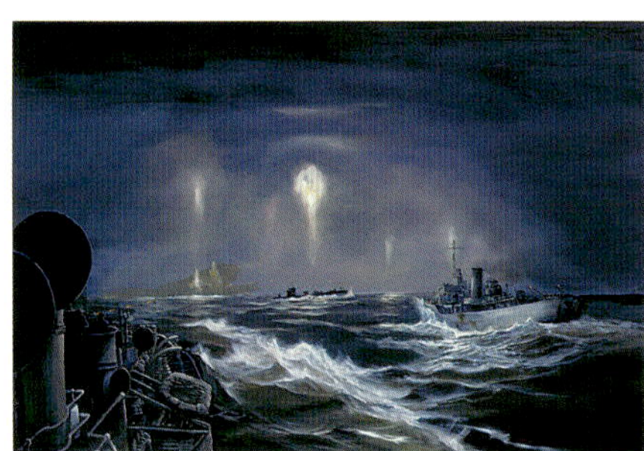

Hamilton, John 1919–1993
Night Action: Crew Abandoning Sinking Submarine U-70, 7 March 1941 1972–1978
oil on panel 60.9 x 91.4
IWM ART LD 7407

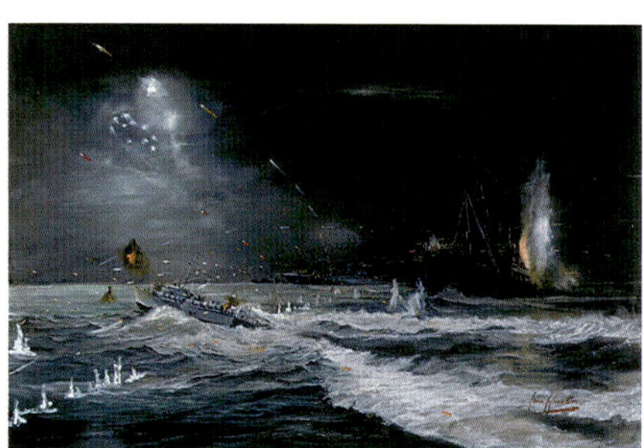

Hamilton, John 1919–1993
Night Battle 1972–1978
oil on panel 60.9 x 91.4
IWM ART LD 7455

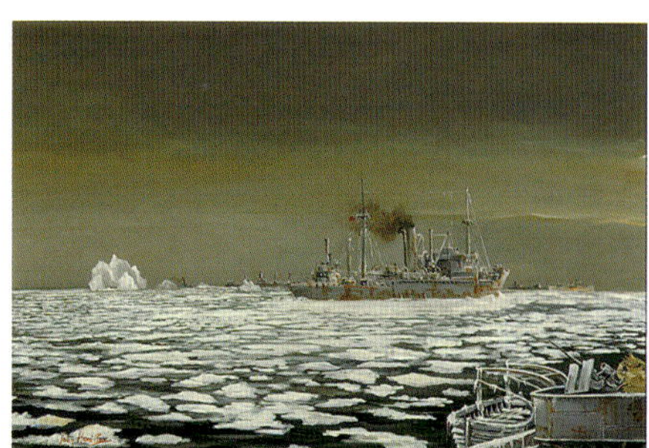

Hamilton, John 1919–1993
Routed North: Arctic Convoys Routed North in Summer, to the Edge of the Ice Pack, to Evade Aircraft Based in North Norway 1972–1978
oil on panel 60.9 x 91.4
IWM ART LD 7420

Facing page: Blyth, Robert Henderson, 1919–1970, *In the Image of Man* (detail), 1947, (p. 14)

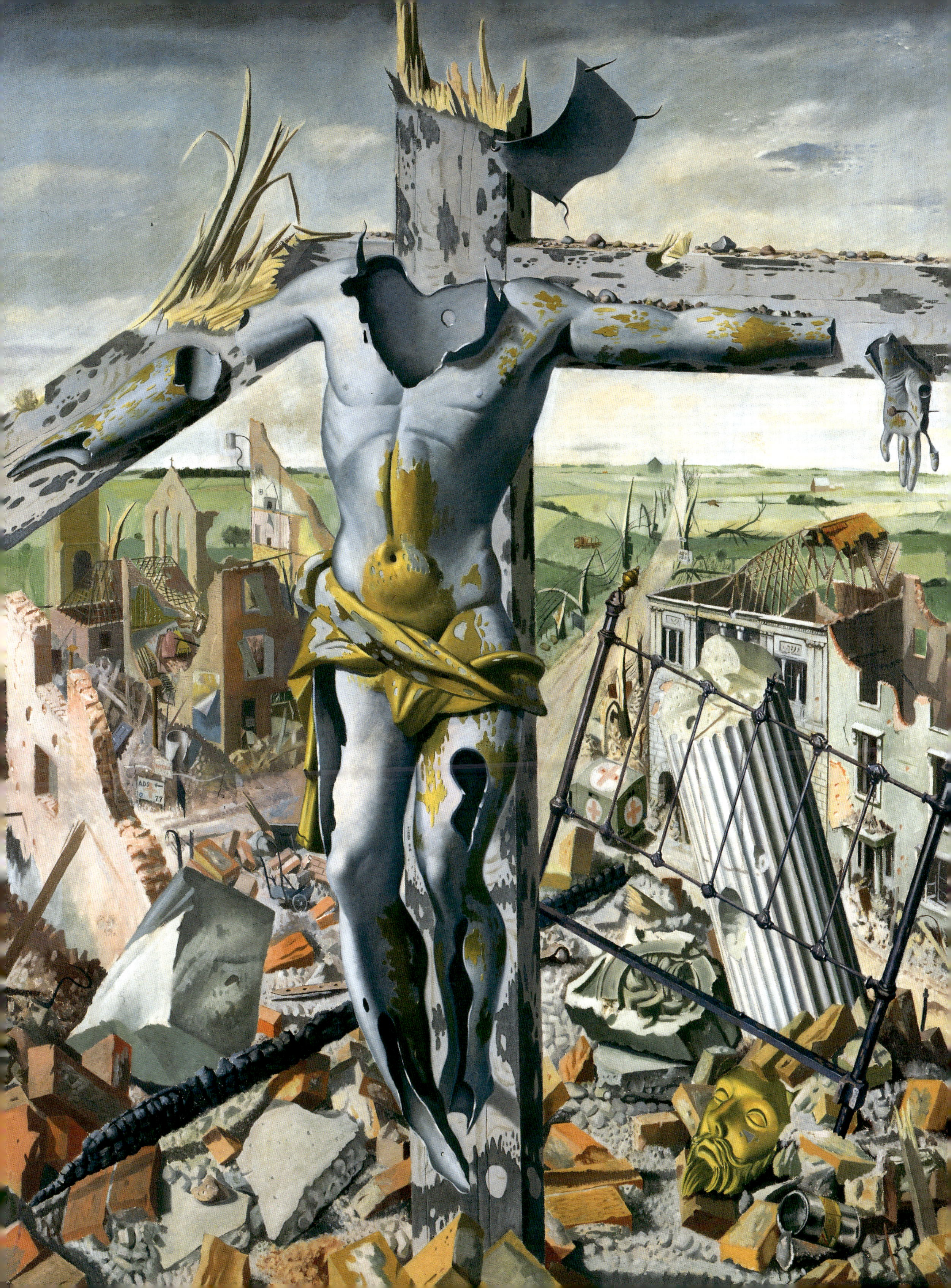

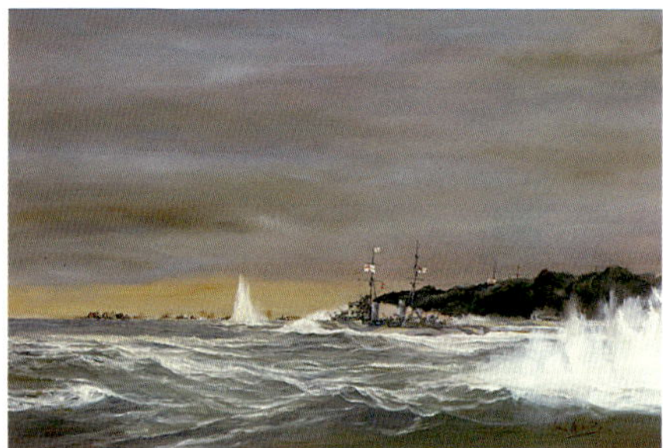

Hamilton, John 1919–1993
Second Battle of Sirte, 22 March 1942
1972–1978
oil on panel 60.9 x 91.4
IWM ART LD 7440

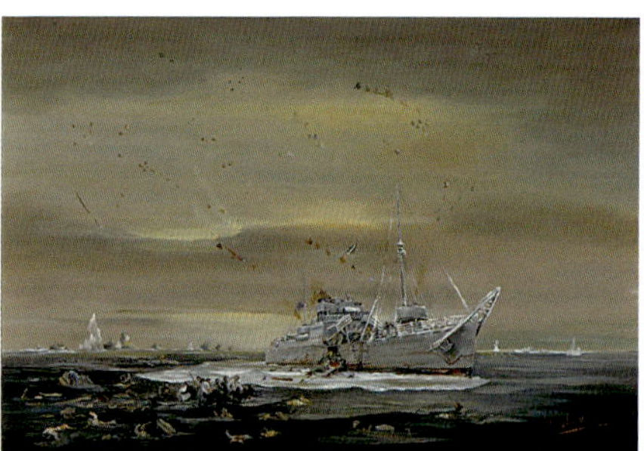

Hamilton, John 1919–1993
'SS Rathlin', Rescue Ship 1972–1978
oil on panel 60.9 x 91.4
IWM ART LD 7423

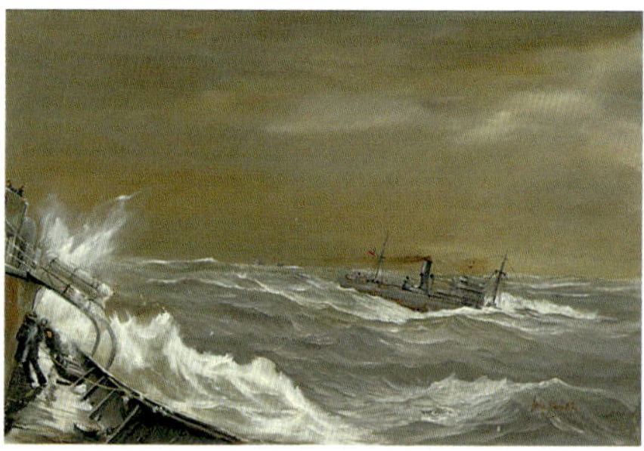

Hamilton, John 1919–1993
Storm at Sea 1972–1978
oil on panel 60.9 x 91.4
IWM ART LD 7456

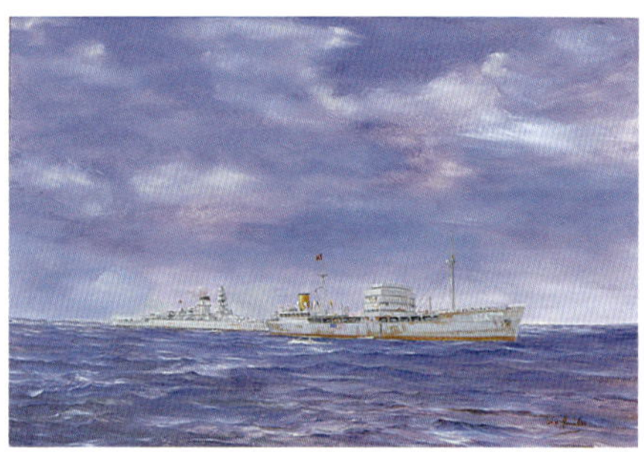

Hamilton, John 1919–1993
*Supplies for the Raiders: The Disguised Supply
Ship 'Nordmark' with the Raider 'Admiral
Scheer', March 1941* 1972–1978
oil on panel 60.9 x 91.4
IWM ART LD 7444

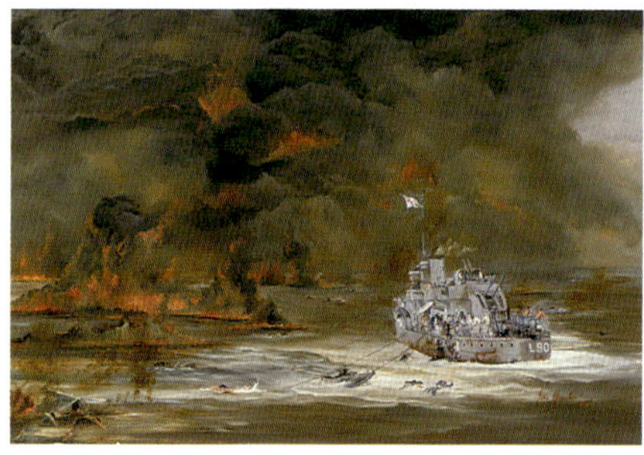

Hamilton, John 1919–1993
*Survivors: 'HMS Ledbury' Rescued 44 Men
from the Merchantman 'SS Waimarama',
Pedestal Convoy, 1942* 1972–1978
oil on panel 60.9 x 91.4
IWM ART LD 7435

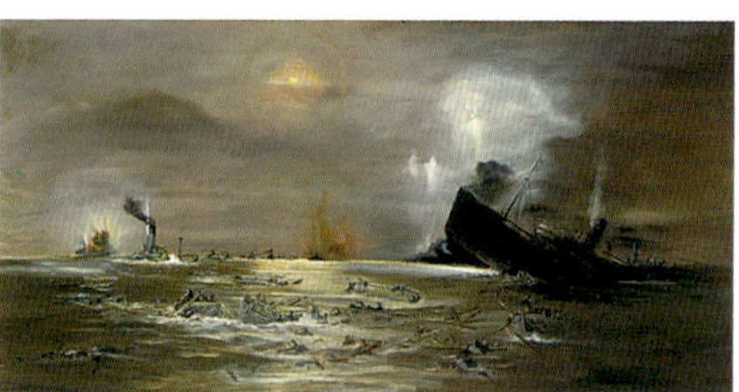

Hamilton, John 1919–1993
*The Attack on Convoy SC7: The Sinking of 'SS
Assyrian'* 1972–1978
oil on panel 60.9 x 121.9
IWM ART LD 7399

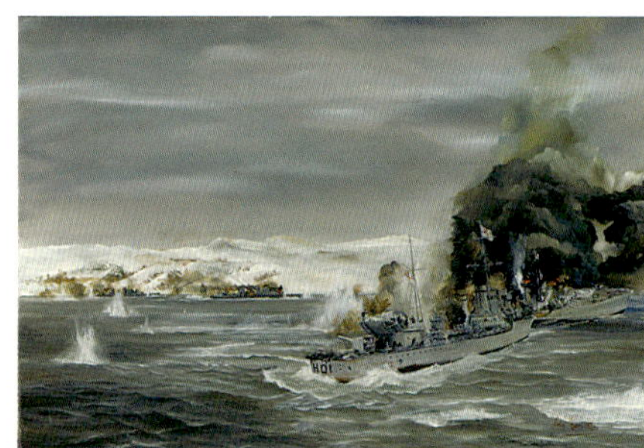

Hamilton, John 1919–1993
*The Battle of the Fjords: In the Running
Destroyer Fight, during the Withdrawal from
Narvik, the Damaged (…)* 1972–1978
oil on panel 60.9 x 91.4
IWM ART LD 7431

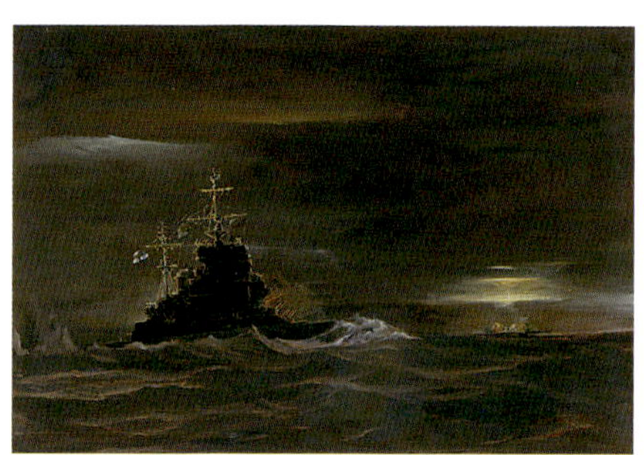

Hamilton, John 1919–1993
*The Battle of the North Cape: 'HMS Duke of
York' in Action against the 'Scharnhorst', 26
December 1943* 1972–1978
oil on panel 60.9 x 91.4
IWM ART LD 7424

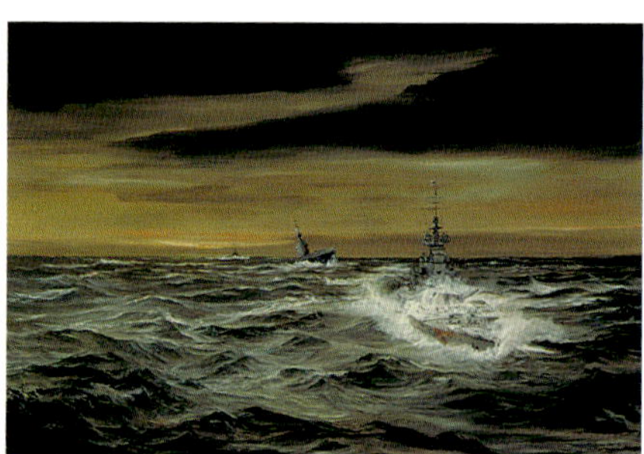

Hamilton, John 1919–1993
The 'Bismarck' Action: The 'Bismarck' Escapes
1972–1978
oil on panel 60.9 x 91.4
IWM ART LD 7416

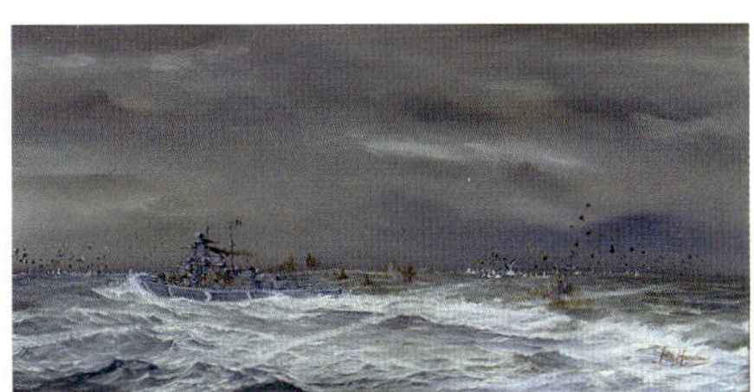

Hamilton, John 1919–1993
The 'Bismarck' Action: The 'Swordfish' Attack, 26 May 1941 1972–1978
oil on panel 60.9 x 121.9
IWM ART LD 7417

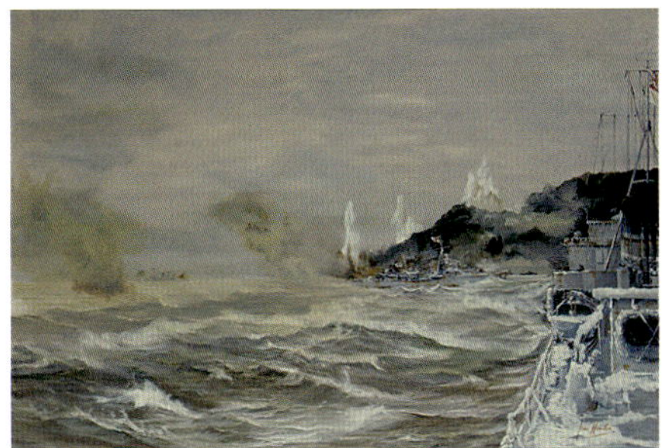

Hamilton, John 1919–1993
The Defence of Convoy JW 51B: Destroyers 'HMS Onslow' and 'HMS Orwell' Defended the Convoy (…) 1972–1978
oil on panel 60.9 x 91.4
IWM ART LD 7422

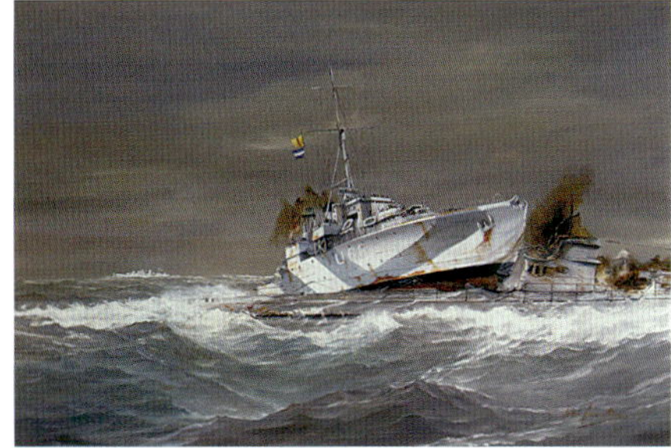

Hamilton, John 1919–1993
The Destruction of U-202 by 'HMS Starling', 1 June 1943 1972–1978
oil on panel 60.9 x 91.4
IWM ART LD 7411

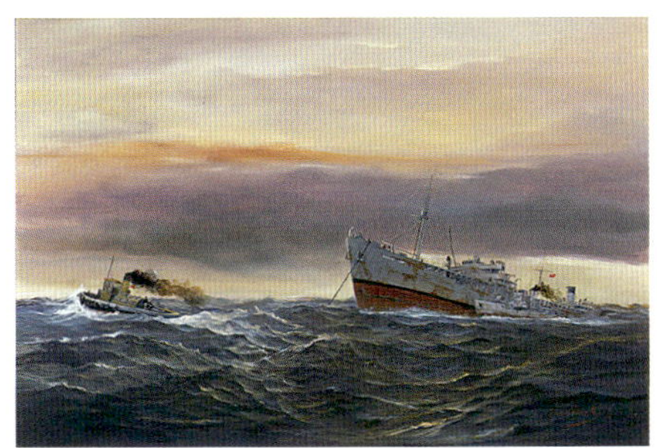

Hamilton, John 1919–1993
The Fight to Save the 'SS Regent Lion' 1972–1978
oil on panel 60.9 x 91.4
IWM ART LD 7405

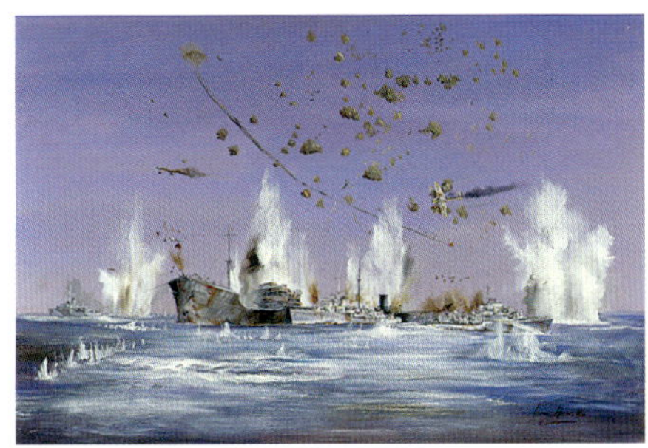

Hamilton, John 1919–1993
The 'Gallant Ohio' 1972–1978
oil on panel 60.9 x 91.4
IWM ART LD 7438

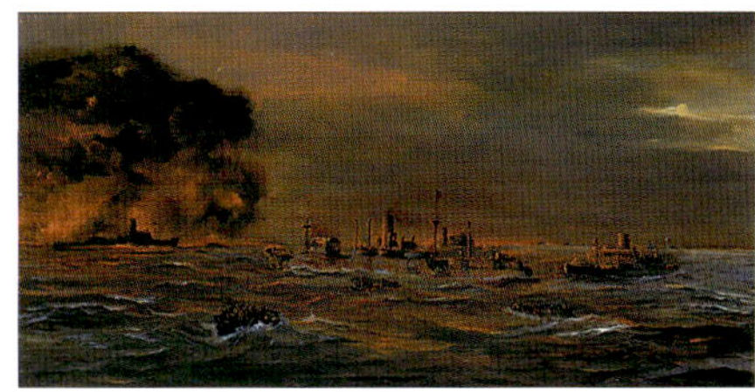

Hamilton, John 1919–1993
The 'Gallant Tekoa', New Zealand Steamship Company, Picking Up Survivors, March 1943 1972–1978
oil on panel 60.9 x 121.9
IWM ART LD 7408

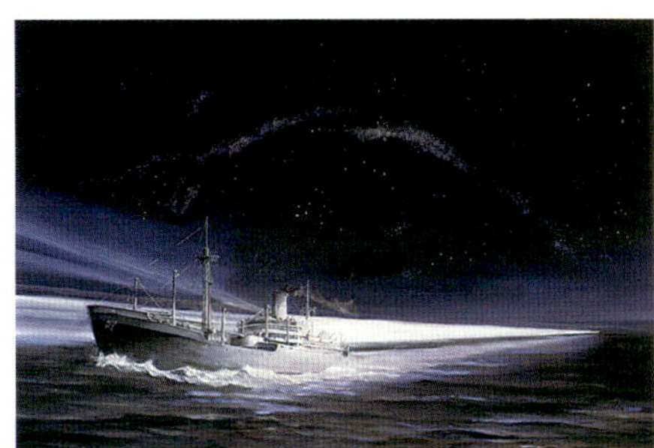

Hamilton, John 1919–1993
The 'Glenorchy' is Spotted, Pedestal Convoy, 13 August 1942 1972–1978
oil on panel 60.9 x 91.4
IWM ART LD 7436

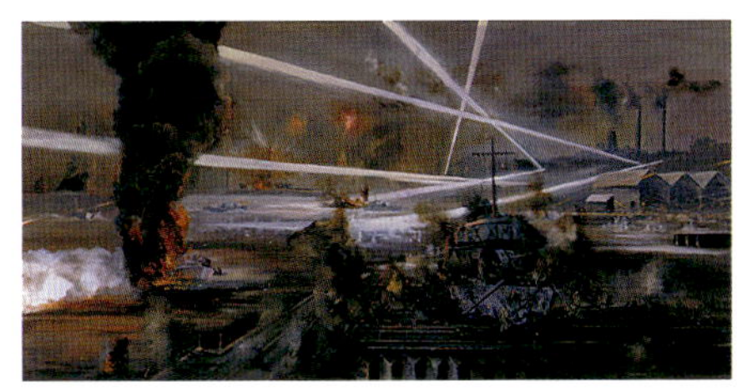

Hamilton, John 1919–1993
The Raid on St Nazaire, 27–28 March 1942 1972–1978
oil on panel 60.9 x 121.9
IWM ART LD 7450

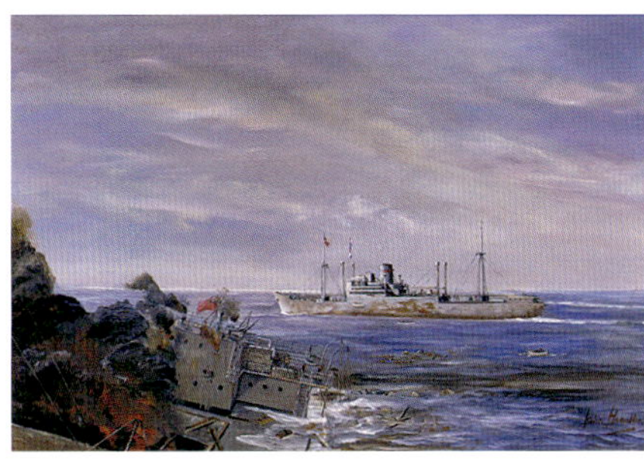

Hamilton, John 1919–1993
The Raider 'Kormoran' 1972–1978
oil on panel 60.9 x 91.4
IWM ART LD 7443

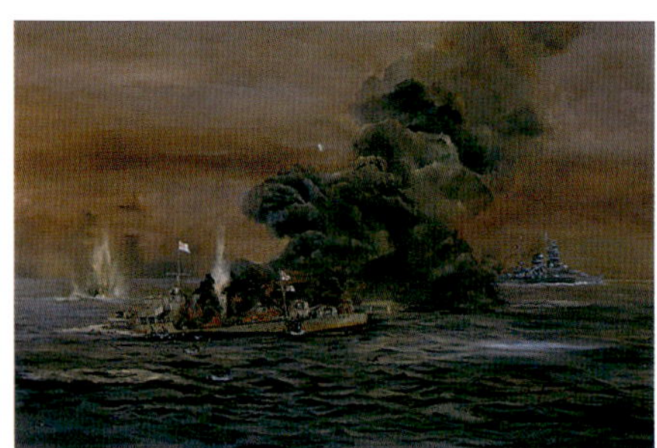

Hamilton, John 1919–1993
*The Sinking of 'HMS Acasta', Attacked by
Battleships 'Scharnhorst' and 'Gneisenau'*
1972–1978
oil on panel 60.9 x 91.4
IWM ART LD 7432

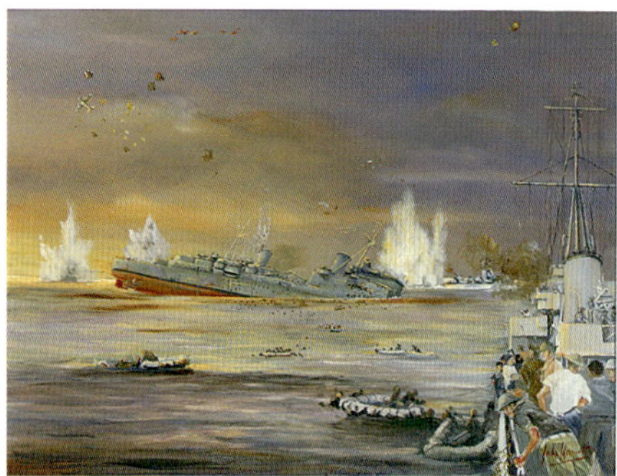

Hamilton, John 1919–1993
*The Sinking of 'HMS Fiji', 'HMS Kingston'
Standing by, 22 May 1941* 1972–1978
oil on panel 45.7 x 60.9
IWM ART LD 7434

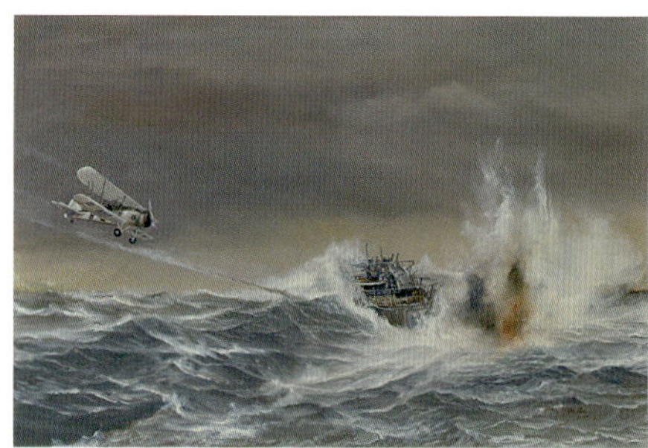

Hamilton, John 1919–1993
The Sinking of U-752, 23 May 1943
1972–1978
oil on panel 60.9 x 91.4
IWM ART LD 7413

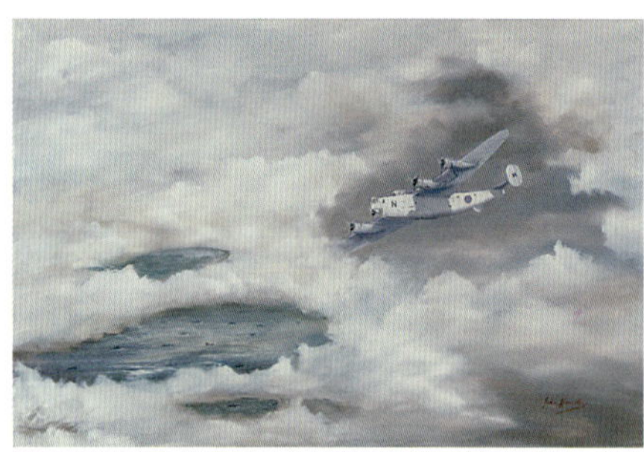

Hamilton, John 1919–1993
*The Tide Begins to Turn: One of the Long
Range Liberators of 120 Squadron, Royal Air
Force, Based in Iceland, (…)* 1972–1978
oil on panel 60.9 x 91.4
IWM ART LD 7409

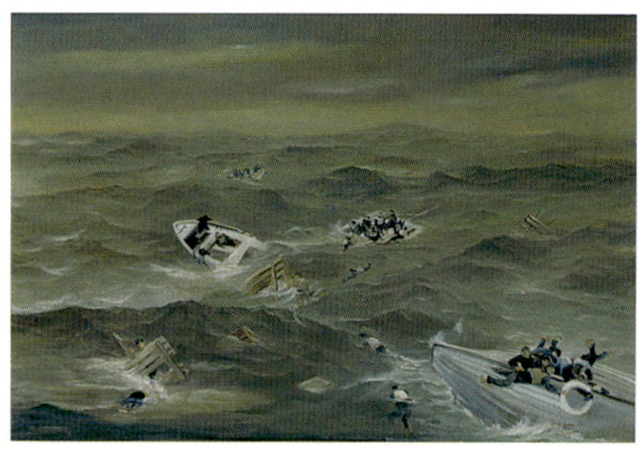

Hamilton, John 1919–1993
The Toll 1972–1978
oil on panel 60.9 x 91.4
IWM ART LD 7402

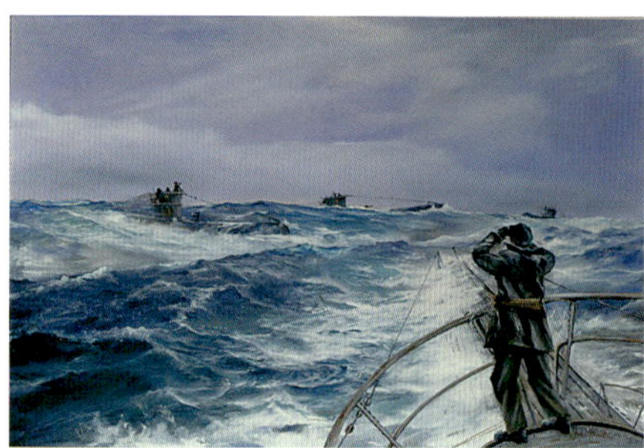

Hamilton, John 1919–1993
*The Wolf Pack Gathers: U-99, U-100, U-101
and U-123 Prepare to Attack Convoy SC7, 18
October 1940* 1972–1978
oil on panel 60.9 x 91.4
IWM ART LD 7452

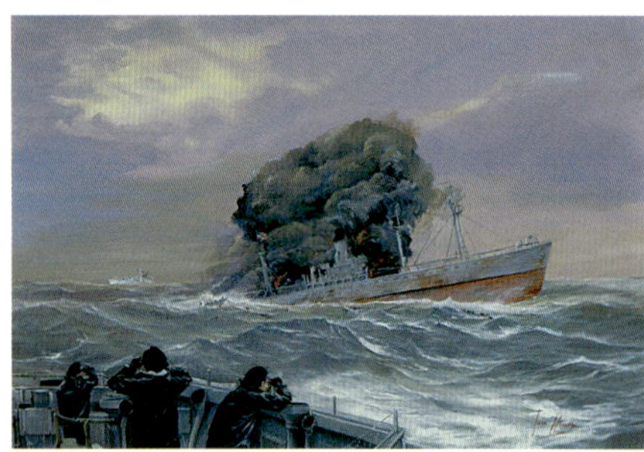

Hamilton, John 1919–1993
*Torpedoed: A Corvette Picks Up Survivors from
a Torpedoed Liberty Ship* 1972–1978
oil on panel 60.9 x 91.4
IWM ART LD 7403

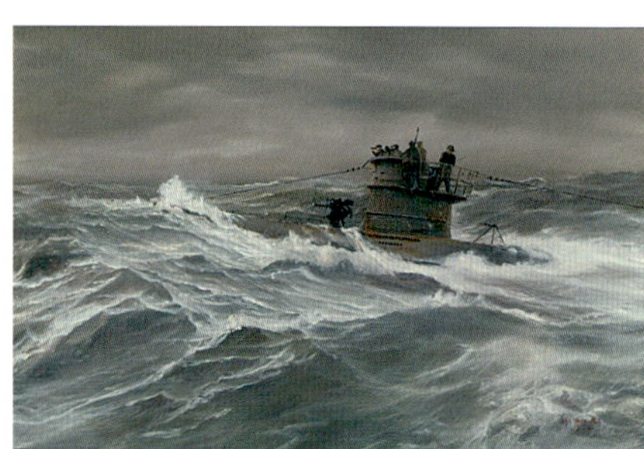

Hamilton, John 1919–1993
U-309 on Atlantic Patrol 1972–1978
oil on panel 60.9 x 91.4
IWM ART LD 7393

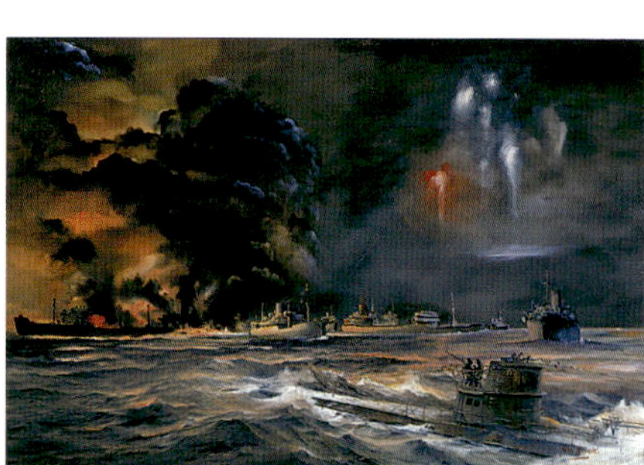

Hamilton, John 1919–1993
*U-Boats inside the Convoy: U-99 on the
Surface Having Torpedoed the Tanker 'Ferm', 7
March 1941* 1972–1978
oil on panel 60.9 x 91.4
IWM ART LD 7404

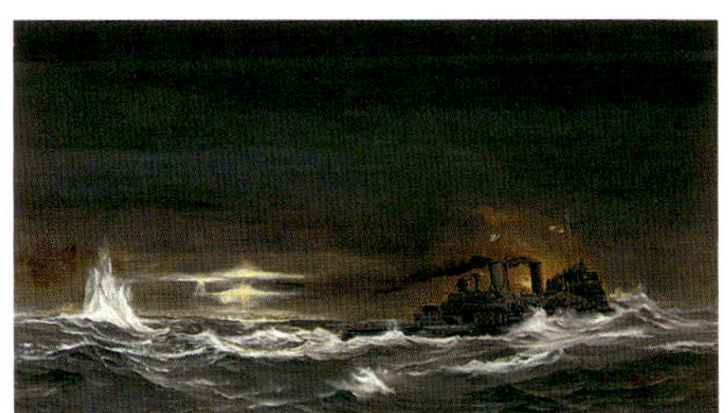

Hamilton, John 1919–1993
'HMS Belfast' in Action against the
'Scharnhorst', 26 December 1943 1974
oil on panel 50.8 x 91.4
IWM ART LD 7425

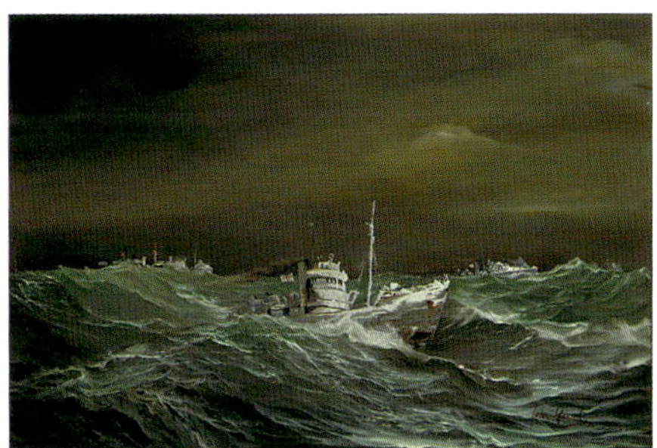

Hamilton, John 1919–1993
'HMS Northern Pride' 1974
oil on panel 60.9 x 91.4
IWM ART LD 7419

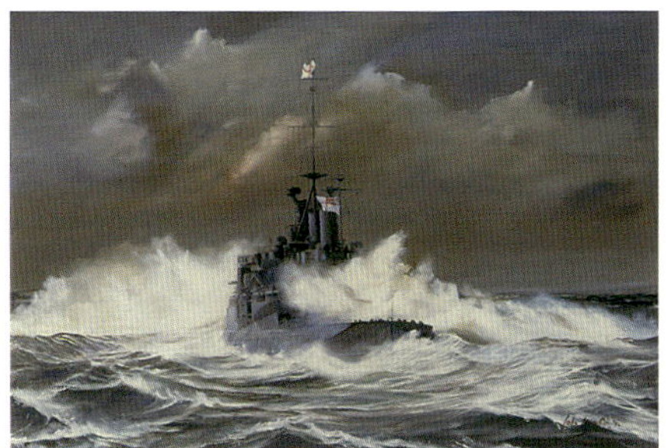

Hamilton, John 1919–1993
'HMS Renown' in a North Sea Gale, April
1940 1975
oil on panel 60.9 x 91.4
IWM ART LD 7396

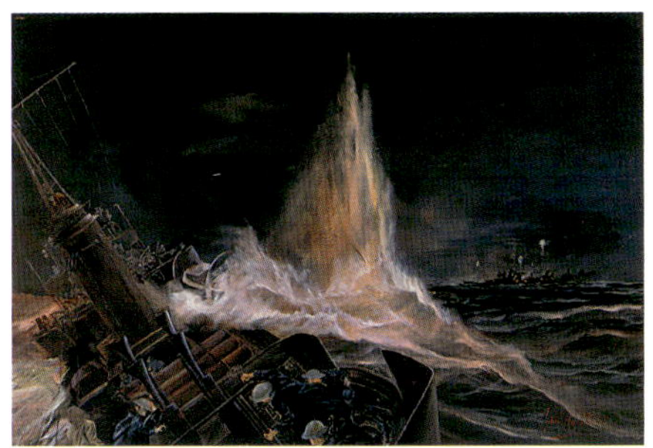

Hamilton, John 1919–1993
The 'Bismarck' Action: 'HMS Zulu' under Fire
1975
oil on panel 60.9 x 91.4
IWM ART LD 7418

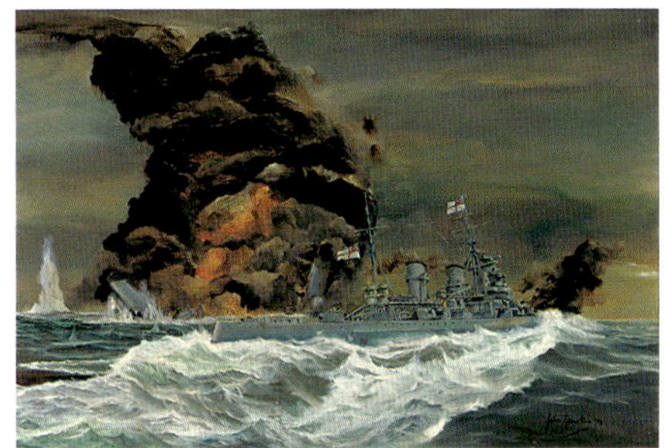

Hamilton, John 1919–1993
The 'Bismarck' Action: The Destruction of
'HMS Hood' 1975
oil on panel 60.9 x 91.4
IWM ART LD 7415

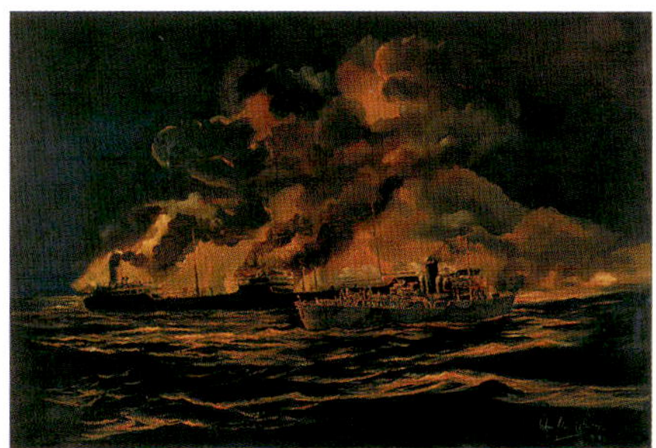

Hamilton, John 1919–1993
The Sinking of 'SS Bedouin', 16 March 1941
1975
oil on panel 60.9 x 91.4
IWM ART LD 7401

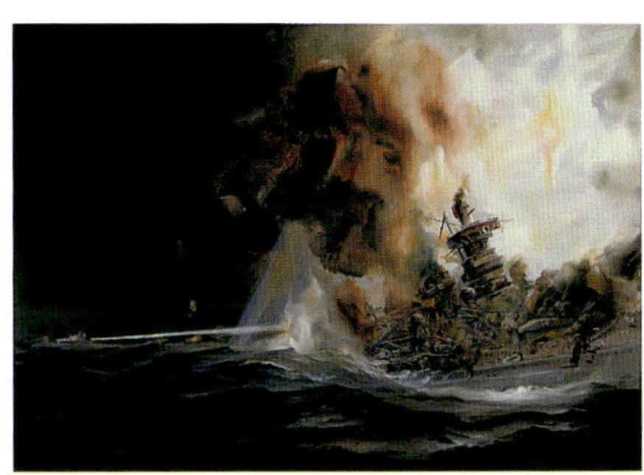

Hamilton, John 1919–1993
The Sinking of the 'Scharnhorst', 26 December
1943 1975
oil on panel 60.9 x 87.6
IWM ART LD 7426

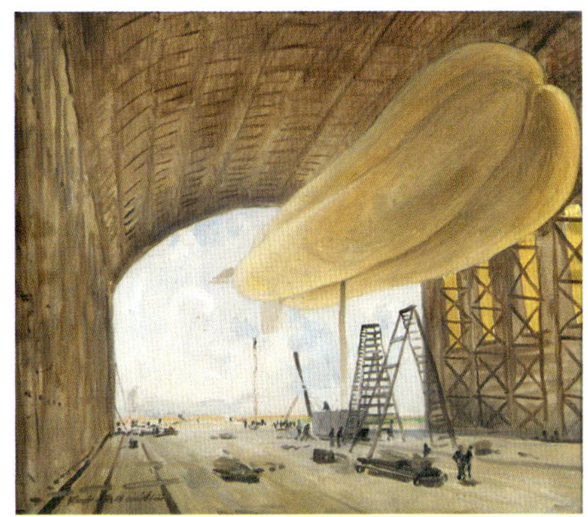

Hamilton, Vereker 1856–1931
HM Airship No.3 at Kingsnorth 1914
oil on canvas 49.5 x 58.4
IWM ART 862

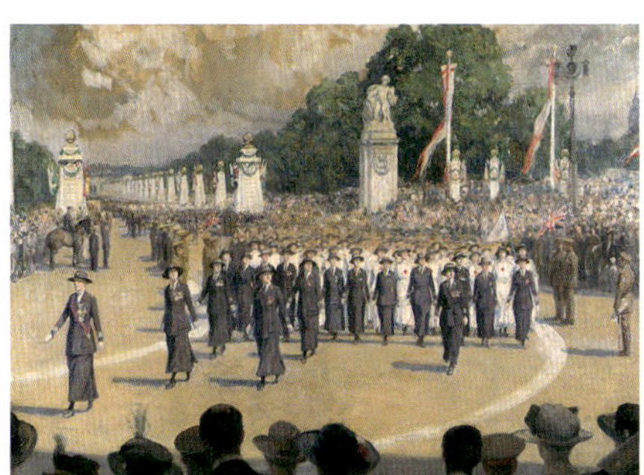

Harcourt, George 1868–1947
The Voluntary Aid Detachments: Peace
Procession, 19 July 1919 1919
oil on canvas 121.9 x 182.8
IWM ART 4037

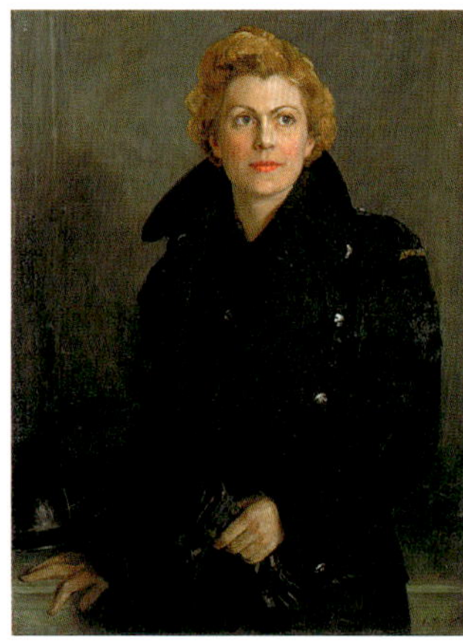

Harcourt, George 1868–1947
Aletha Harcourt, Ambulance Driver, Bushey Heath Air Raid Precautions 1942
oil on canvas 90 x 68.8
IWM ART 15627

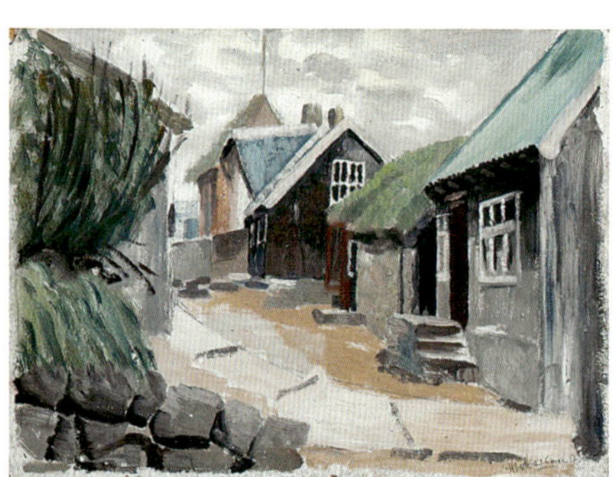

Harcourt, H. L. active 1940s
The Village of Sorvagur, Faroe Islands c.1943
oil on board 27.7 x 37.9
IWM ART 16618

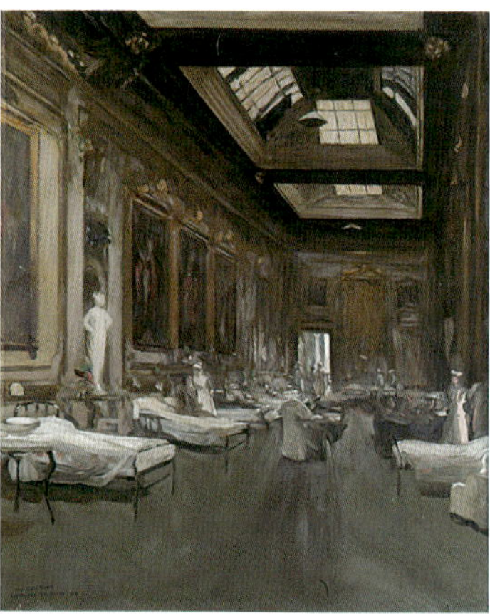

Hardy, Dorofield 1882–1927
The Ballroom, Londonderry House, 1912 (copy of John Lavery)
oil on canvas 75.5 x 62.8
IWM ART 5606

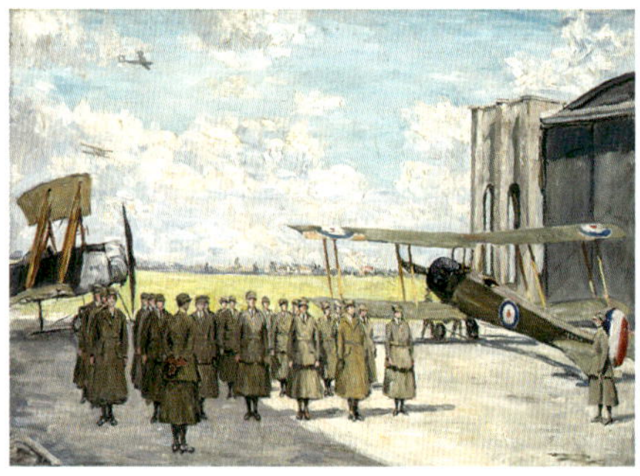

Harmar, Fairlie 1876–1945
Women's Royal Air Force Workers Drilling at Andover Aerodrome c.1917–1918
oil on canvas 50.8 x 71.1
IWM ART 5103

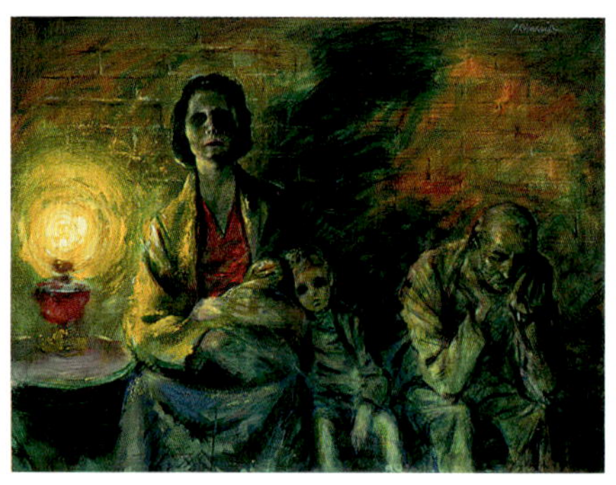

Harrison, Arthur R. active 1935–1976
The Long Night: London Blitz 1942
oil on board 91.4 x 123.1
IWM ART LD 7266

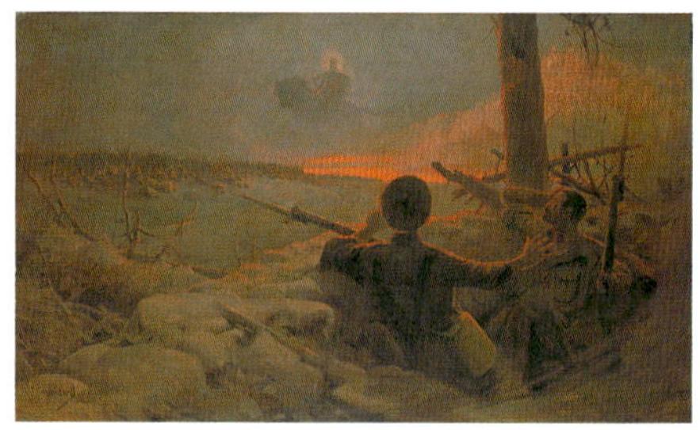

Hassall, John 1868–1948
The Vision of St George over the Battlefield 1915
oil on canvas 76.2 x 130.2
IWM ART 15600

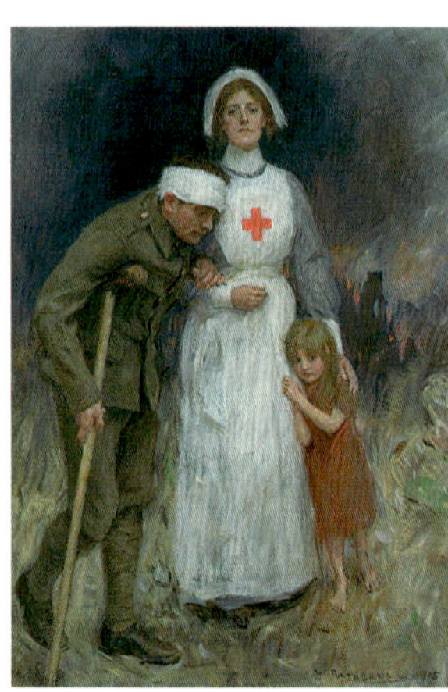

Hatherell, William 1855–1928
Nurse, Wounded Soldier and Child 1915
oil on canvas 45.7 x 32.3
IWM ART 5194

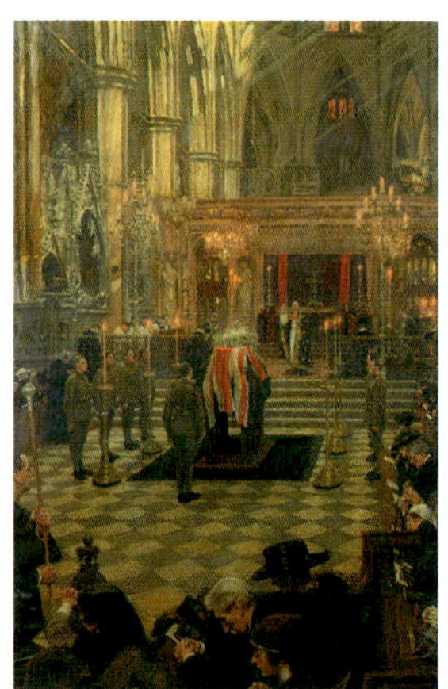

Hatherell, William 1855–1928
The Funeral Service of Edith Cavell at Westminster Abbey, 15 May 1919 1919
oil on canvas 170.8 x 114.9
IWM ART 2624

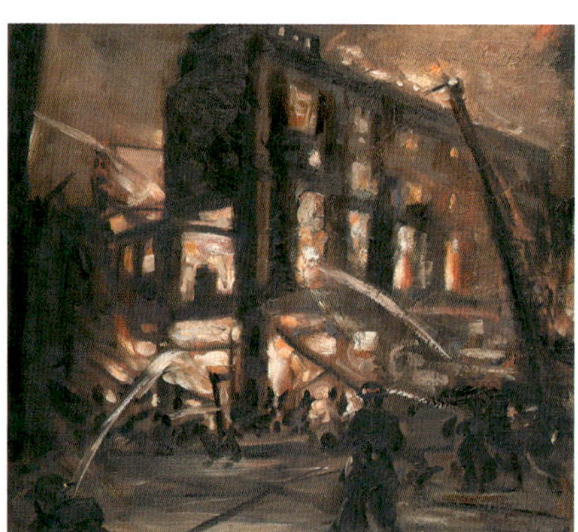

Haybrook, Rudolf 1868–1965
Hampton's 1939–1945
oil on canvas 69 x 76.5
IWM ART 16212

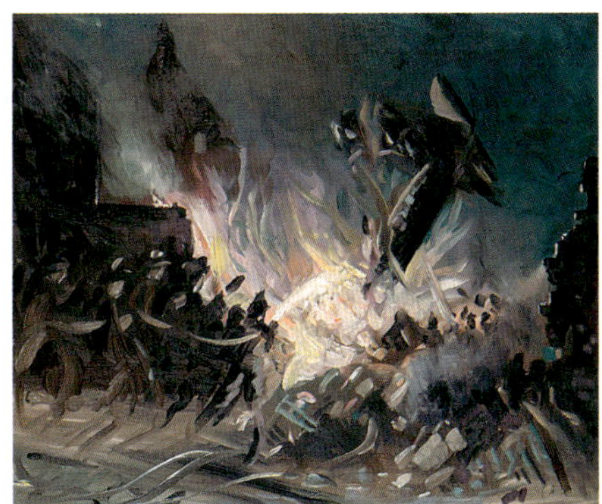

Haybrook, Rudolf 1868–1965
Aeroplane Crash, North London, May 1940
c.1940
oil on canvas 63.5 x 76.5
IWM ART 16211

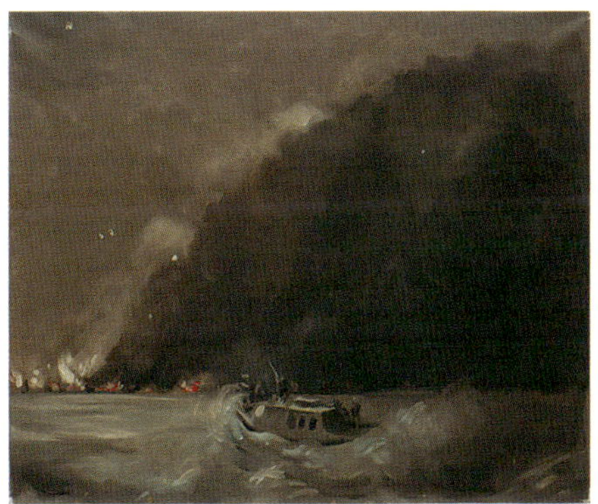

Haybrook, Rudolf 1868–1965
The London Fireboat 'Massey Shaw'
Approaching Dunkirk at 11pm, 2 June 1940
c.1940
oil on canvas 63.5 x 76.2
IWM ART LD 248

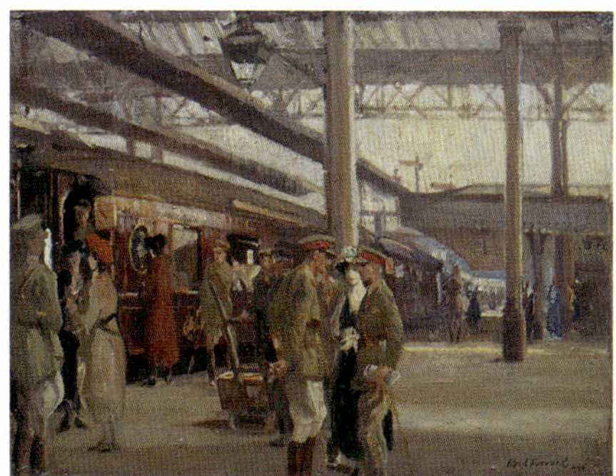

Hayward, Alfred Robert 1875–1971
First Study for 'The Staff Train at Charing
Cross Station' 1918
oil on canvas 38.1 x 50.8
IWM ART 1883

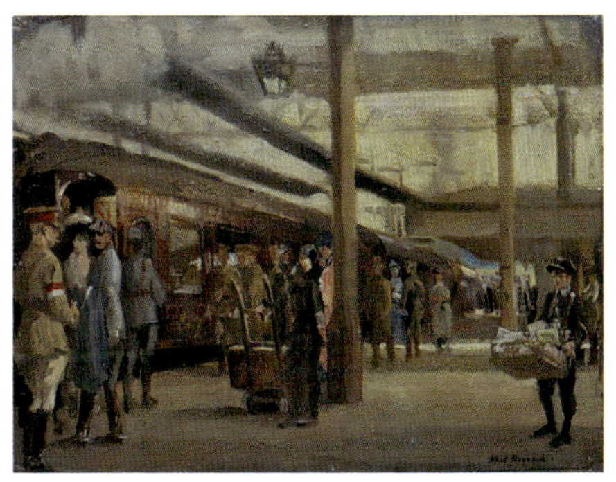

Hayward, Alfred Robert 1875–1971
Second Study for 'The Staff Train at Charing
Cross Station' 1918
oil on canvas 38.1 x 50.8
IWM ART 1884

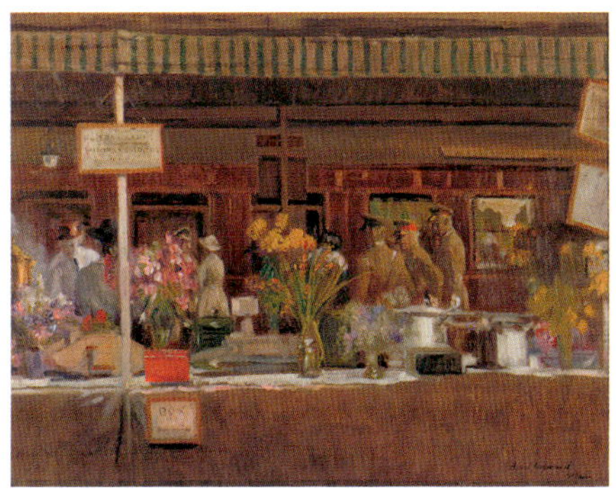

Hayward, Alfred Robert 1875–1971
The Soldiers' Buffet, Charing Cross Station
1918
oil on panel 45.7 x 60.9
IWM ART 1882

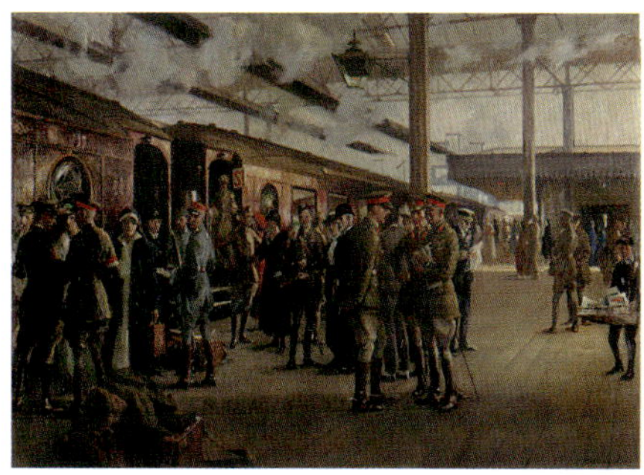

Hayward, Alfred Robert 1875–1971
The Staff Train at Charing Cross Station 1918
oil on canvas 106.6 x 152.4
IWM ART 1881

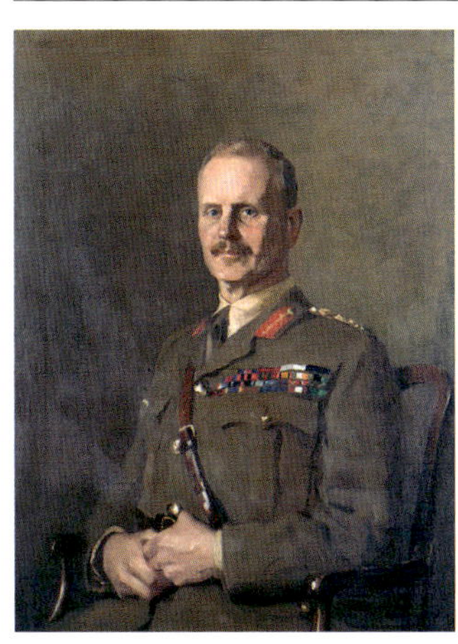

Hayward, Alfred Robert 1875–1971
General Sir William Riddell Birdwood
(1865–1951), GCMG, KCB, KCSI 1919
oil on canvas 91.4 x 71.1
IWM ART 1876

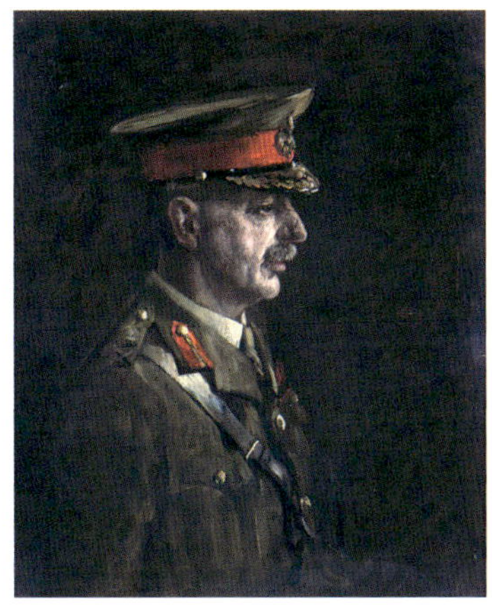

Hayward, Alfred Robert 1875–1971
Lieutenant General Sir William T. Furse
(1865–1953), KCB, DSO 1919
oil on panel 76.2 x 63.5
IWM ART 2277

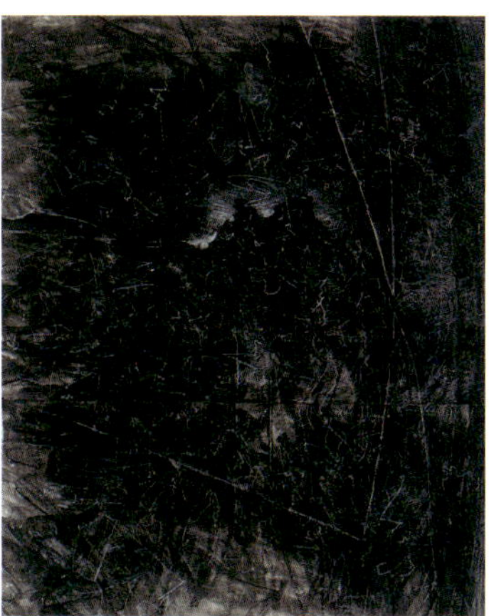

Hellawell, Harry 1921–2004
Untitled
mixed media on paper 88 x 71
IWM ART 17165

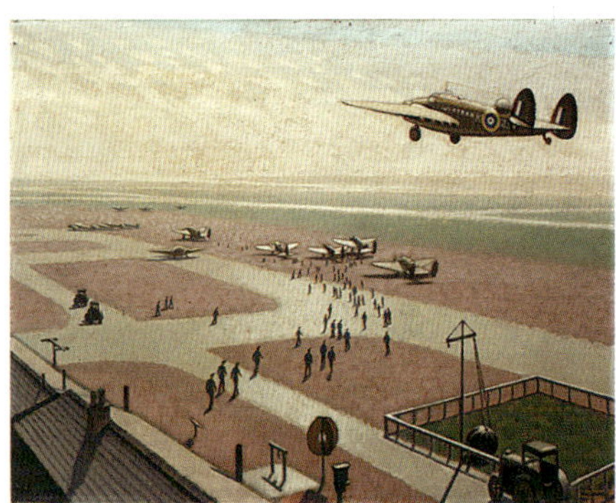

Henderson, Keith 1883–1982
A North-East Coast Aerodrome 1940
oil on canvas 69.8 x 90.1
IWM ART LD 257

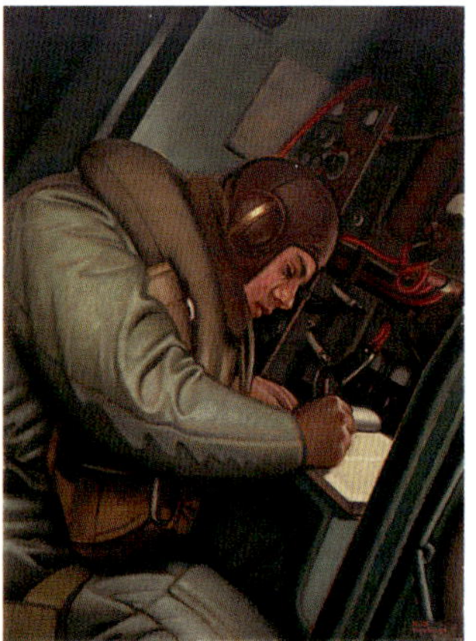

Henderson, Keith 1883–1982
A Sergeant Wireless Operator 1940
oil on canvas 101.9 x 76.2
IWM ART LD 379

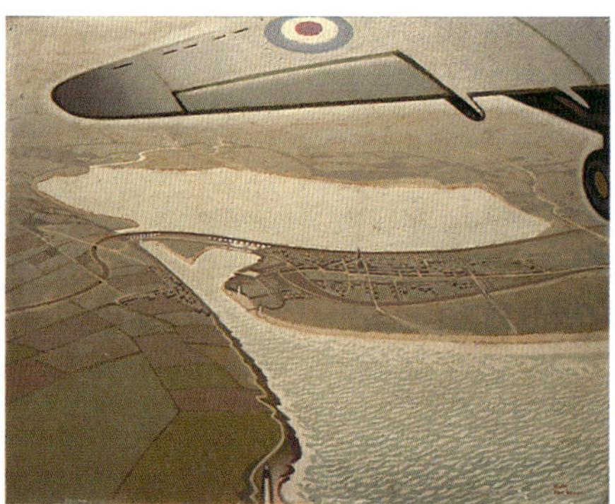

Henderson, Keith 1883–1982
An Air View of Montrose, Angus 1940
oil on panel 66 x 83.8
IWM ART LD 256

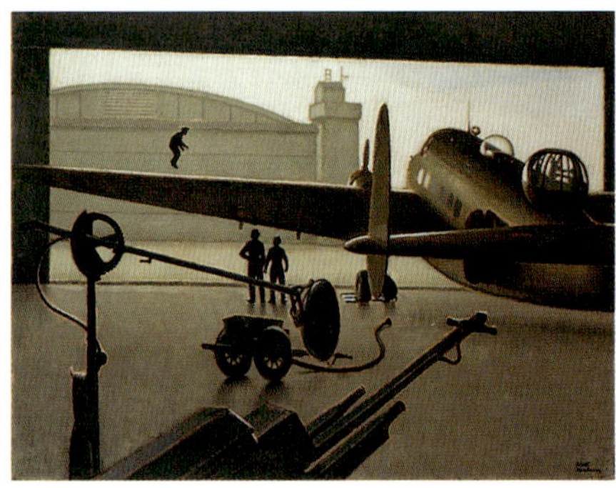

Henderson, Keith 1883–1982
An Improvised Test of an Undercarriage 1940
oil on canvas 76.2 x 101.9
IWM ART LD 380

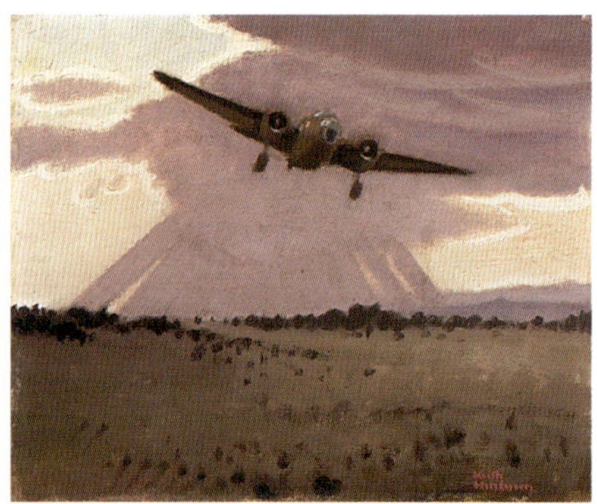

Henderson, Keith 1883–1982
Dawn: Leaving for North Sea Patrol 1940
oil on board 33 x 40.6
IWM ART LD 663

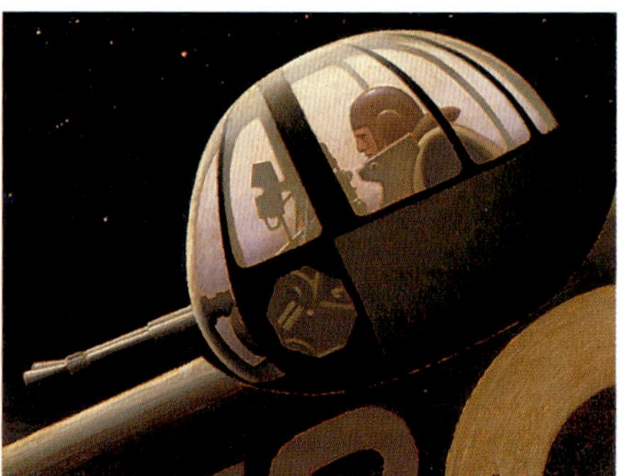

Henderson, Keith 1883–1982
Night: An Air Gunner in Action Turret 1940
oil on canvas 76.2 x 101.9
IWM ART LD 633

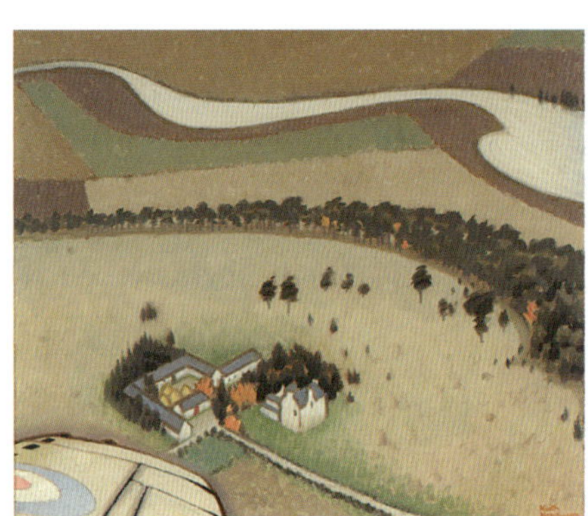

Henderson, Keith 1883–1982
Wings over Scotland 1940
oil on canvas 50.8 x 60.9
IWM ART LD 634

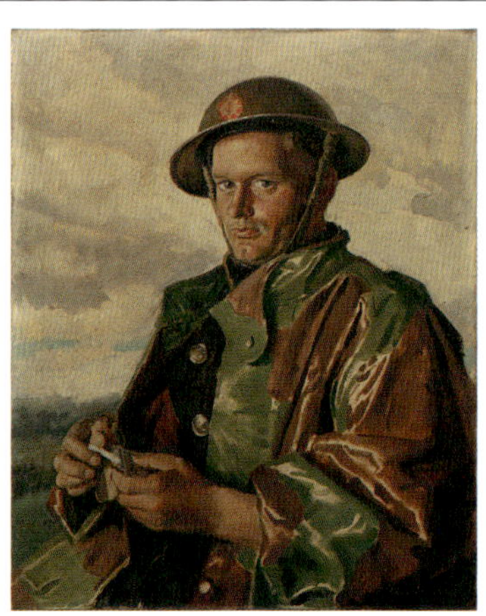

Hepple, Norman 1908–1994
Canadian Fireman, Overseas Contingent 1944
oil on canvas 75.5 x 62.8
IWM ART LD 4721

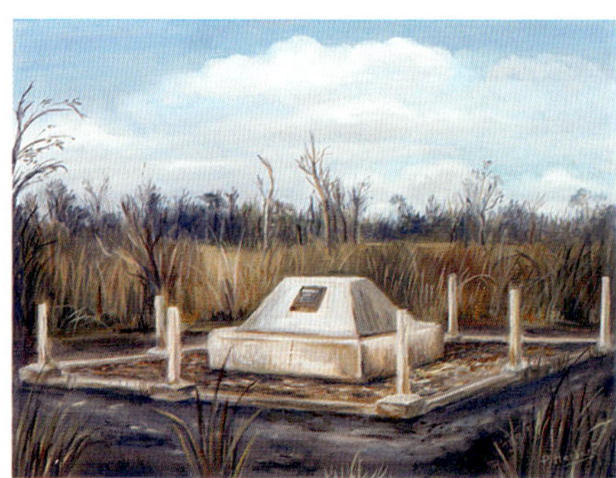

Herbert, P. active 1960s
Judi's Grave c.1960
oil on canvas 30.4 x 40.6
IWM ART LD 6683

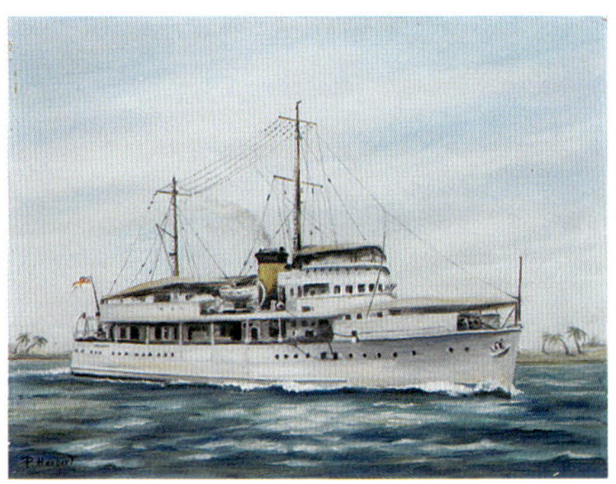

Herbert, P. active 1960s
Royal Navy Ships from the Starboard Bow
c.1960
oil on canvas 30.4 x 40.6
IWM ART LD 6682

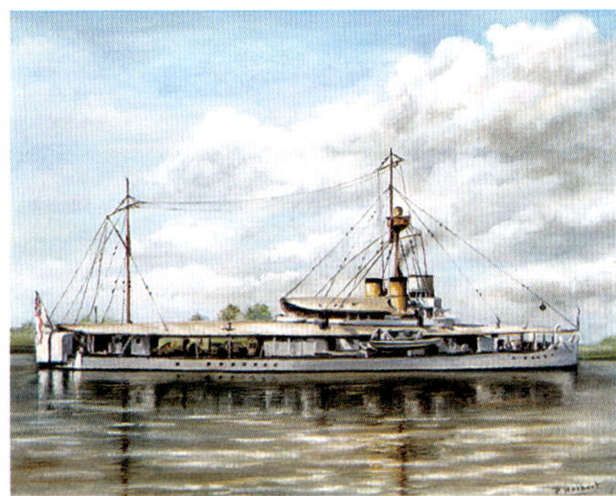

Herbert, P. active 1960s
*Two-Funnelled Royal Navy Ships from the
Starboard Quarter* c.1960
oil on board 40.6 x 50.8
IWM ART LD 6681

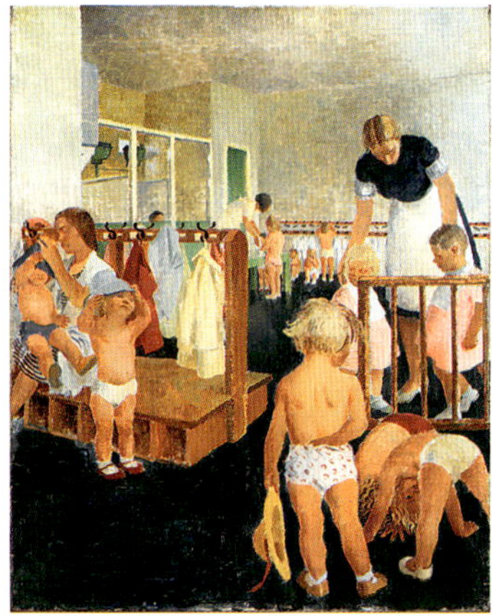

Hewland, Elsie Dalton 1901–1979
A Nursery School for War Workers' Children
1942
oil on canvas 56.8 x 46.8
IWM ART LD 2371

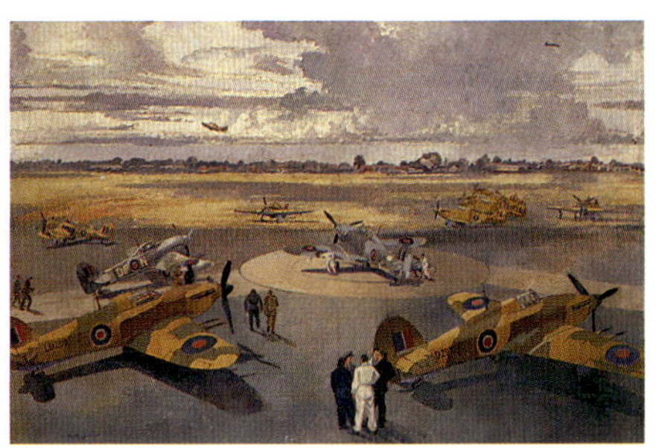

Hewland, Elsie Dalton 1901–1979
*Assembling Hawker Hurricane Aircraft:
Swinging the Compasses and Making Test
Flights* 1943
oil on canvas 50.8 x 76.2
IWM ART LD 3286

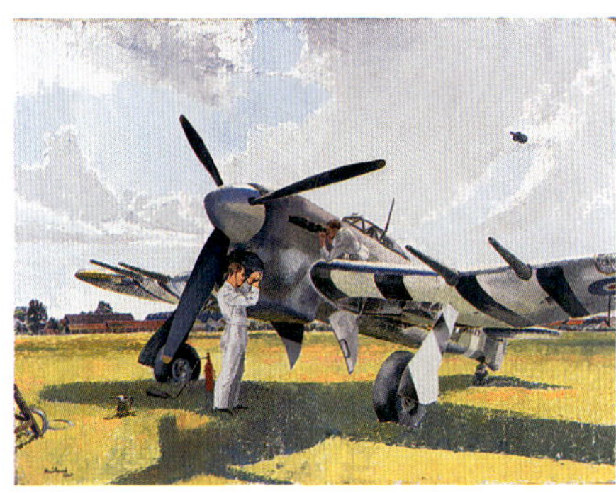

Hewland, Elsie Dalton 1901–1979
Typhoon Aircraft Undergoing Minor Repairs
1943
oil on canvas 45.7 x 60.9
IWM ART LD 3032

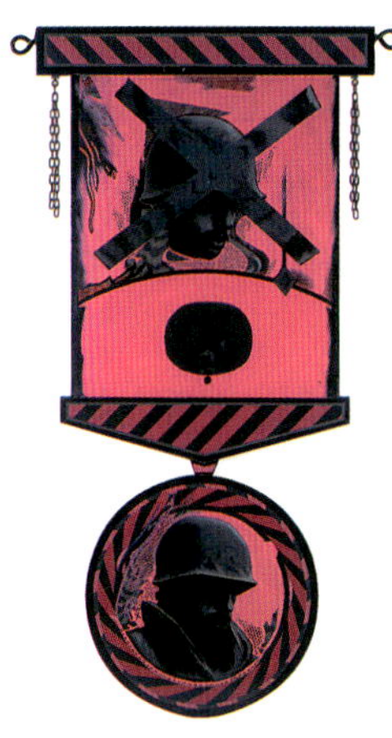

Hicks, Philip b.1928
Evening Blues 1968–1969
oil on metal, board & wood 205.7 x 144.7
IWM ART MW(A) 37

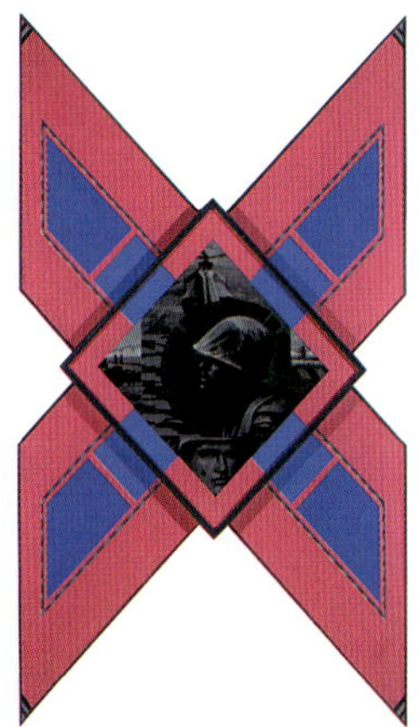

Hicks, Philip b.1928
Posthumous 1 1968–1969
oil on board & wood 210.8 x 116.8
IWM ART MW(A) 31

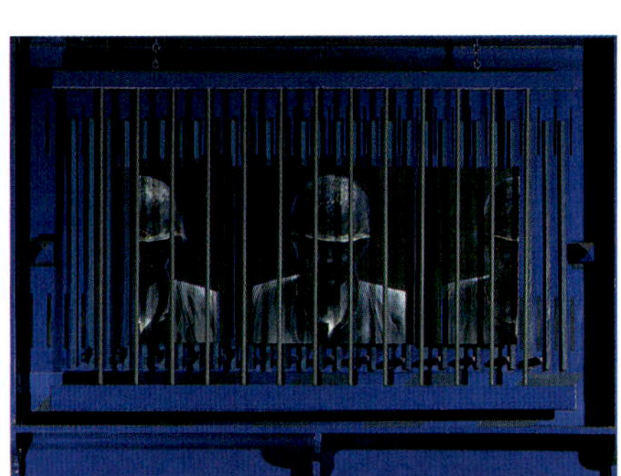

Hicks, Philip b.1928
Posthumous 2 1968–1969
oil on metal & wood 134.6 x 231.1
IWM ART MW(A) 32

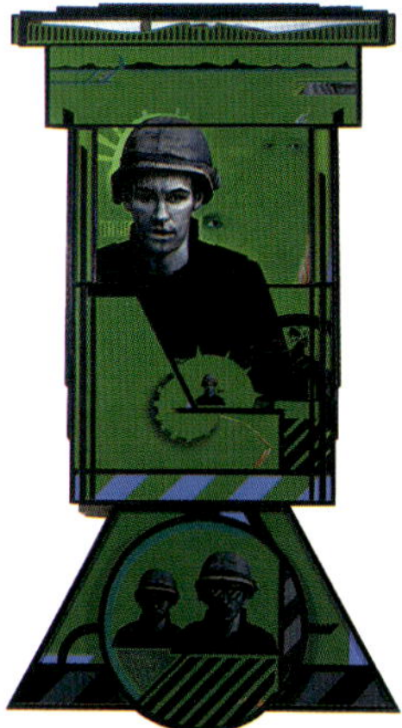

Hicks, Philip b.1928
Boy and Veteran 1969
oil on fibreglass, board & wood 233.6 x 127
IWM ART MW(A) 36

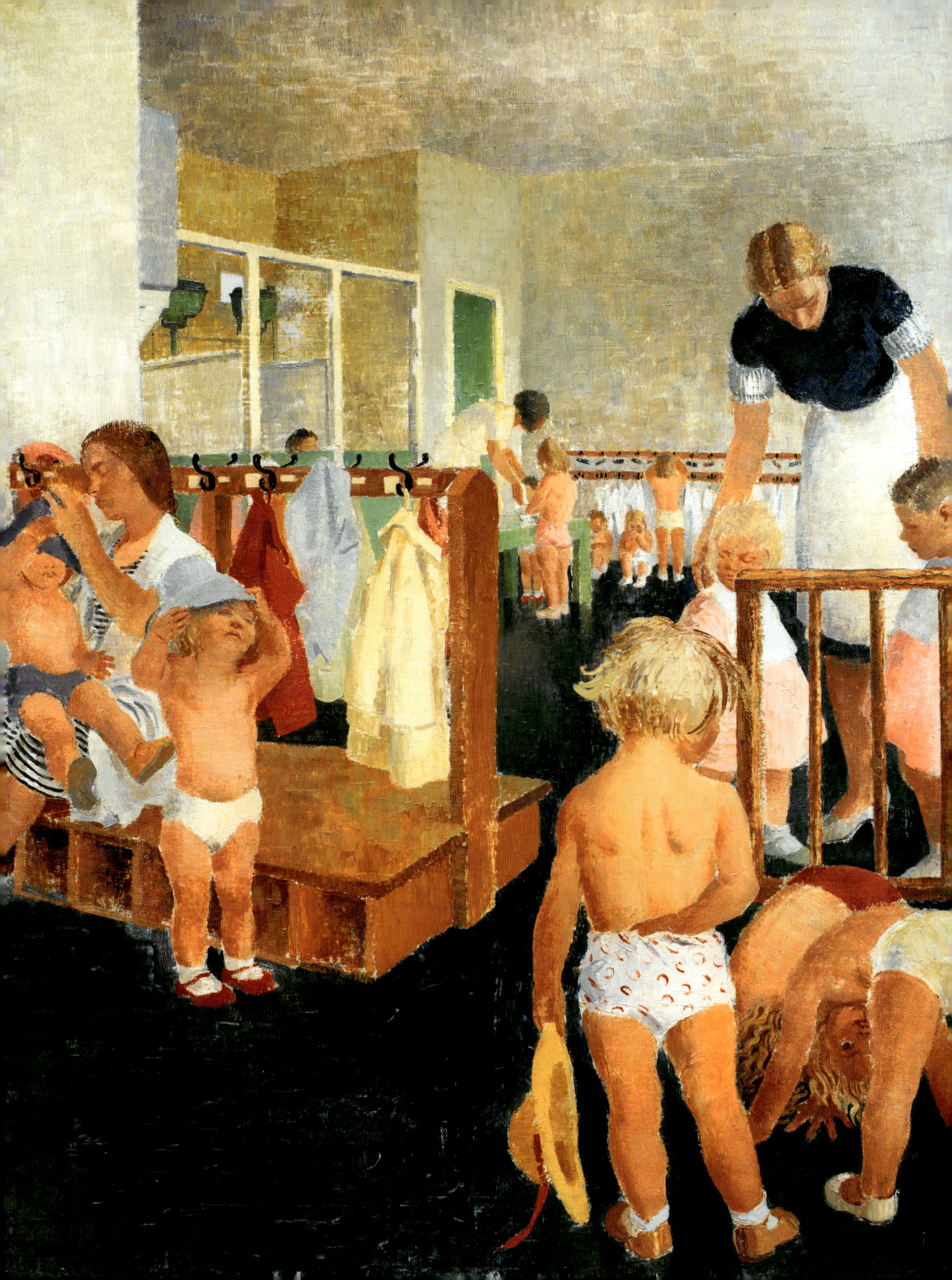

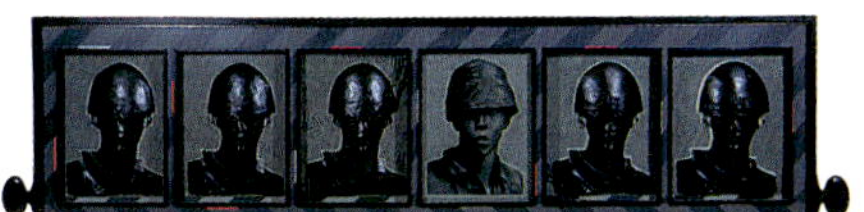

Hicks, Philip b.1928
Boy at War 1969
oil on board, wood & fibreglass 81.3 x 342.9
IWM ART MW(A) 35

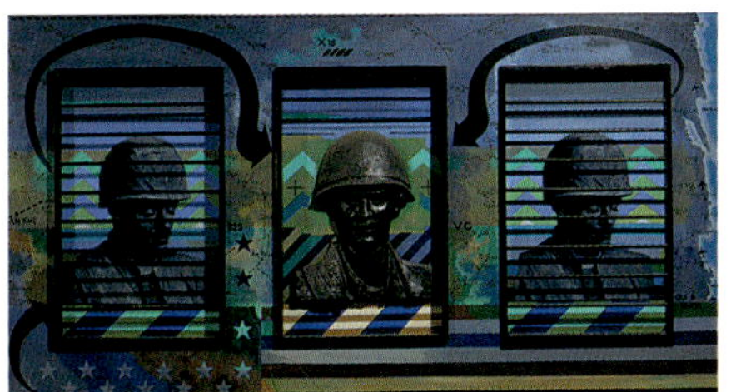

Hicks, Philip b.1928
Anonymous Award 1969–1970
oil on board 124.4 x 228.6
IWM ART MW(A) 38

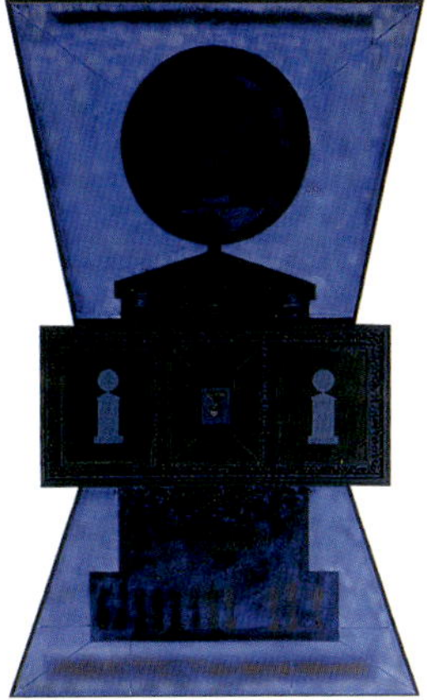

Hicks, Philip b.1928
Posthumous 3 1969–1970
oil & acrylic on board & wood 182.8 x 111.7
IWM ART MW(A) 33

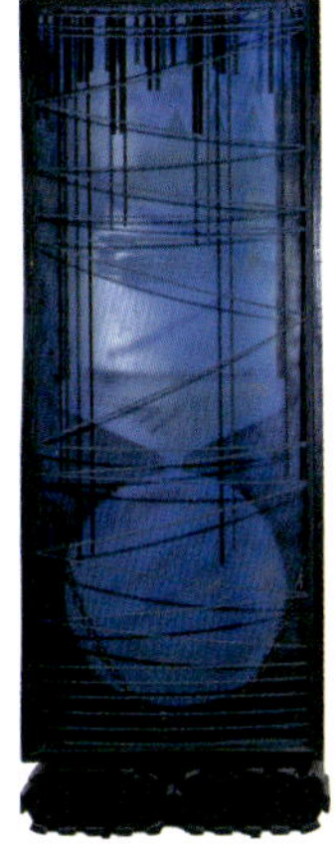

Hicks, Philip b.1928
Posthumous 4 1970
oil & acrylic on board, wood, metal & cord
198.1 x 73.6
IWM ART MW(A) 34

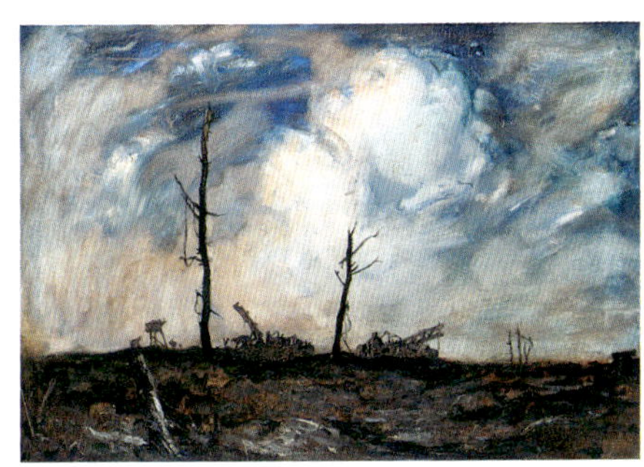

Hill, Adrian Keith Graham 1895–1977
Ruins between Bernafay Wood and Maricourt
1918
oil on canvas 71.1 x 101.9
IWM ART 1663

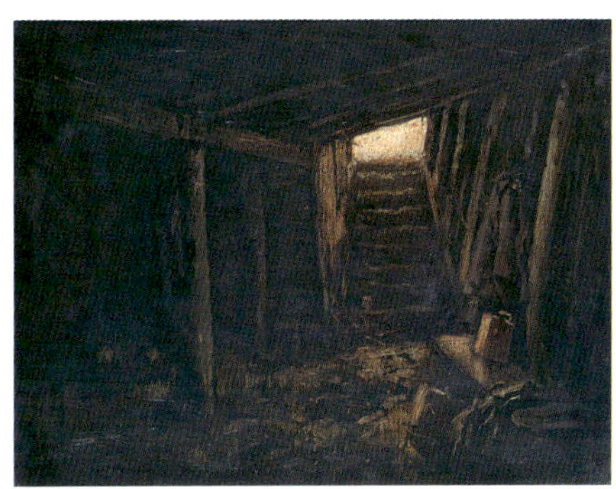

Hill, Adrian Keith Graham 1895–1977
Interior of a Dugout at Gavrelle 1927
oil on canvas 55.2 x 72.3
IWM ART 4432

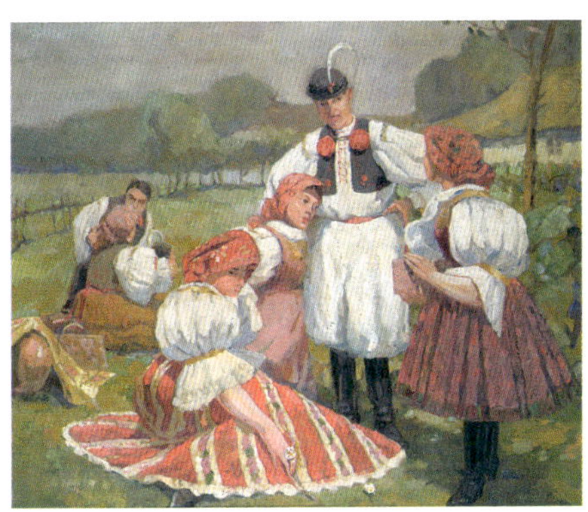

Hlavsa, Oldrich 1889–1936
*Country Life in Moravia: 'To Our Comrades in
Arms (the Officers of 'HMS Suffolk'), from the
Czecho-Slovaks Vladivostok'* 1918
oil on canvas 78.1 x 92
IWM ART 3990

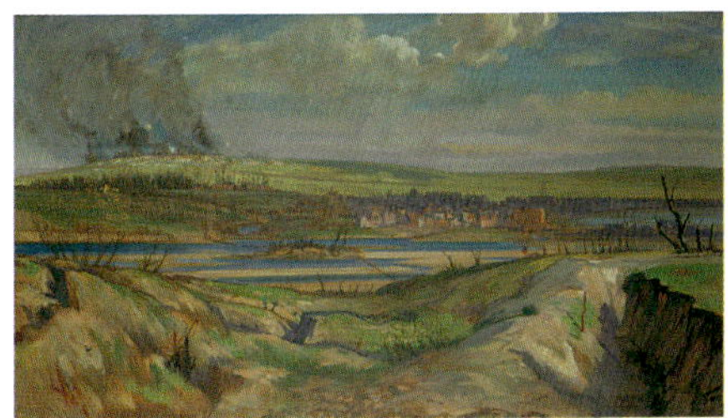

Hodge, Francis Edwin 1883–1949
*Mont St Quentin and Péronne from near
Maisonette, 1918* 1919
oil on canvas 69.2 x 122.5
IWM ART 2289

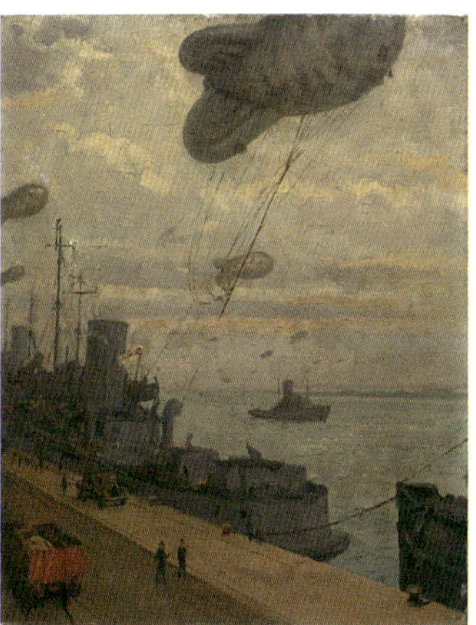

Hodge, Francis Edwin 1883–1949
*A Balloon Being Transferred to a Land Winch
from a Barrage Balloon Vessel* 1941
oil on canvas 50.8 x 40.6
IWM ART LD 1611

Facing page: Hewland, Elsie Dalton, 1901–1979, *A Nursery School for War Workers' Children* (detail), 1942, (p. 109)

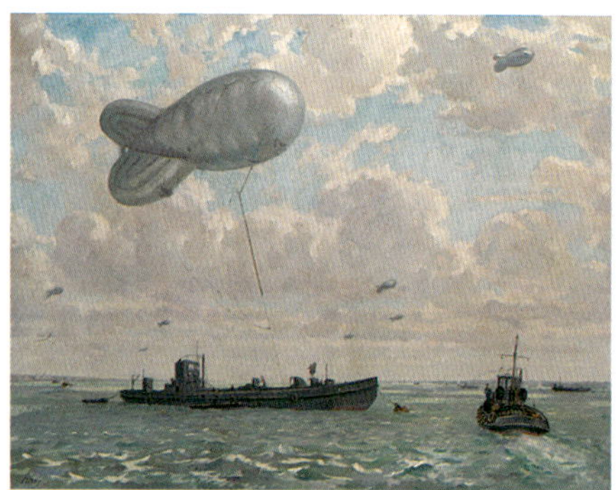

Hodge, Francis Edwin 1883–1949
A Balloon Close: Hauled on a Barge 1941
oil on canvas 71.1 x 91.4
IWM ART LD 1931

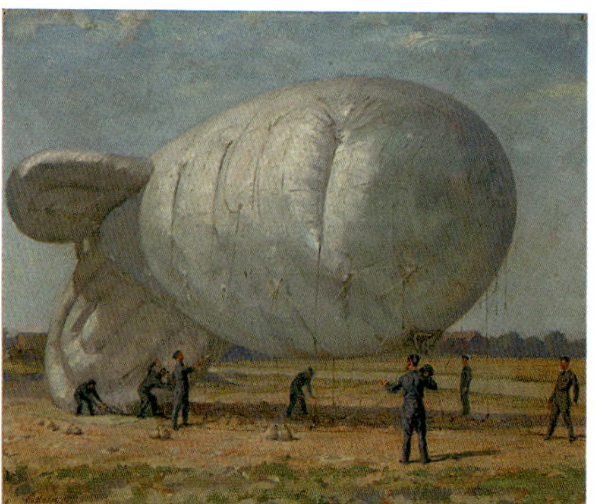

Hodge, Francis Edwin 1883–1949
Bedding Down: A Barrage Balloon 1941
oil on canvas 50.8 x 60.9
IWM ART LD 1612

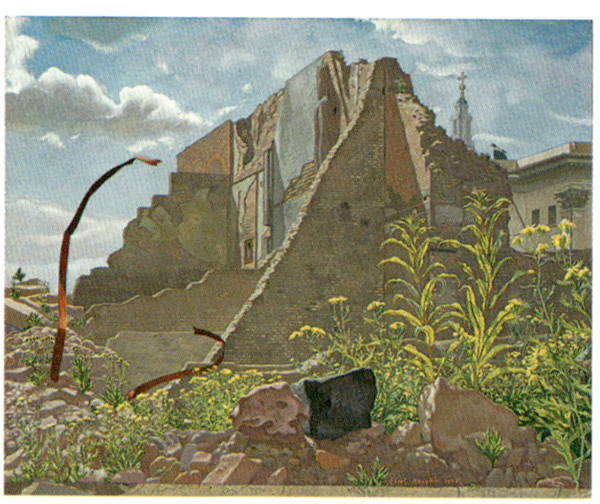

Hodgkin, Eliot 1905–1987
The Haberdashers' Hall, 8 May 1945 1945
tempera on panel 29.2 x 36.8
IWM ART LD 5311

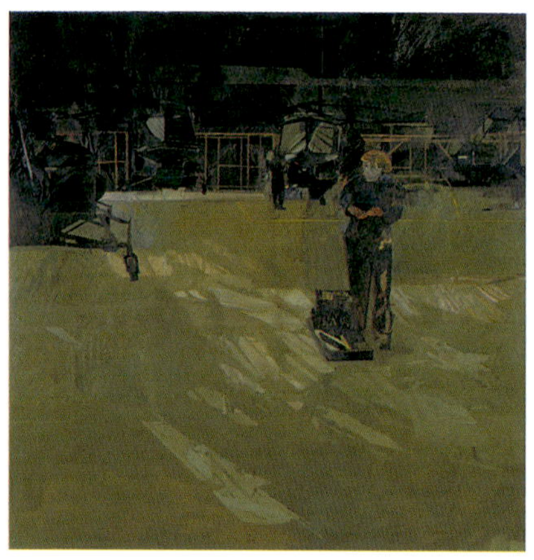

Hogan, Eileen b.1946
*Women's Royal Naval Service Air Mechanic,
Portland* 1983
oil on board 122 x 122
IWM ART 15749

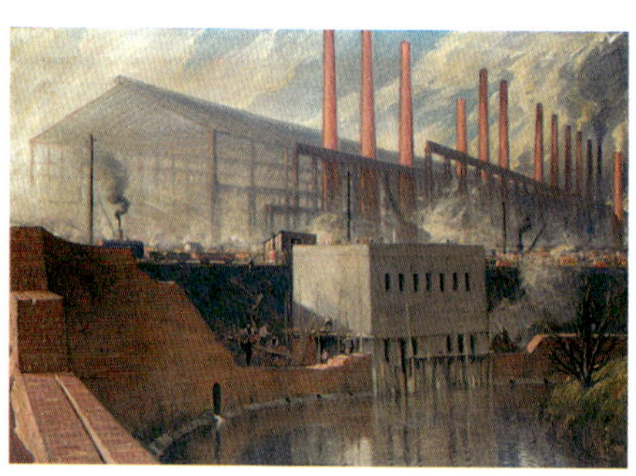

Holmes, Charles John 1868–1936
*A Two-Year-Old Steel Works: Erected during
the War for Messrs. Steel, Peech & Tozer, Ltd,
Phoenix Works, Sheffield* c.1918
oil on canvas 106.6 x 152.4
IWM ART 1216

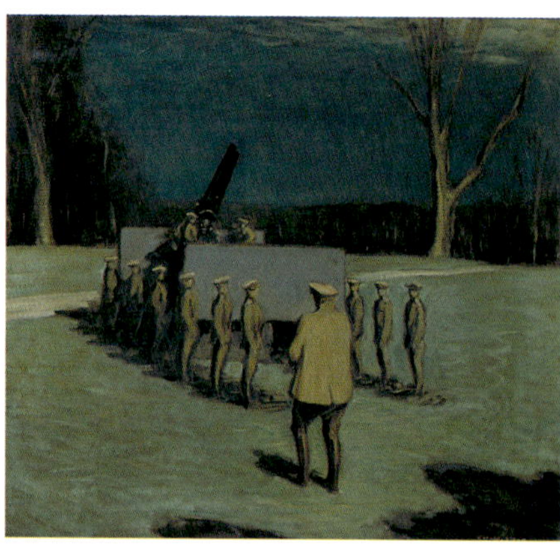

Holmes, Charles John 1868–1936
*Awaiting Zeppelins: Sandringham, January
1915* 1919
oil on canvas 69 x 76.5
IWM ART 2493

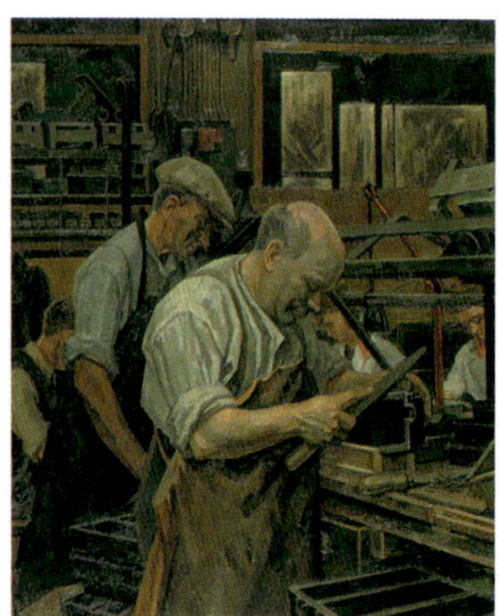

Horton, Percy Frederick 1897–1970
Blind Workers in a Birmingham Factory
c.1942
oil on canvas 60.9 x 50.8
IWM ART LD 3920

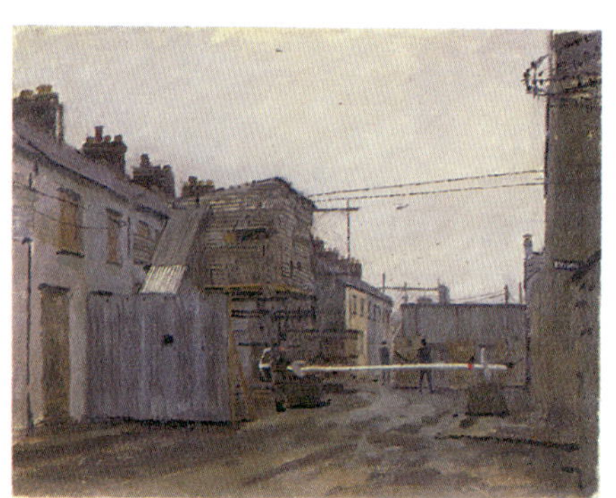

Howard, Ken b.1932
Rosemount 1973
oil on canvas 38.1 x 55.8
IWM ART MW(A) 24

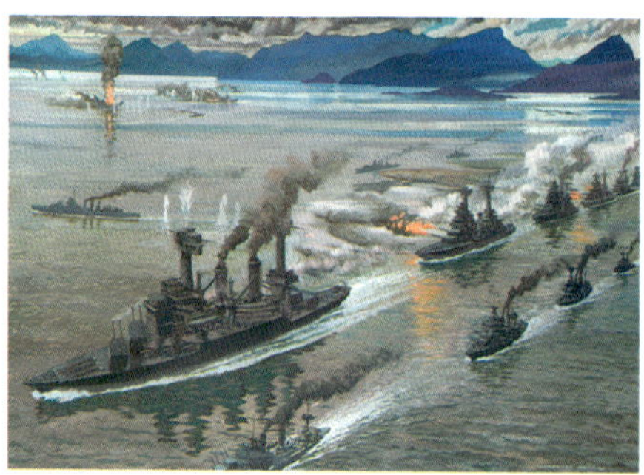

Howard, Norman 1899–1955
The Battle of the Leyte Gulf c.1945–1955
oil on canvas 76.5 x 107
IWM ART 15452

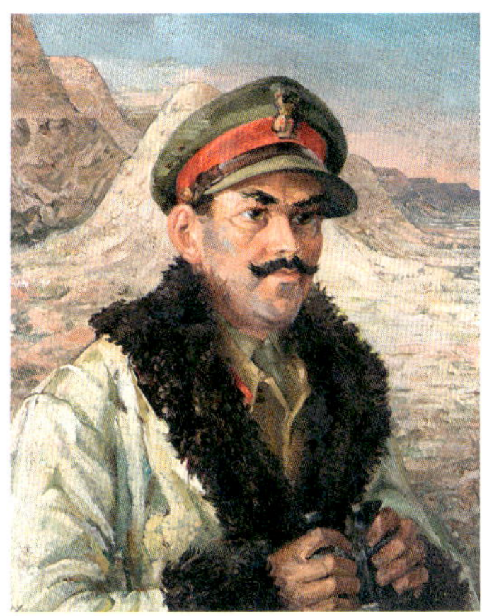

Howard-Jones, Ray 1903–1996
*Brigadier L. Howard-Jones, OBE, Royal
Electrical and Mechanical Engineers, 8th Army
(1942–1943)* 1943
oil on panel 60 x 49.8
IWM ART LD 3766

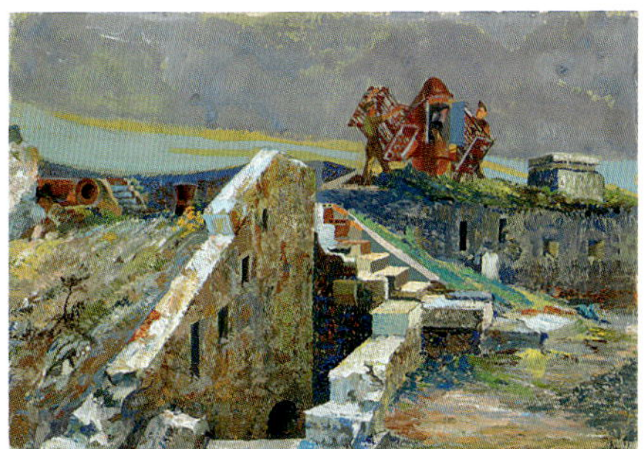

Howard-Jones, Ray 1903–1996
*Fortified Islands in the Bristol Channel: Two
Inch Naval UP-Projector on an Earlier
Fortification* 1943
oil & gouache on board 36.6 x 53.4
IWM ART LD 3527

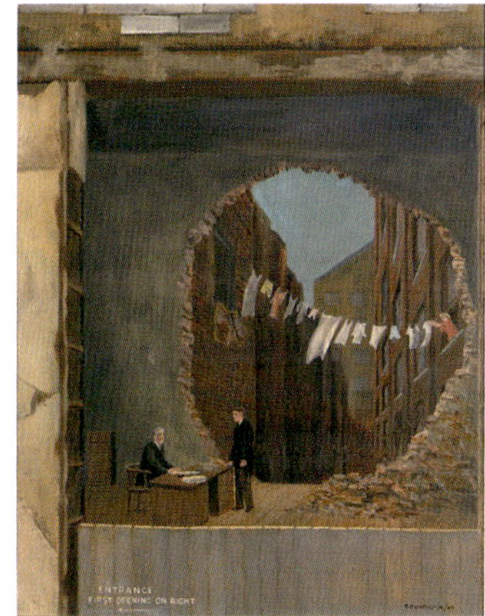

Howitt-Lodge, B. 1883–1948
London 'Carries On' 1940
oil on canvas 50.8 x 40.6
IWM ART LD 1508

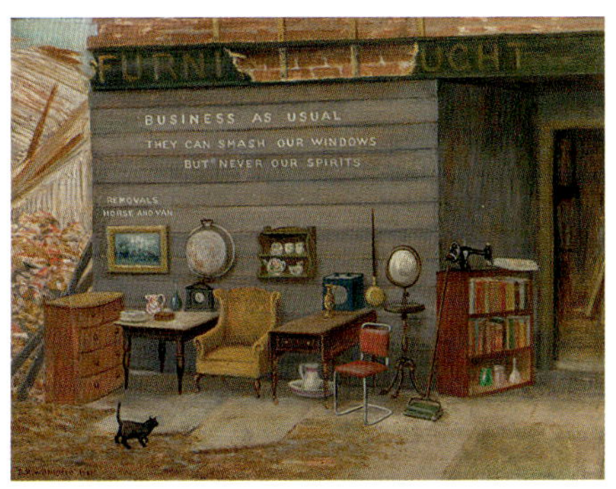

Howitt-Lodge, B. 1883–1948
Business as Usual 1941
oil on canvas 30.4 x 40.6
IWM ART LD 1176

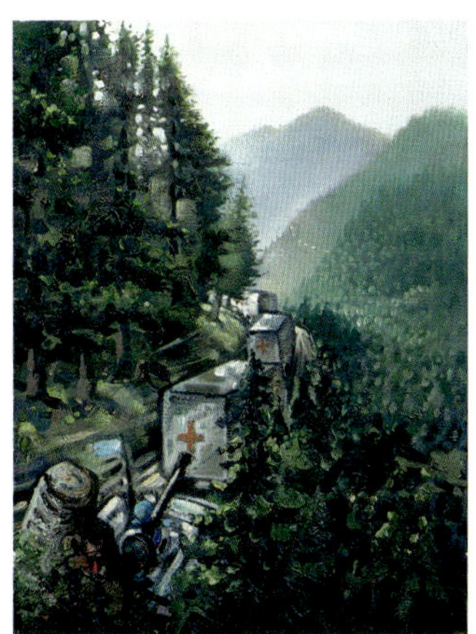

Howson, Peter b.1958
Entering Gornji Vakuf 1993–1994
oil on canvas 40.5 x 30.5
IWM ART 16523

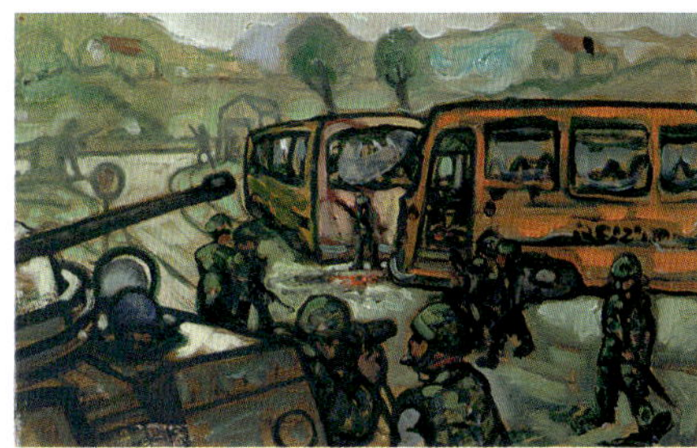

Howson, Peter b.1958
Three Miles from Home 1993–1994
oil on canvas 28 x 46
IWM ART 16524

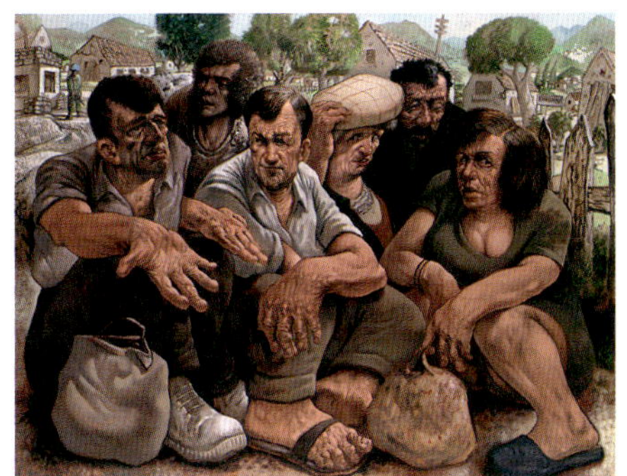

Howson, Peter b.1958
Cleansed 1994
oil on canvas 182.8 x 243.6
IWM ART 16521

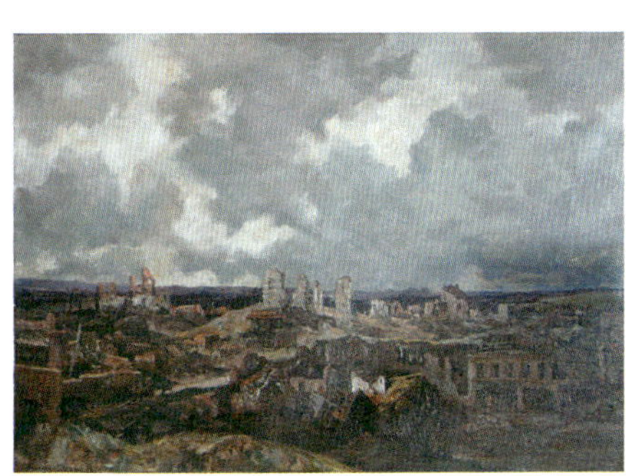

Hughes-Stanton, Herbert Edwin Pelham
1870–1937
Lens 1918
oil on canvas 50.8 x 68.5 (E)
IWM ART 1996

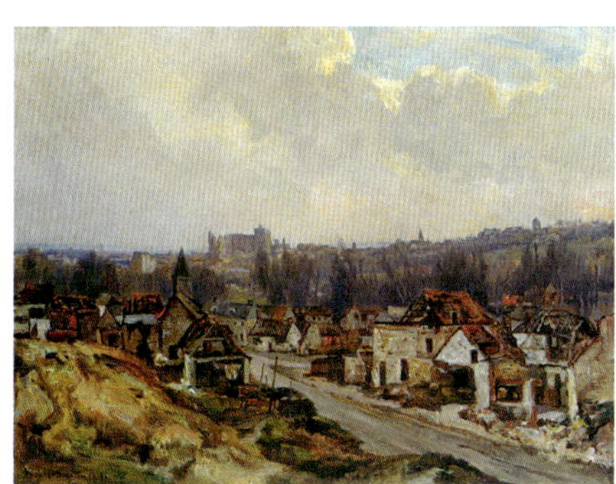

Hughes-Stanton, Herbert Edwin Pelham
1870–1937
*Lens Road, Arras: From the Suburb of St
Nicholas, Arras* 1918
oil on canvas 50.8 x 68.5 (E)
IWM ART 1994

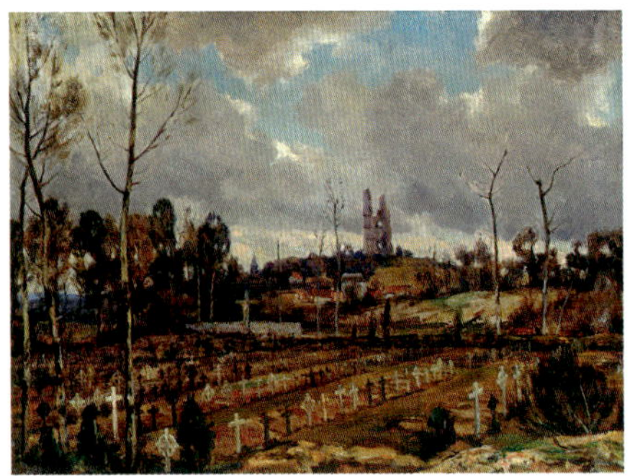

Hughes-Stanton, Herbert Edwin Pelham
1870–1937
The Cemetery at Mont St Eloi 1918
oil on canvas 50.8 x 68.5
IWM ART 1997

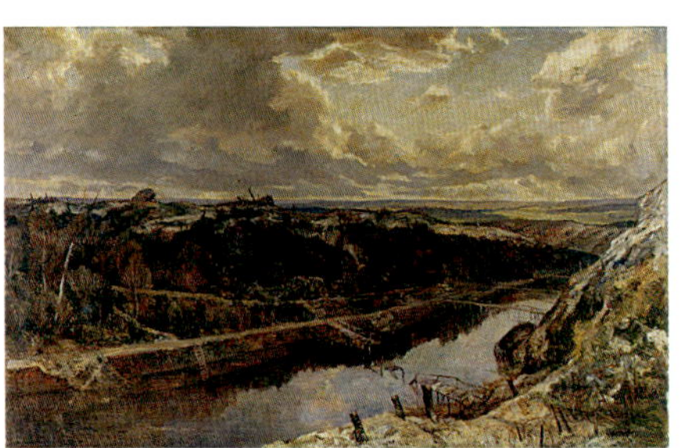

Hughes-Stanton, Herbert Edwin Pelham
1870–1937
The St Quentin Canal from the Temporary Bridge Erected across (…) 1918
oil on canvas 141.8 x 241.3
IWM ART 1998

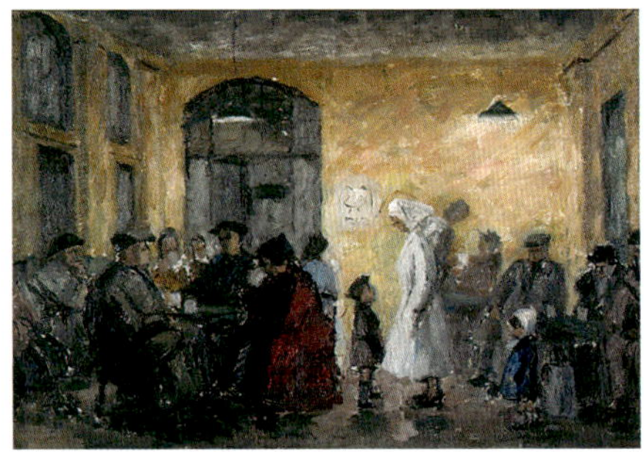

Hutchinson, Mabel b.1903
A Bermondsey Rest Centre 1941
oil on canvas 40.6 x 60.9
IWM ART LD 1376

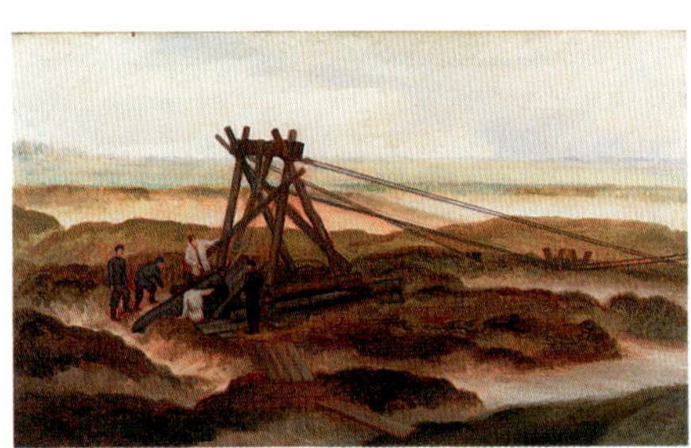

Hutton, Philip active 1940–1945
A Bomb Disposal Squad at Work c.1945
oil on canvas 44.7 x 75.5
IWM ART LD 4978

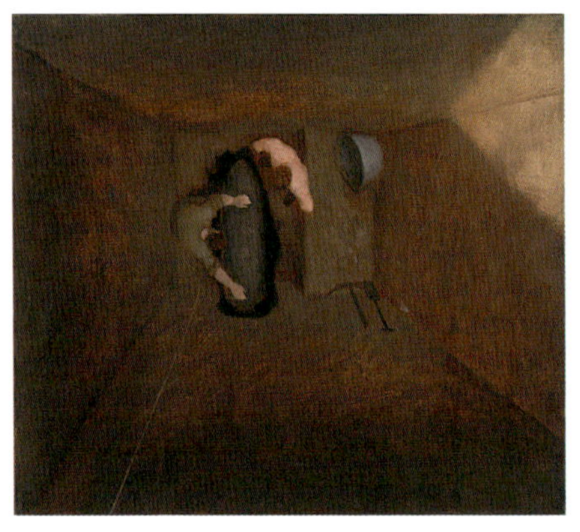

Hutton, Philip active 1940–1945
A Bomb Disposal Squad Digging out an Unexploded Bomb c.1945
oil on canvas 34.9 x 40
IWM ART LD 4979

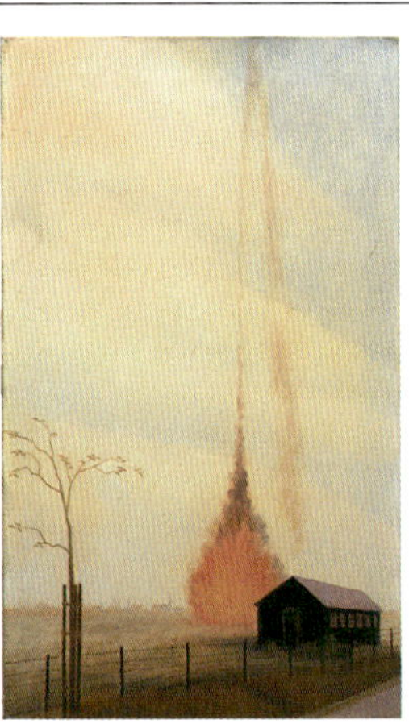

Hutton, Philip active 1940–1945
Destroying an Unexploded Bomb c.1945
oil on canvas 74.9 x 44.7
IWM ART LD 4977

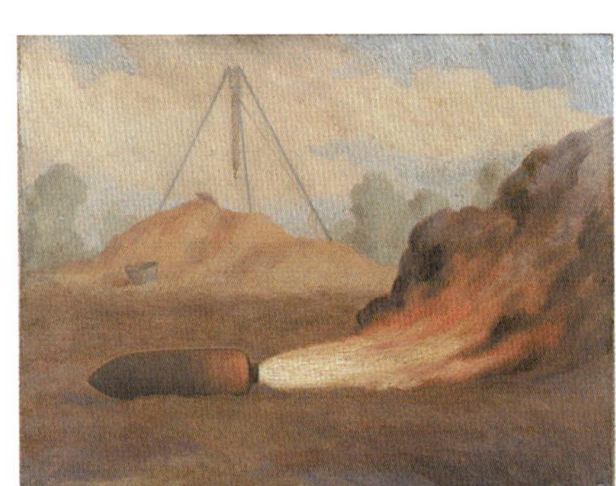

Hutton, Philip active 1940–1945
Destroying an Unexploded Bomb c.1945
oil on canvas 37.1 x 50.1
IWM ART LD 4980

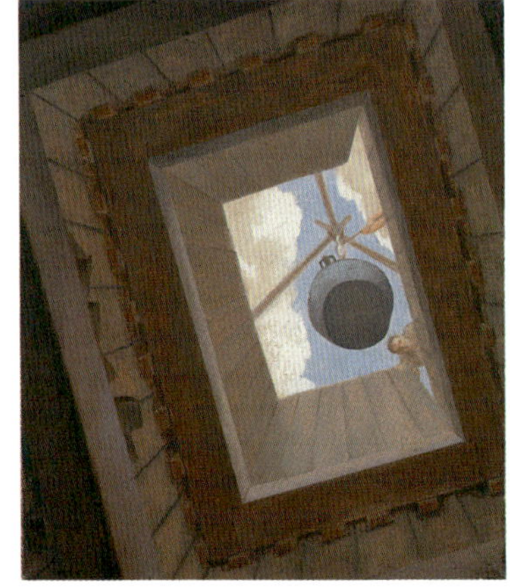

Hutton, Philip active 1940–1945
Preparing a Shaft to Reach an Unexploded Bomb c.1945
oil on canvas 40 x 34.6
IWM ART LD 4981

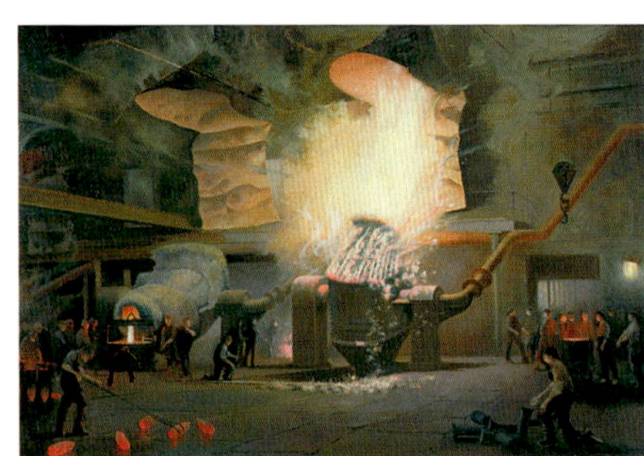

Hyde, William 1859–1925
The Steel Converter at Woolwich Arsenal: The Tropenas Steel Converters at Work in the Royal Laboratory Shell Foundry (…) 1919
oil on canvas 71.1 x 107.9
IWM ART 2275

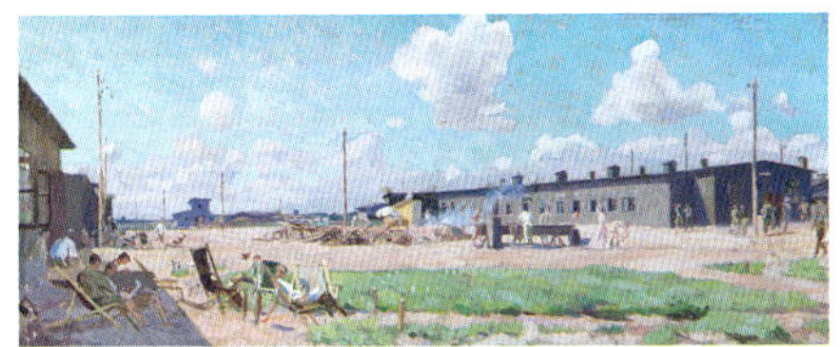

Jackson, Gerald Goddard b.1878
Schwarmstedt Camp I 1915–1918
oil on panel 12 x 30.4
IWM ART 1857

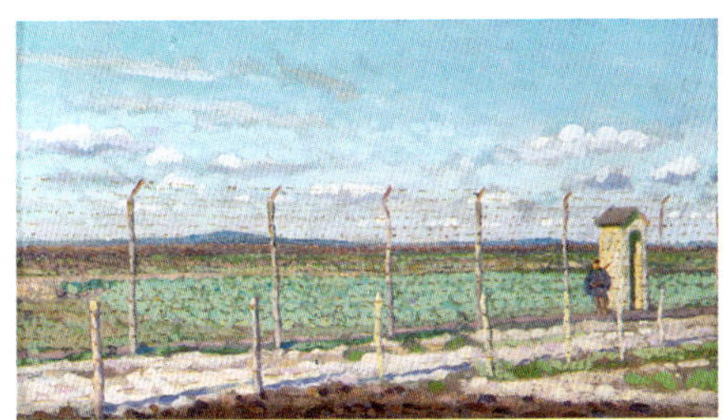

Jackson, Gerald Goddard b.1878
Schwarmstedt Camp II 1915–1918
oil on panel 10.7 x 20.9
IWM ART 1858

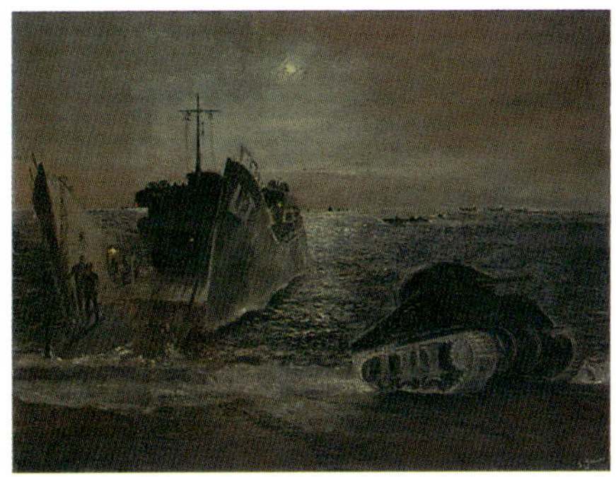

James, Edward Ernest active 1940s
A Tank Landing at Night 1944
oil on canvas 49.5 x 66
IWM ART LD 4282

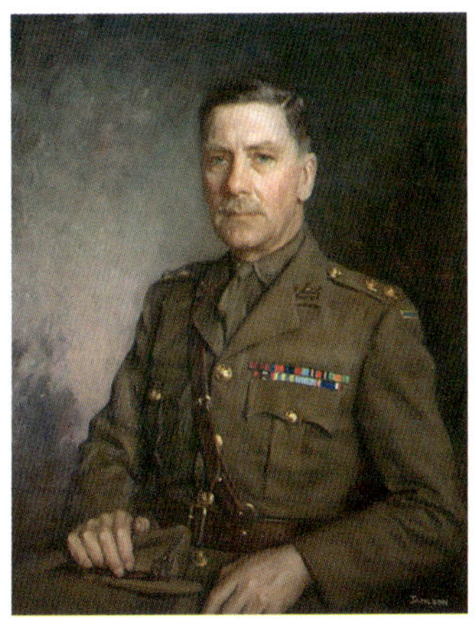

Jameson, Cecil 1883–c.1962
Lieutenant Colonel Carne, VC c.1959
oil on canvas 74.9 x 63.5
IWM ART MW(A) 6

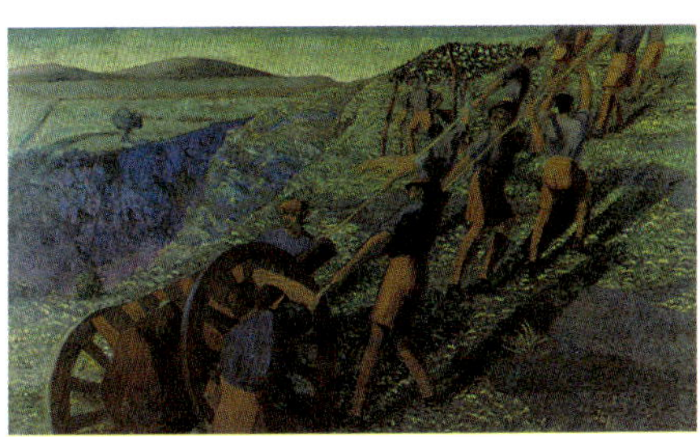

Japp, Darsie 1883–1973
*The Royal Field Artillery in Macedonia, Spring
1918* 1918
oil on canvas 182.8 x 317.5
IWM ART 2625

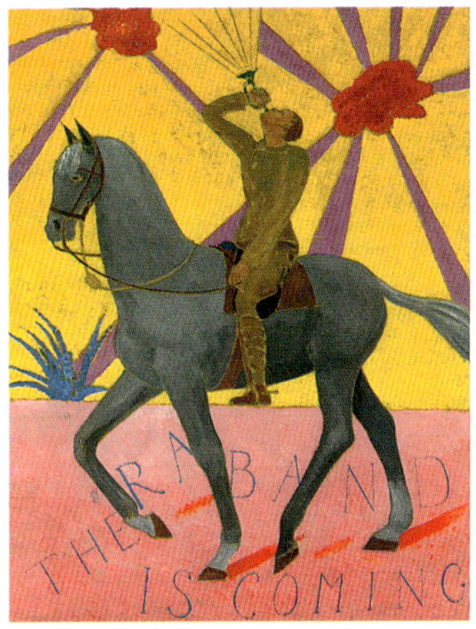

Japp, Darsie 1883–1973
Regimental Band c.1918
oil on panel 91.4 x 71.1
IWM ART 4031

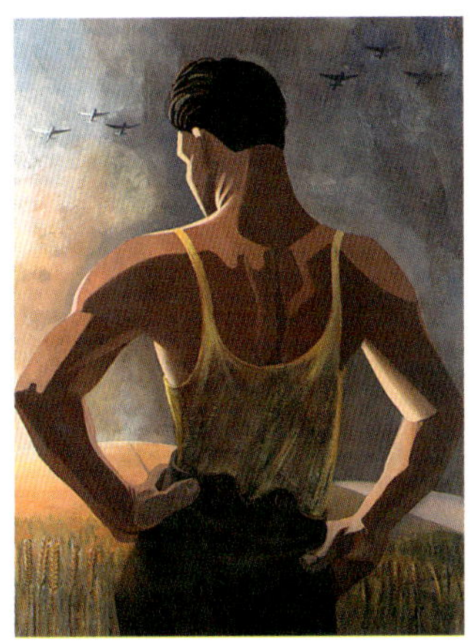

Jillard, Hilda 1899–1975
What Harvest? 1939
oil on panel 122 x 91.5
IWM ART 15201

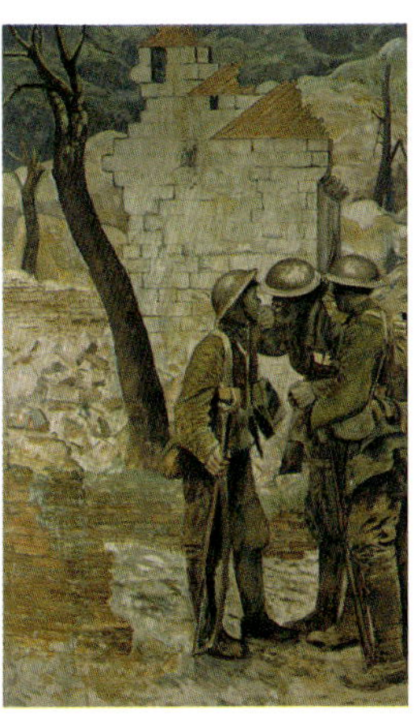

John, Augustus Edwin 1878–1961
Fraternity c.1920
oil on canvas 237.4 x 144.7
IWM ART 3070

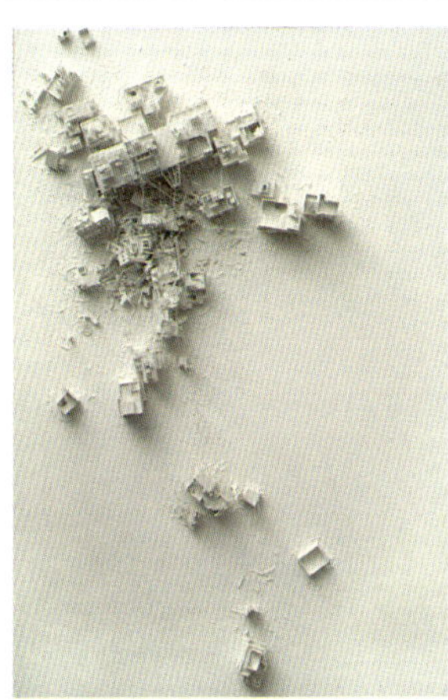

Judah, Gerry b.1951
Frontiers 07 2005
foamboard, brass rod, nylon wire, acrylic &
gesso on canvas 280 x 190
IWM ART 17102

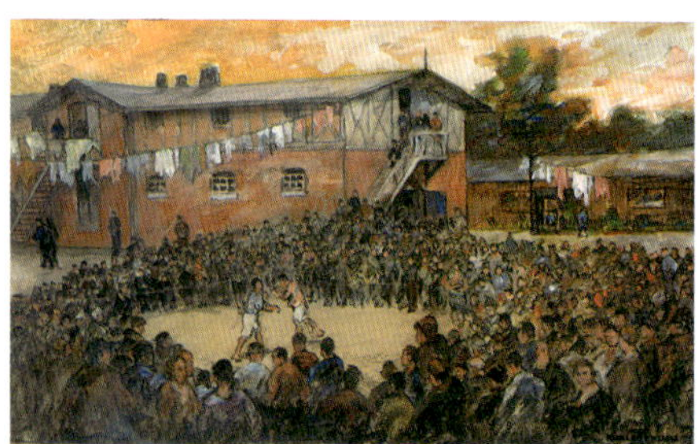

Jungman, Nico 1872–1935
Ruhleben Prison Camp: Slaves of the Ring
1916
tempera & chalk on paper 45.7 x 73.6
IWM ART 529

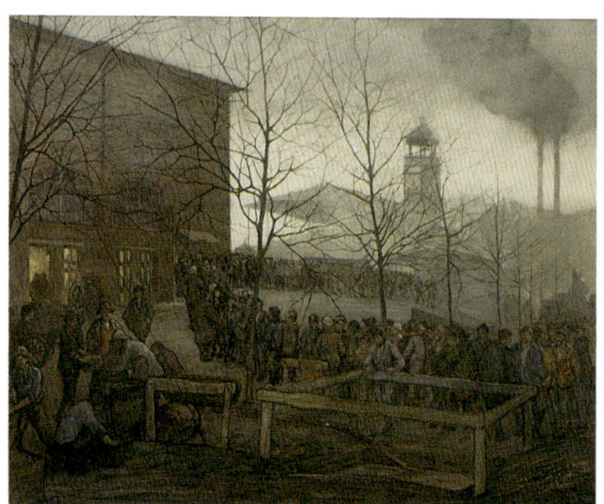

Jungman, Nico 1872–1935
Ruhleben Prison Camp: The Queue for Bread from Denmark 1916
tempera on paper 63.5 x 76.8
IWM ART 526

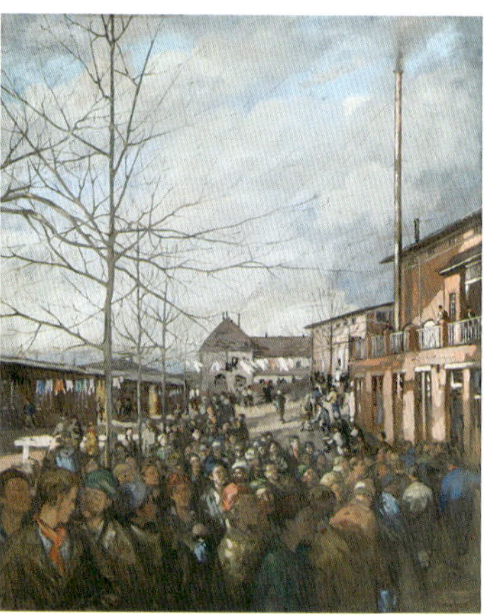

Jungman, Nico 1872–1935
Ruhleben Prison Camp: Christmas Dinner
1917
tempera on paper 76.2 x 63.5
IWM ART 528

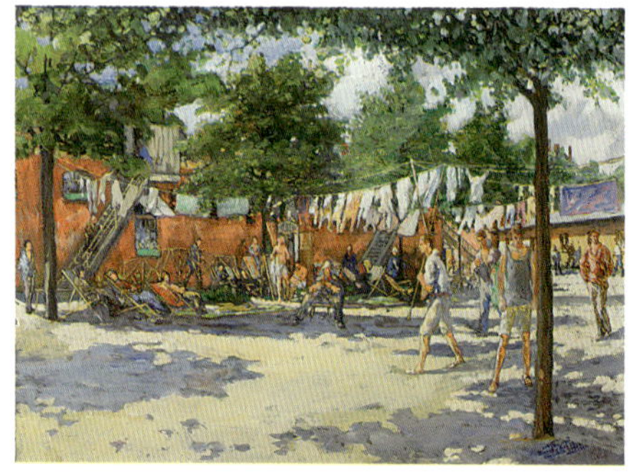

Jungman, Nico 1872–1935
Ruhleben Prison Camp: Hut No.8, on Plan No.530 1917
tempera on paper 46.9 x 62.2
IWM ART 527

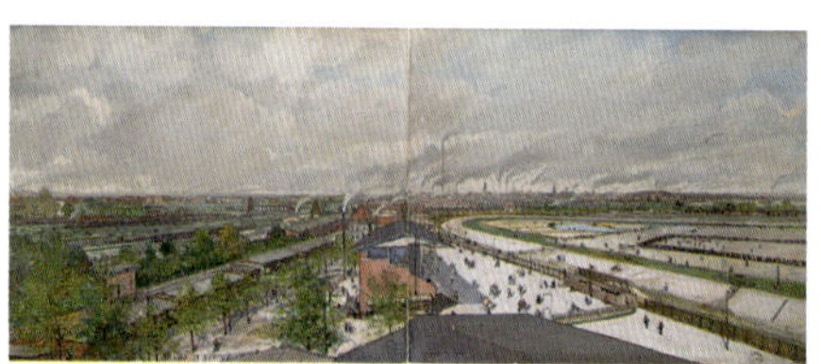

Jungman, Nico 1872–1935
Ruhleben Prison Camp: Panoramic View 1917
tempera on panel 63.5 x 75.5
IWM ART 522

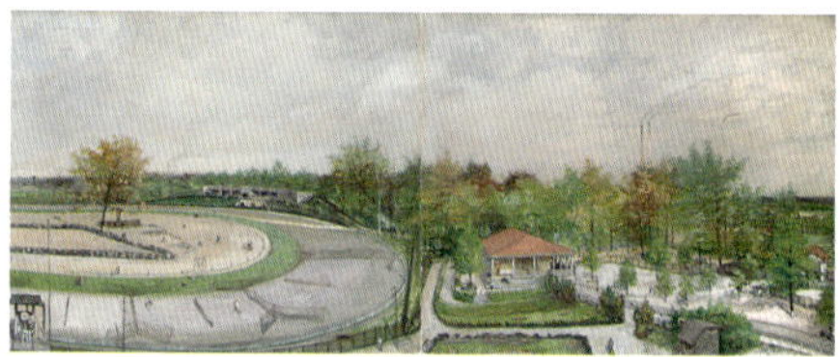

Jungman, Nico 1872–1935
Ruhleben Prison Camp: Panoramic View 1917
tempera on panel 63.5 x 75.5
IWM ART 522

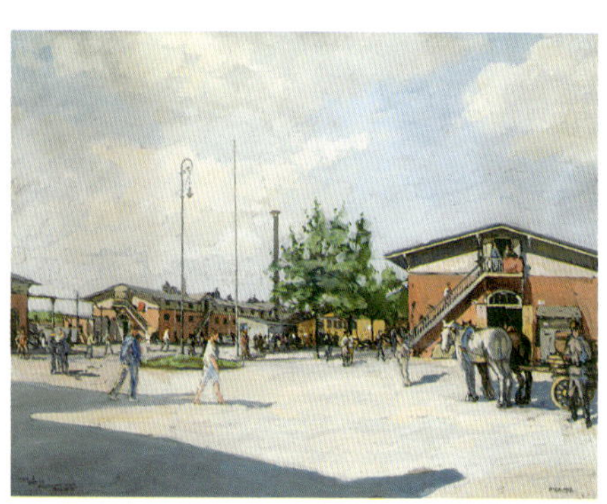

Jungman, Nico 1872–1935
Ruhleben Prison Camp: 'Trafalgar Square'
1917
tempera on paper 54.6 x 71.1
IWM ART 523

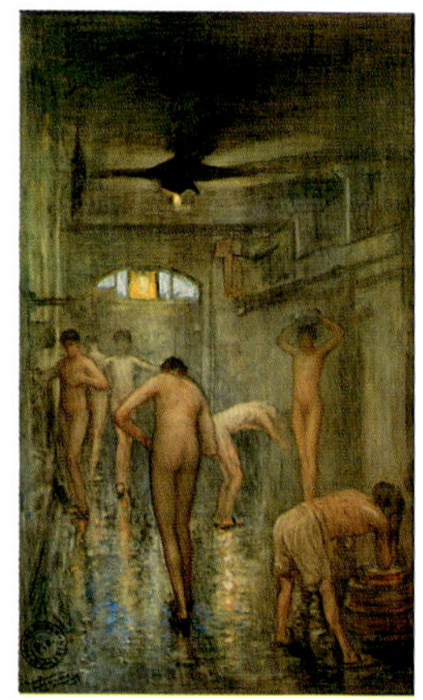

Jungman, Nico 1872–1935
Ruhleben Prison Camp: Bathing 1918
tempera on paper 40 x 24.7
IWM ART 525

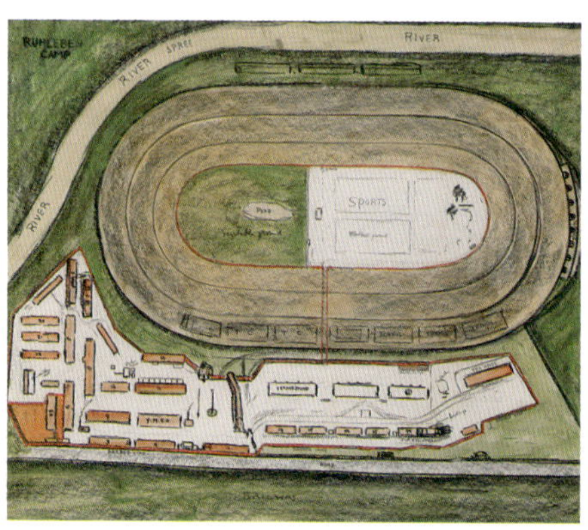

Jungman, Nico 1872–1935
Plan of Ruhleben Camp: Key to Panoramic View
tempera & chalk on paper 61.5 x 71.7
IWM ART 530

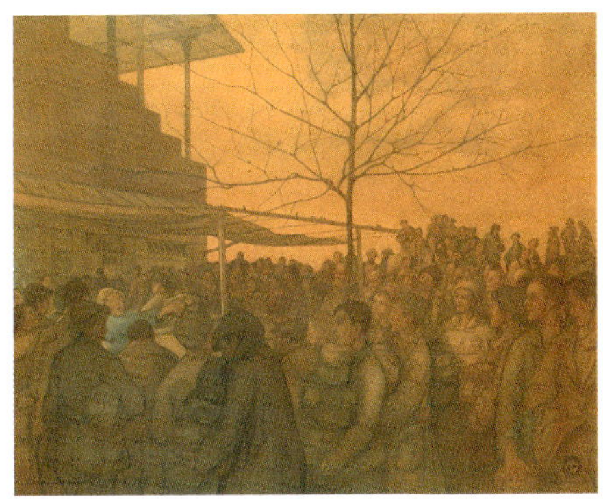

Jungman, Nico 1872–1935
*Ruhleben Prison Camp: The Distribution of
Parcels from Home*
tempera on paper 63.5 x 78.1
IWM ART 524

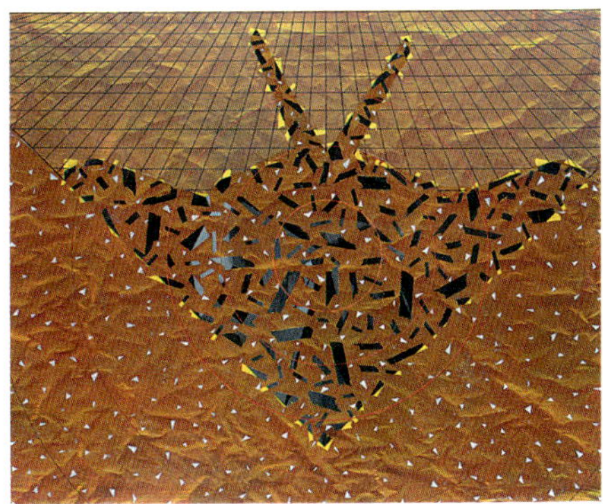

Kalkhof, Peter b.1933
Stealth 1995
acrylic & metal foil on canvas 146 x 180
IWM ART 16824

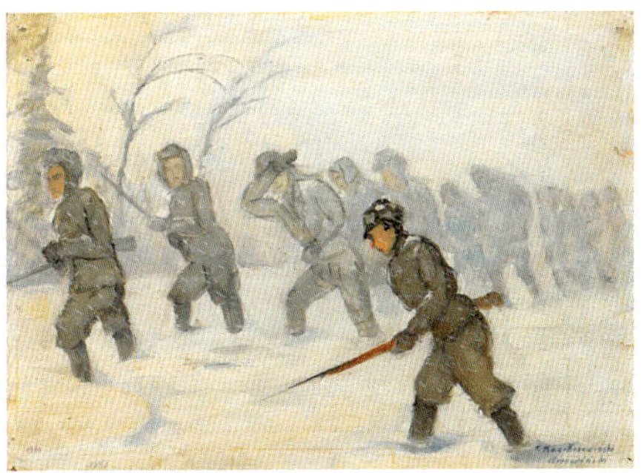

Kay-Krzewinski, Feliks 1900–1981
*Polish Prisoners of War Marching to Siberia,
Kazakhstan* 1940
oil on panel 25 x 34.8
IWM ART 15429

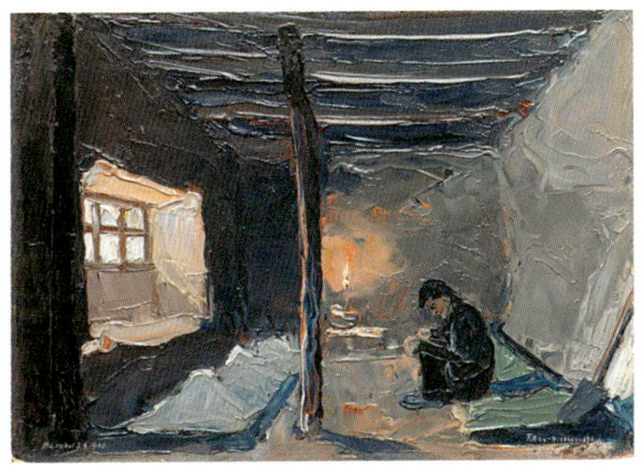

Kay-Krzewinski, Feliks 1900–1981
The Artist, Karakol, Kazakhstan, Russia 1940
oil on panel 25 x 35.2
IWM ART 15430

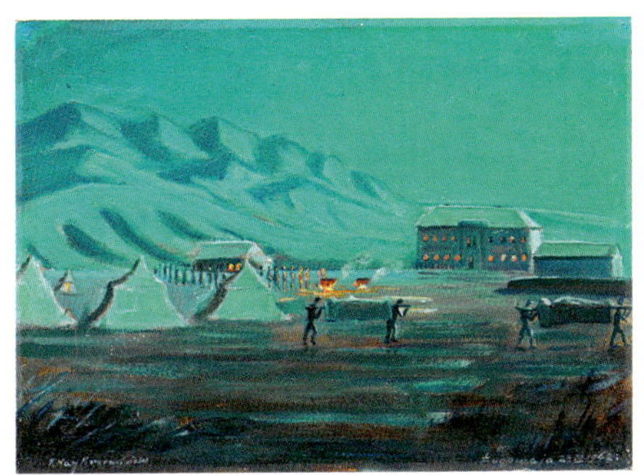

Kay-Krzewinski, Feliks 1900–1981
Typhoid Victims, Lugowaja, South Kazakhstan
1942
oil on panel 24.8 x 34.8
IWM ART 15428

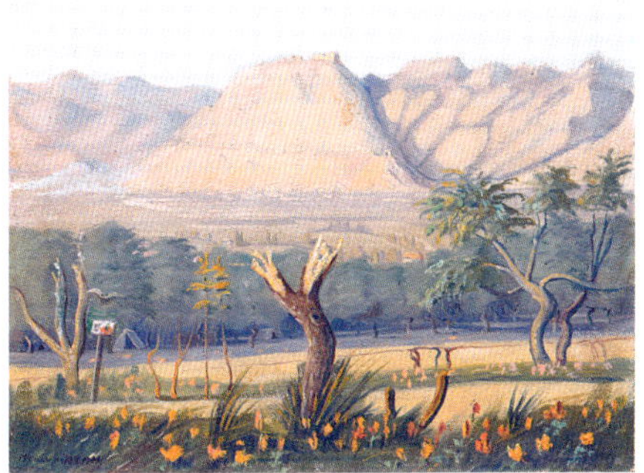

Kay-Krzewinski, Feliks 1900–1981
*Monte Cassino and the Tent of the Military
Police Headquarters* 1944
oil on board 33.7 x 44.8
IWM ART 15425

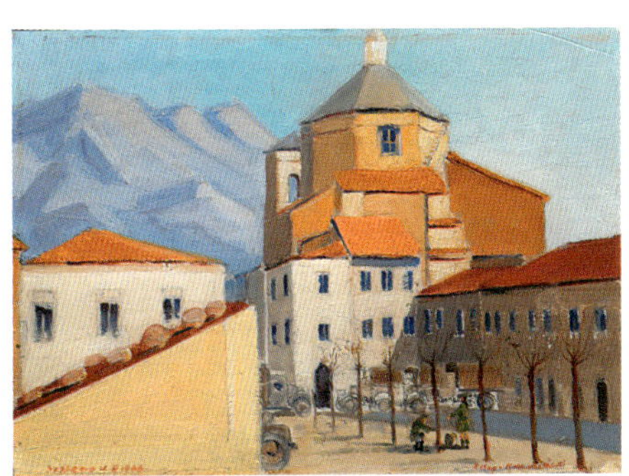

Kay-Krzewinski, Feliks 1900–1981
Sessano, Italy, 12 April 1944 1944
oil on panel 24.7 x 34.4
IWM ART 15431

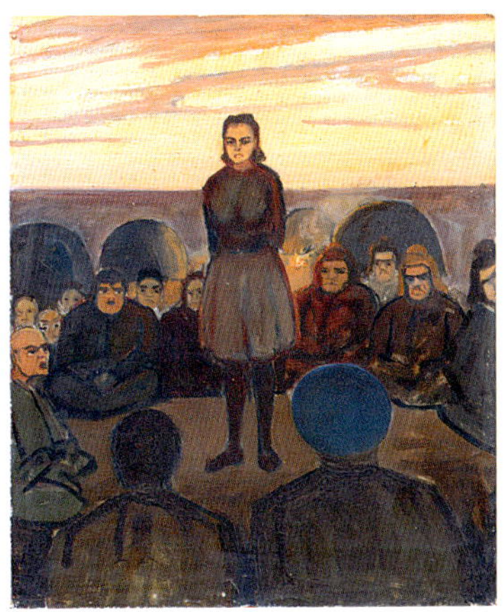

Kay-Krzewinski, Feliks 1900–1981
Hungry Steppe 1945, Kazakhstan, Russia 1945
oil on board 36 x 30.5
IWM ART 15427

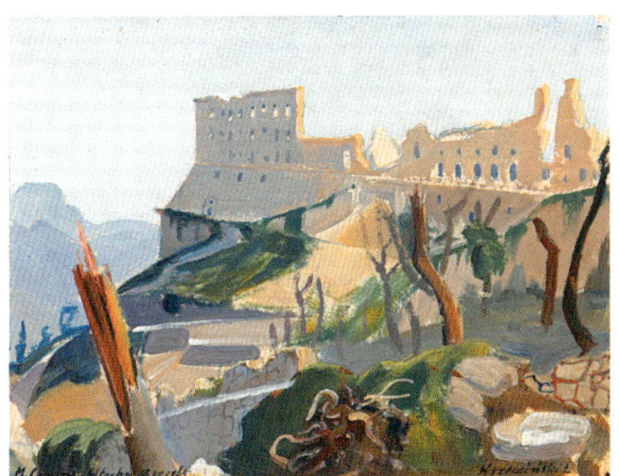

Kay-Krzewinski, Feliks 1900–1981
Monte Cassino One Month after the Battle
1945
oil on board 30.2 x 40.7
IWM ART 15426

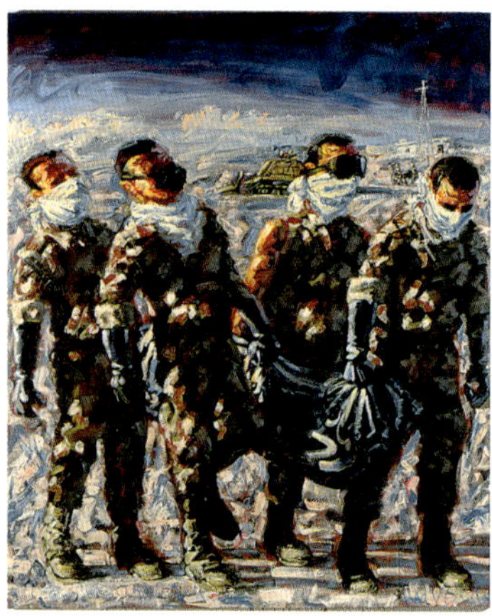

Keane, John b.1954
Death Squad 1991
oil on canvas 203.6 x 173.5
IWM ART 16432

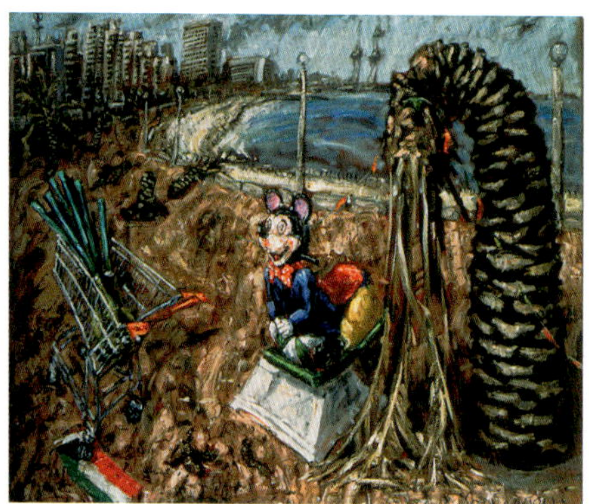

Keane, John b.1954
Mickey Mouse at the Front 1991
oil on canvas 173 x 198.5
IWM ART 16414

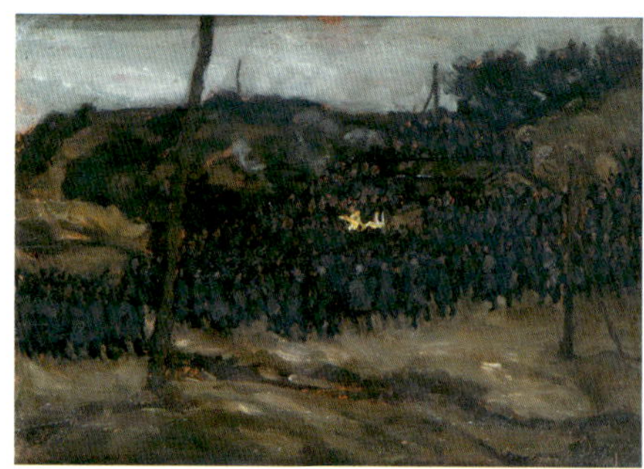

Kemeny, Kalman 1896–1994
Mass in the Field, Russian Front 1917
oil on board 38.1 x 55.8
IWM ART 6244

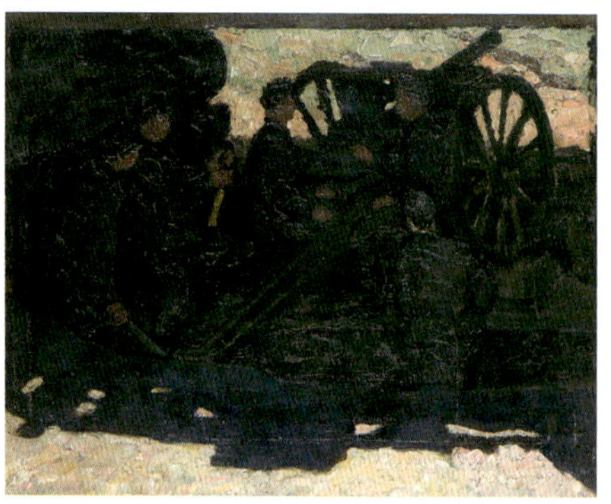

Kemeny, Kalman 1896–1994
Battery in the Field, Russian Front c.1917
oil on board 45 x 53.9
IWM ART 6248

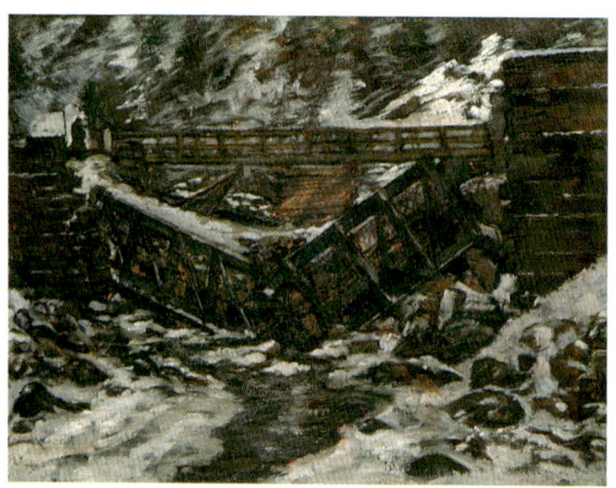

Kemeny, Kalman 1896–1994
*Destroyed Bridge, Carpathian Mountains,
Romanian Front* c.1917
oil on board 39.3 x 50.1
IWM ART 6249

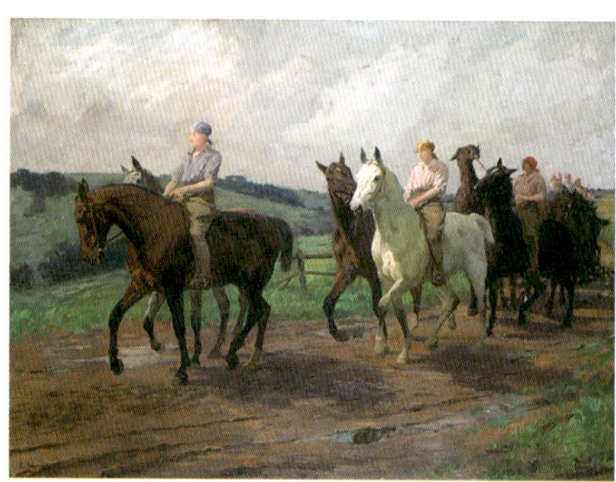

Kemp-Welch, Lucy 1869–1958
*The Ladies' Army Remount Depot, Russley
Park, Wiltshire, 1918* 1919
oil on canvas 111.7 x 148.3
IWM ART 3094

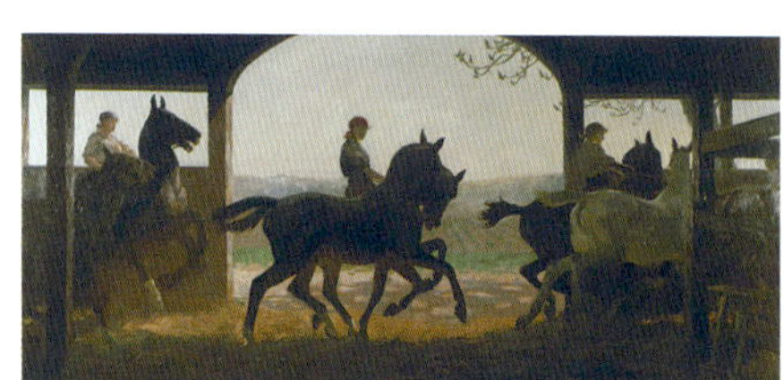

Kemp-Welch, Lucy 1869–1958
*The Straw Ride: Russley Park Remount Depot,
Wiltshire* 1919–1920
oil on canvas 182.8 x 396.2
IWM ART 3160

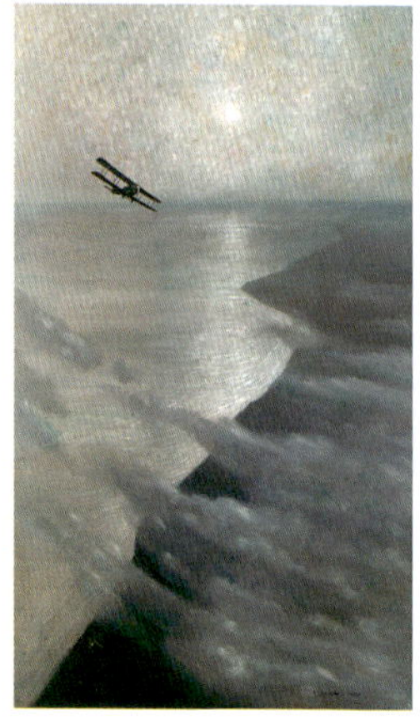

Kennedy, Cedric J. 1898–1968
*The Defence of London against Gothas with a
DH4 on Night Patrol Work over the South-East
Coast* 1919
oil on canvas 127 x 76.2
IWM ART 3078

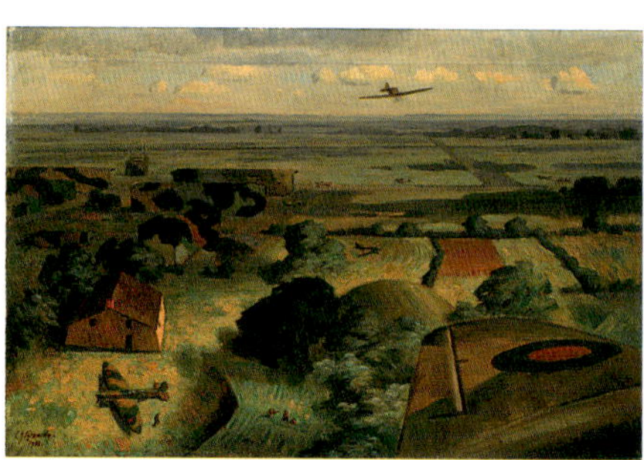

Kennedy, Cedric J. 1898–1968
A Camouflaged Runway 1942
oil on canvas 51 x 76
IWM ART LD 2758

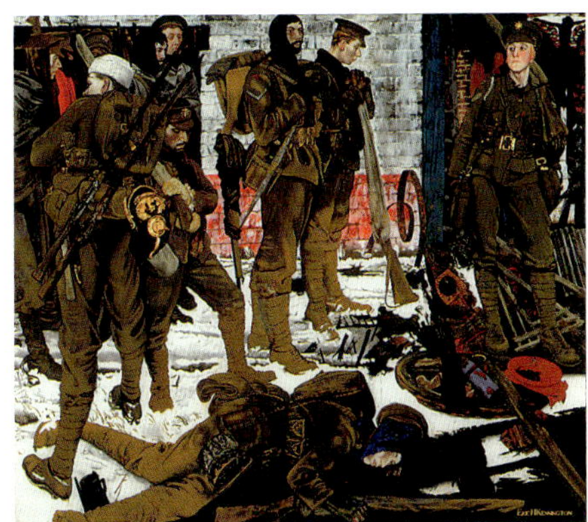

Kennington, Eric 1888–1960
The Kensingtons at Laventie 1915
oil on glass 139.7 x 152.4
IWM ART 15661

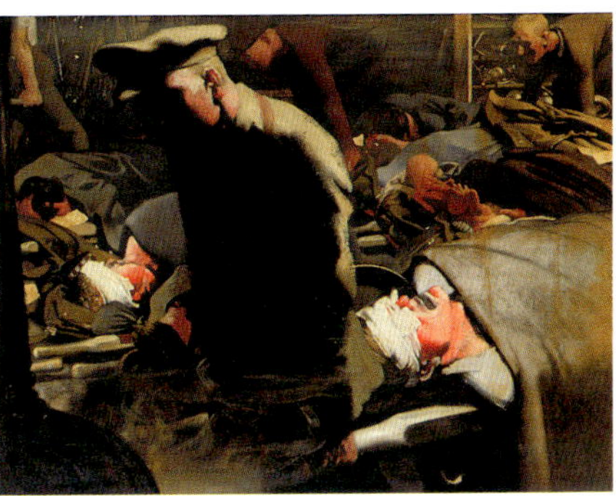

Kennington, Eric 1888–1960
Gassed and Wounded 1918
oil on canvas 71.1 x 91.4
IWM ART 4744

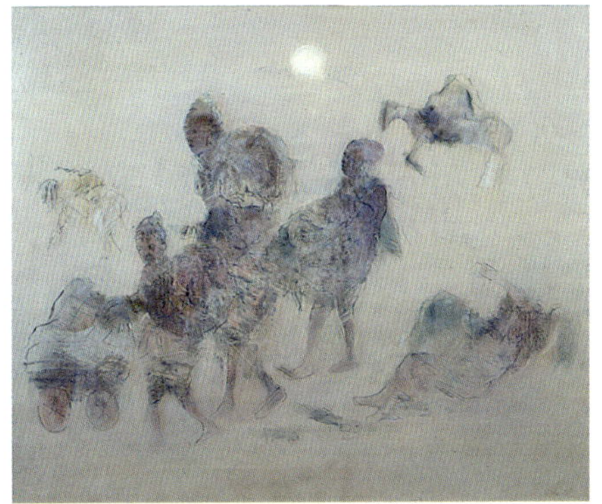

Kessell, Mary 1914–1977
Refugees: '…pray ye that your fight be not in the winter...' Matthew XXIV, 20 1945
oil on canvas 50.8 x 60.9
IWM ART LD 5846

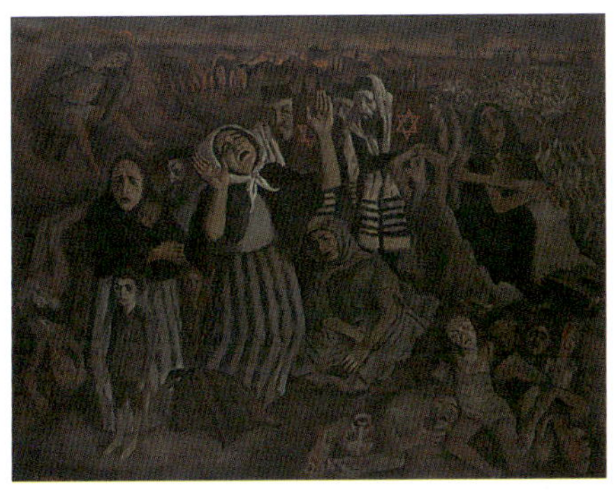

Kestelman, Morris 1905–1998
Lama Sabachthani, Why Have You Forsaken Me? 1943
oil on canvas 117 x 153
IWM ART 16786

Kinley, Peter 1926–1988
Battleship 1985
oil on paper 58.4 x 78.7
IWM ART 16108

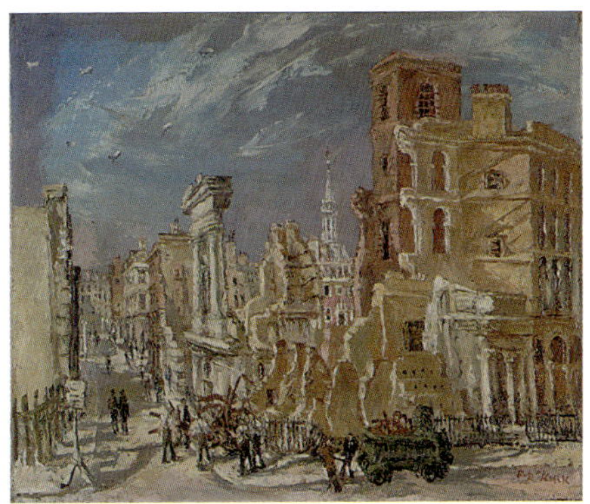

Kirk, Eve 1900–1969
Bomb Damage in the City c.1941
oil on canvas 50.8 x 60.9
IWM ART LD 1874

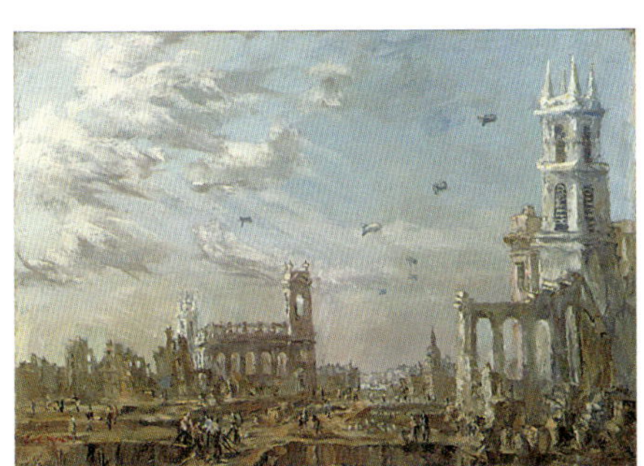

Kirk, Eve 1900–1969
St Nicholas Cole Abbey, EC4 c.1943
oil on canvas 50.8 x 73
IWM ART LD 3703

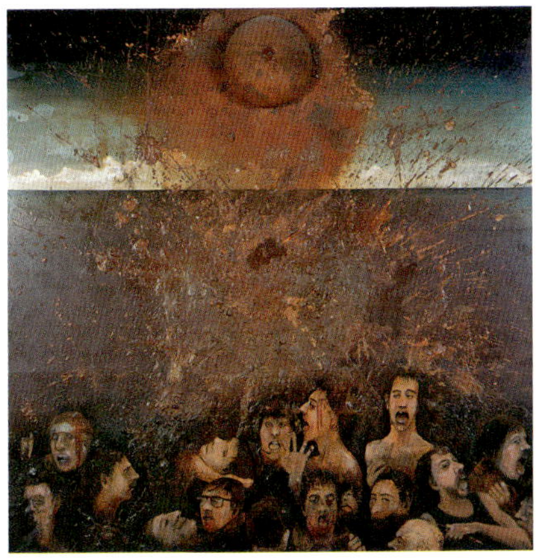

Kirkwood, John b.1947
The Belgrano, 2 and 3 May 1990
oil & collage on canvas 182.8 x 182.8
IWM ART 16583

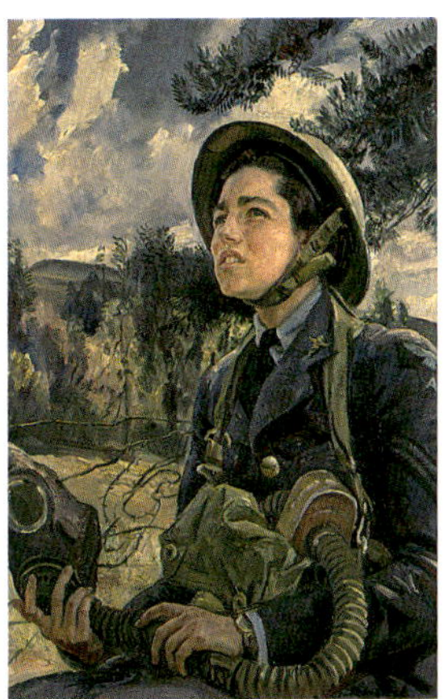

Knight, Laura 1877–1970
Corporal J. D. M. Pearson, GC, Women's Auxiliary Air Force 1940
oil on canvas 91.4 x 60.9
IWM ART LD 626

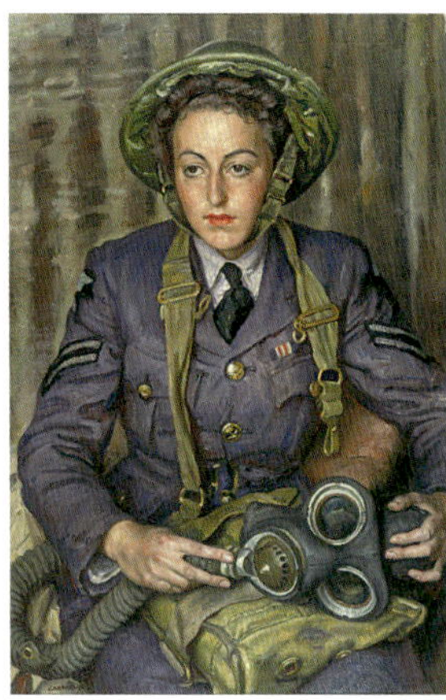

Knight, Laura 1877–1970
*Corporal J. M. Robins, Women's Auxiliary Air
Force* 1941
oil on canvas 91.4 x 60.9
IWM ART LD 1467

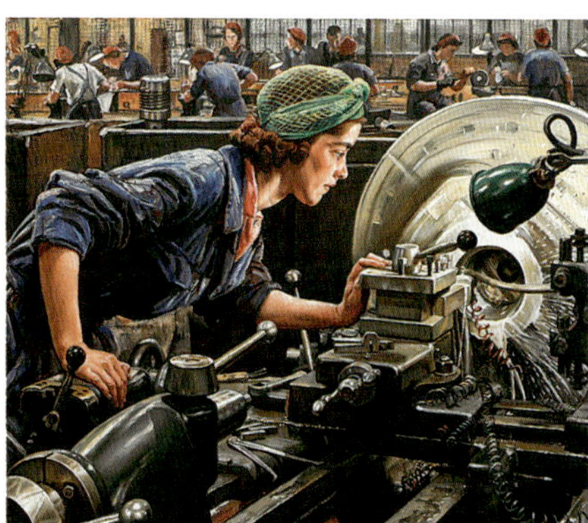

Knight, Laura 1877–1970
Ruby Loftus Screwing a Breech Ring 1942
oil on canvas 86.3 x 101.9
IWM ART LD 2850

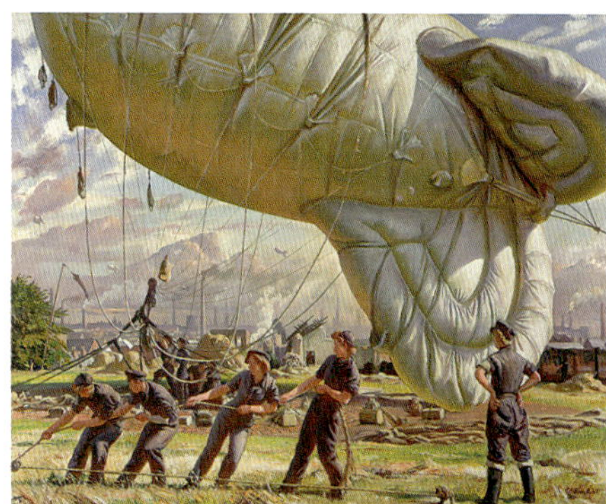

Knight, Laura 1877–1970
A Balloon Site, Coventry 1943
oil on canvas 102.5 x 127
IWM ART LD 2750

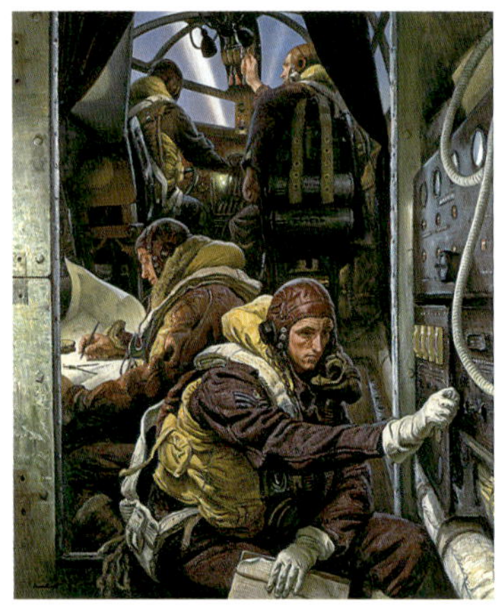

Knight, Laura 1877–1970
Take Off: Interior of a Bomber Aircraft c.1943
oil on canvas 182.8 x 152.4
IWM ART LD 3834

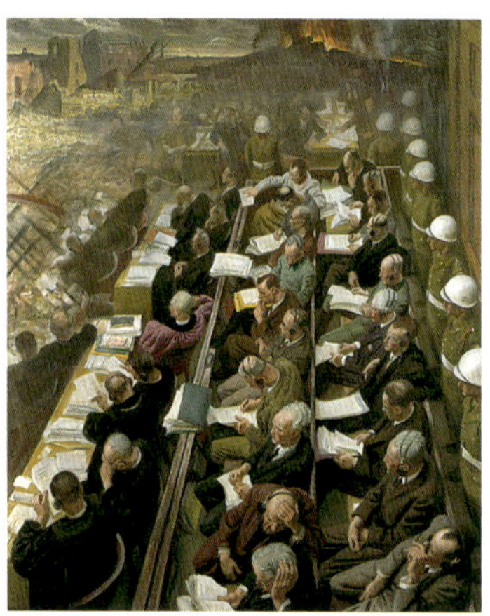

Knight, Laura 1877–1970
The Nuremberg Trial 1946
oil on canvas 182.8 x 152.4
IWM ART LD 5798

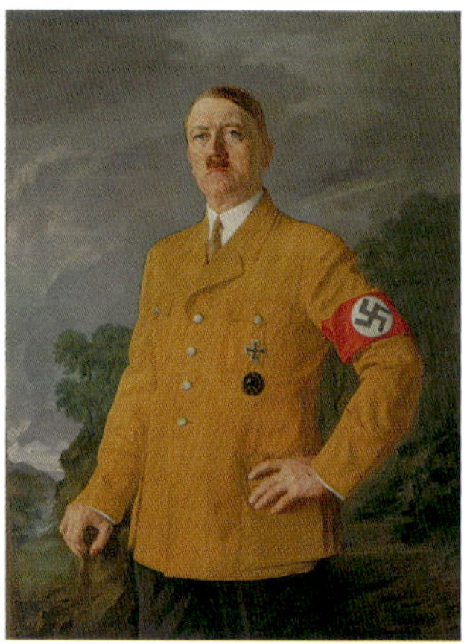

Knirr, Heinrich 1862–1944
Der Führer (1889–1945) 1937
oil on canvas 129.5 x 96.5
IWM ART LD 6217

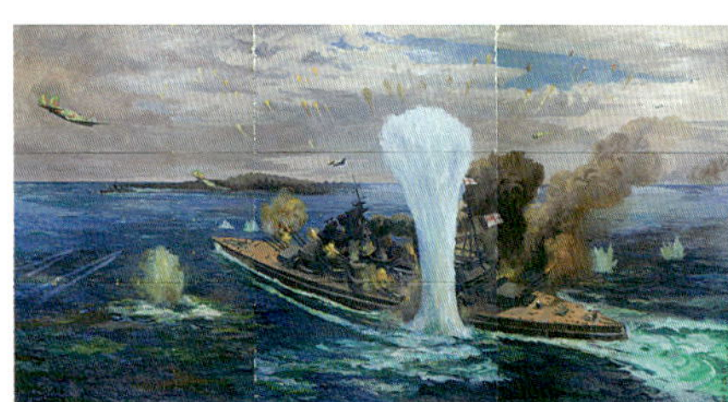

Kojima, Yuunosoke
*The Sinking of the 'Prince of Wales', 10
December 1942, off Kuenten, South China Sea*
1942
oil on board 182.8 x 304.8
IWM ART LD 6722

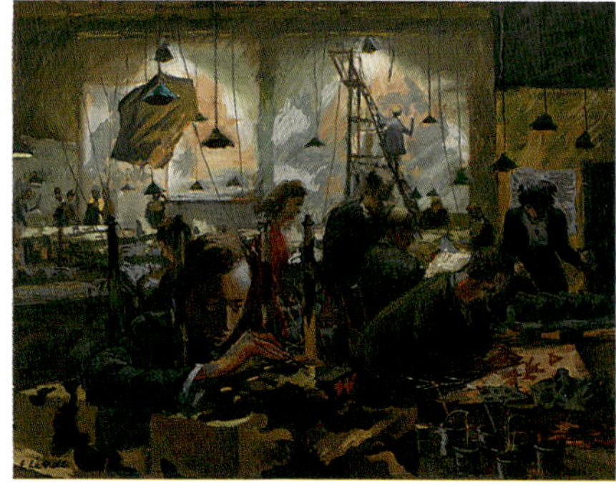

La Dell, Edwin 1914–1970
The Camouflage Workshop, Leamington Spa
1940
oil on panel 43 x 55.6
IWM ART LD 322

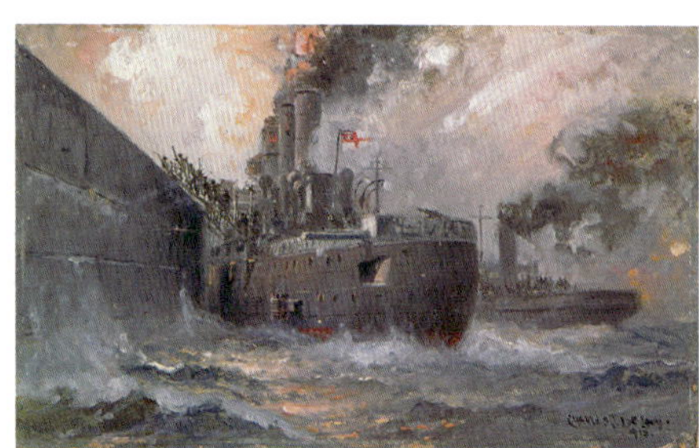

Lacy, Charles John de c.1860–1936
*The 'Vindictive' at Zeebrugge: The Storming of
Zeebrugge Mole* 1918
oil on panel 21.5 x 36.8
IWM ART 871

Facing page: Nevinson, Christopher, 1889–1946, *French Troops Resting* (detail), 1916, (p. 168)

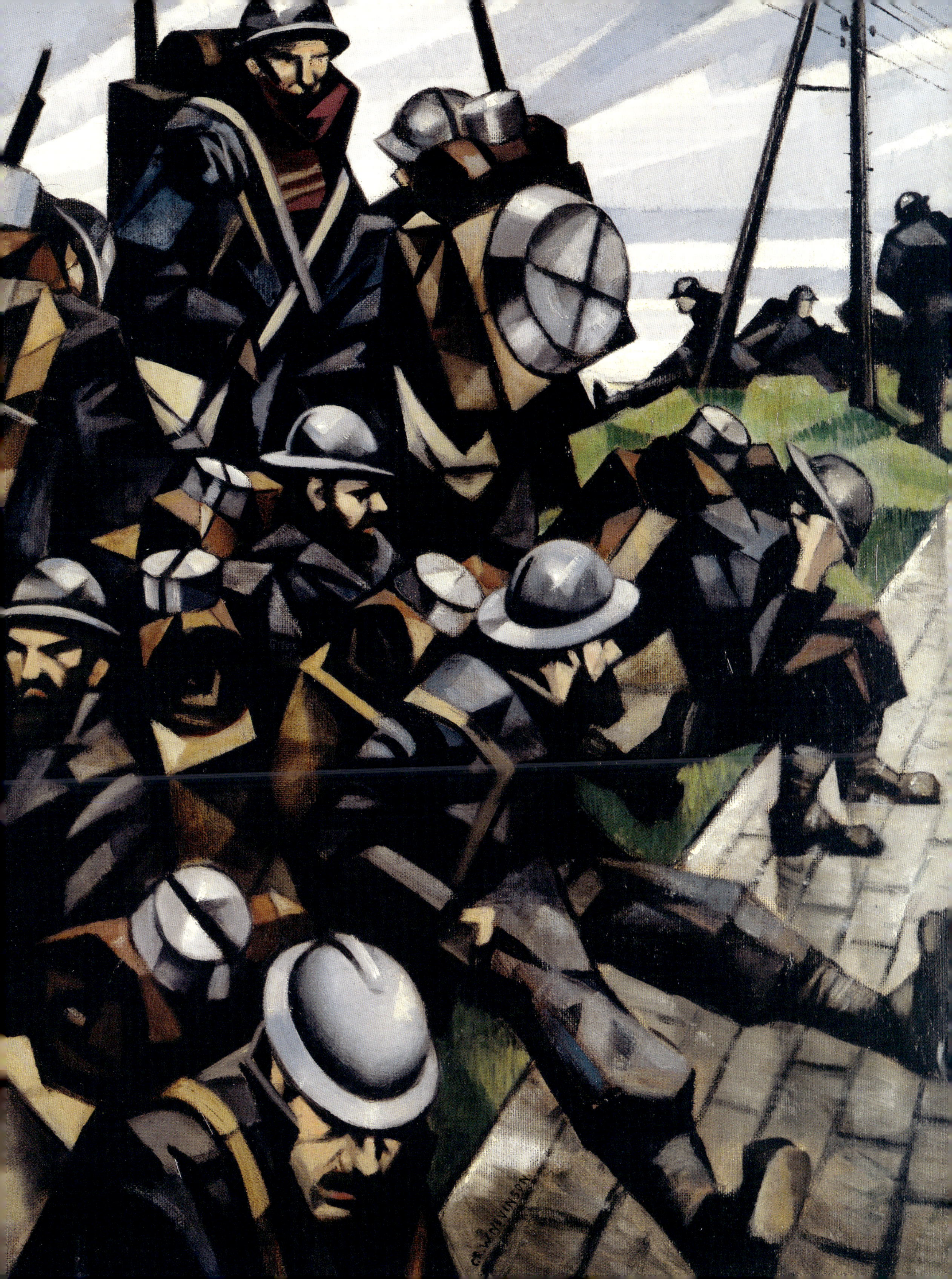
C.R.W. NEVINSON

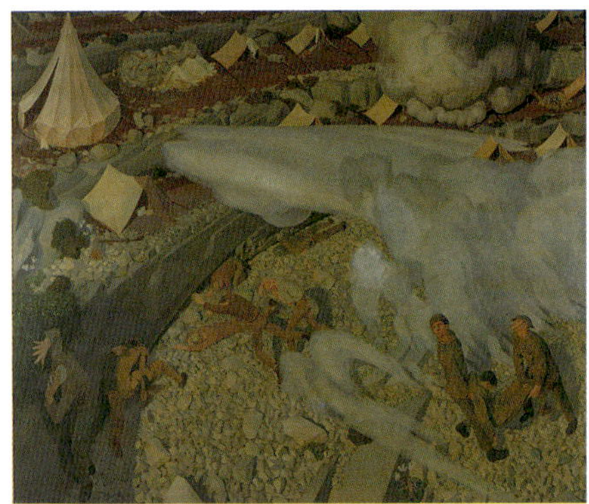

Lamb, Henry 1883–1960
Irish Troops in the Judaean Hills Surprised by a Turkish Bombardment 1919
oil on canvas 183.4 x 219.7
IWM ART 2746

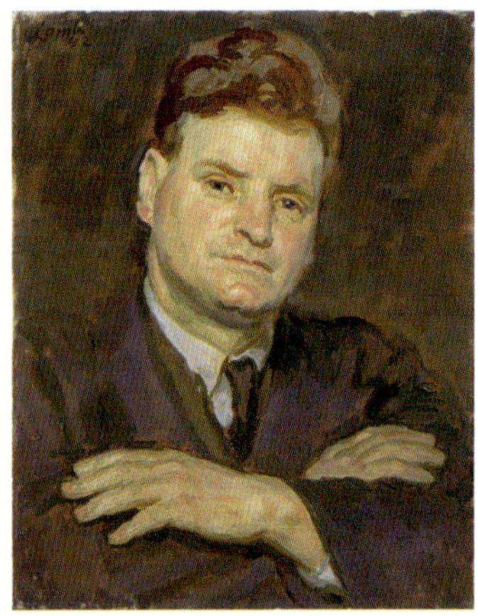

Lamb, Henry 1883–1960
Frederick Bolton, GM, Decorated for Gallantry at Leytonstone, September 1940 1940
oil on canvas 50.8 x 40.6
IWM ART LD 1894

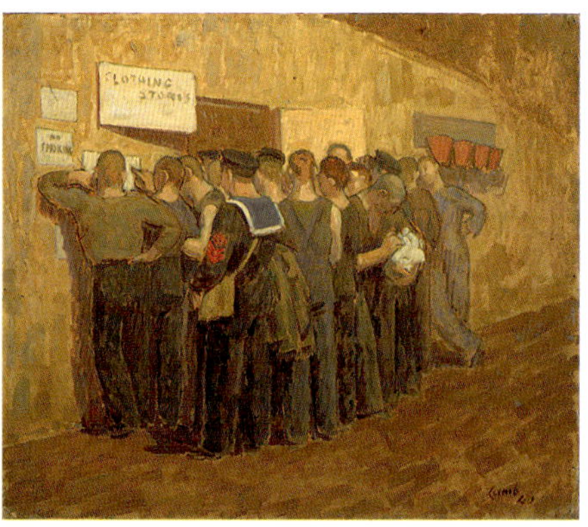

Lamb, Henry 1883–1960
Pay Week at the Clothing Store 1940
oil on panel 41.2 x 48.2
IWM ART LD 429

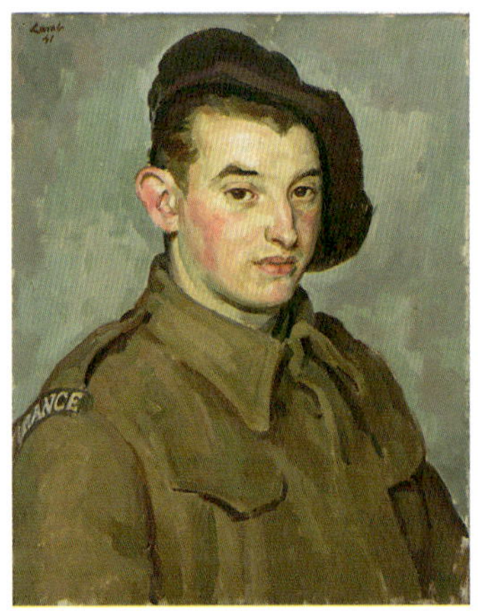

Lamb, Henry 1883–1960
A Soldier of Free France 1941
oil on canvas 50.8 x 40.6
IWM ART LD 888

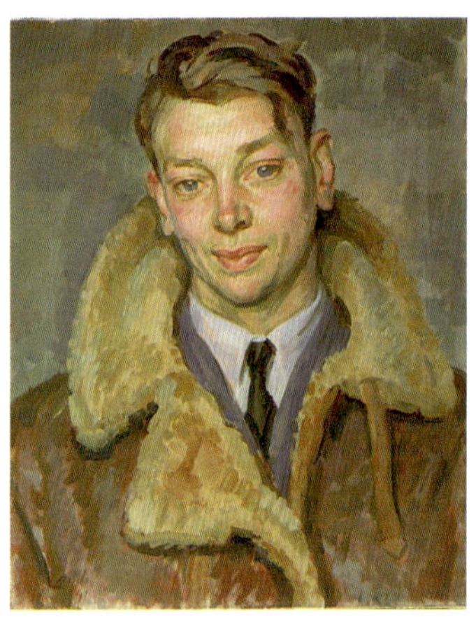

Lamb, Henry 1883–1960
An Instructor at the Army and Royal Air Force Co-Operation School 1941
oil on canvas 55.8 x 45.7
IWM ART LD 1137

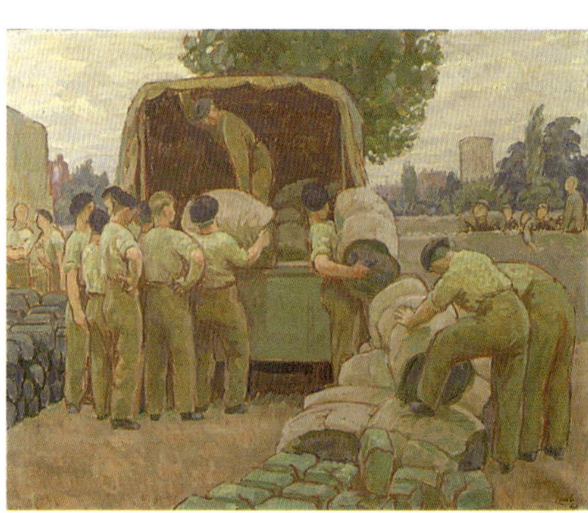

Lamb, Henry 1883–1960
Canadian Forces Reach Their Billets 1941
oil on canvas 48.2 x 59.6
IWM ART LD 1751

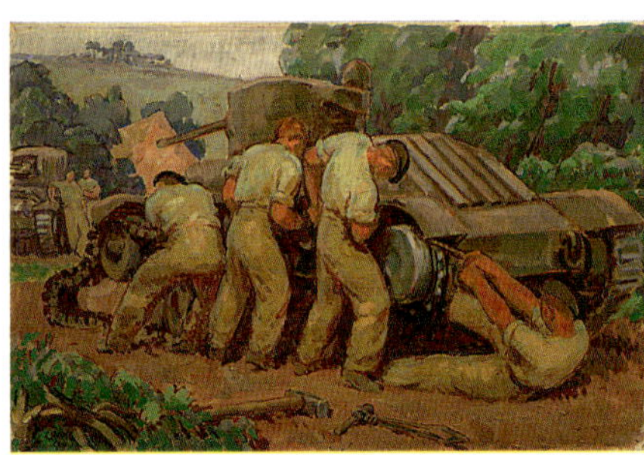

Lamb, Henry 1883–1960
Canadian Troops Replacing Track 1941
oil on canvas 39.3 x 60.9
IWM ART LD 1756

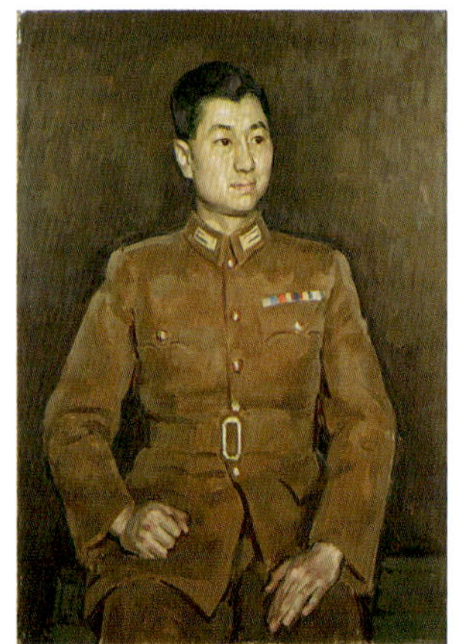

Lamb, Henry 1883–1960
Colonel Tang Paohuang 1941
oil on canvas 90.1 x 62.8
IWM ART LD 4503

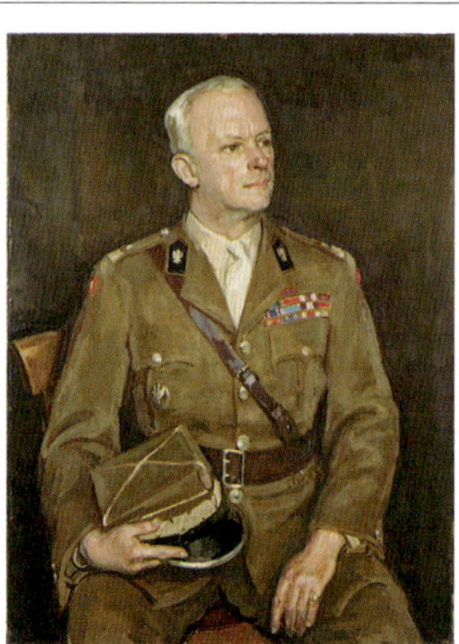

Lamb, Henry 1883–1960
General Bronislaw Regulski (1886–1961), CB 1941
oil on canvas 101.9 x 76.8
IWM ART LD 4505

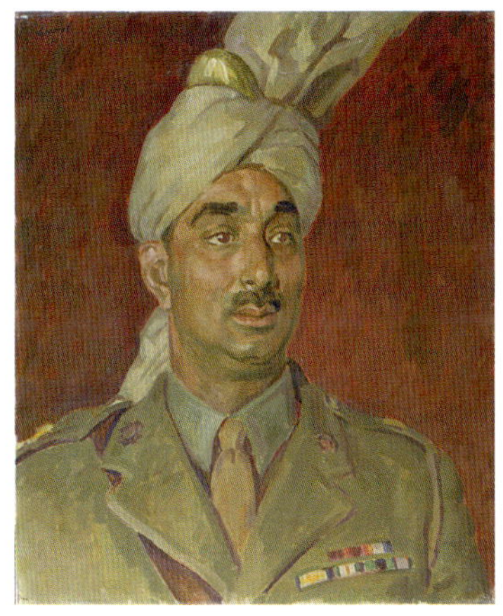

Lamb, Henry 1883–1960
Major Mahomed Akbar Khan, Commanding Officer, 29 Mule Coy, Royal Indian Army Service Corps 1941
oil on canvas 60.9 x 50.8
IWM ART LD 1285

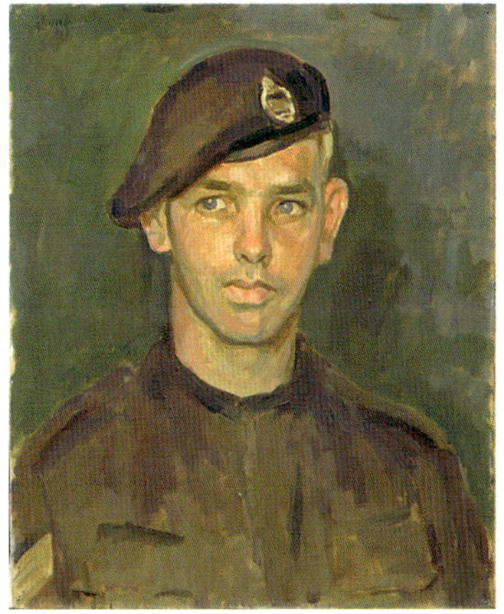

Lamb, Henry 1883–1960
Sergeant Watts, 40th Battalion, Royal Tank Regiment 1941
oil on canvas 55.8 x 45.7
IWM ART LD 1755

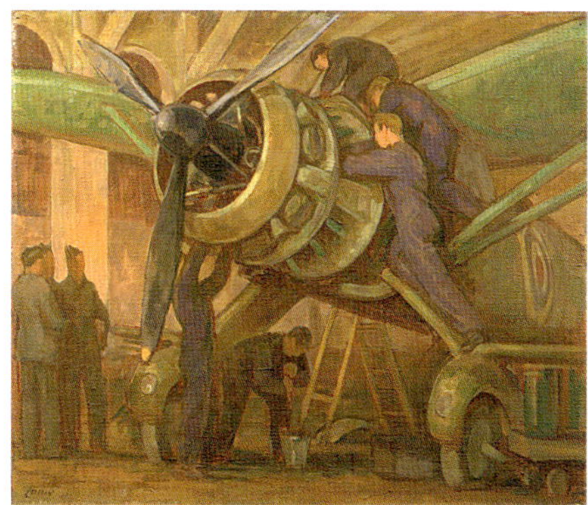

Lamb, Henry 1883–1960
The Overhaul 1941
oil on canvas 50.8 x 60.9
IWM ART LD 1139

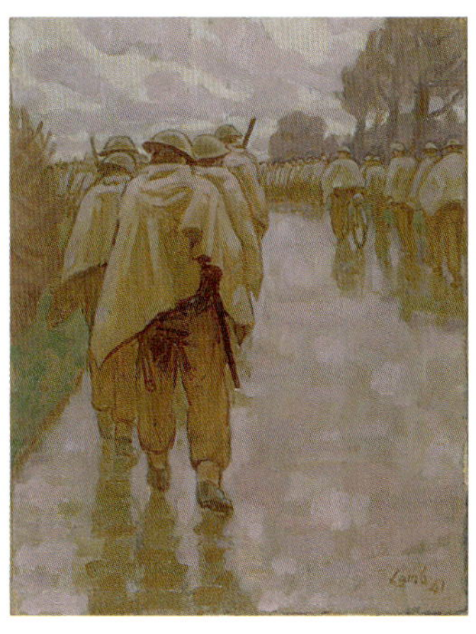

Lamb, Henry 1883–1960
The Poor Bloody Infantry 1941
oil on canvas 45.7 x 35.5
IWM ART LD 1143

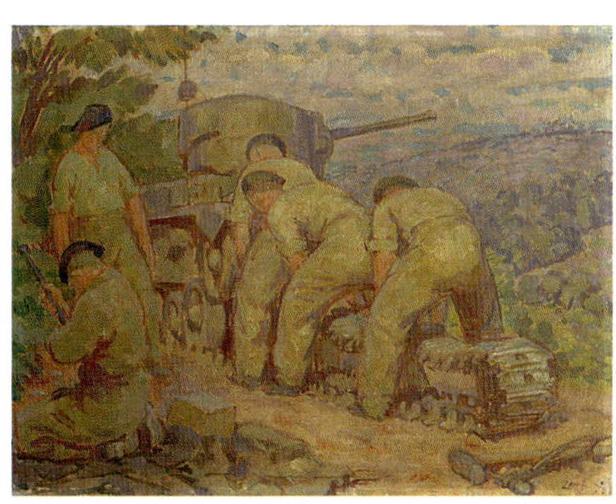

Lamb, Henry 1883–1960
Track Repairs by Canadian Troops 1941
oil on canvas 30.4 x 40.6
IWM ART LD 1759

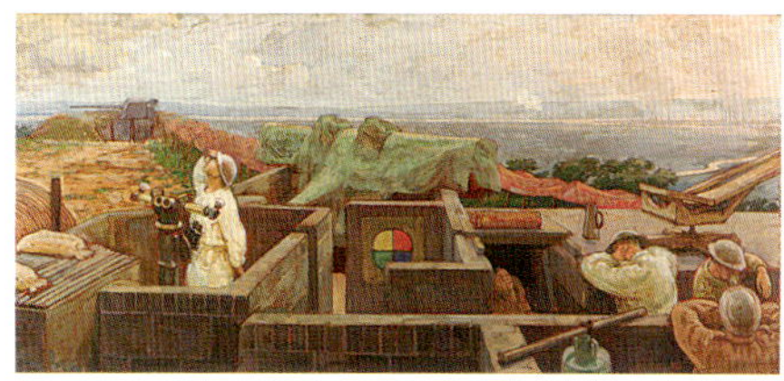

Lamb, Henry 1883–1960
A Command Post, Heavy Anti-Aircraft: Royal Canadian Artillery 1942
oil on wood 62.8 x 137.1
IWM ART LD 2575

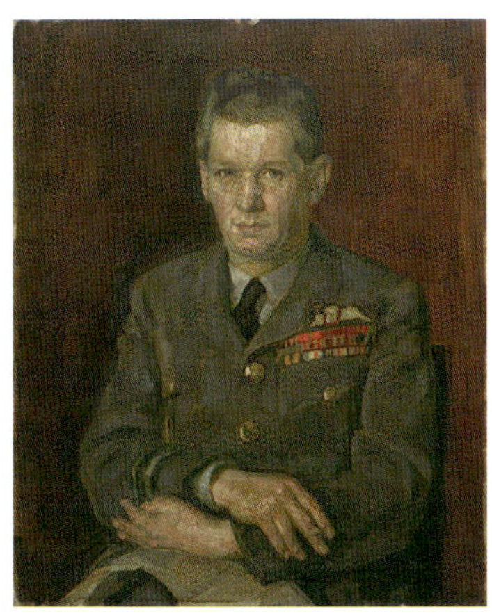

Lamb, Henry 1883–1960
Air Vice-Marshal Karel Janousek (1893–1971), KCB, Inspector General Czechoslovakian Air Force 1942
oil on canvas 74.9 x 61.5
IWM ART LD 3774

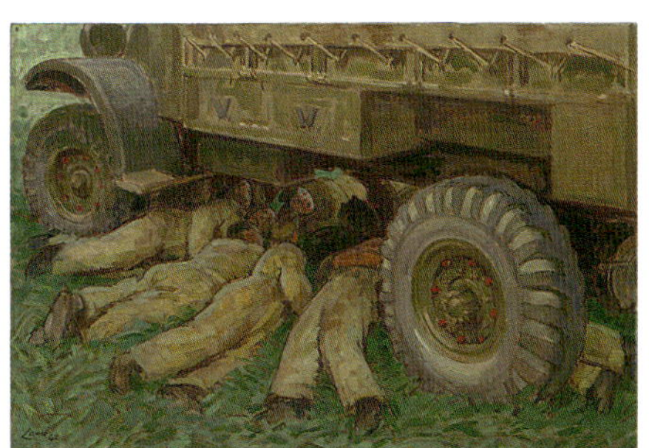

Lamb, Henry 1883–1960
Canadian Troops Undergoing Instruction 1942
oil on canvas 40.6 x 60.9
IWM ART LD 3206

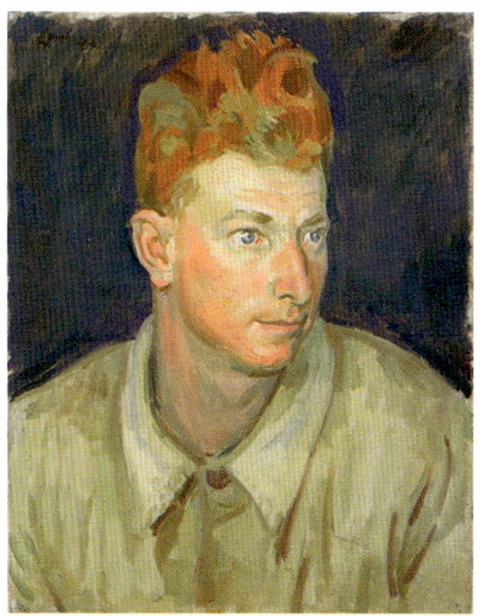

Lamb, Henry 1883–1960
Gunner W. C. Macaloney, Royal Canadian Artillery 1942
oil on canvas 50.8 x 40.6
IWM ART LD 2151

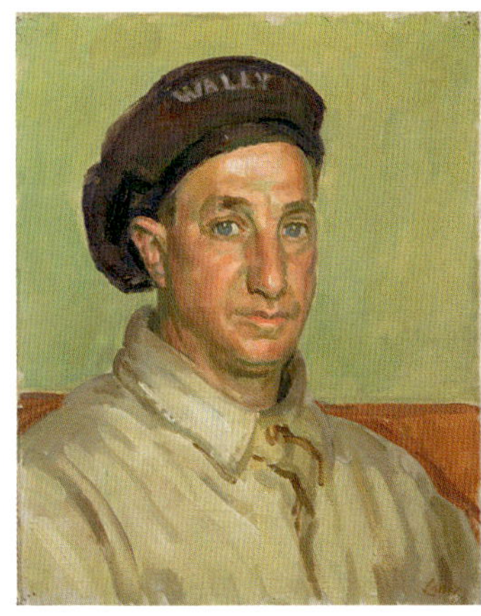

Lamb, Henry 1883–1960
Gunner W. H. St Cyr, Royal Canadian Artillery
1942
oil on canvas 50.8 x 40.6
IWM ART LD 2150

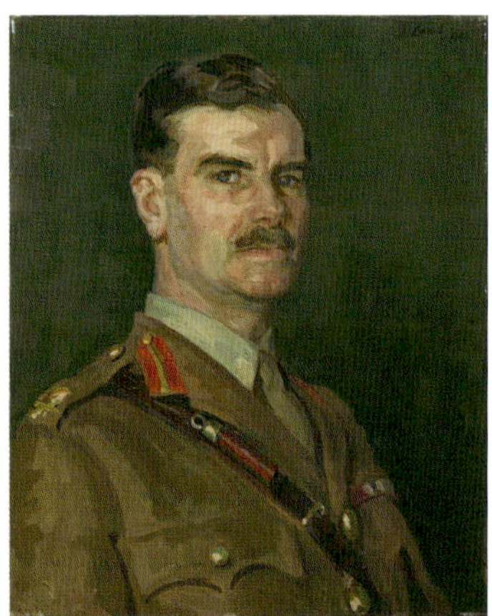

Lamb, Henry 1883–1960
Lieutenant General Archibald Edward Nye
(1895–1967), CB, MC 1942
oil on canvas 55.8 x 45.7
IWM ART LD 3205

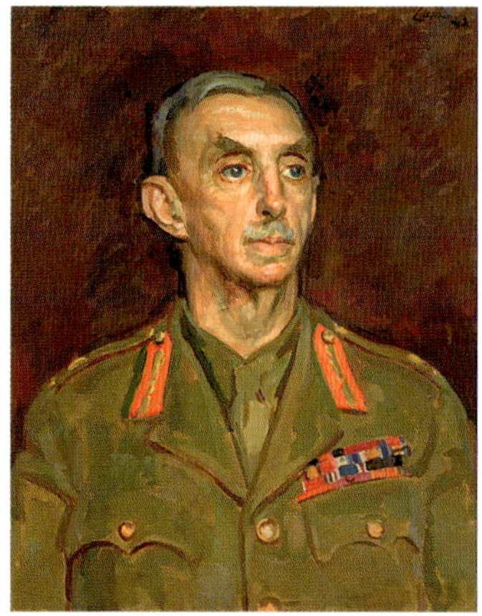

Lamb, Henry 1883–1960
Lieutenant General Sir William Dobbie
(1879–1964), GCMG, KCB, DSO 1942
oil on canvas 68.5 x 55.8
IWM ART LD 2577

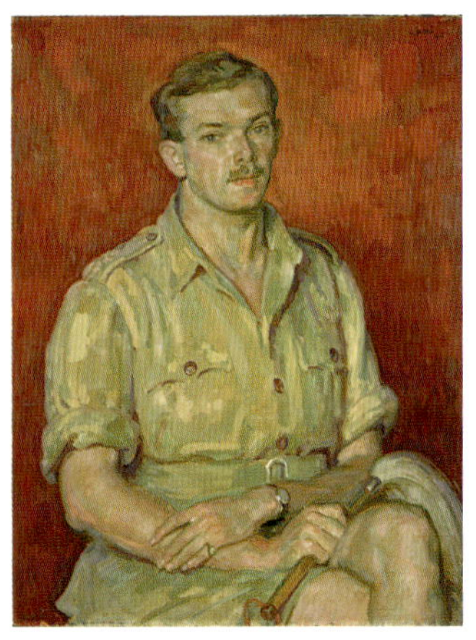

Lamb, Henry 1883–1960
Major E. Wilson, VC, 10th Battalion, East
Surrey Regiment 1942
oil on canvas 91.4 x 71.1
IWM ART LD 2572

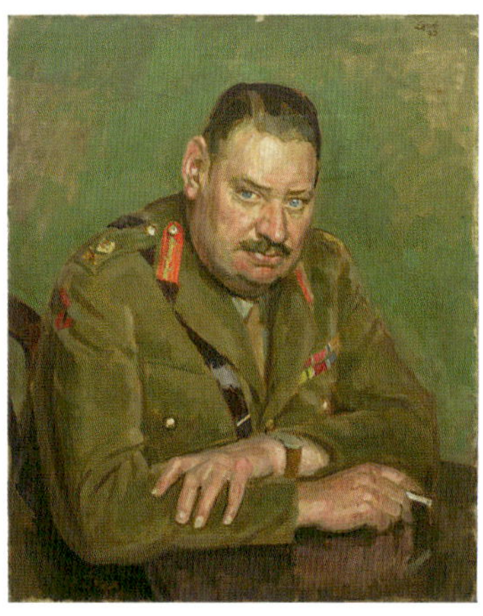

Lamb, Henry 1883–1960
Major General Robert Frederick Edward
Whittaker (1894–1967), CB, OBE, TD, Anti-
Aircraft Command 1942
oil on canvas 76.2 x 63.5
IWM ART LD 3772

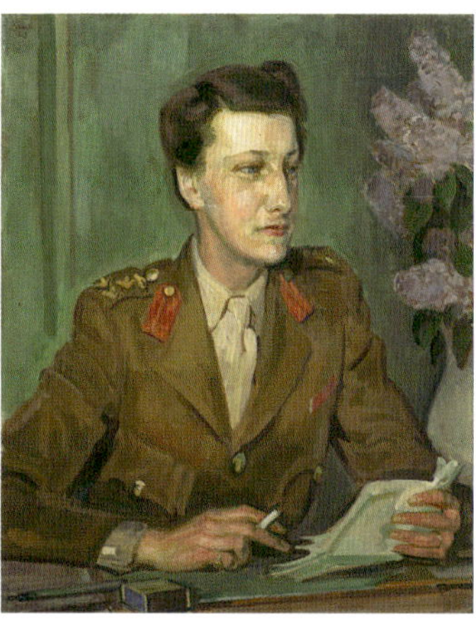

Lamb, Henry 1883–1960
Chief Controller Leslie Violet Lucy Whateley,
CBE, Director of Auxiliary Territorial
Service 1943
oil on canvas 68.5 x 55.8
IWM ART LD 3208

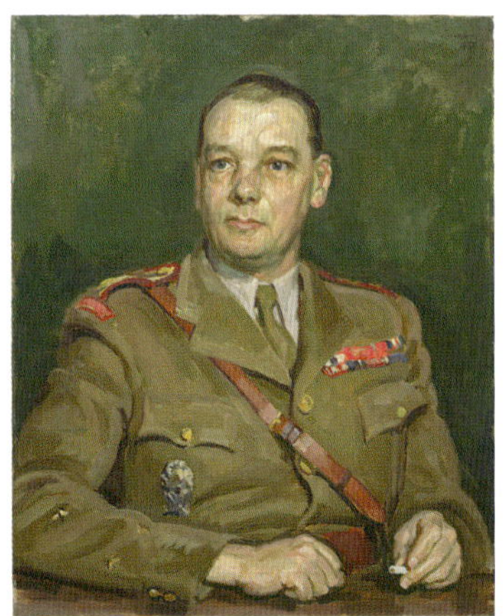

Lamb, Henry 1883–1960
General Rudolf Viest (1890–1944) 1943
oil on canvas 76.2 x 63.5
IWM ART LD 3207

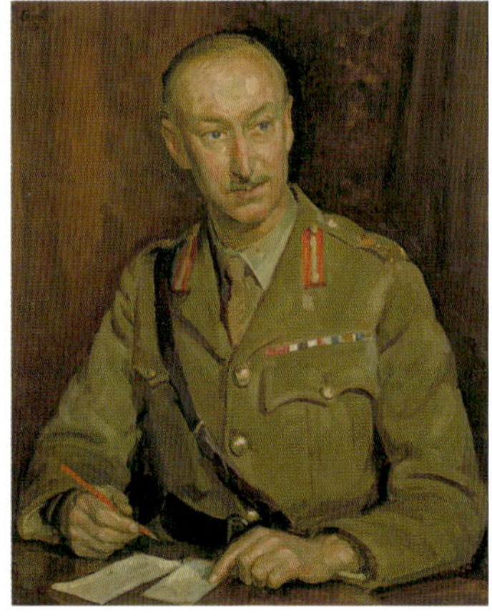

Lamb, Henry 1883–1960
Major General John Noble Kennedy
(1893–1970), CB, MC 1943
oil on canvas 76.2 x 63.5
IWM ART LD 3210

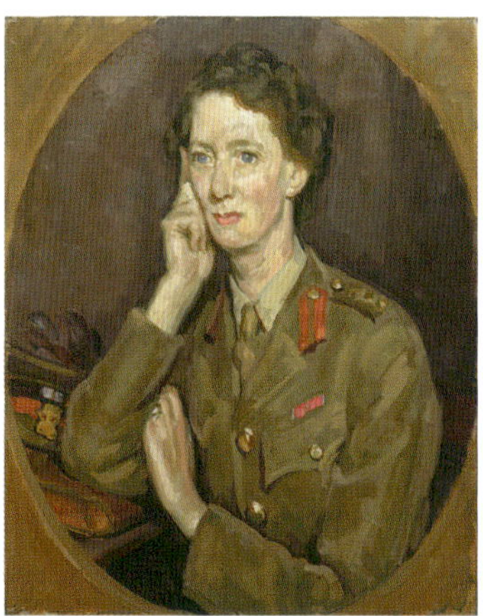

Lamb, Henry 1883–1960
Senior Controller Christian Helen Fraser-
Tytler, CBE, Deputy Director of Anti-Aircraft
Command, Auxiliary Territorial Service 1943
oil on canvas 68.5 x 55.8
IWM ART LD 3209

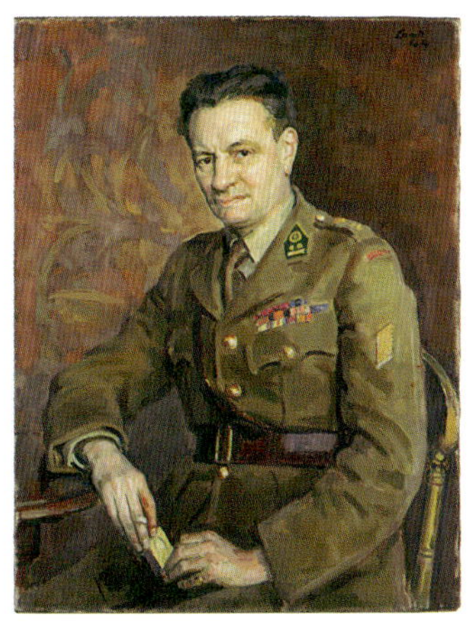

Lamb, Henry 1883–1960
Colonel P. Devaux 1944
oil on canvas 88.9 x 69.8
IWM ART LD 4506

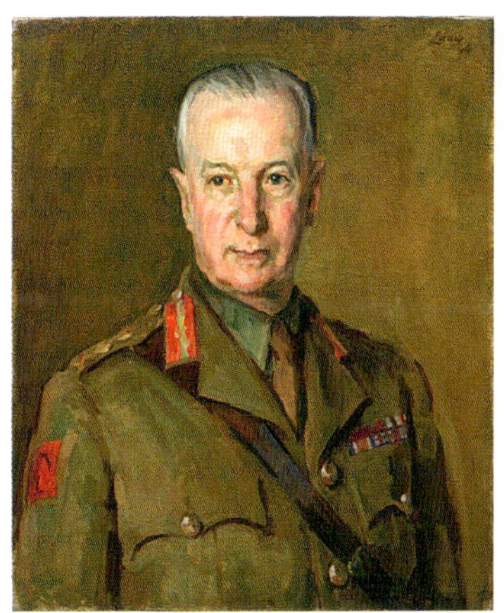

Lamb, Henry 1883–1960
General Sir Frederick Pile (1884–1976), KCB, DSO, MC 1944
oil on canvas 60.9 x 50.8
IWM ART LD 3775

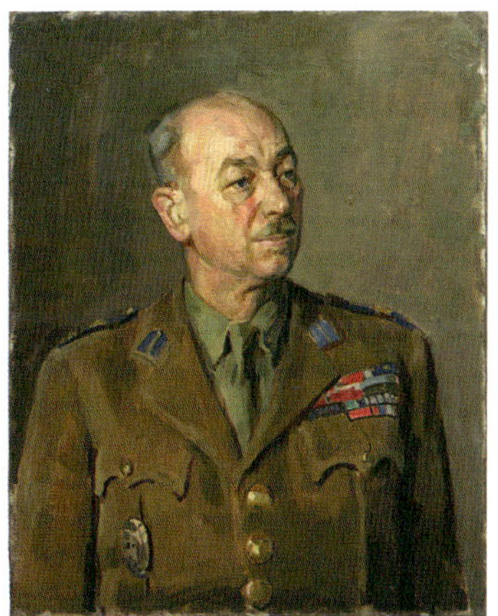

Lamb, Henry 1883–1960
Generale de Division Milorad M. Radovitch 1944
oil on canvas 68.5 x 55.8
IWM ART LD 3893

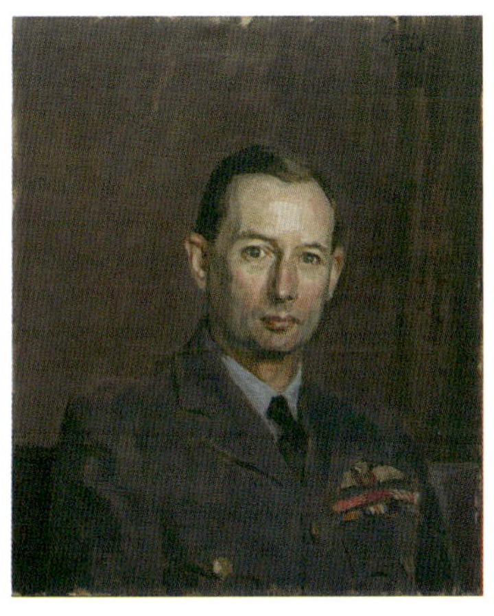

Lamb, Henry 1883–1960
Air Marshal the Honourable Sir Ralph Cochrane (1895–1977), KBE, Aide-de-Camp to His Majesty the King 1946
oil on canvas 60.9 x 50.8
IWM ART LD 5800

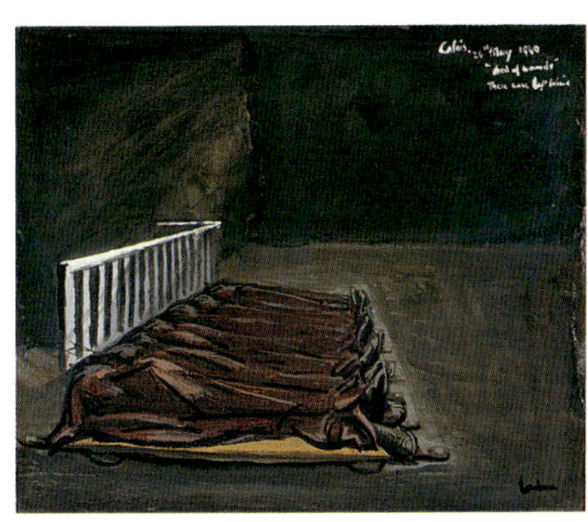

Lambourn, George 1900–1977
Calais, 26 May 1940: Died of Wounds
oil on canvas 50.1 x 60.9
IWM ART LD 970

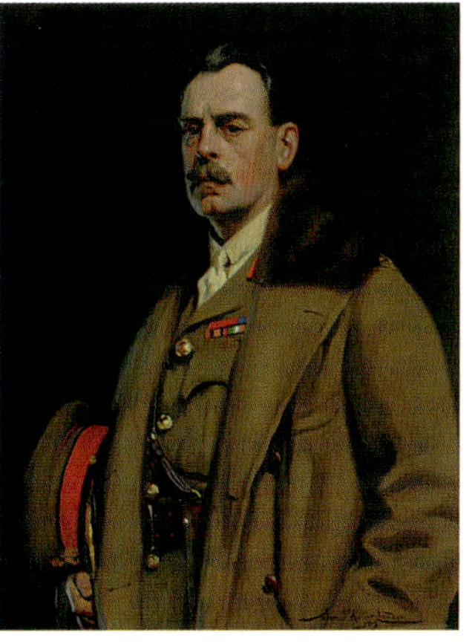

Lander, John Saint-Hélier 1869–1944
General Sir Philip Chetwode (1869–1950), KCMG, CB, DSO 1919
oil on canvas 91.4 x 71.1
IWM ART 5929

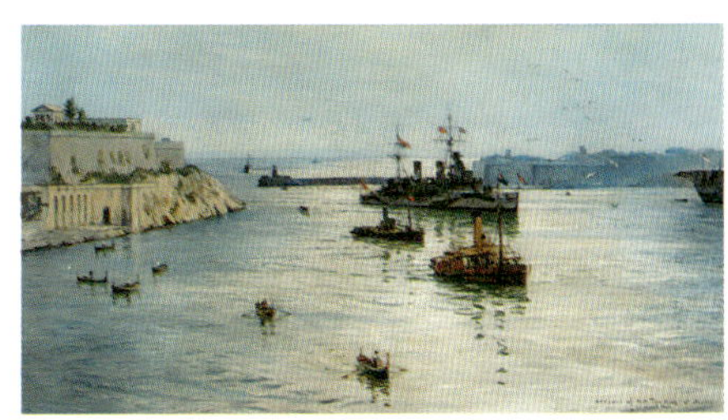

Langmaid, Rowland 1897–1956
Arrival of His Majesty the King at Malta 1943
oil on canvas 51 x 91.4
IWM ART 15082

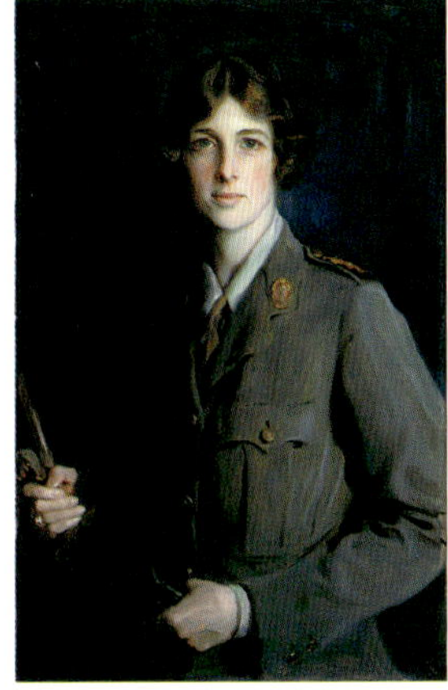

László, Philip Alexius de 1869–1937
Edith Vane-Tempest-Stewart, the Marchioness of Londonderry (1879–1959), DBE 1918
oil on canvas 86.3 x 57.1
IWM ART 3095

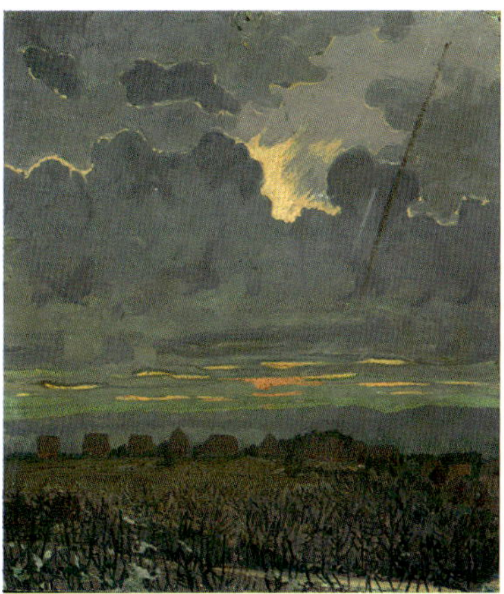

Laveaux, Ludwik de 1891–1969
View from Oflag 2B 1940
oil on board 19 x 17
IWM ART 17119

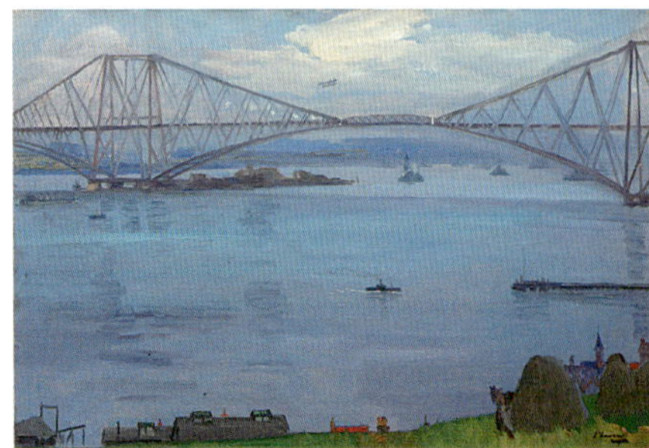

Lavery, John 1856–1941
The Forth Bridge 1914
oil on canvas 50.8 x 76.2
IWM ART 1393

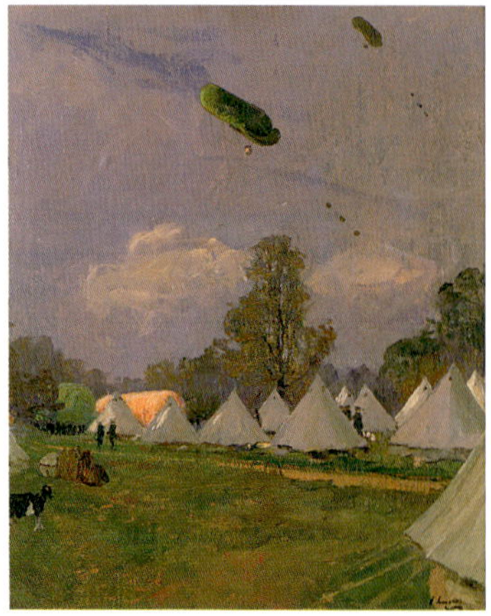

Lavery, John 1856–1941
Kite Balloons, Roehampton 1915
oil on canvas 76.2 x 63.5
IWM ART 1262

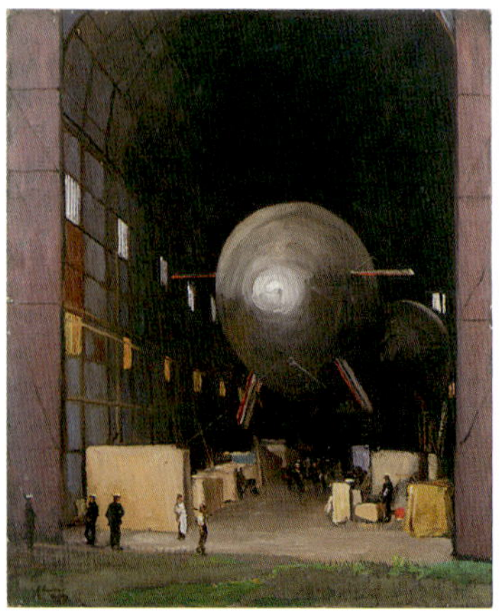

Lavery, John 1856–1941
*'The Silver Queen', Wormwood Scrubs: One of
the Original 'Blimps'* 1915
oil on canvas 76.2 x 63.5
IWM ART 1267

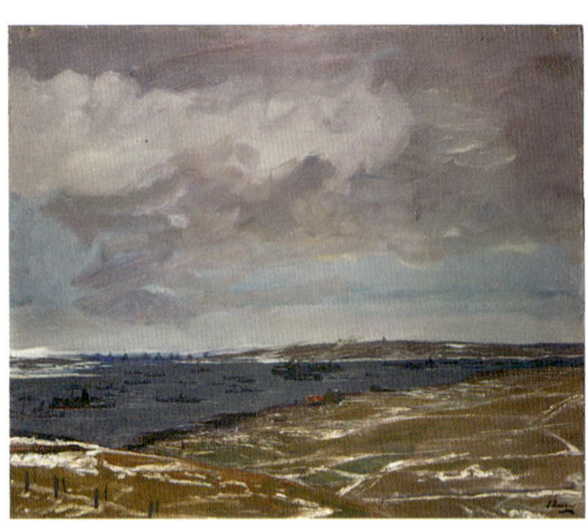

Lavery, John 1856–1941
Flotta and Weddel Sound 1916
oil on canvas 63.5 x 76.2
IWM ART 1249

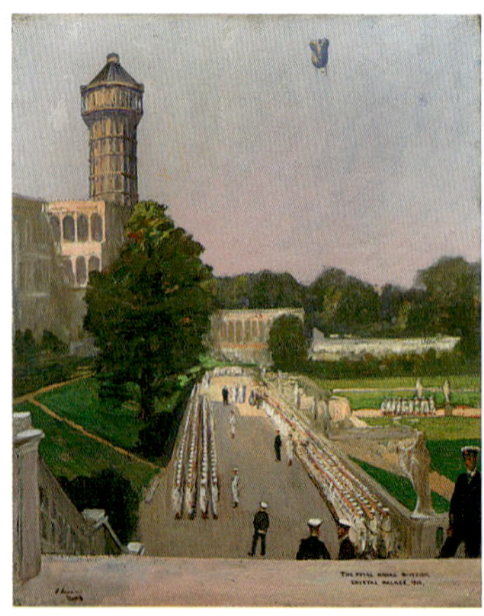

Lavery, John 1856–1941
*Royal Naval Division, Crystal Palace: The Spot
Known as the Quarter-Deck* 1916
oil on canvas 76.2 x 63.5
IWM ART 1268

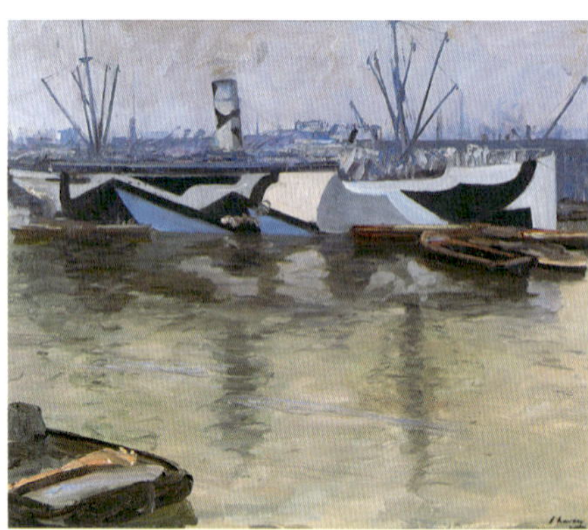

Lavery, John 1856–1941
The 'Appam', London Docks 1916
oil on canvas 63.5 x 76.2
IWM ART 1281

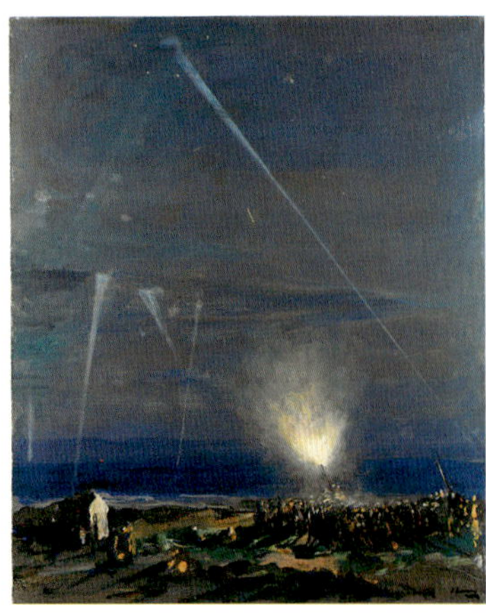

Lavery, John 1856–1941
*A Coast Defence: An 18-Pounder Anti-Aircraft
Gun, Tyneside* 1917
oil on canvas 76.2 x 63.5
IWM ART 1263

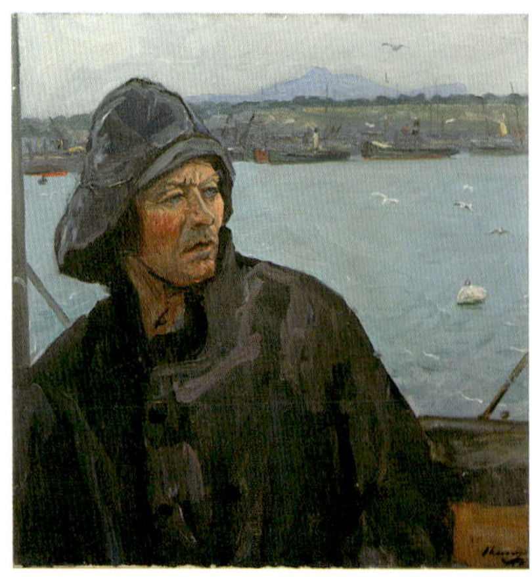

Lavery, John 1856–1941
A Deck Hand, North Sea Patrol 1917
oil on canvas 63.5 x 60.9
IWM ART 1397

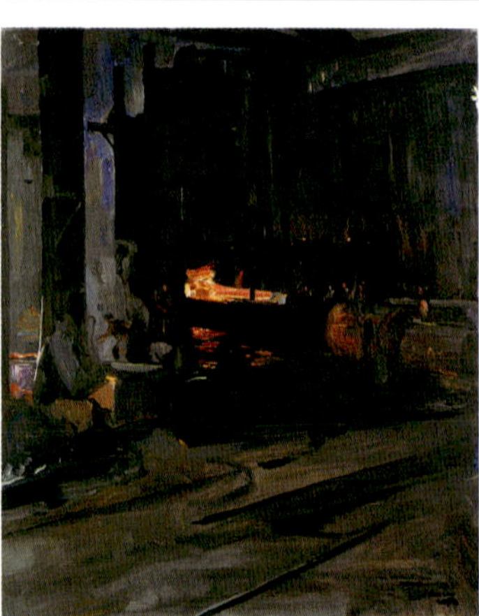

Lavery, John 1856–1941
*A Naval Gun in the Hydraulic Press: Elswick
Works, Newcastle-on-Tyne* 1917
oil on canvas 76.2 x 63.5
IWM ART 1258

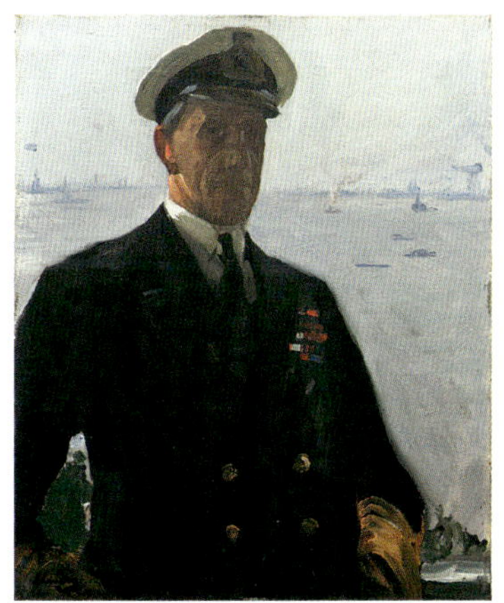

Lavery, John 1856–1941
*Admiral Sir Cecil Burney (1859–1929),
GCMG, KCB, Commander-in-Chief, Coast of
Scotland* 1917
oil on canvas 76.2 x 63.5
IWM ART 1254

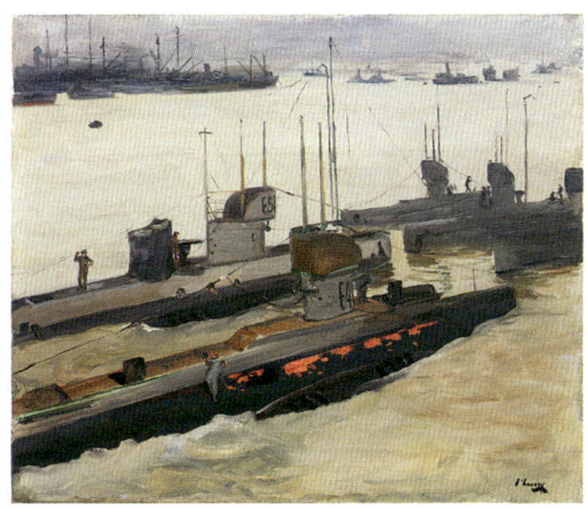

Lavery, John 1856–1941
British Mine-Laying Submarines, Harwich
1917
oil on canvas 64 x 76.2
IWM ART 1259

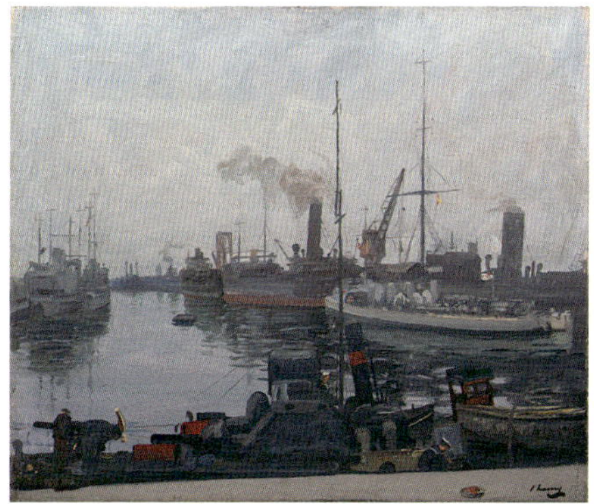

Lavery, John 1856–1941
Leith 1917
oil on canvas 63.5 x 76.2
IWM ART 1391

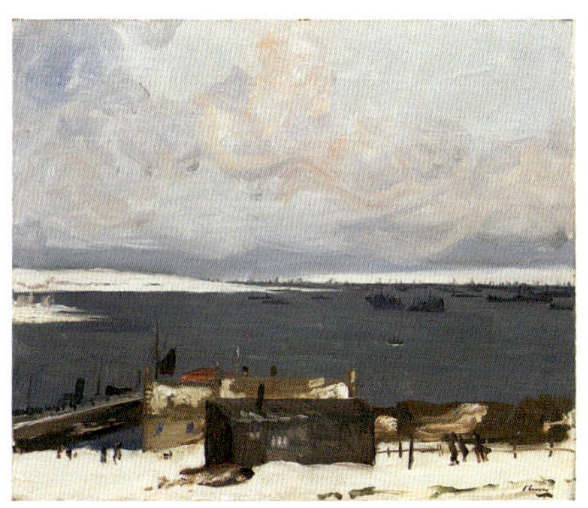

Lavery, John 1856–1941
Long Hope: Orkney 1917
oil on canvas 63.5 x 76.2
IWM ART 1255

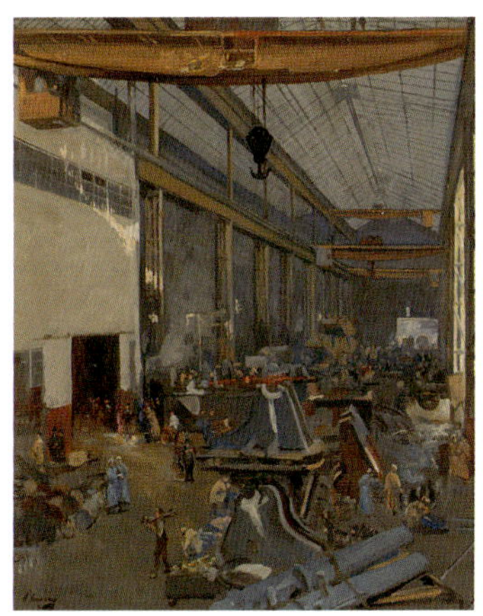

Lavery, John 1856–1941
Munitions, Newcastle 1917
oil on canvas 76.2 x 63.5
IWM ART 1271

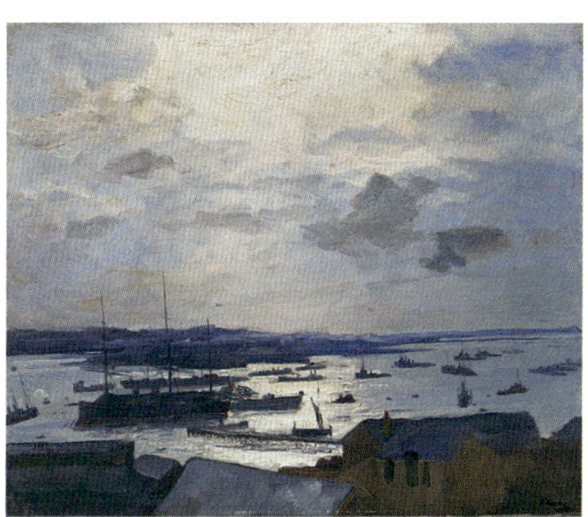

Lavery, John 1856–1941
Parkestone: A Destroyer Base at Harwich 1917
oil on canvas 63.5 x 76.2
IWM ART 1278

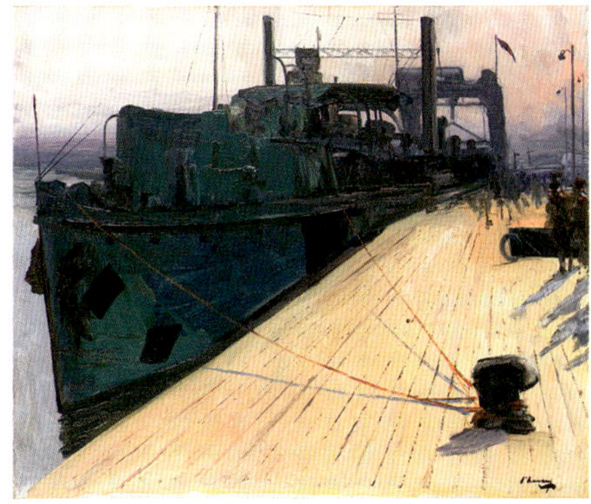

Lavery, John 1856–1941
Richborough: A Cross-Channel Ferry 1917
oil on canvas 63.5 x 76.2
IWM ART 1253

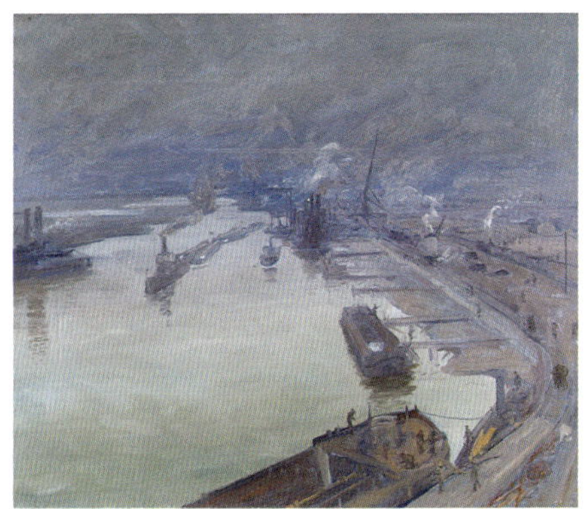

Lavery, John 1856–1941
Richborough in Fog 1917
oil on canvas 63.5 x 76.2
IWM ART 1272

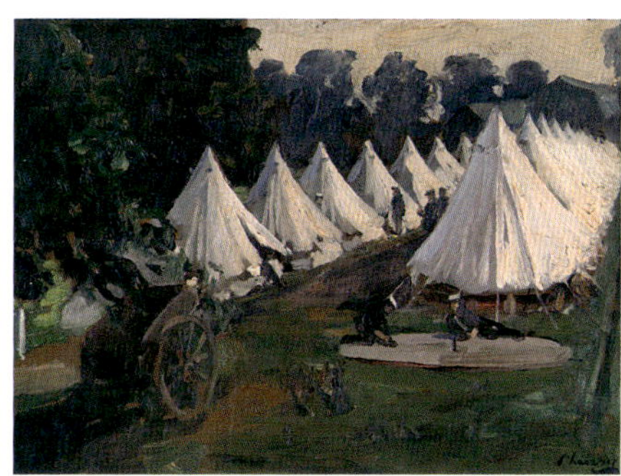

Lavery, John 1856–1941
*Royal Naval Air Service, Roehampton, August
1917* 1917
oil on canvas 25.2 x 35.5
IWM ART 5733

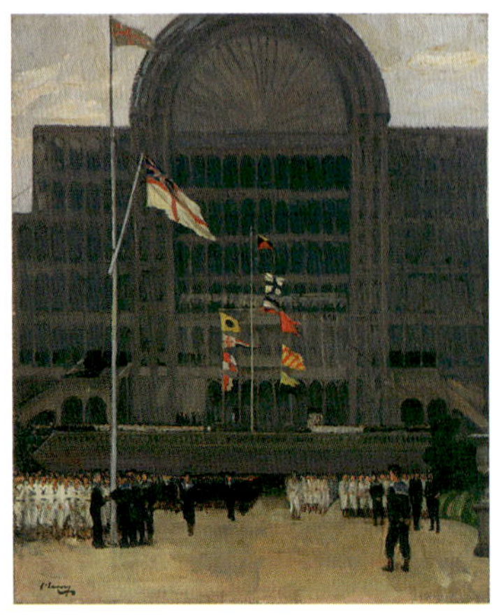

Lavery, John 1856–1941
Royal Naval Volunteer Reserve, Crystal Palace
1917
oil on canvas 76.2 x 63.5
IWM ART 1275

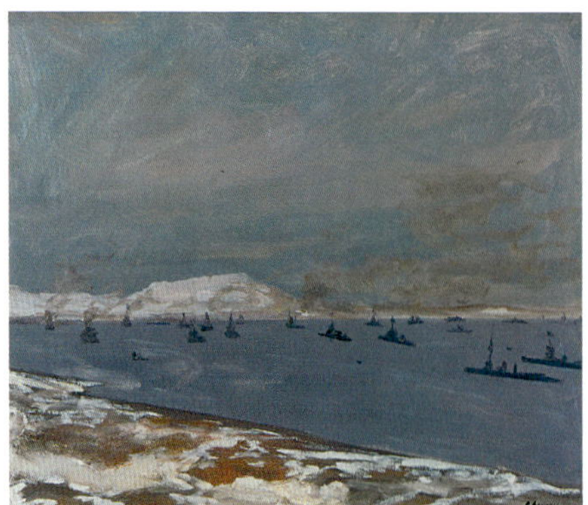

Lavery, John 1856–1941
Scapa Flow 1917
oil on canvas 63.5 x 76.2 (E)
IWM ART 1266

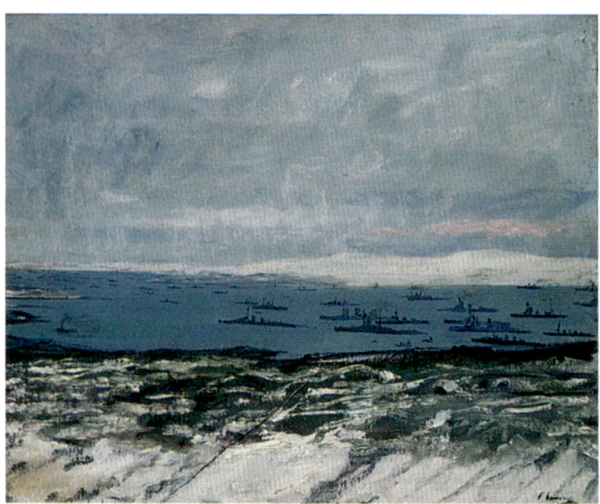

Lavery, John 1856–1941
Scapa Flow, Orkney, from the Signal Station
1917
oil on canvas 63.5 x 76.2 (E)
IWM ART 1264

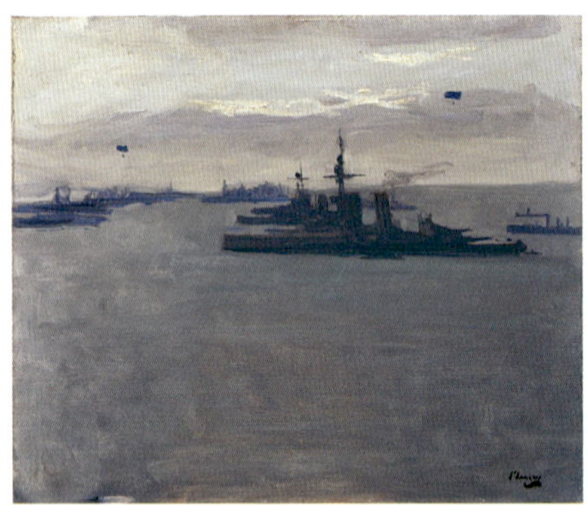

Lavery, John 1856–1941
The Firth of Forth: Wind 1917
oil on canvas 63.5 x 76.2
IWM ART 1269

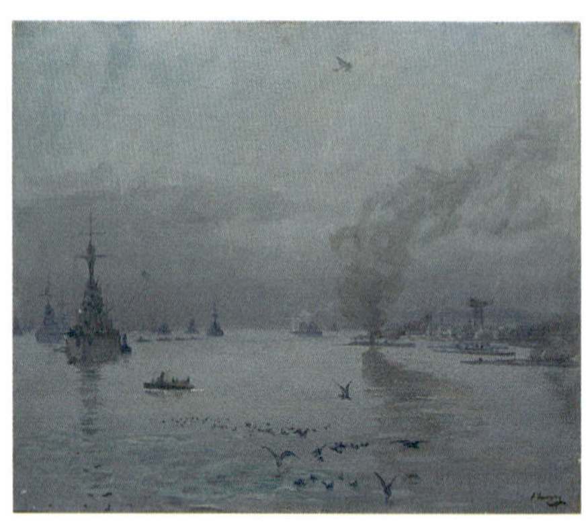

Lavery, John 1856–1941
The Fleet: A Misty Day, the Firth of Forth
1917
oil on canvas 63.5 x 74.9
IWM ART 1274

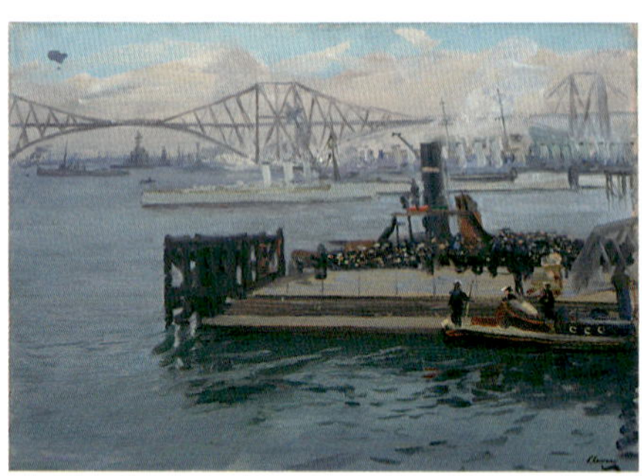

Lavery, John 1856–1941
The Forth Bridge: Bluejackets Landing 1917
oil on canvas 53.3 x 76.2
IWM ART 1389

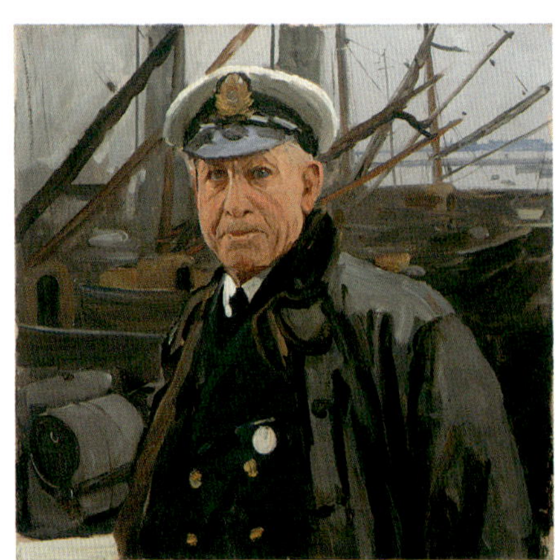

Lavery, John 1856–1941
*The Skipper, Captain William Lyons, 'HMT
Semiramis'* 1917
oil on canvas 60.9 x 63.5
IWM ART 1380

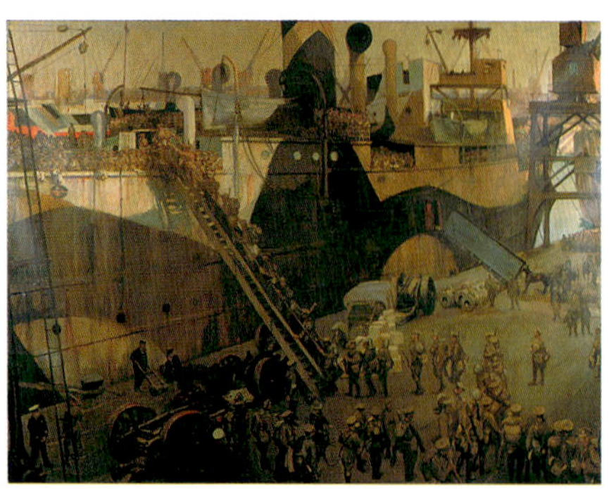

Lavery, John 1856–1941
*Troops Embarking at Southampton for the
Western Front* 1917
oil on canvas 274.3 x 365.7
IWM ART 2616

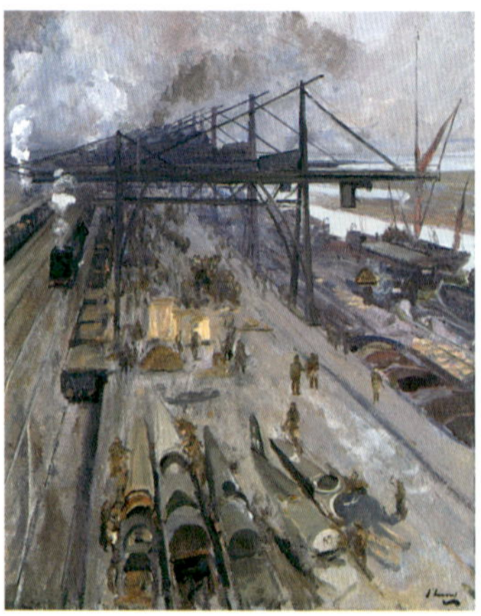

Lavery, John 1856–1941
Richborough: The Gantries c.1917–1918
oil on canvas 76.2 x 63.5
IWM ART 1387

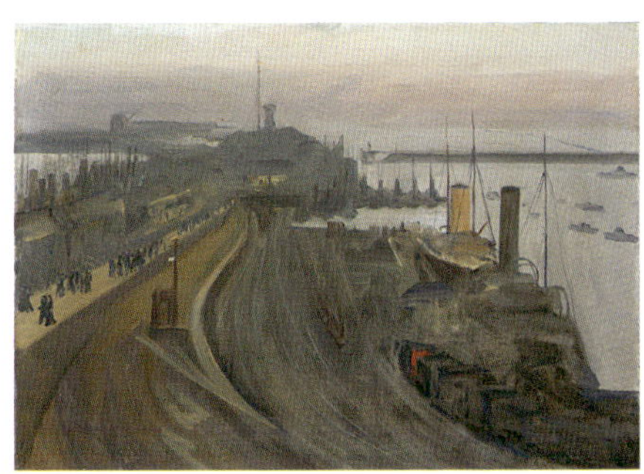

Lavery, John 1856–1941
*Twilight, the Naval Base, Granton: Booms
Guarding the Forth Are Seen in the Distance*
c.1917–1918
oil on canvas 52 x 76.2
IWM ART 1384

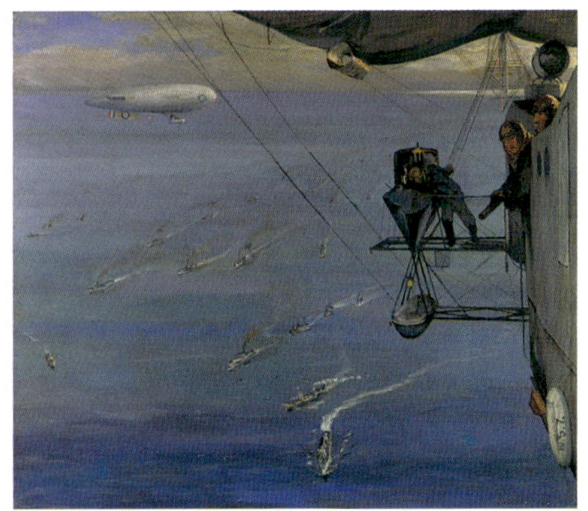

Lavery, John 1856–1941
*A Convoy, North Sea: From NS 7, Painted from
an Airship off the Coast of Norway* 1918
oil on canvas 172.7 x 198.1
IWM ART 1257

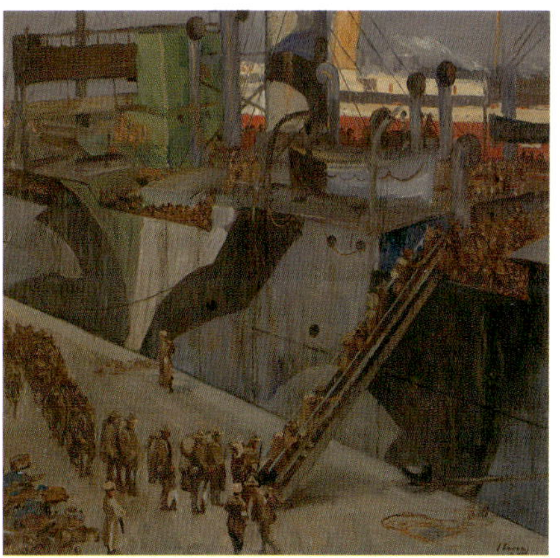

Lavery, John 1856–1941
American Troops Embarking, Southampton
1918
oil on canvas 76.2 x 76.2
IWM ART 1279

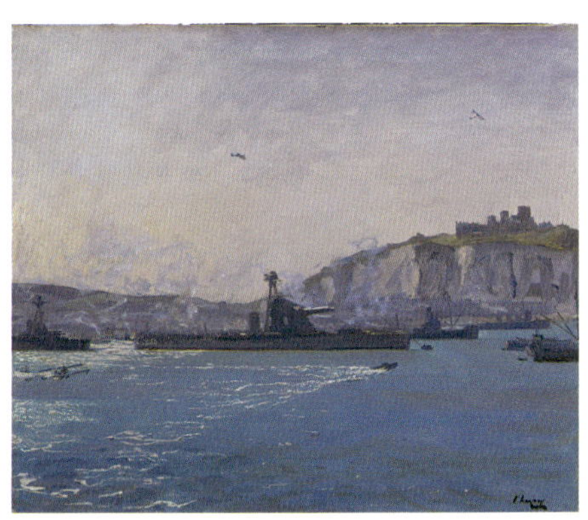

Lavery, John 1856–1941
Monitors, Dover Harbour 1918
oil on canvas 63.5 x 76.2
IWM ART 1280

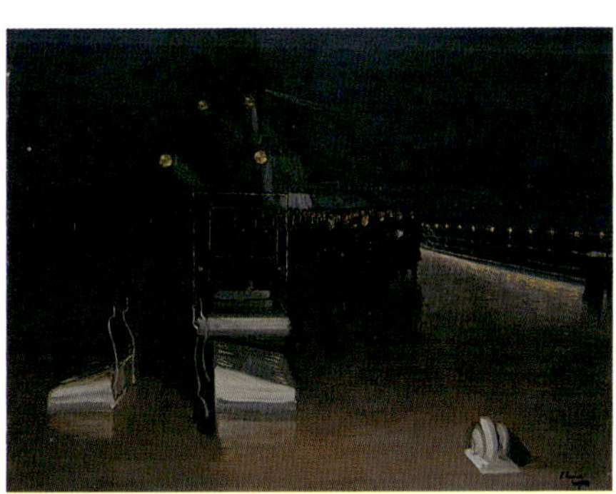

Lavery, John 1856–1941
*Night and the Arrival of the German Delegates:
'HMS Queen Elizabeth', 15 November 1918*
1918
oil on canvas 76.2 x 101.9
IWM ART 1265

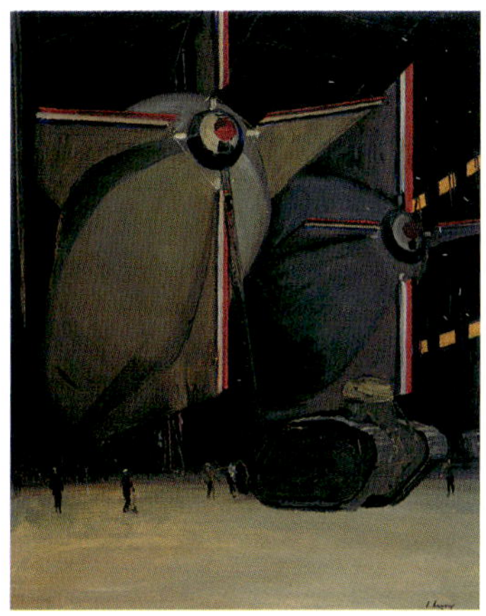

Lavery, John 1856–1941
*'Rigids' at Pulham: 'R 23' Type British Airships
at Pulham St Mary, Norfolk* 1918
oil on canvas 76.2 x 63.5
IWM ART 1256

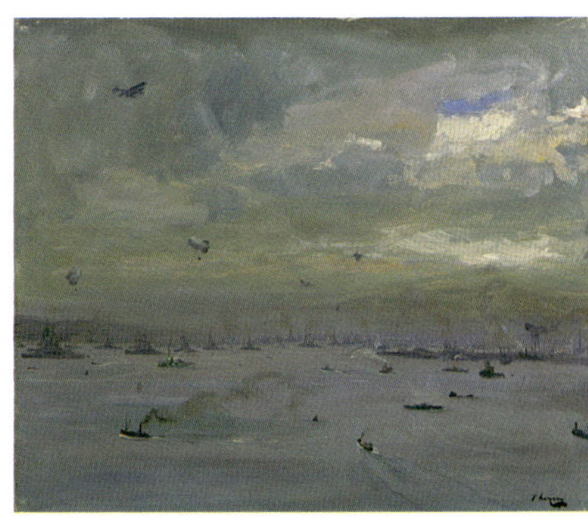

Lavery, John 1856–1941
Rosyth: The Principal Base of the Grand Fleet
1918
oil on canvas 63.5 x 76.2
IWM ART 1252

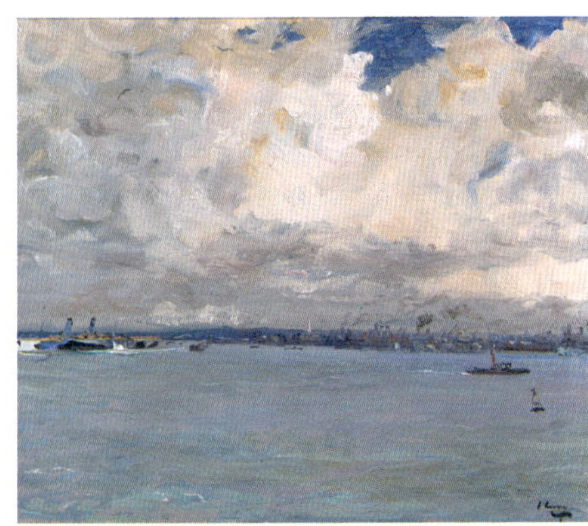

Lavery, John 1856–1941
Southampton Water 1918
oil on canvas 63.5 x 76.2
IWM ART 1270

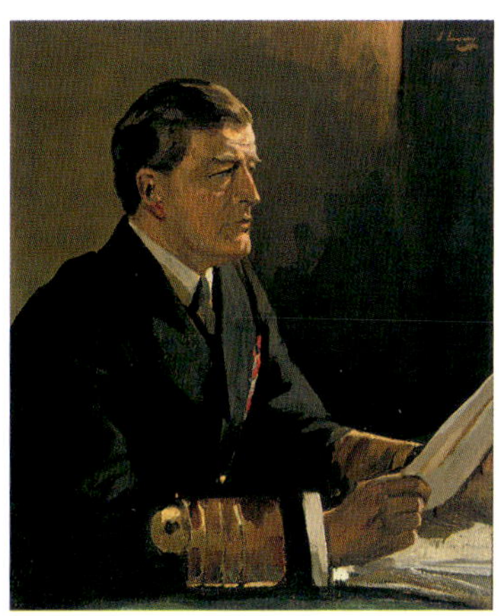

Lavery, John 1856–1941
*Study for 'Admiral Sir David Beatty
(1871–1936), GCB, Reading the Terms of the
Armistice to the German Delegates; (…)* 1918
oil on canvas 74.9 x 62.8
IWM ART 2617

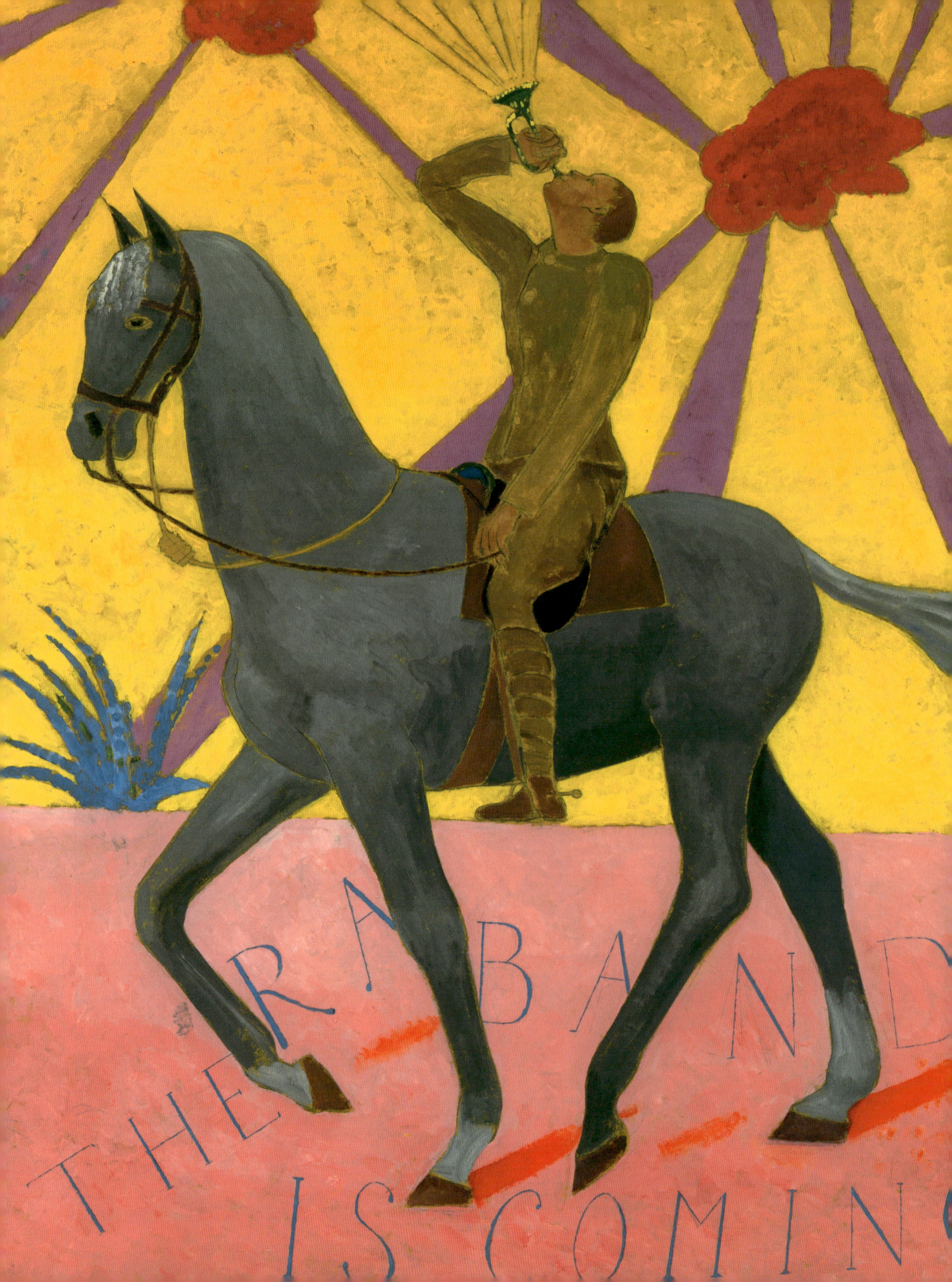
RABAND
THE IS COMING

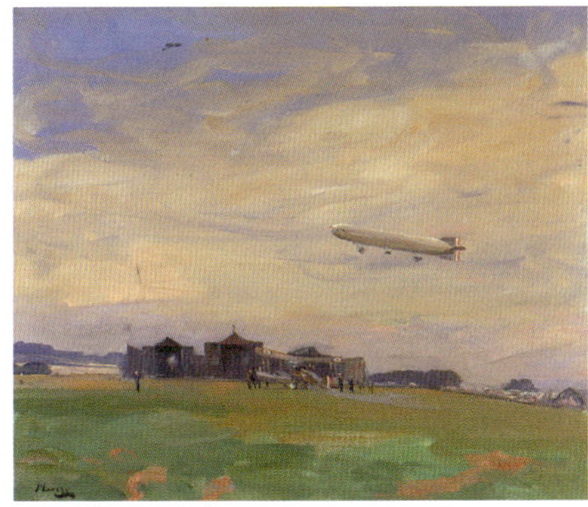

Lavery, John 1856–1941
The Aerodrome, East Fortune, North Berwick:
The Starting Point for British Airships of the
North Sea Air Patrol 1918
oil on canvas 63.5 x 76.2
IWM ART 1276

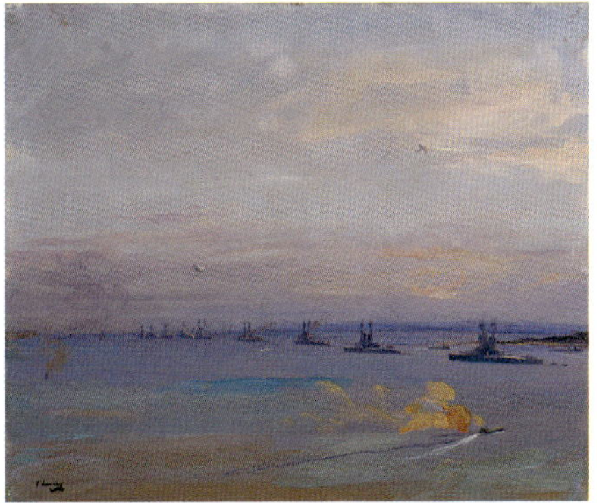

Lavery, John 1856–1941
The American Battle Squadron in the Firth of
Forth: 'New York' (Flagship), 'Texas', 'Florida',
'Wyoming' and 'Delaware' 1918
oil on canvas 63.5 x 76.2
IWM ART 1250

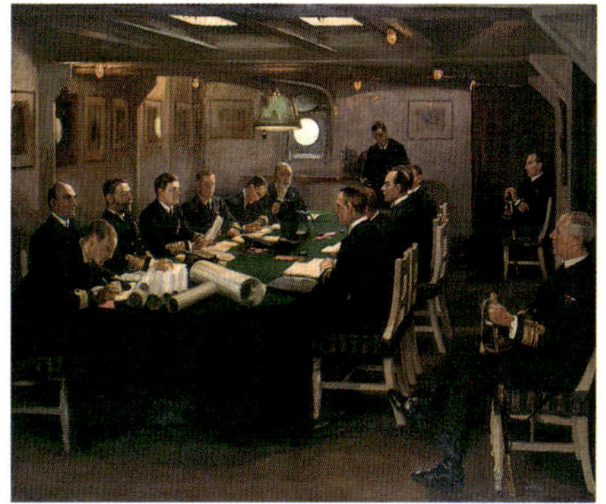

Lavery, John 1856–1941
The End: The Fore-Cabin of 'HMS Queen
Elizabeth' with Admiral Beatty Reading the
Terms of the Surrender (…) 1918
oil on canvas 220.9 x 276.8
IWM ART 4219

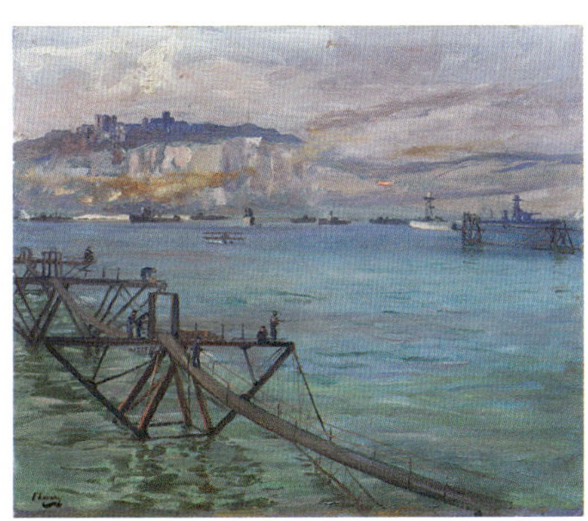

Lavery, John 1856–1941
The Entrance, Dover Harbour, 1918: In the
Foreground Are the Harbour Protection Nets
against Enemy Submarines 1918
oil on canvas 63.5 x 76.2
IWM ART 1261

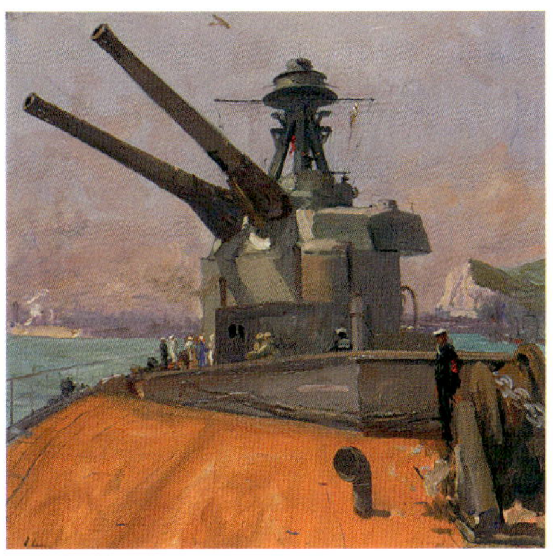

Lavery, John 1856–1941
The Guns, 'HMS Terror' 1918
oil on canvas 61.2 x 63.8
IWM ART 1379

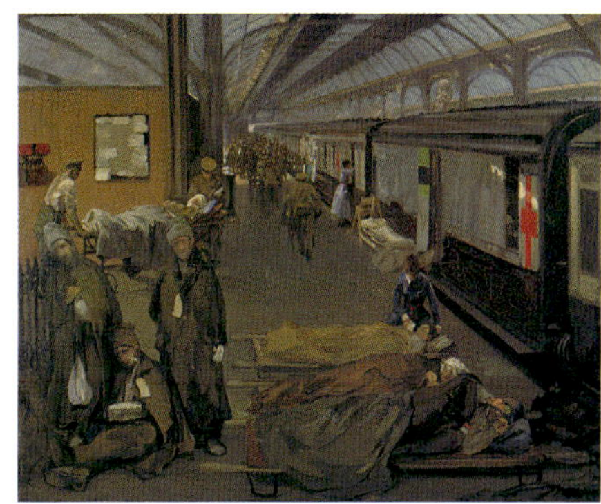

Lavery, John 1856–1941
The Wounded at Dover 1918
oil on canvas 101.9 x 127
IWM ART 1273

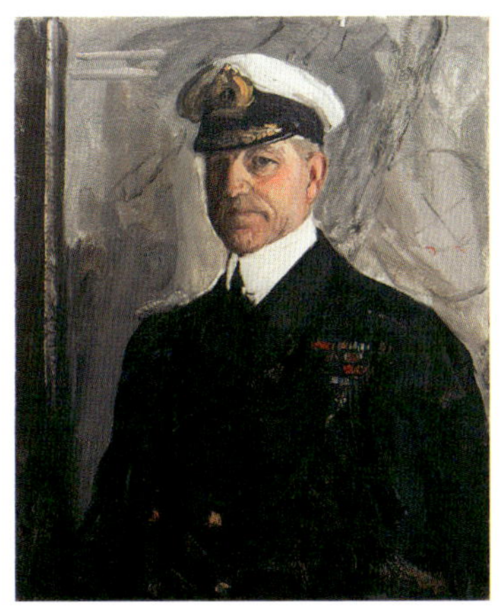

Lavery, John 1856–1941
Admiral Sir James Startin (1855–1948), KCB,
AM, Royal Naval Reserve c.1918
oil on canvas 76.2 x 63.5
IWM ART 1260

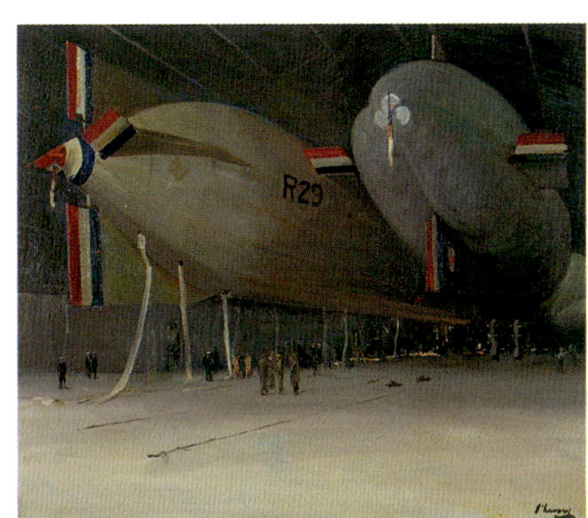

Lavery, John 1856–1941
'Rigid 29' and 'NS 7' at East Fortune c.1918
oil on canvas 63.5 x 76.2
IWM ART 1277

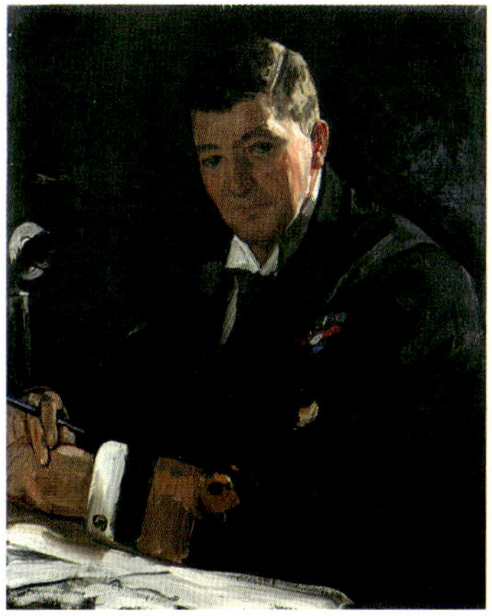

Lavery, John 1856–1941
The Chief Naval Censor: Rear Admiral Sir
Douglas Browning, Bt, CB, Royal Navy c.1918
oil on canvas 73.6 x 62.2
IWM ART 1251

Facing page: Japp, Darsie, 1883–1973, *Regimental Band* (detail), c.1918, (p. 115)

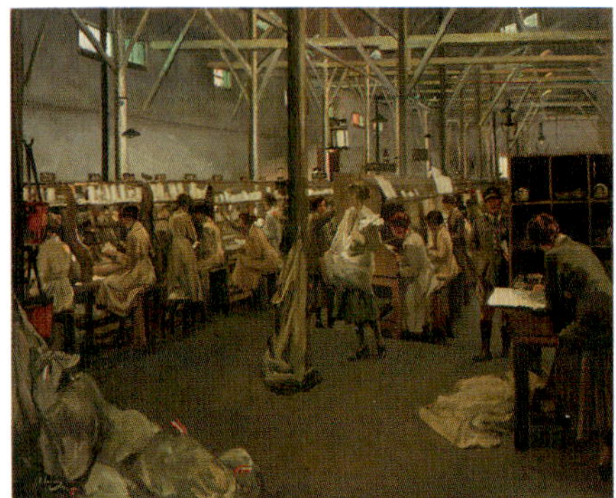

Lavery, John 1856–1941
Army Post Office 3, Boulogne 1919
oil on canvas 101.9 x 127
IWM ART 2881

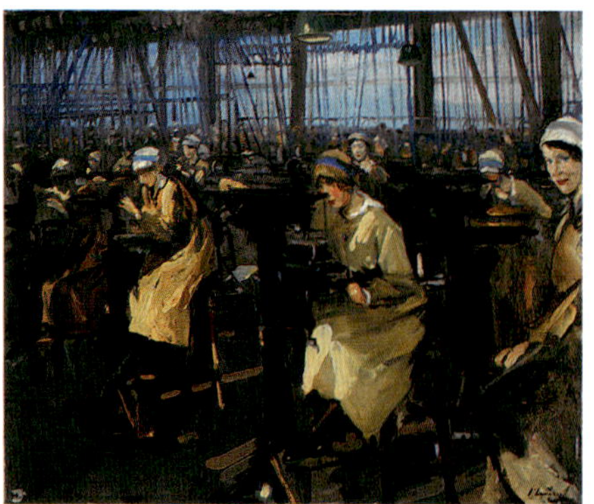

Lavery, John 1856–1941
Elswick, 1917: Messrs. Armstrong, Whitworth & Company 1919
oil on canvas 63.5 x 76.2
IWM ART 2883

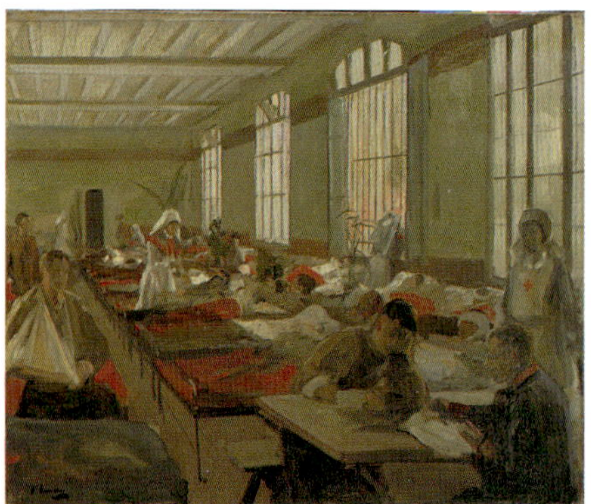

Lavery, John 1856–1941
German Wounded, Le Havre 1919
oil on canvas 63.5 x 76.2
IWM ART 2887

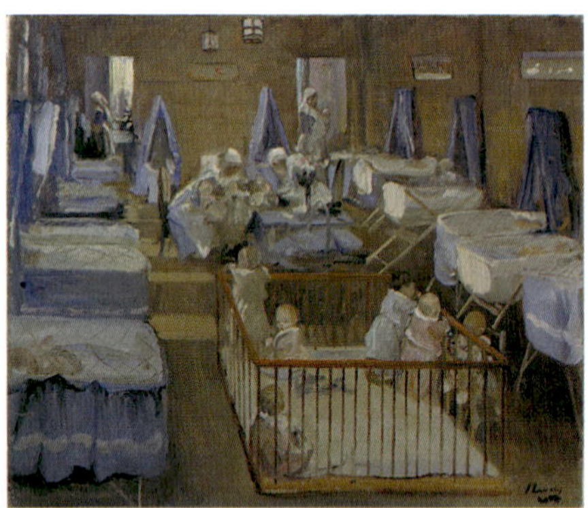

Lavery, John 1856–1941
Lady Henry's Crèche, Woolwich 1919
oil on canvas 63.5 x 76.2
IWM ART 3084

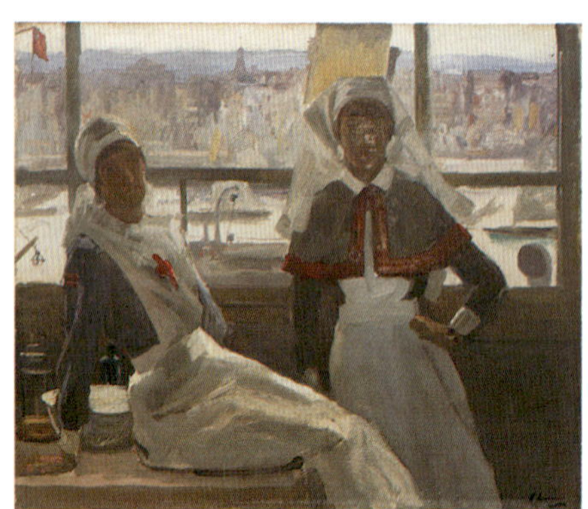

Lavery, John 1856–1941
Le Havre: Nurse Billam and Sister Currier 1919
oil on canvas 63.5 x 76.2
IWM ART 2892

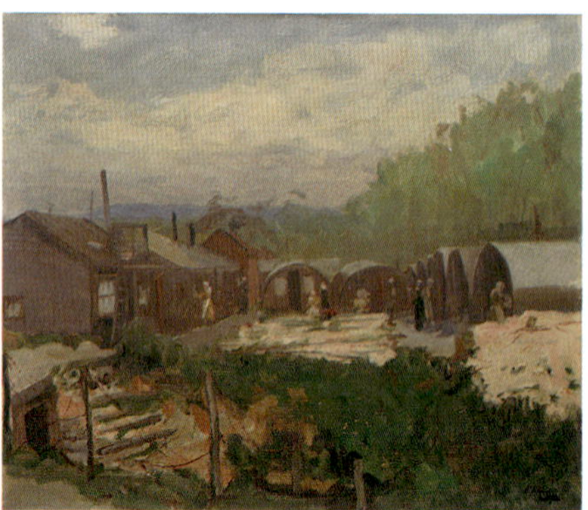

Lavery, John 1856–1941
No.3 GS, Voluntary Aid Detachment Camp, Rouen 1919
oil on canvas 63.5 x 76.2
IWM ART 2886

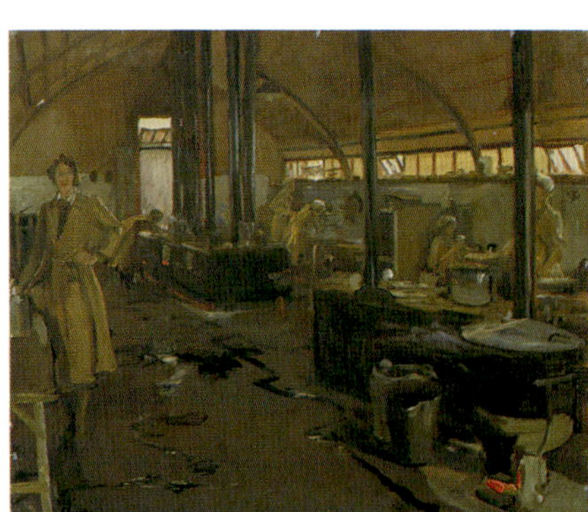

Lavery, John 1856–1941
Queen Mary's Army Auxiliary Corps Cookhouse, Rouxmesnil 1919
oil on canvas 53.3 x 64.7
IWM ART 2891

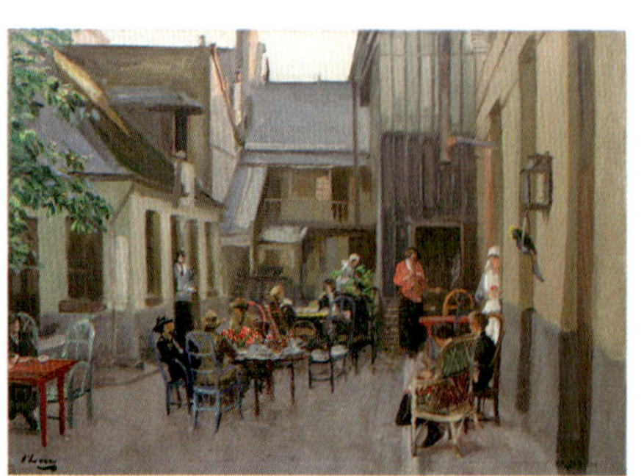

Lavery, John 1856–1941
Red Cross Hostel, Rouen 1919
oil on canvas 53.3 x 76.2
IWM ART 2888

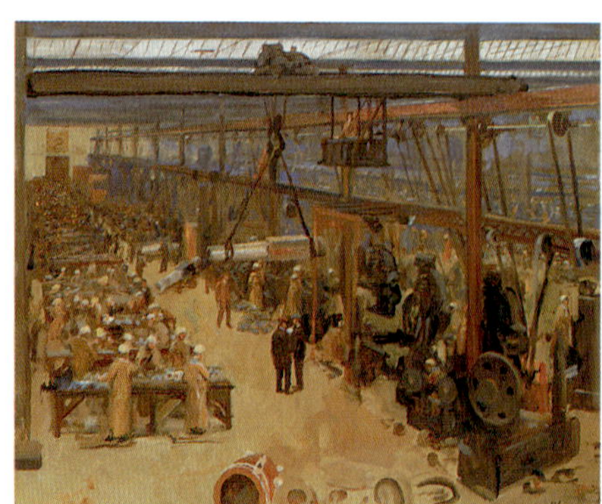

Lavery, John 1856–1941
Scene at a Clyde Shipyard, Messrs. William Beardmore & Co. 1919
oil on canvas 63.5 x 76.2 (E)
IWM ART 3992

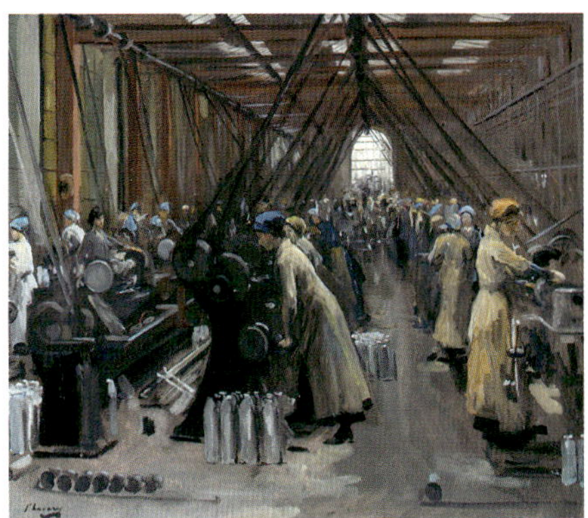

Lavery, John 1856–1941
Shell Making, Edinburgh 1919
oil on canvas 63.5 x 76.2 (E)
IWM ART 4235

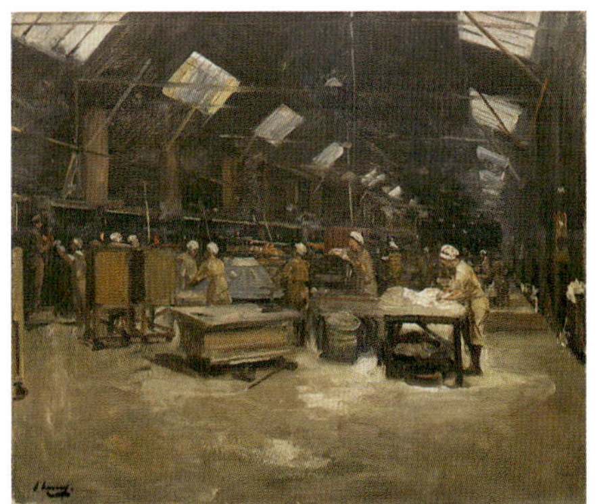

Lavery, John 1856–1941
The Bakeries, Dieppe 1919
oil on canvas 63.5 x 76.2
IWM ART 2889

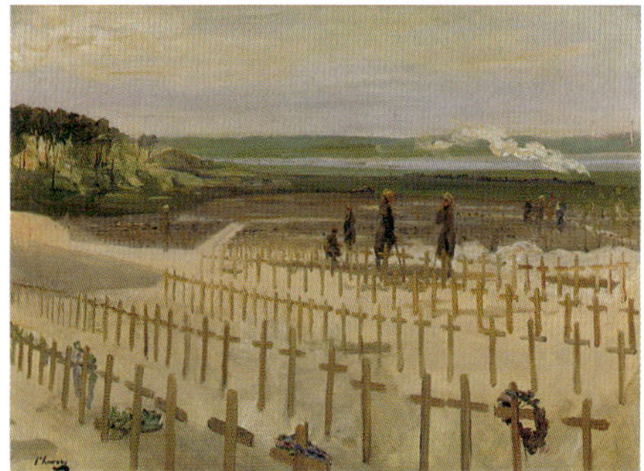

Lavery, John 1856–1941
The Cemetery, Etaples 1919
oil on canvas 52.4 x 72.2
IWM ART 2884

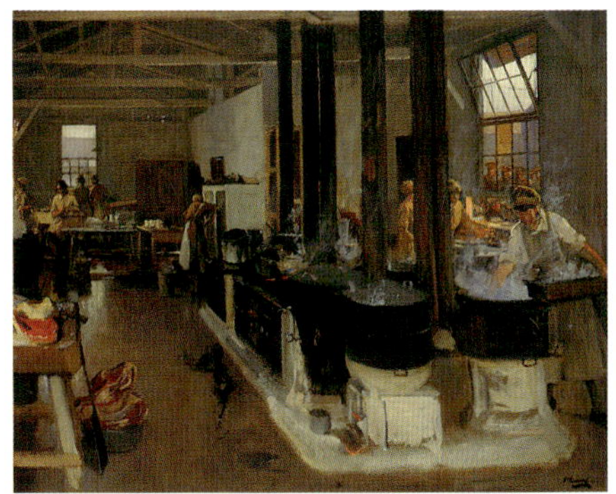

Lavery, John 1856–1941
*The Ordnance Chief Officer's Cookhouse,
Henriville, Boulogne* 1919
oil on canvas 101.9 x 127
IWM ART 2882

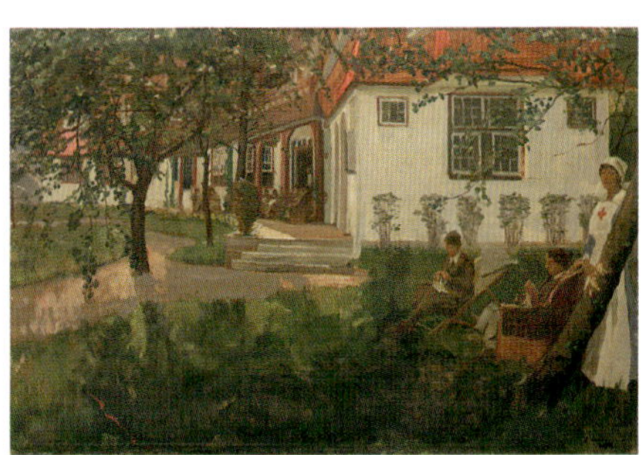

Lavery, John 1856–1941
*The Queen Mary's Army Auxiliary Corps
Convalescent Home, Le Touquet* 1919
oil on canvas 59.6 x 91.4
IWM ART 2885

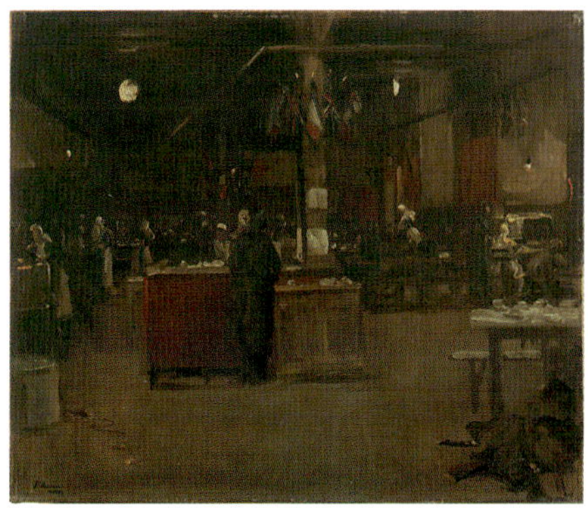

Lavery, John 1856–1941
*The Women's Emergency Canteen, Gare du
Nord, Paris* 1919
oil on canvas 53.3 x 64.7
IWM ART 2890

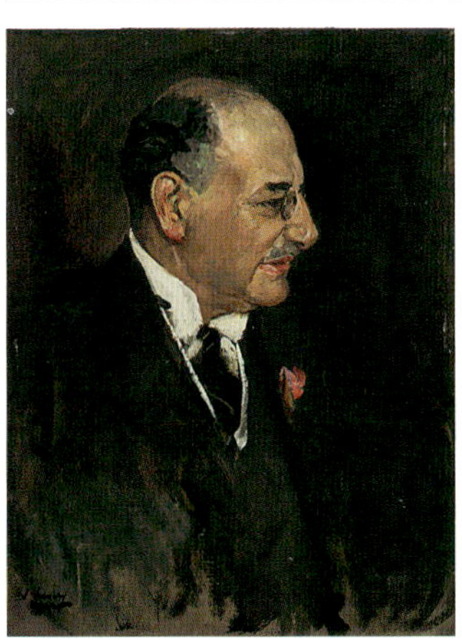

Lavery, John 1856–1941
*Sir Alfred Moritz Mond (1868–1930), First
Lord Melchett* 1929
oil on canvas 60.9 x 45
IWM ART 6222

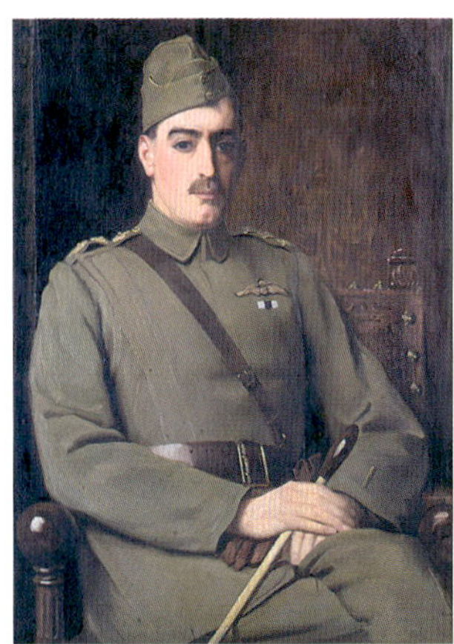

Lawrence, Alfred Kingsley 1893–1975
David Emlyn Evans, Royal Flying Corps Officer
c.1916
oil on canvas 91.4 x 71.1
IWM ART 5565

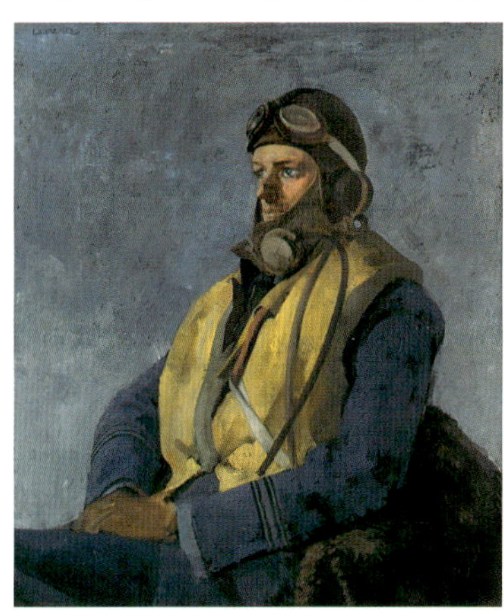

Lawrence, Alfred Kingsley 1893–1975
*Squadron Leader Humphrey Trench Gilbert
(1919–1942), DFC* 1941
oil on canvas 103 x 94
IWM ART 16502

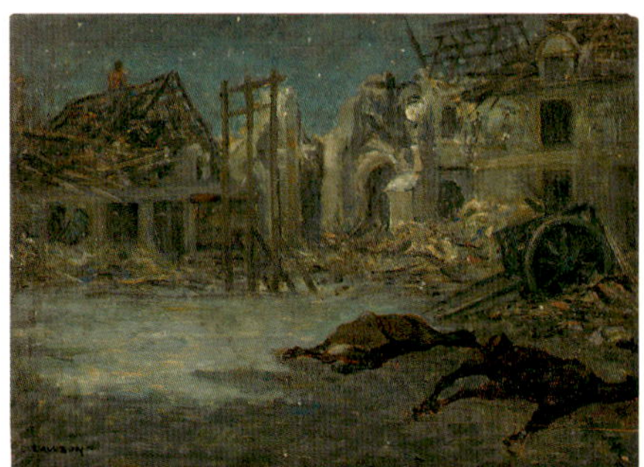

Lawson, Cecil active 1913–1923
Devastated Farm 1915
oil on panel 23.4 x 33
IWM ART 5887

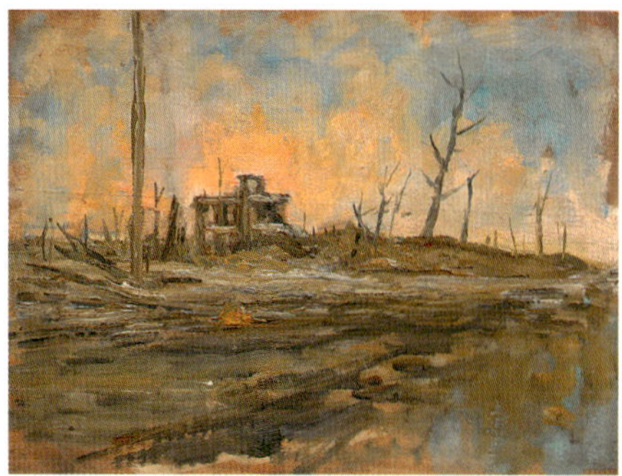

Lawson, Cecil active 1913–1923
Berry-au-Bar c.1916–1918
oil on panel 15.2 x 29.8
IWM ART 5893

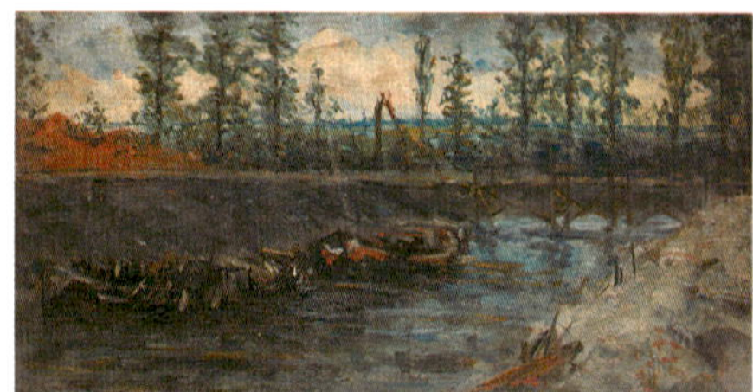

Lawson, Cecil active 1913–1923
Hell Fire Corner c.1916–1918
oil on panel 20.9 x 27.9
IWM ART 5892

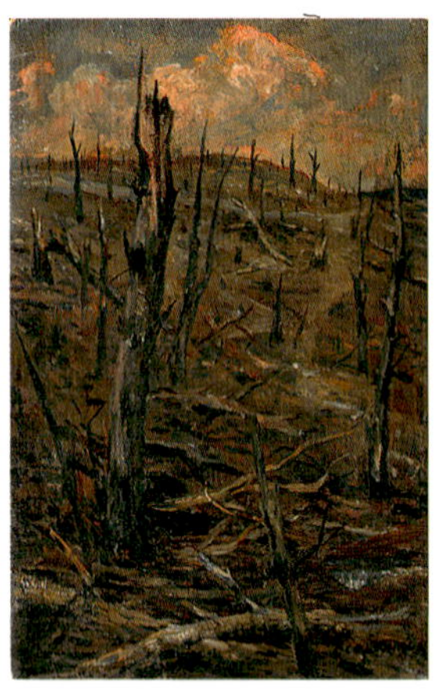

Lawson, Cecil active 1913–1923
Kemilly Hill c.1916–1918
oil on panel 22.8 x 14.6
IWM ART 5897

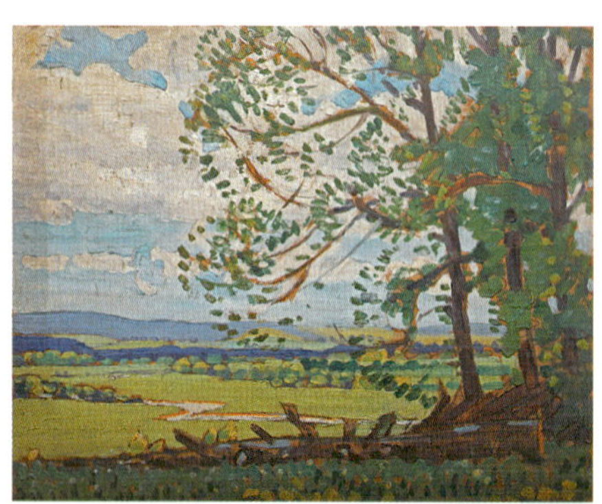

Lawson, Cecil active 1913–1923
Landscape c.1916–1918
oil on panel 31.7 x 41.2
IWM ART 5874

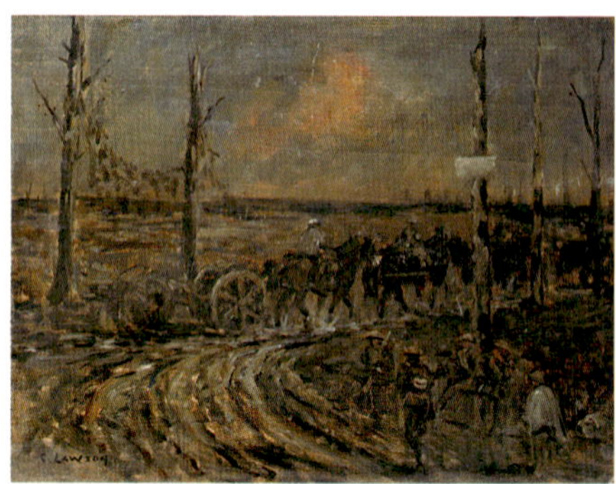

Lawson, Cecil active 1913–1923
Les routes de France c.1916–1918
oil on panel 26.6 x 34.9
IWM ART 5886

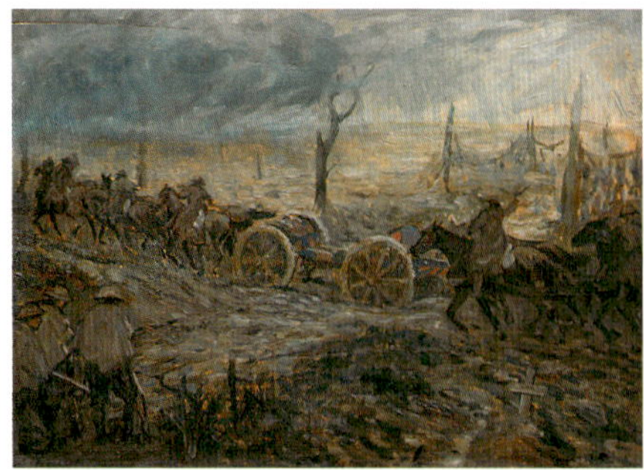

Lawson, Cecil active 1913–1923
Moving Up c.1916–1918
oil on panel 23.4 x 33
IWM ART 5888

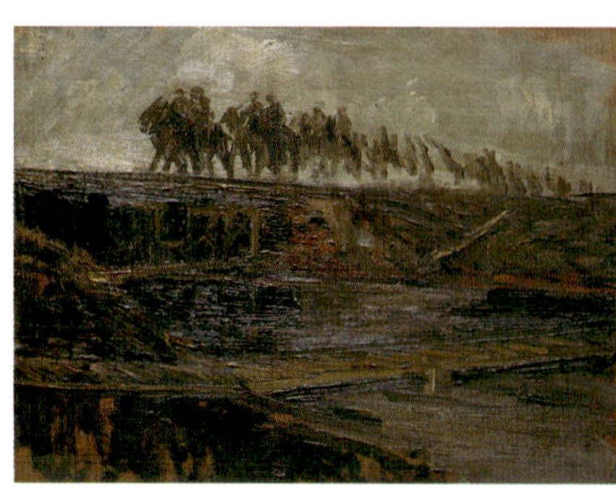

Lawson, Cecil active 1913–1923
Near Albert c.1916–1918
oil on panel 26.6 x 34.9
IWM ART 5882

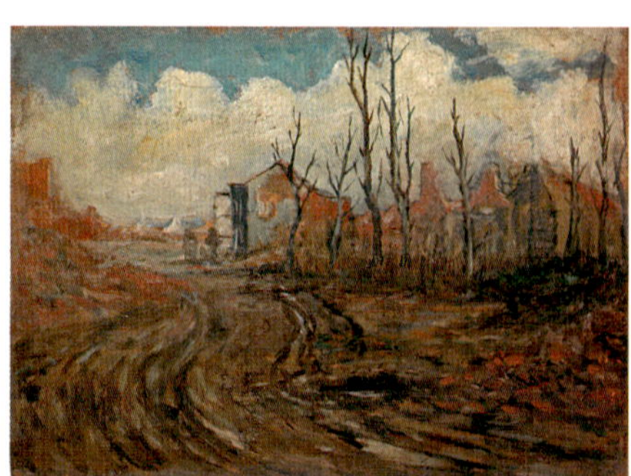

Lawson, Cecil active 1913–1923
Near Salient c.1916–1918
oil on panel 15.8 x 22.2
IWM ART 5895

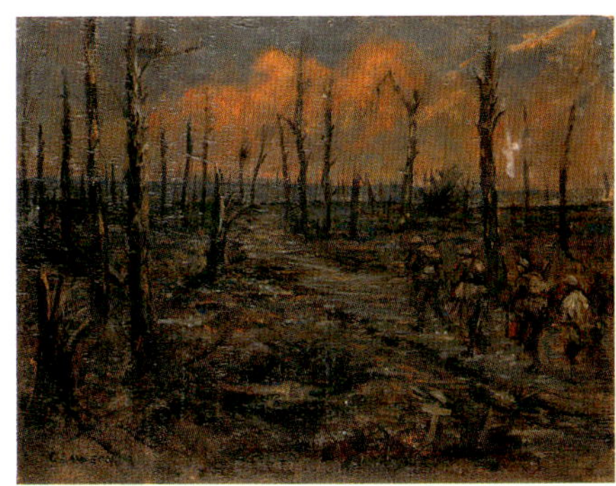

Lawson, Cecil active 1913–1923
Sanctuary Wood c.1916–1918
oil on panel 27.3 x 34.9
IWM ART 5880

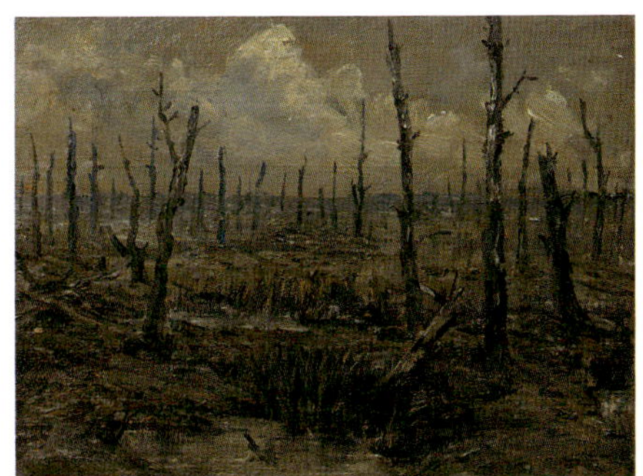

Lawson, Cecil active 1913–1923
Sanctuary Wood c.1916–1918
oil on panel 26 x 34.9
IWM ART 5884

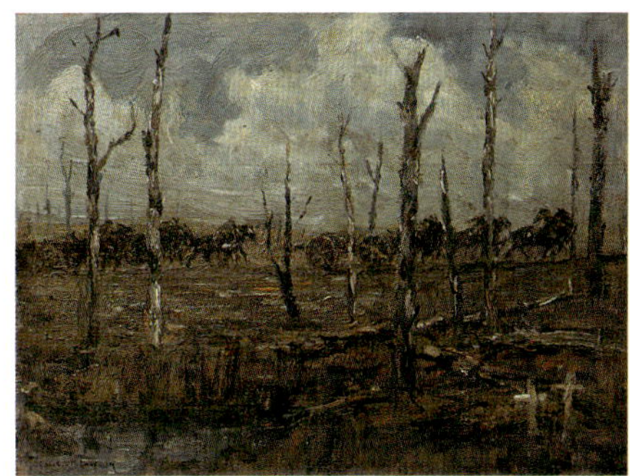

Lawson, Cecil active 1913–1923
Somme c.1916–1918
oil on panel 26 x 34.9
IWM ART 5883

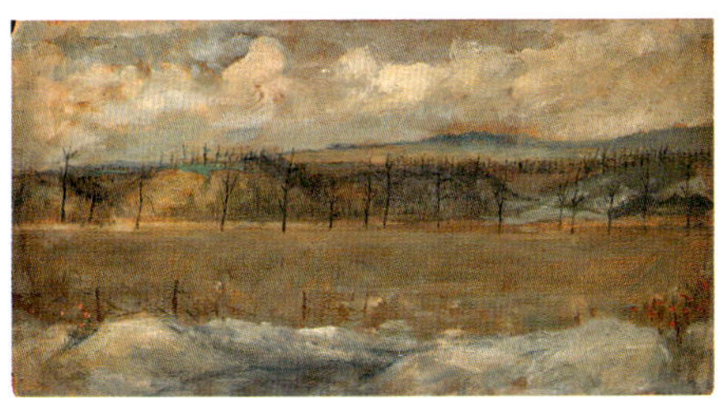

Lawson, Cecil active 1913–1923
Themiss la Daine c.1916–1918
oil on panel 15.2 x 29.2
IWM ART 5896

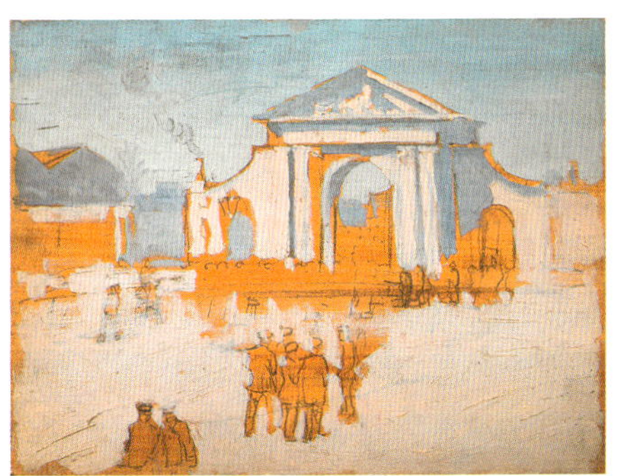

Lawson, Cecil active 1913–1923
Untitled c.1916–1918
oil on panel 29.9 x 40.6
IWM ART 5878

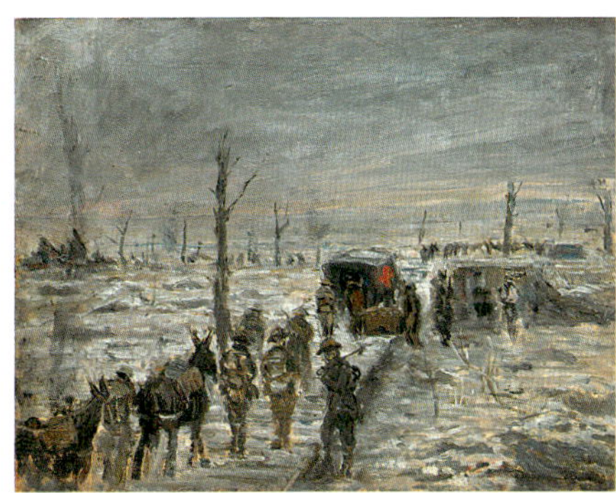

Lawson, Cecil active 1913–1923
Untitled c.1916–1918
oil on panel 26.6 x 34.9
IWM ART 5879

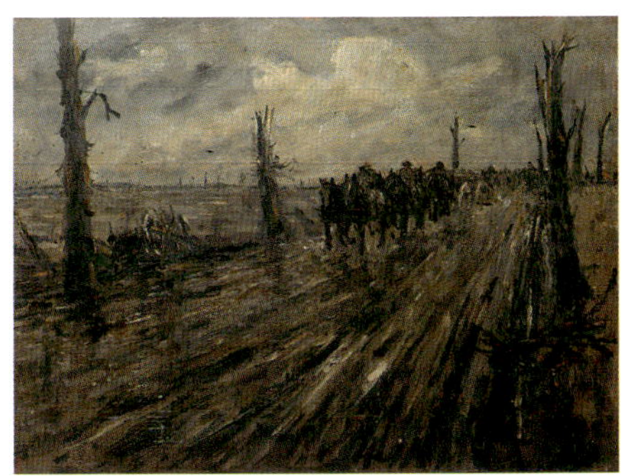

Lawson, Cecil active 1913–1923
Untitled c.1916–1918
oil on panel 26 x 34.9
IWM ART 5885

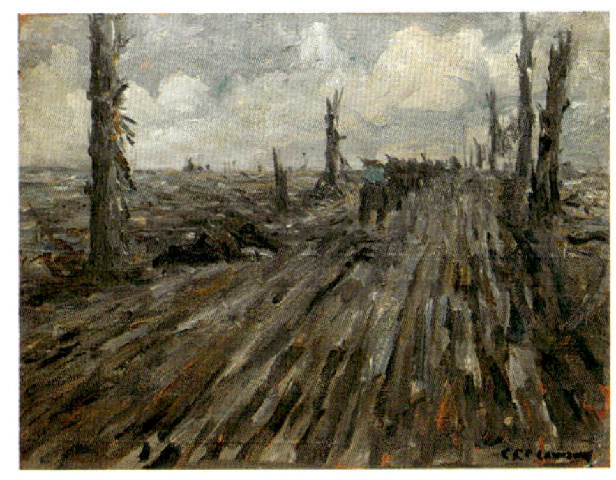

Lawson, Cecil active 1913–1923
Untitled c.1916–1918
oil on panel 22.2 x 27.9
IWM ART 5891

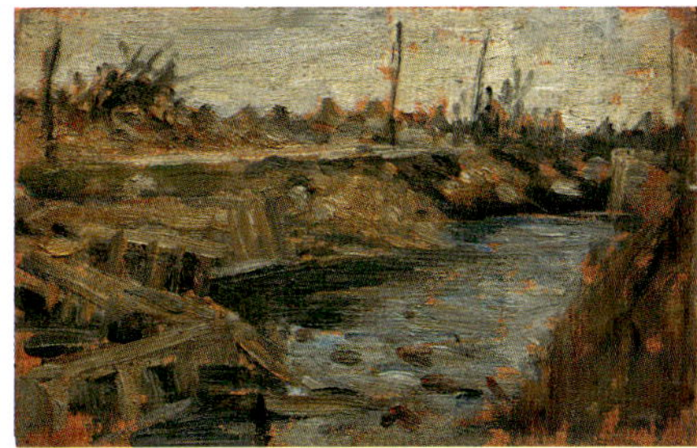

Lawson, Cecil active 1913–1923
Untitled c.1916–1918
oil on panel 14.6 x 24.1
IWM ART 5894

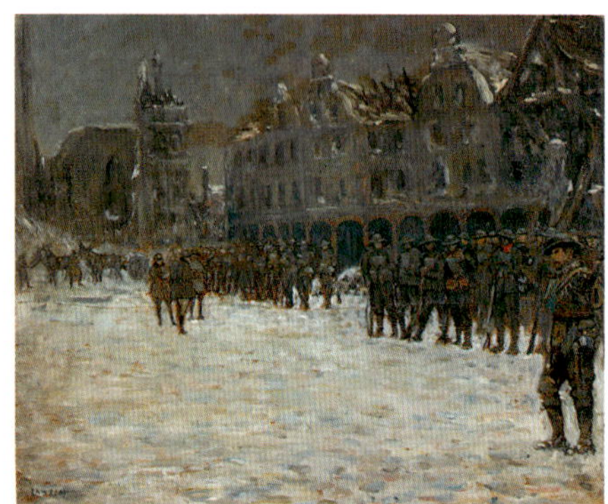

Lawson, Cecil active 1913–1923
Arras 1917–1918
oil on panel 29.8 x 35.5
IWM ART 5877

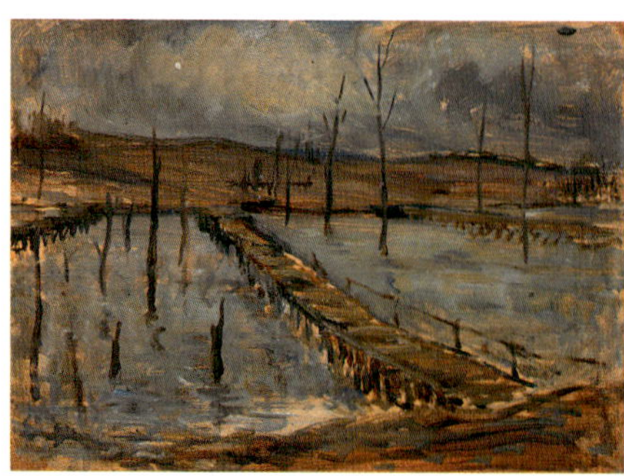

Lawson, Cecil active 1913–1923
Outside Arras 1917–1918
oil on panel 23.4 x 33
IWM ART 5889

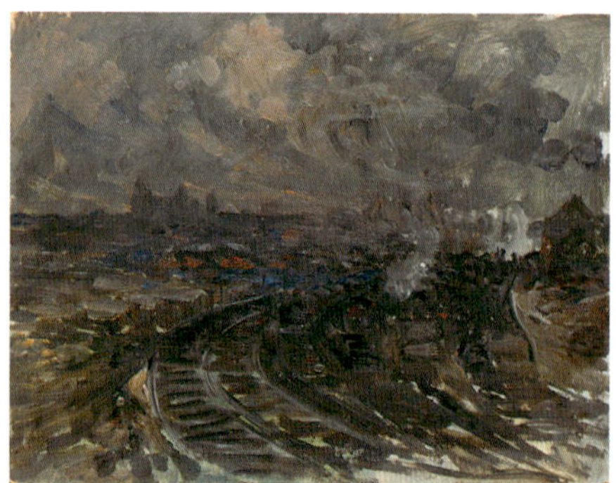

Lawson, Cecil active 1913–1923
Railway Station, Arras 1917–1918
oil on panel 27.3 x 34.9
IWM ART 5881

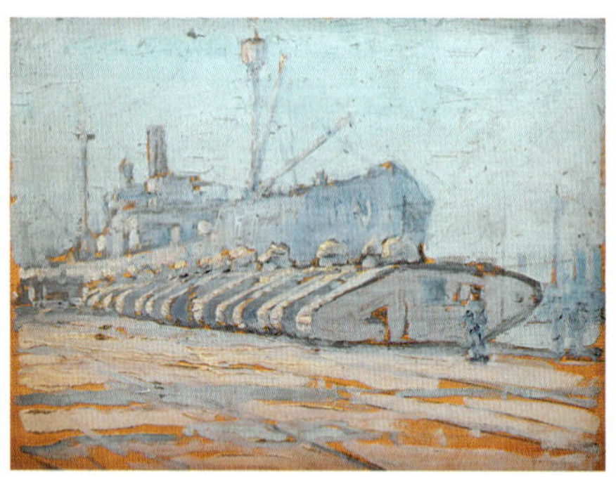

Lawson, Cecil active 1913–1923
A Line of Tanks c.1917
oil on panel 29.8 x 40.6
IWM ART 5875

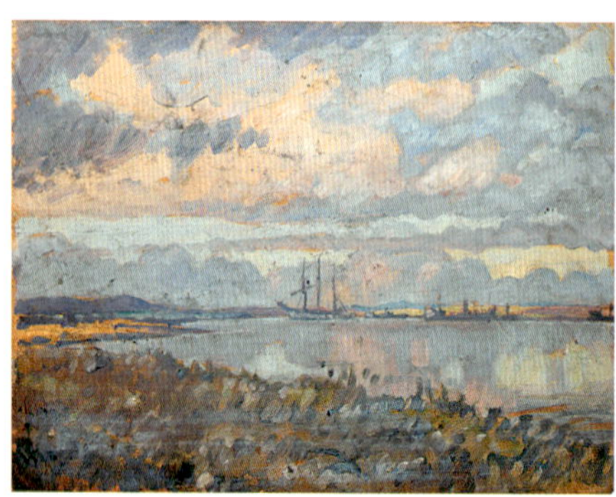

Lawson, Cecil active 1913–1923
Seascape c.1917
oil on panel 31.1 x 40.6
IWM ART 5876

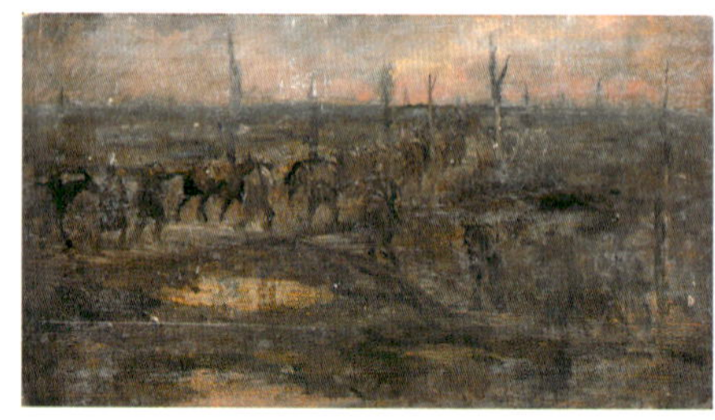

Lawson, Cecil active 1913–1923
Machine Gunners c.1917–1918
oil on panel 19.6 x 35.5
IWM ART 5890

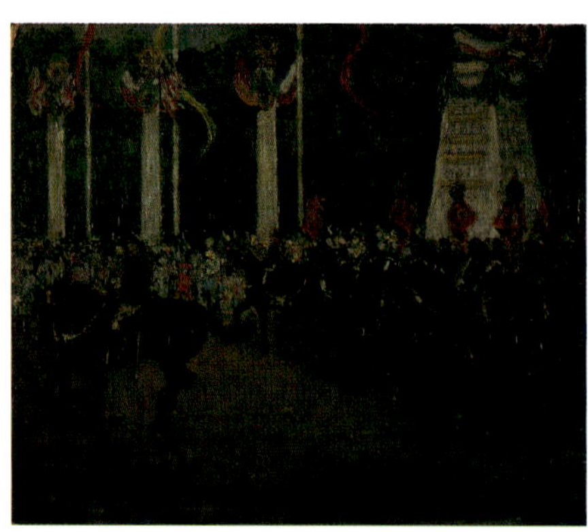

Lawson, Cecil active 1913–1923
Victory Parade c.1918
oil on panel 53.9 x 64.7
IWM ART 5898

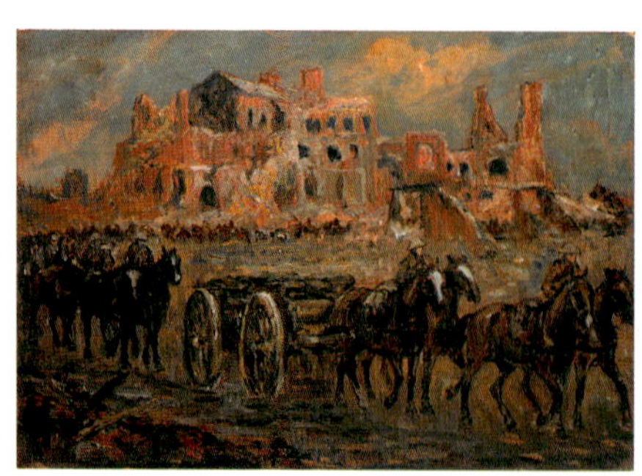

Lawson, P.
Albert
oil on board 17.7 x 25.4
IWM ART 5928

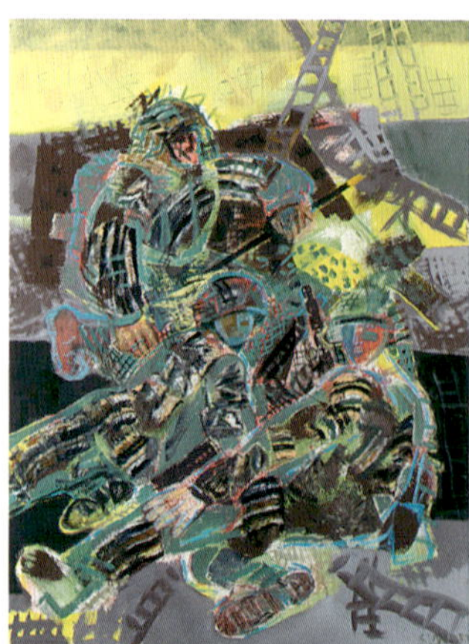

Lawson, Sonia b.1934
Camouflaged Men in a Trench 1984
oil on canvas 121.5 x 91.4
IWM ART 16014

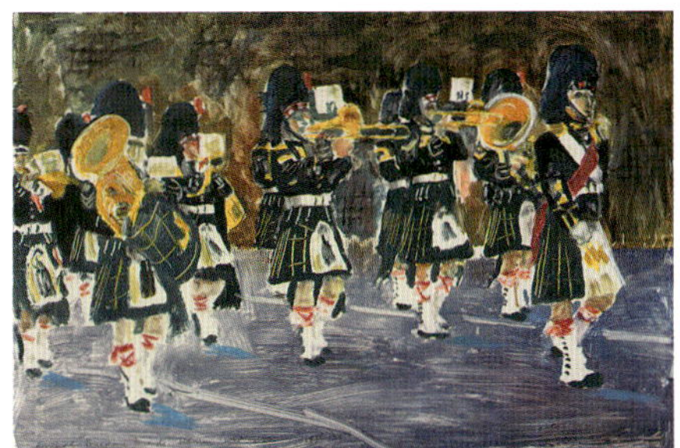

Lawson, Sonia b.1934
Hamm: Freedom Parade with Gordon Highlanders Band Marching, 1 September 1984 1984
oil on paper 43 x 65.8
IWM ART 15954 16

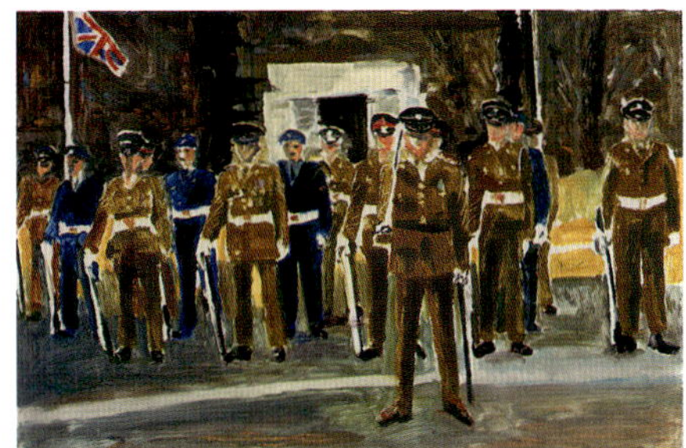

Lawson, Sonia b.1934
Hamm: Freedom Parade with Polish Veterans in Blue and War Memorial at Rear 1984
oil on paper 43 x 65.8
IWM ART 15954 17

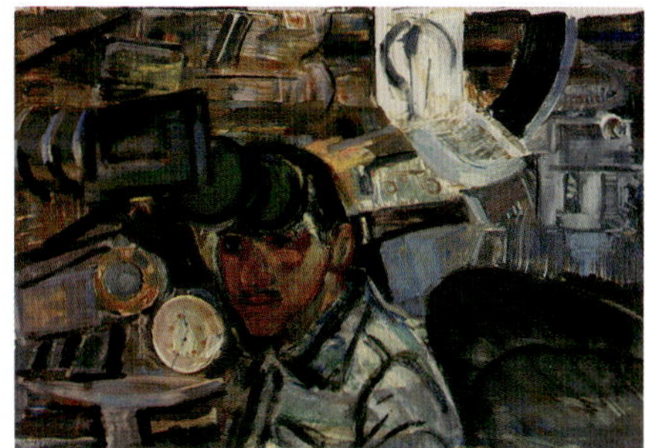

Lawson, Sonia b.1934
Interior, Chieftan Tank 1984
oil on paper 49.5 x 75.5
IWM ART 15954 9

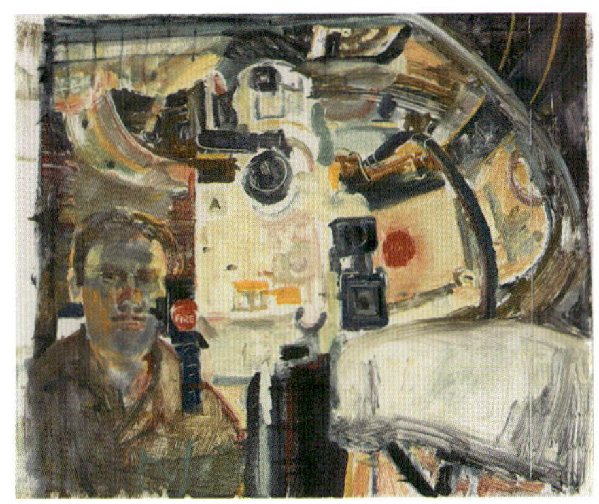

Lawson, Sonia b.1934
Interior, Guided Weapons Vehicle, 'Swingfire' 1984
oil on paper 54 x 64
IWM ART 15954 10

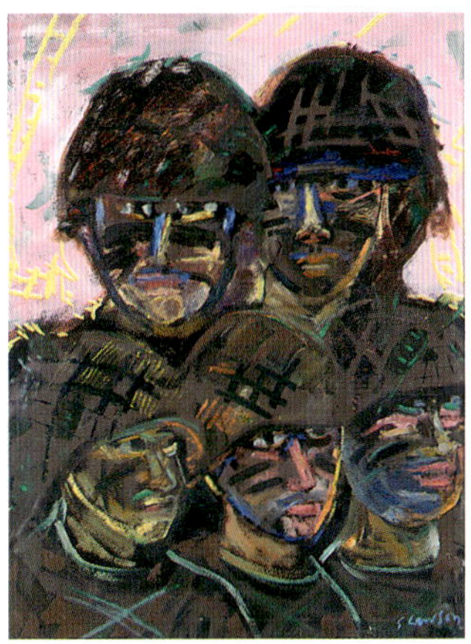

Lawson, Sonia b.1934
Men Disguised as Clods 1984
oil on canvas 77.5 x 59.4
IWM ART 16015

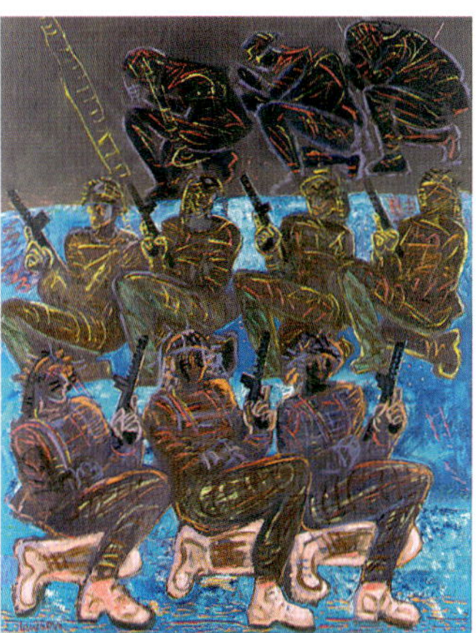

Lawson, Sonia b.1934
Troops in Single File Prepare to Break Cover and Board a Chinook Helicopter 1984
oil on canvas 152.8 x 121.8
IWM ART 16013

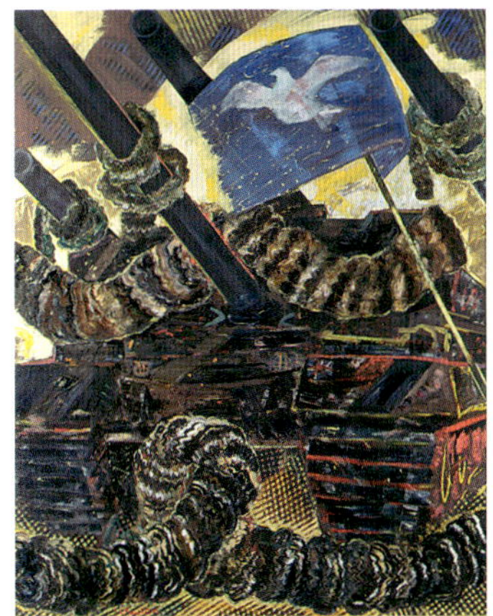

Lawson, Sonia b.1934
Two Minds but with a Single Thought? 1984
oil on canvas 153.2 x 122.6
IWM ART 16012

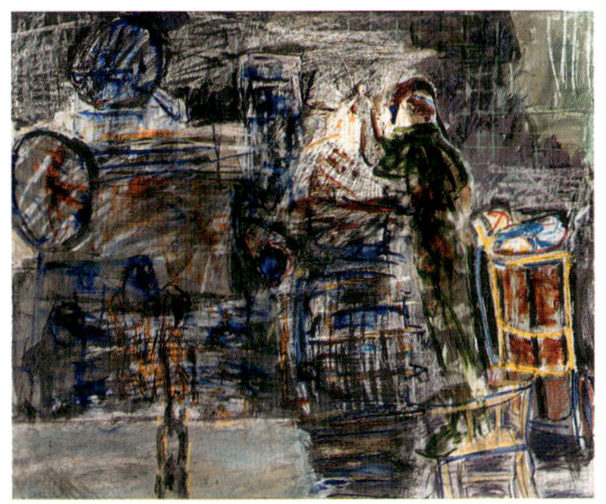

Lawson, Sonia b.1934
Welding: Chieftan Tank, Swinton Barracks, Munster 1984
acrylic & mixed media on paper 76.4 x 94.5
IWM ART 15954 18

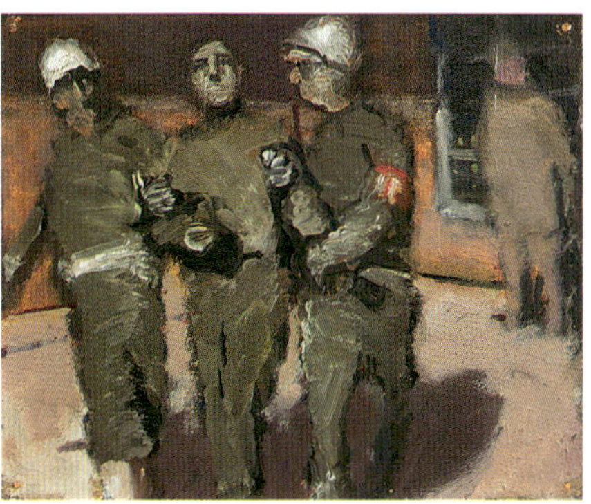

Lee, Dick 1923–2001
Catch-22: Arrest of the Innocent Man 1970s
oil on board 20.2 x 25.2
IWM ART 16784 9

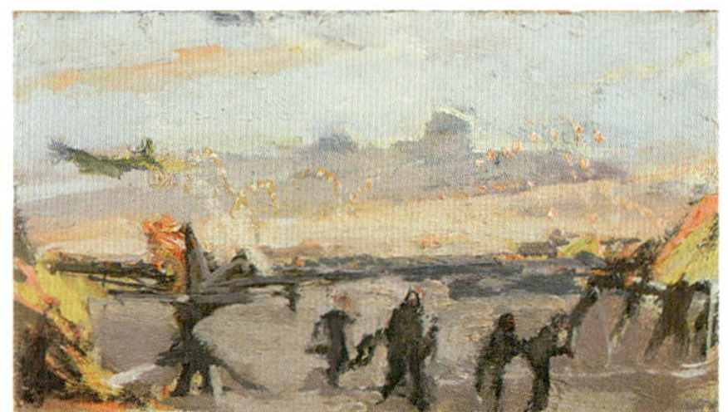

Lee, Dick 1923–2001
Catch-22: Bombing the Airfield 1970s
oil on board 23 x 40.7
IWM ART 16784 13

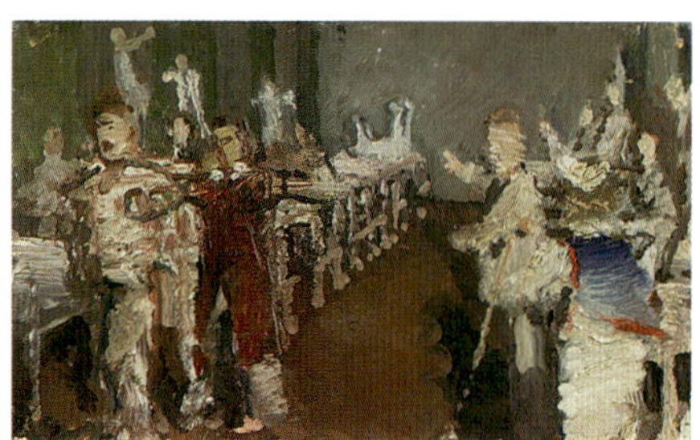

Lee, Dick 1923–2001
Catch-22: 'He's back!' 1970s
oil on board 15.2 x 25.5
IWM ART 16784 4

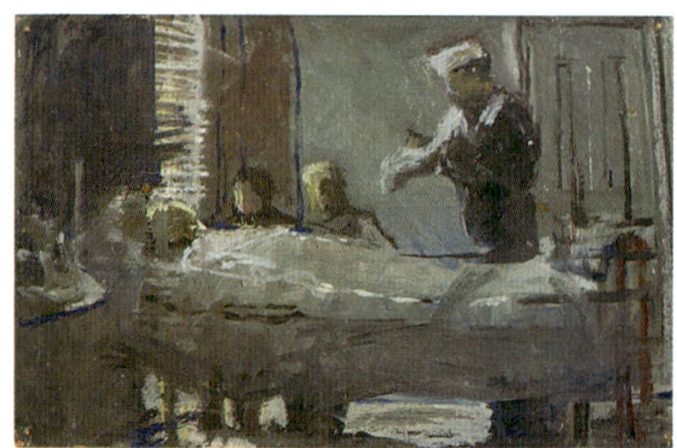

Lee, Dick 1923–2001
Catch-22: Impersonating Giuseppe 1970s
oil on board 22.9 x 35.6
IWM ART 16784 14

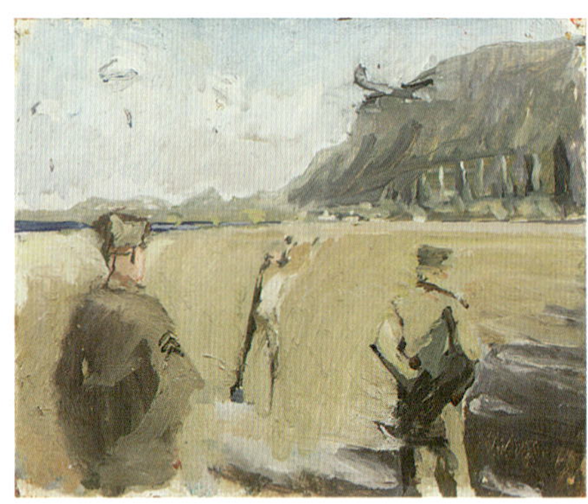

Lee, Dick 1923–2001
Catch-22: McWatt Crashes 1970s
oil on board 21 x 25.9
IWM ART 16784 24

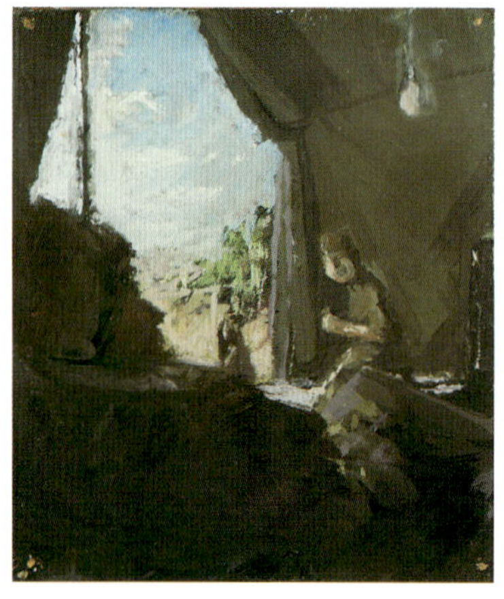

Lee, Dick 1923–2001
Catch-22: Mending the Stove 1970s
oil on board 23 x 20.2
IWM ART 16784 23

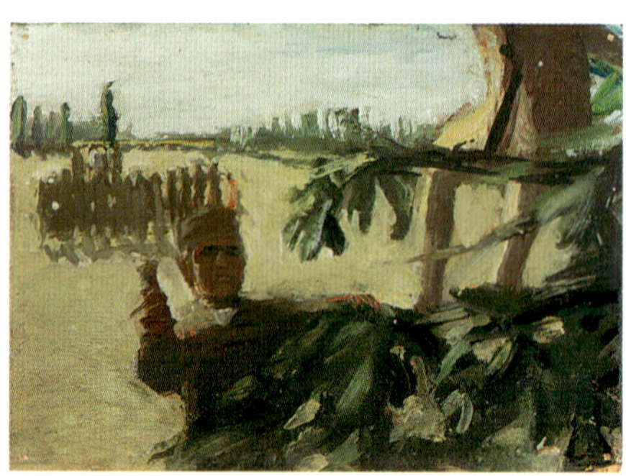

Lee, Dick 1923–2001
Catch-22: Milo's Cotton 1970s
oil on wood 17.8 x 25.7
IWM ART 16784 6

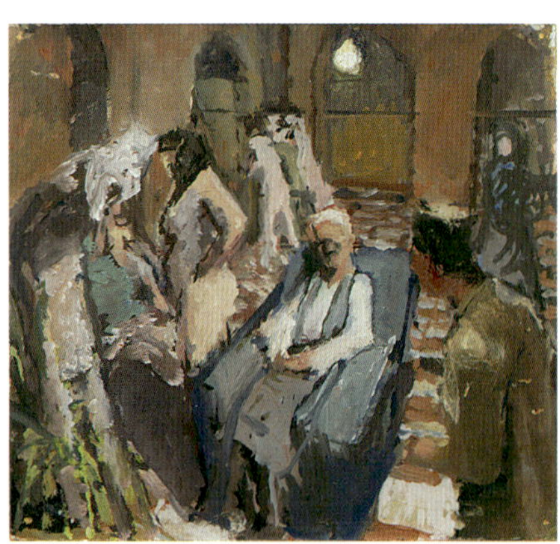

Lee, Dick 1923–2001
Catch-22: Nately and the Old Man 1970s
oil on board 23.2 x 25.5
IWM ART 16784 12

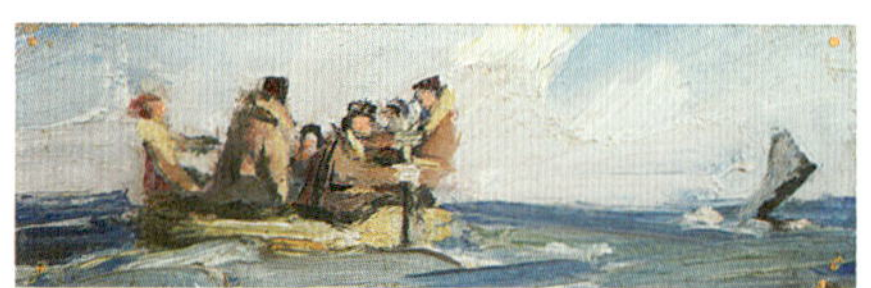

Lee, Dick 1923–2001
Catch-22: Orr 1970s
oil on board 23.6 x 70.3
IWM ART 16784 5

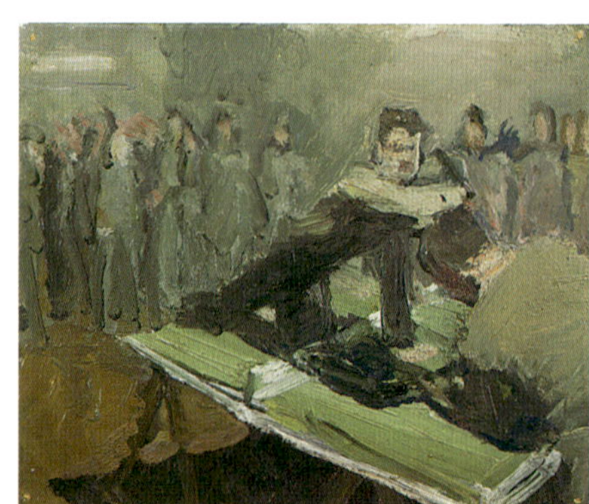

Lee, Dick 1923–2001
Catch-22: Ping Pong 1970s
oil on board 23.2 x 28.2
IWM ART 16784 1

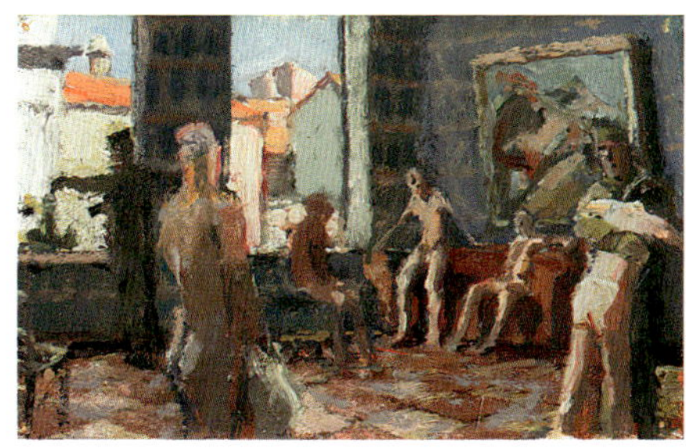

Lee, Dick 1923–2001
Catch-22: Rescuing Nately's Whore from the Generals 1970s
oil on board 17.7 x 28.3
IWM ART 16784 16

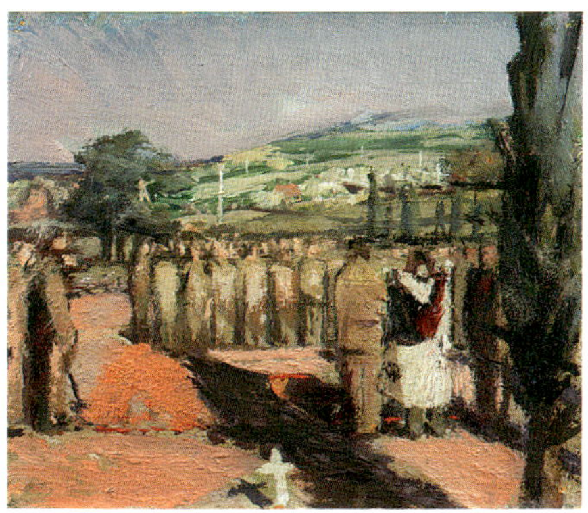

Lee, Dick 1923–2001
Catch-22: Snowden's Funeral 1970s
oil on board 20.5 x 24.7
IWM ART 16784 11

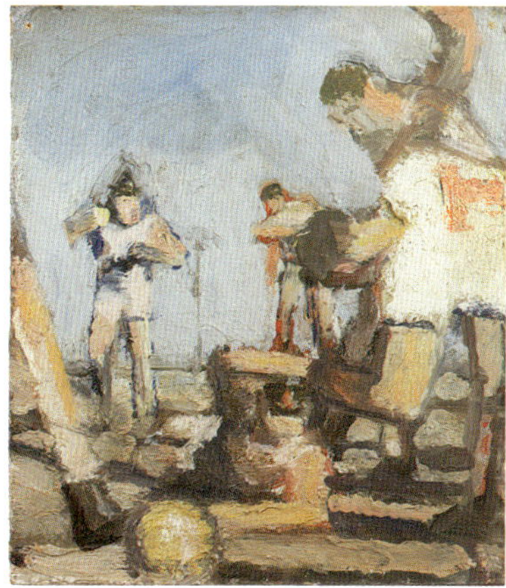

Lee, Dick 1923–2001
Catch-22: The Basketball Game 1970s
oil on board 22.9 x 20.6
IWM ART 16784 22

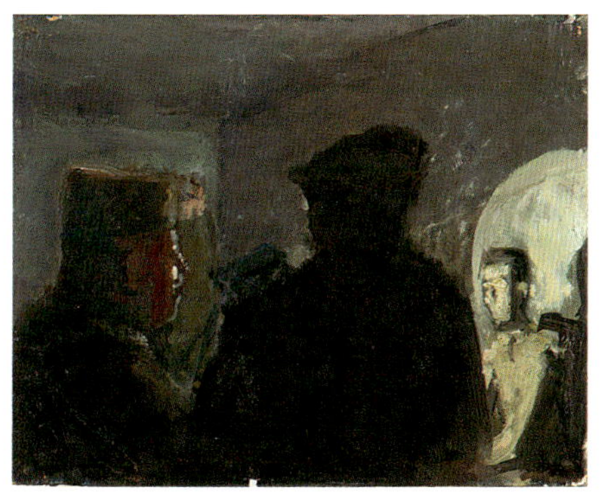

Lee, Dick 1923–2001
Catch-22: The Chaplain Interrogated 1970s
oil on board 20.5 x 25.7
IWM ART 16784 2

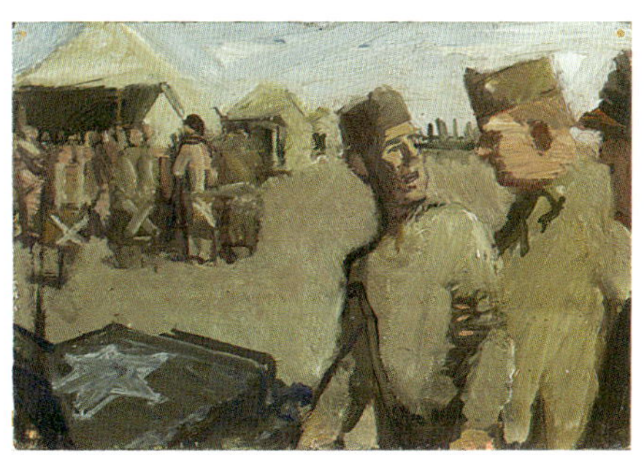

Lee, Dick 1923–2001
Catch-22: The Chaplain Is Arrested 1970s
oil on board 17.8 x 26.6
IWM ART 16784 17

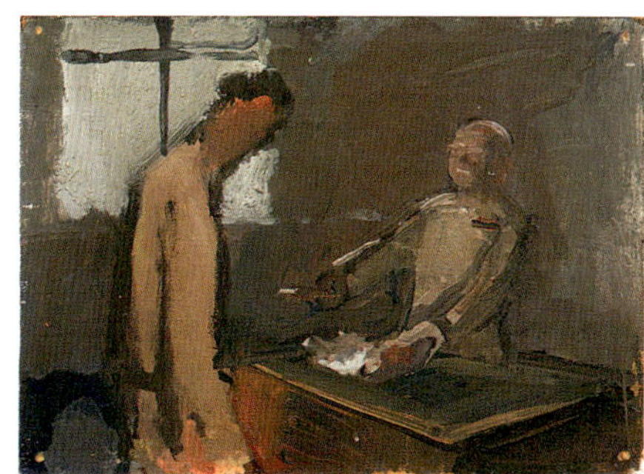

Lee, Dick 1923–2001
Catch-22: The Chaplain's Interview 1970s
oil on board 15.5 x 21.9
IWM ART 16784 10

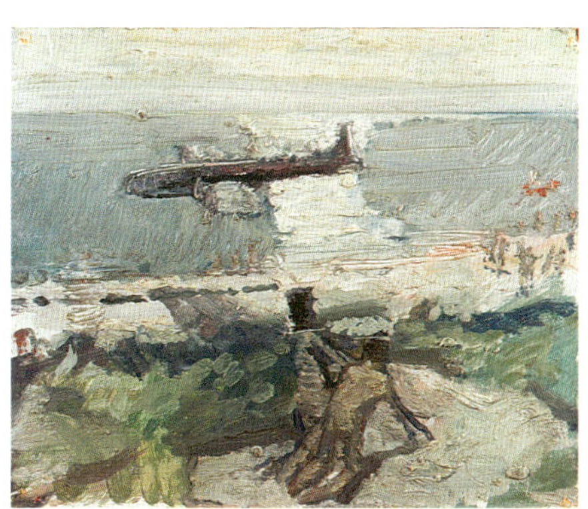

Lee, Dick 1923–2001
Catch-22: The Death of Kid Sampson 1970s
oil on board 23.2 x 28.3
IWM ART 16784 21

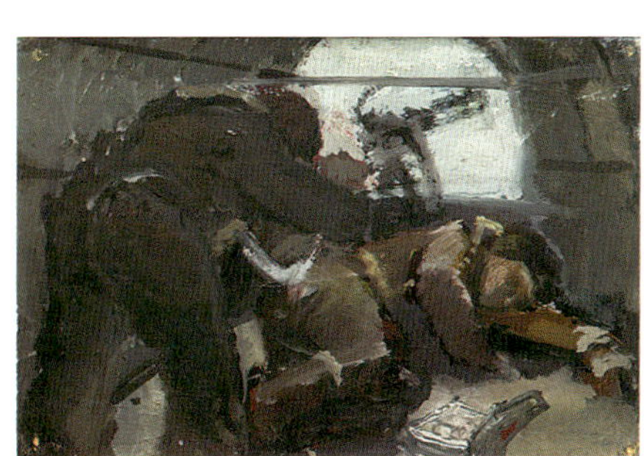

Lee, Dick 1923–2001
Catch-22: The Death of Snowden 1970s
oil on cardboard 15.4 x 23.3
IWM ART 16784 18

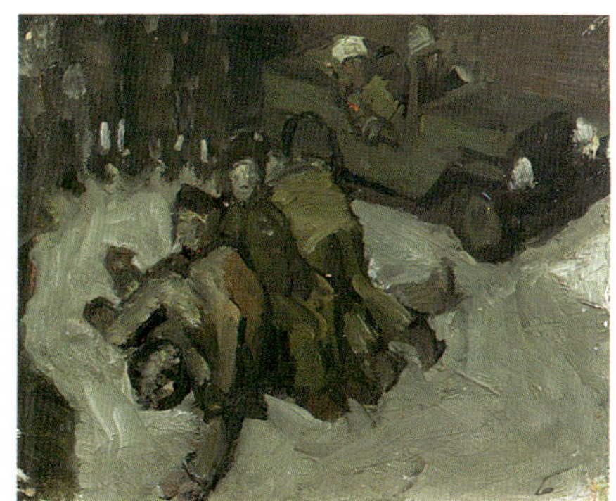

Lee, Dick 1923–2001
Catch-22: The Epileptic Fit 1970s
oil on board 20.2 x 25.4
IWM ART 16784 15

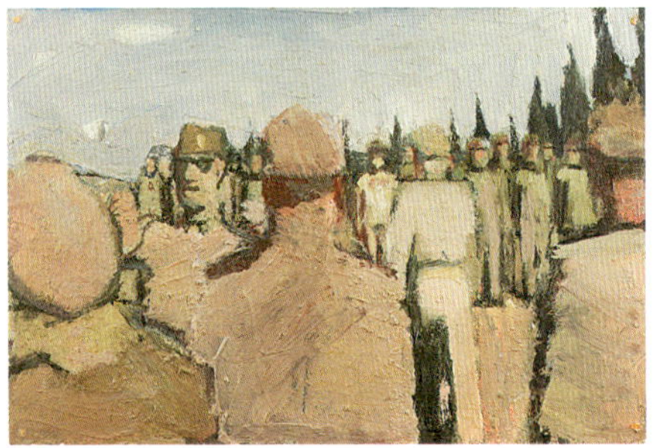

Lee, Dick 1923–2001
Catch-22: The Medal Ceremony 1970s
oil on board 21 x 31.5
IWM ART 16784 3

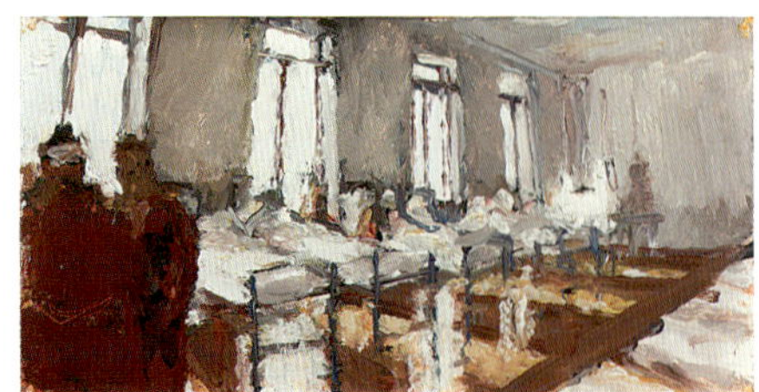

Lee, Dick 1923–2001
Catch-22: The Soldier in White 1970s
oil on board 15.2 x 30.2
IWM ART 16784 7

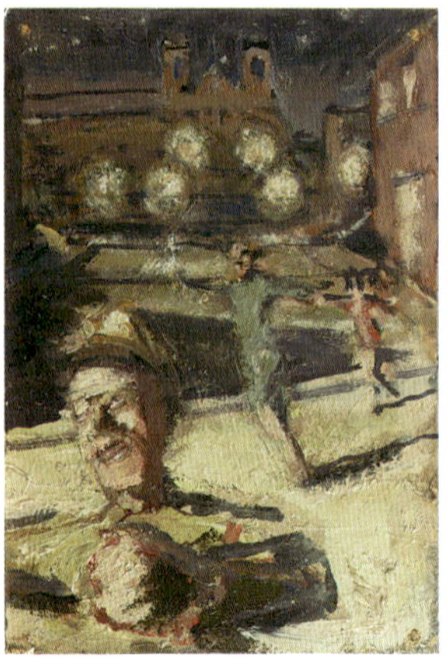

Lee, Dick 1923–2001
Catch-22: Yossarian Escapes 1970s
oil on board 22.2 x 15.2
IWM ART 16784 8

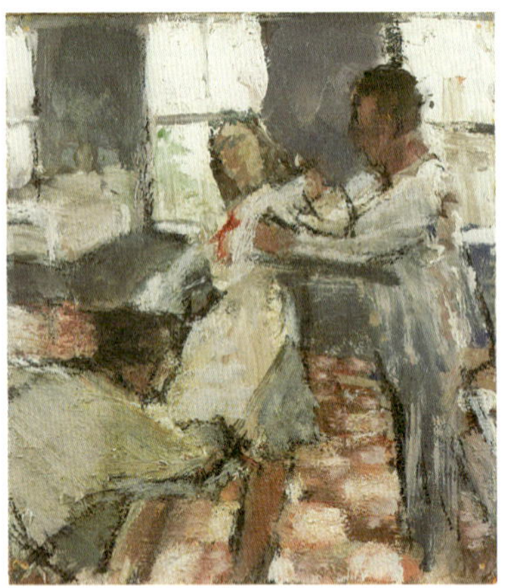

Lee, Dick 1923–2001
Catch-22: Yossarian Grabs Nurse Duckett
1970s
oil on board 23.1 x 20.5
IWM ART 16784 19

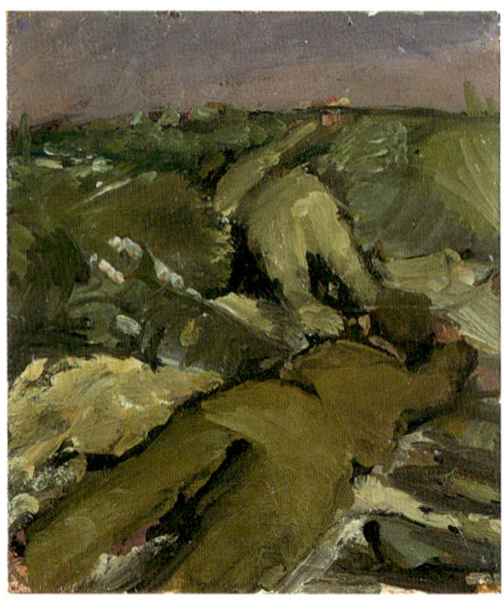

Lee, Dick 1923–2001
Catch-22: Yossarian Tackles Major Major
1970s
oil on board 23.1 x 20.3
IWM ART 16784 20

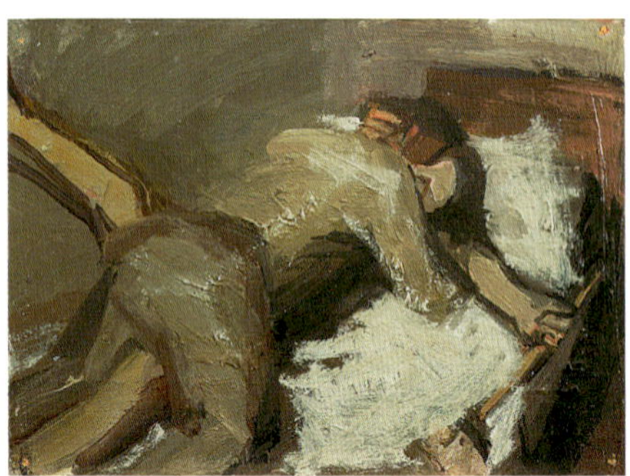

Lee, Dick 1923–2001
Catch-22: Yossarian with the Maid 1970s
oil on wood 17.8 x 24.8
IWM ART 16784 25

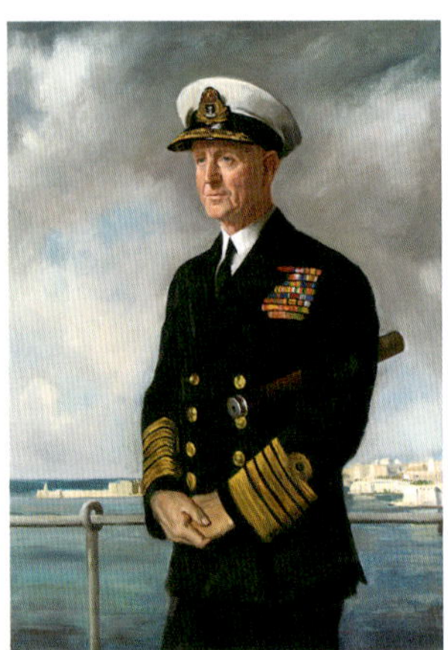

Leigh-Pemberton, John 1911–1997
*Admiral of the Fleet the Viscount Cunningham
of Hyndhope (1883–1963), KT, GCB, DSO*
c.1940–1946
oil on canvas 124.4 x 88.9
IWM ART LD 5917

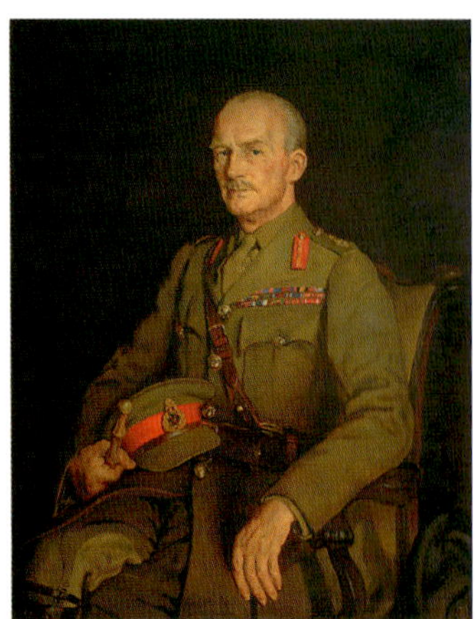

Leigh-Pemberton, John 1911–1997
*Field Marshal Sir John Dill (1881–1944), GCB,
CMG, DSO* c.1940–1946
oil on canvas 127 x 101.9
IWM ART LD 5925

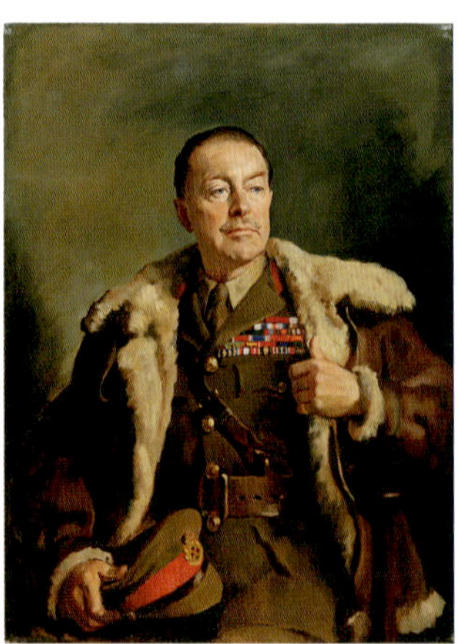

Leigh-Pemberton, John 1911–1997
*Field Marshal the Viscount Alexander of Tunis
(1891–1969), GCB, CSI, DS, MC (copy of
Oswald Hornby Joseph Birley)* c.1940–1946
oil on canvas 99 x 76.2
IWM ART LD 5916

Facing page: Knight, Laura, 1877–1970, *Corporal J. D. M. Pearson, GC, Women's Auxiliary Air Force* (detail), 1940, (p. 119)

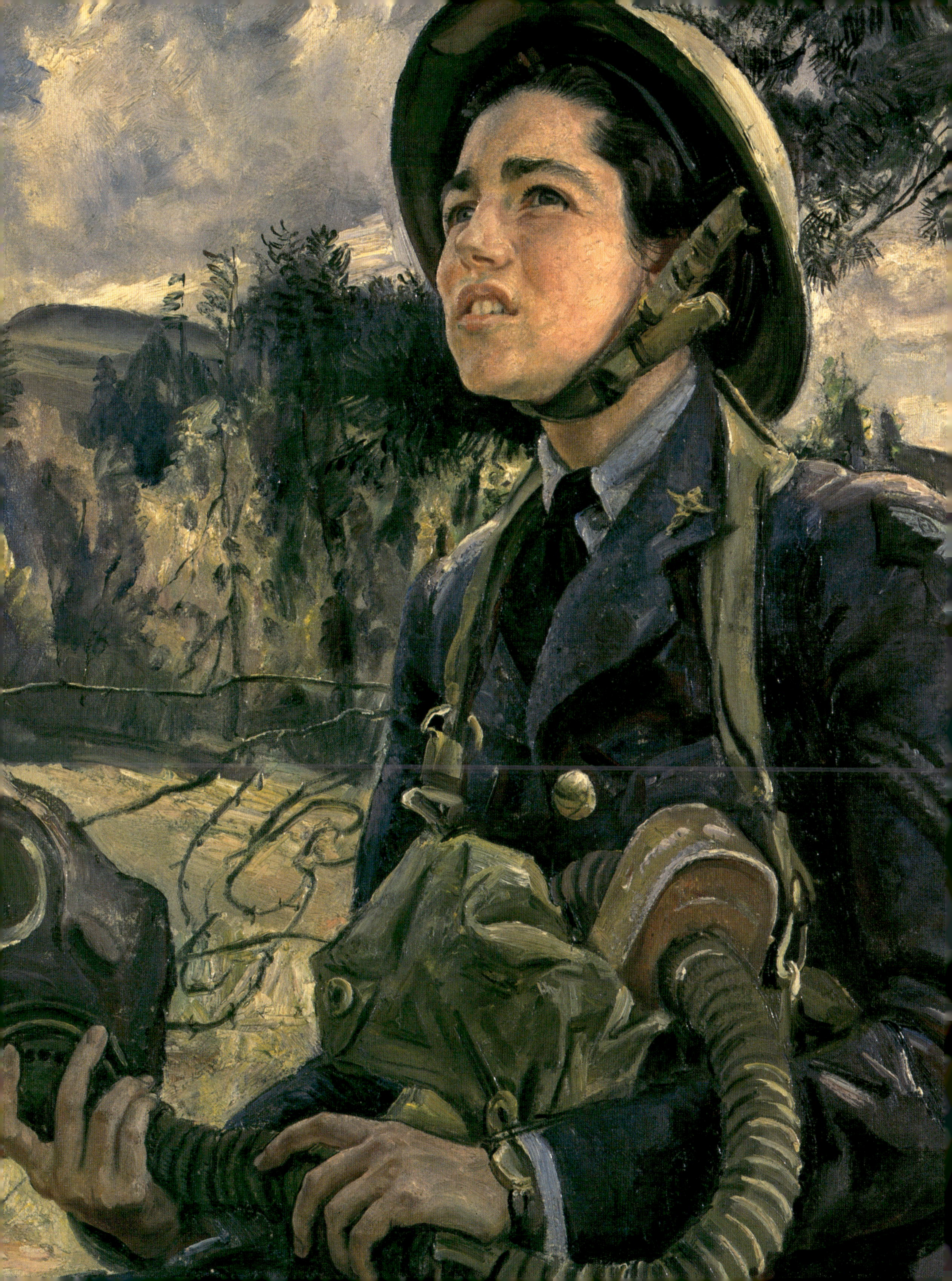

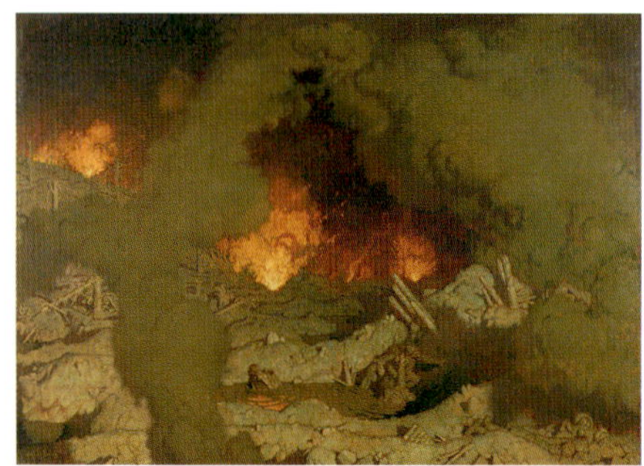

Leroux, Georges Paul 1877–1957
L'enfer 1921
oil on canvas 114.3 x 161.2
IWM ART 4415

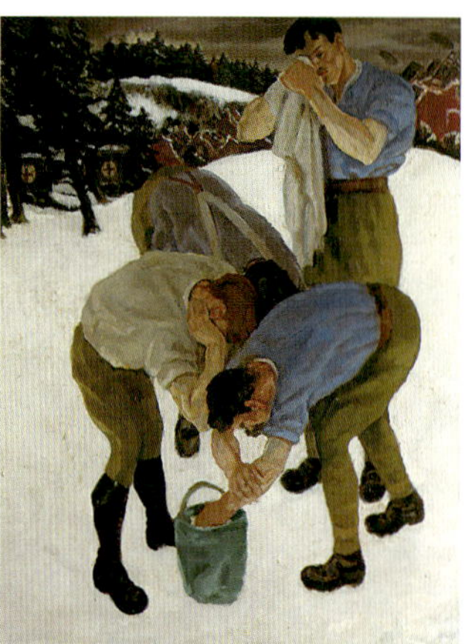

Lewis, Neville 1895–1972
Artillery Drivers in the Snow, Italian Front
c.1914–1918
oil on canvas 91.4 x 71.1
IWM ART 2003

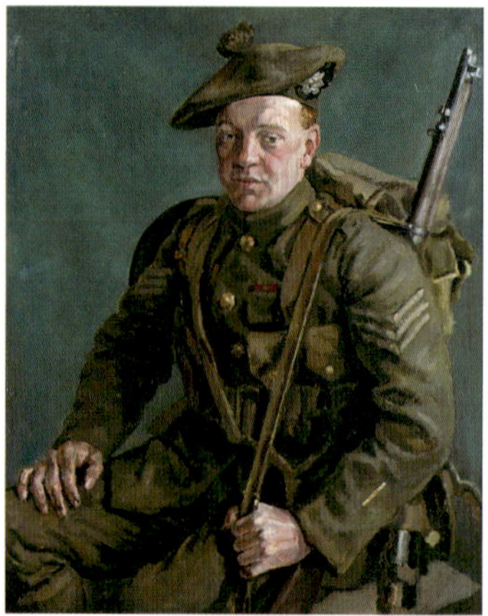

Lewis, Neville 1895–1972
*Sergeant David Ferguson Hunter, VC, 1/5th
Highland Light Infantry* c.1919
oil on canvas 91.4 x 76.2
IWM ART 1631

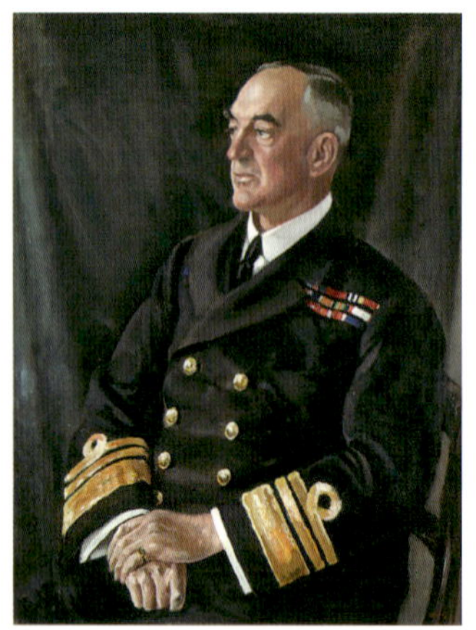

Lewis, Neville 1895–1972
*Vice Admiral Sir Edward F. B. Charlton,
KCMG, CB* 1920
oil on canvas 91.4 x 71.1
IWM ART 3069

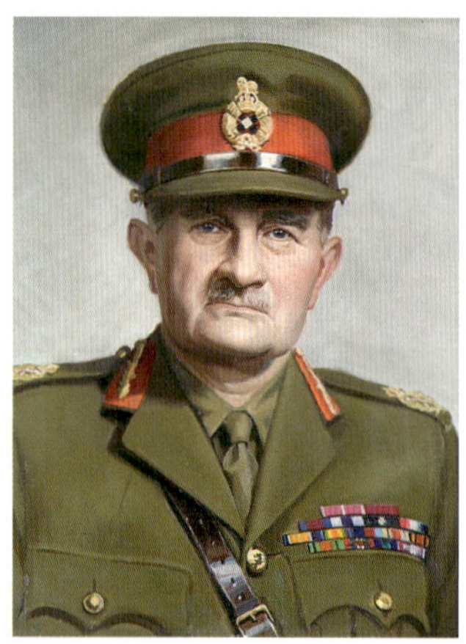

Lewis, Reginald b.1901
General William Slim (1897–1970) 1952
oil on canvas 51 x 41
IWM ART LD 6114

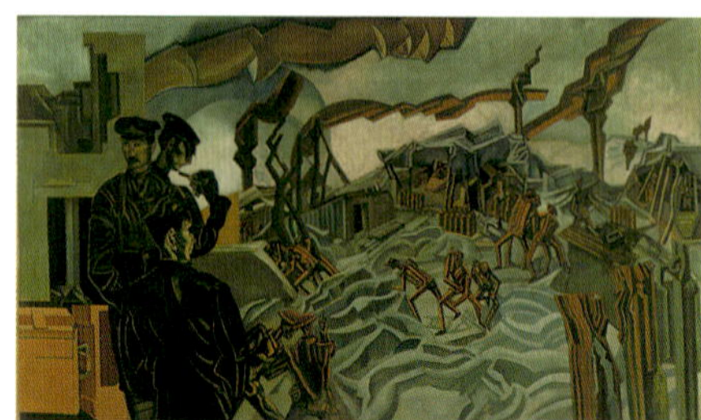

Lewis, Wyndham 1882–1957
A Battery Shelled 1919
oil on canvas 182.8 x 317.5
IWM ART 2747

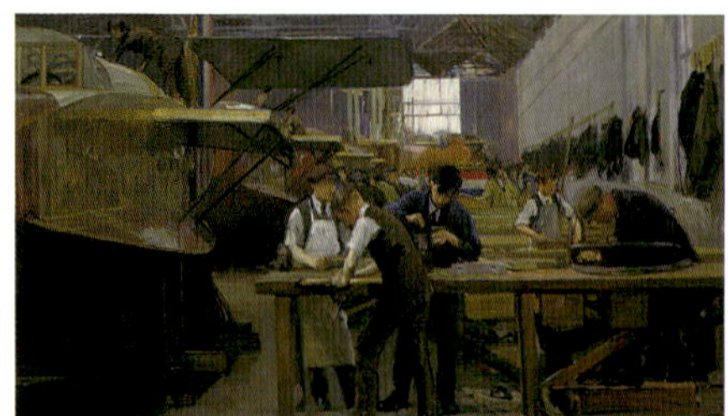

Lion, Flora 1878–1958
Building Flying Boats 1918
oil on canvas 107.6 x 184.2
IWM ART 4435

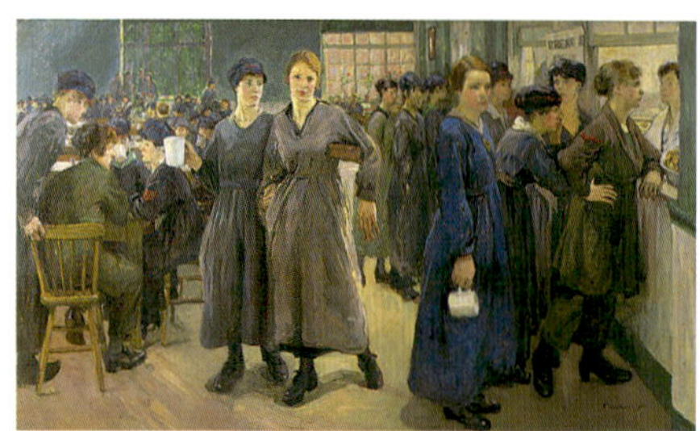

Lion, Flora 1878–1958
Women's Canteen at Phoenix Works, Bradford
1918
oil on canvas 106.6 x 182.8
IWM ART 4434

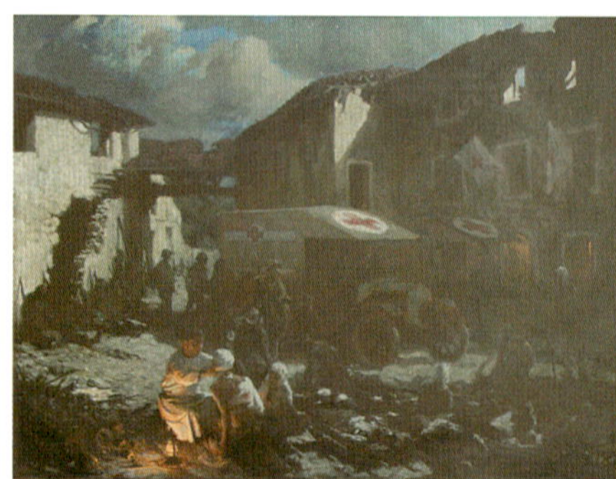

Lipscombe, Guy 1881–1952
*A First-Line Dressing Station, Doberdo, Isonzo
Front, Italy* 1917
oil on canvas 148.3 x 191.7
IWM ART 1218

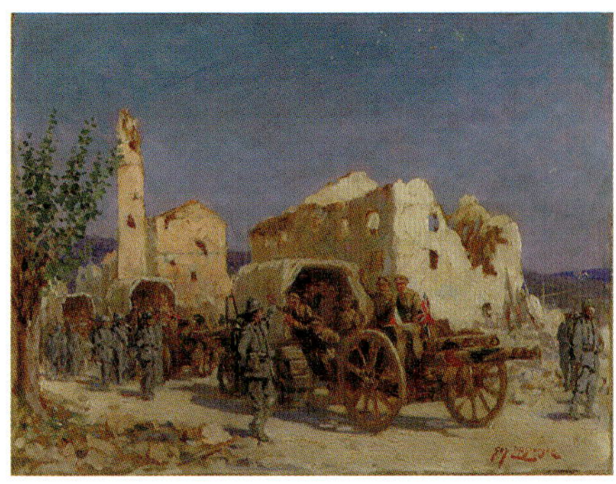

Lipscombe, Guy 1881–1952
The Arrival of the First Guns on the Carso Front, Italy, 1916 c.1917
oil on board 45.7 x 60.9
IWM ART 1856

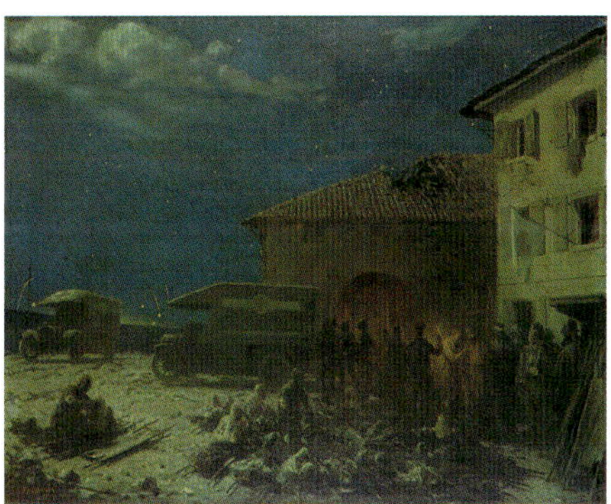

Lipscombe, Guy 1881–1952
British Red Cross Ambulance, Italian Front, 1916 1918
oil on canvas 152.4 x 191.1
IWM ART 1217

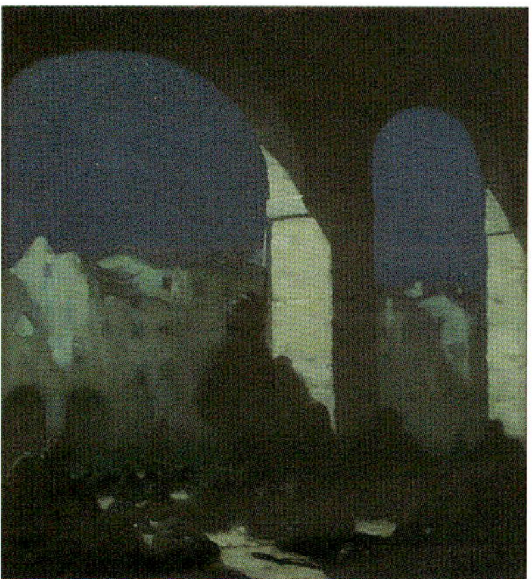

Lipscombe, Guy 1881–1952
Castelfranco: Italian Troops Resting en Route to the Piave Front 1918
oil on canvas 152.4 x 136.5
IWM ART 1855

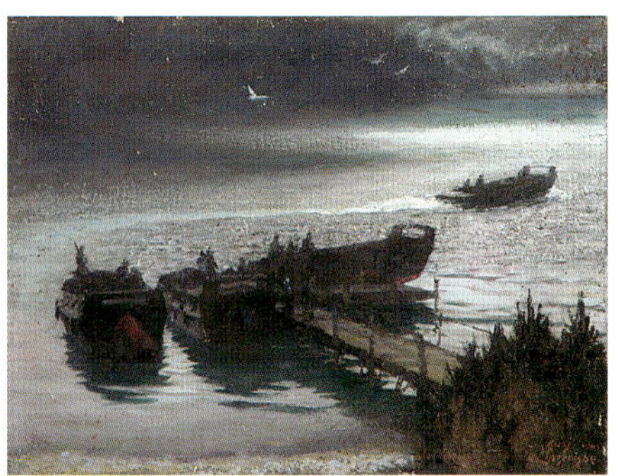

Lipscombe, Guy 1881–1952
Invasion Training in Cornwall 1944
oil on canvas 30.5 x 40.6
IWM ART LD 6028

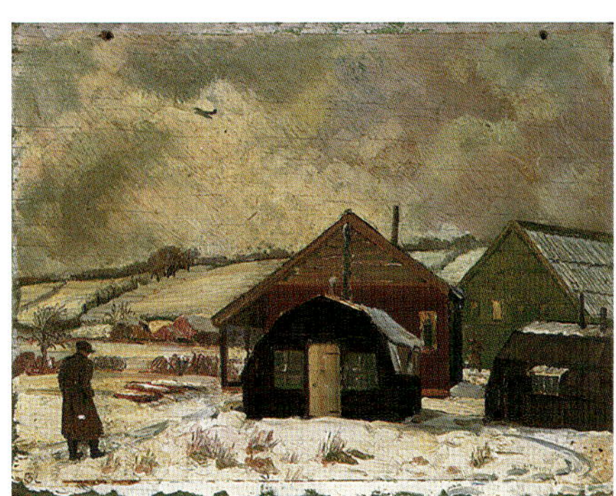

Lithiby, Beatrice Ethel 1889–1966
An Auxiliary Territorial Service Camp at Tuxford, Nottinghamshire 1958
oil on panel 19.6 x 25.4
IWM ART LD 5994

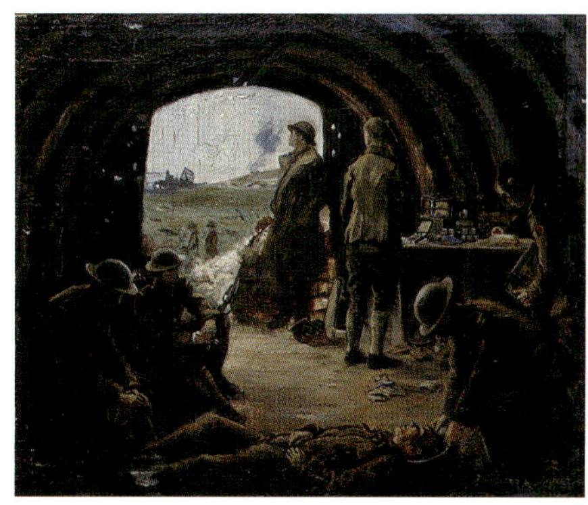

Lobley, John Hodgson 1878–1954
Dugouts in the Railway Embankment, near Le Cateau 1918
oil on panel 33 x 40.6
IWM ART 3674

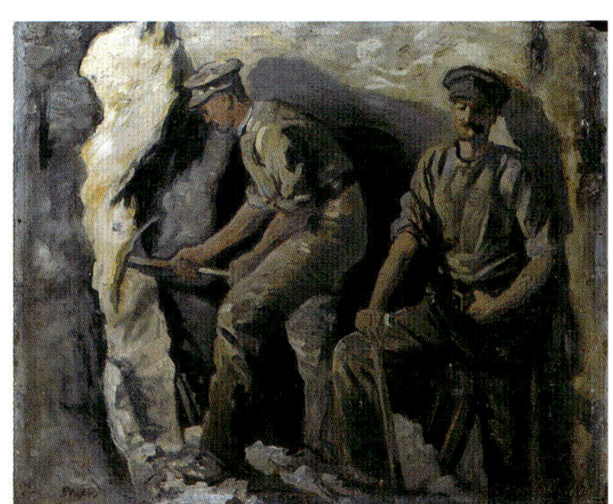

Lobley, John Hodgson 1878–1954
Galleries of Large Dugouts at Etaples 1918
oil on panel 31.7 x 40.6 (E)
IWM ART 3670

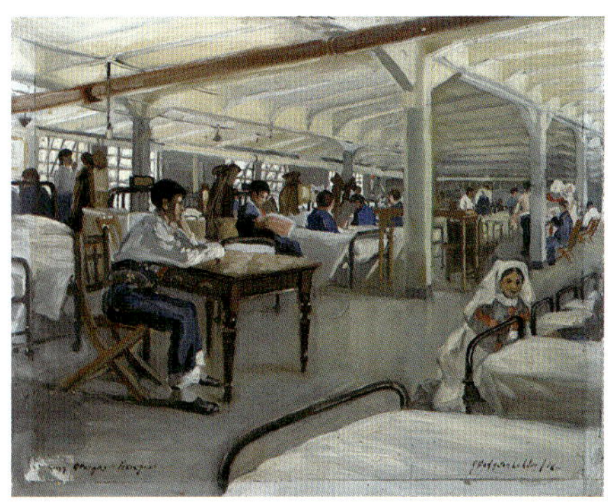

Lobley, John Hodgson 1878–1954
King George's Hospital, Stamford Street, SE: The Largest Ward (71 beds) 1918
oil on panel 31.7 x 40.6 (E)
IWM ART 3821

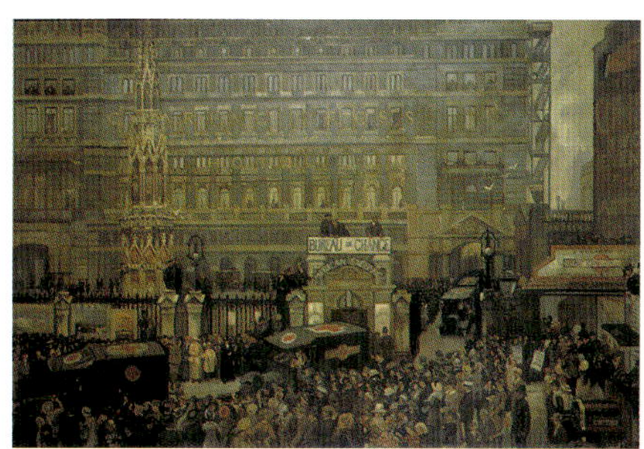

Lobley, John Hodgson 1878–1954
Outside Charing Cross Station, July 1916: Casualties from the Battle of the Somme Arriving in London 1918
oil on canvas 205.7 x 307.3
IWM ART 2759

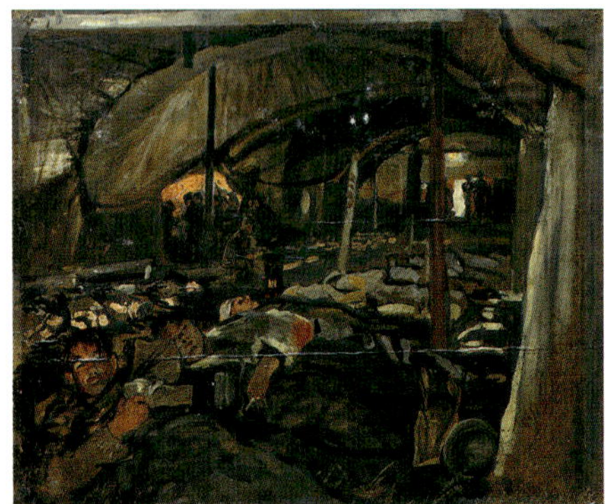

Lobley, John Hodgson 1878–1954
*Reception of the Wounded at the First Casualty
Clearing Station, Le Château, during the
British Advance in October 1918* 1918
oil on panel 33.6 x 40.6
IWM ART 3800

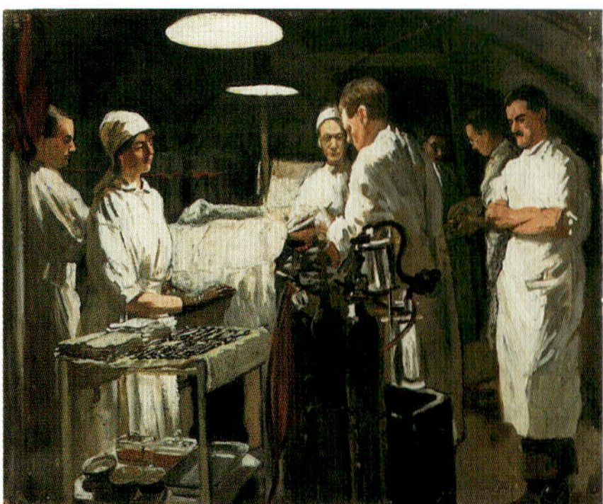

Lobley, John Hodgson 1878–1954
*The Operating Theatre, First Casualty
Clearing Station* 1918
oil on panel 31.1 x 39.3
IWM ART 3750

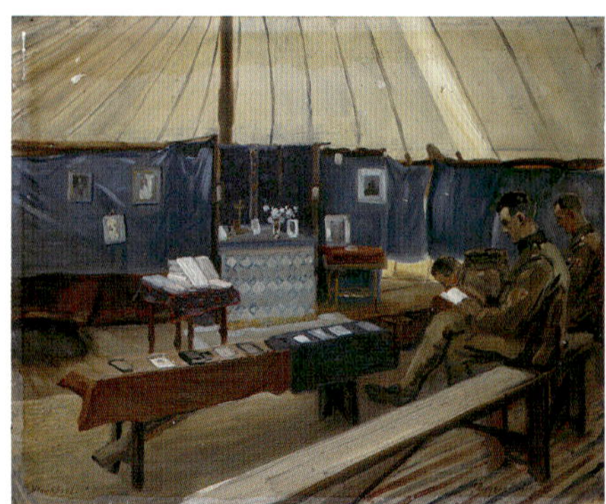

Lobley, John Hodgson 1878–1954
*The Royal Army Medical Corps in Training,
Blackpool: The Church of England Tent* 1918
oil on panel 33 x 40.6
IWM ART 3686

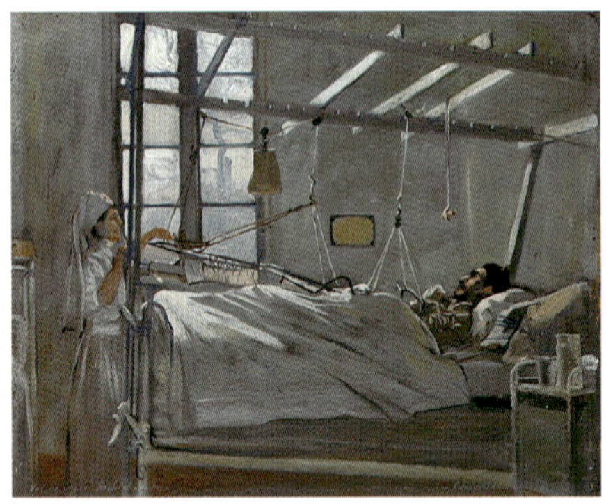

Lobley, John Hodgson 1878–1954
Val de Grâce Hospital, Paris: Interior of a Ward
1918
oil on panel 32.3 x 40.6
IWM ART 3830

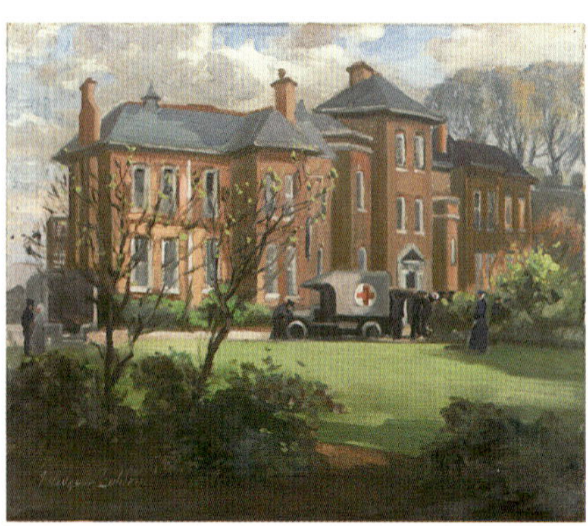

Lobley, John Hodgson 1878–1954
*The Auxiliary Hospital, Children's House,
Exeter Workhouse* c.1918
oil on canvas 50.8 x 60.9
IWM ART 3660

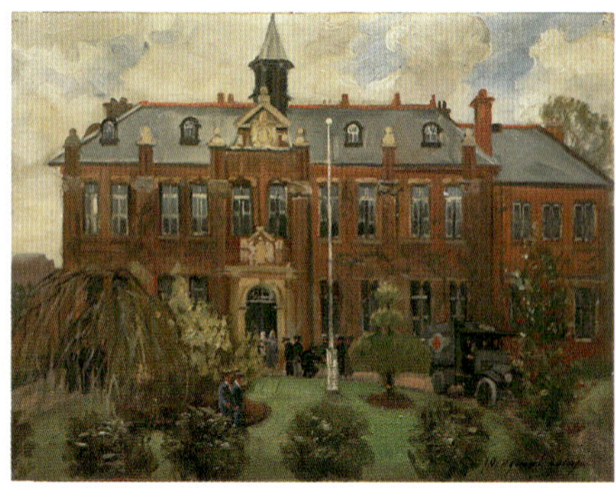

Lobley, John Hodgson 1878–1954
*The British Red Cross Society Hospital at the
Episcopal Modern Schools, Exeter* c.1918
oil on canvas 45.7 x 60.9
IWM ART 3654

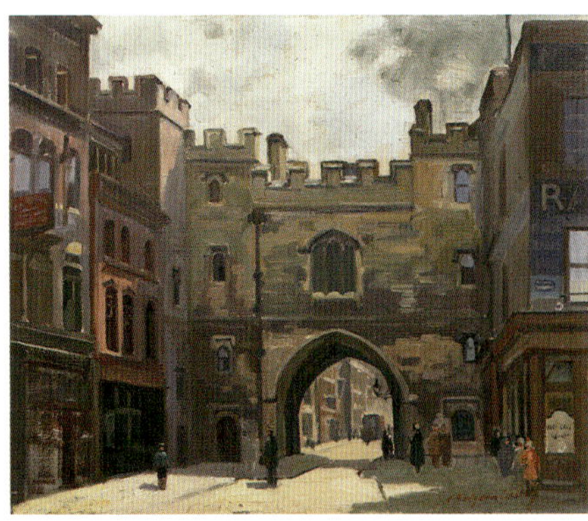

Lobley, John Hodgson 1878–1954
*The Grand Priory of the Order of St John of
Jerusalem in England, St John's Gate,
Clerkenwell, EC* c.1918
oil on canvas 50.8 x 60.9
IWM ART 3693

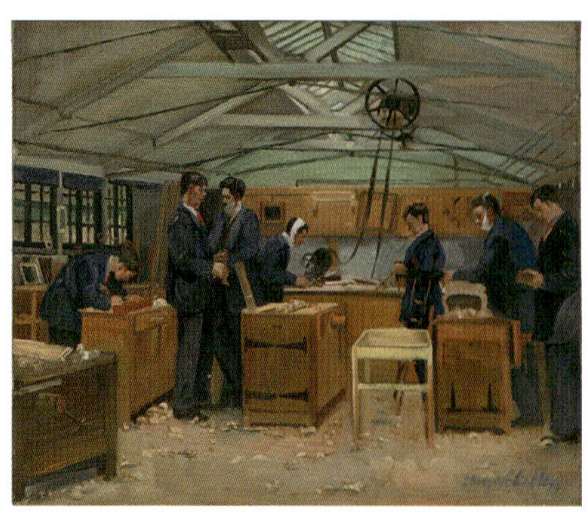

Lobley, John Hodgson 1878–1954
*The Queen's Hospital for Facial Injuries,
Frognal, Sidcup: The Carpenters' Shop* c.1918
oil on canvas 50.8 x 60.9 (E)
IWM ART 3728

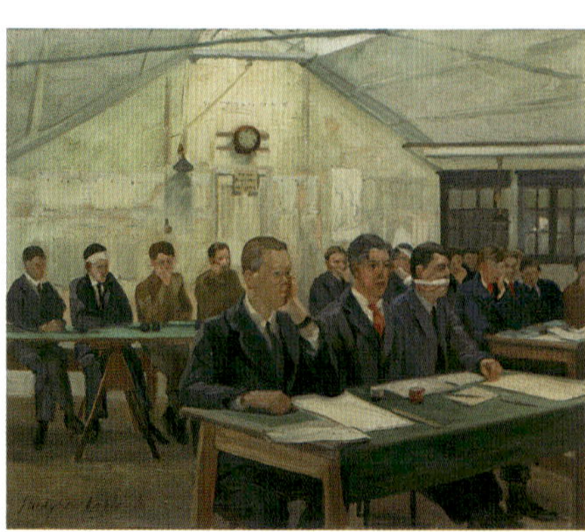

Lobley, John Hodgson 1878–1954
*The Queen's Hospital for Facial Injuries,
Frognal, Sidcup: The Commercial Class* c.1918
oil on canvas 50.8 x 60.9 (E)
IWM ART 3767

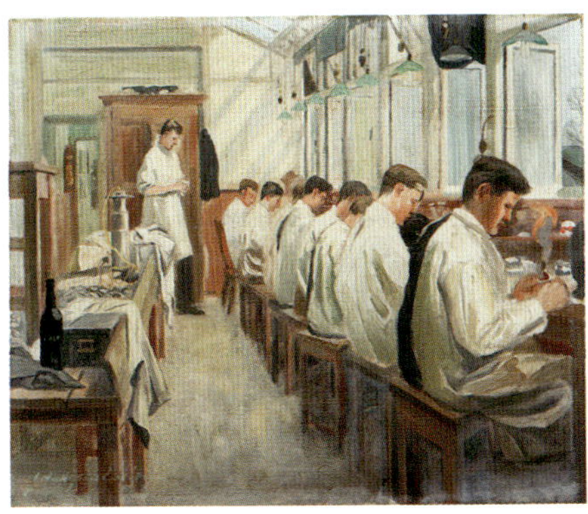

Lobley, John Hodgson 1878–1954
The Queen's Hospital for Facial Injuries, Frognal, Sidcup: The Dental Mechanics' Class c.1918
oil on canvas 50.8 x 60.9
IWM ART 3757

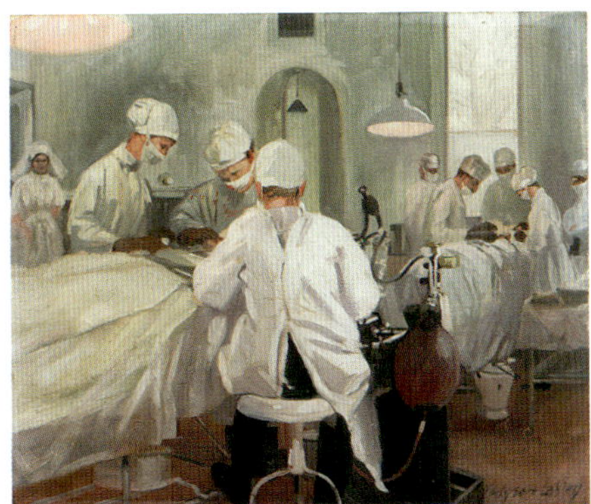

Lobley, John Hodgson 1878–1954
The Queen's Hospital for Facial Injuries, Frognal, Sidcup: The Operating Theatre c.1918
oil on canvas 50.8 x 60.9
IWM ART 3659

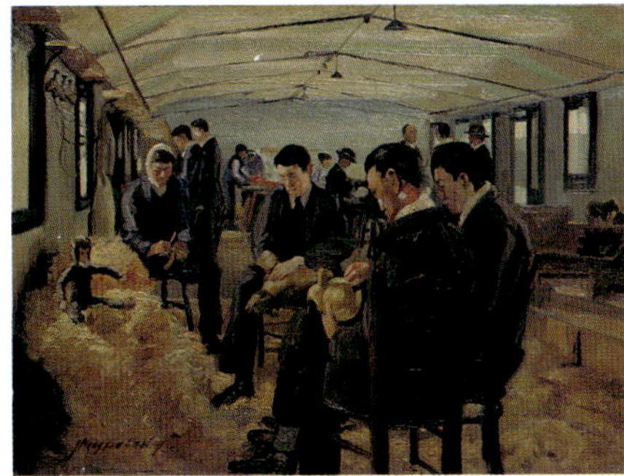

Lobley, John Hodgson 1878–1954
The Queen's Hospital for Facial Injuries, Frognal, Sidcup: The Toy Makers' Shop c.1918
oil on canvas 45 x 60.7
IWM ART 3756

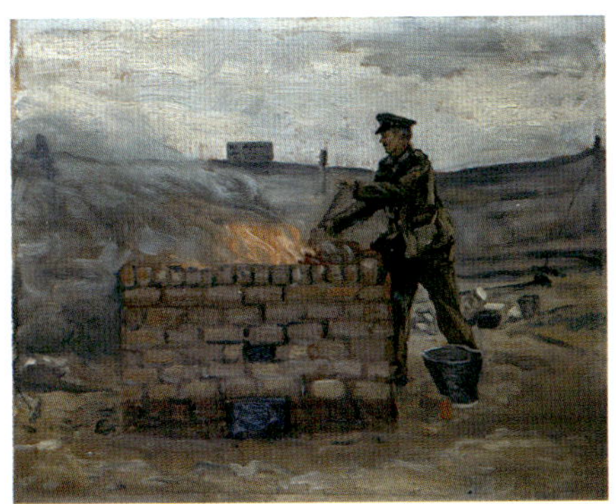

Lobley, John Hodgson 1878–1954
The Royal Army Medical Corps in Training, Blackpool: The Depot Incinerator c.1918
oil on panel 32.3 x 40.6
IWM ART 3731

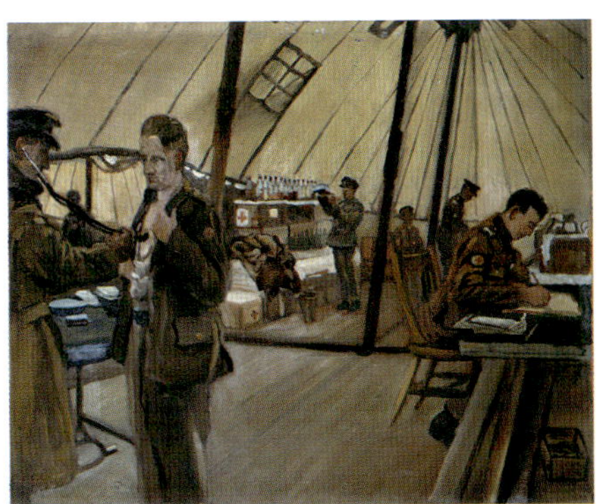

Lobley, John Hodgson 1878–1954
The Royal Army Medical Corps in Training, Blackpool: The Medical Inspection Room and Dispensary c.1918
oil on panel 33 x 40.6
IWM ART 3681

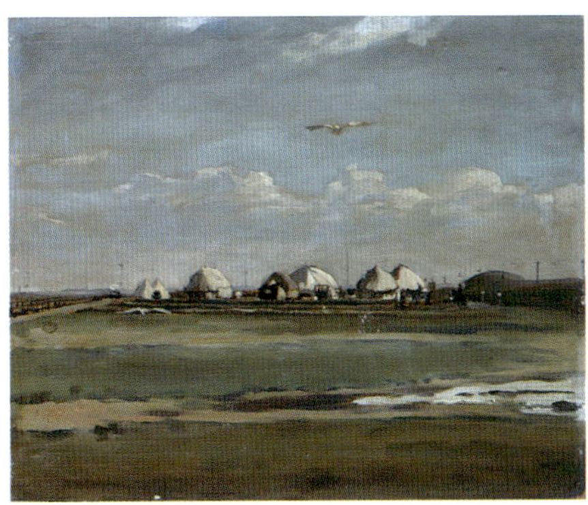

Lobley, John Hodgson 1878–1954
The Royal Army Medical Corps in Training, Blackpool: The Officers' School of Instruction c.1918
oil on panel 33 x 40.6
IWM ART 3698

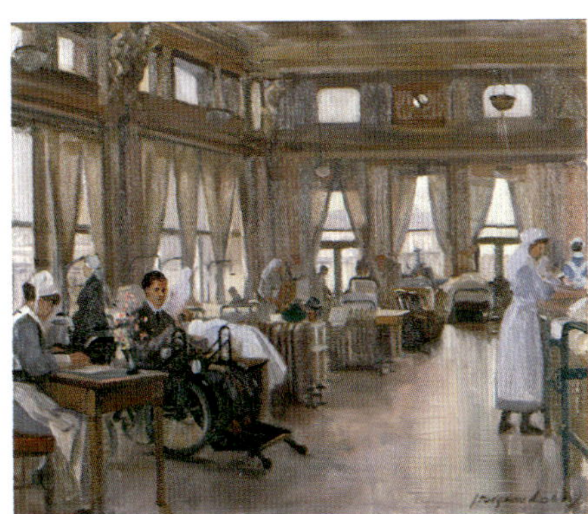

Lobley, John Hodgson 1878–1954
The Special Surgical Auxiliary Hospital at the 'Star and Garter', Richmond: The Dining Room c.1918
oil on canvas 50.8 x 60.9
IWM ART 3763

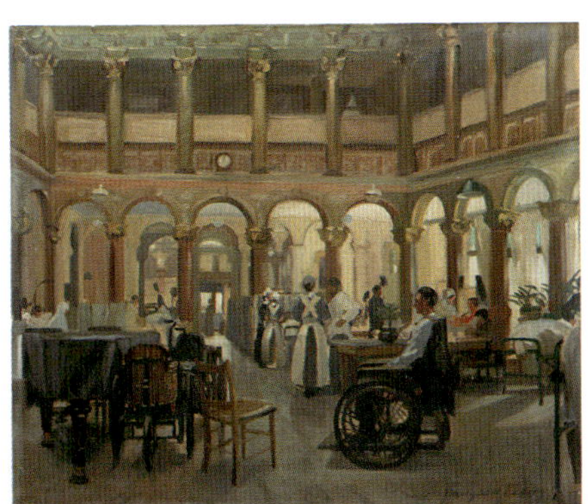

Lobley, John Hodgson 1878–1954
The Special Surgical Hospital at the 'Star and Garter', Richmond: The Ballroom c.1918
oil on canvas 50.8 x 60.9
IWM ART 3768

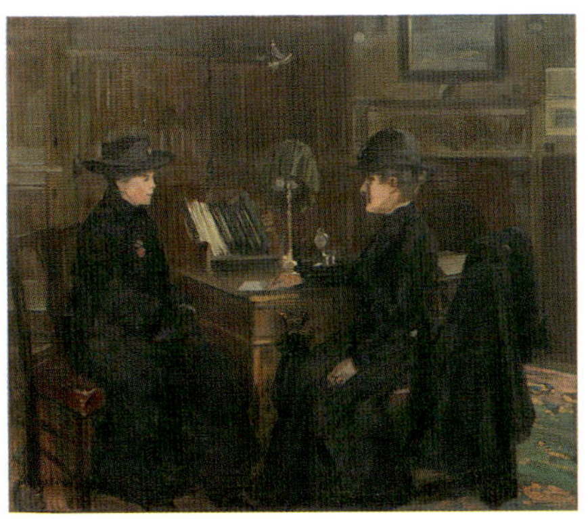

Lobley, John Hodgson 1878–1954
The Superintendent Posting a Sister for Service: The Grand Priory of the Order of St John of Jerusalem in England, (…) c.1918
oil on canvas 50.8 x 60.9
IWM ART 3657

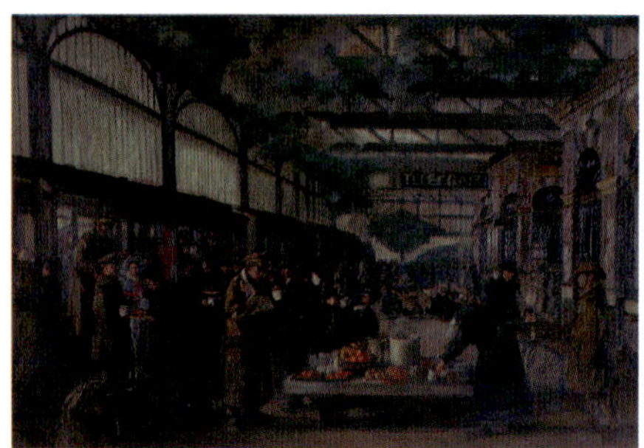

Lobley, John Hodgson 1878–1954
*Wounded Passing through Snow Hill Railway
Station, Birmingham* c.1918
oil on canvas 101.9 x 152.4
IWM ART 3717

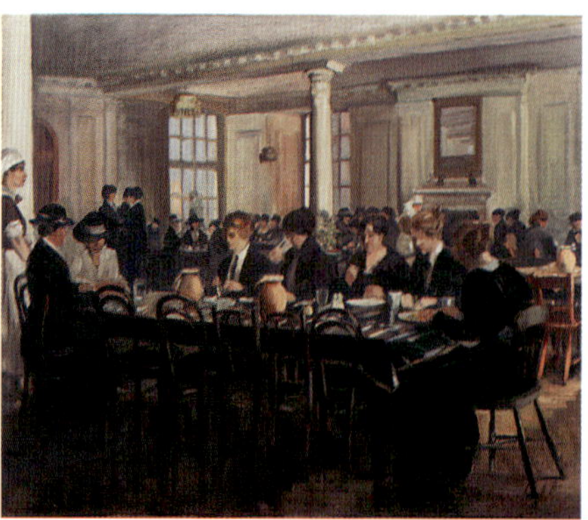

Lobley, John Hodgson 1878–1954
*The Canteen at the Headquarters of the Joint
War Council of the British Red Cross Society
and Order of St John, (…)* c.1918–1919
oil on canvas 50.8 x 60.9
IWM ART 3747

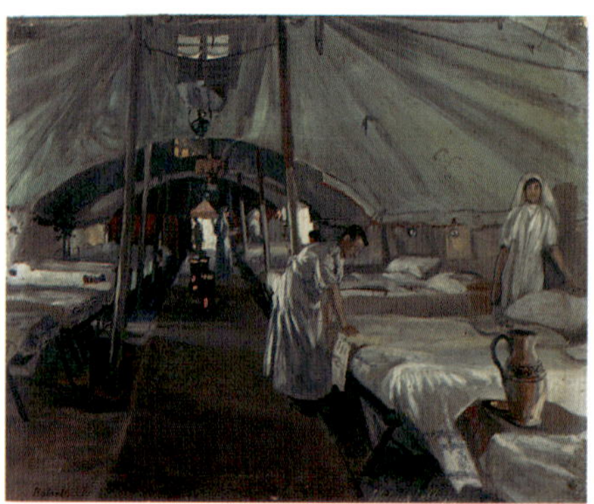

Lobley, John Hodgson 1878–1954
*The Officers' Ward at the 41st Casualty
Clearing Station* c.1918–1919
oil on panel 31.7 x 39.3
IWM ART 3809

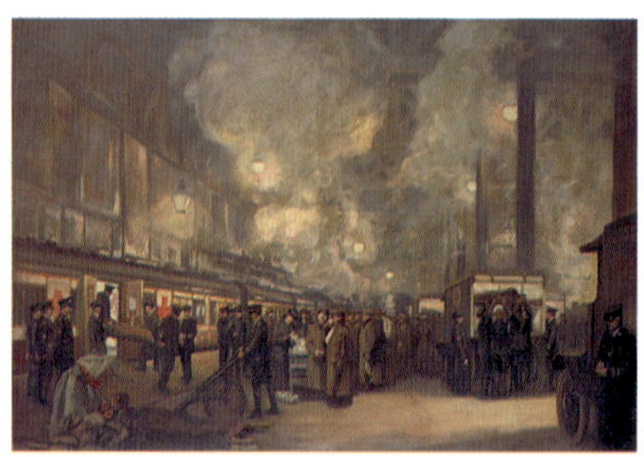

Lobley, John Hodgson 1878–1954
*Charing Cross Station: Detraining Wounded by
the British Red Cross Society and Order of St
John* 1919
oil on canvas 101.9 x 152.4
IWM ART 2758

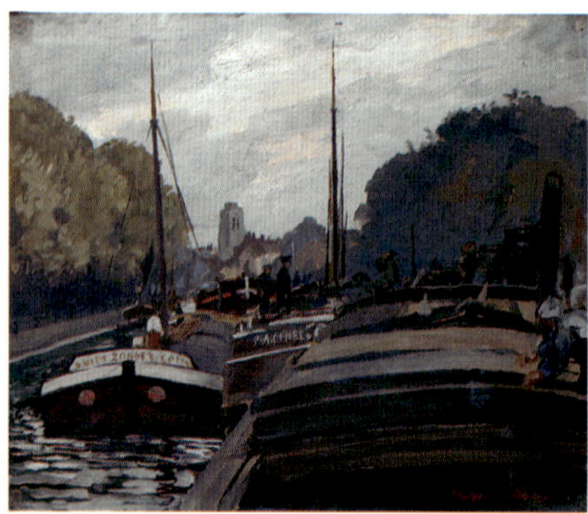

Lobley, John Hodgson 1878–1954
Hospital Barges in Flanders 1919
oil on panel 33 x 40.6
IWM ART 3687

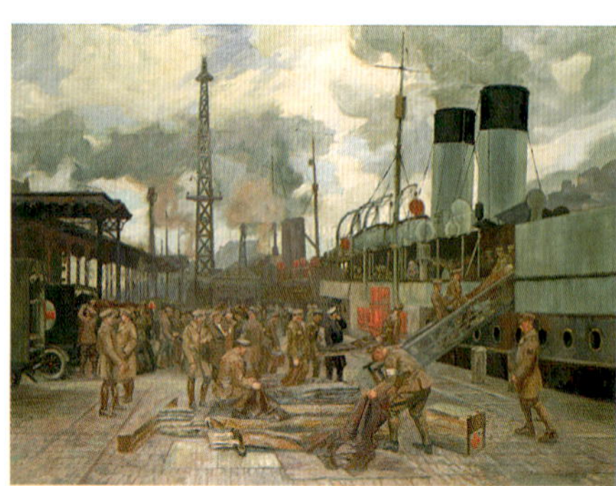

Lobley, John Hodgson 1878–1954
Loading Wounded at Boulogne 1919
oil on canvas 205.7 x 276.8
IWM ART 2760

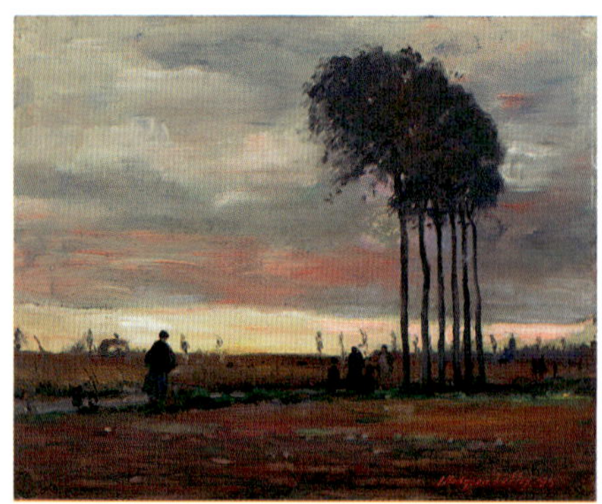

Lobley, John Hodgson 1878–1954
Refugees on the Road from Ascq to Lille 1919
oil on board 31.7 x 40
IWM ART 3711

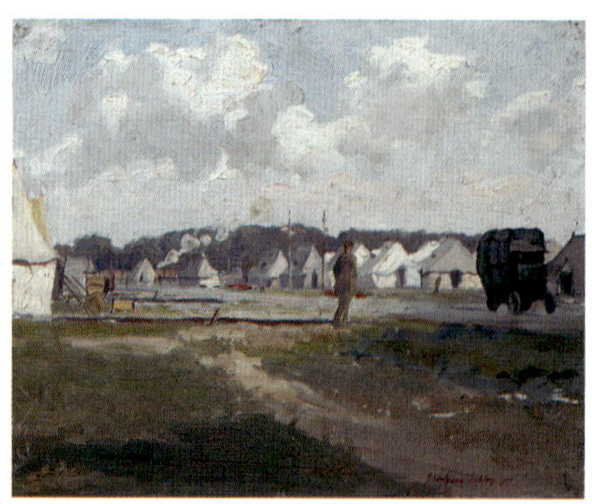

Lobley, John Hodgson 1878–1954
*The 39th Stationary Hospital, Ascq, September
1919* 1919
oil on canvas 31.7 x 40.6
IWM ART 3746

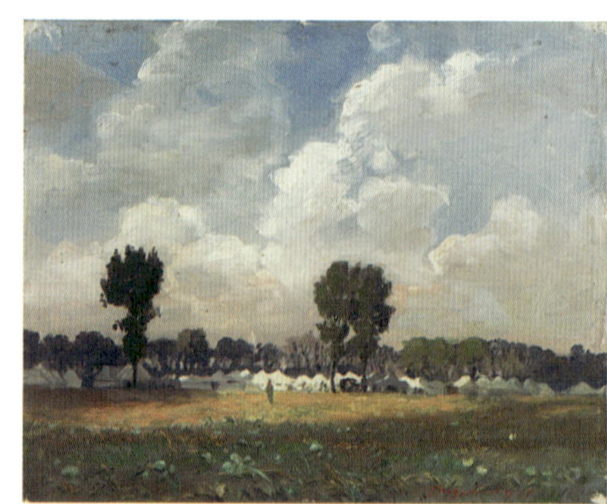

Lobley, John Hodgson 1878–1954
*The Camp of the 42nd Casualty Clearing
Station, Douai* 1919
oil on canvas 33 x 39.3
IWM ART 3765

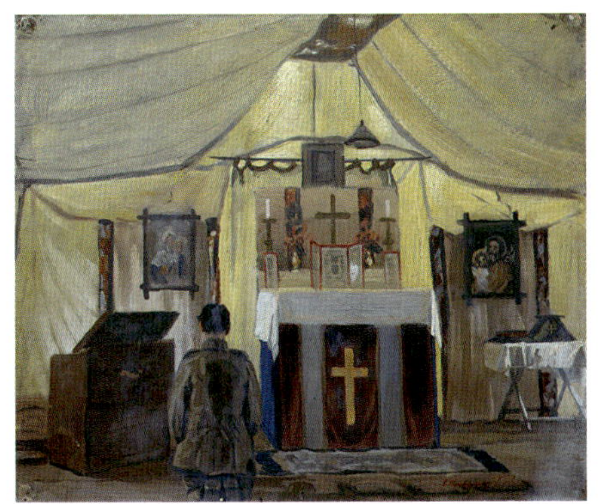

Lobley, John Hodgson 1878–1954
*The Church of England Tent, 39th Stationary
Hospital, Ascq, September 1919* 1919
oil on panel 33 x 40.6
IWM ART 3661

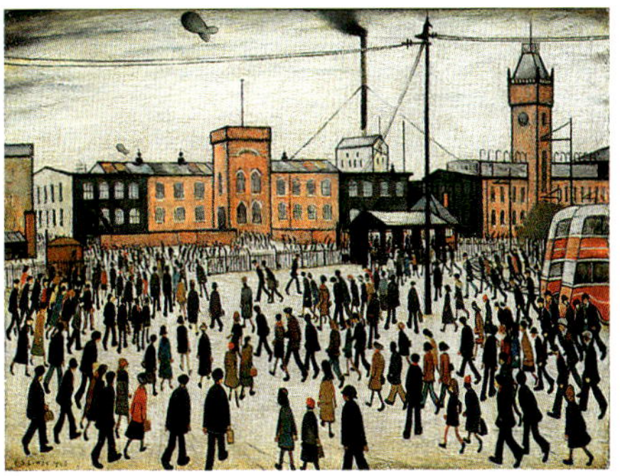

Lowry, Laurence Stephen 1887–1976
Going to Work 1943
oil on canvas 45.7 x 60.9
IWM ART LD 3074

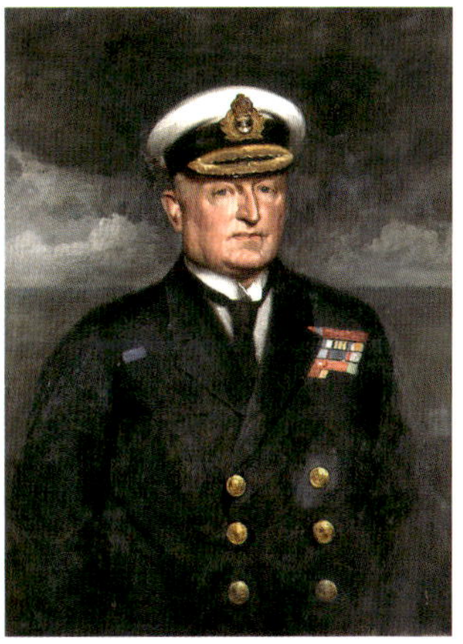

Lytton, Neville Stephen 1879–1951
*Admiral Sir Thomas Henry Martyn Jerram
(1858–1933), GCMG, KCB* 1920
oil on panel 91.4 x 71.1
IWM ART 3141

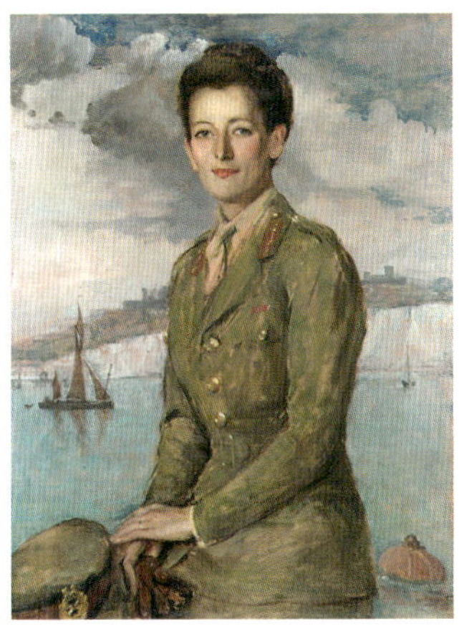

Lytton, Neville Stephen 1879–1951
*Mrs Jean Knox, CBE, Chief Controller and
Director, Auxiliary Territorial Service
1942–1943*
oil on canvas 91.4 x 71.1
IWM ART LD 3671

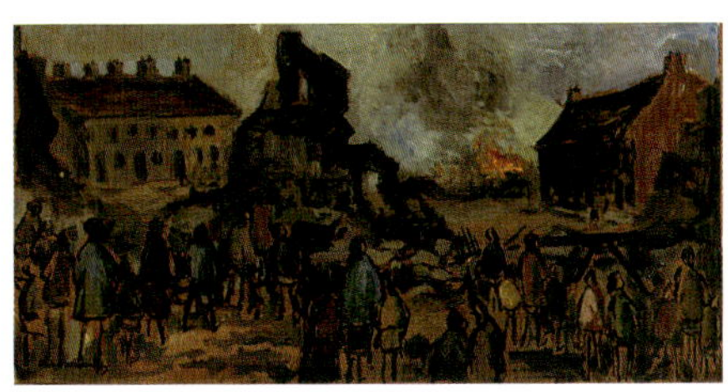

Maccabe, Gladys b.1918
After a Bomb Went Off, Belfast 1979
oil on board 46.7 x 95.5
IWM ART 16152

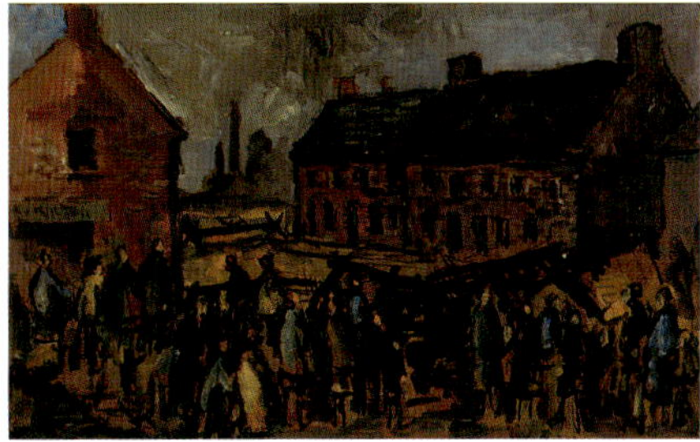

Maccabe, Gladys b.1918
Barricades, Belfast 1979
oil on board 45.5 x 73
IWM ART 16150

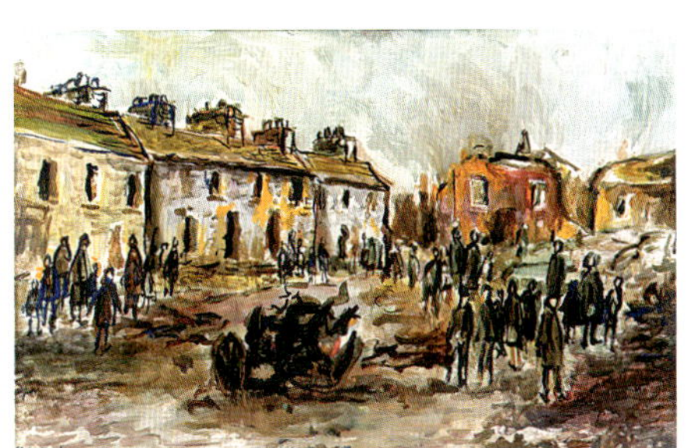

Maccabe, Gladys b.1918
After a Car Bomb Explosion, Ulster Village
c.1979
oil on panel 45 x 71.1
IWM ART MW(A) 42

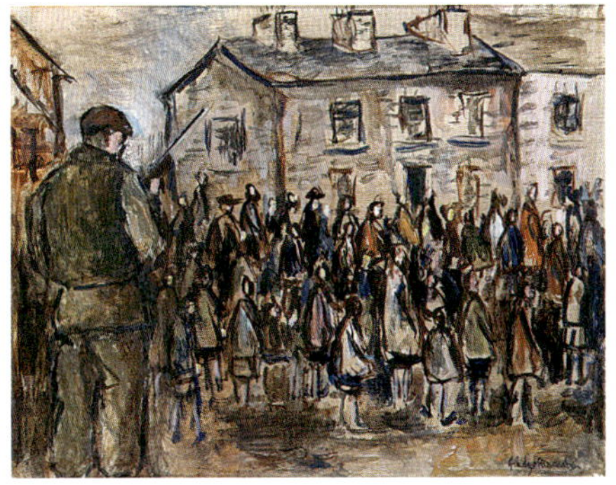

Maccabe, Gladys b.1918
Street Incident, Londonderry c.1979
oil on board 43.1 x 53.3
IWM ART MW(A) 43

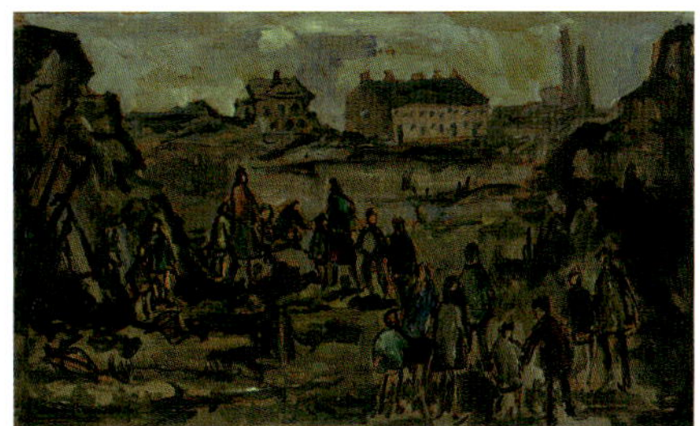

Maccabe, Gladys b.1918
To School via a Bomb Site, Belfast 1980
oil on board 44 x 74.8
IWM ART 16151

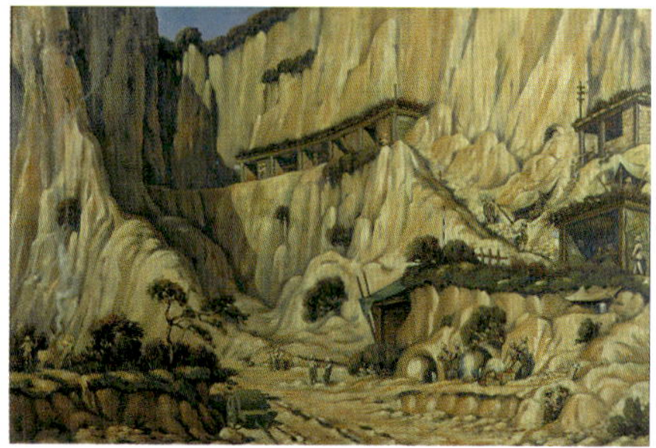

MacClure, Victor 1887–1963
The Headquarters of the 29th Division, Gully Ravine, Cape Helles, Gallipoli c.1915–1918
oil on canvas 101.9 x 152.4
IWM ART 1927

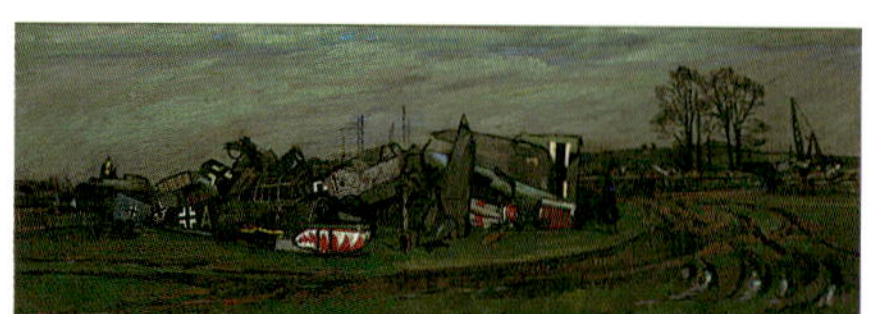

Macdonald, Frances 1914–2002
Graveyard: No.1 Metal and Produce Recovery Depot, Morris Works, Cowley, Oxford 1940
oil on canvas 43.1 x 121.9
IWM ART LD 717

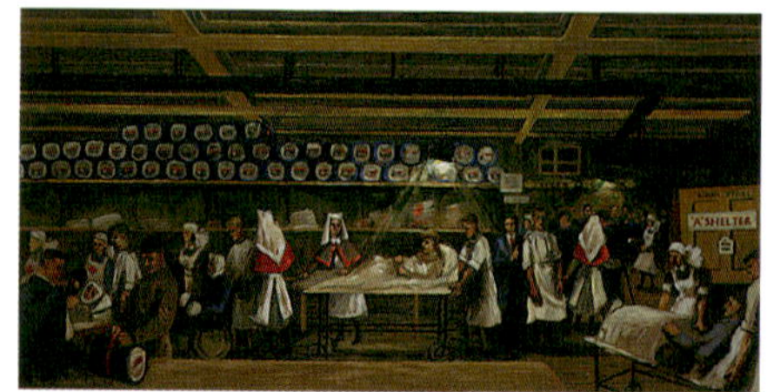

Macdonald, Frances 1914–2002
In the Millbank Hospital during an Air Raid: Patients Being Taken to the Shelter 1940
oil on canvas 60.9 x 121.9
IWM ART LD 1598

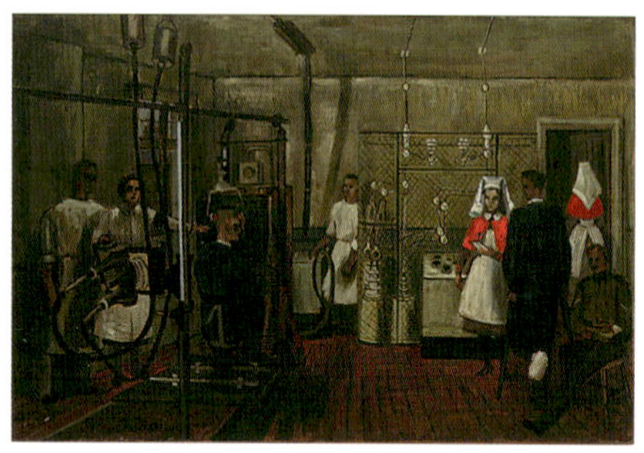

Macdonald, Frances 1914–2002
The X-Ray Department at the Queen Alexandra Military Hospital 1941
oil on canvas 40.6 x 60.9
IWM ART LD 791

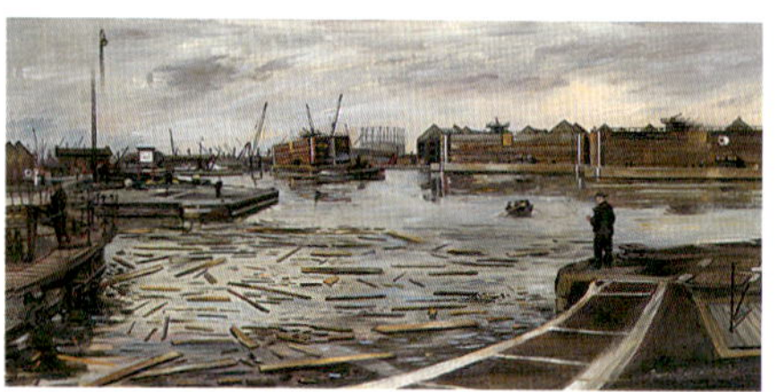

Macdonald, Frances 1914–2002
London Docks 1944
oil on canvas 44.4 x 90.4
IWM ART LD 4039

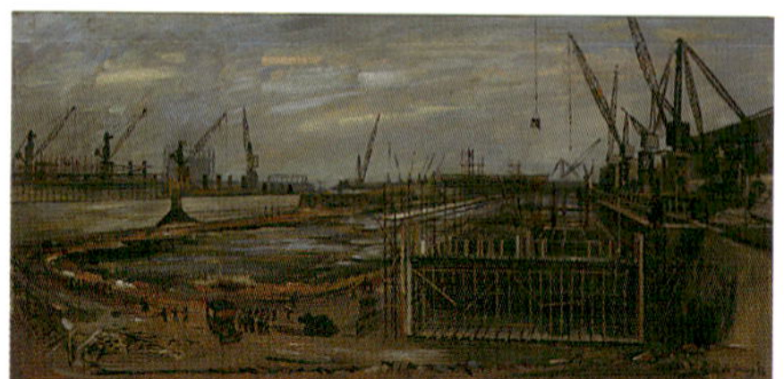

Macdonald, Frances 1914–2002
Sketch for 'London Docks' 1944
oil on panel 37.1 x 78.1
IWM ART LD 3925

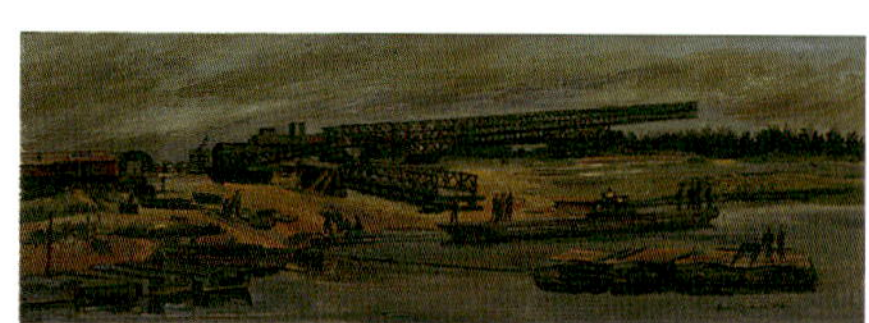

Macdonald, Frances 1914–2002
Testing Jeep Power on Barges 1944
oil on canvas 29.2 x 85
IWM ART LD 4411

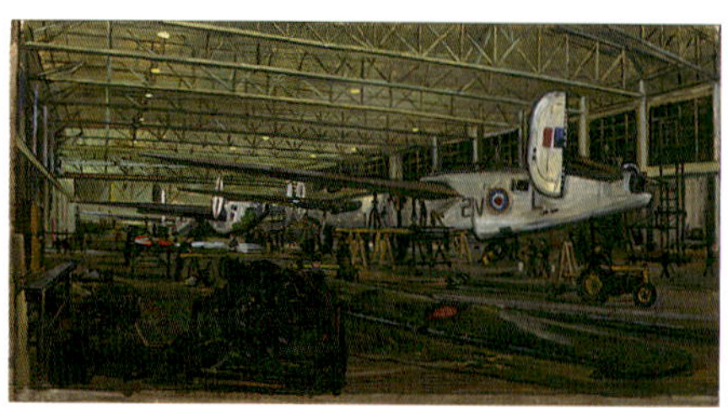

Macdonald, Frances 1914–2002
43 Repair Group, Air Frame Repair Service, Lincoln: Repairing Liberator Aircraft 1945
oil on canvas 38.1 x 74.9
IWM ART LD 5509

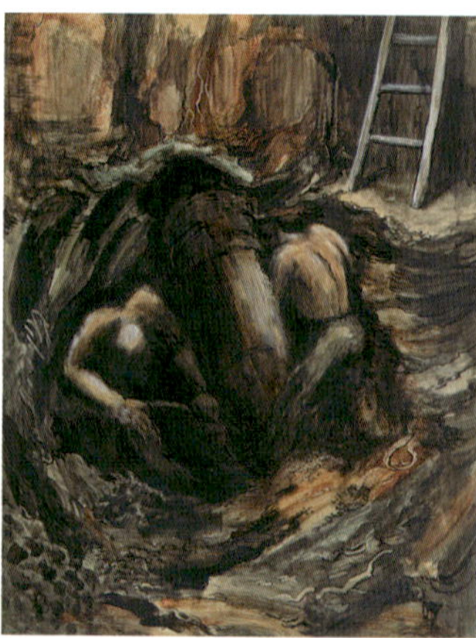

Mackertich, Robin 1921–1993
Bomb Disposal
oil on canvas 62 x 48
IWM ART 17117

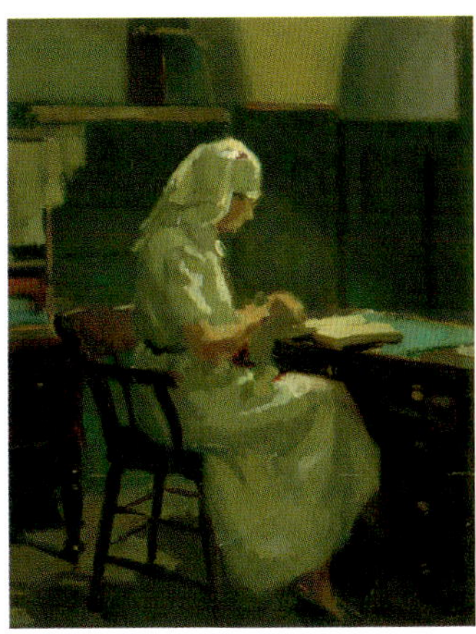

Mackey, Arthur Stewart b.1909
*Sister Buchanan at the Cosway Street Rest
Centre, NW1* c.1941
oil on panel 35.5 x 27.9
IWM ART LD 5978

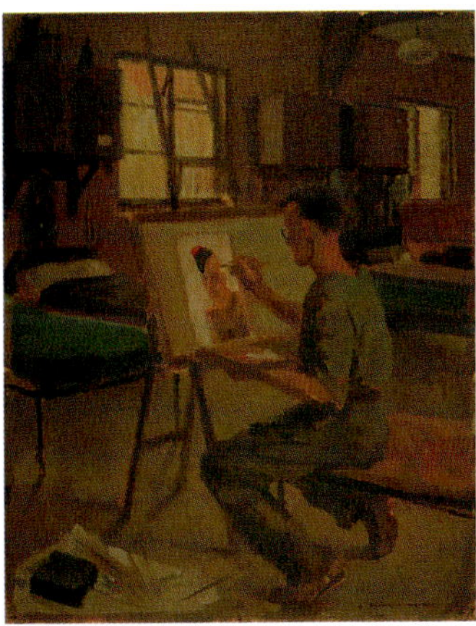

Mackey, Arthur Stewart b.1909
The Barrack Room Artist 1942
oil on board 38 x 30.2
IWM ART 16422

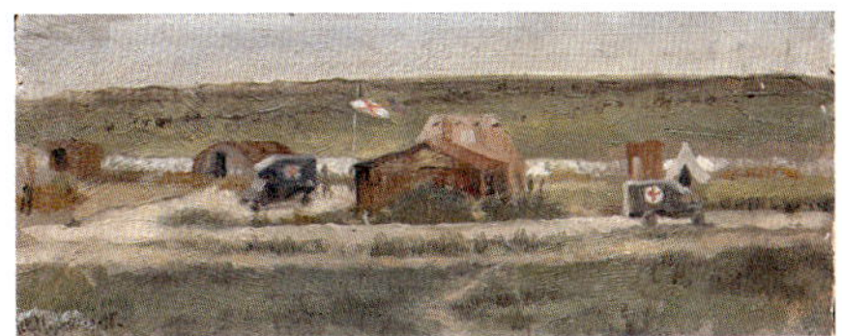

Mackey, Haydn Reynolds 1881–1979
*An Advanced Dressing Station of the 36th Field
Ambulance at Liéramont* 1918
oil on panel 10.1 x 25.4
IWM ART 3785

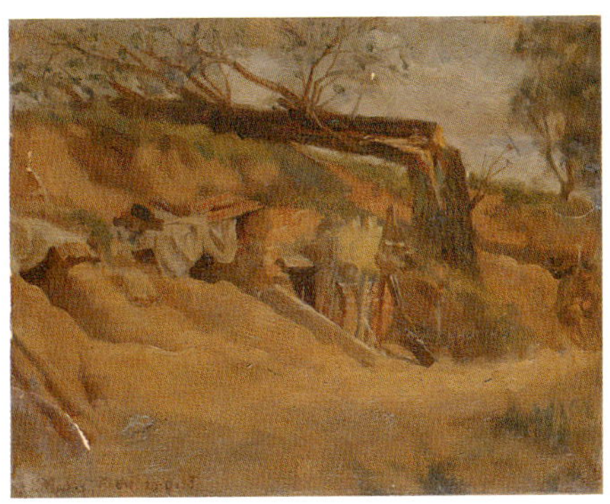

Mackey, Haydn Reynolds 1881–1979
*Epéhy: In a Sunken Roadway near the
Regimental Aid Post of the 7th Battalion Royal
Sussex Regiment* 1918
oil on panel 20.3 x 25.4
IWM ART 3799

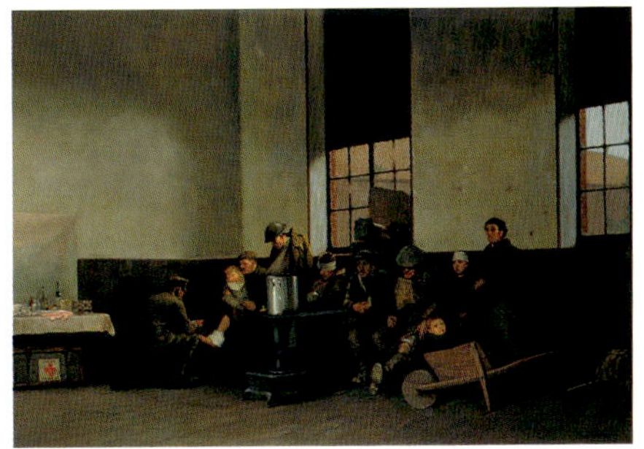

Mackey, Haydn Reynolds 1881–1979
*Some Civilian Casualties at the Main Dressing
Station of the 36th Field Ambulance, Flines-les-
Raches, October 1918* 1918
oil on canvas 170.1 x 247
IWM ART 2770

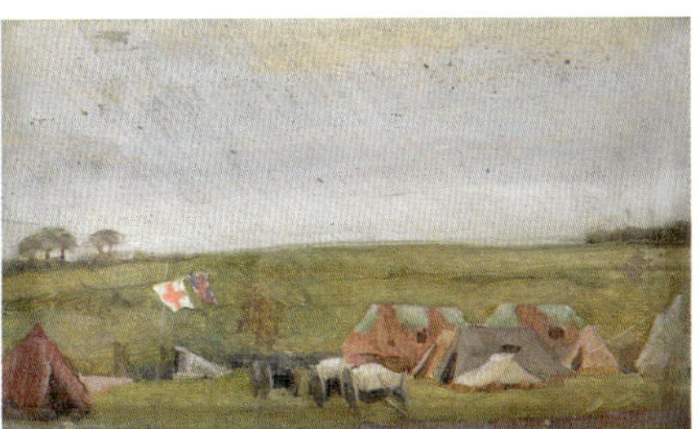

Mackey, Haydn Reynolds 1881–1979
*The Main Dressing Station of a Field
Ambulance: Templeux-la-Fosse, 18 September
1918* 1918
oil on panel 11.4 x 19.6
IWM ART 3790

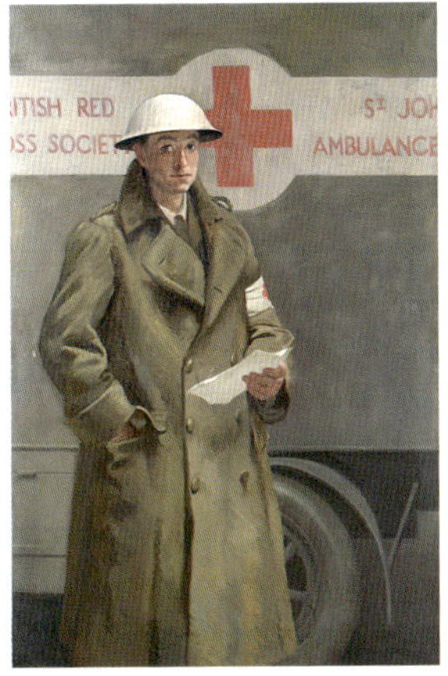

Mackey, Haydn Reynolds 1881–1979
*A British Red Cross Society and Order of St
John of Jerusalem Officer in France* 1918–1919
oil on canvas 152.4 x 101.9
IWM ART 3840

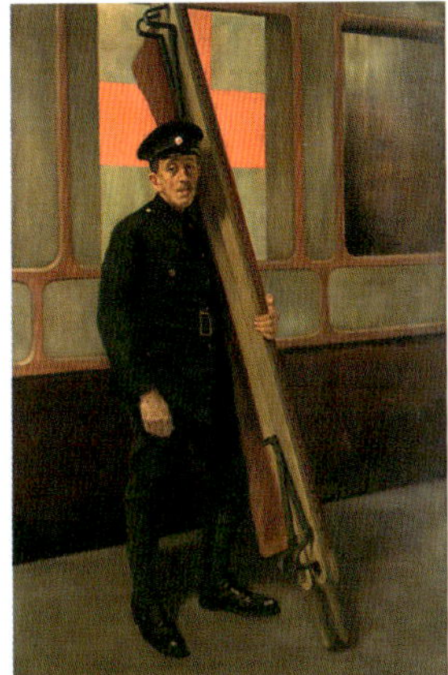

Mackey, Haydn Reynolds 1881–1979
*A British Red Cross Society and Order of St
John of Jerusalem Stretcher-Bearer* 1918–1919
oil on canvas 152.4 x 101.9
IWM ART 3814

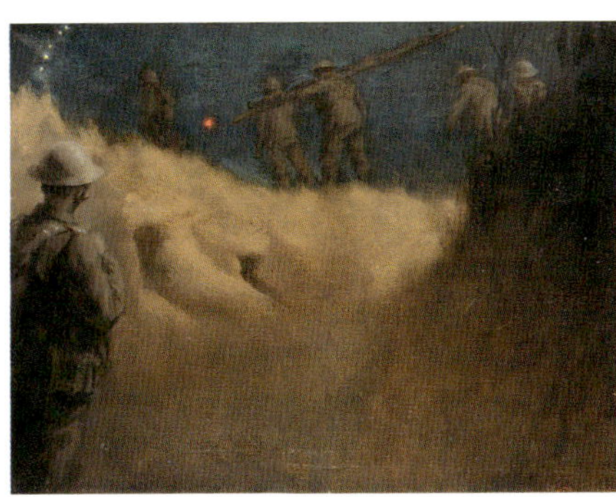

Mackey, Haydn Reynolds 1881–1979
*A Royal Army Medical Corps Squad with
Infantry: Night at Nurlu, October 1918*
1918–1919
oil on canvas 30.4 x 40.6
IWM ART 3795

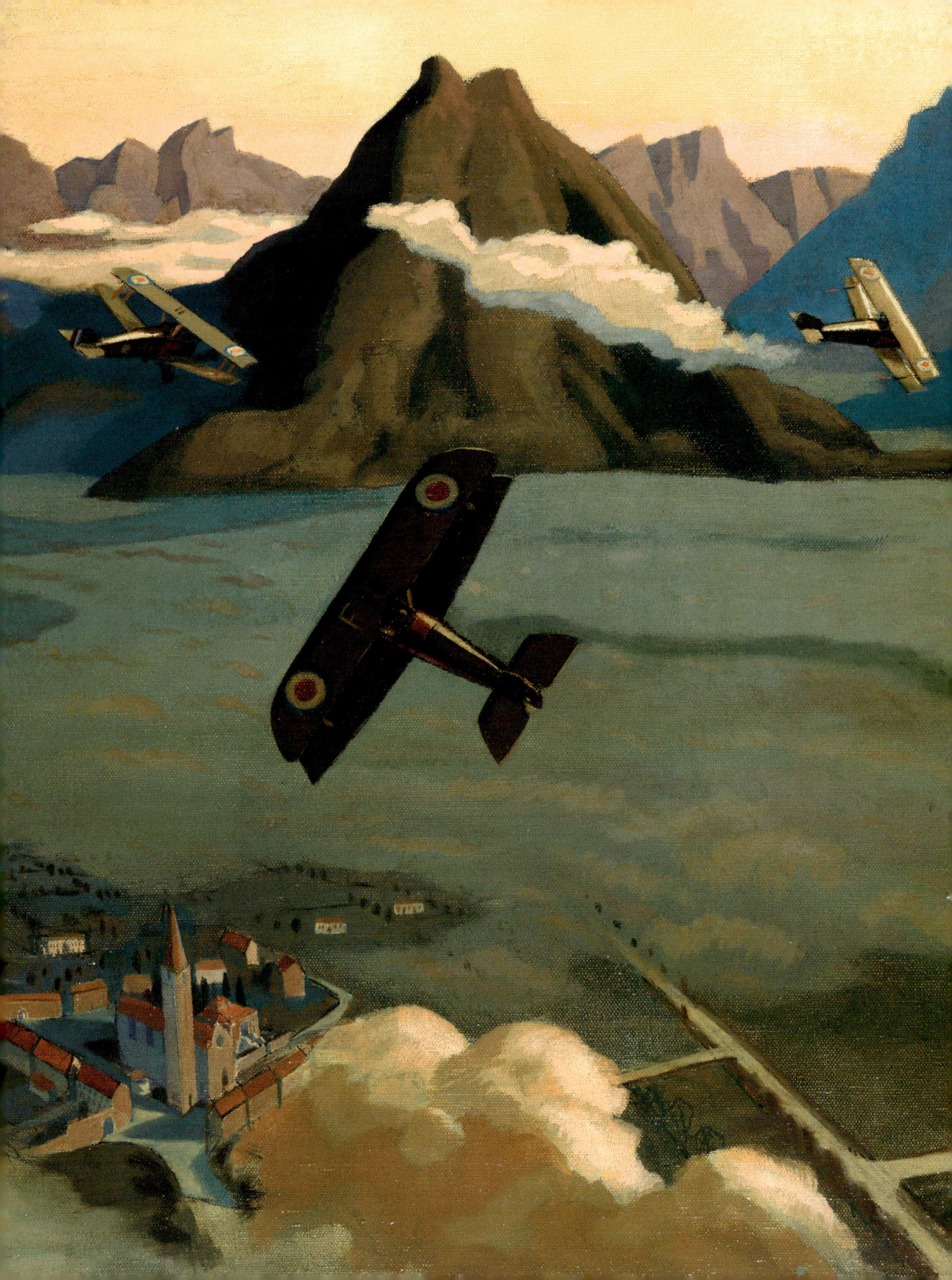

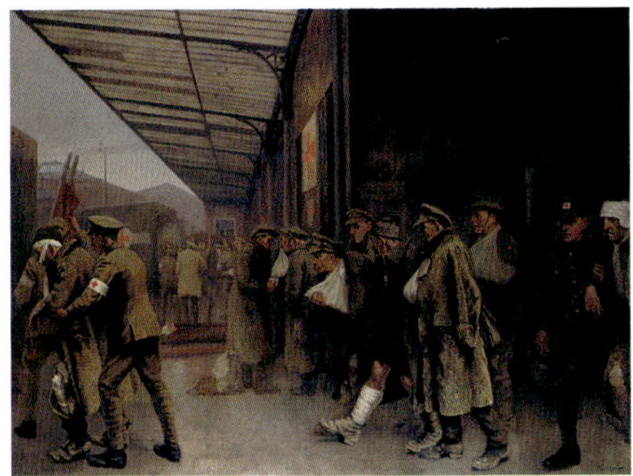

Mackey, Haydn Reynolds 1881–1979
*British Red Cross Society and Order of St John
of Jerusalem Workers Attending Wounded on
their Arrival at Boulogne Station* 1918–1919
oil on canvas 203.2 x 274.3
IWM ART 3820

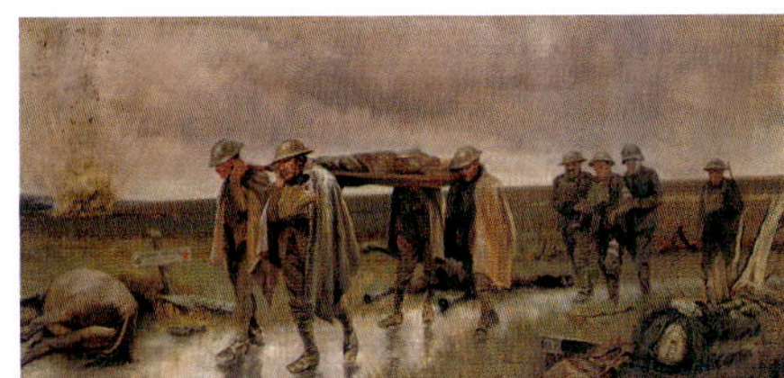

Mackey, Haydn Reynolds 1881–1979
Epéhy, 1918 1918–1919
oil on canvas 67.3 x 137.1
IWM ART 3653

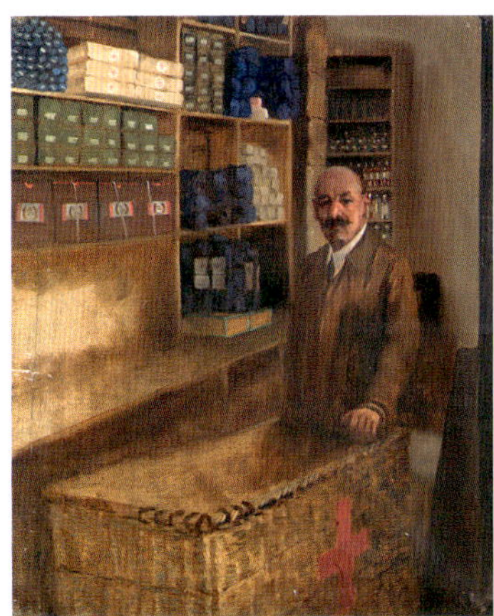

Mackey, Haydn Reynolds 1881–1979
*Medical Storeman: British Red Cross Society
and Order of St John of Jerusalem Medical
Stores, Tottenham Court (…)* 1918–1919
oil on canvas 60.9 x 50.8
IWM ART 3729

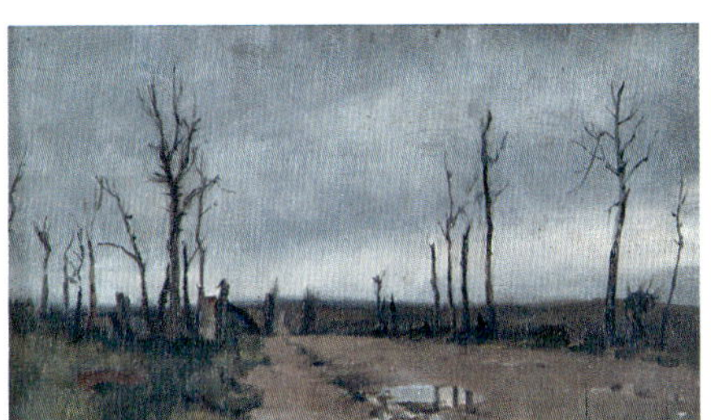

Mackey, Haydn Reynolds 1881–1979
Near 'Hell Fire Corner', Menin Road, Ypres
1918–1919
oil on panel 17.1 x 30.4
IWM ART 3794

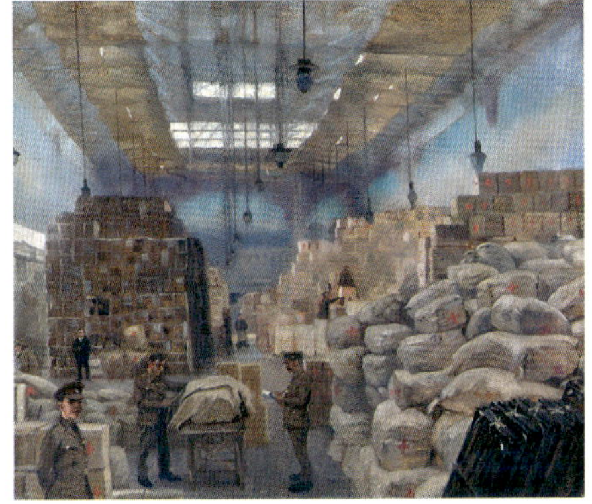

Mackey, Haydn Reynolds 1881–1979
*Prince's Skating Rink, Knightsbridge, London,
during the War: British Red Cross Society Store*
1918–1919
oil on canvas 50.8 x 60.9
IWM ART 3758

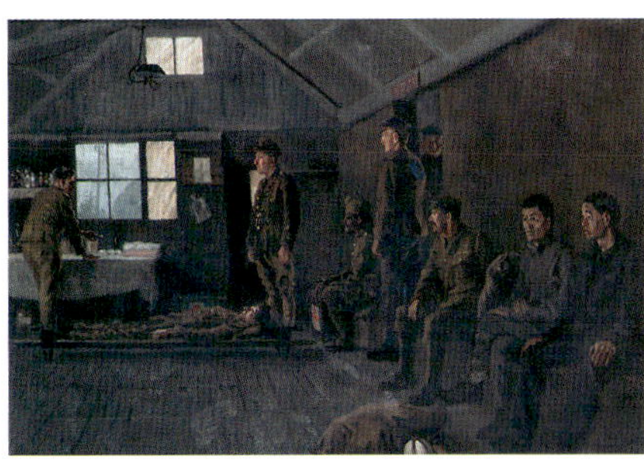

Mackey, Haydn Reynolds 1881–1979
*Sick Parade: British Labour Corps, Indian
Troops, Chinese Labour Corps and German
Prisoners of War, (…)* 1918–1919
oil on canvas 50.8 x 73.6
IWM ART 3781

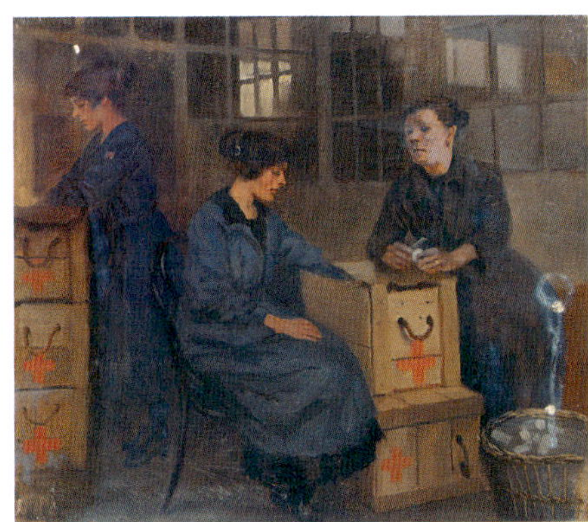

Mackey, Haydn Reynolds 1881–1979
*Sorting Bandages, British Red Cross Society
and Order of St John of Jerusalem Medical
Stores, Tottenham Court (…)* 1918–1919
oil on panel 33 x 39.3
IWM ART 2769

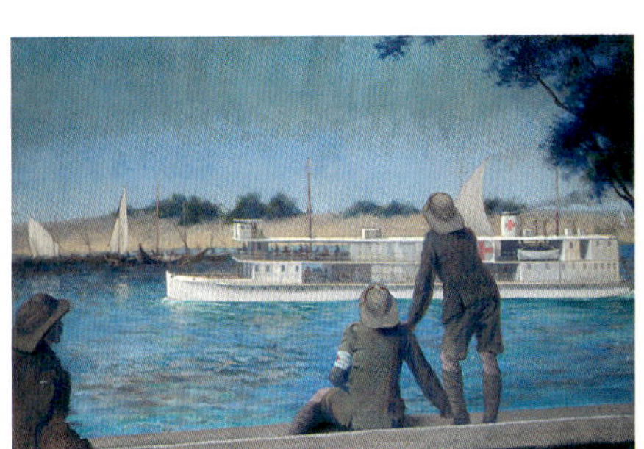

Mackey, Haydn Reynolds 1881–1979
*The British Red Cross Society and Order of St
John of Jerusalem Hospital Ship Passing
through the Suez Canal* 1918–1919
oil on canvas 101.9 x 152.4
IWM ART 3810

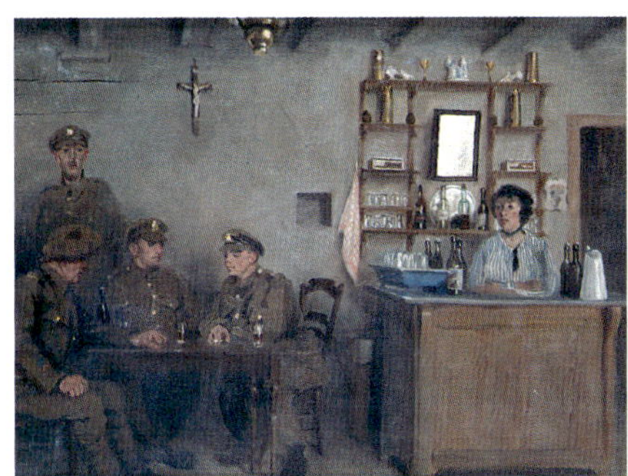

Mackey, Haydn Reynolds 1881–1979
The Estaminet 1918–1919
oil on panel 30.4 x 40.6
IWM ART 3787

Facing page: Carline, Sydney William, 1888–1929, *British Scouts Leaving Their Aerodrome on Patrol over the Asiago Plateau, Italy* (detail),
1918, (p. 29)

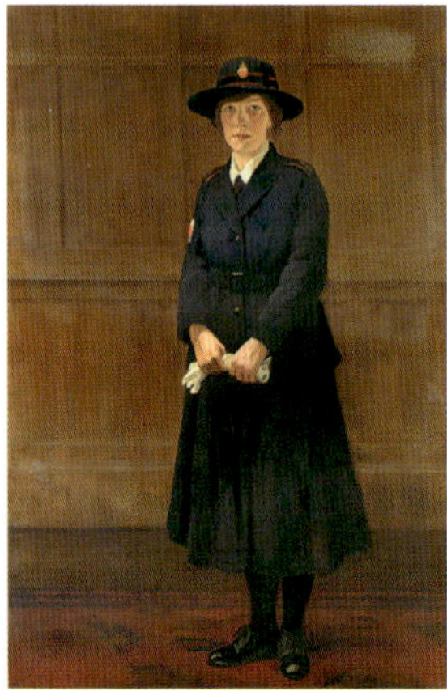

Mackey, Haydn Reynolds 1881–1979
Voluntary Aid Detachment Territorial Force
1918–1919
oil on canvas 152.4 x 101.9
IWM ART 3837

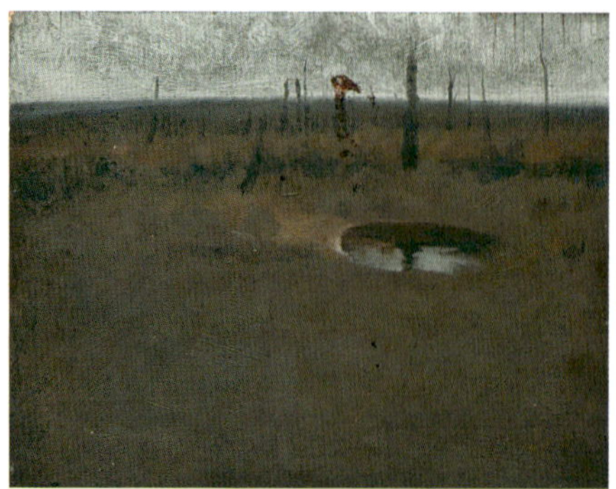

Mackey, Haydn Reynolds 1881–1979
Ypres Landscape 1918–1919
oil on panel 23.6 x 30.5
IWM ART 16326

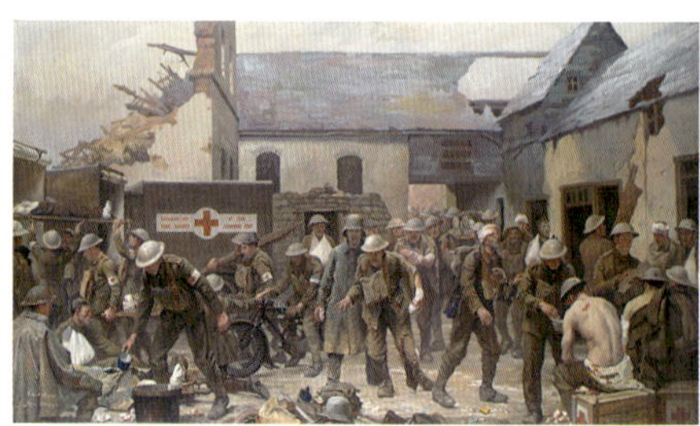

Mackey, Haydn Reynolds 1881–1979 &
Rogers, Gilbert active 1905–1920
*An Advanced Dressing Station, France: Cars
Supplied by the British Red (…)* 1918–1919
oil on canvas 203.2 x 365.7
IWM ART 3835

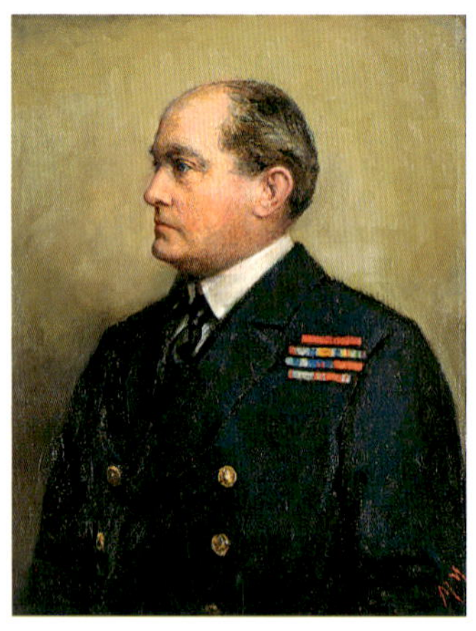

Macleod, Mary active 1914–1933
Admiral Sir Arthur Leveson, GCB 1918–1919
oil on canvas 76.2 x 62.8
IWM ART 4713

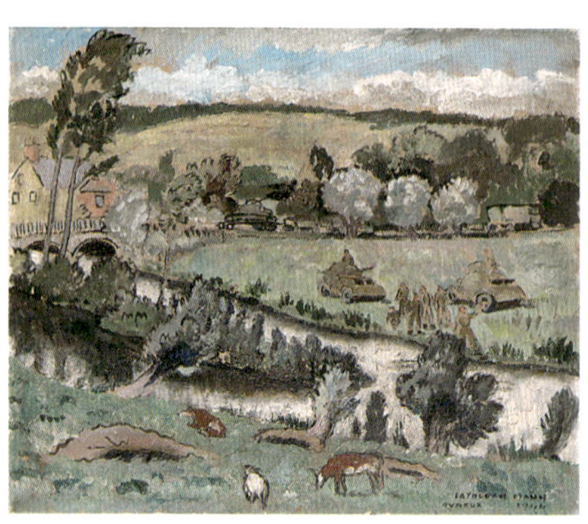

Mann, Cathleen 1896–1959
Evreux 1944
oil on canvas 50.7 x 61
IWM ART 16795

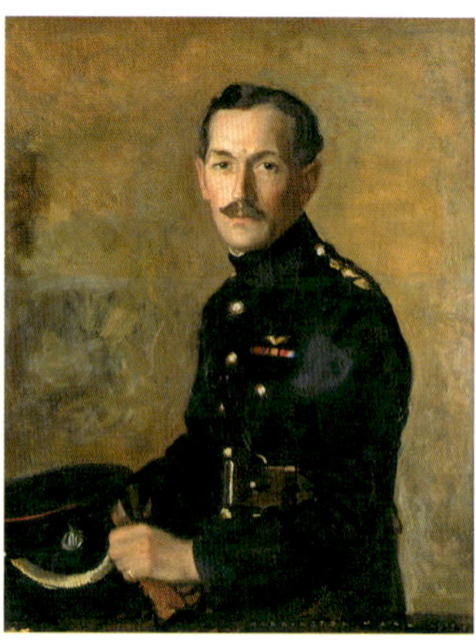

Mann, Harrington 1864–1936
Lieutenant Colonel Maitland, CMG, DSO
1918
oil on canvas 91.4 x 73.6
IWM ART 4414

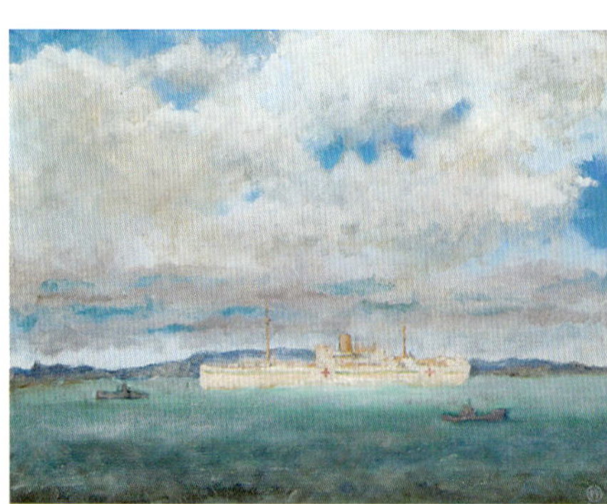

Mann, W. N. active 1940–1971
'HMHS Dorsetshire' at Milford Haven 1940
oil on canvas 40.5 x 50.7
IWM ART LD 6498

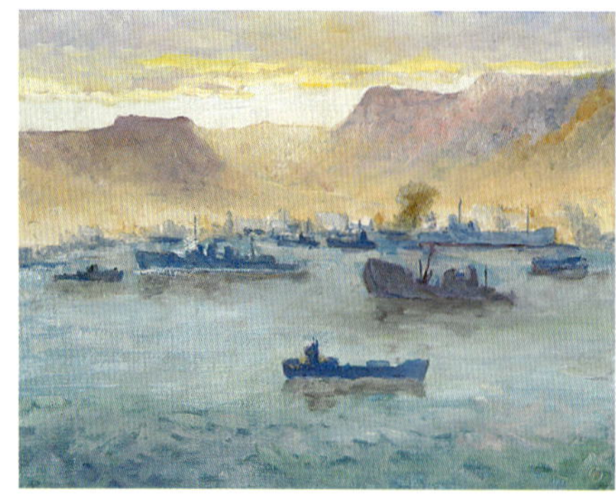

Mann, W. N. active 1940–1971
*Sollum Harbour Seen from the Hospital Ship
'Dorsetshire', 7 January 1941* 1941
oil on canvas 40.3 x 51
IWM ART LD 6497

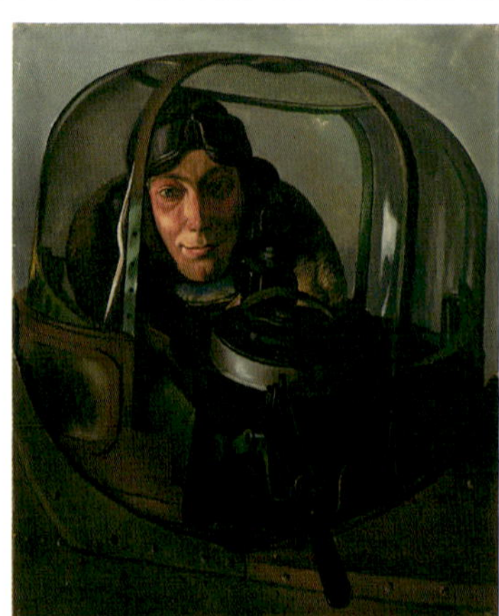

Mansbridge, John 1901–1981
*An Air Gunner in a Gun Turret: Sergeant G.
Holmes, DFM* 1939
oil on canvas 76.2 x 63.5
IWM ART LD 374

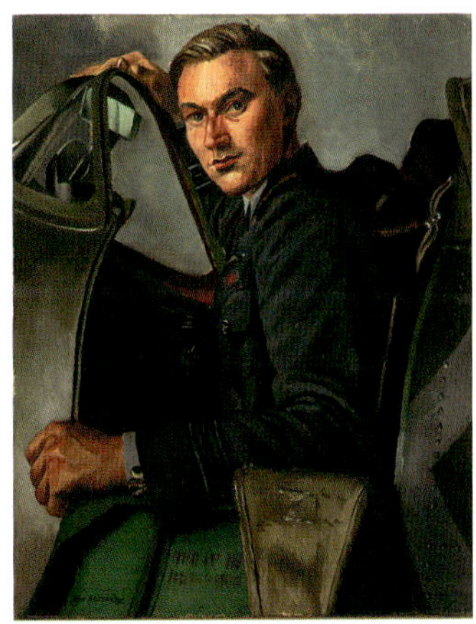

Mansbridge, John 1901–1981
*Squadron Leader J. A. Leathart, DSO, No.54
Squadron* 1939
oil on canvas 66 x 50.8
IWM ART LD 414

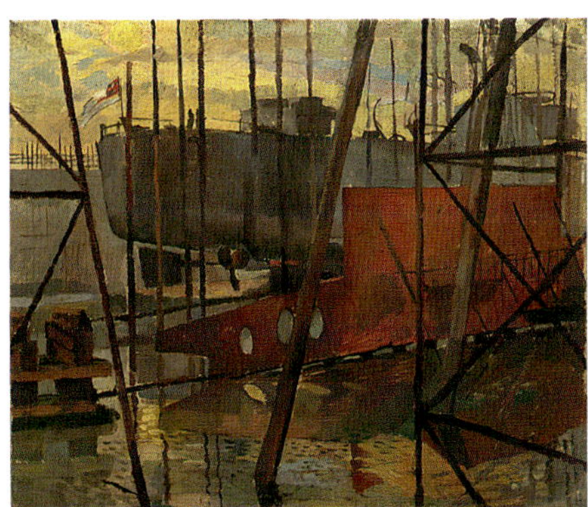

Mansfield, Edward b.1907
*The View across the Musgrave Yard, Belfast,
with the Centre Plate of a Ship in the
Foreground and Ship No.1154 (…)* 1942
oil on canvas 50.8 x 60.9
IWM ART LD 2784

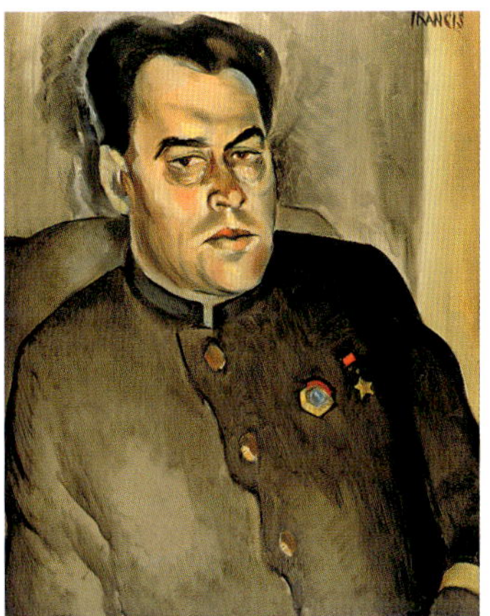

Marshall, Francis 1901–1980
*Commodore Alexander Vladimirvitch
Tripolski, Hero of the Soviet Union, Order of
Lenin, Gold Star* 1943
oil on canvas 66 x 53.3
IWM ART LD 3330

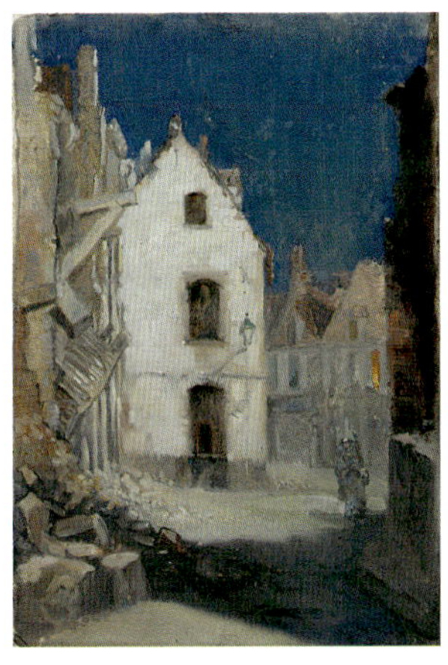

Martin, Edwin active 1913–1938
Arras 1918
oil on panel 34.2 x 24.1
IWM ART 3404

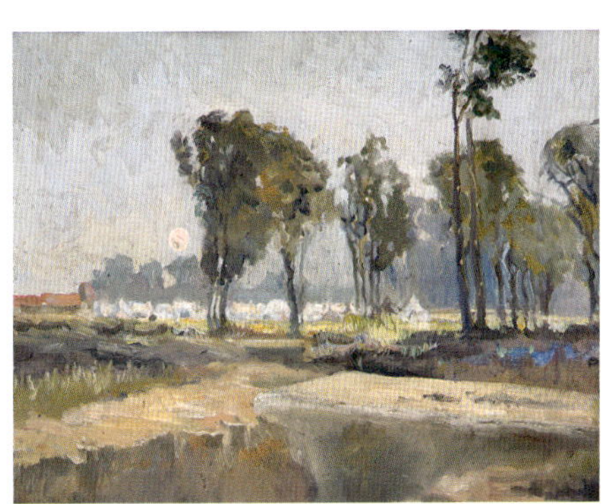

Martin, Edwin active 1913–1938
*German Pillboxes: An Old Regimental Aid
Post, Douai* 1918
oil on canvas 31.7 x 38.7
IWM ART 3716

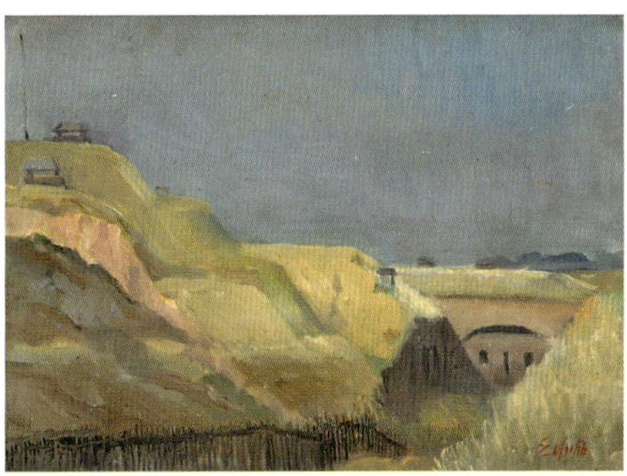

Martin, Edwin active 1913–1938
The 'Black Hole', Lille, (Fort Macdonald) 1918
oil on canvas 22.8 x 33
IWM ART 3760

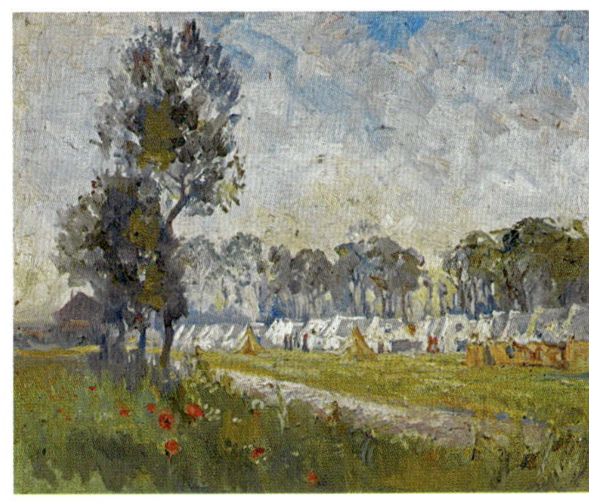

Martin, Edwin active 1913–1938
The Second Casualty Clearing Station, Douai
1919
oil on board 31.7 x 38.7
IWM ART 3662

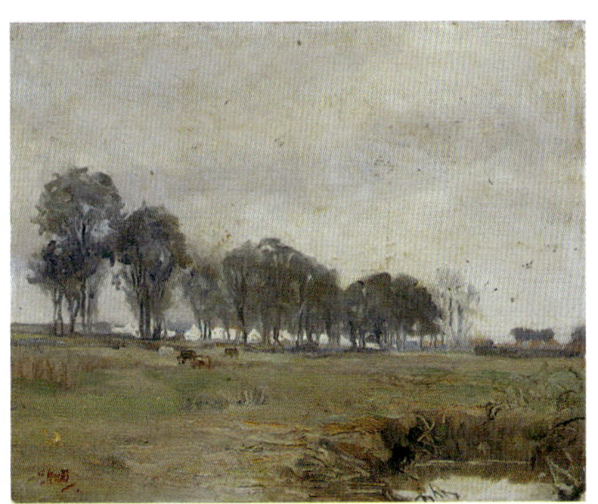

Martin, Edwin active 1913–1938
The Second Casualty Clearing Station, Douai
1919
oil on canvas 31.7 x 39.3
IWM ART 3741

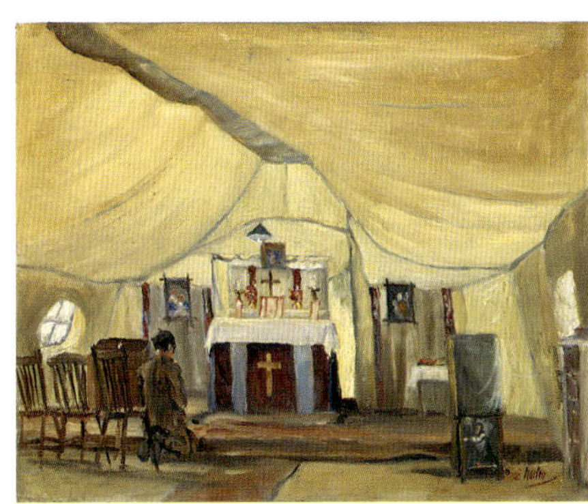

Martin, Edwin active 1913–1938
*Church of England Marquee: 39th Stationary
Hospital, Ascq* c.1919
oil on canvas 31.7 x 38.7
IWM ART 2771

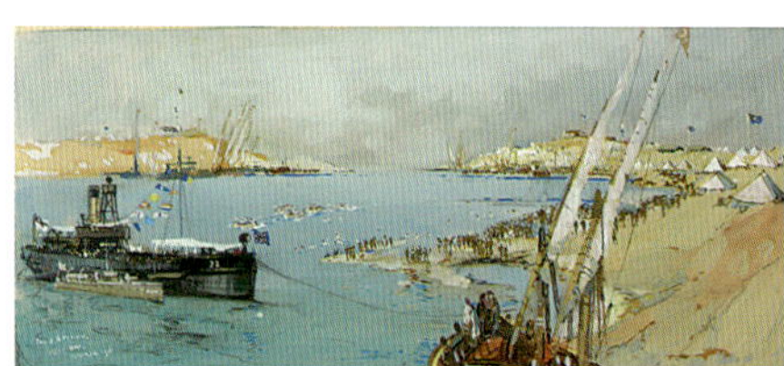

Mason, Frank Henry 1876–1965
Ferry Post, Ballah, Suez Canal: Anzac Day Celebrations, Carley Float Race, 'HM Hopper 32', Official Judge Ship 1916
tempera on paper 20.3 x 47.6
IWM ART 2840

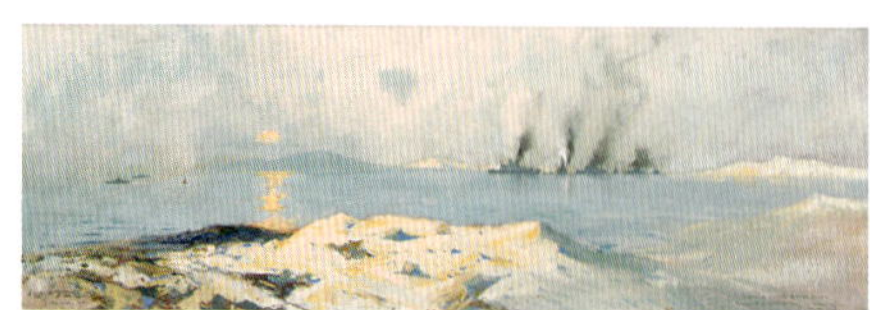

Mason, Frank Henry 1876–1965
Ismailia: Sunrise on the Bitter Lakes 1916
tempera on paper 24.1 x 73
IWM ART 2844

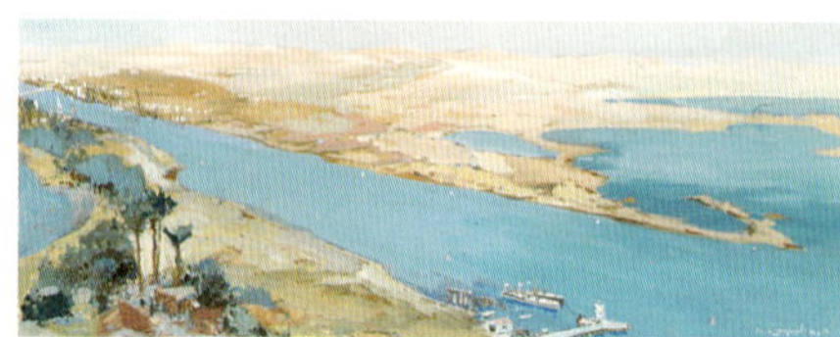

Mason, Frank Henry 1876–1965
Suez Canal, 28 April 1916: From the Crow's Nest of Deversoir Signal Station; Base Camp at Serapeum on the Extreme Left 1916
tempera on paper 21.5 x 55.8
IWM ART 2841

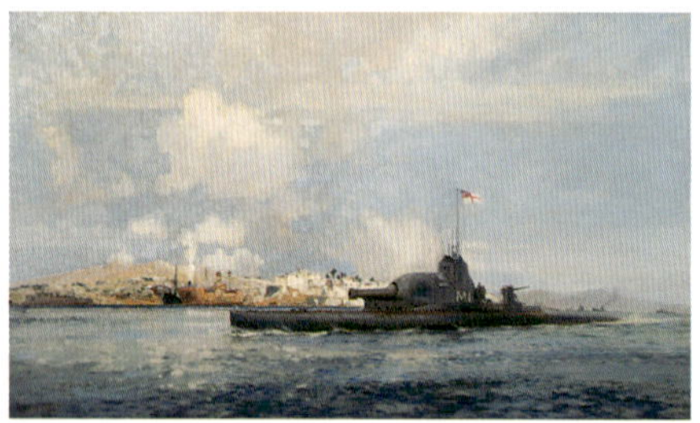

Mason, Frank Henry 1876–1965
'HM Submarine M1' off Sedd-el-Bahr: Salvage Operations in Progress on the Transport 'River Clyde' 1917–1919
oil on canvas 76.2 x 127
IWM ART 3065

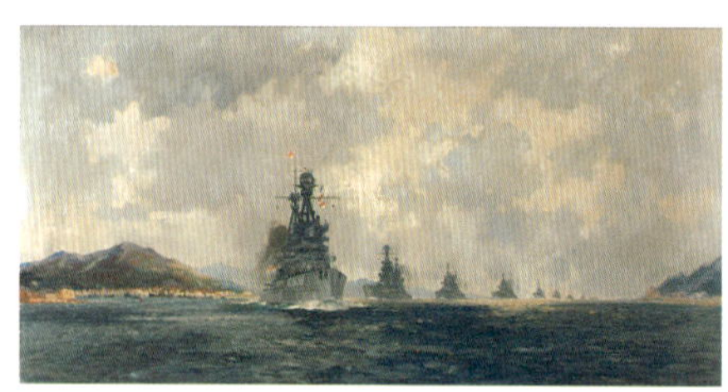

Mason, Frank Henry 1876–1965
'HMS Superb': Flagship of the Commander-in-Chief, Mediterranean, Leading the British Fleet to Constantinople, November 1918 1918
oil on canvas 90.8 x 182.8
IWM ART 2613

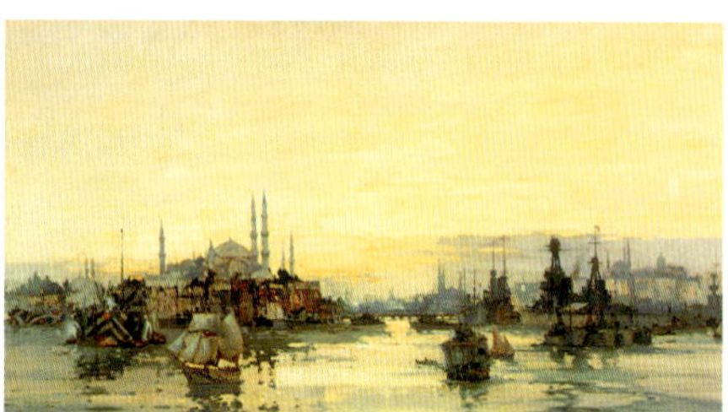

Mason, Frank Henry 1876–1965
The Allied Fleet and Shipping at Constantinople 1919
oil on canvas 75.6 x 152.4
IWM ART 2614

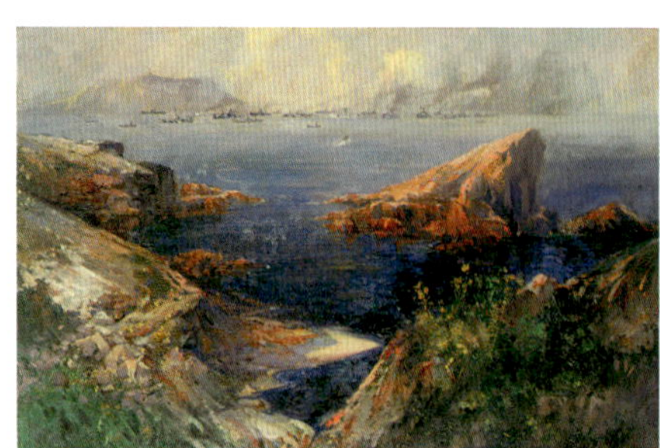

Mason, Frank Henry 1876–1965
The Mediterranean Convoy Passing through the South Comino Channel, Malta 1919
oil on canvas 50.8 x 76.2
IWM ART 2615

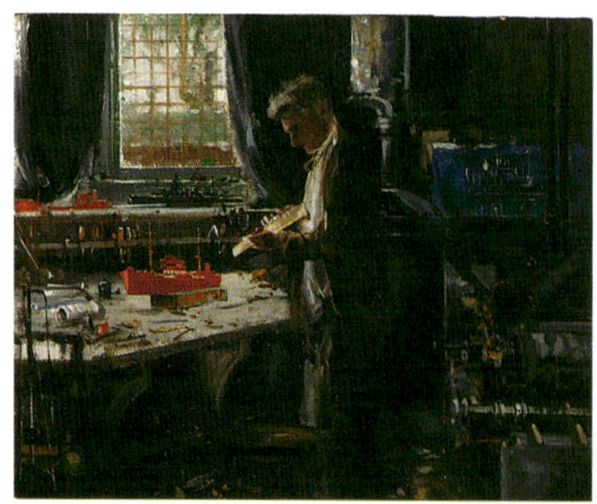

Mason, Frank Henry 1876–1965
The Model Maker's Shop: Directorate of Camouflage (Naval Section), Leamington Spa 1943
oil on panel 41.2 x 50.8
IWM ART LD 2755

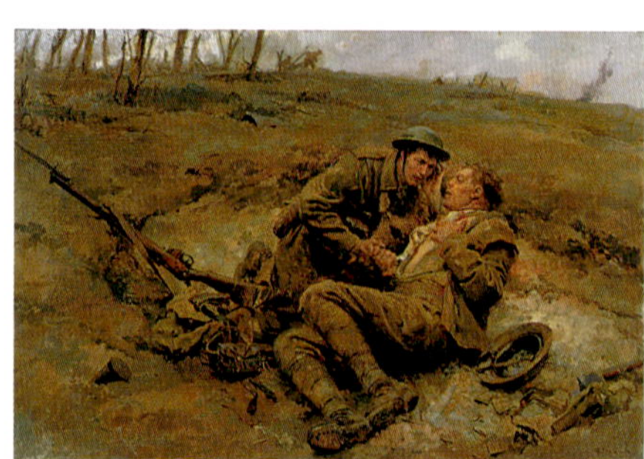

Matania, Fortunino 1881–1963
The Last Message 1917
oil on canvas 50.8 x 76.2
IWM ART 5192

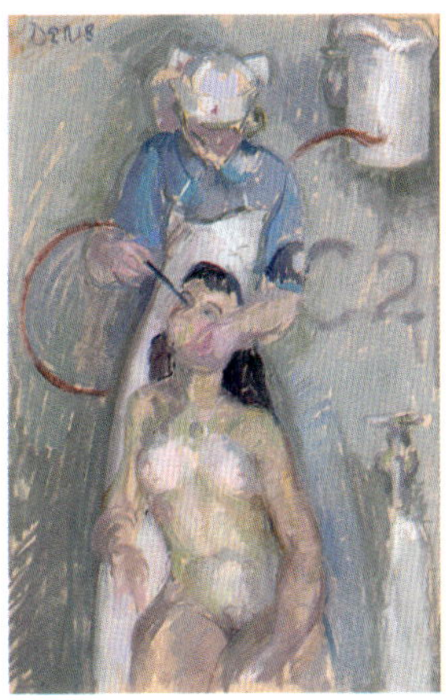

Mathews, Denis 1913–1997
*An Impression of a Gas Cleansing Exercise at a
First Aid Post: Eye Irritation*
tempera on paper 59 x 39.3
IWM ART LD 1966

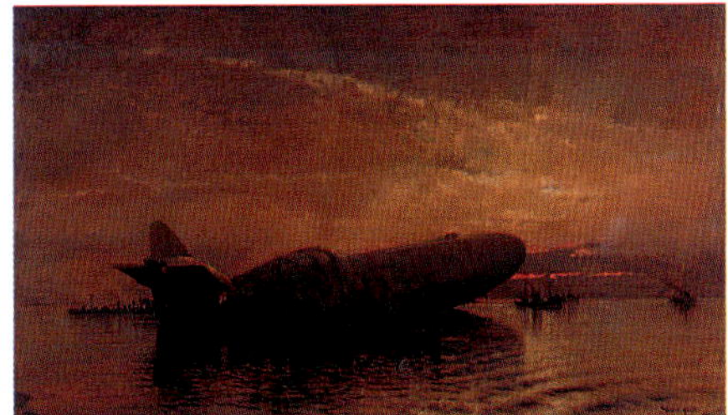

Maxwell, Donald 1877–1936
*St George and the Dragon: Zeppelin L15 in the
Thames, April 1916* 1916
oil on canvas 83 x 144.2
IWM ART 888

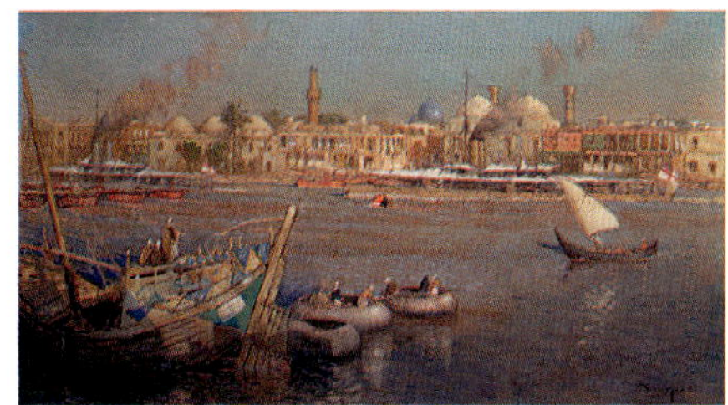

Maxwell, Donald 1877–1936
The Navy in Baghdad 1918
oil on canvas 78.7 x 142.2
IWM ART 1843

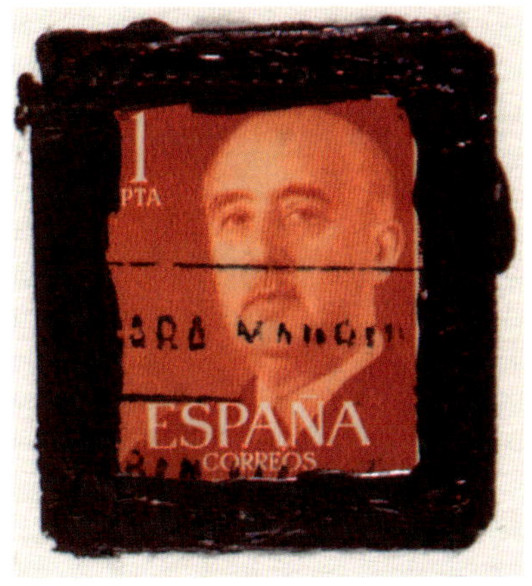

Mayen, Eric b.1953
Heroes of the XXth Century: Franco 1995
acrylic on paper & mixed media 30.4 x 21.5
IWM ART 16585 1

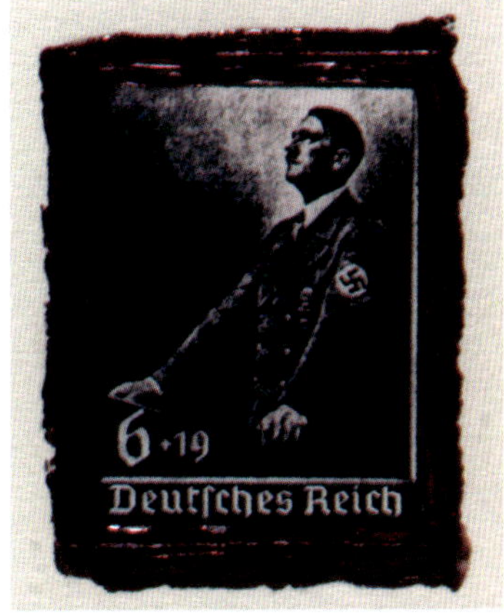

Mayen, Eric b.1953
Heroes of the XXth Century: Hitler 1995
acrylic on paper & mixed media 29.9 x 21.1
IWM ART 16585 4

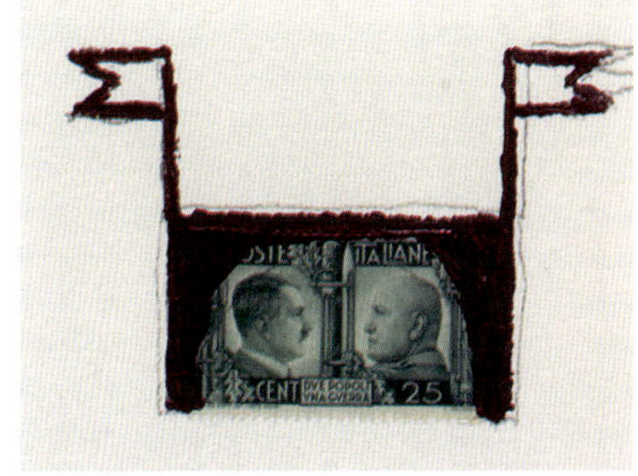

Mayen, Eric b.1953
*Heroes of the XXth Century: Hitler and
Mussolini* 1995
acrylic on paper & mixed media 30.1 x 41.9
IWM ART 16585 7

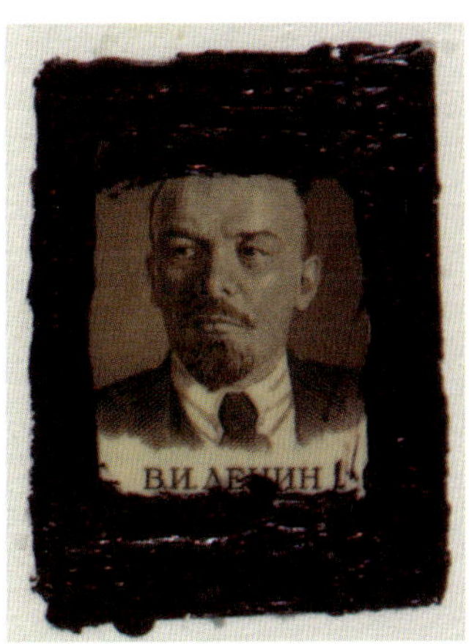

Mayen, Eric b.1953
Heroes of the XXth Century: Lenin 1995
acrylic on paper & mixed media 29.5 x 21.5
IWM ART 16585 3

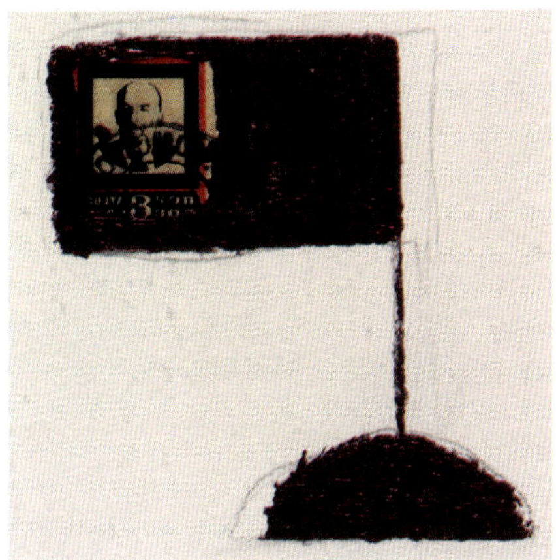

Mayen, Eric b.1953
Heroes of the XXth Century: Lenin 1995
acrylic on paper & mixed media 21.3 x 30.4
IWM ART 16585 6

Mayen, Eric b.1953
Heroes of the XXth Century: Petain 1995
acrylic on paper & mixed media 30.1 x 21.1
IWM ART 16585 5

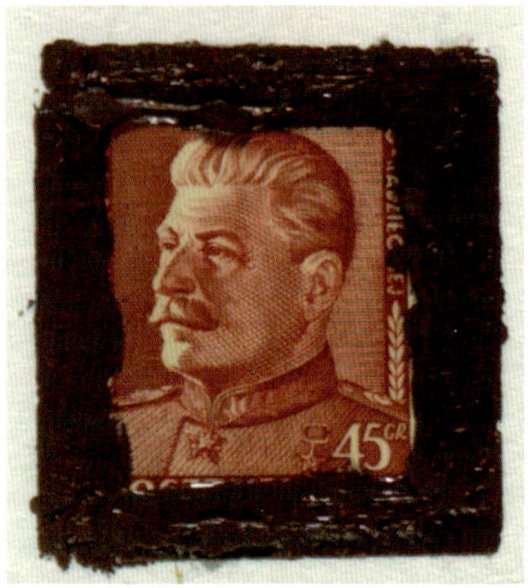

Mayen, Eric b.1953
Heroes of the XXth Century: Stalin 1995
acrylic on paper & mixed media 30.3 x 21.4
IWM ART 16585 2

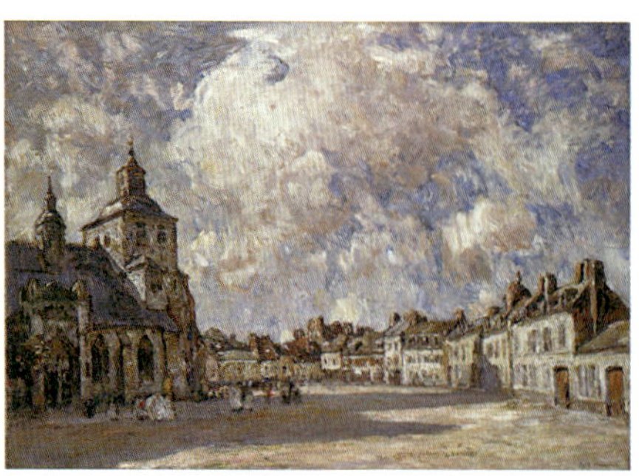

Mayor, Fred 1865–1916
Montreuil c.1913
oil on canvas 111.7 x 162.5
IWM ART 5541

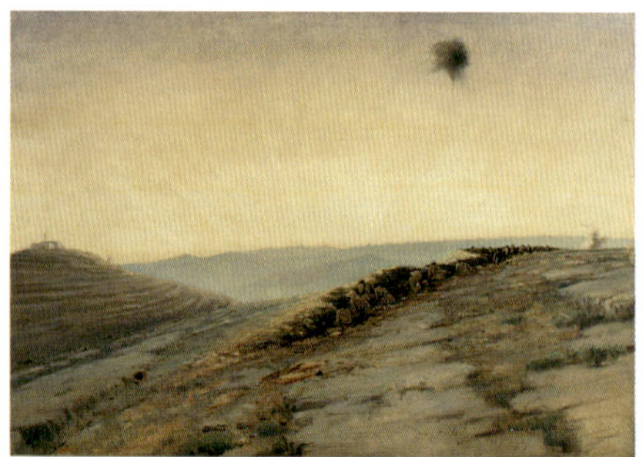

McBey, James 1883–1959
Nebi Samwil: The First Sight of Jerusalem
1917–1919
oil on canvas 106.6 x 152.4
IWM ART 2600

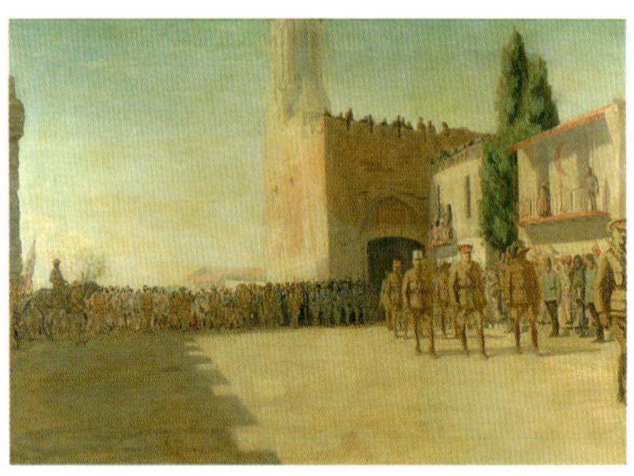

McBey, James 1883–1959
*The Allies Entering Jerusalem, 11 December
1917: General Allenby with Colonel de Piépape
Commanding the French (…)* 1917–1919
oil on canvas 106.6 x 152.4
IWM ART 2599

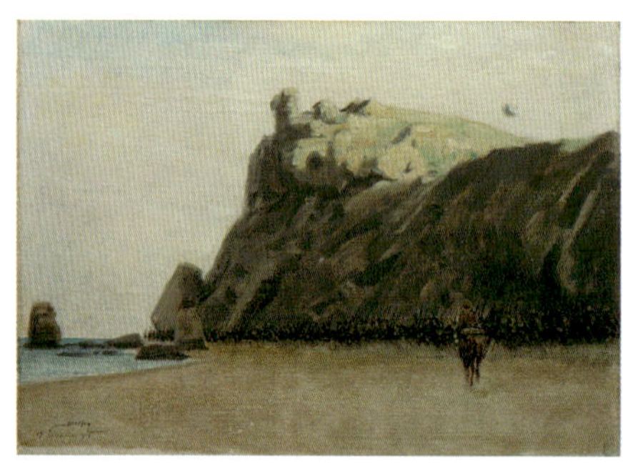

McBey, James 1883–1959
*Arsuf: The Cavalry Dash along the Sea Coast
on the Morning of 19 September 1918* 1918
oil on canvas 42.5 x 60.3
IWM ART 2511

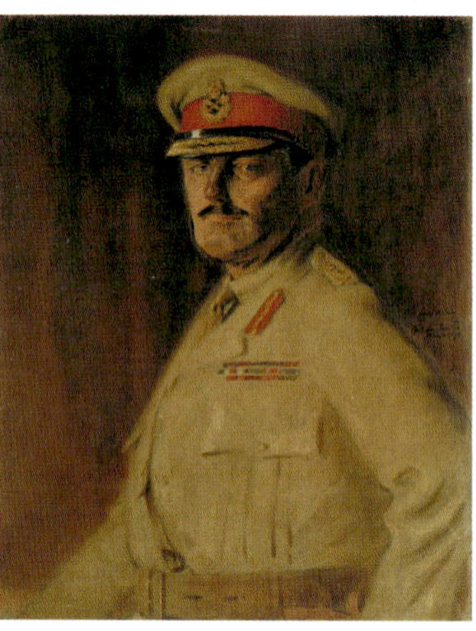

McBey, James 1883–1959
*General Sir Edmund Allenby (1861–1936),
KCB* 1918
oil on canvas 83.8 x 65.4
IWM ART 1553

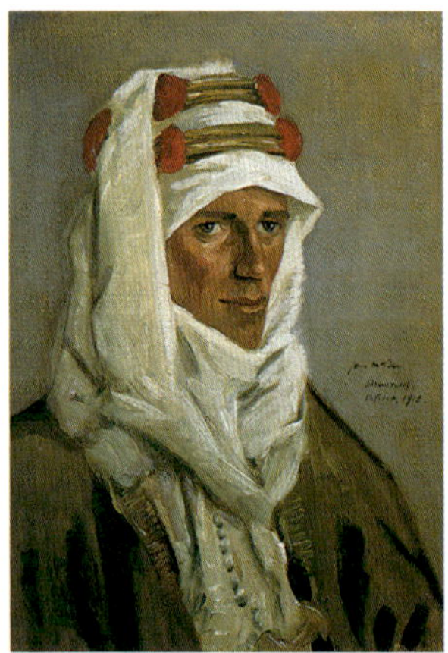

McBey, James 1883–1959
*Lieutenant Colonel T. E. Lawrence
(1888–1935), CB, DSO* 1918
oil on canvas 53.3 x 38.1
IWM ART 2473

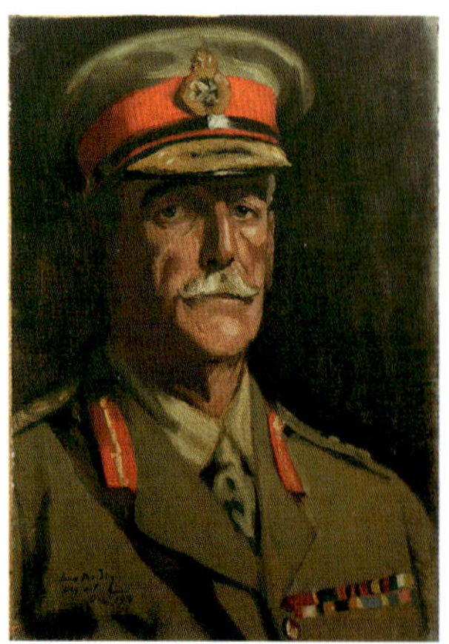

McBey, James 1883–1959
*Lieutenant General Sir Edward S. Bulfin
(1862–1939), KCB, CVO* 1918
oil on canvas 53.3 x 38.1
IWM ART 2472

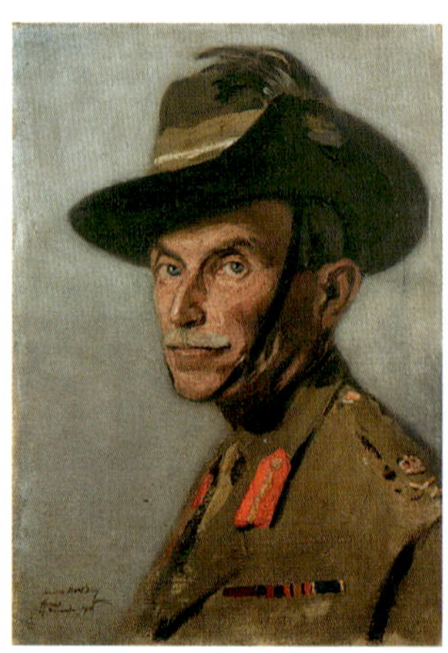

McBey, James 1883–1959
*Lieutenant General Sir Henry George Chauvel
(1865–1945), KCB, KCMG* 1918
oil on canvas 53.3 x 38.1
IWM ART 2471

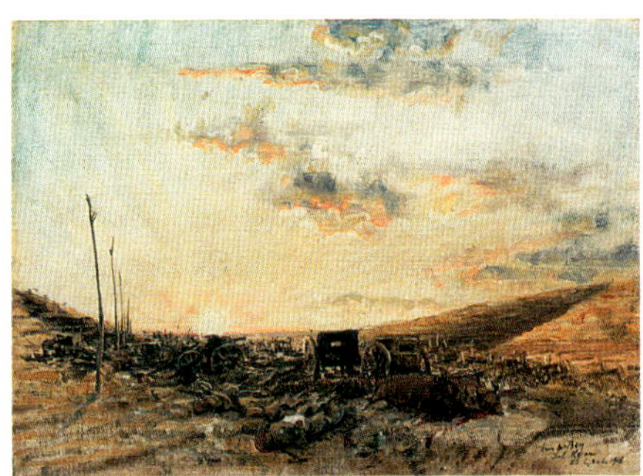

McBey, James 1883–1959
*Tul Keram: A Retreating Turkish Column
Bombed and Machine-Gunned by Airmen in
the Defile at Tul Keram, (…)* 1918
oil on canvas 42.5 x 60.3
IWM ART 2510

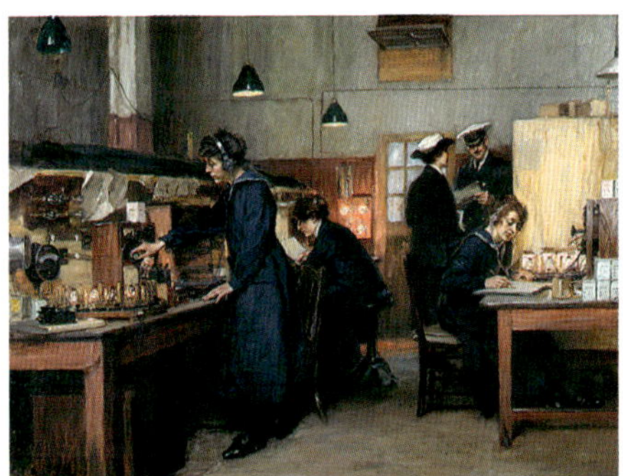

McCormick, Arthur David 1860–1943
*Valve Testing: The Signal School, Royal Navy
Barracks, Portsmouth* 1919
oil on canvas 76.2 x 101.9
IWM ART 2620

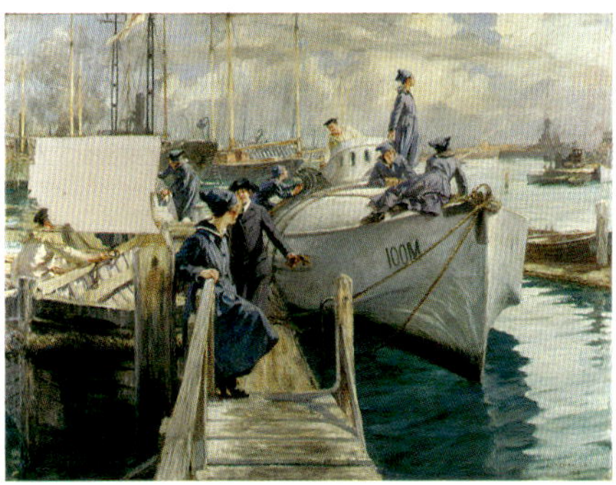

McCormick, Arthur David 1860–1943
*Women's Royal Naval Service Officer and
Ratings: Boat Cleaning at the Coastal Motor
Boat Base, Haslar Creek, Portsmouth* 1919
oil on canvas 152.4 x 203.2
IWM ART 2619

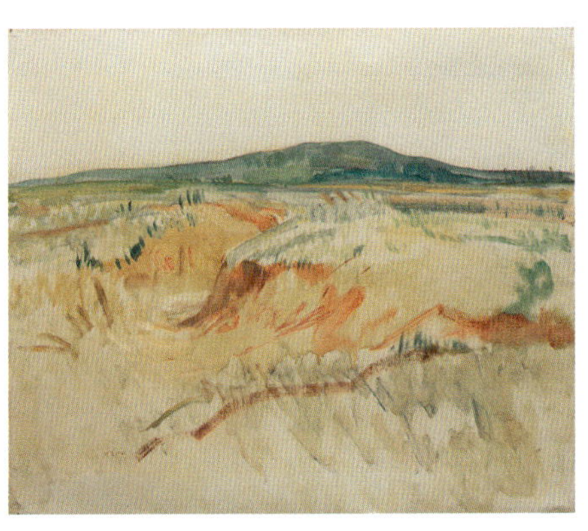

McEvoy, Ambrose 1878–1927
Bourlon Wood, Somme 1918
oil on canvas 63.5 x 76.2
IWM ART 1338

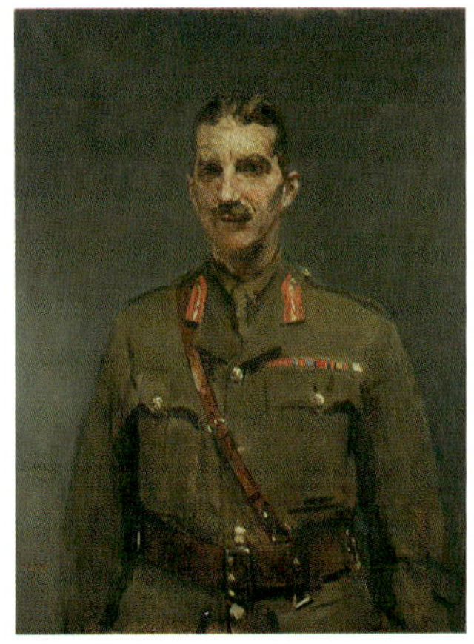

McEvoy, Ambrose 1878–1927
*Brigadier General A. R. H. Hutchinson, CB,
CMG, DSO, Assistant Adjutant General, Royal
Marines* 1918
oil on canvas 101.9 x 76.2
IWM ART 1344

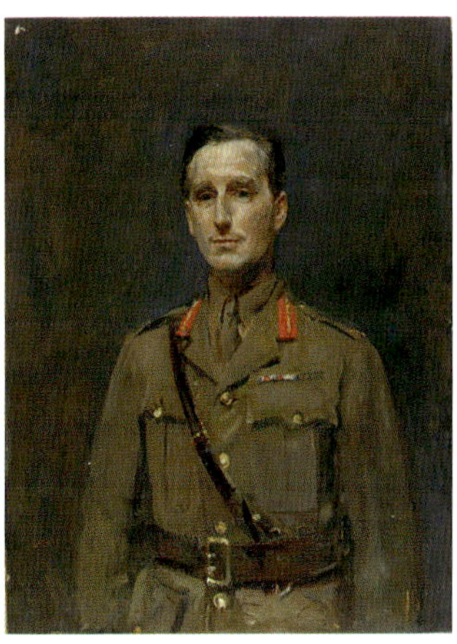

McEvoy, Ambrose 1878–1927
Brigadier General Arthur M. Asquith, DSO
1918
oil on canvas 101.9 x 76.2
IWM ART 1339

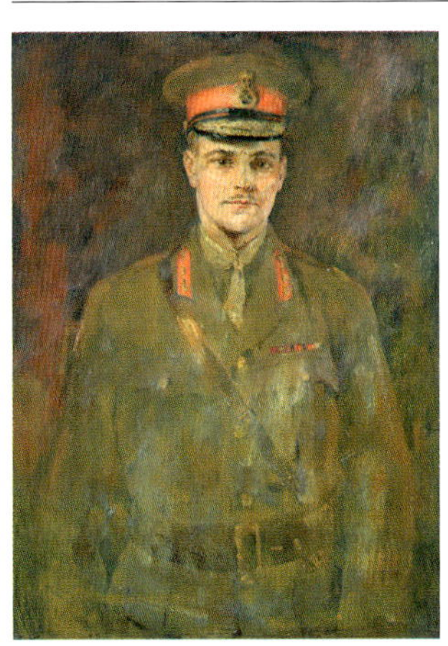

McEvoy, Ambrose 1878–1927
*Brigadier General Bernard Cyril Freyberg
(1889–1963), VC, DSO* 1918
oil on canvas 101.9 x 76.2
IWM ART 1326

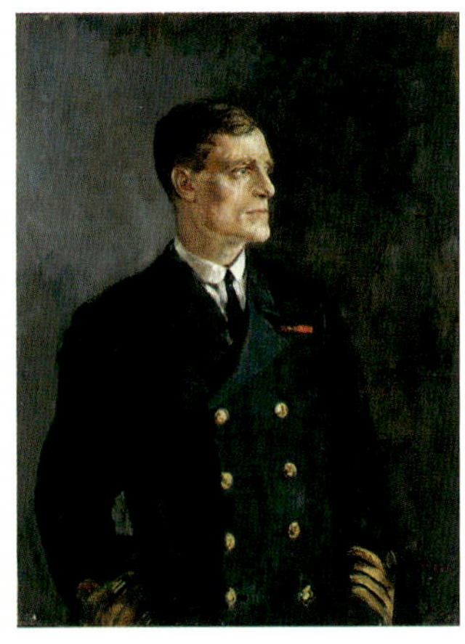

McEvoy, Ambrose 1878–1927
Captain Martin Eric Nasmith, VC, Royal Navy
1918
oil on canvas 101.9 x 76.2
IWM ART 1335

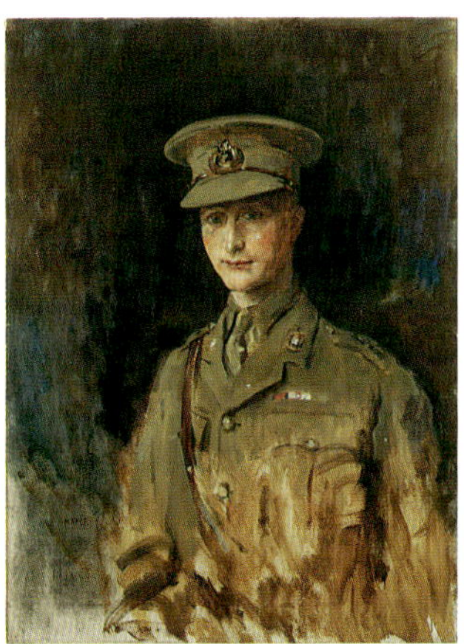

McEvoy, Ambrose 1878–1927
*Commander Daniel Marcus William Beak
(1891–1967), VC, DSO, MC, RNVR* 1918
oil on canvas 101.9 x 76.2
IWM ART 1331

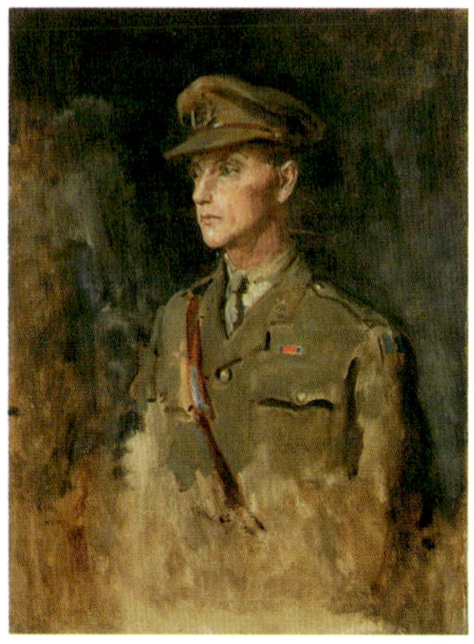

McEvoy, Ambrose 1878–1927
*Commander W. M. Le C. Egerton, DS, Royal
Naval Volunteer Reserve* 1918
oil on canvas 101.9 x 76.2
IWM ART 1341

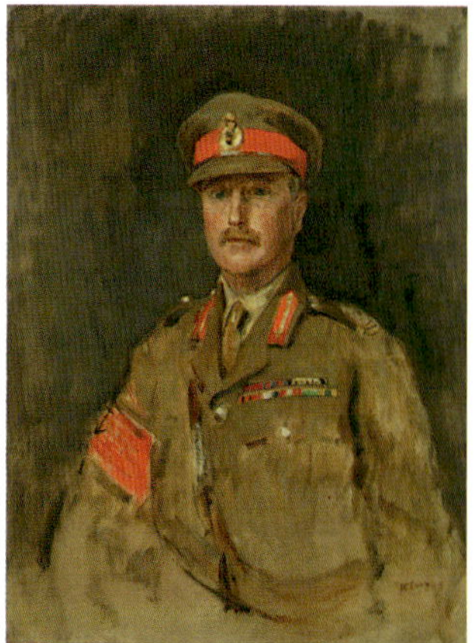

McEvoy, Ambrose 1878–1927
Major General C. E. Lawrie, CB, CMG, DSO
1918
oil on canvas 101.9 x 76.2
IWM ART 1345

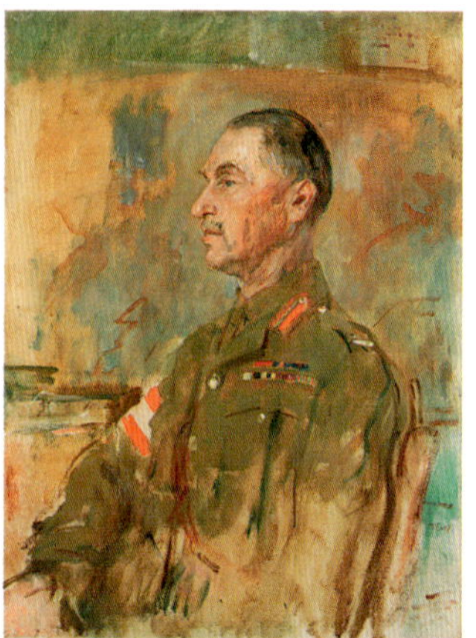

McEvoy, Ambrose 1878–1927
Major General Sir C. D. Shute, KCB, CMG
1918
oil on canvas 101.9 x 76.2
IWM ART 1340

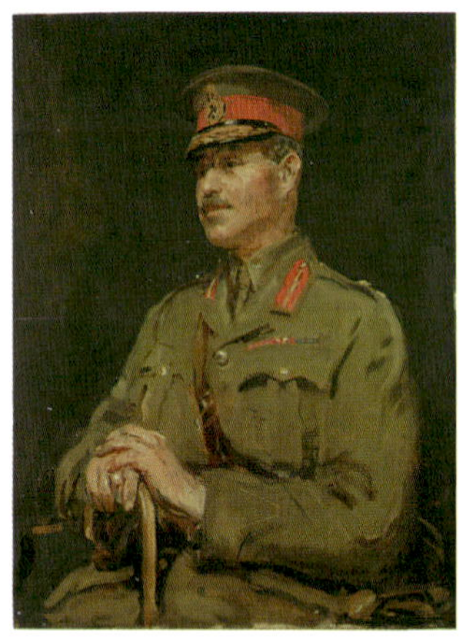

McEvoy, Ambrose 1878–1927
*Major General Sir David Mercer, KCB,
Adjutant General, Royal Marine Forces
(1916–1920)* 1918
oil on canvas 101.9 x 76.2
IWM ART 1336

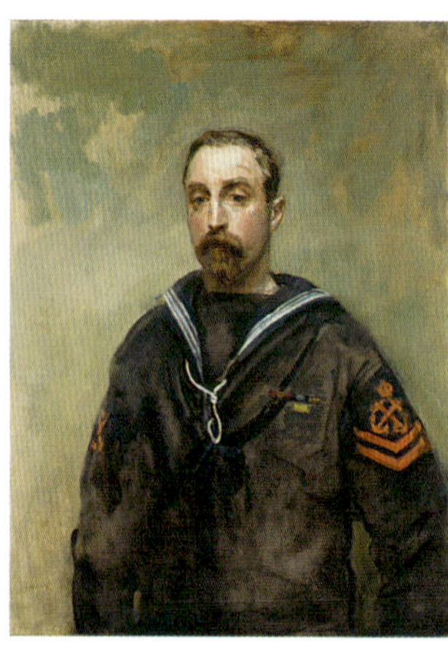

McEvoy, Ambrose 1878–1927
Petty Officer E. Pitcher, VC 1918
oil on canvas 101.9 x 76.2
IWM ART 1327

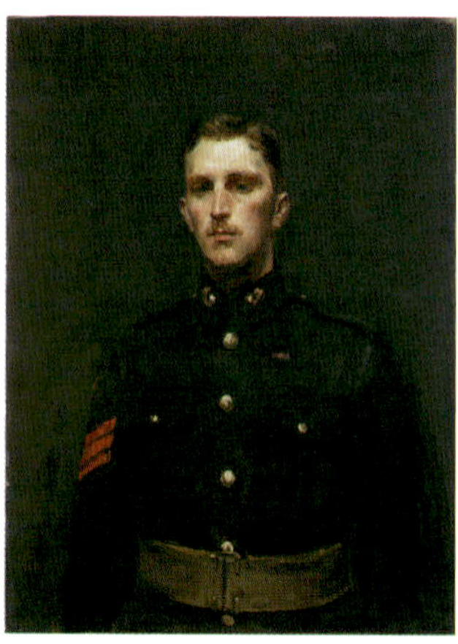

McEvoy, Ambrose 1878–1927
*Sergeant Norman Augustus Finch
(1890–1966), VC, Royal Marine Artillery* 1918
oil on canvas 101.9 x 76.2
IWM ART 1332

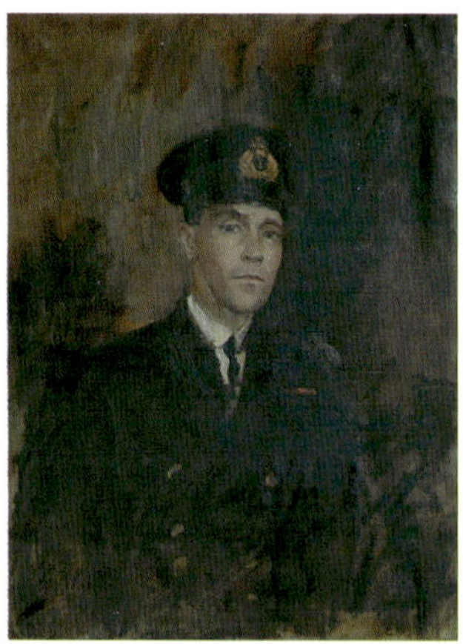

McEvoy, Ambrose 1878–1927
*The Late Lieutenant Richard D. Sandford, VC,
Royal Navy* 1918
oil on canvas 101.9 x 76.2
IWM ART 1330

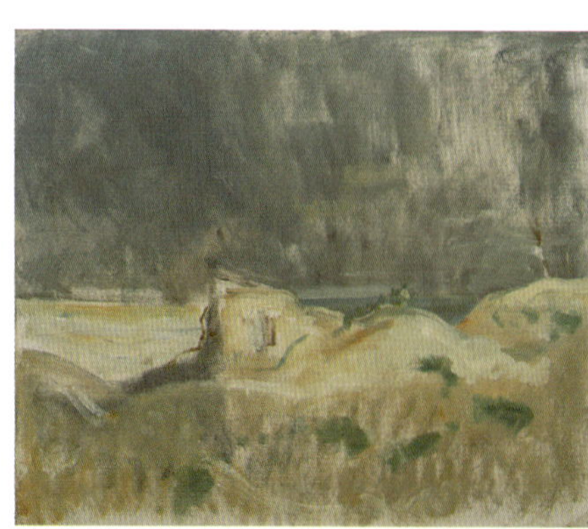

McEvoy, Ambrose 1878–1927
*A Pillbox in the Hindenburg Line near
Fontaine-les-Croisilles, Captured by the Royal
Naval Division* c.1918
oil on canvas 63.5 x 76.2
IWM ART 1334

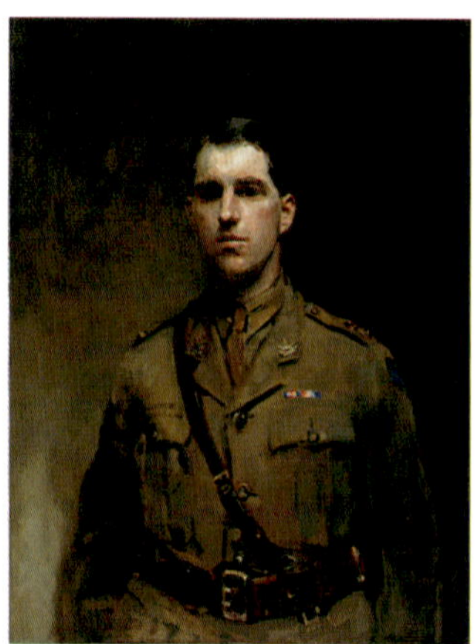

McEvoy, Ambrose 1878–1927
*Commander A. W. Buckle, DSO, Royal Naval
Volunteer Reserve* 1919
oil on canvas 101.9 x 76.2
IWM ART 2693

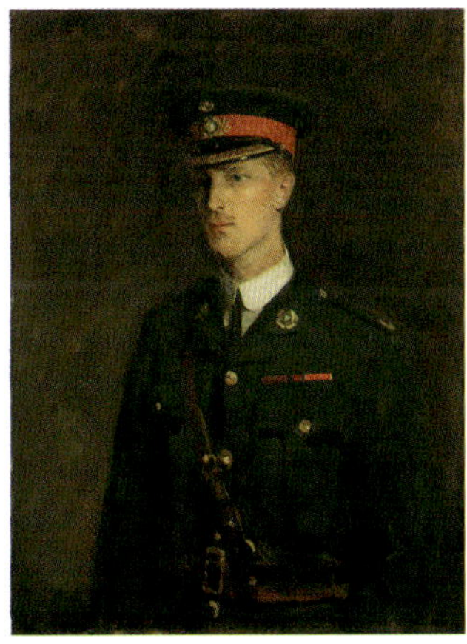

McEvoy, Ambrose 1878–1927
*Major Edward Bamford, VC, DSO, Royal
Marines* 1919
oil on canvas 101.9 x 76.2
IWM ART 2748

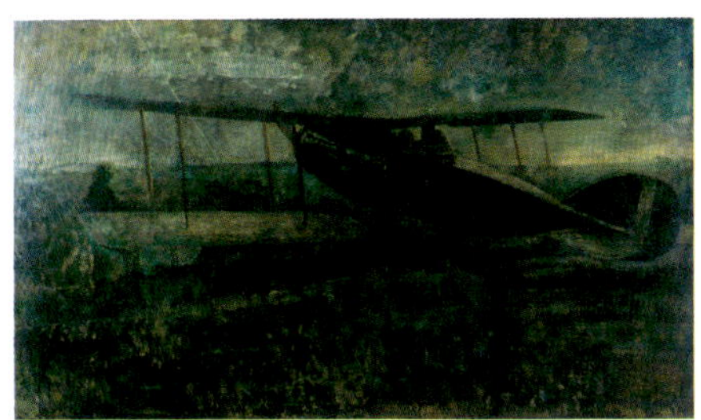

McEvoy, Ambrose 1878–1927
Night Flying 1937
oil on canvas 182.8 x 317.5
IWM ART 5016

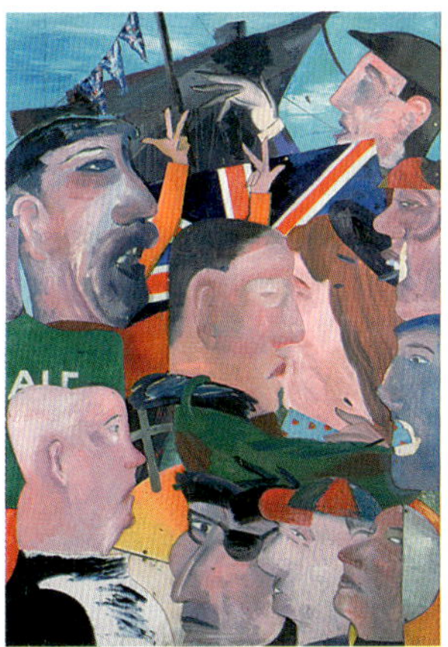

McFadyen, Jock b.1950
'With singing hearts and throaty roarings…'
1983
oil on card & collage 178 x 118
IWM ART 16248

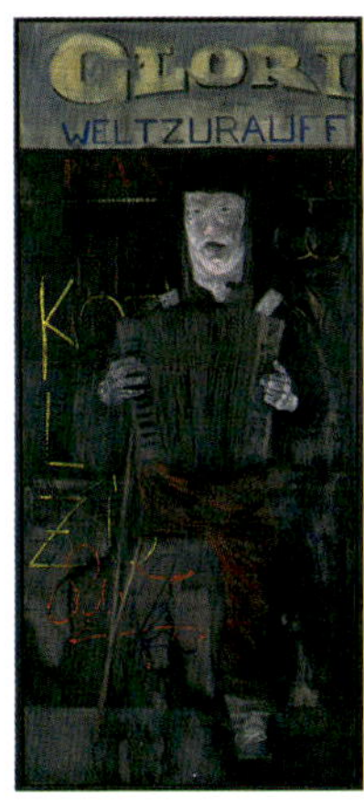

McFadyen, Jock b.1950
Kurfürstendamm 1991
oil on canvas 203.5 x 91.5
IWM ART 16418

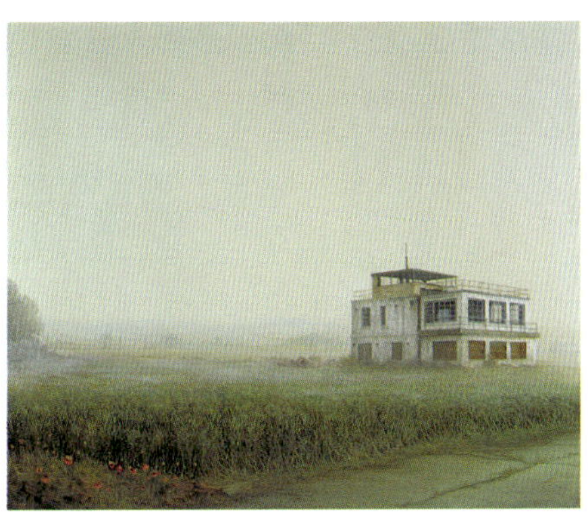

McGill, Ronald William b.1930
After the Battle at RAF Tangmere, Sussex 1980
oil on canvas 50.5 x 61
IWM ART 15519

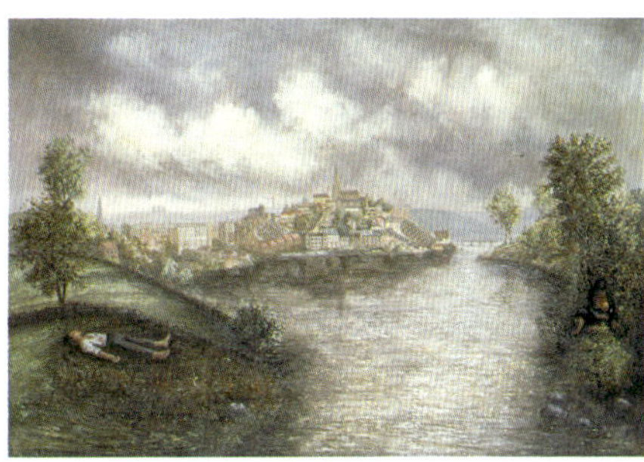

McKenna, Stephen b.1939
City of Derry I 1982
oil on canvas 120 x 180
IWM ART 16097 1

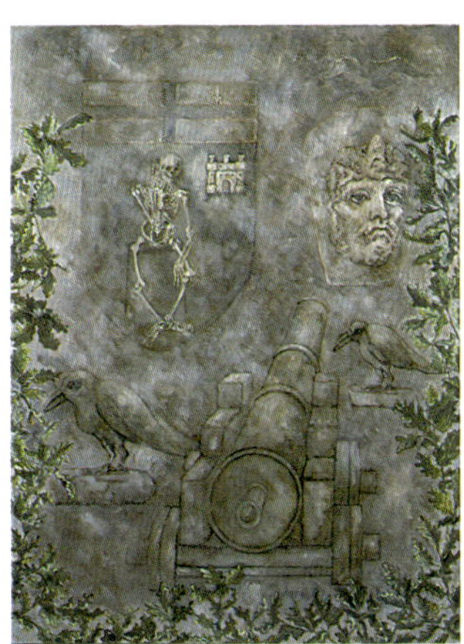

McKenna, Stephen b.1939
City of Derry II 1982
oil on canvas 160 x 120
IWM ART 16097 2

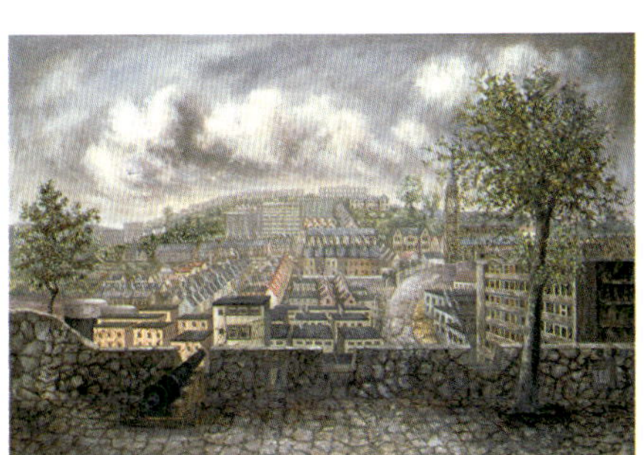

McKenna, Stephen b.1939
City of Derry III 1982
oil on canvas 120 x 180
IWM ART 16097 3

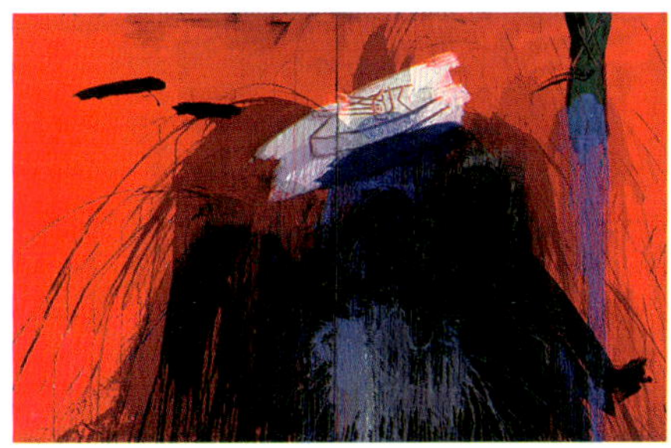

McLean, Bruce b.1944
Broadside 1985
acrylic on canvas 213 x 334
IWM ART 16395

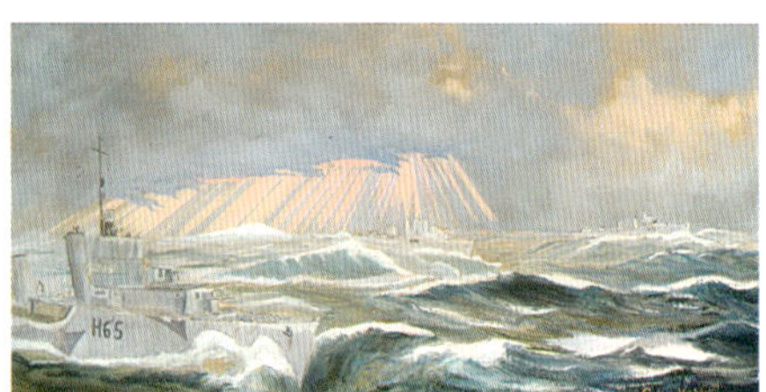

McMillan, Colin active 1940s–1970s
*HMS Ships 'Beagle', 'Boadicea' and 'Bulldog'
off Bear Island* 1943
oil on canvas 51.2 x 101.8
IWM ART 16598 a

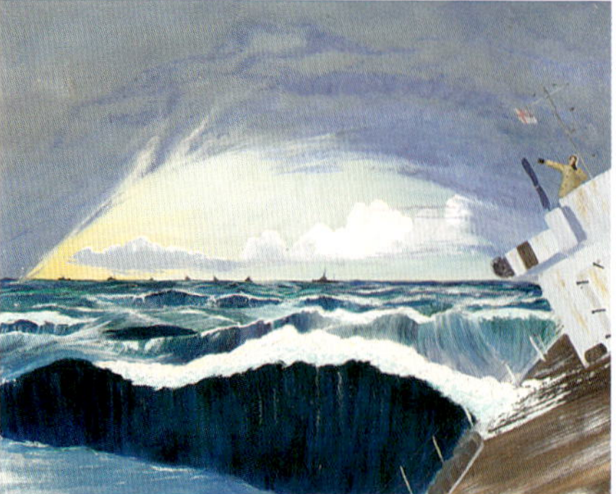

McMillan, Colin active 1940s–1970s
Convoy JW 55a to Russia c.1943
oil on canvas 61 x 75.8
IWM ART 16598 b

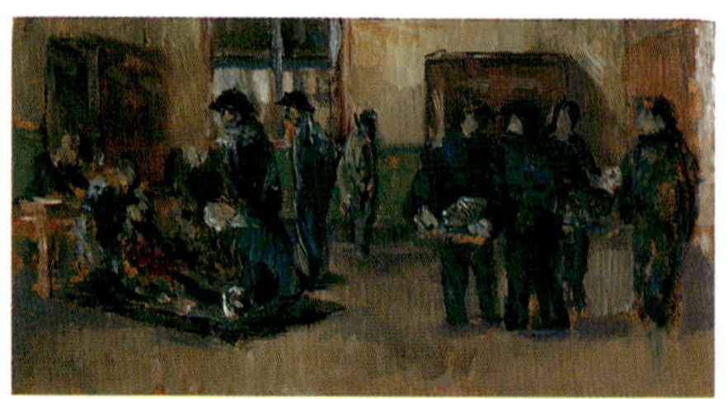

Medley, Robert 1905–1994
*A St John's Ambulance Examination in
Progress* 1940
oil on panel 20.6 x 38.7
IWM ART LD 83

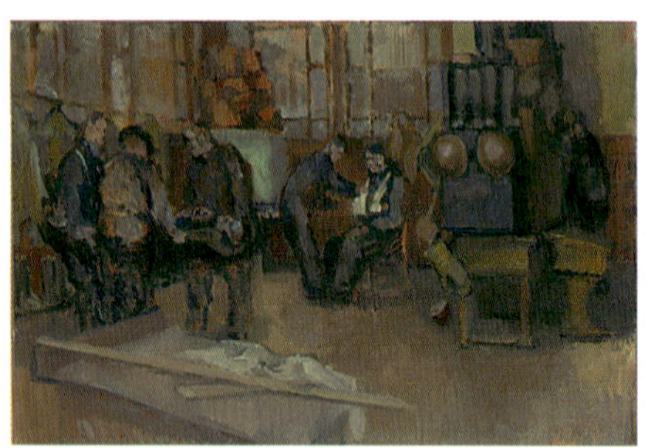

Medley, Robert 1905–1994
First Aid Practice 1940
oil on board 35.5 x 53.3
IWM ART LD 81

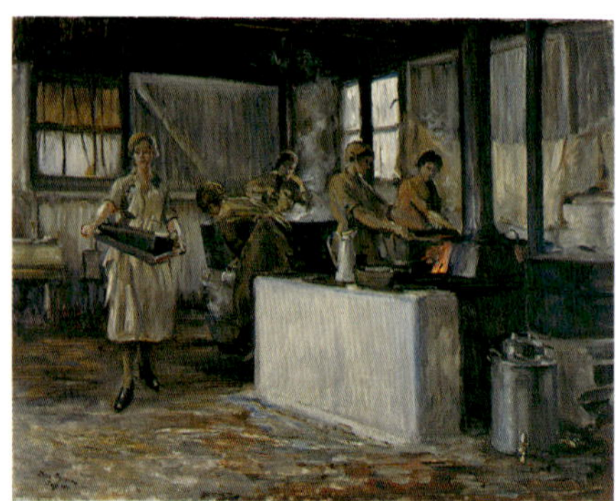

Meeson, Dora 1869–1955
*Members of the Queen Mary's Army Auxiliary
Corps: At Work in the Cookhouse, Royal Air
Force Camp, Charlton Park* 1919
oil on canvas 71.1 x 91.4
IWM ART 2658

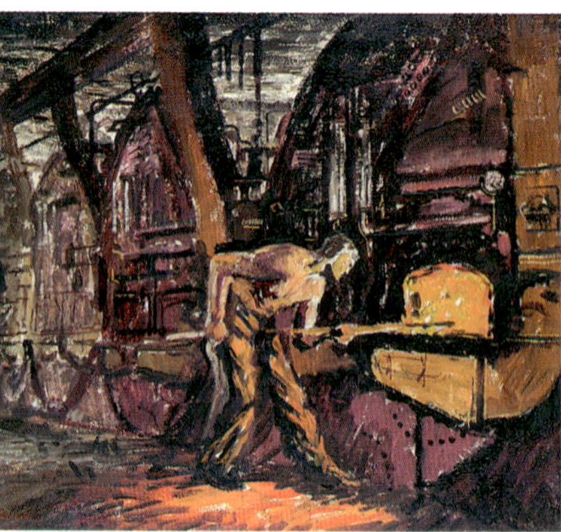

Melhuish, George 1916–1985
Turbine Furnaces 1943
oil on canvas 91.4 x 101.9
IWM ART LD 3636

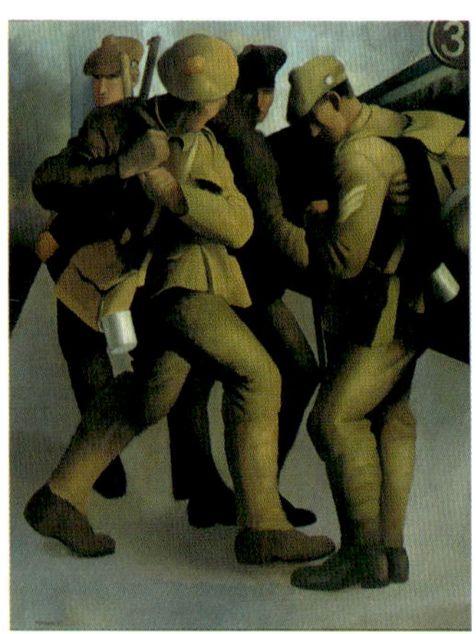

Meninsky, Bernard 1891–1950
On the Departure Platform, Victoria Station
1918
oil on canvas 91.4 x 71.1
IWM ART 1188

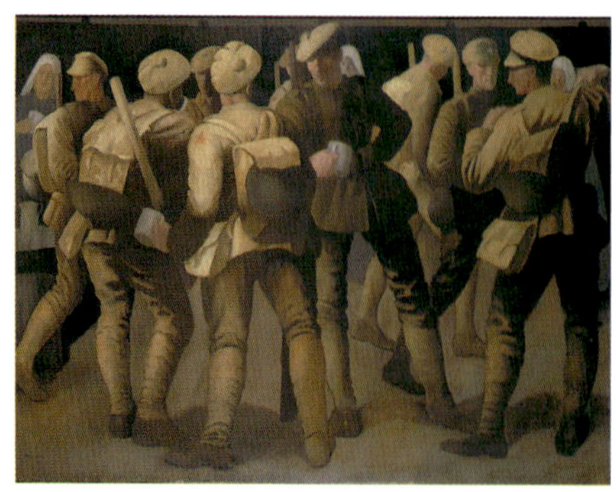

Meninsky, Bernard 1891–1950
The Arrival 1918
oil on canvas 76.2 x 101.9
IWM ART 1186

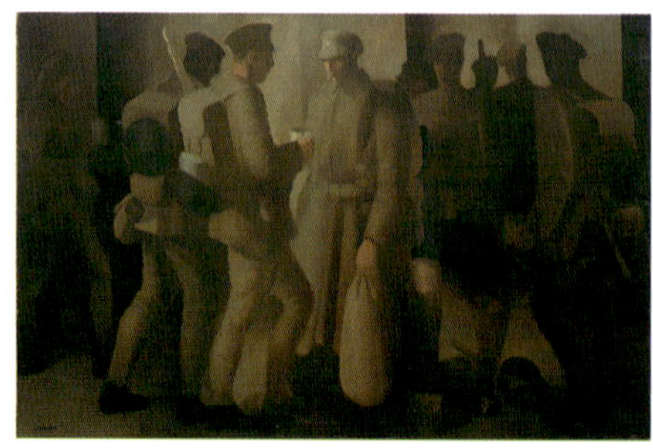

Meninsky, Bernard 1891–1950
The Platform Canteen, Victoria Station 1918
oil on canvas 50.8 x 76.2
IWM ART 1184

Facing page: Piper, John, 1903–1992, *The Passage to the Control Room at South-West Regional Headquarters, Bristol* (detail), 1940, (p. 189)

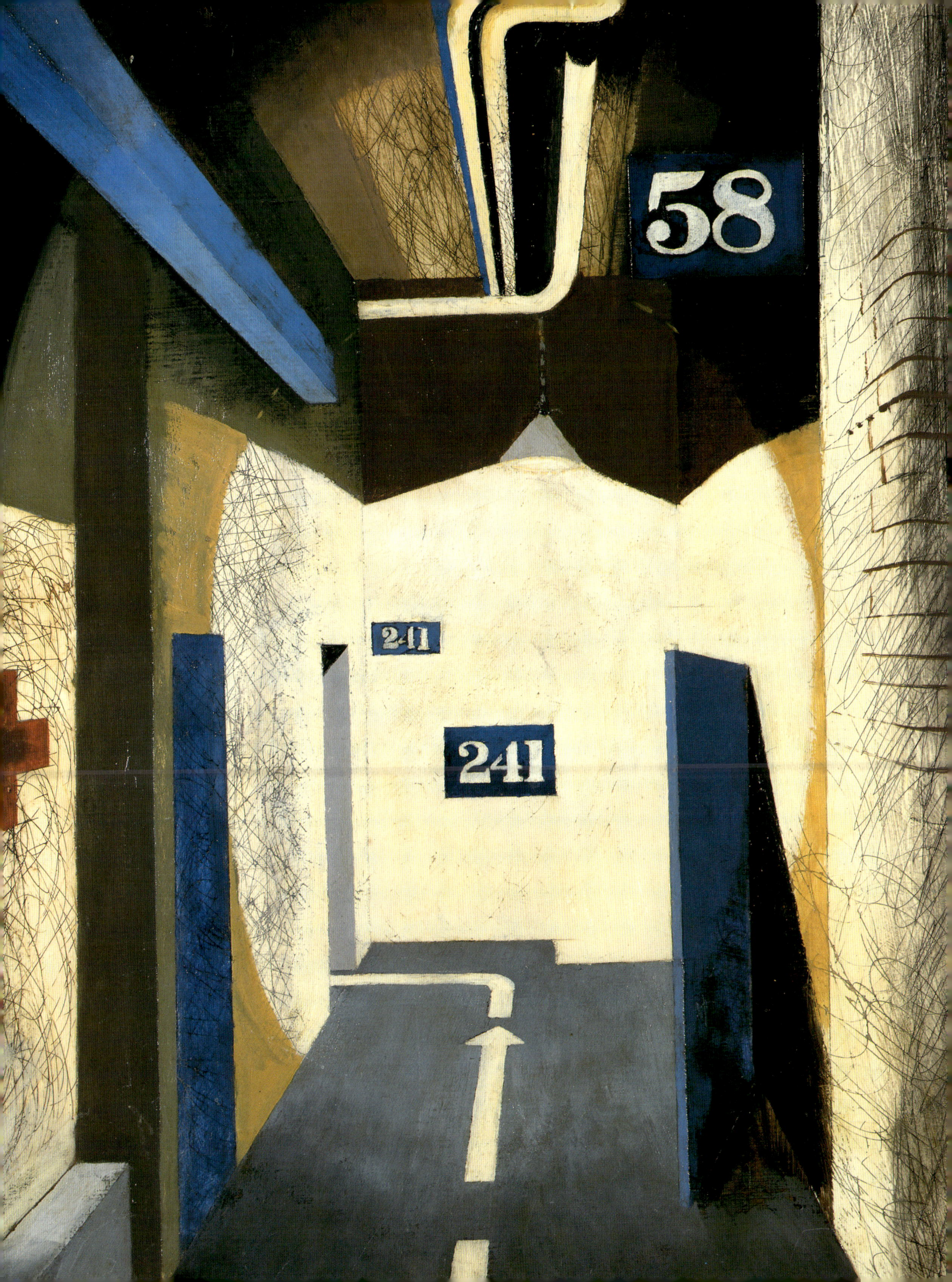

58
241
241

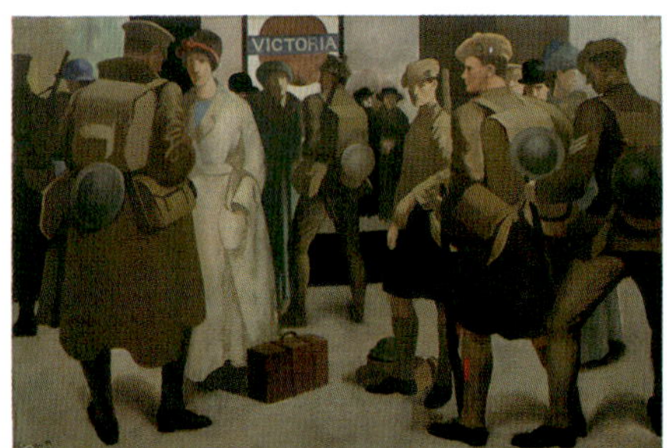

Meninsky, Bernard 1891–1950
Victoria Station, District Railway 1918
oil on canvas 50.8 x 76.5
IWM ART 1185

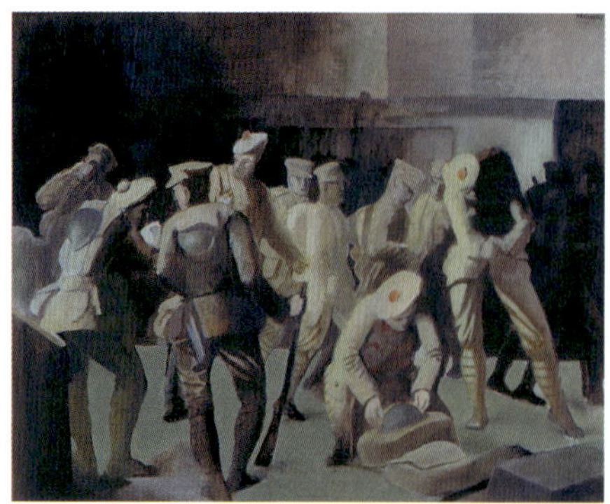

Meninsky, Bernard 1891–1950
Sketch of Soldiers Arriving on Leave c.1918
oil on paper 42.5 x 53.3
IWM ART 1187

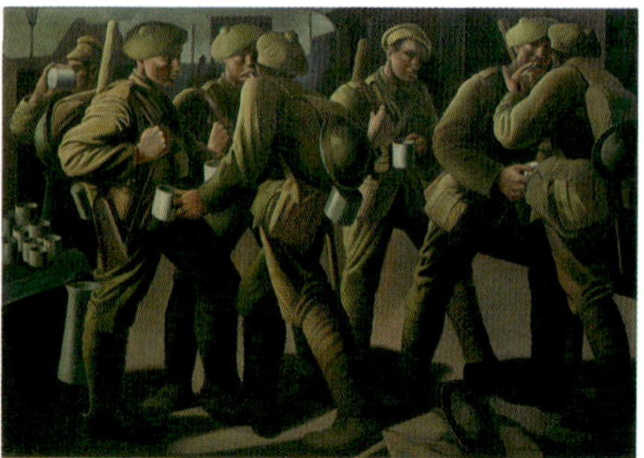

Meninsky, Bernard 1891–1950
The Arrival of a Leave Train, Victoria Station, 1918 1919
oil on canvas 106.6 x 152.4
IWM ART 2241

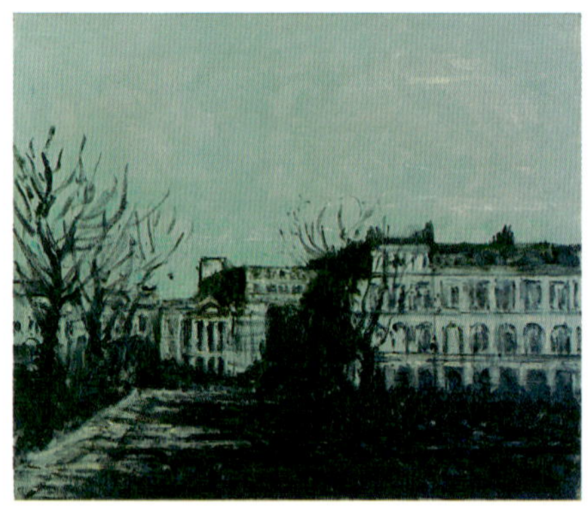

Methuen, Paul Ayshford 1886–1974
London by Moonlight 1940
oil on canvas 50.8 x 60.9
IWM ART LD 622

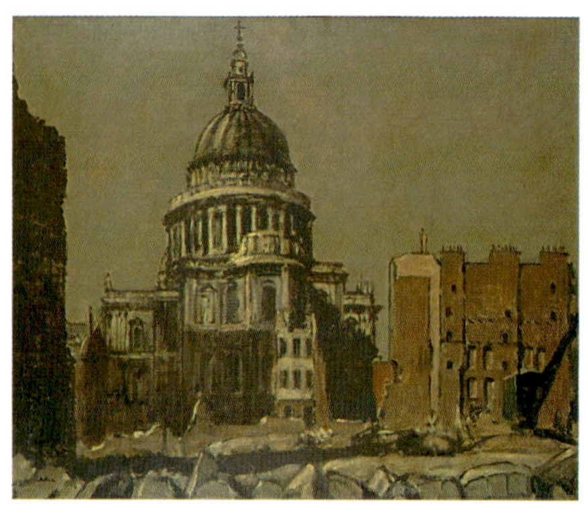

Methuen, Paul Ayshford 1886–1974
St Paul's by Moonlight 1941
oil on canvas 63.5 x 76.2
IWM ART LD 5860

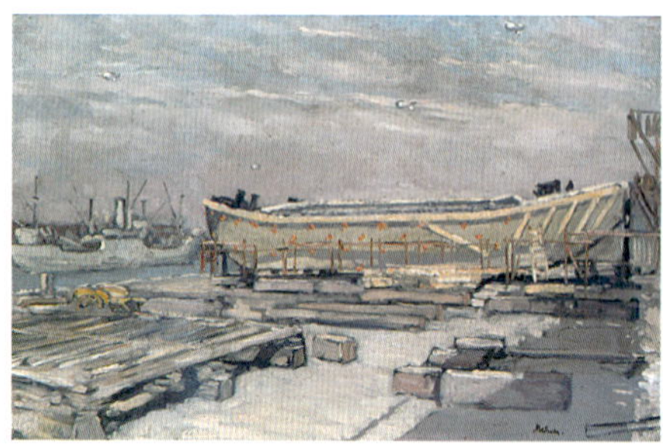

Methuen, Paul Ayshford 1886–1974
Invasion Craft Being Built in the West India Docks, 30 May 1944 1944
oil on canvas 50.1 x 75.7
IWM ART LD 5933

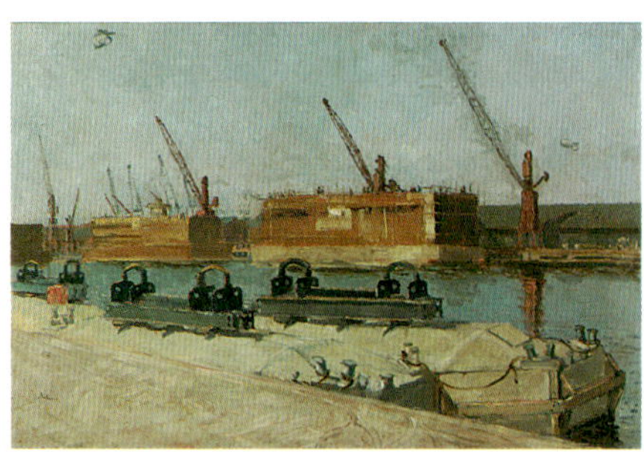

Methuen, Paul Ayshford 1886–1974
Invasion Craft in the West India Docks, April 1944 1944
oil on canvas 63.5 x 99
IWM ART LD 4044

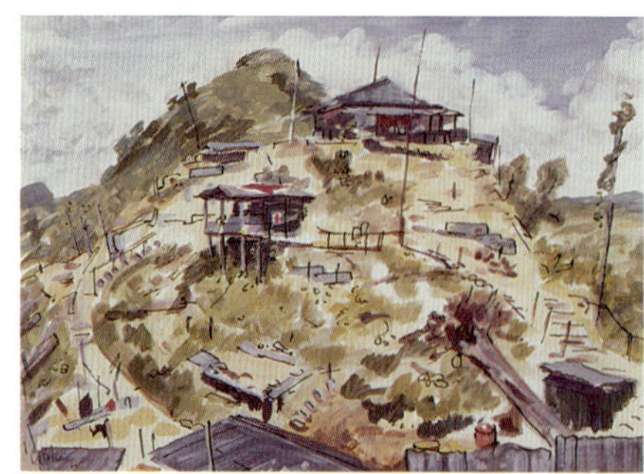

Miers, Christopher b.1941
A Regimental Aid Post near Gumbang, Borneo 1964
tempera on paper 27.9 x 38.1
IWM ART MW(A) 8

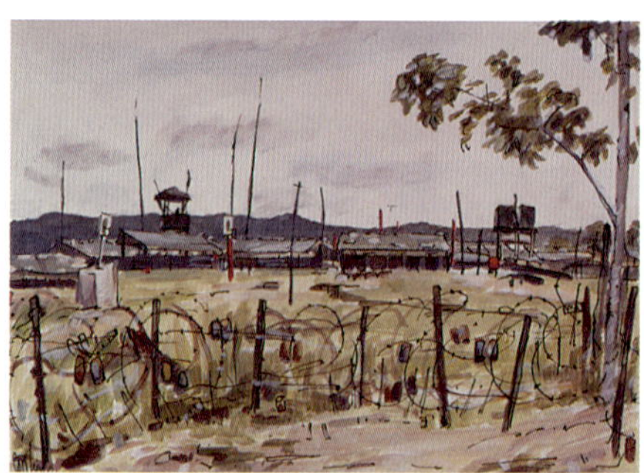

Miers, Christopher b.1941
Camp Area near Stass, Borneo 1964
tempera on paper 26.6 x 38.1
IWM ART MW(A) 9

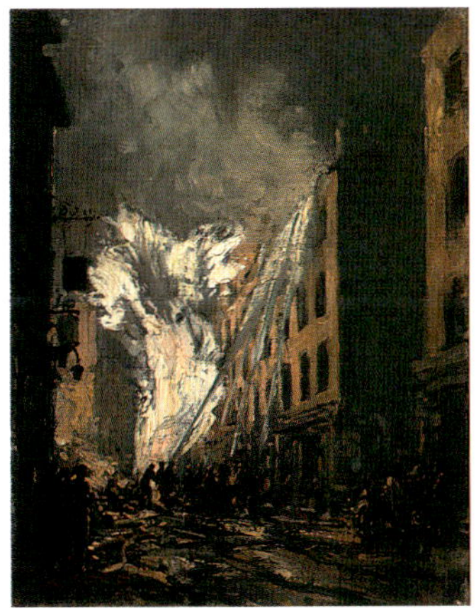

Mills, Reginald b.1896
*A Blazing Gas Main in Old Compton Street,
London W1* 1944
oil on canvas 40.6 x 31.7
IWM ART LD 4038

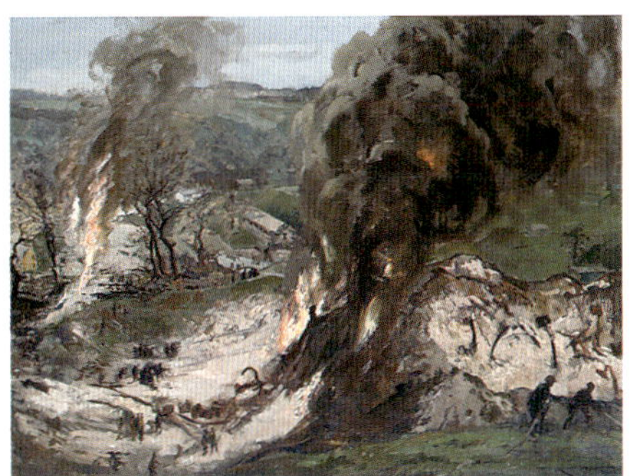

Mills, Reginald b.1896
*Flashback: A Recollection of an Air Raid on an
Ammunition Dump* 1944
oil on canvas 74.9 x 100.3
IWM ART LD 4678

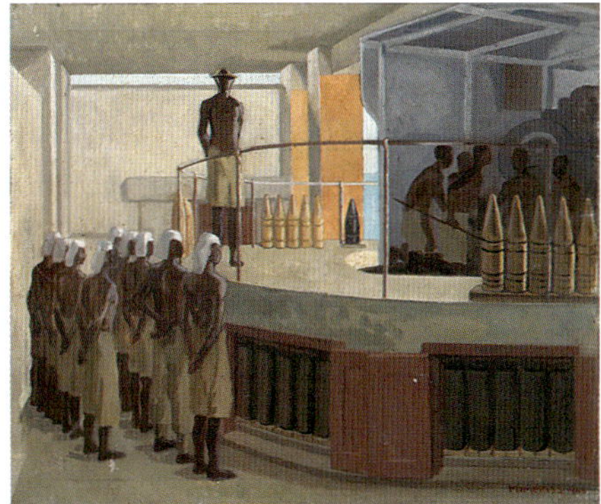

Mimpriss, Violet Barber 1895–1987
Gun Drill: Fort Mombasa, Kenya 1943
oil on canvas 50.8 x 60.9
IWM ART LD 5582

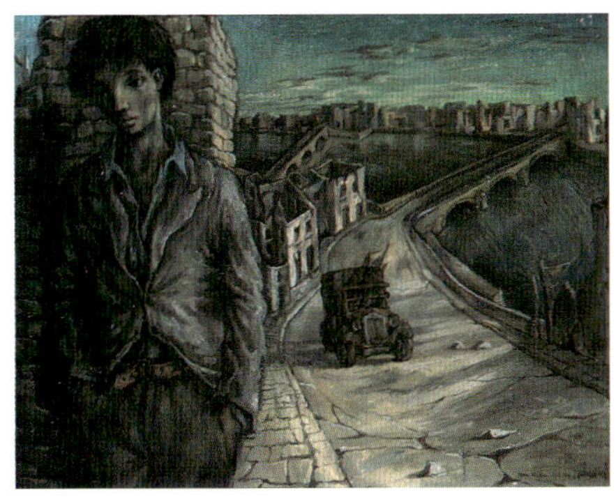

Minton, John 1917–1957
Blitzed City with Self Portrait 1941
oil on board 30.5 x 40
IWM ART 16739

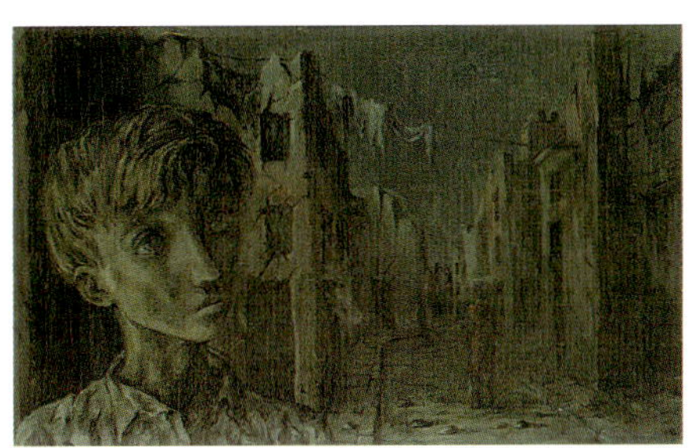

Minton, John 1917–1957
Wapping 1941
oil on board 25 x 40.8
IWM ART 17174

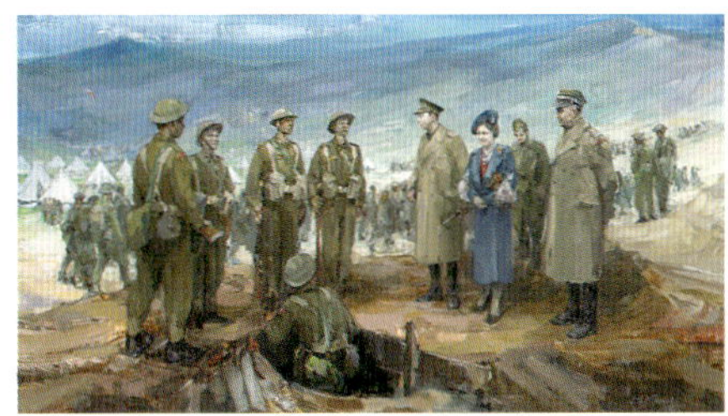

Mlynarski, Josef 1925–1984
*The Royal Family Visiting Polish Troops in
Scotland, 1941* 1981
oil on canvas 100.5 x 180.5
IWM ART 15323

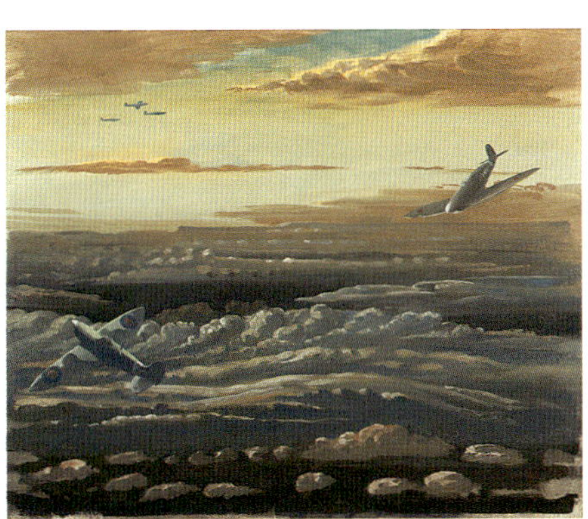

Monnington, Walter Thomas 1902–1976
Clouds and Spitfires 1943
oil on canvas 50.8 x 60.9
IWM ART LD 3767

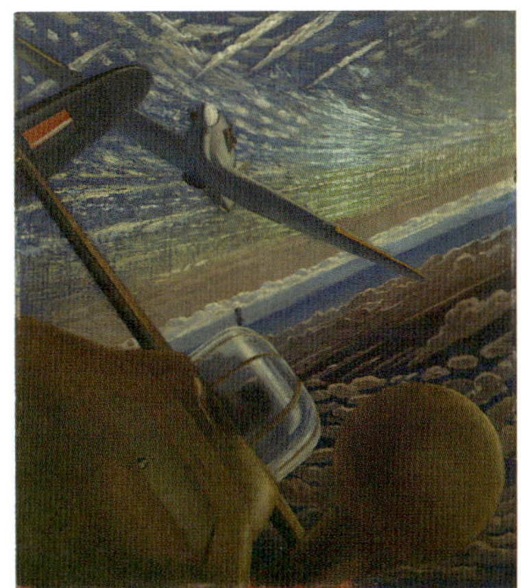

Monnington, Walter Thomas 1902–1976
*Fighter Affiliation: Halifax and Hurricane
Aircraft Co-Operating in Action* 1943
oil on canvas 46.3 x 41.2
IWM ART LD 3769

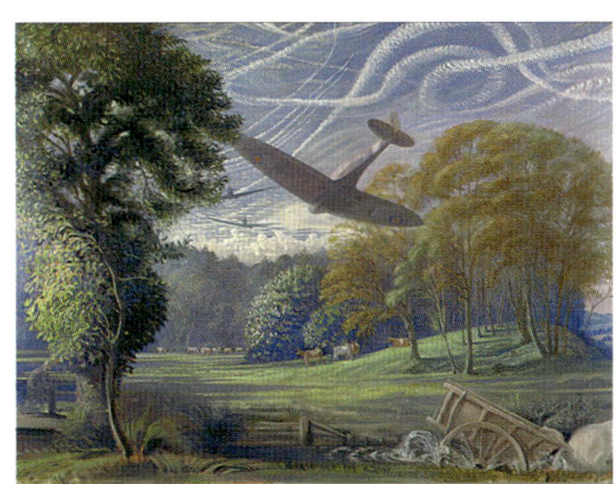

Monnington, Walter Thomas 1902–1976
*Southern England: Spitfires Attacking Flying
Bombs* 1944
oil on canvas 105.4 x 143.3
IWM ART LD 4589

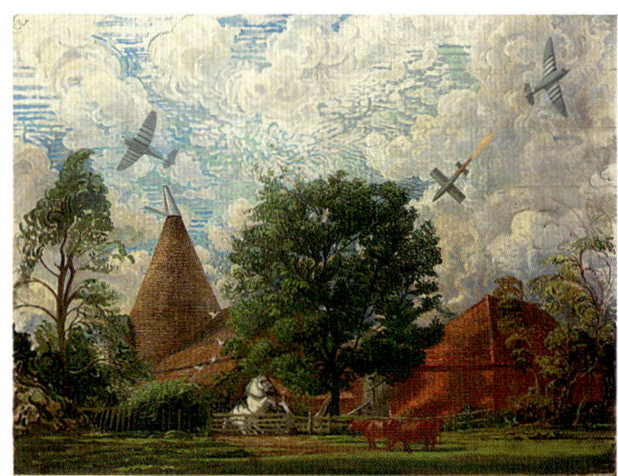

Monnington, Walter Thomas 1902–1976
Tempests Attacking Flying Bombs 1944
oil on canvas 90.1 x 114.3
IWM ART LD 4588

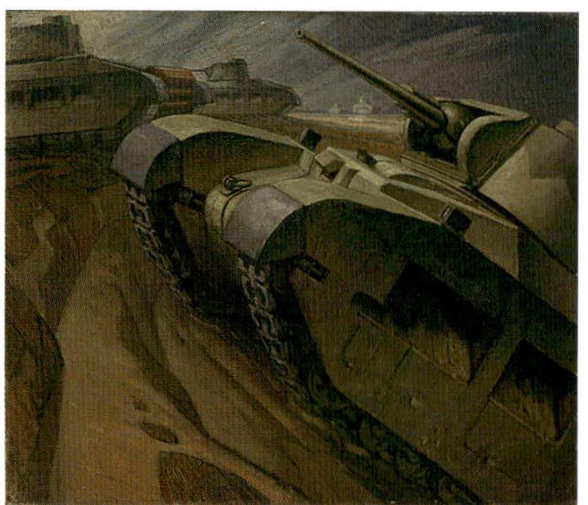

Morley, Harry 1881–1943
On the Driving Ground 1940
oil on canvas 50.8 x 60.9
IWM ART LD 919

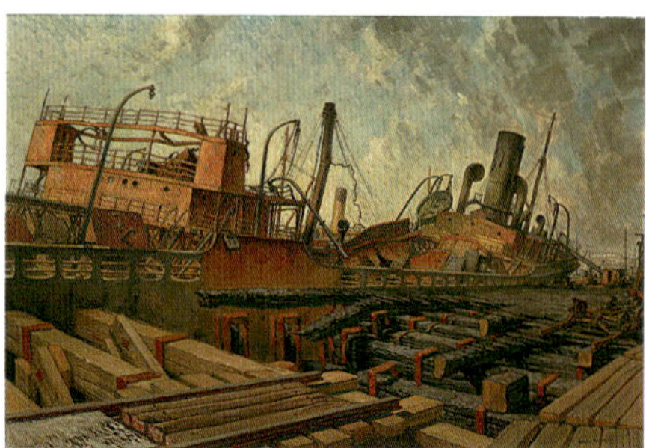

Morley, Harry 1881–1943
The Bombed 'SS Toscalusa' at a Western Port 1940
oil on canvas 50.8 x 76.2
IWM ART LD 665

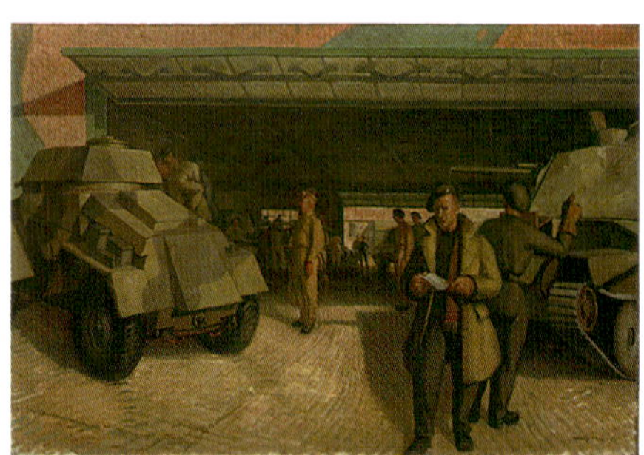

Morley, Harry 1881–1943
The Tank Park 1940
oil on canvas 50.8 x 76.2
IWM ART LD 920

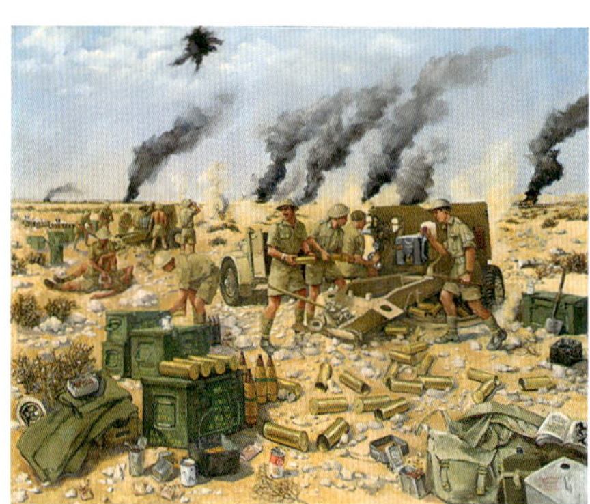

Mount, Cyril b.1920
Guns of the 11th Field Regiment in Action with Robcol, Ruweisat Ridge, El Alamein, July 1942 1992
oil on canvas 80 x 100
IWM ART 17111

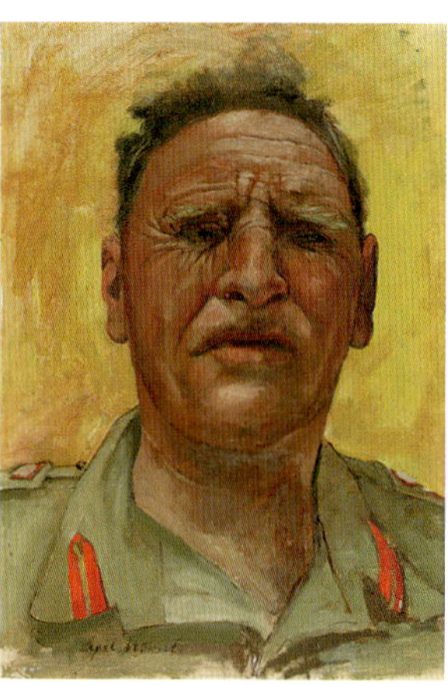

Mount, Cyril b.1920
Lieutenant General C. J. E. Auchinleck (1884–1981), CB, CSI, DSO, OBE
oil on board 64.5 x 45.8
IWM ART LD 6056

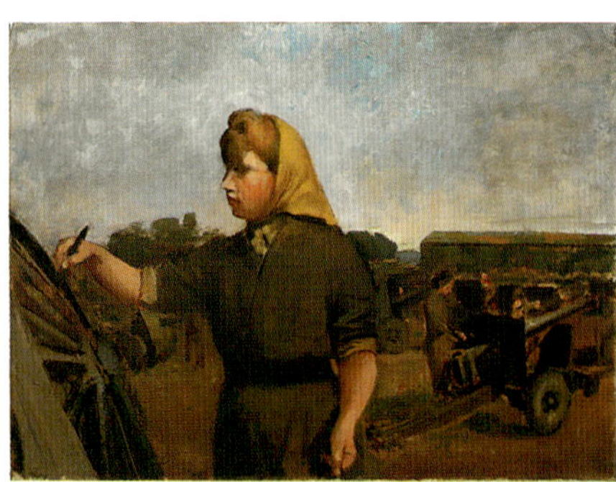

Moynihan, Rodrigo 1910–1990
Auxiliary Territorial Service at Work 1943
oil on canvas 55.8 x 76.2
IWM ART LD 3630

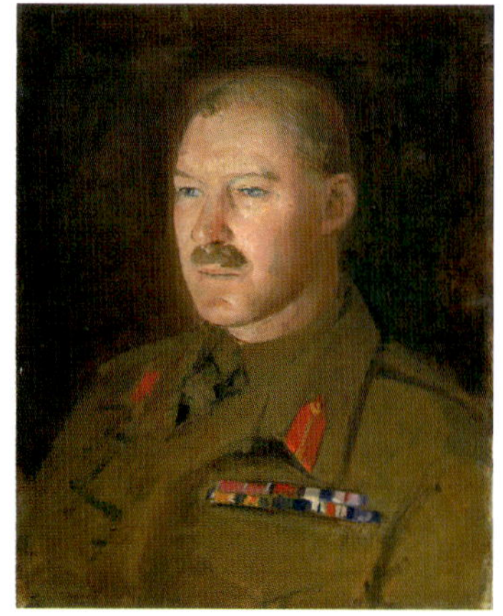

Moynihan, Rodrigo 1910–1990
Lieutenant General Neil M. Ritchie (1897–1983), CBE, DSO, MC 1943
oil on canvas 53.3 x 43.1
IWM ART LD 3711

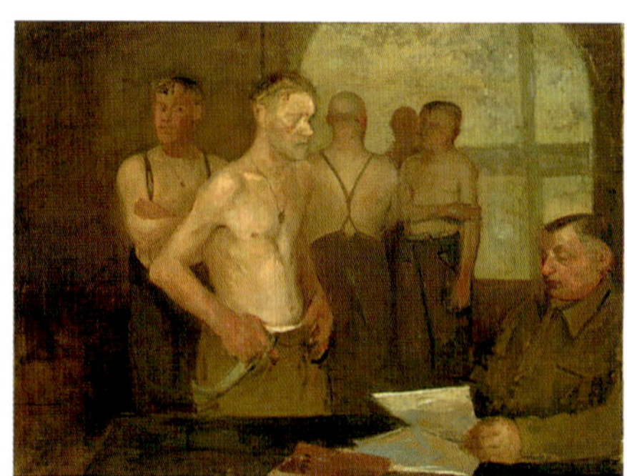

Moynihan, Rodrigo 1910–1990
Medical Inspection 1943
oil on canvas 91.4 x 121.9
IWM ART LD 3259

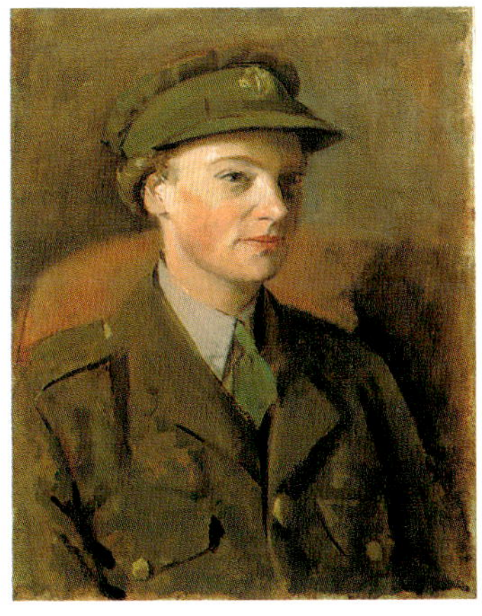

Moynihan, Rodrigo 1910–1990
Regimental Sergeant Major Hadley, Transport Service 1943
oil on canvas 49.5 x 39.3
IWM ART LD 3710

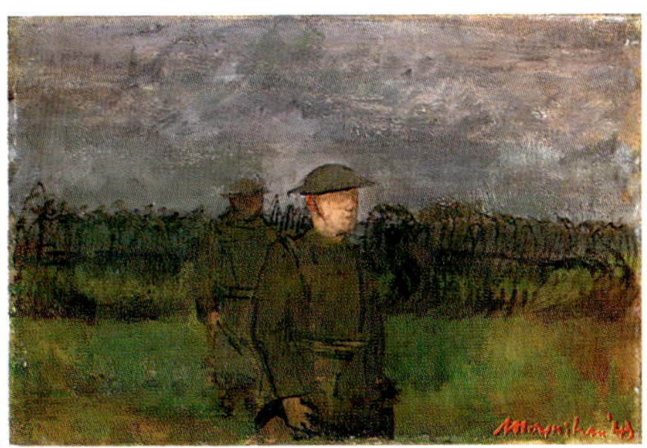

Moynihan, Rodrigo 1910–1990
Soldiers on Manoeuvres in Cornwall 1943
oil on canvas 30.4 x 45.7
IWM ART LD 3581

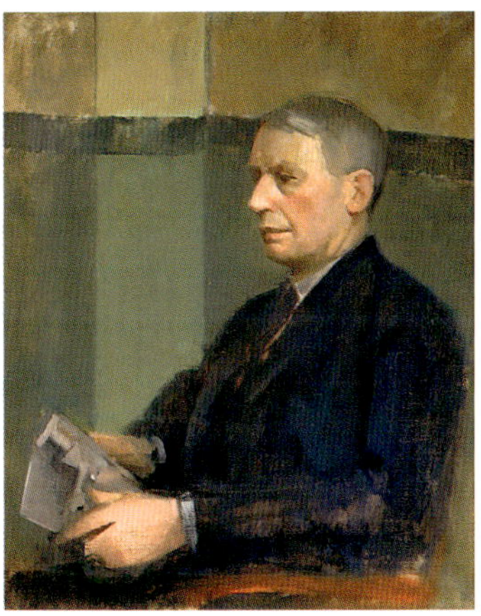

Moynihan, Rodrigo 1910–1990
Sir George Thomson (1892–1975), FRS, Scientific Adviser to the Air Ministry 1943–1944
oil on canvas 76.2 x 63.5
IWM ART LD 5681

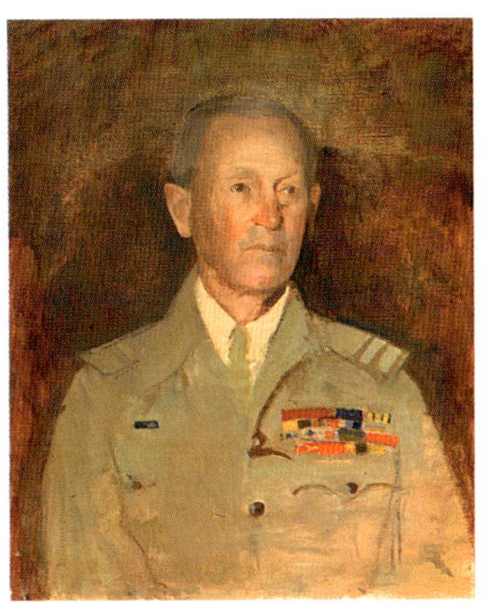

Moynihan, Rodrigo 1910–1990
Admiral Sir Walter Cowan (1871–1956), BT, KCB, DSO, MVO 1944
oil on canvas 62.8 x 50.1
IWM ART LD 4512

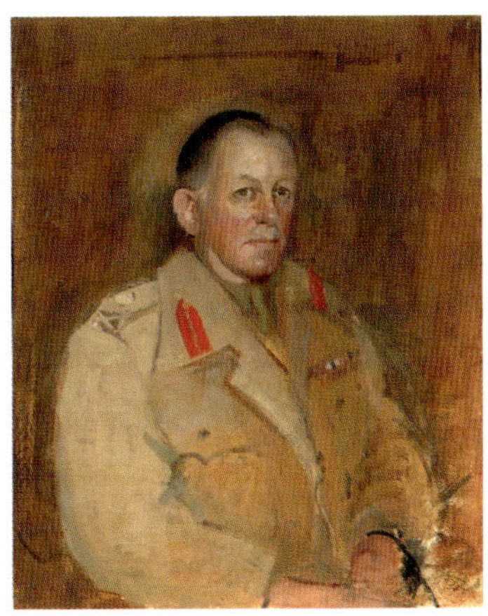

Moynihan, Rodrigo 1910–1990
Lieutenant General Sir Willoughby Norrie (1893–1977), KCMG, CB, DSO, MC 1944
oil on canvas 76.2 x 63.5
IWM ART LD 3993

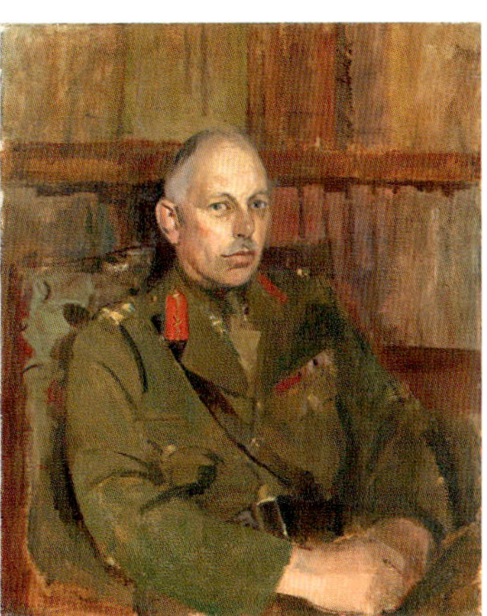

Moynihan, Rodrigo 1910–1990
Major General the Viscount Bridgeman (1896–1982), CB, DSO, MC 1944
oil on canvas 75.2 x 62.8
IWM ART LD 3994

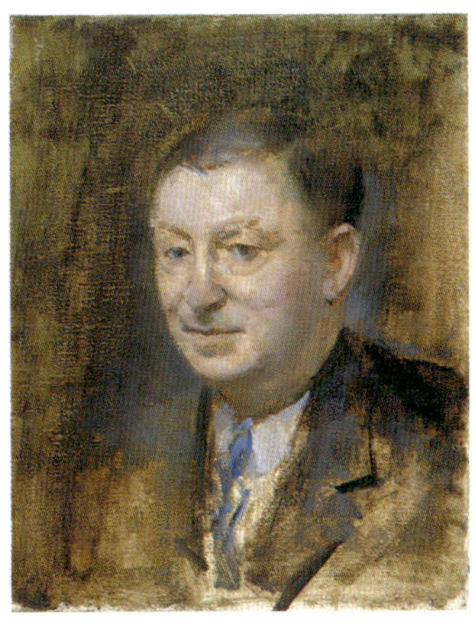

Moynihan, Rodrigo 1910–1990
Professor John Cockcroft (1897–1967), CBE, FRS, Director of the Atomic Energy Division, National Research Council (…) 1944–1946
oil on canvas 50.8 x 40.6
IWM ART LD 5852

Moynihan, Rodrigo 1910–1990
Air Marshal Sir Roderic Hill (1894–1954), KCB, MC, AFC and Bar 1945
oil on canvas 91.4 x 71.1
IWM ART LD 5451

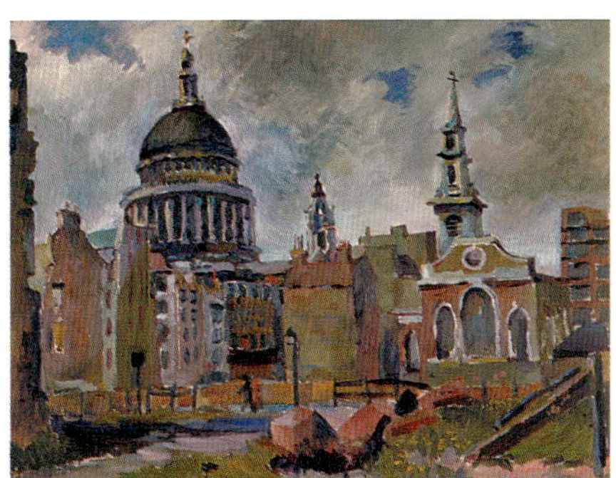

Mozley, Charles 1914–1991
St Paul's Cathedral 1940
oil on canvas 53 x 71.2
IWM ART 15895

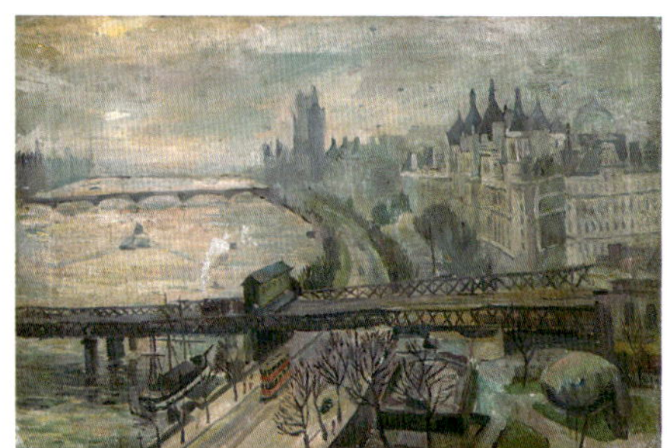

Mozley, Charles 1914–1991
The Thames Embankment 1940
oil on canvas 50.5 x 76
IWM ART 16235

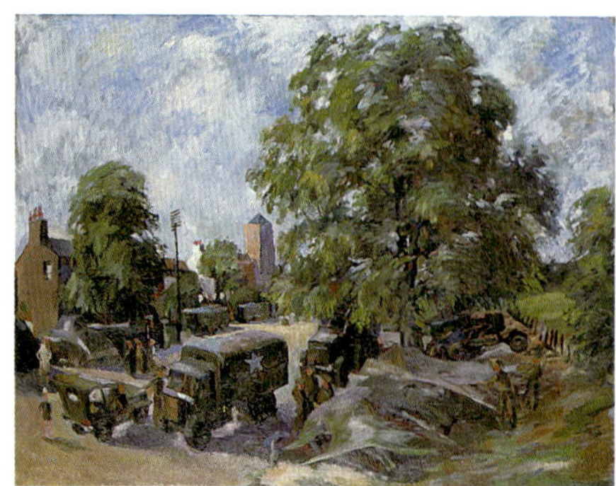

Mozley, Charles 1914–1991
Invasion Preparations in an English Village
c.1944
oil on canvas 76.5 x 100.5
IWM ART 15546

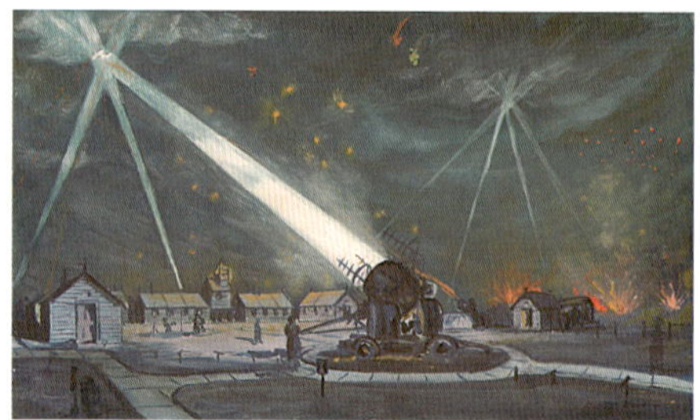

Munro, Alastair active 1950s
Searchlight Troop Headquarters, Royal Artillery 1959
oil on canvas 45.7 x 76.2
IWM ART LD 6002

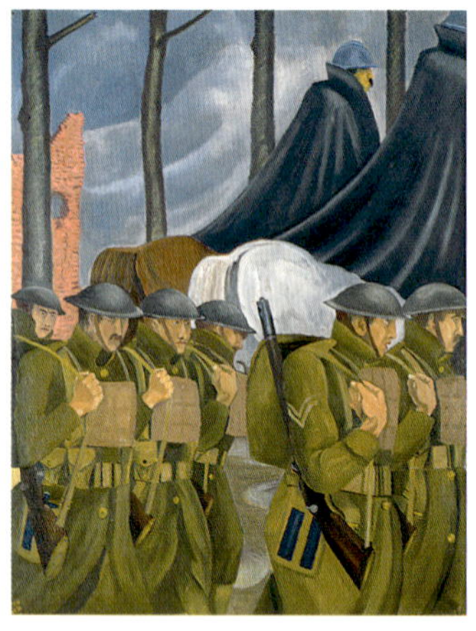

Nash, John Northcote 1893–1977
A French Highway 1918
oil on canvas 91.4 x 71.1
IWM ART 1162

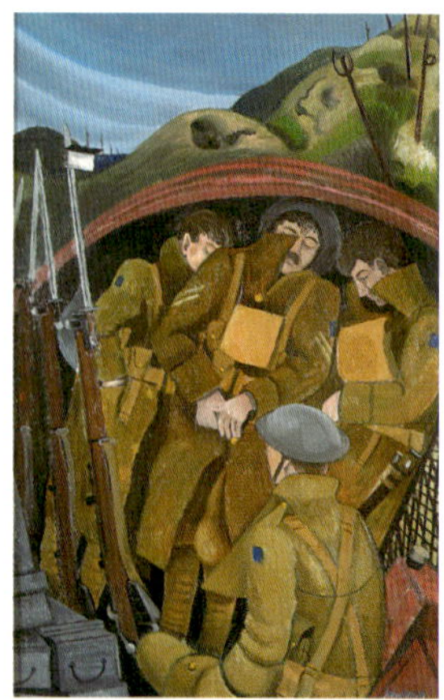

Nash, John Northcote 1893–1977
An Advance Post: Day 1918
oil on canvas 76.2 x 50.8
IWM ART 1157

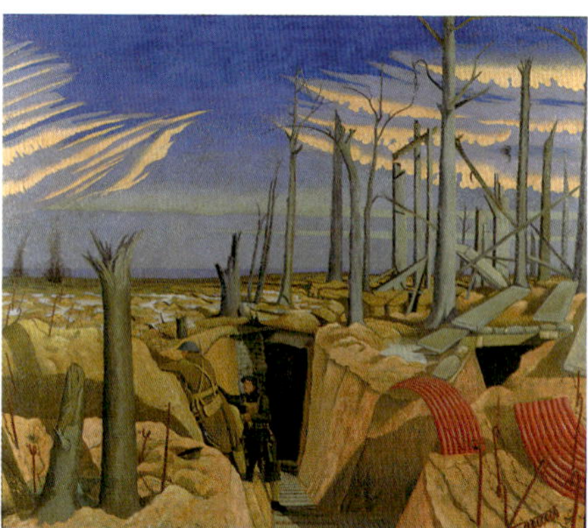

Nash, John Northcote 1893–1977
Oppy Wood, 1917: Evening 1918
oil on canvas 182.8 x 213.3
IWM ART 2243

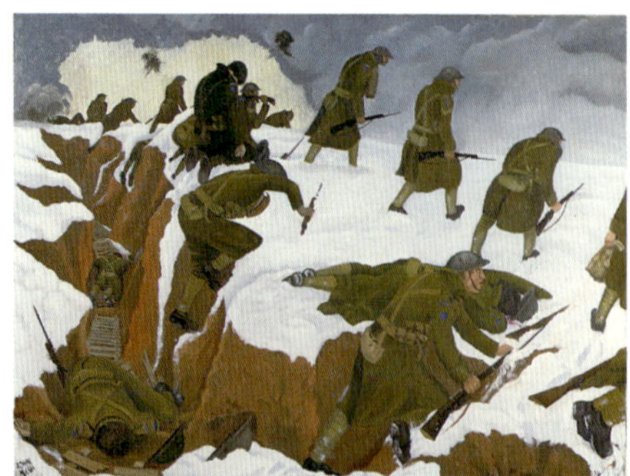

Nash, John Northcote 1893–1977
'Over The Top': First Artists' Rifles at Marcoing, 30 December 1917 1918
oil on canvas 79.8 x 108
IWM ART 1656

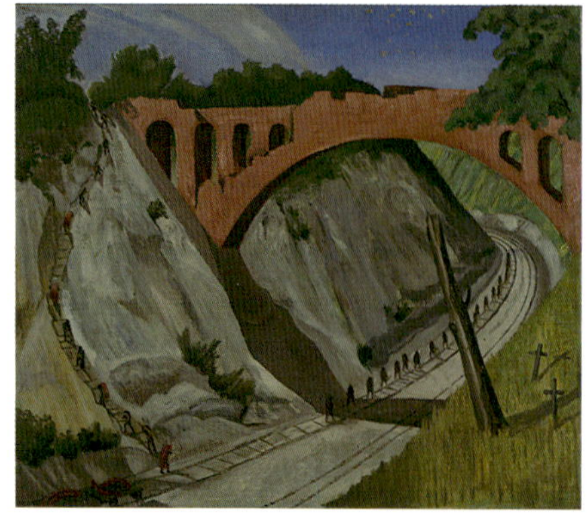

Nash, John Northcote 1893–1977
The Bridge over the Arras-Lens Railway
c.1919
oil on canvas 68.5 x 80
IWM ART 1163

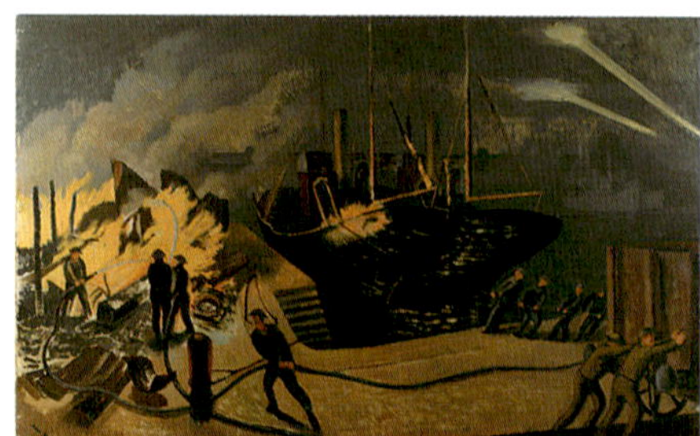

Nash, John Northcote 1893–1977
A Dockyard Fire 1940
oil on canvas 50.8 x 81.2
IWM ART LD 704

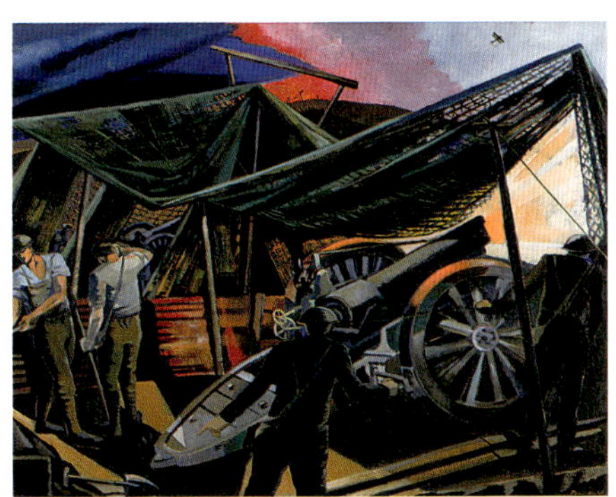

Nash, Paul 1889–1946
A Howitzer Firing 1918
oil on canvas 71.1 x 91.4
IWM ART 1152

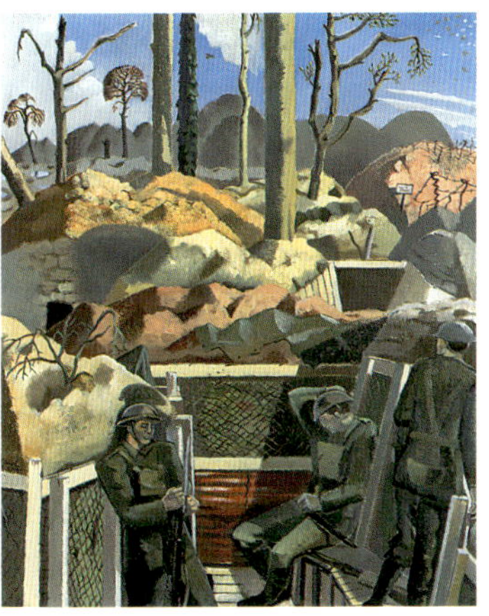

Nash, Paul 1889–1946
Spring in the Trenches, Ridge Wood, 1917
1918
oil on canvas 60.9 x 50.8
IWM ART 1154

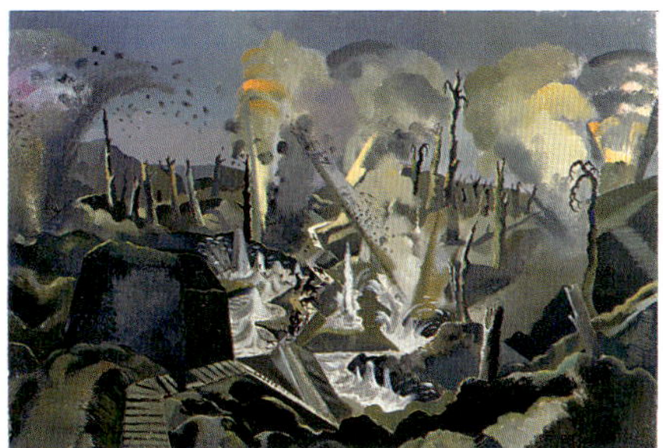

Nash, Paul 1889–1946
The Mule Track 1918
oil on canvas 60.9 x 91.4
IWM ART 1153

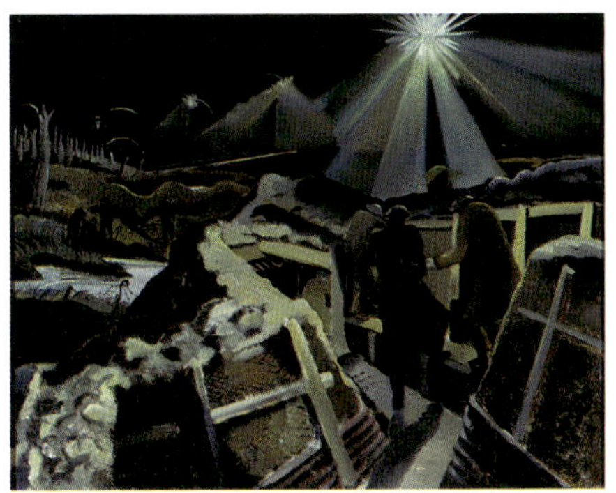

Nash, Paul 1889–1946
The Ypres Salient at Night 1918
oil on panel 71.4 x 92
IWM ART 1145

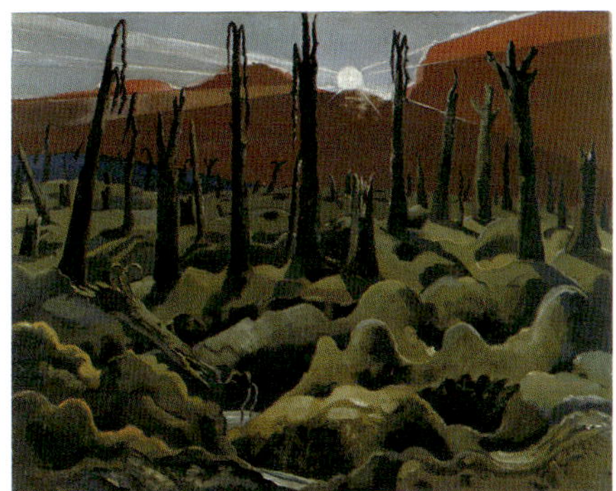

Nash, Paul 1889–1946
We Are Making a New World 1918
oil on canvas 71.1 x 91.4
IWM ART 1146

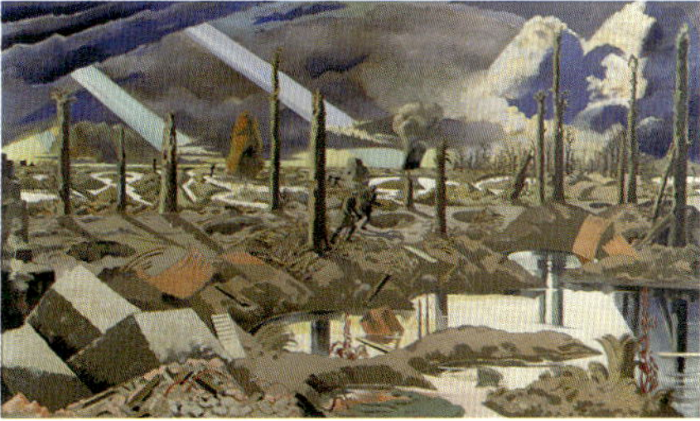

Nash, Paul 1889–1946
The Menin Road 1919
oil on canvas 182.8 x 317.5
IWM ART 2242

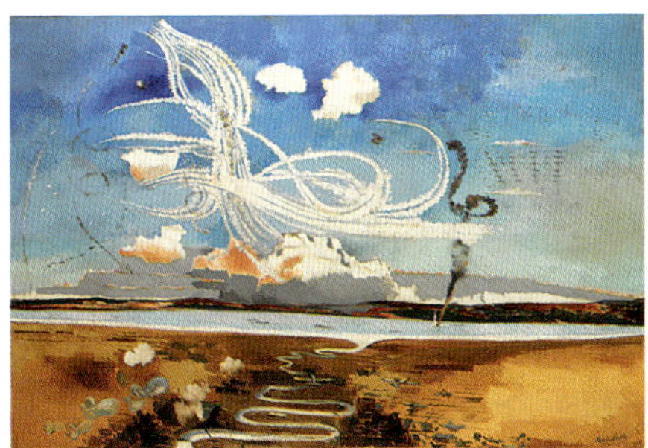

Nash, Paul 1889–1946
Battle of Britain 1941
oil on canvas 122.6 x 183.5
IWM ART LD 1550

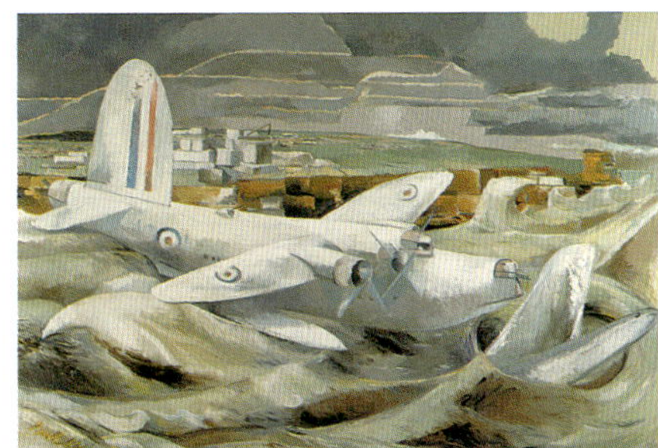

Nash, Paul 1889–1946
Defence of Albion 1942
oil on canvas 121.9 x 182.8
IWM ART LD 1933

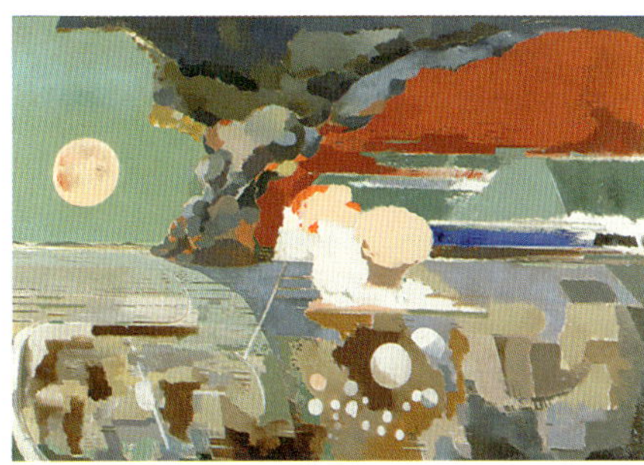

Nash, Paul 1889–1946
Battle of Germany 1944
oil on canvas 121.9 x 182.8
IWM ART LD 4526

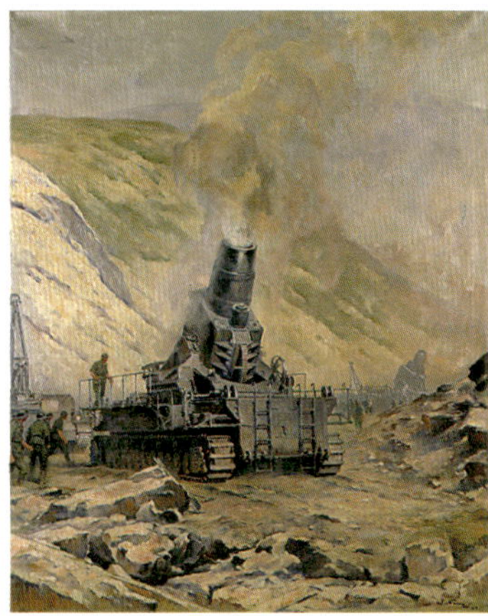

Neuss, W. active 1940s
The Giant Howitzer 'Karl' during the German Offensive in the Crimea, 1943 1944
oil on canvas 169 x 140
IWM ART 15504

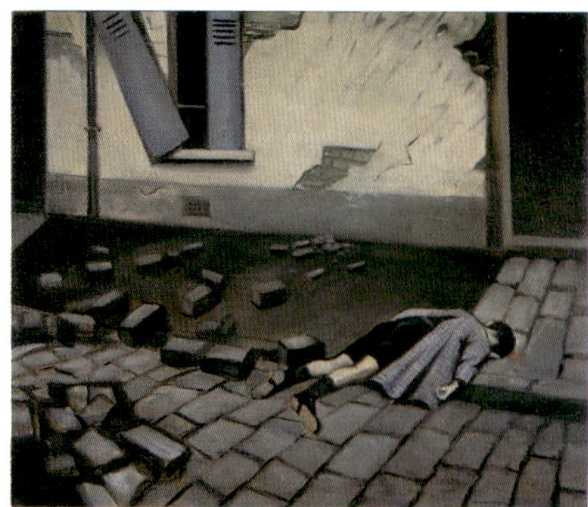

Nevinson, Christopher 1889–1946
A Taube 1916
oil on canvas 63.8 x 76.6
IWM ART 200

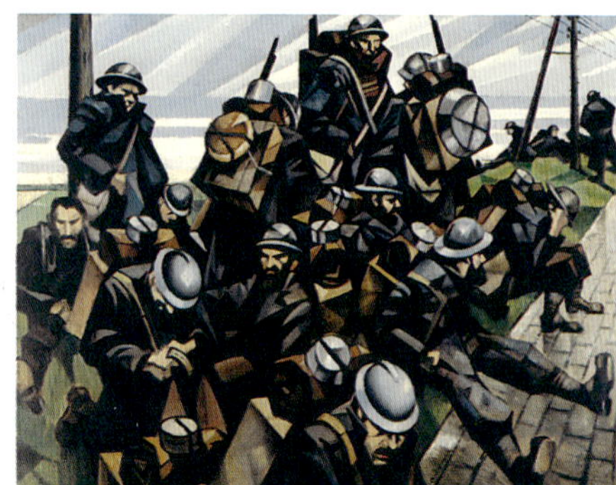

Nevinson, Christopher 1889–1946
French Troops Resting 1916
oil on canvas 71.1 x 91.4
IWM ART 5219

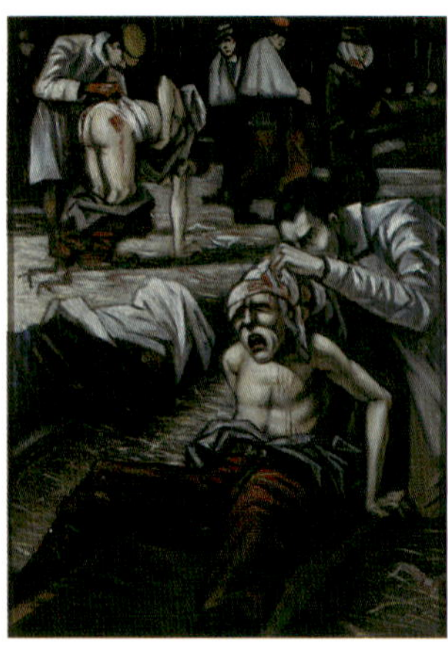

Nevinson, Christopher 1889–1946
The Doctor 1916
oil on canvas 57.1 x 41.2
IWM ART 725

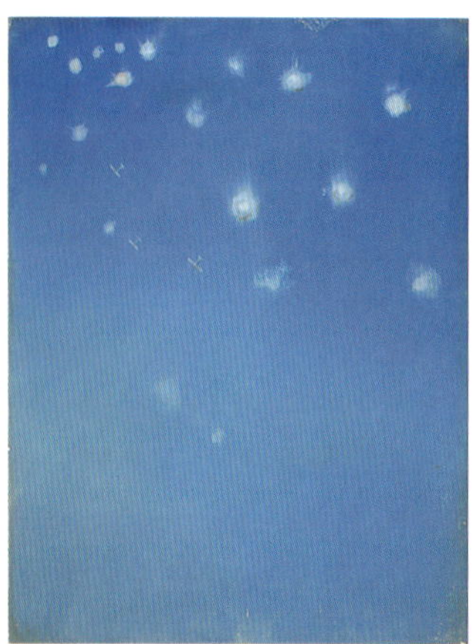

Nevinson, Christopher 1889–1946
Archies c.1916
oil on glass 62.8 x 48.2
IWM ART 6473

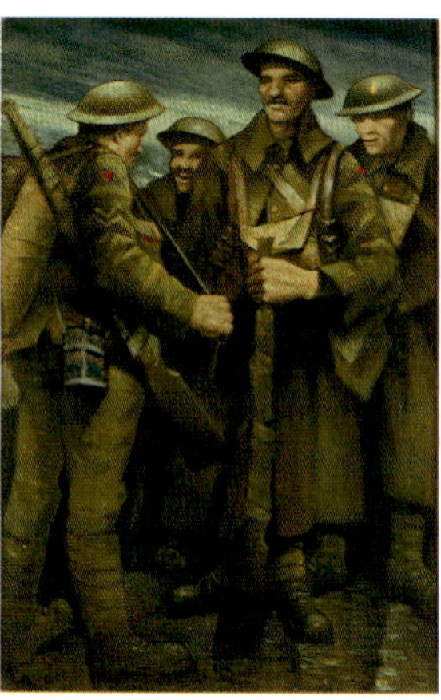

Nevinson, Christopher 1889–1946
A Group of Soldiers 1917
oil on canvas 91.4 x 60.9
IWM ART 520

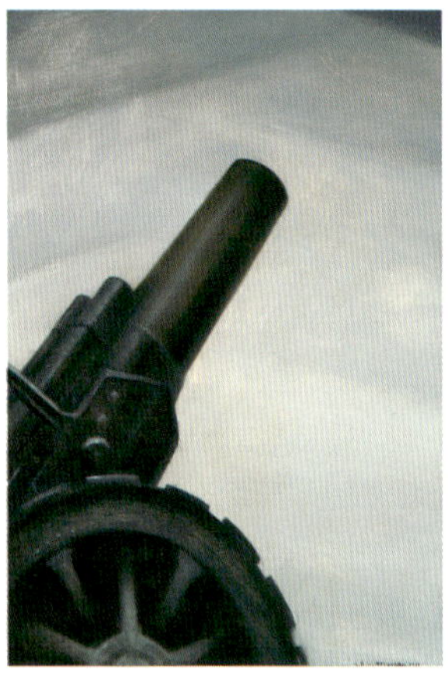

Nevinson, Christopher 1889–1946
A Howitzer Gun in Elevation 1917
oil on canvas 60.9 x 45.7
IWM ART 514

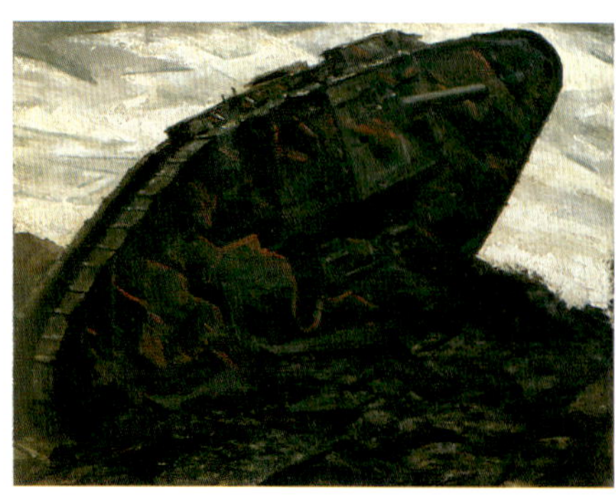

Nevinson, Christopher 1889–1946
A Tank 1917
oil on canvas 44.2 x 59.3
IWM ART 5275

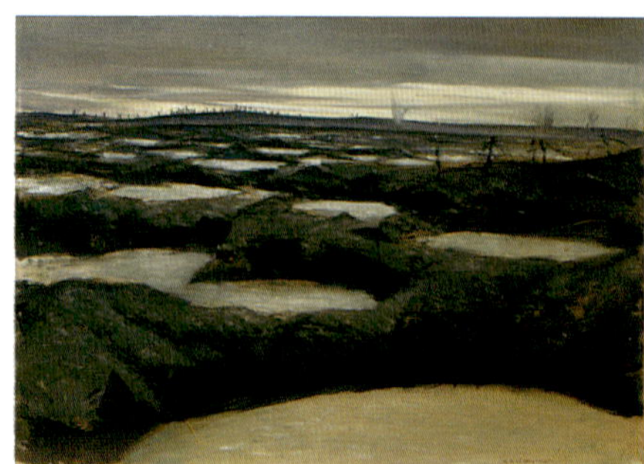

Nevinson, Christopher 1889–1946
After a Push 1917
oil on canvas 57.1 x 80
IWM ART 519

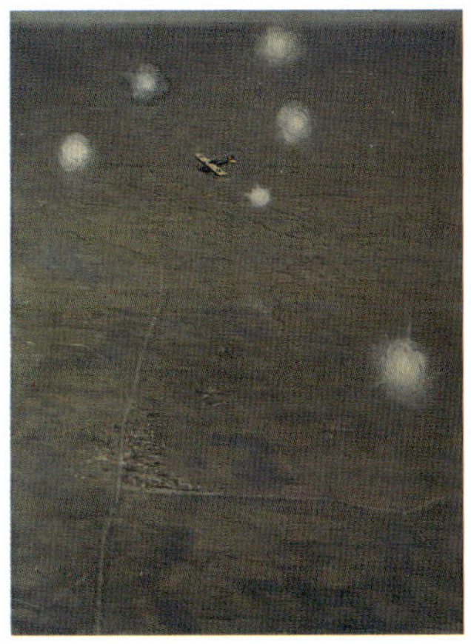

Nevinson, Christopher 1889–1946
Over the Lines 1917
oil on canvas 60.9 x 45.7
IWM ART 515

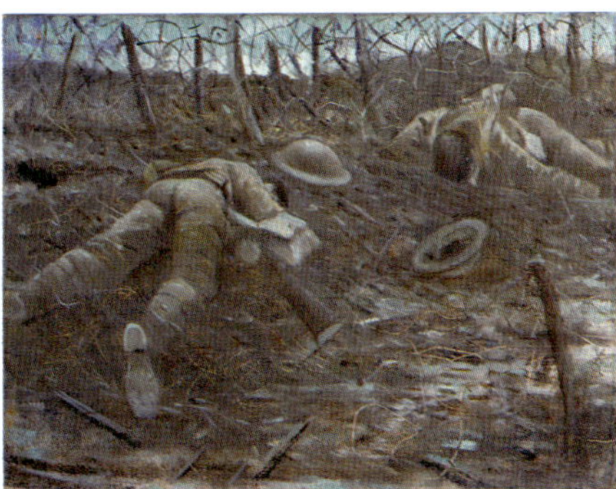

Nevinson, Christopher 1889–1946
Paths of Glory 1917
oil on canvas 45.7 x 60.9
IWM ART 518

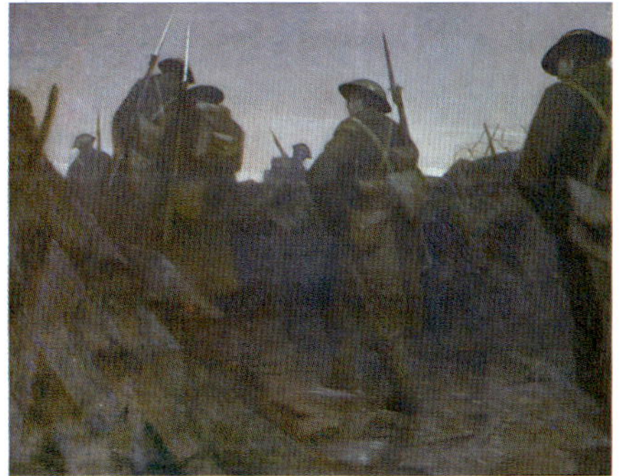

Nevinson, Christopher 1889–1946
Reliefs at Dawn 1917
oil on canvas 71.1 x 91.4
IWM ART 513

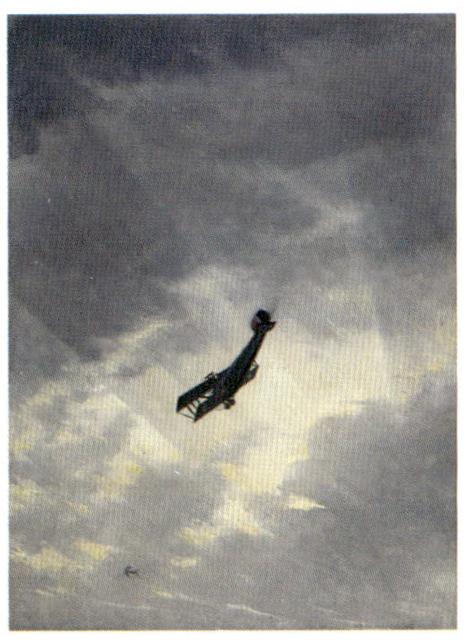

Nevinson, Christopher 1889–1946
Swooping Down on a Hostile Plane 1917
oil on canvas 60.9 x 45.7
IWM ART 517

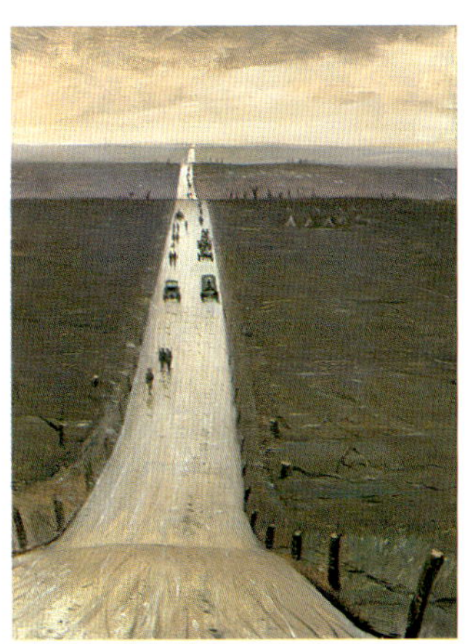

Nevinson, Christopher 1889–1946
The Road from Arras to Bapaume 1917
oil on canvas 60.9 x 45.7
IWM ART 516

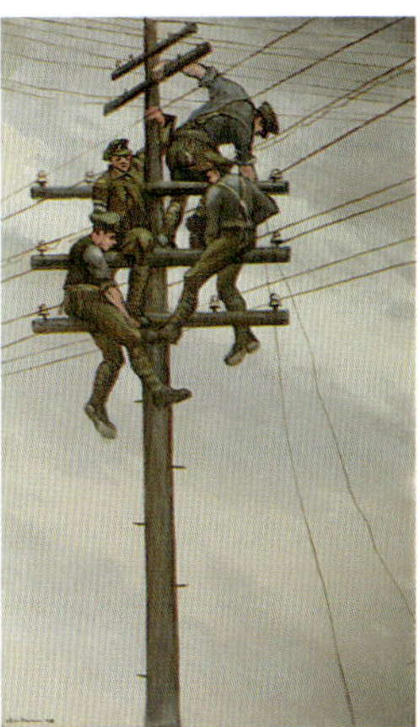

Nevinson, Christopher 1889–1946
Nerves of the Army 1918
oil on canvas 88.9 x 54
IWM ART 5287

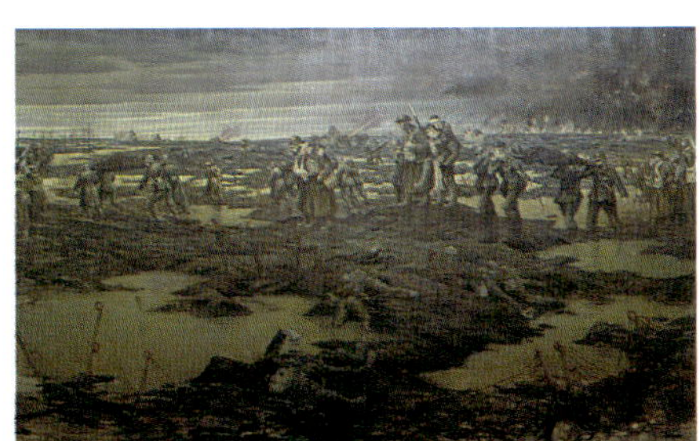

Nevinson, Christopher 1889–1946
The Harvest of Battle 1919
oil on canvas 182.8 x 317.5
IWM ART 1921

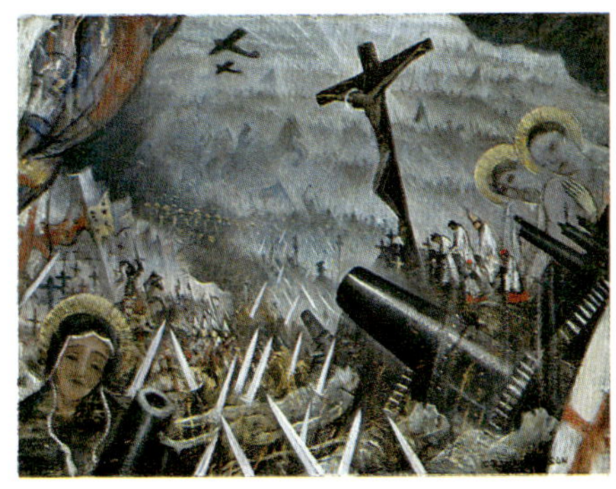

Nevinson, Christopher 1889–1946
The Unending Cult of Human Sacrifice c.1934
oil on canvas 46 x 61
IWM ART 16717

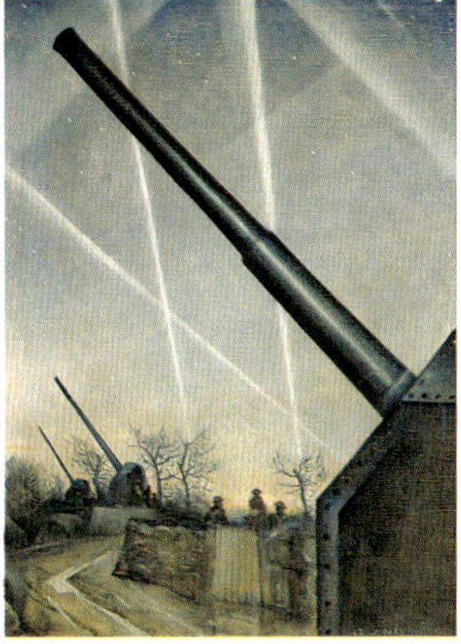

Nevinson, Christopher 1889–1946
Anti-Aircraft Defences 1940
oil on canvas 81.2 x 60.9
IWM ART LD 14

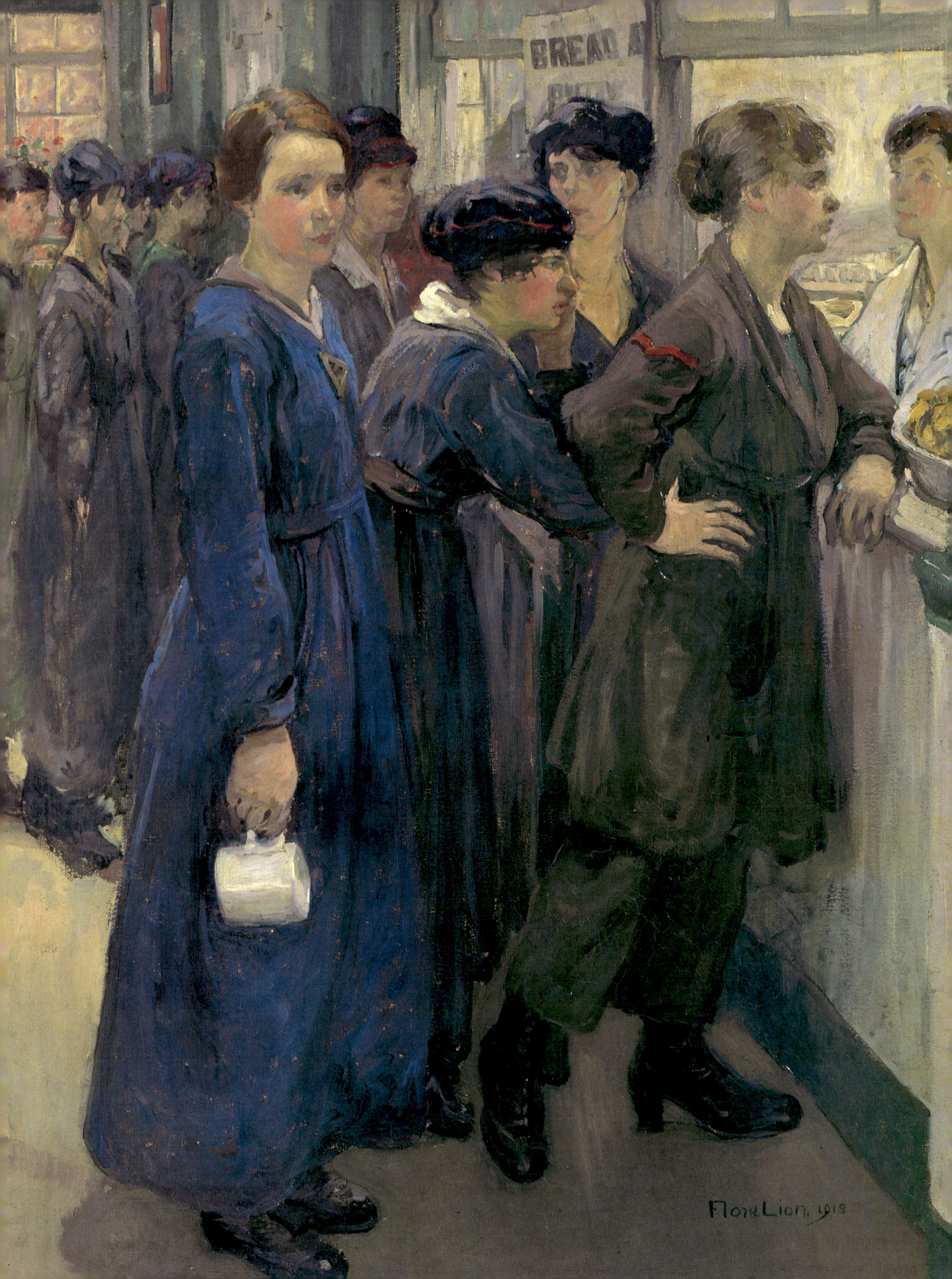
BREAD A
Flora Lion. 1918

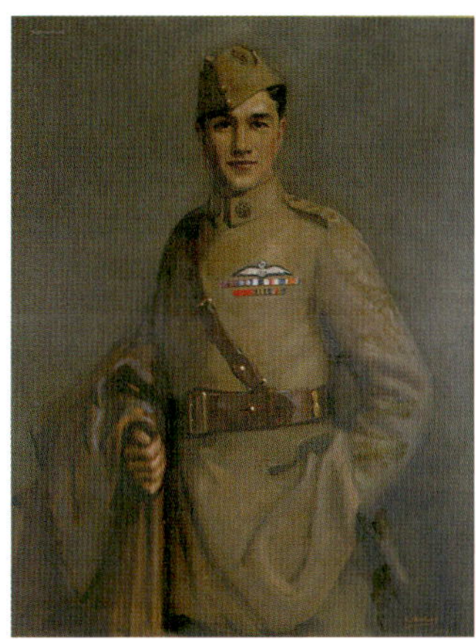

Newling, Edward active 1890–1934
Captain Albert Ball (1896–1917), VC, DSO, MC, Nottinghamshire and Derby Regiment and Royal Flying Corps 1919
oil on canvas 112.3 x 87.2
IWM ART 2628

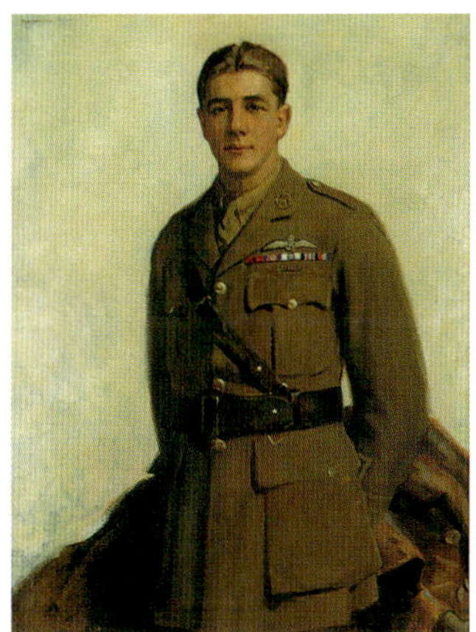

Newling, Edward active 1890–1934
Major James Byford McCudden (1895–1918), VC, SO, MC, RFC 1919
oil on canvas 112.3 x 86.9
IWM ART 2627

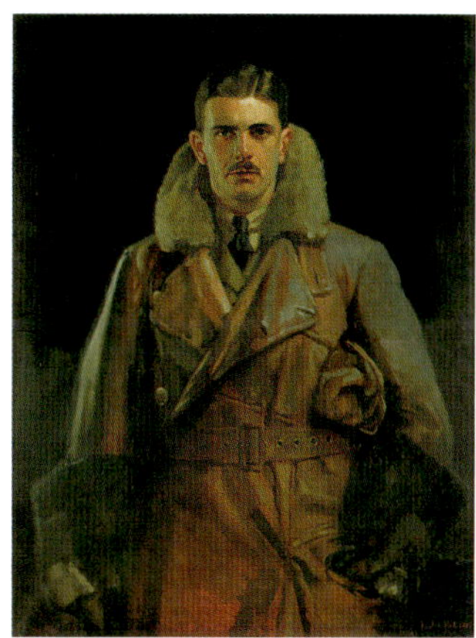

Newling, Edward active 1890–1934
Second Lieutenant Gilbert Stuart Martin Insall (1894–1972), VC, MC, Royal Flying Corps and Later Squadron Leader, Royal Air Force 1919
oil on canvas 112.3 x 86.9
IWM ART 2629

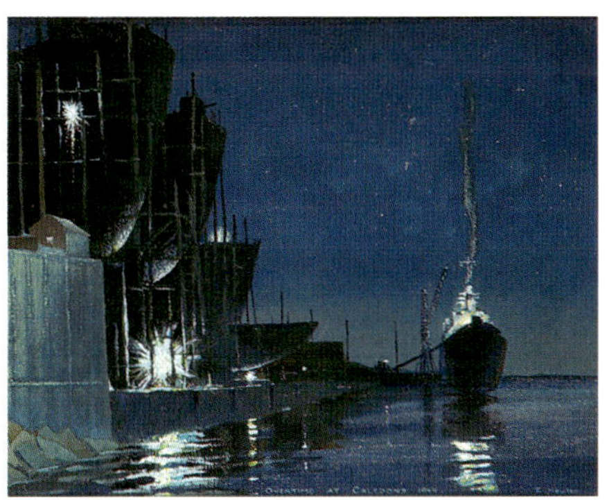

Newton, Eric 1893–1965
Overtime at Caledons 1944
oil on canvas 30.5 x 38
IWM ART LD 7267

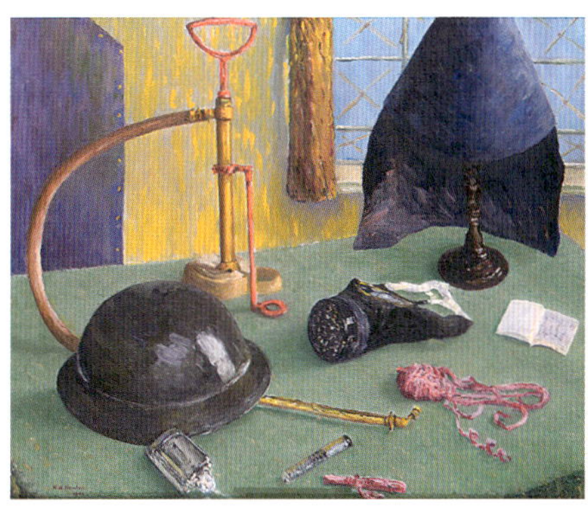

Newton, Herbert H. 1881–1959
War Accessories: A Group of Objects Familiar to Civilians during the War, Including Red Tape! 1940
oil on canvas 63.5 x 76.2
IWM ART LD 5861

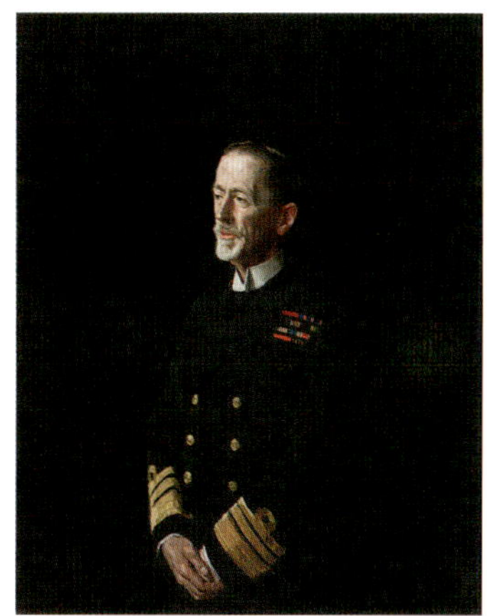

Nicholson, William 1872–1949
Vice Admiral Sir William C. Pakenham (1861–1933), KCB, KCMG, KCVO 1920
oil on canvas 127 x 101.9
IWM ART 3142

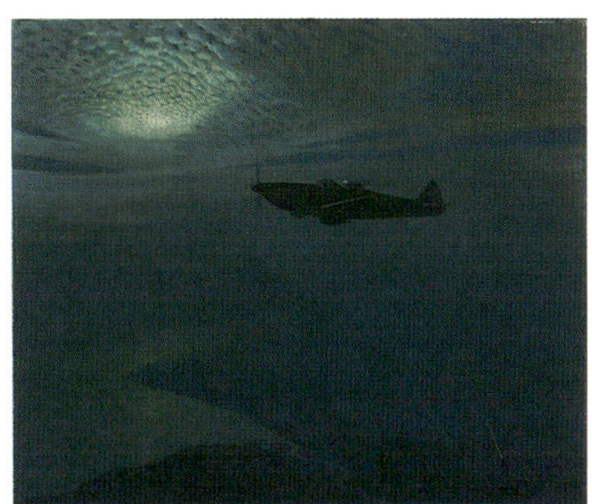

Nockolds, Roy Anthony 1911–1979
Stalking the Night Raider 1941
oil on canvas 63.5 x 76.2
IWM ART LD 1150

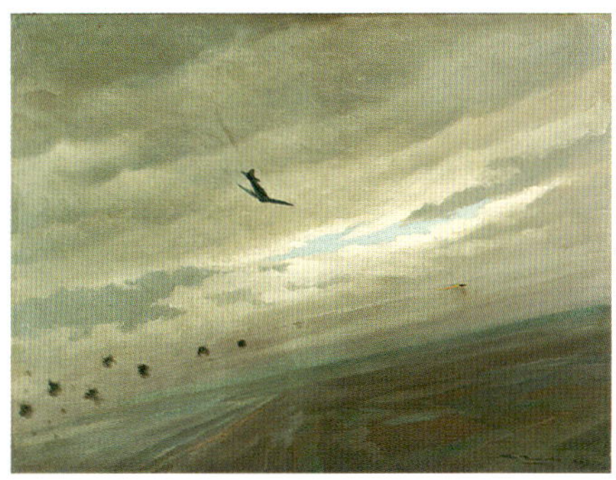

Nockolds, Roy Anthony 1911–1979
A Tempest Shooting Down a Flying Bomb 1944
oil on canvas 75.8 x 100.9
IWM ART LD 4533

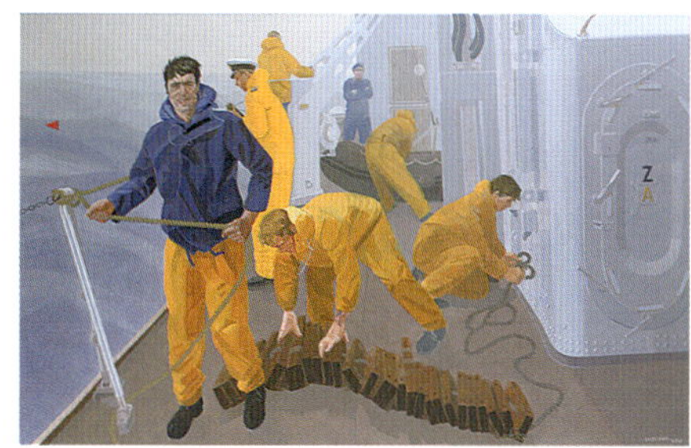

Ocean, Humphrey b.1951
Recovering the Dan Buoy, 'HMS Broadsword' 1979–1980
acrylic on canvas 89 x 143.5
IWM ART 15015

Facing page: Lion, Flora, 1878–1958, *Women's Canteen at Phoenix Works, Bradford* (detail), 1918, (p. 142)

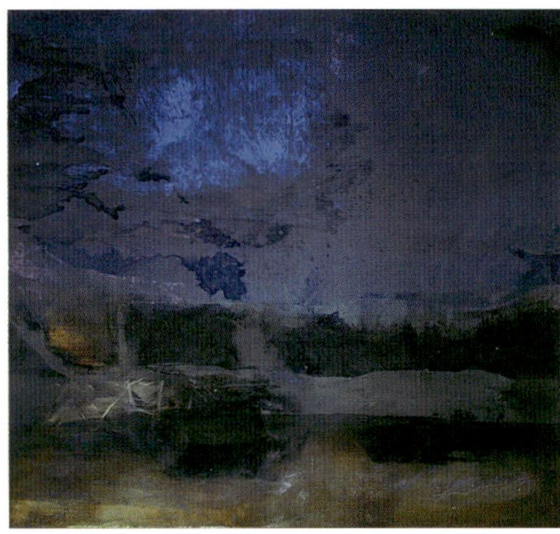

O'Donoghue, Hughie b.1953
German Tanks, Forges-les-Eaux 1996–1999
oil on canvas 195.6 x 218.4
IWM ART 17112

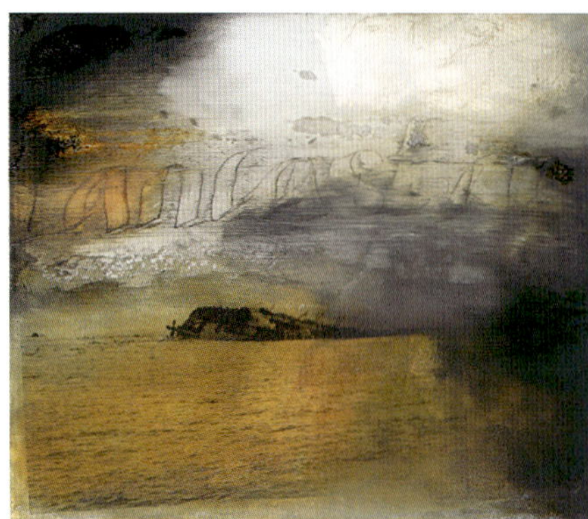

O'Donoghue, Hughie b.1953
'Lancastria' 1999–2000
oil & mixed media on linen & tissue 56 x 67
IWM ART 16790

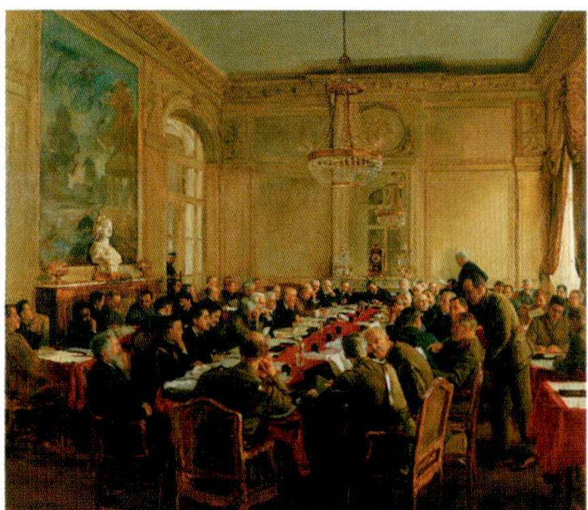

Olivier, Herbert Arnould 1861–1952
The Terms of the Armistice, 3–4 November 1918 1918
oil on canvas 209.5 x 229.2
IWM ART 4208

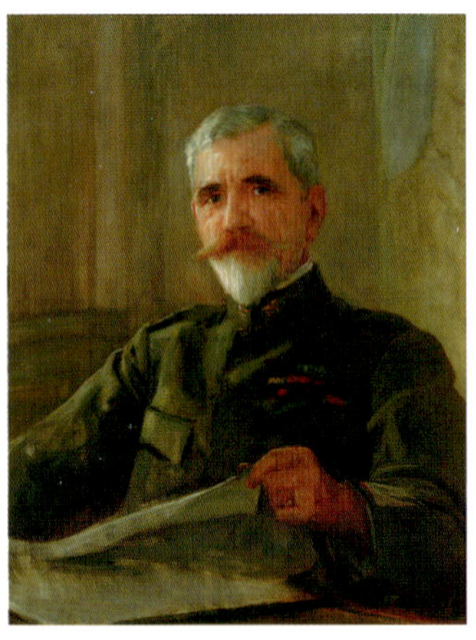

Olivier, Herbert Arnould 1861–1952
General Di Robilant: Italian Military Representative on the Supreme War Council, Versailles 1919
oil on canvas 80.6 x 64.7
IWM ART 4211

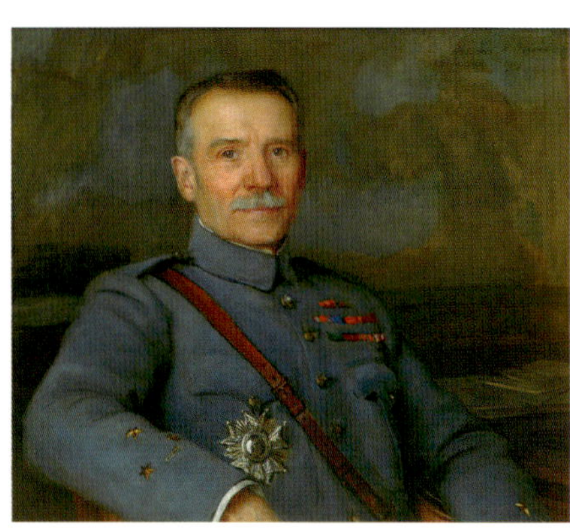

Olivier, Herbert Arnould 1861–1952
General Sir Emile Belin, KCB, French Permanent Military Representative, Supreme War Council, Versailles, (…) 1919
oil on canvas 63.5 x 76.2
IWM ART 4209

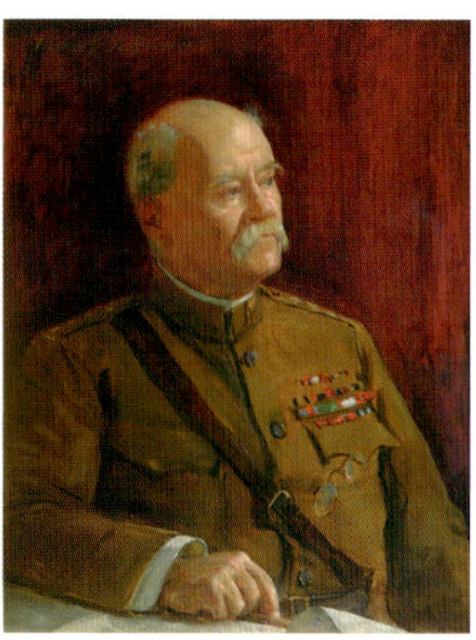

Olivier, Herbert Arnould 1861–1952
General Tasker Bliss (1853–1930): Military Representative of the United States of America at the Supreme War Council, Versailles 1919
oil on canvas 80.6 x 65.4
IWM ART 4212

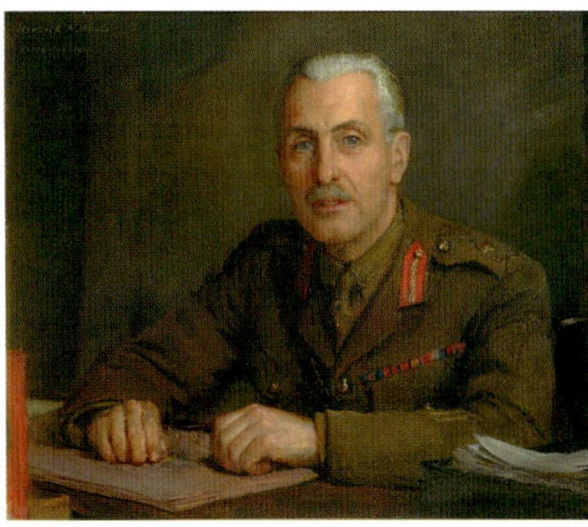

Olivier, Herbert Arnould 1861–1952
Major General the Honourable Charles Sackville-West (1870–1962), CMG, British Permanent Military Representative, (…) 1919
oil on canvas 63.5 x 76.2
IWM ART 4210

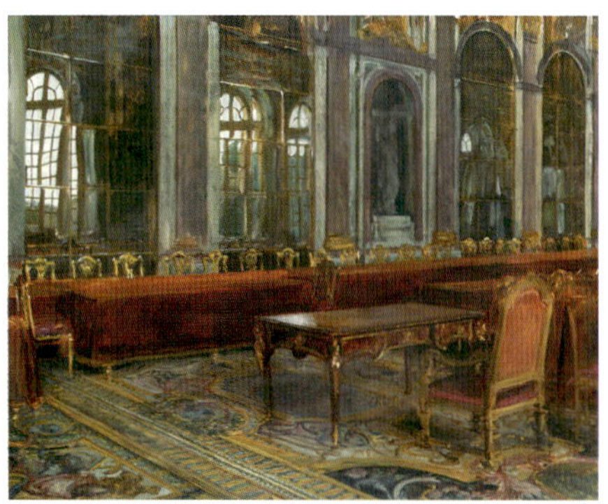

Olivier, Herbert Arnould 1861–1952
Sketch of the Table in the Hall of Mirrors, at Which the Treaty of Versailles Was Signed 1919
oil on canvas 80.9 x 100.3
IWM ART 4213

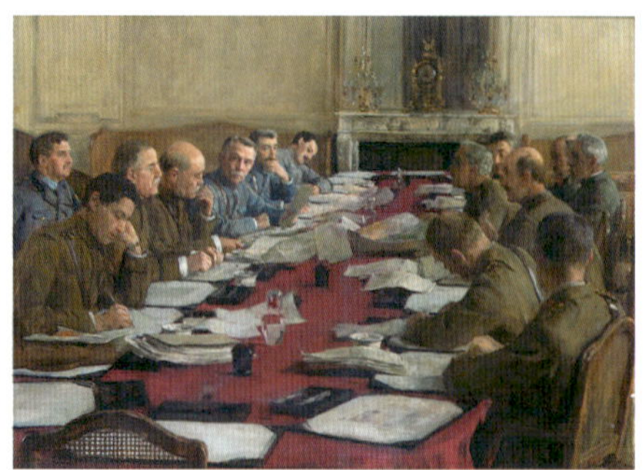

Olivier, Herbert Arnould 1861–1952
The Four Military Representatives of the Supreme War Council, Versailles, Their Chief Officers, Secretaries and (…) 1919
oil on canvas 76.2 x 101.9
IWM ART 4214

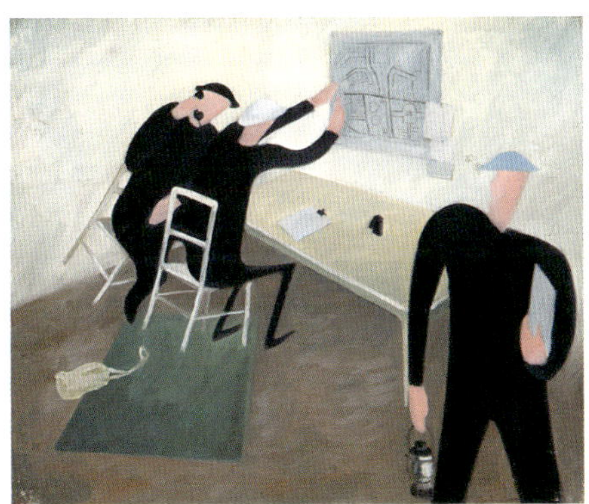

Oppenheim, Duncan 1904–2003
Boredom: Air Raid Wardens on Duty 1940
oil on canvas 51 x 61
IWM ART 16540

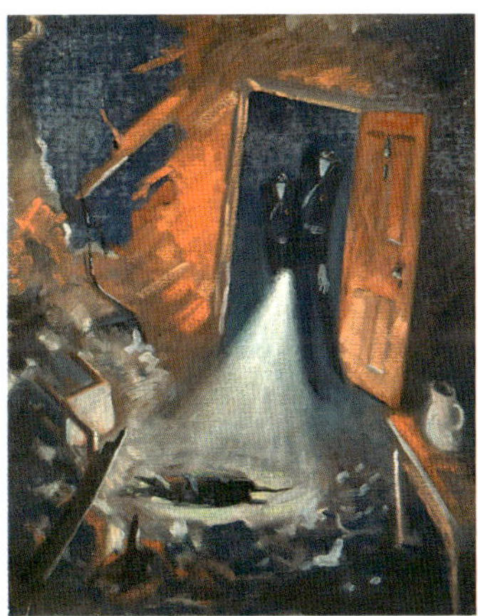

Oppenheim, Duncan 1904–2003
*Finding an Unexploded Bomb, Barton Street,
London SW1* 1940
oil on canvas 51 x 41
IWM ART 16537

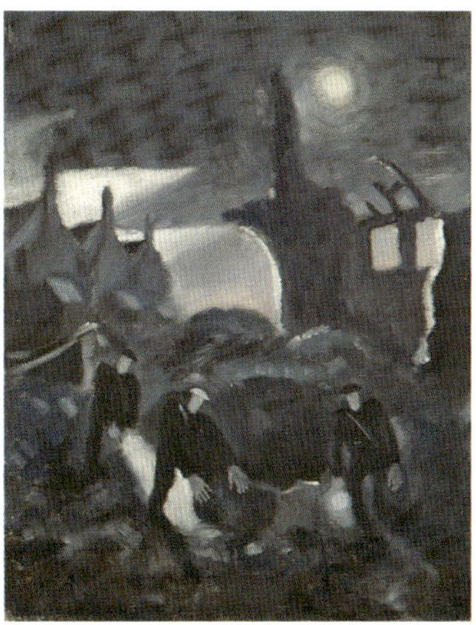

Oppenheim, Duncan 1904–2003
*Searching for Casualties after the Explosion of
a 1,000-Pound Bomb off Great Peter Street,
London SW1* 1940
oil on canvas 51 x 40.9
IWM ART 16538

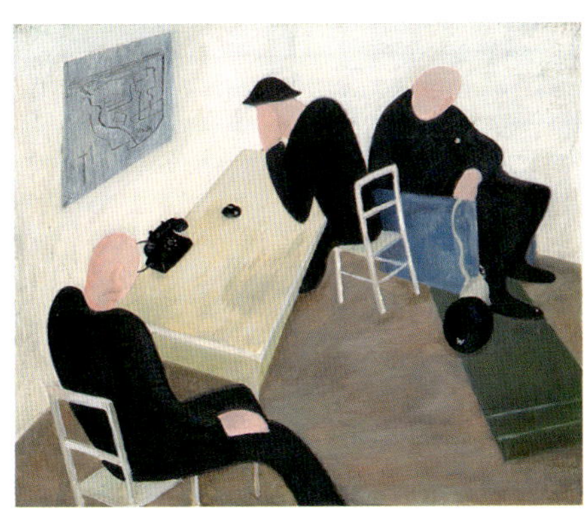

Oppenheim, Duncan 1904–2003
The Terrible Boredom of Waiting for Action
1940
oil on canvas 51 x 61
IWM ART 16541

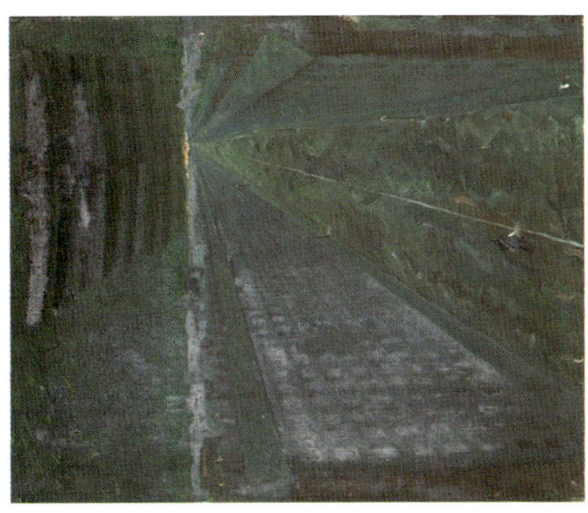

Oppenheim, Duncan 1904–2003
*The Loneliness of an Air Raid Warden on
Patrol during the Night Raids* 1940–1941
oil on canvas 50.8 x 61
IWM ART 16539

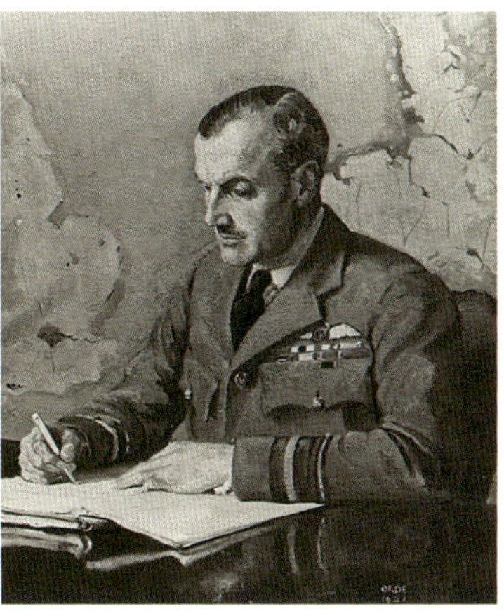

Orde, Cuthbert Julian 1888–1968
*Air Vice-Marshal John Cotesworth Slessor
(1897–1979), DSO, MC* 1941
oil on canvas 76.2 x 63.5
IWM ART LD 1292

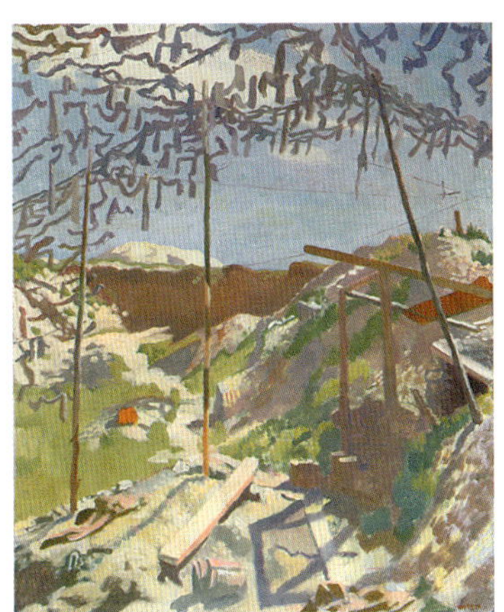

Orpen, William 1878–1931
A German Gunner's Shelter, Warlencourt 1917
oil on canvas 76.2 x 63.5
IWM ART 2965

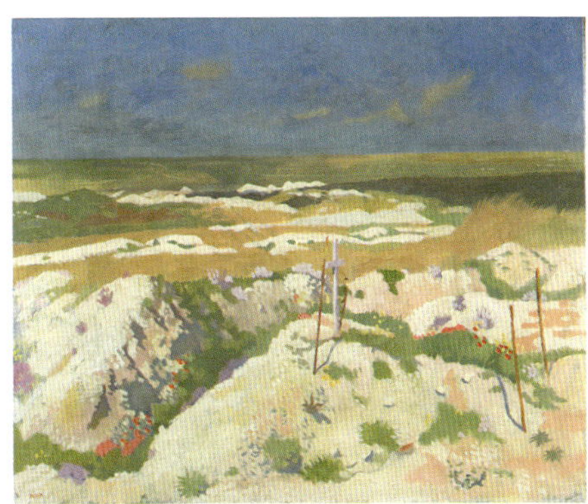

Orpen, William 1878–1931
*A Grave and a Mine Crater at La Boiselle,
August 1917* 1917
oil on canvas 63.5 x 76.2
IWM ART 2378

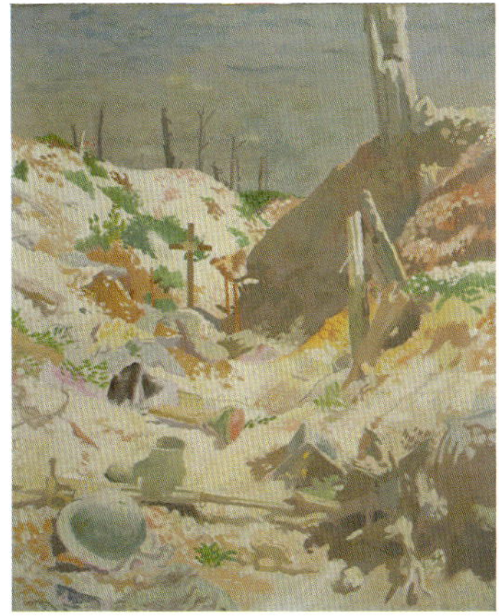

Orpen, William 1878–1931
A Grave in a Trench 1917
oil on canvas 76.2 x 63.5
IWM ART 2976

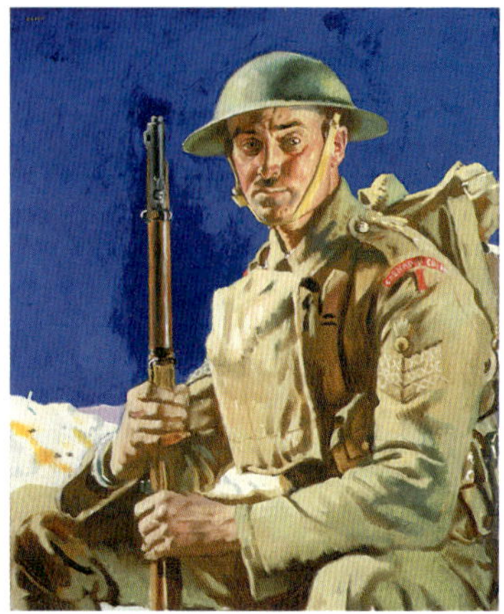

Orpen, William 1878–1931
A Grenadier Guardsman 1917
oil on canvas 91.4 x 76.2
IWM ART 3045

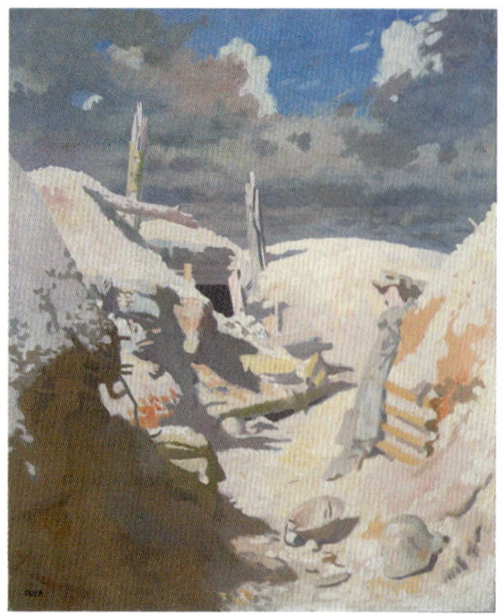

Orpen, William 1878–1931
A Gunner's Shelter in a Trench, Thiepval 1917
oil on canvas 76.2 x 63.5
IWM ART 2963

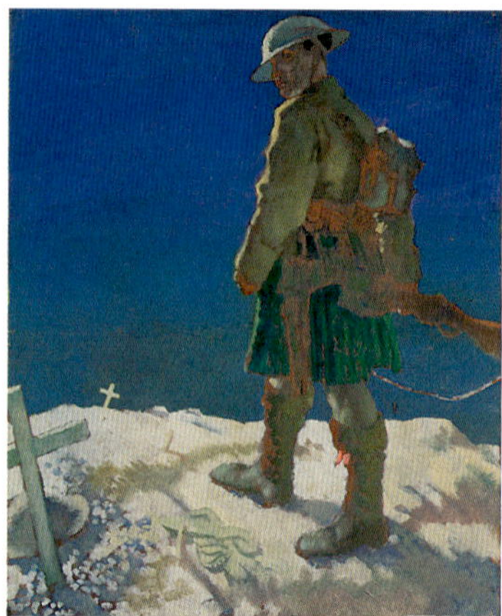

Orpen, William 1878–1931
A Highlander Passing a Grave 1917
oil on panel 60.9 x 50.8
IWM ART 2995

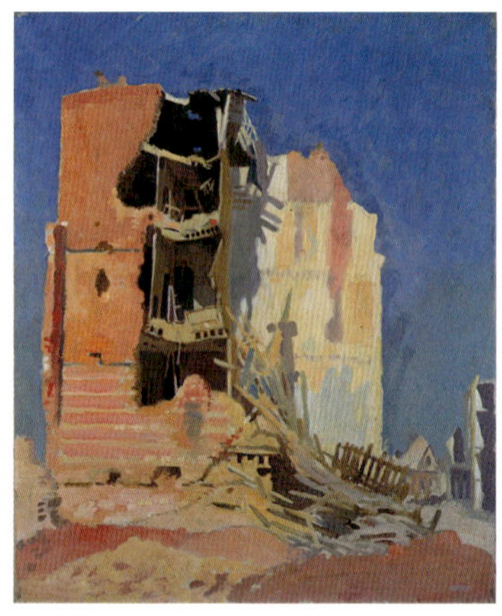

Orpen, William 1878–1931
A House at Péronne 1917
oil on canvas 76.2 x 63.5
IWM ART 2997

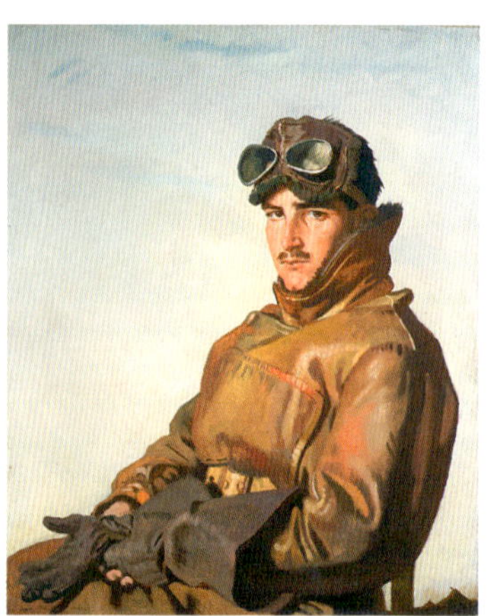

Orpen, William 1878–1931
An Airman: Lieutenant Reginald Theodore Carlos Hoidge (1894–1963), MC 1917
oil on canvas 91.4 x 76.2
IWM ART 2996

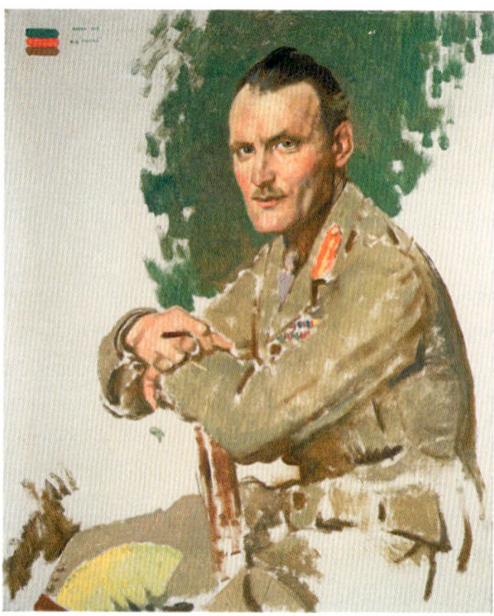

Orpen, William 1878–1931
Brigadier General Hugh Jamieson Elles (1880–1945), CB, DSO 1917
oil on canvas 91.4 x 76.2
IWM ART 2999

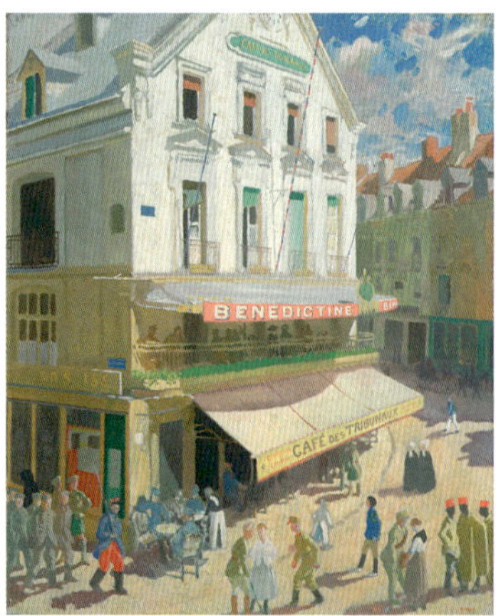

Orpen, William 1878–1931
Dieppe 1917
oil on canvas 76.2 x 63.5
IWM ART 2972

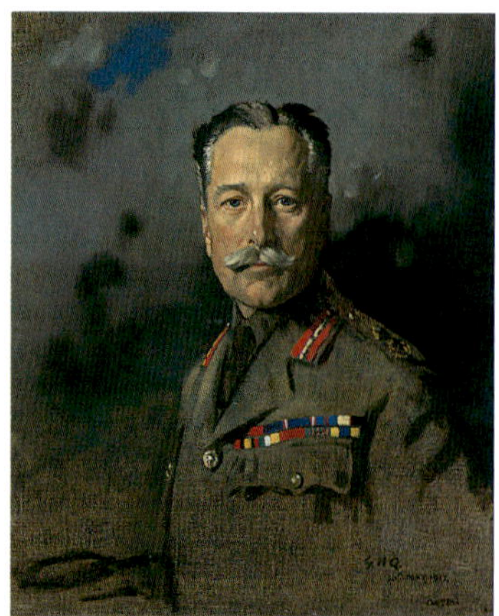

Orpen, William 1878–1931
Field Marshal Sir Douglas Haig (1861–1928), KT, GCB, GCVO, KCIE, Commander-in-Chief, France, from 15 December 1915 1917
oil on canvas 74.9 x 63.5
IWM ART 324

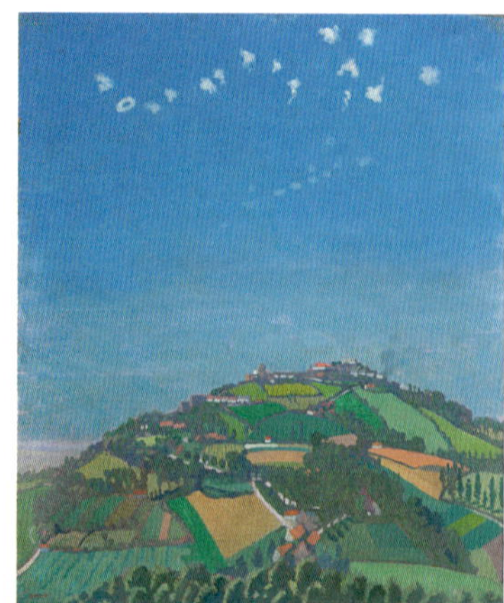

Orpen, William 1878–1931
German Planes Visiting Cassel 1917
oil on canvas 76.2 x 63.5
IWM ART 2960

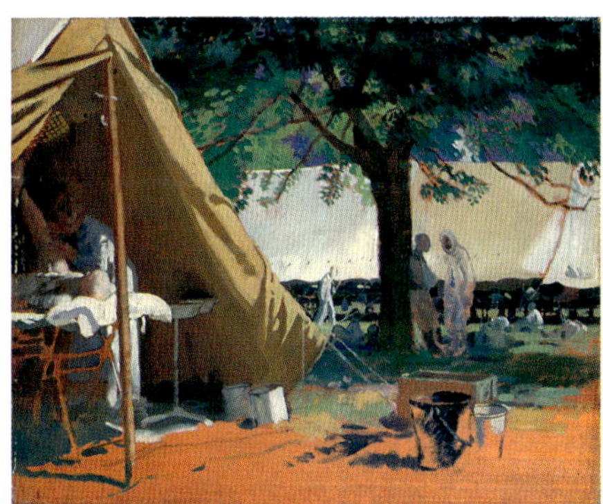

Orpen, William 1878–1931
*German Sick: Captured at Messines, in a
Canadian Hospital* 1917
oil on panel 49.5 x 60.9
IWM ART 3043

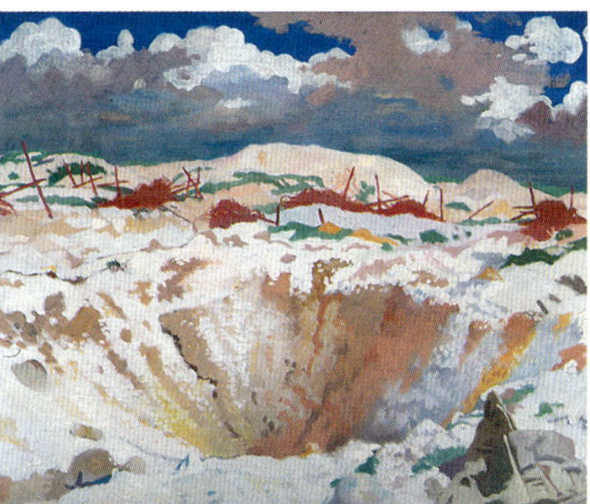

Orpen, William 1878–1931
German Wire, Thiepval 1917
oil on canvas 63.5 x 76.2 (E)
IWM ART 3006

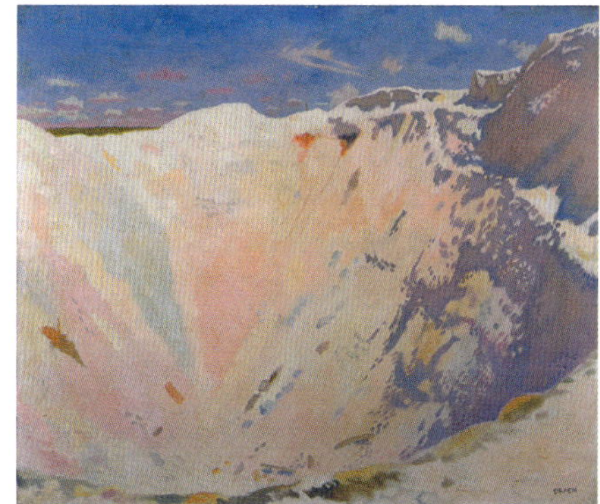

Orpen, William 1878–1931
Inside a Small Mine Crater, La Boisselle 1917
oil on canvas 63.5 x 76.2 (E)
IWM ART 2373

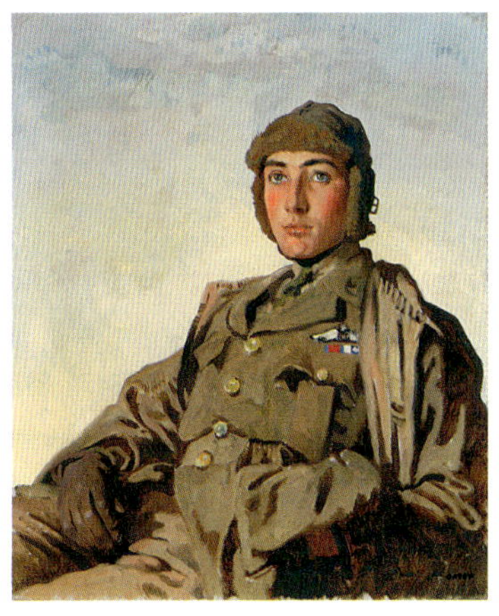

Orpen, William 1878–1931
*Lieutenant Arthur Percival Foley Rhys Davids
(1897–1917), DSO, MC* 1917
oil on canvas 91.4 x 76.2 (E)
IWM ART 3004

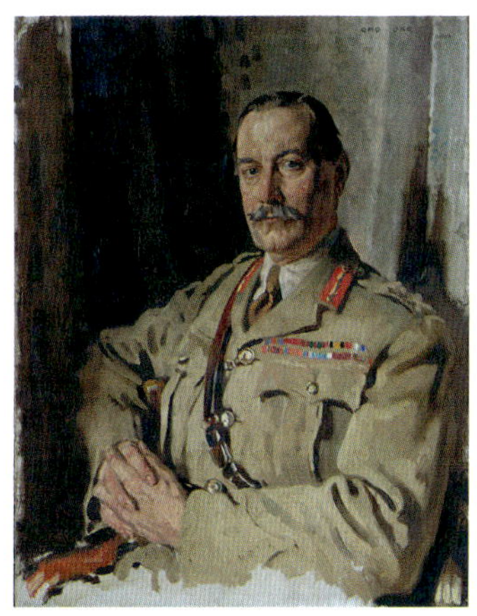

Orpen, William 1878–1931
*Lieutenant General Sir Travers Clarke, KCMG,
CB, Quartermaster General, France, December
1917* 1917
oil on canvas 91.4 x 76.2 (E)
IWM ART 2400

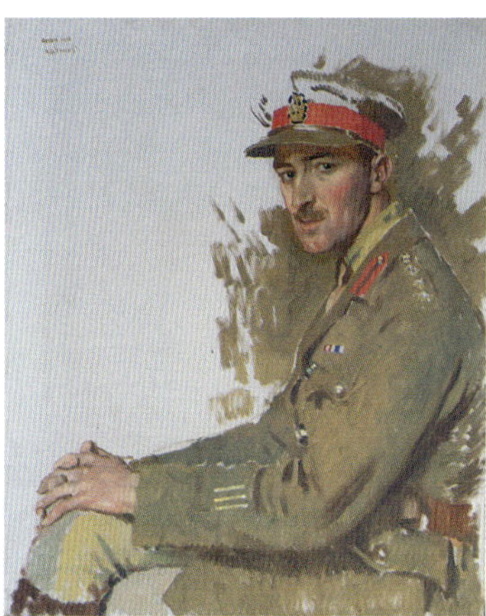

Orpen, William 1878–1931
Major F. E. Hotblack, DSO, MC 1917
oil on canvas 91.4 x 76.2
IWM ART 3007

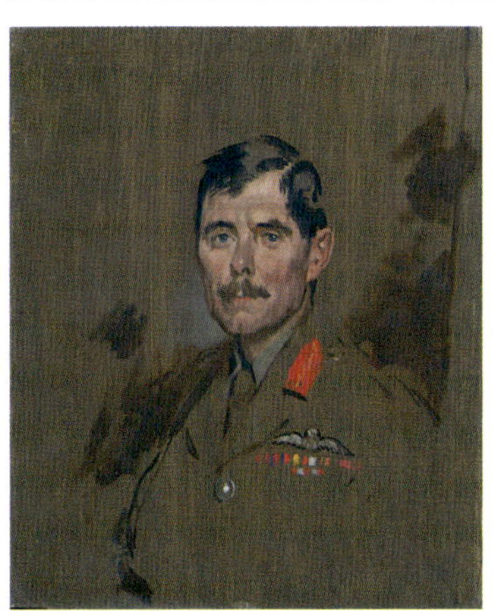

Orpen, William 1878–1931
*Major General Hugh M. Trenchard (1873–
1956), CB, DSO, Royal Flying Corps* 1917
oil on canvas 76.2 x 63.5
IWM ART 325

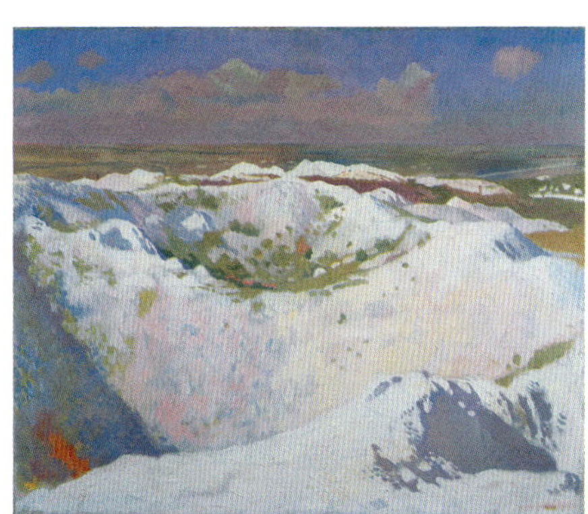

Orpen, William 1878–1931
Mines and the Bapaume Road, La Boisselle
1917
oil on canvas 63.5 x 76.2
IWM ART 2962

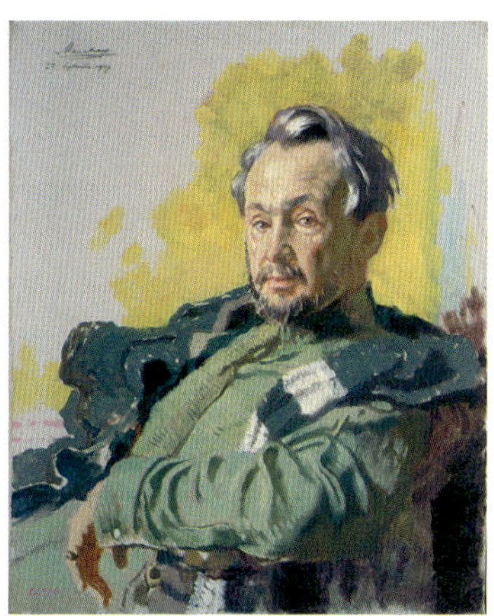

Orpen, William 1878–1931
*Monsieur R. D. De Maratray, French War
Correspondent for 'Le Petit Journal'* 1917
oil on canvas 76.2 x 63.5
IWM ART 3002

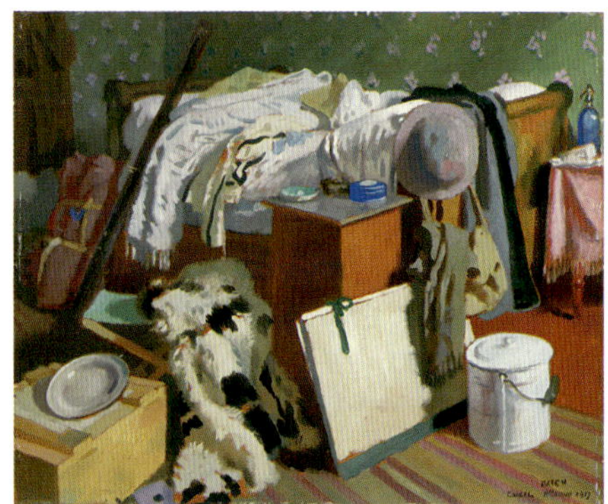

Orpen, William 1878–1931
My Work Room, Cassel 1917
oil on panel 49.5 x 60.9
IWM ART 2967

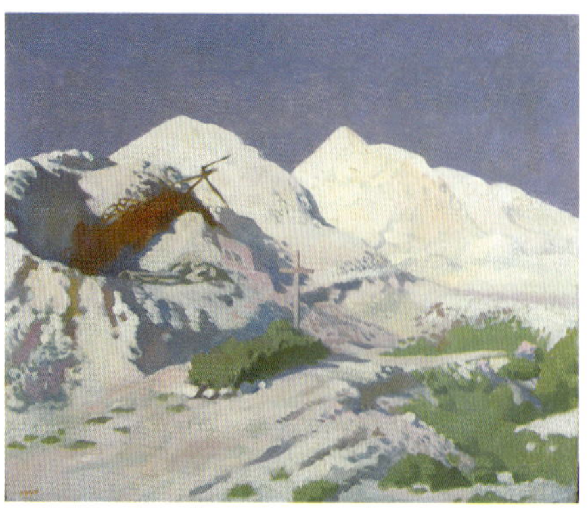

Orpen, William 1878–1931
Outside a Small Mine Crater, Bapaume Road 1917
oil on canvas 63.5 x 76.2
IWM ART 2381

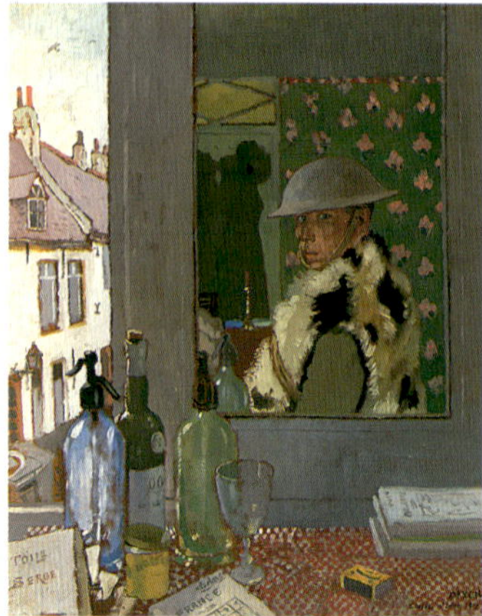

Orpen, William 1878–1931
Ready to Start: Self Portrait 1917
oil on panel 60.8 x 49.4
IWM ART 2380

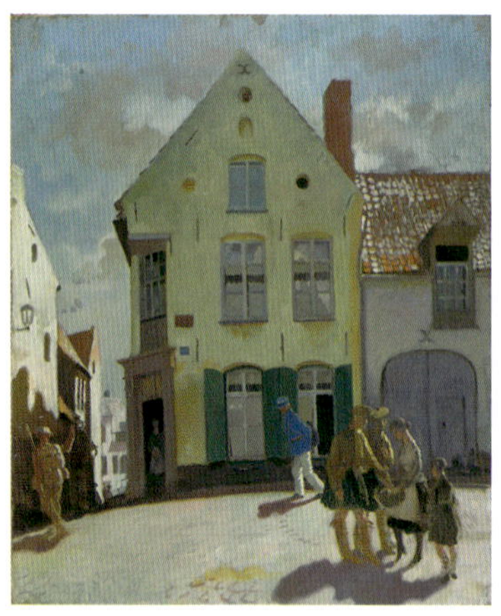

Orpen, William 1878–1931
Soldiers and Peasants, Cassel 1917
oil on canvas 76.2 x 63.5
IWM ART 2975

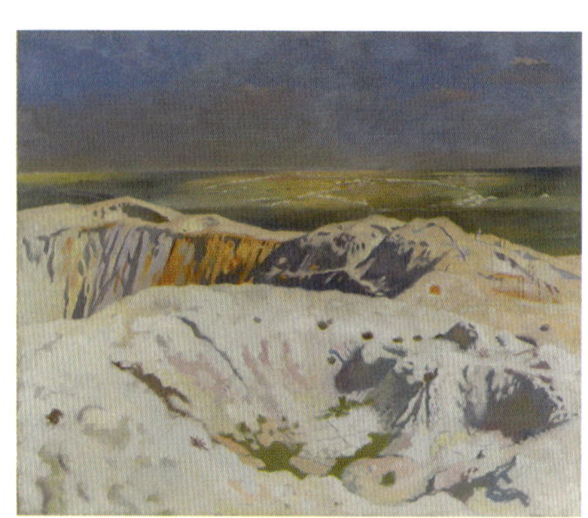

Orpen, William 1878–1931
The Big Crater 1917
oil on canvas 76.2 x 91.4 (E)
IWM ART 3001

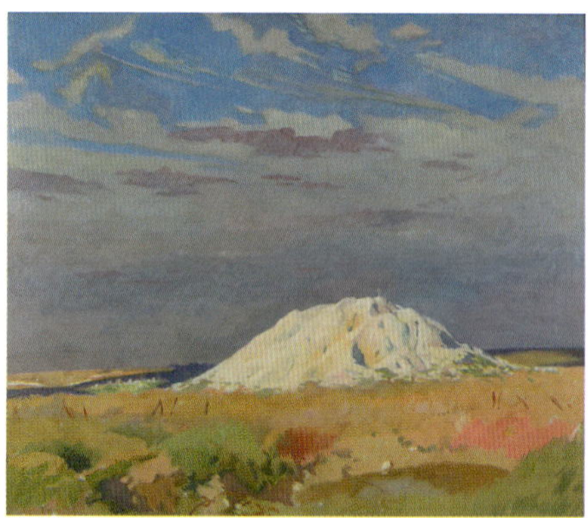

Orpen, William 1878–1931
The Butte de Warlencourt 1917
oil on canvas 76.2 x 91.4 (E)
IWM ART 2973

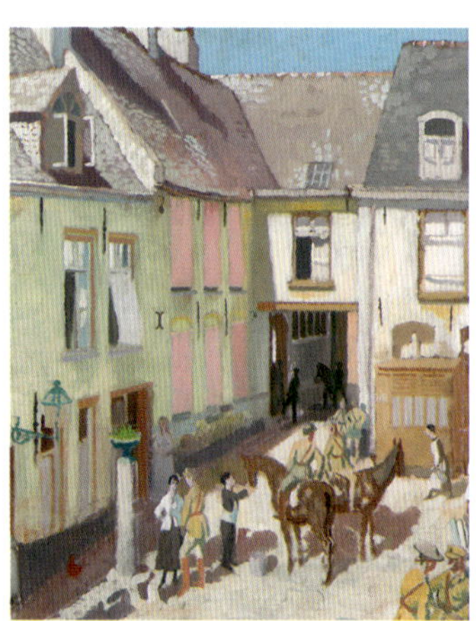

Orpen, William 1878–1931
The Courtyard, Hotel Sauvage, Cassel, Nord 1917
oil on panel 60.9 x 49.5
IWM ART 2992

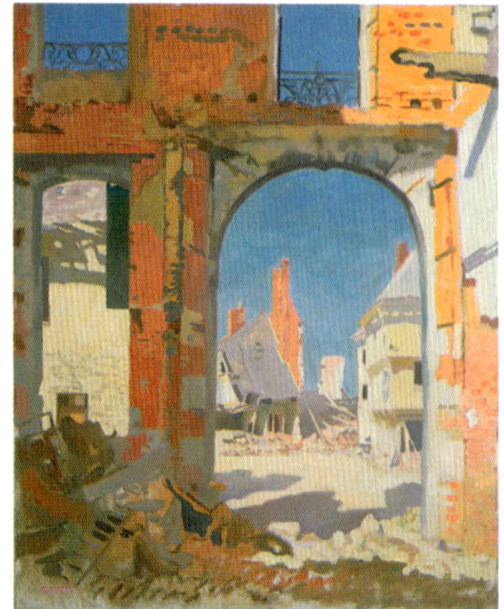

Orpen, William 1878–1931
The Girls' College, Péronne 1917
oil on canvas 76.2 x 63.5
IWM ART 2980

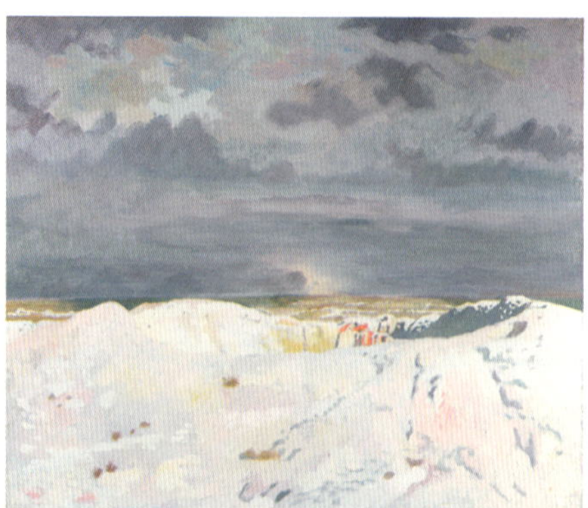

Orpen, William 1878–1931
The Great Mine, La Boisselle 1917
oil on canvas 76.2 x 91.4
IWM ART 2379

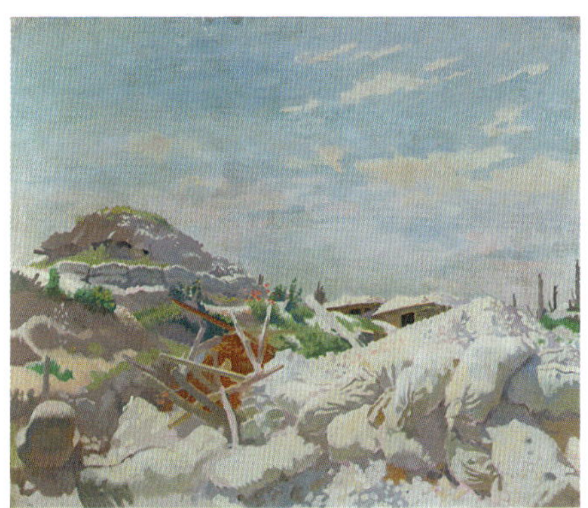

Orpen, William 1878–1931
The Gunners' Shelter, Thiepval 1917
oil on canvas 63.5 x 76.2
IWM ART 2372

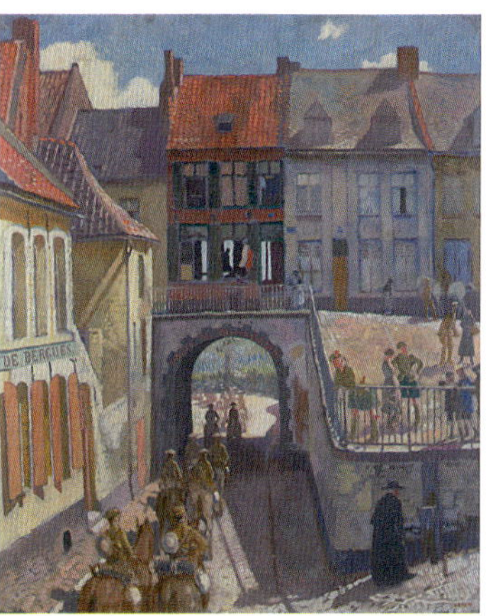

Orpen, William 1878–1931
The Household Brigade Passing to the Ypres Salient, Cassel 1917
oil on canvas 76.2 x 63.5
IWM ART 2968

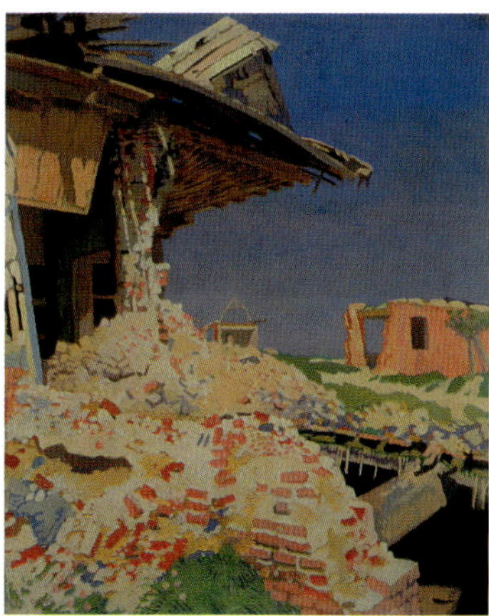

Orpen, William 1878–1931
The Main Street, Combles 1917
oil on canvas 76.2 x 63.5
IWM ART 2969

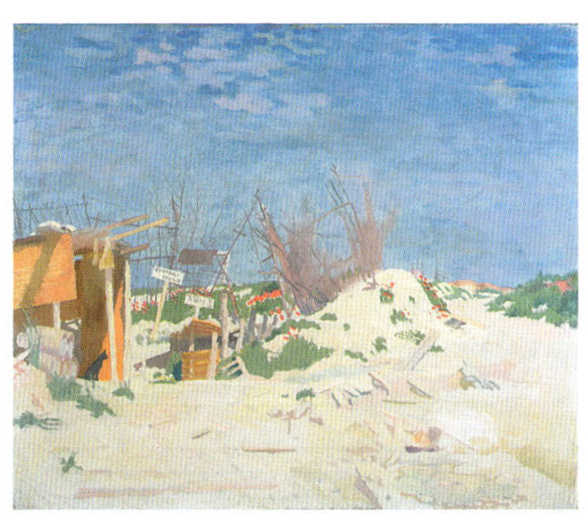

Orpen, William 1878–1931
The Main Street, Thiepval 1917
oil on canvas 63.5 x 76.2
IWM ART 2978

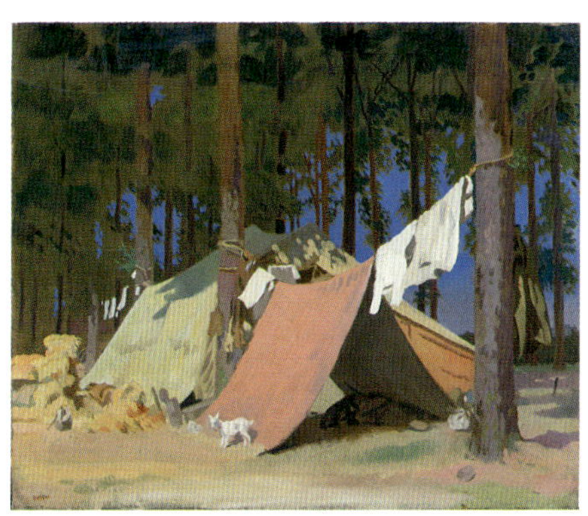

Orpen, William 1878–1931
The Mascot of the Coldstream Guards 1917
oil on canvas 63.5 x 76.2
IWM ART 3003

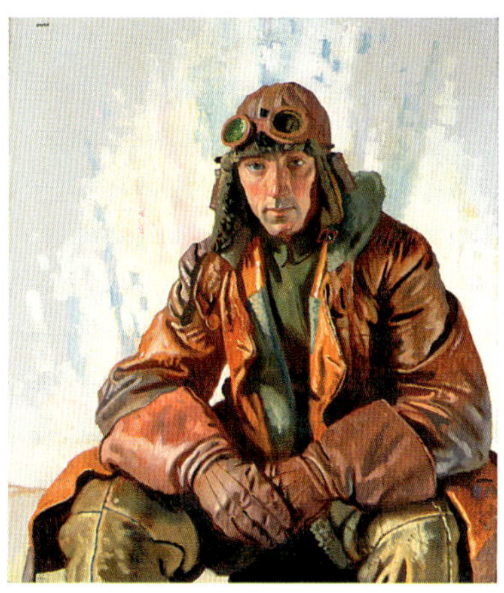

Orpen, William 1878–1931
The Non-Commissioned Officer Pilot, Royal Flying Corps: Flight Sergeant W. G. Bennett 1917
oil on canvas 91.4 x 81.2
IWM ART 2397

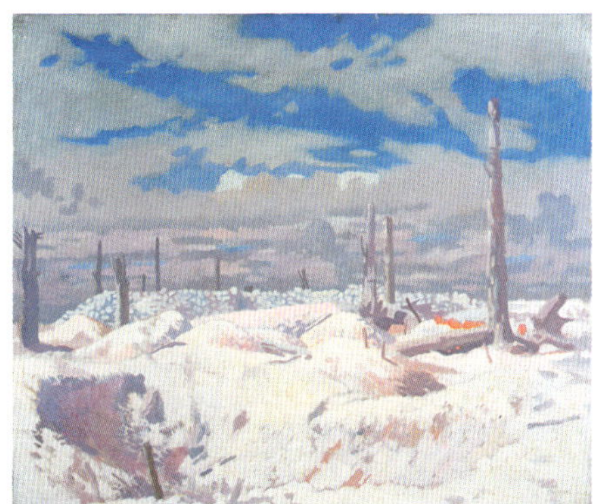

Orpen, William 1878–1931
The Schwaben Redoubt 1917
oil on canvas 63.5 x 76.2
IWM ART 3000

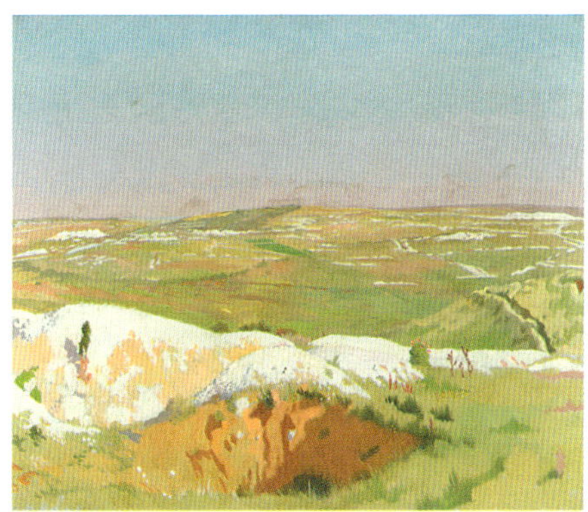

Orpen, William 1878–1931
The Somme: A Clear Day; View from the British Trenches opposite La Boisselle, Showing the German Front Line (…) 1917
oil on canvas 76.2 x 91.4
IWM ART 2970

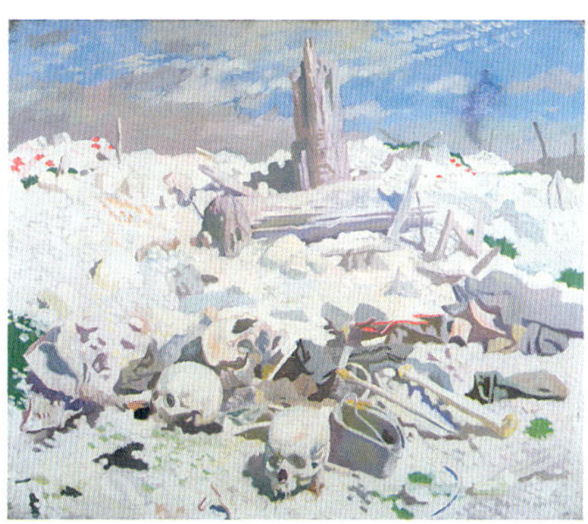

Orpen, William 1878–1931
Thiepval 1917
oil on canvas 63.5 x 76.2
IWM ART 2377

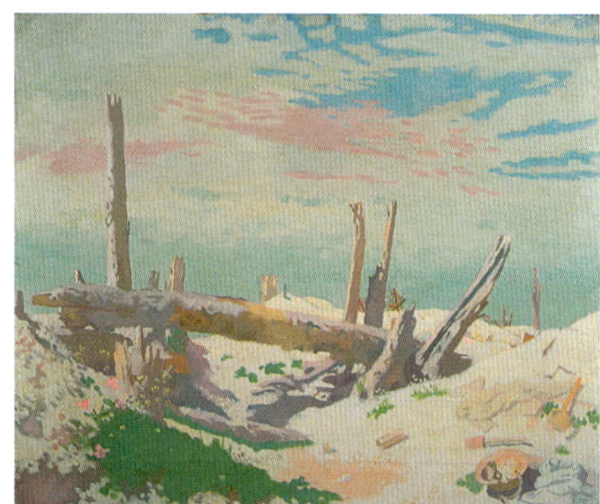

Orpen, William 1878–1931
Thiepval Wood 1917
oil on canvas 63.5 x 76.2
IWM ART 2998

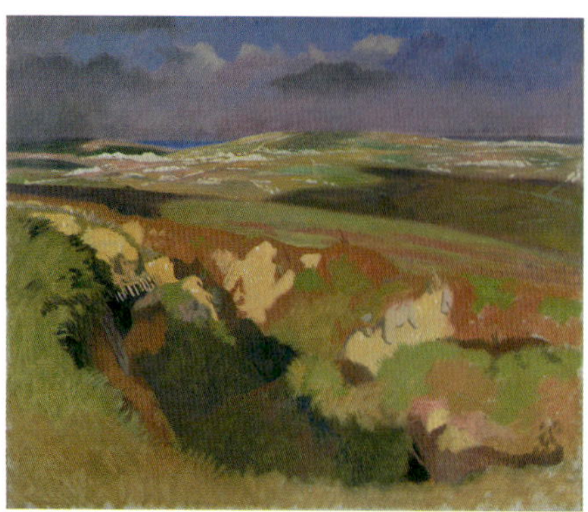

Orpen, William 1878–1931
View from the Old British Trenches: Looking towards La Boisselle, Courcelette on the Left, Martinpuich on the Right 1917
oil on canvas 76.2 x 91.4
IWM ART 2966

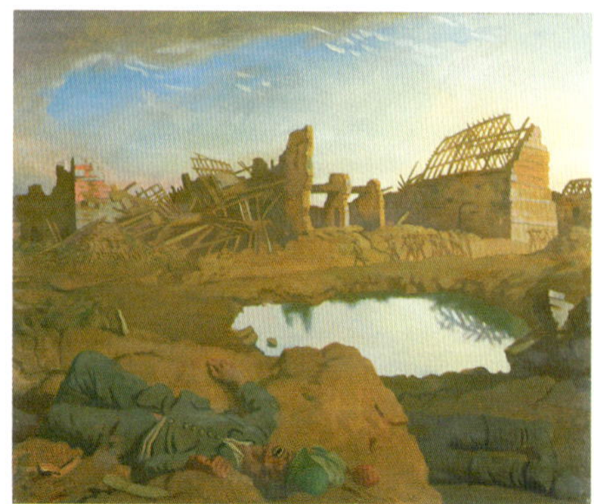

Orpen, William 1878–1931
Village: Evening 1917
oil on canvas 76.2 x 91.4
IWM ART 2977

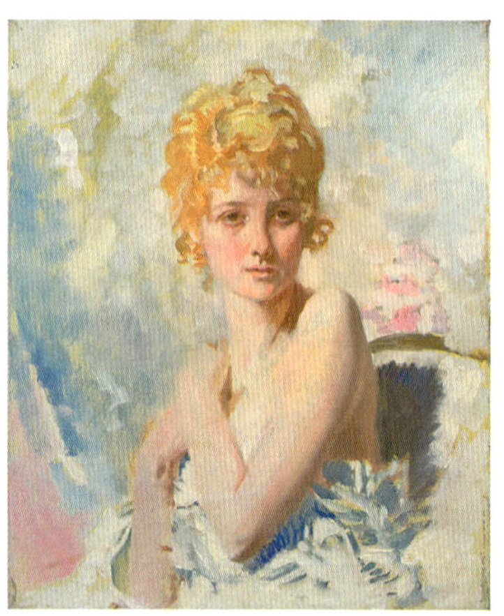

Orpen, William 1878–1931
The Refugee (B) 1917–1918
oil on canvas 76.2 x 63.5
IWM ART 3005

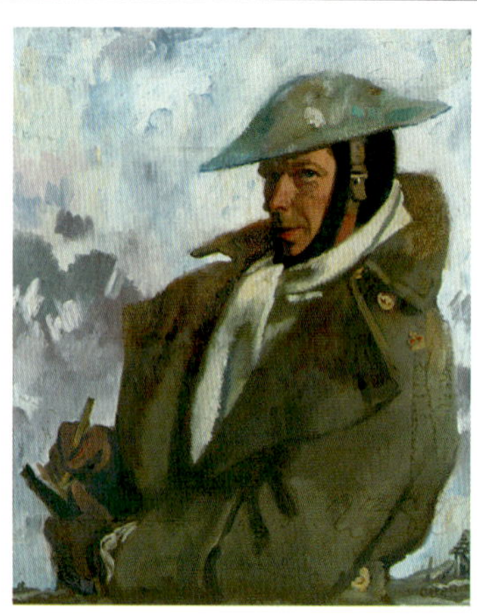

Orpen, William 1878–1931
Self Portrait c.1917
oil on canvas 76.2 x 63.5
IWM ART 2382

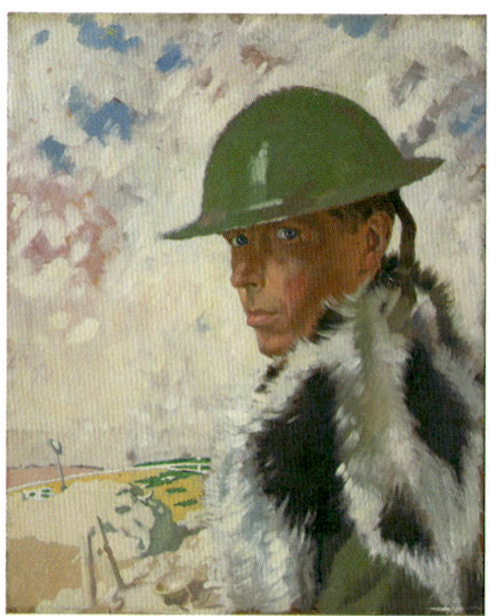

Orpen, William 1878–1931
Self Portrait c.1917
oil on panel 60.9 x 49.5
IWM ART 2993

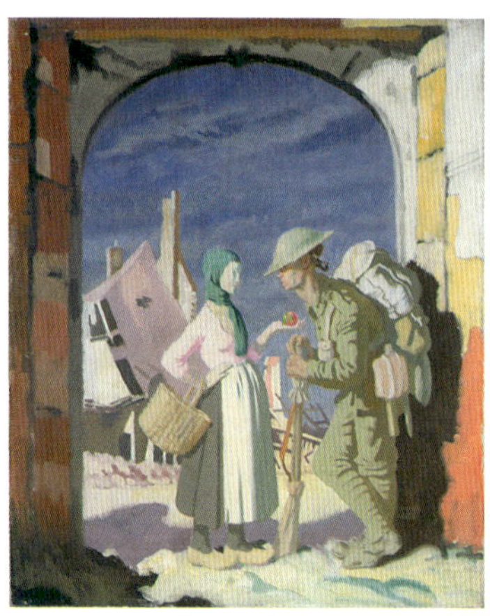

Orpen, William 1878–1931
Adam and Eve at Péronne 1918
oil on canvas 76.2 x 63.5
IWM ART 2981

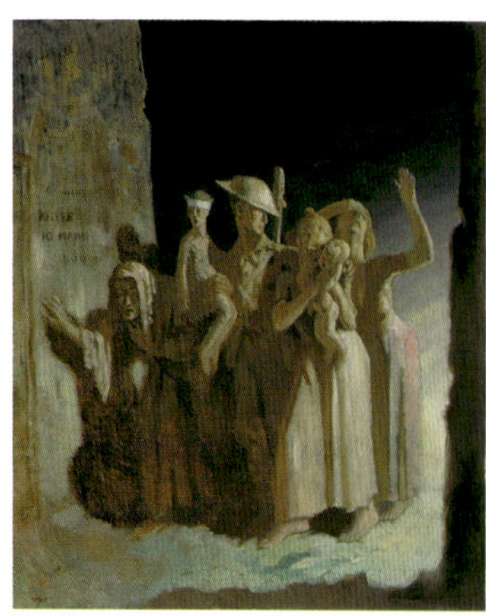

Orpen, William 1878–1931
Bombing: Night 1918
oil on canvas 76.2 x 63.5
IWM ART 2994

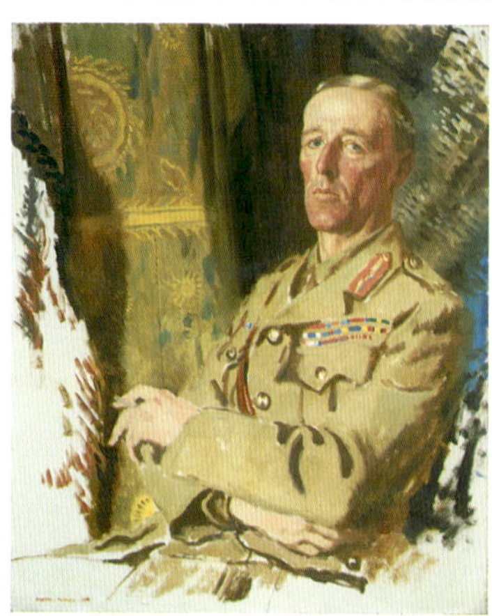

Orpen, William 1878–1931
Brigadier General the Right Honourable John Edward Bernard Seely (1868–1947), CB, DSO, MP 1918
oil on canvas 91.4 x 76.2
IWM ART 2982

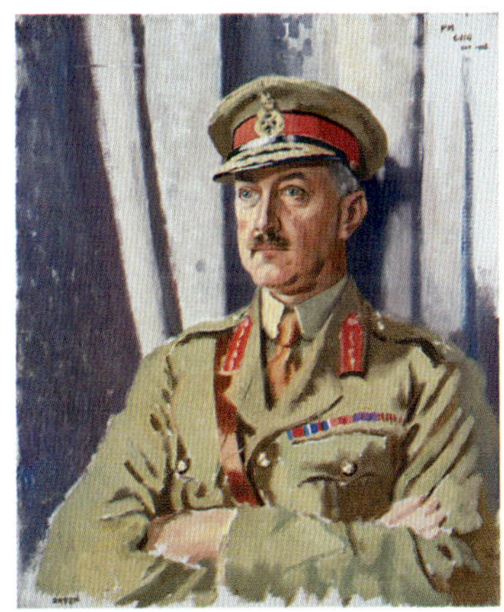

Orpen, William 1878–1931
Brigadier General William Thomas Francis Horwood (1868–1943), DSO, Late Provost-Marshal, General Headquarters, (…) 1918
oil on canvas 76.2 x 63.5
IWM ART 4179

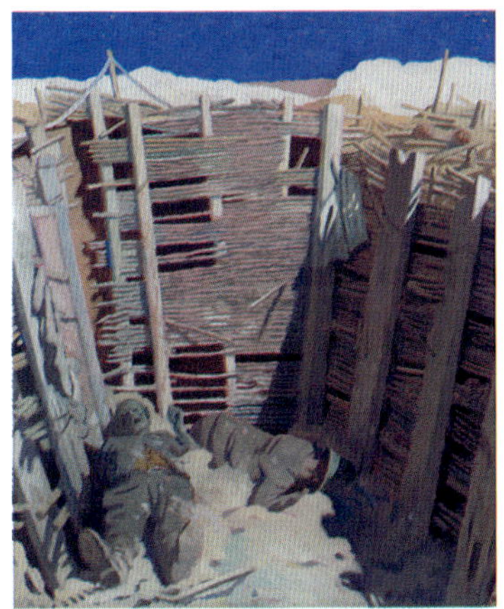

Orpen, William 1878–1931
Dead Germans in a Trench 1918
oil on canvas 91.4 x 76.2
IWM ART 2955

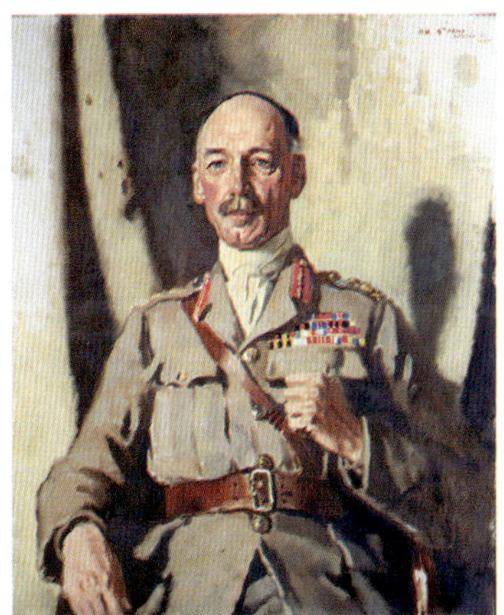

Orpen, William 1878–1931
General Sir Henry Seymour Rawlinson (1864–1925), Bt, GCVO, KCB, KCMG, Fourth Army 1918
oil on canvas 91.4 x 76.2
IWM ART 3047

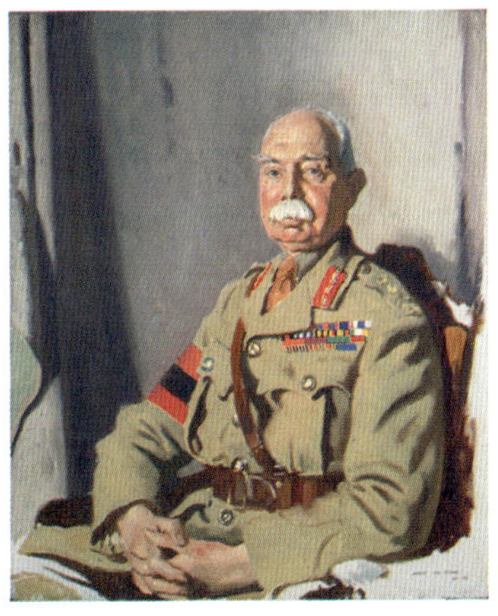

Orpen, William 1878–1931
General Sir Herbert Charles Onslow Plumer (1857–1932), GCMG, GCVO, KCB, Second Army 1918
oil on canvas 91.4 x 76.2
IWM ART 2398

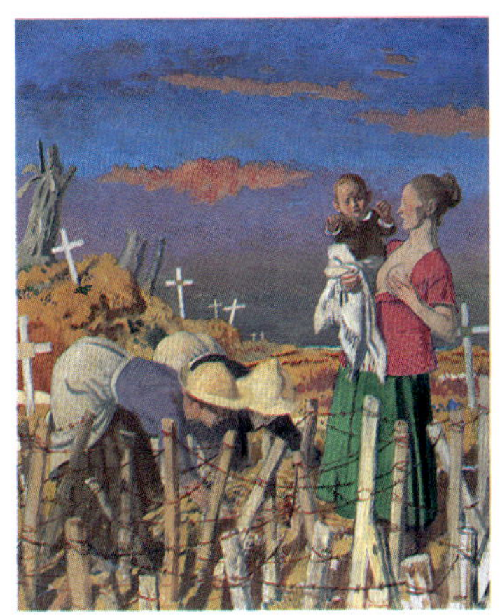

Orpen, William 1878–1931
Harvest 1918
oil on canvas 76.2 x 63.5
IWM ART 4663

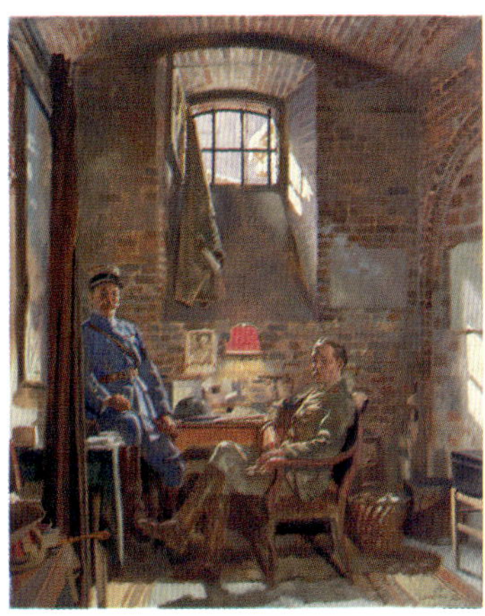

Orpen, William 1878–1931
In Their Cellar in Amiens: Captain R. Maude, Department of the Army, Provost Marshal General, Awarded the Croix de (…) 1918
oil on canvas 76.2 x 63.5
IWM ART 3049

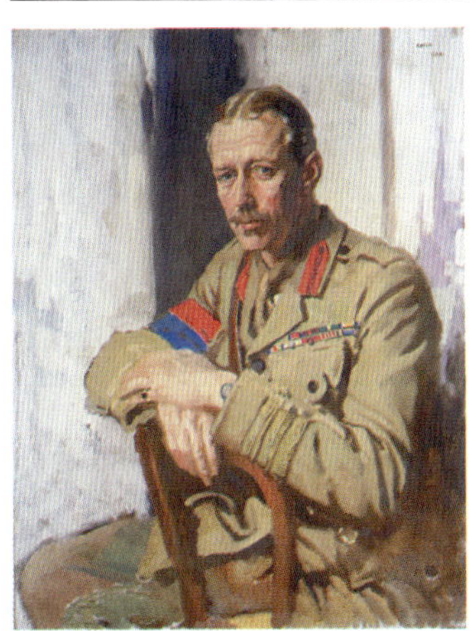

Orpen, William 1878–1931
Lieutenant Colonel A. N. Lee, DSO, OBE, TD, Censor in France of Paintings and Drawings by Artists at the Front 1918
oil on canvas 92 x 71
IWM ART 2399

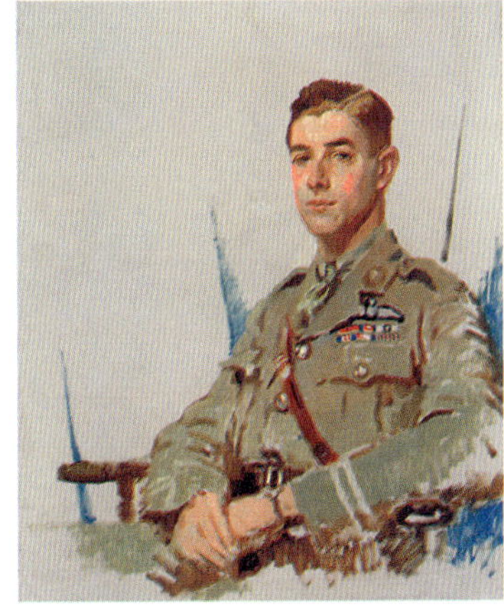

Orpen, William 1878–1931
Major James Byford McCudden (1895–1918), VC, DSO, MC 1918
oil on canvas 91.4 x 76.2
IWM ART 2979

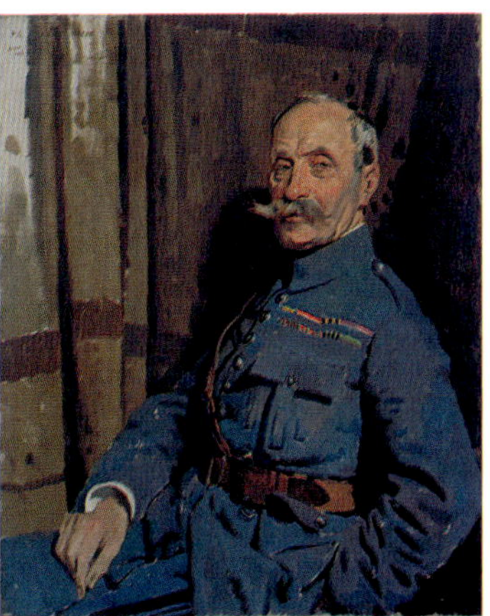

Orpen, William 1878–1931
Marshal Ferdinand Foch (1851–1929), OM 1918
oil on canvas 91.4 x 76.2
IWM ART 3046

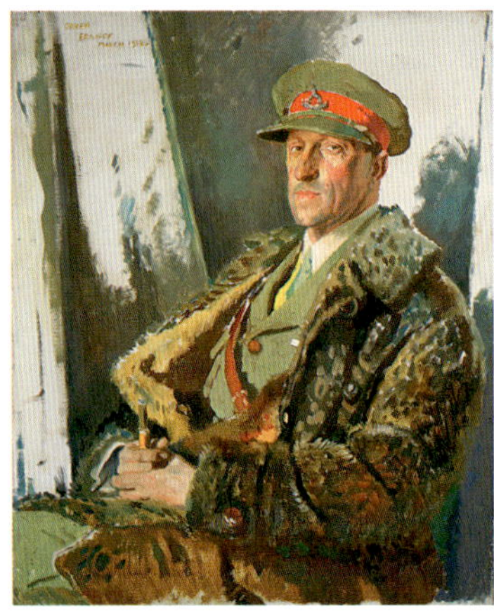

Orpen, William 1878–1931
Prince Antoine d'Orleans et Braganza, MC
1918
oil on canvas 91.4 x 76.2
IWM ART 4654

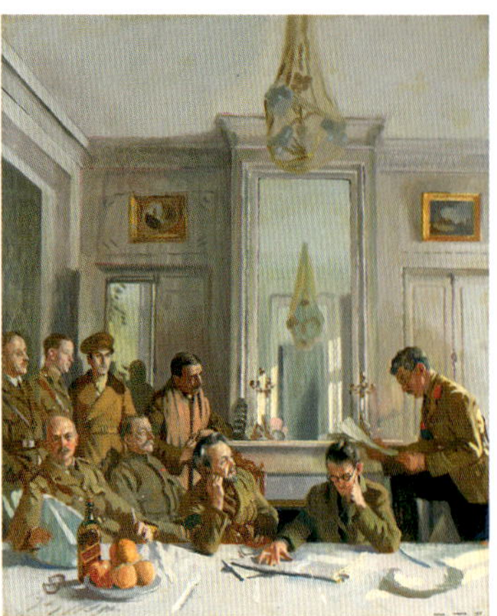

Orpen, William 1878–1931
Some Members of the Allied Press Camp with Their Press Officers 1918
oil on canvas 91.4 x 76.2
IWM ART 2971

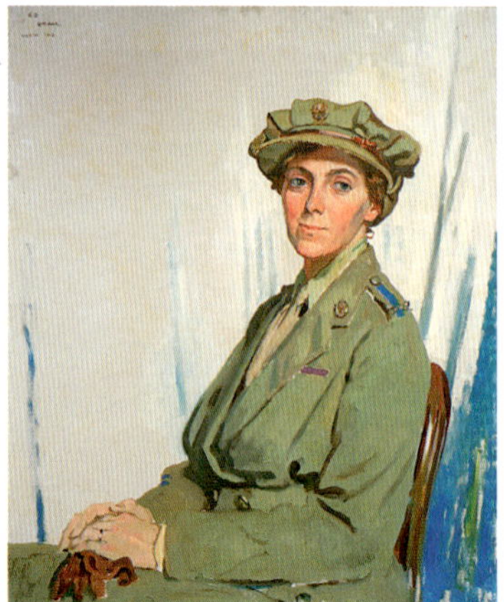

Orpen, William 1878–1931
The First Chief Controller, Queen Mary's Army Auxiliary Corps in France, Dame Helen Gwynne-Vaughan (1879–1967), (…) 1918
oil on canvas 91.4 x 76.2
IWM ART 3048

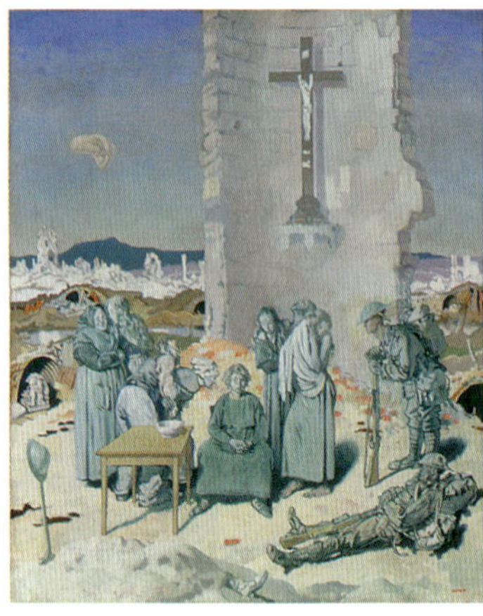

Orpen, William 1878–1931
The Mad Woman of Douai 1918
oil on canvas 91.4 x 76.2
IWM ART 4671

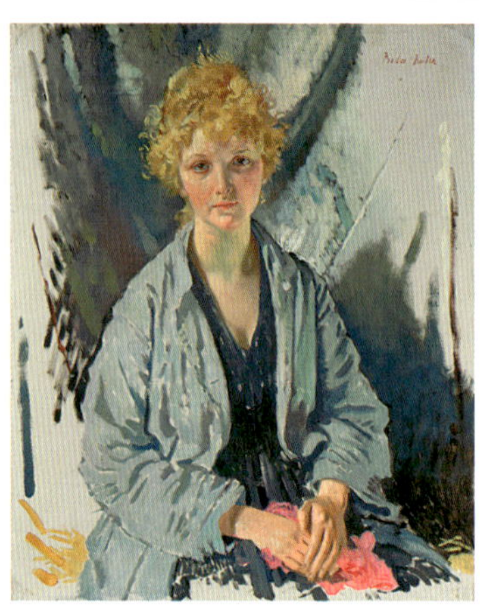

Orpen, William 1878–1931
The Refugee (A) 1918
oil on canvas 91.4 x 76.2
IWM ART 2964

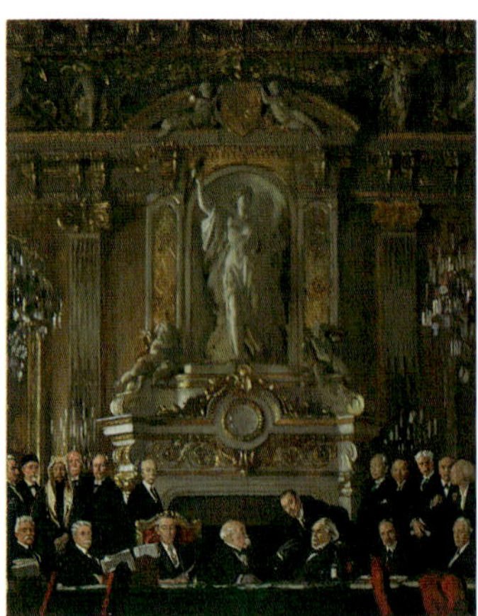

Orpen, William 1878–1931
A Peace Conference at the Quai d'Orsay 1919
oil on canvas 124.4 x 101.9
IWM ART 2855

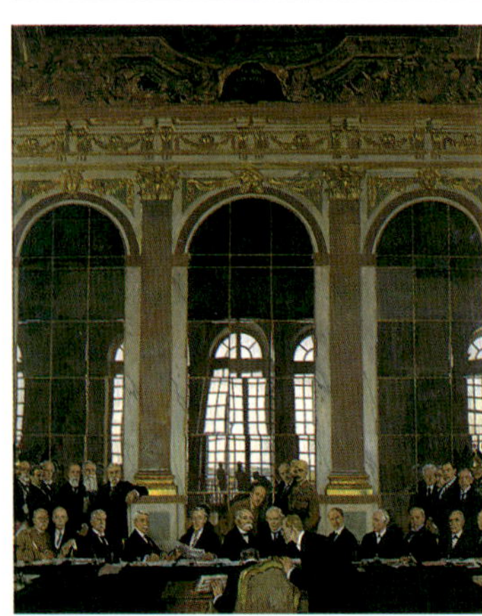

Orpen, William 1878–1931
The Signing of Peace in the Hall of Mirrors, Versailles, 28 June 1919 1919
oil on canvas 152.4 x 127
IWM ART 2856

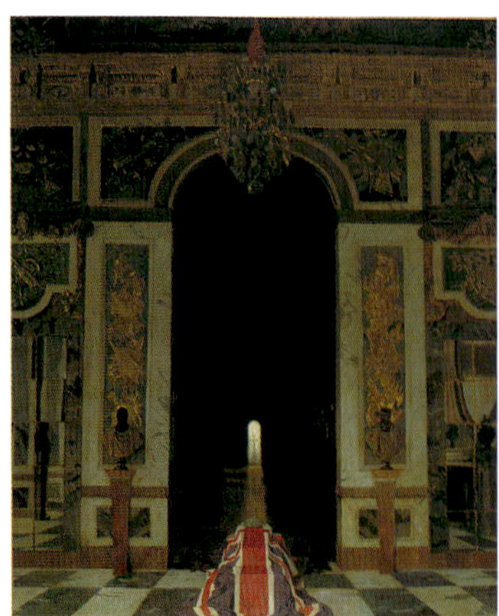

Orpen, William 1878–1931
To the Unknown British Soldier in France
1921–1928
oil on canvas 154.2 x 128.9
IWM ART 4438

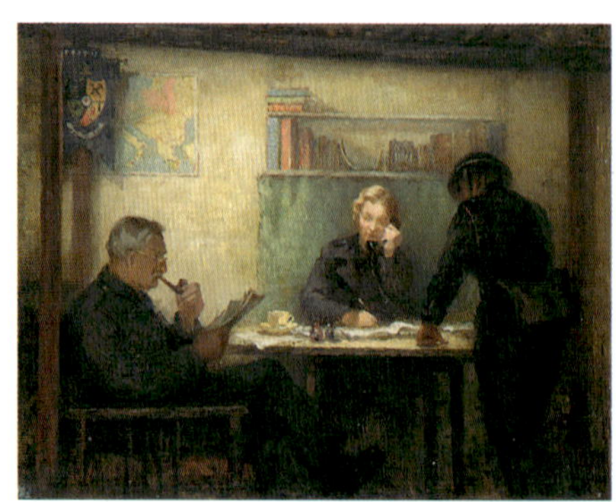

Ouless, Catherine 1879–1961
A Warden's Post in Kensington c.1941–1942
oil on canvas 46 x 58.8
IWM ART LD 6094

Facing Page Text: Jillard, Hilda 1899–1975, *What Harvest?* 1939 (p. 115)

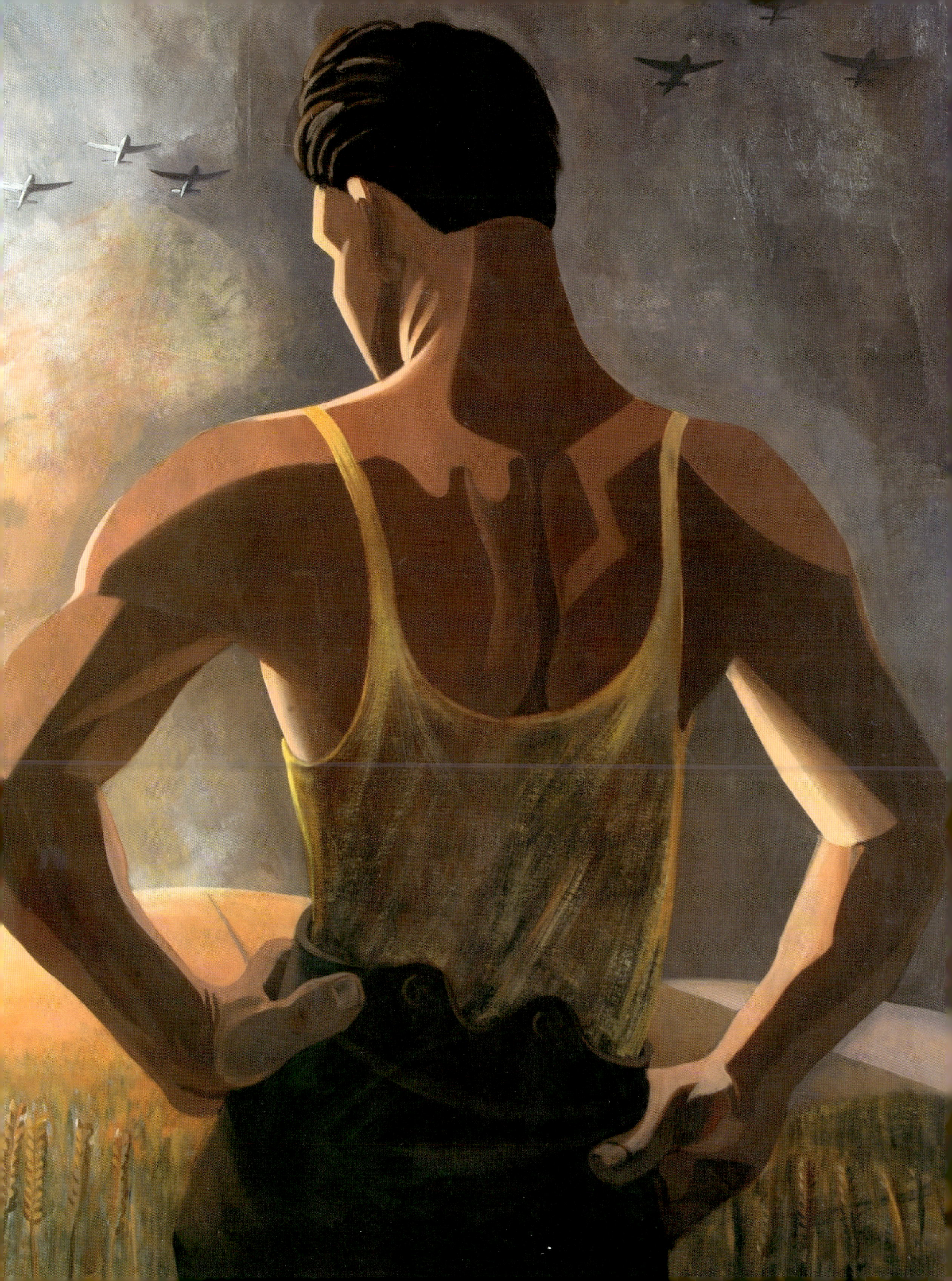

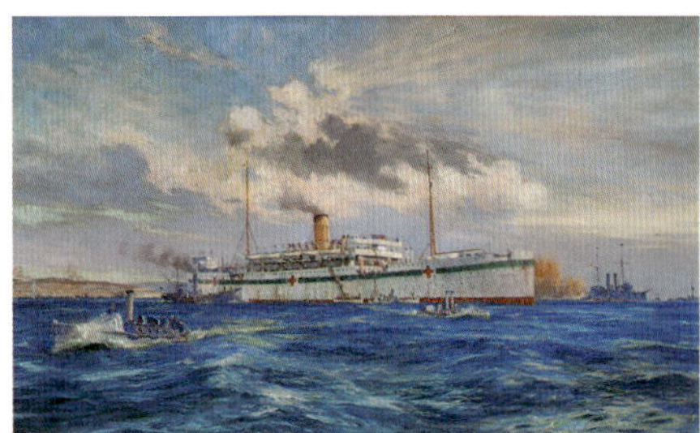

Parkes, Oscar 1885–1958
Royal Navy Hospital Ship 'Somali' off Cape
Helles: Walking Cases Coming on Board 1915
oil on canvas 76.2 x 127.6 (E)
IWM ART 4006

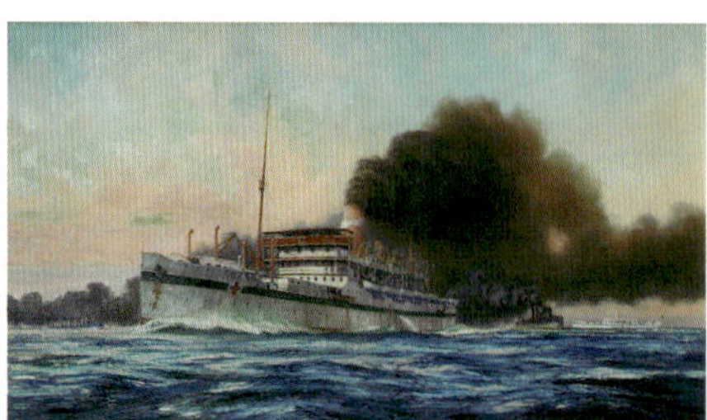

Parkes, Oscar 1885–1958
The Smoke Screen: Destroyers Throwing a
Smoke Screen around Hospital Ship 'Karapara'
after Hospital Ship 'Dover Castle' (…) c.1919
oil on canvas 76.2 x 128.2 (E)
IWM ART 2775

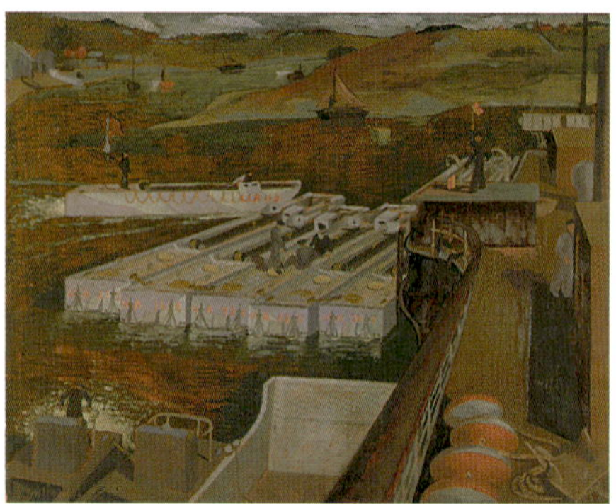

Paterson, G. W. Lennox 1915–1986
A Landing Craft Base: The 'SS Duchess of
Rothesay' at HMS Helder, near Clacton-on-Sea
1942
oil on panel 71.1 x 89.5
IWM ART LD 5755

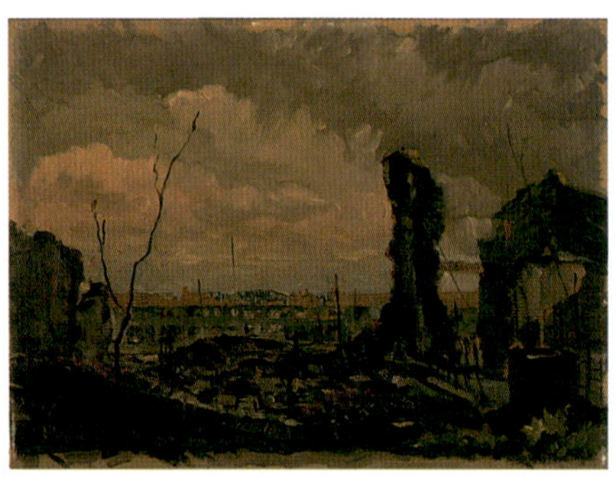

Payne, R. H. b.1921
Bomb Damage at Chingford, Essex 1942
oil on canvas 38.7 x 53.6
IWM ART LD 1832

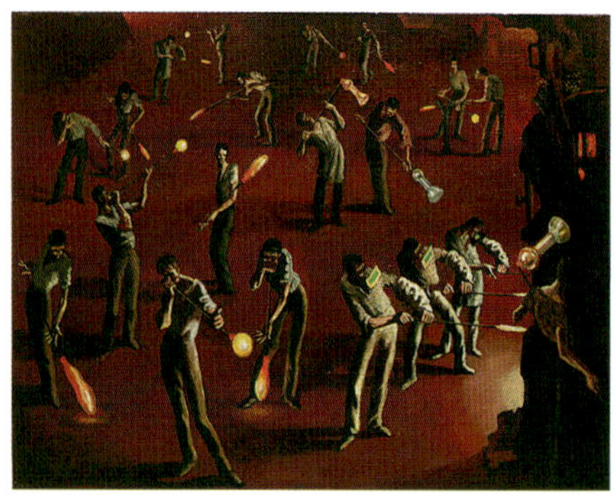

Peake, Mervyn 1911–1968
The Evolution of the Cathode Ray
(Radiolocation) Tube 1943
oil on canvas 85 x 110.4
IWM ART LD 3685

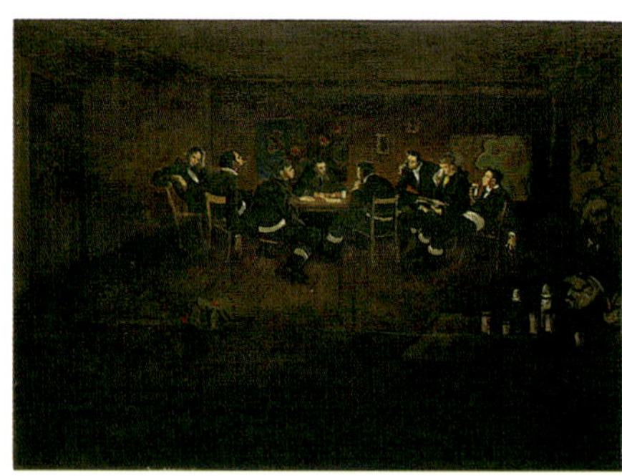

Peake, Mervyn 1911–1968
Interrogation of Pilots 1944
oil on canvas 90.8 x 127
IWM ART LD 4528

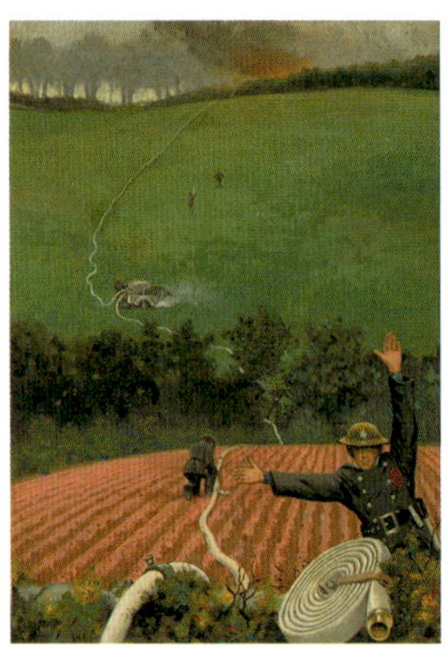

Pearce, C. J. active 1940s
A Crashed Aeroplane, Devon 1943
oil on card 53.3 x 38.7
IWM ART LD 3592

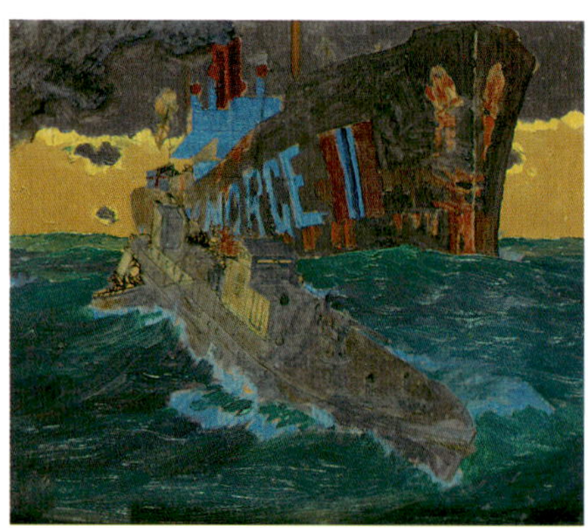

Pears, Charles 1873–1958
An Officer of a Motor Launch about to Board a
Norwegian Steamer 1914–1918
oil on panel 21.5 x 25.4
IWM ART 1049

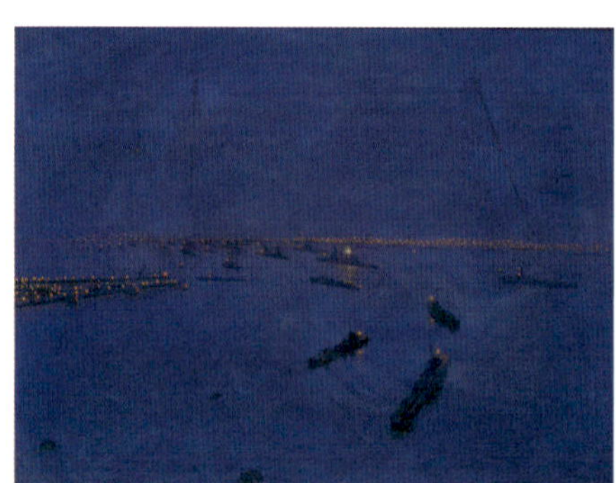

Pears, Charles 1873–1958
The Lights of Rosyth from the Forth Bridge
Footpath: Port Edgar and the Fleet 1914–1918
oil on canvas 71.1 x 91.4
IWM ART 631

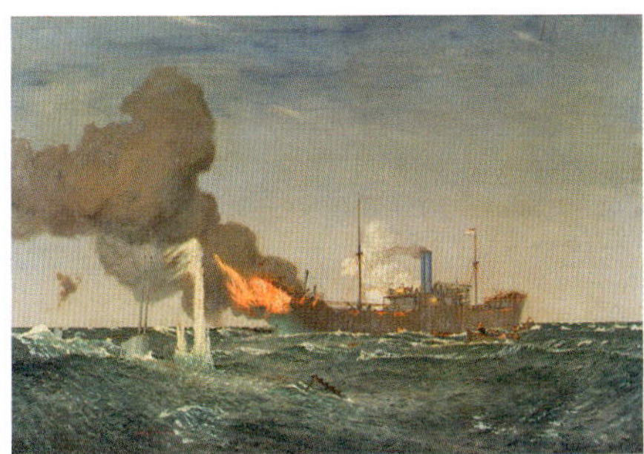

Pears, Charles 1873–1958
'HMS Dunraven VC' in Action against the Submarine That Sank Her, 8 August 1917
1917
oil on canvas 59 x 88.9
IWM ART 5130

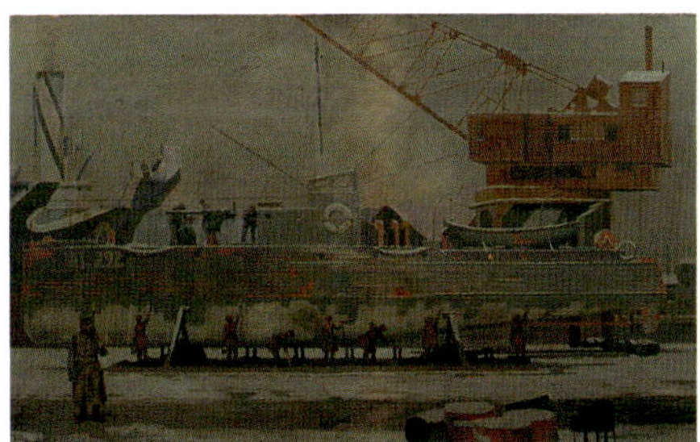

Pears, Charles 1873–1958
Women Putting Anti-Fouling Paint on the Bottom of a Motor Launch, Leith 1917
oil on canvas 66 x 107.9
IWM ART 1364

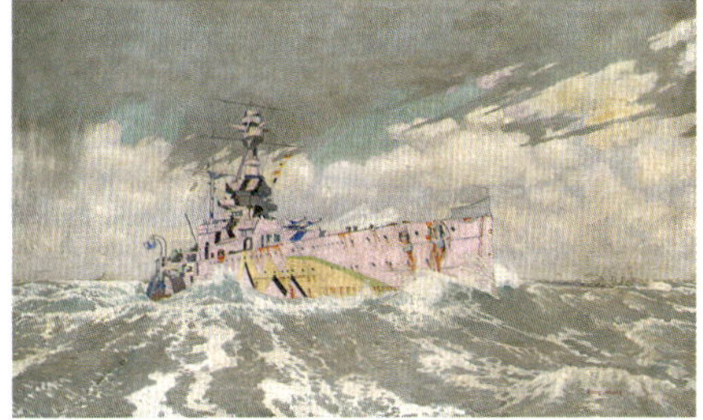

Pears, Charles 1873–1958
Dazzled, a Camouflaged Battleship: 'HMS Ramillies' in a Gale of Wind c.1917
oil on canvas 106.6 x 177.8
IWM ART 1367

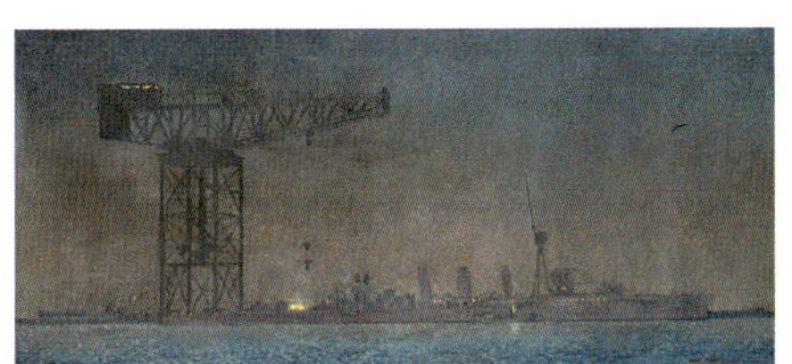

Pears, Charles 1873–1958
A Big Crane at Rosyth Placing a Gun on a Light Cruiser at Night 1918
oil on canvas 58.4 x 129.5
IWM ART 1347

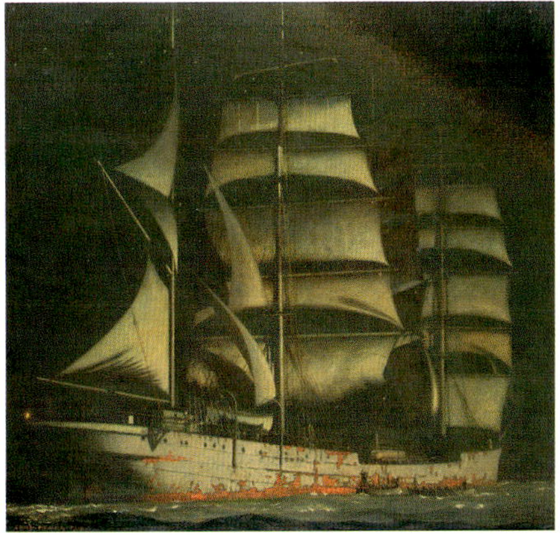

Pears, Charles 1873–1958
A Boarding Party of Royal Naval Reserve Men Going Aboard a Prize under Searchlight 1918
oil on canvas 101.9 x 107.9
IWM ART 1353

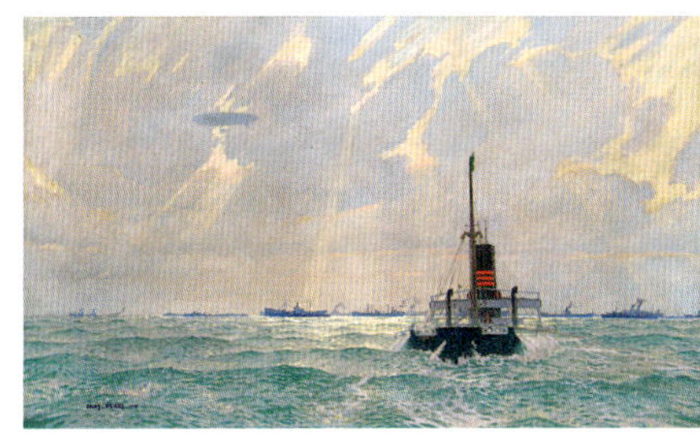

Pears, Charles 1873–1958
A Convoy 1918
oil on canvas 76.2 x 129.5
IWM ART 632

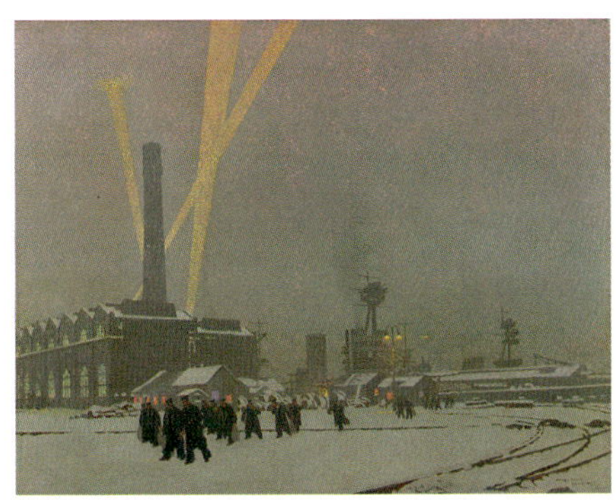

Pears, Charles 1873–1958
A Corner of the Dockyard, Rosyth: Winter
1918
oil on canvas 71.1 x 91.4
IWM ART 1354

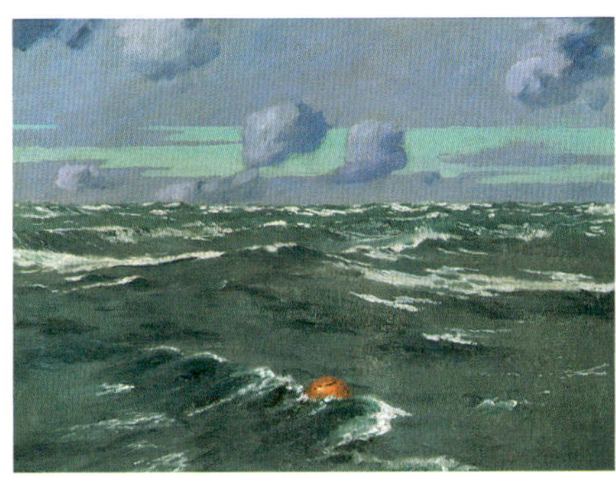

Pears, Charles 1873–1958
A Drifting Mine 1918
oil on panel 35.5 x 45.7
IWM ART 1350

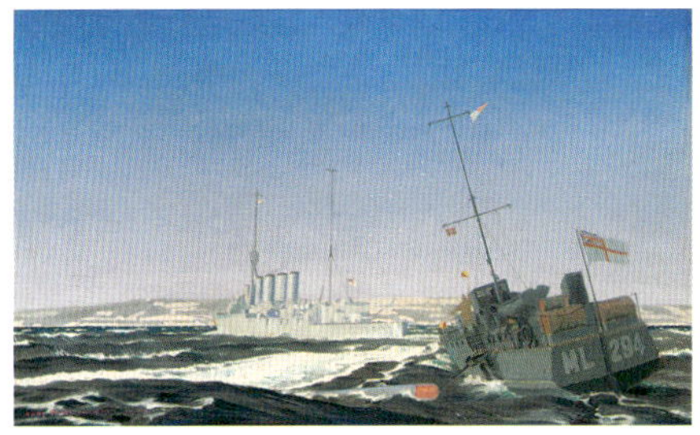

Pears, Charles 1873–1958
A Motor Launch Recovering a Torpedo: 'HMS Yarmouth' at Practice, January 1918 1918
oil on canvas 35.5 x 59.6
IWM ART 1366

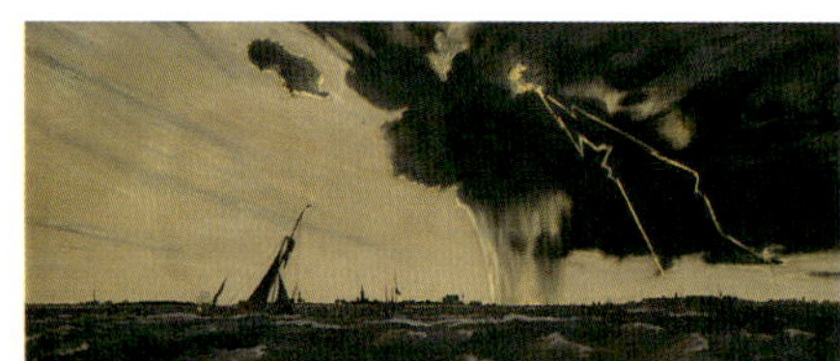

Pears, Charles 1873–1958
*A Thunderstorm, Harwich: Submarines
Leaving Port* 1918
oil on canvas 58.4 x 129.5
IWM ART 1371

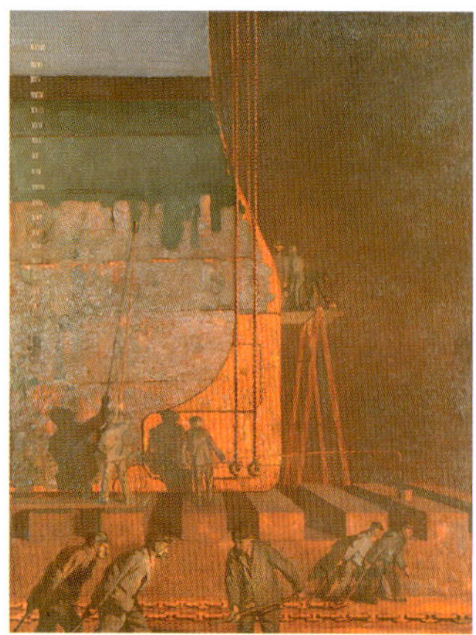

Pears, Charles 1873–1958
*At Work on a Battleship at Rosyth: Testing
Cables at Night by the Light of a Flare Lamp*
1918
oil on canvas 91.4 x 71.1
IWM ART 1365

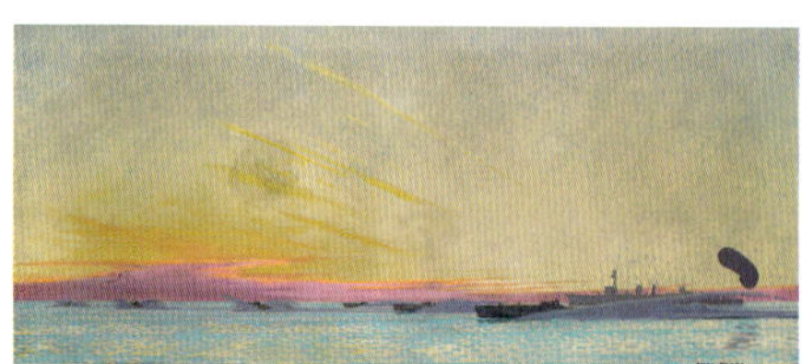

Pears, Charles 1873–1958
*Dawn: Sending away Coastal Motor Boats, 11
August 1918* 1918
oil on canvas 58.4 x 129.5
IWM ART 1362

Pears, Charles 1873–1958
*German Star Shells: Men at the Guns off the
German Coast, 11 August 1918* 1918
oil on canvas 66 x 107.9
IWM ART 1356

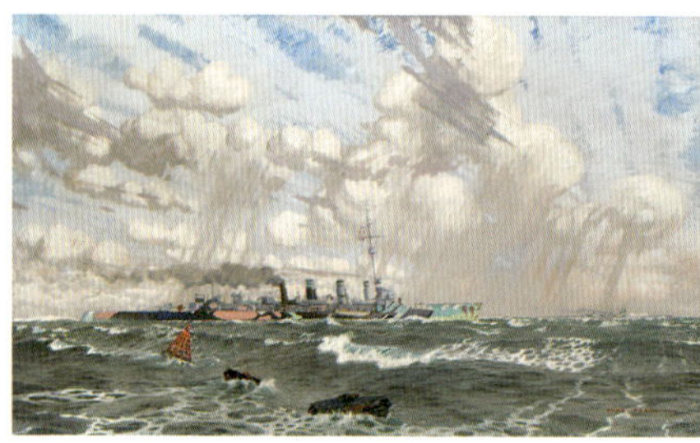

Pears, Charles 1873–1958
‘HMS Fearless’ 1918
oil on canvas 106.6 x 177.8
IWM ART 1360

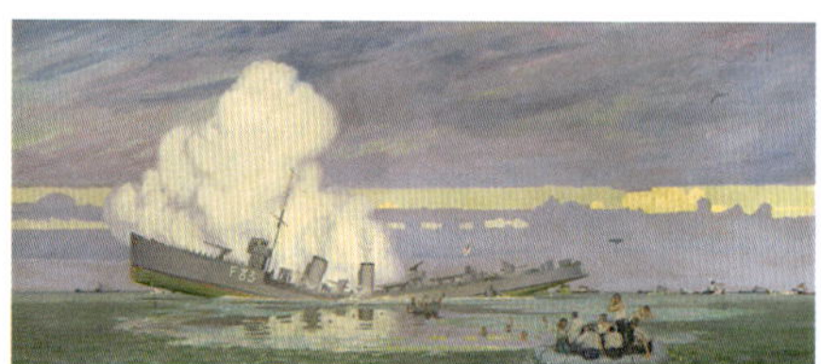

Pears, Charles 1873–1958
‘HMS Ullswater’: A Destroyer Torpedoed 1918
oil on canvas 58.4 x 129.5
IWM ART 1351

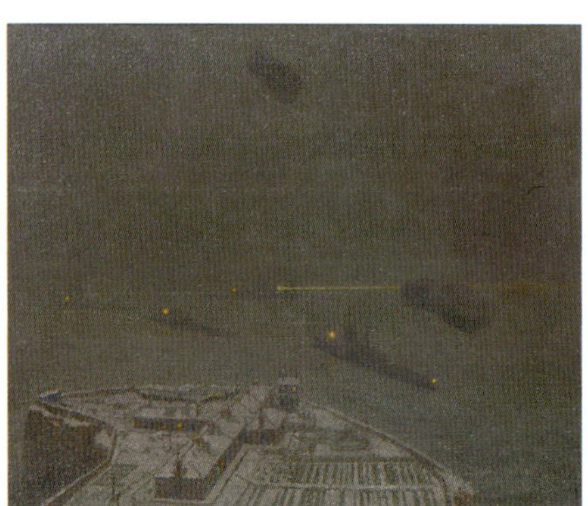

Pears, Charles 1873–1958
*North Queensferry Signal Station, Winter: The
First Battle Cruiser Squadron Seen from the
Forth Bridge* 1918
oil on canvas 50.8 x 60.9
IWM ART 627

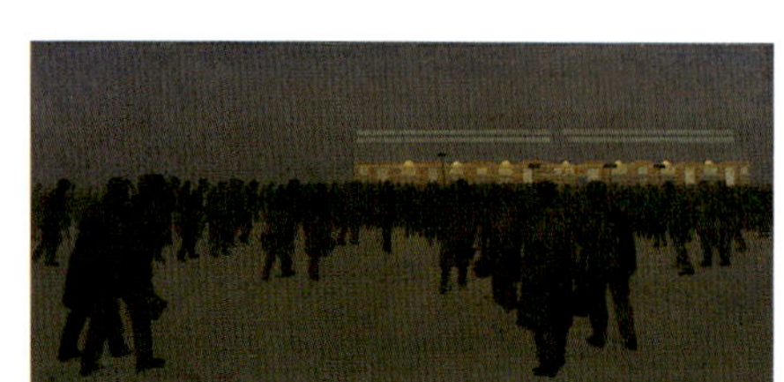

Pears, Charles 1873–1958
Pay Night, Rosyth, in Winter 1918
oil on canvas 58.4 x 129.5
IWM ART 1355

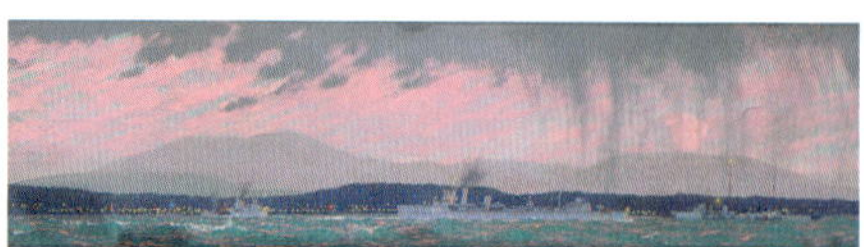

Pears, Charles 1873–1958
*Port Edgar, Firth of Forth, the Destroyer Base
of the Northern Waters: Sunset, V-Class
Destroyers Backing out to Sea* 1918
oil on canvas 29.2 x 95.2
IWM ART 629

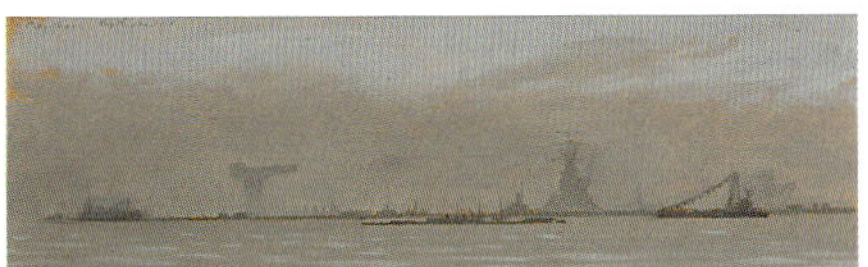

Pears, Charles 1873–1958
Rosyth: Fog Obscuring the Dockyard 1918
oil on panel 11.4 x 37.4
IWM ART 639

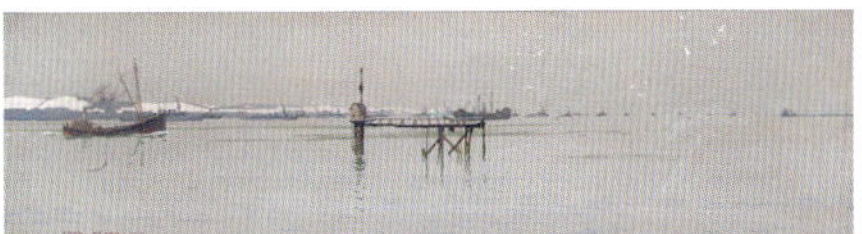

Pears, Charles 1873–1958
Rosyth: Light Cruiser Anchorage 1918
oil on canvas 29.2 x 95.2
IWM ART 628

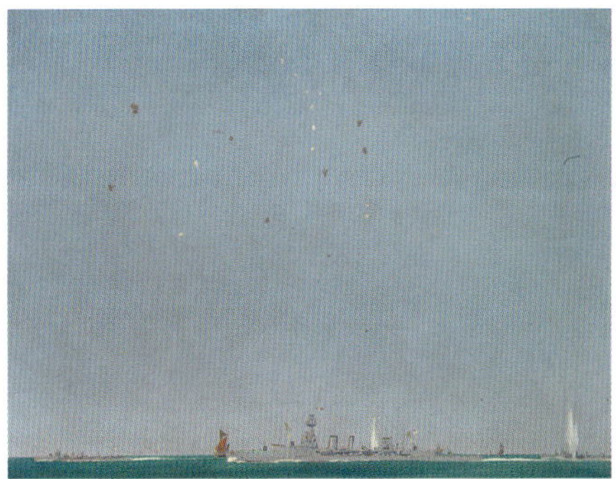

Pears, Charles 1873–1958
Strafed by a German Seaplane off Terschelling 1918
oil on canvas 85 x 111.7
IWM ART 1361

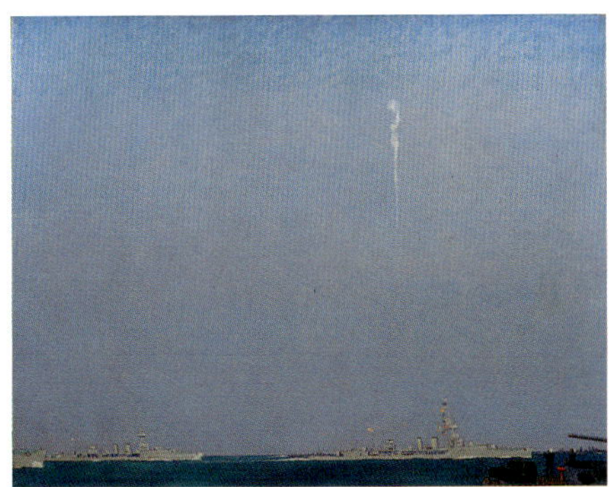

Pears, Charles 1873–1958
The Action of 11 August 1918, Island of Borkum: Zeppelin Falling; the Flagship is Flying the Signal 1918
oil on canvas 85 x 110.4
IWM ART 1357

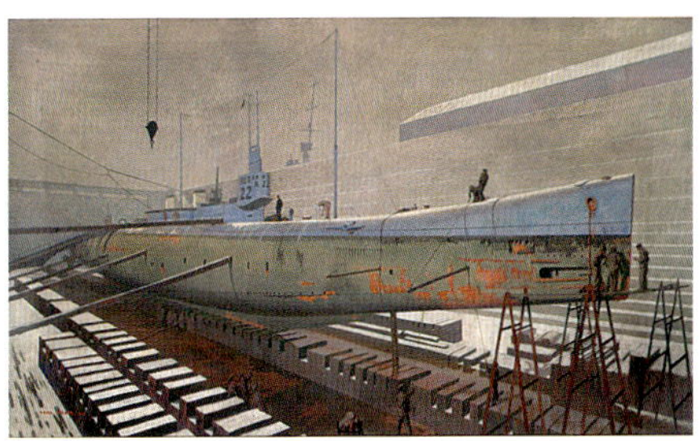

Pears, Charles 1873–1958
The British Submarine K22 in Dry Dock, at Rosyth, in Winter 1918
oil on canvas 106.6 x 177.8
IWM ART 1359

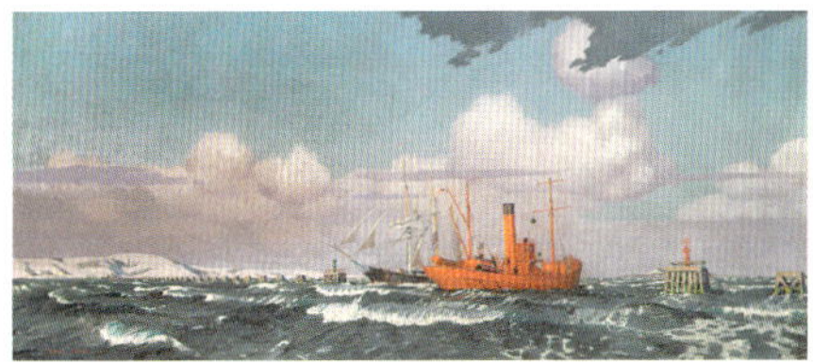

Pears, Charles 1873–1958
The Gate Ship at Granton Painted Scarlet to Indicate the Port Entrance through One of the Barriers across the Firth of Forth 1918
oil on canvas 58.4 x 129.5
IWM ART 1358

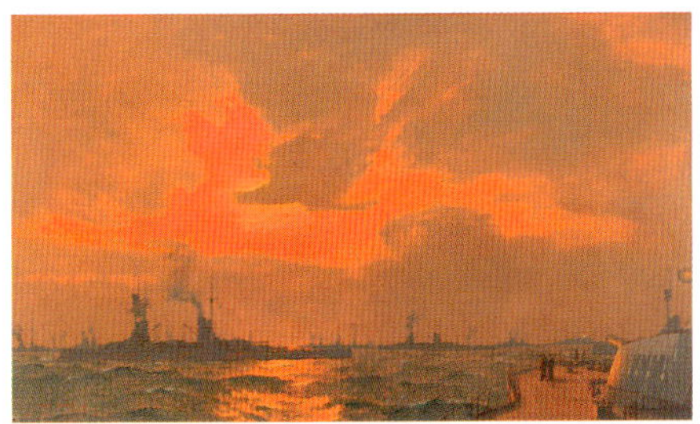

Pears, Charles 1873–1958
The German Fleet at Anchor off Inchkeith, Firth of Forth: After the Surrender, 22 November 1918 1918
oil on canvas 76.8 x 130.1
IWM ART 1926

Pears, Charles 1873–1958
The Harwich Gate Ships, Barrier and Light Cruisers under Searchlight 1918
oil on canvas 58.4 x 129.5
IWM ART 1368

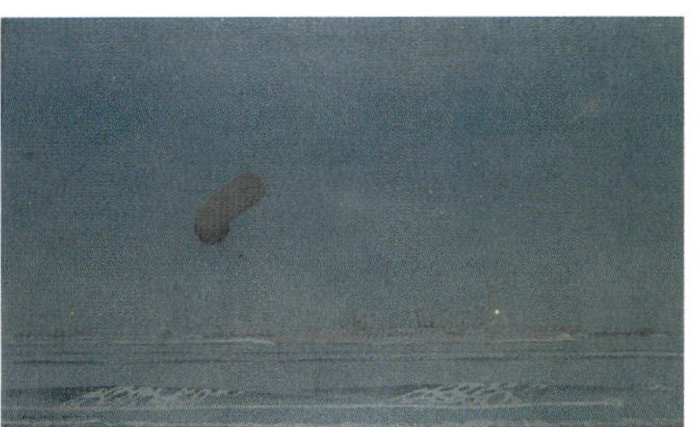

Pears, Charles 1873–1958
The North Sea: The Night of 10 August 1918 1918
oil on canvas 76.2 x 129.5
IWM ART 1363

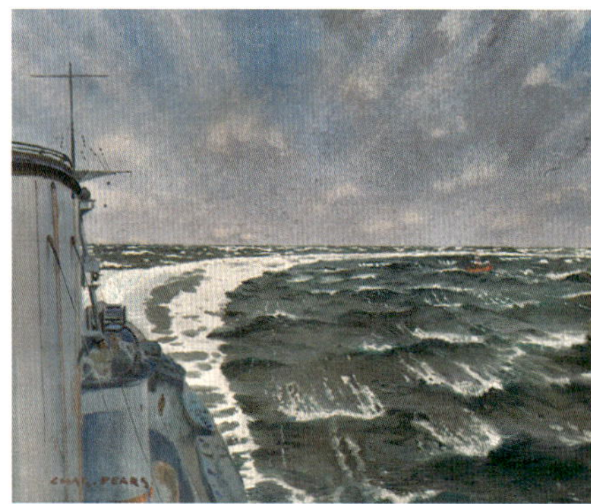

Pears, Charles 1873–1958
The Wake: 'HMS Courageous' at Top Speed
1918
oil on canvas 50.8 x 60.9
IWM ART 1370

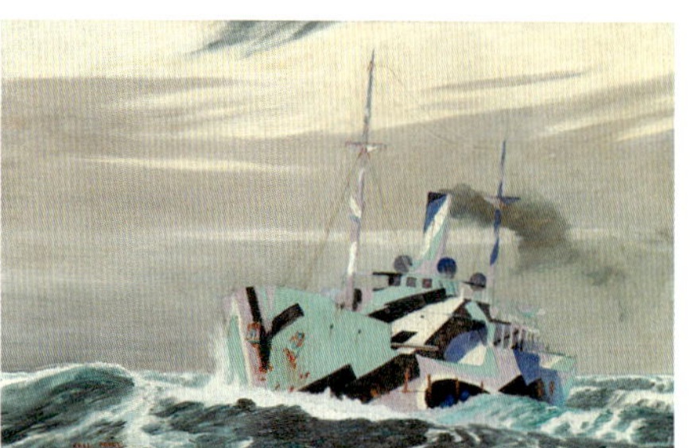

Pears, Charles 1873–1958
A Dazzled Merchantman c.1918
oil on canvas 40.6 x 60.9
IWM ART 2878

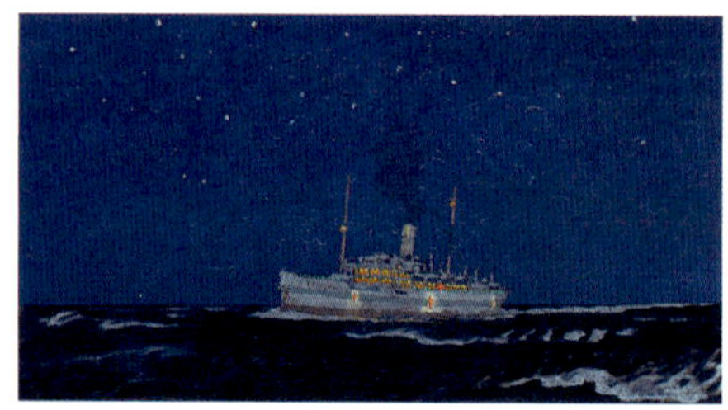

Pears, Charles 1873–1958
A Hospital Ship at Night c.1918
oil on panel 19 x 34.9
IWM ART 645

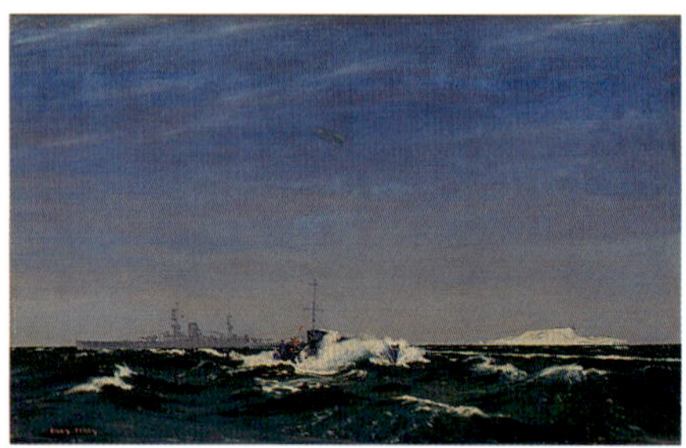

Pears, Charles 1873–1958
Big and Little: 'HMS Glorious' and a Motor Launch at the Island of Inchkeith under Snow c.1918
oil on panel 38.1 x 60.9
IWM ART 626

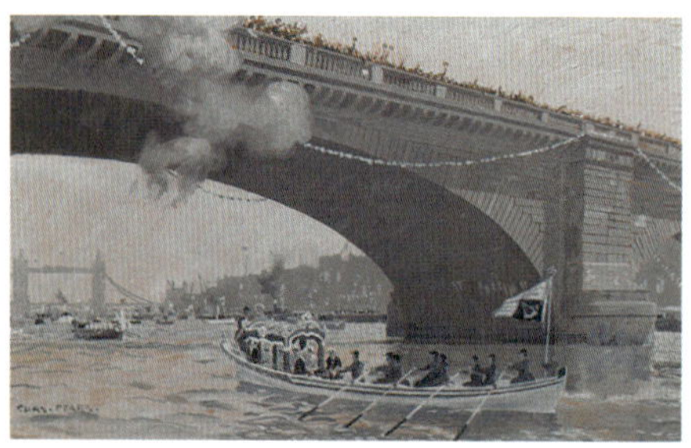

Pears, Charles 1873–1958
River Plate Pageant c.1918
oil on panel 41.9 x 64.7
IWM ART 5443

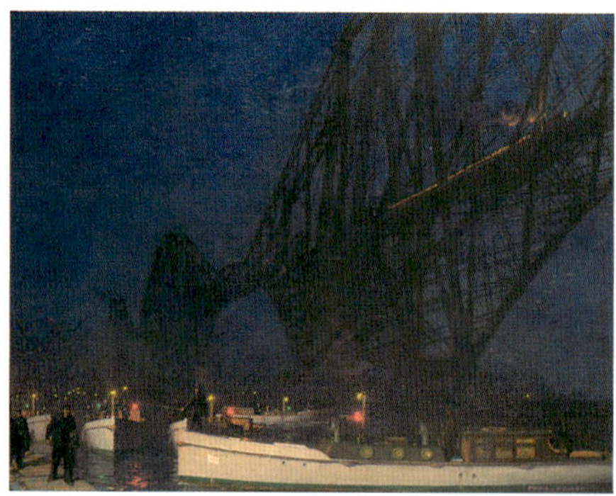

Pears, Charles 1873–1958
Steam Pinnaces at Hawkes Pier c.1918
oil on canvas 71.1 x 91.4
IWM ART 630

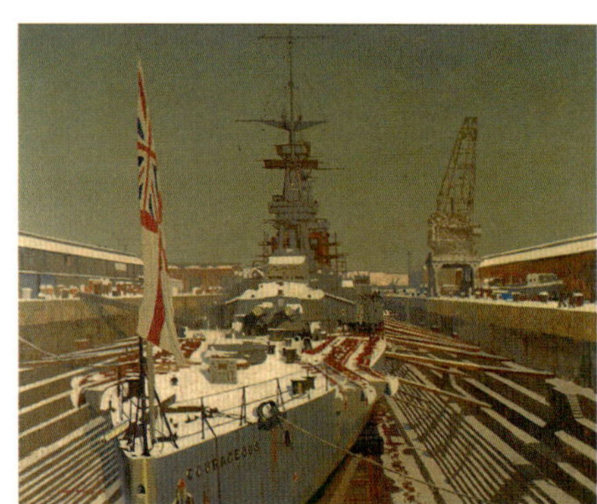

Pears, Charles 1873–1958
'HMS Courageous' in Dry Dock, at Rosyth, in Winter 1919
oil on canvas 101.9 x 127
IWM ART 633

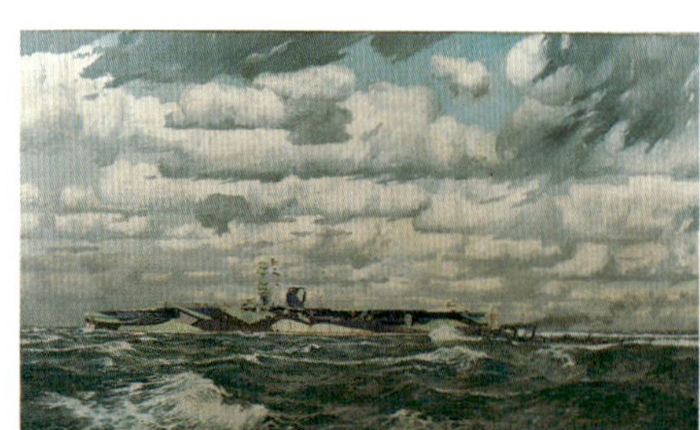

Pears, Charles 1873–1958
'HMS Furious': Aerodrome Ship 1919
oil on canvas 101.9 x 177.8
IWM ART 1629

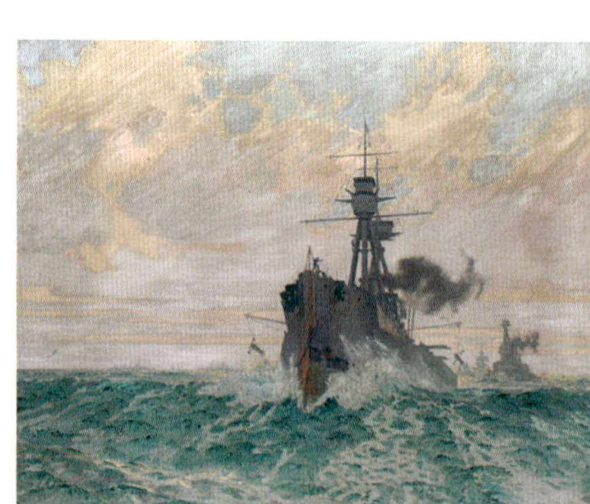

Pears, Charles 1873–1958
Streaming the Paravanes: Paravanes Enable a Ship to Go through Mines in Almost Complete Safety 1919
oil on canvas 101.9 x 127
IWM ART 1232

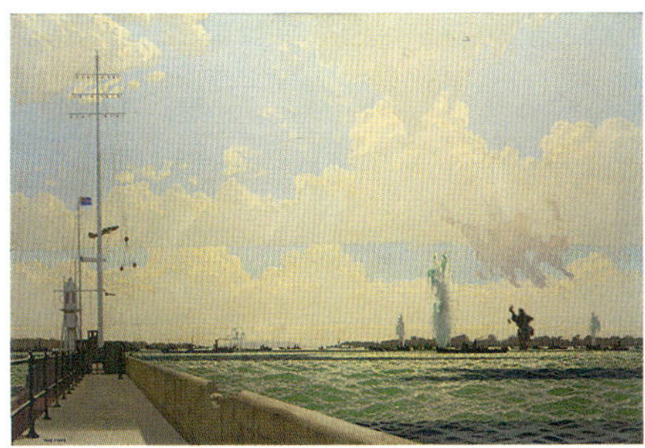

Pears, Charles 1873–1958
*Shelling of a British Convoy by the Germans
from the French Coast* 1940
oil on canvas 101.9 x 152.4
IWM ART LD 761

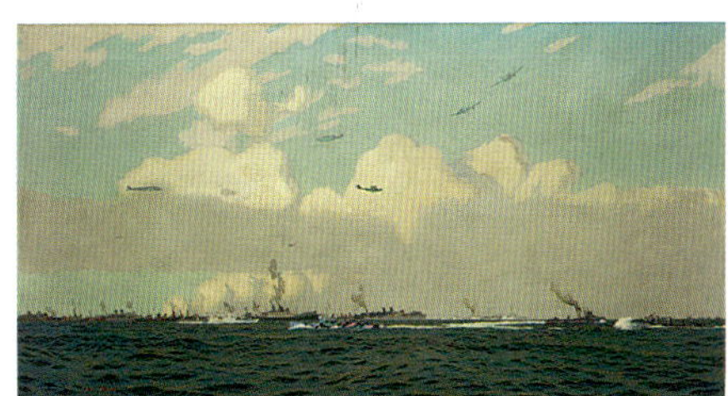

Pears, Charles 1873–1958
*Handing Over a Convoy from American to
British Escorts* 1941
oil on canvas 80 x 152.4
IWM ART LD 1487

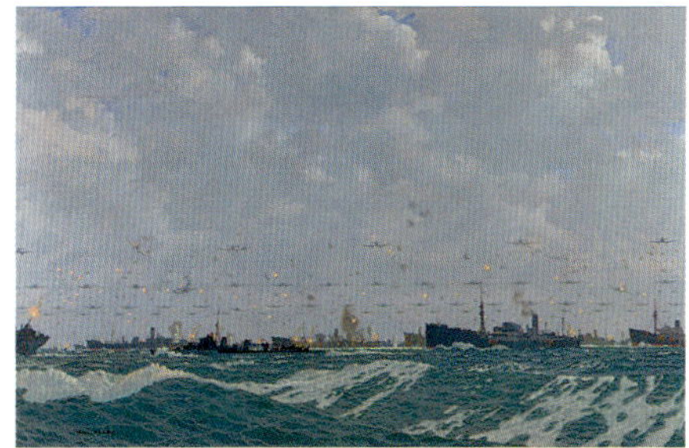

Pears, Charles 1873–1958
A British Convoy on Its Way to Russia 1942
oil on canvas 80.6 x 127
IWM ART LD 2682

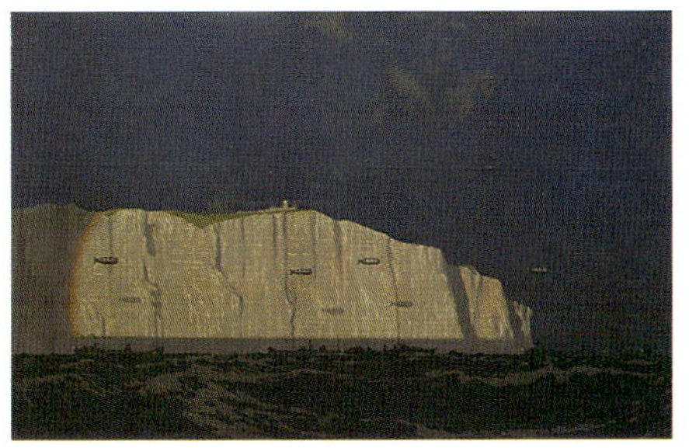

Pears, Charles 1873–1958
*A German Searchlight across the English
Channel* 1942
oil on canvas 81.2 x 127
IWM ART LD 1916

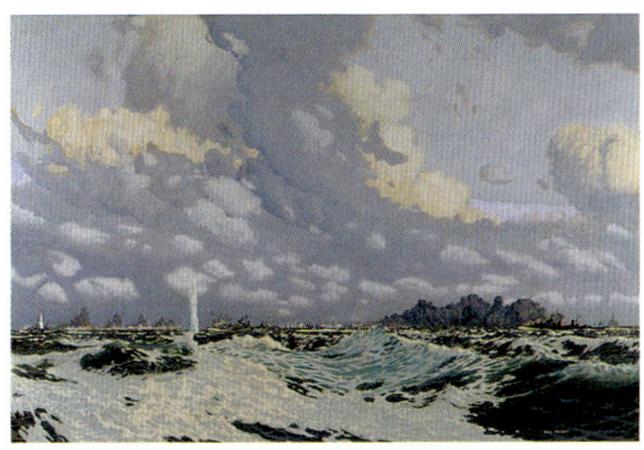

Pears, Charles 1873–1958
*The Convoy Led by Admiral Vian Fighting Its
Way through to Malta* 1942
oil on canvas 101.9 x 152.4
IWM ART LD 2175

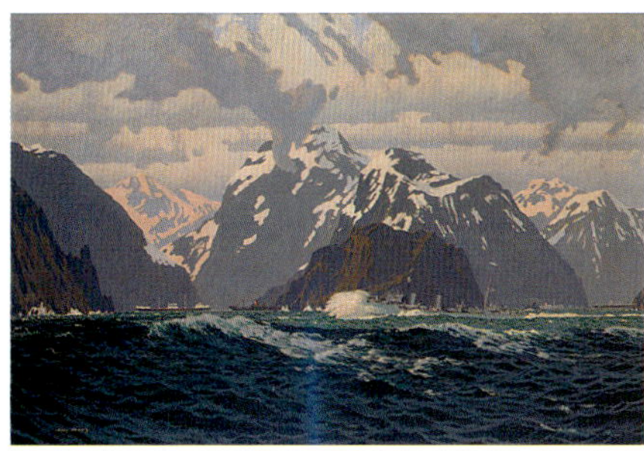

Pears, Charles 1873–1958
The Norwegian Coast, Spring 1940 1943
oil on canvas 101.9 x 152.4
IWM ART LD 662

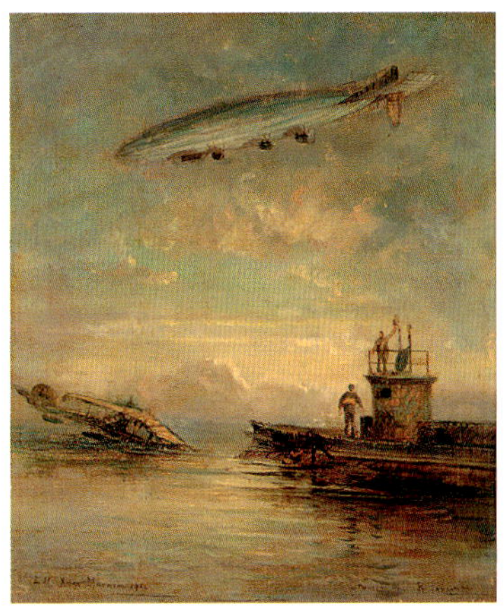

Pearson, R. active 1914–1918
The End of the Cuxhaven Raid: Christmas Day
1914
oil on canvas 64.7 x 54.6
IWM ART 3137

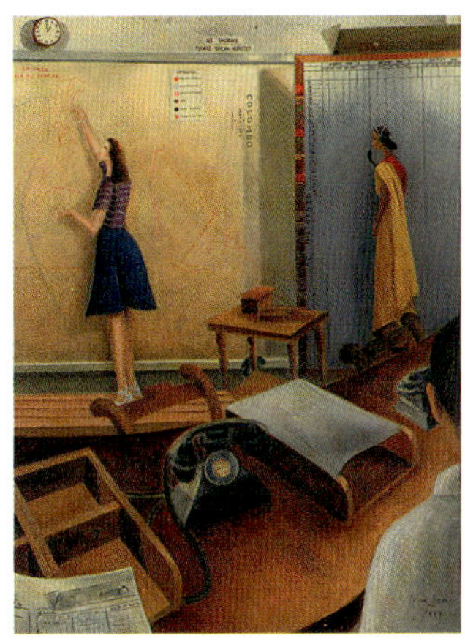

Peries, Ivan 1921–1988
Combined Control and Report Centre 1943
oil on canvas 82.5 x 62.5
IWM ART LD 4201

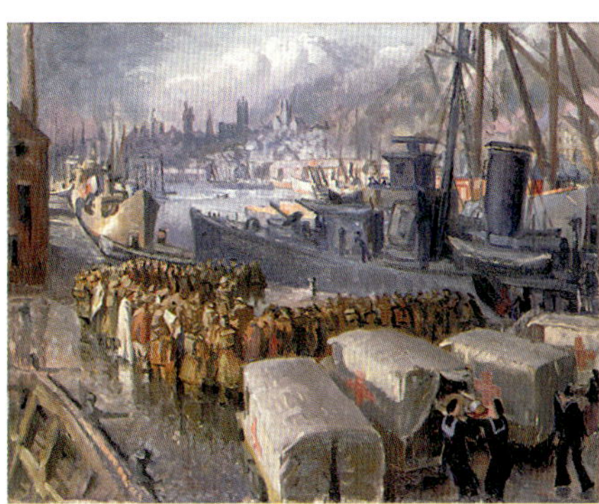

Perkins, Christopher 1891–1968
*Roll-Call of the Survivors of HM Troopship
'Archangel' at Aberdeen* 1941
oil on canvas 71.1 x 91.4
IWM ART LD 1599

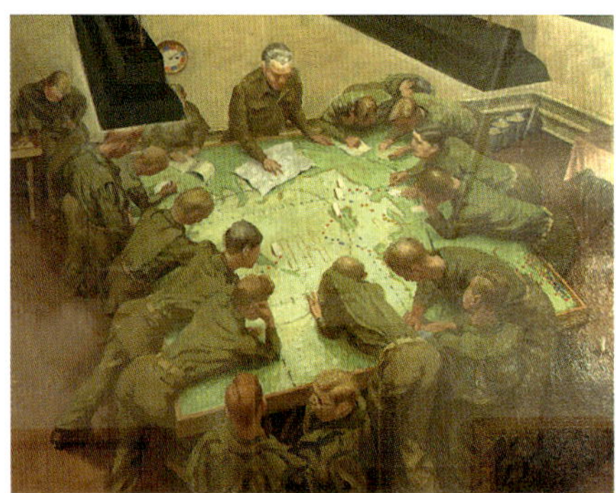

Perkins, Christopher 1891–1968
American Soldiers in an Anti-Aircraft Plotting Room in Northern Ireland 1942
oil on canvas 71.7 x 86.3
IWM ART LD 2465

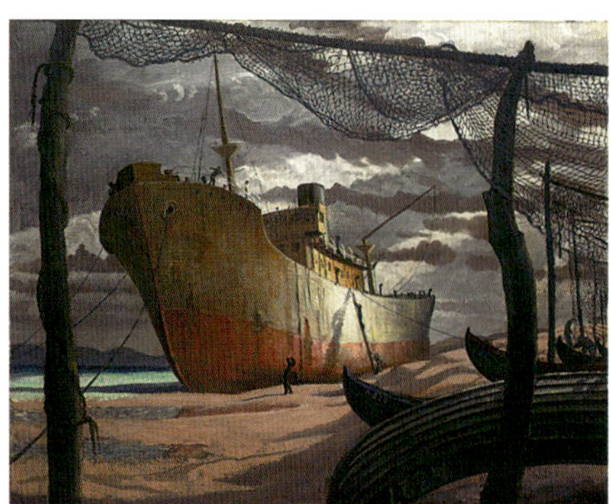

Perkins, Christopher 1891–1968
Torpedoed and Beached 1944
oil on canvas 101.9 x 127
IWM ART LD 3779

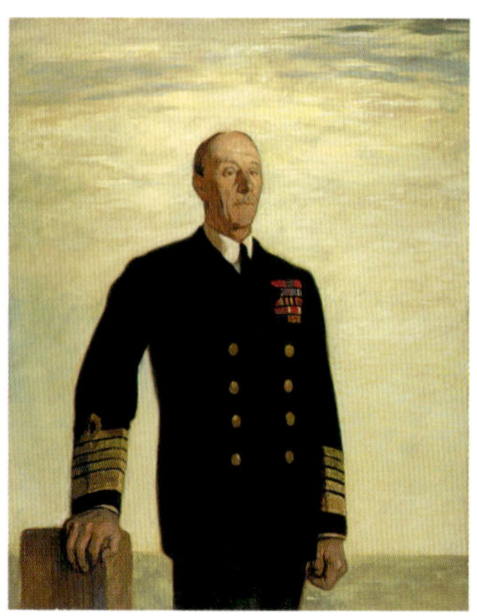

Philpot, Glyn Warren 1884–1937
Admiral of the Fleet Sir John Jellicoe (1859–1935), GCM, OM, GCVO 1918
oil on canvas 127 x 101.9
IWM ART 1322

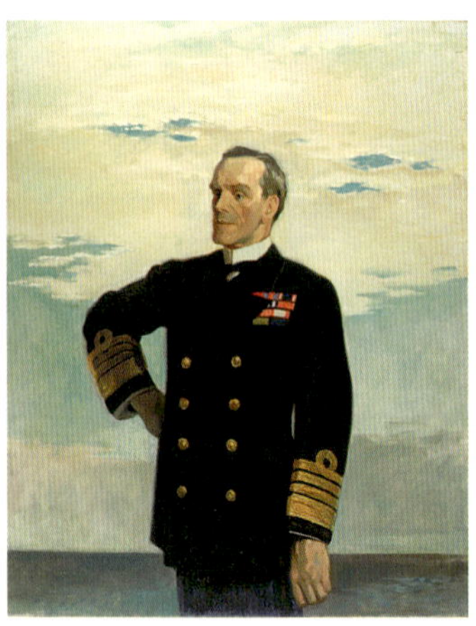

Philpot, Glyn Warren 1884–1937
Admiral Sir Frederick Charles Dove Sturdee (1829–1925), Bt, KCB, KCMG, CVO 1918
oil on canvas 127 x 101.9
IWM ART 1325

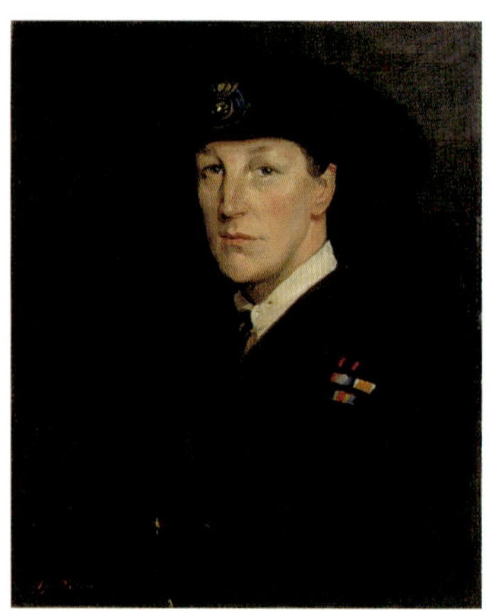

Philpot, Glyn Warren 1884–1937
Dame Katherine Furse, CBE, RRC, Director of the Women's Royal Naval Service (1920) 1918
oil on canvas 60.9 x 50.8
IWM ART 3067

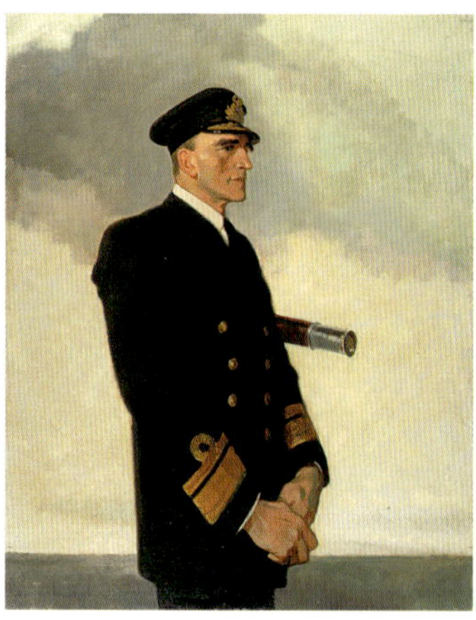

Philpot, Glyn Warren 1884–1937
Rear Admiral Sir Reginald Y. Tyrwhitt (1870–1951), KCB, DSO 1918
oil on canvas 127 x 101.9
IWM ART 1323

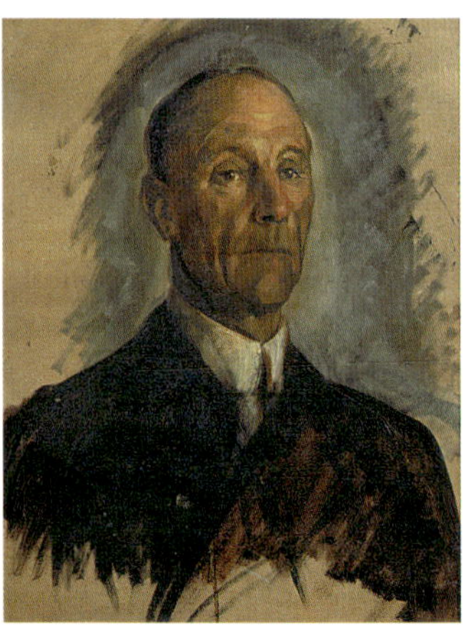

Philpot, Glyn Warren 1884–1937
Sketch of 'Admiral of the Fleet Sir John Jellicoe (1859–1935), GCM, OM, GCVO' 1918
oil on canvas 75 x 47.5
IWM ART 5729

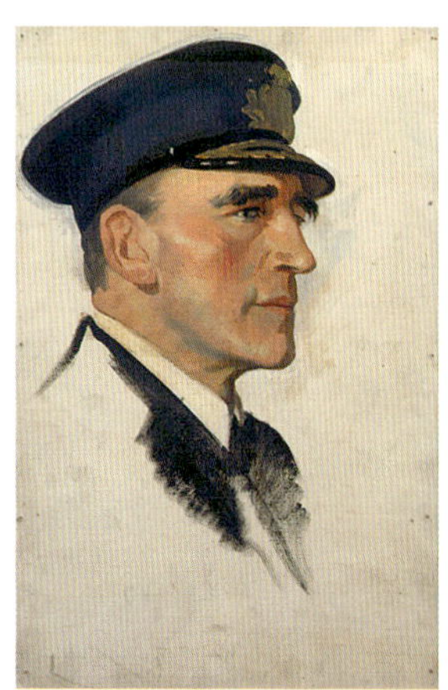

Philpot, Glyn Warren 1884–1937
Sketch of 'Rear Admiral Sir Reginald Y. Tyrwhitt (1870–1951), KCB, DSO' 1918
oil on panel 48.5 x 33.2
IWM ART 5730

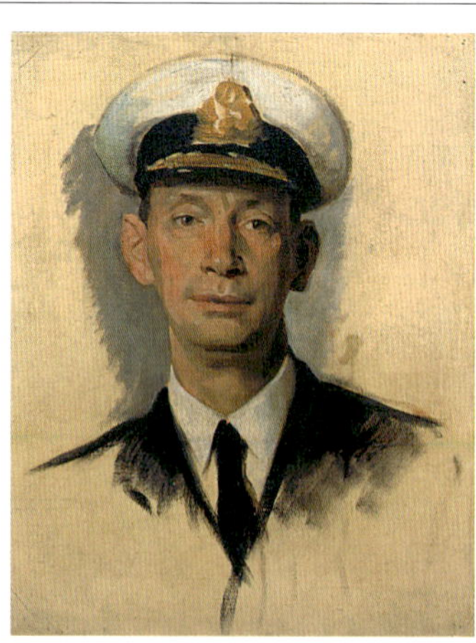

Philpot, Glyn Warren 1884–1937
Sketch of 'Vice Admiral Sir Roger Keyes (1872–1945), KCB, CMG, CVO, DSO' 1918
oil on canvas 50.8 x 40.8
IWM ART 5731

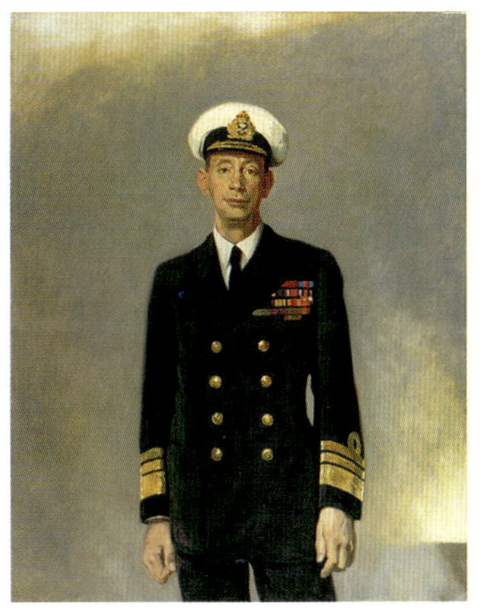

Philpot, Glyn Warren 1884–1937
*Vice Admiral Sir Roger Keyes (1872–1945),
KCB, CMG, CVO, DSO* 1918
oil on canvas 127 x 101.9
IWM ART 1324

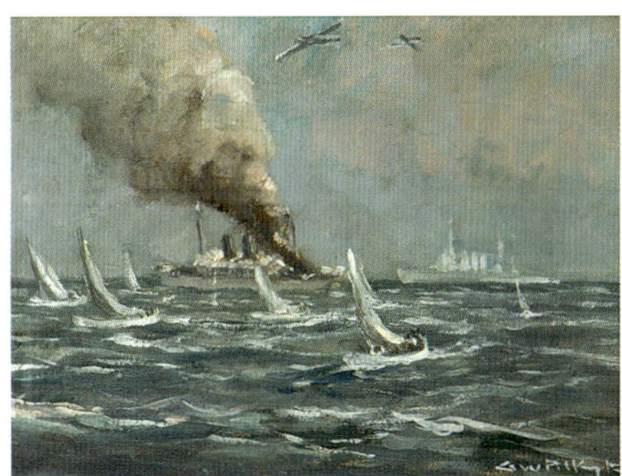

Pilkington, George William 1879–1958
*Scuttling of the 'Watussi' off Cape Point with
'HMS Sussex' and Junkers Aircraft* c.1943
oil on panel 26 x 36.1
IWM ART LD 7488

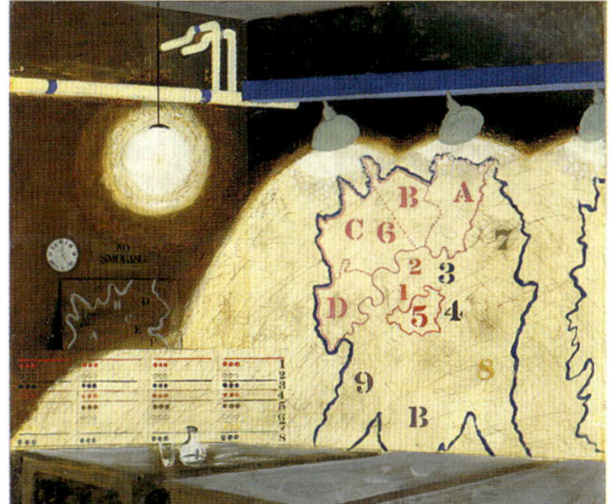

Piper, John 1903–1992
*The Control Room at South-West Regional
Headquarters, Bristol* 1940
oil on panel 63.5 x 76.2
IWM ART LD 169

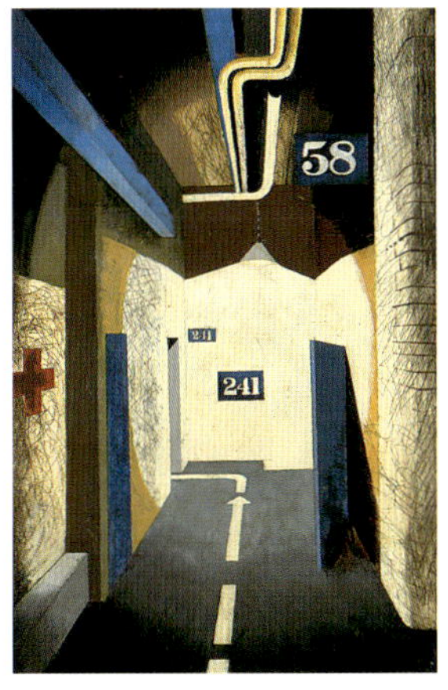

Piper, John 1903–1992
*The Passage to the Control Room at South-
West Regional Headquarters, Bristol* 1940
oil on panel 76.2 x 50.8
IWM ART LD 170

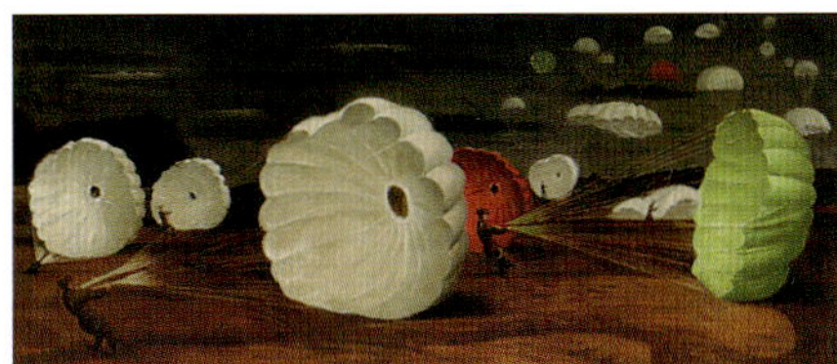

Pitchforth, Roland Vivian 1895–1982
A Parachute Landing c.1940–1945
oil on panel 55.2 x 126.3
IWM ART LD 3189

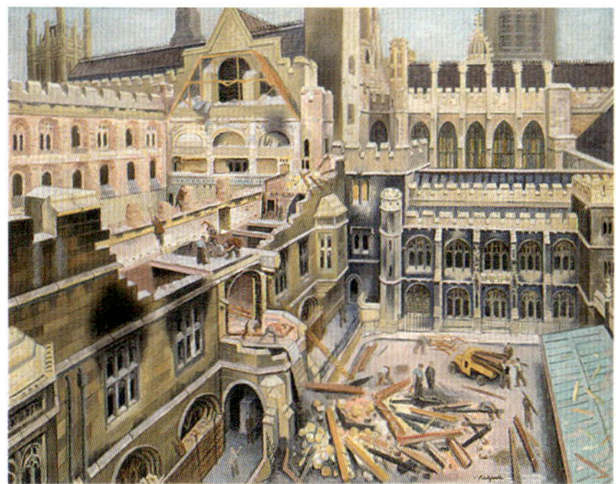

Pitchforth, Roland Vivian 1895–1982
*Chamber of the House of Commons: Bomb
Damage* c.1940–1945
oil on panel 86.3 x 111.8 (E)
IWM ART LD 6113

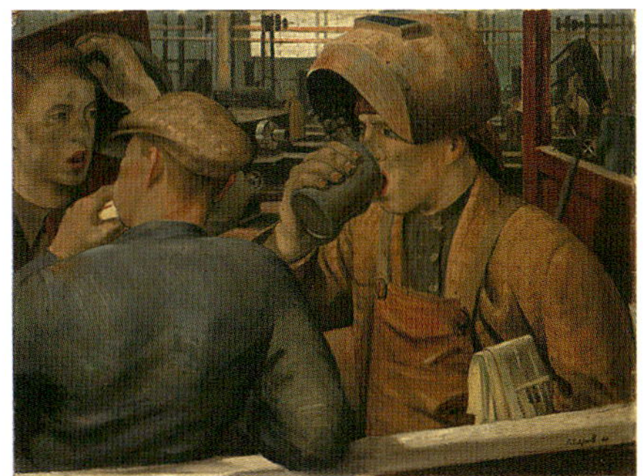

Pitchforth, Roland Vivian 1895–1982
Snack Time in a Factory 1941
oil on panel 55.8 x 76.2
IWM ART LD 1486

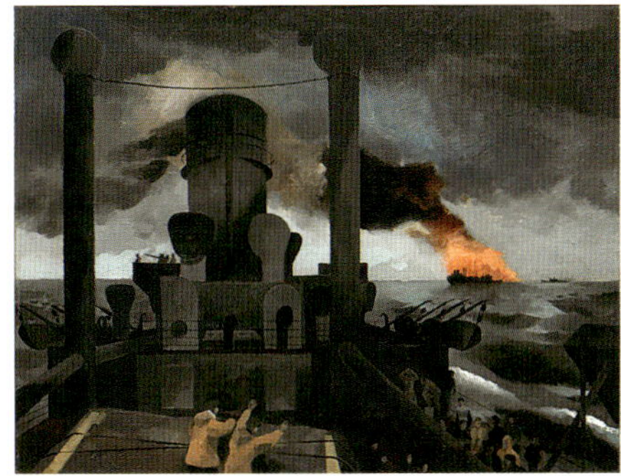

Plante, George 1914–1995
A Rescue Ship in the Atlantic, March 1943
1943
oil on canvas 46 x 61
IWM ART LD 3055

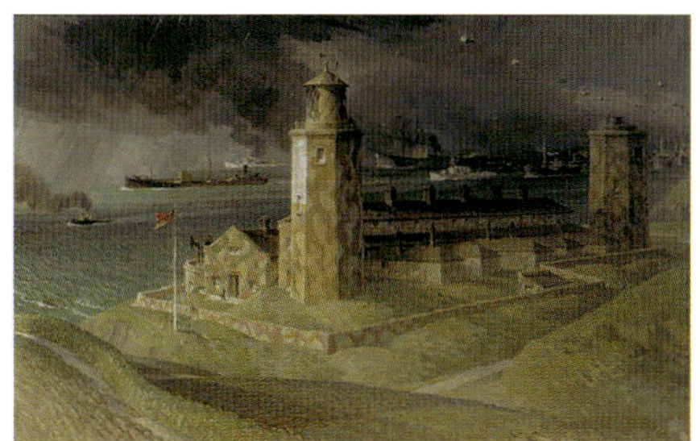

Platt, John Edgar 1886–1967
A Convoy Passing the Lizard, Cornwall 1942
oil on canvas 60.9 x 101.9
IWM ART LD 2416

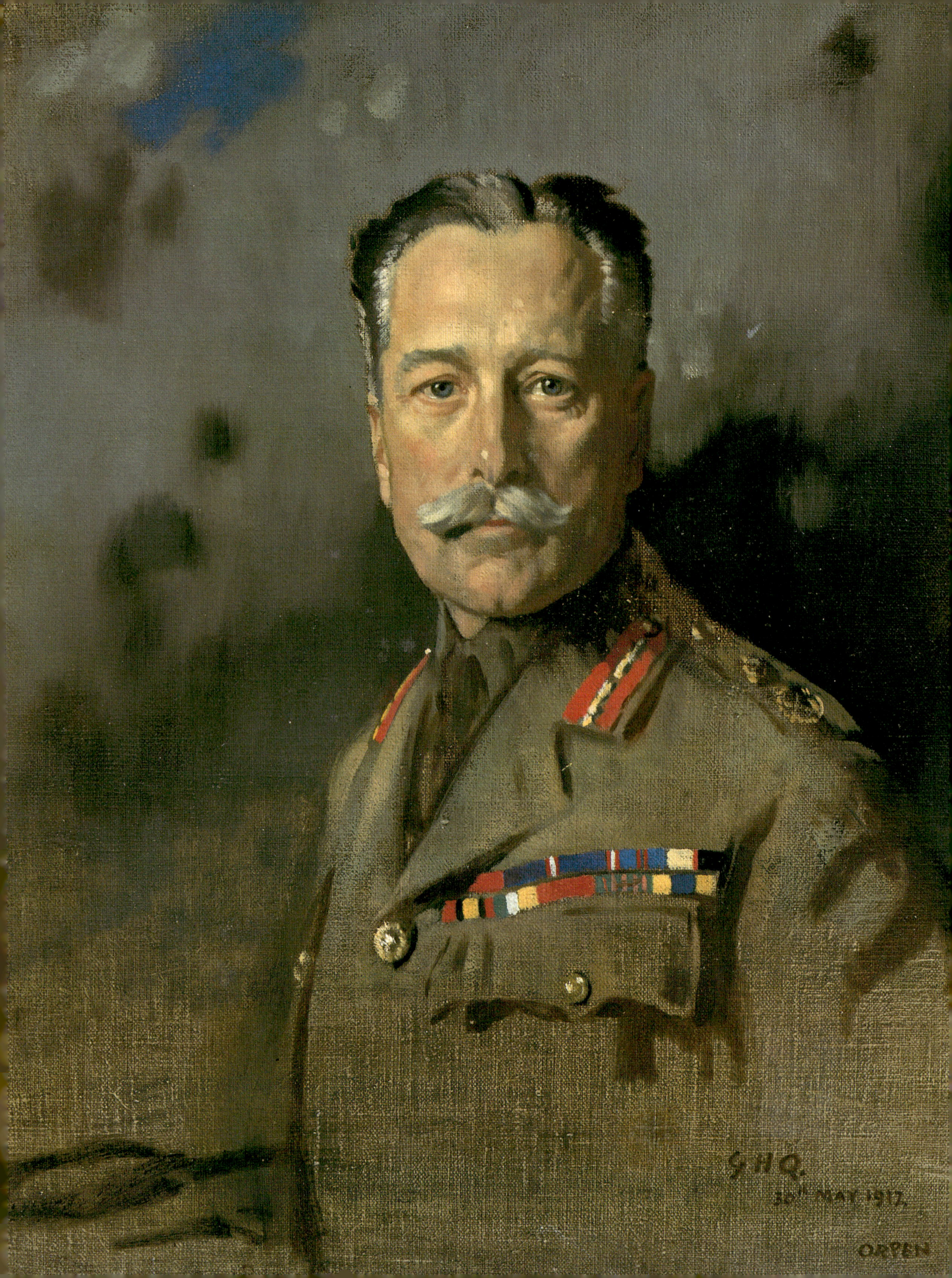
G.H.Q.
30th MAY. 1917.
ORPEN

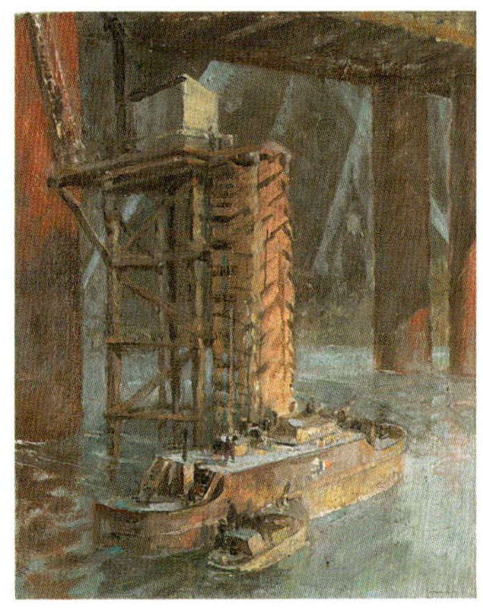

Platt, John Edgar 1886–1967
*Wartime Traffic on the River Thames: Fire
Services, Hungerford Bridge* 1942
oil on panel 22.8 x 19
IWM ART LD 2641

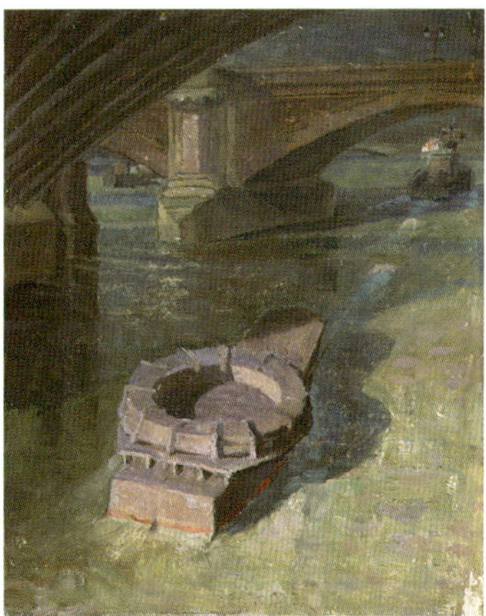

Platt, John Edgar 1886–1967
*Wartime Traffic on the River Thames: River
Minesweepers* 1942
oil on panel 22.8 x 17.7
IWM ART LD 2638

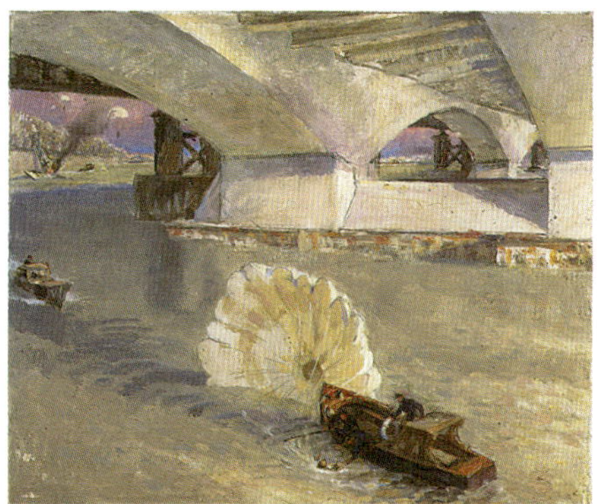

Platt, John Edgar 1886–1967
*Wartime Traffic on the River Thames: River
Police at Waterloo Bridge during the Battle of
Britain* 1942
oil on panel 19 x 22.8
IWM ART LD 2642

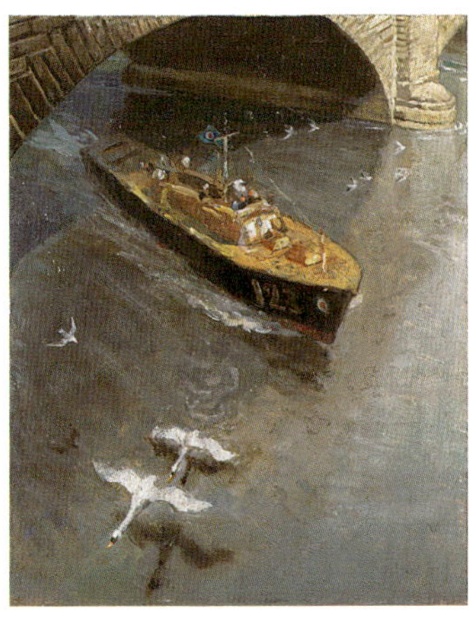

Platt, John Edgar 1886–1967
*Wartime Traffic on the River Thames: Royal
Air Force Sea Rescue Launch, London Bridge*
1942
oil on panel 22.8 x 19
IWM ART LD 2643

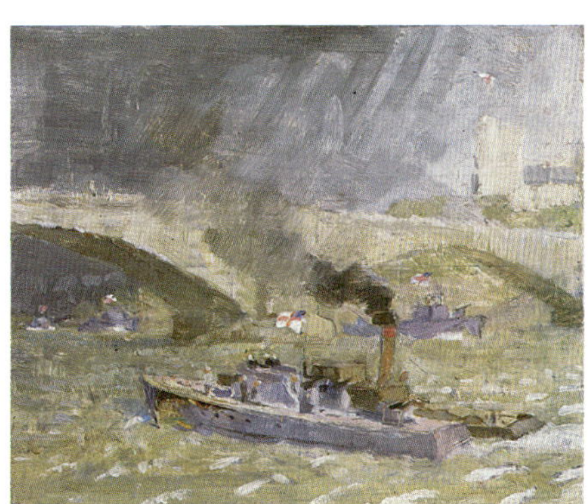

Platt, John Edgar 1886–1967
*Wartime Traffic on the River Thames: Upriver
Repairs after the Dieppe Raid* 1942
oil on panel 19 x 22.8
IWM ART LD 2639

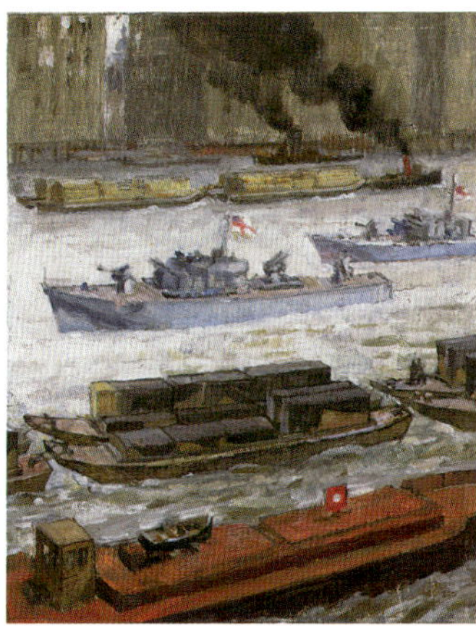

Platt, John Edgar 1886–1967
*Wartime Traffic on the River Thames: War
Supplies at Paul's Wharf* 1942
oil on panel 22.8 x 19
IWM ART LD 2640

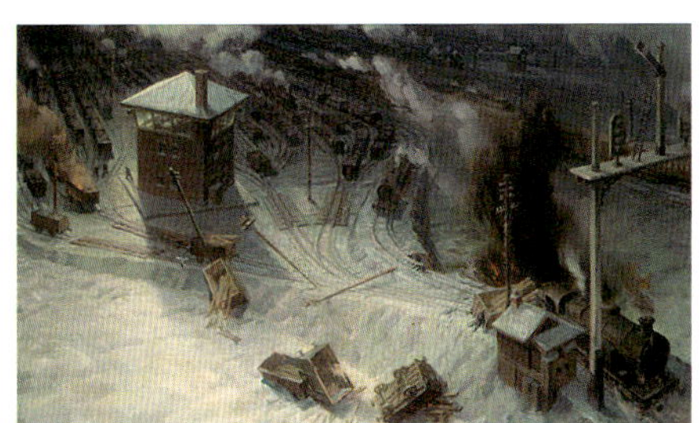

Platt, John Edgar 1886–1967
*A Marshalling Yard in Wartime: 'Bomber's
Moon'* 1943
oil on canvas 60.9 x 101.9
IWM ART LD 3530

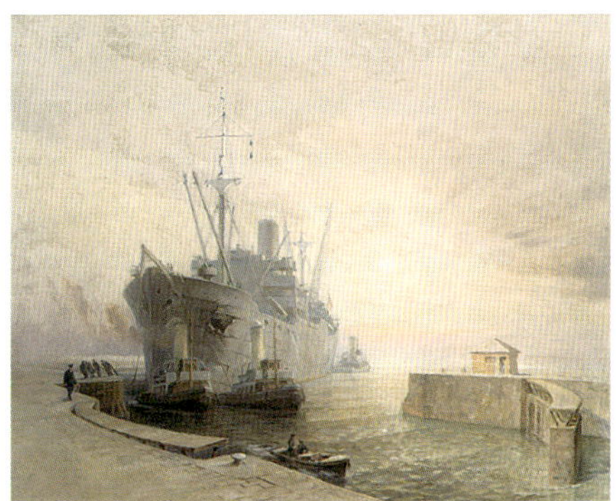

Platt, John Edgar 1886–1967
*The Battle of the Atlantic: A Cargo Ship
Completes Another Crossing* 1943
oil on canvas 54.9 x 67.3
IWM ART LD 4191

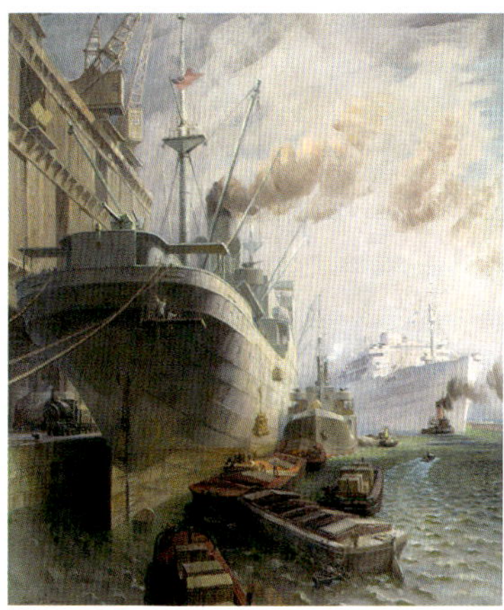

Platt, John Edgar 1886–1967
The Quick Turnround 1943
oil on canvas 81.5 x 81.5 (E)
IWM ART LD 3827

Facing page: Orpen, William, 1878–1931, *Field Marshal Sir Douglas Haig (1861–1928), KT, GCB, GCVO, KCIE, Commander-in-Chief, France, from
15 December 1915 (detail)*, 1917, (p. 174)

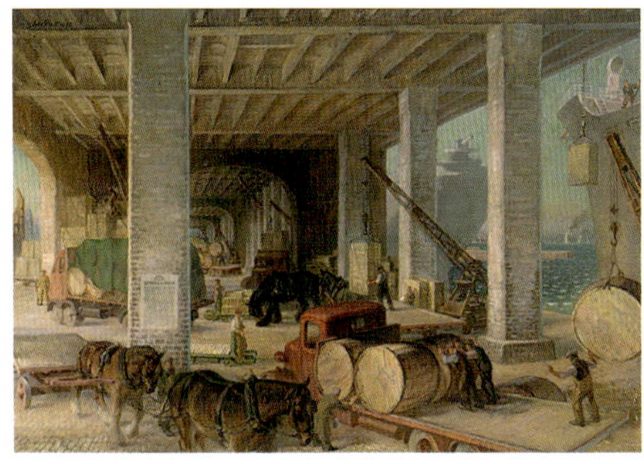

Platt, John Edgar 1886–1967
War Transport: A Dockside Unloading Shed for Tobacco, Ammunition and Machinery 1943
oil on canvas 50.1 x 75.5
IWM ART LD 3777

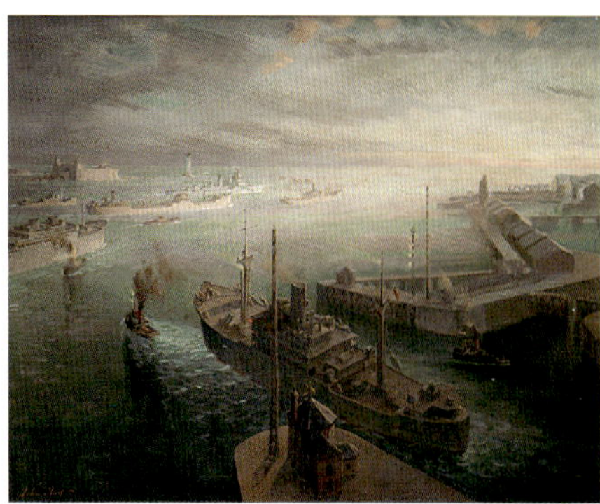

Platt, John Edgar 1886–1967
Ocean Transport: The Gateway to Battle c.1943
oil on canvas 54.9 x 67.9
IWM ART LD 4190

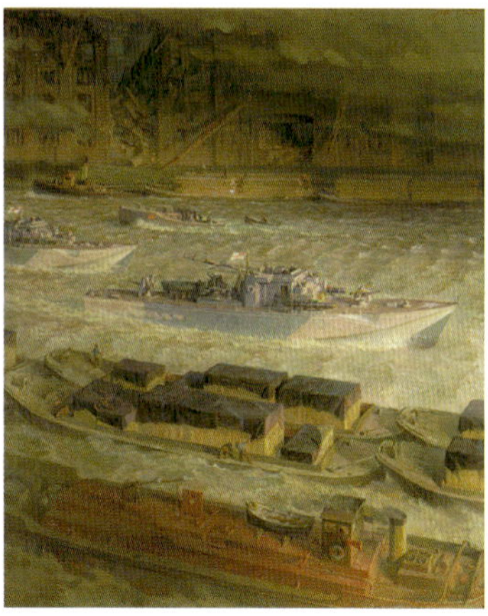

Platt, John Edgar 1886–1967
Wartime Traffic on the River Thames c.1944
oil on canvas 76.2 x 62.8
IWM ART LD 4958

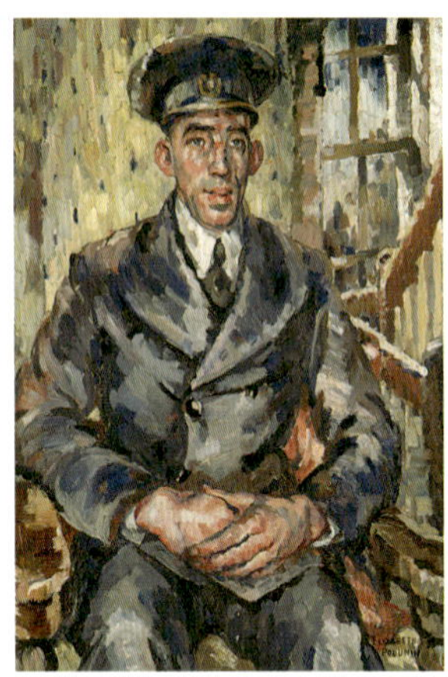

Polunin, Elizabeth V. 1880–1953
Divisional Officer Twyman 1942
oil on canvas 92.7 x 64.1
IWM ART LD 1898

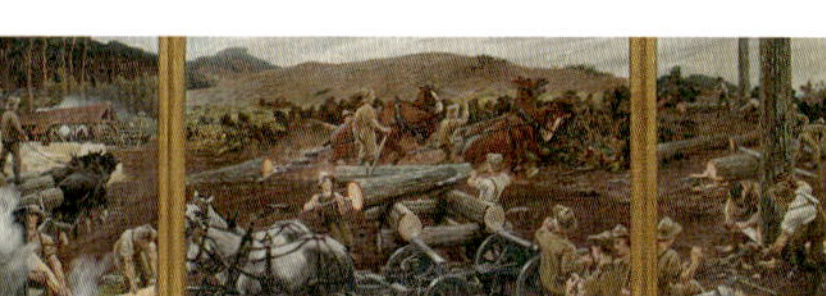

Porter, Alfred Thomas active 1882–1919
Canadians Cutting and Carting Wood, Farnham 1919
oil on panel 50.8 x 227.3
IWM ART 1854

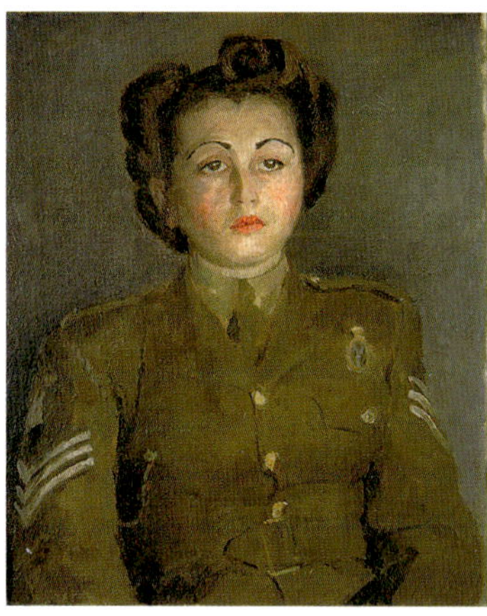

Potter, Mary 1900–1981
Portrait of an Auxiliary Territorial Service Sergeant 1942
oil on canvas 61.5 x 51
IWM ART 16505

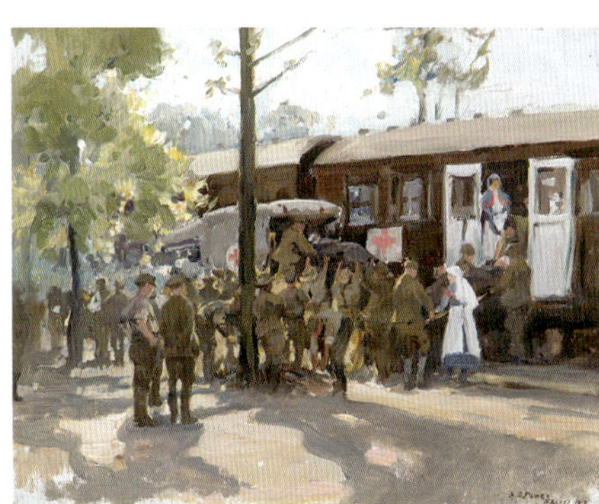

Power, Harold Septimus 1879–1951
A 'Red Cross' Train, France 1918
oil on canvas 40.6 x 50.8
IWM ART 1031

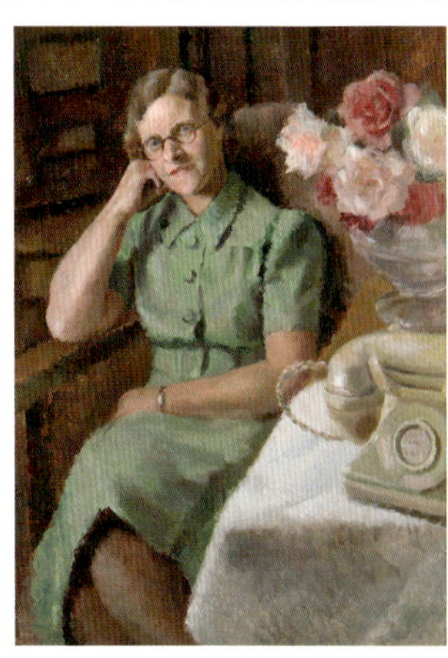

Preece, Patricia 1894–1966
Miss M. Steele 1942
oil on canvas 68.5 x 50.8
IWM ART LD 2404

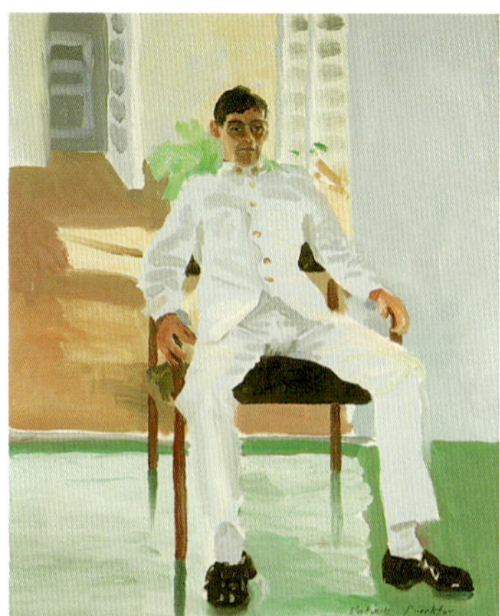

Procktor, Patrick 1936–2003
Corporal Robert James Ransome, 1 Royal Anglian, Belize 1983
oil on canvas 61 x 51
IWM ART 15730

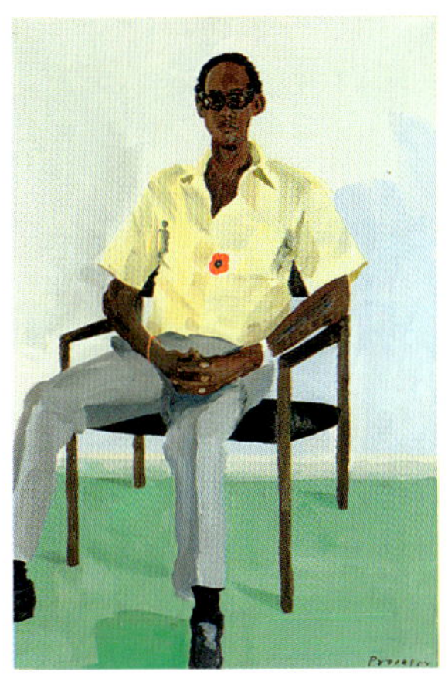

Procktor, Patrick 1936–2003
Edward Jones, Chief Clerk DOE, Belize 1983
oil on canvas 76.2 x 51
IWM ART 15731

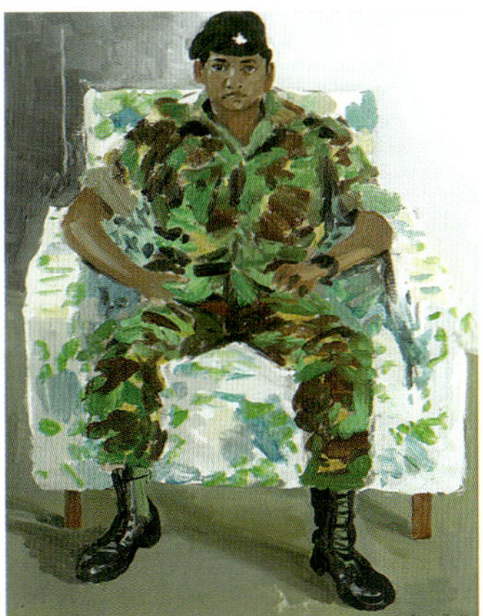

Procktor, Patrick 1936–2003
*R. F. M. Harka Raj Rai, 10th Prime Minister's
Official Representative: Gurkha in Belize* 1983
oil on canvas 61 x 51
IWM ART 15729

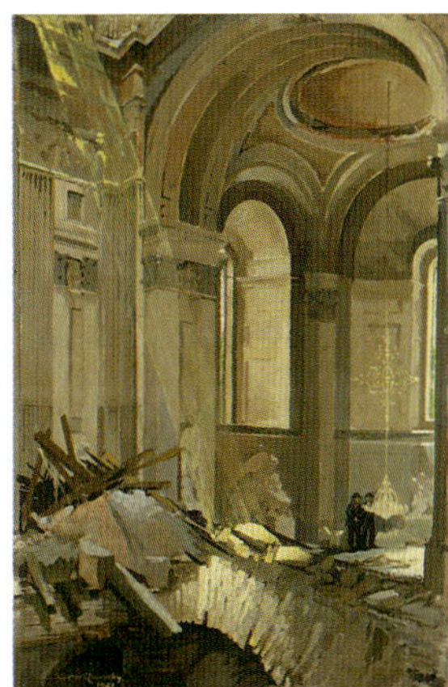

Quarmby, George 1883–1957
Bomb Damage in St Paul's Cathedral, London
1941
oil on canvas 76.2 x 50.8
IWM ART LD 2405

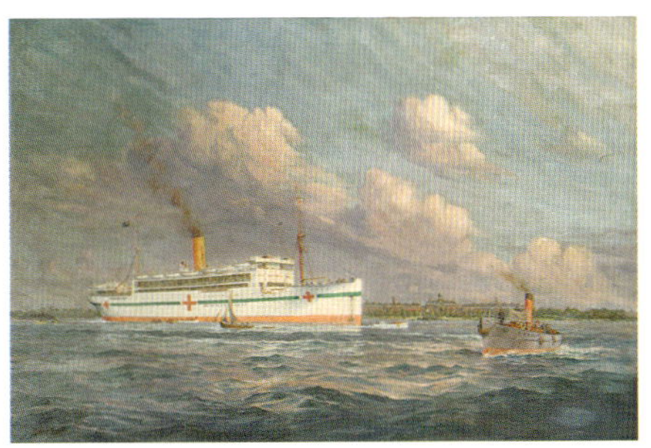

Randall, Maurice active 1890–1935
*HM Hospital Ship 'Llandovery Castle', Union
Castle Line, Sunk by Enemy Submarines, 27
June 1918* c.1919–1920
oil on canvas 101.6 x 152.7
IWM ART 5605

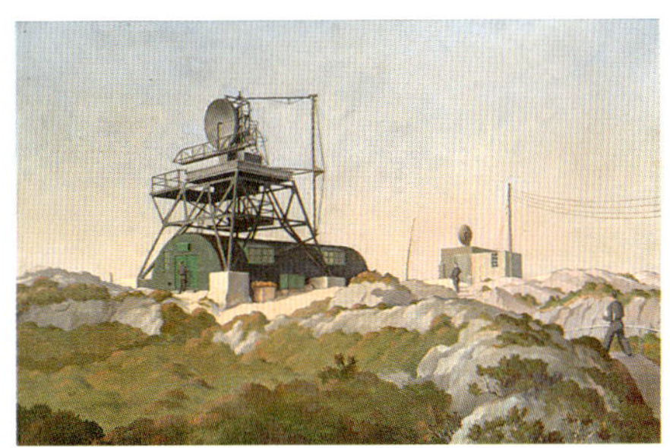

Rawlinson, William Thomas 1912–1993
A Chain Home Extra Low Radar Station 1945
oil on canvas 50.8 x 76.2
IWM ART LD 5732

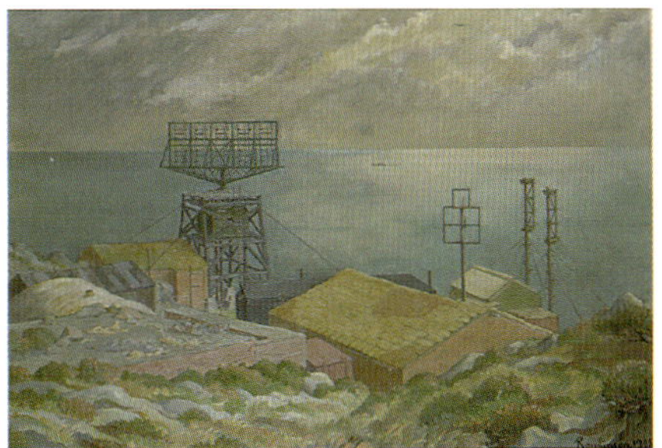

Rawlinson, William Thomas 1912–1993
A 'CHL' (Chain Home Low) Radar Station
1945
oil on canvas 50.8 x 76.2 (E)
IWM ART LD 5731

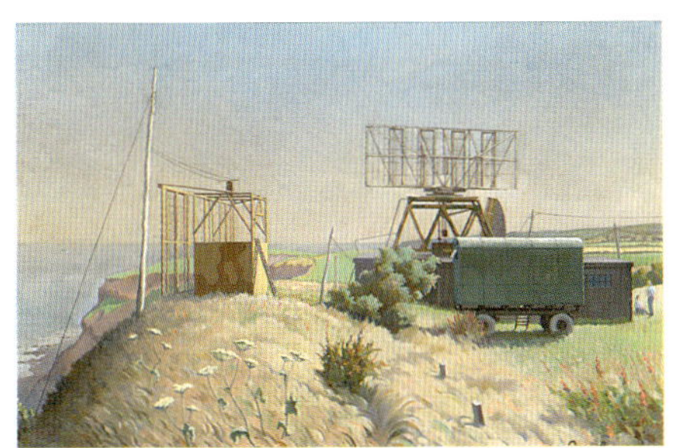

Rawlinson, William Thomas 1912–1993
A 'CHL' (Chain Home Low) Radar Station
1946
oil on canvas 50.8 x 76.2 (E)
IWM ART LD 5734

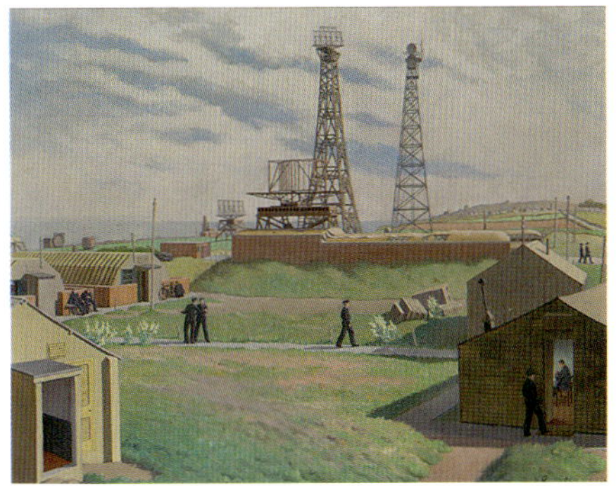

Rawlinson, William Thomas 1912–1993
*A 'Composite' Radar Station for Air Surface
Watching* 1946
oil on canvas 60.9 x 76.2
IWM ART LD 5835

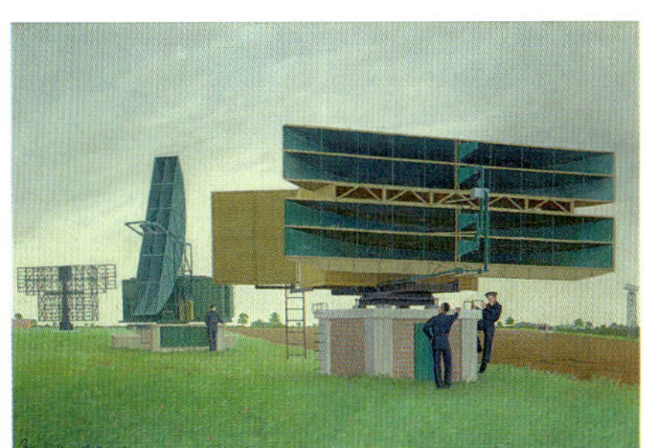

Rawlinson, William Thomas 1912–1993
*A 'Final' GCI (Ground-Controlled
Interception) Radar Station* 1946
oil on canvas 50.8 x 76.2 (E)
IWM ART LD 5836

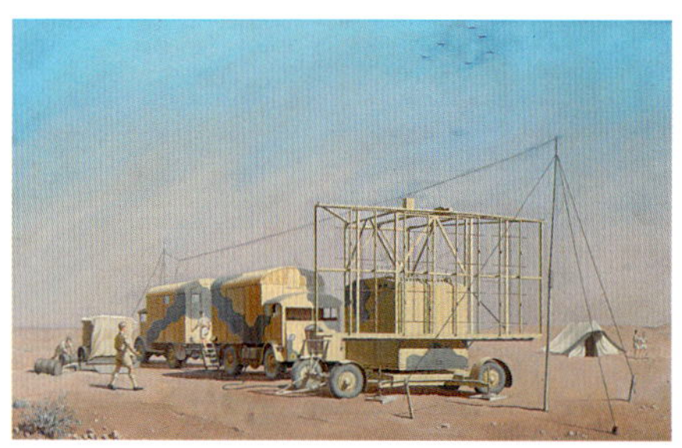

Rawlinson, William Thomas 1912–1993
*A Mobile Ground-Controlled Interception
Radar Station* 1946
oil on canvas 50.8 x 76.2 (E)
IWM ART LD 5779

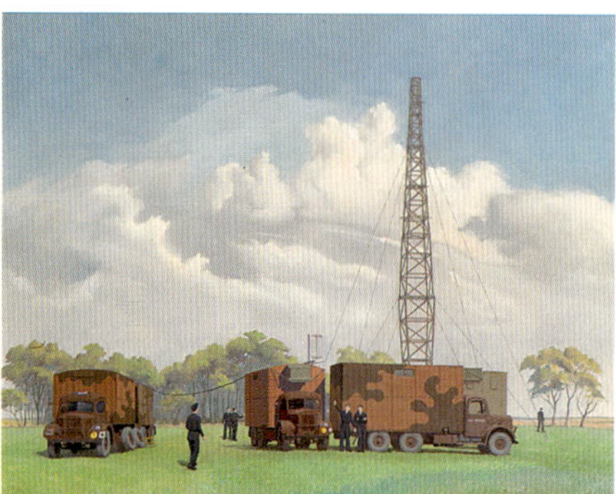

Rawlinson, William Thomas 1912–1993
A Mobile Radio Unit 1946
oil on canvas 60.9 x 76.2
IWM ART LD 5834

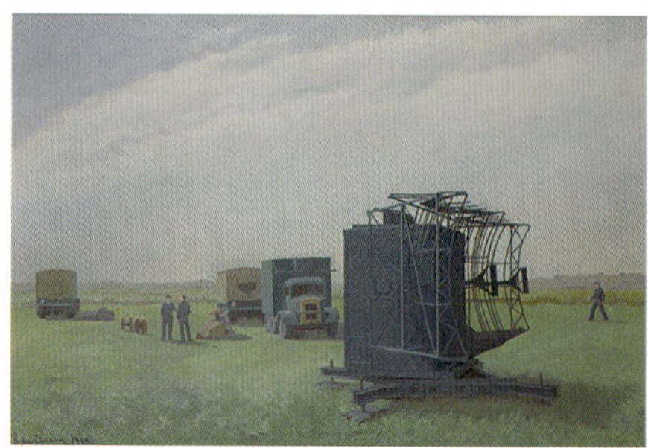

Rawlinson, William Thomas 1912–1993
A 'Type 11' Radar Station 1946
oil on canvas 50.8 x 76.2 (E)
IWM ART LD 5837

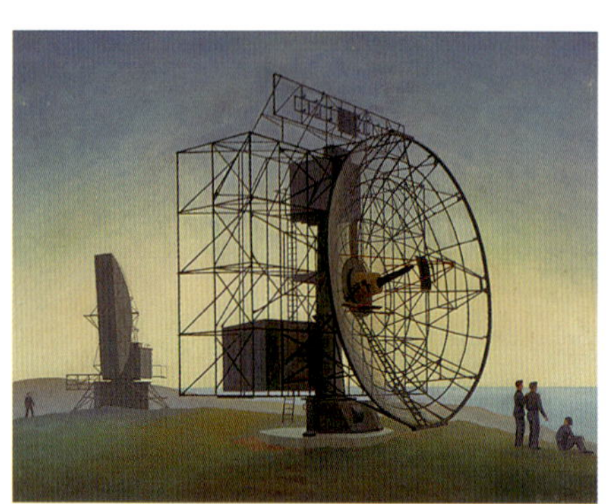

Rawlinson, William Thomas 1912–1993
A 'Type 16' Fighter Direction Radar Station
1946
oil on canvas 60.9 x 76.2
IWM ART LD 5833

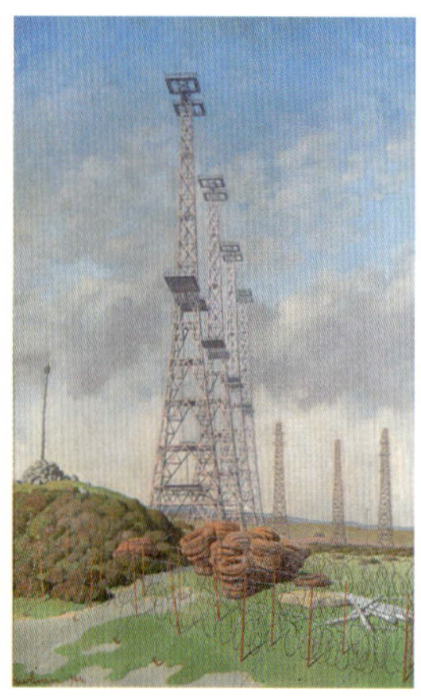

Rawlinson, William Thomas 1912–1993
*A 'Type CH' (Chain Home) Radar Station on
the East Coast* 1946
oil on canvas 76.2 x 50.8 (E)
IWM ART LD 5735

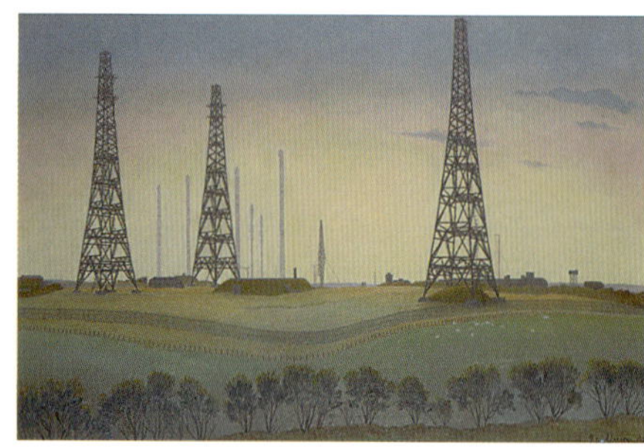

Rawlinson, William Thomas 1912–1993
*A 'Type CH' (Chain Home) Radar Station on
the West Coast* 1946
oil on canvas 50.8 x 76.2
IWM ART LD 5838

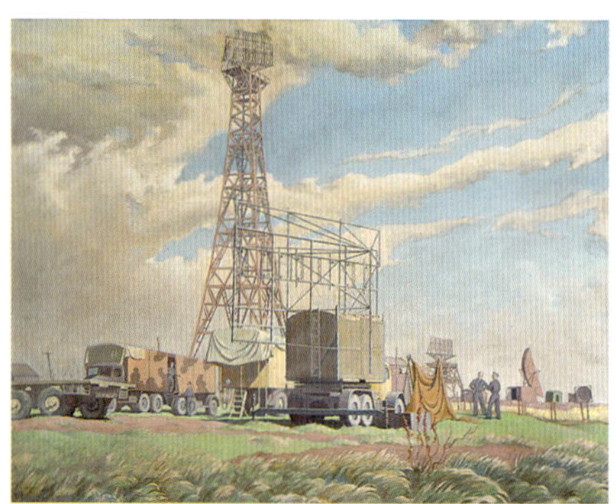

Rawlinson, William Thomas 1912–1993
*An 'Interception Chain Home Low' Radar
Station* 1946
oil on canvas 60.9 x 76.2
IWM ART LD 5733

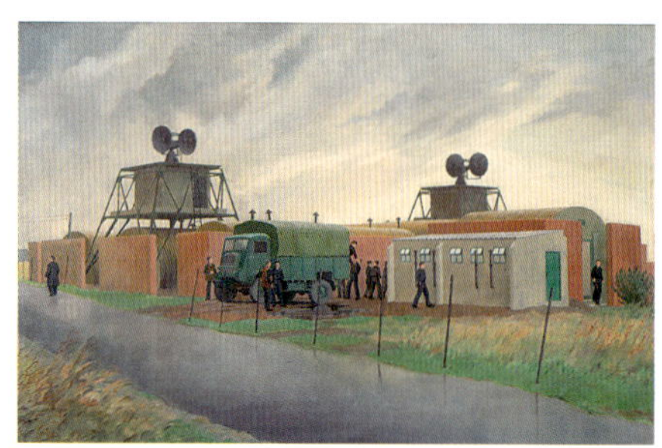

Rawlinson, William Thomas 1912–1993
An 'OBOE/9000' Ground Radar Station 1946
oil on canvas 50.8 x 76.2
IWM ART LD 5780

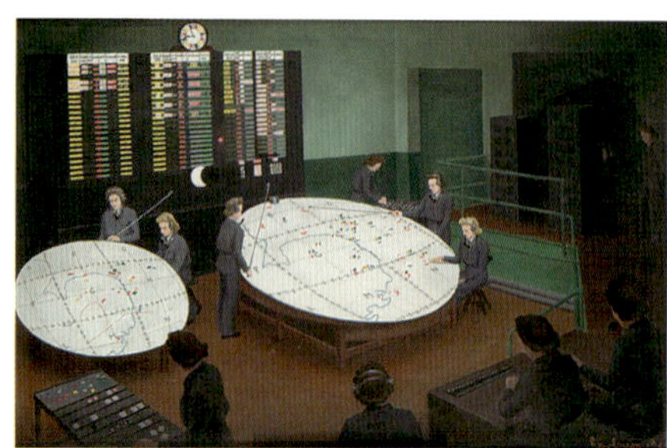

Rawlinson, William Thomas 1912–1993
*The Reporting Room in a 'Final' Ground-
Controlled Interception Station* 1946
oil on canvas 50.8 x 76.2
IWM ART LD 5839

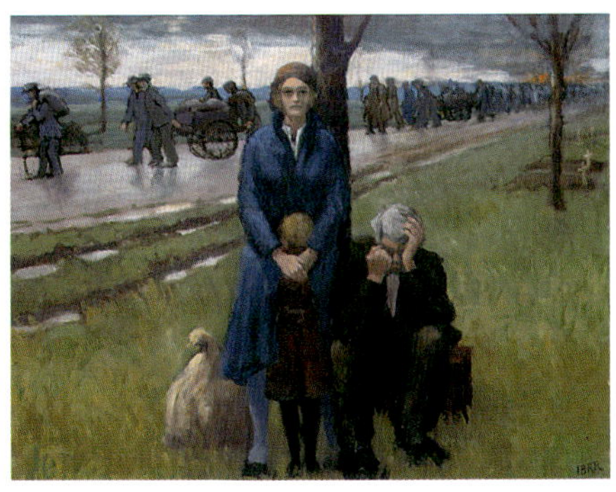

Rees-Roberts, Ivor Bailey b.1915
Displaced Persons
oil on canvas 45 x 58.2
IWM ART 17116

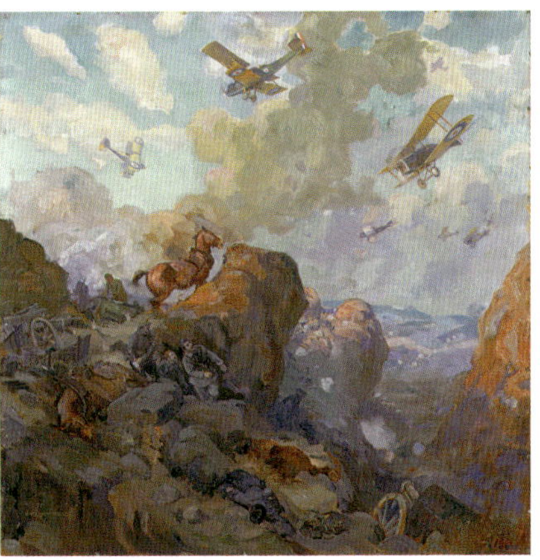

Reid, Stuart 1883–1971
Bombing of the Wadi Fara, 20 September 1918
1918
oil on panel 101.9 x 100.9
IWM ART 3196

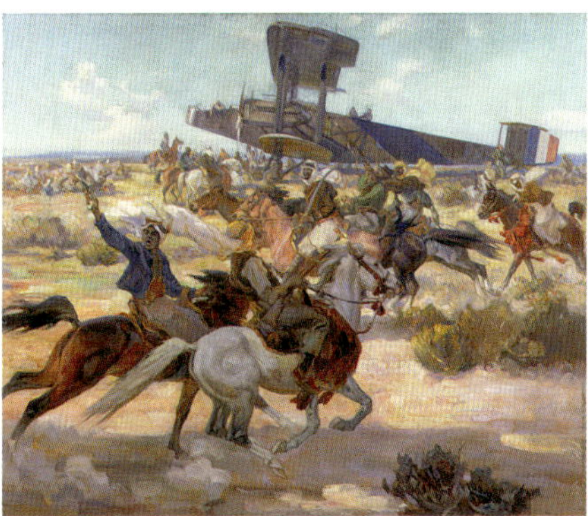

Reid, Stuart 1883–1971
Deraa: The Arab Welcome to the First Handley Page Machine to Arrive in Palestine, 22 September 1918 1918
oil on panel 76.2 x 91.4
IWM ART 3198

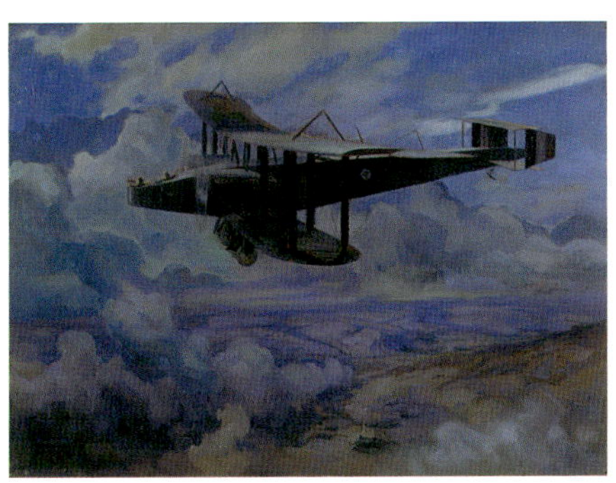

Reid, Stuart 1883–1971
A Handley Page Aeroplane Bombing Nabulus by Night c.1918–1920
oil on canvas 69.8 x 93.9
IWM ART 3073

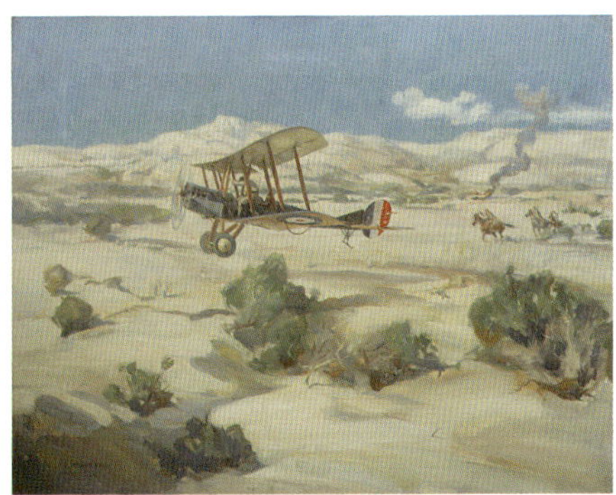

Reid, Stuart 1883–1971
Lieutenant McNamara: Winning the VC in the Course of a Bombing Raid in the Wadi Hesi, 10 Miles East-North-East (…) c.1918–1920
oil on canvas 71.1 x 91.4
IWM ART 3074

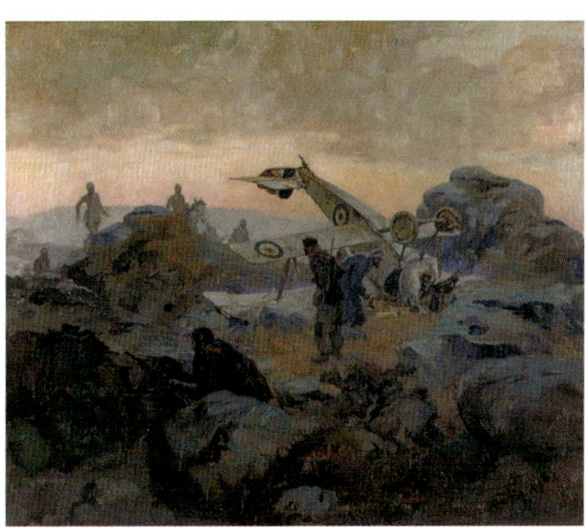

Reid, Stuart 1883–1971
The Bott Incident c.1918–1920
oil on canvas 76.2 x 91.4
IWM ART 3197

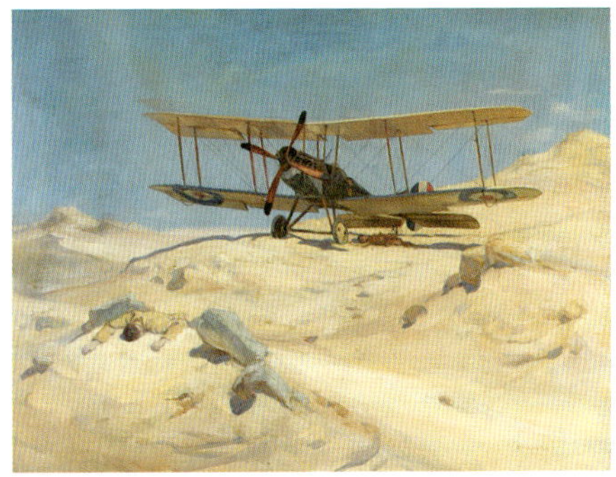

Reid, Stuart 1883–1971
The Ridley Tragedy c.1918–1920
oil on canvas 68.5 x 91.4 (E)
IWM ART 3075

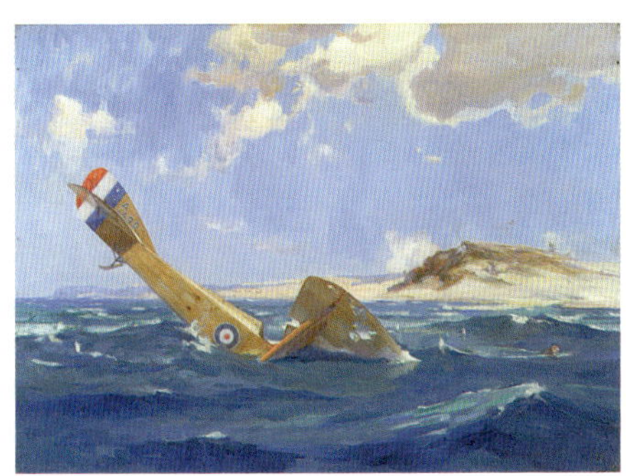

Reid, Stuart 1883–1971
The Seward Exploit: Second Lieutenant W. E. L. Seward, MC, at Ramleh, near Jaffa in Palestine, 24 March 1917 c.1918–1920
oil on canvas 68.5 x 91.4 (E)
IWM ART 3072

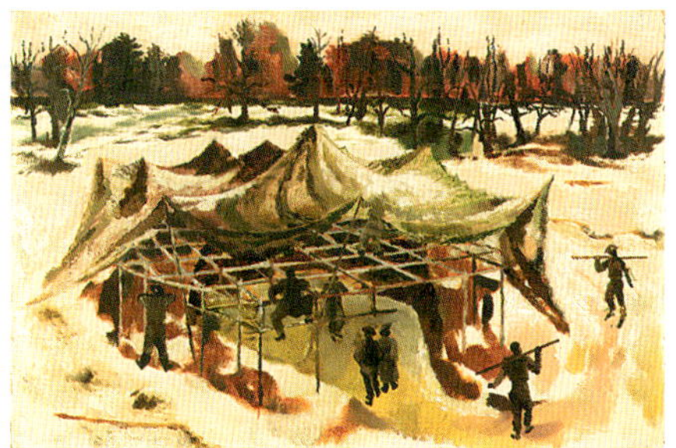

Richards, Albert 1919–1945
A Covering for a Gun Site 1942
oil on panel 44.4 x 67.9
IWM ART LD 1940

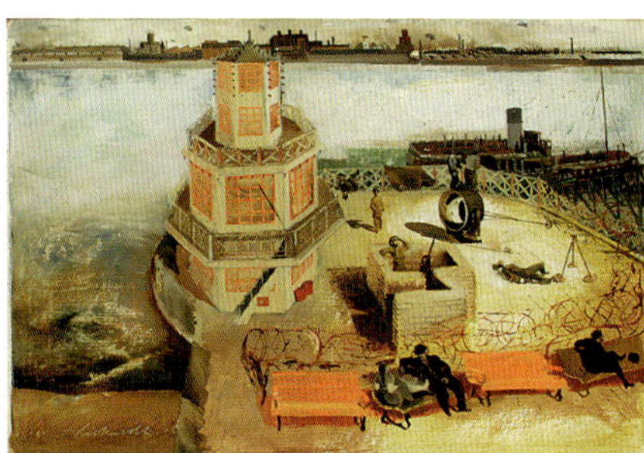

Richards, Albert 1919–1945
A Searchlight Battery 1942
oil on panel 50.8 x 76.2
IWM ART LD 3284

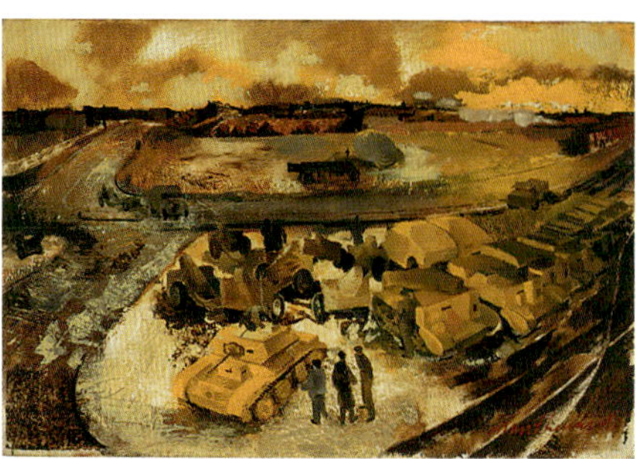

Richards, Albert 1919–1945
*The Industrial Battle: Tanks Ready for
Shipment Overseas* c.1943
oil on panel 50.8 x 76.2
IWM ART LD 3283

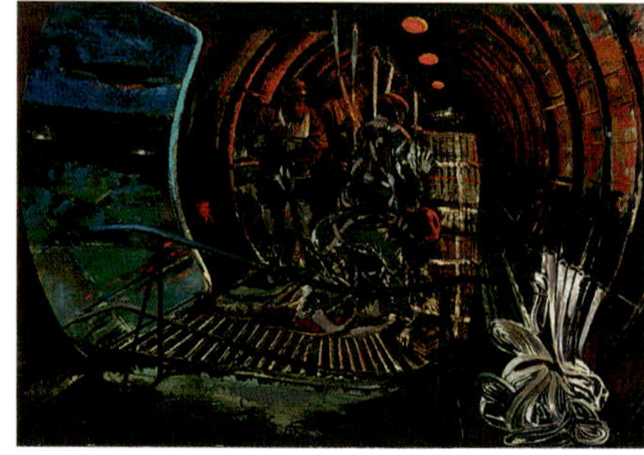

Richards, Albert 1919–1945
*Airborne Royal Army Service Corps Supply
Dropping* 1944
oil on panel 58.1 x 84.7
IWM ART LD 3923

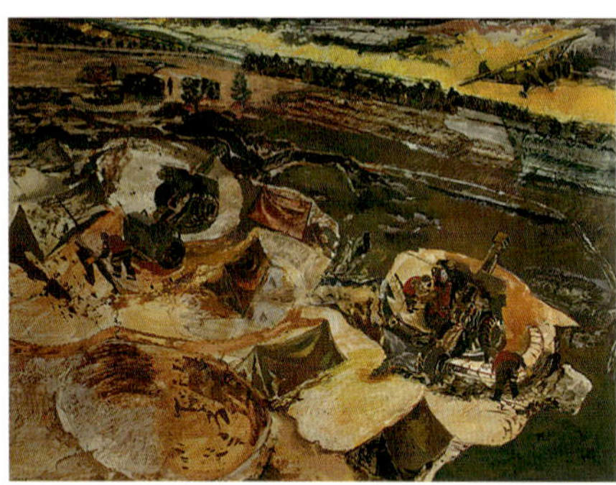

Richards, Albert 1919–1945
*Breaking up the Attack, Holland: 25-Pounders
of the 15th (Scottish) Division Firing towards
Meijel* 1944
oil on panel 55.8 x 76.2
IWM ART LD 4825

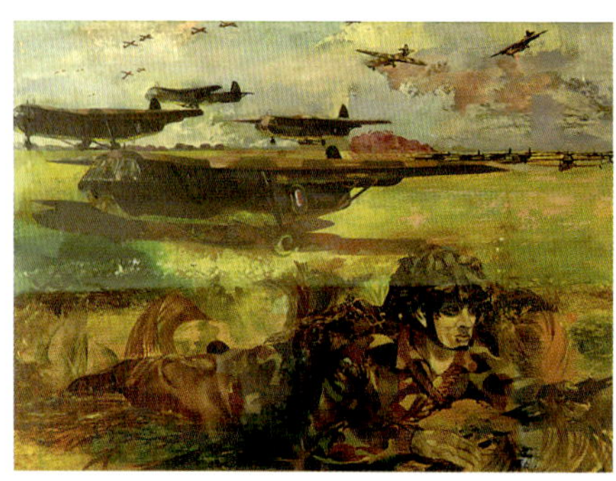

Richards, Albert 1919–1945
*Exercise 'Mush': Gliders Land on a 'Captured'
Airfield and Paratroops Surround the Field,
Waiting for the Unloading of the Gliders* 1944
oil on panel 57.1 x 76.8
IWM ART LD 4176

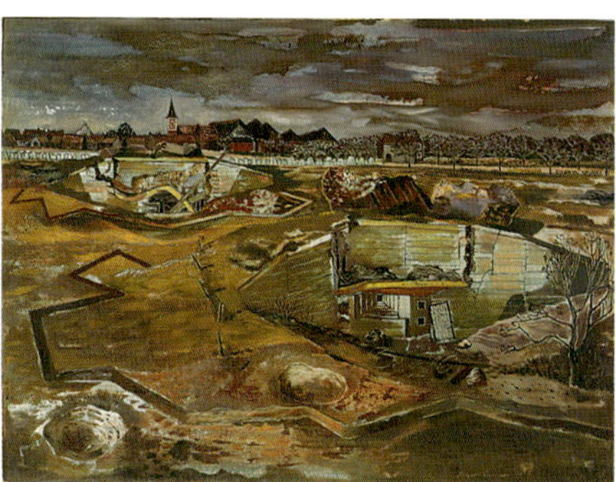

Richards, Albert 1919–1945
*Germany: The Siegfried Line between Heerlen
and Aachen* 1944
oil on panel 56.5 x 76.5
IWM ART LD 4830

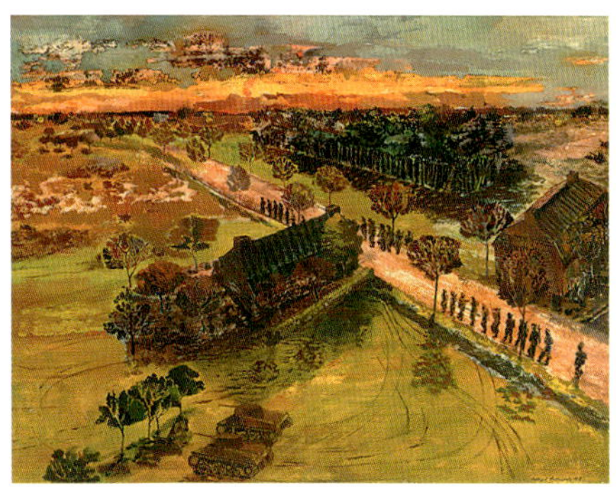

Richards, Albert 1919–1945
*Holland: Infantry of the 15th (Scottish)
Division Taking Over from Hard-Pressed
American Troops during a German (…)* 1944
oil on panel 55.8 x 76.2
IWM ART LD 4829

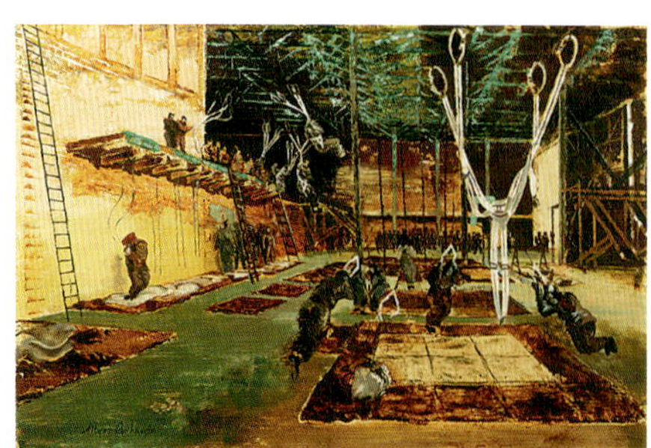

Richards, Albert 1919–1945
*'Kilkenny's Circus': Parachute Training School
Paratroops Undergoing Synthetic Training*
1944
oil on panel 50.4 x 77.4
IWM ART LD 3922

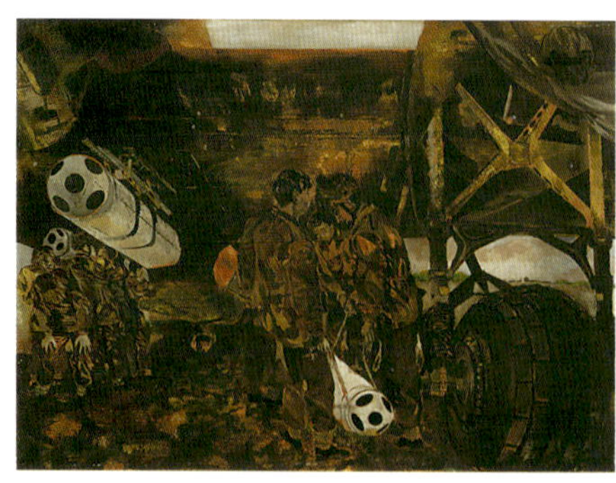

Richards, Albert 1919–1945
Loading Containers on a Dakota Aircraft 1944
oil on panel 55.5 x 75.5
IWM ART LD 4178

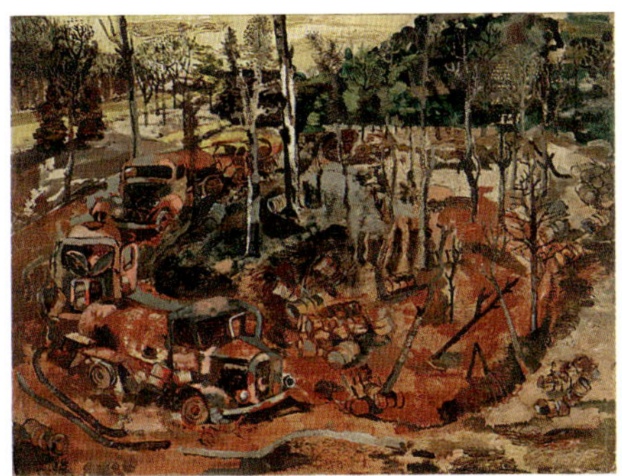

Richards, Albert 1919–1945
*The Advance, France: Burnt Out German
Petrol Tankers* 1944
oil on panel 58.4 x 78.1
IWM ART LD 4665

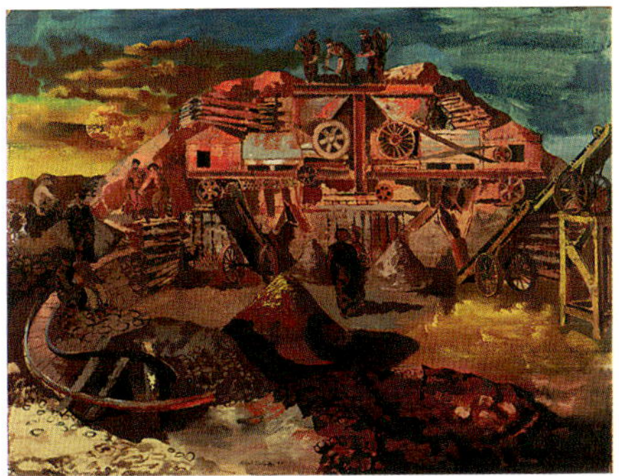

Richards, Albert 1919–1945
*The Beach Head, France: The Search for
Rubble; the Wear and Tear on the Roads
Resulted in a Constant Search for (…)* 1944
oil on panel 58.4 x 77.4
IWM ART LD 4667

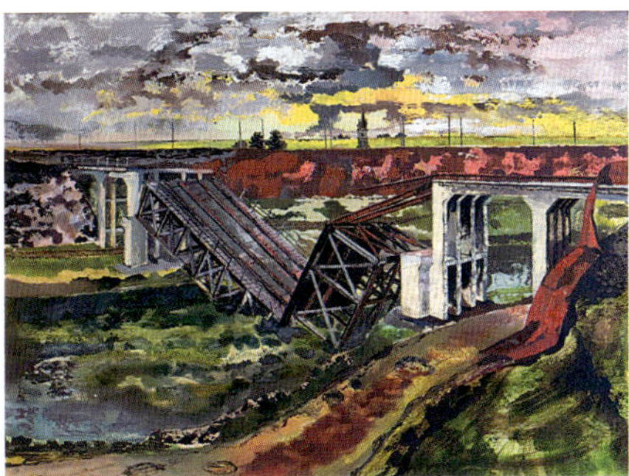

Richards, Albert 1919–1945
*The Beginning of the Advance, France: German
Bridge Demolition* 1944
oil on panel 55.8 x 75.8
IWM ART LD 4666

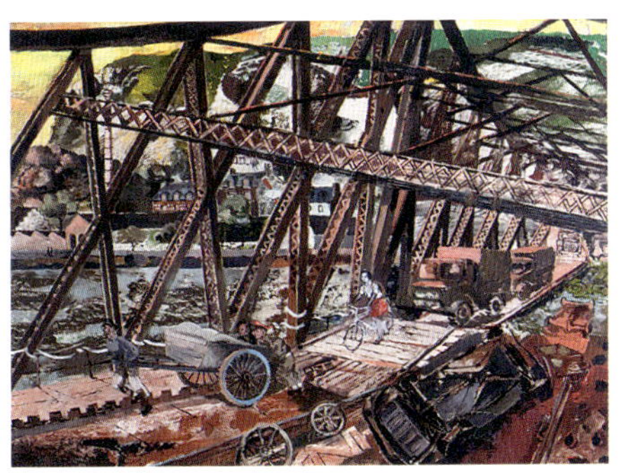

Richards, Albert 1919–1945
*The Break through, France: 'Marmalade
Bridge', A Railway Bridge Crossing the River
Seine at Rouen* 1944
oil on panel 55.8 x 75.5
IWM ART LD 4668

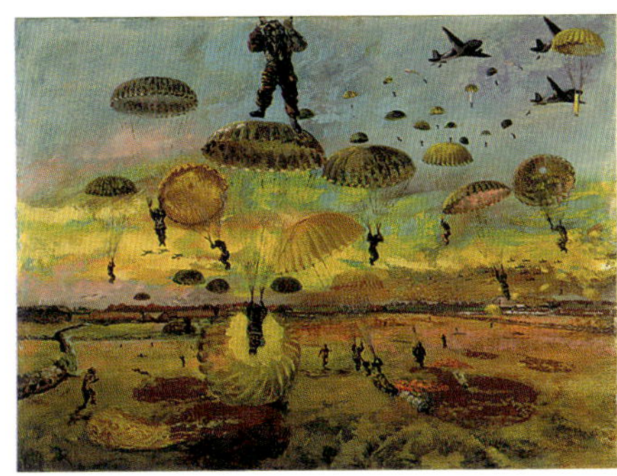

Richards, Albert 1919–1945
The Drop 1944
oil on panel 54.9 x 75.2
IWM ART LD 3924

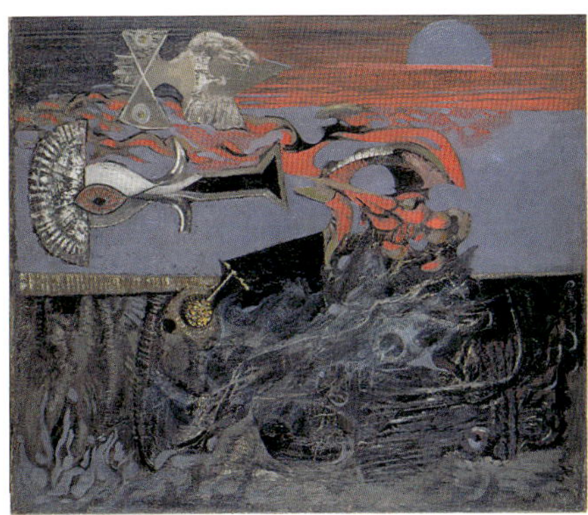

Richards, Ceri Geraldus 1903–1971
Falling Forms 1944
oil on canvas 51 x 61
IWM ART 16504

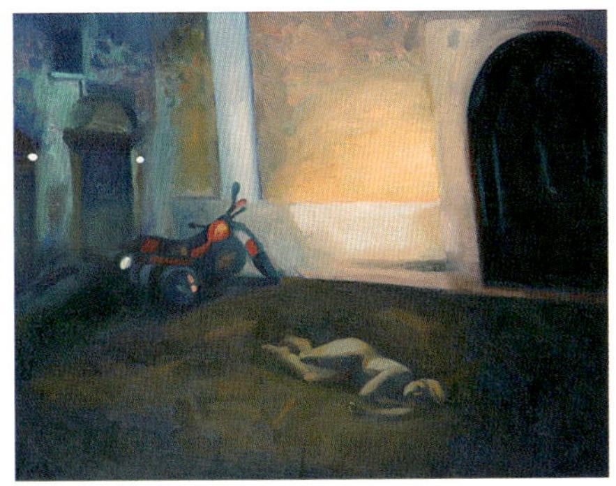

Robb, Carole b.1943
Casualty of War 1995
oil on linen 35.8 x 45.5
IWM ART 16957

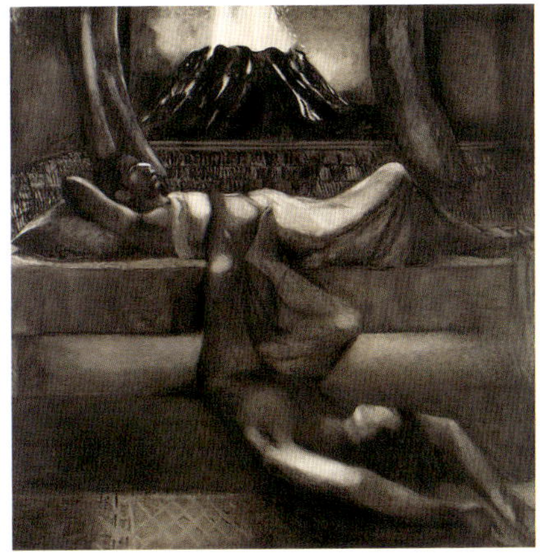

Robb, Carole b.1943
Death of Achilles 1996
oil on linen 157.5 x 157.2
IWM ART 16958

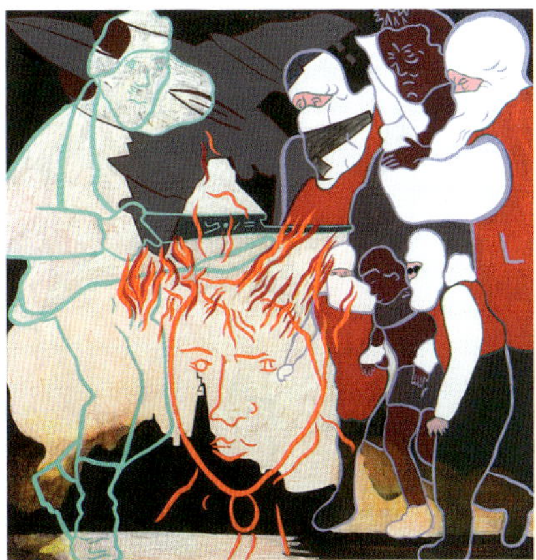

Roberts, Diane b.1956
Falklands War Triptych (left)
acrylic on board 91.5 x 91
IWM ART 16461 1

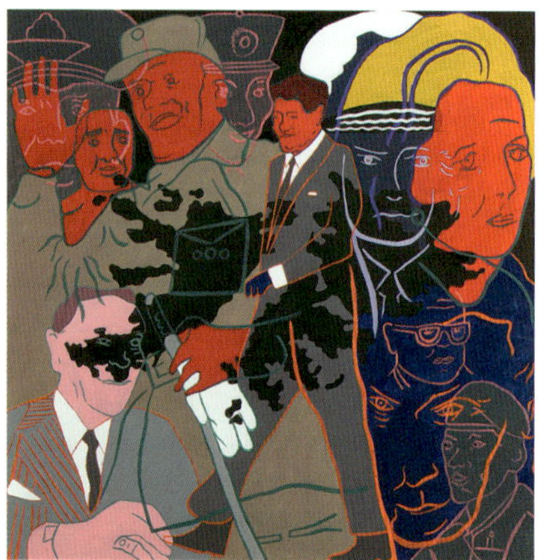

Roberts, Diane b.1956
Falklands War Triptych (centre)
acrylic on board 91.5 x 91
IWM ART 16461 2

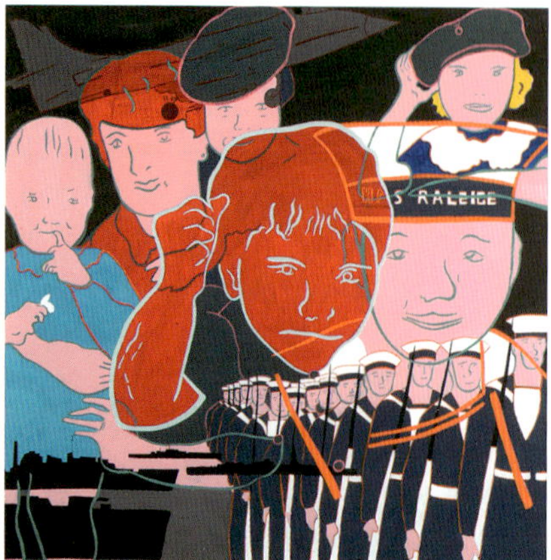

Roberts, Diane b.1956
Falklands War Triptych (right)
acrylic on board 91.5 x 91
IWM ART 16461 3

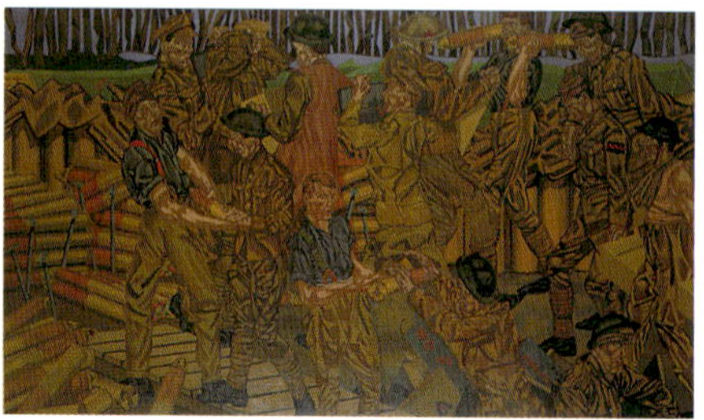

Roberts, William Patrick 1895–1980
A Shell Dump, France 1918
oil on canvas 182.8 x 317.5
IWM ART 2273

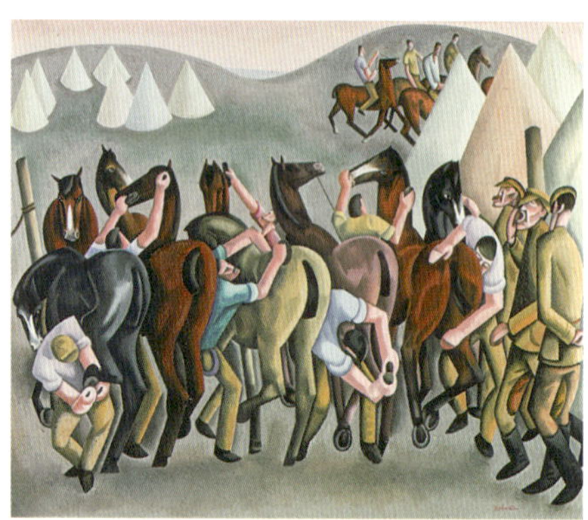

Roberts, William Patrick 1895–1980
'Feeds Round!': Stable Time in the Wagon Lines, France 1922
oil on canvas 51.2 x 61.2
IWM ART 4218

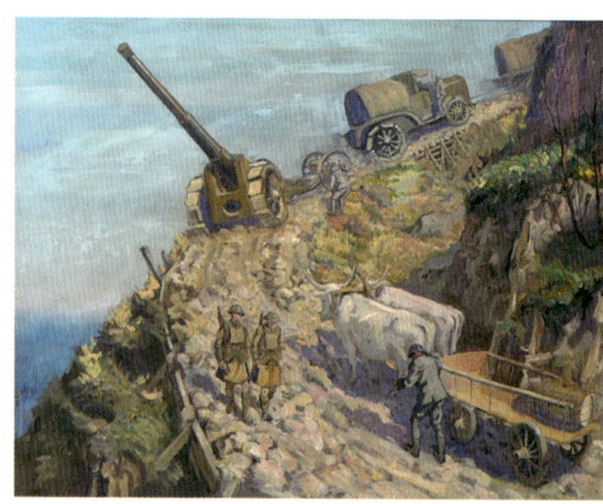

Robertson, Stewart active 1912–1920
Mixed Company on the Montello-Italian Front: An Italian Six-Inch Gun Being Hauled up Road Four by Fiat (…) c.1917–1918
oil on canvas 55.8 x 68.5
IWM ART 1630

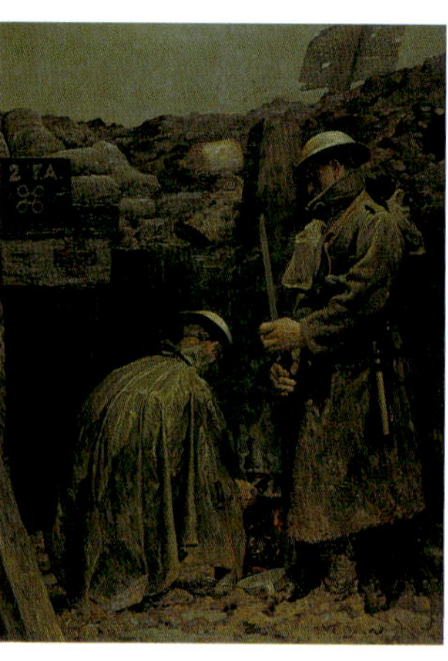

Rogers, Gilbert active 1905–1920
'Humanity' Bearer Post, Cambrin Sector, August 1916: The First Field Ambulance 1916
oil on canvas 276.8 x 203.2
IWM ART 3752

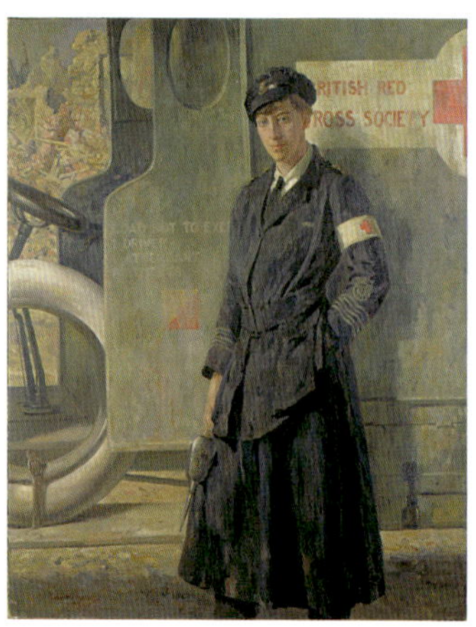

Rogers, Gilbert active 1905–1920
A Voluntary Aid Detachment Motor Driver c.1918–1919
oil on canvas 142.2 x 113
IWM ART 3824

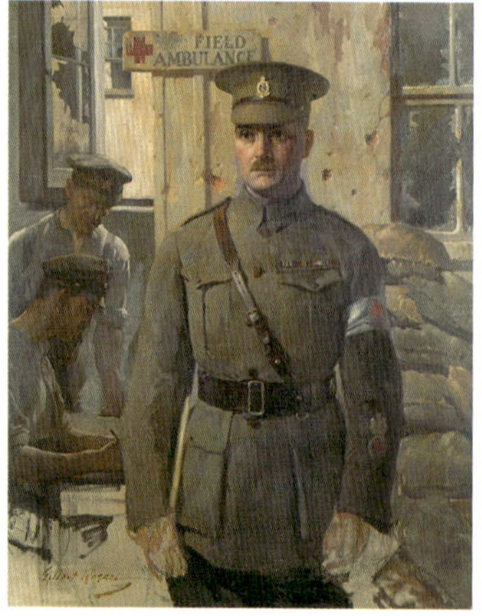

Rogers, Gilbert active 1905–1920
A Royal Army Medical Corps Sergeant Major 1919–1920
oil on canvas 127 x 101.9
IWM ART 3748

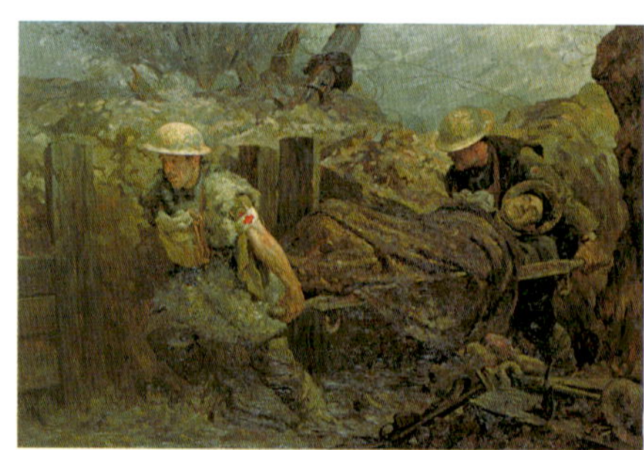

Rogers, Gilbert active 1905–1920
Stretcher Bearing in Difficulties 1919–1920
oil on canvas 203.2 x 306
IWM ART 3801

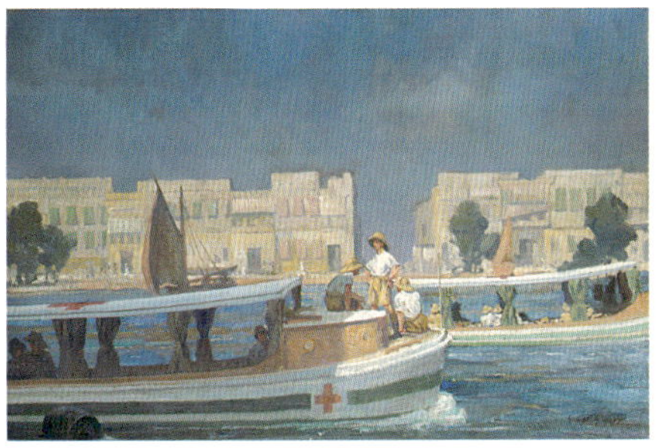

Rogers, Gilbert active 1905–1920
*A British Red Cross Society and Order of St
John of Jerusalem Barge on the Tigris at
Amara: British Red Cross Society (…)* c.1919
oil on canvas 101.9 x 152.4
IWM ART 3721

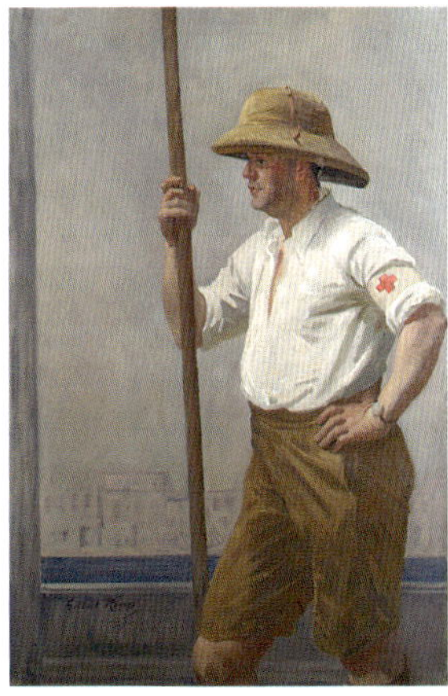

Rogers, Gilbert active 1905–1920
*A British Red Cross Society and Order of St
John of Jerusalem Hospital Barge Orderly on
the Tigris* c.1919
oil on canvas 152.4 x 101.9
IWM ART 3839

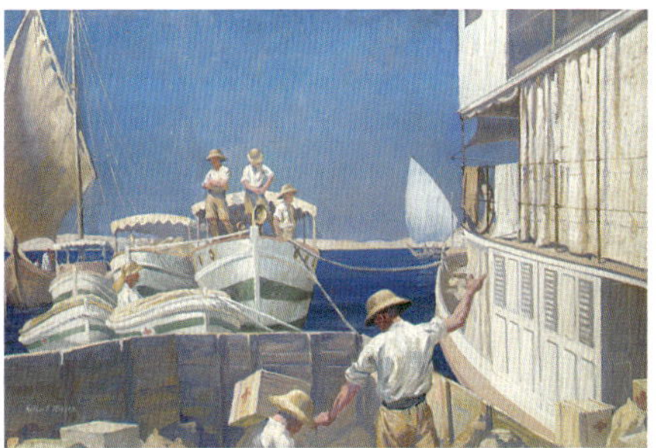

Rogers, Gilbert active 1905–1920
*A British Red Cross Society and Order of St
John of Jerusalem Hospital Ship and Barges on
the Tigris* c.1919
oil on canvas 101.9 x 152.4
IWM ART 3771

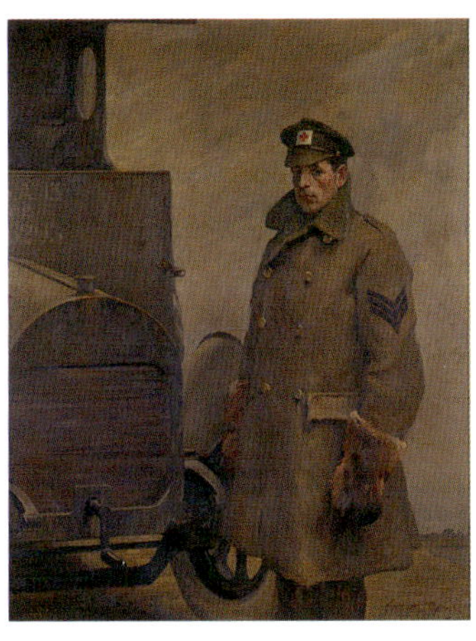

Rogers, Gilbert active 1905–1920
*A British Red Cross Society and Order of St
John of Jerusalem Motor Driver* c.1919
oil on canvas 142.2 x 111.7
IWM ART 3739

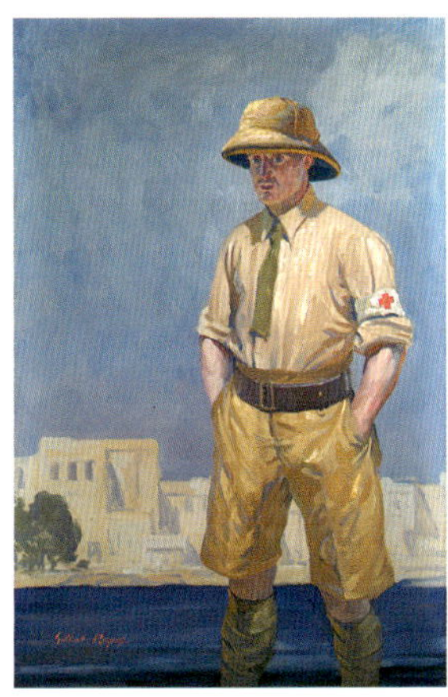

Rogers, Gilbert active 1905–1920
*A British Red Cross Society and Order of St
John of Jerusalem Officer in
Mesopotamia* c.1919
oil on canvas 152.4 x 101.9
IWM ART 3836

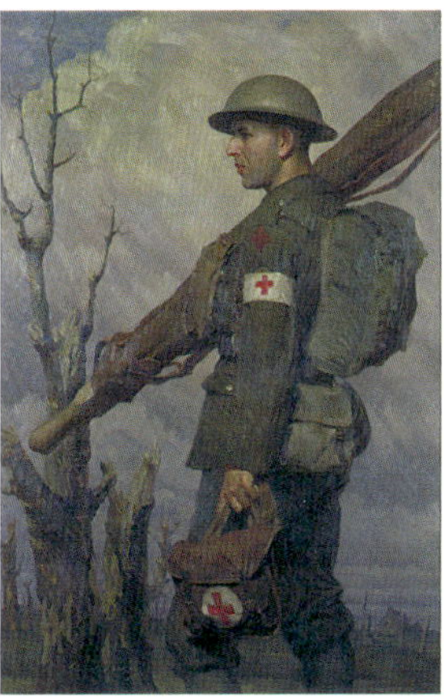

Rogers, Gilbert active 1905–1920
*A Royal Army Medical Corps Stretcher-Bearer,
Fully Equipped* c.1919
oil on canvas 152.4 x 101.9
IWM ART 3775

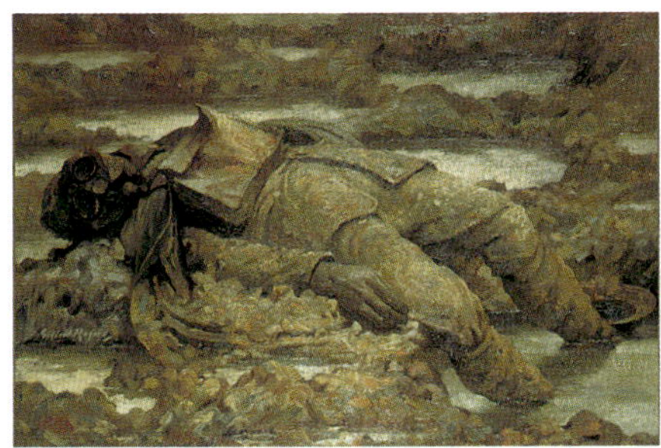

Rogers, Gilbert active 1905–1920
Gassed: 'In arduis fidelis' c.1919
oil on canvas 101.9 x 152.4
IWM ART 3819

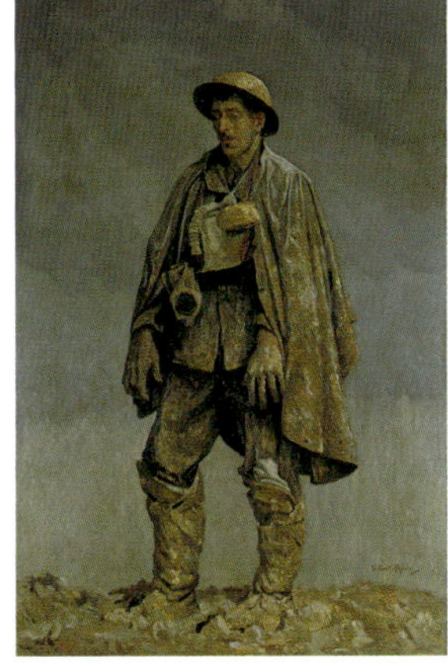

Rogers, Gilbert active 1905–1920
Mud c.1919
oil on canvas 335.2 x 203.2
IWM ART 3734

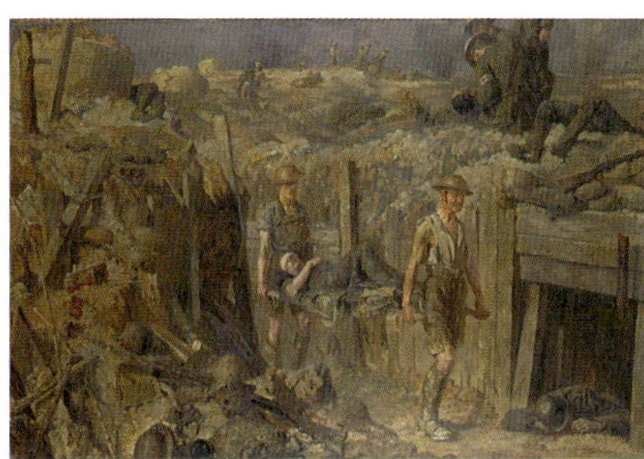

Rogers, Gilbert active 1905–1920
*The Royal Army Medical Corps at Messines
during the 1917 Offensive* c.1919
oil on canvas 101.9 x 152.4
IWM ART 2757

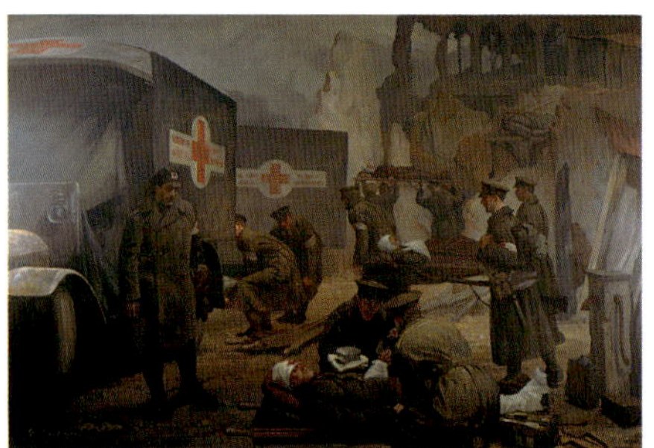

Rogers, Gilbert active 1905–1920
Ypres, 1915 c.1919
oil on canvas 335.2 x 457.2
IWM ART 3792

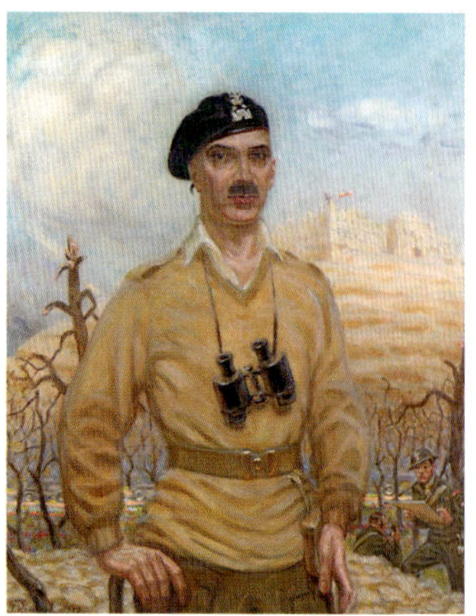

Rommel, T. active 1950s
Lieutenant General Wladyslaw Anders (1892–1970): Commander of Two Polish Corps at Monte Cassino 1954
oil on canvas 76.2 x 60.9
IWM ART LD 5980

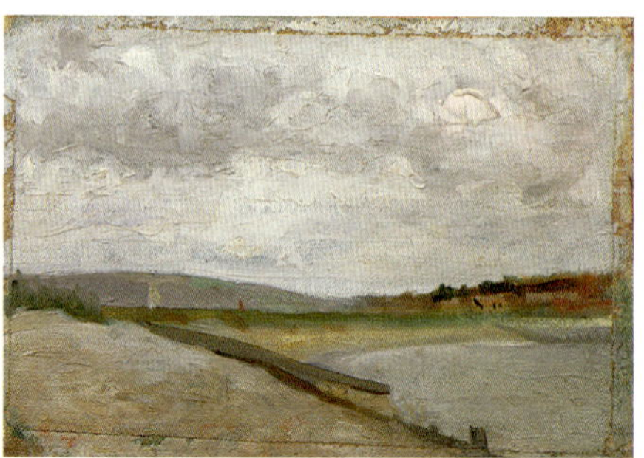

Rosenberg, Isaac 1890–1918
Sea and Beach 1910
oil on board 23.4 x 34.2
IWM ART 6365

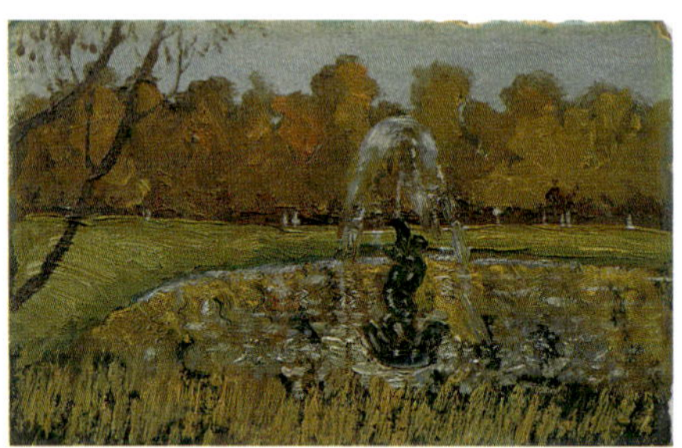

Rosenberg, Isaac 1890–1918
The Fountain 1911
oil on board 15.8 x 26
IWM ART 6366

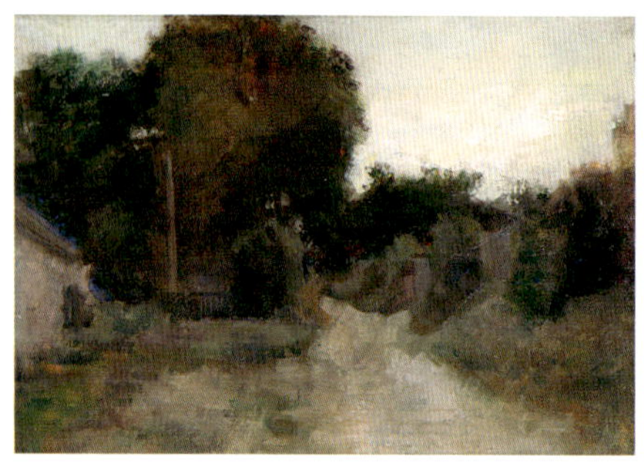

Rosenberg, Isaac 1890–1918
The Road 1911
oil on board 26.6 x 36.1
IWM ART 6359

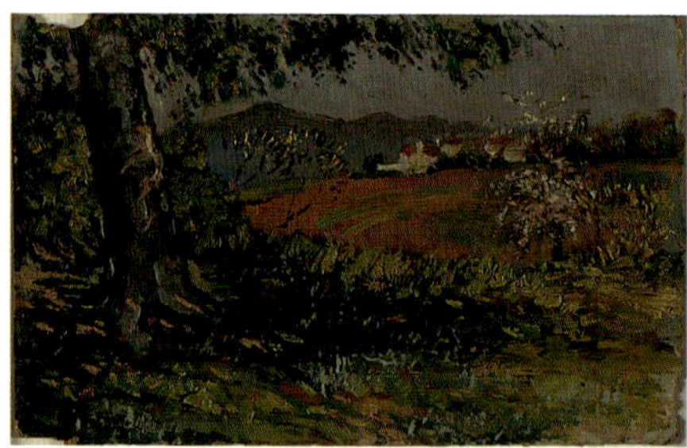

Rosenberg, Isaac 1890–1918
Landscape with Flowering Trees 1911–1912
oil on board 15.2 x 26
IWM ART 6361

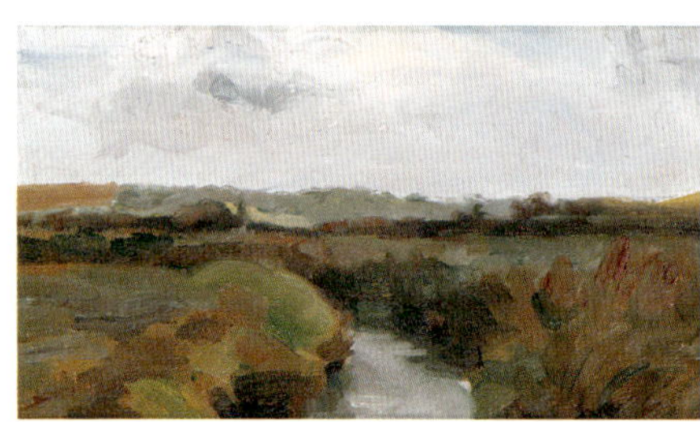

Rosenberg, Isaac 1890–1918
Landscape with River 1911–1912
oil on canvas board 22.8 x 34.9
IWM ART 6360

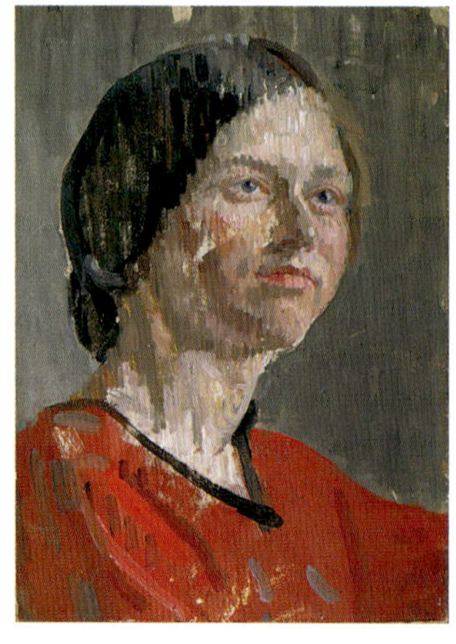

Rosenberg, Isaac 1890–1918
Head of a Woman, 'Grey and Red' 1912
oil on board 41.9 x 30.4
IWM ART 6362

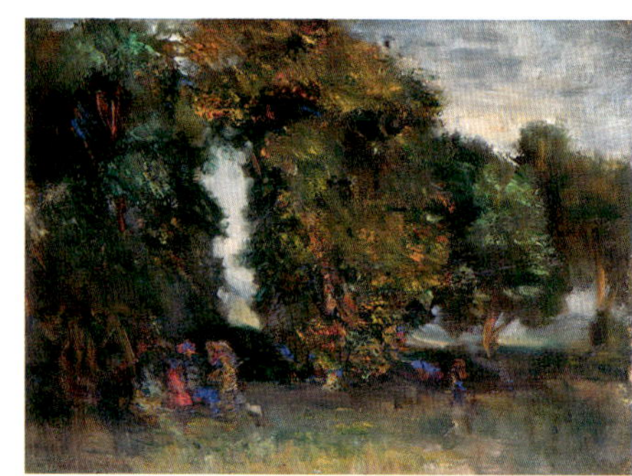

Rosenberg, Isaac 1890–1918
Trees 1912
oil on board 26.6 x 35.5
IWM ART 6363

Facing page: Cole, Leslie, 1910–1976, *Greece, an Orphanage: Curing Scabies with Anachryl* (detail), 1945, (p. 45)

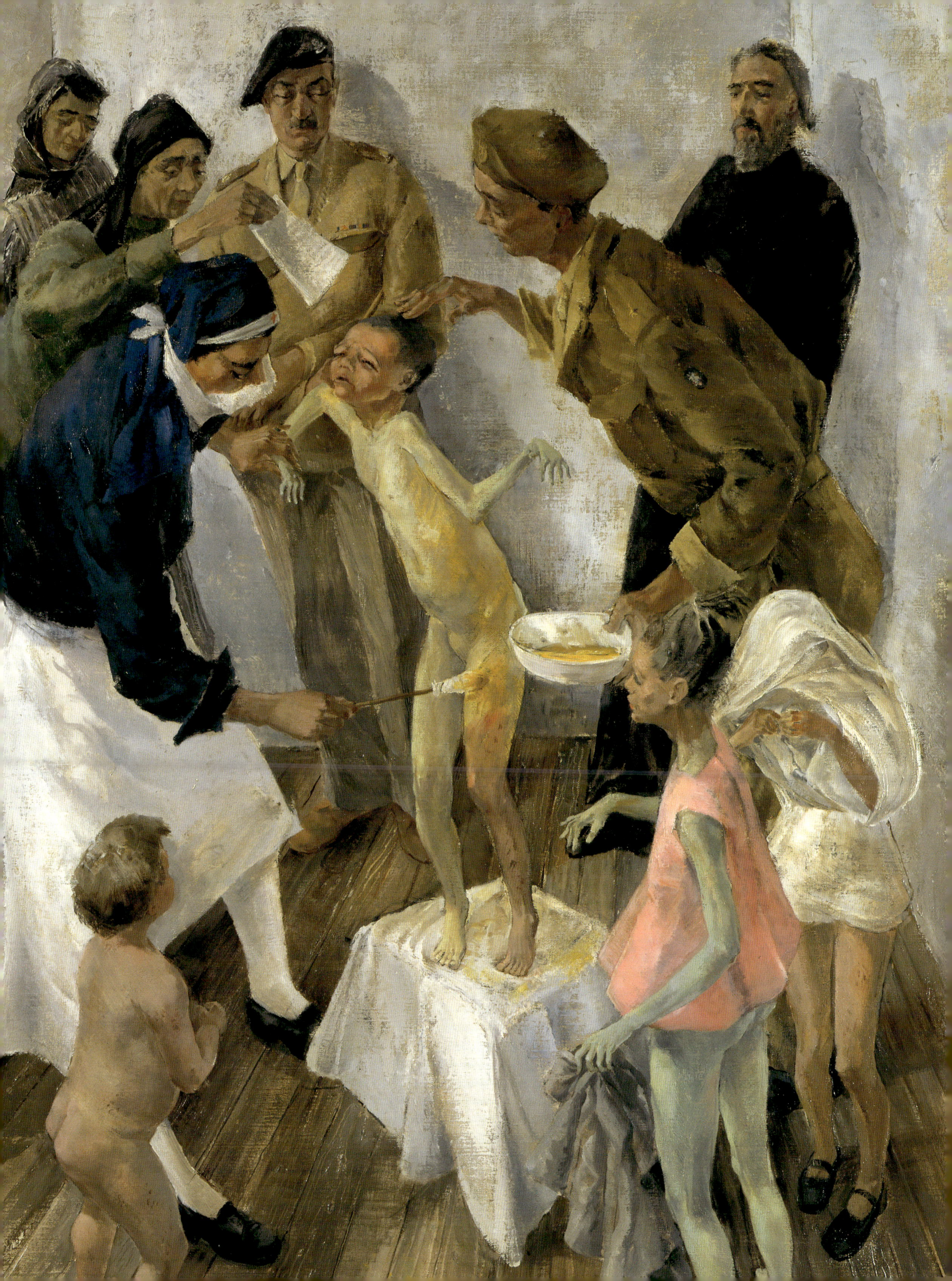

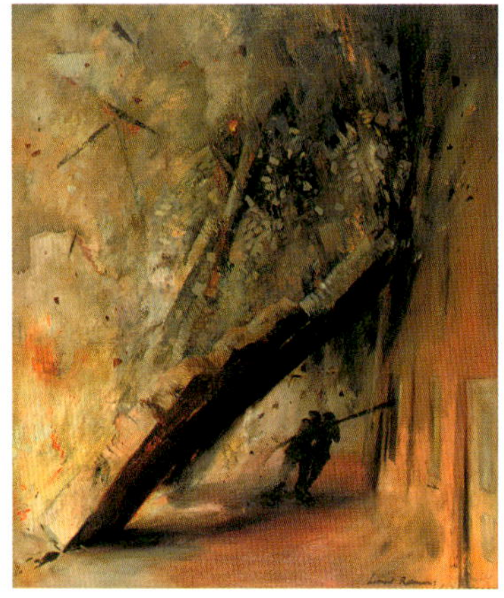

Rosoman, Leonard Henry b.1913
A House Collapsing on Two Firemen, Shoe Lane, London, EC4 1940
oil on canvas 91.8 x 76.8
IWM ART LD 1353

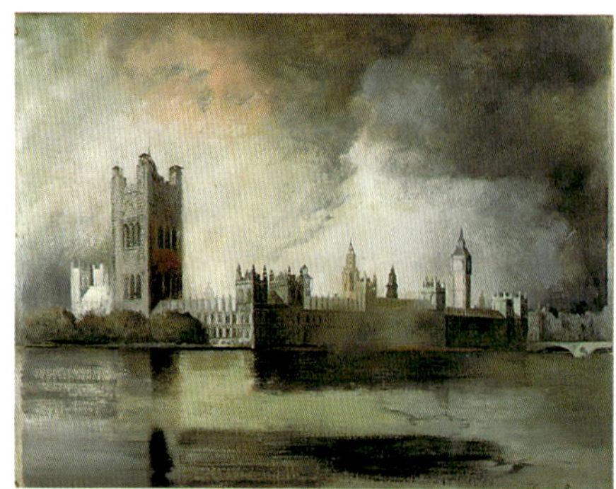

Rosoman, Leonard Henry b.1913
The Houses of Parliament on Fire, May 1941 1941
oil on canvas 97.5 x 123
IWM ART 15962

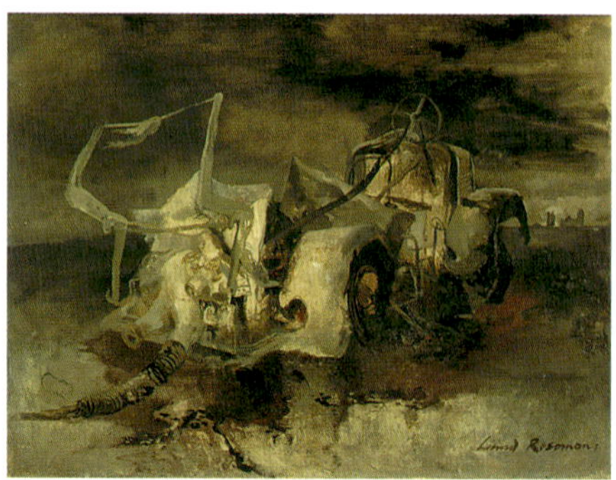

Rosoman, Leonard Henry b.1913
A Burnt Out Fire Appliance 1943
oil on canvas 76.2 x 101.9
IWM ART LD 3591

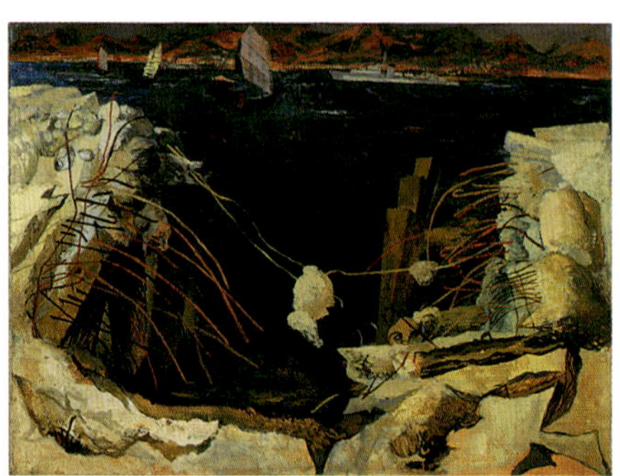

Rosoman, Leonard Henry b.1913
A Crater in the Naval Dockyard, Hong Kong 1945
oil on canvas 56.5 x 76.5
IWM ART LD 5650

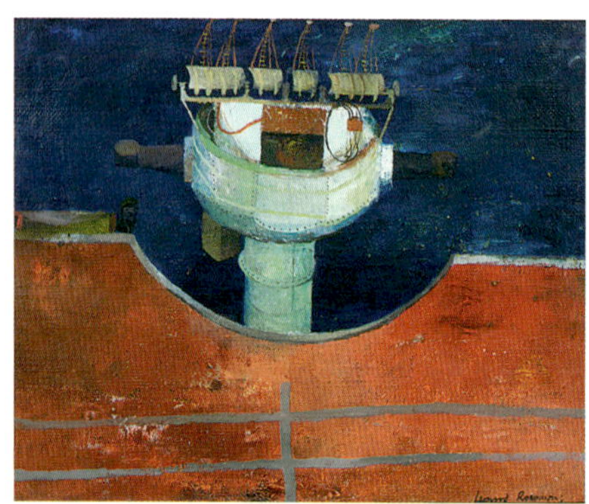

Rosoman, Leonard Henry b.1913
A Radar Predictor 1945
oil on canvas 40.6 x 50.8
IWM ART LD 5627

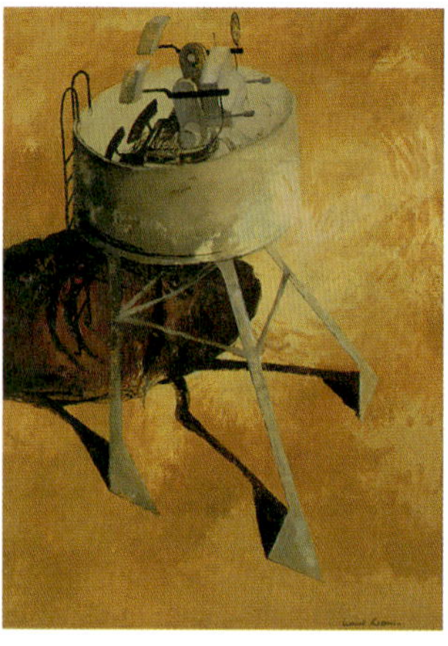

Rosoman, Leonard Henry b.1913
A Rangefinder in Hot Sunlight 1945
oil on canvas 76.2 x 50.8
IWM ART LD 5625

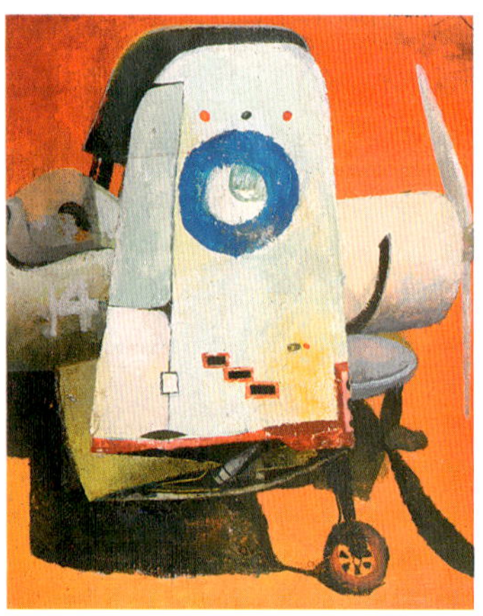

Rosoman, Leonard Henry b.1913
Corsair Aircraft with Folded Wings in Hot Sunlight 1945
oil on canvas 50.8 x 40.6
IWM ART LD 5626

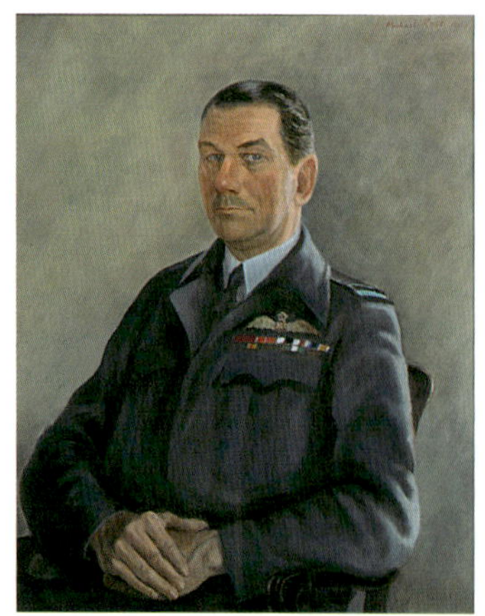

Ross, Michael active 1935–1955
Air Vice-Marshal Simpson, Air Defence Commander, 19 Group, RAF Pitreavie c.1944
oil on canvas 74.5 x 62.6
IWM ART 16179

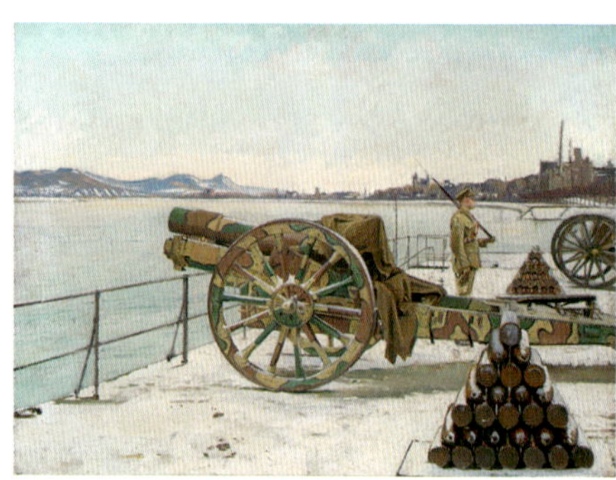

Rothenstein, William 1872–1945
The Watch on the Rhine 1917–1918
oil on canvas 76.2 x 101.9
IWM ART 2623 ✷

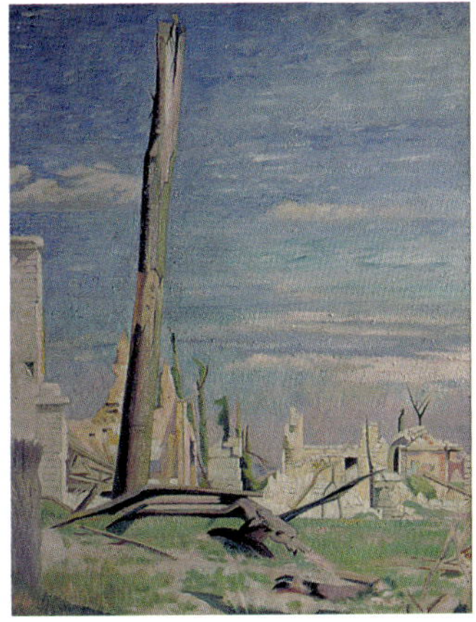

Rothenstein, William 1872–1945
Ypres Salient 1917–1918
oil on canvas 91.5 x 71
IWM ART 15999

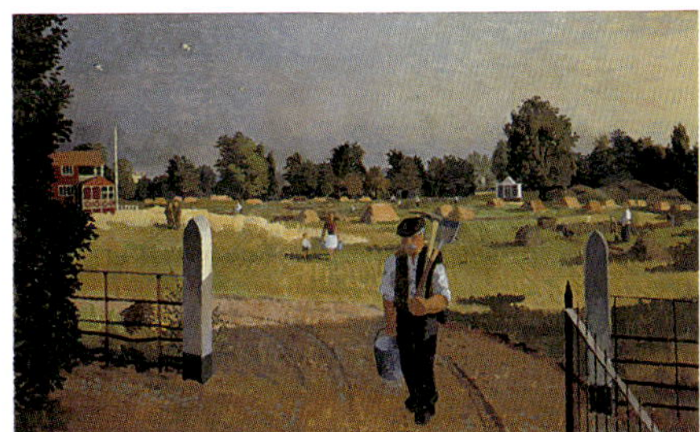

Rowntree, Kenneth 1915–1997
A Polo Ground in Wartime 1940
oil on canvas 55.8 x 91.4
IWM ART LD 637

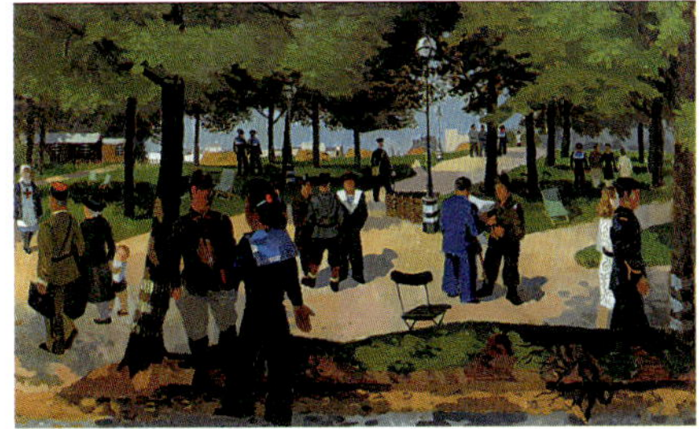

Rowntree, Kenneth 1915–1997
*Foreign Servicemen in Hyde Park: Early
Summer* 1940
oil on canvas 45.7 x 76.2
IWM ART LD 415

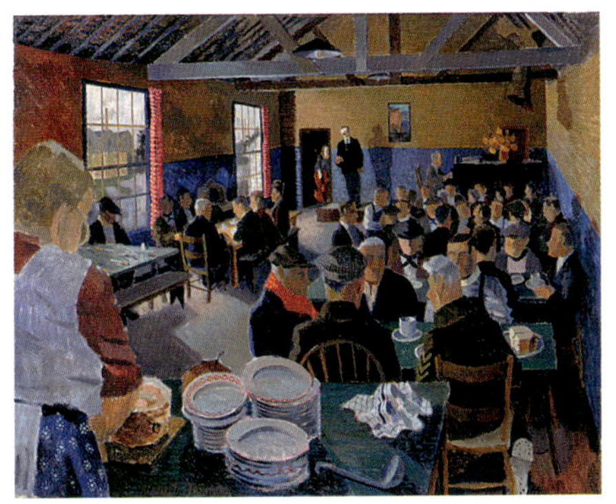

Rowntree, Kenneth 1915–1997
*The Council for the Encouragement of Music
and the Arts Canteen Concert, Isle of Dogs,
London, E14* 1941
oil on canvas 60.9 x 76.2
IWM ART LD 1879

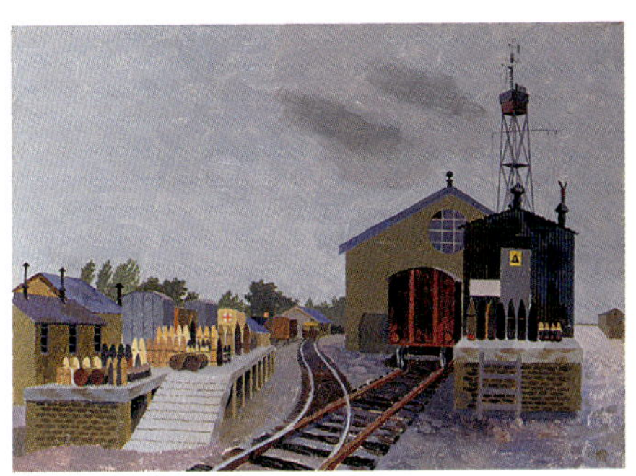

Rowntree, Kenneth 1915–1997
Experimental Establishment, Shoeburyness
1945
oil on canvas 38.1 x 53.3
IWM ART LD 5690

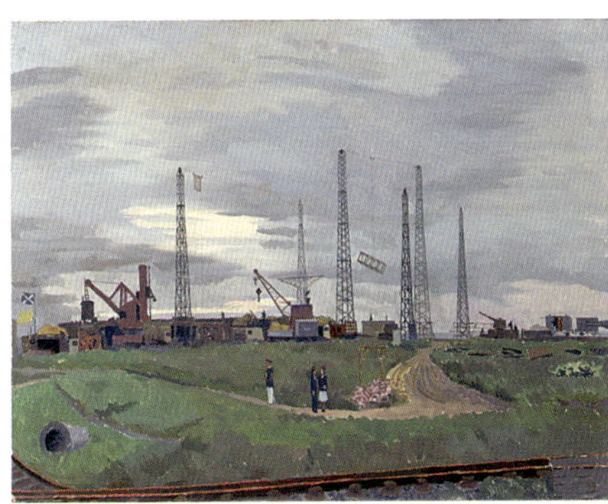

Rowntree, Kenneth 1915–1997
*The Experimental Establishment,
Shoeburyness: Firing through Screens* 1945
oil on canvas 53.3 x 68.5
IWM ART LD 5689

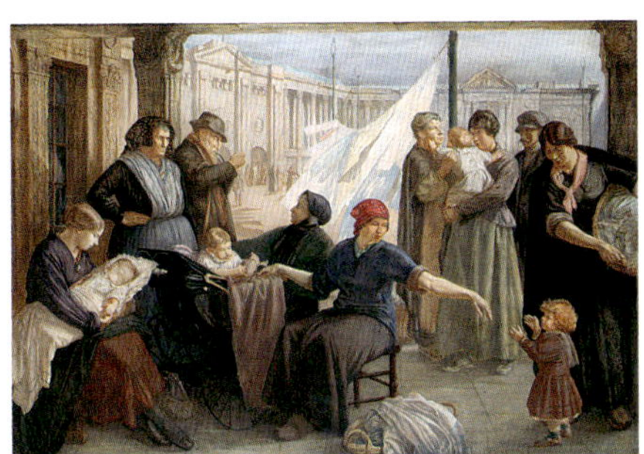

Rushbury, Henry 1889–1968
The War Refugees' Camp, Earl's Court 1918
tempera on canvas 106.6 x 152.4
IWM ART 2449

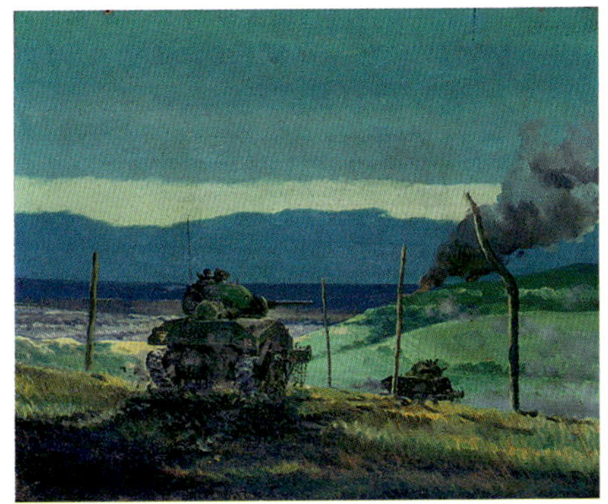

Russell, C. A. active 1940s
'Scorpion' Mine Destroying Tanks in France
1944
oil on panel 49.5 x 59.6
IWM ART LD 5559

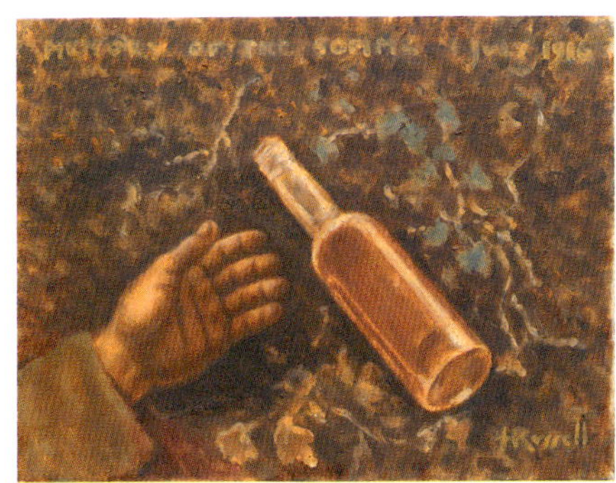

Russell, H. active 1914–1918
Memory of the Somme, 1 July 1916 1916
oil on canvas 30.4 x 40.6
IWM ART 6462

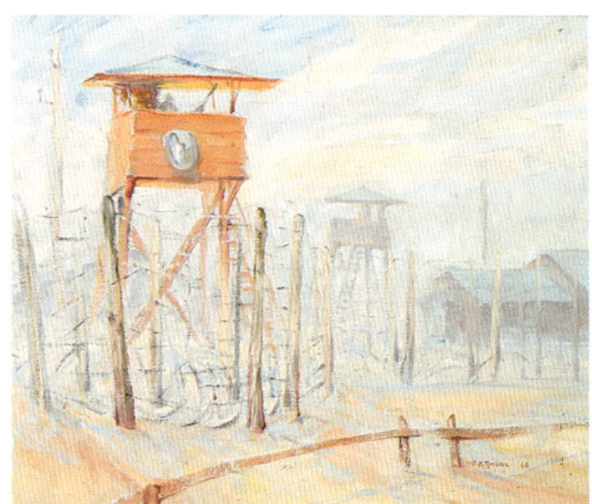

Russell, J. A. b.1920
The Wire 1945
oil on canvas 54.6 x 63.5
IWM ART LD 5304

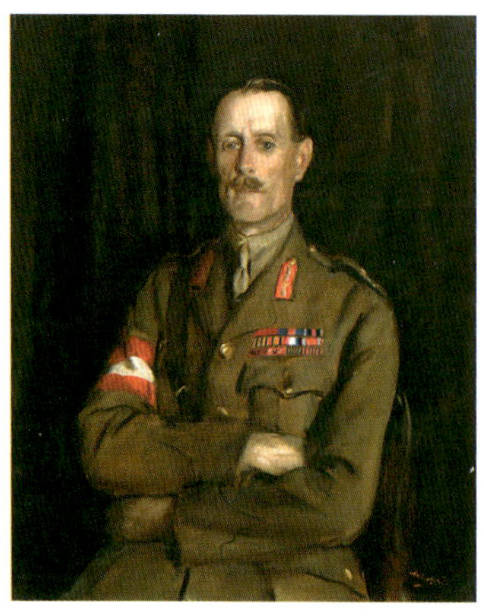

Russell, Walter Westley 1867–1949
General Sir Alexander John Godley
(1867–1957), KCB, KCMG 1919
oil on canvas 91.4 x 76.2
IWM ART 1916

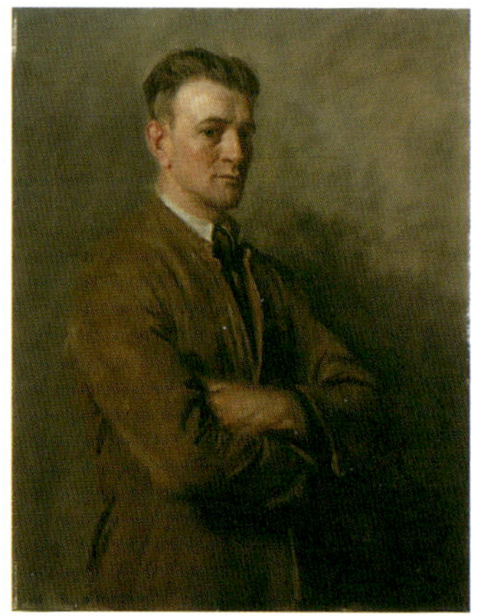

Russell, Walter Westley 1867–1949
Reginald Stone, GM 1941
oil on canvas 91.4 x 71.1
IWM ART LD 1666

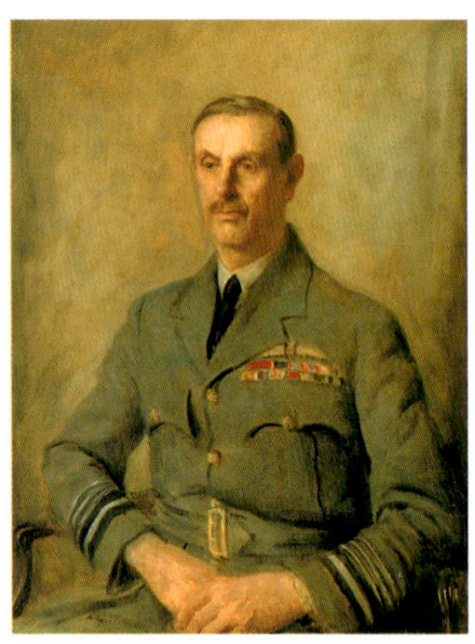

Russell, Walter Westley 1867–1949
Air Chief Marshal Sir Hugh Dowding
(1882–1970), GCB, GCVO, CMG 1942
oil on canvas 91.4 x 71.1
IWM ART LD 1904

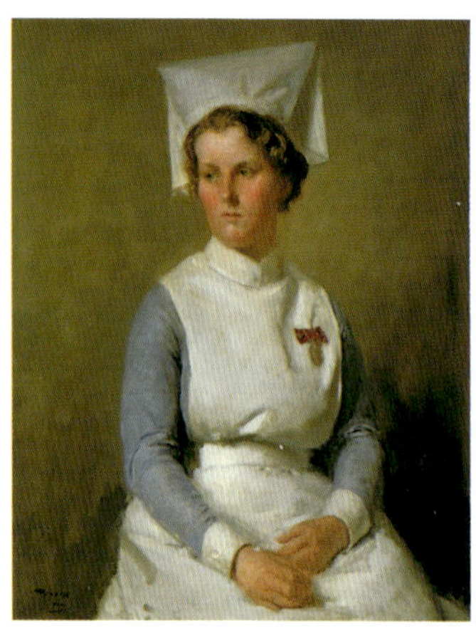

Russell, Walter Westley 1867–1949
Staff Nurse R. Rosser, GM 1942
oil on canvas 91.4 x 71.1
IWM ART LD 2179

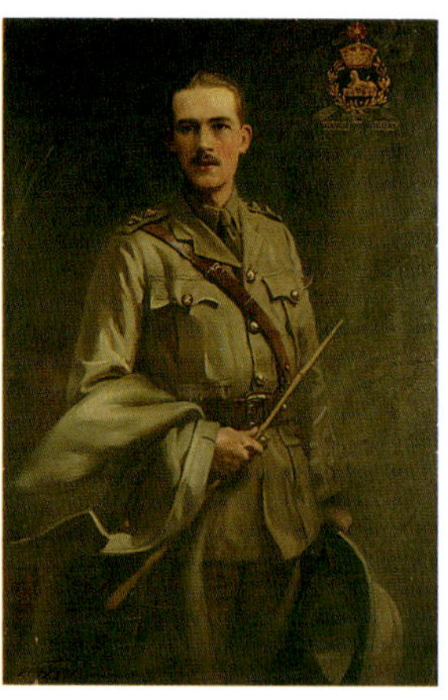

Salisbury, Frank O. 1874–1962
Lieutenant Samuel O'Neill: The Lancashire
Fusiliers, Gallipoli, 10 June 1915 1915
oil on canvas 132 x 88.9
IWM ART 5607

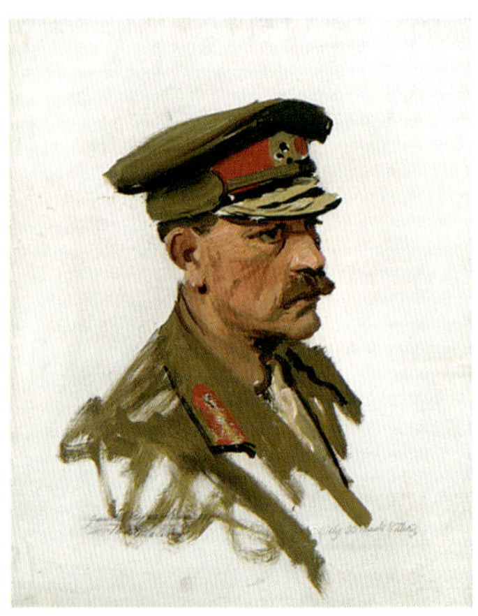

Salisbury, Frank O. 1874–1962
General Julian Byng (1862–1935) 1917
oil on canvas 58.4 x 48.2
IWM ART 5995

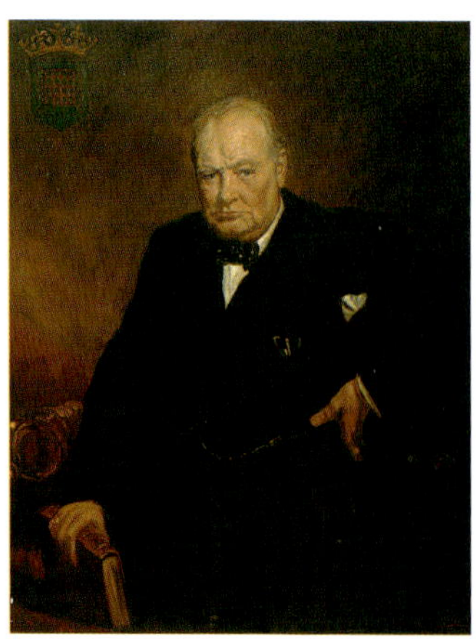

Salisbury, Frank O. (after) 1874–1962
Winston Churchill (1874–1965) c.2000
oil on canvas 120.6 x 95.8 (E)
IWM ART 16839

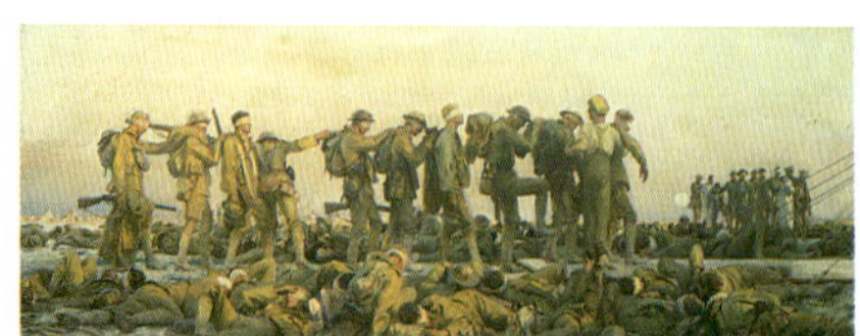

Sargent, John Singer 1856–1925
Gassed 1919
oil on canvas 231 x 611.1
IWM ART 1460

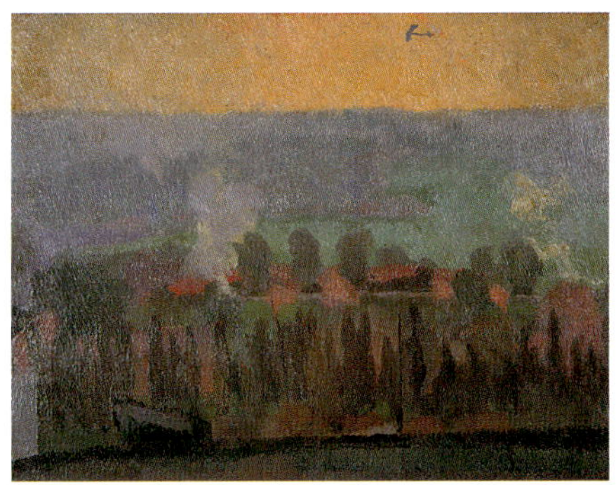

Sauter, Rudolf Helmut 1895–1977
*An Aeroplane: View from the Compound,
Alexandra Palace Civil Internment Camp*
1918
oil on panel 27.5 x 35.4
IWM ART 16491

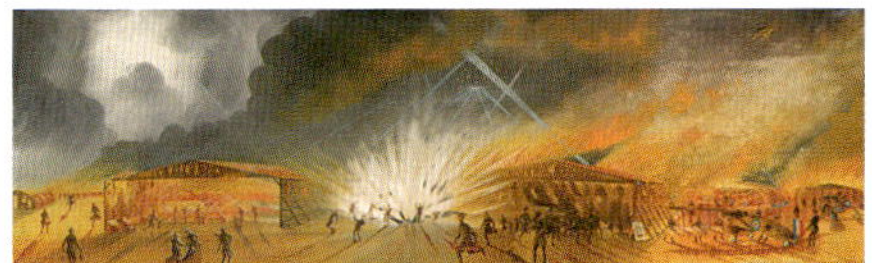

Sawyer, Douglas J. active 1920s
*Bertangles Aerodrome, Somme: The Bombing
of No.48 Squadron's Aerodrome by Four
German Machines, 29 October 1918* 1920
oil on canvas 40.6 x 125.7
IWM ART 3159

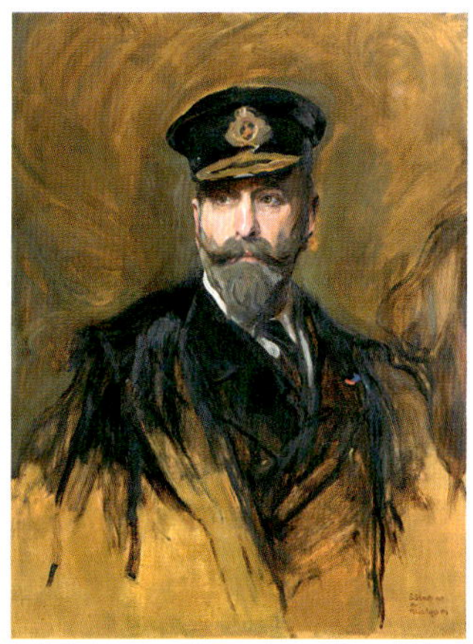

Schmolle, Stella 1908–1975
*Admiral Prince Louis of Battenberg (1854–
1921), Later Admiral of the Fleet of Milford
Haven, First Sea Lord, 9 December (…)* 1968
oil on canvas 91.4 x 71.1
IWM ART LD 6724

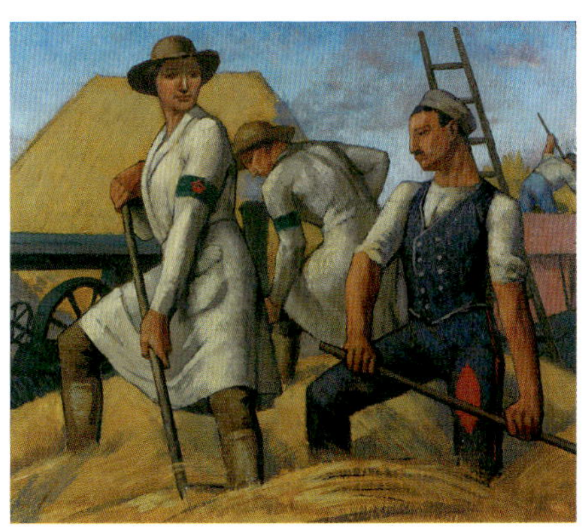

Schwabe, Randolph 1885–1948
*The Women's Land Army and German
Prisoners* 1918
oil on panel 48.2 x 57.1
IWM ART 1179

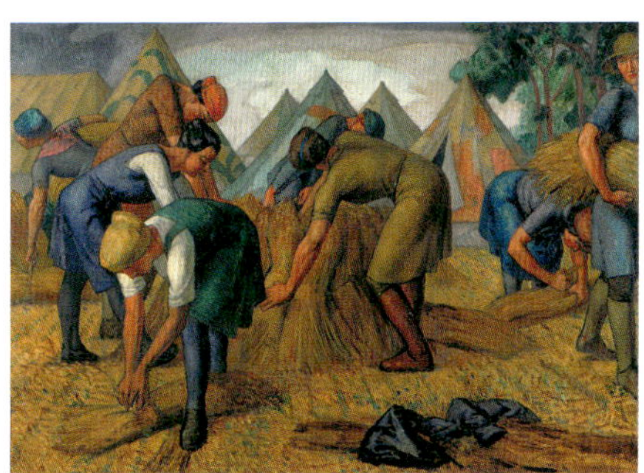

Schwabe, Randolph 1885–1948
*Voluntary Land Workers in a Flax Field,
Podington, Northamptonshire* 1919
oil on canvas 106.6 x 152.4
IWM ART 2288

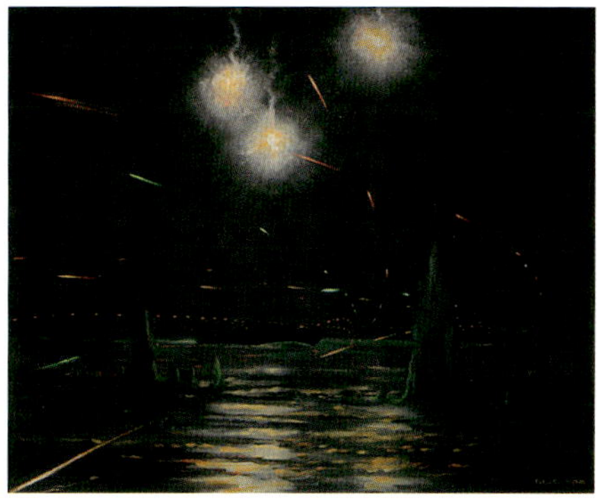

Scott, Peter Markham 1909–1989
*Night Action: Gunboats off Le Tréport, 4
September 1943* 1943
oil on canvas 63.5 x 76.2
IWM ART LD 5680

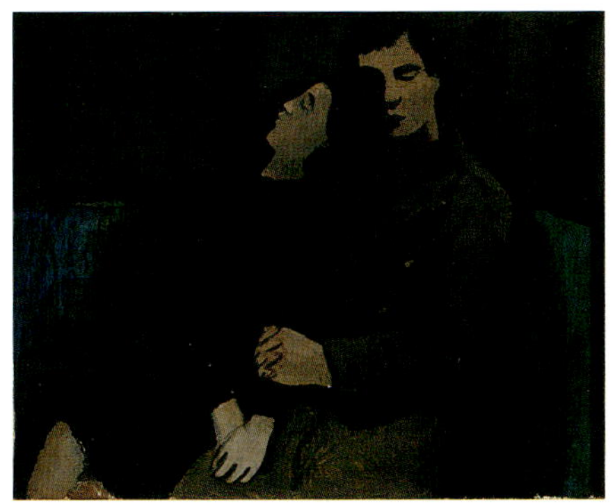

Scott, William George 1913–1989
Soldier and Girl Sleeping 1942
oil on canvas 40.9 x 50.8
IWM ART 16843

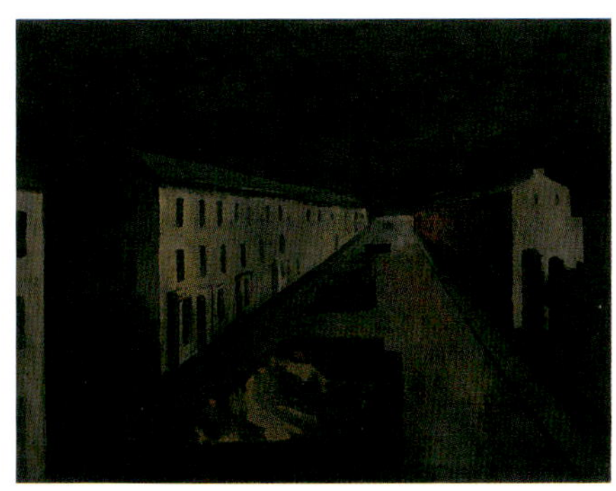

Scott, William George 1913–1989
Night Convoy 1942–1943
oil on canvas 50.5 x 67
IWM ART LD 6514

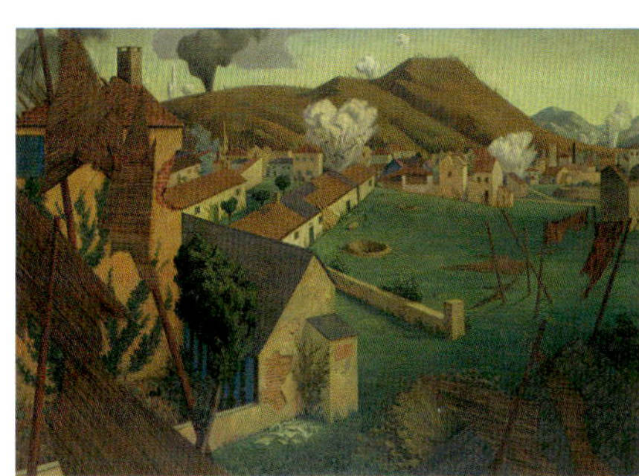

Seabrooke, Elliot 1886–1950
The Bombardment of Gorizia, 21 August 1917
1917
oil on canvas 106.6 x 152.4
IWM ART 2235

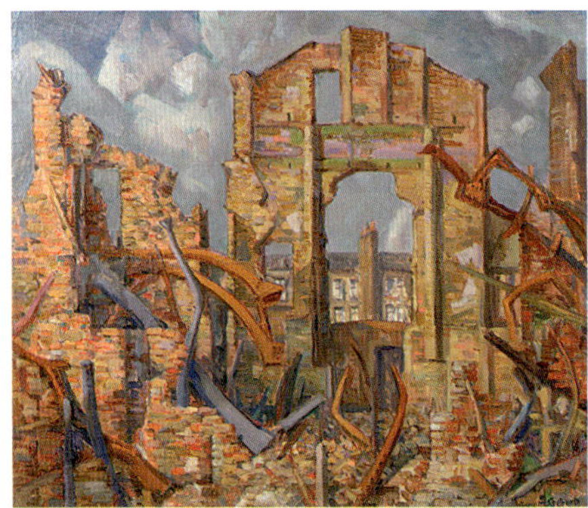

Seabrooke, Elliot 1886–1950
*Bomb Damage: Druce's Store, Baker Street,
London* c.1940–1944
oil on canvas 60.9 x 76.2
IWM ART LD 7547

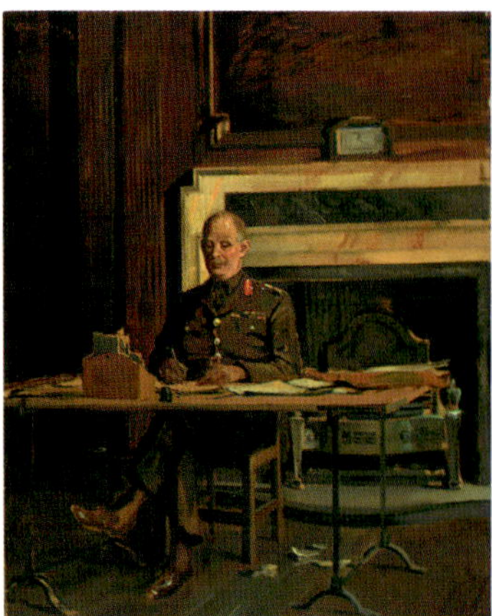

Seago, Edward Brian 1910–1974
*General Lord Gort (1886–1946), VC, at the
Headquarters of the British Expeditionary
Force* 1940
oil on panel 76.2 x 63.5
IWM ART LD 310

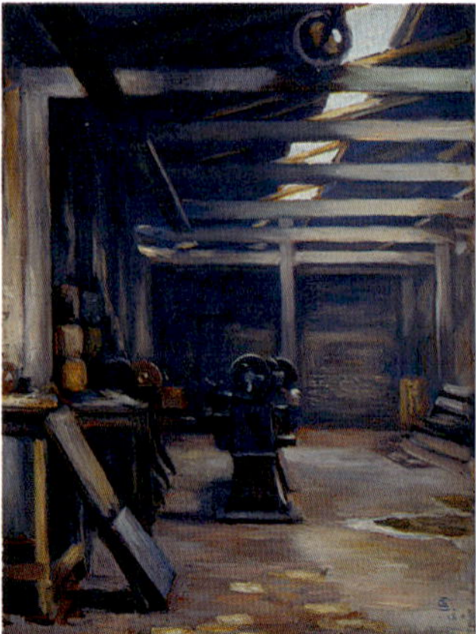

Seligman, Edgar 1867–1958
*After the Armistice: The Belgian Steel Factory,
Goldhawk Road, W12* 1918
oil on panel 44.4 x 33.6
IWM ART 5040

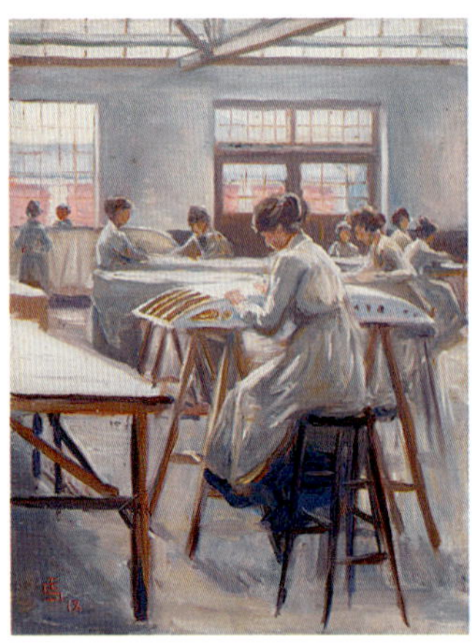

Seligman, Edgar 1867–1958
*Making Aeroplanes: Sizaire-Berwick Motor
Car Factory, Park Royal, NW10* 1918
oil on panel 43.8 x 33.6
IWM ART 5041

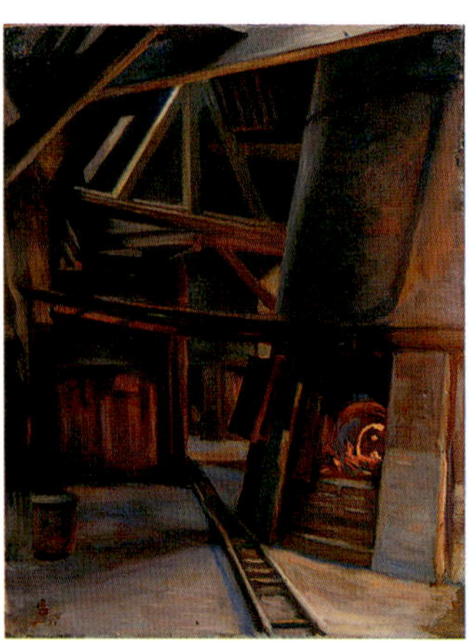

Seligman, Edgar 1867–1958
*Making Glass Floats for Submarine Nets:
Powell's Glass Factory, Whitefriars, EC4* 1918
oil on panel 43.8 x 33.6
IWM ART 5042

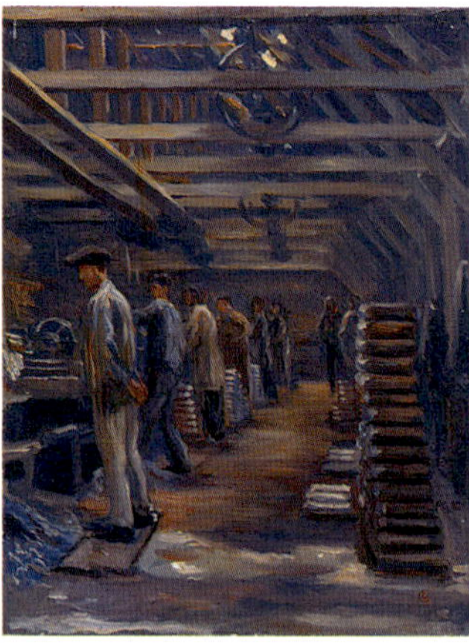

Seligman, Edgar 1867–1958
*Men at Work: The Belgian Steel Factory,
Goldhawk Road, W12* 1918
oil on panel 43.8 x 33.6
IWM ART 5037

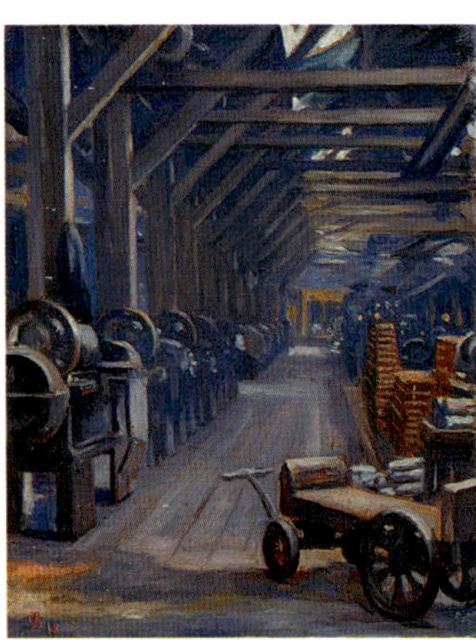

Seligman, Edgar 1867–1958
*The Luncheon Hour: The Belgian Steel Factory,
Goldhawk Road, W12* 1918
oil on panel 42.5 x 33.6
IWM ART 5039

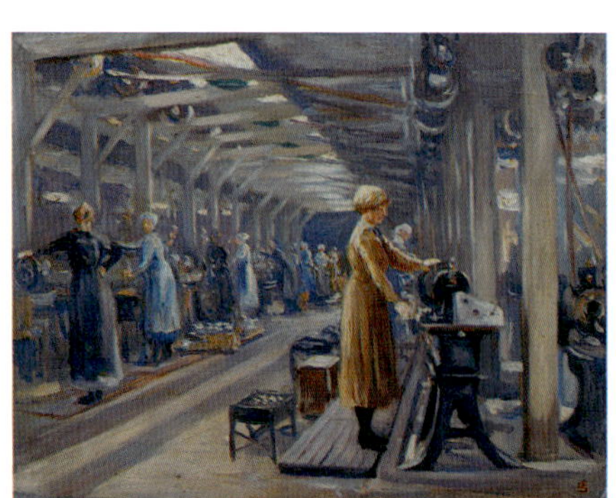

Seligman, Edgar 1867–1958
*Women at Work: The Belgian Steel Factory,
Goldhawk Road, W12* 1918
oil on panel 34.2 x 44.4
IWM ART 5038

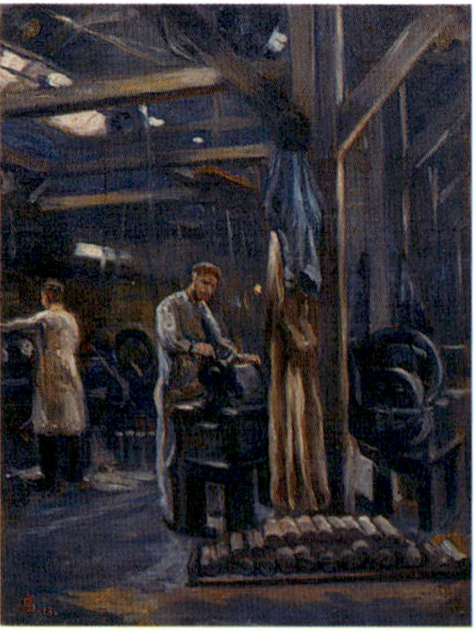

Seligman, Edgar 1867–1958
*Workers: The Belgian Steel Factory, Goldhawk
Road, W12* 1918
oil on panel 43.1 x 33.6
IWM ART 5036

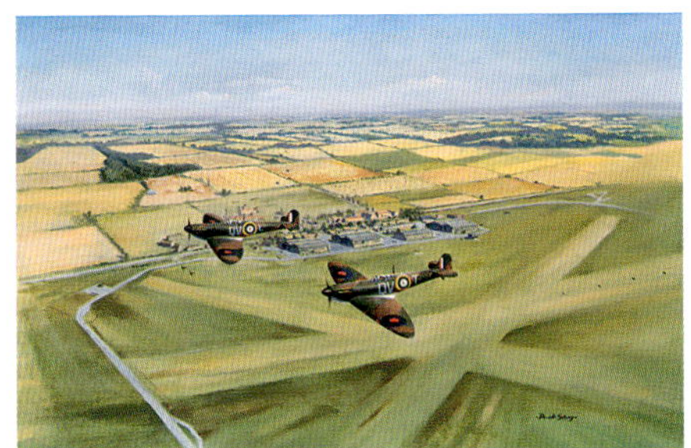

Selway, Donald active 1970s
Spitfires over Duxford: Reconstruction 1975
oil on canvas 59.6 x 90.1
IWM ART LD 7207

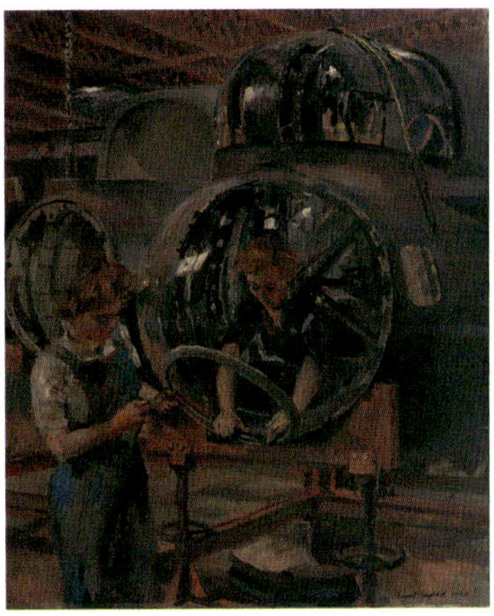

Shephard, Rupert 1909–1992
*A Nose Section after Repair: Girls Fitting
Supports to Take the Bomb Aimer's Window*
1944
oil on canvas 60.3 x 50.1
IWM ART LD 4141

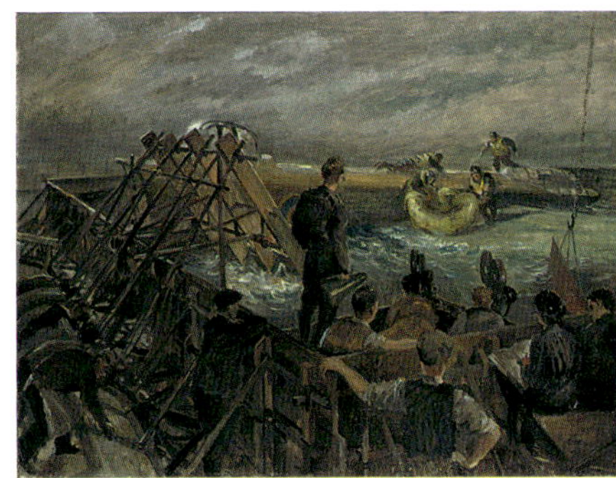

Shephard, Rupert 1909–1992
*Filming a Practice Launching of a Rubber
Dinghy in a Training Pond* 1944
oil on canvas 55.8 x 75.2
IWM ART LD 4647

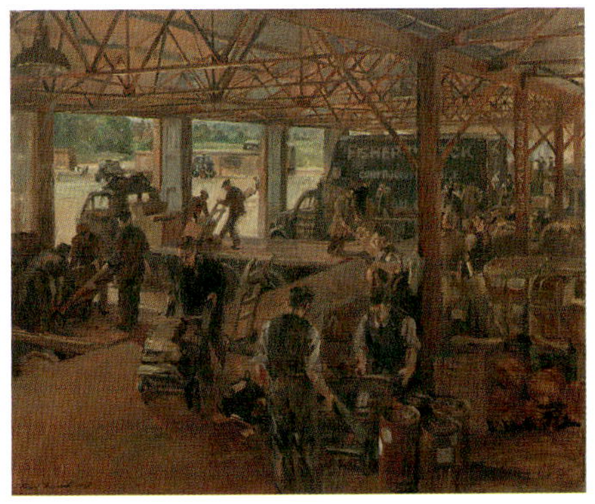

Shephard, Rupert 1909–1992
*A Lorry Depot: Long Distance and Local
Lorries Loading and Unloading at the 'Bank'*
1945
oil on canvas 62.2 x 74.9
IWM ART LD 5556

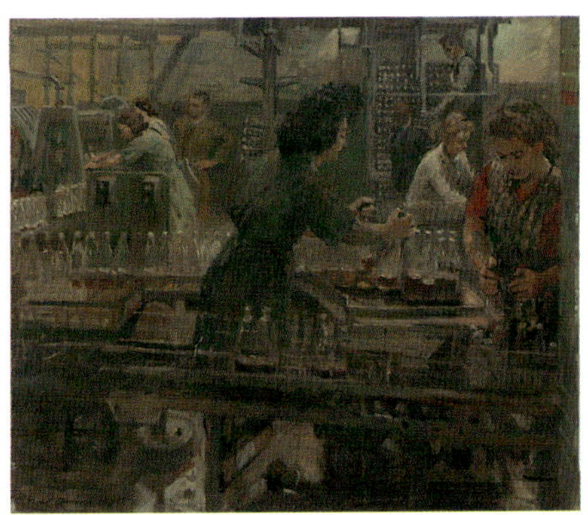

Shephard, Rupert 1909–1992
A Penicillin Factory: Girls Filling Bottles 1945
oil on canvas 58.4 x 69.8
IWM ART LD 5020

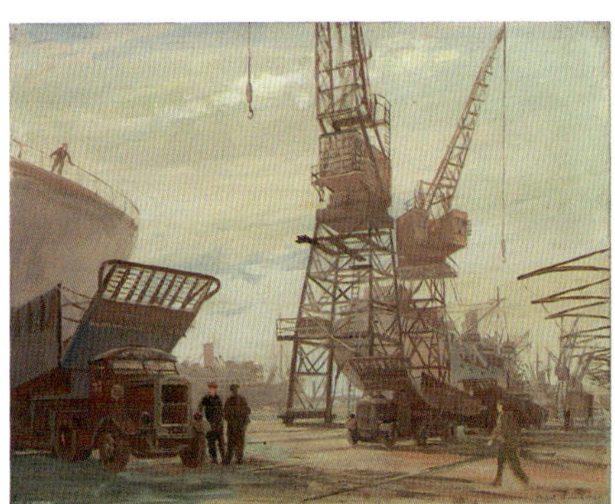

Shephard, Rupert 1909–1992
*Lorries Transporting Landing Craft: Royal
Albert Docks, London* 1945
oil on canvas 55.8 x 71.1
IWM ART LD 5293

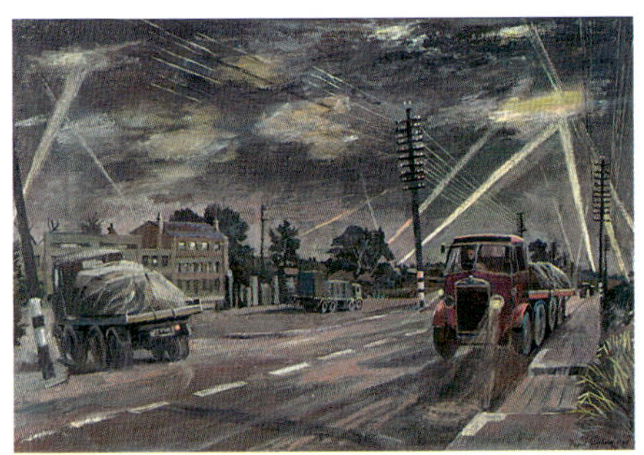

Shephard, Rupert 1909–1992
Road Transport in the Blitz 1945
oil on canvas 50.8 x 76.2
IWM ART LD 5449

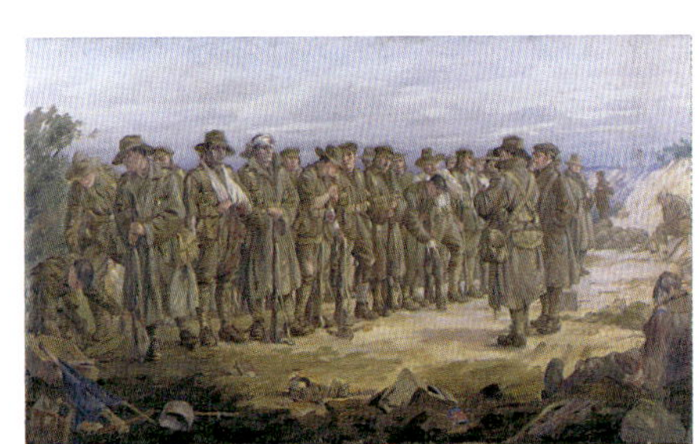

Silas, Ellis 1883–1972
The Last Roll Call c.1914–1918
oil on canvas 74.7 x 125.5
IWM ART 15852

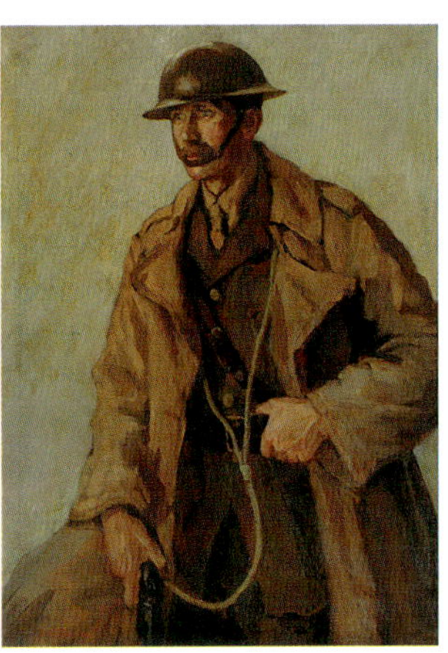

Simpson, Ruth 1889–1964
An Officer 1920s
oil on canvas 102.3 x 76.3
IWM ART 5769

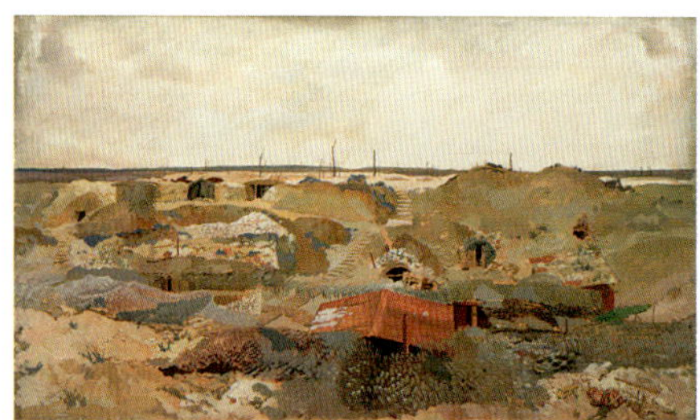

Sims, Charles 1873–1928
A Camouflaged Quarry between Chérisy and Hendecourt 1916
oil on canvas 43.1 x 73.6
IWM ART 2006

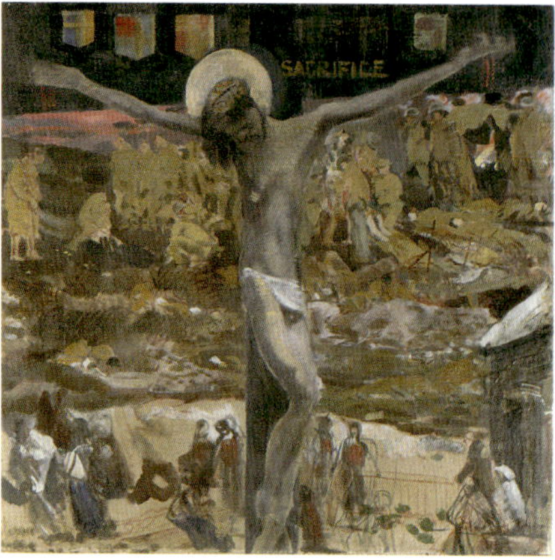

Sims, Charles 1873–1928
'Sacrifice' (study for the painting in Ottawa) 1918
oil on canvas 76.2 x 78.1
IWM ART 5581

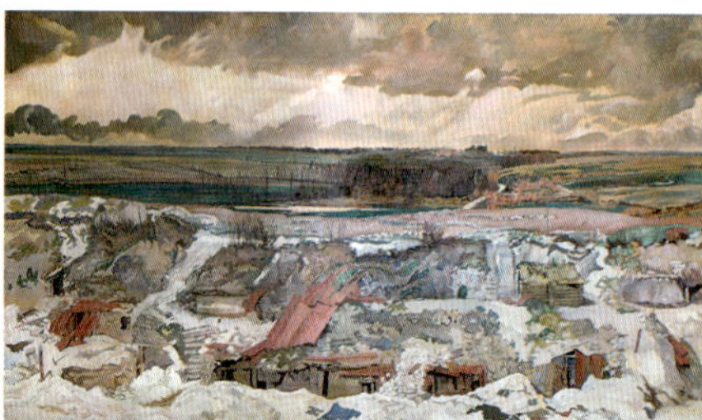

Sims, Charles 1873–1928
The Old German Front Line, Arras, 1916 1919
oil on canvas 182.8 x 317.5
IWM ART 2282

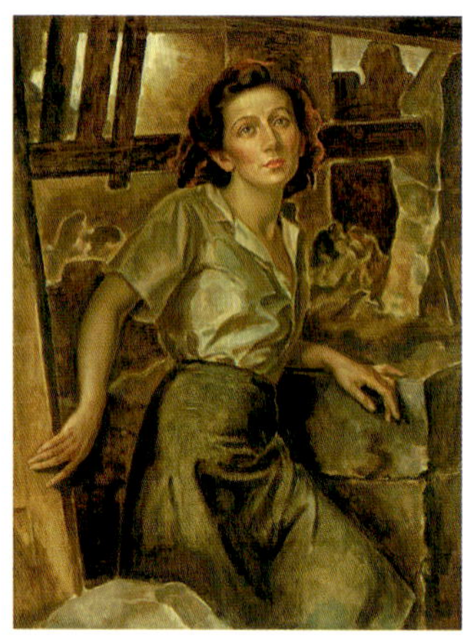

Sivell, Robert 1888–1958
Mrs Marion Patterson, GM c.1942
oil on canvas 91.4 x 71.1
IWM ART LD 3030

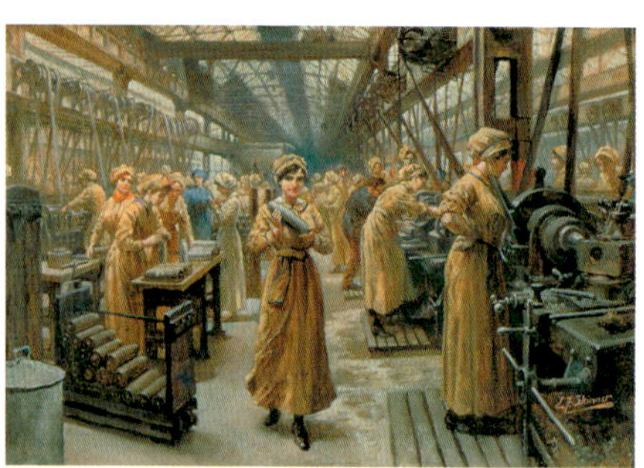

Skinner, Edward F. active 1888–1919
For King and Country c.1918
oil on canvas 30.3 x 45.9
IWM ART 6513

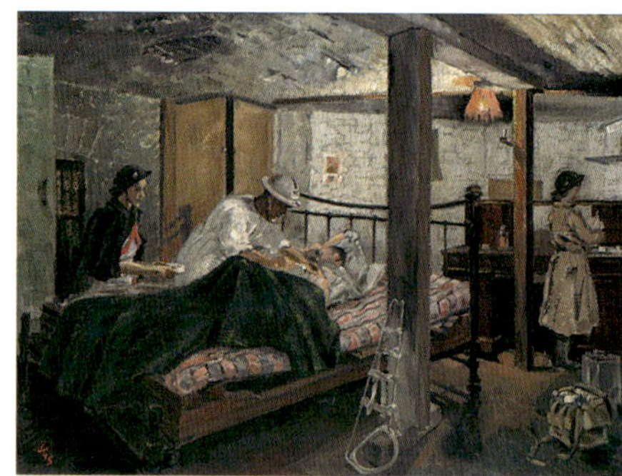

Smith, B. Gordon active 1940s
A Mobile First Aid Unit at Work 1941
oil on canvas 60.3 x 80
IWM ART LD 1519

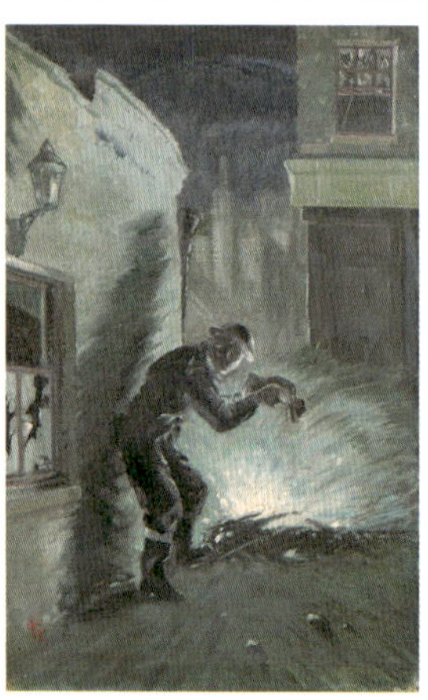

Smith, B. Gordon active 1940s
Incendiary Bomb c.1941
oil on canvas 73.7 x 48.2
IWM ART 16672

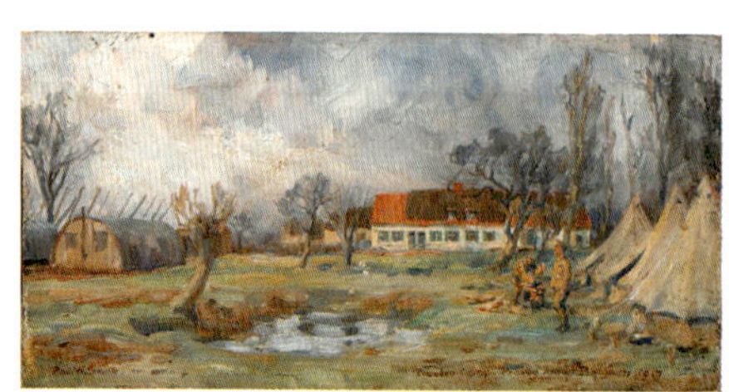

Smith, Phill W. active 1890–1932
Pounden Camp, Proven Area, Belgium 1917
oil on canvas 20 x 40.3
IWM ART 16298

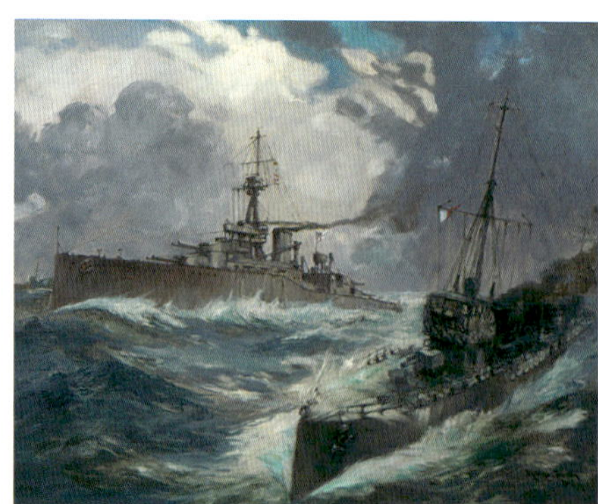

Smith, Robert Henry active 1906–1920
'HMS Conqueror' and Escort in the North Sea 1915
oil on canvas 63.5 x 76.2
IWM ART 1246

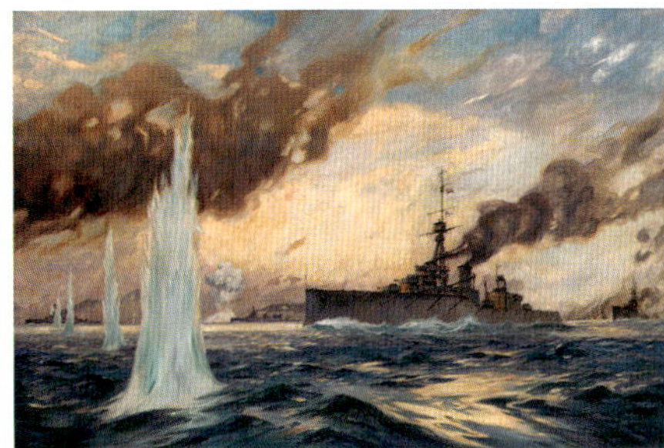

Smith, Robert Henry active 1906–1920
*The Battle of Jutland: Admiral Jellicoe Arrives
with the Battleships and Meets the Battle
Cruisers* c.1915–1919
oil on canvas 121.9 x 182.8
IWM ART 1245

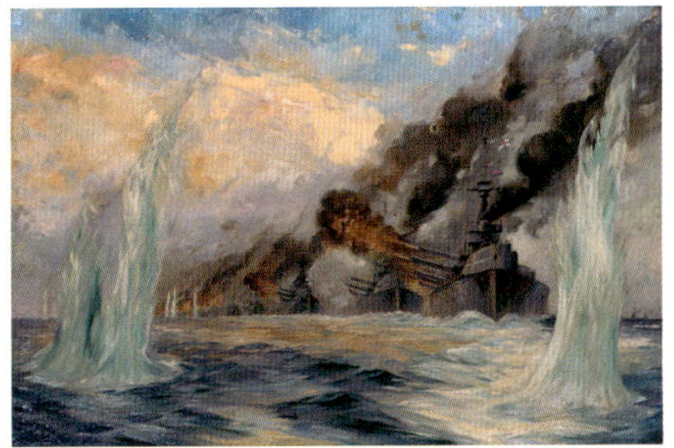

Smith, Robert Henry active 1906–1920
Battleships in Action at Jutland 1919
oil on canvas 121.9 x 182.8
IWM ART 1248

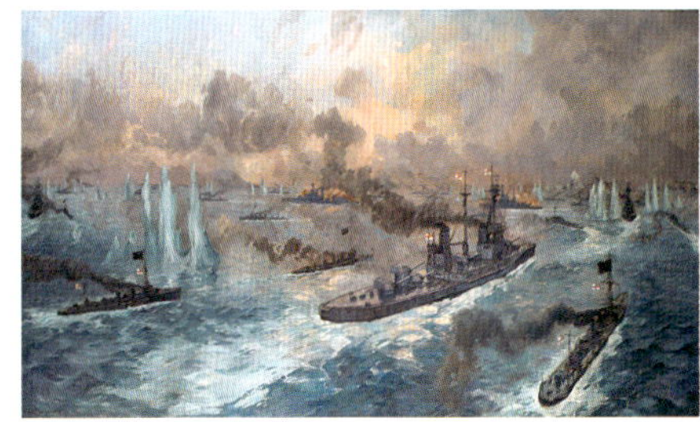

Smith, Robert Henry active 1906–1920
The Battle of Jutland, 31 May to 1 June, 1916
1920
oil on canvas 208.2 x 485.1
IWM ART 5930

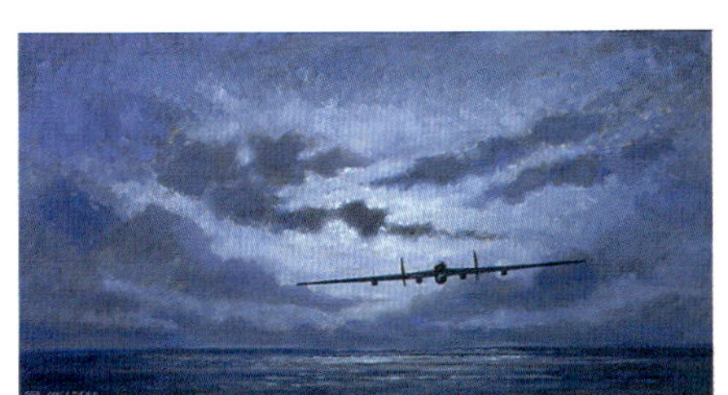

Smulders, Gabriel b.1931
The Last One 1991
oil on board 31.4 x 58.9
IWM ART 16653

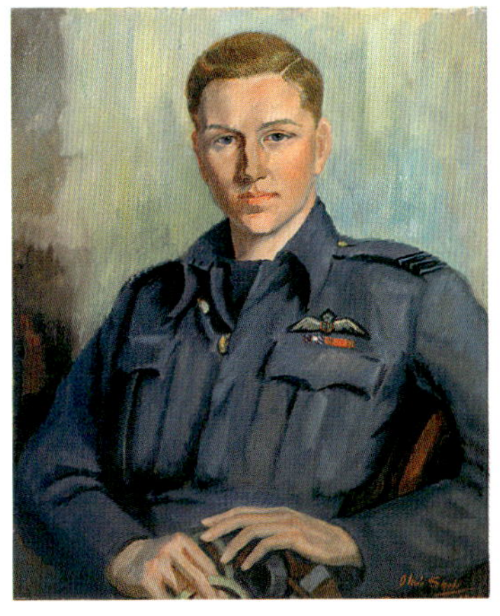

Snell, Olive active c.1910–1955
Wing Commander Paul H. M. Richey, DFC
1942
oil on canvas 76.4 x 64
IWM ART 16543

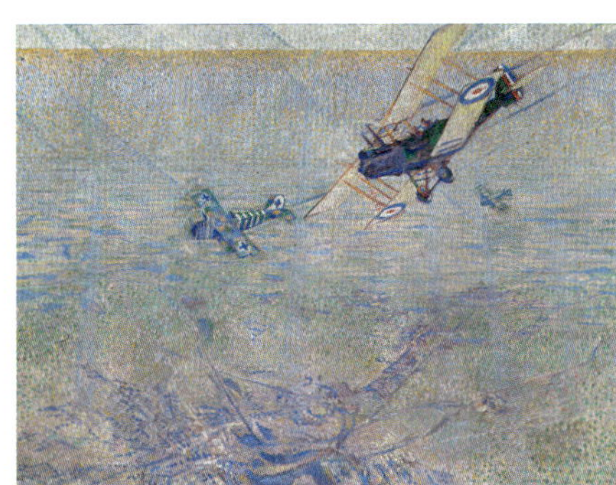

Solomon, Gilbert 1890–1955
*The Mist Curtain: RE 8 (16th Squadron)
Attacked over Lens* 1918
oil on canvas 91.4 x 121.9
IWM ART 2659

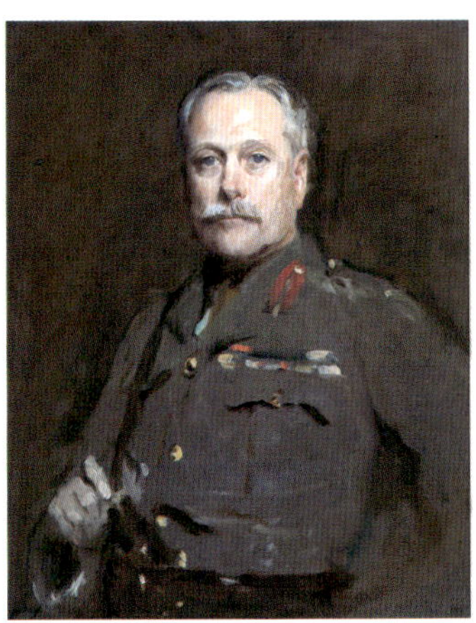

Solomon, J. Solomon 1860–1927
Field Marshal Earl Haig (1861–1928)
c.1919–1920
oil on paper 59.6 x 49.5
IWM ART 4436

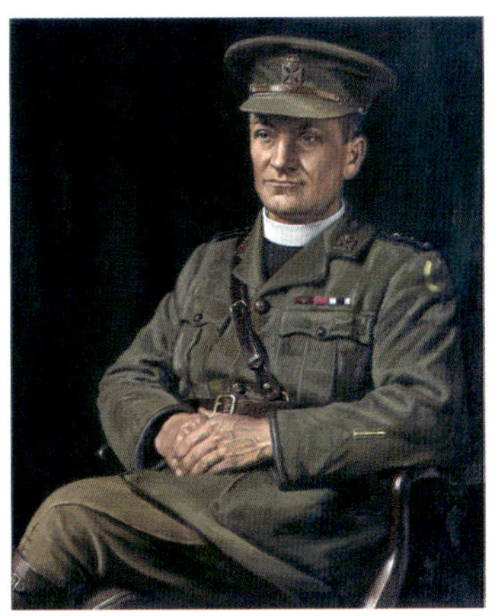

Somerville, Howard 1873–1952
*The Late Reverend Theodore Bailey Hardy
(1863–1918), VC, DSO, MC* 1919
oil on canvas 91.4 x 76.2
IWM ART 1999

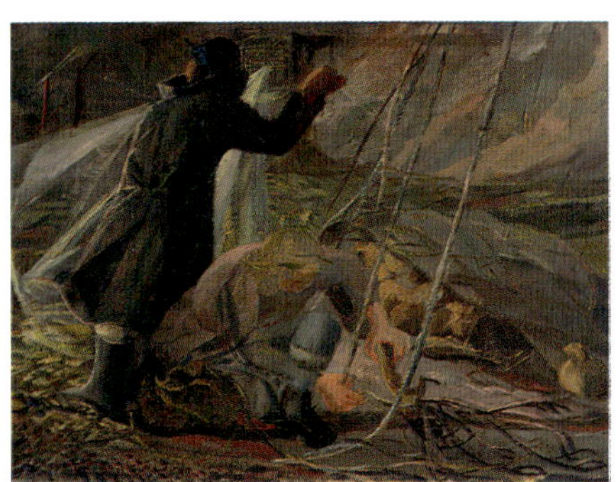

Sonnis, Alexander b.1905
Balloon Operations at Night 1941
oil on canvas 41.2 x 56.2
IWM ART LD 2113

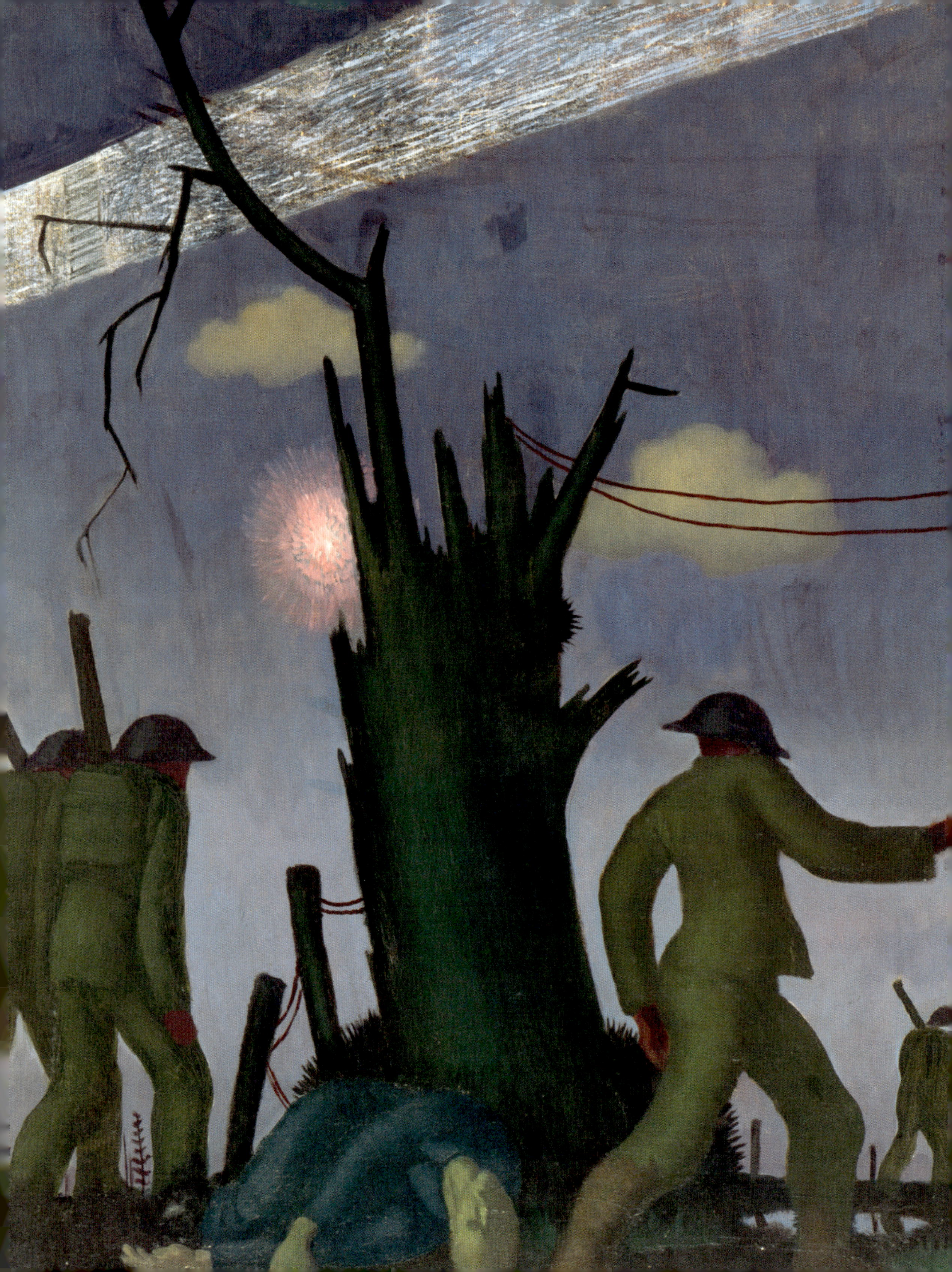

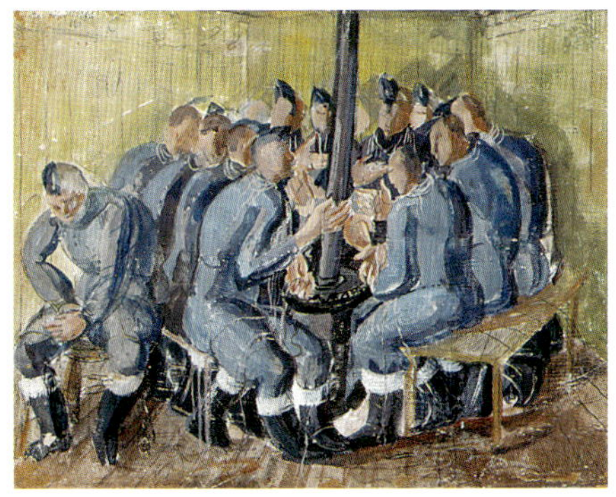

Sonnis, Alexander b.1905
Sitting Round the Stove Splicing Balloon Cords
1941
oil on board 23.8 x 30.4
IWM ART LD 2112

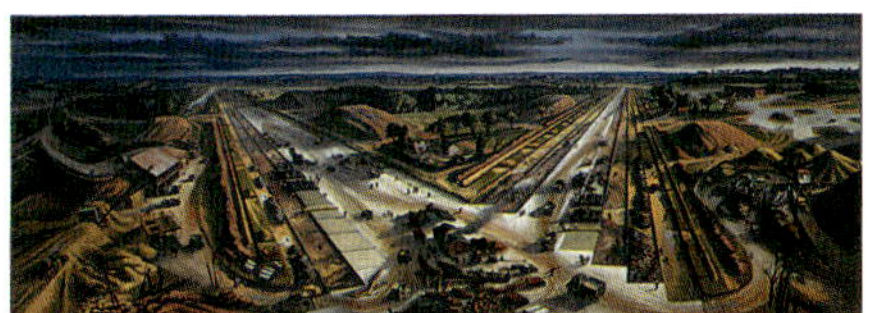

Sorrell, Alan 1904–1974
Construction of a Runway at an Aerodrome
1946
oil on canvas 66.5 x 188.5
IWM ART LD 5674

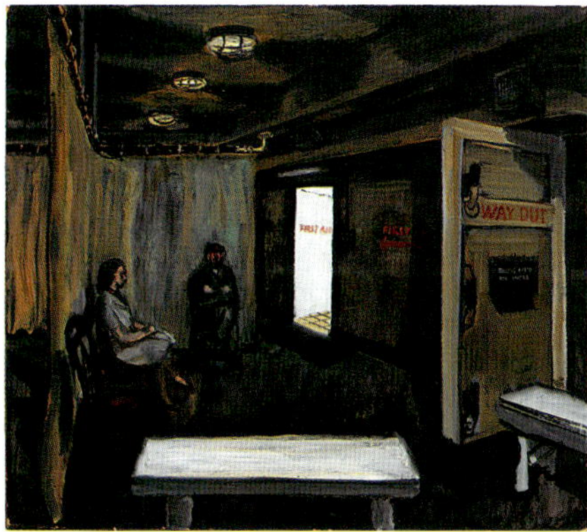

Spear, Ruskin 1911–1990
Patients Waiting outside a First Aid Post in a Factory 1942
oil on panel 68 x 78.5
IWM ART LD 2683

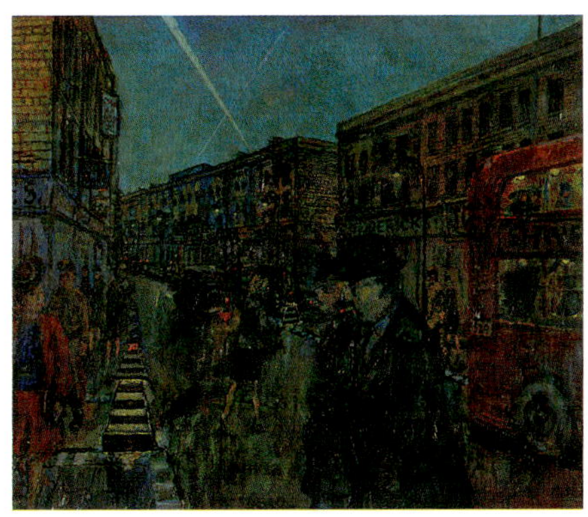

Spear, Ruskin 1911–1990
The Blackout 1942
oil on panel 50.8 x 60.9
IWM ART LD 2581

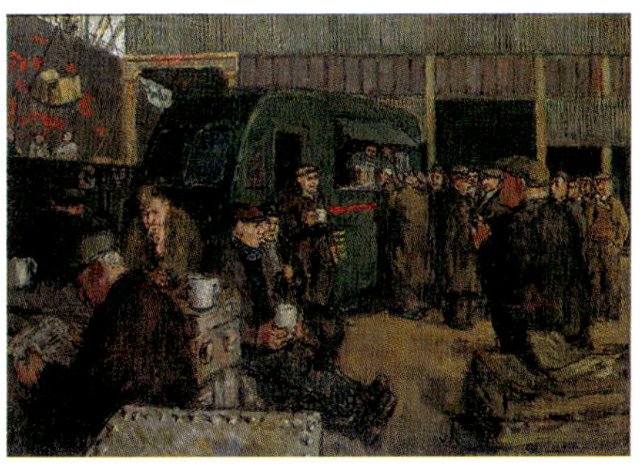

Spear, Ruskin 1911–1990
A Women's Voluntary Services Canteen at the Docks 1943
oil on canvas 71.1 x 101.9
IWM ART LD 3600

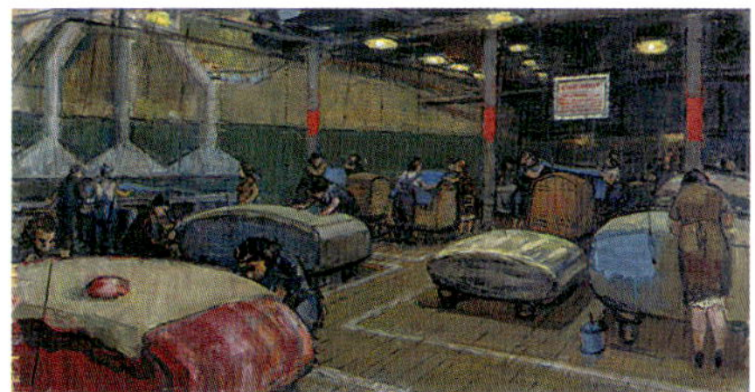

Spear, Ruskin 1911–1990
Deaf Girls Working on the Construction of Petrol Tanks 1943
oil on panel 29.2 x 59.3
IWM ART LD 3810

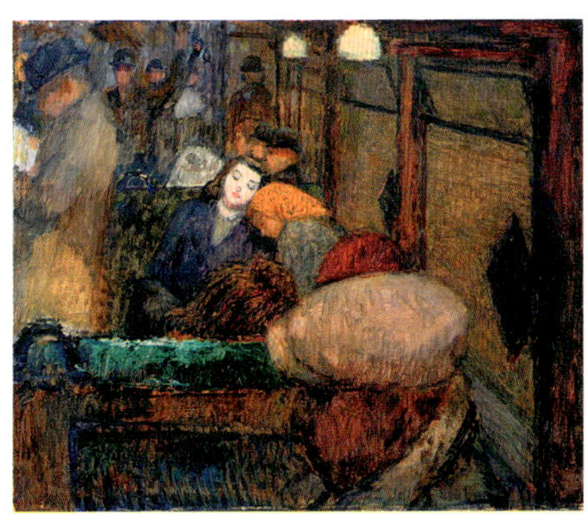

Spear, Ruskin 1911–1990
Scene in an Underground Train: Workers Returning from Night Shift 1943
oil on panel 58.4 x 71.1
IWM ART LD 2798

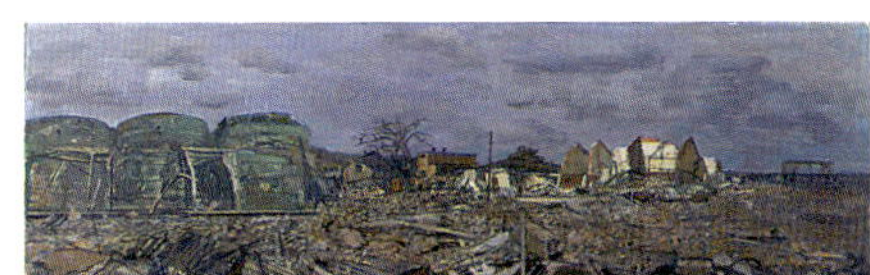

Spear, Ruskin 1911–1990
A Royal Ordnance Factory Explosion, Hereford
1945
oil on panel 45.7 x 147.3
IWM ART LD 5636

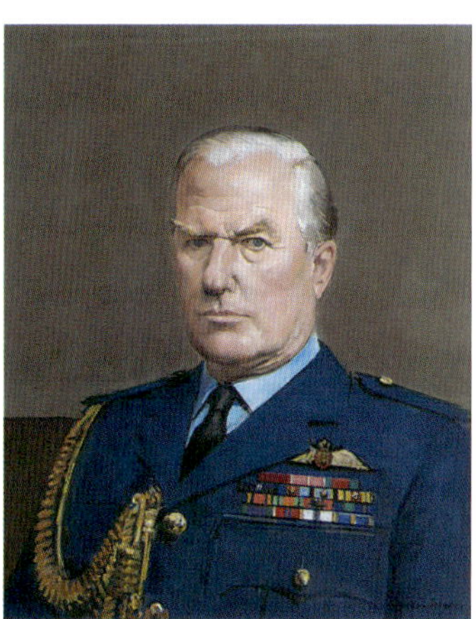

Spear, Ruskin 1911–1990
Marshal of the Royal Air Force Sir John Grandy (1913–2004), GCB, KBE, DSO 1981
oil on canvas 76.3 x 63.5
IWM ART 15418

Facing page: Gill, Colin Unwin, 1892–1940, *Evening after a Push* (detail), 1919, (p. 87)

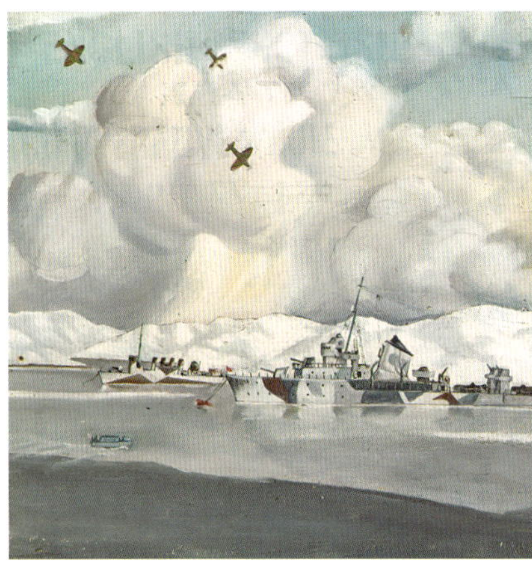

Spence, J. M. active 1940s
*A Russian (Ex-American) Destroyer, Russia,
April 1942* 1942
oil on panel 41.2 x 41.2
IWM ART LD 2115

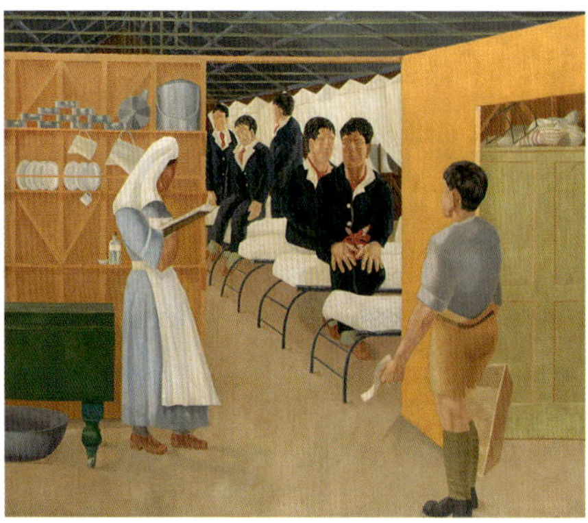

Spencer, Gilbert 1893–1979
*New Arrivals: F4 Ward, No.36 Stationary
Hospital, Mahemdia, Sinai* c.1918
oil on canvas 182.8 x 218.4
IWM ART 2266

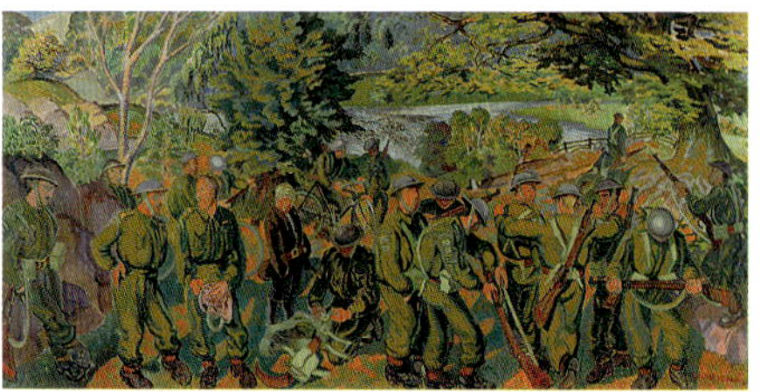

Spencer, Gilbert 1893–1979
Grasmere Home Guard 1943
oil on canvas 61.5 x 121.9
IWM ART LD 3329

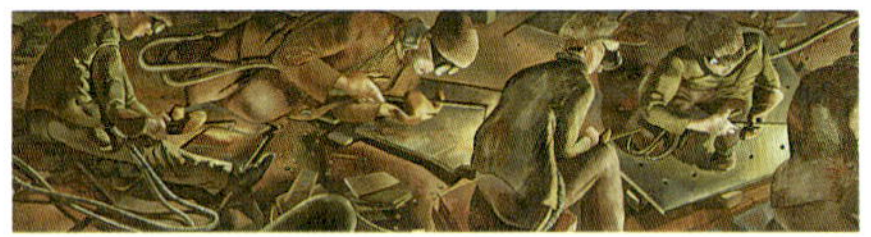

Spencer, Stanley 1891–1959
Shipbuilding on the Clyde: Burners (left) 1940
oil on canvas 106.7 x 555.8 (overall)
IWM ART LD 432

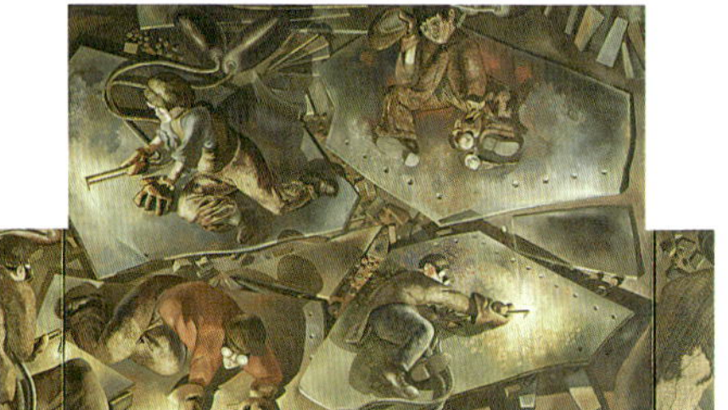

Spencer, Stanley 1891–1959
Shipbuilding on the Clyde: Burners (centre)
1940
oil on canvas 106.7 x 555.8 (overall)
IWM ART LD 433

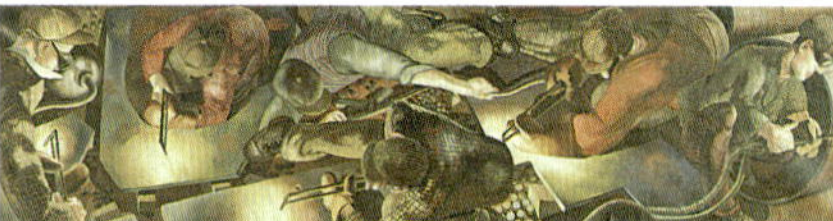

Spencer, Stanley 1891–1959
Shipbuilding on the Clyde: Burners (right)
1940
oil on canvas 106.7 x 555.8 (overall)
IWM ART LD 434

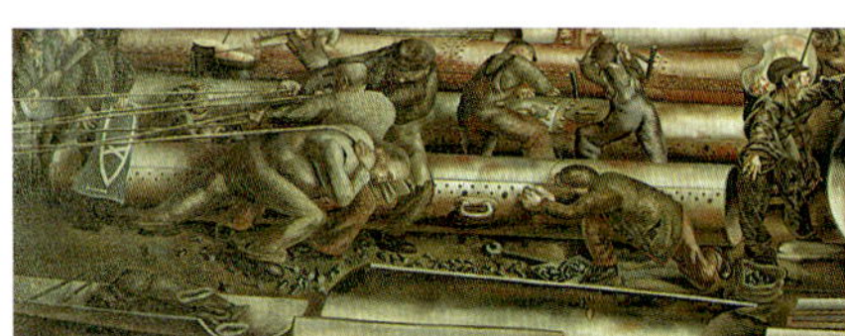

Spencer, Stanley 1891–1959
Shipbuilding on the Clyde: Riveters (left) 1941
oil on canvas 76.2 x 579.1 (overall)
IWM ART LD 1375

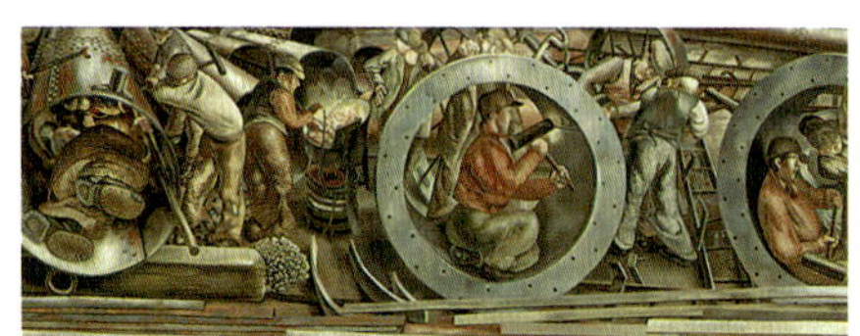

Spencer, Stanley 1891–1959
Shipbuilding on the Clyde: Riveters (centre)
1941
oil on canvas 76.2 x 579.1 (overall)
IWM ART LD 1375

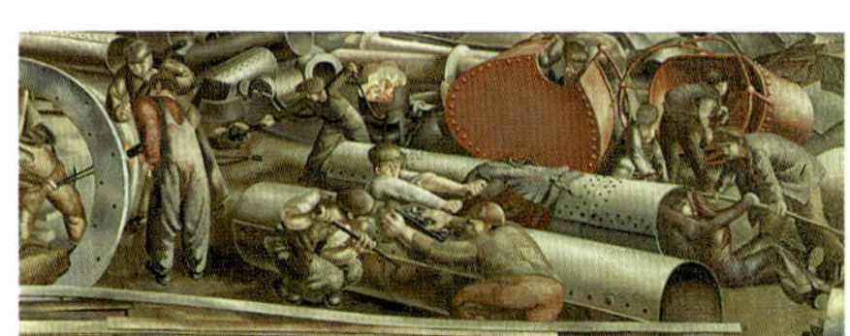

Spencer, Stanley 1891–1959
Shipbuilding on the Clyde: Riveters (right)
1941
oil on canvas 76.2 x 579.1 (overall)
IWM ART LD 1375

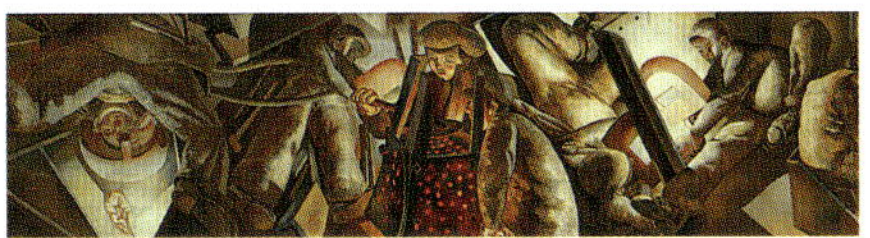

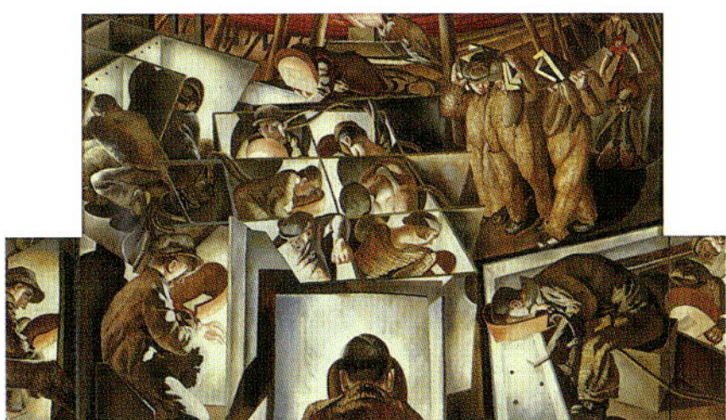

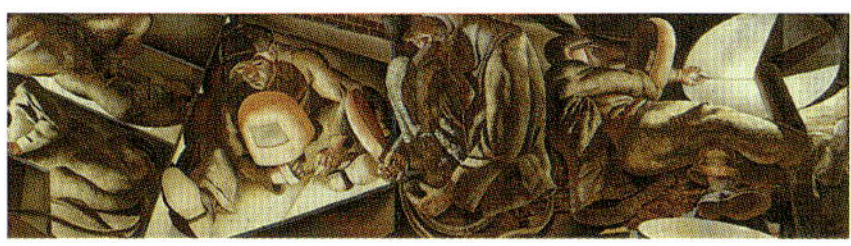

Spencer, Stanley 1891–1959
Shipbuilding on the Clyde: Welders (left) 1941
oil on canvas 106.7 x 555.8 (overall)
IWM ART LD 924

Spencer, Stanley 1891–1959
Shipbuilding on the Clyde: Welders (centre)
1941
oil on canvas 106.7 x 555.8 (overall)
IWM ART LD 925

Spencer, Stanley 1891–1959
Shipbuilding on the Clyde: Welders (right)
1941
oil on canvas 106.7 x 555.8 (overall)
IWM ART LD 926

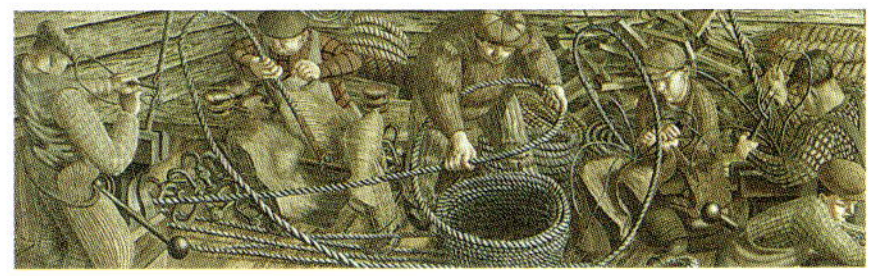

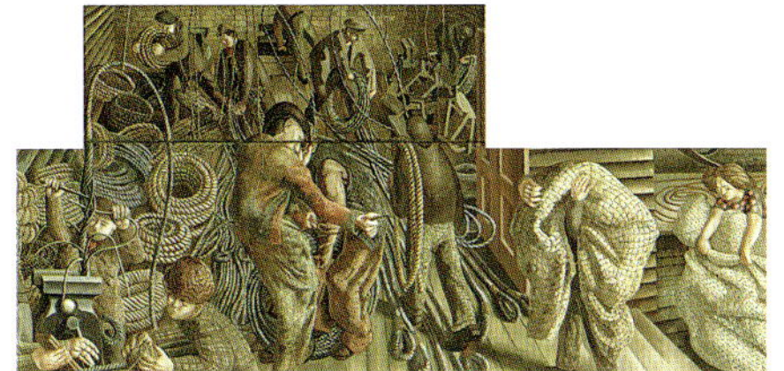

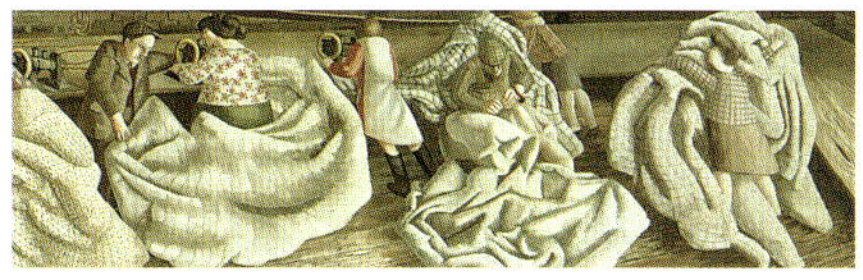

Spencer, Stanley 1891–1959
Shipbuilding on the Clyde: The Riggers (left)
1941–1944
oil on canvas 81.2 x 494 (overall)
IWM ART LD 4284

Spencer, Stanley 1891–1959
Shipbuilding on the Clyde: The Riggers (centre)
1941–1944
oil on canvas 81.2 x 494 (overall)
IWM ART LD 4284

Spencer, Stanley 1891–1959
Shipbuilding on the Clyde: The Riggers (right)
1941–1944
oil on canvas 81.2 x 494 (overall)
IWM ART LD 4284

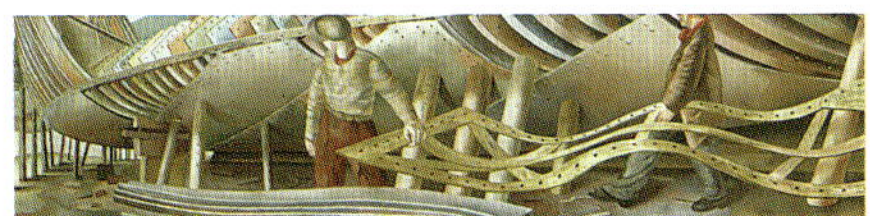

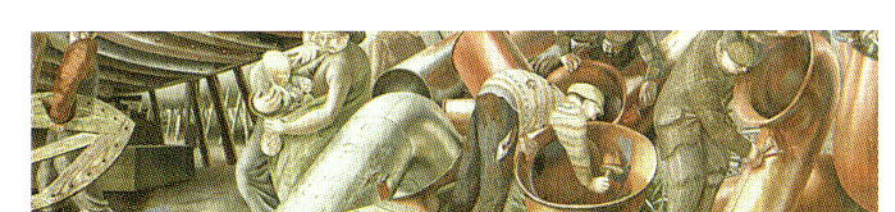

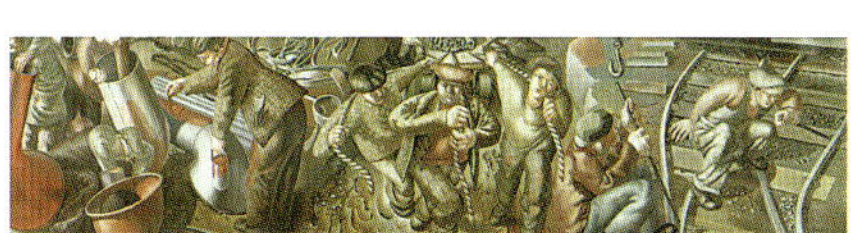

Spencer, Stanley 1891–1959
Shipbuilding on the Clyde: The Template (left)
1942
oil on canvas 50.8 x 579.1 (overall)
IWM ART LD 2000

Spencer, Stanley 1891–1959
Shipbuilding on the Clyde: The Template
(centre) 1942
oil on canvas 50.8 x 579.1 (overall)
IWM ART LD 2000

Spencer, Stanley 1891–1959
Shipbuilding on the Clyde: The Template
(right) 1942
oil on canvas 50.8 x 579.1 (overall)
IWM ART LD 2000

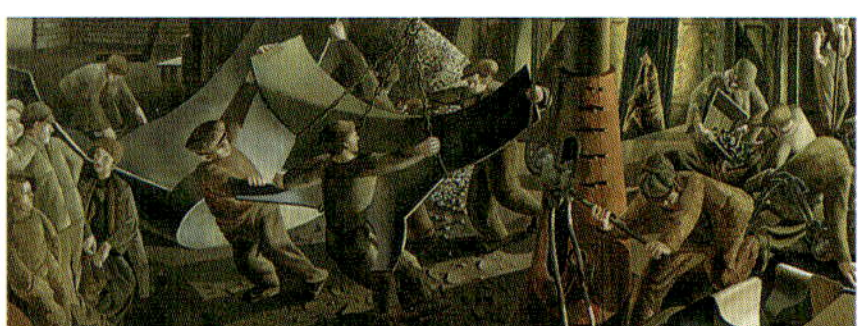

Spencer, Stanley 1891–1959
Shipbuilding on the Clyde: Bending the Keel Plate (left) 1943
oil on canvas 76.2 x 579.1 (overall)
IWM ART LD 3106

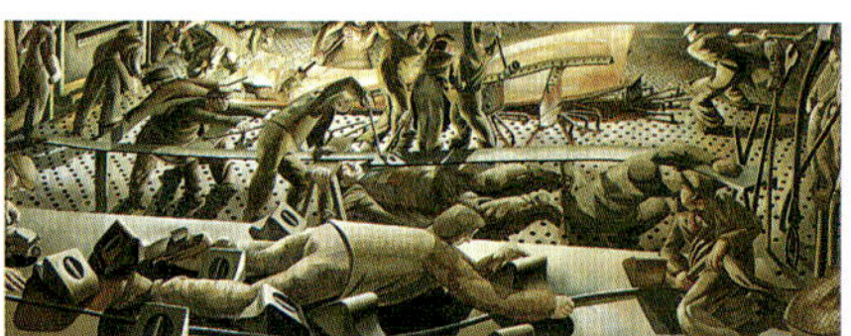

Spencer, Stanley 1891–1959
Shipbuilding on the Clyde: Bending the Keel Plate (centre) 1943
oil on canvas 76.2 x 579.1 (overall)
IWM ART LD 3106

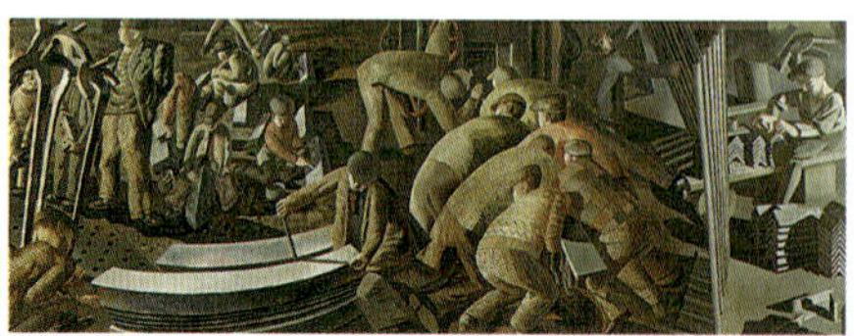

Spencer, Stanley 1891–1959
Shipbuilding on the Clyde: Bending the Keel Plate (right) 1943
oil on canvas 76.2 x 579.1 (overall)
IWM ART LD 3106

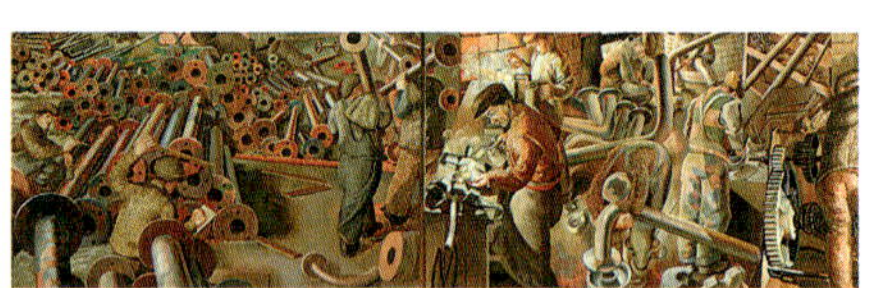

Spencer, Stanley 1891–1959
Shipbuilding on the Clyde: Plumbers (left)
1944–1945
oil on canvas 81.2 x 492.7 (overall)
IWM ART LD 5000

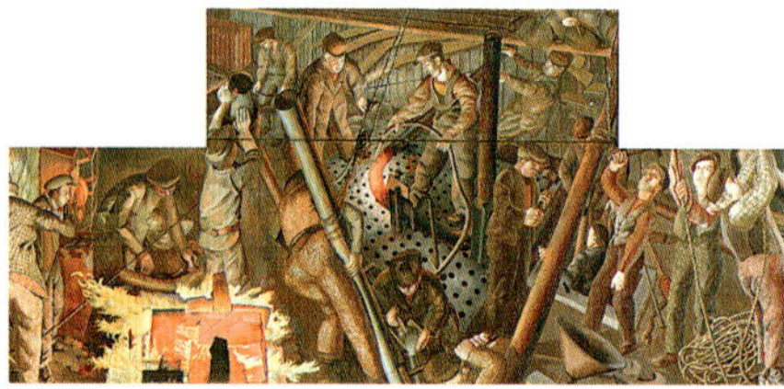

Spencer, Stanley 1891–1959
Shipbuilding on the Clyde: Plumbers (centre)
1944–1945
oil on canvas 81.2 x 492.7 (overall)
IWM ART LD 5000

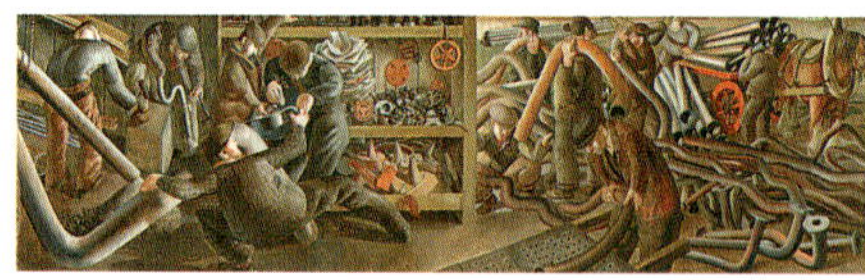

Spencer, Stanley 1891–1959
Shipbuilding on the Clyde: Plumbers (right)
1944–1945
oil on canvas 81.2 x 492.7 (overall)
IWM ART LD 5000

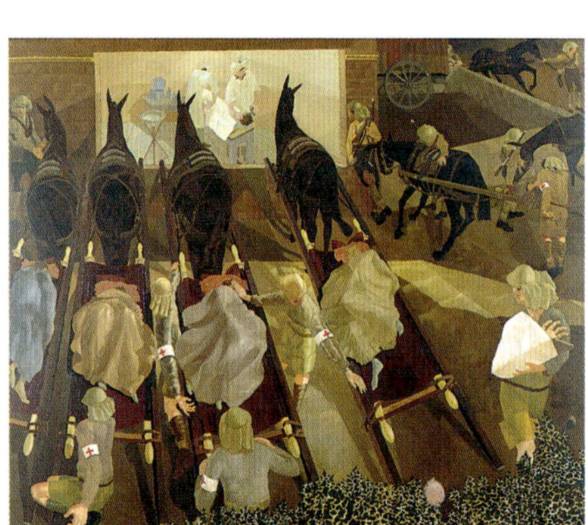

Spencer, Stanley 1891–1959
Travoys Arriving with Wounded at a Dressing Station at Smol, Macedonia, September 1916
1919
oil on canvas 182.8 x 218.4
IWM ART 2268

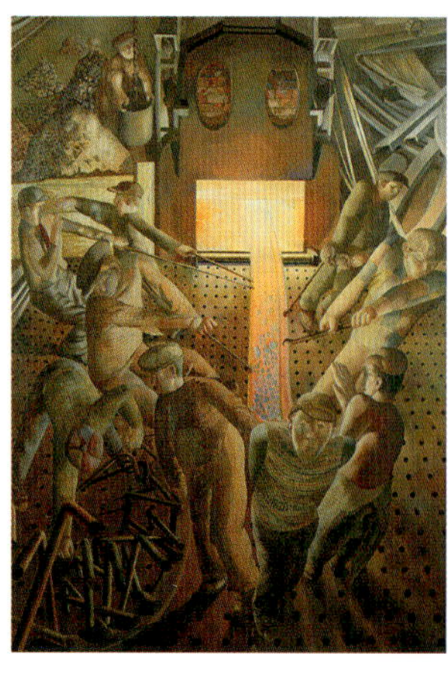

Spencer, Stanley 1891–1959
Shipbuilding on the Clyde: The Furnaces 1946
oil on canvas 156.2 x 113.6
IWM ART LD 5781

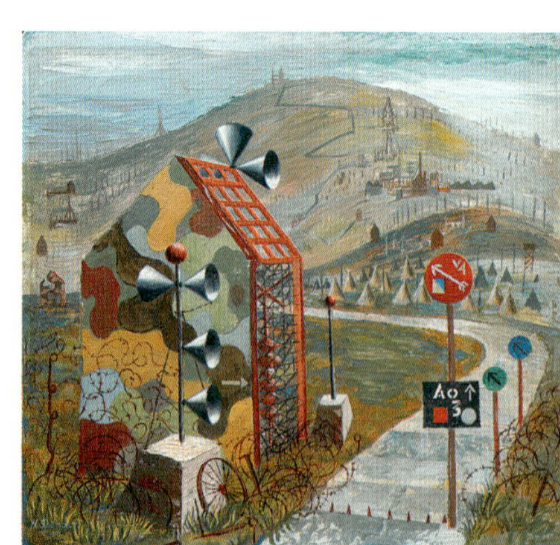

Spender, John Humphrey 1910–2005
Salisbury Plain 1942
oil on board 38.8 x 41.2
IWM ART 15861

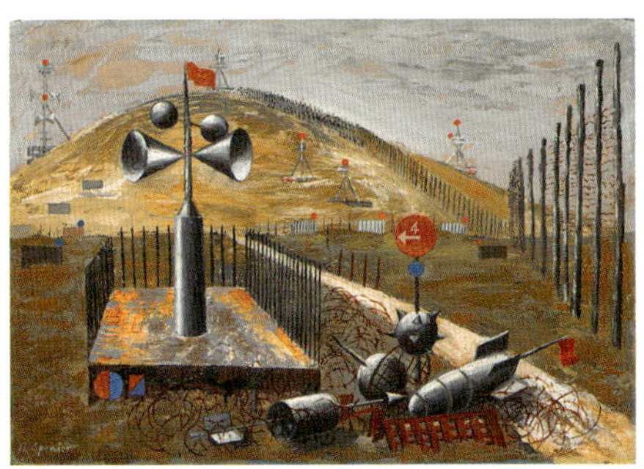

Spender, John Humphrey 1910–2005
Salisbury Plain 1942
oil on board 29.2 x 42.6
IWM ART 15862

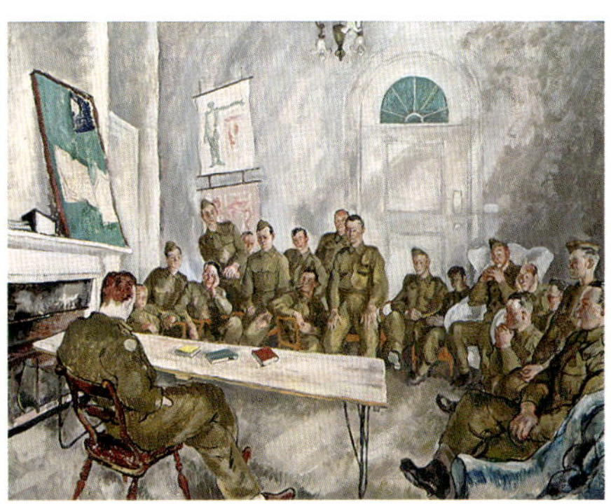

Spurrier, Steven 1878–1961
An Army Discussion Group 1943
oil on canvas 73.6 x 91.4
IWM ART LD 3858

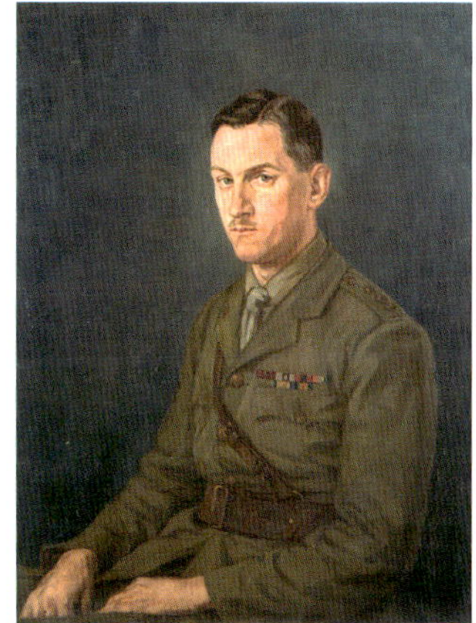

Stabb, Charles T. active 1899–1936
*Captain Alfred Oliver Pollard (1893–1960),
VC, MC, DCM* c.1917–1919
oil on canvas 91.4 x 71.1
IWM ART 2745

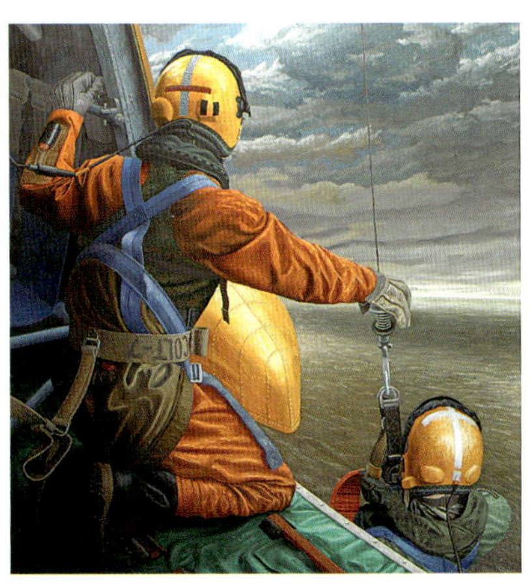

Staden, Geoffrey b.1953
Air-Sea Rescue from RAF Coltishall, Norfolk
1981
acrylic on canvas 131.5 x 126
IWM ART 15288

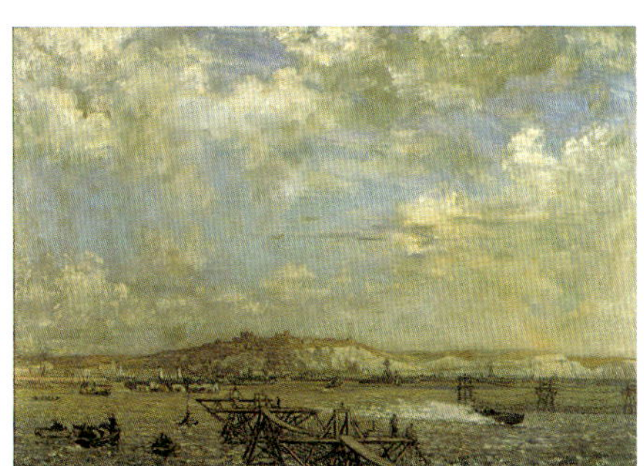

Steer, Philip Wilson 1860–1942
Dover Harbour 1918
oil on canvas 106.6 x 152.4
IWM ART 1233

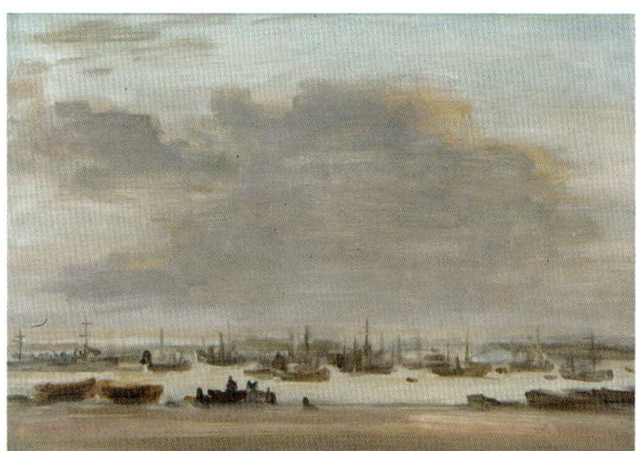

Steer, Philip Wilson 1860–1942
Dover Harbour from the Parade 1918
oil on canvas 40.6 x 60.9

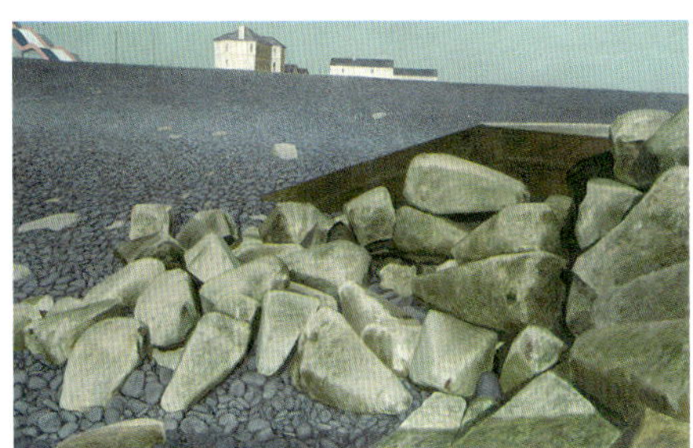

Stevens, Norman 1937–1988
Tank Trap 1979
oil on canvas 76 x 121.5
IWM ART 15860

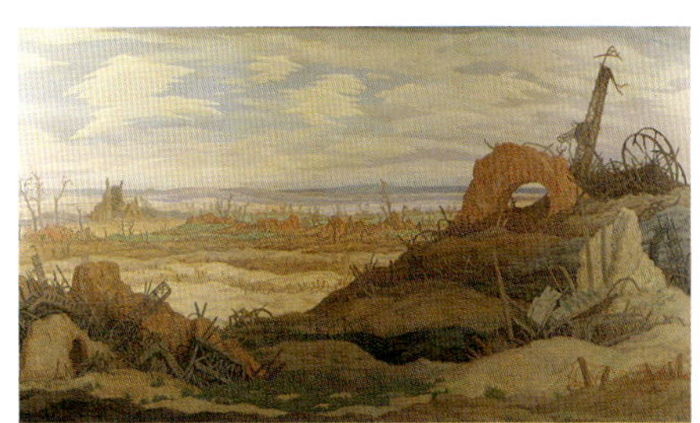

Strang, Ian 1886–1952
*The Outskirts of Lens: In the Foreground Ruins
of the Mine Buildings Known as 'Fosse St Louis'*
1919
oil on canvas 182.8 x 317.5
IWM ART 2284

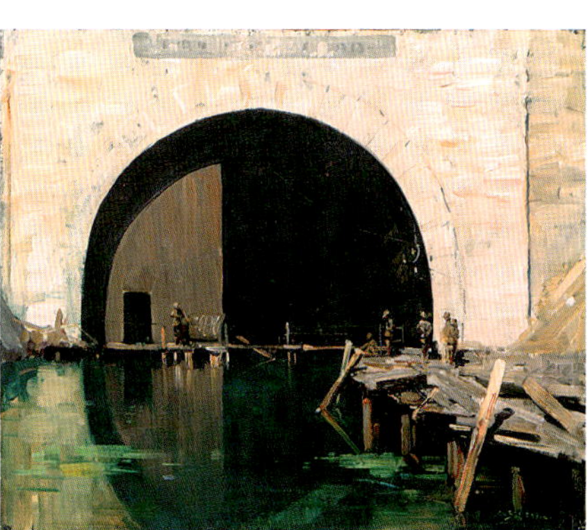

Streeton, Arthur 1876–1943
*The Tunnel Mouth, Bellicourt, the Hindenburg
Line: The Southern Entrance to the Tunnel,
December 1918* 1918
oil on canvas 63.5 x 76.2
IWM ART 2236

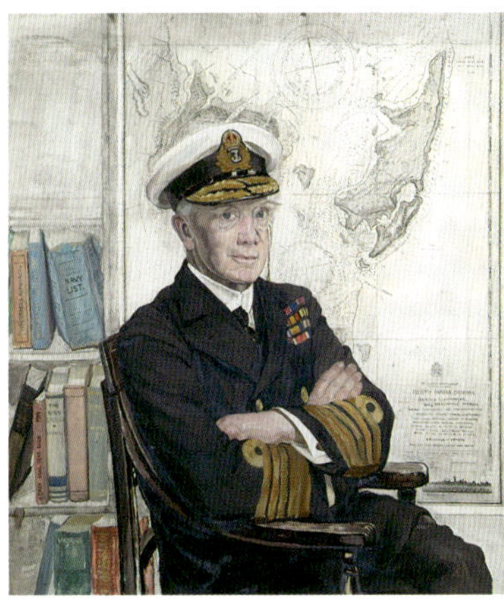

Stuart-Hill, A. c.1918–1950
Admiral Sir H. Goodenough King-Hall, KCB, CVO, DSO 1920
oil on panel 97.1 x 87.6
IWM ART 3144

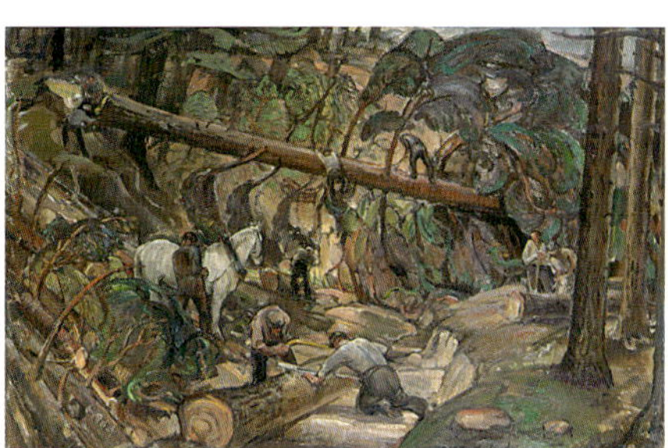

Sutherland, David Macbeth 1883–1973
War in the Forest: Newfoundland Lumberjacks at Work in Scotland 1940
oil on canvas 60.9 x 91.4
IWM ART LD 714

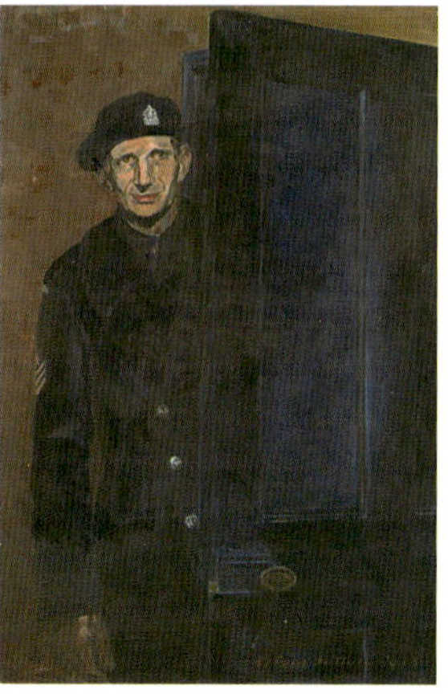

Sutton, R. Fran b.1912
Air Raid Precautions: Civil Defence Worker 1943
oil on linen on panel 113.5 x 75.8
IWM ART 16558

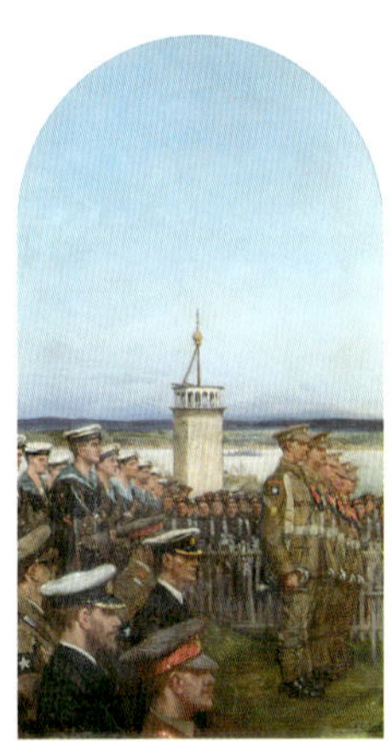

Tayler, Albert Chevallier 1862–1925
The Dwina Relief Force Memorial (left) 1921
oil on canvas 78.7 x 45.7
IWM ART 4099

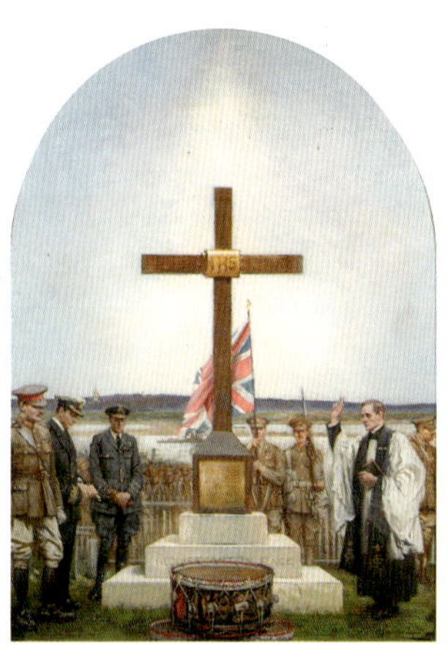

Tayler, Albert Chevallier 1862–1925
The Dwina Relief Force Memorial (centre) 1921
oil on canvas 78.7 x 68.5
IWM ART 4099

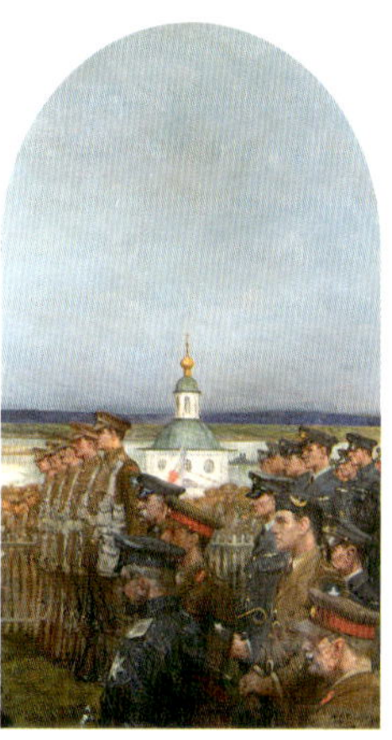

Tayler, Albert Chevallier 1862–1925
The Dwina Relief Force Memorial (right) 1921
oil on canvas 78.7 x 45.7
IWM ART 4099

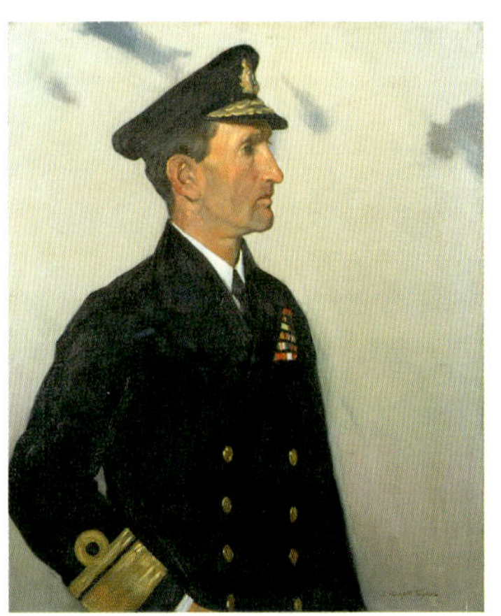

Tayler, Leonard Campbell 1874–1969
Rear Admiral Sir Walter Henry Cowan (1871–1958), KCB, MVO, DSO 1920
oil on canvas 91.4 x 76.2
IWM ART 3143

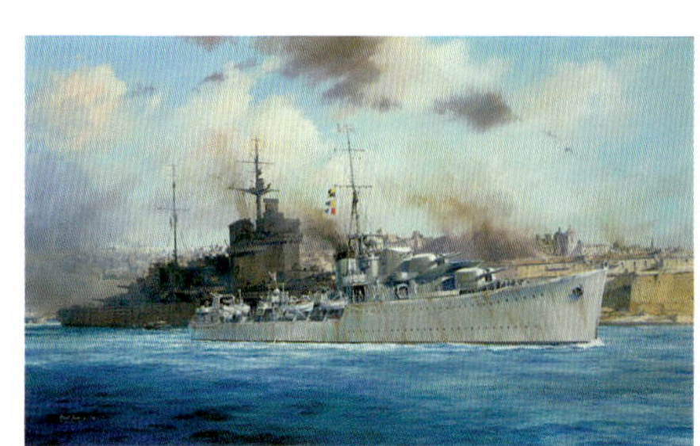

Taylor, Robert b.1946
'HMS Kelly', Grand Harbour, Malta, 1941 1978
oil on canvas 71 x 117
IWM ART 15505

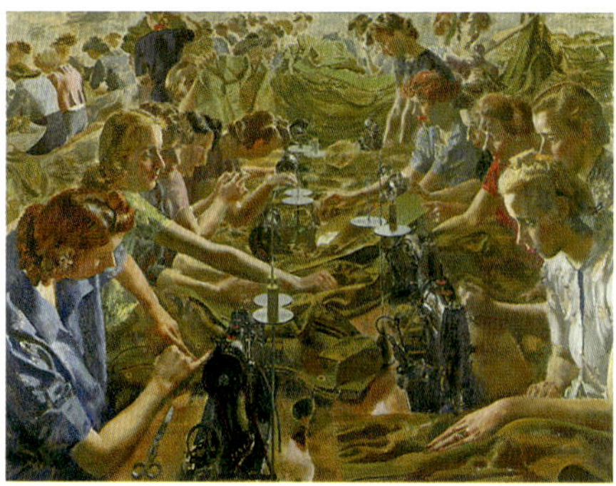

Thomson, Alfred Reginald 1894–1979
The Manufacture of Battle Dress 1940
oil on canvas 76.2 x 101.9
IWM ART LD 209

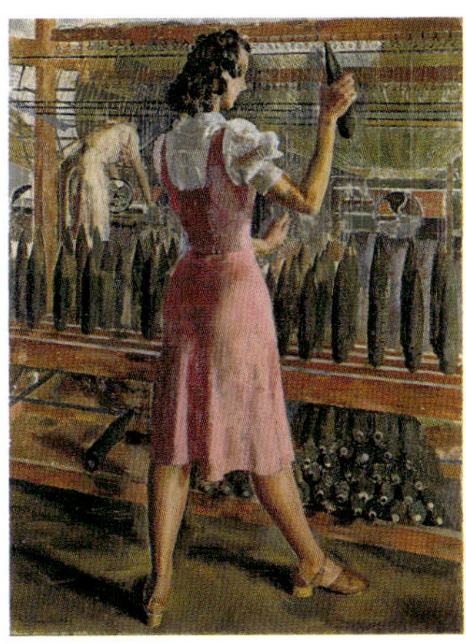

Thomson, Alfred Reginald 1894–1979
Weaving Cloth for Battle Dress 1940
oil on canvas 101.9 x 76.2
IWM ART LD 403

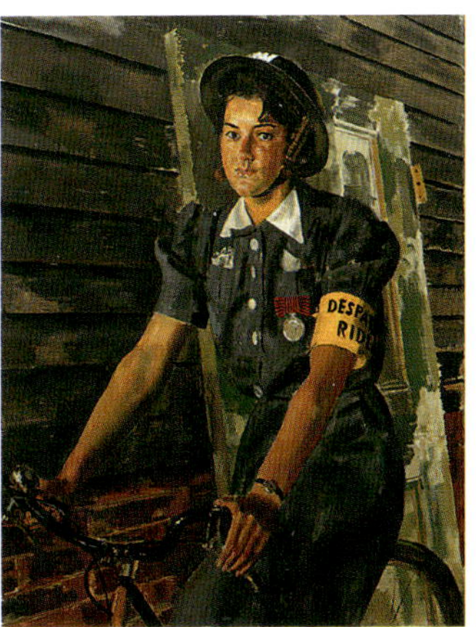

Thomson, Alfred Reginald 1894–1979
*Miss Charity Bick, GM, of West Bromwich, the
Youngest Woman Civil Defence Worker to be
Decorated with the George Medal* 1941
oil on canvas 91.4 x 71.1
IWM ART LD 1207

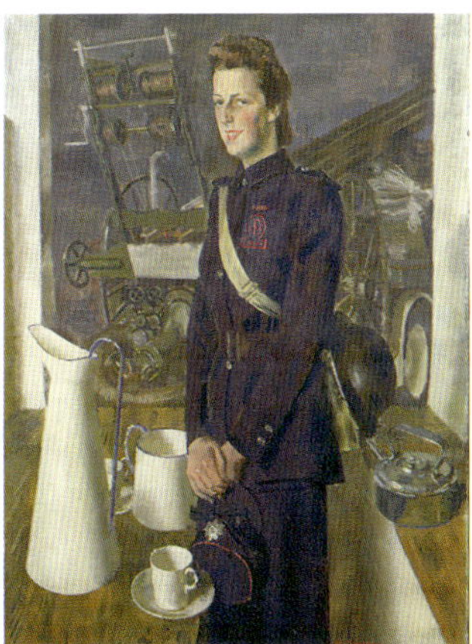

Thomson, Alfred Reginald 1894–1979
Miss Gillian Tanner, GM, of London 1941
oil on canvas 101.9 x 76.2
IWM ART LD 1667

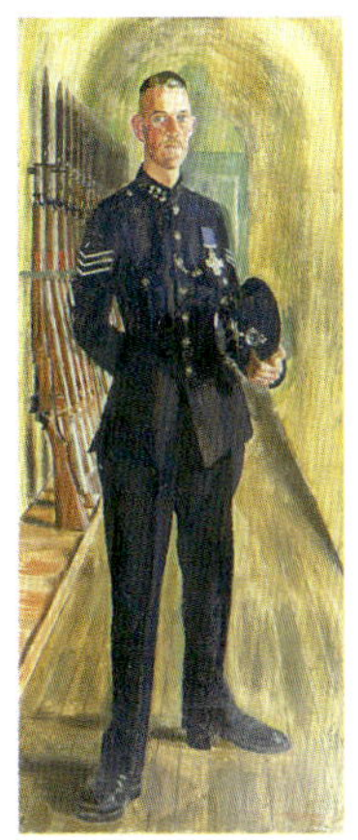

Thomson, Alfred Reginald 1894–1979
Section Leader Brandon Moss, GC, of Coventry
1941
oil on canvas 124.4 x 52
IWM ART LD 1301

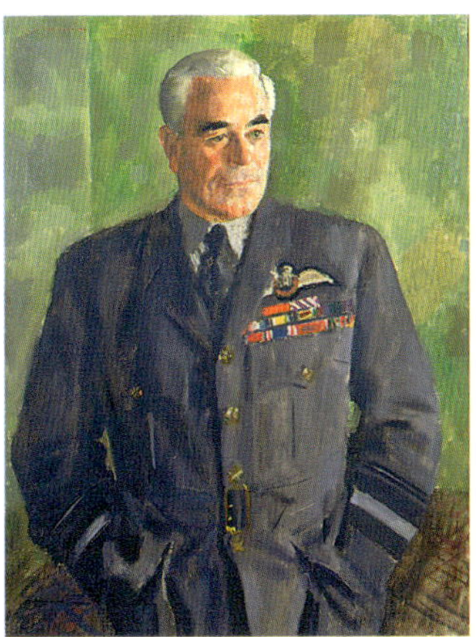

Thomson, Alfred Reginald 1894–1979
Air Vice-Marshal Richard E. Saul, CB, DFC
1942
oil on canvas 91.4 x 71.1
IWM ART LD 1861

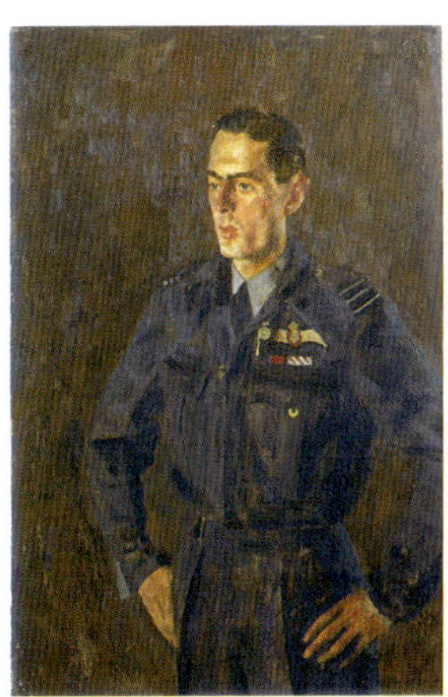

Thomson, Alfred Reginald 1894–1979
*Wing Commander Geoffrey Leonard Cheshire
(1917–1992), DSO, DFC* 1942
oil on canvas 76.2 x 50.8
IWM ART LD 2651

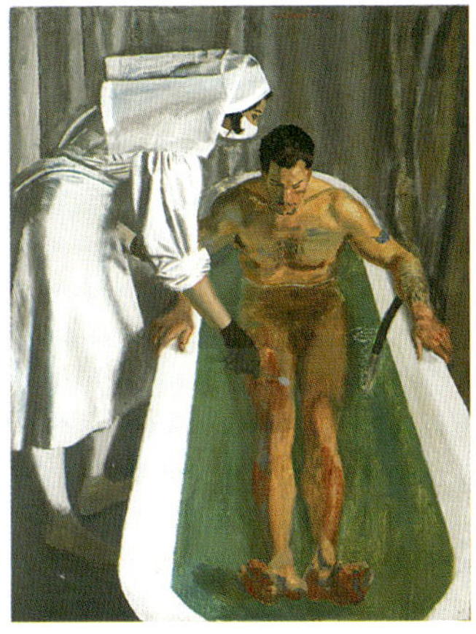

Thomson, Alfred Reginald 1894–1979
A Saline Bath, Royal Air Force Hospital 1943
oil on canvas 111.7 x 86.3
IWM ART LD 3629

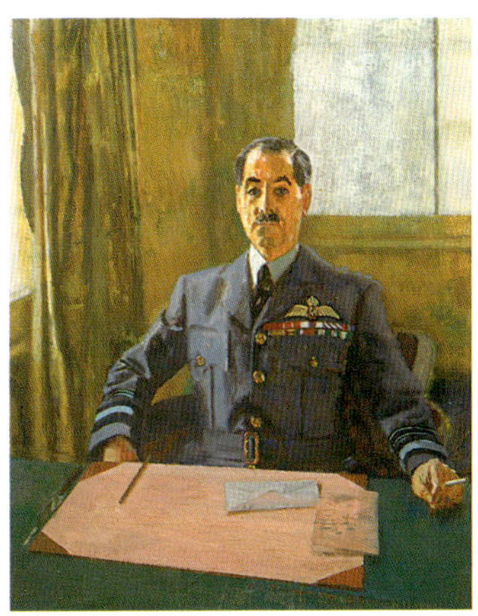

Thomson, Alfred Reginald 1894–1979
*Air Marshal A. Guy R. Garrod (1891–1965),
CB, OBE, MC, DFC* 1943
oil on canvas 76.2 x 63.5
IWM ART LD 2907

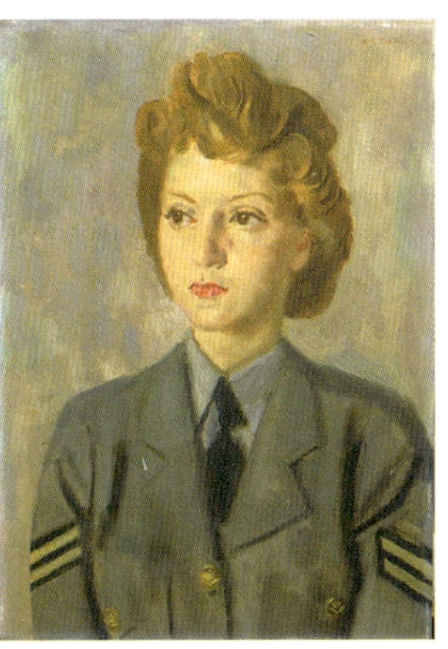

Thomson, Alfred Reginald 1894–1979
*Corporal Lilian Levy, Women's Auxiliary Air
Force* 1943
oil on canvas 54.2 x 39.6
IWM ART LD 2848

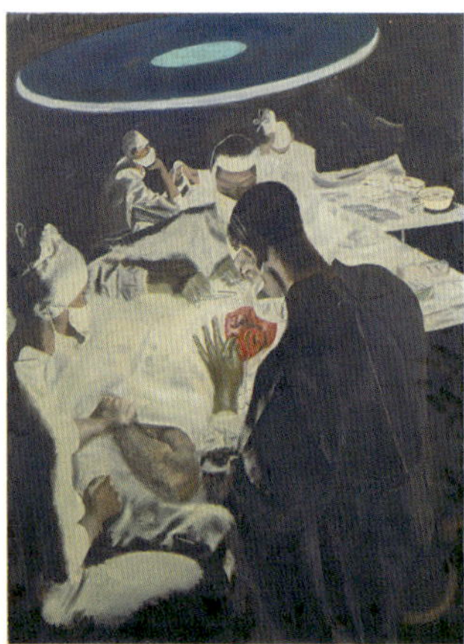

Thomson, Alfred Reginald 1894–1979
Grafting a New Eyelid 1943
oil on canvas 101.9 x 76.2
IWM ART LD 3602

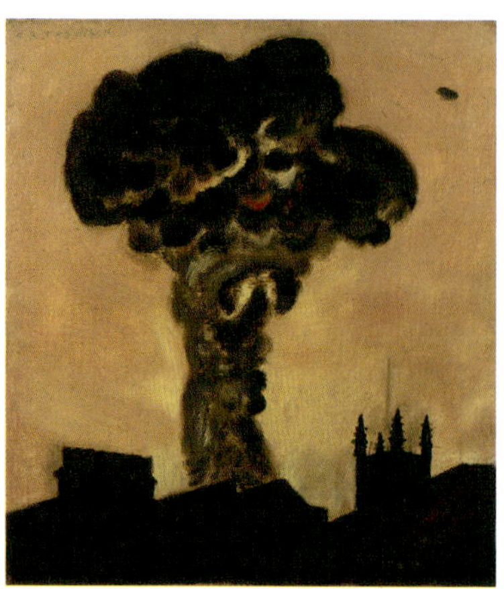

Thomson, Alfred Reginald 1894–1979
*A High Explosive Bomb in High Street,
Kensington, 18 February 1944* 1944
oil on canvas 50.8 x 45.7
IWM ART LD 3812

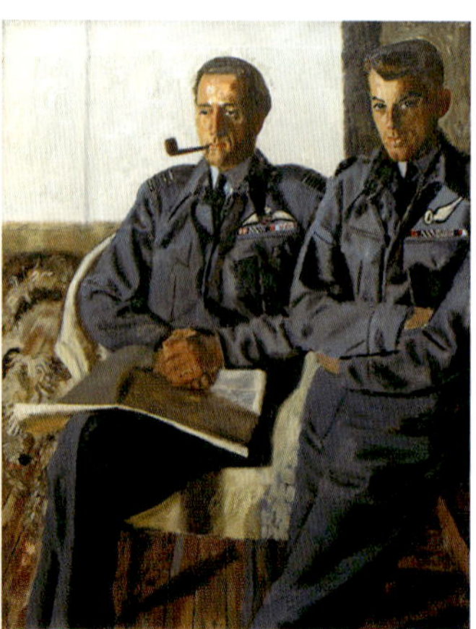

Thomson, Alfred Reginald 1894–1979
*Group Captain P. C. Pickard (1915–1944),
DSO, and Two Bars, DFC, and Flight
Lieutenant J. A. Broadley (…)* 1944
oil on canvas 91.4 x 71.1
IWM ART LD 3814

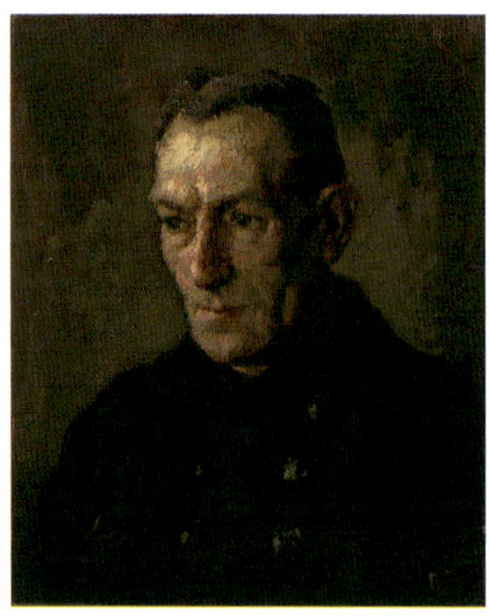

Todd, Arthur Ralph Middleton 1891–1966
Auxiliary Fireman H. Barker, GM 1940
oil on canvas 45.7 x 38.1
IWM ART LD 1958

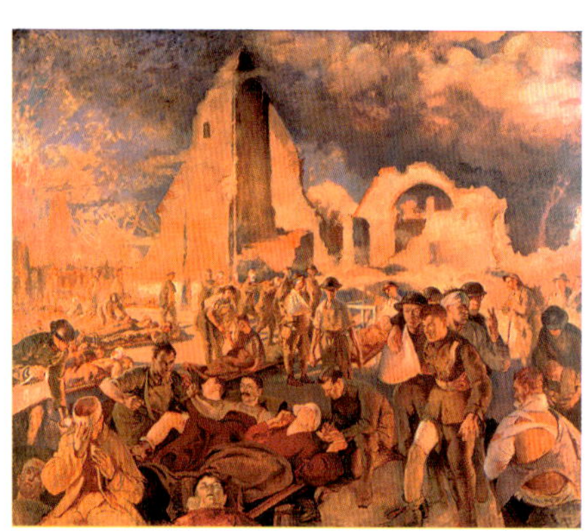

Tonks, Henry 1862–1937
An Advanced Dressing Station in France 1918
oil on canvas 182.8 x 218.4
IWM ART 1922

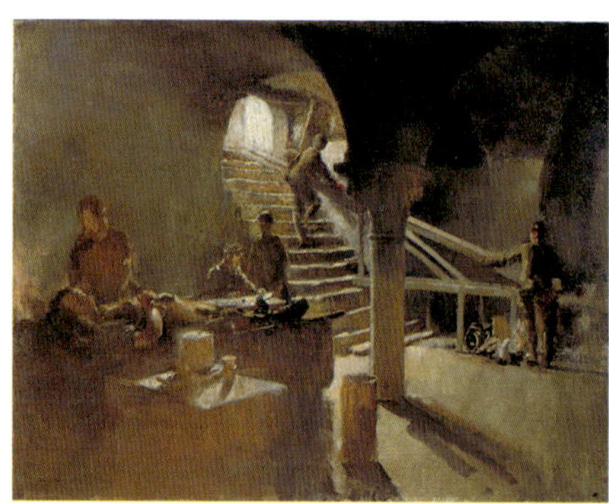

Tonks, Henry 1862–1937
*An Underground Casualty Clearing Station,
Arras* 1918
oil on canvas 56.3 x 71.6
IWM ART 1653

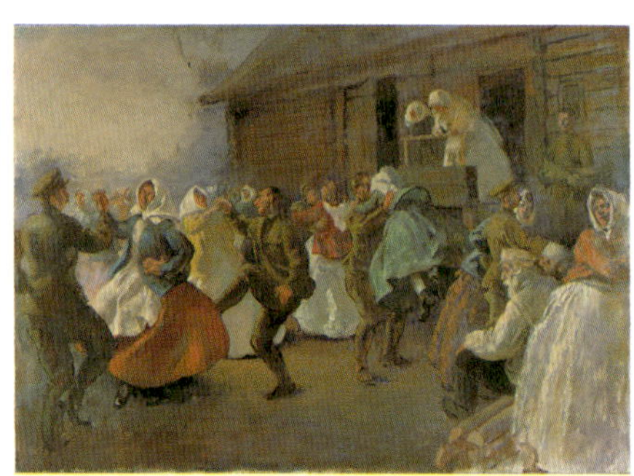

Tonks, Henry 1862–1937
Russian Soldiers Dancing with Peasant Women
1919
oil on canvas 72.3 x 101.6
IWM ART 3064

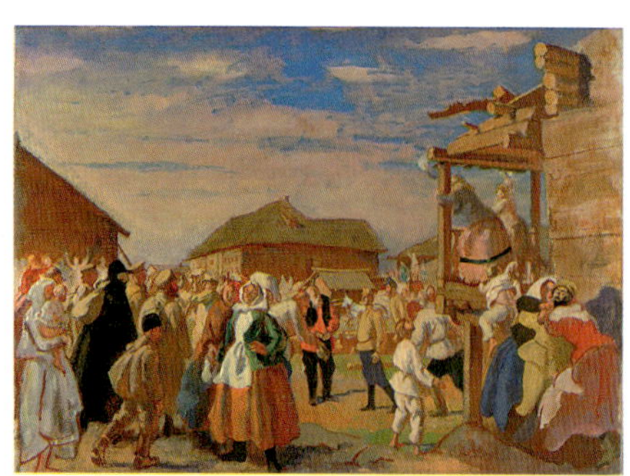

Tonks, Henry 1862–1937
The Surrender of Pujos Gora 1919
oil on canvas 72.3 x 101.9
IWM ART 3063

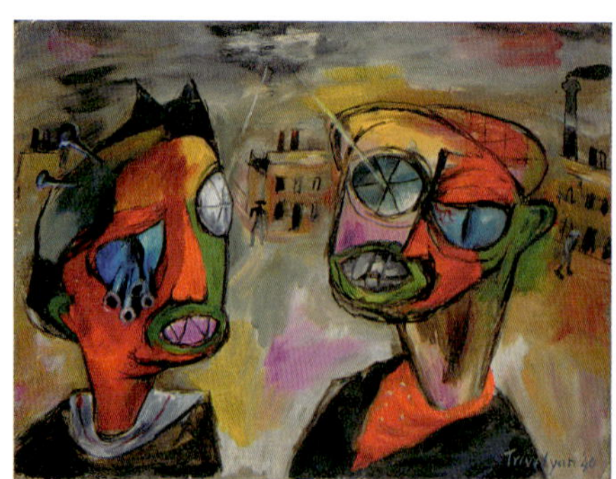

Trevelyan, Julian 1910–1989
Premonitions of the Blitz 1940
oil on canvas 38.5 x 51
IWM ART 15756

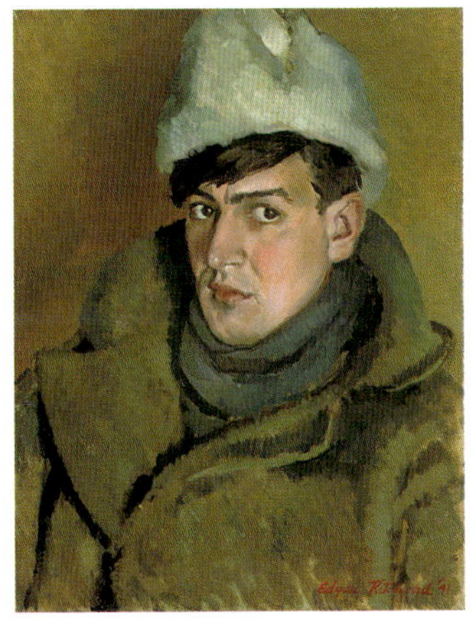

Trimnell-Ritchard, E. active 1940s
Coxwain Davey: Icelandic Patrol 1941
oil on canvas 55.8 x 43.1
IWM ART LD 1853

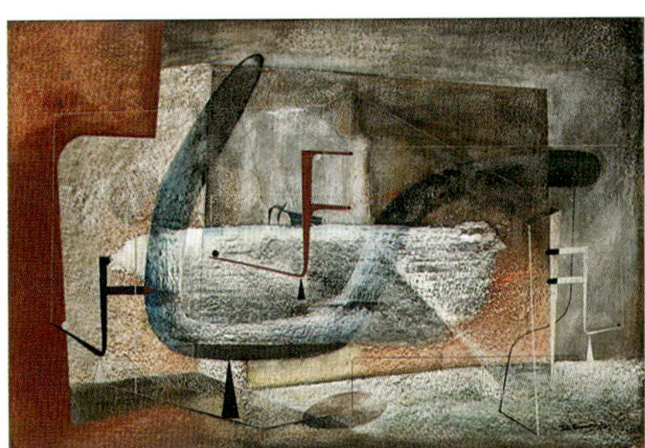

Tunnard, John 1900–1971
Anglo-Dutch 1942
tempera & oil on board 65 x 95
IWM ART 16736

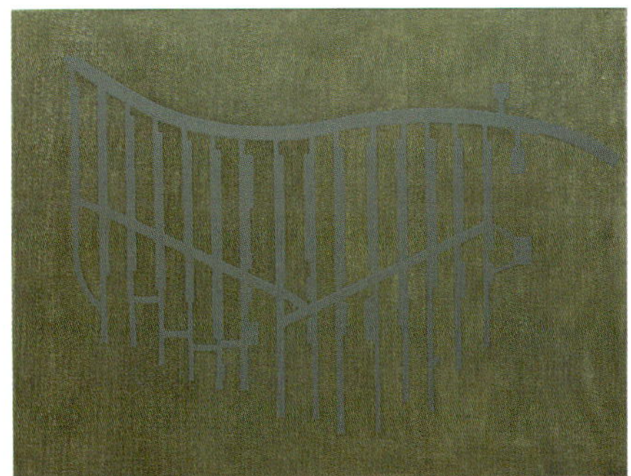

Turnbull, Alison b.1956
Factory 2000
oil on canvas 68.6 x 91.4
IWM ART 16747

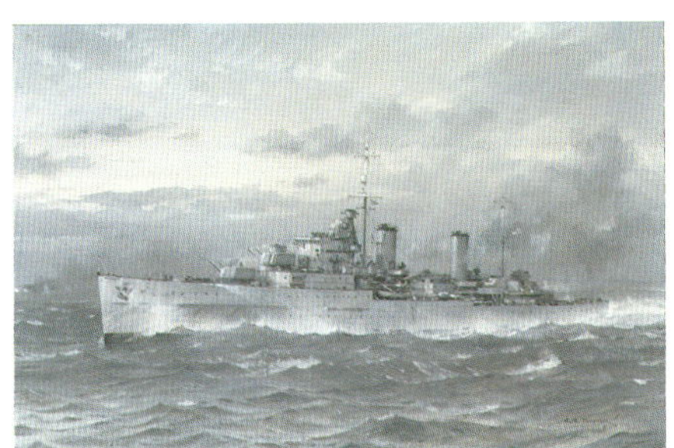

Turner, Charles E. 1883–1965
'HMS Aurora' 1914–1918
oil on canvas 45.6 x 71
IWM ART 15083

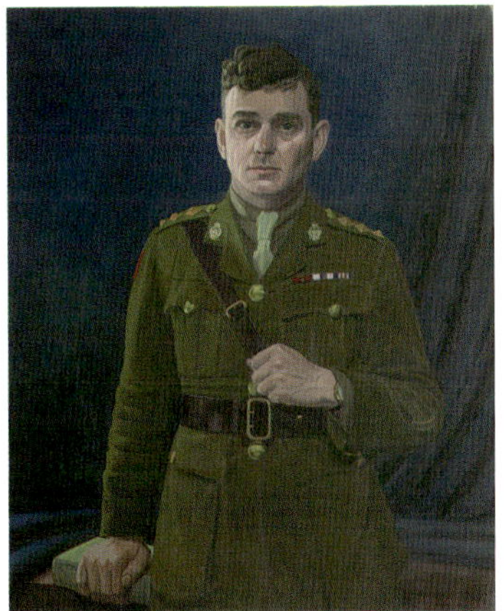

Underwood, Leon 1890–1975
*Captain George Burdon McKean (1888–1926),
VC, MC, 14th Battalion Canadian Infantry*
1919
oil on canvas 91.4 x 76.2
IWM ART 1924

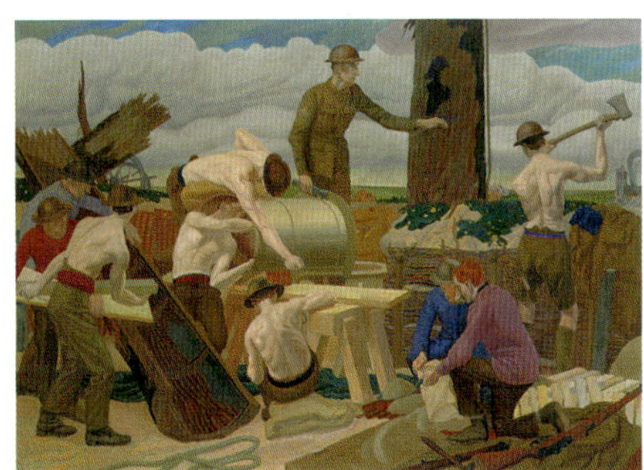

Underwood, Leon 1890–1975
Erecting a Camouflage Tree 1919
oil on canvas 106.6 x 152.4
IWM ART 2283

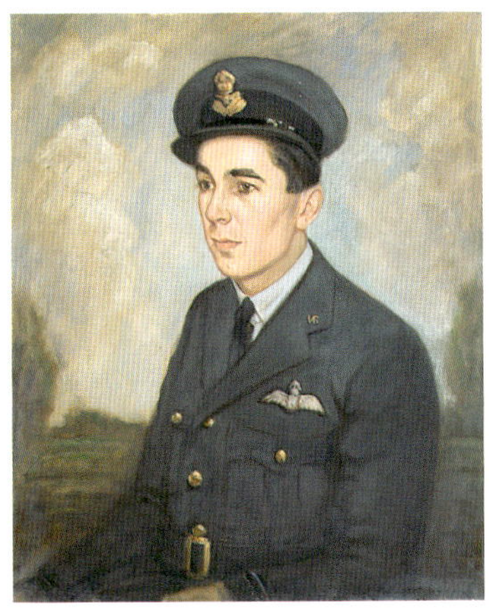

unknown artist
*Maurice Lishman, Royal Air Force Flying
Officer, Shot Down in the Battle of Britain,
Aged 21* 1939–1940
oil on canvas 76.2 x 63.5
IWM ART LD 7378

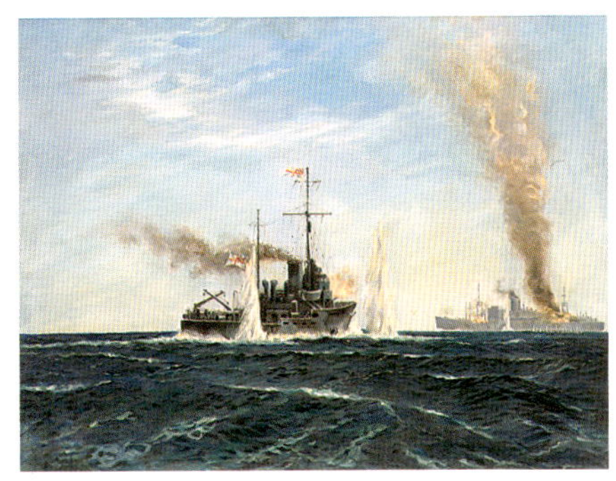

unknown artist
*The Sinking of an Armed Japanese Raider by
HM Minesweeper 'Bengal' in the Indian
Ocean, 11 November 1942* 1942
oil on canvas 91.4 x 121.9
IWM ART LD 5979

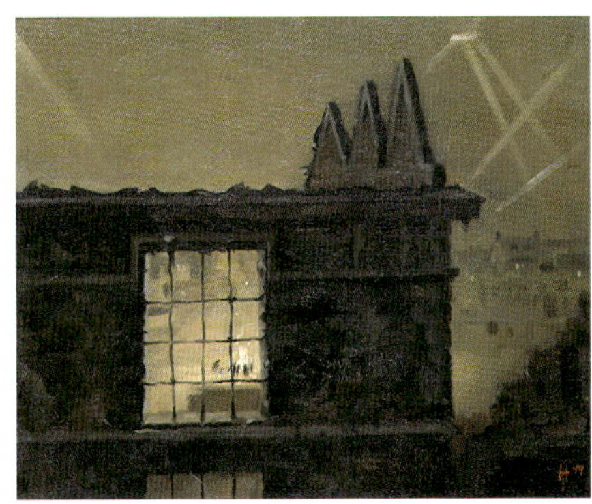

unknown artist
Burning Building during a Zeppelin Raid
1944
oil on board 37.8 x 45.7
IWM ART 15287

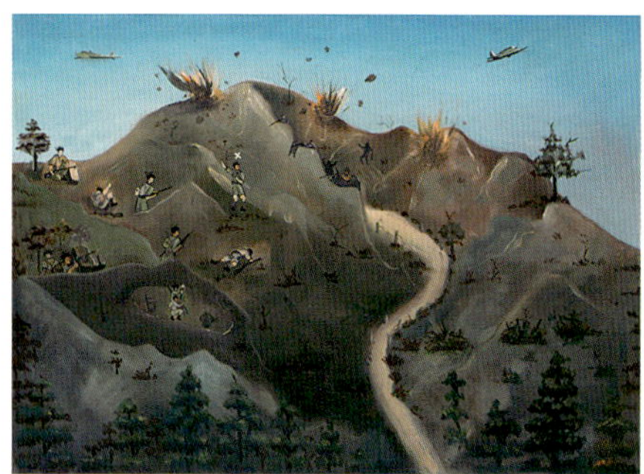

unknown artist
An Episode in the Battle of Sailum Vum (Chin Hills, Burma): Subedar Ram Sarup Singh Winning the VC c.1944–1946
oil on canvas 91.4 x 121.9
IWM ART LD 5981

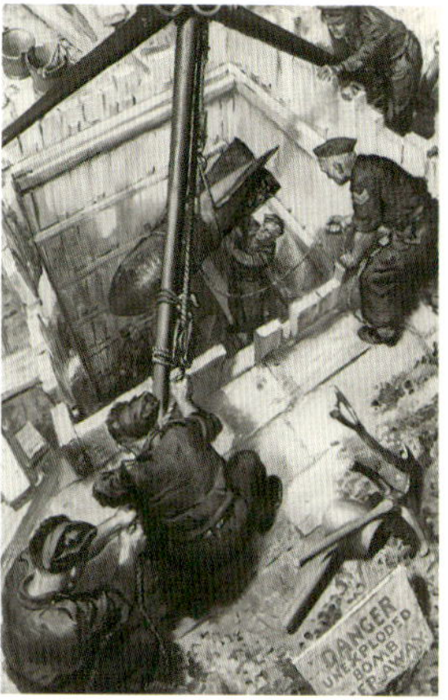

Uptton, Clive 1911–2006
Bomb Disposal: Bringing up a 250-Kilo Bomb 1942
oil on canvas 76.2 x 50.8
IWM ART LD 2275

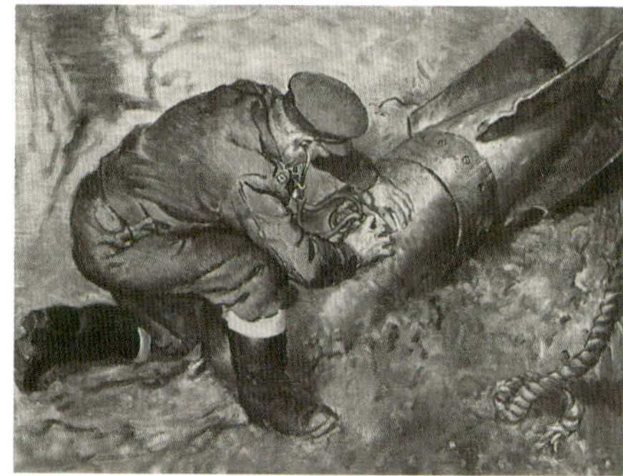

Uptton, Clive 1911–2006
Bomb Disposal: Listening for Ticking 1942
oil on canvas 50.8 x 66
IWM ART LD 2276

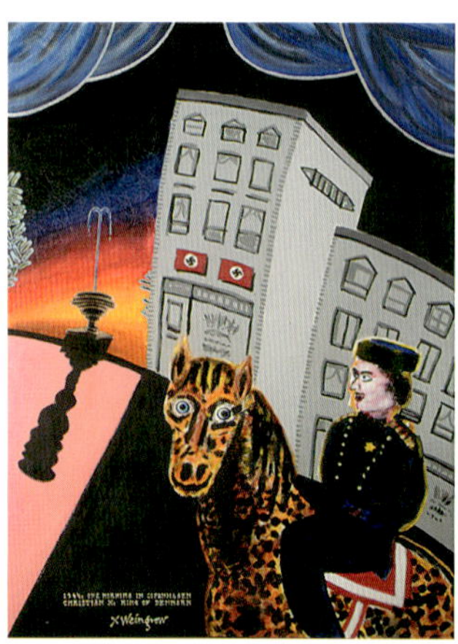

Waingrow, X. Bits b.1951
Early One Morning in Copenhagen: Christian X, King of Denmark
acrylic on canvas 203.3 x 152
IWM ART 16323

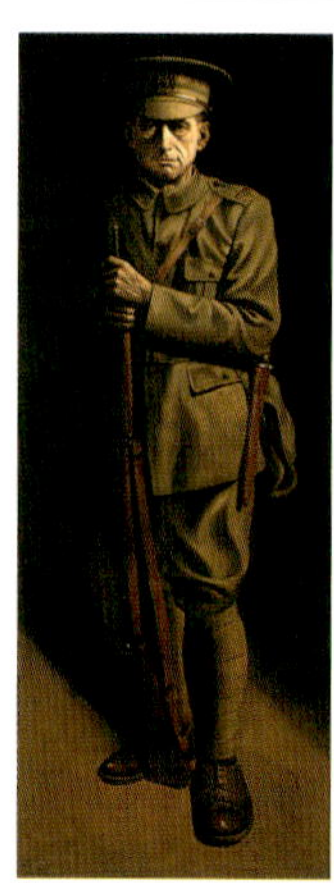

Walker, Claude Alfred Pennington b.1862
The Artist in the Uniform of the City of London National Guard 1916
oil on canvas 195.5 x 76.8
IWM ART 117

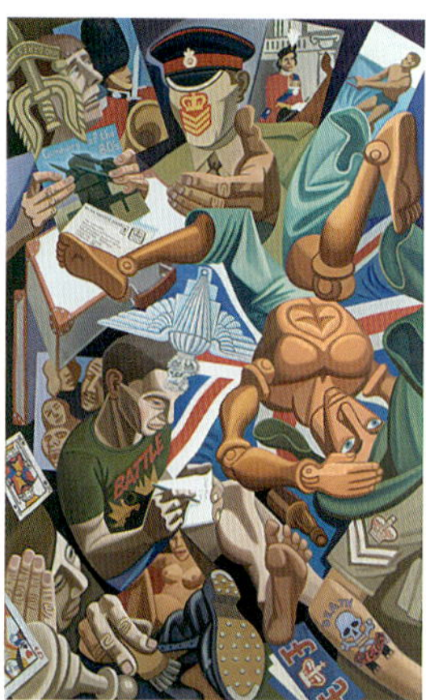

Walker, Ray 1945–1984
Army Recruitment I 1981–1982
oil on canvas 244 x 152.5
IWM ART 15423

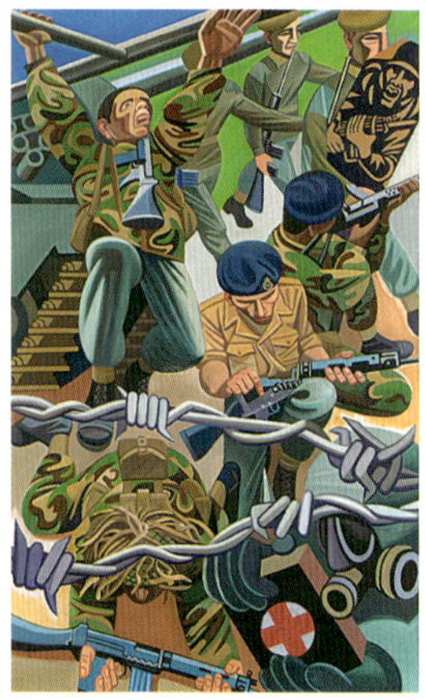

Walker, Ray 1945–1984
Army Recruitment II 1981–1982
oil on canvas 244 x 152.5
IWM ART 15423

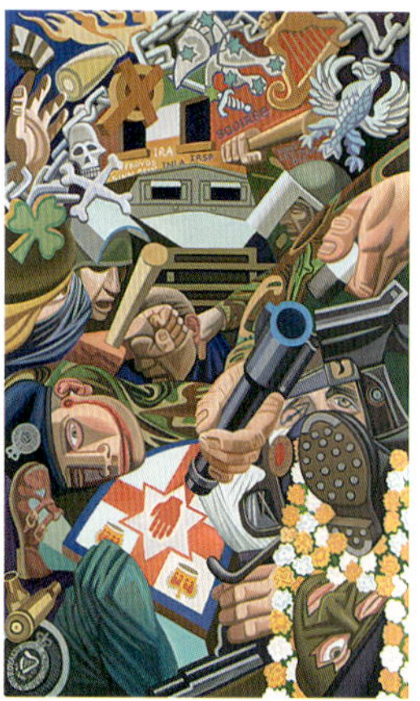

Walker, Ray 1945–1984
Army Recruitment III 1981–1982
oil on canvas 244 x 152.5
IWM ART 15423

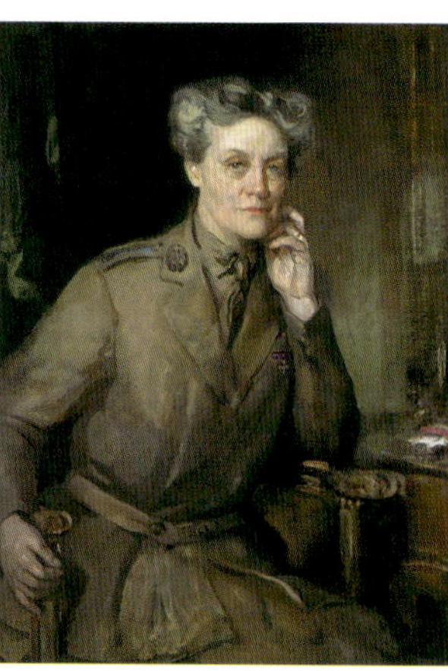

Walton, Edward Arthur 1860–1922 &
Walton, Cecile 1891–1956
Mrs Chalmers, CBE, Director of QMAAC 1921
oil on canvas 98 x 73.8
IWM ART 4172

Facing Page: Lavery, John, 1856–1941, *Elswick, 1917: Messrs. Armstrong, Whitworth & Company* (detail), 1919, (p. 132)

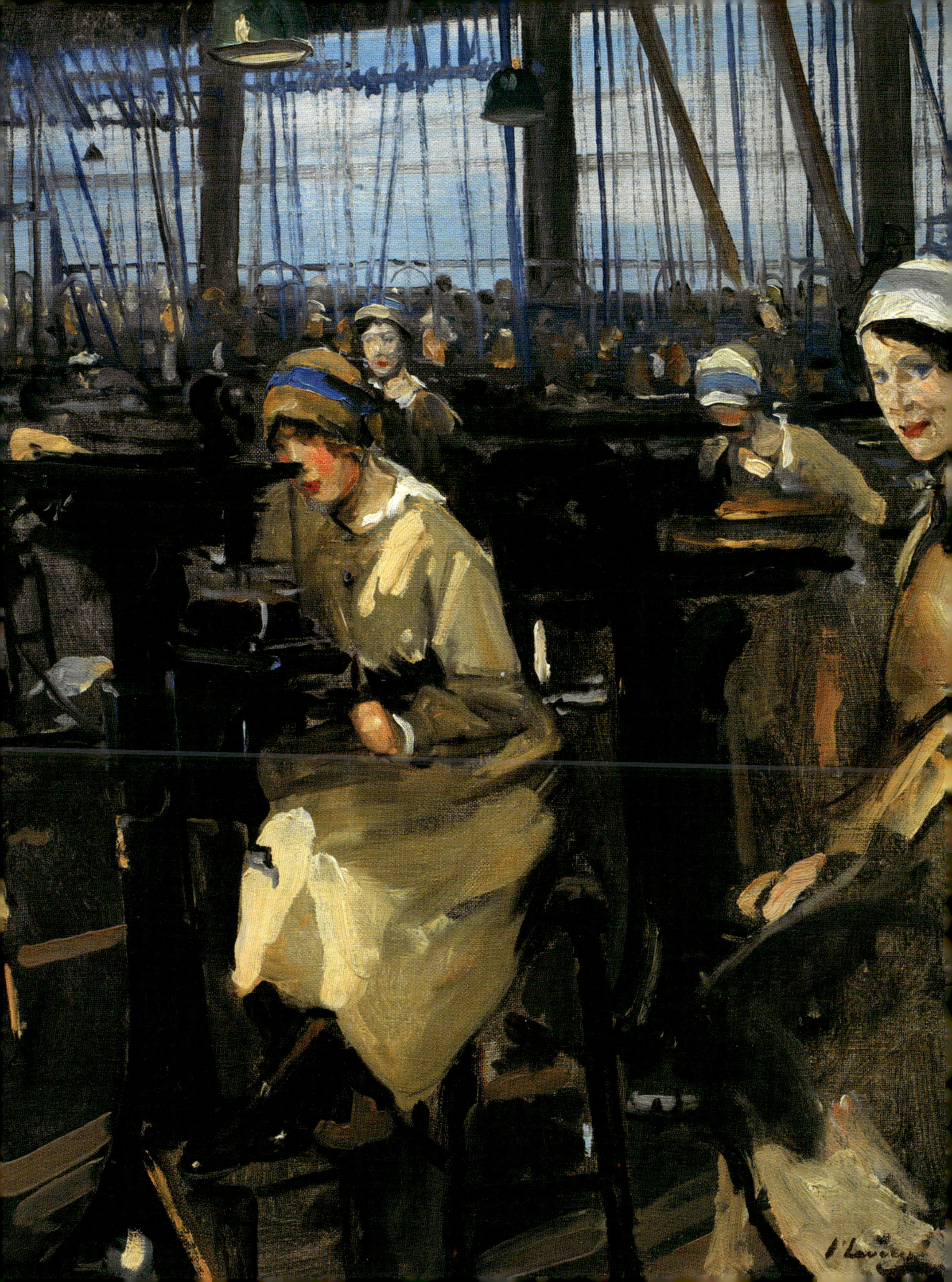

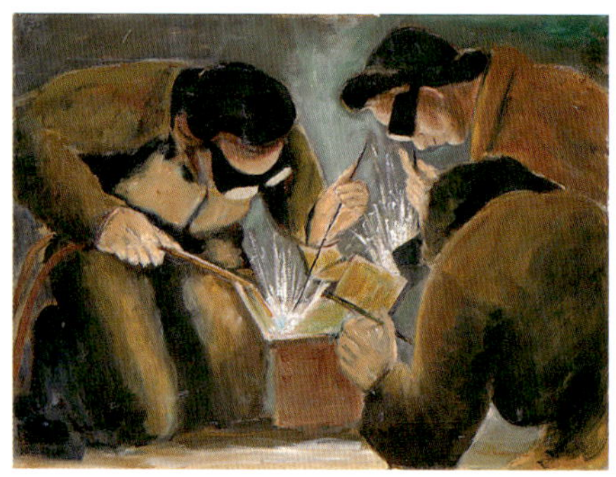

Ward, Grace active 1940s
*Royal Electrical and Mechanical Engineer
Auxiliary Territorial Service Welders* 1944
oil on canvas 46.3 x 61.5
IWM ART LD 7224

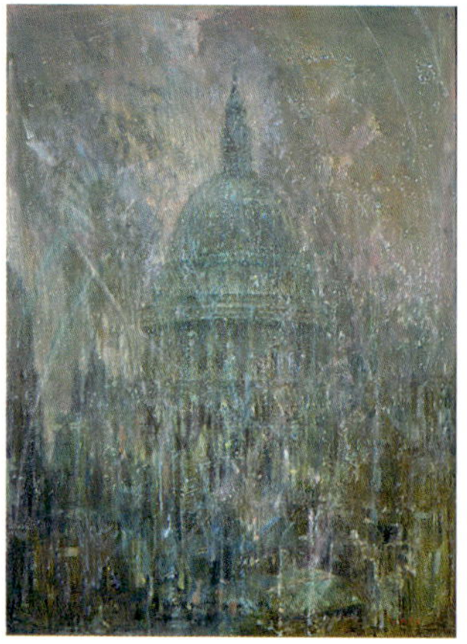

Ware, William 1915–1997
St Paul's Cathedral c.1941
oil on board 100.5 x 74.5
IWM ART 15664

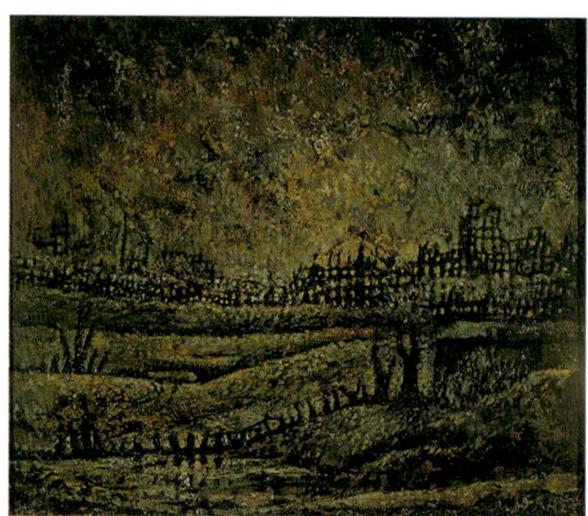

Ware, William 1915–1997
Fired City 1942
oil on panel 53.9 x 64.1
IWM ART LD 2635

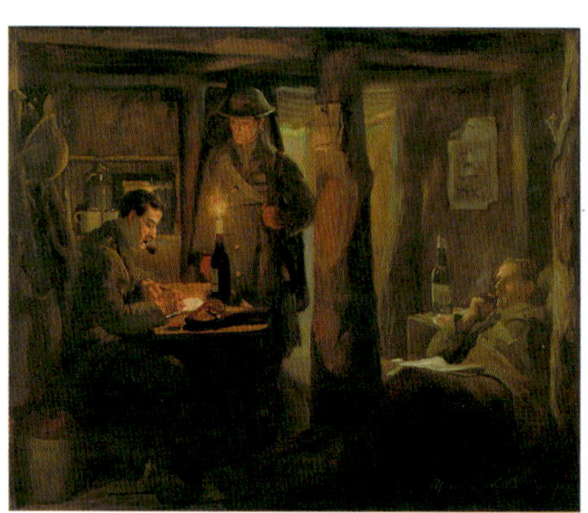

Watherston, Marjorie Violet d.c.1970
The Dispatch: The Captain's Dugout 1917
oil on canvas 102.8 x 127
IWM ART 5199

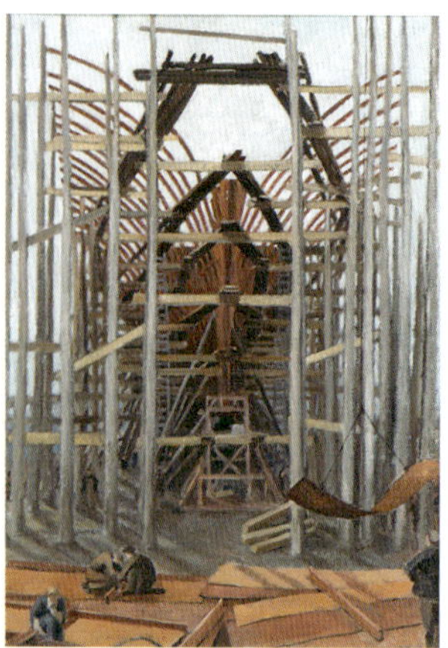

Watson, Barbara 1893–1978
An Aircraft Carrier under Construction 1943
oil on canvas 60.9 x 45.7
IWM ART LD 3603

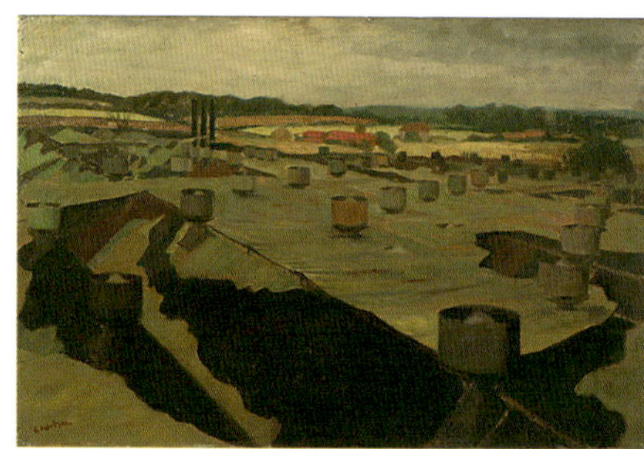

Watson, Geoffrey active 1940s
A View across Camouflaged Roofs 1943
oil on panel 40.9 x 60.9
IWM ART LD 3705

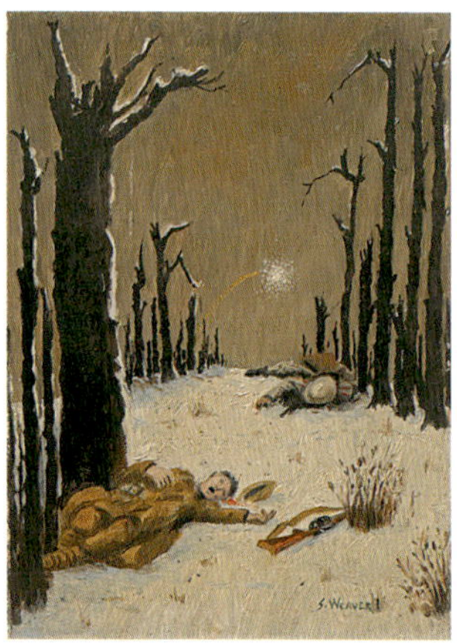

Weaver, S. active 1914–1918
Bourlon Wood, Somme 1917
oil on canvas 23 x 17
IWM ART 5587

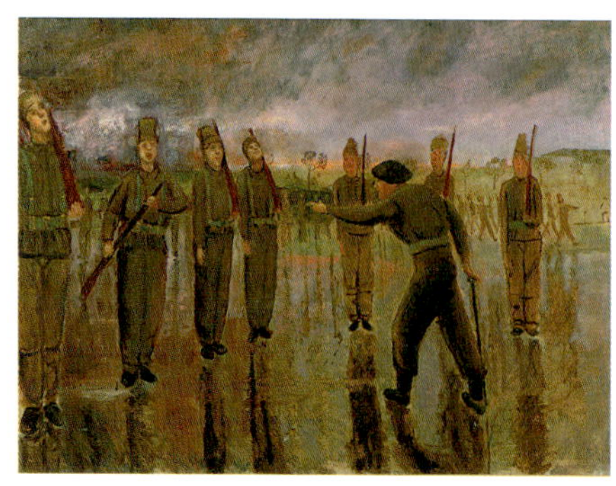

Weight, Carel Victor Morlais 1908–1997
Recruits' Progress: Arms Drill 1942
oil on canvas 50.8 x 68.5
IWM ART LD 2910

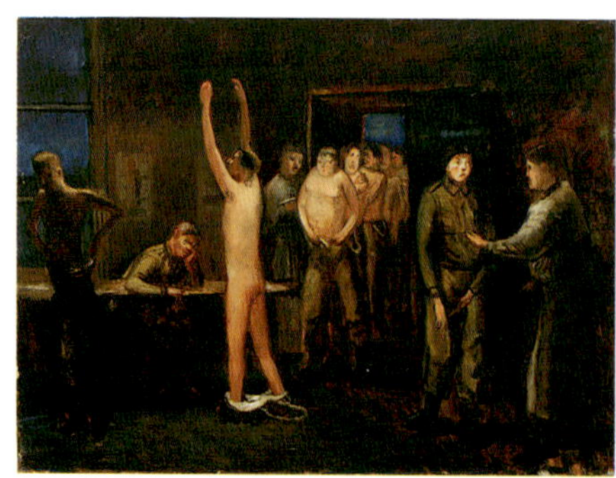

Weight, Carel Victor Morlais 1908–1997
Recruits' Progress: Medical Inspection 1942
oil on canvas 51 x 68.5
IWM ART LD 2909

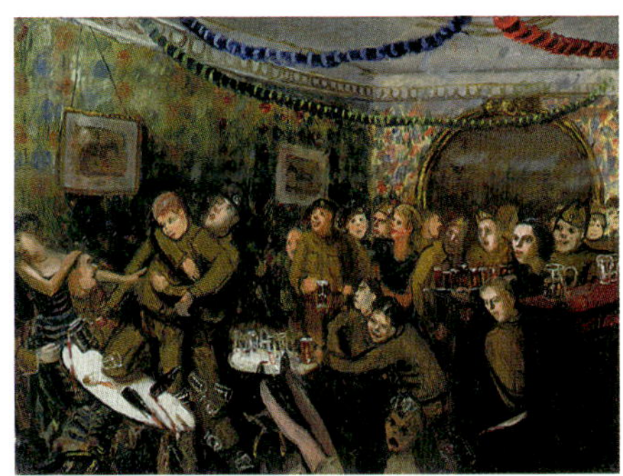

Weight, Carel Victor Morlais 1908–1997
Recruits' Progress: An Evening out, Pub Scene
1943
oil on canvas 50.8 x 68.5
IWM ART LD 2912

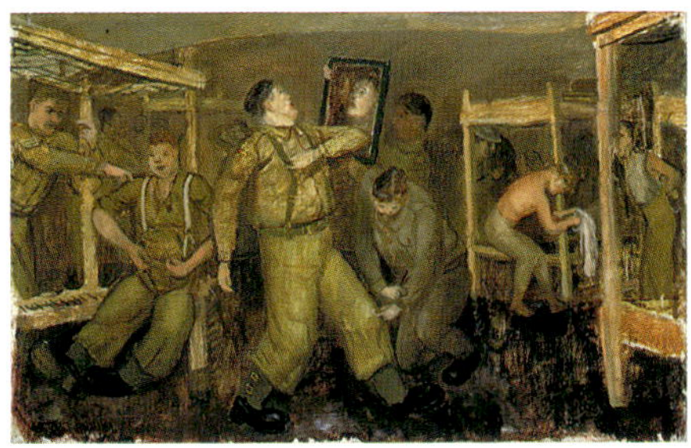

Weight, Carel Victor Morlais 1908–1997
Recruits' Progress: Preparations for an Evening out 1943
oil on canvas 50.8 x 68.5
IWM ART LD 2911

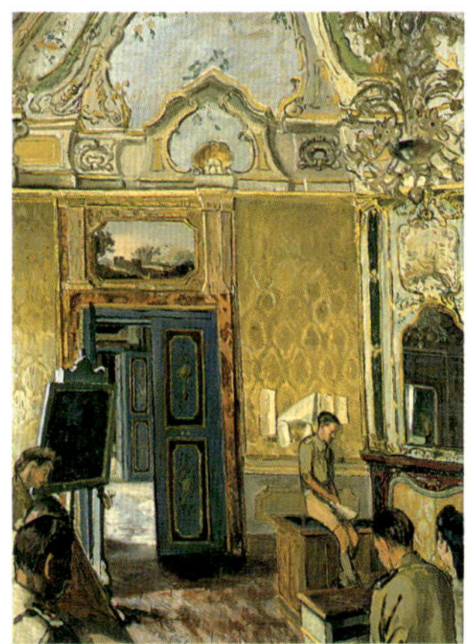

Weight, Carel Victor Morlais 1908–1997
A Classroom in the University, Perugia, Italy
1945
oil on canvas 100.3 x 74.9
IWM ART LD 5501

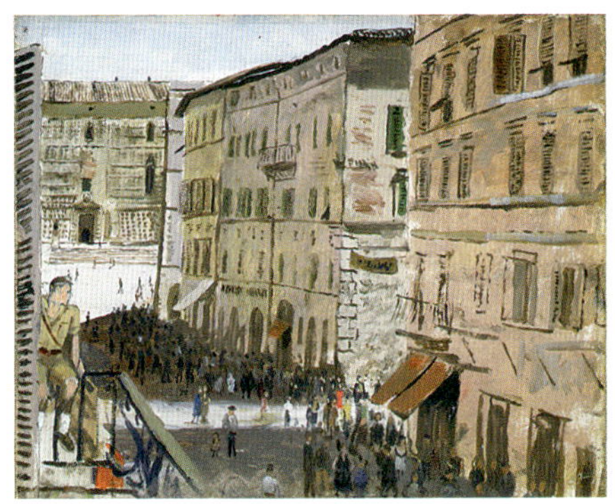

Weight, Carel Victor Morlais 1908–1997
A Street Scene from the Officers' Mess, Perugia, Italy 1945
oil on panel 19.3 x 24.7
IWM ART LD 5506

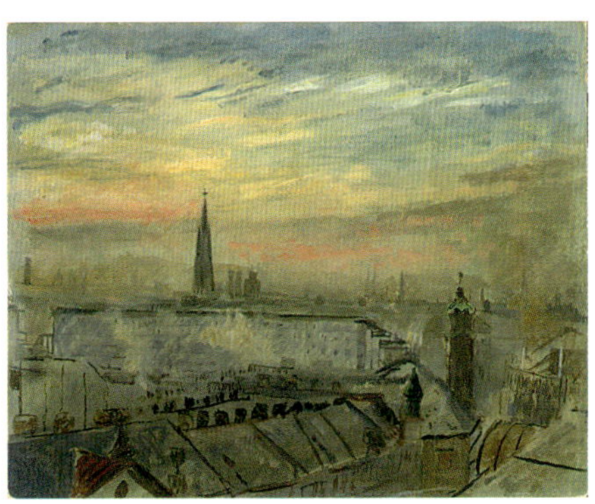

Weight, Carel Victor Morlais 1908–1997
A View of Vienna 1945
oil on panel 24.1 x 30.4
IWM ART LD 5699

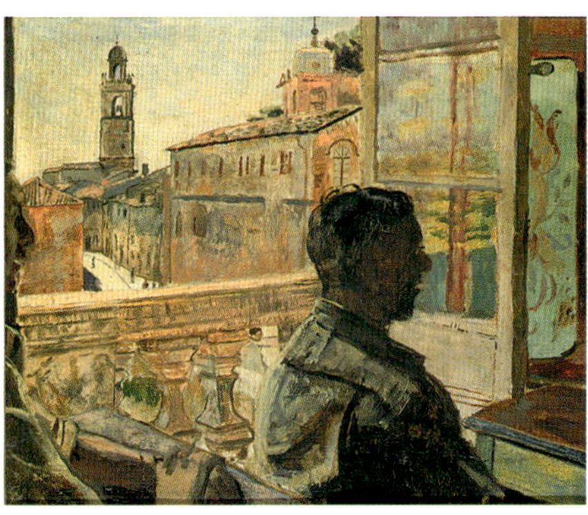

Weight, Carel Victor Morlais 1908–1997
A Window of a Classroom in the Army School of Education, Perugia, Italy 1945
oil on canvas 24.1 x 29.2
IWM ART LD 5498

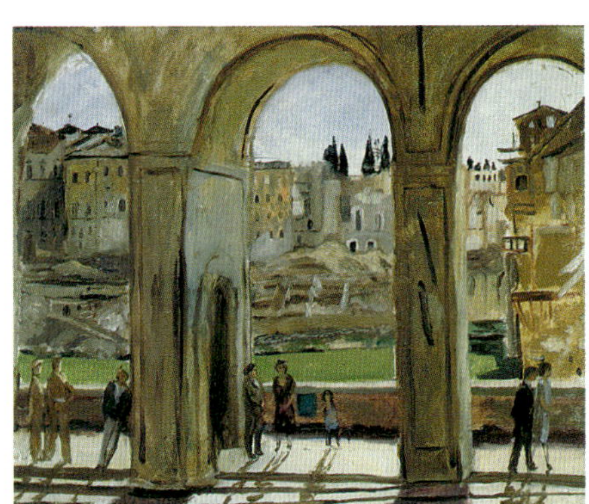

Weight, Carel Victor Morlais 1908–1997
German Demolition Seen from the South Side of the Ponte Vecchio, Florence 1945
oil on canvas 45.7 x 55.8
IWM ART LD 5710

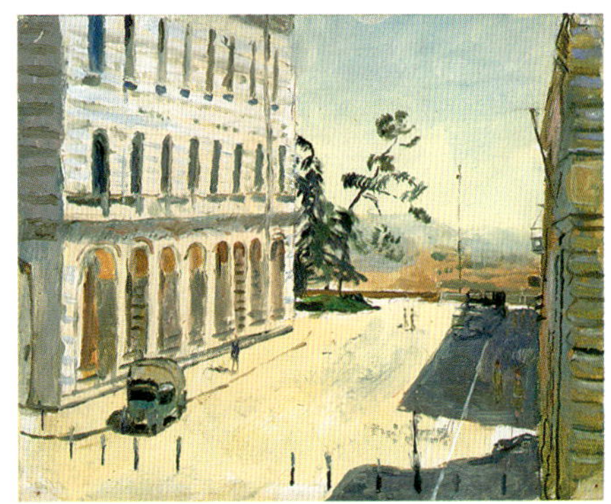

Weight, Carel Victor Morlais 1908–1997
Outside the Officers' Transit Hotel, Perugia, Italy 1945
oil on panel 19.3 x 24.7
IWM ART LD 5505

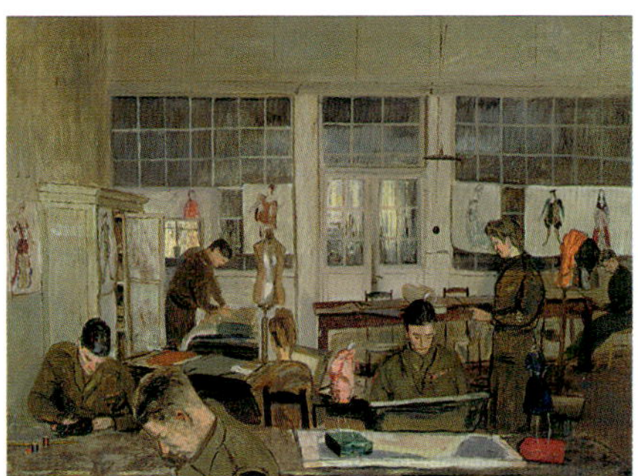

Weight, Carel Victor Morlais 1908–1997
The Dress Design Class, Formation College Arts Wing, Florence 1945
oil on canvas 49.5 x 69.8
IWM ART LD 5713

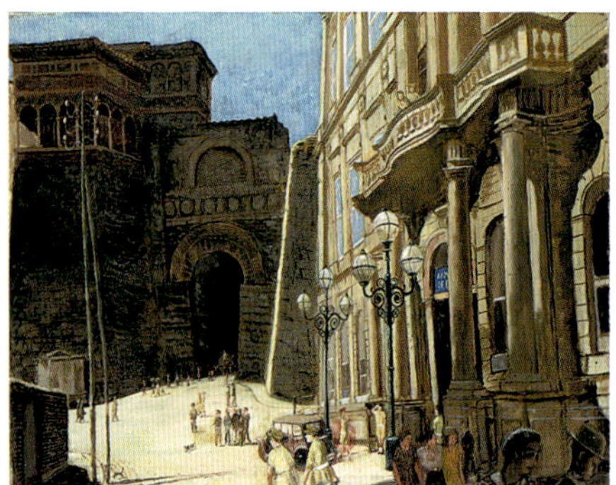

Weight, Carel Victor Morlais 1908–1997
*The Exterior of the Army School of Education,
Perugia, Italy: The Etruscan Gate* 1945
oil on canvas 69.8 x 88.9
IWM ART LD 5502

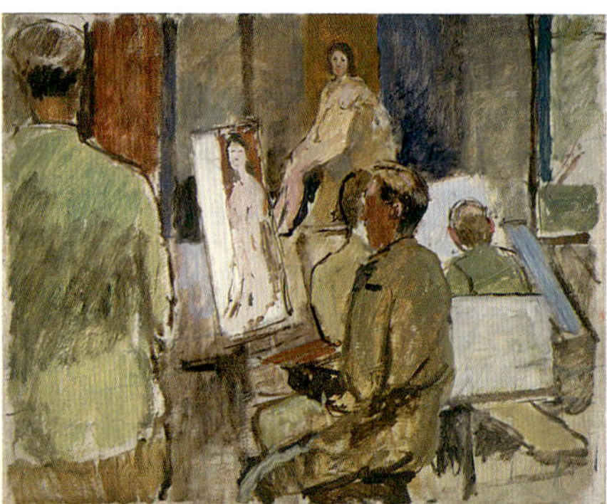

Weight, Carel Victor Morlais 1908–1997
*The Life Class, Formation College Arts Wing,
Florence* 1945
oil on panel 39.3 x 49.5
IWM ART LD 5704

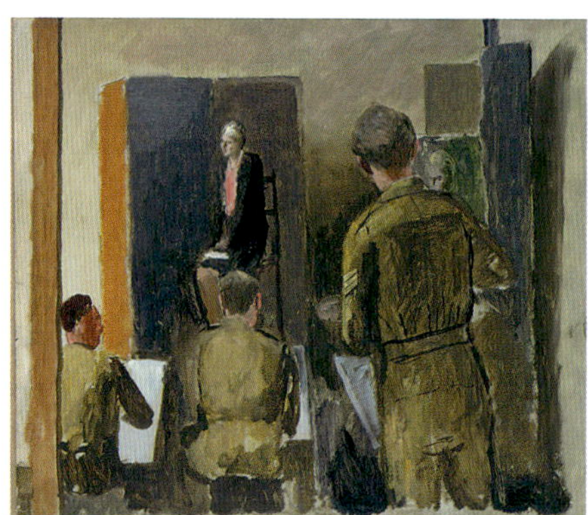

Weight, Carel Victor Morlais 1908–1997
*The Portrait Class, Formation College Arts
Wing, Florence* 1945
oil on panel 36.1 x 42.5
IWM ART LD 5700

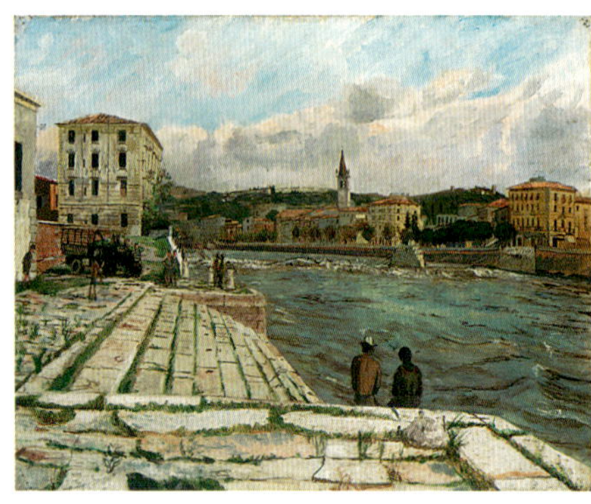

Weight, Carel Victor Morlais 1908–1997
The Remains of Ponte Navi, Verona 1945
oil on canvas 60.9 x 76.2
IWM ART LD 5715

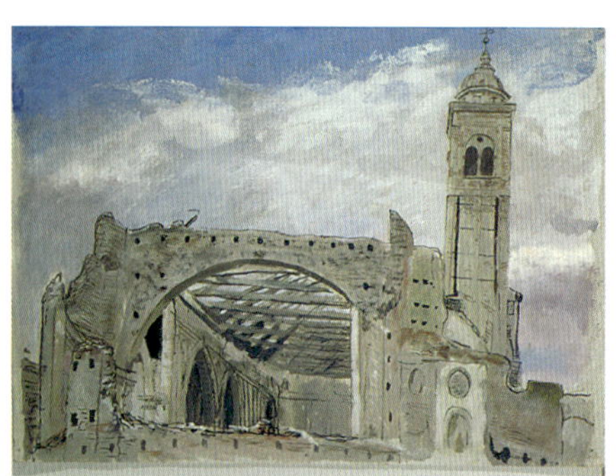

Weight, Carel Victor Morlais 1908–1997
The Temple of Malatesta, Rimini 1945
oil on panel 34.9 x 48.8
IWM ART LD 5703

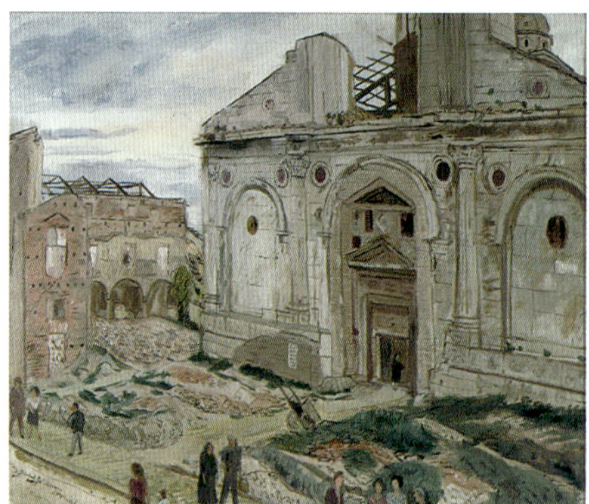

Weight, Carel Victor Morlais 1908–1997
The Temple of Malatesta, Rimini 1945
oil on canvas 54.6 x 65.4
IWM ART LD 5714

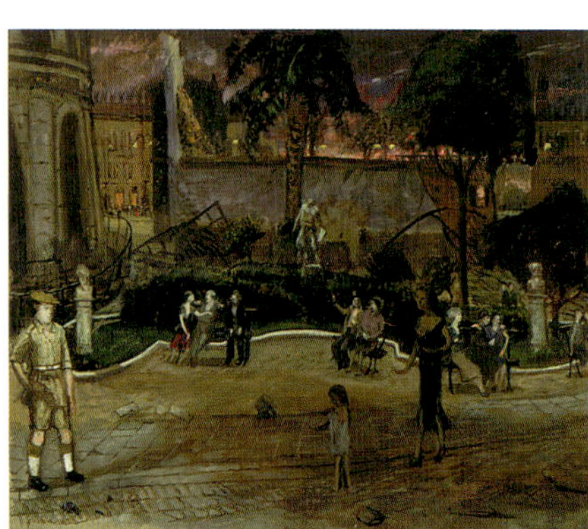

Weight, Carel Victor Morlais 1908–1997
Veronese Night 1945
oil on canvas 50.8 x 60.9
IWM ART LD 5708

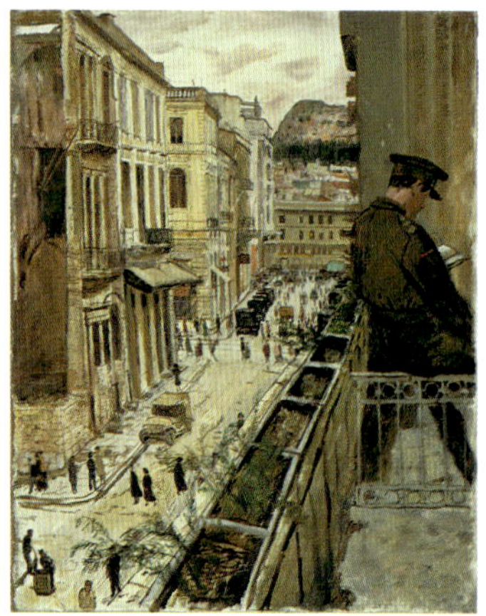

Weight, Carel Victor Morlais 1908–1997
*A Scene in Athens from the British Officers'
Hotel Cosmopolitan* 1946
oil on canvas 50.1 x 40
IWM ART LD 5806

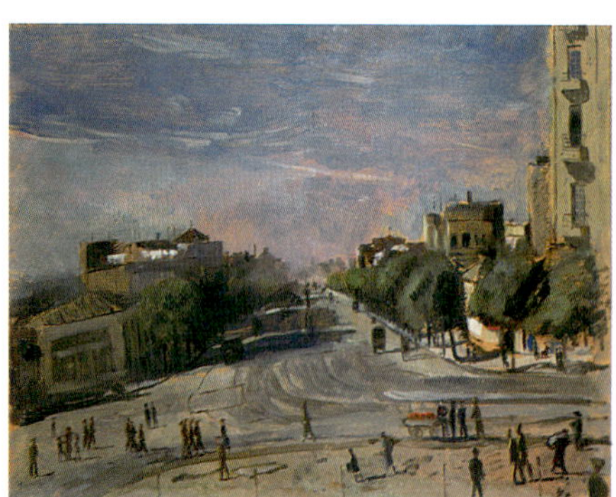

Weight, Carel Victor Morlais 1908–1997
A Street in Athens 1946
oil on panel 34.9 x 44.4 (E)
IWM ART LD 5807

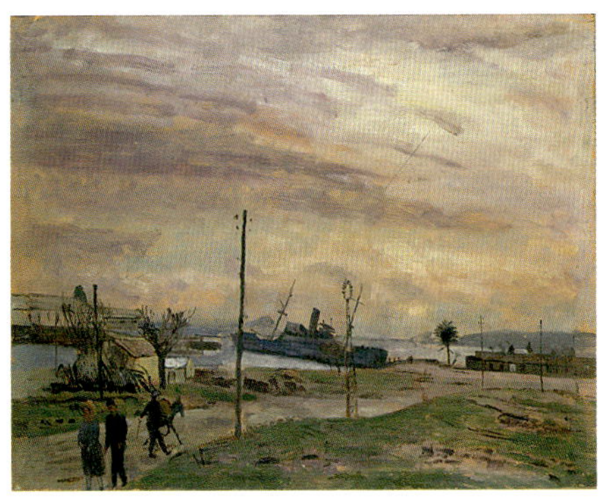

Weight, Carel Victor Morlais 1908–1997
*A Sunken Blockship in the Mouth of the
Corinth Canal* 1946
oil on panel 34.9 x 44.4 (E)
IWM ART LD 5808

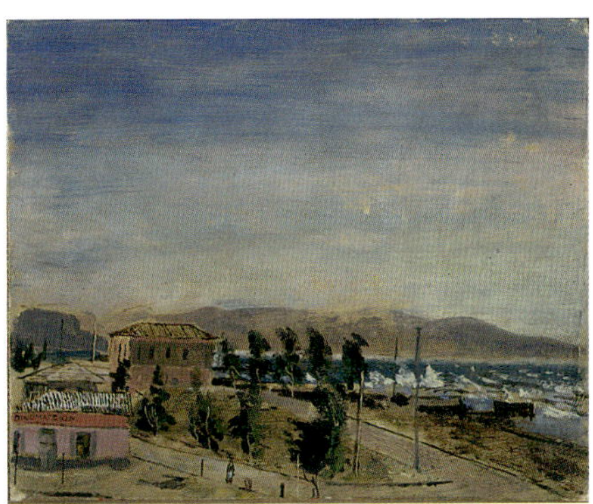

Weight, Carel Victor Morlais 1908–1997
Eleusis 1946
oil on canvas 20.3 x 25.4
IWM ART LD 5811

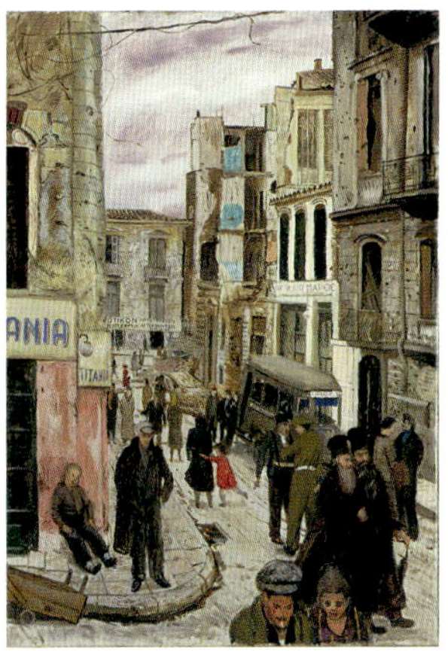

Weight, Carel Victor Morlais 1908–1997
Greece: A Typical Street in Athens 1946
oil on canvas 69.8 x 49.5
IWM ART LD 5805

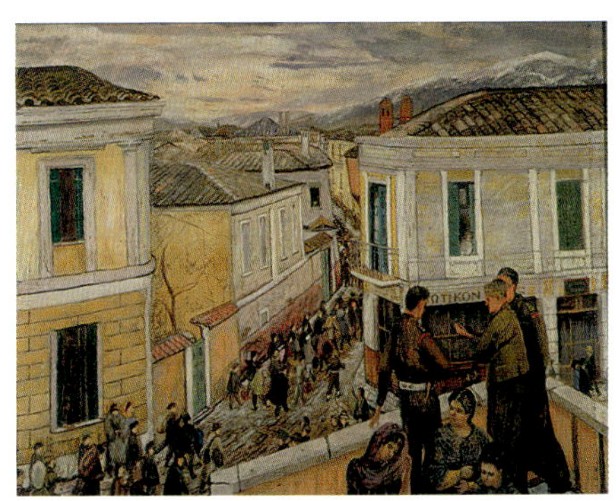

Weight, Carel Victor Morlais 1908–1997
Kosani, Greece 1946
oil on canvas 69.8 x 91.4
IWM ART LD 5867

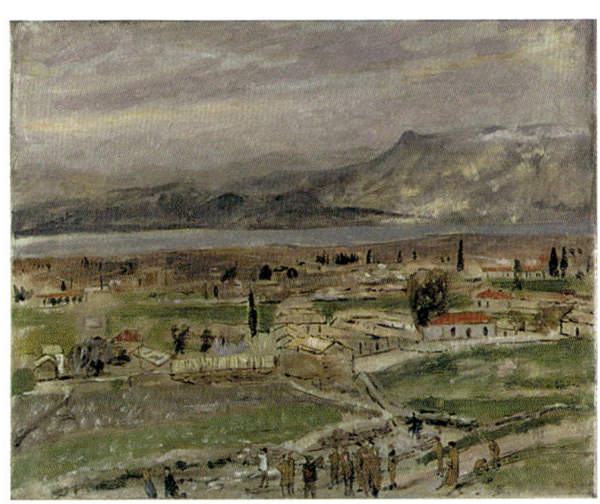

Weight, Carel Victor Morlais 1908–1997
*The Army Education Corps History Course,
Corinth* 1946
oil on canvas 39.3 x 50.1
IWM ART LD 5814

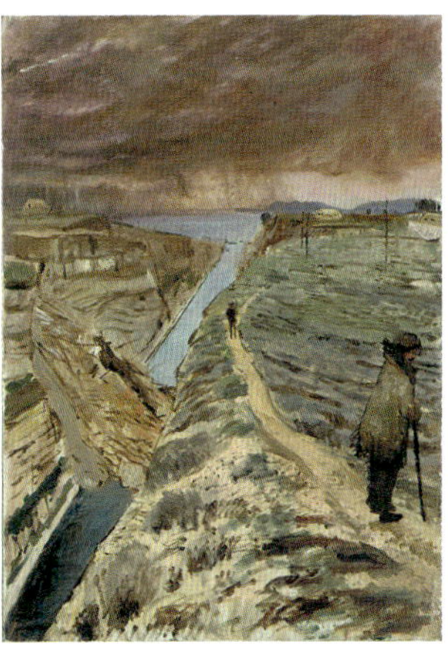

Weight, Carel Victor Morlais 1908–1997
*The Bridge over the Corinth Canal Demolished
by the Germans* 1946
oil on canvas 69.8 x 50.8
IWM ART LD 5809

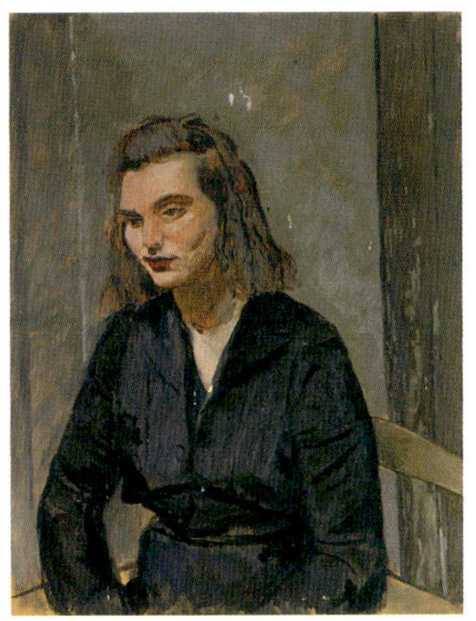

Weight, Carel Victor Morlais 1908–1997
The Girl from Anzio 1946
oil on panel 44.4 x 34.9
IWM ART LD 5815

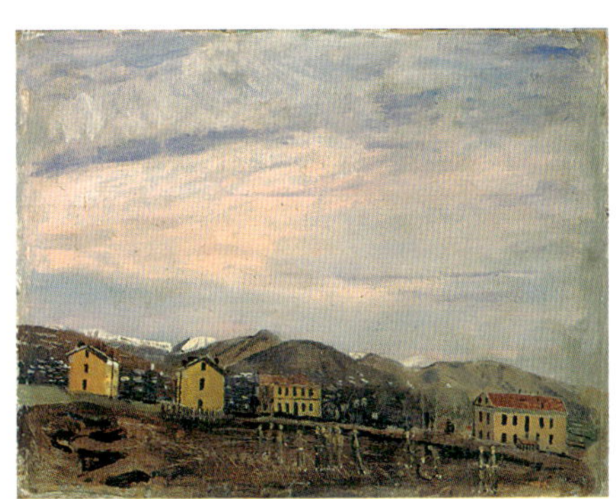

Weight, Carel Victor Morlais 1908–1997
The Greek Barracks at Kosani 1946
oil on panel 33.6 x 44.4
IWM ART LD 5812

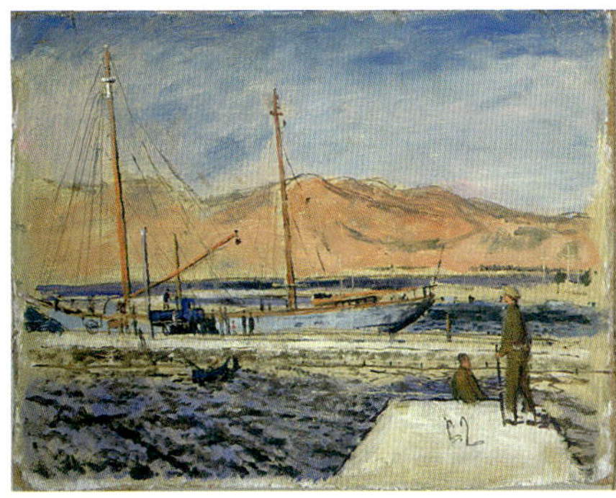

Weight, Carel Victor Morlais 1908–1997
*The Harbour at Eleusis: A Typical Greek
Sailing Ship Bringing United Nations Relief
and Rehabilitation (…)* 1946
oil on panel 34.2 x 44.4
IWM ART LD 5810

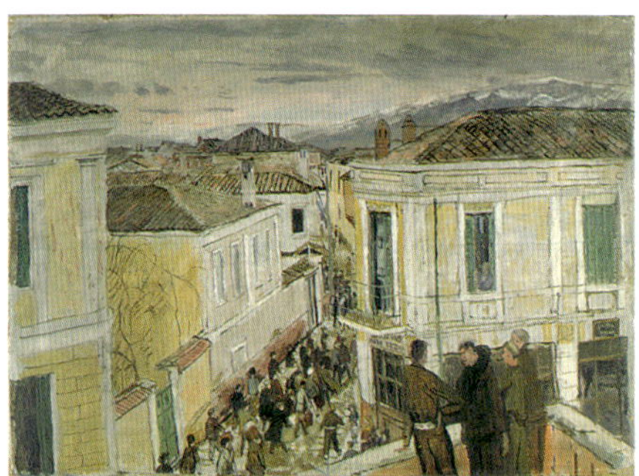

Weight, Carel Victor Morlais 1908–1997
*With the British Military Mission of Kosani:
The Arrival of Army Conscripts Passing the
British Officers' Mess (…)* 1946
oil on panel 44.4 x 62.2
IWM ART LD 5813

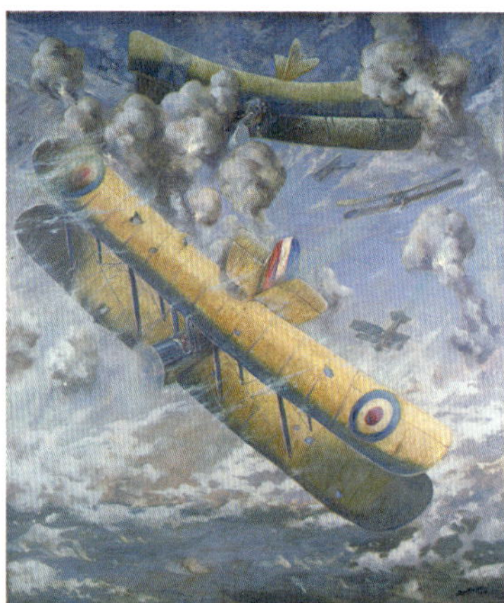

Weirter, Louis 1871–1932
An Aerial Fight 1918
oil on canvas 236.2 x 205.7
IWM ART 654

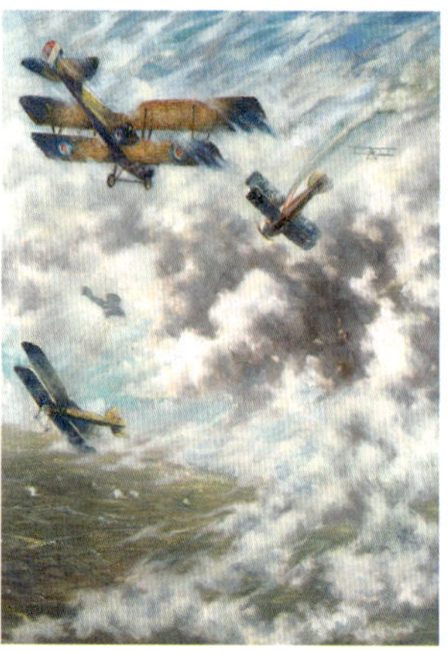

Weirter, Louis 1871–1932
An Incident on the Western Front 1918
oil on canvas 100.3 x 76.2
IWM ART 2660

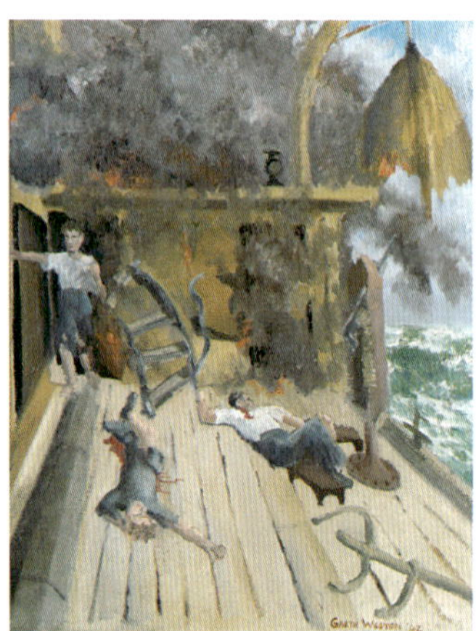

Weston, Garth b.1914
'The admiralty regrets...' 1942
oil on panel 50.8 x 40.6
IWM ART LD 1831

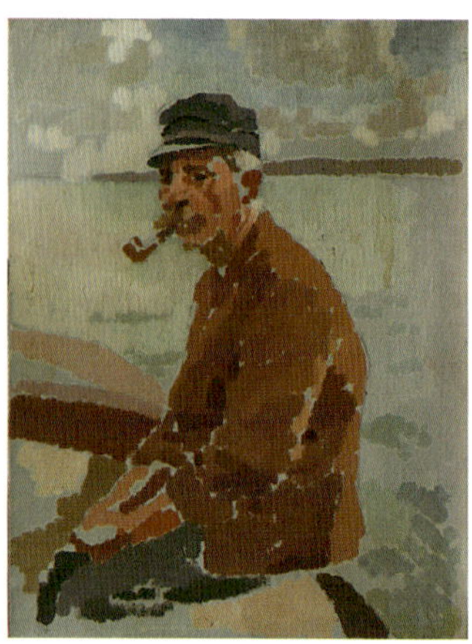

Wheatley, John 1892–1955
A Diver's Tender 1918
oil on canvas 35.5 x 27.3
IWM ART 2255

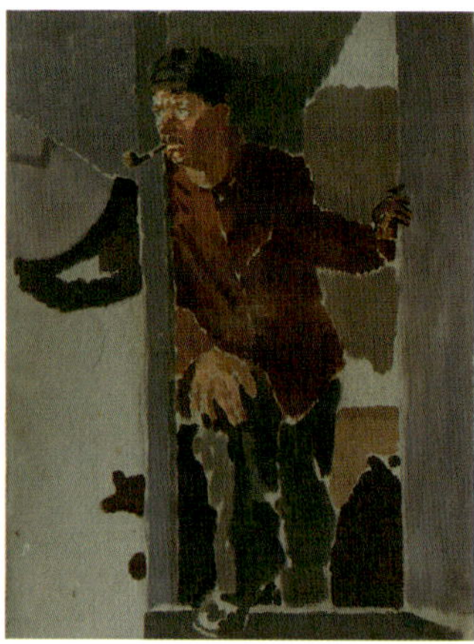

Wheatley, John 1892–1955
A Greaser: Admiralty Salvage Ship 1918
oil on panel 35.5 x 31.1
IWM ART 2252

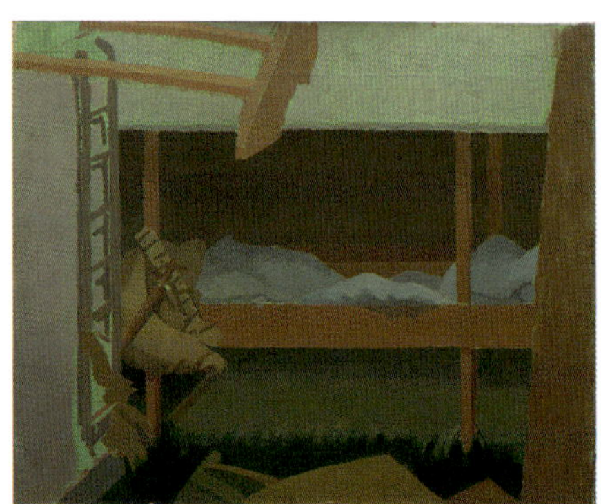

Wheatley, John 1892–1955
A Torpedoed American Troopship Sinking
1918
oil on canvas 43.1 x 53.3
IWM ART 2248

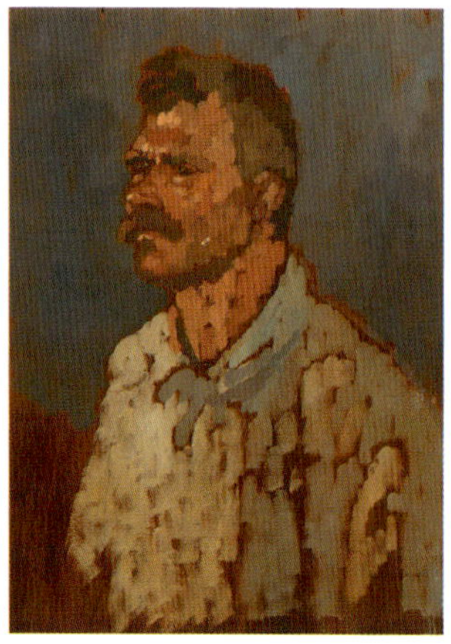

Wheatley, John 1892–1955
An Able Seaman, Royal Naval Reserve 1918
oil on panel 41.2 x 31.1
IWM ART 2254

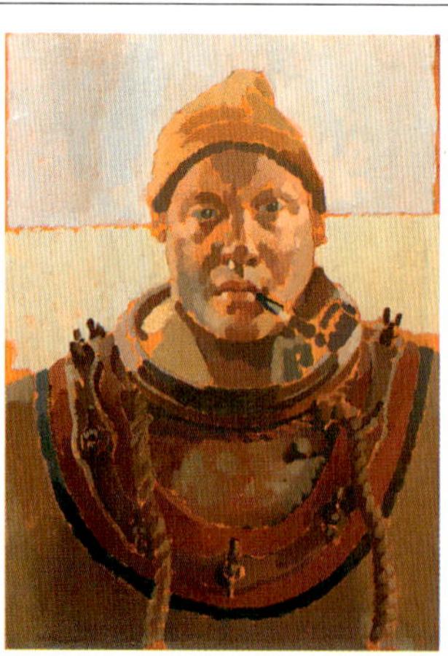

Wheatley, John 1892–1955
An Admiralty Salvage Diver (1) 1918
oil on panel 41.2 x 31.1
IWM ART 2250

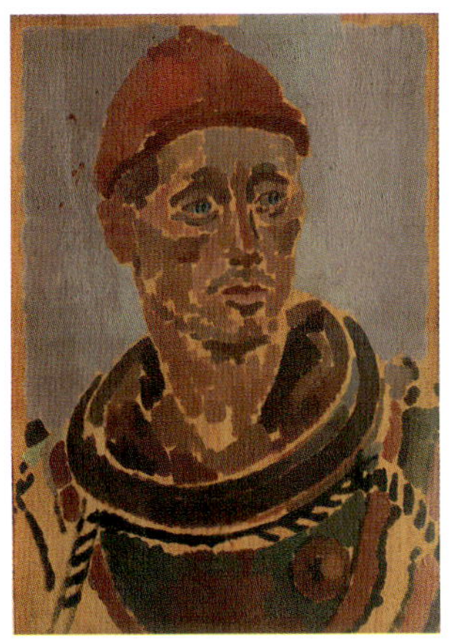

Wheatley, John 1892–1955
An Admiralty Salvage Diver (2) 1918
oil on panel 33.6 x 24.1
IWM ART 2251

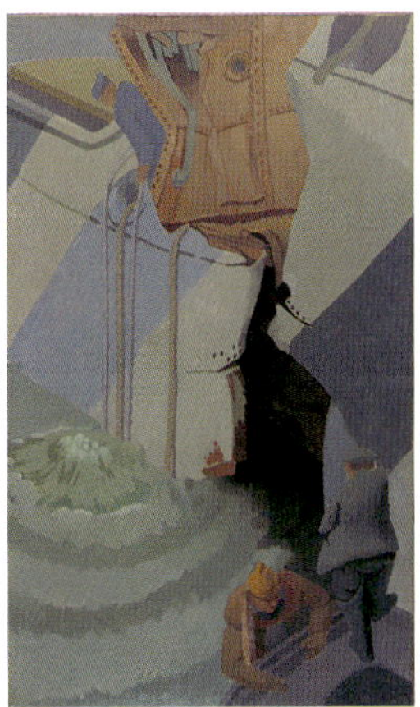

Wheatley, John 1892–1955
An Armoured Cruiser, Showing Fracture:
Divers Going down to Investigate 1918
oil on canvas 76.2 x 45.7
IWM ART 2246

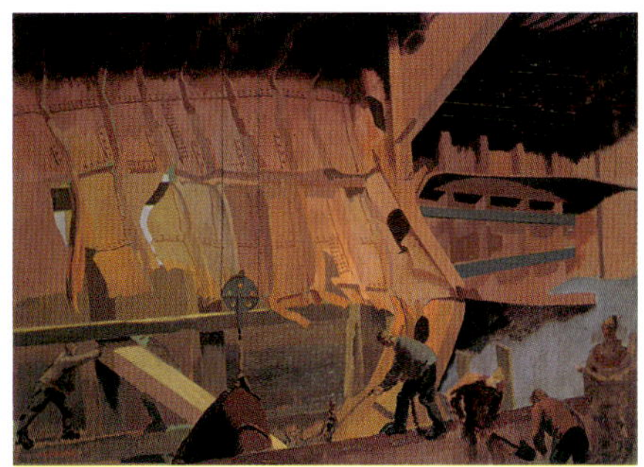

Wheatley, John 1892–1955
Divers at Work Repairing a Torpedoed Ship
1918
oil on canvas 106.6 x 152.4
IWM ART 2245

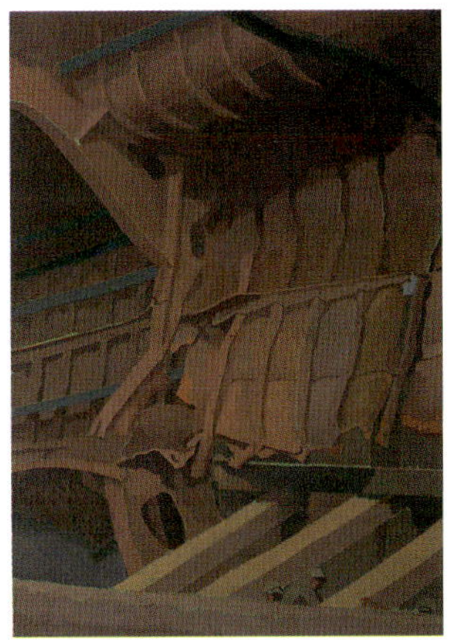

Wheatley, John 1892–1955
Repairing a Fracture in a Torpedoed Merchant
Ship 1918
oil on canvas 106.6 x 76.2
IWM ART 2247

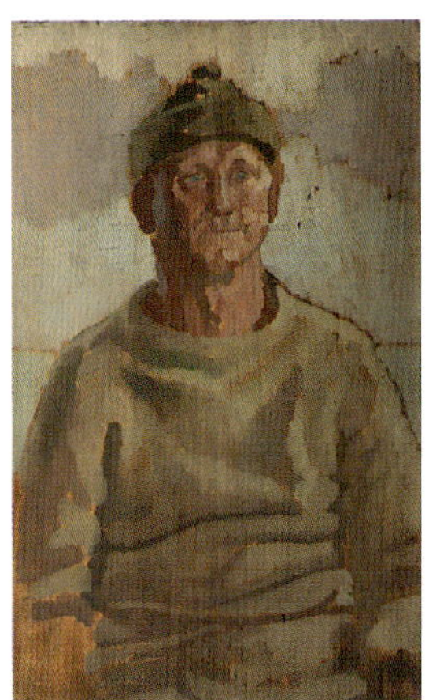

Wheatley, John 1892–1955
The Head Diver: Admiralty Salvage Section
1918
oil on panel 48.8 x 31.1
IWM ART 2253

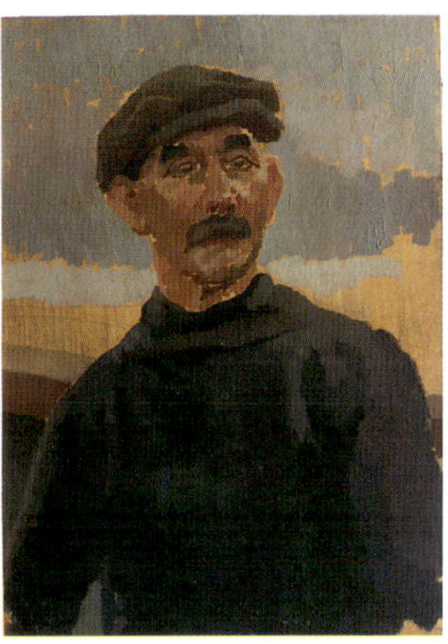

Wheatley, John 1892–1955
The Royal Naval Reserve Skipper 1918
oil on panel 41.2 x 31.1
IWM ART 2249

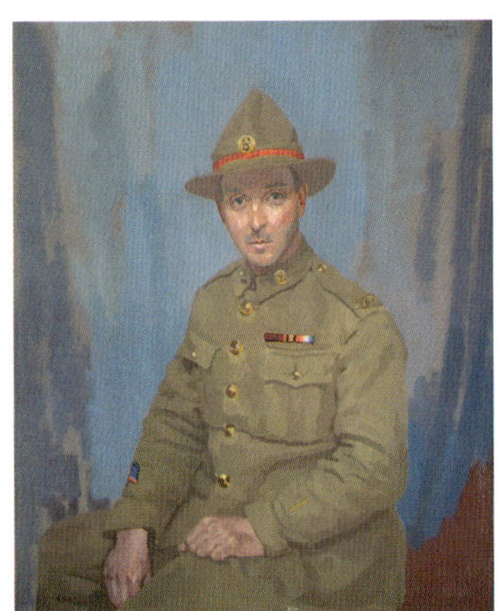

Wheatley, John 1892–1955
Private James Crichton (1879–1961), VC,
Auckland Regiment, New Zealand
Expeditionary Forces 1919
oil on canvas 91.4 x 81.2
IWM ART 1923

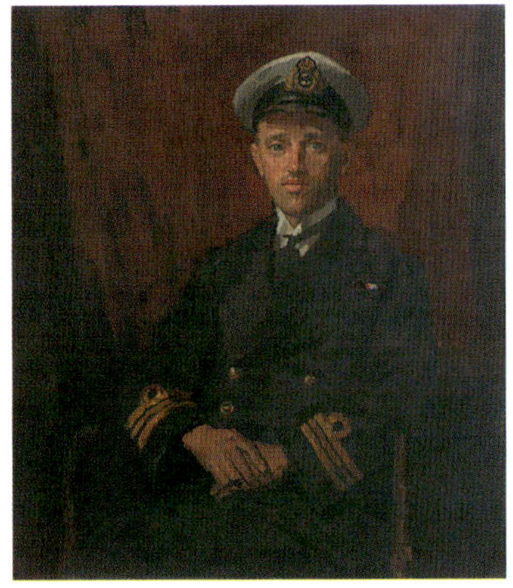

Wheatley, John 1892–1955
Lieutenant Commander Norman Douglas
Holbrook (1888–1976), VC 1920
oil on canvas 91.4 x 81.2
IWM ART 3140

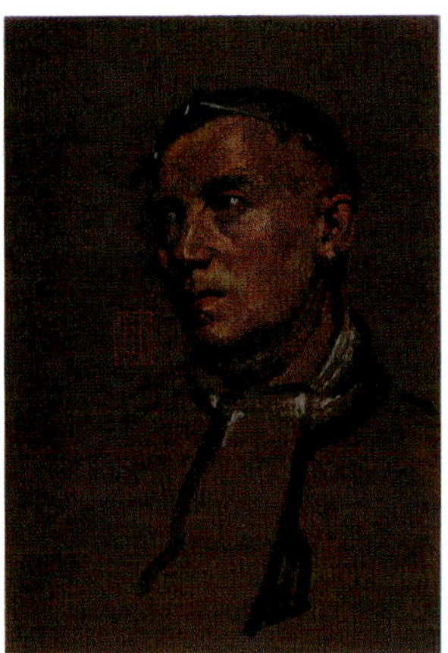

Wheatley, John 1892–1955
Edward Roche: A Head Melter at a Sheffield
Munition Factory
tempera on board 55.7 x 38
IWM ART LD 2483

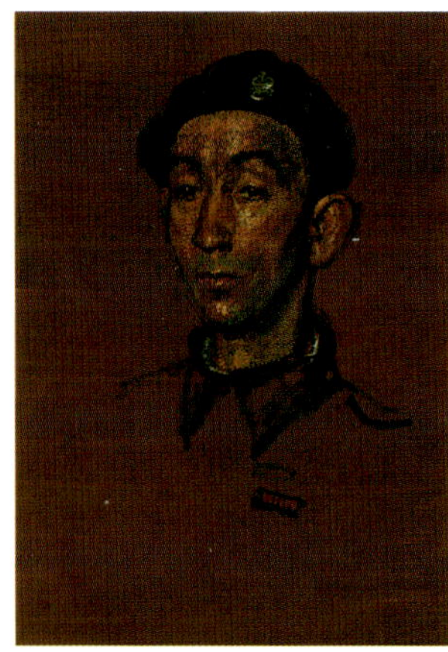

Wheatley, John 1892–1955
Leslie Croft, GM, of Sheffield
tempera on board 45 x 29.8
IWM ART LD 1914

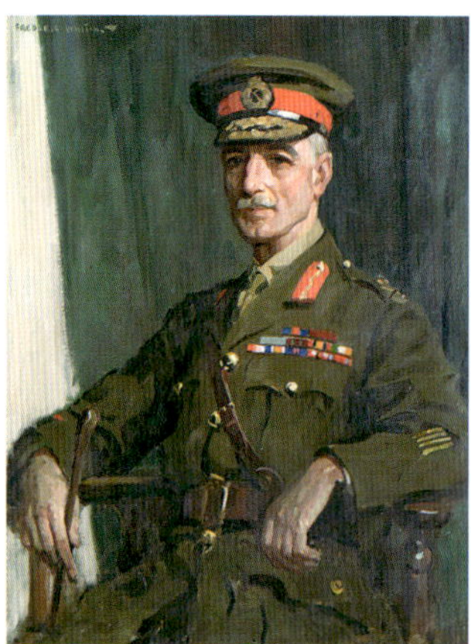

Whiting, Frederic 1874–1962
General Sir W. R. Marshall, KCB 1919
oil on canvas 91.4 x 71.1
IWM ART 2000

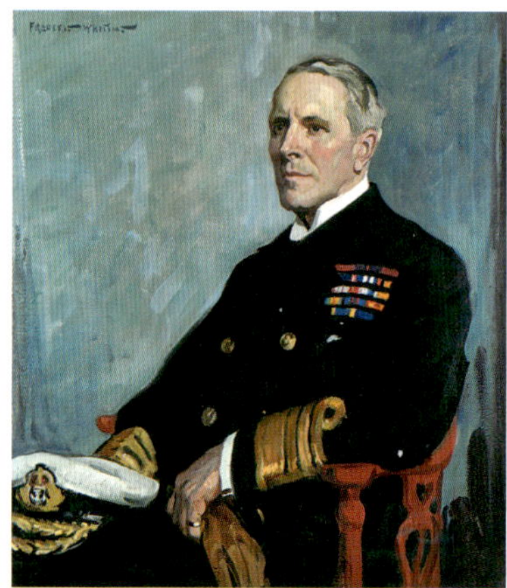

Whiting, Frederic 1874–1962
*Admiral Sir R. H. Pierse, KCB, KBE,
MVO* 1920
oil on canvas 91.4 x 81.2
IWM ART 3056

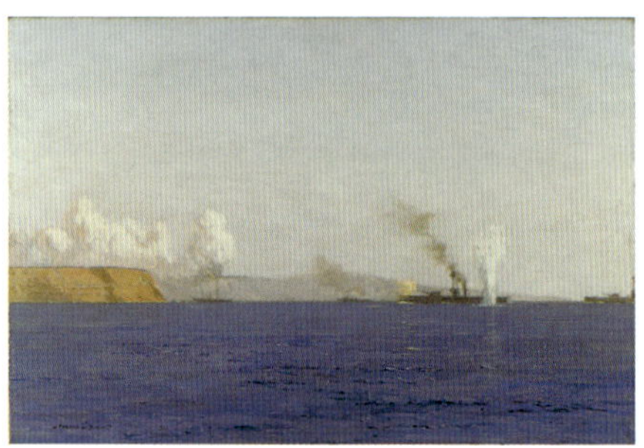

Wilkinson, Norman 1878–1971
*A Monitor with 14-Inch Guns Shelling Yeni
Sher Village and the Asiatic Batteries*
1915–1918
oil on canvas 60.9 x 91.4
IWM ART 2752

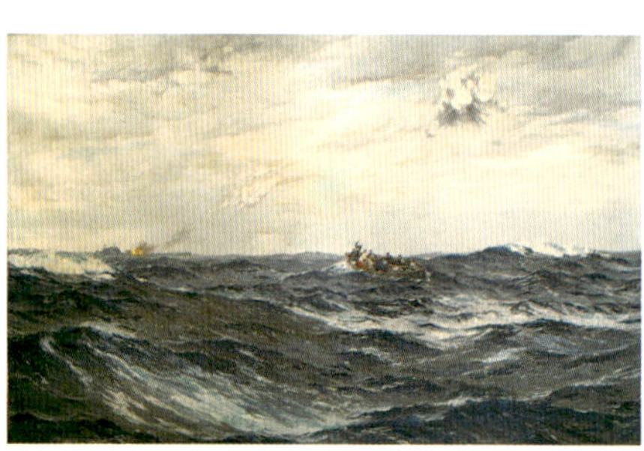

Wilkinson, Norman 1878–1971
Lest We Forget 1915–1918
oil on canvas 215.3 x 337.8
IWM ART 5278

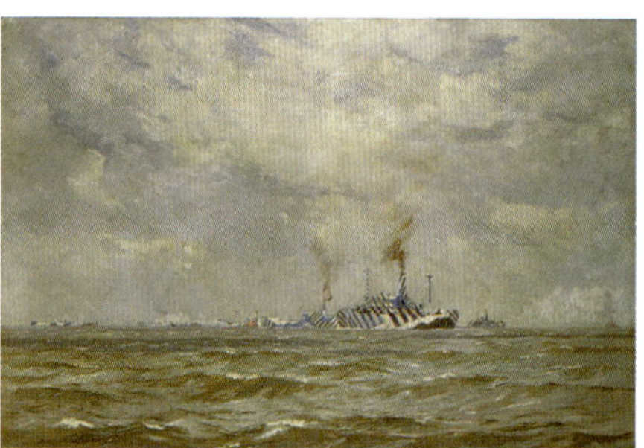

Wilkinson, Norman 1878–1971
A Convoy of Dazzled Ships in the Channel
1918
oil on canvas 101.9 x 152.4
IWM ART 4030

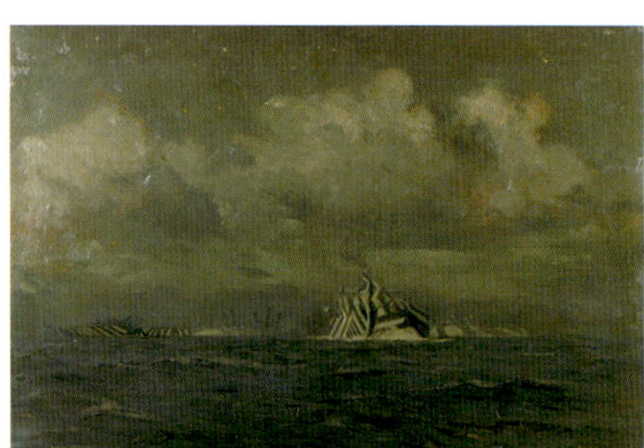

Wilkinson, Norman 1878–1971
Dazzled Ships at Night 1918
oil on canvas 102.5 x 152.5
IWM ART 4029

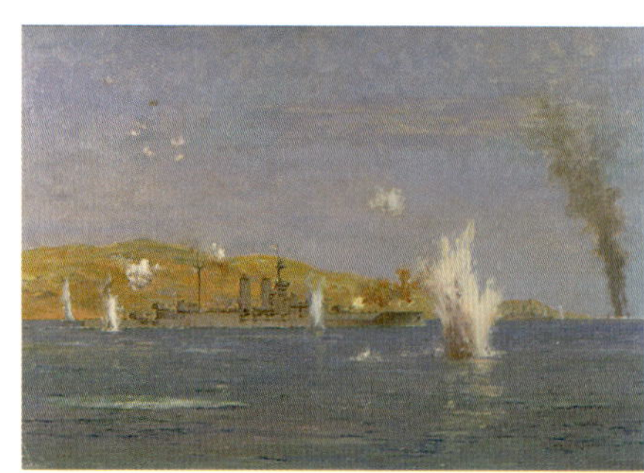

Wilkinson, Norman 1878–1971
*'HMS Queen Elizabeth' Shelling Forts,
Dardanelles: The Attack on the Narrows,
Gallipoli, 18 March 1915* 1919
oil on canvas 63.5 x 93.9
IWM ART 249

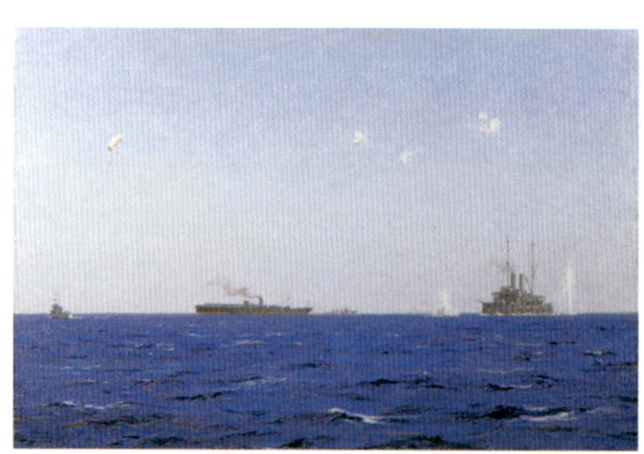

Wilkinson, Norman 1878–1971
*The Balloon Ship Hector with Kite Balloon
Spotting off the Left Flank, Dardanelles
Operations, 1915* 1919
oil on canvas 60.9 x 91.4 (E)
IWM ART 2453

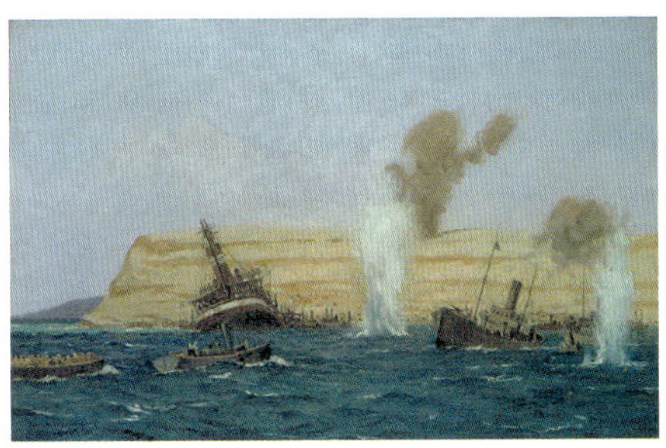

Wilkinson, Norman 1878–1971
The Base Camp, Cape Helles, under Shell Fire, August 1915: The 'SS River Clyde' Aground 1919
oil on canvas 60.9 x 91.4 (E)
IWM ART 2450

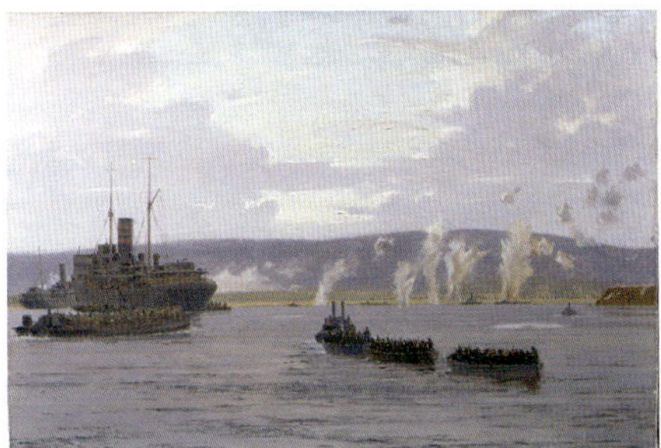

Wilkinson, Norman 1878–1971
The Landing in Suvla Bay: Early Morning, 7 August 1915 1919
oil on canvas 60.9 x 91.4
IWM ART 2451

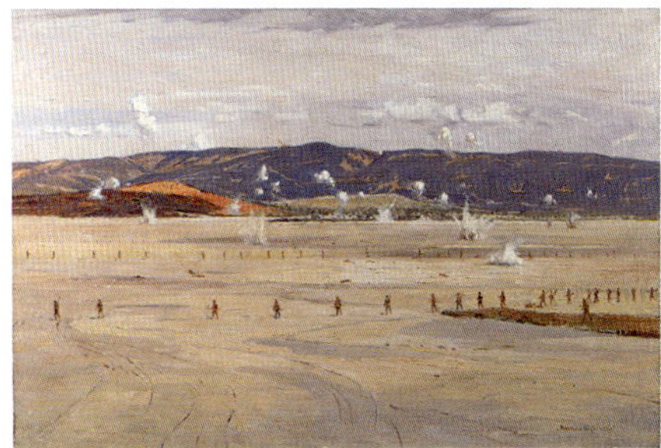

Wilkinson, Norman 1878–1971
The Salt Lake, Suvla Bay: The Advance, 21 August 1915 1919
oil on canvas 60.9 x 91.4 (E)
IWM ART 2326

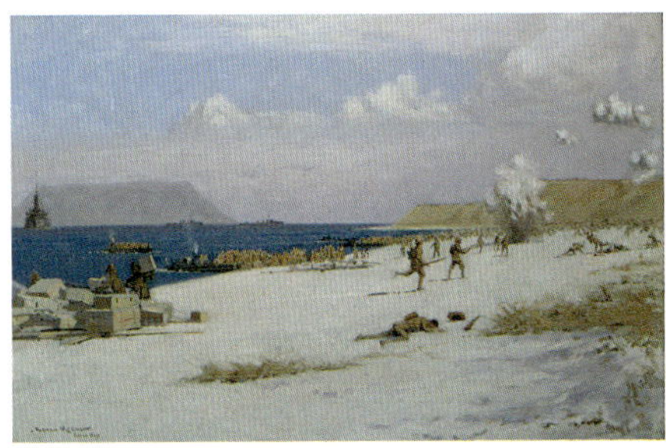

Wilkinson, Norman 1878–1971
Troops Landing on C Beach, Suvla Bay, Later in the Day, 7 August 1915 1919
oil on canvas 60.9 x 91.4 (E)
IWM ART 2452

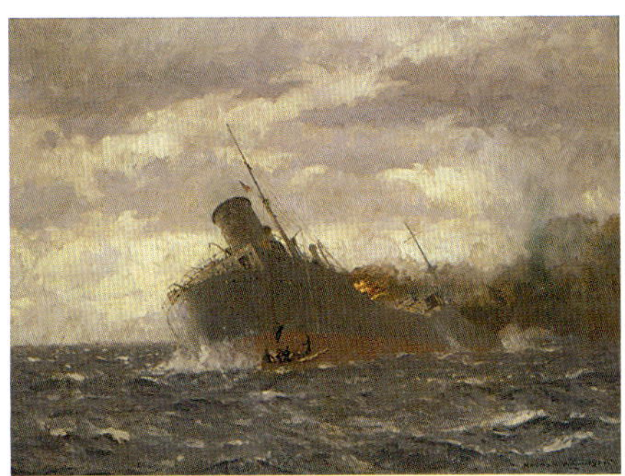

Wilkinson, Norman 1878–1971
The Crew Reboarding the Tanker 'San Demetrio', 7 November 1940 1940
oil on canvas 76.2 x 101.9
IWM ART LD 6006

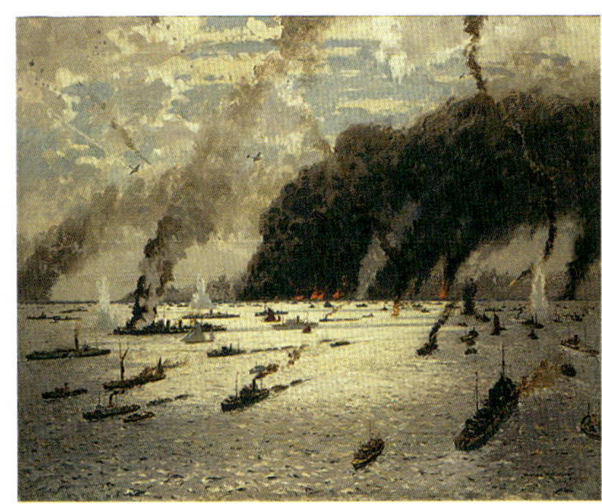

Wilkinson, Norman 1878–1971
The Little Ships at Dunkirk, June 1940 1940
oil on canvas 101.9 x 127
IWM ART LD 6007

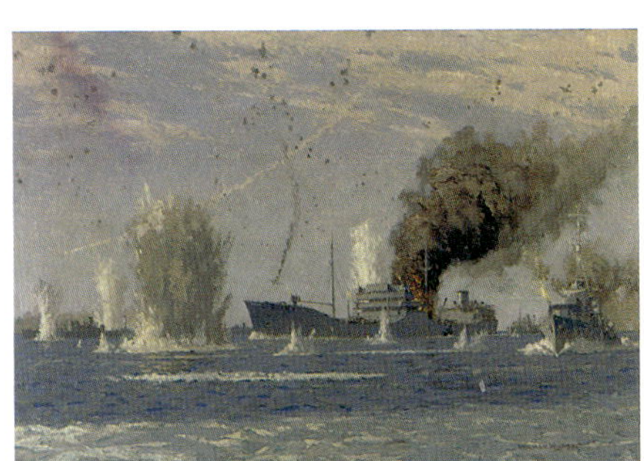

Wilkinson, Norman 1878–1971
The Tanker 'Ohio' in a Malta Convoy: August 1942 1942
oil on canvas 76.2 x 114.3
IWM ART LD 6005

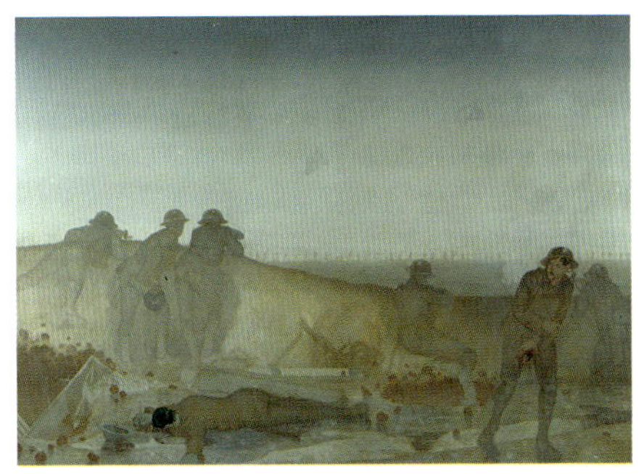

Williamson, Harold Sandys 1892–1978
A German Attack on a Wet Morning, April 1918 1918
oil on canvas 106.6 x 152.4
IWM ART 1986

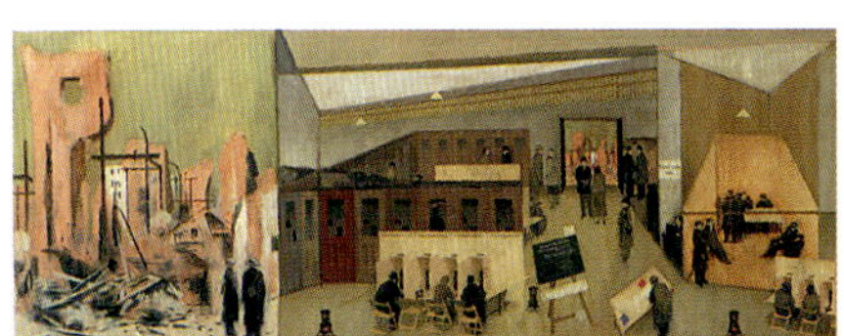

Williamson, Harold Sandys 1892–1978
An Emergency Telephone Office in the City, January 1941 1941
oil on canvas 40.6 x 101.9
IWM ART LD 1189

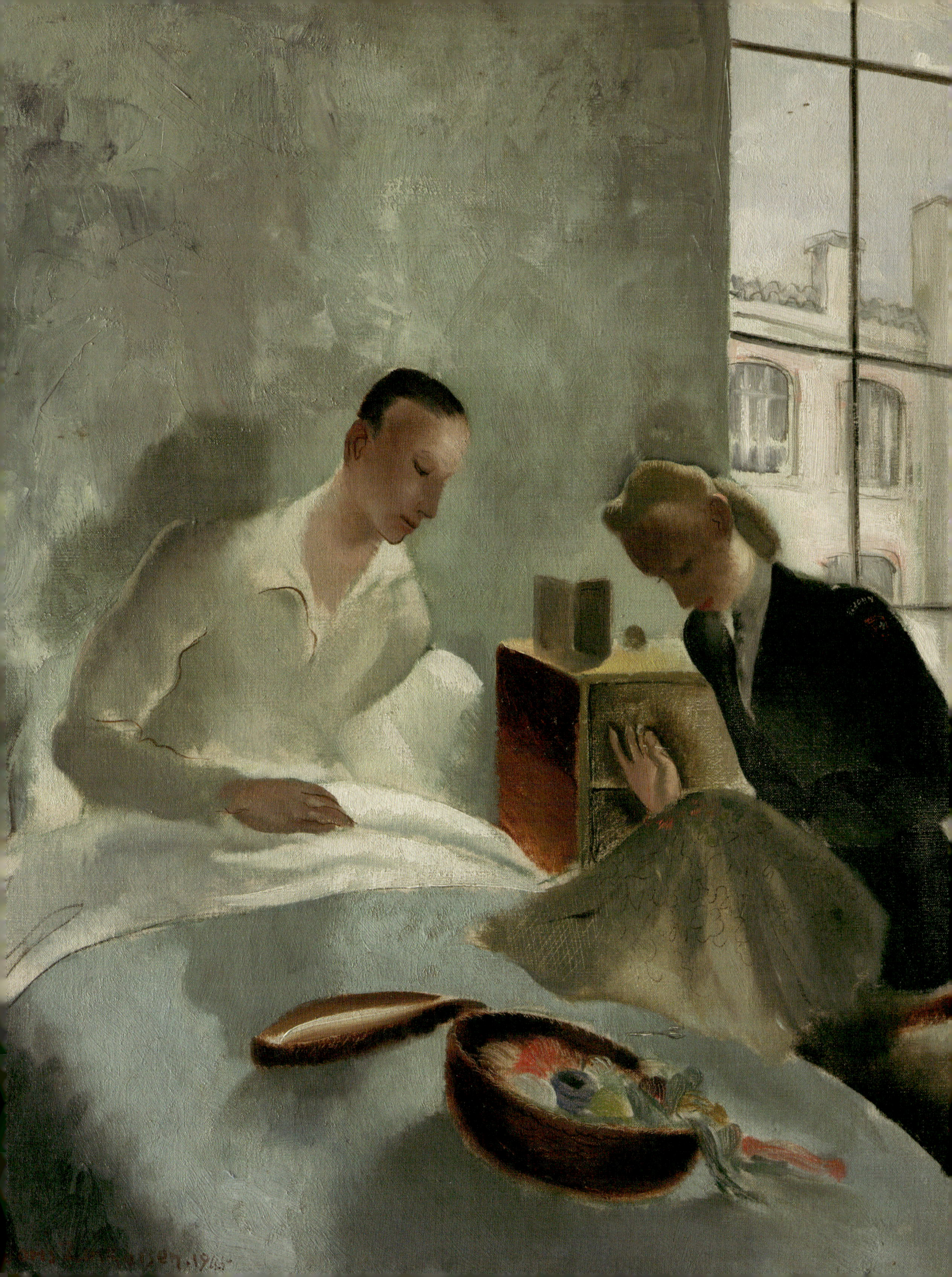

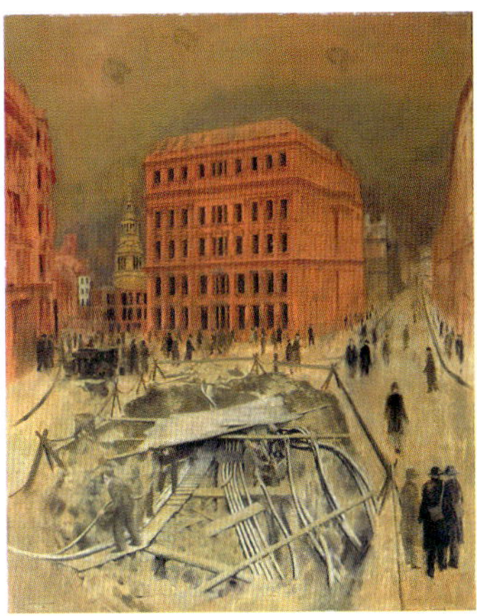

Williamson, Harold Sandys 1892–1978
St Martin's le Grand, London, January 1941
1941
oil on canvas 76.2 x 60.9
IWM ART LD 1188

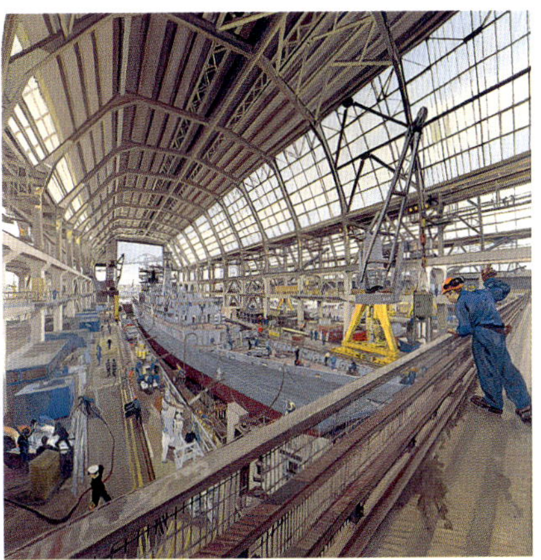

Wonnacott, John b.1940
Refit, Devonport 1990
oil on board 244 x 243
IWM ART 16409

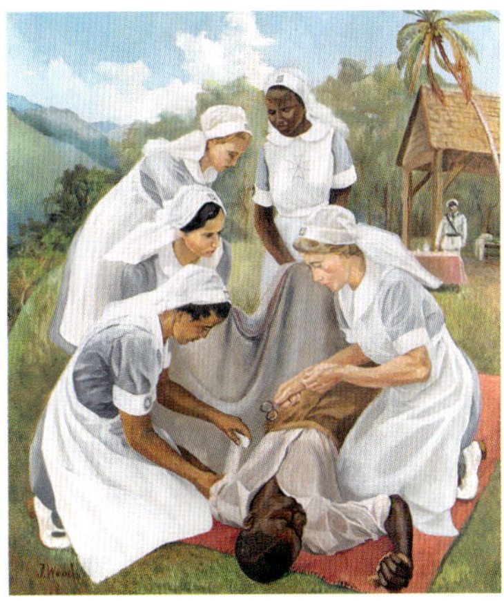

Wood, John active 1940s
Air Raid Precautions in Jamaica c.1941–1945
oil on canvas 95.8 x 85
IWM ART LD 3150

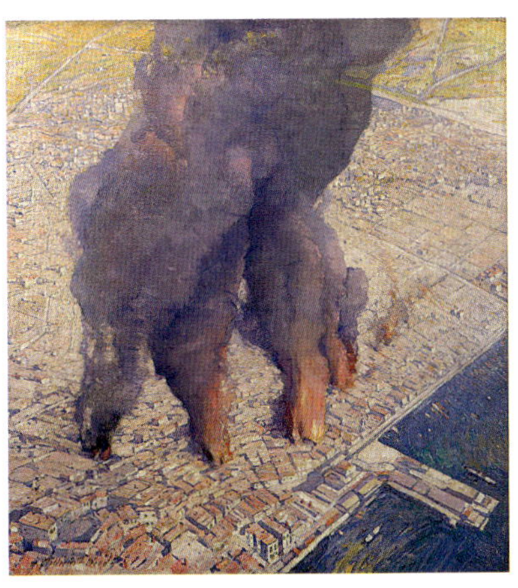

Wood, William Thomas 1877–1958
The Fire, Salonica: The Last Phase 1917–1918
oil on canvas 76.2 x 71.1
IWM ART 877

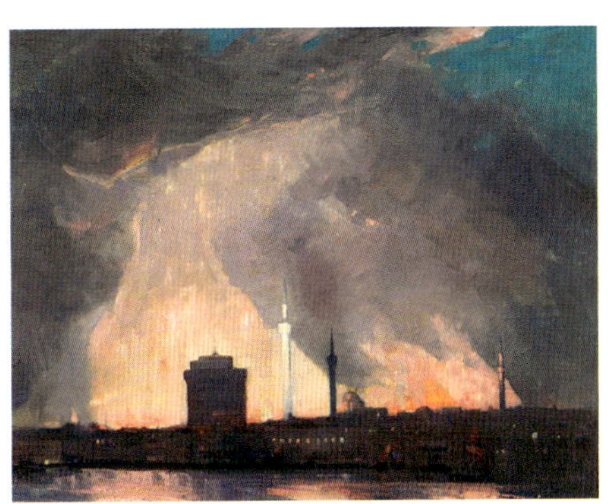

Wood, William Thomas 1877–1958
The Great Fire, Salonica: The Famous White Tower in the Foreground 1917–1918
oil on canvas 60.9 x 76.2
IWM ART 1489

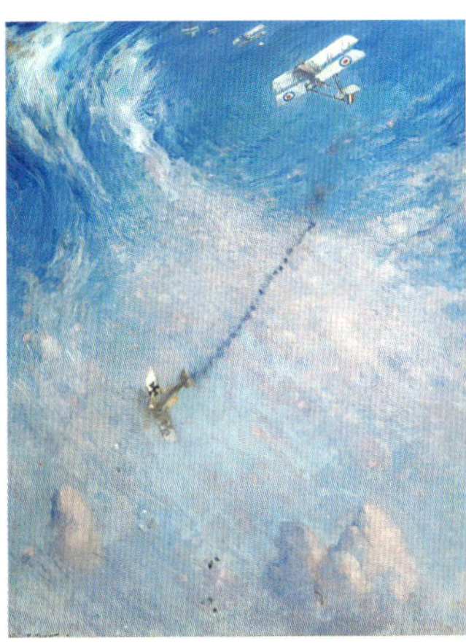

Wood, William Thomas 1877–1958
Crashed!: De Havilland 2 Single-Seater Scout Shooting down a 'Fokker' Monoplane Salonika
1918
oil on panel 76.2 x 60.9
IWM ART 796

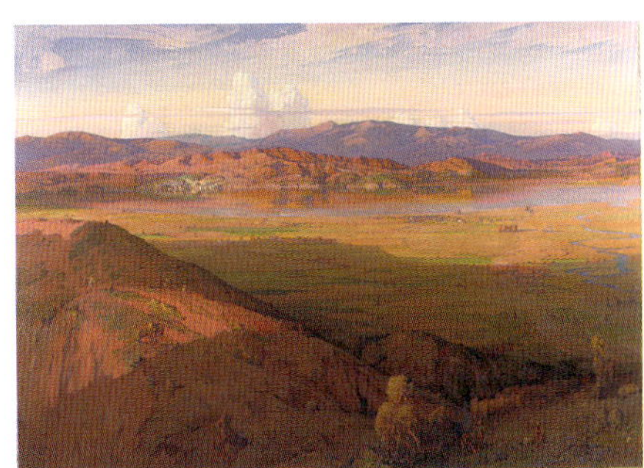

Wood, William Thomas 1877–1958
The Doiran Front, Seen from Sal Grec de Popovo 1918
oil on canvas 106.6 x 152.4
IWM ART 2244

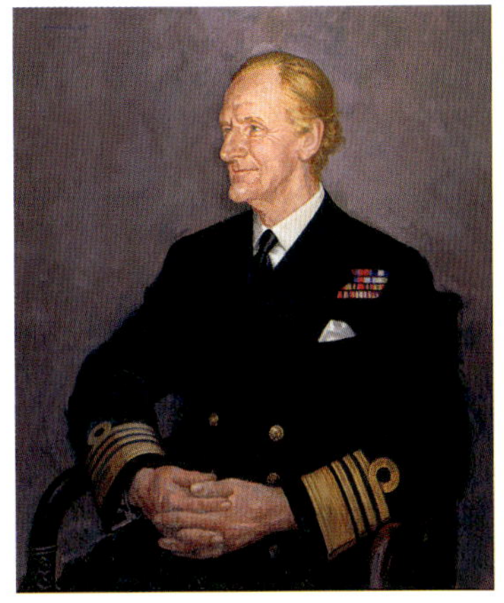

Woodington, Walter 1916–2000
Admiral Sir Deric Holland-Martin, GCB, DSO, DSC, Chairman of the Board of Trustees, Imperial War Museum (1966–1977) 1978
oil on canvas 91.4 x 77.4
IWM ART MW(A) 41

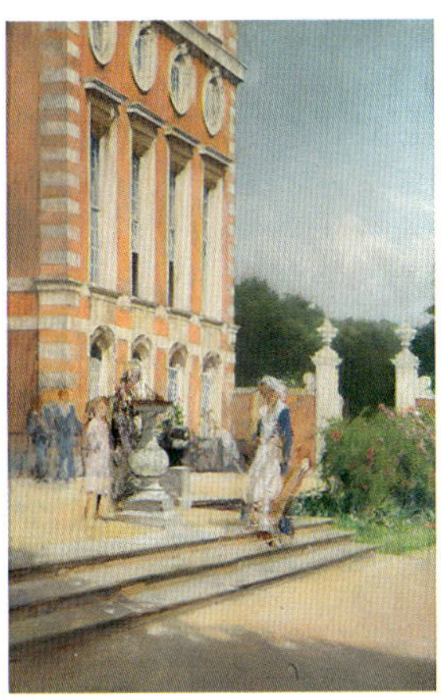

Woods, Henry 1846–1921
Christopher Wren Wing: Hampton Court Palace as a Hospital c.1914–1918
oil on panel 50.9 x 35.2
IWM ART 5250

Facing Page: Zinkeisen, Doris Clare, 1898–1991, *Welfare Work in a Services Hospital* (detail), 1945, (p. 235)

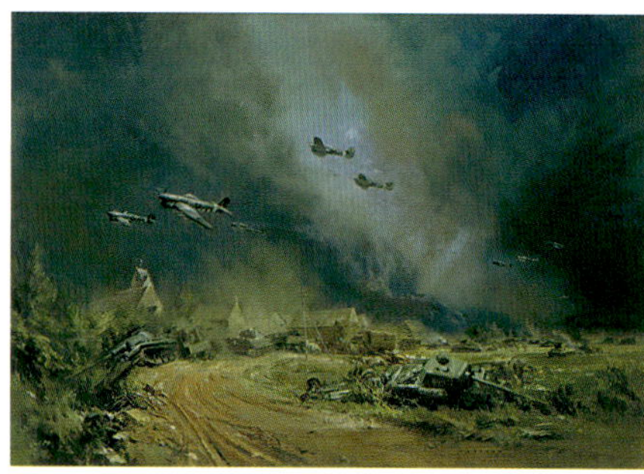

Wootton, Frank 1914–1998
Rocket-Firing Typhoons at the Falaise Gap, Normandy 1944
oil on canvas 105.4 x 151.1
IWM ART LD 4756

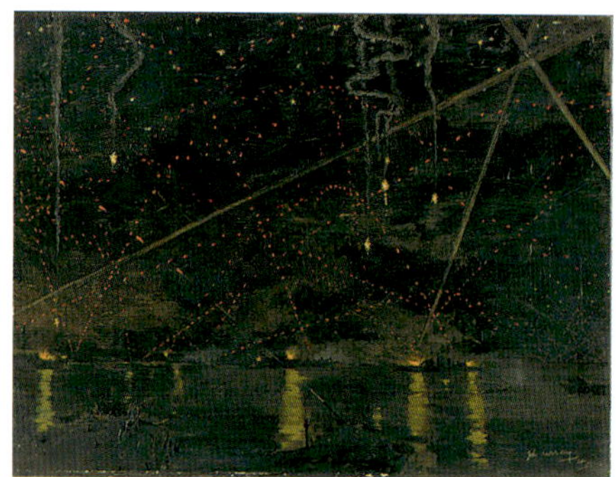

Worsley, John 1919–2000
A Night Air Raid over Augusta 1943
oil on canvas 60.3 x 83.8
IWM ART LD 3380

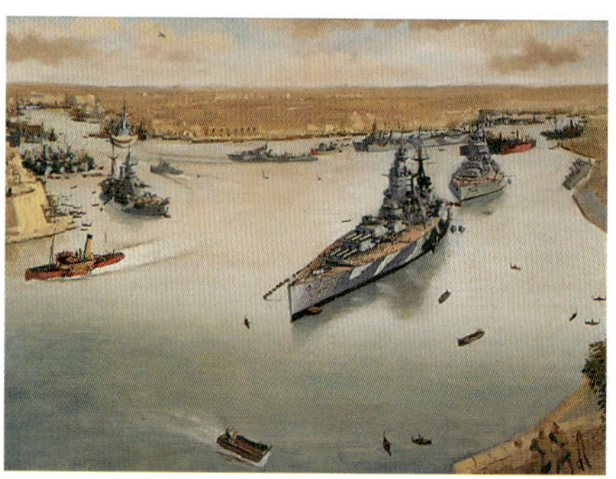

Worsley, John 1919–2000
Grand Harbour, Malta, October 1943 1943
oil on canvas 65.4 x 85
IWM ART LD 5156

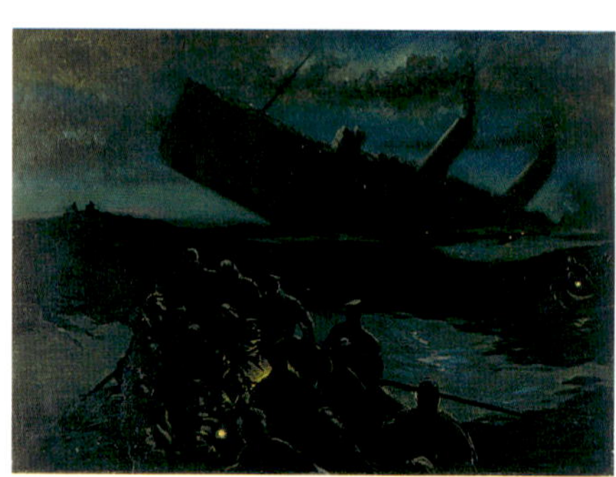

Worsley, John 1919–2000
The Last of the 'Laurentic' 1943
oil on canvas 76.2 x 106.6
IWM ART LD 984

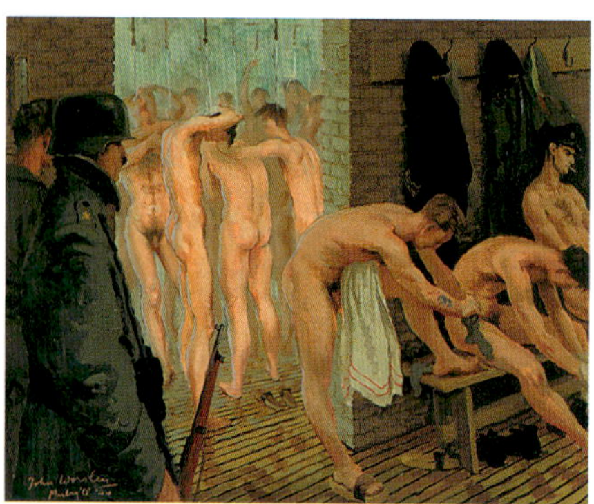

Worsley, John 1919–2000
Shower Room: Marlag 'O' 1944
oil on canvas 59.6 x 74.9
IWM ART LD 5153

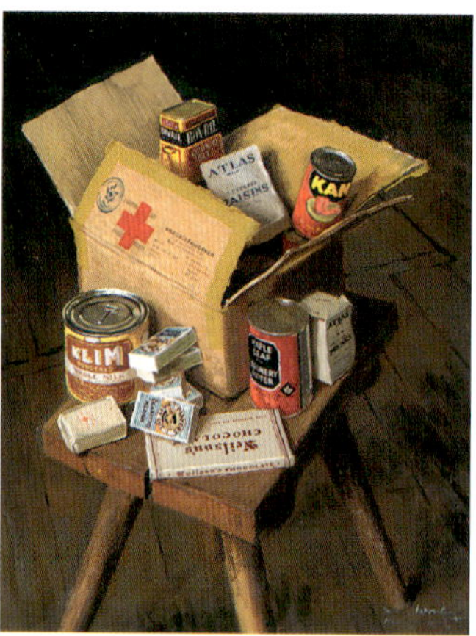

Worsley, John 1919–2000
The Contents of a Red Cross Parcel 1944
oil on linen 76.2 x 60.9
IWM ART LD 5155

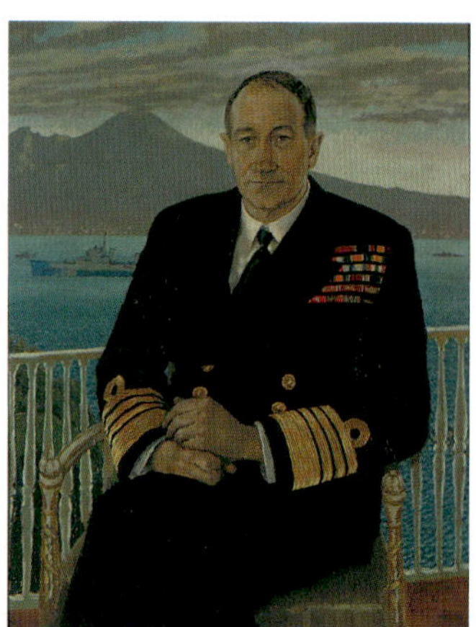

Worsley, John 1919–2000
Admiral Sir John Cunningham, KCB, MVO 1945
oil on canvas 88.9 x 71.1
IWM ART LD 5691

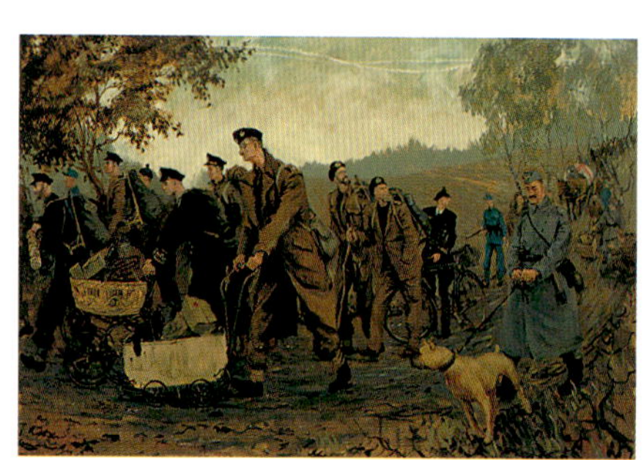

Worsley, John 1919–2000
Naval and Marine Prisoners of War on the March ahead of the Allied Advance in Germany between Bremen and Lübeck 1945
oil on canvas 91.4 x 137.1
IWM ART LD 5219

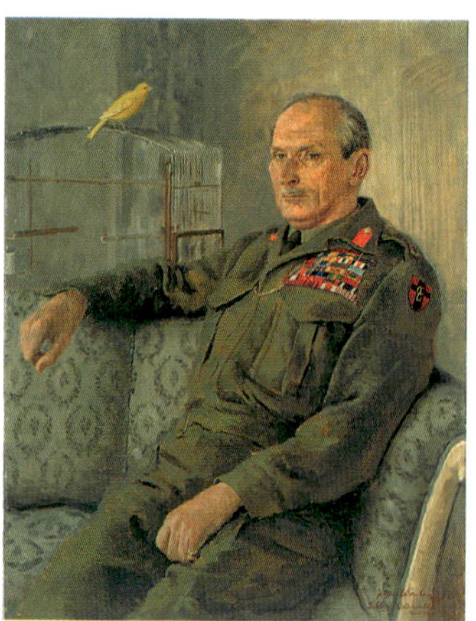

Worsley, John 1919–2000
Field Marshal the Viscount Montgomery of Alamein (1887–1976), GCB, SO 1946
oil on canvas 91.4 x 71.1
IWM ART LD 5802

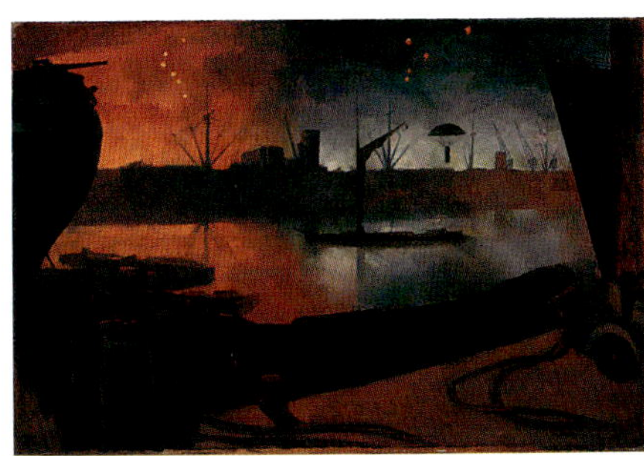

Wright, W. Matvyn b.1910
A Parachute Bomb 1941
oil on canvas 50.8 x 76.2
IWM ART LD 1355

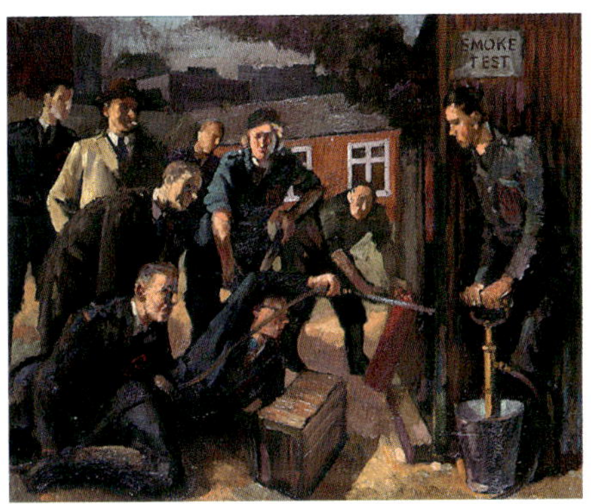

Wright, W. Matvyn b.1910
Fire Guard Training School: The Smoke Test
1943
oil on canvas 63.5 x 76.2
IWM ART LD 3039

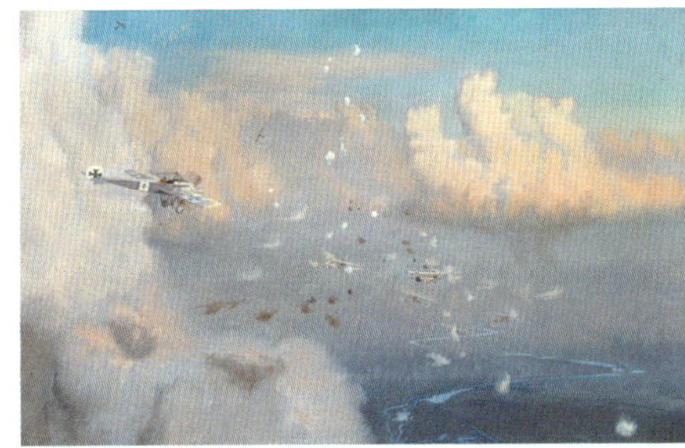

Wyllie, Harold 1880–1973
Army Reconnaissance 1919
oil on canvas 60.9 x 91.4
IWM ART 2754

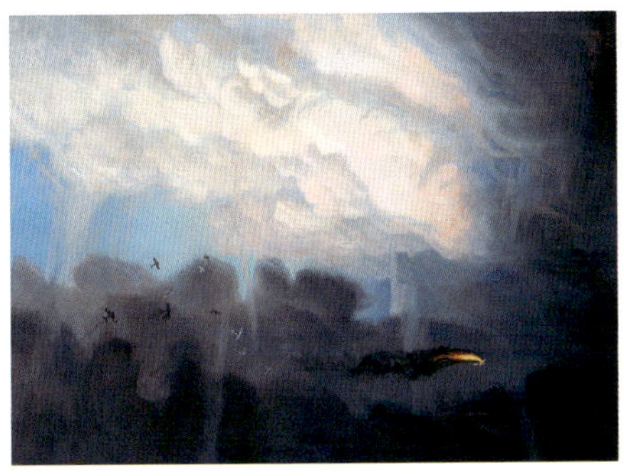

Wyllie, Harold 1880–1973
*An Air Fight, France (1917–1918): Formation
of Six SE5 Machines and Six Albatross Scouts
in Combat* 1920
oil on canvas 76.2 x 101.9
IWM ART 3199

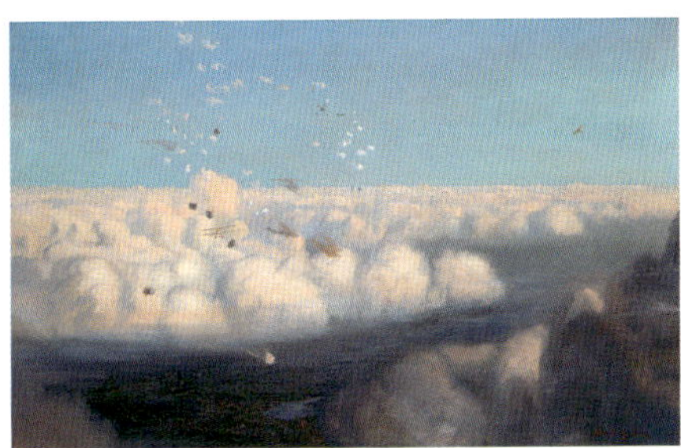

Wyllie, Harold 1880–1973
*Artillery Observation: BE2c Machines over
Hooge Ranging British Guns by Means of
Wireless Telegraphy, 1915* 1920
oil on canvas 60.9 x 91.4 (E)
IWM ART 2920

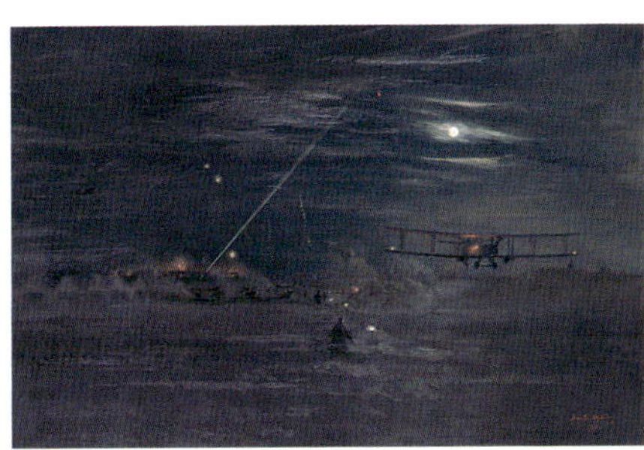

Wyllie, Harold 1880–1973
*Night Bombers Getting Off from Trezennes
Aerodrome, 1917* 1920
oil on canvas 60.9 x 91.4 (E)
IWM ART 4028

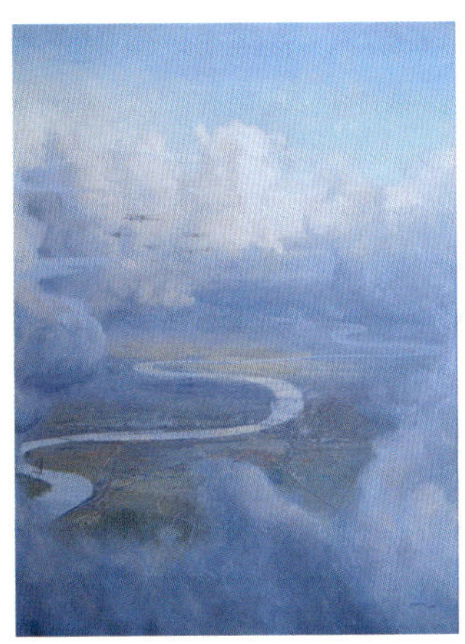

Wyllie, Harold 1880–1973
*The Aerial Watch on the Rhine: A Formation of
DH9a Machines on Patrol over Cologne, Army
of Occupation, 1918* 1920
oil on canvas 101.9 x 76.2
IWM ART 2845

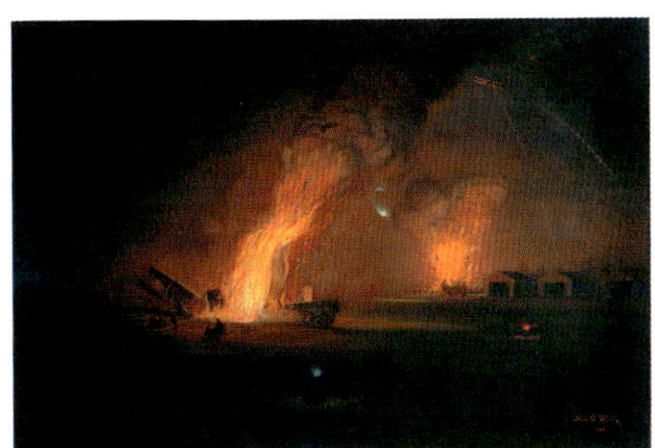

Wyllie, Harold 1880–1973
*The Bombing of Bissheghem Aerodrome: Night,
20 October 1917* 1920
oil on canvas 60.9 x 91.4
IWM ART 3993

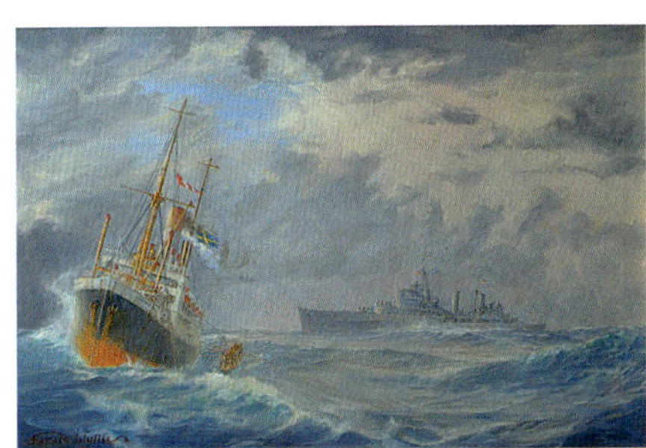

Wyllie, Harold 1880–1973
*'HMS Belfast' on Northern Patrol Captures the
German Blockade Runner 'Cap Norte', 13,615
Tons, 9 October 1939* 1968
oil on canvas 48.5 x 74
IWM ART 16801

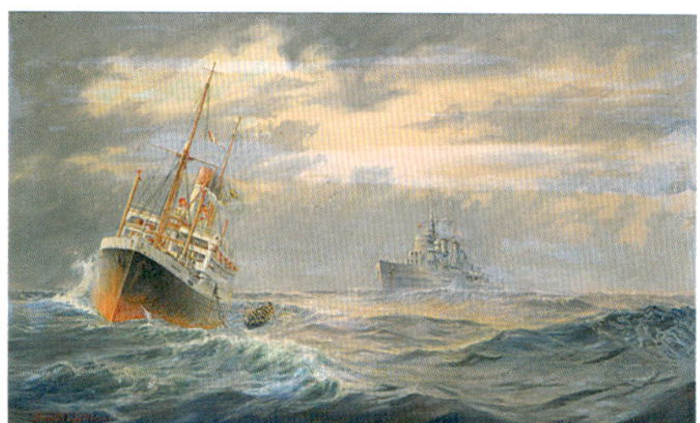

Wyllie, Harold 1880–1973
The 'Belfast' Boarding a German Merchant Ship c.1968
oil on canvas 59.7 x 99.1
IWM ART 17109

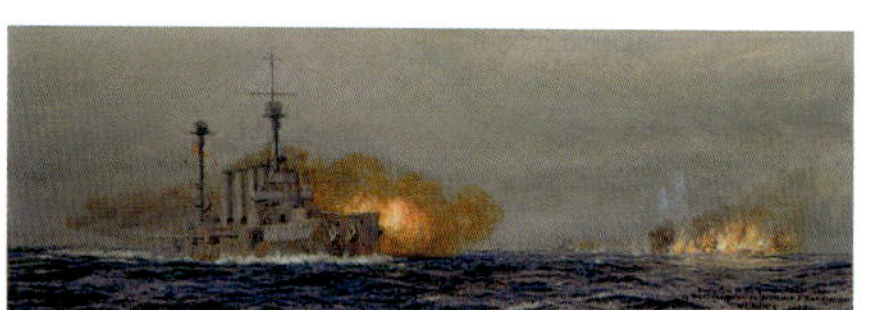

Wyllie, William Lionel 1851–1931
Destruction of the German Raider 'Leopard' by 'HMS Achilles' and 'HMS Dundee' 1920
oil on canvas 30.5 x 89.2
IWM ART 15814

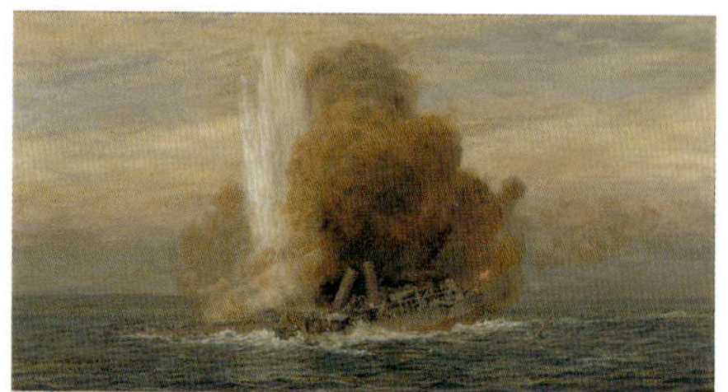

Wyllie, William Lionel 1851–1931
Loss of 'HMS Pathfinder', 5 September 1914 1920
oil on canvas 40.6 x 76.2
IWM ART 5721

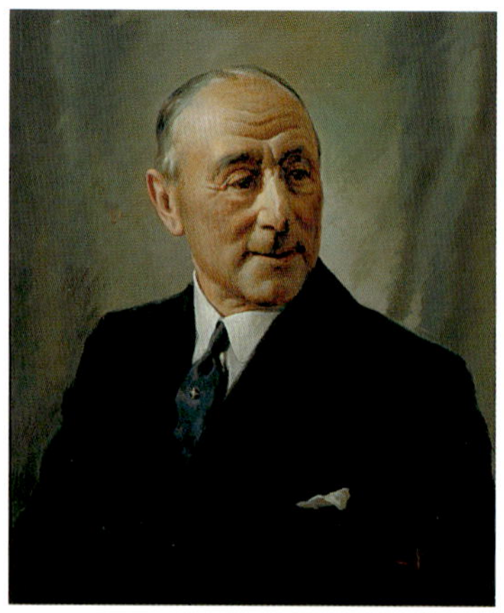

Ximming, Elio active 1940s
Portrait of a Man c.1940–1945
oil on board 61.5 x 51.5
IWM ART 5726

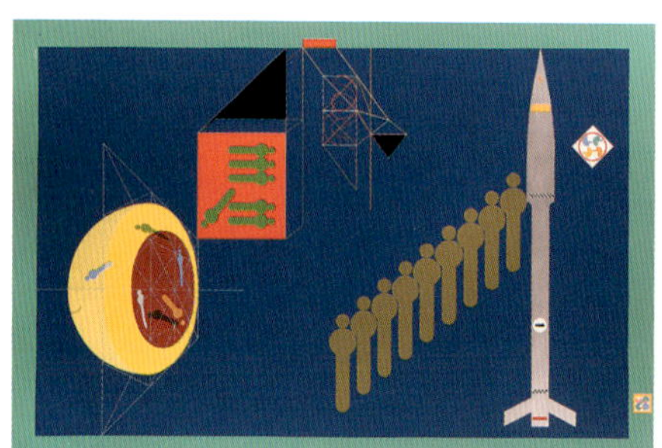

Yale, Brian b.1936
War 1967
oil & house paint on board 122 x 183
IWM ART 15049

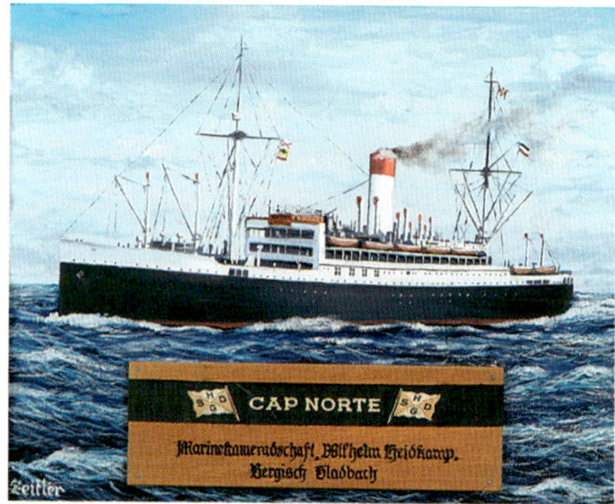

Zeitler
Liner 'Cap Norte'
oil on board 40 x 50.3
IWM ART 16570

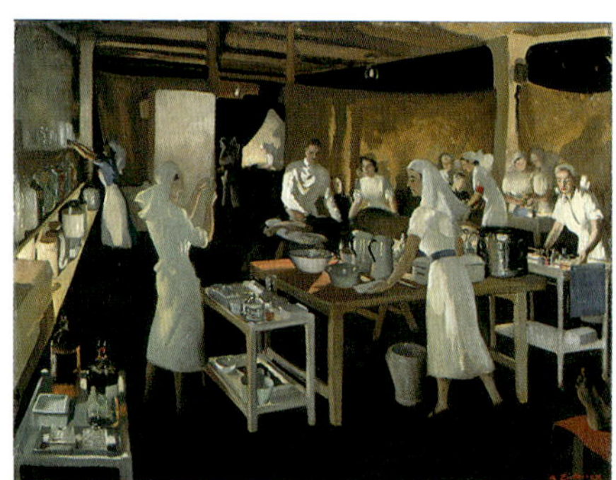

Zinkeisen, Anna Katrina 1901–1976
St Mary's First Aid Post by Candlelight 1941
oil on canvas 76.2 x 101.9
IWM ART LD 1442

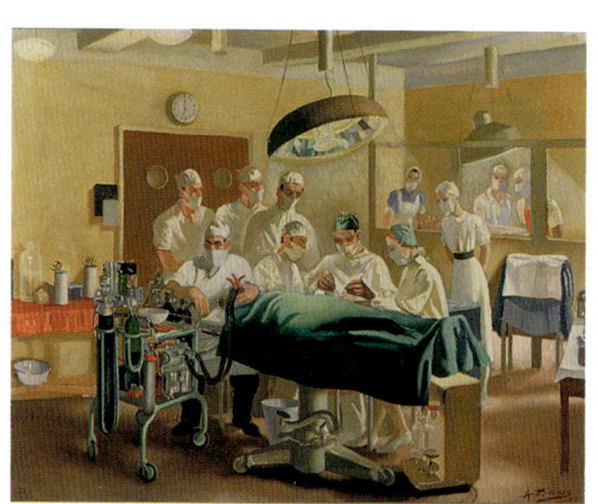

Zinkeisen, Anna Katrina 1901–1976
Archibald McIndoe: Consultant in Plastic Surgery to the Royal Air Force, Operating at the Queen Victoria Plastic (…) 1944
oil on canvas 71.1 x 91.4
IWM ART LD 6001

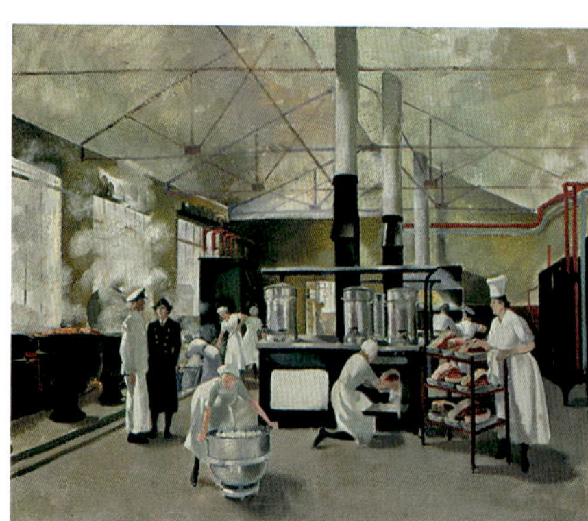

Zinkeisen, Doris Clare 1898–1991
A Women's Royal Naval Service Galley 1945
oil on canvas 63.5 x 76.2
IWM ART LD 2279

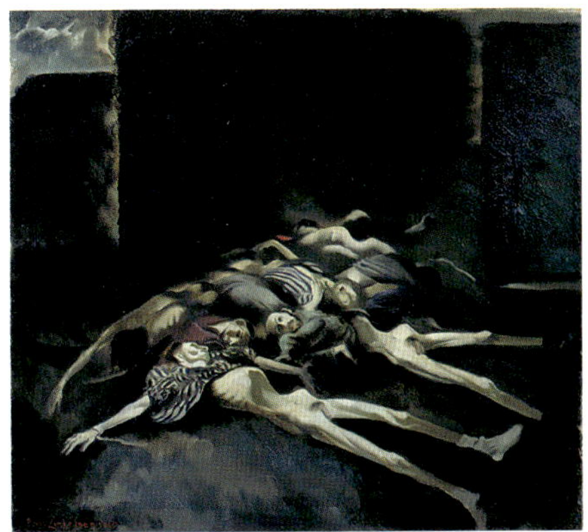

Zinkeisen, Doris Clare 1898–1991
Belsen, April 1945 1945
oil on canvas 62.2 x 69.8
IWM ART LD 5467

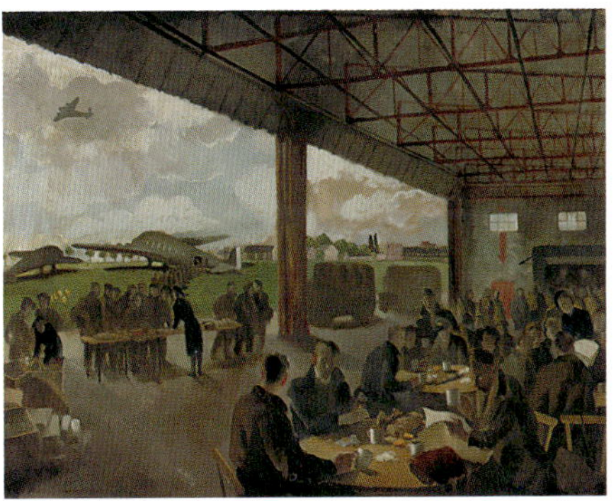

Zinkeisen, Doris Clare 1898–1991
Feeding Liberated Prisoners of War before They Are Flown Home, Brussels Airport 1945
oil on canvas 71.1 x 91.4
IWM ART LD 5998

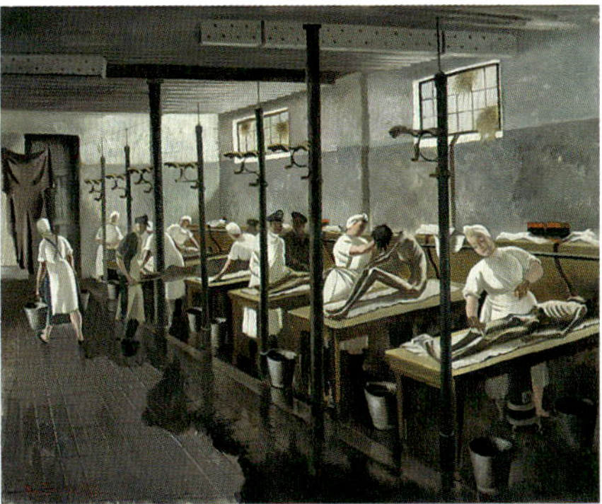

Zinkeisen, Doris Clare 1898–1991
Human Laundry, Belsen, April 1945 1945
oil on canvas 80.4 x 100
IWM ART LD 5468

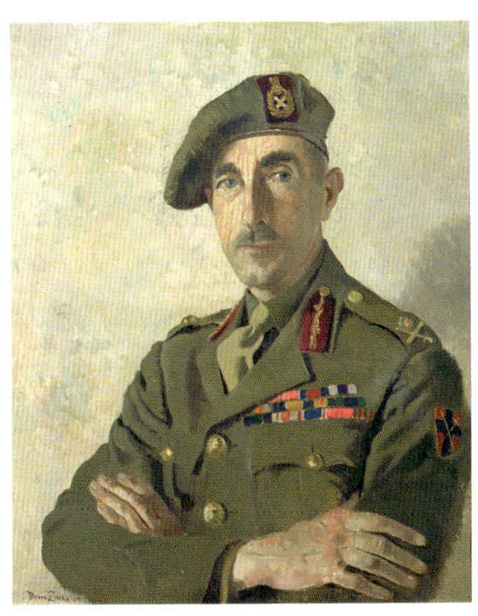

Zinkeisen, Doris Clare 1898–1991
Major General E. Phillips, CBE, DSO, MC, Director of Medical Services, British Liberation Army 1945
oil on canvas 72.3 x 59.6
IWM ART LD 5470

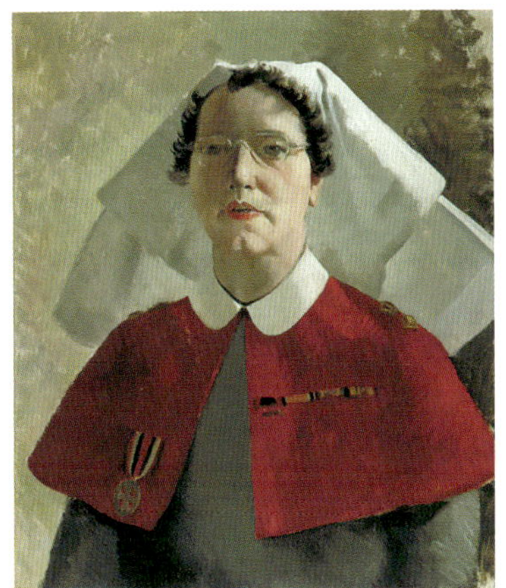

Zinkeisen, Doris Clare 1898–1991
Miss S. A. W. Wade, RRC, Principal Matron, 101 British General Hospital 1945
oil on canvas 72.3 x 59.6
IWM ART LD 5469

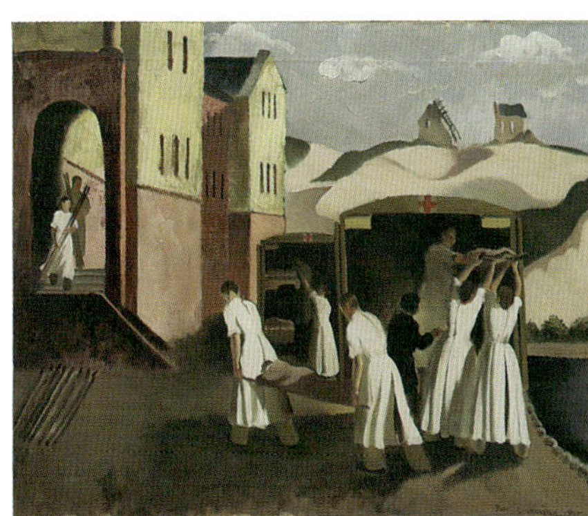

Zinkeisen, Doris Clare 1898–1991
No.115 British General Hospital, Ostend: Unloading Wounded 1945
oil on canvas 63.5 x 76.2
IWM ART LD 5999

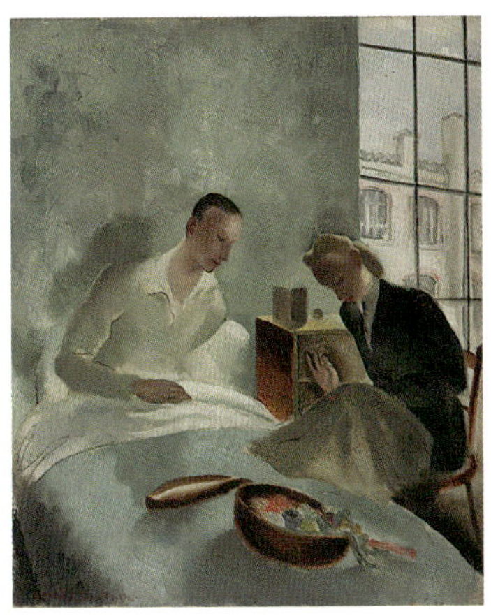

Zinkeisen, Doris Clare 1898–1991
Welfare Work in a Services Hospital 1945
oil on canvas 60.9 x 50.8
IWM ART LD 6000

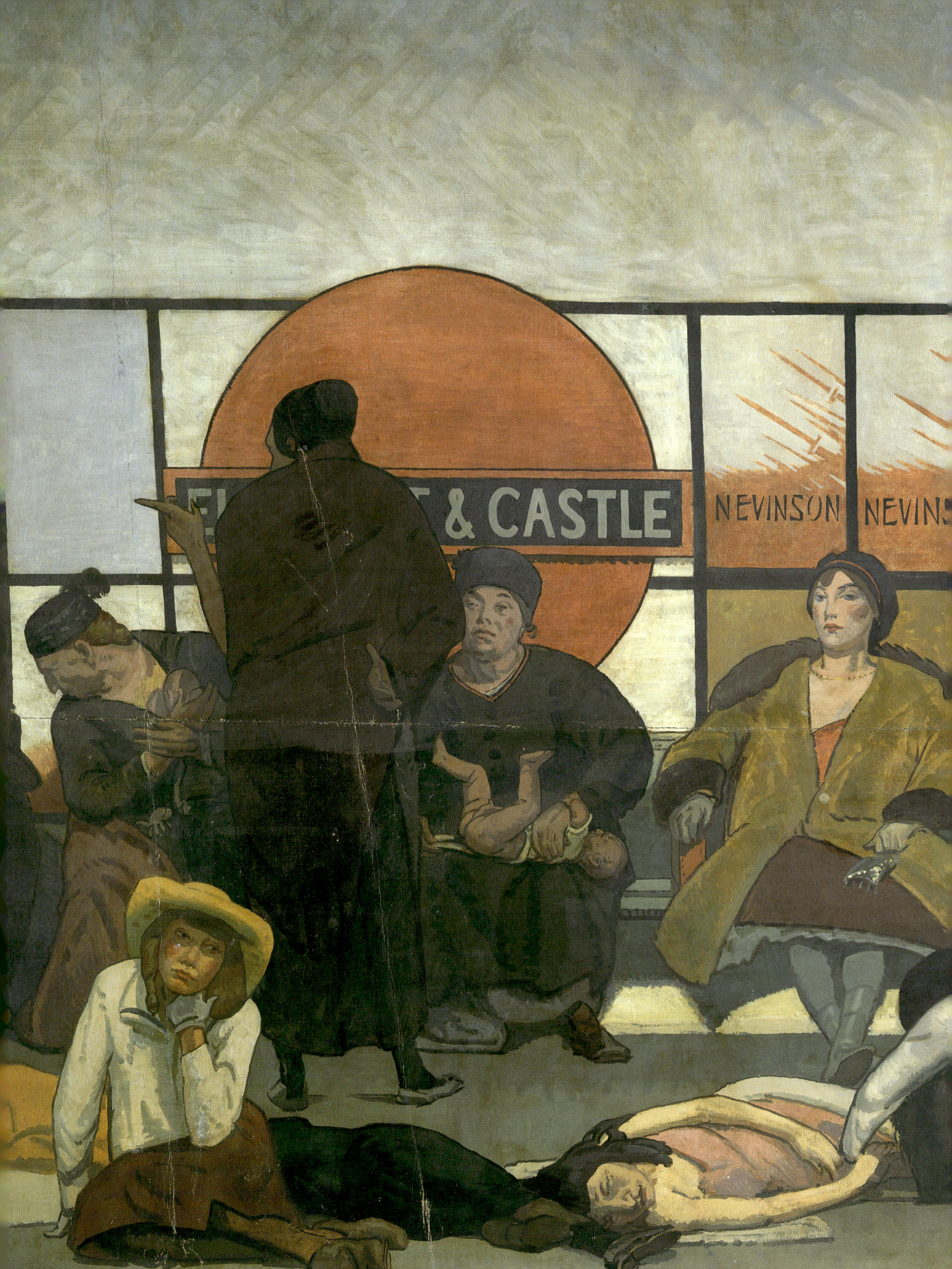

& CASTLE
NEVINSON
NEVINS

Paintings Without Reproductions

This section lists all the paintings that have not been included in the main pages of the catalogue. They were excluded as it was not possible to photograph them for this project. Additional information relating to acquisition credit lines or loan details is also included. For this reason the information below is not repeated in the Further Information section.

Imperial War Museum

Drew, Pamela 1910–1989, *Kenya: Harvards of No.1340 Squadron Diving to Strafe Mau Mau Hideouts in a Gully of the Kipipiri Forest*, 1955, 60.9 x 76.2, oil on aluminium, IWM ART MW(A) 1, purchased, 1956, not available at the time of photography

Drew, Pamela 1910–1989, *Kenya: Harvards of No.1340 Squadron Diving to Strafe Mau Mau Hideouts in a Gully of the Kipipiri Forest II*, 1955, 90.8 x 60.9, oil on aluminium IWM ART MW(A) 2, purchased, 1956, not available at the time of photography

Eastman, Mary active c.1932– 1979, *Sir David P. Maxwell Fyffe*, 1947, 76.2 x 63.5, oil on canvas, IWM ART LD 6513, gift from the artist, 1979, not available at the time of photography

Hine, Stewart active 1970s, *'HMS Belfast' Arriving in the Pool of London*, 1972, 89.5 x 64, oil on board, IWM ART 16596, gift from the artist, not available at the time of photography

Mackey, Haydn Reynolds 1883– 1979, *A British Red Cross Society Nursing Member*, 1918–1919, 152.4 x 101.9, oil on canvas, IWM ART 3938, gift from the British Red Cross and Order of St John of Jerusalem, 1920, not available at the time of photography

Rogers, Gilbert active 1905–1920, *The Dead Stretcher-Bearer*, c.1919, 101.9 x 127, oil on canvas, IWM ART 3688, transferred from the Royal Medical Corps, 1920, not available at the time of photography

Sutton, John b.1935, *'HMS Belfast' Arriving in the Pool of London*, 1974, 60.9 x 91.4, oil on canvas, IWM ART 16610, gift from the artist and Wroxham Galleries Limited, 1974, not available at the time of photography

Facing page: Bayes, Walter, 1869–1956, *The Underworld: Taking Cover in a Tube Station during a London Air Raid* (detail), 1918, (p. 12)

Further Information

The paintings listed in this section have additional information relating to one or more of the five categories outlined below. This extra information is only provided where it is applicable and where it exists. Paintings listed in this section follow the same order as in the illustrated pages of the catalogue.

I	The full name of the artist if this was too long to display in the illustrated pages of the catalogue. Such cases are marked in the catalogue with a (…).
II	The full title of the painting if this was too long to display in the illustrated pages of the catalogue. Such cases are marked in the catalogue with a (…).
III	Acquisition information or acquisition credit lines as well as information about loans, copied from the records of the owner collection.
IV	Artist copyright credit lines where the copyright owner has been traced. Exhaustive efforts have been made to locate the copyright owners of all the images included within this catalogue and to meet their requirements. Any omissions or mistakes brought to our attention will be duly attended to and corrected in future publications.
V	The credit line of the lender of the transparency if the transparency has been borrowed. Bridgeman images are available subject to any relevant copyright approvals from the Bridgeman Art Library at www.bridgeman.co.uk

Imperial War Museum

Adams, Danton 1904–1991, *Vice Admiral Sir Arthur Dowding*, gift from the artist, 1970, © the artist's estate

Adeney, William Bernard 1878–1966, *A 'Mark V' Tank Going into Action*, commissioned, acquired, 1919, © crown copyright

Adeney, William Bernard 1878–1966, *The Advance*, commissioned, acquired, 1919, © crown copyright

Adeney, William Bernard 1878–1966, *The Experimental Depot for Tanks, Dollis Hill, North-West London*, commissioned, acquired, 1919, © crown copyright

Adshead, Mary 1904–1995, *Riding into Barmouth*, purchased, 2003, © the artist's estate

Airy, Anna 1882–1964, *A Shell Forge at a National Projectile Factory, Hackney Marshes, London*, commissioned, acquired, 1920, © crown copyright

Airy, Anna 1882–1964, *An Aircraft Assembly Shop, Hendon*, commissioned, acquired, 1919, © crown copyright

Airy, Anna 1882–1964, *Shop for Machining 15-Inch Shells: Singer Manufacturing Company, Clydebank, Glasgow*, commissioned, acquired, 1919, © crown copyright

Airy, Anna 1882–1964, *The 'L' Press: Forging the Jacket of an 18-Inch Gun, Armstrong-Whitworth Works, Openshaw*, commissioned, acquired, 1919, © crown copyright

Airy, Anna 1882–1964, *Women Working in a Gas Retort House: South Metropolitan Gas Company, London*, commissioned, acquired, 1920, © crown copyright

Aldin, Cecil 1870–1935, *A Land Girl Ploughing*, commissioned, acquired, 1919

Allfree, Geoffrey Stephen 1889–1918, *The Seaplane Station, Scapa Flow, Orkney*, commissioned, acquired, 1917

Allfree, Geoffrey Stephen 1889–1918, *The Wreck of the 'Hampshire'*, gift from Mrs Allfree, 1966

Allfree, Geoffrey Stephen 1889–1918, *A Convoy in the Channel*, commissioned, acquired, 1918

Allfree, Geoffrey Stephen 1889–1918, *A Corner of a Dockyard*, commissioned, acquired, 1918

Allfree, Geoffrey Stephen 1889–1918, *A Dazzled Oiler, with Escort*, commissioned, acquired, 1918

Allfree, Geoffrey Stephen 1889–1918, *A Monitor*, commissioned, acquired, 1918

Allfree, Geoffrey Stephen 1889–1918, *A Monitor's Turret*, commissioned, acquired, 1918

Allfree, Geoffrey Stephen 1889–1918, *A Sketch in Portsmouth Harbour*, commissioned, acquired, 1918

Allfree, Geoffrey Stephen 1889–1918, *A Torpedoed Tramp Steamer off the Longships, Cornwall*, gift from Sir Muirhead Bone, 1919

Allfree, Geoffrey Stephen 1889–1918, *Motor Launches*, commissioned, acquired, 1919

Allfree, Geoffrey Stephen 1889–1918, *Seascape with Convoy and Evening Sky Effect*, commissioned, acquired, 1918

Allfree, Geoffrey Stephen 1889–1918, *Ships in No.1 Basin*, commissioned, acquired, 1918

Allfree, Geoffrey Stephen 1889–1918, *The Quarter-Deck of a Battleship*, commissioned, acquired, 1918

Allfree, Geoffrey Stephen 1889–1918, *The Wake of a 'P' Boat*, commissioned, acquired, 1918

Appelbee, Leonard 1914–2000, *Sir Robert Watson-Watt (1892–1973), CB, FRS, Radar Scientist*, transferred from the War Artists' Advisory Committee, 1947, © crown copyright

Aris, J. active 1940s, *General Sir Richard Nugent O'Connor (1889–1981), KT, GCB, DSO, MC*, gift from Sir Richard Nugent O'Connor, 1979

Armfield, Stuart 1916–2000, *Anti-Invasion Obstacles on a Road*, purchased, 1985

Armstrong, John 1893–1973, *Pro Patria*, purchased with the assistance of the National Heritage Memorial Fund and the National Art Collections Fund, 1995, © the artist's estate

Armstrong, John 1893–1973, *Building Mosquitoes*, transferred from the War Artists' Advisory Committee, 1947, © crown copyright

Atwood, Clare 1866–1962, *Olympia in War Time: Royal Army Clothing Depot*, purchased, 1920, © crown copyright

Atwood, Clare 1866–1962, *Devonshire House, 1918: Voluntary Aid Detachment Workers Filing Papers in the Ballroom*, commissioned, acquired, 1919, © crown copyright

Atwood, Clare 1866–1962, *Victoria Station, 1918: The Green Cross Corps (Women's Reserve Ambulance), Guiding Soldiers on Leave*, commissioned, acquired, 1919, © crown copyright

Atwood, Clare 1866–1962, *Christmas Day in the London Bridge Young Men's Christian Association Canteen: Her Royal Highness Princess Helena Victoria, Mrs Norrie and Miss Ellen Terry*, gift from the artist, 1920, © crown copyright

Auchinleck, Claude J. 1884–1981, *Frontier Hills, Quetta, April 1954*, purchased, 1967

Baker, Alix b.1947, *Royal Navy, World War Two: Leading Wire Man, Landing Party, Home Waters, 1940; Leading Seaman, Beach Party, Royal Naval Reserve Naval Commando, North-West Europe, 1944; Lieutenant Colonel, Royal Naval Volunteer Reserve, 30th Assault Unit, Germany, 1945*, purchased, 2005, artwork by Alix Baker taken from ELITE 79 – The Royal Navy 1939–1945 © Osprey Publishing Ltd www.ospreypublishing.com

Baker, Alix b.1947, *Royal Navy, World War Two: Lieutenant, Home Waters, 1941; Lieutenant Royal Naval Reserve, Home Waters, 1941; Signal Rating, Coastal Waters, 1945*, purchased, 2005, artwork by Alix Baker taken from ELITE 79 – The Royal Navy 1939–1945 © Osprey Publishing Ltd www.ospreypublishing.com

Baker, Alix b.1947, *Air Branch, World War Two: Rating Pilot, Air Branch, Scotland, 1939; Lieutenant (A), Royal New Zealand Navy Volunteer Reserve, Home Waters, 1942; Aircraft Direction Personnel; Aircraft Carrier, 1945*, purchased, 2005, artwork by Alix Baker taken from ELITE 79 – The Royal Navy 1939–1945 © Osprey Publishing Ltd www.ospreypublishing.com

Baker, Alix b.1947, *Anti-Aircraft Home Waters, Royal Navy, World War Two: Rating Home Waters, 1942; Anti-Aircraft Rating Third Class, Home Waters, 1942; Petty Officer Anti-Aircraft Rating First Class, Home Waters, 1944*, purchased, 2005, artwork by Alix Baker taken from ELITE 79 – The Royal Navy 1939–1945 © Osprey Publishing Ltd www.ospreypublishing.com

Baker, Alix b.1947, *Northern Waters, Royal Navy, World War Two: Rating Northern Waters, 1943, Lieutenant, Royal Naval Volunteer Reserve, Northern Waters, 1943, Rating Northern Waters, 1945*, purchased, 2005, artwork by Alix Baker taken from ELITE 79 – The Royal Navy 1939–1945 © Osprey Publishing Ltd www.ospreypublishing.com

Baker, Alix b.1947, *Pacific and Far East, Royal Navy, World War Two: Lieutenant Commander, Pacific, 1945; Women's Royal Naval Service Chief Wireless Telephonist, Far East, 1945; Surgeon Lieutenant Commander, Royal Naval Volunteer Reserve, Pacific, 1945*, purchased, 2005, artwork by Alix Baker taken from ELITE 79 – The Royal Navy 1939–1945 © Osprey Publishing Ltd www.ospreypublishing.com

Baker, Alix b.1947, *Royal Navy, 1939: Captain, Master at Arms, Leading Seaman*, purchased, 2005, artwork by Alix Baker taken from ELITE 79 – The Royal Navy 1939–1945 © Osprey Publishing Ltd www.ospreypublishing.com

Baker, Alix b.1947, *Royal Navy, Far East, World War Two: Petty Officer 1940, Rear Admiral, 1940; Rating, Far East, 1945*, purchased, 2005, artwork by Alix Baker taken from ELITE 79 – The Royal Navy 1939–1945 © Osprey Publishing Ltd www.ospreypublishing.com

Baker, Alix b.1947, *Royal Navy, World War Two: Visual Signalman, 1939; Rating (Overalls) Home Waters, 1944; Rating, Coastal Waters, 1939*, purchased, 2005, artwork by Alix Baker taken from ELITE 79 – The Royal Navy 1939–1945 © Osprey Publishing Ltd www.ospreypublishing.com

Baker, Alix b.1947, *Women's Royal Naval Service and Queen Alexandra's Royal Naval Nursing Service: Women's Royal Naval Service Boats' Crew, Home Waters, 1943; Women's Royal Naval Service Motor Mechanic, Home Waters, 1943; Nursing Sister, Queen Alexandra's Royal Naval Nursing Service Reserve, 1942*, purchased, 2005, artwork by Alix Baker taken from ELITE 79 – The Royal Navy 1939–1945 © Osprey Publishing Ltd www.ospreypublishing.com

Ball, C. S. active 1920s, *The Rescue*

Barberis, Mario, *British 'Nieuport Scout' Destroying an Enemy Biplane in Italy*, transferred from the RAF, 1919

Barnham, Denis A. b.1920, *Battle over Malta: Spitfire Attacking JU 88s but in a Dog-Fight with ME 109s*, transferred from the War Artists' Advisory Committee, 1947, © crown copyright

Bastien, Alfred 1873–1955, *The Battle of Pervyse, 25 October 1914*, gift from Lady Birkenhead, 1930, © DACS

Bateman, John Yunge active 1943–1958, *The Outside Viewing Tank: Directorate of Camouflage, Naval Section*, transferred from the War Artists' Advisory Committee, 1947, © crown copyright

Bayes, Walter 1869–1956, *The Underworld: Taking Cover in a Tube Station during a London Air Raid*, purchased, 1918, © the artist's estate

Bayes, Walter 1869–1956, *The Road to Peace: Design for Tapestry*, gift from Sir Muirhead Bone, 1919, © the artist's estate

Bayes, Walter 1869–1956, *The Armoured Fighting Vehicle School, Bovington: Lunch on the Driving Grounds*, transferred from the War Artists' Advisory Committee, 1947, © crown copyright

Bayes, Walter 1869–1956, *Battle of Britain: Parachutists from an Enemy Aircraft Brought down in an Apparent Attempt to Bomb Buckingham Palace*, transferred from the War Artists' Advisory Committee, 1947, © crown

copyright

Beadle, James Prinsep 1863–1947, *The Breaking of the Hindenburg Line*, purchased, 1977

Beadle, James Prinsep 1863–1947, *Zero Hour*, gift from Lady Kindersley, 1950

Berry, John b.1920, *25-Pounder Gun and Team in Action on the El Alamein Front*, transferred from the War Artists' Advisory Committee, 1947, © crown copyright

Berry, John b.1920, *A Pathfinder*, transferred from the War Artists' Advisory Committee, 1947, © crown copyright

Berry, John b.1920, *A Sikh: Atma Singh*, transferred from the War Artists' Advisory Committee, 1947, © crown copyright

Berry, John b.1920, *Major W. J. Riddell, Chief Instructor of the Mountaineer Wing of the Mountain Warfare School, Marine Expeditionary Force*, transferred from the War Artists' Advisory Committee, 1947, © crown copyright

Birkin, Edith b.1927, *A Camp of Twins: Auschwitz*, gift from the artist, 1983, © the artist

Birkin, Edith b.1927, *Liberation Day*, gift from the artist, 1983, © the artist

Birkin, Edith b.1927, *The Death Cart: Lodz Ghetto*, gift from the artist, 1983, © the artist

Birkin, Edith b.1927, *The Last Gasp: Gas Chamber*, gift from the artist, 1983, © the artist

Birley, Oswald Hornby Joseph 1880–1952, *Air Marshal Sir Richard Peirse (1892–1970), KCB, DSO, AFC*, transferred from the War Artists' Advisory Committee, 1947, © crown copyright

Birley, Oswald Hornby Joseph 1880–1952, *Field Marshal the Viscount Montgomery of Alamein (1887–1976), KG, GCB, DSO*, commissioned, 1948, © crown copyright

Blyth, Robert Henderson 1919–1970, *In the Image of Man*, gift, 1985

Böcher, August 1873–1961, *Field Marshal Von Hindenburg (1847–1934), (formerly hung in the German battle cruiser 'Hindenburg')*, transferred, 1921

Böcher, August 1873–1961, *Kaiser Wilhelm II (1859–1941)*, gift

Bomberg, David 1890–1957, *Bomb Store*, purchased with the assistance of the National Art Collections Fund and the National Heritage Memorial Fund, 1989, © the artist's family

Bone, Muirhead 1876–1953, *Winter Mine-Laying off Iceland*, transferred from the War Artists' Advisory Committee, 1947, © crown copyright

Bone, Stephen 1904–1958, *Camouflaging the Pipeline at the British Aluminium Company's Works at Fort William, October*

1941, transferred from the War Artists' Advisory Committee, 1947, © crown copyright

Bone, Stephen 1904–1958, *A Rescue Motor Launch in the Floating Dock, Stornoway*, transferred from the War Artists' Advisory Committee, 1947, © crown copyright

Bone, Stephen 1904–1958, *Gas Workers*, transferred from the War Artists' Advisory Committee, 1947, © crown copyright

Bone, Stephen 1904–1958, *Drifters at Greenock with Hospital Launches Beyond*, transferred from the War Artists' Advisory Committee, 1947, © crown copyright

Bone, Stephen 1904–1958, *'HMS Truant'*, transferred from the War Artists' Advisory Committee, 1947, © crown copyright

Bone, Stephen 1904–1958, *Monitor: A Snowstorm Approaching*, transferred from the War Artists' Advisory Committee, 1947, © crown copyright

Bone, Stephen 1904–1958, *Air-Sea Rescue*, transferred from the War Artists' Advisory Committee, 1947, © crown copyright

Bone, Stephen 1904–1958, *'HMS Erebus' in Action off Walcheren*, transferred from the War Artists' Advisory Committee, 1947, © crown copyright

Bone, Stephen 1904–1958, *'HMS Paul Rykens' and the Boat Pool, Oban*, transferred from the War Artists' Advisory Committee, 1947, © crown copyright

Bone, Stephen 1904–1958, *Oban Bay: Asdic Trawlers 'HMS Paul Rykens' and 'HMS Southern Star'*, transferred from the War Artists' Advisory Committee, 1947, © crown copyright

Bone, Stephen 1904–1958, *On Board a Minesweeper: Engine-Room Men Take a Breath of Fresh Air*, transferred from the War Artists' Advisory Committee, 1947, © crown copyright

Bone, Stephen 1904–1958, *Royal Air Force Air Sea Rescue Launches, Stornoway: The Fish Quay Beyond*, transferred from the War Artists' Advisory Committee, 1947, © crown copyright

Bone, Stephen 1904–1958, *Royal Air Force Duty Boats and Naval Rescue Launches at Stornoway: A Motor Drifter on Its Way to the Fishing Grounds*, transferred from the War Artists' Advisory Committee, 1947, © crown copyright

Bone, Stephen 1904–1958, *Stornoway: Armed Trawlers and a Coasting Vessel Loading Kippers*, transferred from the War Artists' Advisory Committee, 1947, © crown copyright

Bone, Stephen 1904–1958, *A Motor Launch in a Fog*, transferred from the War Artists' Advisory Committee, 1947, © crown copyright

Bone, Stephen 1904–1958, *A Neutral Drifter in the Minch*, transferred from the War Artists' Advisory Committee, 1947, © crown copyright

Bone, Stephen 1904–1958, *Bathing from a Motor Launch*, transferred from the War Artists' Advisory Committee, 1947, © crown copyright

Bone, Stephen 1904–1958, *Convoy: The Rendezvous*, transferred from the War Artists' Advisory Committee, 1947, © crown copyright

Bone, Stephen 1904–1958, *'HMS Mauritius'*, transferred from the War Artists' Advisory Committee, 1947, © crown copyright

Bone, Stephen 1904–1958, *On Board an Escort Carrier: 'HMS Pursuer' in Belfast Lough*, transferred from the War Artists' Advisory Committee, 1947, © crown copyright

Bone, Stephen 1904–1958, *On Board an Escort Carrier: Lookout at Dawn, 'HMS Pursuer'*, transferred from the War Artists' Advisory Committee, 1947, © crown copyright

Bone, Stephen 1904–1958, *On Board an Escort Carrier: Winter Dusk in Belfast Harbour; Sunderland Flying Boats*, transferred from the War Artists' Advisory Committee, 1947, © crown copyright

Bone, Stephen 1904–1958, *Sinking a Floating Mine with Rifle Fire*, transferred from the War Artists' Advisory Committee, 1947, © crown copyright

Bone, Stephen 1904–1958, *Sunbathing on the Four-Inch Gun*, transferred from the War Artists' Advisory Committee, 1947, © crown copyright

Bone, Stephen 1904–1958, *Tank Landing Craft Just before Dawn*, transferred from the War Artists' Advisory Committee, 1947, © crown copyright

Bone, Stephen 1904–1958, *The Shadow of a Balloon*, transferred from the War Artists' Advisory Committee, 1947, © crown copyright

Bone, Stephen 1904–1958, *Boarding a German U-Boat at Loch Eriboll, Sutherlandshire*, transferred from the War Artists' Advisory Committee, 1947, © crown copyright

Bone, Stephen 1904–1958, *Home Fleet Cruisers in the Firth of Forth*, transferred from the War Artists' Advisory Committee, 1947, © crown copyright

Bone, Stephen 1904–1958, *An Important Tow: A Caisson for Mulberry Harbour Being Towed to Normandy*, transferred from the War Artists' Advisory Committee, 1947, © crown copyright

Bone, Stephen 1904–1958, *Caen*, transferred from the War Artists' Advisory Committee, 1947, ©

crown copyright

Bone, Stephen 1904–1958, *Campbeltown Harbour with 'HMS St Modwyn' and 'HMS Samsonia'*, transferred from the War Artists' Advisory Committee, 1947, © crown copyright

Bone, Stephen 1904–1958, *Coasting Vessel and Barges at Port-en-Bessin*, transferred from the War Artists' Advisory Committee, 1947, © crown copyright

Bone, Stephen 1904–1958, *Commander E. G. Martin, OBE, Royal Naval Volunteer Reserve*, transferred from the War Artists' Advisory Committee, 1947, © crown copyright

Bone, Stephen 1904–1958, *Courseulles Beach*, transferred from the War Artists' Advisory Committee, 1947, © crown copyright

Bone, Stephen 1904–1958, *Embarking Bulldozers*, transferred from the War Artists' Advisory Committee, 1947, © crown copyright

Bone, Stephen 1904–1958, *Fleet Minesweepers off Walcheren: Sunrise, 1 November 1944*, transferred from the War Artists' Advisory Committee, 1947, © crown copyright

Bone, Stephen 1904–1958, *HM Rescue Tug 'Samsonia'*, transferred from the War Artists' Advisory Committee, 1947, © crown copyright

Bone, Stephen 1904–1958, *HM Rescue Tug 'Samsonia': The 20 Inches Manilla Cable*, transferred from the War Artists' Advisory Committee, 1947, © crown copyright

Bone, Stephen 1904–1958, *HM Submarines 'Voracious', 'Sea-Lion' and 'La Cordelière'*, transferred from the War Artists' Advisory Committee, 1947, © crown copyright

Bone, Stephen 1904–1958, *'HMS Malaya' in Tow*, transferred from the War Artists' Advisory Committee, 1947, © crown copyright

Bone, Stephen 1904–1958, *'HMS Mauritius' and 'HMS Roberts' Bombarding Targets near Caen, 18 July 1944*, transferred from the War Artists' Advisory Committee, 1947, © crown copyright

Bone, Stephen 1904–1958, *'HMS Mauritius': Bathing, July 1944*, transferred from the War Artists' Advisory Committee, 1947, © crown copyright

Bone, Stephen 1904–1958, *'HMS Wildgoose' and 'HMS Starling'*, transferred from the War Artists' Advisory Committee, 1947, © crown copyright

Bone, Stephen 1904–1958, *Launch Control Trailer and Medium Landing Ship on Their Way to Normandy*, transferred from the War Artists' Advisory Committee, 1947, © crown copyright

Dead Sea, Palestine', gift from Mrs Sydney Carline and Mr Richard Carline, 1929

Carline, Sydney William 1888–1929, *Study for 'The Destruction of the Turkish Transport in the Gorge of the Wadi Fara, Palestine'*, gift from Mrs Sydney Carline and Mr Richard Carline, 1929

Carline, Sydney William 1888–1929, *The Hills of Judea*, gift from Mrs Sydney Carline and Mr Richard Carline, 1929

Carline, Sydney William 1888–1929, *The Sea of Galilee: Aeroplanes Attacking Turkish Boats*, commissioned, acquired, 1920

Carline, Sydney William 1888–1929, *Two British Planes Attacking the Turkish Army Corps in the Gorge of the Wadi Baroda, Lebanon, 30 September 1918*, gift from Mrs Sydney Carline and Mr Richard Carline, 1929

Carline, Sydney William 1888–1929, *A Destroyed Turkish Aerodrome at Rayak, Lebanon, 1919*, commissioned, acquired, 1920

Carline, Sydney William 1888–1929, *Study for 'The Dead Sea': An Enemy Aeroplane over the Dead Sea, Palestine*, gift from Mrs Sydney Carline and Mr Richard Carline, 1929

Carline, Sydney William 1888–1929, *The Dead Sea: An Enemy Aeroplane over the Dead Sea, Palestine*, commissioned, acquired, 1920

Carline, Sydney William 1888–1929, *The Destruction of the Turkish Transport in the Gorge of the Wadi Fara, Palestine*, commissioned, acquired, 1920

Carnon, Roy 1911–2002, *Seletar, Singapore*, gift, 2005, © the artist's estate

Carr, Henry Marvell 1894–1970, *A Railway Terminus*, transferred from the War Artists' Advisory Committee, 1947, © crown copyright

Carr, Henry Marvell 1894–1970, *Captain Atal: Served at Keren, Eritrea*, transferred from the War Artists' Advisory Committee, 1947, © crown copyright

Carr, Henry Marvell 1894–1970, *Incendiaries in a Suburb*, transferred from the War Artists' Advisory Committee, 1947, © crown copyright

Carr, Henry Marvell 1894–1970, *St Clement Dane's Church on Fire after Being Bombed*, transferred from the War Artists' Advisory Committee, 1947, © crown copyright

Carr, Henry Marvell 1894–1970, *Familiar Silhouettes*, transferred from the War Artists' Advisory Committee, 1947, © crown copyright

Carr, Henry Marvell 1894–1970, *Sir Arthur Street, KCB, KBE, CMG, CIE, MC*, transferred from the War Artists' Advisory Committee, 1947,

© crown copyright

Carr, Henry Marvell 1894–1970, *The Merchant Navy: The Chain Locker*, transferred from the War Artists' Advisory Committee, 1947, © crown copyright

Carr, Henry Marvell 1894–1970, *A Bofors Gun, Algiers*, transferred from the War Artists' Advisory Committee, 1947, © crown copyright

Carr, Henry Marvell 1894–1970, *A Camouflaged 25-Pounder Gun in Action near Medjez-el-Bab with Djebel Djaffa, Tunis, in the Background*, transferred from the War Artists' Advisory Committee, 1947, © crown copyright

Carr, Henry Marvell 1894–1970, *A Member of the Pope's Swiss Guard*, transferred from the War Artists' Advisory Committee, 1947, © crown copyright

Carr, Henry Marvell 1894–1970, *Admiral of the Fleet, Sir Andrew Cunningham (1890–1967), Bt, GCB, DSO*, transferred from the War Artists' Advisory Committee, 1947, © crown copyright

Carr, Henry Marvell 1894–1970, *Air Chief Marshal Sir Arthur Tedder (1890–1967), GCB*, transferred from the War Artists' Advisory Committee, 1947, © crown copyright

Carr, Henry Marvell 1894–1970, *Army Divers: Sappers of a Port Reconstruction and Repair Group*, transferred from the War Artists' Advisory Committee, 1947, © crown copyright

Carr, Henry Marvell 1894–1970, *Arthur E. Mann, War Correspondent, Mutual Broadcasting Company of America*, transferred from the War Artists' Advisory Committee, 1947, © crown copyright

Carr, Henry Marvell 1894–1970, *Carthage*, transferred from the War Artists' Advisory Committee, 1947, © crown copyright

Carr, Henry Marvell 1894–1970, *Charles C. Collingwood, War Correspondent, Columbia Broadcasting System of America*, transferred from the War Artists' Advisory Committee, 1947, © crown copyright

Carr, Henry Marvell 1894–1970, *General Dwight D. Eisenhower (1890–1969)*, transferred from the War Artists' Advisory Committee, 1947, © crown copyright

Carr, Henry Marvell 1894–1970, *General Spaatz (1891–1974), Air Commodore-in-Chief, American Air Force*, transferred from the War Artists' Advisory Committee, 1947, © crown copyright

Carr, Henry Marvell 1894–1970, *General the Honourable Sir Harold Alexander (1891–1969), GCB, CSI, DSO*, transferred from the War Artists' Advisory Committee, 1947, © crown copyright

Carr, Henry Marvell 1894–1970, *Henry Cox, CMG, BEM,*

transferred from the War Artists' Advisory Committee, 1947, © crown copyright

Carr, Henry Marvell 1894–1970, *His Highness the Bey of Tunis*, transferred from the War Artists' Advisory Committee, 1947, © crown copyright

Carr, Henry Marvell 1894–1970, *Howard Marshall, War Correspondent, British Broadcasting Corporation*, transferred from the War Artists' Advisory Committee, 1947, © crown copyright

Carr, Henry Marvell 1894–1970, *Infantry Landing Craft Disembarking Troops*, transferred from the War Artists' Advisory Committee, 1947, © crown copyright

Carr, Henry Marvell 1894–1970, *Major General H. M. Gale, CB, CBE, MC*, transferred from the War Artists' Advisory Committee, 1947, © crown copyright

Carr, Henry Marvell 1894–1970, *Marcel Peyrouton (1887–1983), Governor General, Algeria, 1943*, transferred from the War Artists' Advisory Committee, 1947, © crown copyright

Carr, Henry Marvell 1894–1970, *Mosquito Nets*, transferred from the War Artists' Advisory Committee, 1947, © crown copyright

Carr, Henry Marvell 1894–1970, *Parachute Drop*, transferred from the War Artists' Advisory Committee, 1947, © crown copyright

Carr, Henry Marvell 1894–1970, *Searchlight on Infantry Landing Craft*, transferred from the War Artists' Advisory Committee, 1947, © crown copyright

Carr, Henry Marvell 1894–1970, *Sergeant B. Montague: One of the Desert Rats (7th Armoured Division)*, transferred from the War Artists' Advisory Committee, 1947, © crown copyright

Carr, Henry Marvell 1894–1970, *Sergeant J. P. Kenneally, VC, First Battalion, Irish Guards*, transferred from the War Artists' Advisory Committee, 1947, © crown copyright

Carr, Henry Marvell 1894–1970, *Staff Sergeant Major E. A. Billett*, transferred from the War Artists' Advisory Committee, 1947, © crown copyright

Carr, Henry Marvell 1894–1970, *The Bailey Bridge at Medjez-el-Bab*, transferred from the War Artists' Advisory Committee, 1947, © crown copyright

Carr, Henry Marvell 1894–1970, *The Goumier*, transferred from the War Artists' Advisory Committee, 1947, © crown copyright

Carr, Henry Marvell 1894–1970, *The Gulf of Carthage*, transferred from the War Artists' Advisory Committee, 1947, © crown copyright

Carr, Henry Marvell 1894–1970, *Tirailleur Algérien*, transferred from the War Artists' Advisory Committee, 1947, © crown copyright

Carr, Henry Marvell 1894–1970, *William E. Mundy, Daily Telegraph War Correspondent*, transferred from the War Artists' Advisory Committee, 1947, © crown copyright

Carr, Henry Marvell 1894–1970, *A 3.7 Anti-Aircraft Gun of 393/72 Heavy Anti-Aircraft Regiment, RA, CMF*, transferred from the War Artists' Advisory Committee, 1947, © crown copyright

Carr, Henry Marvell 1894–1970, *Cassino*, transferred from the War Artists' Advisory Committee, 1947, © crown copyright

Carr, Henry Marvell 1894–1970, *Edward Ardizzone (1900–1979), Official War Artist*, transferred from the War Artists' Advisory Committee, 1947, © crown copyright

Carr, Henry Marvell 1894–1970, *General Sir Harold Franklyn, KCB, DSO, MC*, transferred from the War Artists' Advisory Committee, 1947, © crown copyright

Carr, Henry Marvell 1894–1970, *Liberation*, transferred from the War Artists' Advisory Committee, 1947, © crown copyright

Carr, Henry Marvell 1894–1970, *Lieutenant W. F. Smyth, Gunner Officer*, transferred from the War Artists' Advisory Committee, 1947, © crown copyright

Carr, Henry Marvell 1894–1970, *Major Paul Triquet, VC, of Cabano, Province of Quebec*, transferred from the War Artists' Advisory Committee, 1947, © crown copyright

Carr, Henry Marvell 1894–1970, *Major the Viscount Stopford, First Battalion, London Irish Rifles (Royal Ulster Rifles)*, transferred from the War Artists' Advisory Committee, 1947, © crown copyright

Carr, Henry Marvell 1894–1970, *Nurse Giving an Injection of Penicilin to a Wounded Man, 15th Canadian General Hospital*, transferred from the War Artists' Advisory Committee, 1947, © crown copyright

Carr, Henry Marvell 1894–1970, *Paul Wyand, War Correspondent*, transferred from the War Artists' Advisory Committee, 1947, © crown copyright

Carr, Henry Marvell 1894–1970, *Sepoy Kamal Ram (1924–1982), VC, 8th Punjab Regiment*, transferred from the War Artists' Advisory Committee, 1947, © crown copyright

Carr, Henry Marvell 1894–1970, *The Goumier*, transferred from the War Artists' Advisory Committee, 1947, © crown copyright

Carr, Henry Marvell 1894–1970, *Vesuvius in Eruption, March 1944*, transferred from the War Artists' Advisory Committee, 1947, © crown copyright

Carr, Henry Marvell 1894–1970, *A 7.2 Gun Firing at Night*, transferred from the War Artists' Advisory

Carr, Henry Marvell 1894–1970, Committee, 1947, © crown copyright

Carr, Henry Marvell 1894–1970, *A Cockney Soldier*, transferred from the War Artists' Advisory Committee, 1947, © crown copyright

Carr, Henry Marvell 1894–1970, *Air Marshal Sir Leslie Hollinghurst, KBE, CB, DFC*, transferred from the War Artists' Advisory Committee, 1947, © crown copyright

Carr, Henry Marvell 1894–1970, *Frederick Alexander Lindemann (1886–1957), PC, FRS, First Baron Cherwell of Oxford*, transferred from the War Artists' Advisory Committee, 1947, © crown copyright

Carr, Leslie b.1891, *The Navy's Little Ships on the High Seas*, gift from Shirley Carr, in memory of Gordon Carr, Coastal Forces (1943–1946), 2006

Chapman, H. M. active 1914–1918, *Blargies, Arms, France*, unknown provenance

Chapman, H. M. active 1914–1918, *France*, unknown provenance

Chapman, Stephen active 1940s, *Christ Receiving the Stretcher-Bearers*, purchased, 1983

Charlton, Evan 1904–1984, *A Parachute Factory*, transferred from the War Artists' Advisory Committee, 1947, © crown copyright

Christie, Alexander b.1901, *Simon Denis St Leger Fleming, Royal Horse Artillery*, gift from Mayor General D. L. Lloyd Owen, The Long Range Desert Group Association, 1974

Claessen, George 1909–1999, *ARP Practice: Dealing with Casualties*, transferred from the War Artists' Advisory Committee, 1947, © crown copyright

Clause, William Lionel 1887–1946, *A Fire Guard Team, Exeter*, transferred from the War Artists' Advisory Committee, 1947, © crown copyright

Clausen, George 1852–1944, *Youth Mourning*, gift, 1929, © Imperial War Museum

Clausen, George 1852–1944, *In the Gun Factory at Woolwich Arsenal*, commissioned, acquired, 1919, © crown copyright

Codner, Maurice Frederick 1888–1958, *Field Marshal Lord Milne (1866–1948), GCB, GCMG, DSO, DCL, LLD, K.St J.*, gift to commemorate all the men and women who served under Lord Milne in Salonika (1915–1918) from the Salonika Reunion Association, 1959, © Imperial War Museum

Codner, Maurice Frederick 1888–1958, *Charles Ffoulkes (1868–1947), CB, CBE, First Curator and Secretary of the Imperial War Museum, in the Uniform of Master of the Tower Armouries*, gift from Evelyn E. Barron, 1939

Codrington, Isabel 1874–1943,

Cantine Franco-Britannique, Vitry-le-François, gift from the artist, 1919, © Imperial War Museum

Coldstream, William Menzies 1908–1987, *Havildar Kulbir Thapa, 2/3 Gurkha Regiment*, transferred from the War Artists' Advisory Committee, 1947, © crown copyright

Coldstream, William Menzies 1908–1987, *Rifleman Mangal Singh, 2/6 Rajput Rifles*, transferred from the War Artists' Advisory Committee, 1947, © crown copyright

Coldstream, William Menzies 1908–1987, *Subedar Jagat Singh, 2/11 Sikhs*, transferred from the War Artists' Advisory Committee, 1947, © crown copyright

Coldstream, William Menzies 1908–1987, *The Bailey Bridge Built by Royal Engineers over the Volturno River, Italy*, transferred from the War Artists' Advisory Committee, 1947, © crown copyright

Coldstream, William Menzies 1908–1987, *Sir Alwyn Crow, CBE, Director and Controller of Projectile Development (1940–1945)*, transferred from the War Artists' Advisory Committee, 1947, © crown copyright

Cole, Leslie 1910–1976, *Loading Tanks for Russia*, transferred from the War Artists' Advisory Committee, 1947, © crown copyright

Cole, Leslie 1910–1976, *The Interior of an Aircraft in Flight*, transferred from the War Artists' Advisory Committee, 1947, © crown copyright

Cole, Leslie 1910–1976, *16th US Medical Regiment: Field Dental Service Operating during an Attack*, transferred from the War Artists' Advisory Committee, 1947, © crown copyright

Cole, Leslie 1910–1976, *A Glider Pilot at the Controls*, transferred from the War Artists' Advisory Committee, 1947, © crown copyright

Cole, Leslie 1910–1976, *An American Soldier in Fatigue Dress*, transferred from the War Artists' Advisory Committee, 1947, © crown copyright

Cole, Leslie 1910–1976, *Dentistry during the Hour of Gas Practice*, transferred from the War Artists' Advisory Committee, 1947, © crown copyright

Cole, Leslie 1910–1976, *Loading Tanks for Russia II*, transferred from the War Artists' Advisory Committee, 1947, © crown copyright

Cole, Leslie 1910–1976, *Night Scene in a Watch Office*, transferred from the War Artists' Advisory Committee, 1947, © crown copyright

Cole, Leslie 1910–1976, *Admiral C. H. J. Harcourt's Flagship 'HMS Newfoundland' in the Attack on Pantellaria*, transferred from the War Artists' Advisory Committee, 1947, © crown copyright

Cole, Leslie 1910–1976, *Air Vice-Marshal Sir Keith Park (1892–1975), KBE, CB, MC, DFC, Air Officer Commanding Malta in His Plane*, transferred from the War Artists' Advisory Committee, 1947, © crown copyright

Cole, Leslie 1910–1976, *Brigadier Ivan de la Bere, OBE, in Charge of Troops during the Siege of Malta*, transferred from the War Artists' Advisory Committee, 1947, © crown copyright

Cole, Leslie 1910–1976, *Diffone Workers Mending the Roof of the Officers' Mess, Floriana*, transferred from the War Artists' Advisory Committee, 1947, © crown copyright

Cole, Leslie 1910–1976, *Major General G. C. Kemp, CB, MC*, transferred from the War Artists' Advisory Committee, 1947, © crown copyright

Cole, Leslie 1910–1976, *Major General W. H. Oxley, CBE, MC, General Officer Commanding Troops in Malta*, transferred from the War Artists' Advisory Committee, 1947, © crown copyright

Cole, Leslie 1910–1976, *Malta: A Few People Sleep out among the Debris*, transferred from the War Artists' Advisory Committee, 1947, © crown copyright

Cole, Leslie 1910–1976, *Malta Convoy: Basutos Deal with the Overflow Mail on the Causeway, the Palace, Valletta*, transferred from the War Artists' Advisory Committee, 1947, © crown copyright

Cole, Leslie 1910–1976, *Malta: Fighters Take Off from Luca's Bombed Runway*, transferred from the War Artists' Advisory Committee, 1947, © crown copyright

Cole, Leslie 1910–1976, *Malta: Gunners Resting Between Alerts at a Heavy Anti-Aircraft Post*, transferred from the War Artists' Advisory Committee, 1947, © crown copyright

Cole, Leslie 1910–1976, *Malta: No Time to Lose, Soldier Dockers Unloading a Convoy during a Raid*, transferred from the War Artists' Advisory Committee, 1947, © crown copyright

Cole, Leslie 1910–1976, *Malta: Preparing for the Night in the Crypt of St Augustine's, Valletta*, transferred from the War Artists' Advisory Committee, 1947, © crown copyright

Cole, Leslie 1910–1976, *Malta: Shelterers Praying during a Raid*, transferred from the War Artists' Advisory Committee, 1947, © crown copyright

Cole, Leslie 1910–1976, *Malta: The Harbour Barrage from the Upper Barracca*, transferred from the War Artists' Advisory Committee, 1947, © crown copyright

Cole, Leslie 1910–1976, *Malta, the Hypogeum: People of Paula Sheltering during a Raid*, transferred from the War Artists' Advisory Committee, 1947, © crown copyright

Cole, Leslie 1910–1976, *Maltese Fishermen Mending Bombed Dghaisas and Other Boats*, transferred from the War Artists' Advisory Committee, 1947, © crown copyright

Cole, Leslie 1910–1976, *Star Shells over Lampedusa during a Night Bombardment*, transferred from the War Artists' Advisory Committee, 1947, © crown copyright

Cole, Leslie 1910–1976, *Battle of London: Royal Marine Anti-Aircraft Gunners Bring down a Flying Bomb*, transferred from the War Artists' Advisory Committee, 1947, © crown copyright

Cole, Leslie 1910–1976, *Bechuanaland Boys Cleaning Anti-Aircraft Guns in the Twilight after Action, Syracuse, Sicily*, transferred from the War Artists' Advisory Committee, 1947, © crown copyright

Cole, Leslie 1910–1976, *Scene in a Regimental Aid Post: In a Filthy Cellar at Sallenelle, France, after an Action*, transferred from the War Artists' Advisory Committee, 1947, © crown copyright

Cole, Leslie 1910–1976, *Sick Women and the Hooded Men of Belsen*, transferred from the War Artists' Advisory Committee, 1947, © crown copyright

Cole, Leslie 1910–1976, *14th Army: Men of the Royal Berkshire Regiment Form the Spearhead of a Patrol, Cutting through the Jungle on the Toungoo-Manchi Road*, transferred from the War Artists' Advisory Committee, 1947, © crown copyright

Cole, Leslie 1910–1976, *A Greek Refugee Family from Samos at Moses Wells Encampment, Arabia, with Red Cross Workers*, transferred from the War Artists' Advisory Committee, 1947, © crown copyright

Cole, Leslie 1910–1976, *Belsen Camp: The Compound for Women*, transferred from the War Artists' Advisory Committee, 1947, © crown copyright

Cole, Leslie 1910–1976, *British Snipers on the Island of Ubbea near Khakio, 10th Infantry Brigade*, transferred from the War Artists' Advisory Committee, 1947, © crown copyright

Cole, Leslie 1910–1976, *British Women and Children Interned in a Japanese Prison Camp, Syme Road, Singapore*, transferred from the War Artists' Advisory Committee, 1947, © crown copyright

Cole, Leslie 1910–1976, *Burma, 14th Army: The Battle of the Sittang Bend with Men of the Queen's Own (Royal West Kent) Regiment Making an Armed Patrol*, transferred from the War Artists' Advisory Committee, 1947, © crown copyright

Cole, Leslie 1910–1976, *Burmese Guerillas in Action*, transferred from the War Artists' Advisory Committee, 1947, © crown copyright

Cole, Leslie 1910–1976, *Captain L. E. George, MC*, transferred from the War Artists' Advisory Committee, 1947, © crown copyright

Cole, Leslie 1910–1976, *Commandant Marjorie F. Wagstaffe, CBE, Deputy Director, Auxiliary Territorial Service, Middle East Forces*, transferred from the War Artists' Advisory Committee, 1947, © crown copyright

Cole, Leslie 1910–1976, *Company Quartermaster, Sergeant Van Omoheusen of the Auxiliary Territorial Service, Ceylon*, transferred from the War Artists' Advisory Committee, 1947, © crown copyright

Cole, Leslie 1910–1976, *Greece, an Orphanage: Curing Scabies with Anachryl*, transferred from the War Artists' Advisory Committee, 1947, © crown copyright

Cole, Leslie 1910–1976, *Havildar Gurbakhsh Singh, IDSM*, transferred from the War Artists' Advisory Committee, 1947, © crown copyright

Cole, Leslie 1910–1976, *Mother Mourning the Death of a Village Priest*, transferred from the War Artists' Advisory Committee, 1947, © crown copyright

Cole, Leslie 1910–1976, *One of the Death Pits, Belsen: SS Guards Collecting Bodies*, transferred from the War Artists' Advisory Committee, 1947, © crown copyright

Cole, Leslie 1910–1976, *Orderly on His Rounds in X Ward, Changi Gaol, Singapore, with Prisoners of War Suffering from Starvation and Beriberi*, transferred from the War Artists' Advisory Committee, 1947, © crown copyright

Cole, Leslie 1910–1976, *Subedar-Major Musank Khan*, transferred from the War Artists' Advisory Committee, 1947, © crown copyright

Cole, Leslie 1910–1976, *The Greek Civil War: Relatives Mourn Their Dead at Peristeres*, transferred from the War Artists' Advisory Committee, 1947, © crown copyright

Cole, Leslie 1910–1976, *Borneo: Officers' Mess, 3/8 Gurkha Regiment*, transferred from the War Artists' Advisory Committee, 1947, © crown copyright

Cole, Leslie 1910–1976, *Burma, the Guerilla Headquarters: Sergeant Brierley (Ex-Maquis) with Burmese Members of Reindeer Force 136*, transferred from the War Artists' Advisory Committee, 1947, © crown copyright

Cole, Leslie 1910–1976, *Burmese Guerillas in Action*, transferred from the War Artists' Advisory Committee, 1947, © crown copyright

Cole, Leslie 1910–1976, *Scorched Earth: Devastated Rubber Plantations*, transferred from the War Artists' Advisory Committee, 1947, © crown copyright

Cole, Leslie 1910–1976, *Singapore: Limbless Officers and Men Checking out from Changi Gaol*, transferred from the War Artists' Advisory Committee, 1947, © crown copyright

Cole, Leslie 1910–1976, *Singapore: The Cookhouse, Changi Gaol, British Prisoners of War Prepare Their Main Meal of Rice*, transferred from the War Artists' Advisory Committee, 1947, © crown copyright

Cole, Leslie 1910–1976, *Singapore: The Remains of One of the Big Defence Guns*, transferred from the War Artists' Advisory Committee, 1947, © crown copyright

Cole, Leslie 1910–1976, *Subedar-Major of the 3/8 Gurkhas*, transferred from the War Artists' Advisory Committee, 1947, © crown copyright

Cole, Philip Tennyson 1862–1939, *Lord Kitchener of Khartoum (1850–1916)*, gift from the artist, 1925, © Imperial War Museum

Cole, Philip Tennyson 1862–1939, *General Sir Edmund Allenby (1861–1936), KCB*, gift from the artist, 1925, © Imperial War Museum

Connard, Philip 1875–1958, *27 Knots: 'HMS Melampus'*, commissioned, acquired, 1918, © Imperial War Museum

Connard, Philip 1875–1958, *A Destroyer*, commissioned, acquired, 1918, © Imperial War Museum

Connard, Philip 1875–1958, *A Destroyer in a Heavy Sea: From 'HMS Melampus'*, commissioned, acquired, 1918, © Imperial War Museum

Connard, Philip 1875–1958, *Anti-Aircraft Gun*, commissioned, acquired, 1918, © Imperial War Museum

Connard, Philip 1875–1958, *Between Decks*, commissioned, acquired, 1918, © Imperial War Museum

Connard, Philip 1875–1958, *Between Decks, 'HMS Coventry'*, commissioned, acquired, 1918, © Imperial War Museum

Connard, Philip 1875–1958, *Captain P. Boyds, RN*, gift from the artist, 1936, © Imperial War Museum

Connard, Philip 1875–1958, *Cloud Shadows*, commissioned, acquired, 1918, © Imperial War Museum

Connard, Philip 1875–1958, *Coastal Motor Boats off the Frisian Coast, 11 August 1918*, © Imperial War Museum

Connard, Philip 1875–1958, *Cookhouse: 'HMS Maidstone'*, gift from the artist, 1936, © Imperial War Museum

Connard, Philip 1875–1958, *E.44 Making an Attack*, commissioned, acquired, 1918, © Imperial War Museum

Connard, Philip 1875–1958, *E.45: The Commander, Lieutenant-Commander J. E. Gaimes, DSO, RN*, commissioned, acquired, 1918, © Imperial War Museum

Connard, Philip 1875–1958, *Evening*, commissioned, acquired, 1918, © Imperial War Museum

Connard, Philip 1875–1958, *Gun Practice: 'HMS Canterbury'*, commissioned, acquired, 1918, © Imperial War Museum

Connard, Philip 1875–1958, *Harwich*, commissioned, acquired, 1918, © Imperial War Museum

Connard, Philip 1875–1958, *'HMS Canterbury'*, commissioned, acquired, 1918, © Imperial War Museum

Connard, Philip 1875–1958, *'HMS Canterbury'*, commissioned, acquired, 1918, © Imperial War Museum

Connard, Philip 1875–1958, *'HMS Curaçao'*, commissioned, acquired, 1918, © Imperial War Museum

Connard, Philip 1875–1958, *'HMS Curaçao'*, commissioned, acquired, 1918, © Imperial War Museum

Connard, Philip 1875–1958, *'HMS Curlew'*, commissioned, acquired, 1918, © Imperial War Museum

Connard, Philip 1875–1958, *'HMS Curlew'*, commissioned, acquired, 1918, © Imperial War Museum

Connard, Philip 1875–1958, *'HMS Danaë'*, commissioned, acquired, 1918, © Imperial War Museum

Connard, Philip 1875–1958, *Light Cruisers*, commissioned, acquired, 1918, © Imperial War Museum

Connard, Philip 1875–1958, *Lowering the Whaler: 'HMS Coventry'*, commissioned, acquired, 1918, © Imperial War Museum

Connard, Philip 1875–1958, *Near the South Dogger*, commissioned, acquired, 1918, © Imperial War Museum

Connard, Philip 1875–1958, *Off Harwich*, commissioned, acquired, 1918, © Imperial War Museum

Connard, Philip 1875–1958, *Oiler Alongside*, commissioned, acquired, 1918, © Imperial War Museum

Connard, Philip 1875–1958, *Parkestone*, commissioned, acquired, 1918, © Imperial War Museum

Connard, Philip 1875–1958, *Rangefinder in Action, August 1918*, gift from the artist, 1936, © Imperial War Museum

Connard, Philip 1875–1958, *Sailor on the Bridge*, gift from the artist, 1936, © Imperial War Museum

Connard, Philip 1875–1958, *Sketch for '27 Knots: 'HMS Melampus''*, gift from the artist, 1936, © Imperial War Museum

Connard, Philip 1875–1958, *Sketch for 'The Harwich Force at Sea'*, gift from the artist, 1936, © Imperial War Museum

Connard, Philip 1875–1958, *St George's Day: Bridge of 'HMS Canterbury', on Patrol Work when the Great Naval Raid on Zeebrugge and Ostend Took Place*, commissioned, acquired, 1918, © Imperial War Museum

Connard, Philip 1875–1958, *Submarines*, commissioned, acquired, 1918, © Imperial War Museum

Connard, Philip 1875–1958, *Submarines*, commissioned, acquired, 1918, © Imperial War Museum

Connard, Philip 1875–1958, *Submarines*, commissioned, acquired, 1918, © Imperial War Museum

Connard, Philip 1875–1958, *The Bandstand*, commissioned, acquired, 1918, © Imperial War Museum

Connard, Philip 1875–1958, *The Bridge, 'HMS Melampus'*, © Imperial War Museum

Connard, Philip 1875–1958, *The Chief*, commissioned, acquired, 1918, © Imperial War Museum

Connard, Philip 1875–1958, *The Destruction of an Airship off the Frisian Coast, 11 August 1918*, commissioned, acquired, 1918, © Imperial War Museum

Connard, Philip 1875–1958, *The Forecastle, 'HMS Curlew'*, commissioned, acquired, 1918, © Imperial War Museum

Connard, Philip 1875–1958, *The Harwich Force at Sea*, commissioned, acquired, 1918, © Imperial War Museum

Connard, Philip 1875–1958, *The Harwich Force Leaving for Sea*, commissioned, acquired, 1918, © Imperial War Museum

Connard, Philip 1875–1958, *The Harwich Force: Sailing Race*, commissioned, acquired, 1918, © Imperial War Museum

Connard, Philip 1875–1958, *The Quarter-Deck*, commissioned, acquired, 1918, © Imperial War Museum

Connard, Philip 1875–1958, *The Return of a 'Camel' off the Frisian Coast: 'HMS Curaçao', 11 August 1918*, commissioned, acquired, 1918, © Imperial War Museum

Connard, Philip 1875–1958, *Vice Admiral the Honourable Sir Somerset A. Gough-Calthorpe (1864–1937), GCMG, KCB, CVO, on Board 'HMS Superb' at Constantinople*, commissioned, acquired, 1919, © Imperial War Museum

Connard, Philip 1875–1958, *From 'HMS Caesar': 'HMS Superb' at Constantinople, 'HMS Lord Nelson' and the French 'Diderot' in the Distance with Seaforth Highlanders Marching along the Quay*, commissioned, acquired, 1919, © Imperial War Museum

Connard, Philip 1875–1958, *The Guns of 'HMS Caesar': Off Constantinople, Looking towards the Golden Horn*, commissioned, acquired, 1919, © Imperial War Museum

Connard, Philip 1875–1958, *The Port of Constantinople: The Guns of 'HMS Caesar'*, commissioned, acquired, 1919, © Imperial War Museum

Connard, Philip 1875–1958, *The Surrender of the 'Goeben': Passing the German Embassy, Constantinople, Flying the White Flag*, commissioned, acquired, 1919, © Imperial War Museum

Connard, Philip 1875–1958, *Balloon Barrage and Shipping*, transferred from the War Artists' Advisory Committee, 1947, © crown copyright

Connard, Philip 1875–1958, *Air Chief Marshal Sir Edgar Ludlow-Hewitt (1886–1973), KCB, CMG, DSO, MC*, transferred from the War Artists' Advisory Committee, 1947, © crown copyright

Connew, Joan V. b.1915, *Blackout*, transferred from the War Artists' Advisory Committee, 1947, © crown copyright

Cook, Frederick T. W. 1907–1982, *Bristol Beaufighter I*, gift from Mrs M. Anyon Cook, 1986

Cook, Frederick T. W. 1907–1982, *Bristol Beaufighter II*, gift from Mrs M. Anyon Cook, 1986

Cook, Frederick T. W. 1907–1982, *Burlington Arcade*, gift from Mrs M. Anyon Cook, 1986

Cook, Frederick T. W. 1907–1982, *Chancery Lane Fireplaces*, gift from Mrs M. Anyon Cook, 1986

Cook, Frederick T. W. 1907–1982, *Paternoster Row*, gift from Mrs M. Anyon Cook, 1986

Cook, Frederick T. W. 1907–1982, *St Bride's*, gift from Mrs M. Anyon Cook, 1986

Cook, Frederick T. W. 1907–1982, *St Nicholas Cole Abbey*, gift from Mrs M. Anyon Cook, 1986

Cook, Frederick T. W. 1907–1982, *A Flying Bomb over Tower Bridge*, transferred from the War Artists' Advisory Committee, 1947, © crown copyright

Cook, Frederick T. W. 1907–1982, *Aftermath: The Prudential Building, Plymouth*, gift from Mrs M. Anyon Cook, 1987

Cook, James 1904–1960, *Australian Troops: Night Convoy*, accessioned, 1996

Cook, John Kingsley 1911–1994, *French and Arab Prisoners at Mecheria Internment Camp, Algeria*, transferred from the War Artists' Advisory Committee, 1947, © crown copyright

Cooke, Isaac 1846–1922, *Lieutenant Colonel J. R. Webster, DSO, MC*, gift from Mrs Vera Knight, 1974

Cooper, Alfred Egerton 1883–1974, *Airship 9*, purchased, 1919, © Imperial War Museum

Cooper, Alfred Egerton 1883–1974, *Airship 23*, purchased, 1919, © Imperial War Museum

Cooper, Alfred Egerton 1883–1974, *'Rigid 26'*, purchased, 1919, © Imperial War Museum

Cooper, Alfred Egerton 1883–1974, *R.34 and R.29 in the Shed at East Fortune*, gift from the artist, 1921, © Imperial War Museum

Cooper, Alfred Egerton 1883–1974, *Surgeon Major Arthur Martin-Leake (1874–1953), VC, RAMC*, purchased, 1921, © Imperial War Museum

Coventry, Frederick Halford b.1905, *Dummy Figures Used in Training*, transferred from the War Artists' Advisory Committee, 1947, © crown copyright

Cowern, Raymond Teague 1913–1986, *Brussels: VE Day 3*, gift from the Cowern Family, 2005, © Imperial War Museum

Coxon, Raymond James 1896–1997, *Convoy*, transferred from the War Artists' Advisory Committee, 1947, © crown copyright

Coxon, Raymond James 1896–1997, *Ordinary Seaman H. V. Cronyn, GM, RNVR, of 'HMS Mallard'*, transferred from the War Artists' Advisory Committee, 1947, © crown copyright

Craig, Barry 1902–1951, *Camouflage Screens at a Cheshire Factory*, transferred from the War Artists' Advisory Committee, 1947, © crown copyright

Crawford, Hugh Adam 1898–1982, *Company Sergeant Major McLeod, DCM, Seaforth Highlanders, 51st Division*, transferred from the War Artists' Advisory Committee, 1947, © crown copyright

Crook, Pamela b.1945, *Other Mothers' Sons*, gift from Professor and Mrs Kenneth Simmonds, 1992, © Imperial War Museum

Crook, Pamela b.1945, *The Naming of Parts*, gift from Professor and Mrs Kenneth Simmonds, 2004, © courtesy of the artist/www.bridgeman.co.uk

Crosby, Frederick Gordon 1885–1943, *Lieutenant Warneford's Great Exploit: The First Zeppelin to Be Brought down by Allied Aircraft, 7 June 1915*, gift from Edward Lliffe, 1920, © Imperial War Museum

Crowley, Graham b.1950, *Mainframe*, commissioned, 1988, © Imperial War Museum

Cruttwell, Grace active 1903–1945, *Joseph Stalin (1879–1953)*

Cundall, Charles Ernest 1890–1971, *Bordeaux Refugees at Falmouth*, transferred from the War Artists' Advisory Committee, 1947, © crown copyright

Cundall, Charles Ernest 1890–1971, *Building Submarines*, transferred from the War Artists' Advisory Committee, 1947, © crown copyright

Cundall, Charles Ernest 1890–1971, *Dunkirk Paddleboat*, purchased, 1965, © courtesy of the artist's estate/www.bridgeman.co.uk

Cundall, Charles Ernest 1890–1971, *'HMS Exeter' at Plymouth in 1940: Back from the Graf Spee Action*, transferred from the War Artists' Advisory Committee, 1947, © crown copyright

Cundall, Charles Ernest 1890–1971, *'Iron Duke'*, purchased, 1965, © courtesy of the artist's estate/www.bridgeman.co.uk

Cundall, Charles Ernest 1890–1971, *Motor Launches, Dartmouth*, transferred from the War Artists' Advisory Committee, 1947, © crown copyright

Cundall, Charles Ernest 1890–1971, *Sheerness*, transferred from the War Artists' Advisory Committee, 1947, © crown copyright

Cundall, Charles Ernest 1890–1971, *The Withdrawal from Dunkirk, June 1940*, transferred from the War Artists' Advisory Committee, 1947, © crown copyright

Cundall, Charles Ernest 1890–1971, *Our Mechanised Army: Tanks in Action (Ministry of Information poster)*, transferred from the War Artists' Advisory Committee, 1947, © crown copyright

Cundall, Charles Ernest 1890–1971, *A U-Boat Surrenders to a Hudson Aircraft*, transferred from the War Artists' Advisory Committee, 1947, © crown copyright

Cundall, Charles Ernest 1890–1971, *Physical Training at a Royal Air Force Training Centre*, transferred from the War Artists' Advisory Committee, 1947, © crown copyright

Cundall, Charles Ernest 1890–1971, *A. B. Charles: Portrait of a Flyer*, purchased, 1965, © courtesy of the artist's estate/www.bridgeman.co.uk

Cundall, Charles Ernest 1890–1971, *Pilot Officer A. W. I. Jones: Portrait of a Flyer*, purchased, 1965, © courtesy of the artist's estate/www.bridgeman.co.uk

Cundall, Charles Ernest 1890–1971, *Portrait of a Flyer II*, purchased, 1965, © courtesy of the artist's estate/www.bridgeman.co.uk

Cundall, Charles Ernest 1890–1971, *Portrait of a Flyer III*, purchased, 1965, © courtesy of the artist's estate/www.bridgeman.co.uk

Cundall, Charles Ernest 1890–1971, *Pilot Officer Donati: Portrait of a Flyer IV*, purchased, 1965, © courtesy of the artist's estate/www.bridgeman.co.uk

Cundall, Charles Ernest 1890–1971, *Portrait of a Flyer V*, purchased, 1965, © courtesy of the artist's estate/www.bridgeman.co.uk

Cundall, Charles Ernest 1890–1971, *Sergeant Pilot R. H. Higgins, Royal New Zealand Air Force, RAF Wyton*, purchased, 1965, ©

Committee, 1947, © crown copyright

Eves, Reginald Grenville 1876–1941, *Lieutenant General Sir Alan Brooke (1883–1963), KCB, DSO*, transferred from the War Artists' Advisory Committee, 1947, © crown copyright

Eves, Reginald Grenville 1876–1941, *Lieutenant General Sir Ronald Adam (1896–1979), Bt, CB, DSO, OBE*, transferred from the War Artists' Advisory Committee, 1947, © crown copyright

Eves, Reginald Grenville 1876–1941, *Lieutenant General the Honourable H. R. Alexander, CB, CSI, DSO, MC*, transferred from the War Artists' Advisory Committee, 1947, © crown copyright

Eves, Reginald Grenville 1876–1941, *Major C. Tremayne, MC, and Bar*, transferred from the War Artists' Advisory Committee, 1947, © crown copyright

Eves, Reginald Grenville 1876–1941, *Major C. Tremayne, MC and Bar*, transferred from the War Artists' Advisory Committee, 1947

Eves, Reginald Grenville 1876–1941, *Major General Frank Noel Mason-Macfarlane (1889–1953), CB, DSO, MC*, transferred from the War Artists' Advisory Committee, 1947, © crown copyright

Eves, Reginald Grenville 1876–1941, *Major General Frank Noel Mason-Macfarlane (1889–1953), CB, DSO, MC*, transferred from the War Artists' Advisory Committee, 1947

Eves, Reginald Grenville 1876–1941, *Major General W. N. Herbert, CB, CMG, DSO and Bar*, transferred from the War Artists' Advisory Committee, 1947, © crown copyright

Eves, Reginald Grenville 1876–1941, *Sir Cyril Newall (1886–1963), GCB, CMG, CBE*, transferred from the War Artists' Advisory Committee, 1947, © crown copyright

Ewart, David Shanks 1901–1965, *Admiral of the Fleet Sir Dudley Pound (1877–1943), GCB, OM, GCVO*, commissioned, acquired, 1950

Eyton, Anthony John Plowden b.1923, *Reception for Australian and New Zealand Naval Officers at 'HMS Tamar'*, commissioned, 1983, © Imperial War Museum

Faithfull, Leila 1896–1994, *Evacuees Growing Cabbages*, transferred from the War Artists' Advisory Committee, 1947, © crown copyright

Faithfull, Leila 1896–1994, *VE-Day Celebrations outside Buckingham Palace*, transferred from the War Artists' Advisory Committee, 1947, © crown copyright

Feilding, David active 1940s, *Robert Lush, a Prisoner of War*, transferred from the War Artists' Advisory Committee, 1947, © crown copyright

Feilding, David active 1940s, *An Escape Tunnel Built by Prisoners of War*, transferred from the War Artists' Advisory Committee, 1947, © crown copyright

Ferguson, Stuart (Commander) active 1970s, *'HMS Belfast', Bay of Bengal*, transferred from the Belfast Trust, 1978

Ferguson, V. active 1940s, *A Roadside Market Scene*, transferred from the War Artists' Advisory Committee, 1947, © crown copyright

Fergusson, John Duncan 1874–1961, *Dockyard, Portsmouth*, purchased, 1975, © The Fergusson Gallery, Perth and Kinross Council, Scotland

Feteridge, J. F. active 1914–1918, *The FX Six-Inch Gun of 'HMS Chester' (Boy Jack Cornwall)*, gift from Helen Moore, 1975

Ffoulkes, Charles 1868–1947, *St George (1914–1918)*, gift, 1933, © Imperial War Museum

Fischer, Arthur 1872–1948, *Benito Mussolini (1883–1945)*, purchased, 1970

Flint, Francis Russell 1915–1977, *'HMS Belfast', Normandy, 8 July 1944*, gift, 1978

Flint, Francis Russell 1915–1977, *A Rocket Ship Attacking at Walcheren*, transferred from the War Artists' Advisory Committee, 1947, © crown copyright

Flint, Francis Russell 1915–1977, *Rocket Ships in Firing Position off Walcheren*, transferred from the War Artists' Advisory Committee, 1947, © crown copyright

Foot, Victorine b.1920, *Camouflaging a Cruiser in Dock*, transferred from the War Artists' Advisory Committee, 1947, © crown copyright

Forbes, Stanhope Alexander 1857–1947, *Women's Royal Naval Service Ratings Sail-Making: Onboard 'HMS Essex' at Devonport*, commissioned, acquired, 1919, © crown copyright

Ford, Michael b.1920, *Home Guards Brewing Tea Just before Dawn*, transferred from the War Artists' Advisory Committee, 1947, © crown copyright

Ford, Michael b.1920, *War Weapons Week in a Country Town*, transferred from the War Artists' Advisory Committee, 1947, © crown copyright

Ford, Michael b.1920, *Italian Prisoners of War Working on the Land*, transferred from the War Artists' Advisory Committee, 1947, © crown copyright

Fox-Pitt, Douglas 1864–1922, *Indian Army Wounded in Hospital in the Dome, Brighton*, purchased, 1919, © Imperial War Museum

Frampton, Meredith 1894–1984, *Sir Ernest Gowers (1880–1966), KCB, KBE, Senior Regional Commissioner for London, Lieutenant Colonel A. J. Child, OBE, MC, Director of Operations and Intelligence, and K. A. L. Parker, Deputy Chief Administrative Officer, in the London Regional Civil Defence Control Room*, transferred from the War Artists' Advisory Committee, 1947, © crown copyright

Freedman, Barnett 1901–1958, *Aircraft Runway in Course of Construction at Thélus: Near Arras, May 1940*, transferred from the War Artists' Advisory Committee, 1947, © crown copyright

Freedman, Barnett 1901–1958, *Coast Defence Battery, September 1940*, transferred from the War Artists' Advisory Committee, 1947, © crown copyright

Freedman, Barnett 1901–1958, *The Gun*, transferred from the War Artists' Advisory Committee, 1947, © crown copyright

Freedman, Barnett 1901–1958, *15-Inch Gun Turret, 'HMS Repulse'*, transferred from the War Artists' Advisory Committee, 1947, © crown copyright

Freedman, Barnett 1901–1958, *The Landing in Normandy, Arromanches: D-Day Plus 20, 26 June 1944*, transferred from the War Artists' Advisory Committee, 1947, © crown copyright

Freeth, Thomas 1912–1997, *A Wireless Operator in an Armoured Command Vehicle*, transferred from the War Artists' Advisory Committee, 1947, © crown copyright

Freeth, Thomas 1912–1997, *A Liaison Officer Arriving at the Headquarters of an Armoured Division*, transferred from the War Artists' Advisory Committee, 1947, © crown copyright

Freeth, Thomas 1912–1997, *Divisional HQ in Convoy at First Light*, transferred from the War Artists' Advisory Committee, 1947, © crown copyright

Freeth, Thomas 1912–1997, *Twenty Minutes Halt: Divisional HQ in Convoy*, transferred from the War Artists' Advisory Committee, 1947, © crown copyright

Fried, Theodore 1902–1980, *Propagande*, purchased, 1976

Gabain, Ethel 1883–1950, *Sandbag Filling, Islington Borough Council*, transferred from the War Artists' Advisory Committee, 1947, © crown copyright

Gabain, Ethel 1883–1950, *A Crèche*, transferred from the War Artists' Advisory Committee, 1947, © crown copyright

Gabain, Ethel 1883–1950, *A Bunyan-Stannard Irrigation Envelope for the Treatment of Burns, Applied by Sister Roberts in Middlesex Hospital*, transferred from the War Artists' Advisory Committee, 1947, © crown copyright

Gabain, Ethel 1883–1950, *A Bunyan-Stannard First Aid Envelope for Protection against Infection in Burns, as Issued to the Royal Air Force*, transferred from the War Artists' Advisory Committee, 1947, © crown copyright

Gabain, Ethel 1883–1950, *A Child Bomb Victim Receiving Penicillin Treatment*, transferred from the War Artists' Advisory Committee, 1947, © crown copyright

Gabain, Ethel 1883–1950, *Sir Alexander Fleming (1881–1955), FRS, the Discoverer of Penicillin*, transferred from the War Artists' Advisory Committee, 1947, © crown copyright

Gammage, Russell V. 1920–2001, *Anti-Aircraft Gun and Crew*

Garratt, Dorothy A. active 1912–1940, *Dr Charles Ffoulkes, CB*, accessioned, 1987

George, Patrick b.1923, *Early Warning Radar Site, RAF Neatishead*, commissioned, 1981, © Imperial War Museum

Georghiou, Georgios Polybius 1901–1972, *Italians Surrendering at Famagusta, Cyprus, 13 September 1943*, purchased, 1950

Gere, Charles March 1869–1957, *The Standard Prison Ship*, purchased

Gerrard, Kaff 1894–1970, *Bomb Damage with Cows*, gift from Professor A. H. Gerrard, 1991, © Imperial War Museum

Gerrard, Kaff 1894–1970, *Bomb Fragments with Incendiaries*, gift from Professor A. H. Gerrard, 1991, © Imperial War Museum

Gerrard, Kaff 1894–1970, *Twisted Metal and Doodlebug*, gift from Professor A. H. Gerrard, 1991, © Imperial War Museum

Gibbings, Robert 1889–1958, *Gallipoli: Sunset over Lemnos, 'HMS Triumph' and 'HMS Swiftsure'*, commissioned, acquired, 1920

Gibbs, Evelyn 1905–1991, *Women's Voluntary Services Clothing Exchange*, transferred from the War Artists' Advisory Committee, 1947, © crown copyright

Gibbs, J. B. 1859–1935, *Congleton War-Working Party*, gift from the artist, 1919

Gibbs, Nicholas b.1957, *Ruins of War*, gift from the artist, 2006, © the artist

Gill, Colin Unwin 1892–1940, *The Captive*, transferred from the Ministry of Information, 1919, © crown copyright

Gill, Colin Unwin 1892–1940, *A Captured Howitzer at Fampoux*, commissioned, acquired, 1919, © crown copyright

Gill, Colin Unwin 1892–1940, *A Gunner*, commissioned, acquired, 1919, © crown copyright

Gill, Colin Unwin 1892–1940, *Captain Albert Jacka (1893–1932), VC, MC and Bar*, commissioned, acquired, 1919, © crown copyright

Gill, Colin Unwin 1892–1940, *Design for 'Heavy Artillery'*, commissioned, acquired, 1919, © crown copyright

Gill, Colin Unwin 1892–1940, *Evening after a Push*, transferred from the Ministry of Information, 1919, © crown copyright

Gill, Colin Unwin 1892–1940, *Fampoux*, commissioned, acquired, 1919, © crown copyright

Gill, Colin Unwin 1892–1940, *Heavy Artillery*, commissioned, acquired, 1919, © crown copyright

Gill, Colin Unwin 1892–1940, *Observation of Fire: Gunner Officers Correcting Their Battery Fire by Field Telephone from a Disused Trench in No-Man's-Land*, commissioned, acquired, 1919, © crown copyright

Gillot, Eugène Louis 1868–1925, *An Attack by Flamethrowers*, purchased, 1919

Ginner, Charles 1878–1952, *Building a Battleship*, transferred from the War Artists' Advisory Committee, 1947, © crown copyright

Ginner, Charles 1878–1952, *Machine Tools for Russia*, transferred from the War Artists' Advisory Committee, 1947, © crown copyright

Ginner, Charles 1878–1952, *The National Physical Laboratory, Teddington*, transferred from the War Artists' Advisory Committee, 1947, © crown copyright

Ginnett, Louis 1875–1946, *Ypres Salient, Dawn, February 1918*, gift from Mrs L. E. Ginnett, 1960, © the artist's estate

Gledstanes, Elsie 1891–1982, *Her Majesty the Queen Reviewing at County Hall, May 1940*, gift from the artist, 1968

Gledstanes, Elsie 1891–1982, *The Duchess of Kent Reviewing Women's Royal Naval Service Training, Summer 1940*, gift from the artist, 1968

Gledstanes, Elsie 1891–1982, *A Women's Royal Naval Service Officer*, gift from the artist, 1968

Gledstanes, Elsie 1891–1982, *Ambulance Drivers, Non-Commissioned Officers*, gift from the artist, 1968

Gledstanes, Elsie 1891–1982, *Courtyard, Queen Anne's House, Greenwich*, gift from the artist, 1968

Gledstanes, Elsie 1891–1982, *Drivers on Duty at an Ambulance Station*, gift from the artist, 1968

Gledstanes, Elsie 1891–1982, *Food Van at the Royal Docks, London Women's Legion*, gift from the artist, 1968

Gledstanes, Elsie 1891–1982, *No.39a London Auxiliary Ambulance Station*, gift from the artist, 1968

Gledstanes, Elsie 1891–1982, *The Dirty Plate*, gift from the artist, 1968

Gledstanes, Elsie 1891–1982,

Women's Royal Naval Service Ratings Drill and Inspection in the Courtyard of Queen Anne's House, Greenwich, gift from the artist, 1968

Gleichen, Helena 1873–1947, *Troops Moving into Gorizia*, gift from the artist, 1938

Glen, Graham active 1897–1919, *Armament School, Uxbridge: Women's Royal Air Force at Work in Aerial Gun-Testing Shop*, commissioned, acquired, 1919

Glen, Graham active 1897–1919, *No.1 Southern Aircraft Repair Depot, South Farnborough: Women's Royal Air Force at Work on Aeroplane Salvage*, commissioned, acquired, 1919

Golden, Grace Lydia 1904–1993, *An Emergency Food Office*, transferred from the War Artists' Advisory Committee, 1947, © crown copyright

Goodin, Walter 1907–1992, *A Barrage Balloon over a Dock at Hull*, transferred from the War Artists' Advisory Committee, 1947, © crown copyright

Gordon, Jan 1882–1944, *'HMS Castor': Wounded, Received after the Battle of Jutland, 31 May 1916*, commissioned, acquired, 1919, © crown copyright

Gordon, Jan 1882–1944, *Royal Navy Armoured Car Squadron: Transport of Wounded on the Turkish Front*, commissioned, acquired, 1920, © crown copyright

Gordon, Jan 1882–1944, *Royal Navy Armoured Car Squadron: Winter Transport of Wounded at Alexandrovsk*, commissioned, acquired, 1920, © crown copyright

Gordon, Jan 1882–1944, *The Dressing Station in a Man-of-War*, commissioned, acquired, 1920, © crown copyright

Gourdie, Thomas 1913–2005, *De-Icing before a Strike off the Norwegian Coast, during which this Beaufighter was lost*, transferred from the War Artists' Advisory Committee, 1947, © crown copyright

Gow, Andrew Carrick 1848–1920, *The First Zeppelin Seen from Piccadilly Circus, 8 September 1915*, gift from the artist's family, 1961

Gow, Andrew Carrick 1848–1920, *Volunteers Drilling in the Courtyard of Burlington House*, gift from the artist's family, 1961

Grant, Duncan 1885–1978, *Study for 'The Gunnery Lesson'*, purchased, 1982, © 1978 estate of Duncan Grant

Grant, Duncan 1885–1978, *St Paul's*, transferred from the War Artists' Advisory Committee, 1947, © crown copyright

Graves, Frank 1913–2001, *An Entertainments National Service Association Party Travels in a Canvas-Covered Lorry*, transferred from the War Artists' Advisory Committee, 1947, © crown copyright

Graves, Frank 1913–2001, *Ruth Earley Practises on Setting: Entertainments National Service Association Production, Garrison Theatre Stage*, gift from the artist, 1973, © the artist's estate

Graves, Frank 1913–2001, *A Cinema in the Desert: Entertainments National Service Association, Suez*, gift from the artist, 1973, © the artist's estate

Graves, Frank 1913–2001, *American Soldiers Prepare Nissen Hut Stage Prior to Entertainments National Service Association Show*, gift from the artist, 1973, © the artist's estate

Graves, Frank 1913–2001, *An Afternoon Show by an Entertainments National Service Association Company in a Navy Army and Air Force Institutes' Canteen Hut*, transferred from the War Artists' Advisory Committee, 1947, © crown copyright

Gray, Joseph 1890–1962, *A Ration Party of the 4th Black Watch at the Battle of Neuve Chapelle, 1915*, commissioned, acquired, 1919, © crown copyright

Gray, Norah Neilson 1882–1931, *The Scottish Women's Hospital: In the Cloister of the Abbaye at Royaumont, Dr Frances Ivens Inspects a French Patient*, commissioned, acquired, 1920

Gray, Ronald 1868–1951, *Evening Quarters: The Lookout at Cannon Street Anti-Aircraft Station*, purchased, 1917, © Imperial War Museum

Gray, Ronald 1868–1951, *King's Cross Anti-Aircraft Gun in Action*, purchased, 1917, © Imperial War Museum

Green, Leonora Kathleen b.1901, *Coupons Required*, gift from Mrs D. M. Moore, 1988

Green, Leonora Kathleen b.1901, *Lest We Forget*, gift from Mrs Dorothy M. Moore, 1988

Greenwood, Walter Edmund active 1914–1918, *Sunset*

Groom, Arthur G. active 1914–1974, *Review of Silver Badge Men, Hyde Park, 23 November 1918*, gift from the artist, 1974

Gross, Anthony 1905–1984, *Arakan Campaign: The Battle of Rathedaung, 1943 with Six Rajputana Rifles Attacking Hill North 75*, transferred from the War Artists' Advisory Committee, 1947, © crown copyright

Gunn, Herbert James 1893–1964, *Air Marshal Sir Philip Joubert de la Ferté (1887–1965), KCB, CMG, DSO*, transferred from the War Artists' Advisory Committee, 1947, © crown copyright

Gunn, Herbert James 1893–1964, *Air Marshal William Sholto Douglas (1893–1969), CB, MC, DFC*, transferred from the War Artists' Advisory Committee, 1947, © crown copyright

Gunn, Herbert James 1893–1964, *General Henry Graham Crerar (1888–1965), CH, CB, DSO*, gift from the Canadian Government, 1950, © estate of the artist

Guthrie, Kathleen 1905–1981, *A Bombed Hospital Ward*, transferred from the War Artists' Advisory Committee, 1947, © crown copyright

Hailstone, Bernard 1910–1987, *An Evening in the City, April 1941*, transferred from the War Artists' Advisory Committee, 1947, © crown copyright

Hailstone, Bernard 1910–1987, *Andrew Nures Nabarro, GM, Leading Fireman, Portsmouth Auxiliary Fire Service*, transferred from the War Artists' Advisory Committee, 1947, © crown copyright

Hailstone, Bernard 1910–1987, *Barbara Mary Rendell, BEM, Auxiliary Fire Service*, transferred from the War Artists' Advisory Committee, 1947, © crown copyright

Hailstone, Bernard 1910–1987, *Frederick Charles Reville, GM, Bristol Auxiliary Fire Service*, transferred from the War Artists' Advisory Committee, 1947, © crown copyright

Hailstone, Bernard 1910–1987, *Activity at a Hull Dock*, transferred from the War Artists' Advisory Committee, 1947, © crown copyright

Hailstone, Bernard 1910–1987, *Convoy Centre at Augusta, Sicily*, transferred from the War Artists' Advisory Committee, 1947, © crown copyright

Hailstone, Bernard 1910–1987, *Damaged Tanks Being Lowered into the Hold of a Merchant Ship*, transferred from the War Artists' Advisory Committee, 1947, © crown copyright

Hailstone, Bernard 1910–1987, *Escaped Prisoners' Camp, Algiers*, transferred from the War Artists' Advisory Committee, 1947, © crown copyright

Hailstone, Bernard 1910–1987, *Loading Ammuniton at Hull Docks*, transferred from the War Artists' Advisory Committee, 1947, © crown copyright

Hailstone, Bernard 1910–1987, *The Morning after the Big Raid at Bari, Italy*, transferred from the War Artists' Advisory Committee, 1947, © crown copyright

Hailstone, Bernard 1910–1987, *Able Seaman Welcher*, transferred from the War Artists' Advisory Committee, 1947, © crown copyright

Hailstone, Bernard 1910–1987, *Admiral Lord Louis Mountbatten (1900–1979), GCVO, KCB, DSO*, transferred from the War Artists' Advisory Committee, 1947, © crown copyright

Hailstone, Bernard 1910–1987, *Christian Vlasto, a Canal Boat Woman*, transferred from the War Artists' Advisory Committee, 1947,

© crown copyright

Hailstone, Bernard 1910–1987, *Convoy from Malta*, gift from Mrs Thompson, 2002, © the artist's estate

Hailstone, Bernard 1910–1987, *Lieutenant General Sir Frank Messervy (1893–1974), KBE, CB, DSO and Bar*, transferred from the War Artists' Advisory Committee, 1947, © crown copyright

Hailstone, Bernard 1910–1987, *Lieutenant General Sir Miles Dempsey (1896–1969), KCB, KBE, DSO, MC*, transferred from the War Artists' Advisory Committee, 1947, © crown copyright

Hailstone, Bernard 1910–1987, *Lieutenant General Sir Montagu Stopford (1892–1971), KBE, CB, DSO, MC*, transferred from the War Artists' Advisory Committee, 1947, © crown copyright

Hailstone, Bernard 1910–1987, *Major General R. F. S. Denning, CB*, transferred from the War Artists' Advisory Committee, 1947, © crown copyright

Hailstone, Bernard 1910–1987, *R. Dibnah, BEM, Motorman of the 'Nonsuch' Blockade Runner*, transferred from the War Artists' Advisory Committee, 1947, © crown copyright

Hailstone, Bernard 1910–1987, *Sir Edward Appleton (1892–1965), KCB, FRS*, transferred from the War Artists' Advisory Committee, 1947, © crown copyright

Hailstone, Bernard 1910–1987, *Sir Henry Tizard (1885–1959), KCB, AFC, FRS*, transferred from the War Artists' Advisory Committee, 1947, © crown copyright

Hailstone, Bernard 1910–1987, *Brigadier C. P. Jones, CBE, MC, Malaya Command*, transferred from the War Artists' Advisory Committee, 1947, © crown copyright

Hailstone, Bernard 1910–1987, *Rear Admiral C. E. Douglas-Pennant, CB, CBE, DSO, DSC*, transferred from the War Artists' Advisory Committee, 1947, © crown copyright

Hailstone, Bernard 1910–1987, *Air Chief Marshal Sir Keith Park (1892–1975), KCB, KBE, MC, DFC*, transferred from the War Artists' Advisory Committee, 1947, © crown copyright

Hailstone, Bernard 1910–1987, *Lieutenant General Sir Frederick Browning (1896–1965), KBE, CB, SO*, transferred from the War Artists' Advisory Committee, 1947, © crown copyright

Haines, Wilfred Stanley 1905–1944, *Burning Oil on a Slack Tide*, gift from V. Haines, 1980

Haines, Wilfred Stanley 1905–1944, *Fire Blitz on Bath*, transferred from the War Artists' Advisory Committee, 1947, © crown copyright

Haines, Wilfred Stanley 1905–1944, *An Observation Post: Flying*

© crown copyright

Hailstone, Bernard 1910–1987, *Convoy from Malta*, gift from Mrs Thompson, 2002, © the artist's estate

Hambling, Maggi b.1945, *Captain E. P. Forster, Women's Royal Air Corps, Director of Music for the Women's Royal Air Corps Staff Band*, commissioned, 1985, © Imperial War Museum

Hambling, Maggi b.1945, *The Staff Band of the Women's Royal Army Corps*, commissioned, 1985, © Imperial War Museum

Hamilton, John 1919–1993, *A Lone Survivor, Covered in Oil*, transferred from the Belfast Trust, 1978, © the artist's estate

Hamilton, John 1919–1993, *Air Cover: A Typical Escort Carrier, 'HMS Archer' on North Atlantic Escort Duty*, transferred from the Belfast Trust, 1978, © the artist's estate

Hamilton, John 1919–1993, *Aircraft Attacking Four Ships in the Mediterranean*, transferred from the Belfast Trust, 1978, © the artist's estate

Hamilton, John 1919–1993, *Arctic Gale*, transferred from the Belfast Trust, 1978, © the artist's estate

Hamilton, John 1919–1993, *Attack on Taranto, 11 November 1940*, transferred from the Belfast Trust, 1978, © the artist's estate

Hamilton, John 1919–1993, *Battle of Matapan, 28 March 1941*, transferred from the Belfast Trust, 1978, © the artist's estate

Hamilton, John 1919–1993, *Battle of the River Plate*, transferred from the Belfast Trust, 1978, © the artist's estate

Hamilton, John 1919–1993, *Caught on the Surface: A Short Sunderland Flying Boat Attacking a U-Boat*, transferred from the Belfast Trust, 1978, © the artist's estate

Hamilton, John 1919–1993, *Channel Dash: The Attempt to Halt the Progress of the Battleships 'Scharnhorst' and 'Gneisenau' through the Channel, 12–13 February 1942*, transferred from the Belfast Trust, 1978, © the artist's estate

Hamilton, John 1919–1993, *Convoy*, transferred from the Belfast Trust, 1978, © the artist's estate

Hamilton, John 1919–1993, *Convoy PQ18 Attacked by a Junkers 88 and Heinkel III Torpedo Bombers, 13 September 1942*, transferred from the Belfast Trust, 1978, © the artist's estate

Hamilton, John 1919–1993, *D-Day Naval Bombardment: 'HMS Ramillies', 'HMS Warspite' and Monitor 'HMS Roberts' Bombard the Beaches*, transferred from the Belfast Trust, 1978, © the artist's estate

Hamilton, John 1919–1993, *Distant Escort: The Cruisers 'HMS Sheffield' and 'HMS Jamaica' with the Battleship 'HMS Duke of York'*

Patrol the Convoy Route to Russia, transferred from the Belfast Trust, 1978, © the artist's estate

Hamilton, John 1919–1993, *Evacuation of Crete: Cruisers 'HMS Orion' and 'HMS Kimberley' under Attack, May 1941*, transferred from the Belfast Trust, 1978, © the artist's estate

Hamilton, John 1919–1993, *'HMC S Snowberry', a Flower Class Corvette of the Royal Canadian Navy*, transferred from the Belfast Trust, 1978, © the artist's estate

Hamilton, John 1919–1993, *'HMS Biter' in an Arctic Gale*, transferred from the Belfast Trust, 1978, © the artist's estate, © the artist's estate

Hamilton, John 1919–1993, *'HMS Illustrious' under Attack: Excess Convoy, January 1941*, transferred from the Belfast Trust, 1978, © the artist's estate

Hamilton, John 1919–1993, *HMS Submarine 'Trident' on Patrol in Arctic Waters*, transferred from the Belfast Trust, 1978, © the artist's estate

Hamilton, John 1919–1993, *HMS Submarine 'Upholder'*, transferred from the Belfast Trust, 1978, © the artist's estate

Hamilton, John 1919–1993, *'HMS Wallace', 1940*, transferred from the Belfast Trust, 1978, © the artist's estate

Hamilton, John 1919–1993, *'HMS Woodpecker'*, transferred from the Belfast Trust, 1978, © the artist's estate

Hamilton, John 1919–1993, *Large and Small Vessels and a Lifeboat*, transferred from the Belfast Trust, 1978, © the artist's estate

Hamilton, John 1919–1993, *Last Stand of the 'SS Stephen Hopkins'*, transferred from the Belfast Trust, 1978, © the artist's estate

Hamilton, John 1919–1993, *Listening: Motor Torpedo Boats of the Coastal Forces off the Enemy Coast*, transferred from the Belfast Trust, 1978, © the artist's estate

Hamilton, John 1919–1993, *Malta Convoy: 'SS Brisbane Star' and 'SS Rochester Castle'*, transferred from the Belfast Trust, 1978, © the artist's estate

Hamilton, John 1919–1993, *Mines in the Fairway*, transferred from the Belfast Trust, 1978, © the artist's estate

Hamilton, John 1919–1993, *Minesweepers under Attack, Thames Estuary, October 1940*, transferred from the Belfast Trust, 1978, © the artist's estate

Hamilton, John 1919–1993, *Narvik Harbour after the Destroyer Attack, 10 April 1940*, transferred from the Belfast Trust, 1978, © the artist's estate

Hamilton, John 1919–1993, *Night Action: Crew Abandoning Sinking Submarine U-70, 7 March 1941*, transferred from the Belfast Trust, 1978, © the artist's estate

Hamilton, John 1919–1993, *Night Battle*, transferred from the Belfast Trust, 1978, © the artist's estate

Hamilton, John 1919–1993, *Routed North: Arctic Convoys Routed North in Summer, to the Edge of the Ice Pack, to Evade Aircraft Based in North Norway*, transferred from the Belfast Trust, 1978, © the artist's estate

Hamilton, John 1919–1993, *Second Battle of Sirte, 22 March 1942*, transferred from the Belfast Trust, 1978, © the artist's estate

Hamilton, John 1919–1993, *'SS Rathlin', Rescue Ship*, transferred from the Belfast Trust, 1978, © the artist's estate

Hamilton, John 1919–1993, *Storm at Sea*, transferred from the Belfast Trust, 1978, © the artist's estate

Hamilton, John 1919–1993, *Supplies for the Raiders: The Disguised Supply Ship 'Nordmark' with the Raider 'Admiral Scheer', March 1941*, transferred from the Belfast Trust, 1978, © the artist's estate

Hamilton, John 1919–1993, *Survivors: 'HMS Ledbury' Rescued 44 Men from the Merchantman 'SS Waimarama', Pedestal Convoy, 1942*, transferred from the Belfast Trust, 1978, © the artist's estate

Hamilton, John 1919–1993, *The Attack on Convoy SC7: The Sinking of 'SS Assyrian'*, transferred from the Belfast Trust, 1978, © the artist's estate

Hamilton, John 1919–1993, *The Battle of the Fjords: In the Running Destroyer Fight, during the Withdrawal from Narvik, the Damaged 'HMS Hotspur' Collided with 'HMS Hunter'*, transferred from the Belfast Trust, 1978, © the artist's estate

Hamilton, John 1919–1993, *The Battle of the North Cape: 'HMS Duke of York' in Action against the 'Scharnhorst', 26 December 1943*, transferred from the Belfast Trust, 1978, © the artist's estate

Hamilton, John 1919–1993, *The 'Bismarck' Action: The 'Bismarck' Escapes*, transferred from the Belfast Trust, 1978, © the artist's estate

Hamilton, John 1919–1993, *The 'Bismarck' Action: The 'Swordfish' Attack, 26 May 1941*, transferred from the Belfast Trust, 1978, © the artist's estate

Hamilton, John 1919–1993, *The Defence of Convoy JW 51B: Destroyers 'HMS Onslow' and 'HMS Orwell' Defended the Convoy against the Heavy Cruiser 'Hipper', 31 December 1942*, transferred from the Belfast Trust, 1978, © the artist's estate

Hamilton, John 1919–1993, *The Destruction of U-202 by 'HMS Starling', 1 June 1943*, transferred from the Belfast Trust, 1978, © the artist's estate

Hamilton, John 1919–1993, *The Fight to Save the 'SS Regent Lion'*, transferred from the Belfast Trust, 1978, © the artist's estate

Hamilton, John 1919–1993, *The 'Gallant Ohio'*, transferred from the Belfast Trust, 1978, © the artist's estate

Hamilton, John 1919–1993, *The 'Gallant Tekoa', New Zealand Steamship Company, Picking Up Survivors, March 1943*, transferred from the Belfast Trust, 1978, © the artist's estate

Hamilton, John 1919–1993, *The 'Glenorchy' is Spotted, Pedestal Convoy, 13 August 1942*, transferred from the Belfast Trust, 1978, © the artist's estate

Hamilton, John 1919–1993, *The Raid on St Nazaire, 27–28 March 1942*, transferred from the Belfast Trust, 1978, © the artist's estate

Hamilton, John 1919–1993, *The Raider 'Kormoran'*, transferred from the Belfast Trust, 1978, © the artist's estate

Hamilton, John 1919–1993, *The Sinking of 'HMS Acasta', Attacked by Battleships 'Scharnhorst' and 'Gneisenau'*, transferred from the Belfast Trust, 1978, © the artist's estate

Hamilton, John 1919–1993, *The Sinking of 'HMS Fiji', 'HMS Kingston' Standing by, 22 May 1941*, transferred from the Belfast Trust, 1978, © the artist's estate

Hamilton, John 1919–1993, *The Sinking of U-752, 23 May 1943*, transferred from the Belfast Trust, 1978, © the artist's estate

Hamilton, John 1919–1993, *The Tide Begins to Turn: One of the Long Range Liberators of 120 Squadron, Royal Air Force, Based in Iceland, Providing Air Cover in the Mid-Atlantic*, transferred from the Belfast Trust, 1978, © the artist's estate

Hamilton, John 1919–1993, *The Toll*, transferred from the Belfast Trust, 1978, © the artist's estate

Hamilton, John 1919–1993, *The Wolf Pack Gathers: U-99, U-100, U-101 and U-123 Prepare to Attack Convoy SC7, 18 October 1940*, transferred from the Belfast Trust, 1978, © the artist's estate

Hamilton, John 1919–1993, *Torpedoed: A Corvette Picks Up Survivors from a Torpedoed Liberty Ship*, transferred from the Belfast Trust, 1978, © the artist's estate

Hamilton, John 1919–1993, *U-309 on Atlantic Patrol*, transferred from the Belfast Trust, 1978, © the artist's estate

Hamilton, John 1919–1993, *U-Boats inside the Convoy: U-99 on the Surface Having Torpedoed the Tanker 'Ferm', 7 March 1941*, transferred from the Belfast Trust, 1978, © the artist's estate

Hamilton, John 1919–1993, *'HMS Belfast' in Action against the 'Scharnhorst', 26 December 1943*, transferred from the Belfast Trust, 1978, © the artist's estate

Hamilton, John 1919–1993, *'HMS Northern Pride'*, transferred from the Belfast Trust, 1978, © the artist's estate

Hamilton, John 1919–1993, *The 'Gallant Ohio'*, transferred from the Belfast Trust, 1978, © the artist's estate

Hamilton, John 1919–1993, *'HMS Renown' in a North Sea Gale, April 1940*, transferred from the Belfast Trust, 1978, © the artist's estate

Hamilton, John 1919–1993, *The 'Bismarck' Action: 'HMS Zulu' under Fire*, transferred from the Belfast Trust, 1978, © the artist's estate

Hamilton, John 1919–1993, *The 'Bismarck' Action: The Destruction of 'HMS Hood'*, transferred from the Belfast Trust, 1978, © the artist's estate

Hamilton, John 1919–1993, *The Sinking of 'SS Bedouin', 16 March 1941*, transferred from the Belfast Trust, 1978, © the artist's estate

Hamilton, John 1919–1993, *The Sinking of the 'Scharnhorst', 26 December 1943*, transferred from the Belfast Trust, 1978, © the artist's estate

Hamilton, Vereker 1856–1931, *HM Airship No.3 at Kingsnorth*, purchased, 1918

Harcourt, George 1868–1947, *The Voluntary Aid Detachments: Peace Procession, 19 July 1919*, purchased, 1921

Harcourt, George 1868–1947, *Aletha Harcourt, Ambulance Driver, Bushey Heath Air Raid Precautions*, gift from Mrs A. D Manoir, 1982

Harcourt, H. L. active 1940s, *The Village of Sorvagur, Faroe Islands*, gift from Mr D. W. Byers, 1996

Hardy, Dorofield 1882–1927, *The Ballroom, Londonderry House, 1912 (copy of John Lavery)*

Harmar, Fairlie 1876–1945, *Women's Royal Air Force Workers Drilling at Andover Aerodrome*, gift from Randolph Schwabe, 1946

Harrison, Arthur R. active 1935–1976, *The Long Night: London Blitz*, gift from the artist, 1976

Hassall, John 1868–1948, *The Vision of St George over the Battlefield*, purchased, 1983, © the artist's estate

Hatherell, William 1855–1928, *Nurse, Wounded Soldier and Child*, gift from F. H. Deakin, 1957

Hatherell, William 1855–1928, *The Funeral Service of Edith Cavell at Westminster Abbey, 15 May 1919*, commissioned, acquired, 1919

Haybrook, Rudolf 1868–1965, *Hampton's*, bequeathed by John and Nora Wise, 1987

Haybrook, Rudolf 1868–1965, *Aeroplane Crash, North London, May 1940*, bequeathed by John and Nora Wise, 1987

Haybrook, Rudolf 1868–1965, *The London Fireboat 'Massey Shaw' Approaching Dunkirk at 11pm, 2 June 1940*, transferred from the War Artists' Advisory Committee, 1947, © crown copyright

Hayward, Alfred Robert 1875–1971, *First Study for 'The Staff Train at Charing Cross Station'*, commissioned, acquired, 1919, © crown copyright

Hayward, Alfred Robert 1875–1971, *Second Study for 'The Staff Train at Charing Cross Station'*, commissioned, acquired, 1919, © crown copyright

Hayward, Alfred Robert 1875–1971, *The Soldiers' Buffet, Charing Cross Station*, commissioned, 1919, on loan, © crown copyright

Hayward, Alfred Robert 1875–1971, *The Staff Train at Charing Cross Station*, commissioned, acquired, 1919, © crown copyright

Hayward, Alfred Robert 1875–1971, *General Sir William Riddell Birdwood (1865–1951), GCMG, KCB, KCSI*, commissioned, acquired, 1919, © crown copyright

Hayward, Alfred Robert 1875–1971, *Lieutenant General Sir William T. Furse (1865–1953), KCB, DSO*, commissioned, acquired, 1919, © crown copyright

Hellawell, Harry 1921–2004, *Untitled*, gift from the artist's wife, 2006

Henderson, Keith 1883–1982, *A North-East Coast Aerodrome*, transferred from the War Artists' Advisory Committee, 1947, © crown copyright

Henderson, Keith 1883–1982, *A Sergeant Wireless Operator*, transferred from the War Artists' Advisory Committee, 1947, © crown copyright

Henderson, Keith 1883–1982, *An Air View of Montrose, Angus*, transferred from the War Artists' Advisory Committee, 1947, © crown copyright

Henderson, Keith 1883–1982, *An Improvised Test of an Undercarriage*, transferred from the War Artists' Advisory Committee, 1947, © crown copyright

Henderson, Keith 1883–1982, *Dawn: Leaving for North Sea Patrol*, transferred from the War Artists' Advisory Committee, 1947, © crown copyright

Henderson, Keith 1883–1982, *Night: An Air Gunner in Action Turret*, transferred from the War Artists' Advisory Committee, 1947, © crown copyright

Henderson, Keith 1883–1982, *Wings over Scotland*, transferred from the War Artists' Advisory Committee, 1947, © crown copyright

Hepple, Norman 1908–1994, *Canadian Fireman, Overseas Contingent*, transferred from the War Artists' Advisory Committee, 1947, © crown copyright

Herbert, P. active 1960s, *Judi's Grave*, bequeathed by W. F. Wilson, 1974

Herbert, P. active 1960s, *Royal Navy Ships from the Starboard Bow*, bequeathed by W. F. Wilson, 1974

Herbert, P. active 1960s, *Two-Funnelled Royal Navy Ships from the Starboard Quarter*, bequeathed by W. F. Wilson, 1974

Hewland, Elsie Dalton 1901–1979, *A Nursery School for War Workers'*

Children, transferred from the War Artists' Advisory Committee, 1947, © crown copyright

Hewland, Elsie Dalton 1901–1979, *Assembling Hawker Hurricane Aircraft: Swinging the Compasses and Making Test Flights*, transferred from the War Artists' Advisory Committee, 1947, © crown copyright

Hewland, Elsie Dalton 1901–1979, *Typhoon Aircraft Undergoing Minor Repairs*, transferred from the War Artists' Advisory Committee, 1947, © crown copyright

Hicks, Philip b.1928, *Evening Blues*, gift from the artist, 1974, © the artist

Hicks, Philip b.1928, *Posthumous 1*, gift from the artist, 1974, © the artist

Hicks, Philip b.1928, *Posthumous 2*, gift from the artist, 1974, © the artist

Hicks, Philip b.1928, *Boy and Veteran*, gift from the artist, 1974, © the artist

Hicks, Philip b.1928, *Boy at War*, gift from the artist, 1974, © the artist

Hicks, Philip b.1928, *Anonymous Award*, gift from the artist, 1974, © the artist

Hicks, Philip b.1928, *Posthumous 3*, gift from the artist, 1974, © the artist

Hicks, Philip b.1928, *Posthumous 4*, gift from the artist, 1974, © the artist

Hill, Adrian Keith Graham 1895–1977, *Ruins between Bernafay Wood and Maricourt*, commissioned, acquired, 1919, © Imperial War Museum

Hill, Adrian Keith Graham 1895–1977, *Interior of a Dugout at Gavrelle*, gift from the artist, 1927, © Imperial War Museum

Hlavsa, Oldrich 1889–1936, *Country Life in Moravia: 'To Our Comrades in Arms (the Officers of 'HMS Suffolk'), from the Czecho-Slovaks Vladivostok'*, gift, 1920

Hodge, Francis Edwin 1883–1949, *Mont St Quentin and Péronne from near Maisonette, 1918*, purchased, 1919, © crown copyright

Hodge, Francis Edwin 1883–1949, *A Balloon Being Transferred to a Land Winch from a Barrage Balloon Vessel*, transferred from the War Artists' Advisory Committee, 1947, © crown copyright

Hodge, Francis Edwin 1883–1949, *A Balloon Close: Hauled on a Barge*, transferred from the War Artists' Advisory Committee, 1947, © crown copyright

Hodge, Francis Edwin 1883–1949, *Bedding Down: A Barrage Balloon*, transferred from the War Artists' Advisory Committee, 1947, © crown copyright

Hodgkin, Eliot 1905–1987, *The Haberdashers' Hall, 8 May 1945*, transferred from the War Artists' Advisory Committee, 1947, © crown copyright

Hogan, Eileen b.1946, *Women's Royal Naval Service Air Mechanic, Portland*, commissioned, 1984, © Imperial War Museum

Holmes, Charles John 1868–1936, *A Two-Year-Old Steel Works: Erected during the War for Messrs. Steel, Peech & Tozer, Ltd, Phoenix Works, Sheffield*, transferred from the Ministry of Information, 1919, © crown copyright

Holmes, Charles John 1868–1936, *Awaiting Zeppelins: Sandringham, January 1915*, commissioned, acquired, 1919, © crown copyright

Horton, Percy Frederick 1897–1970, *Blind Workers in a Birmingham Factory*, transferred from the War Artists' Advisory Committee, 1947, © crown copyright

Howard, Ken b.1932, *Rosemount*, commissioned, acquired, 1973, © courtesy of the artist/www.bridgeman.co.uk

Howard, Norman 1899–1955, *The Battle of the Leyte Gulf*, gift from Herbert Addison OBE, MSC, 1983

Howard-Jones, Ray 1903–1996, *Brigadier L. Howard-Jones, OBE, Royal Electrical and Mechanical Engineers, 8th Army (1942–1943)*, transferred from the War Artists' Advisory Committee, 1947, © crown copyright

Howard-Jones, Ray 1903–1996, *Fortified Islands in the Bristol Channel: Two Inch Naval UP-Projector on an Earlier Fortification*, transferred from the War Artists' Advisory Committee, 1947, © crown copyright

Howitt-Lodge, B. 1883–1948, *London 'Carries On'*, gift, 1947, © crown copyright

Howitt-Lodge, B. 1883–1948, *Business as Usual*, gift, 1947, © crown copyright

Howson, Peter b.1958, *Entering Gornji Vakuf*, commissioned, acquired, 1994, © Imperial War Museum

Howson, Peter b.1958, *Three Miles from Home*, commissioned, acquired, 1994, © Imperial War Museum

Howson, Peter b.1958, *Cleansed*, commissioned, acquired, 1994, © Imperial War Museum

Hughes-Stanton, Herbert Edwin Pelham 1870–1937, *Lens*, gift, 1919, © crown copyright

Hughes-Stanton, Herbert Edwin Pelham 1870–1937, *Lens Road, Arras: From the Suburb of St Nicholas, Arras*, gift, 1919, © crown copyright

Hughes-Stanton, Herbert Edwin Pelham 1870–1937, *The Cemetery at Mont St Eloi*, purchased, 1919, © crown copyright

Hughes-Stanton, Herbert Edwin Pelham 1870–1937, *The St Quentin Canal from the Temporary Bridge Erected across the St Quentin Canal, North of Bellenglise, Looking towards Bellicourt*, gift from the artist, 1919, © Imperial War Museum

Hutchinson, Mabel b.1903, *A Bermondsey Rest Centre*, transferred from the War Artists' Advisory Committee, 1947, © crown copyright

Hutton, Philip active 1940–1945, *A Bomb Disposal Squad at Work*, transferred from the War Artists' Advisory Committee, 1947, © crown copyright

Hutton, Philip active 1940–1945, *A Bomb Disposal Squad Digging out an Unexploded Bomb*, transferred from the War Artists' Advisory Committee, 1947, © crown copyright

Hutton, Philip active 1940–1945, *Destroying an Unexploded Bomb*, transferred from the War Artists' Advisory Committee, 1947, © crown copyright

Hutton, Philip active 1940–1945, *Destroying an Unexploded Bomb*, transferred from the War Artists' Advisory Committee, 1947, © crown copyright

Hutton, Philip active 1940–1945, *Preparing a Shaft to Reach an Unexploded Bomb*, transferred from the War Artists' Advisory Committee, 1947, © crown copyright

Hyde, William 1859–1925, *The Steel Converter at Woolwich Arsenal: The Tropenas Steel Converters at Work in the Royal Laboratory Shell Foundry at Woolwich Arsenal*, purchased, 1919

Jackson, Gerald Goddard b.1878, *Schwarmstedt Camp I*, purchased, 1919

Jackson, Gerald Goddard b.1878, *Schwarmstedt Camp II*, purchased, 1919

James, Edward Ernest active 1940s, *A Tank Landing at Night*, transferred from the War Artists' Advisory Committee, 1947, © crown copyright

Jameson, Cecil 1883–c.1962, *Lieutenant Colonel Carne, VC*, purchased, 1961, © Imperial War Museum

Japp, Darsie 1883–1973, *The Royal Field Artillery in Macedonia, Spring 1918*, commissioned, 1919, © crown copyright

Japp, Darsie 1883–1973, *Regimental Band*, gift from the artist, 1920, © Imperial War Museum

Jillard, Hilda 1899–1975, *What Harvest?*, gift from Miss I. Keeble, 1980

John, Augustus Edwin 1878–1961, *Fraternity*, purchased, 1920, © Imperial War Museum

Judah, Gerry b.1951, *Frontiers 07*, purchased, 2006, © the artist

Jungman, Nico 1872–1935, *Ruhleben Prison Camp: Slaves of the Ring*, purchased, 1918

Jungman, Nico 1872–1935, *Ruhleben Prison Camp: The Queue for Bread from Denmark*, purchased, 1918

Jungman, Nico 1872–1935,

Ruhleben Prison Camp: Christmas Dinner, purchased, 1918

Jungman, Nico 1872–1935, *Ruhleben Prison Camp: Hut No.8, on Plan No.530*, purchased, 1918

Jungman, Nico 1872–1935, *Ruhleben Prison Camp: Panoramic View*, gift from the artist, 1918

Jungman, Nico 1872–1935, *Ruhleben Prison Camp: Panoramic View*, gift from the artist, 1918

Jungman, Nico 1872–1935, *Ruhleben Prison Camp: 'Trafalgar Square'*, purchased, 1918

Jungman, Nico 1872–1935, *Ruhleben Prison Camp: Bathing*, purchased, 1918

Jungman, Nico 1872–1935, *Plan of Ruhleben Camp: Key to Panoramic View*, gift from the artist, 1918

Jungman, Nico 1872–1935, *Ruhleben Prison Camp: The Distribution of Parcels from Home*, purchased, 1918

Kalkhof, Peter b.1933, *Stealth*, purchased, 2001

Kay-Krzewinski, Feliks 1900–1981, *Polish Prisoners of War Marching to Siberia, Kazakhstan*, gift from Mrs E. Kay-Krzewinski, 1982

Kay-Krzewinski, Feliks 1900–1981, *The Artist, Karakol, Kazakhstan, Russia*, gift from Mrs E. Kay-Krzewinski, 1982

Kay-Krzewinski, Feliks 1900–1981, *Typhoid Victims, Lugowaja, South Kazakhstan*, gift from Mrs E. Kay-Krzewinski, 1982

Kay-Krzewinski, Feliks 1900–1981, *Monte Cassino and the Tent of the Military Police Headquarters*, gift from Mrs E. Kay-Krzewinski, 1982

Kay-Krzewinski, Feliks 1900–1981, *Sessano, Italy, 12 April 1944*, gift from Mrs E. Kay-Krzewinski, 1982

Kay-Krzewinski, Feliks 1900–1981, *Hungry Steppe 1945, Kazakhstan, Russia*, gift from Mrs E. Kay-Krzewinski, 1982

Kay-Krzewinski, Feliks 1900–1981, *Monte Cassino One Month after the Battle*, gift from Mrs E. Kay-Krzewinski, 1982

Keanc, John b.1954, *Death Squad*, commissioned, acquired, 1991, © Imperial War Museum

Keane, John b.1954, *Mickey Mouse at the Front*, commissioned, acquired, 1991, © Imperial War Museum

Kemeny, Kalman 1896–1994, *Mass in the Field, Russian Front*, gift from the artist, 1977

Kemeny, Kalman 1896–1994, *Battery in the Field, Russian Front*, gift from the artist, 1977

Kemeny, Kalman 1896–1994, *Destroyed Bridge, Carpathian Mountains, Romanian Front*, gift from the artist, 1977

Kemp-Welch, Lucy 1869–1958, *The Ladies' Army Remount Depot, Russley Park, Wiltshire, 1918*, commissioned, 1920, © Imperial War Museum

Kemp-Welch, Lucy 1869–1958, *The Straw Ride: Russley Park Remount Depot, Wiltshire*, gift from the artist, 1920

Kennedy, Cedric J. 1898–1968, *The Defence of London against Gothas with a DH4 on Night Patrol Work over the South-East Coast*, gift from the artist, 1920, © Imperial War Museum

Kennedy, Cedric J. 1898–1968, *A Camouflaged Runway*, transferred from the War Artists' Advisory Committee, 1947, © crown copyright

Kennington, Eric 1888–1960, *The Kensingtons at Laventie*, transferred from the Secretary of State for Education & Science, 1983, © Imperial War Museum

Kennington, Eric 1888–1960, *Gassed and Wounded*, gift from the artist, 1934, © Imperial War Museum

Kessell, Mary 1914–1977, *Refugees: '…pray ye that your fight be not in the winter…' Matthew XXIV, 20*, transferred from the War Artists' Advisory Committee, 1947, © crown copyright

Kestelman, Morris 1905–1998, *Lama Sabachthani, Why Have You Forsaken Me?*, gift from Sara Kestelman, 1999

Kinley, Peter 1926–1988, *Battleship*, purchased, 1986

Kirk, Eve 1900–1969, *Bomb Damage in the City*, transferred from the War Artists' Advisory Committee, 1947, © crown copyright

Kirk, Eve 1900–1969, *St Nicholas Cole Abbey, EC4*, transferred from the War Artists' Advisory Committee, 1947, © crown copyright

Kirkwood, John b.1947, *The Belgrano, 2 and 3 May*, purchased, 1994, © the artist

Knight, Laura 1877–1970, *Corporal J. D. M. Pearson, GC, Women's Auxiliary Air Force*, transferred from the War Artists' Advisory Committee, 1947, © crown copyright

Knight, Laura 1877–1970, *Corporal J. M. Robins, Women's Auxiliary Air Force*, transferred from the War Artists' Advisory Committee, 1947, © crown copyright

Knight, Laura 1877–1970, *Ruby Loftus Screwing a Breech Ring*, transferred from the War Artists' Advisory Committee, 1947, © crown copyright

Knight, Laura 1877–1970, *A Balloon Site, Coventry*, transferred from the War Artists' Advisory Committee, 1947, © crown copyright

Knight, Laura 1877–1970, *Take Off: Interior of a Bomber Aircraft*, transferred from the War Artists' Advisory Committee, 1947, © crown copyright

Knight, Laura 1877–1970, *The Nuremberg Trial*, transferred from the War Artists' Advisory Committee, 1947, © crown copyright

Knirr, Heinrich 1862–1944, *Der Führer (1889–1945)*, transferred from the Ministry of Works, c.1946, © DACS

Kojima, Yuunosoke *The Sinking of the 'Prince of Wales', 10 December 1942, off Kuenten, South China Sea*

La Dell, Edwin 1914–1970, *The Camouflage Workshop, Leamington Spa*, transferred from the War Artists' Advisory Committee, 1947, © crown copyright

Lacy, Charles John de c.1860–1936, *The 'Vindictive' at Zeebrugge: The Storming of Zeebrugge Mole*, gift from the artist, 1918

Lamb, Henry 1883–1960, *Irish Troops in the Judaean Hills Surprised by a Turkish Bombardment*, commissioned, acquired, 1919, © crown copyright

Lamb, Henry 1883–1960, *Frederick Bolton, GM, Decorated for Gallantry at Leytonstone, September 1940*, transferred from the War Artists' Advisory Committee, 1947, © crown copyright

Lamb, Henry 1883–1960, *Pay Week at the Clothing Store*, transferred from the War Artists' Advisory Committee, 1947, © crown copyright

Lamb, Henry 1883–1960, *A Soldier of Free France*, transferred from the War Artists' Advisory Committee, 1947, © crown copyright

Lamb, Henry 1883–1960, *An Instructor at the Army and Royal Air Force Co-Operation School*, transferred from the War Artists' Advisory Committee, 1947, © crown copyright

Lamb, Henry 1883–1960, *Canadian Forces Reach Their Billets*, transferred from the War Artists' Advisory Committee, 1947, © crown copyright

Lamb, Henry 1883–1960, *Canadian Troops Replacing Track*, transferred from the War Artists' Advisory Committee, 1947, © crown copyright

Lamb, Henry 1883–1960, *Colonel Tang Paohuang*, transferred from the War Artists' Advisory Committee, 1947, © crown copyright

Lamb, Henry 1883–1960, *General Bronislaw Regulski (1886–1961), CB*, transferred from the War Artists' Advisory Committee, 1947, © crown copyright

Lamb, Henry 1883–1960, *Major Mahomed Akbar Khan, Commanding Officer, 29 Mule Coy, Royal Indian Army Service Corps*, transferred from the War Artists' Advisory Committee, 1947, © crown copyright

Lamb, Henry 1883–1960, *Sergeant Watts, 40th Battalion, Royal Tank Regiment*, transferred from the War Artists' Advisory Committee, 1947, © crown copyright

Lamb, Henry 1883–1960, *The*

Overhaul, transferred from the War Artists' Advisory Committee, 1947, © crown copyright

Lamb, Henry 1883–1960, *The Poor Bloody Infantry*, transferred from the War Artists' Advisory Committee, 1947, © crown copyright

Lamb, Henry 1883–1960, *Track Repairs by Canadian Troops*, transferred from the War Artists' Advisory Committee, 1947, © crown copyright

Lamb, Henry 1883–1960, *A Command Post, Heavy Anti-Aircraft: Royal Canadian Artillery*, transferred from the War Artists' Advisory Committee, 1947, © crown copyright

Lamb, Henry 1883–1960, *Air Vice-Marshal Karel Janousek (1893–19/1), KCB, Inspector General Czechoslovakian Air Force*, transferred from the War Artists' Advisory Committee, 1947, © crown copyright

Lamb, Henry 1883–1960, *Canadian Troops Undergoing Instruction*, transferred from the War Artists' Advisory Committee, 1947, © crown copyright

Lamb, Henry 1883–1960, *Gunner W. C. Macaloney, Royal Canadian Artillery*, transferred from the War Artists' Advisory Committee, 1947, © crown copyright

Lamb, Henry 1883–1960, *Gunner W. H. St Cyr, Royal Canadian Artillery*, transferred from the War Artists' Advisory Committee, 1947, © crown copyright

Lamb, Henry 1883–1960, *Lieutenant General Archibald Edward Nye (1895–1967), CB, MC*, transferred from the War Artists' Advisory Committee, 1947, © crown copyright

Lamb, Henry 1883–1960, *Lieutenant General Sir William Dobbie (1879–1964), GCMG, KCB, DSO*, transferred from the War Artists' Advisory Committee, 1947, © crown copyright

Lamb, Henry 1883–1960, *Major E. Wilson, VC, 10th Battalion, East Surrey Regiment*, transferred from the War Artists' Advisory Committee, 1947, © crown copyright

Lamb, Henry 1883–1960, *Major General Robert Frederick Edward Whittaker (1894–1967), CB, OBE, TD, Anti-Aircraft Command*, transferred from the War Artists' Advisory Committee, 1947, © crown copyright

Lamb, Henry 1883–1960, *Chief Controller Leslie Violet Lucy Whateley, CBE, Director of Auxiliary Territorial Service*, transferred from the War Artists' Advisory Committee, 1947, © crown copyright

Lamb, Henry 1883–1960, *General Rudolf Viest (1890–1944)*, transferred from the War Artists' Advisory Committee, 1947, © crown copyright

Lamb, Henry 1883–1960, *Major General John Noble Kennedy (1893–1970), CB, MC*, transferred from the War Artists' Advisory Committee, 1947, © crown copyright

Lamb, Henry 1883–1960, *Senior Controller Christian Helen Fraser-Tytler, CBE, Deputy Director of Anti-Aircraft Command, Auxiliary Territorial Service*, transferred from the War Artists' Advisory Committee, 1947, © crown copyright

Lamb, Henry 1883–1960, *A Command Post, Heavy Anti-Aircraft: Royal Canadian Artillery*, transferred from the War Artists' Advisory Committee, 1947, © crown copyright

Lamb, Henry 1883–1960, *Colonel P. Devaux*, transferred from the War Artists' Advisory Committee, 1947, © crown copyright

Lamb, Henry 1883–1960, *General Sir Frederick Pile (1884–1976), KCB, DSO, MC*, transferred from the War Artists' Advisory Committee, 1947, © crown copyright

Lamb, Henry 1883–1960, *Generale de Division Milorad M. Radovitch*, transferred from the War Artists' Advisory Committee, 1947, © crown copyright

Lamb, Henry 1883–1960, *Air Marshal the Honourable Sir Ralph Cochrane (1895–1977), KBE, Aide-de-Camp to His Majesty the King*, transferred, 1946, © crown copyright

Lambourn, George 1900–1977, *Calais, 26 May 1940: Died of Wounds*, transferred from the War Artists' Advisory Committee, 1947, © crown copyright

Lander, John Saint-Hélier 1869–1944, *General Sir Philip Chetwode (1869–1950), KCMG, CB, DSO*

Langmaid, Rowland 1897–1956, *Arrival of His Majesty the King at Malta*, gift from Sir Geoffrey Agnew, 1980

László, Philip Alexius de 1869–1937, *Edith Vane-Tempest-Stewart, the Marchioness of Londonderry (1879–1959), DBE*, gift from the artist, 1920, © Imperial War Museum

Laveaux, Ludwik de 1891–1969, *View from Oflag 2B*, purchased, 1976

Lavery, John 1856–1941, *The Forth Bridge*, gift from the artist, 1918, © Imperial War Museum

Lavery, John 1856–1941, *Kite Balloons, Roehampton*, gift from the artist, 1918, © Imperial War Museum

Lavery, John 1856–1941, *'The Silver Queen', Wormwood Scrubs: One of the Original 'Blimps'*, gift from the artist, 1918, © Imperial War Museum

Lavery, John 1856–1941, *Flotta and Weddel Sound*, gift from the artist, 1918, © Imperial War Museum

Lavery, John 1856–1941, *Royal Naval Division, Crystal Palace: The Spot Known as the Quarter-Deck*, gift from the artist, 1918, © Imperial War Museum

Lavery, John 1856–1941, *The 'Appam', London Docks*, gift from

the artist, 1918, © Imperial War Museum

Lavery, John 1856–1941, *A Coast Defence: An 18-Pounder Anti-Aircraft Gun, Tyneside*, gift from the artist, 1918, © the artist's estate

Lavery, John 1856–1941, *A Deck Hand, North Sea Patrol*, gift from the artist, 1918, © Imperial War Museum

Lavery, John 1856–1941, *A Naval Gun in the Hydraulic Press: Elswick Works, Newcastle-on-Tyne*, gift from the artist, 1918, © Imperial War Museum

Lavery, John 1856–1941, *Admiral Sir Cecil Burney (1859–1929), GCMG, KCB, Commander-in-Chief, Coast of Scotland*, gift from the artist, 1918, © Imperial War Museum

Lavery, John 1856–1941, *British Mine-Laying Submarines, Harwich*, gift from the artist, 1918, © Imperial War Museum

Lavery, John 1856–1941, *Leith*, gift from the artist, 1918, © Imperial War Museum

Lavery, John 1856–1941, *Long Hope: Orkney*, gift from the artist, 1918, © Imperial War Museum

Lavery, John 1856–1941, *Munitions, Newcastle*, gift from the artist, 1918, © Imperial War Museum

Lavery, John 1856–1941, *Parkestone: A Destroyer Base at Harwich*, gift from the artist, 1918, © Imperial War Museum

Lavery, John 1856–1941, *Richborough: A Cross-Channel Ferry*, gift from the artist, 1918, © Imperial War Museum

Lavery, John 1856–1941, *Richborough in Fog*, gift from the artist, 1918, © Imperial War Museum

Lavery, John 1856–1941, *Royal Naval Air Service, Roehampton, August 1917*, purchased, 1969, © the artist's estate

Lavery, John 1856–1941, *Royal Naval Volunteer Reserve, Crystal Palace*, gift from the artist, 1918, © Imperial War Museum

Lavery, John 1856–1941, *Scapa Flow*, gift from the artist, 1918, © Imperial War Museum

Lavery, John 1856–1941, *Scapa Flow, Orkney, from the Signal Station*, gift from the artist, 1918, © the artist's estate

Lavery, John 1856–1941, *The Firth of Forth: Wind*, gift from the artist, 1918, © Imperial War Museum

Lavery, John 1856–1941, *The Fleet: A Misty Day, the Firth of Forth*, gift from the artist, 1918, © Imperial War Museum

Lavery, John 1856–1941, *The Forth Bridge: Bluejackets Landing*, gift from the artist, 1918, © Imperial War Museum

Lavery, John 1856–1941, *The Skipper, Captain William Lyons, 'HMT Semiramis'*, gift from the artist, 1918, © Imperial War Museum

Lavery, John 1856–1941, *Troops Embarking at Southampton for the Western Front*, gift from the artist, 1919, © Imperial War Museum

Lavery, John 1856–1941, *Richborough: The Gantries*, gift from the artist, 1918, © Imperial War Museum

Lavery, John 1856–1941, *Twilight, the Naval Base, Granton: Booms Guarding the Forth Are Seen in the Distance*, gift from the artist, 1918, © Imperial War Museum

Lavery, John 1856–1941, *A Convoy, North Sea: From NS 7, Painted from an Airship off the Coast of Norway*, gift from the artist, 1918, © the artist's estate

Lavery, John 1856–1941, *American Troops Embarking, Southampton*, gift from the artist, 1918, © Imperial War Museum

Lavery, John 1856–1941, *Monitors, Dover Harbour*, gift from the artist, 1918, © Imperial War Museum

Lavery, John 1856–1941, *Night and the Arrival of the German Delegates: 'HMS Queen Elizabeth', 15 November 1918*, gift from the artist, 1918, © the artist's estate

Lavery, John 1856–1941, *'Rigids' at Pulham: 'R 23' Type British Airships at Pulham St Mary, Norfolk*, gift from the artist, 1918, © Imperial War Museum

Lavery, John 1856–1941, *Rosyth: The Principal Base of the Grand Fleet*, gift from the artist, 1918, © Imperial War Museum

Lavery, John 1856–1941, *Southampton Water*, gift from the artist, 1918, © Imperial War Museum

Lavery, John 1856–1941, *Study for 'Admiral Sir David Beatty (1871–1936), GCB, Reading the Terms of the Armistice to the German Delegates; 'HMS Queen Elizabeth', Rosyth, 16 November 1918'*, gift from the artist, 1919, © the artist's estate

Lavery, John 1856–1941, *The Aerodrome, East Fortune, North Berwick: The Starting Point for British Airships of the North Sea Air Patrol*, gift from the artist, 1918, © Imperial War Museum

Lavery, John 1856–1941, *The American Battle Squadron in the Firth of Forth: 'New York' (Flagship), 'Texas', 'Florida', 'Wyoming' and 'Delaware'*, gift from the artist, 1918, © Imperial War Museum

Lavery, John 1856–1941, *The End: The Fore-Cabin of 'HMS Queen Elizabeth' with Admiral Beatty Reading the Terms of the Surrender of the German Navy, Rosyth, 16 November 1918*, gift from the artist, 1924, © the artist's estate

Lavery, John 1856–1941, *The Entrance, Dover Harbour, 1918: In the Foreground Are the Harbour Protection Nets against Enemy Submarines*, gift from the artist, 1918, © Imperial War Museum

Lavery, John 1856–1941, *The Guns,*

'HMS Terror', gift from the artist, 1918, © Imperial War Museum
Lavery, John 1856–1941, *The Wounded at Dover*, gift from the artist, 1918, © Imperial War Museum
Lavery, John 1856–1941, *Admiral Sir James Startin (1855–1948), KCB, AM, Royal Naval Reserve*, gift from the artist, 1918, © Imperial War Museum
Lavery, John 1856–1941, *'Rigid 29' and 'NS 7' at East Fortune*, gift from the artist, 1918, © Imperial War Museum
Lavery, John 1856–1941, *The Chief Naval Censor: Rear Admiral Sir Douglas Browning, Bt, CB, Royal Navy*, gift from the artist, 1918, © Imperial War Museum
Lavery, John 1856–1941, *Army Post Office 3, Boulogne*, commissioned, acquired, 1920, © Imperial War Museum
Lavery, John 1856–1941, *Elswick, 1917: Messrs. Armstrong, Whitworth & Company*, commissioned, acquired, 1920, © Imperial War Museum
Lavery, John 1856–1941, *German Wounded, Le Havre*, commissioned, acquired, 1920, © Imperial War Museum
Lavery, John 1856–1941, *Lady Henry's Crèche, Woolwich*, gift from Lady Heny, 1920, © Imperial War Museum
Lavery, John 1856–1941, *Le Havre: Nurse Billam and Sister Currier*, commissioned, acquired, 1920, © Imperial War Museum
Lavery, John 1856–1941, *No.3 GS, Voluntary Aid Detachment Camp, Rouen*, commissioned, acquired, 1920, © Imperial War Museum
Lavery, John 1856–1941, *Queen Mary's Army Auxiliary Corps Cookhouse, Rouxmesnil*, commissioned, acquired, 1920, © Imperial War Museum
Lavery, John 1856–1941, *Red Cross Hostel, Rouen*, commissioned, acquired, 1920, © Imperial War Museum
Lavery, John 1856–1941, *Scene at a Clyde Shipyard, Messrs. William Beardmore & Co.*, gift from William Beardmore, 1920, © Imperial War Museum
Lavery, John 1856–1941, *Shell Making, Edinburgh*, commissioned, acquired, 1920, © Imperial War Museum
Lavery, John 1856–1941, *The Bakeries, Dieppe*, commissioned, acquired, 1920, © Imperial War Museum
Lavery, John 1856–1941, *The Cemetery, Etaples*, commissioned, acquired, 1920, © Imperial War Museum
Lavery, John 1856–1941, *The Ordnance Chief Officer's Cookhouse, Henriville, Boulogne*, commissioned, acquired, 1920, © Imperial War Museum
Lavery, John 1856–1941, *The Queen Mary's Army Auxiliary*

Corps Convalescent Home, Le Touquet, commissioned, acquired, 1920, © Imperial War Museum
Lavery, John 1856–1941, *The Women's Emergency Canteen, Gare du Nord, Paris*, commissioned, acquired, 1920, © Imperial War Museum
Lavery, John 1856–1941, *Sir Alfred Moritz Mond (1868–1930), First Lord Melchett*, gift from 2nd Baron Melchett, 1977, © the artist's estate
Lawrence, Alfred Kingsley 1893–1975, *David Emlyn Evans, Royal Flying Corps Officer*, acquired, c.1972
Lawrence, Alfred Kingsley 1893–1975, *Squadron Leader Humphrey Trench Gilbert (1919–1942), DFC*, unknown provenance
Lawson, Cecil active 1913–1923, *Devastated Farm*, acquired, 1970s
Lawson, Cecil active 1913–1923, *Berry-au-Bar*, acquired, 1970s
Lawson, Cecil active 1913–1923, *Hell Fire Corner*, acquired, 1970s
Lawson, Cecil active 1913–1923, *Kemilly Hill*, acquired, 1970s
Lawson, Cecil active 1913–1923, *Landscape*, gift from the Greater London Council, 1979
Lawson, Cecil active 1913–1923, *Les routes de France*, acquired, 1970s
Lawson, Cecil active 1913–1923, *Moving Up*, acquired, 1970s
Lawson, Cecil active 1913–1923, *Near Albert*, acquired, 1970s
Lawson, Cecil active 1913–1923, *Near Salient*, acquired, 1970s
Lawson, Cecil active 1913–1923, *Sanctuary Wood*, acquired, 1970s
Lawson, Cecil active 1913–1923, *Sanctuary Wood*, acquired, 1970s
Lawson, Cecil active 1913–1923, *Somme*, acquired, 1970s
Lawson, Cecil active 1913–1923, *Themiss la Daine*, acquired, 1970s
Lawson, Cecil active 1913–1923, *Untitled*, acquired, 1970s
Lawson, Cecil active 1913–1923, *Untitled*, acquired, 1970s
Lawson, Cecil active 1913–1923, *Untitled*, acquired, 1970s
Lawson, Cecil active 1913–1923, *Untitled*, acquired, 1970s
Lawson, Cecil active 1913–1923, *Untitled*, acquired, 1970s
Lawson, Cecil active 1913–1923, *Arras*, acquired, 1970s
Lawson, Cecil active 1913–1923, *Outside Arras*, acquired, 1970s
Lawson, Cecil active 1913–1923, *Railway Station, Arras*, acquired, 1970s
Lawson, Cecil active 1913–1923, *A Line of Tanks*, gift from the Greater London Council, 1979
Lawson, Cecil active 1913–1923, *Seascape*, gift from the Greater London Council, 1979
Lawson, Cecil active 1913–1923, *Machine Gunners*, acquired, 1970s
Lawson, Cecil active 1913–1923, *Victory Parade*, acquired, 1970s
Lawson, P. *Albert*, acquired, 1975–1976?
Lawson, Sonia b.1934,

Camouflaged Men in a Trench, commissioned, acquired, 1986, © Imperial War Museum
Lawson, Sonia b.1934, *Hamm: Freedom Parade with Gordon Highlanders Band Marching, 1 September 1984*, commissioned, acquired, 1986, © Imperial War Museum
Lawson, Sonia b.1934, *Hamm: Freedom Parade with Polish Veterans in Blue and War Memorial at Rear*, commissioned, acquired, 1986, © Imperial War Museum
Lawson, Sonia b.1934, *Interior, Chieftan Tank*, commissioned, acquired, 1986, © Imperial War Museum
Lawson, Sonia b.1934, *Interior, Guided Weapons Vehicle, 'Swingfire'*, commissioned, acquired, 1986, © Imperial War Museum
Lawson, Sonia b.1934, *Men Disguised as Clods*, commissioned, acquired, 1986, © Imperial War Museum
Lawson, Sonia b.1934, *Troops in Single File Prepare to Break Cover and Board a Chinook Helicopter*, commissioned, acquired, 1986, © Imperial War Museum
Lawson, Sonia b.1934, *Two Minds but with a Single Thought?*, commissioned, acquired, 1986, © Imperial War Museum
Lawson, Sonia b.1934, *Welding: Chieftan Tank, Swinton Barracks, Munster*, commissioned, acquired, 1986, © Imperial War Museum
Lee, Dick 1923–2001, *Catch-22: Arrest of the Innocent Man*, gift from Mrs Gillian Lee and Family, 2000, © the artist's estate
Lee, Dick 1923–2001, *Catch-22: Bombing the Airfield*, gift from Mrs Gillian Lee and Family, 2000, © the artist's estate
Lee, Dick 1923–2001, *Catch-22: 'He's back!'*, gift from Mrs Gillian Lee and Family, 2000, © the artist's estate
Lee, Dick 1923–2001, *Catch-22: Impersonating Giuseppe*, gift from Mrs Gillian Lee and Family, 2000, © the artist's estate
Lee, Dick 1923–2001, *Catch-22: McWatt Crashes*, gift from Mrs Gillian Lee and Family, 2000, © the artist's estate
Lee, Dick 1923–2001, *Catch-22: Milo's Cotton*, gift from Mrs Gillian Lee and Family, 2000, © the artist's estate
Lee, Dick 1923–2001, *Catch-22: Nately and the Old Man*, gift from Mrs Gillian Lee and Family, 2000, © the artist's estate
Lee, Dick 1923–2001, *Catch-22: Orr*, gift from Mrs Gillian Lee and Family, 2000, © the artist's estate
Lee, Dick 1923–2001, *Catch-22: Ping Pong*, gift from Mrs Gillian Lee and Family, 2000, © the artist's

estate
Lee, Dick 1923–2001, *Catch-22: Rescuing Nately's Whore from the Generals*, gift from Mrs Gillian Lee and Family, 2000, © the artist's estate
Lee, Dick 1923–2001, *Catch-22: Snowden's Funeral*, gift from Mrs Gillian Lee and Family, 2000, © the artist's estate
Lee, Dick 1923–2001, *Catch-22: The Basketball Game*, gift from Mrs Gillian Lee and Family, 2000, © the artist's estate
Lee, Dick 1923–2001, *Catch-22: The Chaplain Interrogated*, gift from Mrs Gillian Lee and Family, 2000, © the artist's estate
Lee, Dick 1923–2001, *Catch-22: The Chaplain Is Arrested*, gift from Mrs Gillian Lee and Family, 2000, © the artist's estate
Lee, Dick 1923–2001, *Catch-22: The Chaplain's Interview*, gift from Mrs Gillian Lee and Family, 2000, © the artist's estate
Lee, Dick 1923–2001, *Catch-22: The Death of Kid Sampson*, gift from Mrs Gillian Lee and Family, 2000, © the artist's estate
Lee, Dick 1923–2001, *Catch-22: The Death of Snowden*, gift from Mrs Gillian Lee and Family, 2000, © the artist's estate
Lee, Dick 1923–2001, *Catch-22: The Epileptic Fit*, gift from Mrs Gillian Lee and Family, 2000, © the artist's estate
Lee, Dick 1923–2001, *Catch-22: The Medal Ceremony*, gift from Mrs Gillian Lee and Family, 2000, © the artist's estate
Lee, Dick 1923–2001, *Catch-22: The Soldier in White*, gift from Mrs Gillian Lee and Family, 2000, © the artist's estate
Lee, Dick 1923–2001, *Catch-22: Yossarian Escapes*, gift from Mrs Gillian Lee and Family, 2000, © the artist's estate
Lee, Dick 1923–2001, *Catch-22: Yossarian Grabs Nurse Duckett*, gift from Mrs Gillian Lee and Family, 2000, © the artist's estate
Lee, Dick 1923–2001, *Catch-22: Yossarian Tackles Major Major*, gift from Mrs Gillian Lee and Family, 2000, © the artist's estate
Lee, Dick 1923–2001, *Catch-22: Yossarian with the Maid*, gift from Mrs Gillian Lee and Family, 2000, © the artist's estate
Leigh-Pemberton, John 1911–1997, *Admiral of the Fleet the Viscount Cunningham of Hyndhope (1883–1963), KT, GCB, DSO*, gift from the Trustees of the Imperial War Museum, 1949
Leigh-Pemberton, John 1911–1997, *Field Marshal Sir John Dill (1881–1944), GCB, CMG, DSO*, gift from the Trustees of the Imperial War Museum, 1949, © Imperial War Museum
Leigh-Pemberton, John 1911–1997, *Field Marshal the Viscount Alexander of Tunis (1891–1969), GCB, CSI, DS, MC (copy of Oswald*

Hornby Joseph Birley), gift from the Trustees of the Imperial War Museum, 1949, © Imperial War Museum
Leroux, Georges Paul 1877–1957, *L'enfer*, gift, 1926, © Imperial War Museum
Lewis, Neville 1895–1972, *Artillery Drivers in the Snow, Italian Front*, gift, 1919, © the artist's estate
Lewis, Neville 1895–1972, *Sergeant David Ferguson Hunter, VC, 1/5th Highland Light Infantry*, commissioned, acquired, 1919, © the artist's estate
Lewis, Neville 1895–1972, *Vice Admiral Sir Edward F. B. Charlton, KCMG, CB*, commissioned, 1920, © the artist's estate
Lewis, Reginald b.1901, *General William Slim (1897–1970)*, gift from Geoffrey Hayman, 1968
Lewis, Wyndham 1882–1957, *A Battery Shelled*, commissioned, acquired, 1919, © crown copyright
Lion, Flora 1878–1958, *Building Flying Boats*, gift, 1927, © Imperial War Museum
Lion, Flora 1878–1958, *Women's Canteen at Phoenix Works, Bradford*, gift, 1927, © Imperial War Museum
Lipscombe, Guy 1881–1952, *A First-Line Dressing Station, Doberdo, Isonzo Front, Italy*, purchased, 1919
Lipscombe, Guy 1881–1952, *The Arrival of the First Guns on the Carso Front, Italy, 1916*, commissioned, acquired, 1919
Lipscombe, Guy 1881–1952, *British Red Cross Ambulance, Italian Front, 1916*, purchased, 1919
Lipscombe, Guy 1881–1952, *Castelfranco: Italian Troops Resting en Route to the Piave Front*, commissioned, 1919
Lipscombe, Guy 1881–1952, *Invasion Training in Cornwall*
Lipscombe, Guy 1881–1952, *Invasion Training in Cornwall*
Lithiby, Beatrice Ethel 1889–1966, *An Auxiliary Territorial Service Camp at Tuxford, Nottinghamshire*, gift, 1958, © Imperial War Museum
Lobley, John Hodgson 1878–1954, *Dugouts in the Railway Embankment, near Le Cateau*, © Imperial War Museum
Lobley, John Hodgson 1878–1954, *Galleries of Large Dugouts at Etaples*, transferred from the Royal Army Medical Corps, 1919, © Imperial War Museum
Lobley, John Hodgson 1878–1954, *King George's Hospital, Stamford Street, SE: The Largest Ward (71 beds)*, transferred from the Royal Army Medical Corps, 1919, © Imperial War Museum
Lobley, John Hodgson 1878–1954, *Outside Charing Cross Station, July 1916: Casualties from the Battle of the Somme Arriving in London*, gift from the British Red Cross Society and the Order of St John of Jerusalem, 1919, © Imperial War

Museum

Lobley, John Hodgson 1878–1954, *Reception of the Wounded at the First Casualty Clearing Station, Le Château, during the British Advance in October 1918*, transferred from the Royal Army Medical Corps, 1919, © Imperial War Museum

Lobley, John Hodgson 1878–1954, *The Operating Theatre, First Casualty Clearing Station*, transferred from the Royal Army Medical Corps, 1919, © Imperial War Museum

Lobley, John Hodgson 1878–1954, *The Royal Army Medical Corps in Training, Blackpool: The Church of England Tent*, transferred from the Royal Army Medical Corps, 1919, © Imperial War Museum

Lobley, John Hodgson 1878–1954, *Val de Grâce Hospital, Paris: Interior of a Ward*, transferred from the Royal Army Medical Corps, 1919, © Imperial War Museum

Lobley, John Hodgson 1878–1954, *The Auxiliary Hospital, Children's House, Exeter Workhouse*, gift from the British Red Cross Society and the Order of St John of Jerusalem, 1919, © Imperial War Museum

Lobley, John Hodgson 1878–1954, *The British Red Cross Society Hospital at the Episcopal Modern Schools, Exeter*, gift from the British Red Cross Society and the Order of St John of Jerusalem, 1919, © Imperial War Museum

Lobley, John Hodgson 1878–1954, *The Grand Priory of the Order of St John of Jerusalem in England, St John's Gate, Clerkenwell, EC*, gift from the British Red Cross Society and the Order of St John of Jerusalem, 1919, © Imperial War Museum

Lobley, John Hodgson 1878–1954, *The Queen's Hospital for Facial Injuries, Frognal, Sidcup: The Carpenters' Shop*, gift from the British Red Cross Society and the Order of St John of Jerusalem, 1919, © Imperial War Museum

Lobley, John Hodgson 1878–1954, *The Queen's Hospital for Facial Injuries, Frognal, Sidcup: The Commercial Class*, gift from the British Red Cross Society and the Order of St John of Jerusalem, 1919, © Imperial War Museum

Lobley, John Hodgson 1878–1954, *The Queen's Hospital for Facial Injuries, Frognal, Sidcup: The Dental Mechanics' Class*, gift from the British Red Cross Society and the Order of St John of Jerusalem, 1919, © Imperial War Museum

Lobley, John Hodgson 1878–1954, *The Queen's Hospital for Facial Injuries, Frognal, Sidcup: The Operating Theatre*, gift from the British Red Cross Society and the Order of St John of Jerusalem, 1919, © Imperial War Museum

Lobley, John Hodgson 1878–1954, *The Queen's Hospital for Facial Injuries, Frognal, Sidcup: The Toy Makers' Shop*, gift from the British

Red Cross Society and the Order of St John of Jerusalem, 1919, © Imperial War Museum

Lobley, John Hodgson 1878–1954, *The Royal Army Medical Corps in Training, Blackpool: The Depot Incinerator*, transferred from the Royal Army Medical Corps, 1919, © Imperial War Museum

Lobley, John Hodgson 1878–1954, *The Royal Army Medical Corps in Training, Blackpool: The Medical Inspection Room and Dispensary*, transferred from the Royal Army Medical Corps, 1919, © Imperial War Museum

Lobley, John Hodgson 1878–1954, *The Royal Army Medical Corps in Training, Blackpool: The Officers' School of Instruction*, transferred from the Royal Army Medical Corps, 1919, © Imperial War Museum

Lobley, John Hodgson 1878–1954, *The Special Surgical Auxiliary Hospital at the 'Star and Garter', Richmond: The Dining Room*, gift from the British Red Cross Society and the Order of St John of Jerusalem, 1919, © Imperial War Museum

Lobley, John Hodgson 1878–1954, *The Special Surgical Hospital at the 'Star and Garter', Richmond: The Ballroom*, gift from the British Red Cross Society and the Order of St John of Jerusalem, 1919, © Imperial War Museum

Lobley, John Hodgson 1878–1954, *The Superintendent Posting a Sister for Service: The Grand Priory of the Order of St John of Jerusalem in England, St John's Gate, Clerkenwell, EC*, gift from the British Red Cross Society and the Order of St John of Jerusalem, 1919, © Imperial War Museum

Lobley, John Hodgson 1878–1954, *Wounded Passing through Snow Hill Railway Station, Birmingham*, gift from the British Red Cross Society and the Order of St John of Jerusalem, 1920, © Imperial War Museum

Lobley, John Hodgson 1878–1954, *The Canteen at the Headquarters of the Joint War Council of the British Red Cross Society and Order of St John, 19 Berkeley Street, W1*, gift from the British Red Cross Society and the Order of St John of Jerusalem, 1919, © Imperial War Museum

Lobley, John Hodgson 1878–1954, *The Officers' Ward at the 41st Casualty Clearing Station*, transferred from the Royal Army Medical Corps, 1919, © Imperial War Museum

Lobley, John Hodgson 1878–1954, *Charing Cross Station: Detraining Wounded by the British Red Cross Society and Order of St John*, gift from the British Red Cross Society and the Order of St John of Jerusalem, 1919, © Imperial War Museum

Lobley, John Hodgson 1878–1954,

Hospital Barges in Flanders, transferred from the Royal Army Medical Corps, 1919, © Imperial War Museum

Lobley, John Hodgson 1878–1954, *Loading Wounded at Boulogne*, gift from the British Red Cross Society and the Order of St John of Jerusalem, 1919, © Imperial War Museum

Lobley, John Hodgson 1878–1954, *Refugees on the Road from Ascq to Lille*, transferred from the Royal Army Medical Corps, 1919, © Imperial War Museum

Lobley, John Hodgson 1878–1954, *The 39th Stationary Hospital, Ascq, September 1919*, transferred from the Royal Army Medical Corps, 1919, © Imperial War Museum

Lobley, John Hodgson 1878–1954, *The Camp of the 42nd Casualty Clearing Station, Douai*, transferred from the Royal Army Medical Corps, 1919, © Imperial War Museum

Lobley, John Hodgson 1878–1954, *The Church of England Tent, 39th Stationary Hospital, Ascq, September 1919*, transferred from the Royal Army Medical Corps, 1919, © Imperial War Museum

Lowry, Laurence Stephen 1887–1976, *Going to Work*, transferred from the War Artists' Advisory Committee, 1947, © crown copyright

Lytton, Neville Stephen 1879–1951, *Admiral Sir Thomas Henry Martyn Jerram (1858–1933), GCMG, KCB*, commissioned, acquired, 1920, © crown copyright

Lytton, Neville Stephen 1879–1951, *Mrs Jean Knox, CBE, Chief Controller and Director, Auxiliary Territorial Service*, transferred from the War Artists' Advisory Committee, 1947, © crown copyright

Maccabe, Gladys b.1918, *After a Bomb Went Off, Belfast*, gift from the artist, 1986, © the artist

Maccabe, Gladys b.1918, *Barricades, Belfast*, gift from the artist, 1986, © the artist

Maccabe, Gladys b.1918, *After a Car Bomb Explosion, Ulster Village*, purchased, 1973, © the artist

Maccabe, Gladys b.1918, *Street Incident, Londonderry*, purchased, 1973, © the artist

Maccabe, Gladys b.1918, *To School via a Bomb Site, Belfast*, gift from the artist, 1986, © the artist

MacClure, Victor 1887–1963, *The Headquarters of the 29th Division, Gully Ravine, Cape Helles, Gallipoli*, purchased, 1919

Macdonald, Frances 1914–2002, *Graveyard: No.1 Metal and Produce Recovery Depot, Morris Works, Cowley, Oxford*, transferred from the War Artists' Advisory Committee, 1947, © crown copyright

Macdonald, Frances 1914–2002, *In the Millbank Hospital during an Air Raid: Patients Being Taken to the*

Shelter, transferred from the War Artists' Advisory Committee, 1947, © crown copyright

Macdonald, Frances 1914–2002, *The X-Ray Department at the Queen Alexandra Military Hospital*, transferred from the War Artists' Advisory Committee, 1947, © crown copyright

Macdonald, Frances 1914–2002, *London Docks*, transferred from the War Artists' Advisory Committee, 1947, © crown copyright

Macdonald, Frances 1914–2002, *Sketch for 'London Docks'*, transferred from the War Artists' Advisory Committee, 1947, © crown copyright

Macdonald, Frances 1914–2002, *Testing Jeep Power on Barges*, transferred from the War Artists' Advisory Committee, 1947, © crown copyright

Macdonald, Frances 1914–2002, *43 Repair Group, Air Frame Repair Service, Lincoln: Repairing Liberator Aircraft*, transferred from the War Artists' Advisory Committee, 1947, © crown copyright

Mackertich, Robin 1921–1993, *Bomb Disposal*, gift, 2006

Mackey, Arthur Stewart b.1909, *Sister Buchanan at the Cosway Street Rest Centre, NW1*, gift from the artist, 1954, © Imperial War Museum

Mackey, Arthur Stewart b.1909, *The Barrack Room Artist*, gift from the artist, 1992

Mackey, Haydn Reynolds 1881–1979, *An Advanced Dressing Station of the 36th Field Ambulance at Liéramont*, gift from the artist, 1920, © the artist's estate

Mackey, Haydn Reynolds 1881–1979, *Epéhy: In a Sunken Roadway near the Regimental Aid Post of the 7th Battalion Royal Sussex Regiment*, gift from the artist, 1920, © the artist's estate

Mackey, Haydn Reynolds 1881–1979, *Some Civilian Casualties at the Main Dressing Station of the 36th Field Ambulance, Flines-les-Raches, October 1918*, gift, 1920, © the artist's estate

Mackey, Haydn Reynolds 1881–1979, *The Main Dressing Station of a Field Ambulance: Templeux-la-Fosse, 18 September 1918*, gift from the artist, 1920, © the artist's estate

Mackey, Haydn Reynolds 1881–1979, *A British Red Cross Society and Order of St John of Jerusalem Officer in France*, gift from the British Red Cross Society and the Order of St John of Jerusalem, 1920, © the artist's estate

Mackey, Haydn Reynolds 1881–1979, *A British Red Cross Society and Order of St John of Jerusalem Stretcher-Bearer*, gift from the British Red Cross Society and the Order of St John of Jerusalem, 1920, © the artist's estate

Mackey, Haydn Reynolds 1881–1979, *A Royal Army Medical*

Corps Squad with Infantry: Night at Nurlu, October 1918, gift from the artist, 1920, © the artist's estate

Mackey, Haydn Reynolds 1881–1979, *British Red Cross Society and Order of St John of Jerusalem Workers Attending Wounded on their Arrival at Boulogne Station*, gift from the British Red Cross Society and the Order of St John of Jerusalem, 1920, © the artist's estate

Mackey, Haydn Reynolds 1881–1979, *Epéhy, 1918*, transferred from the Royal Army Medical Corps, 1920, © the artist's estate

Mackey, Haydn Reynolds 1881–1979, *Medical Storeman: British Red Cross Society and Order of St John of Jerusalem Medical Stores, Tottenham Court Road, London*, gift from the British Red Cross Society and the Order of St John of Jerusalem, 1920, © the artist's estate

Mackey, Haydn Reynolds 1881–1979, *Near 'Hell Fire Corner', Menin Road, Ypres*, transferred from the Royal Army Medical Corps, 1920, © the artist's estate

Mackey, Haydn Reynolds 1881–1979, *Prince's Skating Rink, Knightsbridge, London, during the War: British Red Cross Society Store*, gift from the British Red Cross Society and the Order of St John of Jerusalem, 1920, © the artist's estate

Mackey, Haydn Reynolds 1881–1979, *Sick Parade: British Labour Corps, Indian Troops, Chinese Labour Corps and German Prisoners of War, Menin Road Aid Post, Ypres*, transferred from the Royal Army Medical Corps, 1920, © the artist's estate

Mackey, Haydn Reynolds 1881–1979, *Sorting Bandages, British Red Cross Society and Order of St John of Jerusalem Medical Stores, Tottenham Court Road, London*, gift from the British Red Cross Society and the Order of St John of Jerusalem, 1920, © the artist's estate

Mackey, Haydn Reynolds 1881–1979, *The British Red Cross Society and Order of St John of Jerusalem Hospital Ship Passing through the Suez Canal*, gift from the British Red Cross Society and the Order of St John of Jerusalem, 1920, © the artist's estate

Mackey, Haydn Reynolds 1881–1979, *The Estaminet*, transferred from the Royal Army Medical Corps, 1920, © the artist's estate

Mackey, Haydn Reynolds 1881–1979, *Voluntary Aid Detachment Territorial Force*, gift from the British Red Cross Society and the Order of St John of Jerusalem, 1920, © the artist's estate

Mackey, Haydn Reynolds 1881–1979, *Ypres Landscape*, gift from Mrs S. Power, 1988, © the artist's estate

Mackey, Haydn Reynolds 1881–

1979 & **Rogers, Gilbert** active 1905–1920, *An Advanced Dressing Station, France: Cars Supplied by the British Red Cross Society and Order of St John of Jerusalem, Assisting in the Evacuation of the Wounded*, gift from the British Red Cross Society and the Order of St John of Jerusalem, 1920, Haydn Reynolds Mackey © the artist's estate

Macleod, Mary active 1914–1933, *Admiral Sir Arthur Leveson, GCB*, gift from the artist, 1933, © Imperial War Museum

Mann, Cathleen 1896–1959, *Evreux*, purchased, 2003, © the artist's estate

Mann, Harrington 1864–1936, *Lieutenant Colonel Maitland, CMG, DSO*, gift from Kathleen, Countess of Drogheda, 1926, © Lord Queensberry

Mann, W. N. active 1940–1971, *'HMHS Dorsetshire' at Milford Haven*, gift from the artist, 1971

Mann, W. N. active 1940–1971, *Sollum Harbour Seen from the Hospital Ship 'Dorsetshire', 7 January 1941*, gift from the artist, 1971

Mansbridge, John 1901–1981, *An Air Gunner in a Gun Turret: Sergeant G. Holmes, DFM*, transferred from the War Artists' Advisory Committee, 1947, © crown copyright

Mansbridge, John 1901–1981, *Squadron Leader J. A. Leathart, DSO, No.54 Squadron*, transferred from the War Artists' Advisory Committee, 1947, © crown copyright

Mansfield, Edward b.1907, *The View across the Musgrave Yard, Belfast, with the Centre Plate of a Ship in the Foreground and Ship No.1154 Ready to Leave the Slips*, transferred from the War Artists' Advisory Committee, 1947, © crown copyright

Marshall, Francis 1901–1980, *Commodore Alexander Vladimirvitch Tripolski, Hero of the Soviet Union, Order of Lenin, Gold Star*, transferred from the War Artists' Advisory Committee, 1947, © crown copyright

Martin, Edwin active 1913–1938, *Arras*, transferred from the Royal Army Medical Corps, 1920, © Imperial War Museum

Martin, Edwin active 1913–1938, *German Pillboxes: An Old Regimental Aid Post, Douai*, transferred from the Royal Army Medical Corps, 1920, © Imperial War Museum

Martin, Edwin active 1913–1938, *The 'Black Hole', Lille, (Fort Macdonald)*, transferred from the Royal Army Medical Corps, 1920, © Imperial War Museum

Martin, Edwin active 1913–1938, *The Second Casualty Clearing Station, Douai*, transferred from the Royal Army Medical Corps, 1920, © Imperial War Museum

Martin, Edwin active 1913–1938, *The Second Casualty Clearing Station, Douai*, transferred from the Royal Army Medical Corps, 1920, © Imperial War Museum

Martin, Edwin active 1913–1938, *Church of England Marquee: 39th Stationary Hospital, Ascq*, transferred from the Royal Army Medical Corps, 1919, © Imperial War Museum

Mason, Frank Henry 1876–1965, *Ferry Post, Ballah, Suez Canal: Anzac Day Celebrations, Carley Float Race, 'HM Hopper 32', Official Judge Ship*, purchased, 1920, © Imperial War Museum

Mason, Frank Henry 1876–1965, *Ismailia: Sunrise on the Bitter Lakes*, purchased, 1920, © Imperial War Museum

Mason, Frank Henry 1876–1965, *Suez Canal, 28 April 1916: From the Crow's Nest of Deversoir Signal Station; Base Camp at Serapeum on the Extreme Left*, purchased, 1920, © Imperial War Museum

Mason, Frank Henry 1876–1965, *'HM Submarine M1' off Seddel-Bahr: Salvage Operations in Progress on the Transport 'River Clyde'*, purchased, 1920, © Imperial War Museum

Mason, Frank Henry 1876–1965, *'HMS Superb': Flagship of the Commander-in-Chief, Mediterranean, Leading the British Fleet to Constantinople, November 1918*, commissioned, acquired, 1919, © Imperial War Museum

Mason, Frank Henry 1876–1965, *The Allied Fleet and Shipping at Constantinople*, commissioned, acquired, 1919, © Imperial War Museum

Mason, Frank Henry 1876–1965, *The Mediterranean Convoy Passing through the South Comino Channel, Malta*, commissioned, acquired, 1919, © Imperial War Museum

Mason, Frank Henry 1876–1965, *The Model Maker's Shop: Directorate of Camouflage (Naval Section), Leamington Spa*, transferred from the War Artists' Advisory Committee, 1947, © crown copyright

Matania, Fortunino 1881–1963, *The Last Message*, gift from the artist, 1957, © Imperial War Museum

Mathews, Denis 1913–1997, *An Impression of a Gas Cleansing Exercise at a First Aid Post: Eye Irritation*, transferred from the War Artists' Advisory Committee, 1947, © crown copyright

Maxwell, Donald 1877–1936, *St George and the Dragon: Zeppelin L15 in the Thames, April 1916*, purchased, 1918

Maxwell, Donald 1877–1936, *The Navy in Baghdad*, commissioned, acquired, 1919

Mayen, Eric b.1953, *Heroes of the XXth Century: Franco*, purchased, 1995, © the artist

Mayen, Eric b.1953, *Heroes of the XXth Century: Hitler*, purchased, 1995, © the artist

Mayen, Eric b.1953, *Heroes of the XXth Century: Hitler and Mussolini*, purchased, 1995, © the artist

Mayen, Eric b.1953, *Heroes of the XXth Century: Lenin*, purchased, 1995, © the artist

Mayen, Eric b.1953, *Heroes of the XXth Century: Lenin*, purchased, 1995, © the artist

Mayen, Eric b.1953, *Heroes of the XXth Century: Petain*, purchased, 1995, © the artist

Mayen, Eric b.1953, *Heroes of the XXth Century: Stalin*, purchased, 1995, © the artist

Mayor, Fred 1865–1916, *Montreuil*, gift from Mr F. Mayor and Miss Mayor in memory of their father, 1971

McBey, James 1883–1959, *Nebi Samwil: The First Sight of Jerusalem*, commissioned, acquired, 1919, © crown copyright

McBey, James 1883–1959, *The Allies Entering Jerusalem, 11 December 1917: General Allenby with Colonel de Piépape Commanding the French Detachment and Lieutenant Colonel D'Agostio Commanding the Italian Detachment, Entering the City by the Jaffa Gate*, commissioned, acquired, 1919, © crown copyright

McBey, James 1883–1959, *Arsuf: The Cavalry Dash along the Sea Coast on the Morning of 19 September 1918*, gift from the artist, 1918, © crown copyright

McBey, James 1883–1959, *General Sir Edmund Allenby (1861–1936), KCB*, commissioned, acquired, 1919, © crown copyright

McBey, James 1883–1959, *Lieutenant Colonel T. E. Lawrence (1888–1935), CB, DSO*, gift from the artist, 1919, © crown copyright

McBey, James 1883–1959, *Lieutenant General Sir Edward S. Bulfin (1862–1939), KCB, CVO*, gift from the artist, 1919, © crown copyright

McBey, James 1883–1959, *Lieutenant General Sir Henry George Chauvel (1865–1945), KCB, KCMG*, gift from the artist, 1919, © crown copyright

McBey, James 1883–1959, *Tul Keram: A Retreating Turkish Column Bombed and Machine-Gunned by Airmen in the Defile at Tul Keram, 26 September 1918*, gift from the artist, 1918, © crown copyright

McCormick, Arthur David 1860–1943, *Valve Testing: The Signal School, Royal Navy Barracks, Portsmouth*, commissioned, acquired, 1919, © crown copyright

McCormick, Arthur David 1860–1943, *Women's Royal Naval Service Officer and Ratings: Boat Cleaning at the Coastal Motor Boat Base, Haslar Creek, Portsmouth*, commissioned, acquired, 1919, © crown copyright

McEvoy, Ambrose 1878–1927, *Bourlon Wood, Somme*, commissioned, acquired, 1918

McEvoy, Ambrose 1878–1927, *Brigadier General A. R. H. Hutchinson, CB, CMG, DSO, Assistant Adjutant General, Royal Marines*, commissioned, acquired, 1918

McEvoy, Ambrose 1878–1927, *Brigadier General Arthur M. Asquith, DSO*, commissioned, acquired, 1918

McEvoy, Ambrose 1878–1927, *Brigadier General Bernard Cyril Freyberg (1889–1963), VC, DSO*, commissioned, acquired, 1918

McEvoy, Ambrose 1878–1927, *Captain Martin Eric Nasmith, VC, Royal Navy*, commissioned, acquired, 1918

McEvoy, Ambrose 1878–1927, *Commander Daniel Marcus William Beak (1891–1967), VC, DSO, MC, RNVR*, commissioned, acquired, 1918

McEvoy, Ambrose 1878–1927, *Commander W. M. Le C. Egerton, DS, Royal Naval Volunteer Reserve*, commissioned, acquired, 1918

McEvoy, Ambrose 1878–1927, *Major General C. E. Lawrie, CB, CMG, DSO*, commissioned, acquired, 1918

McEvoy, Ambrose 1878–1927, *Major General Sir C. D. Shute, KCB, CMG*, commissioned, acquired, 1918

McEvoy, Ambrose 1878–1927, *Major General Sir David Mercer, KCB, Adjutant General, Royal Marine Forces (1916–1920)*, commissioned, acquired, 1918

McEvoy, Ambrose 1878–1927, *Petty Officer E. Pitcher, VC*, commissioned, acquired, 1918

McEvoy, Ambrose 1878–1927, *Sergeant Norman Augustus Finch (1890–1966), VC, Royal Marine Artillery*, commissioned, acquired, 1918

McEvoy, Ambrose 1878–1927, *The Late Lieutenant Richard D. Sandford, VC, Royal Navy*, commissioned, acquired, 1918

McEvoy, Ambrose 1878–1927, *A Pillbox in the Hindenburg Line near Fontaine-les-Croisilles, Captured by the Royal Naval Division*, commissioned, acquired, 1918

McEvoy, Ambrose 1878–1927, *Commander A. W. Buckle, DSO, Royal Naval Volunteer Reserve*, gift from the artist, 1919

McEvoy, Ambrose 1878–1927, *Major Edward Bamford, VC, DSO, Royal Marines*, gift from the artist, 1919

McEvoy, Ambrose 1878–1927, *Night Flying*, gift from Mrs Ambrose McEvoy, 1937

McFadyen, Jock b.1950, *'With singing hearts and throaty roarings…'*, purchased, 1987

McFadyen, Jock b.1950, *Kurfürstendamm*, commissioned, 1991, © Imperial War Museum

McGill, Ronald William b.1930, *After the Battle at RAF Tangmere, Sussex*, gift from the artist, 1982, © the artist

McKenna, Stephen b.1939, *City of Derry I*, purchased, 1986, © the artist

McKenna, Stephen b.1939, *City of Derry II*, purchased, 1986, © the artist

McKenna, Stephen b.1939, *City of Derry III*, purchased, 1986, © the artist

McLean, Bruce b.1944, *Broadside*, gift from the artist and the Anthony d'Offay Gallery, 1990

McMillan, Colin active 1940s–1970s, *HMS Ships 'Beagle', 'Boadicea' and 'Bulldog' off Bear Island*, gift, 1996

McMillan, Colin active 1940s–1970s, *Convoy JW 55a to Russia*, gift, 1996

Medley, Robert 1905–1994, *A St John's Ambulance Examination in Progress*, transferred from the War Artists' Advisory Committee, 1947, © crown copyright

Medley, Robert 1905–1994, *First Aid Practice*, transferred from the War Artists' Advisory Committee, 1947, © crown copyright

Meeson, Dora 1869–1955, *Members of the Queen Mary's Army Auxiliary Corps: At Work in the Cookhouse, Royal Air Force Camp, Charlton Park*, gift from the artist, 1919, © crown copyright

Melhuish, George 1916–1985, *Turbine Furnaces*, transferred from the War Artists' Advisory Committee, 1947, © crown copyright

Meninsky, Bernard 1891–1950, *On the Departure Platform, Victoria Station*, transferred, 1919, © crown copyright

Meninsky, Bernard 1891–1950, *The Arrival*, transferred from the Ministry of Information, 1919, © crown copyright

Meninsky, Bernard 1891–1950, *The Platform Canteen, Victoria Station*, transferred from the Ministry of Information, 1919, © crown copyright

Meninsky, Bernard 1891–1950, *Victoria Station, District Railway*, transferred from the Ministry of Information, 1919, © crown copyright

Meninsky, Bernard 1891–1950, *Sketch of Soldiers Arriving on Leave*, transferred from the Ministry of Information, 1919, © crown copyright

Meninsky, Bernard 1891–1950, *The Arrival of a Leave Train, Victoria Station, 1918*, commissioned, acquired, 1919, © crown copyright

Methuen, Paul Ayshford 1886–1974, *London by Moonlight*, transferred from the War Artists' Advisory Committee, 1947, © crown copyright

Methuen, Paul Ayshford 1886–1974, *St Paul's by Moonlight*, gift from the artist, 1947, © the artist's estate

Methuen, Paul Ayshford 1886–1974, *Invasion Craft Being Built in the West India Docks, 30 May 1944*, gift from the artist, 1950, © the artist's estate

Methuen, Paul Ayshford 1886–1974, *Invasion Craft in the West India Docks, April 1944*, transferred from the War Artists' Advisory Committee, 1947, © crown copyright

Miers, Christopher b.1941, *A Regimental Aid Post near Gumbang, Borneo*, purchased, 1967, © Imperial War Museum

Miers, Christopher b.1941, *Camp Area near Stass, Borneo*, purchased, 1967, © Imperial War Museum

Mills, Reginald b.1896, *A Blazing Gas Main in Old Compton Street, London W1*, transferred from the War Artists' Advisory Committee, 1947, © crown copyright

Mills, Reginald b.1896, *Flashback: A Recollection of an Air Raid on an Ammunition Dump*, transferred from the War Artists' Advisory Committee, 1947

Mimpriss, Violet Barber 1895–1987, *Gun Drill: Fort Mombasa, Kenya*, transferred from the War Artists' Advisory Committee, 1947, © crown copyright

Minton, John 1917–1957, *Blitzed City with Self Portrait*, purchased with the assistance of the National Art Collections Fund, 2001, © Royal College of Art

Minton, John 1917–1957, *Wapping*, gift from Mrs Margaret Dale, © Royal College of Art

Mlynarski, Josef 1925–1984, *The Royal Family Visiting Polish Troops in Scotland, 1941*, gift from the Polish Embassy, 1982

Monnington, Walter Thomas 1902–1976, *Clouds and Spitfires*, transferred from the War Artists' Advisory Committee, 1947, © crown copyright

Monnington, Walter Thomas 1902–1976, *Fighter Affiliation: Halifax and Hurricane Aircraft Co-Operating in Action*, transferred from the War Artists' Advisory Committee, 1947, © crown copyright

Monnington, Walter Thomas 1902–1976, *Southern England: Spitfires Attacking Flying Bombs*, transferred from the War Artists' Advisory Committee, 1947, © crown copyright

Monnington, Walter Thomas 1902–1976, *Tempests Attacking Flying Bombs*, transferred from the War Artists' Advisory Committee, 1947, © crown copyright

Morley, Harry 1881–1943, *On the Driving Ground*, transferred from the War Artists' Advisory Committee, 1947, © crown copyright

Morley, Harry 1881–1943, *The Bombed 'SS Toscalusa' at a Western Port*, transferred from the War Artists' Advisory Committee, 1947,

© crown copyright

Morley, Harry 1881–1943, *The Tank Park*, transferred from the War Artists' Advisory Committee, 1947, © crown copyright

Mount, Cyril b.1920, *Guns of the 11th Field Regiment in Action with Robcol, Ruweisat Ridge, El Alamein, July 1942*, gift from the artist, 1999, © the artist

Mount, Cyril b.1920, *Lieutenant General C. J. E. Auchinleck (1884–1981), CB, CSI, DSO, OBE*, gift from the artist, 1967, © the artist

Moynihan, Rodrigo 1910–1990, *Auxiliary Territorial Service at Work*, transferred from the War Artists' Advisory Committee, 1947, © crown copyright

Moynihan, Rodrigo 1910–1990, *Lieutenant General Neil M. Ritchie (1897–1983), CBE, DSO, MC*, transferred from the War Artists' Advisory Committee, 1947, © crown copyright

Moynihan, Rodrigo 1910–1990, *Medical Inspection*, transferred from the War Artists' Advisory Committee, 1947, © crown copyright

Moynihan, Rodrigo 1910–1990, *Regimental Sergeant Major Hadley, Transport Service*, transferred from the War Artists' Advisory Committee, 1947, © crown copyright

Moynihan, Rodrigo 1910–1990, *Soldiers on Manoeuvres in Cornwall*, transferred from the War Artists' Advisory Committee, 1947, © crown copyright

Moynihan, Rodrigo 1910–1990, *Sir George Thomson (1892–1975), FRS, Scientific Adviser to the Air Ministry*, transferred from the War Artists' Advisory Committee, 1947, © crown copyright

Moynihan, Rodrigo 1910–1990, *Admiral Sir Walter Cowan (1871–1956), BT, KCB, DSO, MVO*, transferred from the War Artists' Advisory Committee, 1947, © crown copyright

Moynihan, Rodrigo 1910–1990, *Lieutenant General Sir Willoughby Norrie (1893–1977), KCMG, CB, DSO, MC*, transferred from the War Artists' Advisory Committee, 1947, © crown copyright

Moynihan, Rodrigo 1910–1990, *Major General the Viscount Bridgeman (1896–1982), CB, DSO, MC*, transferred from the War Artists' Advisory Committee, 1947, © crown copyright

Moynihan, Rodrigo 1910–1990, *Professor John Cockcroft (1897–1967), CBE, FRS, Director of the Atomic Energy Division, National Research Council of Canada*, transferred from the War Artists' Advisory Committee, 1947, © crown copyright

Moynihan, Rodrigo 1910–1990, *Air Marshal Sir Roderic Hill (1894–1954), KCB, MC, AFC and BAR*, transferred from the War Artists' Advisory Committee, 1947,

© crown copyright

Mozley, Charles 1914–1991, *St Paul's Cathedral*, accessioned, 1985

Mozley, Charles 1914–1991, *The Thames Embankment*, gift from the artist, 1987

Mozley, Charles 1914–1991, *Invasion Preparations in an English Village*, acquired, c.1982

Munro, Alastair active 1950s, *Searchlight Troop Headquarters, Royal Artillery*, gift from Lieutenant Colonel C. T. Wells, OBE, TD, 1959

Nash, John Northcote 1893–1977, *A French Highway*, transferred, 1919, © crown copyright

Nash, John Northcote 1893–1977, *An Advance Post: Day*, transferred, 1919, © crown copyright

Nash, John Northcote 1893–1977, *Oppy Wood, 1917: Evening*, commissioned, 1919, © crown copyright

Nash, John Northcote 1893–1977, *'Over The Top': First Artists' Rifles at Marcoing, 30 December 1917*, transferred, 1919, © crown copyright

Nash, John Northcote 1893–1977, *The Bridge over the Arras-Lens Railway*, transferred, 1919, © crown copyright

Nash, John Northcote 1893–1977, *A Dockyard Fire*, transferred from the War Artists' Advisory Committee, 1947, © crown copyright

Nash, Paul 1889–1946, *A Howitzer Firing*, transferred, 1919, © crown copyright

Nash, Paul 1889–1946, *Spring in the Trenches, Ridge Wood, 1917*, transferred, 1919, © crown copyright

Nash, Paul 1889–1946, *The Mule Track*, transferred, 1919, © crown copyright

Nash, Paul 1889–1946, *The Ypres Salient at Night*, transferred, 1919, © crown copyright

Nash, Paul 1889–1946, *We Are Making a New World*, transferred, 1919, © crown copyright

Nash, Paul 1889–1946, *The Menin Road*, commissioned, 1919, © crown copyright

Nash, Paul 1889–1946, *Battle of Britain*, transferred from the War Artists' Advisory Committee, 1947, © crown copyright

Nash, Paul 1889–1946, *Defence of Albion*, transferred from the War Artists' Advisory Committee, 1947, © crown copyright

Nash, Paul 1889–1946, *Battle of Germany*, transferred from the RAF, 1947, © crown copyright

Neuss, W. active 1940s, *The Giant Howitzer 'Karl' during the German Offensive in the Crimea, 1943*, purchased, 1982

Nevinson, Christopher 1889–1946, *A Taube*, gift from Sir Alfred Mond, 1917, © Imperial War Museum

Nevinson, Christopher 1889–1946, *French Troops Resting*, gift

from Fulham Borough Council, 1961, © courtesy of the artist's estate/www.bridgeman.co.uk

Nevinson, Christopher 1889–1946, *The Doctor*, commissioned, acquired, 1918, © Imperial War Museum

Nevinson, Christopher 1889–1946, *Archies*, gift from Mrs May Cippico, 1979, © courtesy of the artist's estate/www.bridgeman.co.uk

Nevinson, Christopher 1889–1946, *A Group of Soldiers*, commissioned, acquired, 1918, © Imperial War Museum

Nevinson, Christopher 1889–1946, *A Howitzer Gun in Elevation*, commissioned, acquired, 1918, © Imperial War Museum

Nevinson, Christopher 1889–1946, *A Tank*, purchased, 1968, © courtesy of the artist's estate/www.bridgeman.co.uk

Nevinson, Christopher 1889–1946, *After a Push*, commissioned, acquired, 1918, © Imperial War Museum

Nevinson, Christopher 1889–1946, *Over the Lines*, commissioned, acquired, 1918, © Imperial War Museum

Nevinson, Christopher 1889–1946, *Paths of Glory*, commissioned, acquired, 1918, © Imperial War Museum

Nevinson, Christopher 1889–1946, *Reliefs at Dawn*, commissioned, acquired, 1918, © Imperial War Museum

Nevinson, Christopher 1889–1946, *Swooping Down on a Hostile Plane*, gift from the artist, 1917, © Imperial War Museum

Nevinson, Christopher 1889–1946, *The Road from Arras to Bapaume*, commissioned, acquired, 1918, © Imperial War Museum

Nevinson, Christopher 1889–1946, *Nerves of the Army*, purchased, 1971, © courtesy of the artist's estate/www.bridgeman.co.uk

Nevinson, Christopher 1889–1946, *The Harvest of Battle*, commissioned, acquired, 1919, © crown copyright

Nevinson, Christopher 1889–1946, *The Unending Cult of Human Sacrifice*, purchased, 1998, © courtesy of the artist's estate/www.bridgeman.co.uk

Nevinson, Christopher 1889–1946, *Anti-Aircraft Defences*, transferred from the War Artists' Advisory Committee, 1947, © crown copyright

Newling, Edward active 1890–1934, *Captain Albert Ball (1896–1917), VC, DSO, MC, Nottinghamshire and Derby Regiment and Royal Flying Corps*, commissioned, acquired, 1919, © Imperial War Museum

Newling, Edward active 1890–1934, *Major James Byford McCudden (1895–1918), VC, SO, MC, RFC*, commissioned, acquired,

1919, © Imperial War Museum

Newling, Edward active 1890–1934, *Second Lieutenant Gilbert Stuart Martin Insall (1894–1972), VC, MC, Royal Flying Corps and Later Squadron Leader, Royal Air Force*, commissioned, acquired, 1919, © Imperial War Museum

Newton, Eric 1893–1965, *Overtime at Caledons*, purchased, 1971

Newton, Herbert H. 1881–1959, *War Accessories: A Group of Objects Familiar to Civilians during the War, Including Red Tape!*, gift, 1940

Nicholson, William 1872–1949, *Vice Admiral Sir William C. Pakenham (1861–1933), KCB, KCMG, KCVO*, commissioned, 1920, © Elizabeth Banks

Nockolds, Roy Anthony 1911–1979, *Stalking the Night Raider*, transferred from the War Artists' Advisory Committee, 1947, © crown copyright

Nockolds, Roy Anthony 1911–1979, *A Tempest Shooting Down a Flying Bomb*, transferred from the War Artists' Advisory Committee, 1947, © crown copyright

Ocean, Humphrey b.1951, *Recovering the Dan Buoy, 'HMS Broadsword'*, commissioned, 1980, © Imperial War Museum

O'Donoghue, Hughie b.1953, *German Tanks, Forges-les-Eaux*, purchased, 2003, © the artist

O'Donoghue, Hughie b.1953, *'Lancastria'*, purchased with the assistance of a donation from John Seagrim, 2000, © the artist

Olivier, Herbert Arnould 1861–1952, *The Terms of the Armistice, 3–4 November 1918*, gift from the artist, 1924, © Imperial War Museum

Olivier, Herbert Arnould 1861–1952, *General Di Robilant: Italian Military Representative on the Supreme War Council, Versailles*, gift from the artist, 1924, © Imperial War Museum

Olivier, Herbert Arnould 1861–1952, *General Sir Emile Belin, KCB, French Permanent Military Representative, Supreme War Council, Versailles, Major General of the Armies of the North and North-East*, gift from the artist, 1924, © Imperial War Museum

Olivier, Herbert Arnould 1861–1952, *General Tasker Bliss (1853–1930): Military Representative of the United States of America at the Supreme War Council, Versailles*, gift from the artist, 1924, © Imperial War Museum

Olivier, Herbert Arnould 1861–1952, *Major General the Honourable Charles Sackville-West (1870–1962), CMG, British Permanent Military Representative, Supreme War Council, Versailles*, gift from the artist, 1924, © Imperial War Museum

Olivier, Herbert Arnould 1861–1952, *Sketch of the Table in the Hall of Mirrors, at Which the Treaty of Versailles Was Signed*, gift from the artist, 1924, © Imperial War Museum

Olivier, Herbert Arnould 1861–1952, *The Four Military Representatives of the Supreme War Council, Versailles, Their Chief Officers, Secretaries and Interpreters in Session*, gift from the artist, 1924, © Imperial War Museum

Oppenheim, Duncan 1904–2003, *Boredom: Air Raid Wardens on Duty*, gift from the artist, 1995, © the artist's estate

Oppenheim, Duncan 1904–2003, *Finding an Unexploded Bomb, Barton Street, London SW1, 1940*, gift from the artist, 1995, © the artist's estate

Oppenheim, Duncan 1904–2003, *Searching for Casualties after the Explosion of a 1,000-Pound Bomb off Great Peter Street, London SW1*, gift from the artist, 1995, © the artist's estate

Oppenheim, Duncan 1904–2003, *The Terrible Boredom of Waiting for Action*, gift from the artist, 1995, © the artist's estate

Oppenheim, Duncan 1904–2003, *The Loneliness of an Air Raid Warden on Patrol during the Night Raids*, gift from the artist, 1995, © the artist's estate

Orde, Cuthbert Julian 1888–1968, *Air Vice-Marshal John Cotesworth Slessor (1897–1979), DSO, MC*, transferred from the War Artists' Advisory Committee, 1947, © crown copyright

Orpen, William 1878–1931, *A German Gunner's Shelter, Warlencourt*, gift from the artist, 1918

Orpen, William 1878–1931, *A Grave and a Mine Crater at La Boiselle, August 1917*, gift from the artist, 1918

Orpen, William 1878–1931, *A Grave in a Trench*, gift from the artist, 1918

Orpen, William 1878–1931, *A Grenadier Guardsman*, gift from the artist, 1918

Orpen, William 1878–1931, *A Gunner's Shelter in a Trench, Thiepval*, gift from the artist, 1918

Orpen, William 1878–1931, *A Highlander Passing a Grave*, gift from the artist, 1918

Orpen, William 1878–1931, *A House at Péronne*, gift from the artist, 1918

Orpen, William 1878–1931, *An Airman: Lieutenant Reginald Theodore Carlos Hoidge (1894–1963), MC*, gift from the artist, 1918

Orpen, William 1878–1931, *Brigadier General Hugh Jamieson Elles (1880–1945), CB, DSO*, gift from the artist, 1918

Orpen, William 1878–1931, *Dieppe*, gift from the artist, 1918

Orpen, William 1878–1931, *Field Marshal Sir Douglas Haig (1861–1928), KT, GCB, GCVO, KCIE, Commander-in-Chief, France, from 15 December 1915*, gift from the artist, 1918

Orpen, William 1878–1931, *German Planes Visiting Cassel*, gift from the artist, 1918

Orpen, William 1878–1931, *German Sick: Captured at Messines, in a Canadian Hospital*, gift from the artist, 1918

Orpen, William 1878–1931, *German Wire, Thiepval*, gift from the artist, 1918

Orpen, William 1878–1931, *Inside a Small Mine Crater, La Boiselle*, gift from the artist, 1918

Orpen, William 1878–1931, *Lieutenant Arthur Percival Foley Rhys Davids (1897–1917), DSO, MC*, gift from the artist, 1918

Orpen, William 1878–1931, *Lieutenant General Sir Travers Clarke, KCMG, CB, Quartermaster General, France, December 1917*, gift from the artist, 1918

Orpen, William 1878–1931, *Major F. E. Hotblack, DSO, MC*, gift from the artist, 1918

Orpen, William 1878–1931, *Major General Hugh M. Trenchard (1873–1956), CB, DSO, Royal Flying Corps*, gift from the artist, 1918

Orpen, William 1878–1931, *Mines and the Bapaume Road, La Boiselle*, gift from the artist, 1918

Orpen, William 1878–1931, *Monsieur R. D. De Maratray, French War Correspondent for 'Le Petit Journal'*, gift from the artist, 1918

Orpen, William 1878–1931, *My Work Room, Cassel*, gift from the artist, 1918

Orpen, William 1878–1931, *Outside a Small Mine Crater, Bapaume Road*, gift from the artist, 1919

Orpen, William 1878–1931, *Ready to Start: Self Portrait*, gift from the artist, 1918

Orpen, William 1878–1931, *Soldiers and Peasants, Cassel*, gift from the artist, 1918

Orpen, William 1878–1931, *The Big Crater*, gift from the artist, 1918

Orpen, William 1878–1931, *The Butte de Warlencourt*, gift from the artist, 1918

Orpen, William 1878–1931, *The Courtyard, Hotel Sauvage, Cassel, Nord*, gift from the artist, 1918

Orpen, William 1878–1931, *The Girls' College, Péronne*, gift from the artist, 1918

Orpen, William 1878–1931, *The Great Mine, La Boiselle*, gift from the artist, 1919

Orpen, William 1878–1931, *The Gunners' Shelter, Thiepval*, gift from the artist, 1918

Orpen, William 1878–1931, *The Household Brigade Passing to the Ypres Salient, Cassel*, gift from the artist, 1918

Orpen, William 1878–1931, *The Main Street, Combles*, gift from the artist, 1918

Orpen, William 1878–1931, *The Main Street, Thiepval*, gift from the artist, 1918

Orpen, William 1878–1931, *The Mascot of the Coldstream Guards*, gift from the artist, 1918

Orpen, William 1878–1931, *The Non-Commissioned Officer Pilot, Royal Flying Corps: Flight Sergeant W. G. Bennett*, gift from the artist, 1918

Orpen, William 1878–1931, *The Schwaben Redoubt*, gift from the artist, 1918

Orpen, William 1878–1931, *The Somme: A Clear Day; View from the British Trenches opposite La Boiselle, Showing the German Front Line and Mine Craters*, gift from the artist, 1918

Orpen, William 1878–1931, *Thiepval*, gift from the artist, 1918

Orpen, William 1878–1931, *Thiepval Wood*, gift from the artist, 1918

Orpen, William 1878–1931, *View from the Old British Trenches: Looking towards La Boiselle, Courcelette on the Left, Martinpuich on the Right*, gift from the artist, 1918

Orpen, William 1878–1931, *Village: Evening*, gift from the artist, 1918

Orpen, William 1878–1931, *The Refugee (B)*, gift from the artist, 1918

Orpen, William 1878–1931, *Self Portrait*, gift from the artist, 1918

Orpen, William 1878–1931, *Self Portrait*, gift from the artist, 1918

Orpen, William 1878–1931, *Adam and Eve at Péronne*, gift from the artist, 1918

Orpen, William 1878–1931, *Bombing: Night*, gift from the artist, 1918

Orpen, William 1878–1931, *Brigadier General the Right Honourable John Edward Bernard Seely (1868–1947), CB, DSO, MP*, gift from the artist, 1918

Orpen, William 1878–1931, *Brigadier General William Thomas Francis Horwood (1868–1943), DSO, Late Provost-Marshal, General Headquarters, British Expeditionary Force*, gift from the artist, 1923

Orpen, William 1878–1931, *Dead Germans in a Trench*, gift from the artist, 1918

Orpen, William 1878–1931, *General Sir Henry Seymour Rawlinson (1864–1925), Bt, GCVO, KCB, KCMG, Fourth Army*, gift from the artist, 1918

Orpen, William 1878–1931, *General Sir Herbert Charles Onslow Plumer (1857–1932), GCMG, GCVO, KCB, Second Army*, gift from the artist, 1918

Orpen, William 1878–1931, *Harvest*, gift from the artist, 1930

Orpen, William 1878–1931, *In Their Cellar in Amiens: Captain R. Maude, Department of the Army, Provost Marshal General, Awarded the Croix de Guerre by the French Authorities, and Colonel Du Tiel, Commandant d'Armes, Amiens*, gift from the artist, 1918

Orpen, William 1878–1931, *Lieutenant Colonel A. N. Lee, DSO, OBE, TD, Censor in France of Paintings and Drawings by Artists at the Front*, gift from the artist, 1918

Orpen, William 1878–1931, *Major James Byford McCudden (1895–1918), VC, DSO, MC*, gift from the artist, 1918

Orpen, William 1878–1931, *Marshal Ferdinand Foch (1851–1929), OM*, gift from the artist, 1918

Orpen, William 1878–1931, *Prince Antoine d'Orleans et Braganza, MC*, gift from the artist, 1929

Orpen, William 1878–1931, *Some Members of the Allied Press Camp with Their Press Officers*, gift from the artist, 1918

Orpen, William 1878–1931, *The First Chief Controller, Queen Mary's Army Auxiliary Corps in France, Dame Helen Gwynne-Vaughan (1879–1967), CBE, DSC*, gift from the artist, 1918

Orpen, William 1878–1931, *The Mad Woman of Douai*, gift from the artist, 1931

Orpen, William 1878–1931, *The Refugee (A)*, gift from the artist, 1918

Orpen, William 1878–1931, *A Peace Conference at the Quai d'Orsay*, commissioned, acquired, 1920

Orpen, William 1878–1931, *The Signing of Peace in the Hall of Mirrors, Versailles, 28 June 1919*, commissioned, acquired, 1920

Orpen, William 1878–1931, *To the Unknown British Soldier in France*, gift from the artist in memory of Earl Haig, 1928

Ouless, Catherine 1879–1961, *A Warden's Post in Kensington*, gift, 1968

Parkes, Oscar 1885–1958, *Royal Navy Hospital Ship 'Somali' off Cape Helles: Walking Cases Coming on Board*, purchased, 1921, © Imperial War Museum

Parkes, Oscar 1885–1958, *The Smoke Screen: Destroyers Throwing a Smoke Screen around Hospital Ship 'Karapara' after Hospital Ship 'Dover Castle' Had Been Torpedoed by an Enemy Submarine*, commissioned, acquired, 1919, © Imperial War Museum

Paterson, G. W. Lennox 1915–1986, *A Landing Craft Base: The 'SS Duchess of Rothesay' at HMS Helder, near Clacton-on-Sea*, purchased, 1946, © crown copyright

Payne, R. H. b.1921, *Bomb Damage at Chingford, Essex*, transferred from the War Artists' Advisory Committee, 1947, © crown copyright

Peake, Mervyn 1911–1968, *The Evolution of the Cathode Ray (Radiolocation) Tube*, transferred from the War Artists' Advisory Committee, 1947, © crown copyright

Peake, Mervyn 1911–1968, *Interrogation of Pilots*, transferred from the War Artists' Advisory Committee, 1947, © crown copyright

Pearce, C. J. active 1940s, *A Crashed Aeroplane, Devon*, transferred from the War Artists' Advisory Committee, 1947, © crown copyright

Pears, Charles 1873–1958, *An Officer of a Motor Launch about to Board a Norwegian Steamer*, commissioned, acquired, 1919, © the artist's estate

Pears, Charles 1873–1958, *The Lights of Rosyth from the Forth Bridge Footpath: Port Edgar and the Fleet*, commissioned, acquired, 1918, © the artist's estate

Pears, Charles 1873–1958, *'HMS Dunraven VC' in Action against the Submarine That Sank Her, 8 August 1917*, purchased, 1949, © the artist's estate

Pears, Charles 1873–1958, *Women Putting Anti-Fouling Paint on the Bottom of a Motor Launch, Leith*, commissioned, acquired, 1918, © the artist's estate

Pears, Charles 1873–1958, *Dazzled, a Camouflaged Battleship: 'HMS Ramillies' in a Gale of Wind*, commissioned, acquired, 1918, © the artist's estate

Pears, Charles 1873–1958, *A Big Crane at Rosyth Placing a Gun on a Light Cruiser at Night*, commissioned, acquired, 1918, © the artist's estate

Pears, Charles 1873–1958, *A Boarding Party of Royal Naval Reserve Men Going Aboard a Prize under Searchlight*, commissioned, acquired, 1919, © the artist's estate

Pears, Charles 1873–1958, *A Convoy*, commissioned, acquired, 1918, © the artist's estate

Pears, Charles 1873–1958, *A Corner of the Dockyard, Rosyth: Winter*, commissioned, acquired, 1918, © the artist's estate

Pears, Charles 1873–1958, *A Drifting Mine*, commissioned, acquired, 1918, © the artist's estate

Pears, Charles 1873–1958, *A Motor Launch Recovering a Torpedo: 'HMS Yarmouth' at Practice, January 1918*, commissioned, acquired, 1918, © the artist's estate

Pears, Charles 1873–1958, *A Thunderstorm, Harwich: Submarines Leaving Port*, commissioned, acquired, 1918, © the artist's estate

Pears, Charles 1873–1958, *At Work on a Battleship at Rosyth: Testing Cables at Night by the Light of a Flare Lamp*, commissioned, acquired, 1918, © the artist's estate

Pears, Charles 1873–1958, *Dawn: Sending away Coastal Motor Boats, 11 August 1918*, commissioned, acquired, 1918, © the artist's estate

Pears, Charles 1873–1958, *German Star Shells: Men at the Guns off the*

German Coast, 11 August 1918, commissioned, acquired, 1918, © the artist's estate

Pears, Charles 1873–1958, *'HMS Fearless'*, commissioned, acquired, 1918, © the artist's estate

Pears, Charles 1873–1958, *'HMS Ullswater': A Destroyer Torpedoed*, commissioned, acquired, 1918, © the artist's estate

Pears, Charles 1873–1958, *North Queensferry Signal Station, Winter: The First Battle Cruiser Squadron Seen from the Forth Bridge*, commissioned, acquired, 1918, © the artist's estate

Pears, Charles 1873–1958, *Pay Night, Rosyth, in Winter*, commissioned, acquired, 1918, © the artist's estate

Pears, Charles 1873–1958, *Port Edgar, Firth of Forth, the Destroyer Base of the Northern Waters: Sunset, V-Class Destroyers Backing out to Sea*, commissioned, acquired, 1918, © the artist's estate

Pears, Charles 1873–1958, *Rosyth: Fog Obscuring the Dockyard*, commissioned, acquired, 1918, © the artist's estate

Pears, Charles 1873–1958, *Rosyth: Light Cruiser Anchorage*, commissioned, acquired, 1918, © the artist's estate

Pears, Charles 1873–1958, *Strafed by a German Seaplane off Terschelling*, commissioned, acquired, 1918, © the artist's estate

Pears, Charles 1873–1958, *The Action of 11 August 1918, Island of Borkum: Zeppelin Falling; the Flagship is Flying the Signal*, commissioned, acquired, 1918, © the artist's estate

Pears, Charles 1873–1958, *The British Submarine K22 in Dry Dock, at Rosyth, in Winter*, commissioned, acquired, 1918, © the artist's estate

Pears, Charles 1873–1958, *The Gate Ship at Granton Painted Scarlet to Indicate the Port Entrance through One of the Barriers across the Firth of Forth*, commissioned, acquired, 1918, © the artist's estate

Pears, Charles 1873–1958, *The German Fleet at Anchor off Inchkeith, Firth of Forth: After the Surrender, 22 November 1918*, commissioned, acquired, 1919, © crown copyright

Pears, Charles 1873–1958, *The Harwich Gate Ships, Barrier and Light Cruisers under Searchlight*, commissioned, acquired, 1918, © the artist's estate

Pears, Charles 1873–1958, *The North Sea: The Night of 10 August 1918*, commissioned, acquired, 1918, © the artist's estate

Pears, Charles 1873–1958, *The Wake: 'HMS Courageous' at Top Speed*, commissioned, acquired, 1918, © the artist's estate

Pears, Charles 1873–1958, *A Dazzled Merchantman*, commissioned, acquired, 1920, © the artist's estate

Pears, Charles 1873–1958, *A Hospital Ship at Night*, commissioned, acquired, 1918, © the artist's estate

Pears, Charles 1873–1958, *Big and Little: 'HMS Glorious' and a Motor Launch at the Island of Inchkeith under Snow*, commissioned, acquired, 1918, © the artist's estate

Pears, Charles 1873–1958, *River Plate Pageant*, © the artist's estate

Pears, Charles 1873–1958, *Steam Pinnaces at Hawkes Pier*, commissioned, acquired, 1918, © the artist's estate

Pears, Charles 1873–1958, *'HMS Courageous' in Dry Dock, at Rosyth, in Winter*, commissioned, acquired, 1918, © the artist's estate

Pears, Charles 1873–1958, *'HMS Furious': Aerodrome Ship*, commissioned, acquired, 1919, © crown copyright

Pears, Charles 1873–1958, *Streaming the Paravanes: Paravanes Enable a Ship to Go through Mines in Almost Complete Safety*, commissioned, acquired, 1919, © crown copyright

Pears, Charles 1873–1958, *Shelling of a British Convoy by the Germans from the French Coast*, transferred from the War Artists' Advisory Committee, 1947, © crown copyright

Pears, Charles 1873–1958, *Handing Over a Convoy from American to British Escorts*, transferred from the War Artists' Advisory Committee, 1947, © crown copyright

Pears, Charles 1873–1958, *A British Convoy on Its Way to Russia*, transferred from the War Artists' Advisory Committee, 1947, © crown copyright

Pears, Charles 1873–1958, *A German Searchlight across the English Channel*, transferred from the War Artists' Advisory Committee, 1947, © crown copyright

Pears, Charles 1873–1958, *The Convoy Led by Admiral Vian Fighting Its Way through to Malta*, transferred from the War Artists' Advisory Committee, 1947, © crown copyright

Pears, Charles 1873–1958, *The Norwegian Coast, Spring 1940*, transferred from the War Artists' Advisory Committee, 1947, © crown copyright

Pearson, R. active 1914–1918, *The End of the Cuxhaven Raid: Christmas Day*, gift from H. Gaskell-Blackburn, 1920

Peries, Ivan 1921–1988, *Combined Control and Report Centre*, transferred from the War Artists' Advisory Committee, 1947, © crown copyright

Perkins, Christopher 1891–1968, *Roll-Call of the Survivors of HM Troopship 'Archangel' at Aberdeen*, transferred from the War Artists' Advisory Committee, 1947, © crown copyright

Perkins, Christopher 1891–1968, *American Soldiers in an Anti-Aircraft Plotting Room in Northern Ireland*, transferred from the War Artists' Advisory Committee, 1947, © crown copyright

Perkins, Christopher 1891–1968, *Torpedoed and Beached*, transferred from the War Artists' Advisory Committee, 1947, © crown copyright

Philpot, Glyn Warren 1884–1937, *Admiral of the Fleet Sir John Jellicoe (1859–1935), GCM, OM, GCVO*, commissioned, acquired, 1918, © Imperial War Museum

Philpot, Glyn Warren 1884–1937, *Admiral Sir Frederick Charles Dove Sturdee (1829–1925), Bt, KCB, KCMG, CVO*, commissioned, acquired, 1918, © Imperial War Museum

Philpot, Glyn Warren 1884–1937, *Dame Katherine Furse, CBE, RRC, Director of the Women's Royal Naval Service (1920)*, gift from the artist, 1920, © Imperial War Museum

Philpot, Glyn Warren 1884–1937, *Rear Admiral Sir Reginald Y. Tyrwhitt (1870–1951), KCB, DSO*, commissioned, acquired, 1918, © Imperial War Museum

Philpot, Glyn Warren 1884–1937, *Sketch of 'Admiral of the Fleet Sir John Jellicoe (1859–1935), GCM, OM, GCVO'*, purchased, 1969, © the artist's estate

Philpot, Glyn Warren 1884–1937, *Sketch of 'Rear Admiral Sir Reginald Y. Tyrwhitt (1870–1951), KCB, DSO'*, purchased, 1969, © the artist's estate

Philpot, Glyn Warren 1884–1937, *Sketch of 'Vice Admiral Sir Roger Keyes (1872–1945), KCB, CMG, CVO, DSO'*, purchased, 1969, © the artist's estate

Philpot, Glyn Warren 1884–1937, *Vice Admiral Sir Roger Keyes (1872–1945), KCB, CMG, CVO, DSO*, commissioned, acquired, 1918, © Imperial War Museum

Pilkington, George William 1879–1958, *Scuttling of the 'Watussi' off Cape Point with 'HMS Sussex' and Junkers Aircraft*, gift from Mrs Carol McEwan, 1979

Piper, John 1903–1992, *The Control Room at South-West Regional Headquarters, Bristol*, transferred from the War Artists' Advisory Committee, 1947, © crown copyright

Piper, John 1903–1992, *The Passage to the Control Room at South-West Regional Headquarters, Bristol*, transferred from the War Artists' Advisory Committee, 1947, © crown copyright

Pitchforth, Roland Vivian 1895–1982, *A Parachute Landing*, transferred from the War Artists' Advisory Committee, 1947, © crown copyright

Pitchforth, Roland Vivian 1895–1982, *Chamber of the House of Commons: Bomb Damage*

Pitchforth, Roland Vivian 1895–1982, *Snack Time in a Factory*, transferred from the War Artists' Advisory Committee, 1947, © crown copyright

Plante, George 1914–1995, *A Rescue Ship in the Atlantic, March 1943*, transferred from the War Artists' Advisory Committee, 1947, © crown copyright

Platt, John Edgar 1886–1967, *A Convoy Passing the Lizard, Cornwall*, transferred from the War Artists' Advisory Committee, 1947, © crown copyright

Platt, John Edgar 1886–1967, *Wartime Traffic on the River Thames: Fire Services, Hungerford Bridge*, transferred from the War Artists' Advisory Committee, 1947, © crown copyright

Platt, John Edgar 1886–1967, *Wartime Traffic on the River Thames: River Minesweepers*, transferred from the War Artists' Advisory Committee, 1947, © crown copyright

Platt, John Edgar 1886–1967, *Wartime Traffic on the River Thames: River Police at Waterloo Bridge during the Battle of Britain*, transferred from the War Artists' Advisory Committee, 1947, © crown copyright

Platt, John Edgar 1886–1967, *Wartime Traffic on the River Thames: Royal Air Force Sea Rescue Launch, London Bridge*, transferred from the War Artists' Advisory Committee, 1947, © crown copyright

Platt, John Edgar 1886–1967, *Wartime Traffic on the River Thames: Upriver Repairs after the Dieppe Raid*, transferred from the War Artists' Advisory Committee, 1947, © crown copyright

Platt, John Edgar 1886–1967, *Wartime Traffic on the River Thames: War Supplies at Paul's Wharf*, transferred from the War Artists' Advisory Committee, 1947, © crown copyright

Platt, John Edgar 1886–1967, *A Marshalling Yard in Wartime: 'Bomber's Moon'*, transferred from the War Artists' Advisory Committee, 1947, © crown copyright

Platt, John Edgar 1886–1967, *The Battle of the Atlantic: A Cargo Ship Completes Another Crossing*, transferred from the War Artists' Advisory Committee, 1947, © crown copyright

Platt, John Edgar 1886–1967, *The Quick Turnround*, transferred from the War Artists' Advisory Committee, 1947, © crown copyright

Platt, John Edgar 1886–1967, *War Transport: A Dockside Unloading Shed for Tobacco, Ammunition and Machinery*, transferred from the War Artists' Advisory Committee, 1947, © crown copyright

Platt, John Edgar 1886–1967, *Ocean Transport: The Gateway to Battle*, transferred from the War Artists' Advisory Committee, 1947, © crown copyright

Platt, John Edgar 1886–1967, *Wartime Traffic on the River Thames*, transferred from the War Artists' Advisory Committee, 1947, © crown copyright

Polunin, Elizabeth V. 1880–1953, *Divisional Officer Twyman*, transferred from the War Artists' Advisory Committee, 1947, © crown copyright

Porter, Alfred Thomas active 1882–1919, *Canadians Cutting and Carting Wood, Farnham*, purchased, 1919

Potter, Mary 1900–1981, *Portrait of an Auxiliary Territorial Service Sergeant*, purchased, 1994, © DACS

Power, Harold Septimus 1879–1951, *A 'Red Cross' Train, France*, purchased, 1918, © Imperial War Museum

Preece, Patricia 1894–1966, *Miss M. Steele*, transferred from the War Artists' Advisory Committee, 1947, © crown copyright

Procktor, Patrick 1936–2003, *Corporal Robert James Ransome, 1 Royal Anglian, Belize*, commissioned, 1984, © Imperial War Museum

Procktor, Patrick 1936–2003, *Edward Jones, Chief Clerk DOE, Belize*, commissioned, 1984, © Imperial War Museum

Procktor, Patrick 1936–2003, *R. F. M. Harka Raj Rai, 10th Prime Minister's Official Representative: Gurkha in Belize*, commissioned, 1984, © Imperial War Museum

Quarmby, George 1883–1957, *Bomb Damage in St Paul's Cathedral, London*, gift from Sir Charles Wheeler, PRA, 1942, © crown copyright

Randall, Maurice active 1890–1935, *HM Hospital Ship 'Llandovery Castle', Union Castle Line, Sunk by Enemy Submarines, 27 June 1918*

Rawlinson, William Thomas 1912–1993, *A Chain Home Extra Low Radar Station*, transferred from the War Artists' Advisory Committee, 1947, © crown copyright

Rawlinson, William Thomas 1912–1993, *A 'CHL' (Chain Home Low) Radar Station*, transferred from the War Artists' Advisory Committee, 1947, © crown copyright

Rawlinson, William Thomas 1912–1993, *A 'CHL' (Chain Home Low) Radar Station*, transferred from the War Artists' Advisory Committee, 1947, © crown copyright

Rawlinson, William Thomas 1912–1993, *A 'Composite' Radar Station for Air Surface Watching*, transferred from the War Artists' Advisory Committee, 1947, © crown copyright

Rawlinson, William Thomas 1912–1993, *A 'Final' GCI (Ground-*

Controlled Interception) Radar Station, transferred from the War Artists' Advisory Committee, 1947, © crown copyright

Rawlinson, William Thomas 1912–1993, *A Mobile Ground-Controlled Interception Radar Station*, transferred from the War Artists' Advisory Committee, 1947, © crown copyright

Rawlinson, William Thomas 1912–1993, *A Mobile Radio Unit*, transferred from the War Artists' Advisory Committee, 1947, © crown copyright

Rawlinson, William Thomas 1912–1993, *A 'Type 11' Radar Station*, transferred from the War Artists' Advisory Committee, 1947, © crown copyright

Rawlinson, William Thomas 1912–1993, *A 'Type 16' Fighter Direction Radar Station*, transferred from the War Artists' Advisory Committee, 1947, © crown copyright

Rawlinson, William Thomas 1912–1993, *A 'Type CH' (Chain Home) Radar Station on the East Coast*, transferred from the War Artists' Advisory Committee, 1947, © crown copyright

Rawlinson, William Thomas 1912–1993, *A 'Type CH' (Chain Home) Radar Station on the West Coast*, transferred from the War Artists' Advisory Committee, 1947, © crown copyright

Rawlinson, William Thomas 1912–1993, *An 'Interception Chain Home Low' Radar Station*, transferred from the War Artists' Advisory Committee, 1947, © crown copyright

Rawlinson, William Thomas 1912–1993, *An 'OBOE/9000' Ground Radar Station*, transferred from the War Artists' Advisory Committee, 1947, © crown copyright

Rawlinson, William Thomas 1912–1993, *The Reporting Room in a 'Final' Ground-Controlled Interception Station*, transferred from the War Artists' Advisory Committee, 1947, © crown copyright

Rees-Roberts, Ivor Bailey b.1915, *Displaced Persons*, gift, 2006

Reid, Stuart 1883–1971, *Bombing of the Wadi Fara, 20 September 1918*, commissioned, acquired, 1920

Reid, Stuart 1883–1971, *Deraa: The Arab Welcome to the First Handley Page Machine to Arrive in Palestine, 22 September 1918*, commissioned, acquired, 1920

Reid, Stuart 1883–1971, *A Handley Page Aeroplane Bombing Nabulus by Night*, commissioned, acquired, 1920

Reid, Stuart 1883–1971, *Lieutenant McNamara: Winning the VC in the Course of a Bombing Raid in the Wadi Hesi, 10 Miles East-North-East of Gaza, Palestine, 20 March 1917*, commissioned, acquired, 1920

Reid, Stuart 1883–1971, *The Bott Incident*, commissioned, acquired, 1920

Reid, Stuart 1883–1971, *The Ridley Tragedy*, commissioned, acquired, 1920

Reid, Stuart 1883–1971, *The Seward Exploit: Second Lieutenant W. E. L. Seward, MC, at Ramleh, near Jaffa in Palestine, 24 March 1917*, commissioned, acquired, 1920

Richards, Albert 1919–1945, *A Covering for a Gun Site*, transferred from the War Artists' Advisory Committee, 1947, © crown copyright

Richards, Albert 1919–1945, *A Searchlight Battery*, transferred from the War Artists' Advisory Committee, 1947, © crown copyright

Richards, Albert 1919–1945, *The Industrial Battle: Tanks Ready for Shipment Overseas*, transferred from the War Artists' Advisory Committee, 1947, © crown copyright

Richards, Albert 1919–1945, *Airborne Royal Army Service Corps Supply Dropping*, transferred from the War Artists' Advisory Committee, 1947, © crown copyright

Richards, Albert 1919–1945, *Breaking up the Attack, Holland: 25-Pounders of the 15th (Scottish) Division Firing towards Meijel*, transferred from the War Artists' Advisory Committee, 1947, © crown copyright

Richards, Albert 1919–1945, *Exercise 'Mush': Gliders Land on a 'Captured' Airfield and Paratroops Surround the Field, Waiting for the Unloading of the Gliders*, transferred from the War Artists' Advisory Committee, 1947, © crown copyright

Richards, Albert 1919–1945, *Germany: The Siegfried Line between Heerlen and Aachen*, transferred from the War Artists' Advisory Committee, 1947, © crown copyright

Richards, Albert 1919–1945, *Holland: Infantry of the 15th (Scottish) Division Taking Over from Hard-Pressed American Troops during a German Counterattack on the Village of Meijel*, transferred from the War Artists' Advisory Committee, 1947, © crown copyright

Richards, Albert 1919–1945, *'Kilkenny's Circus': Parachute Training School Paratroops Undergoing Synthetic Training*, transferred from the War Artists' Advisory Committee, 1947, © crown copyright

Richards, Albert 1919–1945, *Loading Containers on a Dakota Aircraft*, transferred from the War Artists' Advisory Committee, 1947, © crown copyright

Richards, Albert 1919–1945, *The Advance, France: Burnt Out German Petrol Tankers*, transferred from the War Artists' Advisory Committee, 1947, © crown copyright

Richards, Albert 1919–1945, *The Beach Head, France: The Search for Rubble; the Wear and Tear on the Roads Resulted in a Constant Search for Materials for Repair, Crushing Iron Ore in the Area of the Colombelles Factory near Caen*, transferred from the War Artists' Advisory Committee, 1947, © crown copyright

Richards, Albert 1919–1945, *The Beginning of the Advance, France: German Bridge Demolition*, transferred from the War Artists' Advisory Committee, 1947, © crown copyright

Richards, Albert 1919–1945, *The Break through, France: 'Marmalade Bridge', A Railway Bridge Crossing the River Seine at Rouen*, transferred from the War Artists' Advisory Committee, 1947, © crown copyright

Richards, Albert 1919–1945, *The Drop*, transferred from the War Artists' Advisory Committee, 1947, © crown copyright

Richards, Ceri Geraldus 1903–1971, *Falling Forms*, purchased, 1994, © estate of Ceri Richard/ DACS 2006

Robb, Carole b.1943, *Casualty of War*, gift in memory of Johanna Davis, 2005, © the artist

Robb, Carole b.1943, *Death of Achilles*, gift in memory of Johanna Davis, 2005, © the artist

Roberts, Diane b.1956, *Falklands War Triptych (left)*, gift from the artist, 1992, © the artist

Roberts, Diane b.1956, *Falklands War Triptych (centre)*, gift from the artist, 1992, © the artist

Roberts, Diane b.1956, *Falklands War Triptych (right)*, gift from the artist, 1992, © the artist

Roberts, William Patrick 1895–1980, *A Shell Dump, France*, commissioned, acquired, 1919, © crown copyright

Roberts, William Patrick 1895–1980, *'Feeds Round!': Stable Time in the Wagon Lines, France*, gift from Sir Muirhead Bone, 1924, © William Roberts Society

Robertson, Stewart active 1912–1920, *Mixed Company on the Montello-Italian Front: An Italian Six-Inch Gun Being Hauled up Road Four by Fiat Tractors; an Ox Wagon Taking up Water for the Infantry*, purchased, 1919

Rogers, Gilbert active 1905–1920, *'Humanity' Bearer Post, Cambrin Sector, August 1916: The First Field Ambulance*, gift from the British Red Cross Society and the Order of St John of Jerusalem, 1920, © Imperial War Museum

Rogers, Gilbert active 1905–1920, *A Voluntary Aid Detachment Motor Driver*, gift from the British Red Cross Society and the Order of St John of Jerusalem, 1920, © Imperial War Museum

Rogers, Gilbert active 1905–1920, *A Royal Army Medical Corps Sergeant Major*, transferred from the Royal Army Medical Corps, 1920, © Imperial War Museum

Rogers, Gilbert active 1905–1920, *Stretcher Bearing in Difficulties*, transferred from the Royal Army Medical Corps, 1920, © Imperial War Museum

Rogers, Gilbert active 1905–1920, *A British Red Cross Society and Order of St John of Jerusalem Barge on the Tigris at Amara: British Red Cross Society and Order of St John Headquarters in the Distance*, gift from the British Red Cross Society and the Order of St John of Jerusalem, 1920, © Imperial War Museum

Rogers, Gilbert active 1905–1920, *A British Red Cross Society and Order of St John of Jerusalem Hospital Barge Orderly on the Tigris*, gift from the British Red Cross Society and the Order of St John of Jerusalem, 1920, © Imperial War Museum

Rogers, Gilbert active 1905–1920, *A British Red Cross Society and Order of St John of Jerusalem Hospital Ship and Barges on the Tigris*, gift from the British Red Cross Society and the Order of St John of Jerusalem, 1920, © Imperial War Museum

Rogers, Gilbert active 1905–1920, *A British Red Cross Society and Order of St John of Jerusalem Motor Driver*, gift from the British Red Cross Society and the Order of St John of Jerusalem, 1920, © Imperial War Museum

Rogers, Gilbert active 1905–1920, *A British Red Cross Society and Order of St John of Jerusalem Officer in Mesopotamia*, gift from the British Red Cross Society and the Order of St John of Jerusalem, 1920, © Imperial War Museum

Rogers, Gilbert active 1905–1920, *A Royal Army Medical Corps Stretcher-Bearer, Fully Equipped*, transferred from the Royal Army Medical Corps, 1920, © Imperial War Museum

Rogers, Gilbert active 1905–1920, *Gassed: 'In arduis fidelis'*, transferred from the Royal Army Medical Corps, 1920, © crown copyright

Rogers, Gilbert active 1905–1920, *Mud*, transferred from the Royal Army Medical Corps, 1920, © Imperial War Museum

Rogers, Gilbert active 1905–1920, *The Royal Army Medical Corps at Messines during the 1917 Offensive*, commissioned, acquired, 1919, © Imperial War Museum

Rogers, Gilbert active 1905–1920, *Ypres, 1915*, gift from the British Red Cross Society and the Order of St John of Jerusalem, 1920, © Imperial War Museum

Rommel, T. active 1950s,

Lieutenant General Wladyslaw Anders (1892–1970): Commander of Two Polish Corps at Monte Cassino, gift, 1954

Rosenberg, Isaac 1890–1918, *Sea and Beach*, gift from Mrs Silver, 1982

Rosenberg, Isaac 1890–1918, *The Fountain*, gift from Mrs Silver, 1982

Rosenberg, Isaac 1890–1918, *The Road*, gift from Mrs Silver, 1982

Rosenberg, Isaac 1890–1918, *Landscape with Flowering Trees*, gift from Mrs Silver, 1982

Rosenberg, Isaac 1890–1918, *Landscape with River*, gift from Mrs Silver, 1982

Rosenberg, Isaac 1890–1918, *Head of a Woman, 'Grey and Red'*, gift from Mrs Silver, 1982

Rosenberg, Isaac 1890–1918, *Trees*, gift from Mrs Silver, 1982

Rosoman, Leonard Henry b.1913, *A House Collapsing on Two Firemen, Shoe Lane, London, EC4*, transferred from the War Artists' Advisory Committee, 1947, © crown copyright

Rosoman, Leonard Henry b.1913, *The Houses of Parliament on Fire, May 1941*, purchased, 1985, © the artist

Rosoman, Leonard Henry b.1913, *A Burnt Out Fire Appliance*, transferred from the War Artists' Advisory Committee, 1947, © crown copyright

Rosoman, Leonard Henry b.1913, *A Crater in the Naval Dockyard, Hong Kong*, transferred from the War Artists' Advisory Committee, 1947, © crown copyright

Rosoman, Leonard Henry b.1913, *A Radar Predictor*, transferred from the War Artists' Advisory Committee, 1947, © crown copyright

Rosoman, Leonard Henry b.1913, *A Rangefinder in Hot Sunlight*, transferred from the War Artists' Advisory Committee, 1947, © crown copyright

Rosoman, Leonard Henry b.1913, *Corsair Aircraft with Folded Wings in Hot Sunlight*, transferred from the War Artists' Advisory Committee, 1947, © crown copyright

Ross, Michael active 1935–1955, *Air Vice-Marshal Simpson, Air Defence Commander, 19 Group, RAF Pitreavie*, gift from Mrs A. Ker, 1987

Rothenstein, William 1872–1945, *The Watch on the Rhine*, gift from Sir Muirhead Bone, 1919, © courtesy of the artist's estate/www.bridgeman.co.uk

Rothenstein, William 1872–1945, *Ypres Salient*, gift from Sir John Rothenstein, 1985, © courtesy of the artist's estate/www.bridgeman.co.uk

Rowntree, Kenneth 1915–1997, *A Polo Ground in Wartime*, transferred from the War Artists' Advisory Committee, 1947, © crown copyright

Rowntree, Kenneth 1915–1997, *Foreign Servicemen in Hyde Park: Early Summer*, transferred from the War Artists' Advisory Committee, 1947, © crown copyright

Rowntree, Kenneth 1915–1997, *The Council for the Encouragement of Music and the Arts Canteen Concert, Isle of Dogs, London, E14*, transferred from the War Artists' Advisory Committee, 1947, © crown copyright

Rowntree, Kenneth 1915–1997, *Experimental Establishment, Shoeburyness*, transferred from the War Artists' Advisory Committee, 1947, © crown copyright

Rowntree, Kenneth 1915–1997, *The Experimental Establishment, Shoeburyness: Firing through Screens*, transferred from the War Artists' Advisory Committee, 1947, © crown copyright

Rushbury, Henry 1889–1968, *The War Refugees' Camp, Earl's Court*, purchased, 1919, © crown copyright

Russell, C. A. active 1940s, *'Scorpion' Mine Destroying Tanks in France*, transferred from the War Artists' Advisory Committee, 1947, © crown copyright

Russell, H. active 1914–1918, *Memory of the Somme, 1 July 1916*, gift, 1976

Russell, J. A. b.1920, *The Wire*, transferred from the War Artists' Advisory Committee, 1947, © crown copyright

Russell, Walter Westley 1867–1949, *General Sir Alexander John Godley (1867–1957), KCB, KCMG*, commissioned, acquired, 1919, © crown copyright

Russell, Walter Westley 1867–1949, *Reginald Stone, GM*, transferred from the War Artists' Advisory Committee, 1947, © crown copyright

Russell, Walter Westley 1867–1949, *Air Chief Marshal Sir Hugh Dowding (1882–1970), GCB, GCVO, CMG*, transferred from the War Artists' Advisory Committee, 1947, © crown copyright

Russell, Walter Westley 1867–1949, *Staff Nurse R. Rosser, GM*, transferred from the War Artists' Advisory Committee, 1947, © crown copyright

Salisbury, Frank O. 1874–1962, *Lieutenant Samuel O'Neill: The Lancashire Fusiliers, Gallipoli, 10 June 1915*, © estate of Frank O. Salisbury/DACS 2006

Salisbury, Frank O. 1874–1962, *General Julian Byng (1862–1935)*, purchased, 1974, © estate of Frank O. Salisbury/DACS 2006

Salisbury, Frank O. (after) 1874–1962, *Winston Churchill (1874–1965)*, gift from David Gilmour, 2004, © estate of Frank O. Salisbury/DACS 2006

Sargent, John Singer 1856–1925, *Gassed*, commissioned, acquired, 1919

Sauter, Rudolf Helmut 1895–1977,

An Aeroplane: View from the Compound, Alexandra Palace Civil Internment Camp, purchased, 1993

Sawyer, Douglas J. active 1920s, *Bertangles Aerodrome, Somme: The Bombing of No.48 Squadron's Aerodrome by Four German Machines, 29 October 1918*, gift from the artist, 1920

Schmolle, Stella 1908–1975, *Admiral Prince Louis of Battenberg (1854–1921), Later Admiral of the Fleet of Milford Haven, First Sea Lord, 9 December 1912 to 29 October 1914 (after Philip Alexius de László)*

Schwabe, Randolph 1885–1948, *The Women's Land Army and German Prisoners*, commissioned, acquired, 1919, © crown copyright

Schwabe, Randolph 1885–1948, *Voluntary Land Workers in a Flax Field, Podington, Northamptonshire*, commissioned, acquired, 1919, © crown copyright

Scott, Peter Markham 1909–1989, *Night Action: Gunboats off Le Tréport, 4 September 1943*, transferred from the War Artists' Advisory Committee, 1947, © crown copyright

Scott, William George 1913–1989, *Soldier and Girl Sleeping*, purchased with assistance from the National Lottery Fund and the National Art Collections Fund, 2004, © William Scott estate

Scott, William George 1913–1989, *Night Convoy*, purchased, 1973, © William Scott estate

Seabrooke, Elliot 1886–1950, *The Bombardment of Gorizia, 21 August 1917*, gift from Sir Muirhead Bone, 1919

Seabrooke, Elliot 1886–1950, *Bomb Damage: Druce's Store, Baker Street, London*, purchased, 1969

Seago, Edward Brian 1910–1974, *General Lord Gort (1886–1946), VC, at the Headquarters of the British Expeditionary Force*, transferred from the War Artists' Advisory Committee, 1947, © crown copyright

Seligman, Edgar 1867–1958, *After the Armistice: The Belgian Steel Factory, Goldhawk Road, W12*, gift from the artist, 1937

Seligman, Edgar 1867–1958, *Making Aeroplanes: Sizaire-Berwick Motor Car Factory, Park Royal, NW10*, gift from the artist, 1937

Seligman, Edgar 1867–1958, *Making Glass Floats for Submarine Nets: Powell's Glass Factory, Whitefriars, EC4*, gift from the artist, 1937

Seligman, Edgar 1867–1958, *Men at Work: The Belgian Steel Factory, Goldhawk Road, W12*, gift from the artist, 1937

Seligman, Edgar 1867–1958, *The Luncheon Hour: The Belgian Steel Factory, Goldhawk Road, W12*, gift from the artist, 1937

Seligman, Edgar 1867–1958, *Women at Work: The Belgian Steel Factory, Goldhawk Road, W12*, gift

from the artist, 1937

Seligman, Edgar 1867–1958, *Workers: The Belgian Steel Factory, Goldhawk Road, W12*, gift from the artist, 1937

Selway, Donald active 1970s, *Spitfires over Duxford: Reconstruction*, purchased, 1975

Shephard, Rupert 1909–1992, *A Nose Section after Repair: Girls Fitting Supports to Take the Bomb Aimer's Window*, transferred from the War Artists' Advisory Committee, 1947, © crown copyright

Shephard, Rupert 1909–1992, *Filming a Practice Launching of a Rubber Dinghy in a Training Pond*, transferred from the War Artists' Advisory Committee, 1947, © crown copyright

Shephard, Rupert 1909–1992, *A Lorry Depot: Long Distance and Local Lorries Loading and Unloading at the 'Bank'*, transferred from the War Artists' Advisory Committee, 1947, © crown copyright

Shephard, Rupert 1909–1992, *A Penicillin Factory: Girls Filling Bottles*, transferred from the War Artists' Advisory Committee, 1947, © crown copyright

Shephard, Rupert 1909–1992, *Lorries Transporting Landing Craft: Royal Albert Docks, London*, transferred from the War Artists' Advisory Committee, 1947, © crown copyright

Shephard, Rupert 1909–1992, *Road Transport in the Blitz*, transferred from the War Artists' Advisory Committee, 1947, © crown copyright

Silas, Ellis 1883–1972, *The Last Roll Call*, gift from Mrs Silas, 1984

Simpson, Ruth 1889–1964, *An Officer*, gift from Miss Leonora Simpson, 1975

Sims, Charles 1873–1928, *A Camouflaged Quarry between Chérisy and Hendecourt*, purchased, 1919

Sims, Charles 1873–1928, *'Sacrifice' (study for the painting in Ottawa)*, purchased, 1928

Sims, Charles 1873–1928, *The Old German Front Line, Arras, 1916*, commissioned, acquired, 1919

Sivell, Robert 1888–1958, *Mrs Marion Patterson, GM*, transferred from the War Artists' Advisory Committee, 1947, © crown copyright

Skinner, Edward F. active 1888–1919, *For King and Country*, gift from Her Majesty the Queen, 1979, © crown copyright

Smith, B. Gordon active 1940s, *A Mobile First Aid Unit at Work*, transferred from the War Artists' Advisory Committee, 1947, © crown copyright

Smith, B. Gordon active 1940s, *Incendiary Bomb*, gift from Mrs M. Smith, 1998

Smith, Phill W. active 1890–1932, *Pounden Camp, Proven Area,*

Belgium, purchased, 1988

Smith, Robert Henry active 1906–1920, *'HMS Conqueror' and Escort in the North Sea*, commissioned, acquired, 1919

Smith, Robert Henry active 1906–1920, *The Battle of Jutland: Admiral Jellicoe Arrives with the Battleships and Meets the Battle Cruisers*, commissioned, acquired, 1919

Smith, Robert Henry active 1906–1920, *Battleships in Action at Jutland*, commissioned, acquired, 1919

Smith, Robert Henry active 1906–1920, *The Battle of Jutland, 31 May to 1 June, 1916*, transferred from the Royal Naval College, Dartmouth, 1975

Smulders, Gabriel b.1931, *The Last One*, gift from the artist, 1998, © the artist

Snell, Olive active c.1910–1955, *Wing Commander Paul H. M. Richey, DFC*, purchased, 1995

Solomon, Gilbert 1890–1955, *The Mist Curtain: RE 8 (16th Squadron) Attacked over Lens*, purchased, 1919, © Imperial War Museum

Solomon, J. Solomon 1860–1927, *Field Marshal Earl Haig (1861–1928)*, purchased, 1928

Somerville, Howard 1873–1952, *The Late Reverend Theodore Bailey Hardy (1863–1918), VC, DSO, MC*, commissioned, acquired, 1919, © crown copyright

Sonnis, Alexander b.1905, *Balloon Operations at Night*, transferred from the War Artists' Advisory Committee, 1947, © crown copyright

Sonnis, Alexander b.1905, *Sitting Round the Stove Splicing Balloon Cords*, transferred from the War Artists' Advisory Committee, 1947, © crown copyright

Sorrell, Alan 1904–1974, *Construction of a Runway at an Aerodrome*, transferred from the War Artists' Advisory Committee, 1947, © crown copyright

Spear, Ruskin 1911–1990, *Patients Waiting outside a First Aid Post in a Factory*, transferred from the War Artists' Advisory Committee, 1947, © crown copyright

Spear, Ruskin 1911–1990, *The Blackout*, transferred from the War Artists' Advisory Committee, 1947, © crown copyright

Spear, Ruskin 1911–1990, *A Women's Voluntary Services Canteen at the Docks*, transferred from the War Artists' Advisory Committee, 1947, © crown copyright

Spear, Ruskin 1911–1990, *Deaf Girls Working on the Construction of Petrol Tanks*, transferred from the War Artists' Advisory Committee, 1947, © crown copyright

Spear, Ruskin 1911–1990, *Scene in an Underground Train: Workers Returning from Night Shift*, transferred from the War Artists'

Advisory Committee, 1947, © crown copyright

Spear, Ruskin 1911–1990, *A Royal Ordnance Factory Explosion, Hereford*, transferred from the War Artists' Advisory Committee, 1947, © crown copyright

Spear, Ruskin 1911–1990, *Marshal of the Royal Air Force Sir John Grandy (1913–2004), GCB, KBE, DSO*, commissioned, acquired, 1981, © crown copyright

Spence, J. M. active 1940s, *A Russian (Ex-American) Destroyer, Russia, April 1942*, transferred from the War Artists' Advisory Committee, 1947, © crown copyright

Spencer, Gilbert 1893–1979, *New Arrivals: F4 Ward, No.36 Stationary Hospital, Mahemdia, Sinai*, commissioned, acquired, 1919, © courtesy of the artist's estate/www.bridgeman.co.uk

Spencer, Gilbert 1893–1979, *Grasmere Home Guard*, transferred from the War Artists' Advisory Committee, 1947, © crown copyright

Spencer, Stanley 1891–1959, *Shipbuilding on the Clyde: Burners (left)*, transferred from the War Artists' Advisory Committee, 1947, © crown copyright

Spencer, Stanley 1891–1959, *Shipbuilding on the Clyde: Burners (centre)*, transferred from the War Artists' Advisory Committee, 1947, © crown copyright

Spencer, Stanley 1891–1959, *Shipbuilding on the Clyde: Burners (right)*, transferred from the War Artists' Advisory Committee, 1947, © crown copyright

Spencer, Stanley 1891–1959, *Shipbuilding on the Clyde: Riveters (left)*, transferred from the War Artists' Advisory Committee, 1947, © crown copyright

Spencer, Stanley 1891–1959, *Shipbuilding on the Clyde: Riveters (centre)*, transferred from the War Artists' Advisory Committee, 1947, © crown copyright

Spencer, Stanley 1891–1959, *Shipbuilding on the Clyde: Riveters (right)*, transferred from the War Artists' Advisory Committee, 1947, © crown copyright

Spencer, Stanley 1891–1959, *Shipbuilding on the Clyde: Welders (left)*, transferred from the War Artists' Advisory Committee, 1947, © crown copyright

Spencer, Stanley 1891–1959, *Shipbuilding on the Clyde: Welders (centre)*, transferred from the War Artists' Advisory Committee, 1947, © crown copyright

Spencer, Stanley 1891–1959, *Shipbuilding on the Clyde: Welders (right)*, transferred from the War Artists' Advisory Committee, 1947, © crown copyright

Spencer, Stanley 1891–1959, *Shipbuilding on the Clyde: The Riggers (left)*, transferred from the War Artists' Advisory Committee,

1947, © crown copyright

Spencer, Stanley 1891–1959, *Shipbuilding on the Clyde: The Riggers (centre)*, transferred from the War Artists' Advisory Committee, 1947, © crown copyright

Spencer, Stanley 1891–1959, *Shipbuilding on the Clyde: The Riggers (right)*, transferred from the War Artists' Advisory Committee, 1947, © crown copyright

Spencer, Stanley 1891–1959, *Shipbuilding on the Clyde: The Template (left)*, transferred from the War Artists' Advisory Committee, 1947, © crown copyright

Spencer, Stanley 1891–1959, *Shipbuilding on the Clyde: The Template (centre)*, transferred from the War Artists' Advisory Committee, 1947, © crown copyright

Spencer, Stanley 1891–1959, *Shipbuilding on the Clyde: The Template (right)*, transferred from the War Artists' Advisory Committee, 1947, © crown copyright

Spencer, Stanley 1891–1959, *Shipbuilding on the Clyde: Bending the Keel Plate (left)*, transferred from the War Artists' Advisory Committee, 1947, © crown copyright

Spencer, Stanley 1891–1959, *Shipbuilding on the Clyde: Bending the Keel Plate (centre)*, transferred from the War Artists' Advisory Committee, 1947, © crown copyright

Spencer, Stanley 1891–1959, *Shipbuilding on the Clyde: Bending the Keel Plate (right)*, transferred from the War Artists' Advisory Committee, 1947, © crown copyright

Spencer, Stanley 1891–1959, *Shipbuilding on the Clyde: Plumbers (left)*, transferred from the War Artists' Advisory Committee, 1947, © Imperial War Museum

Spencer, Stanley 1891–1959, *Shipbuilding on the Clyde: Plumbers (centre)*, transferred from the War Artists' Advisory Committee, 1947, © Imperial War Museum

Spencer, Stanley 1891–1959, *Shipbuilding on the Clyde: Plumbers (right)*, transferred from the War Artists' Advisory Committee, 1947, © Imperial War Museum

Spencer, Stanley 1891–1959, *Travoys Arriving with Wounded at a Dressing Station at Smol, Macedonia, September 1916*, commissioned, acquired, 1919, © crown copyright

Spencer, Stanley 1891–1959, *Shipbuilding on the Clyde: The Furnaces*, transferred from the War Artists' Advisory Committee, 1947, © Imperial War Museum

Spender, John Humphrey 1910–2005, *Salisbury Plain*, purchased, 1984, © the Humphrey Spender Archive

Spender, John Humphrey 1910–2005, *Salisbury Plain*, purchased, 1984, © the Humphrey Spender Archive

Spurrier, Steven 1878–1961, *An Army Discussion Group*, transferred from the War Artists' Advisory Committee, 1947, © crown copyright

Stabb, Charles T. active 1899–1936, *Captain Alfred Oliver Pollard (1893–1960), VC, MC, DCM*, purchased, 1919

Staden, Geoffrey b.1953, *Air-Sea Rescue from RAF Coltishall, Norfolk*, commissioned, acquired, 1981, © Imperial War Museum

Steer, Philip Wilson 1860–1942, *Dover Harbour*, transferred from the Ministry of Information, 1919, © crown copyright

Steer, Philip Wilson 1860–1942, *Dover Harbour from the Parade*, gift from Sir Muirhead Bone, 1919, © Imperial War Museum

Stevens, Norman 1937–1988, *Tank Trap*, gift from the artist, 1984, © the artist's estate

Strang, Ian 1886–1952, *The Outskirts of Lens: In the Foreground Ruins of the Mine Buildings Known as 'Fosse St Louis'*, commissioned, acquired, 1919, © crown copyright

Streeton, Arthur 1876–1943, *The Tunnel Mouth, Bellicourt, the Hindenburg Line: The Southern Entrance to the Tunnel, December 1918*, gift from Herbert F. Cook, 1919, © the artist's estate

Stuart-Hill, A. c.1918–1950, *Admiral Sir H. Goodenough King-Hall, KCB, CVO, DSO*, commissioned, acquired, 1920

Sutherland, David Macbeth 1883–1973, *War in the Forest: Newfoundland Lumberjacks at Work in Scotland*, transferred from the War Artists' Advisory Committee, 1947, © crown copyright

Sutton, R. Fran b.1912, *Air Raid Precautions: Civil Defence Worker*, accessioned, 1996

Tayler, Albert Chevallier 1862–1925, *The Dwina Relief Force Memorial (left)*, gift from the Officers and other Ranks of the Royal Navy, Army and Royal Air Force, Dwina Relief Force, 1921

Tayler, Albert Chevallier 1862–1925, *The Dwina Relief Force Memorial (centre)*, gift from the Officers and other ranks of the Royal Navy, Army and Royal Air Force, Dwina Relief Force, 1921

Tayler, Albert Chevallier 1862–1925, *The Dwina Relief Force Memorial (right)*, gift from the Officers and other ranks of the Royal Navy, Army and Royal Air Force, Dwina Relief Force, 1921

Taylor, Leonard Campbell 1874–1969, *Rear Admiral Sir Walter Henry Cowan (1871–1958), KCB, MVO, DSO*, commissioned, acquired, 1920, © crown copyright

Taylor, Robert b.1946, *'HMS Kelly',*

Grand Harbour, Malta, 1941, gift from the artist, 1982

Thomson, Alfred Reginald 1894–1979, *The Manufacture of Battle Dress*, transferred from the War Artists' Advisory Committee, 1947, © crown copyright

Thomson, Alfred Reginald 1894–1979, *Weaving Cloth for Battle Dress*, transferred from the War Artists' Advisory Committee, 1947, © crown copyright

Thomson, Alfred Reginald 1894–1979, *Miss Charity Bick, GM, of West Bromwich, the Youngest Woman Civil Defence Worker to be Decorated with the George Medal*, transferred from the War Artists' Advisory Committee, 1947, © crown copyright

Thomson, Alfred Reginald 1894–1979, *Miss Gillian Tanner, GM, of London*, transferred from the War Artists' Advisory Committee, 1947, © crown copyright

Thomson, Alfred Reginald 1894–1979, *Section Leader Brandon Moss, GC, of Coventry*, transferred from the War Artists' Advisory Committee, 1947, © crown copyright

Thomson, Alfred Reginald 1894–1979, *Air Vice-Marshal Richard E. Saul, CB, DFC*, transferred from the War Artists' Advisory Committee, 1947, © crown copyright

Thomson, Alfred Reginald 1894–1979, *Wing Commander Geoffrey Leonard Cheshire (1917–1992), DSO, DFC*, transferred from the War Artists' Advisory Committee, 1947, © crown copyright

Thomson, Alfred Reginald 1894–1979, *A Saline Bath, Royal Air Force Hospital*, transferred from the War Artists' Advisory Committee, 1947, © crown copyright

Thomson, Alfred Reginald 1894–1979, *Air Marshal A. Guy R. Garrod (1891–1965), CB, OBE, MC, DFC*, transferred from the War Artists' Advisory Committee, 1947, © crown copyright

Thomson, Alfred Reginald 1894–1979, *Corporal Lilian Levy, Women's Auxiliary Air Force*, transferred from the War Artists' Advisory Committee, 1947, © crown copyright

Thomson, Alfred Reginald 1894–1979, *Grafting a New Eyelid*, transferred from the War Artists' Advisory Committee, 1947, © crown copyright

Thomson, Alfred Reginald 1894–1979, *A High Explosive Bomb in High Street, Kensington, 18 February 1944*, transferred from the War Artists' Advisory Committee, 1947, © crown copyright

Thomson, Alfred Reginald 1894–1979, *Group Captain P. C. Pickard (1915–1944), DSO, and Two Bars, DFC, and Flight Lieutenant J. A. Broadley (1921–1944), DS, DFC, DFM*, transferred from the War

Artists' Advisory Committee, 1947, © crown copyright

Todd, Arthur Ralph Middleton 1891–1966, *Auxiliary Fireman H. Barker, GM*, transferred from the War Artists' Advisory Committee, 1947, © crown copyright

Tonks, Henry 1862–1937, *An Advanced Dressing Station in France*, commissioned, acquired, 1919, © crown copyright

Tonks, Henry 1862–1937, *An Underground Casualty Clearing Station, Arras*, gift from Sir Muirhead Bone, 1919, © family of the artist

Tonks, Henry 1862–1937, *Russian Soldiers Dancing with Peasant Women*, commissioned, acquired, 1920, © crown copyright

Tonks, Henry 1862–1937, *The Surrender of Pujos Gora*, commissioned, acquired, 1920, © crown copyright

Trevelyan, Julian 1910–1989, *Premonitions of the Blitz*, purchased, 1984, © the artist's estate

Trimnell-Ritchard, E. active 1940s, *Coxwain Davey: Icelandic Patrol*, transferred from the War Artists' Advisory Committee, 1947, © crown copyright

Tunnard, John 1900–1971, *Anglo-Dutch*, purchased with the assistance of the National Art Collections Fund, 2001

Turnbull, Alison b.1956, *Factory*, purchased, 2001

Turner, Charles E. 1883–1965, *'HMS Aurora'*, gift from Sir Geoffrey Agnew, 1980

Underwood, Leon 1890–1975, *Captain George Burdon McKean (1888–1926), VC, MC, 14th Battalion Canadian Infantry*, commissioned, acquired, 1919, © crown copyright

Underwood, Leon 1890–1975, *Erecting a Camouflage Tree*, commissioned, acquired, 1919, © crown copyright

unknown artist *Maurice Lishman, Royal Air Force Flying Officer, Shot Down in the Battle of Britain, Aged 21*, gift from Mrs Vera Fitch, 1979

unknown artist *The Sinking of an Armed Japanese Raider by HM Minesweeper 'Bengal' in the Indian Ocean, 11 November 1942*, gift from the Government of India, 1954

unknown artist *Burning Building during a Zeppelin Raid*, gift from Guy's Hospital Medical and Dental Schools, 1981

unknown artist *An Episode in the Battle of Sailum Vum (Chin Hills, Burma): Subedar Ram Sarup Singh Winning the VC*

Uptton, Clive 1911–2006, *Bomb Disposal: Bringing up a 250-Kilo Bomb*, transferred from the War Artists' Advisory Committee, 1947, © crown copyright

Uptton, Clive 1911–2006, *Bomb Disposal: Listening for Ticking*, transferred from the War Artists'

Advisory Committee, 1947, © crown copyright

Waingrow, X. Bits b.1951, *Early One Morning in Copenhagen: Christian X, King of Denmark*, purchased, 1987

Walker, Claude Alfred Pennington b.1862, *The Artist in the Uniform of the City of London National Guard*, gift from the artist, 1917

Walker, Ray 1945–1984, *Army Recruitment I*, commissioned, 1981, © Imperial War Museum

Walker, Ray 1945–1984, *Army Recruitment II*, commissioned, 1981, © Imperial War Museum

Walker, Ray 1945–1984, *Army Recruitment III*, commissioned, 1981, © Imperial War Museum

Walton, Edward Arthur 1860–1922 & **Walton, Cecile** 1891–1956, *Mrs Chalmers, CBE, Director of QMAAC*, purchased, 1922, © crown copyright

Ward, Grace active 1940s, *Royal Electrical and Mechanical Engineer Auxiliary Territorial Service Welders*, gift from Mr G. Gurr, 1977

Ware, William 1915–1997, *St Paul's Cathedral*, gift from the artist, 1983, © the artist's estate

Ware, William 1915–1997, *Fired City*, transferred from the War Artists' Advisory Committee, 1947, © crown copyright

Watherston, Marjorie Violet d.c.1970, *The Dispatch: The Captain's Dugout*, gift from the artist, 1958, © Imperial War Museum

Watson, Barbara 1893–1978, *An Aircraft Carrier under Construction*, transferred from the War Artists' Advisory Committee, 1947, © crown copyright

Watson, Geoffrey active 1940s, *A View across Camouflaged Roofs*, transferred from the War Artists' Advisory Committee, 1947, © crown copyright

Weaver, S. active 1914–1918, *Bourlon Wood, Somme*, unknown provenance

Weight, Carel Victor Morlais 1908–1997, *Recruits' Progress: Arms Drill*, transferred from the War Artists' Advisory Committee, 1947, © crown copyright

Weight, Carel Victor Morlais 1908–1997, *Recruits' Progress: Medical Inspection*, transferred from the War Artists' Advisory Committee, 1947, © crown copyright

Weight, Carel Victor Morlais 1908–1997, *Recruits' Progress: An Evening out, Pub Scene*, transferred from the War Artists' Advisory Committee, 1947, © crown copyright

Weight, Carel Victor Morlais 1908–1997, *Recruits' Progress: Preparations for an Evening out*, transferred from the War Artists' Advisory Committee, 1947, © crown copyright

Weight, Carel Victor Morlais

1908–1997, *A Classroom in the University, Perugia, Italy*, transferred from the War Artists' Advisory Committee, 1947, © crown copyright

Weight, Carel Victor Morlais 1908–1997, *A Street Scene from the Officers' Mess, Perugia, Italy*, transferred from the War Artists' Advisory Committee, 1947, © crown copyright

Weight, Carel Victor Morlais 1908–1997, *A View of Vienna*, transferred from the War Artists' Advisory Committee, 1947, © crown copyright

Weight, Carel Victor Morlais 1908–1997, *A Window of a Classroom in the Army School of Education, Perugia, Italy*, transferred from the War Artists' Advisory Committee, 1947, © crown copyright

Weight, Carel Victor Morlais 1908–1997, *German Demolition Seen from the South Side of the Ponte Vecchio, Florence*, transferred from the War Artists' Advisory Committee, 1947, © crown copyright

Weight, Carel Victor Morlais 1908–1997, *Outside the Officers' Transit Hotel, Perugia, Italy*, transferred from the War Artists' Advisory Committee, 1947, © crown copyright

Weight, Carel Victor Morlais 1908–1997, *The Dress Design Class, Formation College Arts Wing, Florence*, transferred from the War Artists' Advisory Committee, 1947, © crown copyright

Weight, Carel Victor Morlais 1908–1997, *The Exterior of the Army School of Education, Perugia, Italy: The Etruscan Gate*, transferred from the War Artists' Advisory Committee, 1947, © crown copyright

Weight, Carel Victor Morlais 1908–1997, *The Life Class, Formation College Arts Wing, Florence*, transferred from the War Artists' Advisory Committee, 1947, © crown copyright

Weight, Carel Victor Morlais 1908–1997, *The Portrait Class, Formation College Arts Wing, Florence*, transferred from the War Artists' Advisory Committee, 1947, © crown copyright

Weight, Carel Victor Morlais 1908–1997, *The Remains of Ponte Navi, Verona*, transferred from the War Artists' Advisory Committee, 1947, © crown copyright

Weight, Carel Victor Morlais 1908–1997, *The Temple of Malatesta, Rimini*, transferred from the War Artists' Advisory Committee, 1947, © crown copyright

Weight, Carel Victor Morlais 1908–1997, *The Temple of Malatesta, Rimini*, transferred from the War Artists' Advisory Committee, 1947, © crown copyright

Weight, Carel Victor Morlais 1908–1997, *Veronese Night*, transferred from the War Artists' Advisory Committee, 1947, © crown copyright

Weight, Carel Victor Morlais 1908–1997, *A Scene in Athens from the British Officers' Hotel Cosmopolitan*, transferred from the War Artists' Advisory Committee, 1947, © crown copyright

Weight, Carel Victor Morlais 1908–1997, *A Street in Athens*, transferred from the War Artists' Advisory Committee, 1947, © crown copyright

Weight, Carel Victor Morlais 1908–1997, *A Sunken Blockship in the Mouth of the Corinth Canal*, transferred from the War Artists' Advisory Committee, 1947, © crown copyright

Weight, Carel Victor Morlais 1908–1997, *Eleusis*, transferred from the War Artists' Advisory Committee, 1947, © crown copyright

Weight, Carel Victor Morlais 1908–1997, *Greece: A Typical Street in Athens*, transferred from the War Artists' Advisory Committee, 1947, © crown copyright

Weight, Carel Victor Morlais 1908–1997, *Kosani, Greece*, gift from the artist, 1947, © the estate of the artist

Weight, Carel Victor Morlais 1908–1997, *The Army Education Corps History Course, Corinth*, transferred from the War Artists' Advisory Committee, 1947, © crown copyright

Weight, Carel Victor Morlais 1908–1997, *The Bridge over the Corinth Canal Demolished by the Germans*, transferred from the War Artists' Advisory Committee, 1947, © crown copyright

Weight, Carel Victor Morlais 1908–1997, *The Girl from Anzio*, transferred from the War Artists' Advisory Committee, 1947, © crown copyright

Weight, Carel Victor Morlais 1908–1997, *The Greek Barracks at Kosani*, transferred from the War Artists' Advisory Committee, 1947, © crown copyright

Weight, Carel Victor Morlais 1908–1997, *The Harbour at Eleusis: A Typical Greek Sailing Ship Bringing United Nations Relief and Rehabilitation Administration Supplies to Greece*, transferred from the War Artists' Advisory Committee, 1947, © crown copyright

Weight, Carel Victor Morlais 1908–1997, *With the British Military Mission of Kosani: The Arrival of Army Conscripts Passing the British Officers' Mess on their Way to the Barracks*, transferred from the War Artists' Advisory Committee, 1947, © crown copyright

Weirter, Louis 1871–1932, *An Aerial Fight*, commissioned, acquired, 1918

Weirter, Louis 1871–1932, *An Incident on the Western Front*, purchased, 1919

Weston, Garth b.1914, *'The admiralty regrets...'*, transferred from the War Artists' Advisory Committee, 1947, © crown copyright

Wheatley, John 1892–1955, *A Diver's Tender*, commissioned, acquired, 1919, © crown copyright

Wheatley, John 1892–1955, *A Greaser: Admiralty Salvage Ship*, commissioned, acquired, 1919, © crown copyright

Wheatley, John 1892–1955, *A Torpedoed American Troopship Sinking*, commissioned, acquired, 1919, © crown copyright

Wheatley, John 1892–1955, *An Able Seaman, Royal Naval Reserve*, commissioned, acquired, 1919, © crown copyright

Wheatley, John 1892–1955, *An Admiralty Salvage Diver (1)*, commissioned, acquired, 1919, © crown copyright

Wheatley, John 1892–1955, *An Admiralty Salvage Diver (2)*, commissioned, acquired, 1919, © crown copyright

Wheatley, John 1892–1955, *An Armoured Cruiser, Showing Fracture: Divers Going down to Investigate*, commissioned, acquired, 1919, © crown copyright

Wheatley, John 1892–1955, *Divers at Work Repairing a Torpedoed Ship*, commissioned, acquired, 1919, © crown copyright

Wheatley, John 1892–1955, *Repairing a Fracture in a Torpedoed Merchant Ship*, commissioned, acquired, 1919, © crown copyright

Wheatley, John 1892–1955, *The Head Diver: Admiralty Salvage Section*, commissioned, acquired, 1919, © crown copyright

Wheatley, John 1892–1955, *The Royal Naval Reserve Skipper*, commissioned, acquired, 1919, © crown copyright

Wheatley, John 1892–1955, *Private James Crichton (1879–1961), VC, Auckland Regiment, New Zealand Expeditionary Forces*, commissioned, acquired, 1919, © crown copyright

Wheatley, John 1892–1955, *Lieutenant Commander Norman Douglas Holbrook (1888–1976), VC*, commissioned, acquired, 1919, © crown copyright

Wheatley, John 1892–1955, *Edward Roche: A Head Melter at a Sheffield Munition Factory*, transferred from the War Artists' Advisory Committee, 1947, © crown copyright

Wheatley, John 1892–1955, *Leslie Croft, GM, of Sheffield*, transferred from the War Artists' Advisory Committee, 1947, © crown copyright

Whiting, Frederic 1874–1962, *General Sir W. R. Marshall, KCB*, commissioned, acquired, 1919, © crown copyright

Whiting, Frederic 1874–1962, *Admiral Sir R. H. Pierse, KCB, KBE, MVO*, commissioned, acquired, 1920, © crown copyright

Wilkinson, Norman 1878–1971, *A Monitor with 14-Inch Guns Shelling Yeni Sher Village and the Asiatic Batteries*, commissioned, acquired, 1919, © Imperial War Museum

Wilkinson, Norman 1878–1971, *Lest We Forget*, gift from Messrs. Holder, c.1972, © the Norman Wilkinson estate

Wilkinson, Norman 1878–1971, *A Convoy of Dazzled Ships in the Channel*, commissioned, acquired, 1920, © Imperial War Museum

Wilkinson, Norman 1878–1971, *Dazzled Ships at Night*, commissioned, acquired, 1920, © Imperial War Museum

Wilkinson, Norman 1878–1971, *'HMS Queen Elizabeth' Shelling Forts, Dardanelles: The Attack on the Narrows, Gallipoli, 18 March 1915*, purchased, 1919, © Imperial War Museum

Wilkinson, Norman 1878–1971, *The Balloon Ship Hector with Kite Balloon Spotting off the Left Flank, Dardanelles Operations, 1915*, commissioned, acquired, 1919, © Imperial War Museum

Wilkinson, Norman 1878–1971, *The Base Camp, Cape Helles, under Shell Fire, August 1915: The 'SS River Clyde' Aground*, commissioned, acquired, 1919, © Imperial War Museum

Wilkinson, Norman 1878–1971, *The Landing in Suvla Bay: Early Morning, 7 August 1915*, commissioned, acquired, 1919, © Imperial War Museum

Wilkinson, Norman 1878–1971, *The Salt Lake, Suvla Bay: The Advance, 21 August 1915*, commissioned, acquired, 1919, © Imperial War Museum

Wilkinson, Norman 1878–1971, *Troops Landing on C Beach, Suvla Bay, Later in the Day, 7 August 1915*, commissioned, acquired, 1919, © Imperial War Museum

Wilkinson, Norman 1878–1971, *The Crew Reboarding the Tanker 'San Demetrio', 7 November 1940*, gift from the Eagle Oil and Shipping Company, 1959, © Imperial War Museum

Wilkinson, Norman 1878–1971, *The Little Ships at Dunkirk, June 1940*, purchased, 1960, © Imperial War Museum

Wilkinson, Norman 1878–1971, *The Tanker 'Ohio' in a Malta Convoy: August 1942*, gift from the Eagle Oil and Shipping Company, 1959, © Imperial War Museum

Williamson, Harold Sandys 1892–1978, *A German Attack on a Wet Morning, April 1918*, commissioned, acquired, 1919, © Paul Williamson

Williamson, Harold Sandys 1892–1978, *An Emergency Telephone Office in the City, January 1941*, transferred from the War Artists' Advisory Committee, 1947, © crown copyright

Williamson, Harold Sandys 1892–1978, *St Martin's le Grand, London, January 1941*, transferred from the War Artists' Advisory Committee, 1947, © crown copyright

Wonnacott, John b.1940, *Refit, Devonport*, commissioned, acquired, 1989, © Imperial War Museum

Wood, John active 1940s, *Air Raid Precautions in Jamaica*, transferred from the War Artists' Advisory Committee, 1947

Wood, William Thomas 1877–1958, *The Fire, Salonica: The Last Phase*, purchased, 1918, © Imperial War Museum

Wood, William Thomas 1877–1958, *The Great Fire, Salonica: The Famous White Tower in the Foreground*, purchased, 1919, © Imperial War Museum

Wood, William Thomas 1877–1958, *Crashed!: De Havilland 2 Single-Seater Scout Shooting down a 'Fokker' Monoplane Salonika*, purchased, 1918, © Imperial War Museum

Wood, William Thomas 1877–1958, *The Doiran Front, Seen from Sal Grec de Popovo*, transferred from the Ministry of Information, 1919, © Imperial War Museum

Woodington, Walter 1916–2000, *Admiral Sir Deric Holland-Martin, GCB, DSO, DSC, Chairman of the Board of Trustees, Imperial War Museum (1966–1977)*, commissioned, acquired, 1978

Woods, Henry 1846–1921, *Christopher Wren Wing: Hampton Court Palace as a Hospital*, gift, 1966

Wootton, Frank 1914–1998, *Rocket-Firing Typhoons at the Falaise Gap, Normandy*, transferred from the War Artists' Advisory Committee, 1947, © crown copyright

Worsley, John 1919–2000, *A Night Air Raid over Augusta*, transferred from the War Artists' Advisory Committee, 1947, © crown copyright

Worsley, John 1919–2000, *Grand Harbour, Malta, October 1943*, transferred from the War Artists' Advisory Committee, 1947, © crown copyright

Worsley, John 1919–2000, *The Last of the 'Laurentic'*, transferred from the War Artists' Advisory Committee, 1947, © crown copyright

Worsley, John 1919–2000, *Shower Room: Marlag 'O'*, transferred from the War Artists' Advisory Committee, 1947, © crown copyright

Worsley, John 1919–2000, *The Contents of a Red Cross Parcel*, transferred from the War Artists' Advisory Committee, 1947, © crown copyright

Worsley, John 1919–2000, *Admiral*

Sir John Cunningham, KCB, MVO, transferred from the War Artists' Advisory Committee, 1947, © crown copyright

Worsley, John 1919–2000, *Naval and Marine Prisoners of War on the March ahead of the Allied Advance in Germany between Bremen and Lübeck*, transferred from the War Artists' Advisory Committee, 1947, © crown copyright

Worsley, John 1919–2000, *Field Marshal the Viscount Montgomery of Alamein (1887–1976), GCB, SO*, transferred from the War Artists' Advisory Committee, 1947, © crown copyright

Wright, W. Matvyn b.1910, *A Parachute Bomb*, transferred from the War Artists' Advisory Committee, 1947, © crown copyright

Wright, W. Matvyn b.1910, *Fire Guard Training School: The Smoke Test*, transferred from the War Artists' Advisory Committee, 1947, © crown copyright

Wyllie, Harold 1880–1973, *Army Reconnaissance*, commissioned, acquired, 1920, © Imperial War Museum

Wyllie, Harold 1880–1973, *An Air Fight, France (1917–1918): Formation of Six SE5 Machines and Six Albatross Scouts in Combat*, commissioned, acquired, 1920, © Imperial War Museum

Wyllie, Harold 1880–1973, *Artillery Observation: BE2c Machines over Hooge Ranging British Guns by Means of Wireless Telegraphy, 1915*, commissioned, acquired, 1920, © Imperial War Museum

Wyllie, Harold 1880–1973, *Night Bombers Getting Off from Trezennes Aerodrome, 1917*, commissioned, acquired, 1920, © Imperial War Museum

Wyllie, Harold 1880–1973, *The Aerial Watch on the Rhine: A Formation of DH9a Machines on Patrol over Cologne, Army of Occupation, 1918*, commissioned, acquired, 1920, © Imperial War Museum

Wyllie, Harold 1880–1973, *The Bombing of Bissheghem Aerodrome: Night, 20 October 1917*, commissioned, acquired, 1920, © Imperial War Museum

Wyllie, Harold 1880–1973, *'HMS Belfast' on Northern Patrol Captures the German Blockade Runner 'Cap Norte', 13,615 Tons, 9 October 1939*, gift from Mr A. Jeremy Seale, 2003, © Imperial War Museum

Wyllie, Harold 1880–1973, *The 'Belfast' Boarding a German Merchant Ship*, gift from the estate of George Brice Smyth, 2006

Wyllie, William Lionel 1851–1931, *Destruction of the German Raider 'Leopard' by 'HMS Achilles' and 'HMS Dundee'*, gift from K. M. Leake, 1984

Wyllie, William Lionel 1851–1931, *Loss of 'HMS Pathfinder', 5 September 1914*, gift from K. M. Leake, 1973

Ximming, Elio active 1940s, *Portrait of a Man*

Yale, Brian b.1936, *War*, gift from the artist, 1980, © courtesy of the artist/www.bridgeman.co.uk

Zeitler *Liner 'Cap Norte'*

Zinkeisen, Anna Katrina 1901–1976, *St Mary's First Aid Post by Candlelight*, transferred from the War Artists' Advisory Committee, 1947, © crown copyright

Zinkeisen, Anna Katrina 1901–1976, *Archibald McIndoe: Consultant in Plastic Surgery to the Royal Air Force, Operating at the Queen Victoria Plastic and Jaw Injury Centre, East Grinstead*, gift from the artist, 1958, © the artist's estate

Zinkeisen, Doris Clare 1898–1991, *A Women's Royal Naval Service Galley*, transferred from the War Artists' Advisory Committee, 1947, © crown copyright

Zinkeisen, Doris Clare 1898–1991, *Belsen, April 1945*, transferred from the War Artists' Advisory Committee, 1947, © crown copyright

Zinkeisen, Doris Clare 1898–1991, *Feeding Liberated Prisoners of War before They Are Flown Home, Brussels Airport*, gift from the Order of St John of Jerusalem, 1958

Zinkeisen, Doris Clare 1898–1991, *Human Laundry, Belsen, April 1945*, transferred from the War Artists' Advisory Committee, 1947, © crown copyright

Zinkeisen, Doris Clare 1898–1991, *Major General E. Phillips, CBE, DSO, MC, Director of Medical Services, British Liberation Army*, transferred from the War Artists' Advisory Committee, 1947, © crown copyright

Zinkeisen, Doris Clare 1898–1991, *Miss S. A. W. Wade, RRC, Principal Matron, 101 British General Hospital*, transferred from the War Artists' Advisory Committee, 1947, © crown copyright

Zinkeisen, Doris Clare 1898–1991, *No.115 British General Hospital, Ostend: Unloading Wounded*, gift from the Order of St John of Jerusalem, 1958

Zinkeisen, Doris Clare 1898–1991, *Welfare Work in a Services Hospital*, gift from the Order of St John of Jerusalem, 1958

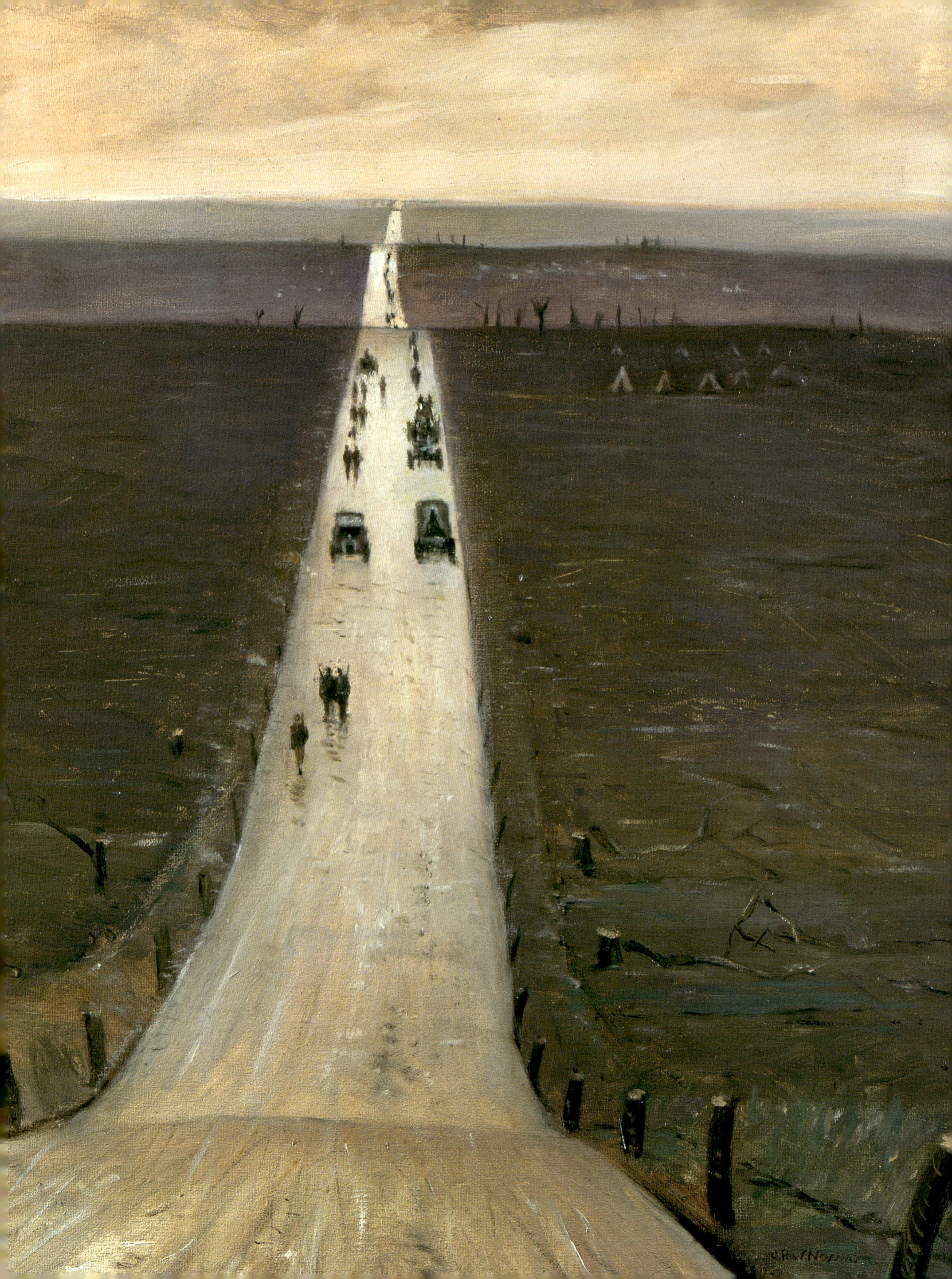

Collection Addresses

Duxford

Imperial War Museum Duxford
Cambridgeshire CB2 4QR
Telephone 01223 835000

London

Churchill Museum & Cabinet War Rooms
Clive Steps, King Charles Street, London SW1A 2AQ
Telephone 020 7930 6961

HMS Belfast
Morgan's Lane, Tooley Street, London SE1 2JH
Telephone 020 7940 6300

Imperial War Museum London
Lambeth Road, London SE1 6HZ
Telephone 020 7416 5320

Manchester

Imperial War Museum North
The Quays, Trafford Wharf, Trafford Park,
Manchester M17 1TE
Telephone 0161 836 4000

Facing page: Nevinson, Christopher, 1889–1946, *The Road from Arras to Bapaume* (detail), 1917, (p. 169)

Index of Artists

In this catalogue, artists' names and the spelling of their names follow the preferred presentation of the name in the Getty Union List of Artist Names (ULAN) as of February 2004, if the artist is listed in ULAN.

The page numbers next to each artist's name below direct readers to paintings that are by the artist; are attributed to the artist; or, in a few cases, are more loosely related to the artist being, for example, 'after', 'the circle of' or copies of a painting by the artist. The precise relationship between the artist and the painting is listed in the catalogue.

Supporters of the Public Catalogue Foundation

Master Patrons

The Public Catalogue Foundation is greatly indebted to the following Master Patrons who have helped it in the past or are currently working with it to raise funds for the publication of their county catalogues. All of them have given freely of their time and have made an enormous contribution to the work of the Foundation.

Peter Andreae, High Sheriff for Hampshire *(Hampshire)*
Sir Nicholas Bacon, DL, High Sheriff for Norfolk *(Norfolk)*
Peter Bretherton *(West Yorkshire: Leeds)*
Richard Compton *(North Yorkshire)*
George Courtauld, Vice Lord Lieutenant for Essex *(Essex)*
The Marquess of Downshire *(North Yorkshire)*

Patricia Grayburn, MBE DL *(Surrey)*
Tommy Jowitt *(West Yorkshire)*
Sir Michael Lickiss *(Cornwall)*
Lord Marlesford, DL *(Suffolk)*
Phyllida Stewart-Roberts, OBE, Lord Lieutenant for East Sussex *(East Sussex)*
Leslie Weller, DL *(West Sussex)*

Financial Support

The Public Catalogue Foundation is particularly grateful to the following organisations and individuals who have given it generous financial support since the project started in 2003.

National Sponsor

Christie's

Benefactors (£10,000–£50,000)

City of Bradford Metropolitan District Council
Deborah Loeb Brice Foundation
The Bulldog Trust
A. & S. Burton 1960 Charitable Trust
The John S. Cohen Foundation
Christie's
Mr Lloyd Dorfman
The Foyle Foundation
Hampshire County Council
Peter Harrison Foundation
Hiscox plc
ICAP plc
Kent County Council
The Linbury Trust

The Manifold Trust
Robert Warren Miller
The Monument Trust
Miles Morland
Stavros S. Niarchos Foundation
Norfolk County Council
Provident Financial
P. F. Charitable Trust
RAB Capital plc
Renaissance West Midlands
Saga Group Ltd
University College, London
University of Leeds
Garfield Weston Foundation

Series Patrons (Minimum donation of £2,500)

Harry Bott
Janey Buchan
Dr Peter Cannon-Brookes
Mrs Greta Fenston
G. Laurence Harbottle
Paul & Kathrine Haworth
Neil Honebon
The Keatley Trust

Michael A. Lambert
David & Amanda Leathers
Miles Morland
Sir Harry & Lady Soloman
Stuart M. Southall
University of Surrey
Mr & Mrs Charles Wyvill